© AP Images/Will Shilling

1908
Ex Parte Sharpe defines more clearly the role of the juvenile court to include *parens patriae*.

Legislation establishes juvenile justice in Canada (Juvenile Delinquents Act) and in England (Children Act).

1890
Children's Aid Society of Pennsylvania, a foster home for the juvenile delinquent used as an alternative to reform schools, is established.

1891
Supreme Court of Minnesota establishes the doctrine of parental immunity.

1897
Ex Parte Becknell, a California decision that reverses the sentence of a juvenile who has not been given a jury trial.

1910
Compulsory school acts.

1870
Illinois Supreme Court reverses Dan O'Connell's vagrancy sentence to the Chicago Reform School due to lack of due process procedures in *People v. Turner*.

1875–1900
Case Law begins to deal with protective statutes.

1899
Illinois Juvenile Court Act.

1870	1880	1890	1900	1910

1868
Passage of the Fourteenth Amendment to the U.S. Constitution.

1889
Board of children's guardians is established in Indiana and given jurisdiction over neglected and dependent children.

1866
Massachusetts establishes that the state has power over children under 16 whose parents are "unfit."

1886
First neglect case is heard in Massachusetts.

1884
The state assumes the authority to take neglected children and place them in an institution. See *Reynolds v. Howe*, 51 Conn. 472, 478 (1884).

© Simon Wheatley/Magnum Photos

1881
Michigan begins child protection with the Michigan Public Acts of

1903–1905
Many other states pass juvenile court acts.

1905
Commonwealth v. Fisher—Pennsylvania Court upholds the constitutionality of the Juvenile Court Act.

1906
Massachusetts passes an act to provide for the treatment of children not as criminals but as children in need of guidance and aid.

© AP Images/Elise Amendola

1959
Standard Family Court Act
of National Council on
Crime and Delinquency
establishes that juvenile
hearings are to be informal.

1918
Chicago area studies are
conducted by Shaw and
McKay.

1930
Children's Charter.

1920 **1930** **1940** **1950** **1960**

1924
Federal Probation Act.

1954
Brown v. Board of Education,
a major school desegregation
decision.

continued on back endsheets…

JUVENILE DELINQUENCY

THEORY, PRACTICE, AND LAW

10th edition

▌ **LARRY J. SIEGEL**
University of Massachusetts—Lowell

▌ **BRANDON C. WELSH**
University of Massachusetts—Lowell

✦ **WADSWORTH**
CENGAGE Learning™

Australia • Brazil • Japan • Korea • Mexico • Singapore
Spain • United Kingdom • United States

Juvenile Delinquency: Theory, Practice, and Law, Tenth Edition
Larry J. Siegel, Brandon C. Welsh

Senior Acquisitions Editor, Criminal Justice:
  Carolyn Henderson Meier

Development Editor: Shelley Murphy

Assistant Editor: Meaghan Banks

Technology Project Manager: Lauren Keyes

Marketing Manager: Terra Schultz

Marketing Assistant: Ileana Shevlin

Marketing Communications Manager:
  Tami Strang

Project Manager, Editorial Production:
  Jennie Redwitz

Creative Director: Rob Hugel

Art Director: Vernon Boes

Print Buyer: Becky Cross

Text Permissions Editor: Bob Kauser

Image Permissions Editor: Don Schlotman

Production Service: Linda Jupiter, Jupiter
  Productions

Text Designers: John Walker and Lisa Delgado,
  Delgado and Company, Inc.

Photo Editor/Researcher: Linda L Rill

Copy Editor: Lunaea Weatherstone

Illustrators: John and Judy Waller,
  Scientific Illustrators

Proofreader: Mary Kanable

Indexer: Katherine Stimson, Stimson Indexing

Cover Designer: Yvo, Riezebos Holzbaur
  Design Group

Cover Image: © Debut Art/Getty Images

Compositor: Pre-Press PMG

For product information and technology assistance, contact us at
Cengage Learning Academic Resource Center, 1–800–423–0563
For permission to use material from this text or product,
submit all requests online at **cengage.com/permissions**
Further permissions questions can be emailed to
permissionrequest@cengage.com

Library of Congress Control Number: 2007938233

Student Edition:

ISBN-13: 978-0-495-50364-4

ISBN-10: 0-495-50364-9

Loose-leaf Edition:

ISBN-13: 978-0-495-50774-1

ISBN-10: 0-495-50774-1

Wadsworth
10 Davis Drive
Belmont, CA 94002–3098
USA

Cengage Learning is a leading provider of customized learning solutions with office locations around the globe, including Singapore, the United Kingdom, Australia, Mexico, Brazil, and Japan. Locate your local office at:
international.cengage.com/region

Cengage Learning products are represented in Canada by Nelson Education, Ltd.

For your course and learning solutions, visit **academic.cengage.com**

Purchase any of our products at your local college store or at our preferred online store **www.ichapters.com**

Printed in Canada
1 2 3 4 5 6 7 12 11 10 09 08

DEDICATIONS

To my wife, Therese J. Libby, and my children,
Julie, Andrew, Eric, and Rachel
         —L.J.S.

To my wife, Jennifer, and our son, Ryan
         —B.C.W.

LARRY J. SIEGEL

Larry J. Siegel was born in the Bronx in 1947. While living on Jerome Avenue and attending City College of New York in the 1960s, he was swept up in the social and political currents of the time. He became intrigued with the influence contemporary culture had on individual behavior: Did people shape society or did society shape people? He applied his interest in social forces and human behavior to the study of crime and justice. After graduating CCNY, he attended the newly opened program in criminal justice at the State University of New York at Albany, earning both his M.A. and Ph.D. degrees there. After completing his graduate work, Dr. Siegel began his teaching career at Northeastern University, where he was a faculty member for nine years. After leaving Northeastern, he held teaching positions at the University of Nebraska, Omaha and Saint Anselm College in New Hampshire. He is currently a professor at the University of Massachusetts, Lowell. Dr. Siegel has written extensively in the area of crime and justice, including books on juvenile law, delinquency, criminology, criminal justice, and criminal procedure. He is a court certified expert on police conduct and has testified in numerous legal cases. The father of four and grandfather of three, Larry Siegel and his wife, Terry, now reside in Bedford, New Hampshire, with their two dogs, Watson and Cody.

BRANDON C. WELSH

Brandon C. Welsh was born in Canada. He received his undergraduate and M.A. degrees at the University of Ottawa and his Ph.D. from Cambridge University in England. Dr. Welsh is currently an associate professor of criminology at the University of Massachusetts, Lowell. He teaches graduate and undergraduate courses on crime prevention, juvenile delinquency, and evidence-based policing. His research interests focus on the prevention of crime and delinquency and the economic analysis of crime prevention programs. Dr. Welsh has published extensively in these areas and is the author or editor of seven books.

PART 2: THEORIES OF DELINQUENCY 67

3 INDIVIDUAL VIEWS OF DELINQUENCY 68

4 SOCIAL STRUCTURE, PROCESS, CULTURE, AND DELINQUENCY 114

PART 4: THE JUVENILE JUSTICE SYSTEM   429

13 JUVENILE JUSTICE: THEN AND NOW   430

14 POLICE WORK WITH JUVENILES   458

In their jointly published report "The Rest of Their Lives: Life without Parole for Child Offenders in the United States," Human Rights Watch and Amnesty International condemn the practice of trying children as adults and sentencing them to life in adult prisons without the possibility of parole. These civil rights watchdog groups found that at least 2,225 child offenders serving life without parole (LWOP) sentences in U.S prisons committed their crimes before age 18; 16 percent were between 13 and 15 years old at the time they committed their crimes; 59 percent were sentenced to life without parole for their first-ever criminal conviction. Forty-two states currently have laws allowing children to receive life without parole sentences.

The report found that significant problems infected the current system. "Kids who commit serious crimes shouldn't go scot-free," said principal author Alison Parker, "but if they are too young to vote or buy cigarettes, they are too young to spend the rest of their lives behind bars." Many of the adolescents serving a life term had gotten mixed up in crimes with older kids that resulted in a death. After being apprehended, their case fell under state laws that allow youths involved in serious crimes to be transferred or waived to the criminal court system where they are tried as adults. Many were then convicted of "felony murder" because in most states anyone involved in the commission of a serious crime during which someone is killed is also guilty of murder, even if he or she did not personally or directly cause the death. In one case 15-year-old Peter A. was sentenced to life without parole for felony murder. Peter had joined two of his older brother's acquaintances to commit a robbery. He was waiting outside in a van when one of the acquaintances botched the robbery and murdered two victims. Peter said, "Although I was present at the scene, I never shot or killed anyone." Under the felony murder law, Peter was held accountable for the double murder because it was established during the trial that he had stolen the van used to drive to the victims' house.

Ironically, the life without parole issue comes at a time when fewer youth are committing serious crimes such as murder, but the likelihood of receiving a life without parole sentence is on the rise. In 1990, 2,234 children were convicted of murder and about 3 percent sentenced to life without parole. By 2000, the conviction rate had dropped by nearly 55 percent (1,006), yet the percentage of children receiving LWOP sentences rose to 9 percent, so that the actual number of kids sentenced to life had increased!* With thousands of juveniles being waived to adult court each year, it is very likely this trend in LWOP sentences will continue.

Should young people be sent to prison for the rest of their lives because of crimes committed before they have reached their maturity? Are teens fully capable of understanding the wrongfulness of their acts? Is it fair to put kids in prison with hardened adult criminals? Should all teens, no matter what their crime, be given the hope of rehabilitation and a return to society? Should the purpose of waivers to adult court be reconsidered?

* Human Rights News, "United States: Thousands of Children Sentenced to Life Without Parole, National Study by Amnesty International and Human Rights Watch Finds Majority Face Life for First Offense," http://hrw.org/english/docs/2005/10/12/usdom11835.htm (accessed November 30, 2007); Amnesty International/Human Rights Watch, The Rest of Their Lives: Life without Parole for Child Offenders in the United States, http://hrw.org/reports/2005/us1005/ (accessed November 30, 2007).

JUVENILE DELINQUENCY: THEORY, PRACTICE, AND LAW

Issues such as sentencing juveniles to life without parole for murder have sparked interest in the study of juvenile delinquency not only in the United States but also around the world. Inexplicable incidents of violence occur all too frequently in schools, homes, and public places. Teen gangs can be found in most major cities. About 1 million youth are the victims of serious neglect and sexual and physical abuse each year. Considering the public concern with the problems of youth, it is not surprising that courses on juvenile delinquency have become popular offerings on the nation's college campuses. We have written *Juvenile Delinquency: Theory, Practice, and Law* to help students understand the nature of juvenile delinquency and its causes and correlates, as well as the current strategies being used to control or eliminate its occurrence. Our text also reviews the legal rules that have been set down to either protect innocent minors or control adolescent misconduct: Can children be required to submit to drug testing in school? Can teachers search suspicious students or use corporal punishment as a method of discipline? Should children be allowed to testify on closed-circuit TV in child abuse cases?

Our primary goals in writing this edition remain the same as in the previous editions:

1. To be as objective as possible, presenting the many diverse views and perspectives that characterize the study of juvenile delinquency and reflect its interdisciplinary nature. We take no single position nor espouse a particular viewpoint or philosophy.

2. To maintain a balance of research, theory, law, policy, and practice. It is essential that a text on delinquency not be solely a theory book without presentation of the juvenile justice system or contain sections on current policies without examining legal issues and cases.

3. To be as thorough and up to date as possible. As always, we have attempted to include the most current data and information available.

4. To make the study of delinquency interesting as well as informative. We want to encourage readers' interest in the study of delinquency so that they will pursue it on an undergraduate or graduate level.

We have tried to provide a text that is both scholarly and informative, comprehensive yet interesting, well organized and objective yet provocative.

ORGANIZATION OF THE TEXT

The 10th edition of *Juvenile Delinquency: Theory, Practice, and Law* has 17 chapters:

I **Chapter 1, Childhood and Delinquency**, contains extensive material on the history of childhood and the legal concept of delinquency and status offending. This material enables the reader to understand how the concept of adolescence evolved over time and how that evolution influenced the development of the juvenile court and the special status of delinquency.

I **Chapter 2, The Nature and Extent of Delinquency**, covers the measurement of delinquent behavior as well as trends and patterns in teen crime, and also discusses the correlates of delinquency, including race, gender, class, age, and chronic offending.

I **Chapter 3, Individual Views of Delinquency**, covers individual-level views of the causes of delinquency, which include choice, biosocial, and psychological theories.

I **Chapter 4, Social Structure, Process, Culture, and Delinquency**, looks at theories that hold that culture and socialization control delinquent behavior.

I **Chapter 5, Social Reaction, Conflict, and Delinquency**, reviews theories that state that delinquency is a product of economic and political forces.

- **Chapter 6, Developmental Theories of Delinquency: Life-Course and Latent Trait**, covers the newly emerging developmental theories of delinquency, including such issues as the onset, continuity, paths, and termination of a delinquent career.

- **Chapter 7, Gender and Delinquency**, explores sex-based differences that are thought to account for gender patterns in the delinquency rate.

- **Chapter 8, The Family and Delinquency**, covers the influence of families on children and delinquency. The concept of child abuse is covered in detail and the steps in the child protection system are reviewed.

- **Chapter 9, Peers and Delinquency: Juvenile Gangs and Groups**, reviews the effects peers have on delinquency and the topic of teen gangs.

- **Chapter 10, Schools and Delinquency**, looks at the influence of schools and the education process as well as delinquency within the school setting.

- **Chapter 11, Drug Use and Delinquency**, reviews the influence drugs and substance abuse have on delinquent behavior and what is being done to reduce teenage drug use.

- **Chapter 12, Delinquency Prevention: Social and Developmental Perspectives**, covers delinquency prevention and efforts to help kids desist from criminal activities.

- **Chapter 13, Juvenile Justice: Then and Now**, gives extensive coverage to the emergence of state control over children in need and the development of the juvenile justice system. It also covers the contemporary juvenile justice system, the major stages in the justice process, the role of the federal government in the juvenile justice system, an analysis of the differences between the adult and juvenile justice systems, and extensive coverage of the legal rights of children.

- **Chapter 14, Police Work with Juveniles**, discusses the role of police in delinquency prevention. It covers legal issues such as major court decisions on searches and *Miranda* rights of juveniles. It also contains material on how race and gender affect police discretion as well as efforts by police departments to control delinquent behavior.

- **Chapter 15, Juvenile Court Process: Pretrial, Trial, and Sentencing**, contains information on plea bargaining in juvenile court, the use of detention, and transfer to adult jails. It contains an analysis of the critical factors that influence the waiver decision, the juvenile trial, and sentencing.

- **Chapter 16, Juvenile Corrections: Probation, Community Treatment, and Institutionalization**, covers material on probation and other community dispositions including restorative justice programs, and secure juvenile corrections with emphasis on legal issues such as right to treatment and unusual programs such as boot camps.

- **Chapter 17, Delinquency and Juvenile Justice Abroad**, looks at delinquency around the world and examines efforts to control antisocial youth in other nations.

WHAT'S NEW IN THIS EDITION

Because the study of juvenile delinquency is a dynamic, ever-changing field of scientific inquiry, and because the theories, concepts, and processes of this area of study are constantly evolving, we have updated *Juvenile Delinquency: Theory, Practice, and Law* to reflect the changes that have taken place in the study of delinquent behavior during the past few years.

Like its predecessors, the 10th edition includes a review of recent legal cases, research studies, and policy initiatives. It aims to provide a groundwork for the study of juvenile delinquency by analyzing and describing the nature and extent of delinquency, the suspected causes of delinquent behavior, and the environmental influences on youthful misbehavior. It also covers what most experts believe are the critical issues in juvenile delinquency and analyzes crucial policy issues, including the use of pretrial detention, waiver to adult court, and restorative justice programs. While these principles remain the backbone of the text, we have also incorporated into the 10th edition the following:

- **Chapter 1** covers new data on the health, education, and welfare challenges faced by youth in American society. It reviews changes in the treatment of status offenders, parental responsibility laws, and curfews. There is new information on programs to reduce the number of status offenders in local juvenile courts.

- **Chapter 2** updates recent trends and patterns in delinquency and juvenile victimization. It contains new information on the victim-offender relationship and new sections on the compatibility of juvenile delinquency data sources and the time and place of delinquency.

- **Chapter 3** contains new research findings on crime as problem solving, false expectations and delinquency, mental illness and delinquency, twin studies, conduct disorders, disruptive behavior disorder, diet and delinquency, and the genetic basis of delinquency.

- **Chapter 4** covers the most recent developments in social structure and social process theories. Among the new research studies covered is one by Kathleen Miller and her associates, which found that kids who join a sports team are more likely to get involved in antisocial acts. There is new material on how living in poor areas magnifies the effects of personal, social, and economic problems. The Policy and Practice feature profiles "Homeboy Industries," a community program that provides kids a way to leave gangs, achieve gainful employment, and, hopefully, live happy, productive, and constructive lives.

- **Chapter 5** is new and focuses on social conflict and social reaction theories. There are new sections on restorative justice and globalization and its effects. Analysis of the concept of retrospective reading occurs through the discussion of the case of John Odgren, a student at upscale Lincoln-Sudbury Regional High School in Massachusetts, who stabbed to death a fellow student whom he barely knew. We cover a recent study by Nadine Lanctôt that reviews the long-term effects of incarceration on youth. A Case Profile entitled "Jay's Story" covers the life of Jay Simmons, the youngest of six children, who was living with his family in an impoverished community when he entered the juvenile justice system.

- **Chapter 6** includes new research on developmental findings that drug use has unique effects and prevents people from desisting from crime. A Policy and Practice feature describes the developmental-based treatment program Across Ages. There is a review of studies looking at the interaction between delinquent propensity and life-course changes. Another new area of research is the effect of impulsivity on noncriminal behavior. We look at evidence, for example, showing that impulsive kids are more prone to become crime victims than their less impulsive peers.

- **Chapter 7** begins with a dramatic story of an abusive prostitution ring in Boston that preyed upon young girls. There is a Focus on Delinquency titled "Human Trafficking and the Sexual Exploitation of Children" that shows how girls in developing nations may become the victims of sexual predators. The Case Profile "Laticia's Story" follows the path of a 15-year-old girl referred to a teen center for her involvement in a gang-related physical assault. There is new material on the view that female delinquency originates with the onset of male supremacy, the subordination of women, male aggression, and the efforts of men to control females sexually. A new Focus on Delinquency box, "The Honor Killing of Girls," shows how male-dominant attitudes can lead to death in some cultures.

- **Chapter 8** begins with the sad saga of a 7-year-old Brooklyn girl, Nixzmary Brown, who was the victim of one of New York City's most notorious child abuse cases. A Focus on Delinquency box called "The Chicken or the Egg?" looks at which comes first, bad parents or bad kids, as well as the issue of whether poor parenting causes delinquency or if delinquents undermine their parents' supervisory abilities. The Case Profile "Joey's Story" describes the life of Joey Williams, who entered the child welfare system at the age of 9 when it was discovered that he and his younger sister and brother were being sexually abused by their stepfather. Because it is suspected that child abuse leads to a cycle of violence, we discuss programs designed to help abusive parents. We also focus on treatment programs designed to help parents become more caring and less violent.

▌ **Chapter 9** discusses new research and scholarship, including the book *Deviant Peer Influences in Programs for Youth: Problems and Solutions*, by Kenneth Dodge, Thomas Dishion, and Jennifer Lansford, who find that public policy is often based on the mistaken and dysfunctional goal of removing delinquent kids from the mainstream and segregating them together in groups. There is a Case Profile called "Luis's Story" that tells how a 16-year-old gang-involved Latino male who was charged with battery and resisting arrest due to a fight at a party with a rival gang member was able to turn his life around. There is new research on gang involvement in crime and discussion of the common stereotype that youth gangs are heavily involved in drug trafficking and violence. We look at how some kids enter the gang life because they want to embrace a "thug" lifestyle. There is a Policy and Practice feature entitled "Gang Control Efforts in the City of Miami" that describes how that community has used both enforcement and community efforts to reduce gang activity.

▌ **Chapter 10** now begins with the story of Eric Hainstock, 15, who shot and killed principal John Klang of the Weston Schools in Cazenovia, Wisconsin. We have updated sections on school performance, highlighting how students in the United States compare to those in other nations. There is new material on the critical school-related issue of dropping out, including new data that compare dropout rates for whites, blacks, and Hispanics. We review research that shows that school failure is linked to learning disabilities, and that reading disabilities might actually be treatable if the proper resources were available. Because the Supreme Court has granted schools the right to test for drugs in all students, the case that made it possible, *Board of Education of Independent School District No. 92 of Pottawatomie County et al. v. Earls et al.*, is set out in a Policy and Practice feature. There is also new and updated information on school crime and safety measures.

▌ **Chapter 11** now opens with a tragic story of the loss of one young teen's life and how the teen who caused the death is repaying society by speaking to others about the dangers of drinking and driving, and the lifelong consequences that this criminal action can cause to victims and their families. The chapter updates recent trends and patterns in juvenile drug use based on three national surveys, including the large-scale Monitoring the Future (MTF) survey. It expands the coverage of the use of methamphetamines by young people and law enforcement efforts to control it. There is a new Focus on Delinquency box that examines the latest research on the question of whether drug dealing pays. The chapter also includes new material on efforts to reduce juvenile drug use through community, education, and treatment strategies.

▌ **Chapter 12** covers the most up-to-date material on what works in delinquency prevention, with new evaluations on the effectiveness of early childhood programs and efforts to prevent juvenile crime in the teenage years. Some of these successful programs, like home visitation and mentoring, have led to changes in local and state policies to provide further preventive services for children and their families. New studies have been added on the financial costs of delinquency as the high costs of juvenile crime are sometimes used to justify more spending on delinquency prevention. There is a new Focus on Delinquency box that examines the latest research findings on public support for delinquency prevention.

▌ **Chapter 13** now begins with the story of Michael Hernandez, 14, who stabbed to death his friend and classmate, Jaime Gough, also 14, in a bathroom at the Southwood Middle School in Miami, Florida, and then returned to class in his blood-soaked clothes. We have updated the section on a comprehensive juvenile justice strategy with new evaluation studies. New material on juvenile drug courts and teen courts is presented. One youth's success in going through a teen court diversion program is described in a Case Profile called "Jennifer's Story."

I **Chapter 14** presents new research on juveniles' attitudes toward the police. It updates statistics on the handling of juvenile offenders by the police, which show that 7 out of 10 juveniles who are arrested are referred to juvenile court. The Case Profile called "Rico's Story" highlights the real-life benefits that can come from the police using their discretion in dealing with some juvenile cases. The chapter covers for the first time the relatively unknown issue of juveniles serving as police informants. It adds a new section on police and procedural justice, highlighting the importance of fair police practices in making arrests. It also brings together the latest research findings on what works when it comes to police efforts to prevent juvenile crime, including new replications of Operation Ceasefire. The chapter ends with a new section that probes the future of policing juveniles.

I **Chapter 15** updates statistics on juvenile court case flow, from the decision to release or detain to juvenile court dispositions. It also provides the latest research and statistics on juvenile transfers to adult or criminal court, including a new Focus on Delinquency box that examines whether transfers are effective in reducing juvenile violence upon return to the community. New material on juvenile diversion programs is presented. The chapter covers the latest Supreme Court ruling on the juvenile death penalty, *Roper v. Simmons*, which put an end to the practice of the death penalty for juveniles in the United States. Key issues facing the future of the juvenile court are examined.

I **Chapter 16** begins with the case of Joseph Daniel Maldonado, 18, and four other juveniles who committed suicide over an 18-month period while in juvenile detention centers in California, and the reforms that have come about to safeguard juvenile inmates and make treatment a priority. It presents up-to-date information on disproportionate minority confinement, new trends in juvenile probation and incarceration, and new material on the mental health needs of incarcerated youth. The latest research findings on what works in treating juvenile offenders are reviewed. A Case Profile shows how one juvenile offender, Karen Gilligan, 16, benefited from an intensive treatment program. The chapter includes new studies on the economics of treating violent juvenile offenders, along with new material on juvenile aftercare and reentry programs.

I **Chapter 17** presents new material on delinquency around the world. It updates statistics on juvenile crime and drug use and brings together the leading theories to explain the trends. It covers new information on the administration of juvenile justice systems around the world, from juvenile gang units in police departments in Canada to aftercare services in China. It updates the section that profiles juvenile justice in England, and a new section looks at the future of international juvenile justice.

LEARNING TOOLS

The text contains the following features designed to help students learn and comprehend the material:

I **Chapter Outline and Objectives** Each chapter begins with an outline and a list of chapter objectives. The summary is now keyed to and corresponds with the chapter objectives.

I **Concept Summary** This new feature is used throughout the text to help students review material in an organized fashion.

I **Focus on Delinquency** As in previous editions, these boxed inserts focus attention on topics of special importance and concern. For example, in Chapter 3, a box called "Diet and Delinquency" discusses whether a child's food intake can affect his or her behavior.

I **Case Profile** This new feature discusses a real-life situation in which an at-risk youth worked his or her way out of delinquency. These cases are then tied to the material in the chapter with thought-provoking critical thinking questions.

I **Policy and Practice** These boxes discuss major initiatives and programs. For example, in Chapter 17, a box entitled "Precourt Diversion Programs around the World" tells how keeping youths who have become involved in minor delinquent acts from being formally processed through the juvenile justice system has become a top priority in many countries.

I **Web Links** In the margins of every chapter are links to websites that can be used to help students enrich their understanding of important issues and concepts found within the text.

I **Key Terms and Running Glossary** The definitions for the key terms appear in the text margin where the concepts are introduced, as well as in the comprehensive glossary at the end of the book.

I **Questions for Discussion** Each chapter includes thought-provoking discussion questions.

I **Viewpoint and Doing Research on the Web** Each chapter ends with a feature called "Viewpoint" that presents a hypothetical case for the student to analyze. The related "Doing Research on the Web" feature suggests appropriate articles on the web to lead students to websites with background on the topics covered by the hypothetical situation.

SUPPLEMENTS

A number of supplements are provided by Wadsworth to help instructors use *Juvenile Delinquency: Theory, Practice, and Law* in their courses and to aid students in preparing for exams. Supplements are available to qualified adopters. Please consult your local sales representative for details.

For the Instructor

Instructor's Resource Manual Fully updated and revised by Lynn Newhart of Rockford College, the *Instructor's Resource Manual* for this edition includes learning objectives, detailed chapter outlines, key terms and figures, class discussion exercises, worksheets, lecture suggestions, and a complete test bank. Each chapter's test bank contains approximately 80 multiple-choice, true-false, fill-in-the-blank, and essay questions, which are coded according to learning objective, and include a full answer key. What's more, most test banks come with our "Instructor Approved" seal on the front cover, which tells you that each question in that test bank has been carefully reviewed by experienced criminal justice instructors for quality, accuracy, and content coverage—so you know that you are working with an assessment and grading resource of the highest caliber. Also included is a Resource Integration Guide, which will help you make maximum use of the rich supplement package available for this text by integrating media, Internet, video, and other resources into each chapter.

ExamView® Computerized Testing The comprehensive *Instructor's Resource Manual* described above is backed up by ExamView, a computerized test bank available for PC and Macintosh computers. With ExamView, an easy-to-use assessment and tutorial system, you can create, deliver, and customize tests and study guides (both print and online) in minutes. You can easily edit and import your own questions and graphics, change test layouts, and reorganize questions. And using ExamView's complete word processing capabilities, you can enter an unlimited number of new questions or edit existing questions.

Lesson Plan New to this edition, the instructor-created Lesson Plan brings accessible, masterful suggestions to every lesson. Prepared by Lynn Newhart of Rockford College, the Lesson Plan includes a sample syllabus, learning objectives, lecture notes, discussion topics, in-class activities, tips for classroom presentation of chapter material, a detailed lecture outline, and assignments.

JoinIn™ Spark discussion and assess your students' comprehension of chapter concepts with interactive classroom quizzes and background polls developed specifically for use with this edition of *Juvenile Delinquency*. Also available are polling/quiz questions that enable you to maximize the educational benefits of the ABC News video clips we custom-selected to accompany this textbook. You can run our tailor-made Microsoft® PowerPoint® slides in conjunction with the "clicker" hardware of your choice. Enhance how your students interact with you, your lecture, and each other. *For college and university adopters only. Contact your local Cengage Learning representative to learn more.*

PowerLecture CD This instructor resource includes Microsoft® PowerPoint® lecture slides with graphics from the text, making it easy for you to assemble, edit, publish, and present custom lectures for your course. The PowerLecture CD also includes video-based polling and quiz questions that can be used with the JoinIn personal response system, and integrates ExamView testing software for customizing tests of up to 250 items that can be delivered in print or online. Finally, all of your media teaching resources in one place!

WebTutor™ ToolBox on Blackboard® and WebCT® A powerful combination: easy-to-use course management tools for whichever program you use combined with content from this text's rich companion website, all in one place. You can use ToolBox as is, from the moment you log on, or if you prefer, you can customize the program with web links, images, and other resources.

The Wadsworth Criminal Justice Video Library So many exciting new videos—so many great ways to enrich your lectures and spark discussion of the material in this text! A list of our unique and expansive video program follows. Or, visit **academic .cengage.com/criminaljustice/media_center** for a complete, up-to-the-minute list of all of Wadsworth's video offerings—available in VHS and DVD format—as well as clip lists and running times. The library includes these selections and many others:

▌ *ABC® Videos.* Featuring short, high-interest clips from current news events specially developed for courses including Introduction to Criminal Justice, Criminology, Corrections, Terrorism, and White Collar Crime, these videos are perfect for use as discussion starters or lecture launchers to spark student interest. The brief video clips provide students with a new lens through which to view the past and present, one that will greatly enhance their knowledge and understanding of significant events and open up to them new dimensions in learning. Clips are drawn from such programs as *World News Tonight, Good Morning America, This Week, Primetime Live, 20/20,* and *Nightline,* as well as numerous ABC News specials and material from the Associated Press Television News and British Movietone News collections.

▌ *The Wadsworth Custom Videos for Criminal Justice.* Produced by Wadsworth and Films for the Humanities, these videos include short (5- to 10-minute) segments that encourage classroom discussion. Topics include white-collar crime, domestic violence, forensics, suicide and the police officer, the court process, the history of corrections, prison society, and juvenile justice.

▌ *Court TV Videos.* One-hour videos presenting seminal and high-profile cases, such as the interrogation of Michael Crowe and serial killer Ted Bundy, as well as crucial and current issues such as cyber crime, double jeopardy, and the management of the prison on Riker's Island.

▌ *A&E American Justice.* Forty videos to choose from, on topics such as deadly force, women on death row, juvenile justice, strange defenses, and Alcatraz.

▌ *Films for the Humanities.* Nearly 200 videos to choose from on a variety of topics such as elder abuse, supermax prisons, suicide and the police officer, the making of an FBI agent, domestic violence, and more.

❚ *Oral History Project.* Developed in association with the American Society of Criminology, the Academy of Criminal Justice Society, and the National Institute of Justice, these videos will help you introduce your students to the scholars who have developed the criminal justice discipline. Compiled over the last several years, each video features a set of guest lecturers—scholars whose thinking has helped to build the foundation of present ideas in the discipline.

Classroom Activities for Criminal Justice This valuable booklet, available to adopters of any Wadsworth criminal justice text, offers instructors the best of the best in criminal justice classroom activities. Containing both tried-and-true favorites and exciting new projects, its activities are drawn from across the spectrum of criminal justice subjects, including introduction to criminal justice, criminology, corrections, criminal law, policing, and juvenile justice, and can be customized to fit any course. Novice and seasoned instructors alike will find it a powerful tool to stimulate classroom engagement.

Internet Activities for Criminal Justice In addition to providing a wide range of activities for any criminal justice class, this useful booklet helps familiarize students with Internet resources they will use both as students of criminal justice and in their criminal justice careers. *Internet Activities for Criminal Justice* allows instructors to integrate Internet resources and addresses important topics such as criminal and police law, policing organizations, policing challenges, corrections systems, juvenile justice, criminal trials, and current issues in criminal justice. Available to adopters of any Wadsworth criminal justice text, and prepared by Christina DeJong of Michigan State University, this booklet will bring current tools and resources to the criminal justice classroom.

The Wadsworth Criminal Justice Resource Center: academic.cengage.com/ criminaljustice Designed with the instructor in mind, this website features information about Wadsworth's technology and teaching solutions, as well as several features created specifically for today's criminal justice student. Supreme Court updates, timelines, and hot-topic polling can all be used to supplement in-class assignments and discussions. You'll also find a wealth of links to careers and news in criminal justice, book-specific sites, and much more.

For the Student

Study Guide An extensive student guide has been developed and updated for this edition by Lynn Newhart of Rockford College. Because students learn in different ways, the guide includes a variety of pedagogical aids. Each chapter is outlined and summarized, major terms are defined, and self-tests coded to the chapter's learning objectives are provided.

Audio Study Tools Lite Students can finally study anytime and anywhere they want using Cengage Learning's eAudio for *Juvenile Delinquency*. Our exclusive eAudio content, which can be downloaded to any MP3 player, includes a review of all key terms and concepts and quizzing items. With this unique supplement, students can quiz themselves on each chapter's vocabulary and key concepts as they go or review important material before tests—even if they don't have their textbook on hand or aren't at their desk.

Careers in Criminal Justice Website: academic.cengage.com/criminaljustice/careers This unique website gives students information on a wide variety of career paths, including requirements, salaries, training, contact information for key agencies, and employment outlooks. Several important tools help students investigate the criminal justice career choices that are right for them.

❚ *Career Profiles.* Video testimonials from a variety of practicing professionals in the field as well as information on many criminal justice careers, including job descriptions, requirements, training, salary and benefits, and the application process.

■ *Interest Assessment.* A self-assessment tool to help students decide which careers suit their personalities and interests.

■ *Career Planner.* Résumé-writing tips and worksheets, interviewing techniques, and successful job search strategies.

■ *Links for Reference.* Direct links to federal, state, and local agencies where students can get contact information and learn more about current job opportunities.

Handbook of Selected Supreme Court Cases, Third Edition This supplementary handbook covers almost 40 landmark cases, each of which includes a full case citation, an introduction, a summary from Westlaw, excerpts from the case, and the decision. The updated edition includes *Hamdi v. Rumsfeld, Roper v. Simmons, Ring v. Arizona, Atkins v. Virginia, Illinois v. Caballes,* and much more.

Current Perspectives: Readings from InfoTrac® College Edition These readers, designed to give students a deeper look at special topics in criminal justice, include free access to InfoTrac College Edition. The timely articles are selected by experts in each topic from within InfoTrac College Edition. They are available for free when bundled with the text.

■ *Terrorism and Homeland Security*

■ *Cyber Crime*

■ *Juvenile Justice*

■ *Public Policy and Criminal Justice*

■ *Crisis Management and National Emergency Response*

■ *Racial Profiling*

■ *New Technologies and Criminal Justice*

■ *White-Collar Crime*

Internet Guide for Criminal Justice, Second Edition Intended for the novice user, this guide provides students with the background and vocabulary necessary to navigate and understand the web, then provides them with a wealth of criminal justice websites and Internet project ideas.

Companion Website The Student Companion website provides chapter outlines and summaries, tutorial quizzing, a final exam, the textbook glossary, flash cards, crossword puzzle, concentration game, InfoTrac College Edition exercises, web links, and the multi-step Concept Builder that includes review, application, and exercise questions on chapter-based key concepts.

InfoTrac® College Edition Students receive four months of real-time access to InfoTrac College Edition's online database of continuously updated, full-length articles from hundreds of journals and periodicals. By doing a simple keyword search, users can quickly generate a list of related articles, then select relevant articles to explore and print out for reference or further study.

Crime Scenes: An Interactive Criminal Justice CD-ROM This highly visual and interactive program casts students as the decision makers in various roles as they explore all aspects of the criminal justice system. Exciting videos and supporting documents put students in the midst of a juvenile murder trial, a prostitution case that turns into manslaughter, and several other scenarios. This product received the gold medal in higher education and silver medal for video interface from *NewMedia Magazine's* Invision Awards.

Crime and Evidence in Action CD-ROM This engaging resource will take your students on an interactive exploration of three criminal investigations. Students will explore each case beginning with crime scene investigation and procedures. They will then delve into the various aspects of trial proceedings, incarceration, and parole. Through each step of the process, students are encouraged to apply what they have learned in the text—they even receive detailed feedback that allows them to pinpoint areas and topics that need further exploration. The related website also includes post-scenario and forensics quizzing, an online resource library, background information on suspects, and much more.

Seeking Employment in Criminal Justice and Related Fields Written by J. Scott Harr and Kären Hess, this practical book helps students develop a search strategy to find employment in criminal justice and related fields. Each chapter includes "insider's views," written by individuals in the field and addressing promotions and career planning.

Guide to Careers in Criminal Justice This concise 60-page booklet provides a brief introduction to the exciting and diverse field of criminal justice. Students can learn about opportunities in law enforcement, courts, and corrections and how they can go about getting these jobs.

ACKNOWLEDGMENTS

We would like to give special thanks to our terrific and supportive editor Carolyn Henderson Meier and our wonderful and fantastic development editor Shelly Murphy. This text would not have been possible to complete without their help and TLC. We love working with the incomparable production manager Jennie Redwitz and production editor Linda Jupiter, who produced a marvelous book. Copy editor Lunaea Weatherstone did a thorough job and it is always a pleasure to work with her. Terra Schultz, marketing manager, is another fabulous member of the Cengage Learning team.

The preparation of this text would not have been possible without the aid of our colleagues who helped by reviewing the previous editions and giving us important suggestions for improvement. Reviewers for the 10th edition were:

Michael Boyko, Cuyahoga Community College

George Burruss, Southern Illinois University Carbondale

Teresa LaGrange, Cleveland State University

Marilyn McShane, University of Houston Downtown

Cynthia Robbins, University of Delaware

Many thanks to all!

Larry Siegel
Brandon Welsh

The Concept of Delinquency

The field of juvenile delinquency has been an important area of study since the turn of the twentieth century. Academicians, practitioners, policy makers, and legal scholars have devoted their attention to basic questions about the nature of youth crime: How should the concept of juvenile delinquency be defined? Who commits delinquent acts? How much delinquency occurs each year? Is the rate of delinquent activity increasing or decreasing? What can we do to prevent delinquency?

Part One reviews these basic questions in detail. Chapter 1 discusses the current state of American youth and the challenges they face. It covers the origins of society's concern for children and the development of the concept of delinquency. It shows how the definition of delinquency was developed and how the legal definition has evolved. While society has chosen to treat adult and juvenile law violators separately, it has also expanded the definition of youthful misbehaviors eligible for social control; these are referred to as *status offenses*. Status offenses include such behaviors as truancy, running away, and incorrigibility. Critics suggest that juveniles' noncriminal behavior is probably not a proper area of concern for law enforcement agencies.

Chapter 2 examines the nature and extent of delinquent behavior. It discusses how social scientists gather information on juvenile delinquency and provides an overview of some of the major trends in juvenile crime. Chapter 2 also discusses some of the critical factors related to delinquency, such as race, gender, class, and age. Finally, it covers the concept of the chronic delinquent, those who continually commit delinquent acts in their youth and continue to offend as adults.

Childhood and Delinquency

Chapter Outline

The Adolescent Dilemma
Youth in Crisis
Adolescent Problems
Are There Reasons for Hope?
FOCUS ON DELINQUENCY: Adolescent Risk Taking
The Study of Juvenile Delinquency
The Development of Childhood
Childhood in the Middle Ages
Development of Concern for Children
Childhood in America
The Concept of Delinquency
Delinquency and *Parens Patriae*
The Legal Status of Delinquency
Legal Responsibility of Youth
Status Offenders
The History of Status Offenses
The Status Offender in the Juvenile Justice System
CASE PROFILE: Aaliyah's Story
Reforming Status Offense Laws
POLICY AND PRACTICE: Orange County's Family Keys Program
POLICY AND PRACTICE: Increasing Social Control over Juveniles and Their Parents
Increasing Social Control

Chapter Objectives

1. Become familiar with the problems of youth in American culture
2. Discuss the specific issues facing American youth
3. Understand the concept of being "at risk" and discuss why so many kids take risks
4. Be familiar with the recent social improvements enjoyed by American teens
5. Discuss why the study of delinquency is so important and what this study entails
6. Describe the life of children during feudal times
7. Know why the treatment of children changed radically after the seventeenth century
8. Discuss childhood in the American colonies
9. Know about the child savers and the creation of delinquency
10. Discuss the elements of juvenile delinquency today
11. Know what is meant by the term "status offender"

Parents and teachers in Laurelvale, County Armagh, Northern Ireland, were in shock in June of 2007 when three schoolboy friends committed suicide just weeks apart.[1] In the aftermath of these deaths, residents were warned to be vigilant amid widespread rumors that other youngsters had entered into suicide pacts. The teens—Lee Walker, Wayne Browne, and James Topley—were classmates; they all attended Craigavon Senior High. A local psychologist, Dr. Arthur Cassidy, who had been working with young people from Laurelvale and the surrounding areas, expressed the opinion that up to a dozen kids were involved in the suicide plot and that the planning and operation were Internet-based.

Laurelvale, a tight-knit community of around 600 people in Northern Ireland, is probably the last place you would expect to find kids troubled enough to hatch a suicide plot. Poverty-stricken, violence-prone urban centers would seem the more likely locale. But as the incident shows, adolescents both here in the United States and abroad are today being forced to confront extremely difficult and emotionally draining life events in almost every kind of environment, whether it be urban, rural, or suburban.

The problems of youth in contemporary society are staggering. Adolescents and young adults often experience stress, confusion, and depression because of trouble and conflict occurring in their families, schools, and communities.[2] Such feelings can overwhelm young people and lead them to consider suicide as a "solution." Though most kids do not take their own life, there are millions who are left troubled and disturbed and at risk for delinquency, drug use, and other forms of antisocial behavior. Acting out or externalized behavior that begins in early adolescence may then persist into adulthood.[3] And as the citizens of Laurelvale found, the stress can cause extreme emotional turmoil. They are not alone. In the United States teen suicide rate remains unacceptably high: Suicide is the third leading cause of death among young people ages 15 to 24, averaging about 4,000 per year. In 2007, the Centers for Disease Control and Prevention announced that after a decade-long rate of more than 28 percent, the suicide rate for 10- to 24-year-olds in the United States increased by 8 percent, the largest single-year rise in 15 years.

▌ For 10- to 14-year-old females, the rate increased from 0.54 per 100,000 in 2003 to 0.95 per 100,000.

▌ For 15- to 19-year-old females, the rate increased from 2.66 to 3.52 per 100,000.

▌ For 15- to 19-year-old males, the rate increased from 11.61 to 12.65 per 100,000.[4]

It may not be surprising to some that this latest generation of adolescents has been described as cynical and preoccupied with material acquisitions.[5] By age 18, American youth have spent more time in front of a television set than in the classroom; each year they may see up to 1,000 rapes, murders, and assaults on TV. Today's teens are listening to rap music, such as 50 Cent's "In Da Club," and Kanye West's "Gold Digger," whose sexually explicit lyrics routinely describe substance abuse and promiscuity. How will this exposure affect them? Should we be concerned? Maybe we should. A recent study by Steven Martino and his colleagues found that kids who listen to music with a sexual content are much more likely to engage in precocious sex than adolescents whose musical tastes run to the Mormon Tabernacle Choir and *The Sound of Music*.[6]

THE ADOLESCENT DILEMMA

The problems of American society and the daily stress of modern life have had a significant effect on our nation's youth as they go through their tumultuous teenage years. Adolescence is unquestionably a time of transition. During this period, the self, or basic personality, is still undergoing a metamorphosis and is vulnerable to a host of external determinants as well as internal physiological changes.[7]

Adolescence is a time of trial and uncertainty for many youths. They may become extremely vulnerable to emotional turmoil and experience anxiety, humiliation, and mood swings. Adolescents also undergo a period of biological development that proceeds at a far faster pace than at any other time in their lives except infancy. Over a period of a few years, their height, weight, and sexual characteristics change dramatically. The average age at which girls reach puberty today is 12.5 years; 150 years ago, girls matured sexually at age 16. But although they may become biologically mature and capable of having children as early as 14, many youngsters remain emotionally and intellectually immature. By the time they reach 15, a significant number of teenagers are approaching adulthood unable to adequately meet the requirements and responsibilities of the workplace, family, and neighborhood. Many suffer from health problems, are educational underachievers, and are already skeptical about their ability to enter the American mainstream.

In later adolescence (ages 16 to 18), youths may experience a life crisis that famed psychologist Erik Erikson labeled the struggle between **ego identity** and **role diffusion**. Ego identity is formed when youths develop a firm sense of who they are and what they stand for. Role diffusion occurs when they experience personal uncertainty, spread themselves too thin, and place themselves at the mercy of leaders who promise to give them a sense of identity they cannot mold for themselves.[8] Psychologists also find that late adolescence is a period dominated by the yearning for independence from parental domination.[9] Given this explosive mixture of biological change and desire for autonomy, it isn't surprising that the teenage years are a time of rebelliousness and conflict with authority at home, at school, and in the community.

ego identity
According to Erik Erikson, ego identity is formed when a person develops a firm sense of who he is and what he stands for.

role diffusion
According to Erik Erikson, role diffusion occurs when youths spread themselves too thin, experience personal uncertainty, and place themselves at the mercy of leaders who promise to give them a sense of identity they cannot develop for themselves.

Youth in Crisis

There are approximately 70 million children in the United States, a number that is projected to increase to about 80 million by 2025 (Figure 1.1).[10] As Figure 1.2 shows, the number of both the oldest and youngest members of society are projected to

FIGURE 1.1

Population Trends by Age

SOURCE: ChildStats.gov, "Children as a Proportion of the Population," www.childstats.gov/americaschildren06/pop2.asp (accessed October 2, 2007).

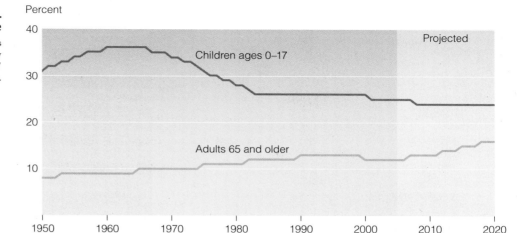

increase between 2000 and 2025 while the middle age population is expected to be reduced.

During the "baby boom" (1946 to 1964), the number of children grew rapidly. Now as the baby boomers are entering their senior years, their needs for support and medical care will be increasing. At the same time, the number of children in the population is also expected to increase, including a significant number of kids who are poor and at risk for delinquency and antisocial behavior. While the number of poor kids and the elderly will be rising, the 30- to 50-year-old population who will be Update urls throughout the chapter and add ending period. expected to care and pay for these groups will constitute a much smaller share of the population.

Adolescent Problems

These population trends take on greater meaning when the special problems of youth are considered. Troubles in the home, the school, and the neighborhood, coupled with health and developmental hazards, have placed a significant portion of American youth "at risk." Youths considered at risk are those dabbling in various forms of dangerous conduct such as drug abuse, alcohol use, and precocious sexuality. They are living in families that, because of economic, health, or social problems, are unable to provide adequate care and discipline. Though it is impossible to determine precisely the number of at-risk youth, the Children's Defense Fund, a Washington, D.C.–based advocacy group, reports that each day in America:

at-risk youth
Young people who are extremely vulnerable to the negative consequences of school failure, substance abuse, and early sexuality.

- 1 mother dies in childbirth.
- 4 children are killed by abuse or neglect.
- 5 children or teens commit suicide.
- 8 children or teens are killed by firearms.
- 33 children or teens die from accidents.
- 77 babies die before their first birthday.
- 192 children are arrested for violent crimes.
- 383 children are arrested for drug abuse.
- 906 babies are born at low birth weight.
- 1,153 babies are born to teen mothers.
- 1,672 public school students are corporally punished.
- 1,839 babies are born without health insurance.
- 2,261 high school students drop out.
- 2,383 children are confirmed as abused or neglected.

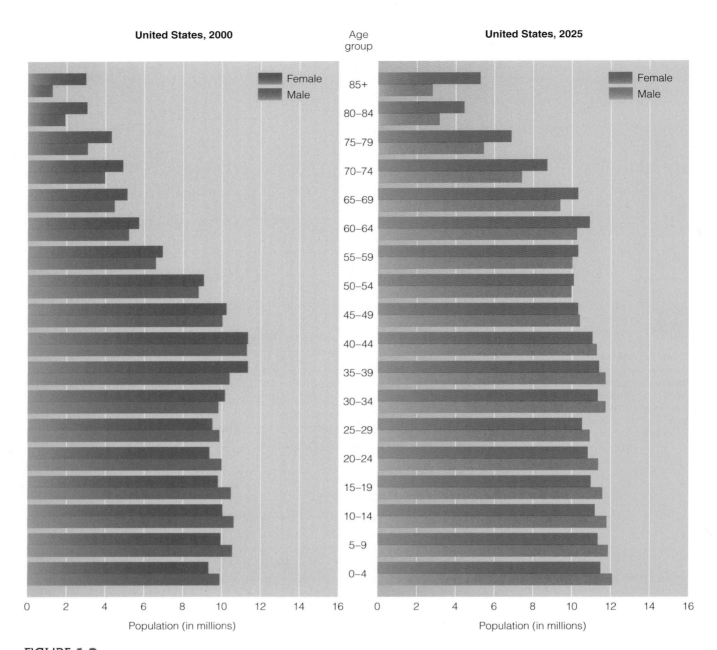

FIGURE 1.2

Population Trends by Age and Gender

SOURCE: U.S. Census Bureau, International Data Base.

Data on population characteristics can be found at the website of the U.S. Census Bureau via academic.cengage.com/criminaljustice/siegel.

| 2,411 babies are born into poverty.
| 2,494 babies are born to mothers who are not high school graduates.
| 4,017 babies are born to unmarried mothers.
| 4,302 children are arrested.
| 17,132 public school students are suspended.[11]

Adolescent Poverty According to the U.S. Census Bureau, more than 37 million Americans still live in poverty, earning an income below $19,900 a year for a family of four. The poverty rate for children under 18 (18 percent) remains higher than that of 18- to 64-year-olds (11 percent) and that of people 65 and older (10 percent). More than 12 million children now live in poverty.

Health Problems Many children are now suffering from chronic health problems and receive inadequate health care. One reason is that so many are living in poverty: Children living below the poverty line are less likely (71 percent) to be in very good or excellent health compared to children in higher-income families (86 percent).[12]

The number of U.S. children covered by health insurance is declining and will continue to do so for the foreseeable future. About 20 percent of children in poverty have no health insurance; minority kids stand the greatest chance of not having health insurance. (See Figure 1.3.)

Family Problems Divorce strikes about half of all new marriages, and many families sacrifice time with each other to afford more affluent lifestyles. Today, about 70 percent of children under age 18 live with two married parents.[13] Kids who live with one parent only are much more likely to experience poverty than those living in two-parent families. Because of family problems, children are being polarized into two distinct economic groups: those in affluent, two-earner, married-couple households and those in poor, single-parent households.[14]

Substandard Living Conditions Many children live in substandard housing—high-rise, multiple-family dwellings—which can have a negative influence on their long-term psychological health.[15] Adolescents living in deteriorated urban areas are prevented from having productive and happy lives. Many die from random bullets and drive-by shootings. Some are homeless and living on the street, where they are at risk of drug addiction and sexually transmitted diseases (STDs), including AIDS. Today about one-third of U.S. households with children have one or more of the following three housing problems: physically inadequate housing, crowded housing, or housing that costs more than 30 percent of the household income.[16]

Inadequate Educational Opportunity Although all young people face stress in the education system, the risks are greatest for the poor, members of racial and ethnic minorities, and recent immigrants. These children usually attend the most underfunded schools, receive inadequate educational opportunities, and have the fewest opportunities to achieve conventional success. For example, by the time they reach the fourth grade, students in poorer public schools have lower achievement scores in mathematics than those in more affluent districts.[17]

Formed in 1985, the **Children's Rights Council (CRC)** is a national nonprofit organization based in Washington, D.C., that works to assure children meaningful and continuing contact with both their parents and extended family regardless of the parents' marital status. Visit this site via academic.cengage.com/criminaljustice/siegel.

FIGURE 1.3 - - - - - - - - - - -
Uninsured Children by Poverty Status, Age, and Race and Hispanic Origin

* Federal surveys now give respondents the option of reporting more than one race.

SOURCE: U.S. Census Bureau, *Current Population Survey, 2006, Annual Social and Economic Supplement*, www.census.gov/cps/ (accessed October 2, 2007).

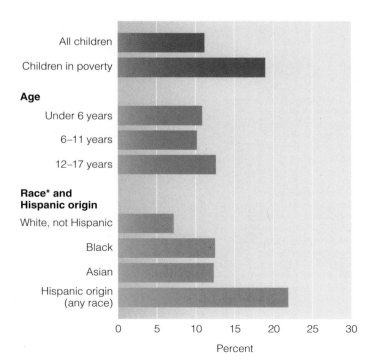

The mission of the **Eisenhower National Clearinghouse** is to identify effective curriculum resources, create high-quality professional development materials, and disseminate useful information and products to improve K–12 mathematics and science teaching and learning. Visit this site via academic.cengage.com/criminaljustice/siegel.

The rate of *retention*—being forced to repeat a grade—is far higher than it should be in most communities. Retention rates are associated with another major educational problem—dropping out.[18]

Considering that youth are at risk during the most tumultuous time of their lives, it comes as no surprise that they are willing to engage in risky, destructive behavior, as the Focus on Delinquency box entitled "Adolescent Risk Taking" suggests.

Are There Reasons for Hope?

Despite the many hazards faced by teens, there are some bright spots on the horizon. Teenage birthrates nationwide have declined substantially during the past decade.[19] The most recent data indicates that about 47 percent of high school students— 6.7 million—reported having had sex, down from 54 percent in 1991. Today, about two-thirds of sexually active adolescents report using condoms; an increase from the 46 percent reported in 1991. Considering this increased use of birth control, it is not surprising that that the U.S. birthrate for teenagers ages 15 to 19 has declined about 30 percent during this period, to about 43 births per 1,000 teen girls (from 62 births per 1,000 in 1991).[20] (See Figure 1.4.) The data indicate that more young girls are using birth control and practicing safe sex, however, there was a slight uptick (3 percent) in the teenage birth rate in 2006.

There are also positive signs of academic and intellectual success—for example, more youngsters are being read to by an adult. Sixty percent of children ages 3 to 5 and not in kindergarten are now read to daily by a family member, an increase from 53 percent in 1993. More young people are completing high school. Today about 88 percent of young people finish high school, compared with 84 percent in 1980.[21]

There are other signs of improvement in adolescent health care. Fewer children with health risks are being born today than in 1990. This probably means that fewer women are drinking alcohol during pregnancy, smoking cigarettes, or receiving late or no prenatal care. Since 1990 the number of children immunized against disease has also increased. Due in large part to improvements in medical technology, the infant mortality rate—the number of children who die before their first birthday—has

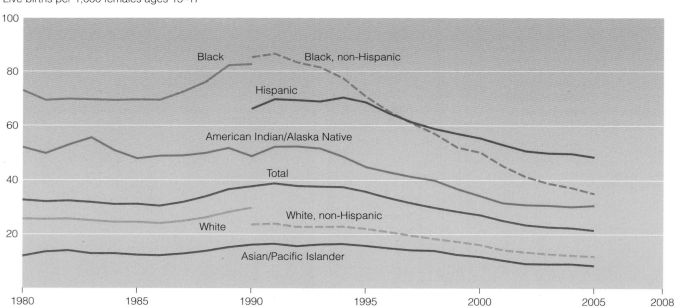

Live births per 1,000 females ages 15–17

FIGURE 1.4

Birthrates for Females Age 15–17 by Race and Hispanic Origin

SOURCE: *Children: Key National Indicators of Well-Being, 2007*, www.childstats.gov/americaschildren/famsoc6.asp (accessed October 2, 2007).

Focus on *delinquency*

Adolescent Risk Taking

We live in uncertain times marked by war, terrorism, and unrest. This uncertainty is not lost on the adolescent population. The Centers for Disease Control and Prevention (CDC) report that, in the United States, 70 percent of all deaths among youth and young adults from 10 to 24 years of age result from only four causes: motor vehicle crashes, unintentional injuries, homicide, and suicide. Though some risk-taking behaviors have declined, kids continue to take chances with their health and safety. More than half are sexually active and of these almost one-third do not use birth control. Ten percent do not exercise and 13 percent are overweight. Twenty percent of teens say they smoke cigarettes and about 17 percent say they have contemplated suicide. Despite these problems, there are some signs of improvement. High school students appear to be getting the message to buckle up for safety. The most recent report finds that only 10 percent of high school students said they rarely or never wore a seat belt when riding in a car, a significant decline from the 18 percent in 2003 and 26 percent in 1991. The percentage of students who report current alcohol use has also declined dramatically (43 percent in 2005 compared to 51 percent in 1991).

The CDC reports significant racial differences in risk taking. Compared with white and Hispanic high school students, black high school students are least likely to use tobacco, alcohol, cocaine and other drugs, but most likely to report sexual risk behaviors and sedentary behaviors such as watching television three or more hours per day. White students are less likely than black or Hispanic high school students to report physical fighting, sexual risk behaviors and being overweight, but more likely to engage in frequent cigarette smoking and episodic heavy drinking. Hispanic students are more likely than black or white students to report attempted suicide and the use of drugs like cocaine, heroin, and methamphetamines.

Why do youths take such chances? Taking risks is normative among teens. They drive fast and recklessly: Motor vehicle crashes are a leading cause of death among young people. Nor is reckless behavior reserved for the class troublemakers. Raymond Bingham and Jean Shope found that kids who are involved in auto accidents are actually among the best students in their class. Although they drank more than average, they smoked less. Their findings suggest that risky driving patterns may be found among any teen group.

Criminologist Nanette Davis suggests that merely trying to survive the adolescent experience in America makes kids prone to take risks. Risk behaviors are emotionally edgy, dangerous, exciting, hazardous, challenging, and volatile. Youths are forced into risky behavior as they try to negotiate the hurdles of adolescent life—learning to drive, date, drink, work, relate, and live. Davis finds that social developments in the United States have increased the risks of growing up for all children. It is a society that is prone to suffer severe economic upswings and downturns. Planning a future is problematic when job elimination and corporate downsizing are accepted business practices and divorce and family restructuring are epidemic. It is a culture that overemphasizes consumerism with often troubling results. In high schools, peer respect is "bought" through the accumulation of material goods; the right clothes, electronic gear, and car are required for popularity. Underprivileged youths are driven to illegal behavior in an effort to gain the material goods they can't afford. Drug deals and theft may be a shortcut to acquiring coveted name-brand clothes and athletic shoes. Kids learn to be part of the "cult of individualism," which makes them self-involved and self-centered. Children are taught to put their own interests above those of others. People occupy their own private worlds without caring for the rights of others. In an effort to fit into this fast-paced environment, some kids become risk takers who engage in chancy behaviors.

Some adolescents may not *choose* to take risks, but are forced into them in order to survive in a hostile environment. Though joining gangs may put kids at risk for drug use and violence, in some neighborhoods choosing not to join may put them in even greater peril. Some kids living in high-crime areas may join with the toughest kids in the neighborhood as a method of coping with a hostile environment; some choose to carry weapons for protection. They believe that the benefits of protection and respect outweigh the dangers of arrest and punishment. In reality, such choices expose them to violence and danger.

Critical Thinking

1. Do kids engage in risky behavior because they feel there is nothing to lose as an adolescent? Would a campaign to inform them of the danger of taking risks, such as early sex, help reduce risky behaviors?

2. What are the benefits of risk taking? Millions of people take risks every day and get involved in risky activities ranging from mountain climbing to diving in shark-infested waters. Why do people take such risks?

SOURCES: Centers for Disease Control and Prevention, "Fewer High School Students Engage in Health Risk Behaviors; Racial and Ethnic Differences Persist," press release, June 8, 2006, www.cdc.gov/od/oc/media/pressrel/r060608.htm (accessed October 2, 2007); Patrick Nickoletti and Heather Taussig, "Outcome Expectancies and Risk Behaviors in Maltreated Adolescents," *Journal of Research on Adolescence* 16:217–228 (2006); Andrew Rasmussen, Mark Aber, and Arvinkumar Bhana, "Adolescent Coping and Neighborhood Violence: Perceptions, Exposure, and Urban Youths' Efforts to Deal with Danger," *American Journal of Community Psychology* 33:61–75 (2004); Raymond Bingham and Jean Shope, "Adolescent Problem Behavior and Problem Driving in Young Adulthood," *Journal of Adolescent Research* 19:205–223 (2004); Jo Anne Grunbaum et al., *Youth Risk Behavior Surveillance: United States, 2001* (Centers for Disease Control and Prevention, *Morbidity and Mortality Weekly Report*, June 28, 2002); Nanette Davis, *Youth Crisis: Growing Up in the High-Risk Society* (New York: Praeger, Greenwood Publishing, 1998).

declined about 30 percent during the past decade (from 11 per 1,000 births in 1991 to 7 per 1,000 births today).[22] Although education is still a problem area, more parents are reading to their young children, and math achievement is rising in grades 4 through 12. And while the dropout problem still exists, the most recent census data (2006) indicate that about 86 percent of all adults 25 and older reported they had completed at least high school. More than one-quarter (28 percent) of adults 25 and older had attained at least a bachelor's degree.

THE STUDY OF JUVENILE DELINQUENCY

juvenile delinquency
Participation in illegal behavior by a minor who falls under a statutory age limit.

chronic delinquent offenders (also known as chronic juvenile offenders, chronic delinquents, or chronic recidivists)
Youths who have been arrested four or more times during their minority and perpetrate a striking majority of serious criminal acts. This small group, known as the "chronic 6 percent," is believed to engage in a significant portion of all delinquent behavior; these youths do not age out of crime but continue their criminal behavior into adulthood.

The problems of youth in modern society are both a major national concern and an important subject for academic study. This text focuses on one area of particular concern: **juvenile delinquency**, or criminal behavior committed by minors. The study of juvenile delinquency is important both because of the damage suffered by its victims and the problems faced by its perpetrators.

More than 2 million youths are now arrested each year for crimes ranging in seriousness from loitering to murder.[23] Though most juvenile law violations are minor, some young offenders are extremely dangerous and violent. More than 700,000 youths belong to more than 20,000 gangs in the United States. Violent street gangs and groups can put fear into an entire city (see Chapter 9 for more on gangs). Youths involved in multiple serious criminal acts—referred to as lifestyle, repeat, or **chronic delinquent offenders**—are now recognized as a serious social problem. State juvenile authorities must deal with these offenders, along with responding to a range of other social problems, including child abuse and neglect, school crime and vandalism, family crises, and drug abuse.

Given the diversity and gravity of these problems, there is an urgent need for strategies to combat such a complex social phenomenon as juvenile delinquency. But formulating effective strategies demands a solid understanding of delinquency's causes and prevention. Is delinquency a function of psychological abnormality?

The study of juvenile delinquency involves a variety of social problems faced by adolescents. Sgt. Vincent Matranga, of the Sacramento City Unified School District, questions Lydia Ochoa, 15, and her boyfriend, Antonio, 17, about why the pair are not in school, in Sacramento, California, on January 30, 2007. Police teamed up with school officials to start rounding up truants in an effort to cut crime as well as prevent kids from dropping out. After questioning the two juveniles, Matranga released Antonio to an adult who confirmed he was enrolled in a home study program. Lydia was taken to an attendance center at Luther Burbank High School where a social worker worked with her to prevent her from becoming one of the estimated 150,000 California students who leave school each year without a diploma. The study of delinquency involves such issues as devising programs to reduce the dropout rate and determining what effect dropping out of school has on delinquency.

© AP Images/Rich Pedroncelli

A collective reaction by youths against destructive social conditions? The product of a disturbed home life and disrupted socialization? Does serious delinquent behavior occur only in large urban areas among lower-class youths? Or is it spread throughout the entire social structure? What impact do family life, substance abuse, school experiences, and peer relations have on youth and their law-violating behaviors? We know that most youthful law violators do not go on to become adult criminals (what is known as the **aging-out process**). Yet we do not know why some youths become chronic delinquents whose careers begin early and persist into their adulthood. Why does the onset of delinquency begin so early in some children? Why does the severity of their offenses escalate? What factors predict the **persistence**, or continuation, of delinquency, and conversely, what are the factors associated with its desistance, or termination? Unless the factors that control the onset and termination of a delinquent career are studied in an orderly and scientific manner, developing effective prevention and control efforts will be difficult.

The study of delinquency also involves analysis of the law enforcement, court, and correctional agencies designed to treat youthful offenders who fall into the arms of the law—known collectively as the **juvenile justice system**. How should police deal with minors who violate the law? What are the legal rights of children? For example, should minors who commit murder receive the death penalty? What kind of correctional programs are most effective with delinquent youths? How useful are educational, community, counseling, and vocational development programs? Is it true, as some critics claim, that most efforts to rehabilitate young offenders are doomed to failure?[24] Should we adopt a punishment or a treatment orientation to combat delinquency, or something in between?

In sum, the scientific study of delinquency requires understanding the nature, extent, and cause of youthful law violations and the methods devised for their control. We also need to study important environmental and social issues associated with delinquent behavior, including substance abuse, child abuse and neglect, education, and peer relations. This text investigates these aspects of juvenile delinquency along with the efforts being made to treat problem youths and prevent the spread of delinquent behavior. Our study begins with a look back to the development of the concept of childhood and how children were first identified as a unique group with its own special needs and behaviors.

aging-out process (also known as desistance or spontaneous remission)
The tendency for youths to reduce the frequency of their offending behavior as they age; aging-out is thought to occur among all groups of offenders.

persistence
The process by which juvenile offenders persist in their delinquent careers rather than aging out of crime.

juvenile justice system
The segment of the justice system, including law enforcement officers, the courts, and correctional agencies, designed to treat youthful offenders.

THE DEVELOPMENT OF CHILDHOOD

The treatment of children as a distinct social group with special needs and behavior is, in historical terms, a relatively new concept. It is only for the past 350 years or so that any mechanism existed to care for even the most needy children, including those left orphaned and destitute. How did this concept of concern for children develop?

Childhood in the Middle Ages

In Europe during the Middle Ages (roughly 500 C.E. to 1500 C.E.), the concept of childhood as we know it today did not exist. In the **paternalistic family** of the time, the father was the final authority on all family matters and exercised complete control over the social, economic, and physical well-being of his wife and children.[25] Children who did not obey were subject to severe physical punishment, even death.

paternalistic family
A family style wherein the father is the final authority on all family matters and exercises complete control over his wife and children.

The Lower Classes For peasant children, the passage into adulthood was abrupt. As soon as they were physically capable, children of all classes were expected to engage in adult roles. Among the working classes, boys engaged in farming and/or learning a skilled trade, such as masonry or metalworking; girls aided in food preparation and/or household maintenance.[26] Some peasant youths went into domestic or agricultural service on the estate of a powerful landowner or into trades or crafts, perhaps as a blacksmith or farrier (horseshoe maker).

As soon as they were physically capable, children of the Middle Ages were expected to engage in adult roles. Among the working classes, males engaged in peasant farming or learned a skilled trade, such as masonry or metalworking; females aided in food preparation or household maintenance. Some peasant youth went into domestic or agricultural service on the estate of a powerful landowner or worked on the estate in such roles as blacksmith or farrier (horseshoer).

This view of medieval childhood was shaped by Philippe Aries, whose influential book *Centuries of Childhood* is considered a classic of historical scholarship. Aries argued that most young people were apprenticed, became agricultural or factory workers, and generally entered adult society at a very early age.[27] According to Aries, high infant mortality rates kept parents emotionally detached from their children. Paintings of the time depict children as mini-adults who were sent off to work as soon as they were capable. Western culture did not have a sense of childhood as a distinct period of life until the very late nineteenth and early twentieth centuries.

Though Aries's view that children in the Middle Ages were treated as "miniature adults" has become the standard view, in a recent book, historian Nicholas Orme puts forth evidence that medieval children may have been valued by their parents and did experience a prolonged period of childhood. In his *Medieval Children*, Orme finds that the medieval mother began to care for her children even before their delivery. Royal ladies borrowed relics of the Virgin Mary from the church to protect their unborn children, while poorer women used jasper stones or drawings of the cross, which were placed across their stomachs to ensure a healthy and uneventful birth. Parents associated their children's birthdays with a saint's feast day. Medieval children devised songs, rhymes, and games. Some simple games made use of cherry pits or hazelnuts, but children also had toys, which included dolls and even mechanical toys made for royalty.[28]

Children of the Nobility Though their lives were quite different, children of the affluent, landholding classes also assumed adult roles at an early age. Girls born into aristocratic families were educated at home and married in their early teens. A few were taught to read, write, and do sufficient mathematics to handle household accounts in addition to typical female duties such as supervising servants and ensuring the food supply of the manor.

At age 7 or 8, boys born to landholding families were either sent to a monastery or cathedral school to be trained for lives in the church or selected to be a member of the warrior class and sent to serve a term as a squire—an apprentice and assistant to an experienced knight. At age 21, young men of the noble classes completed their term as squire, received their own knighthood, and returned home to live with their parents. Many remained single because it was widely believed there should only be one married couple residing in a manor or castle. To pass the time and maintain their fighting edge, many entered the tournament circuit, engaging in melees and jousts to win fame and fortune. Upon the death of their fathers, young nobles assumed their inherited titles, married, and began their own families.

The customs and practices of the time helped shape the lives of children and, in some instances, greatly amplified their hardships and suffering. **Primogeniture** required that the oldest surviving male child inherit family lands and titles. He could then distribute them as he saw fit to younger siblings. There was no absolute requirement, however, that portions of the estate be distributed equally; many youths who received no lands were forced to enter religious orders, become soldiers, or seek wealthy patrons. Primogeniture often caused intense family rivalry that led to blood feuds and tragedy.

primogeniture
During the Middle Ages, the right of firstborn sons to inherit lands and titles, leaving their brothers the option of a military or religious career.

Dower The *dower system* mandated that a woman's family bestow money, land, or other wealth (called a *dowry*) on a potential husband or his family in exchange for his marriage to her. In return, the young woman received a promise of financial assistance, called a *jointure*, from the groom's family. Jointure provided a lifetime income if a wife outlived her mate. The dower system had a significant impact on the role of women in medieval society and consequently on the role of children. Within this system, a father or male guardian had the final say in his daughter's choice of marital partner as he could threaten to withhold her dowry. Some women were denied access to marriage simply because of their position in the family.

A father with many daughters and few sons might find himself financially unable to obtain suitable marriages for them. Consequently, the youngest girls in many families were forced either to enter convents or stay at home, with few prospects for marriage and family.

The dower system had far-reaching effects on the position of women in society, forcing them into the role of second-class citizens dependent upon their fathers, brothers, and guardians. It established a pattern in which females who did not conform to what males considered to be acceptable standards of feminine behavior could receive harsh sanctions; it established a sexual double standard that in part still exists today.

Childrearing The harshness of medieval life influenced childrearing practices. For instance, newborns were almost immediately handed over to *wet nurses*, who fed and cared for them during the first two years of their life. These women often lived away from the family so that parents had little contact with their children. Even the wealthiest families employed wet nurses, because it was considered demeaning for a noblewoman to nurse. Wrapping a newborn entirely in bandages, or **swaddling**, was a common practice. The bandages prevented any movement and enabled the wet nurse to manage the child easily. This practice was thought to protect the child, but it most likely contributed to high infant mortality rates because the child could not be kept clean.

> **swaddling**
> The practice during the Middle Ages of completely wrapping newborns in long bandage-like clothes in order to restrict their movements and make them easier to manage.

Discipline was severe during this period. Young children of all classes, both peasant and wealthy, were subjected to stringent rules and regulations. They were beaten severely for any sign of disobedience or ill temper. Many children of this time would be considered abused by today's standards. The relationship between parent and child was remote. Children were expected to enter the world of adults and to undertake responsibilities early in their lives, sharing in the work of siblings and parents. Children thought to be suffering from disease or retardation were often abandoned to churches, orphanages, or foundling homes.[29]

The roots of the impersonal relationship between parent and child can be traced to high mortality rates, which made sentimental and affectionate relationships risky. Parents were reluctant to invest emotional effort in relationships that could so easily be terminated by violence, accidents, or disease. Many believed that children must be toughened to ensure their survival in a hostile world. Close family relationships were viewed as detrimental to this process. Also, because the oldest male child was viewed as the essential player in a family's well-being, younger male and female siblings were considered economic and social liabilities.

Development of Concern for Children

Throughout the seventeenth and eighteenth centuries, a number of developments in England heralded the march toward the recognition of children's rights. Some of these events eventually affected the juvenile legal system as it emerged in America. They include (a) changes in family style and child care, (b) the English Poor Laws, (c) the apprenticeship movement, and (d) the role of the chancery court.[30]

Changes in Family Structure Family structure and the role of children began to change after the Middle Ages. Extended families, which were created over centuries, gave way to the nuclear family structure with which we are familiar today. It became more common for marriage to be based on love and mutual attraction between men and women rather than on parental consent and paternal dominance. The changing concept of marriage—from an economic arrangement to an emotional commitment—also began to influence the way children were treated within the family structure. Though parents still rigidly disciplined their children, they formed closer parental ties and developed greater concern for their offspring's well-being.

To provide more control over children, grammar and boarding schools were established and began to flourish in many large cities during this time.[31] Children studied grammar, Latin, law, and logic, often beginning at a young age. Teachers in these institutions regularly ruled by fear, and flogging was their main method of discipline. Students were beaten for academic mistakes as well as moral lapses. Such brutal treatment fell on both the rich and the poor throughout all levels of educational life, including universities. This treatment abated in Europe with the rise of the Enlightenment, but it remained in full force in Great Britain until late in the nineteenth century. Although this brutal approach to children may be difficult to understand now, the child in that society was a second-class citizen.

Toward the close of the eighteenth century, the work of such philosophers as Voltaire, Rousseau, and Locke launched a new age for childhood and the family.[32] Their vision produced a period known as the Enlightenment, which stressed a humanistic view of life, freedom, family, reason, and law. The ideal person was sympathetic to others and receptive to new ideas. These new beliefs influenced both the structure and lifestyle of the family. The father's authority was tempered, discipline in the home became more relaxed, and the expression of love and affection became more commonplace among family members. Upper- and middle-class families began to devote attention to childrearing, and the status of children was advanced.

As a result of these changes, in the nineteenth century children began to emerge as a readily distinguishable group with independent needs and interests. Parents often took greater interest in their upbringing. In addition, serious questions arose over the treatment of children in school. Public outcries led to a decrease in excessive physical discipline. Restrictions were placed on the use of the whip, and in some schools, the imposition of academic assignments or the loss of privileges replaced corporal punishment. Despite such reforms, many children still led harsh lives. Girls were still undereducated, punishment was still primarily physical, and schools continued to mistreat children.

Poor Laws Government action to care for needy children can be traced to the Poor Laws of Britain. As early as 1535, England passed statutes allowing for the appointment of overseers to place destitute or neglected children as servants in the homes of the affluent.[33] The Poor Laws forced children to serve during their minority in the care of families who trained them in agricultural, trade, or domestic services. The Elizabethan Poor Laws of 1601 were a model for dealing with poor children for more than 200 years. These laws created a system of church wardens and overseers who, with the consent of justices of the peace, identified vagrant, delinquent, and neglected children and took measures to put them to work. Often this meant placing them in poorhouses or workhouses, or apprenticing them to masters.

The Apprenticeship Movement Under the apprenticeship system, children were placed in the care of adults who trained them to discharge various duties and obtain skills. Voluntary apprentices were bound out by parents or guardians who wished to secure training for their children. Involuntary apprentices were compelled by the authorities to serve until they were 21 or older. The master-apprentice relationship was similar to the parent-child relationship in that the master had complete responsibility for and authority over the apprentice. If an apprentice was unruly, a complaint could be made and the apprentice could be punished. Incarcerated apprentices were often placed in rooms or workshops apart from other prisoners and were generally treated differently from those charged with a criminal offense. Even at this early stage, the conviction was growing that the criminal law and its enforcement should be applied differently to children.

Chancery Court After the fifteenth century, a system of chancery courts became a significant arm of the British legal system. They were originally established as "courts of equity" to handle matters falling outside traditional legal actions. These early courts were based on the traditional English system in which a chancellor acted as the "king's conscience" and had the ability to modify the application of legal rules and provide relief considering the circumstances of individual cases. The courts were not concerned with technical legal issues; rather, they focused on rendering decisions or orders that were fair or equitable. With respect to children, the chancery courts dealt with issues of guardianship of children who were orphaned, their property and inheritance rights, and the appointment of guardians to protect them until they reached the age of majority and could care for themselves. For example, if a wealthy father died prior to his heir's majority, or if there were some dispute as to the identity (or legitimacy) of his heir, the crown might ask the case to be decided by the chancery court in an effort to ensure that inheritance rights were protected (and taxes collected!).

Chancery court decision making rested on the proposition that children and other incompetents were under the protective control of the king; thus, the Latin phrase *parens patriae* was used, referring to the role of the king as the father of his country. The concept was first used by English kings to establish their right to intervene in the lives of the children of their vassals—children whose position and property were of direct concern to the monarch.[34] The concept of *parens patriae* became the theoretical basis for the protective jurisdiction of the chancery courts acting as part of the crown's power. As time passed, the monarchy used *parens patriae* more and more to justify its intervention in the lives of families and children by its interest in their general welfare.[35]

The chancery courts dealt with the property and custody problems of the wealthier classes. They did not have jurisdiction over children charged with criminal conduct. Juveniles who violated the law were handled within the framework of the regular criminal court system. Nonetheless, the concept of *parens patriae* grew to refer primarily to the responsibility of the courts and the state to act in the best interests of the child.

Childhood in America

While England was using its chancery courts and Poor Laws to care for children in need, the American colonies were developing similar concepts. The colonies were a haven for poor and unfortunate people looking for religious and economic opportunities denied them in England and Europe. Along with early settlers, many children came not as citizens but as indentured servants, apprentices, or agricultural workers. They were recruited from the various English workhouses, orphanages, prisons, and asylums that housed vagrant and delinquent youths during the sixteenth and seventeenth centuries.[36]

At the same time, the colonies themselves produced illegitimate, neglected, abandoned, and delinquent children. The colonies' initial response to caring for such unfortunate children was to adopt court and Poor Laws systems similar to those in England. Involuntary apprenticeship, indenture, and binding out of children became integral parts of colonization in America. For example, Poor Law legislation requiring poor and dependent children to serve apprenticeships was passed in Virginia in 1646 and in Massachusetts and Connecticut in 1673.[37]

The master in colonial America acted as a surrogate parent, and in certain instances, apprentices would actually become part of the nuclear family structure. If they disobeyed their masters, apprentices were punished by local tribunals. If masters abused apprentices, courts would make them pay damages, return the children to the parents, or find new guardians. Maryland and Virginia developed an orphan's court that supervised the treatment of youths placed with guardians and ensured that they were not mistreated or taken advantage of by their masters. These courts did not supervise children living with their natural parents, leaving intact the parents' right to care for their children.[38]

chancery courts
Court proceedings created in fifteenth-century England to oversee the lives of highborn minors who were orphaned or otherwise could not care for themselves.

parens patriae
Power of the state to act on behalf of the child and provide care and protection equivalent to that of a parent.

Under the apprenticeship system, children were placed in the care of adults who trained them to discharge various duties and obtain different skills. The young boy shown in this illustration is serving as an apprentice to a blacksmith. The system was brought over to colonial America. Poor Law legislation requiring poor and dependent children to serve apprenticeships was passed in Virginia in 1646 and in Massachusetts and Connecticut in 1673.

By the beginning of the nineteenth century, as the agrarian economy began to be replaced by industry, the apprenticeship system gave way to the factory system. Yet the problems of how to deal effectively with growing numbers of dependent youths increased. Early American settlers believed that hard work, strict discipline, and rigorous education were the only reliable means to salvation. A child's life was marked by work alongside parents, some schooling, prayer, more work, and further study. Work in the factories, however, often taxed young laborers by placing demands on them that they were too young to endure. To alleviate a rapidly developing problem, the Factory Act of the early nineteenth century limited the hours children were permitted to work and the age at which they could begin to work. It also prescribed a minimum amount of schooling to be provided by factory owners.[39] This and related statutes were often violated, and conditions of work and school remained troublesome issues well into the twentieth century. Nevertheless, the statutes were a step in the direction of reform.

Controlling Children In America, as in England, moral discipline was rigidly enforced. "Stubborn child" laws were passed that required children to obey their parents.[40] It was not uncommon in the colonies for children who were disobedient or disrespectful to their families to be whipped or otherwise physically chastised. Children were often required to attend public whippings and executions because these events were thought to be important forms of moral instruction. Parents often referred their children to published works and writings on behavior and discipline and expected them to follow their precepts carefully. Because community and church leaders frowned on harsh punishments, child protection laws were passed as early as 1639 (in New Haven, Connecticut). Nonetheless, these laws were generally symbolic and rarely enforced. They expressed the community's commitment to God to oppose sin; offenders who abused their children usually received lenient sentences.[41]

While most colonies adopted a protectionist stance, few cases of child abuse were actually brought before the courts. There are several explanations for this neglect. The absence of child abuse cases may reflect the nature of life in what were extremely religious households. Children were productive laborers and respected as such by their parents. In addition, large families provided many siblings and kinfolk who could care for children and relieve stress-producing burdens on parents.[42] Another view is that though many children were harshly punished in Early American families, the acceptable limits of discipline were so high that few parents were charged with assault. Any punishment that fell short of maiming or permanently harming a child was considered within the sphere of parental rights.[43]

THE CONCEPT OF DELINQUENCY

Considering the rough treatment handed out to children who misbehaved at home or at school, it should come as no surprise that children who actually broke the law and committed serious criminal acts were dealt with harshly. Before the twentieth century, little distinction was made between adult and juvenile offenders. Although judges considered the age of an offender when deciding punishments, both adults and children were often eligible for the same forms of punishment—prison, corporal punishment, and even the death penalty. In fact, children were treated with extreme cruelty at home, at school, and by the law.[44]

Over the years, this treatment changed, as society became sensitive to the special needs of children. Beginning in the mid-nineteenth century, as immigrant youth poured into America, there was official recognition that children formed a separate group with its own separate needs. Around the nation, in cities such as New York, Boston, and Chicago, groups known as **child savers** were being formed to assist children in need. They created community programs to serve needy children, and lobbied for a separate legal status for children, which ultimately led to the development of a formal juvenile justice system. The child saving movement will be discussed more fully in Chapter 12.

child savers
Nineteenth-century reformers who developed programs for troubled youth and influenced legislation creating the juvenile justice system; today some critics view them as being more concerned with control of the poor than with their welfare.

Delinquency and *Parens Patriae*

The current treatment of juvenile delinquents is a by-product of this developing national consciousness. The designation *delinquent* became popular at the onset of the twentieth century when the first separate juvenile courts were instituted. The child savers believed that treating minors and adults equivalently violated the humanitarian ideals of American society. Consequently, the newly emerging juvenile justice system operated under the *parens patriae* philosophy. Minors who engaged in illegal behavior were viewed as victims of improper care, custody, and treatment at home. Dishonest behavior was a sign that the state should step in and take control of the youths before they committed more serious crimes. The state, through its juvenile authorities, should act in the **best interests of the child**. This means that children should not be punished for their misdeeds but instead should be given the care and custody necessary to remedy and control wayward behavior. It makes no sense to find children guilty of specific crimes, such as burglary or petty larceny, because that stigmatizes them and labels them as thieves or burglars. Instead, the catchall term *juvenile delinquency* should be used, as it indicates that the child needs the care, custody, and treatment of the state.

best interests of the child
A philosophical viewpoint that encourages the state to take control of wayward children and provide care, custody, and treatment to remedy delinquent behavior.

The Legal Status of Delinquency

Though the child savers fought hard for a separate legal status of "juvenile delinquent" early in the twentieth century, the concept that children could be treated differently before the law can actually be traced back much farther to its roots in the British legal tradition. Early English jurisprudence held that children under the age of 7 were legally incapable of committing crimes. Children between the ages of 7 and 14 were responsible for their actions, but their age might be used to excuse or lighten their punishment. Our legal system still recognizes that many young people are incapable of making mature judgments and that responsibility for their acts should be limited. Children can intentionally steal cars and know full well that the act is illegal, but they may be incapable of fully understanding the consequences of their behavior and the harm it may cause. Therefore, the law does not punish a youth as it would an adult, and it sees youthful misconduct as evidence of unreasoned or impaired judgment.

Today, the legal status of "juvenile delinquent" refers to a minor child who has been found to have violated the penal code. Most states define "minor child" as an individual who falls under a statutory age limit, most commonly 17 or 18 years of age (see Exhibit 1.1). Because of their minority status, juveniles are usually kept separate

EXHIBIT 1.1

Oldest Age for Original Juvenile Court Jurisdiction in Delinquency Matters

Age 15	Connecticut, New York, North Carolina
Age 16	Georgia, Illinois, Louisiana, Massachusetts, Michigan, Missouri, New Hampshire, South Carolina, Texas, Wisconsin
Age 17	Alabama, Alaska, Arizona, Arkansas, California, Colorado, Delaware, District of Columbia, Florida, Hawaii, Idaho, Indiana, Iowa, Kansas, Kentucky, Maine, Maryland, Minnesota, Mississippi, Montana, Nebraska, Nevada, New Jersey, New Mexico, North Dakota, Ohio, Oklahoma, Oregon, Pennsylvania, Rhode Island, South Dakota, Tennessee, Utah, Vermont, Virginia, Washington, West Virginia, Wyoming

SOURCE: Howard Snyder and Melissa Sickmund, *Juvenile Offenders and Victims, 2006* (Pittsburgh: National Center for Juvenile Justice, 2006).

from adults and receive different consideration and treatment under the law. For example, most large police departments employ officers whose sole responsibility is youth crime and delinquency. Every state has some form of separate juvenile court with its own judges, probation department, and other facilities. Terminology is also different: Adults are tried in court; children are adjudicated. Adults can be punished; children are treated. If treatment is mandated, children can be sent to secure detention facilities; they cannot normally be committed to adult prisons.

Children also have their own unique legal status. Minors apprehended for a criminal act are usually charged with being a juvenile delinquent regardless of the crime they commit. These charges are usually confidential, trial records are kept secret, and the name, behavior, and background of delinquent offenders are sealed. Eliminating specific crime categories and maintaining secrecy are efforts to shield children from the stigma of a criminal conviction and to prevent youthful misdeeds from becoming a lifelong burden.

Legal Responsibility of Youth

In our society, the actions of adults are controlled by two types of law: criminal and civil. Criminal laws prohibit activities that are injurious to the well-being of society and threaten the social order, such as drug use, theft, and rape; they are legal actions brought by state authorities against private citizens. Civil laws, on the other hand, control interpersonal or private activities and are usually initiated by individual citizens. The ownership and transfer of property, contractual relationships, and personal conflicts (torts) are the subject of the civil law. Also covered under the civil law are provisions for the care and custody of those people who cannot care for themselves—the mentally ill, incompetent, or infirm.

Today, the juvenile delinquency concept occupies a legal status falling somewhere between criminal and civil law. Under *parens patriae*, delinquent acts are not considered criminal violations nor are delinquents considered criminals. Children cannot be found guilty of a crime and punished like adult criminals. The legal action against them is considered more similar (though not identical) to a civil action that determines their "need for treatment." This legal theory recognizes that children who violate the law are in need of the same care and treatment as law-abiding citizens who cannot care for themselves and require state intervention into their lives.

Delinquent behavior is sanctioned less heavily than criminality because the law considers juveniles as being less responsible for their behavior than adults. As a class, adolescents are believed to (a) have a stronger preference for risk and novelty, (b) assess the potentially negative consequences of risky conduct less unfavorably than adults, (c) have a tendency to be impulsive and more concerned with short-term than long-term consequences, (d) have a different appreciation of time and self-control, and (e) be more susceptible to peer pressure.[45] Although many adolescents may be more responsible and calculating than adults, under normal circumstances the law is willing to recognize age as a barrier to having full responsibility over one's actions. The limited moral reasoning ability of very young offenders is taken into consideration when assessing their legal culpability. In one 2007 case, a California appellate court made it clear for the first time that some juvenile defendants may simply be too young to stand trial. The case involved an 11-year-old defendant prosecuted for stealing candy bars. The court ruled that the child was so immature that he could not understand the legal proceedings or assist in his own defense. In doing so, the justices overruled prior case law that held that children must have either a mental disorder or a developmental disability to be deemed incompetent to stand trial. In its ruling, the court said:

> As a matter of law and logic, an adult's incompetence to stand trial must arise from a mental disorder or developmental disability that limits his or her ability to understand the nature of the proceedings and to assist counsel . . . The same may not be said of a young child whose developmental immaturity may result in trial incompetence despite the absence of any underlying mental or developmental abnormality.[46]

Although youths share a lesser degree of legal responsibility than adults, they are subject to arrest, trial, and incarceration. Their legal predicament has prompted the courts to grant them many of the same legal protections granted to adults accused of criminal offenses. These legal protections include the right to consult an attorney, to be free from self-incrimination, and to be protected from illegal searches and seizures. In addition, state legislatures are toughening legal codes and making them more punitive in an effort to "get tough" on dangerous youth.

Although appreciation of the criminal nature of the delinquency concept has helped increase the legal rights of minors, it has also allowed state authorities to declare that some offenders are "beyond control" and cannot be treated as children. This recognition has prompted the policy of waiver, or transferring legal jurisdiction over the most serious and experienced juvenile offenders to the adult court for criminal prosecution. To the dismay of reformers, waived youth may find themselves serving time in adult prisons.[47] It is possible that as many as 200,000 youth have their cases processed in adult criminal court each year as a result of prosecutorial or judicial waiver, statutory exclusion for certain offense categories, or because they reside in states with a lower age of criminal jurisdiction (age 16 or 17). On any given day, an estimated 7,000 youth under the age of 18 are inmates in adult jails; of these, 90 percent are being held "as adults."[48]

So though the *parens patriae* concept is still applied to children whose law violations are not considered serious, the more serious juvenile offenders can be declared "legal adults" and placed outside the jurisdiction of the juvenile court.

waiver (also known as bindover or removal)
Transferring legal jurisdiction over the most serious and experienced juvenile offenders to the adult court for criminal prosecution.

STATUS OFFENDERS

status offense
Conduct that is illegal only because the child is under age.

A child also becomes subject to state authority for committing status offenses—actions that would not be considered illegal if perpetrated by an adult; such conduct is illegal only because the child is under age. For example, more than 40 states now have some form of law prohibiting minors from purchasing, using, or possessing tobacco products. These statutes impose a variety of sanctions, including a monetary fine, suspension from school, and denial of a driver's license. In Florida, repeat offenders may lose their license or be prohibited from obtaining one, and in some communities teens must appear before the judge with their parent or guardian, view an antismoking video, and listen to a lecture from a throat cancer survivor.[49] Exhibit 1.2 describes some typical status offense statutes.

Figure 1.5 illustrates some typical status offenses. It is extremely difficult to evaluate the annual number of status offenses, as most cases escape police detection and those that do not are more often than not handled informally. Yet, according to data compiled by the Federal Bureau of Investigation, more than 250,000 juveniles are

EXHIBIT **1.2**

Status Offense Laws: Maryland, Louisiana, and Wisconsin

Maryland

"Child" means an individual under the age of 18 years. "Child in need of supervision" is a child who requires guidance, treatment, or rehabilitation and:

1. Is required by law to attend school and is habitually truant;
2. Is habitually disobedient, ungovernable, and beyond the control of the person having custody of him;
3. Deports himself so as to injure or endanger himself or others; or
4. Has committed an offense applicable only to children.

Louisiana

"Child in need of supervision" means a child who needs care or rehabilitation because:

1. Being subject to compulsory school attendance, he is habitually truant from school or willfully violates the rules of the school;
2. He habitually disobeys the reasonable and lawful demands of his parents, and is ungovernable and beyond their control;
3. He absents himself from his home or usual place of abode without the consent of his parent;
4. He purposefully, intentionally, and willfully deceives, or misrepresents the true facts to any person holding a retail dealer's permit, or his agent, associate, employee or representative, for the purposes of buying or receiving alcoholic beverages or beer, or visiting or loitering in or about any place where such beverages are the principal commodities sold or handled;
5. His occupation, conduct, environment, or associations are injurious to his welfare; or
6. He has committed an offense applicable only to children.

Wisconsin

The court has exclusive original jurisdiction over a child alleged to be in need of protection or services which can be ordered by the court, and:

1. Who is without a parent or guardian;
2. Who has been abandoned;
3. Who has been the victim of sexual or physical abuse including injury which is self-inflicted or inflicted by another by other than accidental means;
4. Whose parent or guardian signs the petition requesting jurisdiction and states that he or she is unable to care for, control, or provide necessary special care or special treatment for the child;
5. Who has been placed for care or adoption in violation of law;
6. Who is habitually truant from school, after evidence is provided by the school attendance officer that the activities under s. 118.16(5) have been completed;
7. Who is habitually truant from home and either the child or a parent, guardian, or a relative in whose home the child resides signs the petition requesting jurisdiction and attests in court that reconciliation efforts have been attempted and have failed;
8. Who is receiving inadequate care during the period of time a parent is missing, incarcerated, hospitalized, or institutionalized;
9. Who is at least age 12, signs the petition requesting jurisdiction, and attests in court that he or she is in need of special care and treatment which the parent, guardian, or legal custodian is unwilling to provide;
10. Whose parent, guardian, or legal custodian neglects, refuses, or is unable for reasons other than poverty to provide necessary care, food, clothing, medical or dental care, or shelter so as to seriously endanger the physical health of the child;
11. Who is suffering emotional damage for which the parent or guardian is unwilling to provide treatment, which is evidenced by one or more of the following characteristics, exhibited to a severe degree: anxiety, depression, withdrawal, or outward aggressive behavior;
12. Who, being under 12 years of age, has committed a delinquent act as defined in s. 48.12;
13. Who has not been immunized as required by s. 140.05(16) and not exempted under s. 140.05(16)(c); or
14. Who has been determined, under s. 48.30(5)(c), to be not responsible for a delinquent act by reason of mental disease or defect.

SOURCES: MD Courts and Judicial Proceedings Code Ann. § 3-8A-01 (2002), LA Code Juv. Proc. Ann. art. 13 § 12 (West 1979, amended 1987), and WI Stat. Ann. § 48.13 (West 1979, amended 1987).

arrested each year for such status-type offenses as running away from home, breaking curfew, and violating liquor laws.[50]

The History of Status Offenses

A historical basis exists for status offense statutes. It was common practice early in the nation's history to place disobedient or runaway youths in orphan asylums, residential homes, or houses of refuge.[51] In 1646, the Massachusetts Stubborn Child Law was enacted, which provided that "If any man have a stubborne and rebellious sonne of sufficient years and understanding, which will not obey the voice of his father or the voice of his mother, and that when they have chastened him will not harken unto them" they could bring him before the court and testify that he would not obey. If the magistrate then found the child to be unrepentant and incapable of control, such a child could be put to death.[52]

When the first juvenile courts were established in Illinois, the Chicago Bar Association described part of their purpose as follows:

> The whole trend and spirit of the [1899 Juvenile Court Act] is that the State, acting through the Juvenile Court, exercises that tender solicitude and care over its neglected, dependent wards that a wise and loving parent would exercise with reference to his own children under similar circumstances.[53]

FIGURE 1.5
Status Offenses

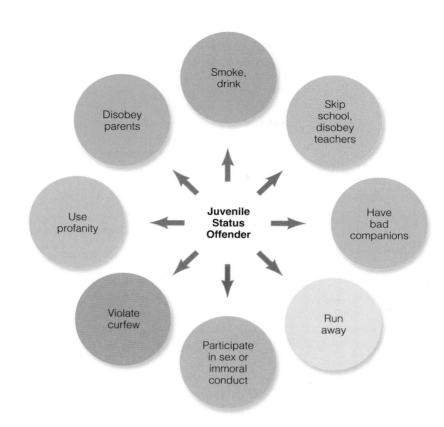

wayward minors
Early legal designation of youths who violate the law because of their minority status; now referred to as status offenders.

Status offenses include running away, being disobedient, and engaging in behavior forbidden to minors, such as drinking. This cheerleader from Danvers High School in Massachusetts is shown at a court hearing after she was arrested after allegedly showing up drunk for a football playoff game with archrival Walpole High.

State control over a child's noncriminal behavior is believed to support and extend the *parens patriae* philosophy because it is assumed to be in the best interests of the child. Typically, status offenders are petitioned to the juvenile court when it is determined that their parents are unable or unwilling to care for or control them and that the offender's behavior is self-destructive or harmful to society. Young teenage girls are much more likely to engage in precocious sex while under the influence of alcohol if they are involved with older teens. Parents may petition their underage daughter to juvenile court if they feel their sexual behavior is getting out of control and they are powerless to stop its occurrence.[54] The case then falls within the jurisdiction of state legal authorities, and failure to heed a judicial command might result in detention in the juvenile correctional system.

At first, juvenile codes referred to status offenders as **wayward minors**, sometimes failing to distinguish them in any significant way from juvenile delinquents. Both classes of children could be detained in the same detention centers and placed in the same youth correctional facilities. A trend begun in the 1960s has resulted in the creation of separate status offense categories—children, minors, persons, youths, or juveniles in need of supervision (CHINS, MINS, PINS, YINS, or JINS)—which vary from state to state. The purpose of creating separate status offender categories was to shield noncriminal youths from the stigma attached to the label "juvenile delinquent" and to signify that they were troubled youths who had special needs and problems.

Most states now have separate categories for juvenile conduct that would not be considered criminal if committed by an adult; these sometimes pertain to neglected or dependent children as well. Of these, more than 10 states use the term "child in need of supervision," while the remainder use such terms as "unruly child," "incorrigible child," and "minor in need of supervision."[55]

Even where there are separate legal categories for delinquents and status offenders, the distinction between them has become blurred. Some noncriminal conduct may be included in the definition of delinquency, and some less serious criminal offenses occasionally may be included within the status offender definition.[56]

In some states, the juvenile court judge is granted discretion to substitute a status offense for a delinquency charge.[57] Replacing a juvenile delinquency charge with a status offense charge can be used as a bargaining chip to encourage youths to admit to the charges against them in return for a promise of being treated as a (less stigmatized) status offender receiving less punitive treatment. Concept Summary 1.1 summarizes the differences among delinquents, adult criminals, and status offenders.

Concept Summary 1.1

Treatment Differences among Juvenile Delinquents, Status Offenders, and Adults

	Juvenile Delinquent	Status Offender	Adult
Act	Delinquent	Behavior forbidden to minors	Criminal
Enforcement	Police	Police	Police
Detention	Secure detention	Nonsecure shelter care	Jail
Adjudication	Juvenile court	Juvenile court	Criminal court
Correctional Alternative	State training school	Community treatment facility	Prison

The Status Offender in the Juvenile Justice System

Separate status offense categories may avoid some of the stigma associated with the delinquency label, but they can have relatively little practical effect on the child's treatment. Youths in either category can be picked up by the police and brought to a police station. They can be petitioned to the same juvenile court, where they have a hearing before the same judge and come under the supervision of the probation department, the court clinic, and the treatment staff. At a hearing, status offenders may see little difference between the treatment they receive and the treatment of the delinquent offenders sitting across the room. Although status offenders are usually not detained or incarcerated with delinquents, they can be transferred to secure facilities if they are repeatedly unruly and considered uncontrollable. Some states are more likely to prosecute status offenses formally in the juvenile court, while others handle most cases informally. Within individual states, some courts make a habit of prosecuting status offenders, and others will divert most cases to treatment institutions.[58]

Efforts have been ongoing to reduce the penalties and stigma borne by status offenders and to help kids avoid becoming status offenders. The Case Profile entitled "Aaliyah's Story" shows how one young status offender was able to overcome her problems.

Office of Juvenile Justice and Delinquency Prevention (OJJDP)
Branch of the U.S. Justice Department charged with shaping national juvenile justice policy through disbursement of federal aid and research funds.

The federal government's Office of Juvenile Justice and Delinquency Prevention (OJJDP), an agency created to identify the needs of youths and fund policy initiatives in the juvenile justice system, has made it a top priority to encourage the removal of status offenders from secure lockups, detention centers, and post-disposition treatment facilities that also house delinquent offenders. States in violation of the initiative are ineligible to receive part of the millions in direct grants for local juvenile justice annually awarded by the federal government.[59] This initiative has been responsible for significantly lowering the number of status offenders kept in secure confinement.

Despite this mandate, juvenile court judges in many states can still detain status offenders in secure lockups if the youths are found in contempt of court. The act that created the OJJDP was amended in 1987 to allow status offenders to be detained and incarcerated for violations of valid court orders.[60] Children have been detained for misbehaving in court or not dressing appropriately for their court appearance.[61] There is also some question whether the valid court order exception disproportionately affects girls, who are much more likely to be arrested for status offenses than boys and receive

Aaliyah's Story

AALIYAH PARKER RAN AWAY FROM HOME AT THE AGE OF 17. SHE HAD STRUGGLED WITH FAMILY ISSUES AND FELT SHE COULD NO LONGER LIVE WITH HER MOTHER, stepfather, and younger siblings in their California home. Arriving in Colorado with no family support, no money, and no place to live, she joined other runaway adolescents, homeless on the streets. Aaliyah was using drugs and was eventually arrested and detained at a juvenile detention center for possession of methamphetamines and providing false information to a police officer. Five feet seven inches tall and weighing only 95 pounds, Aaliyah was an addict. Her health and quality of life were suffering greatly.

When Aaliyah entered the juvenile justice system she was a few months from turning 18. Due to issues of jurisdiction, budget concerns, and Aaliyah's age, system administrators encouraged the caseworker assigned to Aaliyah to make arrangements for her to return to her family in California. After interviewing her at length about her situation and need for treatment, the caseworker could see that Aaliyah had a strong desire to get her life back on track. She needed assistance, but the cost of her treatment would be more than $3,000 per month, and the county agency's budget was already stretched. Despite objections from administrators, the caseworker remained a strong advocate for Aaliyah, convincing them of the harsh reality she would face back at home without first receiving drug treatment. The caseworker's advocacy on her behalf, combined with her own motivation to get her life together, compelled the department to agree to pay for Aaliyah's treatment program, but only until she turned 18. She was transported from the juvenile detention center to a 90-day drug and alcohol treatment program where she was able to detoxify her body and engage in intensive counseling. The program also provided family therapy through phone counseling for Aaliyah's mother, allowing the family to reconnect. Despite this renewed contact, returning home was not an option for Aaliyah.

Nearing the end of the 90-day program, Aaliyah was again faced with being homeless, but she was determined not to return to the streets. She needed an environment where she could make new friends who did not use, and be supported in her sobriety. Due to her age, the county department of human services had to close the case and could no longer assist her with housing or an aftercare program. The caseworker provided Aaliyah with some places to call, but she would have to be her own advocate.

Aaliyah contacted a group home run by a local church that takes runaway adolescents through county placements and provides a variety of services for clients and their families. In Aaliyah's case, no funding was available, so she contacted the therapist at the group home and explained her situation. Initially, they indicated that they would not be able to assist her, but Aaliyah was persistent and determined to find a quality living environment for herself. She continued to contact professionals at the group home to plead her case and was eventually successful. Aaliyah entered the group home, was able to get her high school diploma, and eventually enrolled in an independent living program that assisted her in finding a job and getting her own apartment. Aaliyah has remained in contact with her juvenile caseworker. Though she has struggled with her sobriety on occasion, she has been able to refrain from using methamphetamines and is now at a healthy weight. Her caseworker continues to encourage Aaliyah and has been an ongoing source of support, despite the fact that the client file was closed several years ago. Aaliyah's success can be credited to the initial advocacy of her caseworker, the effective interventions, and the strong determination demonstrated by this young woman. ■

CRITICAL THINKING

1. Housing is a major issue for many teens aging out of the justice system. Often, children placed in alternative care settings, such as foster homes or residential treatment centers, are not prepared to live on their own when they turn 18 or are released from juvenile custody. How can this issue be addressed?

(continued)

2. Many juvenile delinquents commit crimes while under the influence of alcohol or drugs or because they are addicted and need to support their habit. If this is the case, should these juveniles be court-ordered into a treatment program? Why or why not? What can be done to prevent alcohol and drug abuse in the teen population?

3. Teens close to the age of 18, like Aaliyah, may be too old for the juvenile justice system, but too young for the adult system. What should be done with juveniles who are close to 18 when they receive a delinquency charge? Should something be done to bridge the gap between the juvenile justice system and the adult criminal justice system?

4. What should happen to teens who run away from home? This is considered a status offense, but many communities do not charge runaways or require them to be involved in the juvenile justice system. Do you agree with this? Should something more be done and, if so, what?

To learn more about the efforts to remove status offenders from secure lockups, go to Gwen A. Holden and Robert A. Kapler, "**Deinstitutionalizing Status Offenders: A Record of Progress,**" via academic.cengage.com/criminaljustice/siegel.

more severe punishment than boys. Because girls are more likely to be status offenders, criminalization of status offenses through the "violation of court order" exception may contribute to the increasing numbers of girls in the juvenile justice system.[62]

Several studies have found that as a result of deinstitutionalization, children who can no longer be detained are being recycled or relabeled as delinquent offenders so they can be housed in secure facilities. Even more troubling is the charge that some minors no longer subject to detention as status offenders are being committed involuntarily and inappropriately to in-patient drug treatment facilities and psychiatric hospitals.[63]

Change in the treatment of status offenders reflects the current attitude toward children who violate the law. On the one hand, there appears to be a national movement to severely sanction youths who commit serious, violent offenses. On the other hand, a great effort has been made to remove nonserious cases, such as those involving status offenders, from the official agencies of justice and place these youths in informal, community-based treatment programs.

Reforming Status Offense Laws

For the past two decades, national commissions have called for reform of status offense laws. More than 20 years ago, the National Council on Crime and Delinquency, an influential privately funded think tank, recommended removing status offenders from the juvenile court.[64] In 1976, the federal government's National Advisory Commission on Criminal Justice Standards and Goals, a task force created to develop a national crime policy, opted for the nonjudicial treatment of status offenders: "The only conduct that should warrant family court intervention is conduct that is clearly self-destructive or otherwise harmful to the child." To meet this standard, the commission suggested that the nation's juvenile courts confine themselves to controlling five status offenses: habitual truancy, repeated disregard for parental authority, repeated running away, repeated use of intoxicating beverages, and delinquent acts by youths under the age of 10.[65] The American Bar Association's National Juvenile Justice Standards Project, designed to promote significant improvements in the way children are treated by the police and the courts, called for the end of juvenile court jurisdiction over status offenders: "A juvenile's acts of misbehavior, ungovernability, or unruliness which do not violate the criminal law should not constitute a ground for asserting juvenile court jurisdiction over the juvenile committing them."[66] In 2006 the ABA issued this statement about reforming the juvenile status offender process:

> Many teens come before the courts because of behavior that would not otherwise subject them to judicial involvement if they were adults. Lawyers should examine how law, prosecutorial policy, and court practice address youth who are chronic runaways, persistent school truants, or continually out-of-control at home. They should also examine how these interventions differ between boys and girls, since there has been a significant increase in the number of girls entering the juvenile justice system. Special attention also needs to be given to the problem of and solutions to chronic truancy.[67]

Orange County's Family Keys Program

About five years ago, Orange County, located approximately one hour north of New York City, began a significant reform of its PINS (person in need of supervision) intake and diversion processes. Concerned about the projected impact of the state's increasing number of at-risk kids, Orange County wanted to increase its jurisdiction over status offenders to age 18. After much study, and with the legislature's backing, in 2003 the community-based Family Keys program was officially launched. Under the program, the county probation department receives inquiries from parents about PINS. If, after a brief screening, the intake officer finds sufficient allegations to support a PINS complaint, the officer refers the case to Family Keys rather than to probation intake. Depending on the severity of the case, Family Keys dispatches counselors to assess the family's situation 2 to 48 hours after receiving a referral. Based on the assessment, the agency develops an appropriate short-term intervention plan for the youth and family and provides links to community-based programs. Family Keys works with the family for up to three weeks to ensure that the family is engaged in the service plan.

The Family Keys intervention takes place in lieu of filing a PINS complaint, provides intensive, short-term crisis intervention to families, and diverts PINS cases away from the court system. When these short-term interventions do not suffice, cases are referred to an interagency team operated through the mental health department's Network program. Following a family conferencing model, the Network team performs an in-depth assessment and serves as the gateway to the county's most high-end services, such as multisystemic therapy or family functional therapy. Under Orange County's system, a PINS case is referred to court only as a last resort.

The early outcomes of the Family Keys program have been very promising. The time between a parent's first contact with probation and subsequent follow-up has decreased dramatically, from as long as six weeks under the previous system to as low as two hours through the Family Keys process. The number of PINS cases referred to court and the number of PINS placements also have been sharply reduced.

Critical Thinking

1. Can programs such as Family Keys help turn a troubled kid's life around or is there a danger that participation will label and stigmatize them as "at risk" and "troubled" children who should be avoided?

2. Should we spend scarce government funds on kids in trouble with the law or would such funding be better spent on educational programs for adolescents who are crime-free and who therefore have a chance at a promising future?

SOURCE: Tina Chiu and Sara Mogulescu, *Changing the Status Quo for Status Offenders: New York State's Efforts to Support Troubled Teens* (Vera Foundation, New York, 2004), www.vera.org/publication_pdf/253_496.pdf (accessed September 6, 2007).

Catie, 15, is seen at the Renfrew Center, a clinic for eating disorders in Coconut Creek, Florida. Catie started cutting herself after meals in the seventh grade. She has carved designs into her flesh, such as the Japanese symbol for pain. Kids like Catie may need the help of the juvenile justice system, yet they are not really delinquents or status offenders. A few states have attempted to eliminate status offense laws and treat these youths as neglected or dependent children, giving child protective services the primary responsibility for their care.

These calls for reform prompted a number of states to experiment with replacing juvenile court jurisdiction over most status offenders with community-based treatment programs. Some states, such as New York, now require that all alleged status offenders and their families be offered intervention and diversion services before status offense petitions may be filed. Only after intervention services have been offered and failed may the social service agency or juvenile justice agency designated to provide prevention services determine if it is appropriate to seek court involvement. New York has also increased the age limit for status offense jurisdiction from 16 to 18 so that thousands of more needy kids fall under the jurisdiction of the New York family court each year.[68] The Policy and Practice feature entitled "Orange County's Family Keys Program" shows how one county dealt with the influx of new cases.

Other states have amended their laws to eliminate vague terms and language. Instead of labeling a child who is "beyond control of school" as a status offender, the state is now required to show that a student has repeatedly violated "lawful regulations for the government of the school," with the petition describing the behaviors "and all intervention strategies attempted by the school."[69] A few states have tried to eliminate status offense laws and treat these youths as neglected or dependent children, giving child protective services the primary responsibility for their care. However, juvenile court judges strongly resist removal of

Increasing Social Control over Juveniles and Their Parents

Those in favor of retaining the status offense category point to society's responsibility to care for troubled youths. Others maintain that the status offense should remain a legal category so that juvenile courts can force a youth to receive treatment. Although it is recognized that a court appearance can produce a stigma, the taint may be less important than the need for treatment. Many state jurisdictions, prompted by concern over serious delinquency, have enacted laws that actually expand social control over juveniles.

CURFEW LAWS

From the 1880s through the 1920s, American cities created curfew laws designed to limit the presence of children on city streets after dark. Today, about two-thirds of large U.S. cities have curfew laws.

As a general rule, the courts have upheld the use of juvenile curfew laws as long as (a) the language of the statute shows a compelling government interest for use of the curfew and (b) the language of the curfew law is consistent with this narrowly defined interest. Curfew ordinances must also allow youth to be out during curfew hours under certain circumstances (for example, in the company of their parents, coming or going to work or school, and in the event of an emergency).

Evaluations of the benefits of curfews yield mixed results. Andra Bannister and her associates surveyed more than 400 police agencies and found that most had curfew ordinances in effect for several years. In the majority of cases, police felt that curfew was an effective tool to control vandalism, graffiti, nighttime burglary, and auto theft. Those jurisdictions that did not have curfew laws reported that their absence was a result of political objections rather than perceived ineffectiveness. In an important analysis of the effectiveness of curfews on gang crime, Eric Fritsch, Troy Caeti, and Robert Taylor found that passage of a curfew law in Dallas, coupled with police use of aggressive curfew and truancy enforcement, appeared to reduce violent gang crimes. Though gang crimes did increase somewhat in areas of the city with less aggressive policing, the *displacement effect* was not significant.

Although these findings are persuasive, other research efforts failed to find such dramatic effects. For example, one study conducted by Mike Males and Dan Macallair, which focused on curfew laws in California, found that youth curfews do not reduce youth crime and if anything may actually increase delinquent activities. For the entire state of California there was no category of crime (misdemeanors, violent crime, property crime, etc.) that significantly declined in association with youth curfews. In a comprehensive systematic review of the existing literature on curfews, criminologist Ken Adams found little evidence that juvenile crime and victimization were influenced in any way by the implementation of curfew laws.

These results indicate that juvenile curfews are not the panacea some people believe. It is possible that after curfews are implemented, victimization levels increase significantly during non-curfew hours, an indication that rather than suppressing delinquency, curfews merely shift the time of occurrence of the offenses.

PARENTAL RESPONSIBILITY LAWS

Since the early twentieth century, there have been laws aimed at disciplining parents for contributing to the delinquency of a

---

status jurisdiction. They believe that reducing their authority over children leads to limiting juvenile court jurisdiction to only the most hard-core juvenile offenders and interferes with their ability to help youths before they commit serious antisocial acts.[70] Their concerns are fueled by research that shows that many status offenders, especially runaways living on the street, have serious emotional problems and engage in self-destructive behaviors ranging from substance abuse to self-mutilation and suicide.[71]

Legislative changes may be cosmetic because when efforts to remedy the child's problems through a social welfare approach fail, the case may be referred to the juvenile court for more formal processing.[72] Those who favor removing status offenders from juvenile court authority charge that their experience with the legal system further stigmatizes these already troubled youths, exposes them to the influence of "true" delinquents, and enmeshes them in a system that cannot really afford to help them.[73] Reformer Ira Schwartz, for one, argues that status offenders "should be removed from the jurisdiction of the courts altogether."[74] Schwartz maintains that status offenders would best be served not by juvenile courts but by dispute resolution and mediation programs designed to strengthen family ties, as "status offense cases are often rooted in family problems."[75]

Do **curfew laws** work in reducing the rate of youth crime? To find out, visit the Center for Juvenile and Criminal Justice via academic.cengage.com/criminaljustice/siegel.

Increasing Social Control

Those in favor of retaining the status offense category point to society's responsibility to care for troubled youths. Some have suggested that the failure of the courts to extend social control over wayward youths neglects the rights of concerned parents who minor. The first of these was enacted in Colorado in 1903, and most states and the District of Columbia maintain similar laws. Such laws allow parents to be sanctioned in juvenile courts for behaviors associated with their child's misbehavior. Some states require parents to reimburse the government for the costs of detention or care of their children. Others demand that parents make restitution payments, such as paying for damage caused by their children who vandalized a school. All states except New Hampshire have incorporated parental liability laws within their statutes, though most recent legislation places limits on recovery somewhere between $250 (Vermont) and $15,000 (Texas); the average is $2,500. Other states (Colorado, Texas, Louisiana) require parents as well as children to participate in counseling and community service activities.

Parents may also be held civilly liable, under the concept of vicarious liability, for the damages caused by a child. In some states, parents are responsible for up to $300,000 in damages; in others the liability cap is $3,500 (sometimes home-owner's insurance covers at least some of the liability). Parents can also be charged with civil negligence if they should have known of the damage a child was about to inflict but did nothing to stop the child—for example, when they give a weapon to an emotionally unstable youth. Juries have levied awards of up to $500,000 in such cases. The United States is not alone in enforcing parental responsibility. Parental responsibility legislation has been enacted in Canada, where the small claims court may order parents to compensate those suffering any loss or damage intentionally caused by their child, unless the parent was exercising reasonable supervision over the child at the time the child engaged in the activity that caused the loss or damage and made reasonable efforts to prevent or discourage the child from engaging in the kind of activity that resulted in the loss or damage.

An extreme form of discipline for parents makes them criminally liable for the illegal acts of their children. There have been numerous cases in which parents have been ordered to serve time in jail because their children have been truant from school. Civil libertarians charge that these laws violate the constitutional right to due process and seem to be used only against lower-class parents. They find little evidence that punishing parents can deter delinquency. State laws of this kind have been successfully challenged in the lower courts.

Critical Thinking

1. Is it fair to punish parents for the misdeeds of their children? What happens if parents tried to control their teenager and failed? Should they be held liable?

2. Why should all youths be forced to meet a curfew simply because a few are rowdy and get in trouble with the law? Is it fair to punish the innocent for the acts of the guilty?

SOURCES: Kenneth Adams, "The Effectiveness of Juvenile Curfews at Crime Prevention," *Annals of the American Academy of Political and Social Science* 587:136–159 (2003); Canadian Parental Responsibility Act, 2000 S.O. 2000, Chapter 4, www.e-laws.gov.on.ca/html/statutes/english/elaws_statutes_00p04_e.htm (accessed September 6, 2007); Mike Males and Dan Macallair, *The Impact of Juvenile Curfew Laws in California* (San Francisco: Justice Policy Institute, 1998); Jerry Tyler, Thomas Segady, and Stephen Austin, "Parental Liability Laws: Rationale, Theory, and Effectiveness," *Social Science Journal* 37:79–97 (2000); Andra Bannister, David Carter, and Joseph Schafer, "A National Police Survey on the Use of Juvenile Curfews," *Journal of Criminal Justice* 29:233–240 (2001); Mike Reynolds, Ruth Seydlitz, and Pamela Jenkins, "Do Juvenile Curfew Laws Work? A Time-Series Analysis of the New Orleans Law," *Justice Quarterly* (2000); Mike Males and Dan Macallair, "An Analysis of Curfew Enforcement and Juvenile Crime in California," *Western Criminology Review* 1(2), online at http://wcr.sonoma.edu/v1n2/males.html (accessed September 6, 2007); David McDowall and Colin Loftin, "The Impact of Youth Curfew Laws on Juvenile Crime Rates," *Crime and Delinquency* 46:76–92 (2000).

Mayor Frank Melton speaks with reporters on June 20, 2006, at City Hall in Jackson, Mississippi, telling them that he plans to issue a civil emergency proclamation to enforce a stricter curfew and hold parents accountable for their children's criminal acts. Can such measures reduce delinquency in high-crime areas?

© AP Images/Rogelio V. Solis

are not able to care for and correct their children.[76] Others maintain that the status offense should remain a legal category so that juvenile courts can "force" a youth into receiving treatment.[77] Although it is recognized that a court appearance can produce negative stigma, the taint may be less important than the need for treatment.[78] Many state jurisdictions, prompted by concern over serious delinquency, have enacted laws that actually expand social control over juveniles.[79] The Policy and Practice box entitled "Increasing Social Control over Juveniles and Their Parents" discusses this issue in greater detail.

Research shows that a majority of youth routinely engage in some form of status offenses and that those who refrain form an atypical minority.[80] "Illegal" acts such as teen sex and substance abuse have become normative and commonplace. It makes little sense to have the juvenile court intervene with kids who are caught in what has become routine teenage behavior. In contrast, juvenile court jurisdiction over status offenders may be defended if in fact the youths' offending patterns are similar to those of delinquents. Is their current offense only the tip of an antisocial iceberg, or are they actually noncriminal youths who need only the loving hand of a substitute parent-figure interested in their welfare? Some find that status offenders are quite different from delinquents, but others note that many status offenders also had prior arrests for delinquent acts and that many delinquents exhibited behaviors that would define them as status offenders.[81]

These disparate findings may be explained in part by the fact that there may be different types of status offenders, some similar to delinquents and others who are quite different.[82] It might be more realistic to divide status offenders into three groups: first-time status offenders, chronic status offenders, and those with both a delinquent record and a status offense record.[83] The fact that many young offenders have mixed delinquent–status offender records indicates that these legal categories are not entirely independent. It is also recognized that some "pure" first-time status offenders are quite different from delinquents and that a juvenile court experience can be harmful to them and escalate the frequency and seriousness of their law-violating behaviors.[84]

The removal of these status offenders from the juvenile court is an issue that continues to be debated. The predominant view today is that many status offenders and delinquents share similar social and developmental problems and that consequently both categories should fall under the jurisdiction of the juvenile court. Not surprisingly, research does show that the legal processing of delinquents and status offenders remains quite similar.[85]

Summary

1. Become familiar with the problems of youth in American culture

I The problems of youth in contemporary society are staggering.

I Young people are extremely vulnerable to the negative consequences of school failure, substance abuse, and early sexuality.

I Adolescents and young adults often experience stress, confusion, and depression because of trouble and conflict occurring in their families, schools, and communities.

I It is not surprising that this latest generation of adolescents has been described as cynical and preoccupied with material acquisitions.

I The problems of American society and the daily stress of modern life have had a significant effect on our nation's youth as they go through their tumultuous teenage years.

I According to Erik Erikson, ego identity is formed when a person develops a firm sense of who he is and what he stands for.

I Role diffusion occurs when youths spread themselves too thin, experience personal uncertainty, and place themselves at the mercy of leaders who promise to give them a sense of identity they cannot develop for themselves.

2. Discuss the specific issues facing American youth

I Adolescence is a time of trial and uncertainty for many youths.

I Many suffer from health problems, are educational underachievers, and are already skeptical about their ability to enter the American mainstream.

I There are approximately 70 million children in the United States, a number that is projected to increase to about 80 million by 2025.

I According to the U.S. Census Bureau, the poverty rate for children under 18 remains higher than that of 18- to 64-year-olds. More than 12 million children now live in poverty.

I Many children are now suffering from chronic health problems and receive inadequate health care.

- Divorce strikes about half of all new marriages, and many families sacrifice time with each other to afford more affluent lifestyles.

- Many children live in substandard housing—high-rise, multiple-family dwellings—which can have a negative influence on their long-term psychological health.

- Although all young people face stress in the education system, the risks are greatest for the poor, members of racial and ethnic minorities, and recent immigrants.

- Minority kids usually attend the most underfunded schools, receive inadequate educational opportunities, and have the fewest opportunities to achieve conventional success.

3. Understand the concept of being "at risk" and discuss why so many kids take risks

- Troubles in the home, the school, and the neighborhood, coupled with health and developmental hazards, have placed a significant portion of American youth at risk.

- Youths considered at risk are those dabbling in various forms of dangerous conduct such as drug abuse, alcohol use, and precocious sexuality.

- Taking risks is normative among teens.

- Kids drive fast and recklessly: Motor vehicle crashes are a leading cause of death among young people.

4. Be familiar with the recent social improvements enjoyed by American teens

- Despite the many hazards faced by teens, there are some bright spots on the horizon.

- Teenage birthrates nationwide have declined substantially during the past decade.

- More youngsters are being read to by their parents than ever before.

- Today about 88 percent of young people finish high school, compared with 84 percent in 1980.

- Fewer children with health risks are being born today than in 1990.

- Census data indicate that about 86 percent of all adults 25 and older have completed high school.

- More than one-quarter of adults 25 and older have attained at least a bachelor's degree.

5. Discuss why the study of delinquency is so important and what this study entails

- The problems of youth in modern society are both a major national concern and an important subject for academic study.

- More than 2 million youths are now arrested each year for crimes ranging in seriousness from loitering to murder.

- Though most juvenile law violations are minor, some young offenders are extremely dangerous and violent.

- More than 700,000 youths belong to more than 20,000 gangs in the United States.

- Some youths are involved in multiple serious criminal acts—referred to as lifestyle, repeat, or chronic delinquent offenders.

- State juvenile authorities must deal with these offenders, along with responding to a range of other social problems, including child abuse and neglect, school crime and vandalism, family crises, and drug abuse.

- The scientific study of delinquency requires understanding the nature, extent, and cause of youthful law violations and the methods devised for their control.

- The study of delinquency also involves analysis of the law enforcement, court, and correctional agencies designed to treat youthful offenders who fall into the arms of the law—known collectively as the juvenile justice system.

6. Describe the life of children during feudal times

- The treatment of children as a distinct social group with special needs and behavior is, in historical terms, a relatively new concept.

- In Europe during the Middle Ages (roughly 500 C.E. to 1500 C.E.), the concept of childhood as we know it today did not exist.

- In the paternalistic family of the time, the father was the final authority on all family matters and exercised complete control over the social, economic, and physical well-being of the family.

- As soon as they were physically capable, children of all classes were expected to engage in adult roles.

- Western culture did not have a sense of childhood as a distinct period of life until the very late nineteenth and early twentieth centuries.

- Primogeniture required that the oldest surviving male child inherit family lands and titles.

- The dower system mandated that a woman's family bestow money, land, or other wealth on a potential husband or his family in exchange for his marriage to her.

- Newborns were almost immediately handed over to wet nurses, who fed and cared for them during the first two years of their life.

- Discipline was severe during this period. Young children of all classes were subjected to stringent rules and regulations. They were beaten severely for any sign of disobedience or ill temper.

- The roots of the impersonal relationship between parent and child can be traced to high mortality rates, which made sentimental and affectionate relationships risky.

7. Know why the treatment of children changed radically after the seventeenth century

- Throughout the seventeenth and eighteenth centuries, a number of developments in England heralded the march toward the recognition of children's rights.

- Extended families, which were created over centuries, gave way to the nuclear family structure with which we are familiar today.

- To provide more control over children, grammar and boarding schools were established and began to flourish in many large cities during this time.

- The philosophy of the Enlightenment stressed a humanistic view of life, freedom, family, reason, and law. The ideal person was sympathetic to others and receptive to new ideas.

- Government action to care for needy children developed.

- The Poor Laws forced children to serve during their minority in the care of families who trained them in agricultural, trade, or domestic services.

- Under the apprenticeship system, children were placed in the care of adults who trained them to discharge various duties and obtain skills.

- Chancery courts became a significant arm of the British legal system.

- Court proceedings were created in fifteenth-century England to oversee the lives of highborn minors who were orphaned or otherwise could not care for themselves.

- The *parens patriae* concept gave the state the power to act on behalf of the child and provide care and protection equivalent to that of a parent.

8. Discuss childhood in the American colonies

- The colonies were a haven for poor and unfortunate people looking for religious and economic opportunities denied them in England and Europe.

- The colonies' initial response to caring for such unfortunate children was to adopt court and Poor Laws systems similar to those in England.

- Involuntary apprenticeship, indenture, and binding out of children became integral parts of colonization in America.

- By the beginning of the nineteenth century, as the agrarian economy began to be replaced by industry, the apprenticeship system gave way to the factory system.

- In America, as in England, moral discipline was rigidly enforced. "Stubborn child" laws were passed that required children to obey their parents.

- While most colonies adopted a protectionist stance, few cases of child abuse were actually brought before the courts.

- Before the twentieth century, little distinction was made between adult and juvenile offenders.

- Although judges considered the age of an offender when deciding punishments, both adults and children were often eligible for the same forms of punishment—prison, corporal punishment, and even the death penalty.

9. Know about the child savers and the creation of delinquency

- Child savers were nineteenth-century reformers who developed programs for troubled youth and influenced legislation creating the juvenile justice system; today some critics view them as being more concerned with control of the poor than with their welfare.

- The designation *delinquent* became popular at the onset of the twentieth century when the first separate juvenile courts were instituted.

- The state, through its juvenile authorities, was expected to act in the best interests of the child.

- This philosophical viewpoint encouraged the state to take control of wayward children and provide care, custody, and treatment to remedy delinquent behavior.

- Children should not be punished for their misdeeds but instead should be given the care and custody necessary to remedy and control wayward behavior.

10. Discuss the elements of juvenile delinquency today

- Today, the legal status of "juvenile delinquent" refers to a minor child who has been found to have violated the penal code.

- Most states define "minor child" as an individual who falls under a statutory age limit, most commonly 17 or 18 years of age.

- Because of their minority status, juvenile offenders are usually kept separate from adults and receive different consideration and treatment under the law.

- The juvenile delinquency concept occupies a legal status falling somewhere between criminal and civil law.

- Under *parens patriae*, delinquent acts are not considered criminal violations nor are delinquents considered criminals. Children cannot be found guilty of a crime and punished like adult criminals.

- Delinquent behavior is sanctioned less heavily than criminality because the law considers juveniles as being less responsible for their behavior than adults.

- Although youths share a lesser degree of legal responsibility than adults, they are subject to arrest, trial, and incarceration.

- Children can be waived or transferred to the adult court for criminal prosecution.

11. Know what is meant by the term "status offender"

- A child becomes subject to state authority for committing status offenses—actions that would not be considered illegal if perpetrated by an adult; such conduct is illegal only because the child is under age.

- Status offenses have a long history. It was common practice early in the nation's history to place disobedient or runaway youths in orphan asylums, residential homes, or houses of refuge.

- State control over a child's noncriminal behavior is believed to support and extend the *parens patriae* philosophy because it is assumed to be in the best interests of the child.

- Most states now have separate categories for juvenile conduct that would not be considered criminal if committed by an adult; these sometimes pertain to neglected or dependent children as well.

- Even where there are separate legal categories for delinquents and status offenders, the distinction between them has become blurred.

- Some noncriminal conduct may be included in the definition of delinquency, and some less serious criminal offenses occasionally may be included within the status offender definition.

- Separate status offense categories may avoid some of the stigma associated with the delinquency label, but they can have relatively little practical effect on the child's treatment.

- The Office of Juvenile Justice and Delinquency Prevention (OJJDP) has made it a top priority to encourage the removal of status offenders from secure lockups, detention centers, and postdisposition treatment facilities that also house delinquent offenders.

- Those in favor of retaining the status offense category point to society's responsibility to care for troubled youths.

Key Terms

Viewpoint

As the governor of a large southern state, you have been asked to grant a pardon to a young man by his family and friends. Nathaniel B. was convicted of second-degree murder in 1995 and received a sentence of 28 years in the state penal system. Tried as an adult, he was found guilty of murder for intentionally killing Mr. Barry G., his English teacher, because he was angry over receiving a failing grade and being suspended for throwing water balloons. During trial, Nathaniel's attorney claimed that the gun Nathaniel brought to school had gone off accidentally after he pointed it at Mr. G. in an attempt to force him to let Nathaniel talk to two girls in the classroom.

"As he's holding the gun up, he's overwhelmed with tears," Nathaniel's lawyer told the jury. "His hand begins to shake, and the gun discharges. The gun discharged in the hands of an inexperienced 13-year-old with a junk gun." The prosecutor countered that Nathaniel's act was premeditated. He was frustrated because he was receiving an F in the class, and he was angry because he was being barred from talking to the girls. His victim "had no idea of the rage, hate, the anger, the frustration" filling the young man. There was also damaging information from police, who reported that Nathaniel told a classmate he was going to return to school and shoot the teacher; he said he'd be "all over the news."

At his sentencing hearing, Nathaniel read a statement: "Words cannot really explain how sorry I am, but they're all I have." His mother, Polly, blamed herself for her son's actions, claiming that he was surrounded by domestic abuse and alcoholism at home.

Now that he has served seven years in prison, Nathaniel's case has come to your attention. As governor, you recognize that his conviction and punishment raise a number of important issues. His mother claims that his actions were a product of abuse and violence in the home. You have read research showing that many habitually aggressive children have been raised in homes in which they were physically brutalized by their parents; this violence then persists into adulthood. Even though he was only 13 at the time of the crime, Nathaniel has been sentenced to nearly 30 years in an adult prison.

- Should children who are subject to brutal treatment, such as Nathaniel, be punished again by the justice system?

- Should Nathaniel be held personally responsible for actions that may in fact have been caused by a home life beyond his control?

- Even though he was only 13 years old when he committed his crime, Nathaniel's case was heard in an adult court, and he received a long sentence to an adult prison. Should minor children who commit serious crimes, as Nathaniel did, be treated as adults, or should they be tried within an independent juvenile justice system oriented to treatment and rehabilitation?

- Would you pardon Nathaniel now that he has served more than seven years in prison?

Doing Research on the Web

Before you make your decision in Nathaniel's case, you might want to look at the following websites:

I Bibliography of Children's Rights, at University of North Carolina

I The Coalition for Juvenile Justice (CJJ) has championed children and promoted community safety. The coalition's website provides information on judicial waiver.

Both sites can be accessed via
www.thomsonedu.com/criminaljustice/siegel

Questions for Discussion

1. Is it fair to have a separate legal category for youths? Considering how dangerous young people can be, does it make more sense to group offenders on the basis of what they have done and not their age?

2. At what age are juveniles truly capable of understanding the seriousness of their actions?

3. Is it fair to institutionalize a minor simply for being truant or running away from home? Should the jurisdiction of status offenders be removed from juvenile court and placed with the state department of social services or some other welfare organization?

4. Should delinquency proceedings be secret? Does the public have the right to know who juvenile criminals are?

5. Can a "get tough" policy help control juvenile misbehavior, or should *parens patriae* remain the standard?

6. Should juveniles who commit felonies such as rape or robbery be treated as adults?

Notes

1. Sky News, "Suicide Pact Feared as Third Teen Buried," 19 June 2007 http://news.sky.com/skynews/article/0,,30100-1271119,00.html (accessed September 4, 2007); Johnny Caldwell, "Teen Suicide Pact 'in Operation,'" BBC News, www.newsalerts.com/news/article/support-meeting-follows-suicides.html:world14:941770 (accessed June 18, 2007).

2. Ibid.

3. Robin Malinosky-Rummell and David Hansen, "Long-Term Consequences of Childhood Physical Abuse," *Psychological Bulletin* 114:68–79 (1993).

4. Centers for Disease Control and Prevention, "CDC Report Shows Largest One-Year Increase in Youth Suicide Rate in 15 Years," www.cdc.gov/od/oc/media/pressrel/2007/r070906.htm (accessed September 13, 2007).

5. Nanette Davis, *Youth Crisis: Growing Up in the High-Risk Society* (New York: Praeger, Greenwood Publishing, 1998).

6. Steven Martino, Rebecca Collins, Marc Elliott, Amy Strachman, David Kanouse, and Sandra Berry, "Exposure to Degrading versus Nondegrading Music Lyrics and Sexual Behavior Among Youth," *Pediatrics* 118:430–441 (2006).

7. Susan Crimmins and Michael Foley, "The Threshold of Violence in Urban Adolescents," paper presented at the annual meeting of the American Society of Criminology, Reno, Nevada, November 1989.

8. Erik Erikson, *Childhood and Society* (New York: W. W. Norton, 1963).

9. Roger Gould, "Adult Life Stages: Growth toward Self-Tolerance," *Psychology Today* 8:74–78 (1975).

10. U.S. Bureau of the Census, *Population Estimates and Projections* (Washington, DC: U.S. Census Bureau, 2007).

11. Children's Defense Fund, 2007, www.childrensdefense.org/site/PageServer?pagename=research_national_data_each_day (accessed September 4, 2007).

12. Interagency Forum on Child and Family Statistics, "America's Children: Key National Indicators of Well-Being, 2006," www.childstats.gov/americaschildren/ (accessed September 4, 2007).

13. Ibid.

14. David Eggebeen and Daniel Lichter, "Race, Family Structure, and Changing Poverty among American Children," *American Sociological Review* 56:801–817 (1991).

15. Gary Evans, Nancy Wells, and Annie Moch, "Housing and Mental Health: A Review of the Evidence and a Methodological and Conceptual Critique," *Journal of Social Issues* 59:475–501 (2003).

16. Interagency Forum on Child and Family Statistics, "America's Children."

17. National Center for Education Statistics, "Poverty and Student Mathematics Achievement," 2006, http://nces.ed.gov/programs/coe/2006/section2/indicator15.asp (accessed August 22, 2007).

18. National Center for Education Statistics, *Fast Facts* (Washington, DC: U.S. Department of Education, 2001).

19. Centers for Disease Control and Prevention news release, "New CDC Report Shows Teen Birth Rate Hits Record Low: U.S. Births Top 4 Million in 2000," 24 July 2001.

20. Interagency Forum on Child and Family Statistics, "America's Children."

21. Ibid.

22. Kenneth Kochanek and Joyce Martin, *Supplemental Analyses of Recent Trends in Infant Mortality* (Washington, DC: National Center for Health Statistics, 2004), http://firstcandle.org/FC-PDF4/Research_Recent%20Studies/Analyses%20of%20Recent%20Trends%20in%20Infant%20Mortality.pdf (accessed August 22, 2007).

23. Federal Bureau of Investigation, *Crime in the United States, 2002* (Washington, DC: Government Printing Office, 2003), p. 228.

24. John Whitehead and Steven Lab, "A Meta-Analysis of Juvenile Correctional Treatment," *Journal of Research in Crime and Delinquency* 26:276–295 (1989).

25. See Lawrence Stone, *The Family, Sex, and Marriage in England: 1500-1800* (New York: Harper & Row, 1977).

26. This section relies on Jackson Spielvogel, *Western Civilization* (St. Paul: West, 1991), pp. 279-286.

27. Philippe Aries, *Centuries of Childhood: A Social History of Family Life* (New York: Knopf, 1962).

28. Nicholas Orme, *Medieval Children* (New Haven: Yale University Press, 2003).

29. Aries, *Centuries of Childhood*.

30. See Douglas R. Rendleman, "Parens Patriae: From Chancery to the Juvenile Court," *South Carolina Law Review* 23:205 (1971).

31. See Stone, *The Family, Sex, and Marriage in England*, and Lawrence Stone, ed., *Schooling and Society: Studies in the History of Education* (Baltimore: Johns Hopkins University Press, 1970).

32. Ibid.
33. See Wiley B. Sanders, "Some Early Beginnings of the Children's Court Movement in England," *National Probation Association Yearbook* (New York: National Council on Crime and Delinquency, 1945).
34. Douglas Besharov, *Juvenile Justice Advocacy—Practice in a Unique Court* (New York: Practicing Law Institute, 1974), p. 2.
35. Rendleman, "Parens Patriae," p. 209.
36. See Anthony Platt, "The Rise of the Child Saving Movement: A Study in Social Policy and Correctional Reform," *Annals of the American Academy of Political and Social Science* 381:21–38 (1969).
37. Robert H. Bremner, ed., and John Barnard, Tamara K. Hareven, and Robert M. Mennel, asst. eds., *Children and Youth in America* (Cambridge: Harvard University Press, 1970), p. 64.
38. Elizabeth Pleck, "Criminal Approaches to Family Violence, 1640-1980," in Lloyd Ohlin and Michael Tonry, eds., *Family Violence* (Chicago: University of Chicago Press, 1989), pp. 19–58.
39. Ibid.
40. John R. Sutton, *Stubborn Children: Controlling Delinquency in the United States, 1640-1981* (Berkeley: University of California Press, 1988).
41. Pleck, "Criminal Approaches to Family Violence," p. 29.
42. John Demos, *Past, Present and Personal* (New York: Oxford University Press, 1986), pp. 80–88.
43. Elizabeth Pleck, *Domestic Tyranny: The Making of Social Policy against Family Violence from Colonial Times to the Present* (New York: Oxford University Press, 1987), pp. 28–30.
44. Graeme Newman, *The Punishment Response* (Philadelphia: J. B. Lippincott, 1978), pp. 53–79; Aries, *Centuries of Childhood*.
45. Stephen J. Morse, "Immaturity and Irresponsibility," *Journal of Criminal Law and Criminology* 88:15–67 (1997).
46. Hudson Sangree, "Juvenile Defendants May Be Too Immature to Stand Trial, Appeals Panel Says," *Sacramento Bee*, 11 May 2007, www.sacbee.com/391/story/175878.html (accessed September 4, 2007).
47. Shay Bilchik, "Sentencing Juveniles to Adult Facilities Fails Youths and Society," *Corrections Today* 65:21 (2003).
48. Campaign for Youth Justice, www.campaignforyouthjustice.org/Downloads/Resources/jjdpafactbook.pdf (accessed September 4, 2007).
49. M. Wakefield and G. Giovino, "Teen Penalties for Tobacco Possession, Use, and Purchase: Evidence and Issues," *Tobacco Control* 12:6–13 (2003).
50. Federal Bureau of Investigation, *Crime in the United States, 2005* (Washington, DC: U.S. Government Printing Office, 2007).
51. See David Rothman, *The Discovery of the Asylum* (Boston: Little, Brown, 1971).
52. Quote from Jerry Tyler, Thomas Segady, and Stephen Austin, "Parental Liability Laws: Rationale, Theory, and Effectiveness" *Social Science Journal* 37:79–97 (2000).
53. Reports of the Chicago Bar Association Committee, 1899, cited in Anthony Platt, *The Child Savers* (Chicago: University of Chicago Press, 1969), p. 119.
54. L. Kris Gowen, S. Shirley Feldman, Rafael Diaz, and Donnovan Somera Yisrael, "A Comparison of the Sexual Behaviors and Attitudes of Adolescent Girls with Older vs. Similar-Aged Boyfriends," *Journal of Youth and Adolescence* 33:167–176 (2004).
55. Ibid.
56. Susan Datesman and Mikel Aickin, "Offense Specialization and Escalation among Status Offenders," *Journal of Criminal Law and Criminology* 75:1246–1275 (1985).
57. Ibid.
58. David J. Steinharthe, *Status Offenses: The Future of Children* 6(3) (The David and Lucile Packard Foundation, Winter 1996).
59. OJJDP Annual Report 2000 (June 2001).
60. 42 U.S.C.A. 5601–5751 (1983 and Supp. 1987).
61. Claudia Wright, "Contempt No Excuse for Locking Up Status Offenders, Says Florida Supreme Court," *Youth Law News* 13:1–3 (1992).
62. Susanna Zawacki, "Girls' Involvement in Pennsylvania's Juvenile Justice System," *Pennsylvania Juvenile Justice Statistical Bulletin*, October 2005, www.pccd.state.pa.us/pccd/lib/pccd/publications/juvenilejustice/pastat_october2005.pdf (accessed September 4, 2007).
63. Steinharthe, *Status Offenses*, p. 5.
64. National Council on Crime and Delinquency, "Juvenile Curfews—A Policy Statement," *Crime and Delinquency* 18:132–133 (1972).
65. National Advisory Commission on Criminal Justice Standards and Goals, *Juvenile Justice and Delinquency Prevention* (Washington, DC: Government Printing Office, 1977), p. 311.
66. American Bar Association Joint Commission on Juvenile Justice Standards, *Summary and Analysis* (Cambridge: Ballinger, 1977), sect. 1.1.
67. American Bar Association, Youth at Risk Initiative Planning Conference, March 22, 2006, www.ocfs.state.ny.us/main/legal/statewide/ABAYARrecs.doc (accessed September 4, 2007).
68. New York State Office of Children and Family Services, "Chapter 57 of the Laws of 2005, PINS Reform Legislation Summary, Effective April 1, 2005," www.ocfs.state.ny.us/main/legal/legislation/pins/ (accessed September 4, 2007).
69. Gail Robinson and Tim Arnold, "Changes in Laws Impacting Juveniles—An Overview," *The Advocate* 22(4):14–15 (2000).
70. Barry Feld, "Criminalizing the American Juvenile Court," in Michael Tonry, ed., *Crime and Justice, A Review of Research* (Chicago: University of Chicago Press, 1993), p. 232.
71. Sean Kidd, "Factors Precipitating Suicidality Among Homeless Youth: A Quantitative Follow-up," *Youth and Society* 37:393–422 (2006); Kimberly Tyler et al., "Self-Mutilation and Homeless Youth: The Role of Family Abuse, Street Experiences, and Mental Disorders," *Journal of Research on Adolescence* 13:457–474 (2003).
72. Marc Miller, "Changing Legal Paradigms in Juvenile Justice," in Peter Greenwood, ed., *The Juvenile Rehabilitation Reader* (Santa Monica, CA: Rand Corporation, 1985) p. 44.
73. Thomas Kelley, "Status Offenders Can Be Different: A Comparative Study of Delinquent Careers," *Crime and Delinquency* 29:365–380 (1983).
74. Ira Schwartz, *(In)justice for Juveniles: Rethinking the Best Interests of the Child* (Lexington, MA: Lexington Books, 1989), p. 171.
75. Ibid.
76. Lawrence Martin and Phyllis Snyder, "Jurisdiction over Status Offenses Should Not Be Removed from the Juvenile Court," *Crime and Delinquency* 22:44–47 (1976).
77. Lindsay Arthur, "Status Offenders Need a Court of Last Resort," *Boston University Law Review* 57:631–644 (1977).
78. Martin and Snyder, "Jurisdiction over Status Offenses Should Not Be Removed from the Juvenile Court," p. 47.
79. David McDowall and Colin Loftin, "The Impact of Youth Curfew Laws on Juvenile Crime Rates," *Crime and Delinquency* 46:76–92 (2000).
80. Carolyn Smith, "Factors Associated with Early Sexual Activity among Urban Adolescents," *Social Work* 42:334–346 (1997).
81. Charles Thomas, "Are Status Offenders Really So Different?" *Crime and Delinquency* 22:438–455 (1976); Howard Snyder, *Court Careers of Juvenile Offenders* (Washington, DC: Office of Juvenile Justice and Delinquency Prevention, 1988), p. 65.
82. Randall Shelden, John Horvath, and Sharon Tracy, "Do Status Offenders Get Worse? Some Clarifications on the Question of Escalation," *Crime and Delinquency* 35:202–216 (1989).
83. Solomon Kobrin, Frank Hellum, and John Peterson, "Offense Patterns of Status Offenders," in D. Shichor and D. Kelly, eds., *Critical Issues in Juvenile Delinquency* (Lexington, MA: Lexington Books, 1980), pp. 203–235.
84. Schwartz, *(In)justice for Juveniles*, pp. 378–379.
85. Chris Marshall, Ineke Marshall, and Charles Thomas, "The Implementation of Formal Procedures in Juvenile Court Processing of Status Offenders," *Journal of Criminal Justice* 11:195–211 (1983).

2

The Nature and Extent of Delinquency

Chapter Outline

Chapter Objectives

1. Be familiar with how the UCR data are gathered and used
2. Discuss the concept of self-reported delinquency
3. Be familiar with the National Crime Victimization Survey
4. Discuss alternative measures of delinquent activity and behavior
5. Be familiar with recent trends in juvenile delinquency
6. Recognize the factors that affect the juvenile crime rate
7. List and discuss the social and personal correlates of delinquency
8. Discuss the concept of the chronic offender
9. Identify the causes of chronic offending
10. Be familiar with the factors that predict teen victimization

Jesse Timmendequas

Richard and Maureen Kanka thought that their daughter Megan was safe in their quiet, suburban neighborhood in Hamilton Township, New Jersey. Then on July 29, 1994, their lives were shattered when their 7-year-old daughter Megan went missing. Maureen Kanka searched the neighborhood and met 33-year-old Jesse Timmendequas, who lived across the street. Timmendequas told her that he had seen Megan earlier that evening while he was working on his car. The police were called in and soon focused their attention on Timmendequas's house when they learned that he and two other residents were convicted sex offenders who had met at a treatment center and decided to live together upon their release. Timmendequas soon confessed to luring Megan into his home by telling her she could see his puppy dog and then raping and strangling her to death.

Megan's death led to a national crusade to develop laws that require sex offenders to register with local police when they move into a neighborhood and require local authorities to provide community notification of the sex offender's presence. On the federal level, the Jacob Wetterling Crimes Against Children Law passed in May 1996, which requires states to pass some version of "Megan's Law" or lose federal aid. At least 47 states plus the District of Columbia have complied. Jesse Timmendequas was sentenced to death on June 20, 1997, and remains on death row today.

While many people are concerned about juvenile delinquency and youth crime, the case of Megan Kanka illustrates only too well that children face a disproportionate share of victimization. How many juveniles are the victims of crime and which ones stand the greatest chance of becoming victimized? Conversely, who commits delinquent acts, and where are they most likely to occur? Is the juvenile crime rate increasing or decreasing? Are juveniles more likely than adults to become the victims of crime? To understand the causes of delinquent behavior and to devise effective means to reduce its occurrence, we must seek answers to these questions.

Delinquency experts have devised a variety of methods to measure the nature and extent of delinquency. We begin with a description of the most widely used sources of data on crime and delinquency. We also examine the information these resources furnish on juvenile crime rates and trends. These data sources will then be used to provide information on the characteristics of adolescent law violators.

GATHERING INFORMATION ON DELINQUENCY

When they want to find out more about the nature and extent of delinquency, experts rely on three primary sources of data: official records, victim surveys, and self-report surveys. To gain insight into how delinquency is measured and what the data sources tell us about youth crime and victimization, it is important to understand how these data sets are collected. Each is discussed in some detail below.

Official Records of Delinquency: The Uniform Crime Report

One of the most important sources of information about delinquent behavior comes from data collected from local law enforcement agencies by the **Federal Bureau of Investigation** and published yearly in their **Uniform Crime Report (UCR)**. The UCR includes both criminal acts reported to local law enforcement departments and the number of arrests made by police agencies.[1] The FBI receives and compiles records from more than 17,000 police departments serving a majority of the U.S. population. The FBI tallies and annually publishes the number of reported offenses by city, county, standard metropolitan statistical area, and geographical divisions of the United States for the most serious crimes, referred to as **Part I crimes**: murder and non-negligent manslaughter, forcible rape, robbery, aggravated assault, burglary, larceny, arson, and motor vehicle theft.

In addition to these statistics, the UCR gathers data on the number and characteristics (age, race, and gender) of individuals who have been arrested for these and all other crimes, referred to as **Part II crimes**. This is particularly important for delinquency research because it shows how many underage minors are arrested each year.

Compiling the Uniform Crime Report The methods used to compile the UCR are quite complex. Each month law enforcement agencies report the number of crimes known to them. These data are collected from records of all crime complaints that victims, officers who discovered the infractions, or other sources reported to these agencies.

Whenever criminal complaints are found through investigation to be unfounded or false, they are eliminated from the actual count. However, the number of actual offenses known is reported to the FBI whether or not anyone is arrested for the crime, the stolen property is recovered, or prosecution ensues.

In addition, each month law enforcement agencies also report how many crimes were cleared. Crimes are cleared in two ways: (1) when at least one person is arrested, charged, and turned over to the court for prosecution, or (2) by exceptional means, when some element beyond police control precludes the physical arrest of an offender (such as when the offender leaves the country). Data on the number of clearances involving the arrest of only juvenile offenders, data on the value of property stolen and recovered in connection with Part I offenses, and detailed information pertaining to criminal homicide are also reported. Traditionally, slightly more than 20 percent of all reported Part I crimes are cleared by arrest each year (Figure 2.1).

Violent crimes are more likely to be solved than property crimes because police devote more resources to these more serious acts. For these types of crime, witnesses (including the victim) are frequently available to identify offenders, and in many instances the victim and offender were previously acquainted.

Validity of the UCR The accuracy of the UCR is somewhat suspect. Surveys indicate that fewer than half of all crime victims report incidents to police. Those who

Federal Bureau of Investigation (FBI)
Arm of the U.S. Department of Justice that investigates violations of federal law, gathers crime statistics, runs a comprehensive crime laboratory, and helps train local law enforcement officers.

Uniform Crime Report (UCR)
Compiled by the FBI, the UCR is the most widely used source of national crime and delinquency statistics.

Part I crimes
Offenses including homicide and non-negligent manslaughter, forcible rape, robbery, aggravated assault, burglary, larceny, arson, and motor vehicle theft; recorded by local law enforcement officers, these crimes are tallied quarterly and sent to the FBI for inclusion in the UCR.

Part II crimes
All crimes other than Part I crimes; recorded by local law enforcement officers, arrests for these crimes are tallied quarterly and sent to the FBI for inclusion in the UCR.

FIGURE 2.1
Crimes Cleared by Arrest
SOURCE: FBI, *Crime in the United States, 2006*, www.fbi.gov/ucr/cius2006/offenses/clearances/ (accessed November 8, 2007).

Percentage of Part I crimes cleared by arrest

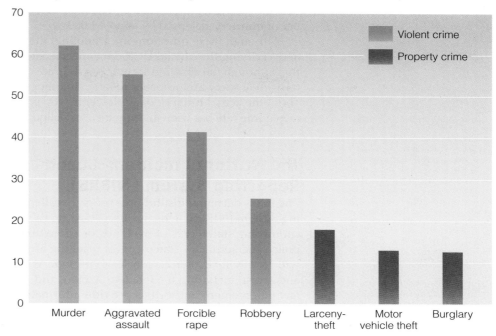

don't report may believe that the victimization was "a private matter," that "nothing could be done," or that the victimization was "not important enough."[2] Some victims do not trust the police or have confidence in their ability to solve crimes. Others do not have property insurance and therefore believe it is useless to report theft. In other cases, victims fear reprisals from an offender's friends or family or, in the case of family violence, from their spouse, boyfriend, or girlfriend.[3] They may believe that they are themselves somehow responsible for the crime: for example, the date rape victim who was drinking or had taken drugs prior to the attack.[4] Some crimes that directly influence children, such as child abuse, may be underreported considering the age of the victims and their ability to contact police authorities.

There is also evidence that local law enforcement agencies make errors in their reporting practices. Some departments may define crimes loosely—for example, reporting an assault on a woman as an attempted rape—whereas others pay strict attention to FBI guidelines.[5] Ironically, what appears to be a rising crime rate may simply be an artifact of improved police record-keeping ability.[6]

Methodological issues also contribute to questions regarding the UCR's validity. The complex scoring procedure used by the FBI means that many serious crimes are not counted. For example, during an armed bank robbery, the offender strikes a teller with the butt of a handgun. The offender then runs from the bank and steals an automobile at the curb. Although the offender has technically committed robbery, aggravated assault, and motor vehicle theft, because robbery is the most serious offense, it is the only one recorded in the UCR.[7] The UCR uses three methods to express crime data. First, the number of crimes reported to the police and arrests made are expressed as raw figures (for instance, 17,034 murders occurred in 2006). Second, crime rates per 100,000 people are computed. That is, when the UCR indicates that the murder rate was 5.7 in 2006, it means that almost 6 people in every 100,000 were murdered between January 1 and December 31, 2006. This is the equation used:

$$\frac{\text{Number of Reported Crimes}}{\text{Total U.S. Population}} \times 100{,}000 = \text{Rate per } 100{,}000$$

Third, the FBI computes changes in the number and rate of crime over time. Murder rates increased more than 5 percent between 2004 and 2006, and the annual number of murders increased by almost 1,000.

Although these questions are troubling, the problems associated with collecting and verifying the official UCR data are consistent and stable over time. This means that although the absolute accuracy of the data can be questioned, the trends and patterns they show are probably reliable. In other words, we cannot be absolutely sure about the actual number of adolescents who commit crimes, but it is likely that the teen crime rate has been in a significant decline.

The National Incident-Based Reporting System (NIBRS)

The FBI is currently instituting a program called the National Incident-Based Reporting System (NIBRS), which collects data on each reported crime incident. Instead of submitting statements of the kinds of crime that individual citizens reported to the police and summary statements of resulting arrests, when fully implemented NIBRS will require local police agencies to provide at least a brief account of each incident and arrest, including the incident, victim, and offender information. Under NIBRS, law enforcement authorities provide information to the FBI on each criminal incident, involving 46 specific offenses, including the eight Part I crimes, that occur in their jurisdiction; arrest information on the 46 offenses plus 11 lesser offenses is also provided in NIBRS. These expanded crime categories include numerous additional crimes, such as blackmail, embezzlement, drug offenses, and bribery; this allows a national database on the nature of crime, victims, and criminals to be developed. So far, 26 states have implemented their NIBRS program and 12 others are in the process of finalizing their data collections. When NIBRS is fully implemented and adopted across the nation, it should provide significantly better data on juvenile crime than exists today.

While official data are used quite often in delinquency research, the data only represent the number of kids arrested and not how many are actually committing delinquent acts. To remedy this flaw, researchers often rely on self-report data in their research.

It is often difficult to measure the full extent of delinquency, because many acts are not included in the UCR. Here, a young man is escorted past his family after a court appearance on a charge of making a false bomb threat while boarding a flight. Would this act be reported to the FBI's program?

© AP Images/Michael Dwyer

SELF-REPORT SURVEYS

self-report survey
Questionnaire or survey technique that asks subjects to reveal their own participation in delinquent or criminal acts.

One of the most important tools to measure delinquency and youthful misconduct is the **self-report survey**. These surveys ask kids to describe, in detail, their recent and lifetime participation in antisocial activity—for example, "How many times in the past year did you take something worth more than $50?" In many instances, but not always, self-reports are given in groups, and the respondents are promised anonymity in order to ensure the validity and honesty of the responses.[8] But even when the reports are given on an individual basis, respondents are guaranteed that their answers will remain confidential.

In addition to questions about delinquent behavior, most self-report surveys contain questions about attitudes, values, and behaviors. There may be questions about a participant's substance abuse history (e.g., how many times have you used marijuana?) and the participant's family history (e.g., did your parents ever strike you with a stick or a belt?). By correlating the responses, delinquency experts are able to analyze the relationships among values, attitudes, personal factors, and delinquent behaviors. Statistical analysis of the responses can be used to determine such issues as whether people who report being abused as children are also more likely to use drugs as adults or if school failure leads to delinquency.[9]

Validity of Self-Reports

Critics of self-report studies frequently suggest that it is unreasonable to expect kids to candidly admit illegal acts. Some surveys contain an overabundance of trivial offenses, such as shoplifting small items or using false identification to obtain alcohol, often lumped together with serious crimes to form a total crime index. Consequently, comparisons between groups can be highly misleading.

Responses may be embellished by some subjects who wish to exaggerate the extent of their deviant activities, and understated by others who want to shield themselves from possible exposure. Recent (2006) research by David Kirk shows that some kids with an official arrest record deny legal involvement while others who remain arrest-free report having an official record. Why would adolescents claim to have engaged in antisocial behaviors such as getting arrested or using drugs when in fact they had not? One reason is that they may live in a subculture that requires kids to be tough rule-breakers, unafraid of conventional authority. Kids may fear that they would be taunted or harassed if anyone found out they were not really "experienced" delinquents.[10]

Other factors that influence self-report validity are age, criminal history, recency of the reported event, IQ, education level, and variety of criminal acts. Despite these caveats, some of the most recent research supports the validity of the self-report method with both occasional and committed (e.g., gang members) delinquents.[11]

The "missing cases" phenomenon is also a concern. Even if 90 percent of a school population voluntarily participate in a self-report study, researchers can never be sure whether the few who refuse to participate or are absent that day comprise a significant portion of the school's population of persistent high-rate offenders. Research indicates that offenders with the most extensive prior criminality are the most likely "to be poor historians of their own crime commission rates."[12] It is also unlikely that the most serious chronic offenders in the teenage population are willing to cooperate with researchers administering self-report tests.[13] Institutionalized youths, who are not generally represented in the self-report surveys, are not only more delinquent than the general youth population but are also considerably more misbehaving than the most delinquent youths identified in the typical self-report survey.[14] Consequently, self-reports may measure only nonserious, occasional delinquents while ignoring hard-core chronic offenders who may be institutionalized and unavailable for self-reports.

To address these criticisms, various techniques have been used to verify self-report data.[15] The "known group" method compares youths who are known to be offenders with those who are not to see whether the former report more delinquency. Research shows that when kids are asked if they have ever been arrested or sent to court, their responses accurately reflect their true-life experiences.[16]

While these studies are supportive, self-report data must be interpreted with some caution. Asking subjects about their past behavior may capture more serious crimes but miss minor criminal acts; that is, people remember armed robberies and rapes better than they do minor assaults and altercations.[17] In addition, some classes of offenders (for example, substance abusers) may have a tough time accounting for their prior misbehavior.[18]

National Crime Victimization Survey (NCVS)

National Crime Victimization Survey (NCVS)
The ongoing victimization study conducted jointly by the Justice Department and the U.S. Census Bureau that surveys victims about their experiences with law violation.

An important issue for delinquency scholars is juvenile victimization. How many kids are victims each year and who are the adolescents most likely to become crime victims? To address this issue, the federal government sponsors the National Crime Victimization Survey (NCVS), a comprehensive, nationwide survey of victimization in the United States.

Each year data are obtained from a large nationally representative sample; typically more than 75,000 households with more than 130,000 people age 12 or older are interviewed.[19] People are asked to report their experiences with such crimes as rape, sexual assault, robbery, assault, theft, household burglary, and motor vehicle theft. Due to the care with which the samples are drawn and the high completion rate, NCVS data are considered a relatively unbiased, valid estimate of all victimizations for the target crimes included in the survey.

The NCVS finds that fewer than half of violent crimes, fewer than one-third of personal theft crimes (such as pocket picking), and fewer than half of household thefts are reported to police. Victims seem to report to the police only crimes that involve considerable loss or injury. If we are to believe NCVS findings, the official UCR statistics do not provide an accurate picture of the crime problem because many crimes go unreported to the police.

While it contains many underreported incidents, the NCVS may also suffer from some methodological problems. As a result, its findings must be interpreted with caution. Among the potential problems are the following:

I Overreporting due to victims' misinterpretation of events. A lost wallet may be reported as stolen, or an open door may be viewed as a burglary attempt.

I Underreporting due to the embarrassment of reporting crime to interviewers, fear of getting in trouble, or simply forgetting an incident.

I Inability to record the personal criminal activity of those interviewed, such as drug use or gambling; murder is also not included, for obvious reasons.

I Sampling errors, which produce a group of respondents who do not represent the nation as a whole.

I Inadequate question format that invalidates responses. Some groups, such as adolescents, may be particularly susceptible to error because of question format and wording.[20]

SECONDARY SOURCES OF DELINQUENCY DATA

In addition to the primary sources of delinquency and victim data—UCR, NCVS, self-report surveys—delinquency experts routinely use a number of other methods to acquire data on youth crime and delinquency. While not exhaustive, the following methods are routinely used in delinquency research.

Cohort Research Data

Collecting cohort data involves observing over time a group of kids who share a like characteristic. Researchers might select all girls born in Boston in 1970 and then follow their behavior patterns for 20 years. The research data might include their school experiences, arrests, hospitalizations, and information about their family life (such as marriages, divorces, parental relations). Data may also be collected directly from the subjects during interviews and meetings with family members. If the cohort is carefully drawn, it may be possible to accumulate a complex array of data that can be used to determine which life experiences produce criminal careers.

Another approach is to take a contemporary cohort, such as kids in school in New York in 2007, and then look back into their past and collect data from educational, family, police, and hospital records, a format known as a *retrospective cohort study*. If they wanted to identify childhood and adolescent risk factors for delinquency, researchers might acquire the juveniles' prior police and court records, school records, and so on.

Experimental Data

Sometimes researchers are able to conduct controlled experiments to collect data on the cause of delinquency. To conduct their experiments, researchers manipulate or intervene in the lives of their subjects to see the outcome or the effect of the intervention. True experiments usually have three elements: (1) random selection of subjects, (2) a control or comparison group, and (3) an experimental condition. For example, in order to determine if viewing violent media content is a cause of violence, a delinquency expert might randomly select one group of kids and have them watch an extremely violent and gory film (*Hostel* or *Saw*) and then compare their behavior to a second randomly selected group who watches something more mellow (*The Princess Diaries*). The behavior of both groups would be monitored; if the subjects who had watched the violent film were significantly more aggressive than those who had watched the nonviolent film, an association between media content and behavior would be supported. The fact that both groups were randomly selected would prevent some preexisting condition from invalidating the results of the experiment.

Delinquency experiments are relatively rare because they are difficult and expensive to conduct; they involve manipulating subjects' lives, which can cause ethical and legal roadblocks; and they require long follow-up periods to verify results. Nonetheless, they have been an important source of criminological data.

Observational and Interview Research

Sometimes researchers focus their research on relatively few subjects, interviewing them in depth or observing them as they go about their activities. This research often results in the kind of in-depth data absent in large-scale surveys. Another common criminological method is to observe criminals firsthand to gain insight into their motives and activities. This may involve going into the field and participating in group activities, as was done in sociologist William Whyte's famous study of a Boston gang, *Street Corner Society*. Other observers conduct field studies but remain in the background, observing but not being part of the ongoing activity.

Meta-analysis and Systematic Review

meta-analysis
A research technique that uses the grouped data from several different studies.

systematic review
A research technique that involves collecting the findings from previously conducted studies, appraising and synthesizing the evidence, and using the collective evidence to address a particular scientific question.

Meta-analysis involves gathering data from a number of previous studies. Compatible information and data are extracted and pooled together. When analyzed, the grouped data from several different studies provide a more powerful and valid indicator of relationships than the results provided from a single study. A systematic review is another widely accepted means of evaluating the effectiveness of public policy interventions. It involves collecting the findings from previously conducted scientific studies that address a particular problem, appraising and synthesizing the evidence, and using the collective evidence to address a particular scientific question.

Data Mining

A relatively new criminological technique, data mining uses multiple advanced computational methods, including artificial intelligence (the use of computers to perform logical functions), to analyze large data sets usually involving one or more data sources. The goal is to identify significant and recognizable patterns, trends, and relationships that are not easily detected through traditional analytical techniques.

Data mining might be employed to help a police department determine if burglaries in their jurisdiction have a particular pattern. To determine if such a pattern exists, a criminologist might employ data mining techniques with a variety of sources, including calls for service data, delinquency or incident reports, witness statements, suspect interviews, tip information, telephone toll analysis, or Internet activity. The data mining might uncover a strong relationship between the time of day and place of occurrence. The police could use the findings to plan an effective burglary elimination strategy.

Crime Mapping

crime mapping
A research technique that employs computerized crime maps and other graphic representations of crime data patterns.

Researchers now use crime mapping to create graphic representations of the spatial geography of delinquency. Computerized crime maps allow researchers to analyze and correlate a wide array of data to create immediate, detailed visuals of delinquency patterns. The simplest maps display delinquency locations or concentrations and can be used to help law enforcement agencies increase the effectiveness of their patrol efforts. More complex maps can be used to chart trends in criminal activity. Researchers might be able to determine if certain neighborhoods in a city have significantly higher delinquency rates than others, so-called hot spots of delinquency.

CRIME AND DELINQUENCY TRENDS IN THE UNITED STATES

What do these data sources tell us about recent trends in the crime rate? Crime and delinquency rates trended upward between 1960 and 1991, when police recorded about 15 million crimes. Since then the number of crimes has been in decline; Figure 2.2 illustrates crime rate trends between 1960 and 2006, the last data available. Although the general crime rates did not increase in 2006, violent crimes—especially murder—ticked upwards, increasing almost 2 percent between 2005 and 2006. While this recent increase in violence is disturbing, it is too soon to tell whether it is the beginning of a new long-term trend or a single year aberration.

These data indicate that crime and delinquency rates ebb and flow and are rarely constant. Experts believe that social, economic, and individual factors all influence the direction delinquency rates take.

FIGURE **2.2**
Crime Rate Trends

SOURCE: FBI, *Crime in the United States, 2006.*

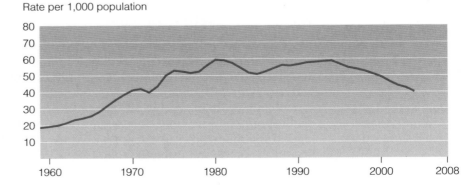

Rate per 1,000 population

What the UCR Tells Us about Delinquency

disaggregated
Analyzing the relationship between two or more independent variables (such as murder convictions and death sentence) while controlling for the influence of a dependent variable (such as race).

Because the UCR arrest statistics are disaggregated (broken down) by suspect's age, they can be used to estimate adolescent delinquency. Juvenile arrest data must be interpreted with caution, however. First, the number of teenagers arrested does not represent the actual number of youths who have committed delinquent acts. Some offenders are never counted because they are never caught. Others are counted more than once because multiple arrests of the same individual for different crimes are counted separately in the UCR. Consequently, the total number of arrests does not equal the number of people who have been arrested. Put another way, if 2 million arrests of youths under 18 years of age were made in a given year, we could not be sure if 2 million individuals had been arrested once or if 500,000 chronic offenders had been arrested four times each. In addition, when an arrested offender commits multiple crimes, only the most serious one is recorded. Therefore, if 2 million juveniles are arrested, the number of crimes committed is at least 2 million, but it may be much higher.

Despite these limitations, the nature of arrest data remains constant over time. Consequently, arrest data can provide some indication of the nature and trends in juvenile crime. What does the UCR tell us about delinquency?

Official Delinquency In 2006 (the latest data available), more than 14 million arrests were made, or about 5,000 per 100,000 population. Of these, more than 2 million were for serious Part I crimes and 12 million for less serious Part II crimes.

In 2006, juveniles were responsible for about 16 percent of the Part I violent crime arrests and about 26 percent of the property crime arrests (see Table 2.1). Because kids ages 14 to 17 who account for almost all underage arrests constitute only about 6 percent of the population, these data show that teens account for a significantly disproportionate share of all arrests. In all, more than 1.6 million kids were arrested in 2006.

About 1.3 million juvenile arrests were made in 2006 for Part II offenses. Included in this total were 83,000 arrests for running away from home, 153,000 for disorderly conduct, 143,000 for drug-abuse violations, and 114,000 for curfew violations.

Juvenile Delinquency Trends Juvenile delinquency continues to have a significant influence on the nation's overall crime statistics. The juvenile arrest rate began to climb in the 1980s, peaked during the mid-1990s, and then began to fall; it has since been in decline. Even the teen murder rate, which had remained stubbornly high, has undergone a decline during the past few years.[21] For example, 1,700 youths were arrested for murder in 1997, a number that by 2006 had declined by almost half (to about 950). Similarly, 3,800 juveniles were arrested for rape in 1997, and about 2,500 in 2006. However, while juvenile violence rates have declined over the past 10 years, there was a disturbing recent uptick in juvenile violent crime arrests during the past year. Arrests of juveniles (under 18 years of age) for murder climbed about 3 percent between 2005 and 2006; for robbery, arrests of juveniles rose an astounding 19 percent over the same year period. The number of juvenile violent crime arrests rose 4 percent between 2005 and 2006. It is uncertain whether this uptick portends a long-term trend in juvenile violence.

TABLE 2.1

Persons Arrested, by Age

	Under 15	Under 18	Over 18
Serious violent crime	4%	16%	84%
Serious property crime	9%	26%	74%
Total all crimes	4%	15%	85%

SOURCE: FBI, *Crime in the United States, 2006*, www.fbi.gov/ucr/cius2006/data/table_36.html (accessed September 27, 2007).

Shaping Delinquency Trends

Crime experts have identified a variety of social, economic, personal, and demographic factors that influence crime rate trends. Although crime experts are still uncertain about how these factors affect these trends, directional change seems to be associated with changes in crime rates.

AGE

Because teenagers have extremely high crime rates, crime experts view changes in the population age distribution as having the greatest influence on crime trends: As a general rule, the crime rate follows the proportion of young males in the population. Kids who commit a lot of crime early in childhood are also likely to continue to commit crime in their adolescence and into adulthood. The more teens in the population, the higher the crime rate. The number of juveniles should be increasing over the next decade, and some crime experts fear that this will signal a return to escalating crime rates. However, the number of senior citizens is also expanding, and their presence in the population may have a moderating effect on crime rates (seniors do not commit much crime), offsetting the effect of teens.

ECONOMY/JOBS

There is debate over the effect the economy has on crime rates. It seems logical that when the economy turns down, people (especially those who are unemployed) will become more motivated to commit theft crimes. Kids who find it hard to get after-school jobs or find employment after they leave school may be motivated to seek other forms of income such as theft and drug dealing. As the economy heats up, delinquency rates should decline because people can secure good jobs; why risk breaking the law when there are legitimate opportunities? Recent (2006) research by Thomas Arvanites and Robert Defina found that the delinquency rate drop in the 1990s could be linked to a strong economy.

However, some experts believe that a poor economy may actually help lower delinquency rates because it limits the opportunity kids have to commit crime: Unemployed parents are at home to supervise children and guard their possessions, and because there is less money to spend, people have fewer valuables worth stealing. Moreover, law-abiding people do not begin to violate the law just because there is an economic downturn.

Although the effect of the economy on delinquency rates is still in question, it is possible that over the long haul a strong economy will help lower delinquency rates, while long periods of sustained economic weakness and unemployment may eventually lead to increased rates. Crime skyrocketed in the 1930s during the Great Depression; crime rates fell when the economy surged for almost a decade during the 1990s. Also, economic effects may be very localized: People in one area of the city are doing well, but people living in another part of town may be suffering unemployment. The economic effect on the delinquency rates may vary by neighborhood or even by street.

IMMIGRATION

Immigration has become one of the most controversial issues in American society. One reason given by those who want to tighten immigration laws is that immigrants have high crime rates and should be prevented from entering the country. Contradicting such concern has been research by Robert Sampson, which indicates that immigrants are actually less violent than the general population, especially when they live in concentrated immigrant areas. Sampson and colleagues found that Mexican immigrants experienced lower rates of violence compared to their native-born counterparts. Ramiro Martinez and his colleagues examined the influence on drug crimes and violence produced by recent immigration in Miami and San Diego and found that overall immigration has a *negative* effect on overall levels of homicides and drug-related homicides specifically. This research indicates that as the number of immigrants in the population increases, the overall delinquency may decline.

SOCIAL MALAISE

As the level of social problems increases—such as single-parent families, dropout rates, racial conflict, and teen pregnancies—so do delinquency rates. Delinquency rates are correlated with the number of unwed mothers in the population. It is possible that children of unwed mothers need more social services than children in two-parent families. As the number of kids born to single mothers increases, the child welfare system is taxed and services depleted. The teenage birth rate has trended downward in recent years, and so have delinquency rates.

Racial conflict may also increase delinquency rates. Areas undergoing racial change, especially those experiencing a migration of minorities into predominantly white neighborhoods, seem prone to significant increases in their delinquency rate. Whites in these areas may be using violence to protect what they view as their home turf. Racially motivated crimes actually diminish as neighborhoods become more integrated and power struggles are resolved.

ABORTION

In a controversial work, John J. Donohue III and Steven D. Levitt found empirical evidence that the recent drop in the delinquency rate can be attributed to the availability of legalized abortion. In 1973, *Roe v. Wade* legalized abortion nationwide. Within a few years of *Roe v. Wade*, more than 1 million abortions were being performed annually, or roughly one abortion for every three live births. Donohue and Levitt suggest that the delinquency rate drop, which began approximately 18 years later, in 1991, can be tied to the fact that at that point the first groups of potential offenders affected by the abortion decision began reaching the peak age of criminal activity. The researchers found that states that legalized abortion before the rest of the nation were the first to experience decreasing delinquency rates and that states with high abortion rates have seen a greater drop in delinquency since 1985.

It is possible that the link between delinquency rates and abortion is the result of three mechanisms: (1) selective abortion on the part of women most at risk to have children who would engage in delinquent activity, (2) improved child-rearing or environmental circumstances because women are having fewer children, and (3) absence of unwanted children who stand the greatest risk of delinquency. If abortion were illegal, Donohue and Levitt find, delinquency rates might be 10 to 20 percent higher than they currently are with legal abortion.

Understandably, Donohue and Levitt's views have sparked considerable controversy and continued research. One recent (2006) effort by Carter Hay and Michelle Evans found that children unwanted by their mothers do in fact commit more delinquency than children who were wanted or planned. However, the effect was only modest and temporary. By their late teens and 20s unwanted kids commit as much crime as their wanted brothers and sisters, a finding that seems to contradict Donohue and Levitt.

GUNS

The availability of firearms may influence the delinquency rate, especially the proliferation of weapons in the hands of teens. Surveys of high school students indicate that between 6 and 10 percent carry guns at least some of the time. Guns also cause escalation in the seriousness of delinquency. As the number of gun-toting students increases, so does the seriousness of violent delinquency: A school yard fight may well turn into murder.

GANGS

Another factor that affects delinquency rates is the explosive growth in teenage gangs. Surveys indicate that there are about 750,000 gang members in the United States. Boys who are members of gangs are far more likely to possess guns than nongang members; criminal activity increases when kids join gangs.

DRUG USE

Some experts tie increases in the violent delinquency rate between 1980 and 1990 to the crack epidemic, which swept the nation's largest cities, and to drug-trafficking gangs that fought over drug turf. These well-armed gangs did not hesitate to use violence to control territory, intimidate rivals, and increase market share. As the crack epidemic has subsided, so has the violence in New York City and other metropolitan areas where crack use was rampant. A sudden increase in drug use, on the other hand, may be a harbinger of future increases in the delinquency rate.

MEDIA

Some experts argue that violent media can influence the direction of delinquency rates. The introduction of home video players, DVDs, cable TV, computers, and video games coincided with increasing teen violence rates. Perhaps the increased availability of media violence on these platforms produced more aggressive teens? Watching violence on TV may be correlated with aggressive behaviors, especially when viewers have a pre-existing tendency toward delinquency and violence. Research shows that the more kids watch TV, the more often they get into violent encounters.

JUVENILE JUSTICE POLICY

Some law enforcement experts have suggested that a reduction in delinquency rates may be attributed to adding large numbers of police officers and using them in aggressive police practices aimed at reducing gang membership, gun possession, and substance abuse. It is also possible that tough laws such as waiving juveniles to adult courts or sending them to adult prisons can affect crime rates. The fear of punishment may inhibit some would-be delinquents, and tough laws place a significant number of chronic juvenile offenders behind bars, lowering delinquency rates.

Critical Thinking

Although juvenile delinquency rates have been declining in the United States, they have been increasing in Europe. Is it possible that factors that correlate with delinquency rate changes in the United States have little utility in predicting changes in other cultures? What other factors may increase or reduce delinquency rates?

SOURCES: Robert Sampson and Lydia Bean, "Cultural Mechanisms and Killing Fields: A Revised Theory of Community-Level Racial Inequality," in Ruth D. Peterson, Lauren Krivo, and John Hagan, eds., *The Many Colors of Crime: Inequalities of Race, Ethnicity, and Crime in America* (New York: New York University Press, 2006): 8–36; Ramiro Martinez, Jr., and Matthew Amie Nielsen, "Local Context and Determinants of Drug Violence in Miami and San Diego: Does Ethnicity and Immigration Matter?" *International Migration Review* 38:131–157 (2004); Rob White and Ron Mason, "Youth Gangs and Youth Violence: Charting the Key Dimensions," *Australian and New Zealand Journal of Criminology* 39:54–70 (2006); Carter Hay and Michelle Evans, "Has *Roe v. Wade* Reduced U.S. Crime Rates? Examining the Link Between Mothers' Pregnancy Intentions and Children's Later Involvement in Law-Violating Behavior," *Journal of Research in Crime and Delinquency* 43:36–66 (2006); Thomas Arvanites and Robert Defina, "Business Cycles and Street Crime," *Criminology* 44:139–164 (2006); David Fergusson, L. John Horwood, and Elizabeth Ridder, "Show Me the Child at Seven: The Consequences of Conduct Problems in Childhood for Psychosocial Functioning in Adulthood," *Journal of Child Psychology and Psychiatry and Allied Disciplines* 46:837–849 (2005); Fahui Wang, "Job Access and Homicide Patterns in Chicago: An Analysis at Multiple Geographic Levels Based on Scale-Space Theory," *Journal of Quantitative Criminology* 21:195–217 (2005); Gary Kleck and Ted Chiricos, "Unemployment and Property Crime: A Target-Specific Assessment of Opportunity and Motivation as Mediating Factors," *Criminology* 40:649–680 (2002); Steven Levitt, "Understanding Why Crime Fell in the 1990s: Four Factors that Explain the Decline and Six that Do Not," *Journal of Economic Perspectives* 18:163–190 (2004); Jeffrey Johnson, Patricia Cohen, Elizabeth Smailes, Stephanie Kasen, and Judith Brook, "Television Viewing and Aggressive Behavior During Adolescence and Adulthood," *Science* 295:2468–2471 (2002); Brad Bushman and Craig Anderson, "Media Violence and the American Public," *American Psychologist* 56:477–489 (2001); Steven Messner, Lawrence Raffalovich, and Richard McMillan, "Economic Deprivation and Changes in Homicide Arrest Rates for White and Black Youths, 1967–1998: A National Time-Series Analysis," *Criminology* 39:591–614 (2001); John J. Donohue III and Steven D. Levitt, "The Impact of Legalized Abortion on Crime," *Quarterly Journal of Economics* 116:379–420 (2001).

What factors account for change in the crime and delinquency rates? This is the topic of the Focus on Delinquency box entitled "Shaping Delinquency Trends."

Self-Reported Findings

Most self-report studies indicate that the number of children who break the law is far greater than official statistics would lead us to believe.[22] In fact, when truancy, alcohol consumption, petty theft, and recreational drug use are included in self-report scales, delinquency appears to be almost universal. The most common offenses are truancy, drinking alcohol, using a false ID, shoplifting or larceny under five dollars, fighting, using marijuana, and damaging the property of others. In Chapter 10, self-report data will be used to gauge trends in adolescent drug abuse.

Researchers at the University of Michigan's Institute for Social Research (ISR) conducted an annual national self-report survey, called Monitoring the Future (MTF), that involves a sample of about three thousand youths.[23] Table 2.2 contains some of the data from the 2006 MTF survey.

A surprising number of these *typical* teenagers reported involvement in serious criminal behavior. About 12 percent reported hurting someone badly enough that the victim needed medical care (6 percent said they did it more than once); about 29 percent reported stealing something worth less than $50, and another 10 percent stole something worth more than $50; 28 percent reported shoplifting; 11 percent had damaged school property.

If the MTF data are accurate, the juvenile crime problem is much greater than official statistics would lead us to believe. There are approximately 40 million youths between the ages of 10 and 18. Extrapolating from the MTF findings, this group accounts for more than 100 percent of all the theft offenses reported in the UCR.

Lydia Ochoa, 15, waits to meet with a social worker at an intervention center for truants at Luther Burbank High School in Sacramento, California, after she was picked up for skipping school. Ochoa's mother was called and the pair met with the social worker. Delinquency experts believe that social factors such as the dropout rate contribute to the ebb and flow of delinquent behavior. A positive social climate can reduce delinquency rates.

TABLE 2.2

Survey of Criminal Activity of High School Seniors, 2006

Crime	Percentage Engaging in Offenses	
	Committed at Least Once	Committed More than Once
Set fire on purpose	2	2
Damaged school property	6	5
Damaged work property	3	3
Auto theft	3	2
Auto part theft	2	2
Break and enter	12	13
Theft, less than $50	12	15
Theft, more than $50	5	5
Shoplift	11	14
Gang fight	9	8
Hurt someone badly enough to require medical care	6	5
Used force or a weapon to steal	2	2
Hit teacher or supervisor	1	2
Participated in serious fight	7	5

SOURCE: *Monitoring the Future, 2006* (Ann Arbor, MI: Institute for Social Research, 2006).

More than 3 percent of high school students said they had used force to steal (which is the legal definition of a robbery). At this rate, high school students alone commit 1.2 million robberies per year. In comparison, the UCR tallied about 440,000 robberies for all age groups in 2006. Over the past decade, the MTF surveys indicate that with a few exceptions, self-reported teenage participation in theft, violence, and damage-related crimes seems to be more stable than the trends reported in the UCR arrest data.

There is also some question about the accuracy of self-report data. Reporting practices differ among racial, ethnic, and gender groups. One study found that while girls are generally more willing to report drug use than boys, Hispanic girls tend to underreport substance abuse. Such gender/cultural differences in self-reporting can skew data and provide misleading results.[24]

Are the Data Sources Compatible?

Each source of crime data has strengths and weaknesses. The FBI survey contains data on the number and characteristics of people arrested, information that the other data sources lack. It is also the source of information on particular crimes such as murder, which no other data source can provide.[25] While used extensively, the UCR omits the many crimes that victims choose not to report to police, and relies on the reporting accuracy of individual police departments.

The NCVS includes unreported crime missed by the UCR and also contains important information on the personal characteristics of victims. However, the data consist of estimates made from relatively limited samples of the total U.S. population, so that even narrow fluctuations in the rates of some crimes can have a major impact on findings. The NCVS also relies on personal recollections that may be inaccurate. It does not include data on important crime patterns, including murder and drug abuse.

Self-report surveys provide useful information because questions on delinquent activity are often supplemented with items measuring the personal characteristics of offenders, such as their attitudes, values, beliefs, and psychological profiles. It can also be used to measure drug and alcohol abuse; this data is not included in the UCR and NCVS. Yet, at their core, self-reports rely on the honesty of criminal offenders and drug abusers, a population not generally known for accuracy and integrity.

Although their tallies of delinquency are certainly not in synch, the patterns and trends measured by various data sources are often quite similar: When the UCR shows a drop in illegal activity, so too does the NCVS.[26] They all generally agree about the personal characteristics of serious delinquents (i.e., age and gender) and where and when delinquency occurs (i.e., urban areas, nighttime, and summer months). Because the measurement problems inherent in each source are consistent over time, they are reliable indicators of changes and fluctuations in delinquency rates.

What the Future Holds

Some experts predict a significant increase in teen violence if current population trends persist. The nation's teenage population will increase by 15 percent, or more than 9 million, between now and 2010; the number in the high-risk ages of 15 to 17 will increase by more than 3 million, or 31 percent. There are approximately 53 million school-age children in the United States, many younger than 10—more than we have had for decades. Although many come from stable homes, others lack stable families and adequate supervision; these are some of the children who will soon enter their prime crime years.[27]

In contrast, other experts argue that even though teen crime rates may eventually rise, their influence on the nation's total crime rate may be offset by the growing number of relatively crime-free senior citizens.[28] Steven Levitt suggests that punitive policies such as putting more kids behind bars and adding police may help control delinquency. One problem on the horizon remains the maturation of "crack babies," who spent their early childhood years in families and neighborhoods ravaged by crack cocaine. Coupled with a difficult home environment, these children may turn out to be extremely prone to delinquent activity, producing an increase in the delinquency now predicted by such experts as criminologist James A. Fox.[29]

Of course, prognostications, predictions, and forecasts are based on contemporary conditions that can change at any time due to the sudden emergence of war, terrorism, social unrest, economic meltdown, and the like. While the number of adolescents in the population may shape crime rates under current conditions, the mere fact of a large juvenile population may have less of an impact as serious social and economic conditions emerge in the future.[30]

CORRELATES OF DELINQUENCY

An important aspect of delinquency research is measurement of the personal traits and social characteristics associated with adolescent misbehavior. If, for example, a strong association exists between delinquent behavior and family income, then poverty and economic deprivation must be considered in any explanation of the onset of adolescent criminality. If the delinquency-income association is not present, then other forces may be responsible for producing antisocial behavior. It would be fruitless to concentrate delinquency control efforts in areas such as job creation and vocational training if social status were found to be unrelated to delinquent behavior. Similarly, if only a handful of delinquents are responsible for most serious crimes, then crime control policies might be made more effective by identifying and treating these offenders. The next sections discuss where and when delinquent acts take place, as well as the relationship between delinquency and the characteristics of gender, race, social class, and age.

The Time and Place of Delinquency

Most delinquent acts occur during the warm summer months of July and August. Weather may affect delinquent behavior in a number of different ways. During the summer, teenagers are out of school and have greater opportunity to commit crime. Homes are left vacant more often during the summer, making them more vulnerable to property crimes. Weather may also have a direct effect on behavior: As it gets warmer kids get more violent.[31] However, some experts believe if it gets too hot, over 85 degrees, the frequency of some violent acts such as sexual assault will begin to decline.[32]

There are also geographic differences in the incidence of delinquent behaviors. Large urban areas have by far the highest juvenile violence rates; rural areas have the lowest. Typically, the western and southern states have had consistently higher delinquency rates than the Midwest and Northeast, which have been linked to differences in cultural values, population makeup, gun ownership, and economic differences.

Gender and Delinquency

With a few exceptions, males are significantly more delinquent than females. The teenage gender ratio for serious violent crime is approximately four to one, and for property crime approximately two to one, male to female.

The only exception to this pattern is arrests for being a runaway: Girls are more likely than boys to be arrested as runaways. There are two possible explanations for this. Girls could be more likely than boys to run away from home, or police may view the female runaway as the more serious problem and therefore are more likely to process girls through official justice channels. This may reflect paternalistic attitudes toward girls, who are viewed as likely to "get in trouble" if they are on the street.

Girls are increasing their involvement in violence at a faster pace than boys. It is no longer surprising when young women commit armed robberies and murders. Police say 15-year-old Holly Harvey (right), and 16-year-old Sandy Ketchum of Fayetteville, Georgia, were involved in a romantic relationship and that Harvey's family had tried to keep them apart. The two are accused of stabbing to death Harvey's grandparents. Harvey had a list inked on her arm that read, "kill, keys, money, jewelry."

Between 1997 and 2006, during a period of rapidly declining crime rates, the number of arrests of male delinquents decreased about 26 percent, whereas the number of female delinquents arrested declined by 17 percent.

Self-report data also seem to show that the incidence of female delinquency is much higher than believed earlier, and that the most common crimes committed by males are also the ones most female offenders commit.[33] Table 2.3 shows the percentages of male and female high school seniors who admitted engaging in delinquent acts during the past 12 months in the latest MTF survey. As the table indicates, about 25 percent of all boys and girls admitted to shoplifting; 11 percent of boys and 6 percent of girls said they stole something worth more than $50, and 18 percent of boys and 6 percent of girls said they hurt someone badly enough that they required medical care. Over the past decade girls have increased their self-reported delinquency whereas boys report somewhat less involvement. Because the relationship between gender and delinquency rate is so important, this topic will be discussed further in Chapter 6.

These trends indicate that gender differences in the crime rate may be eroding. However, it is also possible that changes in female arrest trends may be explained

TABLE 2.3

Percentage of High School Seniors Admitting to at Least One Offense during the Past 12 Months, by Gender

Delinquent Acts	Males	Females
Serious fight	13	9
Gang fight	22	16
Hurt someone badly	18	6
Used a weapon to steal	5	1
Stole less than $50	33	22
Stole more than $50	16	7
Shoplift	35	22
Breaking and entering	30	22
Arson	5	1
Damaged school property	17	7

SOURCE: *Monitoring the Future, 2005* (Ann Arbor, MI: Institute for Social Research, 2005).

Case Profile

Jamesetta's Story

JAMESETTA WAS BORN IN A POOR, URBAN NEIGHBORHOOD. AS HER PARENTS STRUGGLED WITH SUBSTANCE ABUSE, POVERTY, AND UNEMPLOYMENT, JAMESETTA suffered both physical and sexual abuse before being placed in foster care at the age of 5. By the age of 9, Jamesetta was shoplifting, skipping school, and violating curfew. At age 13 she physically assaulted her foster mother and entered the juvenile justice system with charges of disorderly conduct and being a habitual delinquent. Her foster home placement was terminated and Jamesetta was sent to live with her aunt, uncle, and six cousins. It wasn't long before her relatives began to have additional concerns that Jamesetta was exhibiting sexualized behavior, "sneaking around" with her 17-year-old boyfriend, staying out all night, and being disrespectful. They felt she was out of control.

Jamesetta had been ordered by the juvenile court to cooperate with her family's household rules, attend school on a regular basis, have no further law violations, complete 25 hours of community service, and pay restitution for the shoplifting, but she refused to cooperate with any of the programs or services, continuing to come and go as she pleased. The family was receiving support from Jamesetta's intensive supervision program counselor, as well as a family therapist, but during the second month of placement with her relatives, at the age of 14, Jamesetta disclosed that she was pregnant and planning to keep her baby. The program counselor and other professionals involved in Jamesetta's case had to work with her and her family to reevaluate their plan.

Jamesetta was enrolled in a school specifically designed to support teens who are pregnant or already parenting, where in addition to her academic studies to complete high school, she would receive help from parenting classes, independent living courses, and relationship counseling. Jamesetta also received services from a neighborhood intervention program that focused on providing structure and accountability for her through counselors and daily group meetings to encourage her. Even with these additional supports and interventions, Jamesetta continued to have status offenses. She skipped school, didn't come home on time, and would not follow household rules, though she did not have any further delinquent activities.

Jamesetta continued to live with her aunt and uncle, and did eventually complete her community service and restitution payment. After the baby was born Jamesetta began to understand the consequences of her actions. With continued services and support from her counselors, she started following the rules and expectations of her family. Upon taking responsibility to find the necessary medical and child care for her daughter, Jamesetta found employment, a position in retail, and started planning for her future. Despite being at high risk for dropping out of school, Jamesetta was able to complete her high school education and have a positive view of her future. The team of involved professionals continued to provide the needed supports and encouraged Jamesetta to make good decisions for both herself and her new baby. She still struggles at times, but has remained free of further law violations. ■

CRITICAL THINKING

1. Jamesetta received a number of interventions to address her issues, but it still took a long time for her to reduce her delinquent behavior. How long should the juvenile justice system give a young person to change? How many chances should a teen get? Do you think she would have likely been removed from her aunt and uncle's home if her criminal behavior had continued?

2. As Jamesetta grew older, she was less involved in criminal activity. Discuss the reasons for the "aging-out" process and apply them to this case example.

3. What childhood risk factors did Jamesetta have regarding the possibility of becoming a persistent delinquent? How was this avoided? What can be done to reduce chronic offending among at-risk youth?

more by changes in police activity than in criminal activity: Police today may be more willing to arrest girls for crimes than ever before.[34] What appears to be increases in female delinquency may be a function of changes in police activity rather than changes in female behavior patterns.

The Case Profile entitled "Jamesetta's Story" tells the true story of how one young girl was able to overcome the adversities that had made her "at risk" for delinquency.

50   **Part 1** The Concept of Delinquency

Race and Delinquency

There are approximately 41 million white and 9 million African American youths ages 5 to 17, a ratio of about five to one. Yet racial minorities are disproportionately represented in the arrest statistics (see Exhibit 2.1).

These official statistics show that minority youths are arrested for serious criminal behavior at a rate that is disproportionate to their representation in the population. To many delinquency experts, this pattern reflects discrimination in the juvenile justice system. In other words, African American youths are more likely to be formally arrested by the police, who, in contrast, will treat white youths informally. One way to examine this issue is to compare the racial differences in self-reported data with those found in the official delinquency records. Given the disproportionate numbers of African Americans arrested, charges of racial discrimination would be supported if we found little difference between the number of self-reported minority and white crimes.

Early researchers found that the relationship between race and self-reported delinquency was virtually nonexistent.[35] This suggests that racial differences in the official crime data may reflect the fact that African American youths have a much greater chance of being arrested and officially processed.[36] Self-report studies also suggest that the delinquent behavior rates of African American and white teenagers are generally similar and that differences in arrest statistics may indicate discrimination by police.[37] The MTF survey, for example, generally shows that offending differences between African American and white youths are marginal.[38] However, some experts warn that African American youths may underreport more serious crimes, limiting the ability of self-reports to be a valid indicator of racial differences in the crime rate.[39]

Bias Effects? How can the disproportionate number of African American youngsters arrested for serious crimes be explained? One view is that it is a result of bias by the police and courts. Minority group members are more likely to be formally arrested than whites.[40] According to the **racial threat theory**, as the size of the black population increases, the perceived threat to the white population increases, resulting in a greater amount of social control imposed against blacks by police.[41] Police will then routinely search, question, and detain all African American males in an area if a violent criminal has been described as "looking or sounding black"; this is called *racial profiling*. African American youth who develop a police record are more likely to be severely punished if they are picked up again and sent back to juvenile court.[42] Consequently, the racial discrimination that is present at the early stages of the justice system ensures that minorities receive greater punishments at its conclusion.[43]

Juvenile court judges may see the offenses committed by African American youths as more serious than those committed by white offenders. Consequently, they are

> **racial threat theory**
> As the size of the black population increases, the perceived threat to the white population increases, resulting in a greater amount of social control imposed against blacks.

EXHIBIT 2.1

Racial Trends in the Arrest Data

▮ About 70 percent of all persons arrested were white, 28 percent were black.

▮ About 60 percent of persons arrested for violent crime were white, 40 percent African American.

▮ About 70 percent of persons arrested for property crime were white, 30 percent black.

▮ Black juveniles comprised about half of all juveniles arrested in 2006 for serious violent crime and about 31 percent of all juveniles arrested for serious property crime.

▮ White juveniles comprised 67 percent of the total of all juveniles arrested in 2006, African American youth about 30 percent, and the remainder were Pacific Islanders, Asians, and Native Americans.

SOURCE: FBI, *Uniform Crime Report, 2006,* www.fbi.gov/ucr/cius2006/data/table_43.html (accessed September 27, 2007).

more likely to keep minority juveniles in detention pending trial in juvenile court than they are white youth with similar backgrounds.[44] White juveniles are more likely to receive lenient sentences or have their cases dismissed.[45] As a result, African American youths are more likely to get an official record.

According to this view, the disproportionate number of minority youth who are arrested is less a function of their involvement in serious crime and more the result of the race-based decision making that is found in the juvenile justice system.[46] Institutional racism by police and the courts is still an element of daily life in the African American community, a factor that undermines faith in social and political institutions and weakens confidence in the justice system.[47]

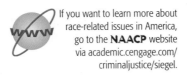

If you want to learn more about race-related issues in America, go to the **NAACP** website via academic.cengage.com/criminaljustice/siegel.

Race Matters The other point of view holds that although evidence of racial bias does exist in the justice system, there is enough correspondence between official and self-report data to conclude that racial differences in the crime rate are real.[48] If African American youths are arrested at a disproportionately high rate for crimes such as robbery and assault, it is a result of actual offending rates rather than bias on the part of the criminal justice system.[49]

If they exist, how can racial differences in the delinquency rate be explained? One view is that racial differentials are tied to the social and economic disparity suffered by African American youths. Too many are forced to live in the nation's poorest areas that suffer high crime rates.[50] Many black youth are forced to attend essentially segregated schools that are underfunded and deteriorated, a condition that increases the likelihood of their being incarcerated in adulthood.[51] The burden of social and economic marginalization has weakened the African American family structure. When families are weakened or disrupted, their ability to act as social control agents is compromised.[52]

Even during times of economic growth, lower-class African Americans are left out of the economic mainstream, causing a growing sense of frustration and failure.[53] As a result of being shut out of educational and economic opportunities enjoyed by the rest of society, this population may be prone, some believe, to the lure of illegitimate gain and criminality. However, even among at-risk African American kids growing up in communities characterized by poverty, high unemployment levels, and single-parent households, those who do live in stable families with reasonable incomes and educational achievement are much less likely to engage in violent behaviors than those lacking family support.[54] Consequently, racial differences in the delinquency rate would evaporate if the social and economic characteristics of racial minorities were improved to levels currently enjoyed by whites, and African American kids could enjoy the same social, economic, and educational privileges.[55]

In summary, official data indicate that African American youths are arrested for more serious crimes than whites. But self-report studies show that the differences in the rates of delinquency between the races are insignificant. Therefore, some experts believe that official differences in the delinquency rate are an artifact of bias in the justice system: Police are more likely to arrest and courts are more likely to convict young African Americans.[56] To those who believe that the official data have validity, the participation of African American youths in serious criminal behavior is generally viewed as a function of their socioeconomic position and the racism they face.

Socioeconomic Status (SES) and Delinquency

Determining the true association between SES and delinquency is critical and a key element in the study of delinquency. If youth crime is purely a lower-class phenomenon, its cause must be rooted in the social forces that are found solely in lower-class areas: poverty, unemployment, social disorganization, culture conflict,

To get information on the **economic status of America's children**, go to the federal government's website via academic.cengage.com/criminaljustice/siegel.

and alienation. However, if delinquent behavior is spread throughout the social structure, its cause must be related to some noneconomic factor: intelligence, personality, socialization, family dysfunction, educational failure, or peer influence. According to this line of reasoning, providing jobs or economic incentives would have little effect on the crime rate.

At first glance, the relationship between socioeconomic status (SES) and delinquency should be clear-cut:

I Youths who lack wealth or social standing should be the ones who use illegal means to achieve their goals and compensate for their lack of economic resources.

I Communities that lack economic and social opportunities should have the highest delinquency rates.

I Kids who live in these areas believe that they can never compete socially or economically with adolescents being raised in more affluent areas. They may turn to illegal behavior for monetary gain and psychological satisfaction.[57]

I Family life is most likely to be frayed and disrupted in low-income areas. As a consequence, gangs and law-violating youth groups should thrive in a climate that undermines and neutralizes the adult supervision that families provide.[58]

I Kids who live in poor families who live within poor communities are doubly at risk for delinquency and find it hard to resist the lure of streets.[59]

Research on Social Class and Delinquency The social class–delinquency relationship was challenged by pioneering self-report studies, specifically those that revealed no direct relationship between social class and the commission of delinquent acts.[60] Instead, socioeconomic class was related to the manner of official processing by police, court, and correctional agencies.[61] In other words, although both poor and affluent kids get into fights, shoplift, and take drugs, only the indigent are likely to be arrested and sent to juvenile court.[62] This finding casts doubt on the assumption that poverty and lower-class position are significant causes of delinquent behavior.

Those who fault self-report studies point to the inclusion of trivial offenses—for example, using a false ID—in most self-report instruments. Although middle- and upper-class youths may appear to be as delinquent as those in the lower class, it is because they engage in significant amounts of such status offenses. Lower-class youths are more likely to engage in serious delinquent acts.[63]

In sum, there are those experts who believe that antisocial behavior occurs at all levels of the social strata. Other experts argue that, while some middle- and upper-class youths engage in some forms of minor illegal activity and theft offenses, it is members of the underclass who are responsible for the majority of serious delinquent acts.[64] The prevailing wisdom is that kids who engage in the most serious forms of delinquency (such as gang violence) are more likely to be members of the lower class.

Age and Delinquency

It is generally believed that age is inversely related to criminality: As people age, the likelihood that they will commit crime declines.[65] Official statistics tell us that young people are arrested at a disproportionate rate to their numbers in the population, and this finding is supported by victim surveys. As you may recall, youths ages 14 to 17 make up about 6 percent of the total U.S. population, but account for about 15 percent for all arrests. In contrast, adults age 50 and older, who make up slightly less than a third of the population, account for only about 6 percent of arrests. Figure 2.3 shows that even though the number of arrests have been in decline, the peak age for arrest remains the teen years.

Why Age Matters Why do people commit less crime as they age? One view is that the relationship is constant: Regardless of race, sex, social class, intelligence, or any other social variable, people commit less crime as they age.[66] This is referred to as the **aging-out process**, sometimes called **desistance from crime** or **spontaneous remission**. According to some experts, even the most chronic juvenile offenders will commit less crime as they age.[67] Because almost everyone commits less crime as they age, it is difficult to predict or identify the relatively few offenders who will continue to commit crime as they travel through their life course.[68]

There are also experts who disagree with the concept of spontaneous remission. They suggest that age is one important determinant of crime but that other factors directly associated with a person's lifestyle, such as peer relations, also affect offending rates.[69] The probability that a person will become a persistent career criminal is influenced by a number of personal and environmental factors.[70] Evidence exists, for example, that the **age of onset** of a delinquent career has an important effect on its length: Those who demonstrate antisocial tendencies at a very early age are more likely to commit more crimes for a longer period of time. This is referred to as the *developmental view of delinquency*.

In summary, some criminologists believe youths who get involved with delinquency at a very early age are most likely to become career criminals. These researchers believe age is a key determinant of delinquency.[71] Those opposed to this view find that all people commit less crime as they age and that because the relationship between age and crime is constant, it is irrelevant to the study of delinquency.[72]

Why Does Crime Decline with Age? Although there is certainly disagreement about the nature of the aging-out process, there is no question that people commit fewer crimes as they grow older. Delinquency experts have developed a number of reasons for the aging-out process:

▌ *Growing older means having to face the future.* Young people, especially the indigent and antisocial, tend to "discount the future."[73] Why should they delay gratification when faced with an uncertain future?

▌ *With maturity comes the ability to resist the "quick fix" to their problems.*[74] Research shows that some kids may turn to crime as a way to solve the problems of adolescence, loneliness, frustration, and fear of peer rejection. As they mature, conventional means of problem solving become available. Life experience helps former delinquents seek out nondestructive solutions to their personal problems.[75]

---

aging-out process (also known as desistance from crime or spontaneous remission)
The tendency for youths to reduce the frequency of their offending behavior as they age; aging out is thought to occur among all groups of offenders.

age of onset
Age at which youths begin their delinquent careers; early onset is believed to be linked with chronic offending patterns.

FIGURE 2.3
The Relationship between Age and Serious Crime Arrests

SOURCE: FBI, *Uniform Crime Report, 2006*, www.fbi.gov/ucr/cius2006/data/table_32.html (accessed October 3, 2007).

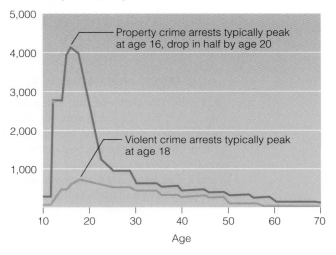

- *Maturation coincides with increased levels of responsibility.* Petty crimes are risky and exciting social activities that provide adventure in an otherwise boring world. As youths grow older, they take on new responsibilities that are inconsistent with criminality.[76] For example, young people who marry, enlist in the armed services, or enroll in vocational training courses are less likely to pursue criminal activities.[77]

- *Personalities can change with age.* As youths mature, rebellious youngsters may develop increased self-control and be able to resist antisocial behavior.[78]

- *Young adults become more aware of the risks that accompany crime.* As adults, they are no longer protected by the relatively kindly arms of the juvenile justice system.[79]

Of course, not all juvenile criminals desist as they age; some go on to become chronic adult offenders. Yet by and large most offenders slow down as they age. Crime is too dangerous, physically taxing, and unrewarding, and punishments too harsh and long lasting, to become a way of life for most people.[80]

CHRONIC OFFENDING: CAREERS IN DELINQUENCY

Although most adolescents age out of crime, a relatively small number of youths begin to violate the law early in their lives (early onset) and continue at a high rate well into adulthood (persistence).[81] The association between early onset and high-rate persistent offending has been demonstrated in samples drawn from a variety of cultures, time periods, and offender types.[82] These offenders are resistant to change and seem immune to the effects of punishment. Arrest, prosecution, and conviction do little to slow down their offending careers. These chronic offenders are responsible for a significant amount of all delinquent and criminal activity.

Current interest in the delinquent life cycle was prompted in part by the "discovery" in the 1970s of the chronic juvenile (or delinquent) offender. According to this view, a relatively small number of youthful offenders commit a significant percentage of all serious crimes, and many of these same offenders grow up to become chronic adult criminals.

chronic juvenile offenders (also known as chronic delinquent offenders, chronic delinquents, or chronic recidivists)
A subset of juvenile offenders who begin their delinquent careers at a young age, have serious and persistent brushes with the law, including five or more arrests, are excessively violent and destructive, and do not age out of crime but continue their law-violating behavior into adulthood.

Chronic offenders can be distinguished from other delinquent youths. Many youthful law violators are apprehended for a single instance of criminal behavior, such as shoplifting or joyriding. Chronic offenders begin their delinquent careers at a young age (under 10 years, referred to as early onset), have serious and persistent brushes with the law, and may be excessively violent and destructive. They do not age out of crime but continue their law-violating behavior into adulthood.[83] Most research shows that early, repeated delinquent activity is the best predictor of future adult criminality.

A number of research efforts have set out to chronicle the careers of serious delinquent offenders. The next sections describe these initiatives.

Delinquency in a Birth Cohort

The concept of the chronic career offender is most closely associated with the research efforts of Marvin Wolfgang.[84] In 1972, Wolfgang, Robert Figlio, and Thorsten Sellin published a landmark study, *Delinquency in a Birth Cohort.* They followed the delinquent careers of a cohort of 9,945 boys born in Philadelphia from birth until they reached age 18. Data were obtained from police files and school records. Socioeconomic status was determined by locating the residence of each member of the cohort and assigning him the median family income for that area. About one-third of the boys (3,475) had some police contact. The remaining two-thirds (6,470) had none. Those boys who had at least one contact with the police committed a total of 10,214 offenses.

The most significant discovery of Wolfgang and his associates was that of the so-called chronic offender. The data indicated that 54 percent (1,862) of the sample's delinquent youths were repeat offenders. The repeaters could be further categorized as nonchronic recidivists and chronic recidivists. *Nonchronic recidivists* had been arrested more than once but fewer than five times. In contrast, the 627 boys labeled *chronic recidivists* had been arrested five times or more. Although these offenders accounted for only 18 percent of the delinquent population (6 percent of the total sample), they were responsible for 52 percent of all offenses. Known today as the "chronic 6 percent," this group perpetrated 71 percent of the homicides, 82 percent of the robberies, and 64 percent of the aggravated assaults (see Figure 2.4).

Arrest and juvenile court experience did little to deter chronic offenders. In fact, the greater the punishment, the more likely they were to engage in repeat delinquent behavior. Strict punishment also increased the probability that further court action would be taken. Two factors stood out as encouraging recidivism: the seriousness of the original offense and the severity of the punishment. The researchers concluded that efforts of the juvenile justice system to eliminate delinquent behavior may be futile.

Wolfgang and his colleagues conducted a second cohort study with children born in 1958 and substantiated the finding that a relatively few chronic offenders are responsible for a significant portion of all delinquent acts.[85] Wolfgang's results have been duplicated in a number of research studies conducted in locales across the United States and

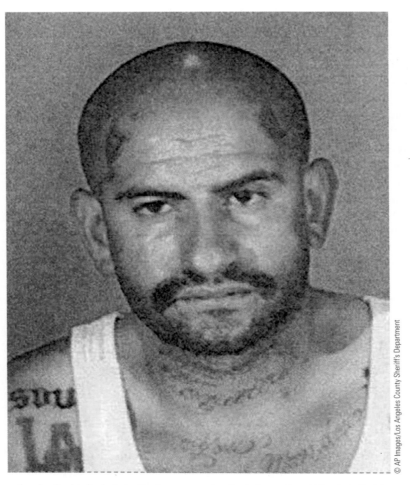

Chronic offenders begin their offending career early, offend often, and persist in criminality into their adulthood. Chronic offender Jose Luis Orozco, 27, was convicted of the fatal shooting of Los Angeles County Sheriff's Deputy Jerry Ortiz. As a teen, Orozco was arrested for possession of marijuana and cocaine as well as for assault with a deadly weapon, resisting arrest, and burglary. As an adult, Orozco was put on three years' probation for vehicle burglary and later jailed for being in possession of a firearm. In 2004, Orozco drew a 16-month prison sentence for resisting arrest and obstruction. Orozco was sentenced to death on May 3, 2007, for the Ortiz murder.

also in Great Britain.[86] Some have used the records of court-processed youths and others have employed self-report data.

Stability in Crime: From Delinquent to Criminal

Do chronic juvenile offenders grow up to become chronic adult criminals? One study that followed a 10 percent sample of the original Pennsylvania cohort (974 subjects) to age 30 found that 70 percent of the persistent adult offenders had also been chronic juvenile offenders. Chronic juvenile offenders had an 80 percent chance of becoming adult offenders and a 50 percent chance of being arrested four or more times as adults.[87] Paul Tracy and Kimberly Kempf-Leonard conducted a follow-up study of all the subjects in the second 1958 cohort. By age 26, Cohort II subjects were displaying the same behavior patterns as their older peers. Kids who started their delinquent careers early, committed a violent crime, and continued offending throughout adolescence were most likely to persist in criminal behavior as adults. Delinquents who began their offending careers with serious offenses

FIGURE 2.4
Distribution of Offenses in the
Philadelphia Cohort

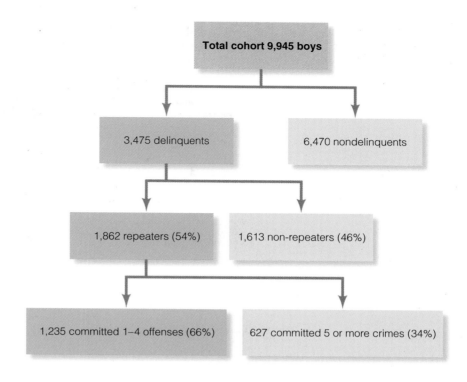

or who quickly increased the severity of their offending early in life were most likely to persist in their criminal behavior into adulthood. Severity of offending rather than frequency of criminal behavior had the greatest impact on later adult criminality.[88]

continuity of crime
The idea that chronic juvenile offenders are likely to continue violating the law as adults.

These studies indicate that chronic juvenile offenders continue their law-violating careers as adults, a concept referred to as the continuity of crime. Kids who are disruptive as early as age 5 or 6 are most likely to exhibit disruptive behavior throughout adolescence.[89]

What Causes Chronic Offending?

Research indicates that chronic offenders suffer from a number of personal, environmental, social, and developmental deficits, as shown in Exhibit 2.2. Other research studies have found that involvement in criminal activity (for example, getting arrested before age 15), relatively low intellectual development, and parental drug involvement were key predictive factors for future chronic offending.[90] Measurable problems in learning and motor skills, cognitive abilities, family relations, and other areas also predict chronicity.[91] Youthful offenders who persist are more likely to abuse alcohol, become economically dependent, have lower aspirations, and have a weak employment record.[92] Apprehension and punishment seem to have little effect on their offending behavior. Youths who have long juvenile records will most likely continue their offending careers into adulthood.

Policy Implications

Efforts to chart the life cycle of crime and delinquency will have a major influence on both theory and policy. Rather than simply asking why youths become delinquent or commit antisocial acts, theorists are charting the onset, escalation, frequency, and

EXHIBIT 2.2

Childhood Risk Factors for Persistent Delinquency

Individual Factors

▌ Early antisocial behavior

▌ Emotional factors such as high behavioral activation and low behavioral inhibition

▌ Poor cognitive development

▌ Low intelligence

▌ Hyperactivity

School and Community Factors

▌ Failure to bond to school

▌ Poor academic performance

▌ Low academic aspirations

▌ Living in a poor family

▌ Neighborhood disadvantage

▌ Disorganized neighborhoods

▌ Concentration of delinquent peer groups

▌ Access to weapons

Family Factors

▌ Parenting

▌ Maltreatment

▌ Family violence

▌ Divorce

▌ Parental psychopathology

▌ Familial antisocial behaviors

▌ Teenage parenthood

▌ Family structure

▌ Large family size

Peer Factors

▌ Association with deviant peers

▌ Peer rejection

SOURCE: Gail Wasserman, Kate Keenan, Richard Tremblay, John Coie, Todd Herrenkohl, Rolf Loeber, and David Petechuk, "Risk and Protective Factors of Child Delinquency," *Child Delinquency Bulletin Series* (Washington, DC: Office of Juvenile Justice and Delinquency Prevention, 2003).

cessation of delinquent behavior. Research on delinquent careers has also influenced policy. If relatively few offenders commit a great proportion of all delinquent acts and then persist as adult criminals, it follows that steps should be taken to limit their criminal opportunities.[93] One approach is to identify persistent offenders at the beginning of their offending careers and provide early treatment.[94] This might be facilitated by research aimed at identifying traits (for example, impulsive personalities) that can be used to classify high-risk offenders.[95] Because many of these youths suffer from a variety of problems, treatment must be aimed at a broad range of educational, family, vocational, and psychological problems. Focusing on a single problem, such as a lack of employment, may be ineffective.[96]

JUVENILE VICTIMIZATION

victimization
The number of people who are victims of criminal acts; young teens are 15 times more likely than older adults (age 65 and over) to be victims of crimes.

Juveniles are also victims of crime, and data from victim surveys can help us understand the nature of juvenile **victimization**.[97] According to the NCVS, young people are much more likely to be the victims of crime than adults. The chance of victimization declines with age. The difference is particularly striking when we compare teens under age 19 with people over age 65. Today, teens are more than 15 times as likely to become victims than their grandparents. The data also indicate that male teenagers have a significantly higher chance than females of becoming victims of most violent crime, and that African American youth have a greater chance of becoming victims of violent crimes than whites of the same age.[98] However, as Figures 2.5 and 2.6 show, young girls are much more likely to be the victim of sexual assaults, while boys are much more likely to be the victims of robbery. In either event, the likelihood of victimization for both crimes declines after the teenage years.

Teen Victims

NCVS data can also tell us something about the relationship between victims and offenders. This information is available because victims of violent personal crimes, such as assault and robbery, can identify the age, sex, and race of their attackers.

In general, teens tend to be victimized by their peers. A majority of teens were shown to have been victimized by other teens, whereas victims age 20 and over identified their attackers as being 21 or older. However, people in almost all age groups who were victimized by *groups* of offenders identified their attackers as teenagers. Violent crime victims report that a disproportionate number of their attackers are young, ranging in age from 16 to 25.

The data also tell us that victimization is intraracial (that is, within race). White teenagers tend to be victimized by white teens, and African American teenagers tend to be victimized by African American teens.

FIGURE 2.5
The Association between Gender and Sexual Assault

In sexual assaults reported to law enforcement, 67% of female victims and 88% of male victims were under age 18.

The modal age for sexual assault victims was age 14 for female victims but age 5 for male victims.

SOURCE: Howard Snyder and Melissa Sickmund, *Juvenile Offenders and Victims, 2006 National Report* (Washington, DC: U.S. Department of Justice, Office of Justice Programs, Office of Juvenile Justice and Delinquency Prevention), http://ojjdp.ncjrs.gov/ojstatbb/nr2006/downloads/chapter2.pdf (accessed October 5, 2007).

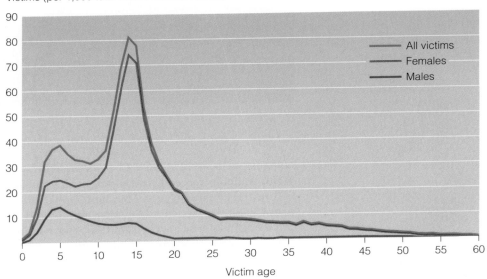

Victims (per 1,000 total sexual assault victims)

— All victims
— Females
— Males

Victim age

FIGURE **2.6**

The Association between Gender and Robbery Victimization

The number of robbery victims known to law enforcement increased with age through the juvenile years, peaking at age 19.

Persons under age 18 accounted for 14% of all male robbery victims and 6% of all female robbery victims.

SOURCE: Howard Snyder and Melissa Sickmund, *Juvenile Offenders and Victims, 2006 National Report* (Washington, DC: U.S. Department of Justice, Office of Justice Programs, Office of Juvenile Justice and Delinquency Prevention), http://ojjdp.ncjrs.gov/ojstatbb/nr2006/downloads/chapter2.pdf (accessed October 5, 2007).

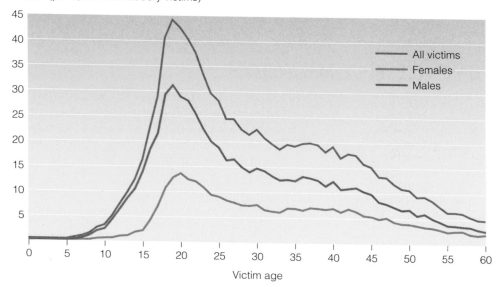

Victims (per 1,000 total robbery victims)

Victim age

All victims
Females
Males

Despite some sensational cases, the number of children abducted or murdered by strangers is less than commonly thought. However, when a young child is victimized the impact can devastate an entire community. Here, kidnap victim Carlie Brucia, 11, is shown being led away by an unidentified man on February 1, 2004. This image was taken by an exterior motion-sensor surveillance camera at a car wash. Carlie's body was found five days after she was abducted. This tragic case sadly shows the vulnerability of children to predatory criminals.

Photo from Sarasota County Sheriff's Office via Getty Images

Most teens are victimized by people with whom they are acquainted, and their victimization is more likely to occur during the day. In contrast, adults are more often victimized by strangers and at night. One explanation for this pattern is that youths are at greatest risk from their own family and relatives. (Chapter 8 deals with the issue of child abuse and neglect.) Another possibility is that many teenage victimizations occur at school, in school buildings, or on school grounds. The issue of teen victimization is discussed further in the Focus on Delinquency feature "Adolescent Victims of Violence."

Adolescent Victims of Violence

How many adolescents experience extreme physical and sexual violence and what effect does the experience have on their lives? To answer these critical questions, Dean Kilpatrick, Benjamin Saunders, and Daniel Smith conducted interviews with 4,023 adolescents ages 12 to 17 to obtain information on their substance use, abuse, delinquency, and post-traumatic stress disorder (PTSD) as well as their experiences with sexual assault, physical assault, physically abusive punishment, and witnessing acts of violence.

Kilpatrick and his colleagues found that rates of interpersonal violence and victimization among adolescents in the United States are extremely high. Approximately 1.8 million adolescents ages 12 to 17 have been sexually assaulted and 3.9 million have been severely physically assaulted. Another 2.1 million have been punished by physical abuse. The most common form of youth victimization was witnessing violence, with approximately 8.8 million youths indicating that they had seen someone else being shot, stabbed, sexually assaulted, physically assaulted, or threatened with a weapon.

There were distinct racial and ethnic patterns in youth victimization. There is a much higher incidence of all types of victimization among African American and Native American adolescents; more than half of African American, Hispanic, and Native American adolescents had witnessed violence in their lifetimes. Native American adolescents had the highest rate for sexual assault victimizations; whites and Asians reported the lowest. Native Americans, African Americans, and Hispanics also reported the highest rate of physical assault victimization—20 to 25 percent of each group reported experiencing at least one physical assault.

Gender also played a role in increasing the exposure to violence. Girls were at greater risk of sexual assault than boys (13.0 percent versus 3.4 percent). Boys were at significantly greater risk of physical assault than girls (21.3 percent versus 13.4 percent). A substantial number of all adolescents (43.6 percent of boys and 35 percent of girls) reported having witnessed violence. Physically abusive punishment was similar for boys (8.5 percent) and girls (10.2 percent).

WHAT ARE THE OUTCOMES OF ABUSE AND VIOLENCE?

The research discovered a clear relationship exists between youth victimization and mental health problems and delinquent behavior. For example:

I Negative outcomes in victims of sexual assault were three to five times the rates observed in nonvictims.

I The lifetime prevalence of post-traumatic stress disorder (PTSD) is 8 percent, indicating that approximately 1.8 million adolescents had met the criteria for PTSD at some point during their lifetime.

I Girls were significantly more likely than boys to have lifetime PTSD (10 percent versus 6 percent).

I Among boys who had experienced sexual assault, 28 percent had PTSD at some point in their lives. The rate of lifetime PTSD among boys who had not been sexually assaulted was 5 percent.

I Sexually assaulted girls had a lifetime PTSD rate of 30 percent, compared with only 7 percent of girls with no sexual assault history.

I Experiencing either a physical assault or physically abusive punishment was associated with a lifetime PTSD rate of 15 percent for boys. The rate of lifetime PTSD in boys who had not been physically assaulted or abusively punished was 3.1 percent.

I Approximately 25 percent of physically assaulted or abused adolescents reported lifetime substance abuse or dependence. Rates of substance problems among nonphysically assaulted or abused adolescents were roughly 6 percent.

I The percentage of boys who were physically assaulted and had ever committed an offense was 47 percent, compared with 10 percent of boys who were not assaulted. Similarly, 29 percent of physically assaulted girls reported having engaged in serious delinquent acts at some point in their lives, compared with 3 percent of girls who had not been assaulted.

The Kilpatrick research shows that youths ages 12 to 17 are at great risk for violent acts and that those who experience violent victimizations suffer significant social problems. Protecting adolescents must become a national priority.

Critical Thinking

1. Should people who abuse or harm adolescent children be punished more severely than those who harm adults?

2. Would you advocate the death penalty for someone who rapes an adolescent female?

SOURCES: Shawna Lee and Richard Tolman, "Childhood Sexual Abuse and Adult Work Outcomes," *Social Work Research* 30:83–92 (2006); Christine Bogar and Diana Hulse-Killacky, "Resiliency Determinants and Resiliency Processes among Female Adult Survivors of Childhood Sexual Abuse," *Journal of Counseling and Development* 84:318–327 (2006); Dean Kilpatrick, Benjamin Saunders, and Daniel Smith, *Youth Victimization: Prevalence and Implications* (Washington, DC: National Institute of Justice, 2003).

Summary

1. Be familiar with how the UCR data are gathered and used

I Delinquency experts have devised a variety of methods to measure the nature and extent of delinquency.

I Experts rely on three primary sources of data: official records, victim surveys, and self-report surveys.

I Official data on delinquent behavior are gathered in the Uniform Crime Report (UCR).

I UCR gathers data on the number and characteristics (age, race, and gender) of individuals who have been arrested. This is particularly important for delinquency research because it shows how many underage minors are arrested each year.

I The accuracy of the UCR is somewhat suspect because surveys indicate that fewer than half of all crime victims report incidents to police.

I The FBI is currently instituting a new program that collects data on each reported crime incident.

2. Discuss the concept of self-reported delinquency

I One of the most important tools to measure delinquency and youthful misconduct is the self-report survey.

I These surveys ask kids to describe, in detail, their recent and lifetime participation in antisocial activity.

I Self-reports are given in groups, and the respondents are promised anonymity in order to ensure the validity and honesty of the responses.

I In addition to questions about delinquent behavior, most self-report surveys contain questions about attitudes, values, and behaviors.

I Critics of self-report studies frequently suggest that it is unreasonable to expect kids to candidly admit illegal acts.

3. Be familiar with the National Crime Victimization Survey

I The federal government sponsors the National Crime Victimization Survey (NCVS), a comprehensive, nationwide survey of victimization in the United States.

I Each year data are obtained from a large nationally representative sample who are asked to report their experiences with crimes.

I Due to the care with which the samples are drawn and the high completion rate, NCVS data are considered a relatively unbiased, valid estimate of all victimizations for the target crimes included in the survey.

I While it contains many underreported incidents, the NCVS may also suffer from some methodological problems. As a result, its findings must be interpreted with caution.

4. Discuss alternative measures of delinquent activity and behavior

I Delinquency experts routinely use a number of methods to acquire data on youth crime and delinquency.

I Collecting cohort data involves observing over time a group of kids who share a like characteristic.

I Researchers are sometimes able to conduct controlled experiments to collect data on the cause of delinquency.

I Sometimes researchers focus their research on relatively few subjects, interviewing them in depth or observing them as they go about their activities.

I Meta-analysis involves gathering data from a number of previous studies.

I Data mining uses multiple advanced computational methods, including artificial intelligence (the use of computers to perform logical functions) to analyze large data sets usually involving one or more data sources.

I Researchers now use mapping to create graphic representations of the spatial geography of delinquency.

5. Be familiar with recent trends in juvenile delinquency

I Crime and delinquency rates trended upward between 1960 and 1991, when police recorded about 15 million crimes. Since then the number of crimes has been in decline.

I While the general crime rates did not increase in 2006, violent crimes, especially murder, ticked upwards. Though this recent increase in violence is disturbing, it is too soon to tell whether it is the beginning of a new long-term trend or a single year aberration.

I Today, about 14 million arrests are made each year, or about 5,000 per 100,000 population. Of these, more than 2 million were for serious Part I crimes and 12 million for less serious Part II crimes.

I About 1.2 million juvenile arrests were for Part II offenses.

I Juvenile delinquency continues to have a significant influence on the nation's overall crime statistics.

6. Recognize the factors that affect the juvenile crime rate

I Because teenagers have extremely high crime rates, crime experts view changes in the population age distribution as having the greatest influence on crime trends.

I As a general rule, the crime rate follows the proportion of young males in the population.

I There is debate over the effect the economy has on crime rates.

I A drop in the delinquency rate has been linked to a strong economy.

- Some believe that a poor economy may actually help lower delinquency rates because it limits the opportunity kids have to commit crime.
- As the level of social problems increases—such as single-parent families, dropout rates, racial conflict, and teen pregnancies—so do delinquency rates.
- Racial conflict may also increase delinquency rates.
- There is evidence that the recent drop in the delinquency rate can be attributed to the availability of legalized abortion.
- The availability of firearms may influence the delinquency rate, especially the proliferation of weapons in the hands of teens.
- Another factor that affects delinquency rates is the explosive growth in teenage gangs.
- Some experts argue that violent media can influence the direction of delinquency rates.

7. List and discuss the social and personal correlates of delinquency

- Delinquents are disproportionately male, although female delinquency rates are rising faster than those for males.
- Minority youth are overrepresented in the delinquency rate, especially for violent crime.
- Experts are split on the cause of racial differences. Some believe they are a function of system bias, others see them as representing actual differences in the delinquency rate.
- Disagreement also exists over the relationship between class position and delinquency.
- Some experts believe that adolescent crime is a lower-class phenomenon, whereas others see it throughout the social structure.
- Problems in methodology have obscured the true class-crime relationship. However, official statistics indicate that lower-class youths are responsible for the most serious delinquent acts.
- There is general agreement that delinquency rates decline with age.

8. Discuss the concept of the chronic offender

- Some experts believe this phenomenon is universal, whereas others believe a small group of offenders persist in crime at a high rate.

- The age-crime relationship has spurred research on the nature of delinquency over the life course.
- Delinquency data show the existence of a chronic persistent offender who begins his or her offending career early in life and persists as an adult.
- Marvin Wolfgang and his colleagues identified chronic offenders in a series of cohort studies conducted in Philadelphia.

9. Identify the causes of chronic offending

- Ongoing research has identified the characteristics of persistent offenders as they mature, and both personality and social factors help us predict long-term offending patterns.
- Early involvement in criminal activity, relatively low intellectual development, and parental drug involvement have been linked to later chronic offending.
- Measurable problems in learning and motor skills, cognitive abilities, family relations, and other areas also predict chronicity.
- Apprehension and punishment seem to have little effect on offending behavior. Youths who have long juvenile records will most likely continue their offending careers into adulthood.

10. Be familiar with the factors that predict teen victimization

- The National Crime Victimization Survey (NCVS) is an annual national survey of the victims of crime that is conducted by agencies of the federal government.
- Teenagers are much more likely to become victims of crime than are people in other age groups.
- Teens tend to be victimized by their peers.
- A majority of teens have been victimized by other teens, whereas victims age 20 and over identified their attackers as being 21 or older.
- Teen victimization is intraracial. White teenagers tend to be victimized by white teens, and African American teenagers tend to be victimized by African American teens.

Key Terms

Federal Bureau of Investigation (FBI), p. 36

Uniform Crime Report (UCR), p. 36

Part I crimes, p. 36

Part II crimes, p. 36

self-report survey, p. 39

National Crime Victimization Survey (NCVS), p. 40

meta-analysis, p. 41

systematic review, p. 41

crime mapping, p. 42

disaggregated, p. 43

racial threat theory, p. 51

aging-out process, p. 54

age of onset, p. 54

chronic juvenile or delinquent offenders, p. 55

continuity of crime, p. 57

victimization, p. 59

Viewpoint

As a juvenile court judge you are forced to make a tough decision during a hearing: whether a juvenile should be waived to the adult court. It seems that gang activity has become a way of life for residents living in local public housing projects. The Bloods sell crack, and the Wolfpack controls the drug market. When the rivalry between the two gangs exploded, 16-year-old Shatiek Johnson, a Wolfpack member, shot and killed a member of the Bloods; in retaliation, the Bloods put out a contract on his life. While in hiding, Shatiek was confronted by two undercover detectives who recognized the young fugitive. Fearing for his life, Shatiek pulled a pistol and began firing, fatally wounding one of the officers. During the hearing, you learn that Shatiek's story is not dissimilar from that of many other children raised in tough housing projects. With an absent father and a single mother who could not control her five sons, Shatiek lived in a world of drugs, gangs, and shootouts long before he was old enough to vote. By age 13, Shatiek had been involved in the gang-beating death of a homeless man in a dispute over ten dollars, for which he was given a one-year sentence at a youth detention center and released after six months.

Now charged with a crime that could be considered first-degree murder if committed by an adult, Shatiek could—if waived to the adult court—be sentenced to life in prison or even face the death penalty.

At the hearing, Shatiek seems like a lost soul. He claims he thought the police officers were killers out to collect the bounty put on his life by the Bloods. He says that killing the rival gang boy was an act of self-defense. The DA confirms that the victim was in fact a known gang assassin with numerous criminal convictions. Shatiek's mother begs you to consider the fact that her son is only 16 years old, that he has had a very difficult childhood, and that he is a victim of society's indifference to the poor.

▌ Would you treat Shatiek as a juvenile and see if a prolonged stay in a youth facility could help this troubled young man, or would you transfer (waive) him to the adult justice system?

▌ Does a 16-year-old like Shatiek deserve a second chance?

▌ Is Shatiek's behavior common among adolescent boys or unusual and disturbing?

Doing Research on the Web

To help you answer these questions and to learn more about gang membership, go to the federal site for the National Criminal Justice Reference Service, a U.N. site that offers important information, and Three Springs, a private treatment center; these sites can be accessed via

academic.cengage.com/criminaljustice/siegel

Questions for Discussion

1. What factors contribute to the aging-out process?

2. Why are males more delinquent than females? Is it a matter of lifestyle, culture, or physical properties?

3. Discuss the racial differences found in the crime rate. What factors account for differences in the African American and white crime rates?

4. Should kids who have been arrested more than three times be given mandatory incarceration sentences?

5. Do you believe that self-reports are an accurate method of gauging the nature and extent of delinquent behavior?

Notes

1. Federal Bureau of Investigation, *Crime in the United States, 2006* (Washington, DC: U.S. Government Printing Office, 2007).

2. Callie Marie Rennison, *Criminal Victimization 1999: Changes 1998–99 with Trends 1993–98* (Washington, DC: Bureau of Justice Statistics, 2000).

3. Richard Felson, Steven Messner, Anthony Hoskin, and Glenn Deane, "Reasons for Reporting and Not Reporting Domestic Violence to the Police." *Criminology* 40:617–648 (2002).

4. Bonnie Fisher, Leah Daigle, Francis Cullen, and Michael Turner, "Reporting Sexual Victimization to the Police and Others: Results from a National-Level Study of College Women," *Criminal Justice and Behavior* 30:6–39 (2003).

5. Duncan Chappell, Gilbert Geis, Stephen Schafer, and Larry Siegel, "Forcible Rape: A Comparative Study of Offenses Known to the Police in Boston and Los Angeles," in James Henslin, ed., *Studies in the Sociology of Sex* (New York: Appleton Century Crofts, 1971), pp. 169–193.

6. Robert O'Brien, "Police Productivity and Crime Rates: 1973–1992," *Criminology* 34:183–207 (1996).

7. FBI, *UCR Handbook* (Washington, DC: U.S. Government Printing Office, 1998), p. 33.

8. A pioneering effort in self-report research is A. L. Porterfield, *Youth in Trouble* (Fort Worth, TX: Leo Potishman Foundation, 1946); for a review, see Robert Hardt and George Bodine, *Development of Self-Report Instruments in Delinquency Research: A Conference Report* (Syracuse, NY: Syracuse University Youth Development Center, 1965). See also Fred Murphy, Mary Shirley, and Helen Witner, "The

Incidence of Hidden Delinquency," *American Journal of Orthopsychology* 16:686–696 (1946).

9. Christiane Brems, Mark Johnson, David Neal, and Melinda Freemon, "Childhood Abuse History and Substance Use among Men and Women Receiving Detoxification Services," *American Journal of Drug and Alcohol Abuse* 30:799–821 (2004).

10. David Kirk, "Examining the Divergence Across Self-Report and Official Data Sources on Inferences about the Adolescent Life-Course of Crime," *Journal of Quantitative Criminology* 22:107–129 (2006).

11. Vincent Webb, Charles Katz, and Scott Decker, "Assessing the Validity of Self-Reports by Gang Members: Results from the Arrestee Drug Abuse Monitoring Program," *Crime and Delinquency* 52:232–252 (2006).

12. Leonore Simon, "Validity and Reliability of Violent Juveniles: A Comparison of Juvenile Self-Reports with Adult Self-Reports Incarcerated in Adult Prisons," paper presented at the annual meeting of the American Society of Criminology, Boston, November 1995, p. 26.

13. Stephen Cernkovich, Peggy Giordano, and Meredith Pugh, "Chronic Offenders: The Missing Cases in Self-Report Delinquency Research," *Journal of Criminal Law and Criminology* 76:705–732 (1985).

14. Terence Thornberry, Beth Bjerregaard, and William Miles, "The Consequences of Respondent Attrition in Panel Studies: A Simulation Based on the Rochester Youth Development Study," *Journal of Quantitative Criminology* 9:127–158 (1993).

15. See Spencer Rathus and Larry Siegel, "Crime and Personality Revisited: Effects of MMPI Sets on Self-Report Studies," *Criminology* 18:245–251 (1980); John Clark and Larry Tifft, "Polygraph and Interview Validation of Self-Reported Deviant Behavior," *American Sociological Review* 31:516–523 (1966).

16. Mallie Paschall, Miriam Ornstein, and Robert Flewelling, "African-American Male Adolescents' Involvement in the Criminal Justice System: The Criterion Validity of Self-Report Measures in Prospective Study," *Journal of Research in Crime and Delinquency* 38:174–187 (2001).

17. Jennifer Roberts, Edward Mulvey, Julie Horney, John Lewis, and Michael Arter, "A Test of Two Methods of Recall for Violent Events," *Journal of Quantitative Criminology* 21:175–193 (2005).

18. Lila Kazemian and David Farrington, "Comparing the Validity of Prospective, Retrospective, and Official Onset for Different Offending Categories," *Journal of Quantitative Criminology* 21:127–147 (2005).

19. Shannan Catalano, *Criminal Victimization 2005* (Washington, DC: Bureau of Justice Statistics, 2006). Data in this section come from this report.

20. L. Edward Wells and Joseph Rankin, "Juvenile Victimization: Convergent Validation of Alternative Measurements," *Journal of Research in Crime and Delinquency* 32:287–307 (1995).

21. Thomas Bernard, "Juvenile Crime and the Transformation of Juvenile Justice: Is There a Juvenile Crime Wave?" *Justice Quarterly* 16:336–356 (1999).

22. For example, the following studies have noted the great discrepancy between official statistics and self-report studies: Maynard Erickson and LaMar Empey, "Court Records, Undetected Delinquency, and Decision Making," *Journal of Criminal Law, Criminology, and Police Science* 54:456–469 (1963); Martin Gold, "Undetected Delinquent Behavior," *Journal of Research in Crime and Delinquency* 3:27–46 (1966); James Short and F. Ivan Nye, "Extent of Unrecorded Delinquency, Tentative Conclusions," *Journal of Criminal Law, Criminology, and Police Science* 49:296–302 (1958).

23. Jerald Bachman, Lloyd Johnston, and Patrick O'Malley, *Monitoring the Future: Questionnaire Responses from the Nation's High School Seniors, 2002* (Ann Arbor, MI: Institute for Social Research, 2003).

24. Julia Yun Soo Kim, Michael Fendrich, and Joseph S. Wislar, "The Validity of Juvenile Arrestees' Drug Use Reporting: A Gender Comparison," *Journal of Research in Crime and Delinquency* 37:419–432 (2000).

25. Barbara Warner and Brandi Wilson Coomer, "Neighborhood Drug Arrest Rates: Are They a Meaningful Indicator of Drug Activity? A Research Note," *Journal of Research in Crime and Delinquency* 40:123–139 (2003).

26. Alfred Blumstein, Jacqueline Cohen, and Richard Rosenfeld, "Trend and Deviation in Crime Rates: A Comparison of UCR and NCVS Data for Burglary and Robbery," *Criminology* 29:237–248 (1991). See also Michael Hindelang, Travis Hirschi, and Joseph Weis, *Measuring Delinquency* (Beverly Hills, CA: Sage, 1981).

27. James A. Fox, *Trends in Juvenile Violence: A Report to the United States Attorney General on Current and Future Rates of Juvenile Offending* (Boston: Northeastern University, 1996).

28. Steven Levitt, "The Limited Role of Changing Age Structure in Explaining Aggregate Crime Rates," *Criminology* 37:581–599 (1999).

29. Steven Levitt, "Understanding Why Crime Fell in the 1990s: Four Factors that Explain the Decline and Six that Do Not," *Journal of Economic Perspectives* 18 (2004).

30. Julie Phillips, "The Relationship between Age Structure and Homicide Rates in the United States, 1970 to 1999," *Journal of Research in Crime and Delinquency* 43:230–260 (2006).

31. Brad Bushman, Morgan Wang, and Craig Anderson, "Is the Curve Relating Temperature to Aggression Linear or Curvilinear? Assaults and Temperature in Minneapolis Reexamined," *Journal of Personality and Social Psychology* 89:62–66 (2005).

32. Paul Bell, "Reanalysis and Perspective in the Heat-Aggression Debate," *Journal of Personality and Social Psychology* 89:71–73 (2005); Ellen Cohn, "The Prediction of Police Calls for Service: The Influence of Weather and Temporal Variables on Rape and Domestic Violence," *Journal of Environmental Psychology* 13:71–83 (1993).

33. Michael Hindelang, Travis Hirschi, and Joseph Weis, *Measuring Delinquency* (Beverly Hills, CA: Sage, 1981); Gary Jensen and Raymond Eve, "Sex Differences in Delinquency: An Examination of Popular Sociological Explanation," *Criminology* 13:427–448 (1976); Michael Hindelang, "Age, Sex, and the Versatility of Delinquent Involvements," *Social Problems* 18:522–535 (1979); James Short and F. Ivan Nye, "Extent of Unrecorded Juvenile Delinquency, Tentative Conclusions," *Journal of Criminal Law, Criminology, and Police Science* 49:296–302 (1958).

34. Darrell Steffensmeier, Jennifer Schwartz, Hua Zhong, and Jeff Ackerman, "An Assessment of Recent Trends in Girls' Violence Using Diverse Longitudinal Sources: Is the Gender Gap Closing?" *Criminology* 43:355–406 (2005).

35. Leroy Gould, "Who Defines Delinquency? A Comparison of Self-Report and Officially Reported Indices of Delinquency for Three Racial Groups," *Social Problems* 16:325–336 (1969); Harwin Voss, "Ethnic Differentials in Delinquency in Honolulu," *Journal of Criminal Law, Criminology, and Police Science* 54:322–327 (1963); Ronald Akers, Marvin Krohn, Marcia Radosevich, and Lonn Lanza-Kaduce, "Social Characteristics and Self-Reported Delinquency," in Gary Jensen, ed., *Sociology of Delinquency* (Beverly Hills, CA: Sage, 1981), pp. 48–62.

36. David Huizinga and Delbert Elliott, "Juvenile Offenders: Prevalence, Offender Incidence, and Arrest Rates by Race," *Crime and Delinquency* 33:206–223 (1987); see also Dale Dannefer and Russell Schutt, "Race and Juvenile Justice Processing in Court and Police Agencies," *American Journal of Sociology* 87:1113–1132 (1982).

37. Paul Tracy, "Race and Class Differences in Official and Self-Reported Delinquency," in Marvin Wolfgang, Terrence Thornberry, and Robert Figlio, eds., *From Boy to Man, from Delinquency to Crime* (Chicago: University of Chicago Press, 1987), p. 120.

38. Bachman, Johnston, and O'Malley, *Monitoring the Future*, pp. 102–104.

39. Samuel Walker, Cassia Spohn, and Miriam DeLone, *The Color of Justice: Race, Ethnicity, and Crime in America* (Belmont, CA: Brooks/Cole, 1992), pp. 46–47.

40. Miriam Sealock and Sally Simpson, "Unraveling Bias in Arrest Decisions: The Role of Juvenile Offender Typescripts," *Justice Quarterly* 15:427–457 (1998).

41. Hubert Blalock, Jr., *Toward a Theory of Minority-Group Relations* (New York: Capricorn Books, 1967).

42. Rodney Engen, Sara Steen, and George Bridges, "Racial Disparities in the Punishment of Youth: A Theoretical and Empirical Assessment of the Literature," *Social Problems* 49:194–221 (2002).

43. Karen Parker, Briam Stults, and Stephen Rice, "Racial Threat, Concentrated Disadvantage and Social Control: Considering the Macro-Level Sources of Variation in Arrests," *Criminology* 43:1111–1134 (2005); Lisa Stolzenberg, J. Stewart D'Alessio, and David Eitle, "A Multilevel Test of Racial Threat Theory," *Criminology* 42:673–698 (2004).

44. Michael Leiber and Kristan Fox, "Race and the Impact of Detention on Juvenile Justice Decision Making," *Crime and Delinquency* 51:470–497 (2005); Traci Schlesinger, "Racial and Ethnic Disparity in Pretrial Criminal Processing," *Justice Quarterly* 22:170–192 (2005).

45. Christina DeJong and Kenneth Jackson, "Putting Race into Context: Race, Juvenile Justice Processing, and Urbanization," *Justice Quarterly* 15:487–504 (1998).

46. Engen, Steen, and Bridges, "Racial Disparities in the Punishment of Youth."

47. David Eitle, Stewart D'Alessio, and Lisa Stolzenberg, "Racial Threat and Social Control: A Test of the Political, Economic, and Threat of Black Crime Hypotheses," *Social Forces* 81:557–576 (2002); Michael Leiber and Jayne Stairs, "Race, Contexts, and the Use of Intake Diversion," *Journal of Research in Crime and Delinquency* 36:56–86 (1999); Darrell Steffensmeier, Jeffery Ulmer, and John Kramer, "The Interaction of Race, Gender, and Age in Criminal Sentencing: The Punishment Cost of Being Young, Black, and Male," *Criminology* 36:763–798 (1998).

48. For a general review, see William Wilbanks, *The Myth of a Racist Criminal Justice System* (Pacific Grove, CA: Brooks/Cole, 1987).

49. Walker, Spohn, and DeLone, *The Color of Justice*, pp. 47–48.

50. Mallie Paschall, Robert Flewelling, and Susan Ennett, "Racial Differences in Violent Behavior among Young Adults: Moderating and Confounding Effects," *Journal of Research in Crime and Delinquency* 35:148–165 (1998).

51. Gary LaFree and Richard Arum, "The Impact of Racially Inclusive Schooling on Adult Incarceration Rates among U.S. Cohorts of African Americans and Whites Since 1930," *Criminology* 44:73–103 (2006).

52. Julie Phillips, "Variation in African-American Homicide Rates: An Assessment of Potential Explanations," *Criminology* 35:527–559 (1997).

53. Melvin Thomas, "Race, Class, and Personal Income: An Empirical Test of the Declining Significance of Race Thesis, 1968–1988," *Social Problems* 40:328–339 (1993).

54. Thomas McNulty and Paul Bellair, "Explaining Racial and Ethnic Differences in Adolescent Violence: Structural Disadvantage, Family Well-Being, and Social Capital," *Justice Quarterly* 20:1–32 (2003).

55. Julie Phillips, "White, Black, and Latino Homicide Rates: Why the Difference?" *Social Problems* 49:349–374 (2002).

56. Carl Pope and William Feyerherm, "Minority Status and Juvenile Processing: An Assessment of the Research Literature," paper presented at the annual meeting of the American Society of Criminology, Reno, Nevada, November 1989.

57. Robert Agnew, "A General Strain Theory of Community Differences in Crime Rates," *Journal of Research in Crime and Delinquency* 36:123–155 (1999).

58. Bonita Veysey and Steven Messner, "Further Testing of Social Disorganization Theory: An Elaboration of Sampson and Groves's 'Community Structure and Crime,'" *Journal of Research in Crime and Delinquency* 36:156–174 (1999).

59. Carter Hay, Edward Fortson, Dusten Hollist, Irshad Altheimer, and Lonnie Schaible, "Compounded Risk: The Implications for Delinquency of Coming from a Poor Family that Lives in a Poor Community," *Journal of Youth and Adolescence* 36:593–605 (2007).

60. James Short and Ivan Nye, "Reported Behavior as a Criterion of Deviant Behavior," *Social Problems* 5:207–213 (1958).

61. Classic studies include Ivan Nye, James Short, and Virgil Olsen, "Socioeconomic Status and Delinquent Behavior," *American Journal of Sociology* 63:381–389 (1958); Robert Dentler and Lawrence Monroe, "Social Correlates of Early Adolescent Theft," *American Sociological Review* 26:733–743 (1961); Charles Tittle, Wayne Villemez, and Douglas Smith, "The Myth of Social Class and Criminality: An Empirical Assessment of the Empirical Evidence," *American Sociological Review* 43:643–656 (1978).

62. R. Gregory Dunaway, Francis Cullen, Velmer Burton, and T. David Evans, "The Myth of Social Class and Crime Revisited: An Examination of Class and Adult Criminality," *Criminology* 38:589–632 (2000).

63. Margaret Farnworth, Terence Thornberry, Marvin Krohn, and Alan Lizotte, *Measurement in the Study of Class and Delinquency: Integrating Theory and Research.* Working paper no. 4, rev. (Albany, NY: Rochester Youth Development Survey, 1992), p. 19.

64. G. Roger Jarjoura and Ruth Triplett, "Delinquency and Class: A Test of the Proximity Principle," *Justice Quarterly* 14:765–792 (1997).

65. See, generally, David Farrington, "Age and Crime," in Michael Tonry and Norval Morris, eds., *Crime and Justice: An Annual Review*, vol. 7 (Chicago: University of Chicago Press, 1986), pp. 189–250.

66. Travis Hirschi and Michael Gottfredson, "Age and the Explanation of Crime," *American Journal of Sociology* 89:552–584 (1983).

67. Michael Gottfredson and Travis Hirschi, "The True Value of Lambda Would Appear to Be Zero: An Essay on Career Criminals, Criminal Careers, Selective Incapacitation, Cohort Studies, and Related Topics," *Criminology* 24:213–234 (1986); further support for their position can be found in Lawrence Cohen and Kenneth Land, "Age Structure and Crime," *American Sociological Review* 52:170–183 (1987).

68. Lila Kazemian and David Farrington, "Exploring Residual Career Length and Residual Number of Offenses for Two Generations of Repeat Offenders," *Journal of Research in Crime and Delinquency* 43:89–113 (2006).

69. David Greenberg, "Age, Crime, and Social Explanation," *American Journal of Sociology* 91:1–21 (1985).

70. Robert Sampson and John Laub, *Crime in the Making: Pathways and Turning Points Through Life* (Cambridge, MA: Harvard University Press, 1993).

71. Marvin Wolfgang, Robert Figlio, and Thorsten Sellin, *Delinquency in a Birth Cohort* (Chicago: University of Chicago Press, 1972); Lyle Shannon, *Assessing the Relationship of Adult Criminal Careers to Juvenile Careers: A Summary* (Washington, DC: U.S. Department of Justice, 1982); D. J. West and David P. Farrington, *The Delinquent Way of Life* (London: Heinemann,

1977); Donna Hamparian, Richard Schuster, Simon Dinitz, and John Conrad, *The Violent Few* (Lexington, MA: Lexington Books, 1978).

72. Rolf Loeber and Howard Snyder, "Rate of Offending in Juvenile Careers: Findings of Constancy and Change in Lambda," *Criminology* 28:97–109 (1990).

73. Margo Wilson and Martin Daly, "Life Expectancy, Economic Inequality, Homicide, and Reproductive Timing in Chicago Neighbourhoods," *British Journal of Medicine* 31:1271–1274 (1997).

74. Edward Mulvey and John LaRosa, "Delinquency Cessation and Adolescent Development: Preliminary Data," *American Journal of Orthopsychiatry* 56:212–224 (1986).

75. Timothy Brezina, "Delinquent Problem-Solving: An Interpretive Framework for Criminological Theory and Research," *Journal of Research in Crime and Delinquency* 37:3–30 (2000).

76. Gordon Trasler, "Cautions for a Biological Approach to Crime," in Sarnoff Mednick, Terrie Moffitt, and Susan Stack, eds., *The Causes of Crime, New Biological Approaches* (Cambridge: Cambridge University Press, 1987), pp. 7–25.

77. Alicia Rand, "Transitional Life Events and Desistance from Delinquency and Crime," in Wolfgang, Thornberry, and Figlio, eds., *From Boy to Man*, pp. 134–163.

78. Marc LeBlanc, "Late Adolescence Deceleration of Criminal Activity and Development of Self- and Social-Control," *Studies on Crime and Crime Prevention* 2:51–68 (1993).

79. Barry Glassner, Margaret Ksander, Bruce Berg, and Bruce Johnson, "Note on the Deterrent Effect of Juvenile vs. Adult Jurisdiction," *Social Problems* 31:219–221 (1983).

80. Neal Shover and Carol Thompson, "Age, Differential Expectations, and Crime Desistance," *Criminology* 30:89–104 (1992).

81. D. Wayne Osgood, "The Covariation among Adolescent Problem Behaviors," paper presented at the annual meeting of the American Society of Criminology, Baltimore, November 1990.

82. Stephen Tibbetts, "Low Birth Weight, Disadvantaged Environment, and Early Onset: A Test of Moffitt's Interactional Hypothesis," paper presented at the annual meeting of the American Society of Criminology, Boston, November 1995.

83. Arnold Barnett, Alfred Blumstein, and David Farrington, "A Prospective Test of a Criminal Career Model," *Criminology* 27:373–388 (1989).

84. Wolfgang, Figlio, and Sellin, *Delinquency in a Birth Cohort.*

85. Paul Tracy, Marvin Wolfgang, and Robert Figlio, *Delinquency in Two Birth Cohorts, Executive Summary* (Washington, DC: U.S. Department of Justice, 1985).

86. Shannon, *Assessing the Relationship of Adult Criminal Careers to Juvenile Careers*; Howard Snyder, *Court Careers of Juvenile Offenders* (Washington, DC: Office of Juvenile Justice and Delinquency Prevention, 1988); Donald J. West and David P. Farrington, *The Delinquent Way of Life* (London: Heinemann, 1977); Hamparian, Schuster, Dinitz, and Conrad, *The Violent Few.*

87. See, generally, Wolfgang, Thornberry, and Figlio, *From Boy to Man.*

88. Paul Tracy and Kimberly Kempf-Leonard, *Continuity and Discontinuity in Criminal Careers* (New York: Plenum, 1996).

89. R. Tremblay, R. Loeber, C. Gagnon, P. Charlebois, S. Larivee, and M. LeBlanc, "Disruptive Boys with Stable and Unstable High Fighting Behavior Patterns During Junior Elementary School," *Journal of Abnormal Child Psychology* 19:285–300 (1991).

90. Peter Jones, Philip Harris, James Fader, and Lori Grubstein, "Identifying Chronic Juvenile Offenders," *Justice Quarterly* 18:478–507 (2001).

91. Jennifer White, Terrie Moffitt, Felton Earls, Lee Robins, and Phil Silva, "How Early Can We Tell? Predictors of Childhood Conduct Disorder and Adolescent Delinquency," *Criminology* 28:507–535 (1990).

92. Kimberly Kempf-Leonard, Paul Tracy, and James Howell, "Serious, Violent, and Chronic Juvenile Offenders: The Relationship of Delinquency Career Types to Adult Criminality," *Justice Quarterly* 18:449–478 (2001).

93. Kimberly Kempf, "Crime Severity and Criminal Career Progression," *Journal of Criminal Law and Criminology* 79:524–540 (1988).

94. Jeffrey Fagan, "Social and Legal Policy Dimensions of Violent Juvenile Crime," *Criminal Justice and Behavior* 17:93–133 (1990).

95. Peter Greenwood, *Selective Incapacitation* (Santa Monica, CA: Rand, 1982).

96. Terence Thornberry, David Huizinga, and Rolf Loeber, "The Prevention of Serious Delinquency and Violence," in James Howell, Barry Krisberg, J. David Hawkins, and John Wilson, eds., *Sourcebook on Serious, Violent, and Chronic Juvenile Offenders* (Thousand Oaks, CA: Sage, 1995).

97. Data here come from Shannan Catalano, *Criminal Victimization, 2005* (Washington, DC: Bureau of Justice Statistics, 2006).

98. Craig A. Perkins, *Age Patterns of Victims of Serious Violent Crime* (Washington, DC: Bureau of Justice Statistics, 1997).

Theories of Delinquency

2

What causes delinquent behavior? Why do some youths enter a life of crime that persists into their adulthood? Are people products of their environment, or is the likelihood of their becoming a delinquent determined at birth?

Social scientists have speculated on the cause of delinquency for 200 years. They have observed facts about delinquent behavior and organized them into complex theoretical models. A *theory* is a statement that explains the relationship between abstract concepts in a meaningful way. For example, if scientists observe that delinquency rates are usually higher in neighborhoods with high unemployment rates, poor housing, and inadequate schools, they might theorize that environmental conditions influence delinquent behavior. This theory suggests that social conditions can exert a powerful influence on human behavior.

Since the study of delinquency is essentially interdisciplinary, it is not surprising that a variety of theoretical models have been formulated to explain juvenile misbehavior. Each reflects the training and orientation of its creator. Consequently, theories of delinquency reflect many different avenues of inquiry, including biology, psychology, sociology, political science, and economics. Chapter 3 reviews theories that hold that delinquency is essentially caused by individual-level factors, such as personal choices and decision making or by psychological and biological factors. Chapter 4 reviews social theories of delinquency that hold that youthful misbehavior is caused by children's place in the social structure and/or their relationships with social institutions and processes. Chapter 5 reviews those theories of delinquency that regard youthful misbehavior as a function of stigma and labeling and also those theories that link both stigma and delinquency to the effects of social conflict. Chapter 6 discusses the theories of delinquency that regard it as a developmental process, reflecting the changes that occur in young people's lives as they evolve during their life course.

Logic dictates that the competing theoretical models presented here cannot all be correct and that some of these may be barking up the wrong tree. Yet every branch of social science—sociology, psychology, political science, economics—contains competing theoretical models. Why people behave the way they do and how society functions are issues that are far from settled. So do not lose patience! Explaining delinquency is a highly complex phenomenon with many points of view.

Individual Views of Delinquency

Chapter Objectives

1. Be familiar with and distinguish between the two branches of individual-level theories of delinquency
2. Know the principles of choice theory
3. Discuss the routine activities theory of delinquency
4. Know the principles of general deterrence theory
5. Distinguish between the effects of punishment and incarceration
6. Discuss the concept of situational crime prevention
7. Trace the history and development of trait theory
8. Be familiar with the branches and substance of biological trait theory
9. Know the various psychological theories of delinquency
10. Be familiar with the psychological traits that have been linked to delinquency

© AP Images/Alamogordo Daily News/Ellis Neel

On July 6, 2004, law enforcement authorities were summoned to the New Mexico ranch of ABC newsman Sam Donaldson. There they discovered the bodies of foreman Delbert Paul Posey, his wife, Tryone Posey, and her daughter, Mary Lee Schmid, 14. A day later, Posey's 14-year-old son, Cody, was arrested on charges of killing his father, stepmother, and stepsister.[1]

The Posey family seemed to be happy and well-adjusted. They had been running one of Donaldson's southern New Mexico ranches for more than two years. Yet Donaldson and neighbors knew that Posey was a tough father who did not shy away from discipline. Cody Posey had seemed withdrawn and moody. Later, law enforcement officials learned that Cody may have been the victim of abuse and that he often showed up at school bruised and battered. He told police that his father had beaten him once too often and that after the last time he took a gun from the barn and shot his family.

Tried as an adult, on February 7, 2006, Cody was convicted of first-degree murder in the death of his stepsister, second-degree murder in the death of his stepmother, and voluntary manslaughter in the death of his father. He was also found guilty of four charges of evidence tampering. Though he could have been put behind bars until he was in his 60s, at least half of the jurors wrote letters to the presiding judge, James Waylon Counts, asking him to sentence Cody as a juvenile. Agreeing with these jurors, Judge Counts gave Cody a juvenile sentence that requires him to remain in the custody of juvenile authorities until he reaches the age of 21.

The Cody Posey case illustrates the fact that many delinquent acts are not caused by some environmental factor such as poverty or hopelessness but must be viewed within the context of individual behaviors and emotions. The Posey family did not live in an inner-city area but on the ranch of a wealthy TV personality. Cody's behavior was motivated not by his environment but by his own mental state, experiences, and decision making.

Some delinquency experts believe that the decision to commit an illegal act is a product of an individual decision-making process shaped by the personal characteristics of the decision maker. Others reject the notion that delinquents are a product of their environment and instead search for an individual trait—selfish temperament, impulsive personality, abnormal hormones—to explain why some people may choose antisocial over conventional behaviors. If social and economic factors alone determine behavior, how is it that many youths residing in the most dangerous and deteriorated neighborhoods live law-abiding lives? According to the U.S. Census Bureau, more than 37 million Americans live in poverty, yet the vast majority of people do not become delinquents and criminals.[2] Research indicates that relatively few youths in any population, even the most economically disadvantaged, actually become hard-core, chronic delinquents.[3] If poverty and environment were solely responsible for antisocial behaviors then there would be many more delinquent youth and their numbers would be increasing.

If social factors are not responsible for the onset of delinquency, what is? To some theorists, the locus of delinquency is rooted in the *individual:* how the individual makes decisions, the quality of his or her biological makeup, and his or her personality and psychological profile.

Individual-level explanations of delinquency can be divided into two distinct categories. One position, referred to as **choice theory**, suggests that young offenders *choose* to engage in antisocial activity because they believe their actions will be beneficial and profitable. Whether they join a gang, steal cars, or sell drugs, their delinquent acts are motivated by the reasoned belief that illegal acts can be profitable and relatively risk-free. They have little fear of getting caught and, if they are apprehended, discount the legal consequences. Some are motivated by fantasies of riches, whereas others may simply enjoy the excitement and short-term gratification produced by delinquent acts such as beating up an opponent or stealing a car.

All youthful misbehavior, however, cannot be traced to rational choice, profit motive, or criminal entrepreneurship. Some delinquent acts, especially violent ones, seem irrational, selfish, and/or hedonistic. Some delinquency experts believe that these seemingly irrational and destructive antisocial behaviors may be inspired by aberrant physical or psychological traits rather than rational thought and decision making While it may be true some youths choose to get involved in delinquent behaviors, others may be driven by biological or psychological abnormalities, such as hyperactivity, low intelligence, biochemical imbalance, or genetic defects. This view of delinquency is referred to here generally as **trait theory** because it links delinquency to biological and psychological traits that control human development.

Choice and trait theories, though independent, are linked here because they share some common ground:

| Both focus on mental and behavioral processes at the individual level. Delinquency is an individual problem, not a social problem.

| Both recognize that because all people are constitutionally different, each reacts to the same set of environmental and social conditions in a unique way. Not all people living under the same socioeconomic conditions behave in the same manner or react in the same manner.

| Because the root cause of delinquency is located at the individual level, delinquency prevention and control efforts must be directed at the individual offender. We must change people rather than society.

This chapter first covers those theoretical models that focus on individual choice. Then it discusses the view that biological and psychological development controls youngsters' ability to make choices, rendering some of them violent, aggressive, and antisocial.

choice theory
Holds that youths will engage in delinquent and criminal behavior after weighing the consequences and benefits of their actions; delinquent behavior is a rational choice made by a motivated offender who perceives that the chances of gain outweigh any possible punishment or loss.

trait theory
Holds that youths engage in delinquent or criminal behavior due to aberrant physical or psychological traits that govern behavioral choices; delinquent actions are impulsive or instinctual rather than rational choices.

RATIONAL CHOICE THEORY

free will
View that youths are in charge of their own destinies and are free to make personal behavior choices unencumbered by environmental factors.

The first formal explanations of crime and delinquency held that human behavior was a matter of choice. Because it was assumed that people had **free will** to choose their behavior, those who violated the law were motivated by personal needs such as greed, revenge, survival, and hedonism. Over 200 years ago, **utilitarian** philosophers Cesare Beccaria and Jeremy Bentham argued that people weigh the benefits

To read more about **Cesare Beccaria**, go to academic .cengage.com/criminaljustice/ siegel.

and consequences of their future actions before deciding on a course of behavior.[4] Their writings formed the core of what is referred to today as classical criminology.

The classical view of crime and delinquency holds that the decision to violate the law comes after a careful weighing of the benefits and costs of criminal behaviors. Most potential law violators would cease their actions if the potential pain associated with a behavior outweighed its anticipated gain; conversely, law-violating behavior seems attractive if the future rewards seem far greater than the potential punishment.[5]

Classical criminologists argued that punishment should be only severe enough to deter a particular offense and that punishments should be graded according to the seriousness of particular crimes: "Let the punishment fit the crime." In his famous analysis, Beccaria stated that to be effective, punishment must be sufficiently severe, certain, and swift to control crime. If rapists and murderers were punished in a similar fashion—put to death—it might encourage a rapist to kill his victims in order to prevent them from calling the police or testifying in court.[6]

The Rational Delinquent

According to this view, delinquents are rational decision makers who choose to violate the law. Before they decide to commit a delinquent act, they weigh the possible benefits or profits, such as cash to buy cars, clothes, and other luxury items, with the potential costs or penalties, such as arrest followed by a long stay in a juvenile facility. If, for instance, they believe that drug dealers are rarely caught and even then usually avoid severe punishments, the youths will more likely choose to become dealers than if they believe that dealers are almost always caught and punished by lengthy prison terms. Some kids may know people or hear about criminals who make a significant income from illegal activities and want to follow in their footsteps.[7]

If kids choose delinquency because "it pays," then it stands to reason that they will forgo illegal behavior if they can be convinced that "crime does not pay."[8] Such measures as adding police officers and having them aggressively patrol the streets, adding school resource officers, and creating anti-gang units are all measures designed to convince would-be delinquents that the chances of apprehension are too great to risk crime. Another approach is to threaten harsh punishments such as waiver to adult court and a sentence to prison. Many kids know that as they age they will no longer be treated as a juvenile, and that an adult prison sentence is much more serious than a stay in a juvenile correctional center. Soon they may begin to realize that the risks of crime are greater than the potential profits and decide to go straight.

Shaping Delinquent Choices

Choice theorists believe that law-violating behavior occurs when a reasoning offender decides to take the chance of violating the law after considering his or her personal situation (need for money, learning experiences, opportunities for conventional success), values (conscience, moral values, need for peer approval), and situation (overcoming some immediate problem). What are some of the most important social developments that produce or influence delinquent decision making?

Personal Problems Kids may be forced to choose delinquent behavior to help them solve problems that defy conventional solutions.[9] Adolescents may find themselves feeling "out of control" because society limits their opportunities and resources. Delinquency may allow some adolescents to exert control over their own lives and destinies, by helping them avoid situations they find uncomfortable or repellant by cutting school or running away from an abusive home. Delinquency may also enable them to obtain things they desire by stealing or selling drugs to buy

Do delinquents choose to commit illegal acts? The evidence shows that most do and that delinquency is a matter of planning as well. Andrew Elisha Staley, a teenager accused of burning a U.S. flag on the Fourth of July, is released after spending nine days in custody. It would be difficult to believe that an act such as flag burning was not planned.

stylish outfits, or deal with rivals or adversaries by getting a gun for self-protection from a local gang.

Parental Controls Adolescents whose parents are poor supervisors and allow them the freedom to socialize with peers are more likely to engage in deviant behaviors.[10] Gender differences in delinquency may be explained in part by variation in parental controls: Teenage boys may have the highest crime rates because they, rather than girls, have the freedom to engage in unsupervised socialization.[11] Though girls are more closely supervised than boys, those who are physically mature seem to have more freedom. Physically mature girls have a lifestyle more similar to boys, and without parental supervision they are the ones most likely to have the opportunity to engage in antisocial acts.[12]

Financial Needs The choice of delinquency may be shaped by economic needs. Kids who use drugs may increase their delinquent activities proportionate to the costs of their habit. As the cost of their drug habit increases, the lure of illegal profits becomes overwhelmingly attractive.[13] Kids may choose delinquency because they believe they have little chance of becoming successful in the conventional world. In the long run, they view drug dealing and car thefts as their ticket to a better life; in the short run, delinquency can provide them with the cash for bling. When Steven Levitt and Sudhir Alladi Venkatesh studied the financial rewards of being in a drug gang, they found that despite enormous risks to their health, life, and freedom, the average gang member earned slightly more than what they could in the legitimate labor market (about six to eleven dollars per hour).[14] Why did they stay in the gang? Gang members believed that there was a strong potential for future riches if they stayed in the drug business and achieved a "management" position as a gang leader who earned quite a bit more than the rank and file members.[15] In reality the likelihood of becoming a well-off gang leader was actually pretty remote, but kids based their behavior on what they believed would happen in the future and not upon what was really likely to occur—for example, the likelihood that they would get shot, go to jail, and never actually become a gang leader.

Getting a Job While economic necessity may propel some kids into delinquent modes of behavior, others may seek a more conventional solution to their problems, such as getting an after-school or weekend job. While gainful employment sounds like a healthy choice, research efforts show that adolescent work experience may actually increase delinquency rather than limit its occurrence. Rather than saving for college as their parents hope, kids who get jobs may be looking for an easy opportunity to acquire cash to buy drugs and alcohol; after-school jobs may attract teens who are more impulsive than ambitious.[16] At work, they will have the opportunity to socialize with deviant peers. This influence, combined with lack of parental supervision, increases criminal motivation.[17] Though some adults may think that providing teens with a job will reduce criminal activity—under the theory that "idle hands are the devil's workshop"—some aspects of the work experience, such as autonomy, increased social status among peers, and increased income, may neutralize the positive effects of working. While the effect of teen employment may not be what is expected or desired, work experiences may have a beneficial influence under some conditions:

▌ Work has proven beneficial if the employment opportunity provides a positive learning experience and can be used to support academic achievement.[18]

| Teen work may have a constructive effect on those individuals who have already been involved in criminal activity or substance abuse prior to their working for the first time. For previously delinquent kids, an after-school job seems to have benefit, an outcome not enjoyed by those who have never been involved in delinquency.[19]

Routine Activities

Given the fact that youthful behavior may be shaped by life experiences, why do some kids choose to commit crimes while others are resigned to a conventional lifestyle? And are there structural factors that influence delinquent decision making? According to **routine activities theory**, originally developed by Lawrence Cohen and Marcus Felson, the volume and distribution of **predatory crime** (violent crimes against the person and crimes in which an offender attempts to steal an object directly from its holder) are influenced by the interaction of three variables that reflect the routine activities found in everyday American life: the *lack of capable guardians* (such as home owners and their neighbors, friends, and relatives); the availability of *suitable targets* (such as homes containing easily salable goods); and the presence of *motivated offenders* (such as unemployed teenagers). If each of these components is present, there is greater likelihood that a predatory crime will take place (see Figure 3.1).[20]

routine activities theory
View that crime is a "normal" function of the routine activities of modern living; offenses can be expected if there is a motivated offender and a suitable target that is not protected by capable guardians.

predatory crime
Violent crimes against people, and crimes in which an offender attempts to steal an object directly from its holder.

| *Lack of capable guardians.* The presence of capable guardians who can protect homes and possessions can reduce the motivation to commit delinquent acts. Even the most motivated offenders may ignore valuable targets if they are well guarded. Private homes and/or public businesses may be considered off-limits if they are well protected by capable guardians and efficient security systems.[21] Since 1970, the number of adult caretakers at home during the day decreased because more women entered the workforce. Because mothers are at work and children are in daycare, homes are left unguarded and become suitable targets. Similarly, with the growth of suburbia and the decline of the traditional neighborhood, the number of such familiar guardians as family, neighbors, and friends has diminished.[22] Research shows that crime levels are relatively low in

FIGURE 3.1
Routine Activities Theory Posits the Interaction of Three Factors Helps Explain Fluctuations in the Delinquency Rate

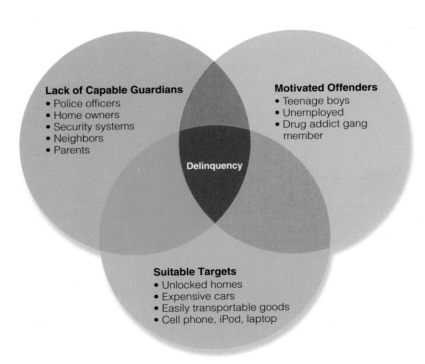

neighborhoods where residents keep a watchful eye on their neighbors' property.[23] Parents who monitor their children's activities serve as guardians. The more time kids spend with their parents and the less time with their friends, the more limited their opportunity to commit delinquent activities.[24]

Delinquent youth are also wary of police guardianship. In order to convince them that "crime does not pay," cities have been putting more police on the street. Proactive, aggressive law enforcement officers who quickly get to the scene of the crime help deter would-be delinquents by reducing their criminal motivation.[25]

- *Suitable targets.* Routine activities theory suggests that the availability of suitable targets such as easily transportable commodities will increase delinquency rates.[26] Research has generally supported the fact that the more wealth a home contains, the more likely it will become a target.[27] As laptop computers, cell phones, portable media players, and digital cameras become more commonplace, burglary rates have risen. The more high-priced, easily transported, and easily resold goods are made available, the more offenders will be motivated to profit from their theft.[28]

- *Motivated offenders.* As the number and motivation of offenders increase, so too do delinquency rates. What increases delinquent motivation? One possible source is scarcity of resources. Delinquency rates may increase if there is a surplus of youths of the same age category competing for a limited number of jobs and educational opportunities.

Motivated offenders, suitable targets, and the lack of guardianship have an interactive effect. Delinquency rates will increase if these motivated offenders are placed in close proximity to unguarded, suitable targets. Take after-school programs, for example. While many adults believe that such programs can reduce delinquency levels, after-school programs designed to reduce criminal activity may produce higher crime rates because they lump together motivated offenders—teen boys—with vulnerable victims, other teen boys.[29]

CONTROLLING DELINQUENCY

If delinquency is a rational choice as some believe, then delinquency prevention is a matter of three general strategies: (1) It stands to reason that it can be prevented by convincing potential delinquents that they will be severely punished for committing delinquent acts; then (2) they must be punished so severely that they never again commit crimes; or (3) it must be so difficult to commit crimes that the potential gain is not worth the risk. This vision has generated four strategies of control: *general deterrence, specific deterrence, incapacitation,* and *situational crime prevention.* Each is discussed below.

General Deterrence

general deterrence
Crime control policies that depend on the fear of criminal penalties, such as long prison sentences for violent crimes; the aim is to convince law violators that the pain outweighs the benefit of criminal activity.

The general deterrence concept holds that the choice to commit delinquent acts is structured by the threat of punishment. If kids believe they will get away with illegal behavior, they may choose to commit crime.[30] If, on the other hand, kids believe that their illegal behavior will result in apprehension and severe punishment, then only the truly irrational will commit crime; the rest will be *deterred.*[31]

One of the guiding principles of deterrence theory is that *the more severe, certain, and swift the punishment, the greater its deterrent effect will be.*[32] Even if a particular crime carries a severe punishment, there will be relatively little deterrent effect if most people do not believe they will be caught.[33] Conversely, even a mild sanction may deter delinquency if kids believe punishment is certain.[34] So if the juvenile justice system can convince would-be delinquents that they will be caught—for example, by putting more police officers on the street—they may decide that delinquency simply does not pay.[35]

Deterrence and Delinquency One might argue that kids are not deterred by the fear of punishment because, traditionally, juvenile justice is based on the *parens patriae* philosophy, which mandates that children be treated and not punished. This limits the power of the law to deter juvenile crime. Yet, in recent years, the increase in teenage violence, gang activity, and drug abuse has prompted a reevaluation of deterrence strategies. One approach has been to put more cops on the street and have them aggressively enforce the law. Proactive, aggressive law enforcement officers who quickly get to the scene of the crime may help deter delinquent activities.[36]

Focusing police activity on particular problems seems to work best.[37] Police are now more willing to use aggressive tactics, such as gang-busting units, to deter membership in drug-trafficking gangs. Youthful-looking officers have been sent undercover into high schools in order to identify, contact, and arrest student drug dealers.[38]

Juvenile courts have also attempted to initiate a deterrence strategy. Juvenile court judges have been willing to waive youths to adult courts; prior record may outweigh an offender's need for services in making this decision.[39] Legislators seem willing to pass more restrictive juvenile codes featuring mandatory incarceration sentences in juvenile facilities, and the number of incarcerated juveniles continues to increase; some states allow life sentences for minors waived to the adult court. The trend toward a more punitive, deterrence-based juvenile process will be discussed further in Chapters 12 through 15.

Do General Deterrence Strategies Work? While the general deterrence concept makes logical sense, there is actually little conclusive evidence that the threat of apprehension and punishment alone can deter delinquency.[40] There are a number of reasons why strategies that attempt to frighten teens may not work:

- Deterrence strategies are based on the idea of a rational, calculating offender; they may not be effective when applied to immature young people. Minors tend to be less capable of making mature judgments about their behavior choices. Many younger offenders are unaware of the content of juvenile legal codes, so that imposition of a deterrence policy, such as mandatory waiver to the adult court for violent crimes, will have little effect on delinquency rates.[41] It seems futile, therefore, to try to deter delinquency through fear of legal punishment. Teens seem more fearful of being punished by their parents or of being the target of disapproval from their friends than they are of the police.[42]

- The deterrent threat of punishment may have little influence on the highest-risk group of young offenders—teens living in economically depressed neighborhoods. Inner-city youngsters may not have internalized the norms of society, which hold that getting arrested is wrong. Young people in these areas have less to lose if arrested; they have a limited stake in society and are not worried about their future. They also may not make connections between delinquency behavior and punishment because they see many people in their neighborhood commit crimes and not get caught or punished.[43]

- It is also possible that experience with the law and punishment actually defuses fear of punishment, thus neutralizing its deterrent effect. Greg Pogarsky and his associates have found that getting arrested had little deterrent effect on youth and that kids who experienced punishment were the ones most likely to continue committing crime. One reason may be that crime-prone youth, the ones who have a long history of delinquency, know that crime provides immediate gratification whereas the threat of punishment remains far in the future.[44] Kids who have already committed crime in the past may maintain a risk-taking personality that is less likely to be impacted by the threat of punishment and more immune from the moral dilemmas caused by crime (i.e., it's bad to steal and attack) than kids who have so far remained delinquency-free.

In sum, deterring delinquency through the fear of punishment may be of limited value because children may not fully comprehend the seriousness of their acts or the consequences they may face.[45] Though on the surface deterrence appears to have benefit as a delinquency control device, there is also reason to believe that it has limited demonstrable effectiveness.

Specific Deterrence

The theory of **specific deterrence** holds that if offenders are punished severely, the experience will convince them not to repeat their illegal acts. Although general deterrence focuses on potential offenders, specific deterrence targets offenders who have already been convicted. Juveniles are sent to secure incarceration facilities with the understanding that their ordeal will deter future misbehavior.

Specific deterrence is a popular approach to crime control today. Unfortunately, relying on punitive measures may expand rather than reduce future delinquency. Institutions quickly become overcrowded, and chronic violent offenders are packed into swollen facilities with juveniles who have committed nonserious and nonviolent crimes. The use of mandatory sentences for some crimes (usually violent crimes or drug dealing) means that all kids who are found to have committed those crimes must be institutionalized; first-time offenders may be treated the same as chronic recidivists.

The evidence on specific deterrence has so far been mixed. Some research studies show that arrest and conviction may under some circumstances lower the frequency of reoffending.[46] However, other studies indicate that punishment has little real effect on reoffending and in some instances may in fact increase the likelihood that first-time offenders will commit new crimes (recidivate).[47] Kids who are placed in a juvenile justice facility are just as likely to become adult criminals as those treated with greater leniency.[48] In fact, a history of prior arrests, convictions, and punishments has proven to be the best predictor of rearrest among young offenders released from correctional institutions. Rather than deterring future offending, punishment may in fact encourage reoffending.[49] One reason is that there seems to be a gap between experiencing punishment and fearing future punishment. That is, just because a kid is punished in the present does not necessarily mean he or she fears punishment in the future.[50]

Why does punishment sometimes encourage rather than reduce delinquency? Being labeled delinquent may cut youth off from prosocial supports in the community, making them more reliant on deviant peers. Being labeled delinquent may also diminish chances for successful future employment, reducing access to legitimate opportunities. Punishment strategies may help lock offenders into a delinquent career. Kids who are punished may also believe that the likelihood of getting caught twice for the same type of crime is remote. "Lightning never strikes twice in the same spot," they may reason; no one is that unlucky. This attitude helps explain the disjunction between current punishment and expectations of future sanctions.[51]

Incapacitation

It stands to reason that that ability of delinquents to commit illegal acts will be eliminated or at least curtailed by putting them behind bars. About 100,000 young people are now housed in juvenile correctional facilities and others, because their case has been waived to the adult court, are incarcerated in adult prisons. There are now more than 25,000 teenagers serving time in adult prisons.[52]

While it seems logical that incarcerating the most dangerous repeat juvenile offenders will reduce their ability to commit delinquent acts, a strict incapacitation policy does not always produce the desired effect:

- Incarceration, especially in an adult prison, exposes younger offenders to higher-risk, more experienced inmates who can influence their lifestyle and help shape their attitudes. They are "schools for crime." The short-term delinquency-reduction effect of incapacitating offenders is negated if the experience has the long-term effect of escalating the frequency and severity of their future criminality upon release.

- If crime and delinquency are functions of rational choice, then the profits of illegal activity are sure to convince kids that "crime pays." Therefore, there will always be someone ready to take the place of the incarcerated offenders and replace them in the gang, group, or clique. New delinquents will be recruited and trained, offsetting any benefit accrued by incarceration.

- Imprisoning established offenders may open new opportunities for competitors who were either suppressed or controlled by more experienced delinquents and tougher rivals. Incarcerating gang members may open illegal markets to new groups and gangs who are even hungrier and more aggressive than the ones they replaced.

- Teens are unlikely to be incarcerated in a juvenile facility or sent to prison until well into their offending career. By the time they are arrested, waived, and sent to an adult prison they are already past the age when they are likely to commit crime. As a result, a strict incarceration policy may keep people in prison beyond the time they are a threat to society while a new cohort of high-risk adolescents is on the street.[53]

- An incapacitation strategy is also terribly expensive. The prison system costs billions of dollars each year, and incarcerating a juvenile in some jurisdictions costs in excess of $50,000 per year. Even if incarceration could reduce the crime rate, the costs would be enormous.

- Even if incarceration can have a short-term effect, almost all delinquents eventually return to society. Because many of these kids are drug- and gang-involved, most come from comparatively few urban inner-city areas. Their return may contribute to family disruption, undermine social institutions, and create community disorganization. Rather than acting as a crime suppressant, incarceration may have the long-term effect of accelerating crime rates.[54]

So while it is logically correct that a stay in a secure facility can reduce the length of a criminal career, there is some question whether increasing the size of the prison population reduces crime rates.[55]

Situational Crime Prevention

situational crime prevention
Crime prevention method that relies on reducing the opportunity to commit criminal acts by (a) making them more difficult to perform, (b) reducing their reward, and (c) increasing their risks.

According to the concept of situational crime prevention, in order to reduce delinquent activity, planners must be aware of the characteristics of sites and situations that are at risk to crime; the things that draw or push kids toward these sites and situations; what equips potential delinquents to take advantage of illegal opportunities offered by these sites and situations; and what constitutes the immediate triggers for delinquent actions.[56] Delinquency can be neutralized if (a) potential targets are carefully guarded, (b) the means to commit crime are controlled, and (c) potential offenders are carefully monitored. Desperate people may contemplate crime, but only the truly irrational will attack a well-defended, inaccessible target and risk strict punishment.

Rather than deterring or punishing individuals in order to reduce delinquency rates, situational crime prevention strategies aim to reduce the opportunities people have to commit particular crimes. The idea is to make it so difficult to commit specific criminal acts that would-be delinquent offenders will be convinced that the risks of crime are greater than the rewards.[57] Controlling the situation of crime can be accomplished by increasing the effort, increasing the risks, and/or reducing the rewards attached to delinquent acts.

Typically, situational crime prevention programs are divided into six separate categories:

1. Increasing the effort to commit delinquent acts
2. Increasing the risks of delinquent activity
3. Reducing the rewards attached to delinquent acts
4. Increasing the shame of committing a delinquent act
5. Reducing provocations that produce delinquent acts
6. Removing excuses for committing a delinquent act

target-hardening technique
Crime prevention technique that makes it more difficult for a would-be delinquent to carry out the illegal act, for example, by installing a security device in a home.

Increasing the effort required to commit delinquency can involve target-hardening techniques such as placing steering locks on cars, putting unbreakable glass on storefronts, or installing a locking device on cars that prevents drunken drivers from starting the vehicle (breath-analyzed ignition interlock device).[58] *Access control* can be maintained by locking gates and fencing yards.[59] The *facilitators of crime* can be controlled by such measures as banning the sale of spray paint to adolescents in an effort to cut down on graffiti, or having photos put on credit cards to reduce their value if stolen.

Increasing the risks of delinquency might involve such measures as improving surveillance lighting, utilizing closed-circuit TV monitoring, creating neighborhood watch programs, controlling building entrances and exits, installing burglar alarms and security systems, and increasing the number of private security officers and police patrols. Research conducted in the United States and England indicates that the installation of street lights may convince would-be burglars that their entries will be seen and reported.[60] Closed-circuit TV cameras have been shown to reduce the amount of car theft from parking lots while reducing the need for higher-cost security personnel.[61] Delinquency rate reductions seem to be maximized when CCTV and improved street lighting are used in tandem.[62]

To find **situational crime prevention resources**, go to a website maintained by Rutgers University via academic .cengage.com/criminaljustice/siegel.

Reducing the rewards of delinquency include strategies such as making car radios removable so they can be kept at home at night, marking property so that it is more difficult to sell when stolen, and having gender-neutral phone listings to discourage obscene phone calls. Tracking systems, such as those made by the LoJack Corporation, help police locate and return stolen vehicles.

Because delinquent acts are sometimes the result of extreme provocation, it might be possible to reduce delinquency rates by creating programs that reduce conflict. Posting guards outside schools at closing time might prevent childish taunts from escalating into full-blown brawls. Antibullying programs that have been implemented in schools are another method of reducing provocation.

Some delinquents neutralize their responsibility for their acts by learning to excuse their behavior by saying things like "I didn't know that was illegal" or "I had no choice." It might be possible to reduce delinquency by eliminating excuses. Teenage vandalism may be reduced by setting up brightly colored litter receptacles that help eliminate the excuse "I just didn't know where to throw my trash." Reducing or eliminating excuses in this way also makes it physically easy for people to comply with laws and regulations, thereby reducing the likelihood they will choose crime. (See Concept Summary 3.1 for a summary of the different delinquency prevention strategies.)

Why Do Delinquents Choose Crime?

All the delinquency control methods based on choice theory assume the delinquent to be a motivated offender who breaks the law because he or she perceives an abundance of benefits and an absence of threat. Increase the threat and reduce the benefits, and the delinquency rate should decline.

Concept Summary 3.1
Crime Control Strategies Based on Rational Choice

Situational Crime Prevention

▌ This strategy is aimed at convincing would-be delinquents to avoid specific targets. It relies on the doctrine that crime can be avoided if motivated offenders are denied access to suitable targets.

▌ Operationalizations of this strategy are home security systems or guards, which broadcast the message that guardianship is great here, stay away; the potential reward is not worth the risk of apprehension.

▌ Problems with the strategy are the extinction of the effect and displacement of crime.

General Deterrence Strategies

▌ These strategies are aimed at making potential delinquents fear the consequences of their acts. The threat of punishment is meant to convince rational delinquents that crime does not pay.

▌ Operationalizations of these strategies are mandatory sentences, waiver to adult court, and aggressive policing.

▌ Problems with these strategies are that delinquents are immature and may not fear punishment, and the certainty of arrest and punishment is low.

Specific Deterrence Strategy

▌ This strategy refers to punishing known delinquents so severely that they will never be tempted to repeat their offenses. If delinquency is rational, then painful punishment should reduce its future allure.

▌ Operationalization of this strategy is placement in a punitive juvenile detention facility or secure institution.

▌ A problem with this strategy is that punishment may increase reoffending rates rather than deter future delinquency.

Incapacitation Strategies

▌ These strategies attempt to reduce crime rates by denying motivated offenders the opportunity to commit crime. If, despite the threat of law and punishment, some people still find crime attractive, then the only way to control their behavior is to incarcerate them for extended periods.

▌ Operationalization of these strategies is long, tough, mandatory sentences, putting more kids behind bars.

▌ A problem with these strategies is that people are kept in prison beyond the years they may commit crime. Minor, nondangerous offenders are locked up, and this is a very costly strategy.

This logic is hard to refute. After all, by definition, a person who commits an illegal act but is not rational cannot be considered a criminal or delinquent but instead is "not guilty by reason of insanity." To say that delinquents choose their crimes is for the most part entirely logical. Yet several questions remain unanswered by choice theorists. First, why do some people continually choose to break the law, even after suffering its consequences? Why are some kids law abiding even though they are indigent and have little chance of gaining economic success? Conversely, why do some affluent youths break the law when they have everything to lose and little more to gain?

Choice theorists also have problems explaining seemingly irrational crimes, such as vandalism, arson, and even drug abuse. To say a teenager who painted swastikas on a synagogue or attacked a gay couple was making a "rational choice" seems inadequate to explain such a destructive, purposeless act.

The relationships observed by rational choice theorists can also be explained in other ways. For example, though the high victimization rates in lower-class neighborhoods can be explained by an oversupply of motivated offenders, they may also be due to other factors, such as social conflict and disorganization.[63]

In sum, although choice theories can contribute to understanding criminal events and victim patterns, they leave a major question unanswered: Why do some people choose crime over legal activities?

TRAIT THEORIES: BIOSOCIAL AND PSYCHOLOGICAL VIEWS

A faithful and loyal choice theorist believes that selecting crime is usually part of an economic strategy, a function of carefully weighing the benefits of criminal over legal behavior. For example, youths decide to commit a robbery if they believe they will make a good profit, have a good chance of getting away with it, and, even if caught, stand little chance of being severely punished.

A number of delinquency experts believe that this model is incomplete. They believe it is wrong to infer that all youths choose crime simply because they believe its advantages outweigh its risks. If that were the case, how could senseless and profitless crimes such as vandalism and random violence be explained? These experts argue that human behavioral choices are a function of an individual's mental and/or physical makeup. Most law-abiding youths have personal traits that keep them within the mainstream of conventional society. In contrast, youths who choose to engage in repeated aggressive, antisocial, or conflict-oriented behavior manifest abnormal traits that influence their behavior choices.[64] Uncontrollable, impulsive behavior patterns place some youths at odds with society, and they soon find themselves in trouble with the law. Although delinquents may choose their actions, the decision is a product of all but uncontrollable mental and physical properties and traits.

The view that delinquents are somehow "abnormal" is not a new one. Some of the earliest theories of criminal and delinquent behavior stressed that crime was a product of personal traits and that measurable physical and mental conditions, such as IQ and body build, determined behavior. This view is generally referred to today as *positivism*. Positivists believe that the scientific method can be used to measure the causes of human behavior and that behavior is a function of often uncontrollable factors, such as mental illness.

The source of behavioral control is one significant difference between trait and choice theories. Whereas the former reasons that behavior is controlled by personal traits, the latter views behavior as purely a product of human reasoning. To a choice theorist, reducing the benefits of crime by increasing the likelihood and severity of punishment will eventually lower the crime rate. Biosocial, or trait, theory focuses less on the effects of punishment and more on the treatment of abnormal mental and physical conditions as a crime-reduction method. In the following section, the primary components of trait theory are reviewed.

Origins of Trait Theory

The first attempts to discover why criminal tendencies develop focused on the physical makeup of offenders. Biological traits present at birth were thought to predetermine whether people would live a life of crime.

The origin of this school of thought is generally credited to the Italian physician Cesare Lombroso (1835–1909).[65] Known as the father of criminology, Lombroso put his many years of medical research to use in his theory of criminal atavism.[66] Lombroso found that delinquents manifest physical anomalies that make them biologically and physiologically similar to our primitive ancestors. These atavistic individuals are savage throwbacks to an earlier stage of human evolution. Because of this link, the "born criminal" has such physical traits as enormous jaws, strong canines, a flattened nose, and supernumerary teeth (double rows, as in snakes). Lombroso made such statements as "It was easy to understand why the span of the arms in criminals so often exceeds the height, for this is a characteristic of apes, whose forelimbs are used in walking and climbing."[67]

Contemporaries of Lombroso refined the notion of a physical basis of crime. Rafaele Garofalo (1851–1934) shared Lombroso's belief that certain physical characteristics indicate a criminal or delinquent nature.[68] Enrico Ferri (1856–1929), a student of Lombroso, believed that a number of biological, social, and organic factors caused delinquency and crime.[69]

These early views portrayed delinquent behavior as a function of a single factor or trait, such as body build or defective intelligence. They had a significant impact on early American criminology, which relied heavily on developing a science of "criminal anthropology."[70] Eventually, these views evoked criticism for their unsound methodology and lack of proper scientific controls. Some researchers used captive offender populations and failed to compare experimental subjects with control groups of nondelinquents or undetected delinquents. These methodological flaws made it impossible to determine whether biological traits produce delinquency. It is equally plausible that police are more likely to arrest, and courts convict, the mentally and

criminal atavism
The idea that delinquents manifest physical anomalies that make them biologically and physiologically similar to our primitive ancestors, savage throwbacks to an earlier stage of human evolution.

A complete list of the **crime-producing physical traits** identified by Lombroso is available online via academic .cengage.com/criminaljustice/siegel.

physically abnormal. By the middle of the twentieth century, biological theories had fallen out of favor as an explanation of delinquency.

CONTEMPORARY BIOSOCIAL THEORY

For most of the twentieth century, delinquency experts scoffed at the notion that a youth's behavior was controlled by physical conditions present at birth. During this period, the majority of delinquency research focused on social factors, such as poverty and family life, which were believed to be responsible for law-violating behavior. However, a small group of criminologists and penologists kept alive the biological approach. Some embraced sociobiology, a perspective that suggests behavior will adapt to the environment in which it evolved. Creatures of all species are influenced by their genetic inheritance and their innate need to survive and dominate others. Sociobiology had a tremendous effect on reviving interest in a biological basis for crime and delinquency, because if biological (genetic) makeup controls all human behavior, it follows that a person's genes should also be responsible for determining whether he or she chooses law-violating or conventional behavior.

Today, those who embrace trait theory reject the traditional assumptions that all humans are born with equal potential to learn and achieve (**equipotentiality**) and that thereafter their behavior is controlled by external or social forces. Traditional criminologists suggest (either explicitly or implicitly) that all people are born equal and that parents, schools, neighborhoods, and friends control subsequent development. Trait theorists argue that no two people (with rare exceptions, such as identical twins) are alike, and therefore each will react to environmental stimuli in a distinct way. They assume that a combination of personal traits and the environment produces individual behavior patterns. People with pathological traits such as brain damage, an abnormal personality, or a low IQ may have a heightened risk for crime. This risk is elevated by environmental stresses such as poor family life, educational failure, substance abuse, and exposure to delinquent peers. These conditions may be interactive. For example, low-birthweight babies have been found to suffer poor educational achievement later in life; academic deficiency has been linked to delinquency and drug abuse.[71] A mother's dietary intake during pregnancy can influence a child's IQ level later in life, and intelligence levels have been linked to delinquency.[72] The reverse may also apply: A supportive environment may be strong enough to counteract adverse biological and psychological traits.

Contemporary **biosocial theorists** seek to explain the onset of antisocial behaviors, such as aggression and violence, by focusing on the physical qualities of the offenders.[73] The majority of major research efforts appear to be concentrated in three distinct areas of study: biochemical factors, neurological dysfunction, and genetic influences. These three views are discussed in some detail below.

equipotentiality
View that all people are equal at birth and are thereafter influenced by their environment.

biosocial theory
The view that both thought and behavior have biological and social bases.

Biochemical Factors

There is a suspected relationship between antisocial behavior and biochemical makeup.[74] One view is that body chemistry can govern behavior and personality, including levels of aggression and depression.[75] Adolescents may be exposed to damaging chemical contaminants from the point of conception when their mothers ingest harmful substances during pregnancy.[76] Maternal alcohol abuse during gestation has long been linked to prenatal damage and subsequent antisocial behavior in adolescence.[77]

Another view is that abnormal body chemistry is an indirect cause of antisocial behavior through its association with abnormal psychological and mental conditions. Research conducted over the past decade shows that an over- or undersupply of certain chemicals and minerals, including sodium, mercury, potassium,

Biochemical research has linked diet to behavior. Excessive intake of certain substances, such as sugar, and the lack of proper vitamins and proteins have been tied to aggression and antisocial behaviors. Considering this connection, should teen diets be closely monitored?

calcium, amino acids, and/or iron, can lead to depression, hyperactivity, cognitive problems, intelligence deficits, memory loss, or abnormal sexual activity; these conditions have been associated with crime and delinquency.[78] Attention deficit/hyperactivity disorder (ADHD), believed to be a precursor of delinquent behaviors, has been linked to the presence of excessive iron.[79] (For more on ADHD see later in this chapter.)

Environmental Contaminants One area of concern is that overexposure to particular environmental contaminants, including metals and minerals such as iron and manganese, may produce effects that put kids at risk for antisocial behavior.[80] Exposure to the now-banned PCB (polychlorinated biphenyls), a chemical once used in insulation materials, has been shown to influence brain functioning and intelligence levels.[81] Pesticides such as chlorpyrifos, once used heavily in inner-city neighborhoods, has also been linked to behaviors associated with delinquency. Children exposed to large amounts of chlorpyrifos before birth are at elevated risk for developmental delays and symptoms of ADHD.[82]

Of all these contaminants, exposure to lead is the one that has been linked most often to antisocial behaviors on both the individual and group levels.[83] When criminologists Paul Stretesky and Michael Lynch examined lead concentrations in air across counties in the United States, they found that areas with the highest concentrations of lead also reported the highest level of homicide.[84] On the individual level, research has shown that exposure to lead can have significant detrimental effects, such as lowering IQ levels.[85] Young children (age 7) with high blood lead levels later display antisocial behavioral symptoms such as "externalizing" (acting-out) behaviors and school problems.[86]

Diet and Delinquency There is also evidence that diet may influence behavior through its impact on body chemistry. Of particular concern is an unusually high intake of such items as artificial food coloring, milk, and sweets. Some scientists believe that chronic under- or oversupply of vitamins, such as C, B3, and B6, may be related to restlessness and antisocial behavior in youths. Evidence also exists that allergies to foods can influence mood and behavior, resulting in personality swings between hyperactivity and depression.[87] This relationship is further explored in the Focus on Delinquency box entitled "Diet and Delinquency."

Hormonal Levels Hormonal levels are another area of biochemical research. Antisocial behavior allegedly peaks in the teenage years because hormonal activity is at its highest level during this period. Research suggests that increased levels of the male androgen testosterone are responsible for excessive levels of violence among teenage boys.[88]

Adolescents who experience more intense moods, mood swings, anxiety, and restlessness than people at other points in development also have the highest crime rates.[89] These mood and behavior changes have been associated with family conflict and antisocial behavior.

An association between hormonal activity and antisocial behavior is suggested because rates of both factors peak in adolescence.[90] Hormonal sensitivity may begin at the very early stages of life when the fetus can be exposed to abnormally high levels of testosterone while in the uterus. This may trigger a heightened response to the release of testosterone when an adolescent male reaches puberty. Although testosterone levels appear normal, the young male is at risk for overaggressive behavior responses.

Hormonal activity as an explanation of gender differences in the delinquency crime rate will be discussed further in Chapter 6.

Neurological Dysfunction

neurological
Pertaining to the brain and nervous system structure.

minimal brain dysfunction (MBD)
Damage to the brain itself that causes antisocial behavior injurious to the individual's lifestyle and social adjustment.

Another focus of biosocial theory is the neurological—or brain and nervous system—structure of offenders. It has been suggested that children who manifest behavioral disturbances may have neurological deficits, such as damage to the hemispheres of the brain; this is sometimes referred to as minimal brain dysfunction (MBD).[91] Impairment in brain functioning may be present at birth, produced by factors such as low birthweight, brain injury during pregnancy, birth complications, and inherited abnormalities. Brain injuries can also occur later in life as a result of brutal beatings or sexual abuse by a parent. According to research conducted by Dr. Martin Teicher of the McLean Hospital in Massachusetts, emotional trauma such as child abuse can actually cause adverse physical changes in the brain, and these deformities can lead to depression, anxiety, and other serious emotional conditions.[92]

Children who suffer from measurable neurological deficits at birth also may experience a number of antisocial traits throughout their life course. Research has even linked this type of deficit to becoming a habitual liar.[93] Later they are more likely to become criminals as adults. Clinical analysis of convicted murderers has found that a significant number had suffered head injuries as children that resulted in neurological impairment.[94] In an important study by Adrian Raine, researchers looked at the medical histories of 4,269 Danish males born between 1959 and 1961. By age 18, boys whose mothers had experienced birth complications and who had also experienced maternal rejection later in life were more than twice as likely to commit a violent crime than boys who did not experience birth trauma and maternal rejection. Raine concluded that birth complications and maternal rejection seemed to predispose offenders to some kinds of criminal offenses.[95]

Supporting Research A number of research efforts have attempted to substantiate a link between neurological impairment and crime. There is evidence that this relationship can be detected quite early and that children who suffer from measurable neurological deficits at birth are more likely to become criminals later in life.[96] For example, low-birthweight children are also likely to be early onset delinquents; low birthweight is highly correlated with neurological impairment.[97] Clinical analysis of death row inmates found that a significant number had suffered head injuries as children, resulting in damage to their central nervous system and neurological impairment.[98] Measurement of the brain activity of antisocial youths has revealed impairments that might cause them to experience otherwise unexplainable outbursts of anger, hostility, and aggression. Evidence has been found linking brain damage to mental disorders such as schizophrenia and depression.[99] Cross-national studies also support a link between neurological dysfunction and antisocial behavior.[100]

Researchers have used the electroencephalogram to measure the brain waves and activity of delinquents and then compared them with those of law-abiding adolescents. Behaviors believed to be highly correlated with abnormal EEG functions include poor impulse control, inadequate social ability, hostility, temper tantrums, destructiveness, and hyperactivity.[101] The Focus on Delinquency box on page 86 entitled "Attention Deficit/Hyperactivity Disorder" discusses this neurological condition, associated with antisocial behavior, in some detail.

Diet and Delinquency

Research conducted in the United States and abroad has linked youth violence and misbehavior to dietary intake. A number of specific food products have been linked to antisocial behaviors, such as the omega-6 fats found in corn, safflower, soybean, cottonseed, and sunflower oils. National Institutes of Health scientists have found that the murder rate is 20 times higher in countries with the highest omega-6 intake, compared with those with the lowest.

There have been a number of controlled experiments linking diet to delinquency. Stephen Schoenthaler conducted three randomized controlled studies in which 66 elementary school children, 62 confined teenage delinquents, and 402 confined adult felons received dietary supplements—the equivalent of a diet providing more fruits, vegetables, and whole grains. In order to remove experimental bias, neither subjects nor researchers knew who received the supplement and who received a placebo. In each study, the subjects receiving the dietary supplement demonstrated significantly less violent and nonviolent antisocial behavior when compared to the control subjects who received placebos. The carefully collected data verified that a very good diet, as defined by the World Health Organization, has significant behavioral benefits beyond its health effects.

In another study, Adrian Raine and his colleagues charted the long-term effects of a two-year diet enrichment program for 3-year-olds in the African nation of Mauritania. One hundred randomly selected children were placed in a program providing them with nutritious lunches, physical exercise, and enhanced education. They were then compared with a control group made up of children who did not participate in the program. By age 17, kids who had been malnourished before they entered the nutrition program had higher scores on physical and psychological well-being than malnourished kids who had not been in the program. By age 23, the malnourished kids who had been in the program 20 years earlier still did better on personality tests and had lower levels of self-reported crimes than the malnourished children who not been placed in the program. Overall, the results showed that providing children with nutritious diets and enriched environments is associated with greater mental health and reduced antisocial activities later in life.

A recent British review of existing research on the association between diet and crime, conducted by Courtney Van de Weyer, found that the combination of nutrients significantly associated with good mental health and well-being is as follows:

▌ Polyunsaturated fatty acids (particularly the omega-3 types found in oily fish and some plants)

▌ Minerals, such as zinc (in whole grains, legumes, meat and milk), magnesium (in green leafy vegetables, nuts, and whole grains), and iron (in red meat, green leafy vegetables, eggs and some fruit)

▌ Vitamins, such as folate (in green leafy vegetables and fortified cereals), a range of B vitamins (in whole grain products, yeast, and dairy products), and antioxidant vitamins such as C and E (in a wide range of fruits and vegetables)

Kids whose diets lack one or more of this combination of polyunsaturated fats, minerals, and vitamins, and/or contain too much saturated fat (or other elements, including sugar and a range of food and agricultural chemicals) seem to be at higher risk of developing the following conditions:

▌ Attention deficit/hyperactivity disorder (ADHD)

▌ A range of depressive conditions

▌ Schizophrenia

▌ Dementia, including Alzheimer's disease

The survey found that people are eating too much saturated fat, sugar, and salt and not enough vitamins and minerals. This diet is not only fueling obesity, cardiovascular disease, diabetes, and some cancers, but may also be contributing to rising rates of mental ill-health and antisocial behavior.

Though more research is needed before the scientific community reaches a consensus on the specific association between diet and crime, there is mounting evidence that vitamins, minerals, chemicals, and other nutrients from a diet rich in fruits, vegetables, and whole grains can improve brain function, basic intelligence, and academic performance. In contrast, those lacking in proper diet seem at greatest risk to antisocial behaviors.

Critical Thinking

1. If this research is correct, should schools be required to provide a proper and nutritious lunch for all children in order to reduce disorder and delinquency?

2. Is it possible that antisocial behaviors decline with age because people eat better as they mature? What about after they get married? Does home cooking reduce deviant behaviors?

SOURCES: Nandini Chakrabarti and V. K. Sinha, "A Study of Serum Lipid Profile and Serum Apolipoproteins A1 and B in Indian Male Violent Criminal Offenders," *Criminal Behaviour and Mental Health* 16:177–182 (2006); Courtney Van de Weyer, "Changing Diets, Changing Minds: How Food Affects Mental Well-Being and Behaviour," Sustain: The Alliance for Better Food and Farming, www.sustainweb.org/pdf/MHRep_LowRes.pdf (accessed March 26, 2006); Adrian Raine, Kjetil Mellingen, Jianghong Liu, Peter Venables, and Sarnoff Mednick, "Effects of Environmental Enrichment at Age Three to Five Years on Schizotypal Personality and Antisocial Behavior at Ages Seventeen and Twenty-Three Years," *American Journal of Psychiatry* 160:1–9 (2003); C. Bernard Gesch, Sean M. Hammond, Sarah E. Hampson, Anita Eves, and Martin J. Crowder, "Influence of Supplementary Vitamins, Minerals, and Essential Fatty Acids on the Antisocial Behaviour of Young Adult Prisoners: Randomized, Placebo-Controlled Trial," *British Journal of Psychiatry* 181:22–28 (2002); Stephen Schoenthaler and Ian Bier, "The Effect of Vitamin–Mineral Supplementation on Juvenile Delinquency among American Schoolchildren: A Randomized Double-Blind Placebo-Controlled Trial," *Journal of Alternative and Complementary Medicine: Research on Paradigm, Practice, and Policy* 6:7–18 (2000).

learning disability (LD)
Neurological dysfunction that prevents an individual from learning to his or her potential.

The **Learning Disabilities Association of America** aims to advance the education and general welfare of children and adults of normal or potentially normal intelligence who manifest disabilities of a perceptual, conceptual, or coordinative nature. To learn more about them, go to academic.cengage.com/criminaljustice/siegel.

Learning Disabilities One specific type of MBD that has generated considerable interest is **learning disability (LD)**, a term that has been defined by the National Advisory Committee on Handicapped Children:

> *Children with special learning disabilities exhibit a disorder in one or more of the basic psychological processes involved in understanding or using spoken or written languages. They may be manifested in disorders of listening, thinking, talking, reading, writing or arithmetic. They include conditions which have been referred to as perceptual handicaps, brain injury, minimal brain dysfunction, dyslexia, developmental aphasia, etc. They do not include learning problems which are due to visual, hearing or motor handicaps, to mental retardation, emotional disturbance, or to environmental disadvantages.*[102]

Learning-disabled kids usually exhibit poor motor coordination (for example, problems with poor hand/eye coordination, trouble climbing stairs, clumsiness), have behavior problems (lack of emotional control, hostility, cannot stay on task), and have improper auditory and vocal responses (do not seem to hear, cannot differentiate sounds and noises).

The relationship between learning disabilities and delinquency has been highlighted by studies showing that arrested and incarcerated children have a far higher LD rate than do children in the general population.[103] Though learning disabilities are quite common (approximately 10 percent of all youths have some form of learning disorder), estimates of LD among adjudicated delinquents range from 26 percent to 73 percent.[104] Do these statistics necessarily mean that learning disabilities somehow cause delinquent behavior?

Typically, there are two possible explanations of the link between learning disabilities and delinquency.[105] One view, known as the *susceptibility rationale*, argues that the link is caused by certain side effects of learning disabilities, such as impulsiveness, poor ability to learn from experience, and inability to take social cues. In contrast, the *school failure rationale* assumes that the frustration caused by the LD child's poor school performance will lead to a negative self-image and acting-out behavior.

A number of recent research efforts have found that the LD child may not be any more susceptible to delinquent behavior than the non-LD child and that the proposed link between learning disabilities and delinquency may be an artifact of bias in the way the juvenile justice system treats LD youths.[106] Because of social bias, LD kids are more likely to get arrested, and if petitioned to juvenile court, their poor school record can influence the outcome of the case. LD youths bring with them to court a record of school problems and low grades and a history of frustrating efforts by agents of the educational system to help them. When information is gleaned from the school personnel at juvenile trials, LD children's poor performance may work against them in the court. Consequently, the view that learning disabilities cause delinquency has been questioned, and the view that LD children are more likely to be arrested and officially labeled delinquent demands further inquiry. Self-reports show little differences between the behavior of LD and non-LD youth, a finding that supports the social bias view.[107]

The **National Center for Learning Disabilities (NCLD)** provides national leadership in support of children and adults with learning disabilities. Find out about their work via academic.cengage.com/criminaljustice/siegel.

Arousal Theory It has long been suspected that obtaining "thrills" is a motivator of crime. Adolescents may engage in such crimes as shoplifting and vandalism simply because they offer the attraction of getting away with it; delinquency is a thrilling demonstration of personal competence.[108] Is it possible that thrill seekers are people who have some form of abnormal brain functioning that directs their behavior?

Arousal theorists believe that, for a variety of genetic and environmental reasons, some people's brains function differently in response to environmental stimuli. All of us seek to maintain a preferred or optimal level of arousal: Too much stimulation leaves us anxious and stressed out; too little makes us feel bored and weary. There is, however, variation in the way children's brains process sensory input. Some nearly always feel comfortable with little stimulation, while others require a high degree of environmental input to feel comfortable. The latter group

arousal theorists
Delinquency experts who believe that aggression is a function of the level of an individual's need for stimulation or arousal from the environment. Those who require more stimulation may act in an aggressive manner to meet their needs.

Attention Deficit/Hyperactivity Disorder

Many parents have noticed that their children do not pay attention to them—they run around and do things in their own way. Sometimes this inattention is a function of age; in other instances it is a symptom of a common learning disability referred to as attention deficit/hyperactivity disorder (ADHD), a condition in which a child shows a developmentally inappropriate lack of attention, distractibility, impulsivity, and hyperactivity. The various symptoms of ADHD are listed below.

LACK OF ATTENTION

- Frequently fails to finish projects
- Does not seem to pay attention
- Does not sustain interest in play activities
- Cannot sustain concentration on schoolwork or related tasks
- Is easily distracted

IMPULSIVITY

- Frequently acts without thinking
- Often "calls out" in class
- Does not want to wait his or her turn
- Shifts from activity to activity
- Cannot organize tasks or work
- Requires constant supervision in line or games

HYPERACTIVITY

- Constantly runs around and climbs on things
- Shows excessive motor activity while asleep
- Cannot sit still; is constantly fidgeting
- Does not remain in his or her seat in class
- Is constantly on the go like a "motor"
- Has difficulty regulating emotions
- Has difficulty getting started
- Has difficulty staying on track
- Has difficulty adjusting to social demands

No one is really sure how ADHD develops, but some psychologists believe it is tied to dysfunction in a section of the lower portion of the brain known as the reticular activating system. This area keeps the higher brain centers alert and ready for input. There is some evidence that this area is not working properly in ADHD kids and that their behavior is really the brain's attempt to generate new stimulation to maintain alertness. Other suspected origins are neurological damage to the frontal lobes of the brain, prenatal stress, and even food additives and chemical allergies. Some experts suggest that the condition might be traced to the neurological effects of abnormal levels of the chemicals dopamine and norepinephrine.

Children from any background can develop ADHD, but it is five to seven times more common in boys than girls. It does not affect intelligence, and ADHD children often show considerable ability with artistic endeavors. More common in the United States than elsewhere, ADHD tends to run in families, and there is some suggestion of an association with a family history of alcoholism or depression.

Estimates of ADHD in the general population range from 3 to 12 percent, but it is much more prevalent in adolescents, where some estimates reach as high as one-third of the population.

Some delinquency experts believe that aggression is a function of the level of an individual's need for stimulation or arousal from the environment. Those who require more stimulation may act in an aggressive manner to meet their needs. They become "sensation seekers" who seek out stimulating activities that may include aggressive, violent behavior patterns.

© Alexandre Simoes/vario images GmbH & Co.KG/Alamy

become "sensation seekers," who seek out stimulating activities that may include aggressive, violent behavior patterns.[109]

The factors that determine a person's level of arousal have not been fully determined. Suspected sources include brain chemistry (for example, serotonin levels) and brain structure. The number of nerve cells with receptor sites for neurotransmitters in the brain differs among people; some have many more than others. Another view is that adolescents with low heart rates are more likely to commit crimes because they seek stimulation to increase their arousal levels to normal levels.[110]

Genetic Influences

Individuals who share genes are alike in personality regardless of how they are reared, whereas rearing environment induces little or no personality resemblance.[111]

ADHD children are most often treated by giving them doses of stimulants, most commonly Ritalin and Dexedrine (or dextroamphetamine), which, ironically, help these children control their emotional and behavioral outbursts. The antimanic, anticonvulsant drug Tegretol has also been used effectively.

ADHD usually results in poor school performance, including a high dropout rate, bullying, stubbornness, mental disorder, and a lack of response to discipline; these conditions are highly correlated with delinquent behavior. Children with ADHD are more likely to use illicit drugs, alcohol, and cigarettes in adolescence. They are more likely to be arrested, to be charged with a felony, and to have multiple arrests than non-ADHD youths. A series of research studies now links ADHD to the onset and continuance of a delinquent career and increased risk for antisocial behavior and substance abuse in adulthood. Symptoms of childhood ADHD are common in adults with opiate dependence. Joseph Biederman and colleagues conducted a 10-year study of more than 100 boys with ADHD and compared them to non-ADHD boys. By age 21, ADHD youth were at high risk for markedly elevated lifetime prevalences of antisocial, addictive, mood and anxiety disorders. ADHD subjects had higher levels of psychopathology despite the fact that 93 percent had received treatment for the disorder at some point during their lives. Of those, 86 percent had received both medication and counseling, while 6 percent received medication alone and 1 percent received counseling alone.

Critical Thinking

Even if it could be proven that kids suffering from ADHD were more likely to engage in antisocial behaviors than non-ADHD kids:

1. Should those diagnosed with the condition be closely monitored by the school system?

2. Would that be fair to the majority of ADHD kids who never violate the law?

3. Would paying special attention to the ADHD population stigmatize them and actually encourage their law-violating behaviors?

SOURCES: Jason Luty, Arghya Sarkhel, Colin O'Gara, and Okon Umoh, "Prevalence of Childhood Attention Deficit Hyperactivity Disorder in Opiate-Dependent Adults," *International Journal of Psychiatry in Clinical Practice*, 11:157–162 (2007): Joseph Biederman, Michael Monuteaux, Eric Mick, Thomas Spencer, Timothy Wilens, Julie Silva, Lindsey Snyder, and Stephen Faraone, "Young Adult Outcome of Attention Deficit Hyperactivity Disorder: A Controlled 10-year Follow-up Study," *Psychological Medicine*, 36:167–179 (2007); Russell Barkley, Mariellen Fischer, Lori Smallish, and Kenneth Fletcher, "Young Adult Follow-up of Hyperactive Children: Antisocial Activities and Drug Use," *Journal of Child Psychology and Psychiatry* 45:195–211 (2004); Molina Pelham, Jr., "Childhood Predictors of Adolescent Substance Use in a Longitudinal Study of Children with ADHD," *Journal of Abnormal Psychology* 112:497–507 (2003); Peter Muris and Cor Meesters, "The Validity of Attention Deficit Hyperactivity and Hyperkinetic Disorder Symptom Domains in Nonclinical Dutch Children," *Journal of Clinical Child and Adolescent Psychology* 32:460–466 (2003); D. R. Blachman and S. P. Hinshaw, "Patterns of Friendship among Girls with and without Attention Deficit/Hyperactivity Disorder," *Journal of Abnormal Child Psychology* 30:625–640 (2002); Terrie Moffitt and Phil Silva, "Self-Reported Delinquency, Neuropsychological Deficit, and History of Attention Deficit Disorder," *Journal of Abnormal Child Psychology* 16:553–569 (1988); Karen Harding, Richard Judah, and Charles Gant, "Outcome-Based Comparison of Ritalin[R] versus Food-Supplement Treated Children with AD/HD," *Alternative Medicine Review* 8:319–330 (2003).

Biosocial theorists also study the genetic makeup of delinquents.[112] According to this view, (a) antisocial behavior is inherited, (b) the genetic makeup of parents is passed on to children, and (c) genetic abnormality is linked to a variety of antisocial behaviors.[113] It has been hypothesized that youths, both males and females, maintain a heritable genetic configuration that predisposes them to delinquent behaviors.[114] Biosocial theorists believe that in the same way that people inherit genes for height and eye color, antisocial behavior characteristics and mental disorders may be passed down from one generation to the next. To test this assumption, parent-child and sibling behavior have been studied.

Parent-Child Similarities If antisocial tendencies are inherited, then the children of criminal parents should be more likely to become law violators than the offspring of conventional parents. A number of studies have found that parental criminality and deviance do, in fact, powerfully influence delinquent behavior.[115] For example, there is a significant relationship between parent and child suicide attempts.[116] Some of the most important data on parental deviance were gathered by Donald J. West and David P. Farrington as part of the long-term Cambridge Youth Survey. These cohort data indicate that a significant number of delinquent youths have criminal fathers.[117] Whereas 8 percent of the sons of noncriminal fathers eventually became chronic offenders, about 37 percent of youths with criminal fathers were multiple offenders.[118] In another important analysis, Farrington found that one type of parental deviance, school yard aggression or bullying, may be both inter- and intragenerational. Bullies have children who bully others, and these second-generation bullies grow up to father children who are also bullies, in a never-ending cycle.[119]

Farrington's findings are supported by some recent research data from the Rochester Youth Development Study (RYDS), a longitudinal analysis that has been monitoring the behavior of 1,000 area youths since 1988. RYDS researchers have also found an intergenerational continuity in antisocial behavior: Criminal fathers produce delinquent sons who grow up to have delinquent children themselves.[120] It is possible that at least part of the association is genetic.[121]

Sibling and Twin Similarities It stands to reason that if the cause of delinquency is in part genetic, the behavior of siblings should be similar because they share genetic material. Research does show that if one sibling engages in antisocial behavior, so do his/her brothers and sisters. The effect is greatest among same-sex sibs.[122]

Because siblings are usually brought up in the same household and share common life experiences, however, any similarity in their delinquent behavior might be a function of comparable environmental influences and not genetics at all. To control for environmental effects, biosocial theorists have compared the behavior of twins and non-twin siblings and found that the twins, who share more genetic material, are also more similar in their behavior. This indicates that it is heredity and not environment that controls behavior.[123] Recent twin studies have found that a highly significant association in childhood antisocial and aggressive behaviors, including conduct disorder, ratings of aggression, delinquency, and psychopathic traits, a finding that supports a genetic basis to antisocial behavior.[124]

An even more rigorous test of genetic theory involves comparison of the behavior of identical monozygotic (MZ) twins with same-sex fraternal dizygotic (DZ) twins; although the former have an identical genetic makeup, the latter share only about 50 percent of their genetic combinations. Research has shown that MZ twins are significantly closer in their personal characteristics, such as intelligence, than are DZ twins.[125] Other relevant findings include:

| There is a significantly higher risk for suicidal behavior among monozygotic twin pairs than dizygotic twin pairs.[126]

| Differences between MZ and DZ twins have been found in tests measuring psychological dysfunctions, such as conduct disorders, impulsivity, and antisocial behavior.[127]

| MZ twins are closer than DZ twins in level of aggression and verbal skills.[128]

| Both members of MZ twin pairs who suffer child abuse are more likely to engage in later antisocial activity than DZ pairs.[129]

| Callous, unemotional traits in very young children can be a warning sign for future psychopathy and antisocial behavior. MZ twin pairs are more likely to be similar in levels of callous, unemotional behavior than DZ pairs.[130]

One famous study of twin behavior still underway is the Minnesota Study of Twins Reared Apart (also called the Minnesota Twin Family Study). This research compares the behavior of MZ and DZ twin pairs who were raised together with others who were separated at birth and in some cases did not even know of each other's existence. The study shows some striking similarities in behavior and ability for twin pairs raised apart. An MZ twin reared away from a co-twin has about as good a chance of being similar to the co-twin in terms of personality, interests, and attitudes as one who has been reared with his or her co-twin. The conclusion: Similarities between twins are due to genes, not the environment. Because twins reared apart are so similar, the environment, if anything, makes them different (see Exhibit 3.1).[131]

Adoption Studies Another way to determine whether delinquency is an inherited trait is to compare the behavior of adopted children with that of their biological parents. If the criminal behavior of children is more like that of their biological parents (whom they

EXHIBIT 3.1

Findings from the Minnesota Study of Twins Reared Apart

❙ MZ twins become *more* similar with respect to abilities such as vocabularies and arithmetic scores as they age. As DZ (fraternal) twins get older they become less similar with respect to vocabularies and arithmetic scores.

❙ Identical (MZ) twin children have very similar brain wave patterns. By comparison, children who are fraternal (DZ) twins do not show as much similarity. These results indicate that the way the brain processes information may be greatly influenced by genes.

❙ An EEG is a measure of brain activity or brain waves that can be used to monitor a person's state of arousal. MZ twins tend to produce strikingly similar EEG spectra; DZ twins show far less similarity.

❙ MZ twins tend to have more similar ages at the time of death than DZ twins do. That is, MZ twins are more likely to die at about the same age, and DZ twins are more likely to die at different ages.

SOURCE: Minnesota Twin Family Study, www.psych.umn.edu/psylabs/mtfs/special.htm (accessed June 8, 2007).

have never met) than that of their adopted parents (who brought them up), it would indicate that the tendency toward delinquency is inherited, rather than shaped by the environment.

Studies of this kind have generally supported the hypothesis that there is a link between genetics and behavior.[132] Adoptees share many of the behavioral and intellectual characteristics of their biological parents despite the social and environmental conditions found in their adoptive homes. Genetic makeup is sufficient to counteract and/or negate even the most extreme environmental conditions, such as malnutrition and abuse.[133]

Some of the most influential research in this area has been conducted by Sarnoff Mednick. In one study, Mednick and Bernard Hutchings found that although only 13 percent of the adoptive fathers of a sample of adjudicated delinquent youths had criminal records, 31 percent of their biological fathers had criminal records.[134] Analysis of a control group's background indicated that about 11 percent of all fathers will have criminal records. Hutchings and Mednick were forced to conclude that genetics played at least some role in creating delinquent tendencies, because the biological fathers of delinquents were much more likely than the fathers of noncriminal youths to be criminals.[135]

In addition to a direct link between heredity and delinquency, the literature also shows that behavior traits indirectly linked to delinquency may be at least in part inherited. Biological parents of adopted hyperactive children are more likely to show symptoms of hyperactivity than are the adoptive parents.[136] Several studies have reported a higher incidence of psychological problems in parents of hyperactive children when compared to control groups. Although not all hyperactive children become delinquent, the link between this neurological condition and delinquency has long been suspected.

Similarly, there is evidence (disputed) that intelligence is related to heredity and that low intelligence is a cause of impulsive delinquent acts that are easier to detect and more likely to result in arrest.[137] This connection can create the appearance of a relationship between heredity and delinquency. (See later in this chapter for more on IQ and delinquency.)

Connecting delinquent behavior to heredity is quite controversial because it implies that the cause of delinquency is (a) present at birth, and (b) "transmitted" from one generation to the next and immune to treatment efforts (because genes cannot be altered). Recent evaluations of the gene-crime relationship find that though a relationship can be detected, the better-designed research efforts provide less support than earlier and weaker studies.[138] If there is a genetic basis of delinquency, it is likely that genetic factors contribute to certain individual differences that interact with specific social and environmental conditions to bring about antisocial behavior.[139]

Evolutionary Theory

Some theorists have speculated that the human traits producing violence and aggression have been nurtured and produced through the long process of human evolution.[140]

evolutionary theory
Explaining the existence of aggression and violent behavior as positive adaptive behaviors in human evolution; these traits allowed their bearers to reproduce disproportionately, which has had an effect on the human gene pool.

According to this **evolutionary theory**, the competition for scarce resources has influenced and shaped the human species.[141] Over the course of human existence, people have been shaped to engage in actions that promote their well-being and ensure the survival and reproduction of their genetic line. Males who are impulsive risk takers may be able to father more children; impulsive behavior is inherited and becomes intergenerational. It is not surprising that human history has been marked by war, violence, and aggression.

Crime rate differences between the genders then are less a matter of socialization than inherent differences in the mating patterns that have developed between the sexes over time.[142] Among young men, reckless, life-threatening "risk-proneness" is especially likely to evolve in societies where choosing not to compete means the inability to find suitable mates and to reproduce.[143] Aggressive males have had the greatest impact on the gene pool. The descendants of these aggressive males now account for the disproportionate amount of male aggression and violence.[144]

This evolutionary model suggests that a subpopulation of men has evolved with genes that incline them toward extremely low parental involvement. Sexually aggressive, they use their cunning to gain sexual conquests with as many females as possible. Because females would not willingly choose them as mates, they use stealth to gain sexual access—cheating—including such tactics as mimicking the behavior of more stable males.[145] Psychologist Byron Roth notes that these flamboyant, sexually aggressive males are especially attractive to younger, less intelligent women who begin having children at a very early age.[146] Their fleeting courtship process produces children with low IQs, aggressive personalities, and little chance of proper socialization in father-absent families. Because the criminal justice system treats them leniently, argues Roth, sexually irresponsible men are free to prey upon young girls. Over time, their offspring will yield an ever-expanding supply of offspring who are both antisocial and sexually aggressive.

Concept Summary 3.2 offers a summary of the major biosocial theories of delinquency.

Concept Summary 3.2
Biosocial Theories

Biochemical	Premise	Crime, especially violence, is a function of diet, vitamin intake, hormonal imbalance, and/or food allergies.
	Strengths	Explains irrational violence. Shows how the environment interacts with personal traits to influence behavior.
Neurological	Premise	Criminals and delinquents often suffer brain impairment, as measured by the EEG. Learning disabilities such as attention deficit/hyperactive disorder and minimum brain dysfunction are related to antisocial behavior.
	Strengths	Helps explain relationship between child abuse and crime, and why there is a relationship between victimization and violence (i.e., people who suffer head trauma may become violent).
Genetic	Premise	Delinquent traits and predispositions are inherited. Criminality of parents can predict the delinquency of children.
	Strengths	Explains why only a small percentage of youths in a high-crime area become chronic offenders.
Evolutionary	Premise	Behavior patterns and reproductive traits, developed over the millennia, control behavior.
	Strengths	Explains male aggressiveness. Helps us understand why violence is so common.

PSYCHOLOGICAL THEORIES OF DELINQUENCY

Some experts view the cause of delinquency as essentially psychological.[147] After all, most behaviors labeled delinquent—for example, violence, theft, sexual misconduct—seem to be symptomatic of some underlying psychological problem.

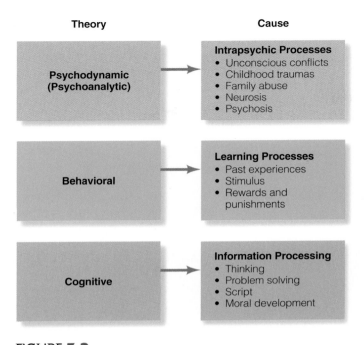

Theory	Cause
Psychodynamic (Psychoanalytic) →	**Intrapsychic Processes** • Unconscious conflicts • Childhood traumas • Family abuse • Neurosis • Psychosis
Behavioral →	**Learning Processes** • Past experiences • Stimulus • Rewards and punishments
Cognitive →	**Information Processing** • Thinking • Problem solving • Script • Moral development

FIGURE 3.2
Psychological Theories of Delinquency

Psychologists point out that many delinquent youths have poor home lives, destructive relationships with neighbors, friends, and teachers, and conflicts with authority figures in general. These relationships seem to indicate a disturbed personality structure. Furthermore, numerous studies of incarcerated youths indicate that the youths' personalities are marked by negative, antisocial behavior characteristics. And because delinquent behavior occurs among youths in every racial, ethnic, and socioeconomic group, psychologists view it as a function of emotional and mental disturbance, rather than purely a result of social factors, such as racism, poverty, and class conflict. Although many delinquents do not manifest significant psychological problems, enough do to give clinicians a powerful influence on delinquency theory.

Because psychology is a complex and diversified discipline, more than one psychological perspective on crime exists. Three prominent psychological perspectives on delinquency are the psychodynamic, the behavioral, and the cognitive.[148] (See Figure 3.2.)

Psychodynamic Theory

According to **psychodynamic theory**, whose basis is the pioneering work of the Austrian physician Sigmund Freud (1856–1939), law violations are a product of an abnormal personality structure formed early in life and which thereafter controls human behavior choices.[149] In extreme cases, mental torment drives people into violence and aggression. The basis of psychodynamic theory is the assumption that human behavior is controlled by unconscious mental processes developed early in childhood.

According to Freud, the human personality contains three major components. The *id* is the unrestrained, primitive, pleasure-seeking component with which each child is born. The *ego* develops through the reality of living in the world and helps manage and restrain the id's need for immediate gratification. The *superego* develops through interactions with parents and other significant people and represents the development of conscience and the moral rules shared by most adults.

Unconscious motivations for behavior come from the id's action in response to two primal needs—sex and aggression. Human behavior is often marked by symbolic actions that reflect hidden feelings about these needs. For example, stealing a car may reflect a person's unconscious need for shelter and mobility to escape from hostile enemies (aggression) or perhaps an urge to enter a closed, dark, womblike structure that reflects the earliest memories (sex).

All three segments of the personality operate simultaneously. The id dictates needs and desires, the superego counteracts the id by fostering feelings of morality and righteousness, and the ego evaluates the reality of a position between these two extremes. If these components are properly balanced, the individual can lead a normal life. If one aspect of the personality becomes dominant at the expense of the others, the individual exhibits abnormal personality traits (see Figure 3.3).

A number of psychologists and psychiatrists expanded upon Freud's original model to explain the onset of antisocial behaviors. Erik Erikson speculated that many adolescents experience a life crisis in which they feel emotional, impulsive, and uncertain of their role and purpose.[150] He coined the phrase **identity crisis** to denote this period of inner turmoil and confusion. Erikson's approach might characterize the behavior of youthful drug abusers as an expression of confusion over their place

FIGURE 3.3
The Structure of the Id, Ego, and Superego

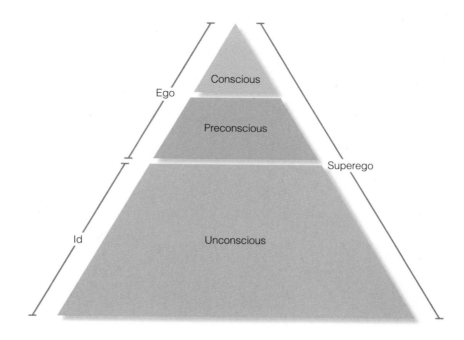

in society, their inability to direct behavior toward useful outlets, and perhaps their dependency on others to offer them solutions to their problems.

In his classic work, psychoanalyst August Aichorn found that social stress alone could not produce such an emotional state. He identifies **latent delinquents**—youths whose troubled family life leads them to seek immediate gratification without consideration of right and wrong or the feelings of others.[151] In its most extreme form, delinquency may be viewed as a form of psychosis that prevents delinquent youths from appreciating the feelings of their victims or controlling their own impulsive needs for gratification.

Psychodynamics of Delinquency Applying these concepts, psychodynamic theory holds that youth crime is a result of unresolved mental anguish and internal conflict. Some children, especially those who have been abused or mistreated, may experience unconscious feelings associated with resentment, fear, and hatred. If this conflict cannot be reconciled, the children may regress to a state in which they become id dominated. This regression may be considered responsible for a great number of mental diseases, from neuroses to psychoses, and in many cases it may be related to criminal behavior.[152]

Delinquents are id-dominated people who suffer from the inability to control impulsive drives. Perhaps because they suffered unhappy experiences in childhood or had families who could not provide proper love and care, delinquents suffer from weak or damaged egos that make them unable to cope with conventional society.[153] Adolescent antisocial behavior is a consequence of feeling unable to cope with feelings of oppression. Criminality actually allows youths to strive by producing positive psychic results: helping them to feel free and independent; giving them the possibility of excitement and the chance to use their skills and imagination; providing the promise of positive gain; allowing them to blame others for their predicament (for example, the police); and giving them a chance to rationalize their own sense of failure ("If I hadn't gotten into trouble, I could have been a success").[154]

The psychodynamic approach places heavy emphasis on the family's role. Antisocial youths frequently come from families in which parents are unable to provide the controls that allow children to develop the personal tools they need to cope with the world.[155] If neglectful parents fail to develop a child's superego adequately, the child's id may become the predominant personality force; the absence of a strong

latent delinquents
Youths whose troubled family life leads them to seek immediate gratification without consideration of right and wrong or the feelings of others.

superego results in an inability to distinguish clearly between right and wrong. Their destructive behavior may actually be a call for help. In fact, some psychoanalysts view delinquent behaviors as motivated by an unconscious urge to be punished. These children, who feel unloved, assume the reason must be their own inadequacy; hence, they deserve punishment. Later, the youth may demand immediate gratification, lack compassion and sensitivity for the needs of others, disassociate feelings, act aggressively and impulsively, and demonstrate other psychotic symptoms. Antisocial behavior, then, may be the result of conflict or trauma occurring early in a child's development, and delinquent activity may become an outlet for violent and antisocial feelings.

Mental Disorders and Crime

According to the psychodynamic approach, delinquent behavior is a function of unconscious mental instability and turmoil. People who have lost control and are dominated by their id are known as *psychotics*; their behavior may be marked by hallucinations and inappropriate responses.

Psychosis takes many forms, the most common being *schizophrenia*, a condition marked by illogical thought processes, distorted perceptions, and abnormal emotional expression. The most serious types of violence and antisocial behavior might be motivated by psychosis.[156]

Of a less serious nature are a variety of mood and/or behavior disorders that render people histrionic, depressed, antisocial, or narcissistic.[157] These **mood disorders** are characterized by disturbance in expressed emotions.[158] Some suffer from **alexithymia**, a deficit in emotional cognition that prevents people from being aware of their feelings or being able to understand or talk about their thoughts and emotions; they seem robotic and emotionally dead.[159] Others may suffer from eating disorders and are likely to use fasting, vomiting, and drugs to lose weight or to keep from gaining weight.[160] One such disorder is discussed more fully in the Focus on Delinquency feature "Disruptive Behavior Disorder."

mood disorder
A condition in which the prevailing emotional mood is distorted or inappropriate to the circumstances.

alexithymia
A deficit in emotional cognition that prevents people from being aware of their feelings or being able to understand or talk about their thoughts and emotions; sufferers from alexithymia seem robotic and emotionally dead.

Is the Psychodynamic View Valid? There is a great deal of empirical evidence showing that kids who suffer from these and other psychological deficits are prone to violence and antisocial behavior.[161] Violent youths have been clinically diagnosed as "overtly hostile," "explosive or volatile," "anxious," and "depressed."[162] Many delinquents exhibit indications of such psychological abnormalities as schizophrenia, paranoia, and obsessive behaviors; female offenders seem to have more serious mental health symptoms and psychological disturbances than male offenders.[163] Antisocial youths frequently come from families in which parents are unable to give love, set consistent limits, and provide the controls that allow children to develop the necessary personal tools to cope with the world in which they live.[164]

Although this evidence is persuasive, the association between mental disturbance and delinquency is unresolved. It is possible that any link is caused by some intervening variable or factor:

I Psychologically troubled youth do poorly in school, and school failure leads to delinquency.[165]

I Psychologically troubled youth have conflict-ridden social relationships that make them prone to commit delinquent acts.[166]

I While good parenting is considered a barrier against delinquency, youth who maintain abnormal psychological characteristics such as low self-control, a hostile view of relationships, and acceptance of deviant norms may neutralize the influence of positive parenting on controlling their conduct.[167]

I Kids who suffer child abuse are more likely to have mental anguish and commit violent acts; child abuse is the actual cause of both problems.[168]

Disruptive Behavior Disorder

Most kids act out, especially when they are under stress. Younger children may become difficult when they are tired or hungry. They may defy parents and talk back to teachers. It would be unusual for a child not to go through the "terrible twos" or be reasonable and mature when they are three years old! However, kids who are frequently uncooperative and hostile and who seem to be much more difficult than other children the same age may be suffering from a psychological condition known as disruptive behavior disorder (DBD). If left untreated, this condition can have long-term effects on the child's social, family, and academic life.

DBD has two components. The first and more mild condition is referred to as oppositional defiant disorder (ODD). Children suffering from ODD experience an ongoing pattern of uncooperative, defiant, and hostile behavior toward authority figures that seriously interferes with the youngster's day-to-day functioning. Symptoms of ODD may include frequent loss of temper; constant arguing with adults; defying adults or refusing adult requests or rules; deliberately annoying others; blaming others for mistakes or misbehavior; being angry and resentful; being spiteful or vindictive; or swearing or using obscene language. The person with ODD is moody and easily frustrated, has a low opinion of him- or herself, and may abuse drugs as a form of self-medication.

Kids with ODD act out in multiple settings, but their behavior is more noticeable at home or at school. It is estimated that 5 to 15 percent of all school-age children have ODD. Though the causes of ODD are unknown, both biosocial and psychological sources are suspected.

The second element of DBD is conduct disorder (CD), which comprises a more serious group of behavioral and emotional problems in youngsters. Children and adolescents with CD have great difficulty following rules and behaving in a socially acceptable way. They are often viewed by other children, adults, and social agencies as severely antisocial. Research shows that they are frequently involved in such activities as bullying, fighting, and cruelty to animals. Kids suffering from CD are more likely to carry weapons than other kids. Sexual assault and arson are common activities. Children with CD have trouble being truthful and think nothing of lying to cover up their activities. When they defy their parents, their activities are more serious than the ODD child: They cut school, stay out all night, or run away from home.

What causes CD? Numerous biosocial and psychological factors are suspected. There is evidence, for example, that interconnections between the frontal lobes and other brain regions may influence CD. There is also research showing that levels of serotonin can influence the onset of CD. CD has been shown to aggregate in families, suggesting a genetic basis of the disorder.

It is generally assumed that ODD is more treatable than CD. Treatment might include parent training programs to help manage the child's behavior, individual psychotherapy, anger management, family psychotherapy, and cognitive-behavioral therapy to assist problem solving.

Critical Thinking

1. Is it possible that kids who are routinely aggressive and seemingly "out of control" are suffering from some form of chemical deficiency? Or do you believe that such behavior is a result of significant psychological deficits?

2. Could kids who are routinely hostile and defiant toward authority figures be controlled by the threat of physical punishment? Which works better: fear or love?

SOURCES: Paul Rohde, Gregory N. Clarke, David E. Mace, Jenel S. Jorgensen, and John R. Seeley, "An Efficacy/Effectiveness Study of Cognitive-Behavioral Treatment for Adolescents with Comorbid Major Depression and Conduct Disorder," *Journal of the American Academy of Child and Adolescent Psychiatry* 43:660–669 (2004); Ellen Kjelsberg, "Gender and Disorder Specific Criminal Career Profiles in Former Adolescent Psychiatric In-Patients," *Journal of Youth and Adolescence* 33:261–270 (2004); Barbara Maughan, Richard Rowe, Julie Messer, Robert Goodman, and Howard Meltzer, "Conduct Disorder and Oppositional Defiant Disorder in a National Sample: Developmental Epidemiology," *Journal of Child Psychology and Psychiatry and Allied Disciplines* 45:609–621 (2004); the American Academy of Child and Adolescent Psychiatry (AACAP), www.aacap.org (accessed September 25, 2007); Jeffrey Burke, Rolf Loeber, and Boris Birmaher, "Oppositional Defiant Disorder and Conduct Disorder: A Review of the Past 10 Years, Part II," *Journal of the American Academy of Child and Adolescent Psychiatry* 41:1275–1294 (2002).

❙ Living in a stress-filled urban environment may produce symptoms of both mental illness and crime.[169]

❙ Kids who are delinquent have reduced life chances. They do poorly in school and as adults are relegated to lower-class economic status. Educational failure and status deprivation are related to depression and other psychological deficits.[170]

It is also possible that the link is spurious and caused by the treatment of the mentally ill: The police may be more likely to arrest the mentally ill, giving the illusion that they are crime prone.[171] However, some recent research by Paul Hirschfield and his associates gives only mixed support to this view: while some mental health problems increase the risk of arrest, others bring out more cautious or compassionate police responses that may result in treatment rather than arrest.[172]

Behavioral Theory

Not all psychologists agree that behavior is controlled by unconscious mental processes determined by parental relationships developed early in childhood. Behavioral psychologists argue that a person's personality is learned throughout life during interaction with others. Based primarily on the works of the American psychologist John B. Watson (1878–1958) and popularized by Harvard professor B. F. Skinner (1904–1990), behaviorism concerns itself solely with measurable events and not the unobservable psychic phenomena described by psychoanalysts.

behaviorism
Branch of psychology concerned with the study of observable behavior rather than unconscious processes; focuses on particular stimuli and responses to them.

Behaviorists suggest that individuals learn by observing how people react to their behavior. Behavior is triggered initially by a stimulus or change in the environment. If a particular behavior is reinforced by some positive reaction or event, that behavior will be continued and eventually learned. However, behaviors that are not reinforced or are punished will be extinguished or become extinct. For example, if children are given a reward (ice cream for dessert) for eating their entire dinner, eventually they will learn to eat properly as a matter of habit. Conversely, if children are punished for some misbehavior, they will eventually learn to associate disapproval with that act and avoid it.

Social Learning Theory Not all behaviorists strictly follow the teachings of Watson and Skinner. Some hold that a person's learning and social experiences, coupled with his or her values and expectations, determine behavior. This is known as the social learning approach. The most widely read social learning theorists are Albert Bandura, Walter Mischel, and Richard Walters.[173] In general, they hold that children will model their behavior according to the reactions they receive from others, either positive or negative; the behavior of those adults they are in close contact with, especially parents; and the behavior they view on television and in movies. If children observe aggression and see that the aggressive behavior, such as an adult slapping or punching someone during an argument, is approved or rewarded, they will likely react violently during a similar incident. Eventually, the children will master the techniques of aggression and become more confident that their behavior will bring tangible rewards.[174]

social learning theory
The view that behavior is modeled through observation, either directly through intimate contact with others or indirectly through media; interactions that are rewarded are copied, whereas those that are punished are avoided.

By implication, social learning suggests that children who grow up in a home where violence is a way of life may learn to believe that such behavior is acceptable and rewarding. Even if parents tell children not to be violent and punish them if they are, the children will still model their behavior on the observed parental violence.

Thus, children are more likely to heed what parents *do* than what they *say*. By mid-childhood, some children have already acquired an association between their use of aggression against others and the physical punishment they receive at home. Often their aggressive responses are directed at other family members and siblings. The family may serve as a training ground for violence because the child perceives physical punishment as the norm during conflict situations with others.[175]

Adolescent aggression is a result of disrupted dependency relations with parents. This refers to the frustration and anger a child feels when parents provide poor role models and hold back affection and nurturing. Children who lack close dependent ties to their parents may have little opportunity or desire to model themselves after them or to internalize their standards of behavior. In the absence of such internalized controls, the child's aggression is likely to be expressed in an immediate, direct, and socially unacceptable fashion such as violence and aggression.[176]

The Media and Delinquency One aspect of social learning theory that has received a great deal of attention is the belief that children will model their behavior after characters they observe on TV or see in movies. This phenomenon is especially critical considering the findings of the recent Henry J. Kaiser Family Foundation study, *Zero to Six: Electronic Media in the Lives of Infants, Toddlers, and Preschoolers* (2003).[177] This research found that children aged 6 and under spend an average of two hours a day using screen media such as TV and computers, about the same amount of time they spend playing outside, and significantly more than the amount they spend reading or being read to (about 39 minutes per day).

Nearly half of all children aged 6 and under have used a computer and just under a third have played video games. Even the youngest children—those under 2—are exposed to electronic media for more than two hours per day; more than 40 percent of those under 2 watch TV every day. But what do they watch? Marketing research indicates that adolescents aged 11 to 14 rent violent horror movies at a higher rate than any other age group; kids this age use older peers and siblings and apathetic parents to gain access to R-rated films. More than 40 percent of U.S. households now have cable TV, which features violent films and shows. Even children's programming is saturated with violence. Violent video games are also a problem. Americans now spend twice as much money on video games as they spend going to the movies. The core gaming audience is 8- to 14-year-old males. Eighty percent of the games produced are violent, with realistic graphics that include blood, decapitation, guns, knives, mutilation, and death. Video games may have a greater impact on their audience than TV and movies because they immerse the players visually, auditorily, and physically rather than have them remain passive observers.[178] There is evidence that violent video game exposure increases aggressive thoughts, angry feelings, physiological arousal, aggressive behaviors, and decreases helpful behaviors. One reason may be because exposure to violence in the virtual world desensitizes kids to violence in the real world, making it appear less threatening and foreboding.[179]

A well-publicized study conducted by researchers at UCLA found that at least 10 network shows made heavy use of violence. Of the 161 television movies monitored (every one that aired that season), 23 raised concerns from viewers about their use of violence, violent theme, violent title, or inappropriate graphicness of a scene. Of the 118 theatrical films monitored, 50 raised concerns about their use of violence. Some television series may contain limited depictions of violence, each of which may be appropriate in its context.

However, it was found that commercials for these programs emphasized only the violent scenes with little in the way of context. Even some children's television programs were found to feature "sinister combat" as the theme of the show. The characters were portrayed as happy to fight with little provocation.[180] It is estimated that the average child views 8,000 TV murders before finishing elementary school.

Does the media, including films, TV, and violent video games, influence violent behavior? The jury is still out on this controversial issue. While lab-based studies seem to show an association between violence and the media, millions of kids watch violent TV shows each day, go to see violent films, and play violent videos without suffering negative consequences or changes in their behavior.

TV and Violence Children are particularly susceptible to TV imagery. It is believed that many children consider television images to be real, especially when the images are authoritatively presented by adults (as in commercials). Some children, especially those who are considered "emotionally disturbed," may be unable to distinguish between fantasy and reality when watching TV shows.[181]

A number of research methods have been used to measure the effect of TV viewing on violent behavior. One method is to expose groups of subjects to violent TV shows in a laboratory setting and then compare their behavior to control groups who viewed nonviolent programming; observations have also been made in playgrounds, athletic fields, and residences. Other experiments require subjects to answer attitude surveys after watching violent TV shows. Still another approach is to use aggregate measures of TV viewing; for example, the number of violent TV shows on the air during a given time period is compared to crime rates during the same period.

Most evaluations of experimental data gathered using these techniques indicate that watching violence on TV is correlated with aggressive behaviors.[182] Such august bodies as the American Psychological Association and the National Institute of Mental Health support the TV-violence link.[183] Subjects who view violent TV shows are likely to commence aggressive behavior almost immediately. This phenomenon is demonstrated by numerous reports of copycat behavior after a particularly violent film or TV show is aired.

According to a recent analysis of all scientific data since 1975, Brad Bushman and Craig Anderson found that the weight of the evidence shows that watching violence on TV is correlated to aggressive behaviors and that the newest, most methodologically sophisticated work shows the greatest amount of association. Put another way, the weight of the experimental results indicates that violent media have an immediate impact on people with a preexisting tendency toward crime and violence.

There is also evidence that watching violent media may create changes in personality and cognition, which in the long term produces negative behavioral changes. Some recent research by Dimitri Christakis and his associates found that for every hour of television watched daily between the ages of 1 and 3, the risk of developing attention problems increased by 9 percent over the life course; attention problems have been linked to antisocial behaviors.[184] A study conducted by researchers at Columbia University found that kids who watched more than an hour of TV each day showed an increase in assaults, fights, robberies, and other acts of aggression later in life. About 6 percent of 14-year-olds who watched less than an hour of television a day became involved in aggressive acts between the ages of 16 and 22. The rate of aggressive acts skyrocketed to 22.5 percent when kids watched between one to three hours of TV. For kids who viewed more than three hours of TV per day, 28.8 percent were later involved in aggressive acts as adults. This association remained significant after previous aggressive behavior, childhood neglect, family income, neighborhood violence, parental education, and psychiatric disorders were controlled statistically. This research provides a direct link between TV viewing in adolescence and later aggressive behavior in adulthood.[185]

A joint statement by the American Academy of Pediatrics, American Academy of Child and Adolescent Psychiatry, American Academy of Family Physicians, American Medical Association, American Psychological Association, and American Psychiatric Association summarized the effects of media violence on adolescent behavior:

I   Viewing violence can lead to emotional desensitization toward violence in real life.

I   Children exposed to violent programming at a young age have a higher tendency for violent and aggressive behavior later in life than children who are not so exposed.

I   Children exposed to violence are more likely to assume that acts of violence are acceptable behavior.

I   Viewing violence increases fear of becoming a victim of violence, with a resultant increase in self-protective behaviors and a mistrust of others.[186]

Alternative Explanations Though this evidence is persuasive, the relationship between TV viewing and violence is still uncertain. A number of critics claim that the evidence simply does not support the claim that TV viewing is related to antisocial behavior.[187] Some critics assert that experimental results are inconclusive and short-lived. Kids may have an immediate reaction to viewing violence on TV, but aggression is quickly extinguished once the viewing ends.[188] Experiments showing that kids act aggressively after watching violent TV shows fail to link aggression to actual criminal behaviors, such as rape or assault. Aggregate data are also inconclusive. Little evidence exists that areas with the highest levels of violent TV viewing also have rates of violent crime that are above the norm.[189] Millions of children watch violence every night yet fail to become violent criminals. And even if a violent behavior–TV link could be established, it would be difficult to show that antisocial people develop aggressive traits merely from watching TV. Aggressive youths may simply enjoy watching TV shows that conform to and support their behavioral orientation. Further research is needed to clarify this important issue.

Cognitive Theory

cognitive theory
The branch of psychology that studies the perception of reality and the mental processes required to understand the world we live in.

A third area of psychology that has received increasing recognition in recent years is cognitive theory. Psychologists with a cognitive perspective focus on mental processes—the way people perceive and mentally represent the world around them, and how they solve problems. The pioneers of this school were Wilhelm Wundt (1832–1920), Edward Titchener (1867–1927), and William James (1842–1920). The cognitive perspective contains several subgroups. Perhaps the most important for criminological theory is the moral and intellectual development branch, which is concerned with how people morally represent and reason about the world.

Jean Piaget (1896–1980), the founder of this approach, hypothesized that a child's reasoning processes develop in an orderly fashion, beginning at birth and continuing until age 12 and older.[190] At first, during the *sensorimotor stage*, children respond to the environment in a simple manner, seeking interesting objects and developing their reflexes. By the fourth and final stage, the *formal operational stage*, they have developed into mature adults who can use logic and abstract thought.

Lawrence Kohlberg applied the concept of developmental stages to issues in criminology.[191] He suggested that people travel through stages of moral development, during which the basis for moral and ethical decision making changes. It is possible that serious offenders have a moral orientation that differs from that of law-abiding citizens. Kohlberg's stages of development are as follows:

Stage 1. Right is obedience to power and avoidance of punishment.
Stage 2. Right is taking responsibility for oneself, meeting one's own needs, and leaving to others the responsibility for themselves.
Stage 3. Right is being good in the sense of having good motives, having concern for others, and "putting yourself in the other person's shoes."
Stage 4. Right is maintaining the rules of a society and serving the welfare of the group or society.
Stage 5. Right is based on recognized individual rights within a society with agreed-upon rules—a social contract.
Stage 6. Right is an assumed obligation to principles applying to all humankind—principles of justice, equality, and respect for human personality.

Kohlberg classified people according to the stage on this continuum at which their moral development has ceased to grow. In studies conducted by Kohlberg and his associates, criminals were found to be significantly lower in their moral judgment development than noncriminals of the same social background.[192] The majority of noncriminals were classified in stages 3 and 4, whereas a majority of criminals were in stages 1 and 2. Moral development theory, then, suggests that people who obey the law simply to avoid punishment or who have outlooks mainly characterized by self-interest are more likely to commit crimes than those who view the law as something that benefits all of society and who honor the rights of others. Subsequent research with delinquent youths has found that a significant number were in the first two moral development categories, whereas nondelinquents were ranked higher.[193] In addition, higher stages of moral reasoning are associated with such behaviors as honesty, generosity, and nonviolence, which are considered incompatible with delinquency.[194]

Information Processing Cognitive theorists who study information processing try to explain antisocial behavior in terms of perception and analysis of data. When people make decisions, they engage in a sequence of cognitive thought processes. They first *encode* information so that it can be interpreted. They then search for a proper response and decide upon the most appropriate action; finally, they act on their decision.[195]

According to this approach, adolescents who use information properly, who are better conditioned to make reasoned judgments, and who can make quick and reasoned decisions when facing emotion-laden events are the ones best able to avoid antisocial behavior choices.[196] In contrast, delinquency-prone adolescents may have cognitive deficits and use information incorrectly when they make decisions.[197] They have difficulty making the "right decision" while under stress. One reason is that they may be relying on mental "scripts" learned in their early childhood that tell them how to interpret events, what to expect, how they should react, and what the outcome of the interaction should be.[198] Hostile children may have learned improper scripts by observing how others react to events; their own parents' aggressive and inappropriate behavior would have considerable impact. Some children may have had early and prolonged exposure to violence, such as child abuse, which increases their sensitivity to teasing and maltreatment. They may misperceive behavioral cues because their decision making was shaped by traumatic life events.[199]

Oversensitivity to rejection by their peers is a continuation of sensitivity to rejection by parents.[200] Violence becomes a stable behavior because the scripts that emphasize aggressive responses are repeatedly rehearsed as the child matures. They view crime as an appropriate means to satisfy their immediate personal needs, which take precedent over more distant social needs such as obedience to the law.[201]

Violence-prone kids see the world around them as filled with aggressive people. They are overly sensitive and tend to overreact to provocation. As these children mature, they use fewer cues than most people to process information. Some use violence in a calculating fashion as a means of getting what they want; others react in an overly volatile fashion to the slightest provocation. When they attack victims, they may believe they are defending themselves, even though they are misreading the situation.[202] Adolescents who use violence as a coping technique with others are also more likely to exhibit other social problems, such as drug and alcohol abuse.[203]

There is also evidence that delinquent boys who engage in theft are more likely to exhibit cognitive deficits than nondelinquent youth. For example, they have a poor sense of time, leaving them incapable of dealing with or solving social problems in an effective manner.[204]

PSYCHOLOGICAL CHARACTERISTICS AND DELINQUENCY

Personality and Delinquency

Personality can be defined as the reasonably stable patterns of behavior, including thoughts and emotions, that distinguish one person from another.[205] An individual's personality reflects characteristic ways of adapting to life's demands and problems. The way we behave is a function of how our personality enables us to interpret life events and make appropriate behavioral choices.

Can the cause of delinquency be linked to personality? There has been a great deal of research on this subject and an equal amount of controversy and debate over the findings.[206] In their early work, Sheldon Glueck and Eleanor Glueck identified a number of personality traits that characterize delinquents:

self-assertiveness	suspicion
extroversion	poor personal skills
defiance	destructiveness
ambivalence	mental instability
impulsiveness	sadism
feeling unappreciated	hostility
narcissism	lack of concern for others
distrust of authority	resentment[207]

The Gluecks' research is representative of the view that delinquents maintain a distinct personality whose characteristics increase the probability that (a) they will be aggressive and antisocial and (b) their actions will involve them with agents of social control, ranging from teachers to police.

Personality and Antisocial Behaviors Since the Gluecks' findings were published, other research efforts have attempted to identify personality traits that would increase the chances for a delinquent career.[208] A common theme is that delinquents are hyperactive, impulsive individuals with short attention spans (attention deficit disorder), who frequently manifest conduct disorders, anxiety disorders, and depression.[209] These traits make them prone to problems ranging from psychopathology to drug abuse, sexual promiscuity, and violence.[210] Suspected traits include impulsivity, hostility, and aggressiveness.[211] The psychologist Hans Eysenck identified two important personality traits that he associated with antisocial behavior: extraversion and neuroticism. Eysenck defines extraverts as impulsive individuals who lack the ability to examine their own motives and behaviors; neuroticism produces anxiety, tension, and emotional instability.[212] Youths who lack self-insight and are impulsive and emotionally unstable are likely to interpret events differently than youths who are able to give reasoned judgments to life events. Though the former may act destructively, for example, by using drugs, the latter will be able to reason that such behavior is ultimately self-defeating and life threatening. Youths who are both neurotic and extraverted often lack insight, are highly impulsive, and more likely than other delinquents to become chronic offenders.[213]

extravert
A person who behaves impulsively and doesn't have the ability to examine motives and behavior.

neuroticism
A personality trait marked by unfounded anxiety, tension, and emotional instability.

The Antisocial Personality It has also been suggested that chronic delinquency may result from a personality pattern or syndrome commonly referred to as the psychopathic or sociopathic personality (the terms are used interchangeably).[214] Though no more than 3 percent of the male offending population may be classified as sociopathic, it is possible that a large segment of the persistent chronic offenders share this trait.[215]

Psychopathic (sociopathic) youths exhibit a low level of guilt and anxiety and persistently violate the rights of others.[216] Although they may exhibit superficial charm and above-average intelligence, these often mask a disturbed personality that makes them incapable of forming enduring relationships with others.[217] Frequently involved in such deviant behaviors as truancy, running away, lying, substance abuse, and impulsivity, psychopaths lack the ability to empathize with others. From an early age, the psychopath's home life is filled with frustrations, bitterness, and quarreling.

Consequently, throughout life, the sociopath is unreliable, unstable, demanding, and egocentric. Hervey Cleckley, a leading authority on psychopathy, uses this definition:

psychopathic personality
(also known as sociopathic personality)
A person lacking in warmth and affection, exhibiting inappropriate behavior responses, and unable to learn from experience.

> *[Psychopaths are] chronically antisocial individuals who are always in trouble, profiting neither from experience nor punishment, and maintaining no real loyalties to any person, group, or code. They are frequently callous and hedonistic, showing marked emotional immaturity, with lack of responsibility, lack of judgment, and an ability to rationalize their behavior so that it appears warranted, reasonable, and justified.[218]*

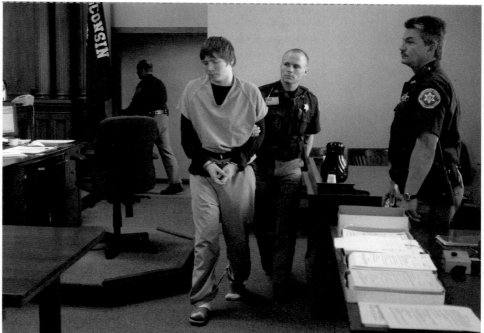

People with antisocial personalities lack remorse and maintain their innocence even when caught red-handed committing horrific crimes. Brendan Dassey, 16, is escorted into a Manitowoc County, Wisconsin, courthouse on May 26, 2006. Dassey was accused of murder and sexual assault after admitting to investigators that he and his uncle, Steven Avery, raped and killed 25-year-old photographer Teresa Halbach and then burned her body in a fire pit. Although Dassey recanted his confession and denied guilt and responsibility he was found guilty of rape and murder on April 25, 2007.

Youths diagnosed as psychopaths are believed to be thrill seekers who engage in violent, destructive behavior. Some become gang members and engage in violent and destructive sexual escapades to compensate for a fear of responsibility and an inability to maintain interpersonal relationships.[219] Delinquents have been described as sensation seekers who desire a hedonistic pursuit of pleasure, an extraverted lifestyle, partying, drinking, and a variety of sexual partners. They may constantly engage in risky behaviors such as car theft and joy riding.[220]

A number of factors have been found to contribute to the development of psychopathic/sociopathic personalities. They include having an emotionally disturbed parent, a lack of love, parental rejection during childhood, and inconsistent discipline. Another view is that psychopathy has its basis in a measurable physical condition—psychopaths suffer from levels of arousal that are lower than those of the general population. Consequently, psychopathic youths may need greater-than-average stimulation to bring them up to comfortable levels. The road to psychopathy may be entered by people with abnormal brain structures.[221] Psychologists have attempted to treat patients diagnosed as psychopaths by giving them adrenaline, which increases their arousal levels.

Intelligence and Delinquency

Psychologists have long been concerned with the development of intelligence and its subsequent relationship to behavior. It has been charged that children with low IQs are responsible for a disproportionate share of delinquency.

Early criminologists believed that low intelligence was a major cause of delinquency. They thought that if it could be determined which individuals were less intelligent, it might be possible to identify potential delinquents before they committed socially harmful acts.[222] Because social scientists had a captive group of subjects in training schools and penal institutions, studies began to appear that measured the correlation between IQ and crime by testing adjudicated juvenile delinquents. Delinquent juveniles were believed to be inherently substandard in intelligence and naturally inclined to commit more crimes than more intelligent people. Thus, juvenile delinquents were used as a test group around which numerous theories about intelligence were built.

Nature Theory When the newly developed IQ tests were administered to inmates of prisons and juvenile training schools in the first decades of the twentieth century, a large proportion of the inmates scored low on the tests. Henry Goddard found in his studies in 1920 that many institutionalized people were what he considered "feebleminded" and thus concluded that at least half of all juvenile delinquents were mental defectives.[223]

Similarly, in 1926, William Healy and Augusta Bronner tested a group of delinquents in Chicago and Boston and found that 37 percent were subnormal in intelligence.[224] They concluded that delinquents were 5 to 10 times more likely to be mentally deficient than nondelinquent boys.

These and other early studies were embraced as proof that low IQ scores indicated potentially delinquent children and that a correlation existed between innate low intelligence and deviant behavior. IQ tests were believed to measure the inborn genetic makeup of individuals, and many criminologists accepted the predisposition of substandard individuals toward delinquency. This view is referred to as nature theory of intelligence.

nature theory
Holds that low intelligence is genetically determined and inherited.

nurture theory
Holds that intelligence is partly biological but mostly sociological; negative environmental factors encourage delinquent behavior and depress intelligence scores for many youths.

Nurture Theory Development of culturally sensitive explanations of human behavior in the 1930s led to the nurture theory of intelligence. This school of thought holds that intelligence must be viewed as partly biological but primarily sociological. Nurture theory argues that intelligence is not inherited and that low-IQ parents do not necessarily produce low-IQ children.[225] It discredits the notion that people commit crimes because they have low IQ scores. Instead, it holds that environmental stimulation from parents, relatives, schools, peer groups, and innumerable others creates a child's IQ level and that low IQs result from an environment that also encourages delinquent and criminal behavior.[226] For example, if educational environments could be improved, the result might be both an elevation in IQ scores and a decrease in delinquency.[227] Studies challenging the assumption that people automatically committed delinquent acts because they had below-average IQs began to appear as early as the 1920s. John Slawson's study of 1,543 delinquent boys in New York institutions found that although 80 percent of the delinquents achieved lower scores in abstract verbal intelligence than the general population, delinquents were about normal in mechanical aptitude and nonverbal intelligence. Slawson found no relationship between the number of arrests, the types of offenses, and IQ.[228] In 1931, Edwin Sutherland also evaluated IQ studies of criminals and delinquents and found evidence disputing the association between intelligence and criminality.[229] These findings did much to discredit the notion that a strong relationship existed between IQ and criminality, and for many years the IQ-delinquency link was ignored.

IQ and Delinquency Today A study published in the 1970s by Travis Hirschi and Michael Hindelang revived interest in the association between IQ and delinquency.[230] After conducting a thorough statistical analysis of IQ and delinquency data sets, Hirschi and Hindelang concluded both that IQ tests are a valid predictor of intelligence and that "the weight of evidence is that IQ is more important than race and social class" for predicting delinquent involvement. They argued that a low IQ increases the likelihood of delinquent behavior through its effect on school performance: Youths with low IQs do poorly in school, and school failure and academic incompetence are highly related to delinquency.

The Hirschi-Hindelang findings have been supported by a number of research efforts.[231] In their widely read *Crime and Human Nature*, James Q. Wilson and Richard Herrnstein concluded

> . . . there appears to be a clear and consistent link between criminality and low intelligence. That is, taking all offenders as a group, and ignoring differences among kinds of crime, criminals seem, on the average, to be a bit less bright and to have a different set of intellectual strengths and weaknesses than do noncriminals as a group.[232]

Contemporary research efforts have continued to uncover an association between low IQ scores and antisocial behavior. Scores on intelligence tests have been used to predict violent behavior and to distinguish between groups of violent and nonviolent offenders.[233] However, among those social scientists that believe that IQ scores predict criminality, there is still disagreement on the direction of the association. Some believe that IQ has an *indirect* influence on delinquency. Children with a low IQ are more likely to engage in delinquent behavior because their poor verbal ability creates a frustrating school experience. According to this view, low IQ leads to school failure, and academic deficiency and failure is associated with delinquency. In contrast, some experts believe that IQ may have a *direct* influence on the onset of delinquent involvement. The key linkage between IQ and delinquency is the ability to manipulate abstract concepts. Low intelligence limits adolescents' ability to "foresee the consequences of their offending and to appreciate the feelings of victims."[234] Therefore, youths with limited intelligence are more likely to misinterpret events and gestures, act foolishly, take risks, and engage in harmful behavior.

IQ and Delinquency Controversy The relationship between IQ and delinquency is extremely controversial. It implies there is a condition present at birth that accounts for a child's delinquent behavior throughout the life cycle and that this condition is not easily changed or improved. By implication, if delinquency is not spread evenly through the social structure, neither is intelligence.

The controversy has been fueled by charges that tests are culturally biased and invalid, which makes any existing evidence at best inconclusive. There is also research indicating that IQ level has negligible influence on delinquent behavior.[235] If, as some believe, the linkage between IQ and crime is indirect, then delinquency may be a reflection of poor school performance and educational failure. As Wilson and Herrnstein put it, "A child who chronically loses standing in the competition of the classroom may feel justified in settling the score outside, by violence, theft, and other forms of defiant illegality."[236] Because the relationship runs from low IQ to poor school performance to frustration to delinquency, school officials need to recognize the problem and plan programs to help underachievers perform better in school. As the hypothesized relationship between IQ and delinquency, even if proved to be valid, is an indirect one, educational enrichment programs can help counteract any influence intellectual impairment has on the predilection of young people to commit crime.

Critiquing Individual-Level Theories

Individual-level studies have been criticized on a number of grounds. One view is that the research methodologies they employ are weak and invalid. Most research efforts use adjudicated or incarcerated offenders. It is often difficult to determine whether findings represent the delinquent population or merely those most likely to be arrested and adjudicated by officials of the justice system. For example, some critics have described the methods used in heredity studies as "poorly designed, ambiguously reported and exceedingly inadequate in addressing the relevant issues."[237]

Some critics also fear that individual-level research can be socially and politically damaging. If an above-average number of indigent youth become delinquent offenders, can it be assumed that the less affluent are impulsive, greedy, have low IQs, or are genetically inferior? To many social scientists, the implications of this conclusion are unacceptable in light of what is known about race, gender, and class bias.

Critics also suggest that individual-level theory is limited as a generalized explanation of delinquent behavior because it fails to account for the known patterns of criminal behavior. Delinquent behavior trends seem to conform to certain patterns linked to social-ecological rather than individual factors—social class, seasonality, population density, and gender roles. Social forces that appear to be influencing the onset and maintenance of delinquent behavior are not accounted for by explanations of delinquency that focus on the individual. If, as is often the case, the delinquent rate is higher in one neighborhood than another, are we to conclude that youths in the high-crime area are more likely to be watching violent TV shows or eating more sugar-coated cereals than those in low-crime neighborhoods? How can individual traits explain the fact that crime rates vary between cities and between regions?

Defending Individual-Level Theory The legitimization of social-psychological, psychiatric, and biosocial approaches to explaining deviant behavior may prove to be an important and productive paradigm shift in the decades ahead.[238]

Theorists who focus on individual behavior contend that critics overlook the fact that their research often gives equal weight to environmental and social as well as mental and physical factors.[239] For example, some people may have particular developmental problems that place them at a disadvantage in society, limit their chances of conventional success, and heighten their feelings of anger, frustration, and rage. Though the incidence of these personal traits may be spread evenly across the social structure, families in one segment of the population have the financial wherewithal to help treat the problem, whereas families in another segment may lack the economic means and the institutional support needed to help their children. Delinquency rate differences may be a result of differential access to opportunities either to commit crime or receive the care and treatment needed to correct and compensate for developmental problems.

In addition, individual-level theorists believe that, like it or not, youths are in fact different and may have differing potentials for antisocial acts. For example, gender differences in the violence rate may be explained by the fact that after centuries of aggressive mating behavior, males have become naturally more violent than females.[240] Male aggression may be more a matter of genetic transfer than socialization or cultural patterns.

Trait Theory and Delinquency Prevention

Because many individual-oriented theorists are also practitioners and clinicians, it is not surprising that a great deal of delinquency prevention efforts are based in psychological and biosocial theory.

As a group, individual perspectives on delinquency suggest that prevention efforts should be directed at strengthening a youth's home life and personal relationships. Almost all of these theoretical efforts point to the child's home life as a key factor in delinquent behavior. If parents cannot supply proper nurturing, love, care, discipline, nutrition, and so on, the child cannot develop properly. Whether one believes that delinquency has a biosocial basis, a psychological basis, or a combination of both, it is evident that delinquency prevention efforts should be oriented to reach children early in their development.

It is, therefore, not surprising that county welfare agencies and privately funded treatment centers have offered counseling and other mental health services to families referred by schools, welfare agents, and juvenile court authorities. In some instances, intervention is focused on a particular family problem that has the potential for producing delinquent behavior, such as alcohol and drug problems, child abuse, and sexual abuse. In other situations, intervention is more generalized and oriented toward developing the self-image of parents and children or improving discipline in the family. These programs are covered in Chapter 11.

In addition, individual approaches have been used to prevent court-adjudicated youths from engaging in further criminal activities. It has become almost universal practice for incarcerated and court-adjudicated youths to be given some form of mental and physical evaluation before they begin their term of correctional treatment. Such rehabilitation methods as psychological counseling and psychotropic medication (involving such drugs as Valium or Ritalin) are often prescribed. In some instances, rehabilitation programs are provided through drop-in centers that service youths who are able to remain in their homes, while more intensive programs require residential care and treatment. The creation of such programs illustrates how agents of the juvenile justice system believe that many delinquent youths and status offenders have psychological or physical problems and that their successful treatment can help reduce repeat criminal behavior. Faith in this treatment approach suggests widespread agreement among juvenile justice system professionals that the cause of delinquency can be traced to individual pathology; if not, why bother treating them?

Some questions remain about the effectiveness of individual treatment as a delinquency prevention technique. Little hard evidence exists that clinical treatment alone can prevent delinquency or rehabilitate known delinquents. It is possible that programs designed to help youths may actually stigmatize and label them, hindering their efforts to live conventional lives.[241] Because this issue is so critical, it will be discussed further in Chapter 4.

Summary

1. Be familiar with and distinguish between the two branches of individual-level theories of delinquency

▌ Some delinquency experts, referred to as choice theorists, believe that delinquency is a product of an individual decision-making process.

▌ Other experts believe that delinquency is the product of some individual trait such as temperament, personality, or hormones.

▌ Choice theory suggests that young offenders choose to engage in antisocial activity because they believe their actions will be beneficial and profitable.

▌ Delinquents have little fear of getting caught and, if they are apprehended, discount the legal consequences.

▌ All youthful misbehavior, however, cannot be traced to rational choice, profit motive, or criminal entrepreneurship.

▌ Some delinquent acts, especially violent ones, seem irrational, selfish, and/or hedonistic.

▌ Trait theory suggests that youthful misbehavior is driven by biological or psychological abnormalities, such as hyperactivity, low intelligence, biochemical imbalance, or genetic defects.

▌ Both views share some common ground:

— Both focus on mental and behavioral processes at the individual level.

— Delinquency is an individual problem, not a social problem.

— Both recognize that people react to the same set of environmental and social conditions in a unique way.

— Both suggest that delinquency prevention and control efforts must be directed at the individual offender.

2. Know the principles of choice theory

▌ Choice theory assumes that people have free will to choose their behavior.

▌ Those who violate the law are motivated by personal needs such as greed, revenge, survival, and hedonism.

▌ The classical view of crime and delinquency holds that the decision to violate the law is based on a careful weighing of the benefits and costs of criminal behaviors.

▌ Punishment should be only severe enough to deter a particular offense

▌ According to this view, delinquents are rational decision makers who choose to violate the law.

▌ Choice theorists believe that law-violating behavior occurs when a reasoning offender decides to take the chance of violating the law after considering his or her personal situation, values, and situation.

▌ Kids may be forced to choose delinquent behavior to help them solve problems that defy conventional solutions.

▌ The choice of delinquency may be shaped by economic needs.

3. Discuss the routine activities theory of delinquency

▌ Routine activities theory holds that delinquency is caused by the lack of capable guardians, the availability of suitable targets, and the presence of motivated offenders (such as unemployed teenagers).

▌ The presence of capable guardians who can protect homes and possessions can reduce the motivation to commit delinquent acts.

▌ Delinquent youth are also wary of police guardianship.

▌ Routine activities theory suggests that the availability of suitable targets such as easily transportable commodities will increase delinquency rates.

▌ As the number and motivation of offenders increase, so too do delinquency rates.

▌ Motivated offenders, suitable targets, and the lack of guardianship have an interactive effect.

4. Know the principles of general deterrence theory

▌ The general deterrence concept holds that the choice to commit delinquent acts is structured by the threat of punishment.

▌ One of the guiding principles of deterrence theory is that the more severe, certain, and swift the punishment, the greater its deterrent effect will be.

▌ One approach has been to put more cops on the street and have them aggressively enforce the law.

Proactive, aggressive law enforcement officers who quickly get to the scene of the crime may help deter delinquent activities.

I Juvenile courts have also attempted to initiate a deterrence strategy by waiving youths to adult courts.

I Deterrence strategies are based on the idea of a rational, calculating offender; they may not be effective when applied to immature young people.

I The deterrent threat of punishment may have little influence on the highest-risk group of young offenders—teens living in economically depressed neighborhoods.

I It is also possible that experience with the law and punishment actually defuses fear of punishment, thus neutralizing its deterrent effect.

5. Distinguish between the effects of punishment and incarceration

I The theory of specific deterrence holds that if offenders are punished severely, the experience will convince them not to repeat their illegal acts.

I Some research studies show that arrest and conviction may under some circumstances lower the frequency of reoffending.

I Rather than deterring future offending, punishment may in fact encourage reoffending.

I It stands to reason that that ability of delinquents to commit illegal acts will be eliminated or at least curtailed by putting them behind bars.

I Incarceration, especially in an adult prison, exposes younger offenders to higher-risk, more experienced inmates who can influence their lifestyle and help shape their attitudes.

I If crime and delinquency are functions of rational choice, then the profits of illegal activity are sure to convince kids that "crime pays," offsetting any benefit accrued by incarceration.

I Imprisoning established offenders may open new opportunities for competitors who were suppressed by more experienced delinquents or controlled by their tougher rivals.

I By the time they are arrested, waived, and sent to an adult prison some offenders are already past the age when they are likely to commit crime.

I An incapacitation strategy is also terribly expensive.

I Even if incarceration can have a short-term effect, almost all delinquents eventually return to society.

6. Discuss the concept of situational crime prevention

I According to the concept of situational crime prevention, in order to reduce delinquent activity, planners must be aware of the characteristics of sites and situations that are at risk to crime.

I Delinquency can be neutralized if (a) potential targets are carefully guarded, (b) the means to commit crime are controlled, and (c) potential offenders are carefully monitored.

I Situational crime prevention strategies aim to reduce the opportunities people have to commit particular crimes.

I Increasing the effort required to commit delinquency can involve target-hardening techniques.

I Increasing the risks of delinquency might involve such measures as improving surveillance lighting, utilizing closed-circuit TV monitoring, and creating neighborhood watch programs.

I Reducing the rewards of delinquency include strategies such as making car radios removable so they can be kept at home at night.

7. Trace the history and development of trait theory

I A number of delinquency experts argue that human behavioral choices are a function of an individual's mental and/or physical makeup.

I The first attempts to discover why criminal tendencies develop focused on the physical makeup of offenders.

I Biological traits present at birth were thought to predetermine whether people would live a life of crime.

I The origin of this school of thought is generally credited to the Italian physician Cesare Lombroso.

I These early views portrayed delinquent behavior as a function of a single factor or trait, such as body build or defective intelligence.

I Trait theorists argue that no two people (with rare exceptions, such as identical twins) are alike, and therefore each will react to environmental stimuli in a distinct way.

8. Be familiar with the branches and substance of biological trait theory

I There is a suspected relationship between antisocial behavior and biochemical makeup.

I One view is that body chemistry can govern behavior and personality, including levels of aggression and depression.

I One area of concern is that overexposure to particular environmental contaminants, including metals and minerals such as iron and manganese, may produce effects that put kids at risk for antisocial behavior.

I Of all these contaminants, exposure to lead is the one that has been linked most often to antisocial behaviors on both the individual and group levels.

I There is also evidence that diet may influence behavior through its impact on body chemistry.

I Hormonal levels are another area of biochemical research. Antisocial behavior allegedly peaks in the teenage years because hormonal activity is at its highest level during this period.

- Another focus of biosocial theory is the neurological—or brain and nervous system—structure of offenders.
- It has been suggested that children who manifest behavioral disturbances may have neurological deficits, such as damage to the hemispheres of the brain; this is sometimes referred to as minimal brain dysfunction (MBD).
- The relationship between learning disabilities and delinquency has been highlighted by studies showing that arrested and incarcerated children have a far higher LD rate than do children in the general population.
- Arousal theorists believe that aggression is related to an individual's need for stimulation from the environment.
- Due to genetic and environmental reasons, some people's brains function differently in response to environmental stimuli.
- The factors that determine a person's level of arousal have not been fully determined. Suspected sources include brain chemistry and brain structure.
- Biosocial theorists also study the genetic makeup of delinquents. Studies of this kind have generally supported the hypothesis that there is a link between genetics and behavior.
- In addition to a direct link between heredity and delinquency, the literature also shows that behavior traits indirectly linked to delinquency may be at least in part inherited.
- Connecting delinquent behavior to heredity is quite controversial because it implies that the cause of delinquency is (a) present at birth, and (b) "transmitted" from one generation to the next and immune to treatment efforts.

9. **Know the various psychological theories of delinquency**

- Some experts view the cause of delinquency as essentially psychological.
- According to psychodynamic theory, law violations are a product of an abnormal personality structure formed early in life and which thereafter controls human behavior choices.
- In extreme cases, mental torment drives people into violence and aggression.
- The basis of psychodynamic theory is the assumption that human behavior is controlled by unconscious mental processes developed early in childhood.
- Applying these concepts, psychodynamic theory holds that youth crime is a result of unresolved mental anguish and internal conflict.
- Some children, especially those who have been abused or mistreated, may experience unconscious feelings associated with resentment, fear, and hatred.

- Delinquents are id-dominated people who suffer from the inability to control impulsive drives.
- People who have lost control and are dominated by their id are known as psychotics; their behavior may be marked by hallucinations and inappropriate responses.
- Behavioral psychologists argue that a person's personality is learned throughout life during interaction with others.
- Behaviorists suggest that individuals learn by observing how people react to their behavior.
- Behavior is triggered initially by a stimulus or change in the environment.
- Children will model their behavior after characters they observe on TV or see in movies.
- The weight of the evidence shows that watching violence on TV is correlated to aggressive behaviors and that the newest, most methodologically sophisticated work shows the greatest amount of association.
- Cognitive theorists who study information processing try to explain antisocial behavior in terms of perception and analysis of data.
- When people make decisions, they engage in a sequence of cognitive thought processes.
- Delinquency-prone adolescents may have cognitive deficits and use information incorrectly when they make decisions.

10. **Be familiar with the psychological traits that have been linked to delinquency**

- Personality can be defined as the reasonably stable patterns of behavior, including thoughts and emotions, that distinguish one person from another.
- Delinquents are hyperactive, impulsive individuals with short attention spans (attention deficit disorder), who frequently manifest conduct disorders, anxiety disorders, and depression.
- Psychopathic (sociopathic) youths exhibit a low level of guilt and anxiety and persistently violate the rights of others.
- Psychologists have long been concerned with the development of intelligence and its subsequent relationship to behavior.
- It has been charged that children with low IQs are responsible for a disproportionate share of delinquency.
- Scores on intelligence tests have been used to predict violent behavior and to distinguish between groups of violent and nonviolent offenders
- The relationship between IQ and delinquency is extremely controversial.

Key Terms

Viewpoint

You are a state legislator who is a member of the subcommittee on juvenile justice. Your committee has been asked to redesign the state's juvenile code because of public outrage over serious juvenile crime. At an open hearing, a professor from the local university testifies that she has devised a surefire test to predict violence-prone delinquents. The procedure involves brain scans, DNA testing, and blood analysis. Used with samples of incarcerated adolescents, her procedure has been able to distinguish with 90 percent accuracy between youths with a history of violence and those who are exclusively property offenders. The professor testifies that if each juvenile offender was tested with her techniques, the violence-prone career offender could easily be identified and given special treatment.

Opponents argue that this type of testing is unconstitutional because it violates the Fifth Amendment protection against self-incrimination and can unjustly label nonviolent offenders. Any attempt to base policy on biosocial makeup seems inherently wrong and unfair.

Those who favor the professor's approach maintain that it is not uncommon to single out the insane or mentally incompetent for special treatment and that these conditions often have a biological basis. It is better that a few delinquents be unfairly labeled than seriously violent offenders be ignored until it is too late.

- Is it possible that some kids are born to be delinquents? Or do kids "choose" crime?

- Is it fair to test kids to see if they have biological traits related to crime, even if they have never committed a single offense?

- Should special laws be created to deal with the potentially dangerous offender?

- Should offenders be typed on the basis of their biological characteristics?

Doing Research on the Web

Before you address this issue, you may want to research the law by using the keyword *self-incrimination*. You can also search the web for information on *criminal profiling*.

Read relevant articles via
academic.cengage.com/criminaljustice/siegel

Questions for Discussion

1. Is there such a thing as the "born criminal"? Are some people programmed at birth to commit crimes?

2. Is crime psychologically abnormal? Can there be "normal" crimes?

3. Apply psychodynamic theory to such delinquent acts as shoplifting and breaking and entering a house.

4. Can delinquent behavior be deterred by the threat of punishment? If not, how can it be controlled?

5. Should we incarcerate violent juvenile offenders for long periods of time—10 years or more?

6. Does watching violent TV and films encourage youth to be aggressive and antisocial? Do advertisements for beer featuring attractive, provocatively dressed young men and women encourage drinking and precocious sex? If not, why bother advertising?

7. Discuss the characteristics of psychopaths. Do you know anyone who fits the description?

Notes

1. CourtTV news, *New Mexico vs. Cody Posey*, www.courttv.com/trials/posey/ (accessed September 17, 2007).

2. U.S. Census Bureau, *Poverty Data, 2005*, www.census.gov/hhes/www/poverty/poverty.html (accessed June 11, 2007).

3. Marvin Wolfgang, Robert Figlio, and Thorsten Sellin, *Delinquency in a Birth Cohort* (Chicago: University of Chicago Press, 1972).

4. Jeremy Bentham, *A Fragment on Government and an Introduction to the Principles of Morals and Legislation*, Wilfred Harrison, ed. (Oxford: Basic Blackwell, 1967).

5. See Ernest Van den Haag, *Punishing Criminals* (New York: Basic Books, 1975).

6. Cesare Beccaria, *On Crimes and Punishments*, 6th ed., Henry Paolucci, trans. (Indianapolis: Bobbs-Merrill, 1977), p. 43.

7. Pierre Tremblay and Carlo Morselli, "Patterns in Criminal Achievement: Wilson and Abrahamsen Revisited," *Criminology* 38:633–660 (2000).

8. James Q. Wilson and Richard Herrnstein, *Crime and Human Nature* (New York: Simon and Schuster, 1985), p. 396.

9. Timothy Brezina, "Delinquent Problem-Solving: An Interpretive Framework for Criminological Theory and Research," *Journal of Research in Crime and Delinquency* 37:3–30 (2000).

10. D. Wayne Osgood, Janet Wilson, Patrick O'Malley, Jerald Bachman, and Lloyd Johnston, "Routine Activities and Individual Deviant Behavior," *American Sociological Review* 61:635–655 (1996).

11. Brenda Sims Blackwell, "Perceived Sanction Threats, Gender, and Crime: A Test and Elaboration of Power-Control Theory," *Criminology* 38:439–488 (2000).

12. Dana Haynie, "Contexts of Risk: Explaining the Link between Girls' Pubertal Development and Their Delinquency Involvement," *Social Forces* 82:355–397 (2003).

13. Christopher Uggen and Melissa Thompson, "The Socioeconomic Determinants of Ill-Gotten Gains: Within-Person Changes in Drug Use and Illegal Earnings," *American Journal of Sociology* 109:146–185 (2003).

14. Steven Levitt and Sudhir Alladi Venkatesh, "An Economic Analysis of a Drug-Selling Gang's Finances," NBER Working Papers 6592 (Cambridge, MA: National Bureau of Economic Research, Inc., 1998).

15. Bill McCarthy, "New Economics of Sociological Criminology," *Annual Review of Sociology* 28:417–442 (2002).

16. Raymond Paternoster, Shawn Bushway, Robert Brame, and Robert Apel, "The Effect of Teenage Employment on Delinquency and Problem Behaviors," *Social Forces* 82:297–336 (2003).

17. Matthew Ploeger, "Youth Employment and Delinquency: Reconsidering a Problematic Relationship," *Criminology* 35:659–675 (1997).

18. Jeremy Staff and Christopher Uggen, "The Fruits of Good Work: Early Work Experiences and Adolescent Deviance," *Journal of Research in Crime and Delinquency* 40:263–290 (2003).

19. Robert Apel, Shawn Bushway, Robert Brame, Amelia Haviland, Daniel Nagin, and Ray Paternoster, "Unpacking the Relationship Between Adolescent Employment and Antisocial Behavior: A Matched Samples Comparison," *Criminology* 45:67–97 (2007).

20. Lawrence Cohen and Marcus Felson, "Social Change and Crime Rate Trends: A Routine Activities Approach," *American Sociological Review* 44:588–608 (1979).

21. Brandon Welsh and David Farrington, "Surveillance for Crime Prevention in Public Space: Results and Policy Choices in Britain and America," *Criminology and Public Policy* 3:701–730 (2004).

22. Denise Osborn, Alan Trickett, and Rob Elder, "Area Characteristics and Regional Variates as Determinants of Area Property Crime Levels," *Journal of Quantitative Criminology* 8:265–282 (1992).

23. Paul Bellair, "Informal Surveillance and Street Crime: A Complex Relationship," *Criminology* 38:137–167 (2000).

24. Grace Barnes, Joseph Hoffman, John Welte, Michael Farrell, and Barbara Dintcheff, "Adolescents' Time Use: Effects on Substance Use, Delinquency and Sexual Activity," *Journal of Youth and Adolescence* 36 (2007): 697–710.

25. Richard Timothy Coupe and Laurence Blake, "The Effects of Patrol Workloads and Response Strength on Arrests at Burglary Emergencies," *Journal of Criminal Justice* 33:239–255 (2005).

26. William Smith, Sharon Glave Frazee, and Elizabeth Davison, "Furthering the Integration of Routine Activity and Social Disorganization Theories: Small Units of Analysis and the Study of Street Robbery as a Diffusion Process," *Criminology* 38:489–521 (2000).

27. James Massey, Marvin Krohn, and Lisa Bonati, "Property Crime and Routine Activities of Individuals," *Journal of Research in Crime and Delinquency* 26:397 (1989).

28. Lawrence Cohen, Marcus Felson, and Kenneth Land, "Property Crime Rates in the United States: A Macrodynamic Analysis, 1947–1977, with Ex-Ante Forecasts for the Mid-1980s," *American Journal of Sociology* 86:90–118 (1980).

29. Denise Gottfredson and David Soulé, "The Timing of Property Crime, Violent Crime, and Substance Use Among Juveniles," *Journal of Research in Crime and Delinquency* 42:110–120 (2005).

30. Rolf Becker and Guido Mehlkop, "Social Class and Delinquency: An Empirical Utilization of Rational Choice Theory with Cross-Sectional Data of the 1990 and 2000 German General Population Surveys (Allbus)," *Rationality and Society* 18:193–235 (2006); Daniel Nagin and Greg Pogarsky, "Integrating Celerity, Impulsivity, and Extralegal Sanction Threats into a Model of General Deterrence: Theory and Evidence," *Criminology* 39:865–892 (2001).

31. Nagin and Pogarsky, "Integrating Celerity, Impulsivity, and Extralegal Sanction Threats into a Model of General Deterrence: Theory and Evidence."

32. Beccaria, *On Crimes and Punishments*.

33. For the classic analysis on the subject, see Johannes Andenaes, *Punishment and Deterrence* (Ann Arbor: University of Michigan Press, 1974).

34. Daniel Nagin and Greg Pogarsky, "An Experimental Investigation of Deterrence: Cheating, Self-Serving Bias and Impulsivity," *Criminology* 41:167–195 (2003).

35. Tomislav V. Kovandzic and John J. Sloan, "Police Levels and Crime Rates Revisited: A County-Level Analysis from Florida (1980–1998)," *Journal of Criminal Justice* 30:65–76 (2002).

36. Richard Timothy Coupe and Laurence Blake, "The Effects of Patrol Workloads and Response Strength on Arrests at Burglary Emergencies," *Journal of Criminal Justice* 33:239–255 (2005).

37. Michael White, James Fyfe, Suzanne Campbell, and John Goldkamp, "The Police Role in Preventing Homicide: Considering the Impact of Problem-Oriented Policing on the Prevalence of Murder," *Journal of Research in Crime and Delinquency* 40:194–226 (2003).

38. Bruce Jacobs, "Anticipatory Undercover Targeting in High Schools," *Journal of Criminal Justice* 22:445–457 (1994).

39. Leona Lee, "Factors Determining Waiver in a Juvenile Court," *Journal of Criminal Justice* 22:329–339 (1994).

40. See Raymond Paternoster, "The Deterrent Effect of Perceived Certainty and Severity of Punishment: A Review of the Evidence and Issues," *Justice Quarterly* 42:173–217 (1987); Paternoster, "Absolute and Restrictive Deterrence in a Panel of Youth: Explaining the Onset, Persistence/Desistance, and Frequency of Delinquent Offending," *Social Problems* 36:289–307 (1989).

41. Eric Jensen and Linda Metsger, "A Test of the Deterrent Effect of Legislative Waiver on Violent Juvenile Crime," *Crime and Delinquency* 40:96–104 (1994).

42. Wanda D. Foglia, "Perceptual Deterrence and the Mediating Effect of Internalized Norms among Inner-City Teenagers," *Journal of Research in Crime and Delinquency* 34:414–442 (1997).

43. Ibid.

44. Greg Pogarsky, KiDeuk Kim, and Ray Paternoster, "Perceptual Change in the National Youth Survey: Lessons for Deterrence Theory and Offender Decision-Making," *Justice Quarterly* 22:1–29 (2005).

45. Maynard Erickson and Jack Gibbs, "Punishment, Deterrence, and Juvenile Justice," in D. Shichor and D. Kelly, eds., *Critical Issues in Juvenile Justice* (Lexington, MA: Lexington Books, 1980), pp. 183–202.

46. Doris Layton MacKenzie and Spencer De Li, "The Impact of Formal and Informal Social Controls on the Criminal Activities of Probationers," *Journal of Research in Crime and Delinquency* 39:243–276 (2002).

47. Christina DeJong, "Survival Analysis and Specific Deterrence: Integrating Theoretical and Empirical Models of Recidivism," *Criminology* 35:561–576 (1997).

48. Paul Tracy and Kimberly Kempf-Leonard, *Continuity and Discontinuity in Criminal Careers* (New York: Plenum, 1996).

49. Pamela Lattimore, Christy Visher, and Richard Linster, "Predicting Rearrest for Violence among Serious Youthful Offenders," *Journal of Research in Crime and Delinquency* 32:54–83 (1995).

50. Alicia Sitren and Brandon Applegate, "Testing the Deterrent Effects of Personal and Vicarious Experience with Punishment and Punishment Avoidance," *Deviant Behavior* 28:29–55 (2007).

51. Greg Pogarsky and Alex R. Piquero, "Can Punishment Encourage Offending? Investigating the 'Resetting' Effect," *Journal of Research in Crime and Delinquency* 40:92–117 (2003).

52. Paige Harrison and Allen Beck, *Prisoners in 2005* (Washington, DC: Bureau of Justice Statistics, 2006).

53. Jose Canela-Cacho, Alfred Blumstein, and Jacqueline Cohen, "Relationship between the Offending Frequency of Imprisoned and Free Offenders," *Criminology* 35:133–171 (1997).

54. James Lynch and William Sabol, "Prisoner Reentry in Perspective," Urban Institute: www.urban.org/UploadedPDF/410213_reentry.PDF (accessed August 27, 2007).

55. Rudy Haapanen, Lee Britton, and Tim Croisdale, "Persistent Criminality and Career Length," *Crime and Delinquency* 53:133–155 (2007).

56. Patricia Brantingham, Paul Brantingham, and Wendy Taylor, "Situational Crime Prevention as a Key Component in Embedded Crime Prevention," *Canadian Journal of Criminology and Criminal Justice* 47:271–292 (2005).

57. Marcus Felson, "Routine Activities and Crime Prevention," in National Council for Crime Prevention, *Studies on Crime and Crime Prevention, Annual Review*, vol. 1 (Stockholm: Scandinavian University Press, 1992), pp. 30–34.

58. Andrew Fulkerson, "Blow and Go: The Breath-Analyzed Ignition Interlock Device as a Technological Response to DWI," *American Journal of Drug and Alcohol Abuse* 29:219–235 (2003).

59. Barry Webb, "Steering Column Locks and Motor Vehicle Theft: Evaluations for Three Countries," in Ronald Clarke, ed., *Crime Prevention Studies* (Monsey, NY: Criminal Justice Press, 1994), pp. 71–89.

60. David Farrington and Brandon Welsh, "Improved Street Lighting and Crime Prevention," *Justice Quarterly* 19:313–343 (2002).

61. Brandon Welsh and David Farrington, "Effects of Closed-Circuit Television on Crime," *Annals of the American Academy of Political and Social Science* 587:110–136 (2003).

62. Brandon Welsh and David Farrington, "Crime Prevention and Hard Technology: The Case of CCTV and Improved Street Lighting," in James Byrne and Donald Rebovich, eds., *The New Technology of Crime, Law, and Social Control* (Monsey, NY: Criminal Justice Press, 2007).

63. Massey, Krohn, and Bonati, "Property Crime and the Routine Activities of Individuals."

64. David Shantz, "Conflict, Aggression, and Peer Status: An Observational Study," *Child Development* 57:1322–1332 (1986).

65. For an excellent review of Lombroso's work, as well as that of other well-known theorists, see Randy Martin, Robert Mutchnick, and W. Timothy Austin, *Criminological Thought, Pioneers Past and Present* (New York: Macmillan, 1990).

66. Marvin Wolfgang, "Cesare Lombroso," in Herman Mannheim, ed., *Pioneers in Criminology* (Montclair, NJ: Patterson Smith, 1970), pp. 232–271.

67. Gina Lombroso-Ferrero, *Criminal Man According to the Classification of Cesare Lombroso* (1911), reprint edition (Montclair, NJ: Patterson Smith, 1972), p. 7.

68. Rafaele Garofalo, *Criminology* (1914), reprint edition (Glen Ridge, NJ: Patterson Smith, 1968).

69. See Thorsten Sellin, "Enrico Ferri," in Mannheim, ed., *Pioneers in Criminology*, pp. 361–384.

70. Nicole Hahn Rafter, "Criminal Anthropology in the United States," *Criminology* 30:525–547 (1992).

71. Dalton Conley and Neil Bennett, "Is Biology Destiny? Birth Weight and Life Chances," *American Sociological Review* 65:458–467 (2000).

72. Ingrid Helland, Lars Smith, Kristin Saarem, Ola Saugstad, and Christian Drevon, "Maternal Supplementation with Very-Long-Chain n-3 Fatty Acids During Pregnancy and Lactation Augments Children's IQ at 4 Years of Age," *Pediatrics* 111:39–44 (2003).

73. For a thorough review of the biosocial perspective, see Diana Fishbein, "Biological Perspectives in Criminology," *Criminology* 28:27–72 (1990); Fishbein, "Selected Studies on the Biology of Antisocial Behavior," in Conklin, ed., *New Perspectives in Criminology*, pp. 26–38.

74. See Adrian Raine, *The Psychopathology of Crime* (San Diego: Academic Press, 1993).

75. Paul Marshall, "Allergy and Depression: A Neurochemical Threshold Model of the Relation between the Illnesses," *Psychological Bulletin* 113:23–43 (1993).

76. "Diet and the Unborn Child: The Omega Point," *The Economist*, January 19, 2006.

77. Amy Schonfeld, Sarah Mattson, and Edward Riley, "Moral Maturity and Delinquency After Prenatal Alcohol Exposure," *Journal of Studies on Alcohol* 66:545–554 (2005).

78. K. Murata, P. Weihe, E. Budtz-Jorgensen, P. J. Jorgensen, and P. Grandjean, "Delayed Brainstem Auditory Evoked Potential Latencies in 14-Year-Old Children Exposed to Methylmercury," *Journal of Pediatrics* 144:177–183 (2004); Eric Konofal, Samuele Cortese, Michel Lecendreux, Isabelle Arnulf, and Marie Christine Mouren, "Effectiveness of Iron Supplementation in a Young Child with Attention-Deficit/Hyperactivity Disorder," *Pediatrics* 116:732–734 (2005).

79. Eric Konofal, Michel Lecendreux, Isabelle Arnulf, and Marie-Christine Mouren, "Iron Deficiency in Children with Attention-Deficit/Hyperactivity Disorder," *Archives of Pediatric and Adolescent Medicine* 158:1113–1115 (2004).

80. Gail Wasserman, Xinhua Liu, Faruque Parvez, Habibul Ahsan, Diane Levy, Pam Factor-Litvak, Jennie Kline, Alexander van Geen, Vesna Slavkovich, Nancy J. Lolacono, Zhongqi Cheng, Yan Zheng, and Joseph Graziano, "Water Manganese Exposure and Children's Intellectual Function in Araihazar, Bangladesh," *Environmental Health Perspectives* 114(1):124–129 (2006).

81. Jens Walkowiak, Jörg-A. Wiener, Annemarie Fastabend, Birger Heinzow, Ursula Krämer, Eberhard Schmidt, Hans-J. Steingürber, Sabine Wundram, and Gerhard Winneke, "Environmental Exposure to Polychlorinated Biphenyls and Quality of the Home Environment: Effects on Psychodevelopment in Early Childhood," *The Lancet* 358:92–93 (2001).

82. Virginia Rauh, Robin Garfinkel, Frederica Perera, Howard Andrews, Lori Hoepner, Dana B. Barr, Ralph Whitehead, Deliang Tang, and Robin W. Whyatt, "Impact of Prenatal Chlorpyrifos Exposure on Neurodevelopment in the First 3 Years of Life Among Inner-City Children," *Pediatrics* 118:1845–1859 (2006).

83. David Bellinger, "Lead," *Pediatrics* 113:1016–1022 (2004); Jeff Evans, "Asymptomatic, High Lead Levels Tied to Delinquency," *Pediatric News* 37:13 (2003); Herbert Needleman, Christine McFarland, Roberta Ness, Stephen Fienberg, and Michael Tobin, "Bone Lead Levels in Adjudicated Delinquents: A Case Control Study," *Neurotoxicology and Teratology* 24:711–717 (2002).

84. Paul Stretesky and Michael Lynch, "The Relationship between Lead Exposure and Homicide," *Archives of Pediatric Adolescent Medicine* 155:579–582 (2001).

85. Bruce P. Lanphear, Richard Hornung, Jane Khoury, Kimberly Yolton, Peter Baghurst, David C. Bellinger, Richard L. Canfield, Kim N. Dietrich, Robert Bornschein, Tom Greene, Stephen J. Rothenberg, Herbert L. Needleman, Lourdes Schnaas, Gail Wasserman, Joseph Graziano, and Russell Roberts, "Low-Level Environmental Lead Exposure and Children's Intellectual Function: An International Pooled Analysis," *Environmental Health Perspectives* 113 (2005), www.ehponline.org/docs/2005/7688/abstract.html (accessed June 11, 2007).

86. Aimin Chen, Bo Cai, Kim Dietrich, Jerilynn Radcliffe, and Walter Rogan, "Lead Exposure, IQ, and Behavior in Urban 5- to 7-Year-Olds: Does Lead Affect Behavior Only by Lowering IQ?" *Pediatrics* 119: 650–658 (2007).

87. Marshall, "Allergy and Depression: A Neurochemical Threshold Model of the Relation between the Illnesses," pp. 23–29.

88. A. Maras, M. Laucht, D. Gerdes, C. Wilhelm, S. Lewicka, D. Haack, L. Malisova, and M. H. Schmidt, "Association of Testosterone and Dihydrotestosterone with Externalizing Behavior in Adolescent Boys and Girls," *Psychoneuroendocrinology* 28:932–940 (2003).

89. Christy Miller Buchanan, Jacquelynne Eccles, and Jill Becker, "Are Adolescents the Victims of Raging Hormones? Evidence for Activational Effects of Hormones on Moods and Behavior at Adolescence," *Psychological Bulletin* 111:62–107 (1992).

90. Alex Piquero and Timothy Brezina, "Testing Moffitt's Account of Adolescent-Limited Delinquency," *Criminology* 39:353–370 (2001).

91. Laurence Tancredi, *Hardwired Behavior: What Neuroscience Reveals about Morality* (London: Cambridge University Press, 2005).

92. "McLean Researchers Document Brain Damage Linked to Child Abuse and Neglect." Information provided by newsletter of McLean's Hospital, Belmont, MA, December 14, 2000.

93. Yaling Yang, Adrian Raine, Todd Lencz, Susan Bihrle, Lori Lacasse, and Patrick Colletti, "Prefrontal White Matter in Pathological Liars," *British Journal of Psychiatry* 187:320–325 (2005).

94. Peer Briken, Niels Habermann, Wolfgang Berner, and Andreas Hill, "The Influence of Brain Abnormalities on Psychosocial Development, Criminal History and Paraphilias in Sexual Murderers," *Journal of Forensic Sciences* 50:1–5 (2005).

95. Adrian Raine, P. Brennan, and S. Mednick, "Interaction Between Birth Complications and Early Maternal Rejection in Predisposing to Adult Violence: Specificity to Serious, Early Onset Violence," *American Journal of Psychiatry* 154:1265–1271 (1997).

96. Raine et al., "High Rates of Violence, Crime, Academic Problems, and Behavioral Problems in Males with Both Early Neuromotor Deficits and Unstable Family Environments."

97. Stephen Tibbetts, "Low Birth Weight, Disadvantaged Environment and Early Onset: A Test of Moffitt's Interactional Hypothesis," paper presented at the annual meeting of the American Society of Criminology, Boston, November 1995.

98. Dorothy Otnow Lewis, Jonathan Pincus, Marilyn Feldman, Lori Jackson, and Barbara Bard, "Psychiatric, Neurological, and Psychoeducational Characteristics of 15 Death Row Inmates in the United States," *American Journal of Psychiatry* 143:838–845 (1986).

99. Adrian Raine et al., "Interhemispheric Transfer in Schizophrenics, Depressives and Normals with Schizoid Tendencies," *Journal of Abnormal Psychology* 98:35–41 (1989).

100. Jean Seguin, Robert Pihl, Philip Harden, Richard Tremblay, and Bernard Boulerice, "Cognitive and Neuropsychological Characteristics of Physically Aggressive Boys," *Journal of Abnormal Psychology* 104:614–624 (1995).

101. Charlotte Johnson and William Pelham, "Teacher Ratings Predict Peer Ratings of Aggression at 3-Year Follow-Up in Boys with Attention Deficit Disorder with Hyperactivity," *Journal of Consulting and Clinical Psychology* 54:571–572 (1987).

102. Cited in Charles Post, "The Link between Learning Disabilities and Juvenile Delinquency: Cause, Effect, and 'Present Solutions,'" *Juvenile and Family Court Journal* 31:59 (1981).

103. For a general review, see Concetta Culliver, "Juvenile Delinquency and Learning Disability: Any Link?" Paper presented at the Academy of Criminal Justice Sciences, San Francisco, April 1988.

104. Joel Zimmerman, William Rich, Ingo Keilitz, and Paul Broder, "Some Observations on the Link between Learning Disabilities and Juvenile Delinquency," *Journal of Criminal Justice* 9:9–17 (1981); J. W. Podboy and W. A. Mallory, "The Diagnosis of Specific Learning Disabilities in a Juvenile Delinquent Population," *Juvenile and Family Court Journal* 30:11–13 (1978).

105. Charles Murray, *The Link between Learning Disabilities and Juvenile Delinquency: A Current Theory and Knowledge* (Washington, DC: Government Printing Office, 1976).

106. Robert Pasternak and Reid Lyon, "Clinical and Empirical Identification of Learning Disabled Juvenile Delinquents," *Journal of Correctional Education* 33:7–13 (1982).

107. Zimmerman et al., "Some Observations on the Link between Learning Disabilities and Juvenile Delinquency."

108. Katz, *Seductions of Crime*, pp. 12–15.

109. Lee Ellis, "Arousal Theory and the Religiosity-Criminality Relationship," in Peter Cordella and Larry Siegel, eds., *Contemporary Criminological Theory* (Boston: Northeastern University, 1996), pp. 65–84.

110. Adrian Raine, Peter Venables, and Sarnoff Mednick, "Low Resting Heart Rate at Age 3 Years Predisposes to Aggression at Age 11 Years: Evidence from the Mauritius Child Health Project," *Journal of the American Academy of Adolescent Psychiatry* 36:1457–1464 (1997).

111. David Rowe, *The Limits of Family Influence: Genes, Experiences and Behavior* (New York: Guilford Press, 1995), p. 64.

112. For a review, see Lisabeth Fisher DiLalla and Irving Gottesman, "Biological and Genetic Contributors to Violence—Widom's Untold Tale," *Psychological Bulletin* 109:125–129 (1991).

113. Anita Thapar, Kate Langley, Tom Fowler, Frances Rice, Darko Turic, Naureen Whittinger, John Aggleton, Marianne Van den Bree, Michael Owen, and Michael O'Donovan, "Catechol O-methyltransferase Gene Variant and Birth Weight Predict Early-Onset Antisocial Behavior in Children with Attention-Deficit/Hyperactivity Disorder," *Archives of General Psychiatry* 62:1275–1278 (2005).

114. Carol Van Hulle, Brian D'Onfrio, Joseph Rodgers, Irwin Waldman, and Benjamin Lahey, "Sex Differences in the Causes of Self-Reported Adolescent Delinquency," *Journal of Abnormal Psychology* 116:236–248 (2007).

115. For an early review, see Barbara Wooton, *Social Science and Social Pathology* (London: Allen and Unwin, 1959); John Laub and Robert Sampson, "Unraveling Families and Delinquency: A Reanalysis of the Gluecks' Data," *Criminology* 26:355–380 (1988).

116. Ping Qin, "The Relationship of Suicide Risk to Family History of Suicide and Psychiatric Disorders," *Psychiatric Times* 20 (2003), www.psychiatrictimes.com/p031262.html (accessed August 27, 2007).

117. D. J. West and D. P. Farrington, "Who Becomes Delinquent?" in D. J. West and D. P. Farrington, eds., *The Delinquent Way of Life* (London: Heinemann, 1977) pp. 1–28; D. J. West, *Delinquency: Its Roots, Careers, and Prospects* (Cambridge, MA: Harvard University Press, 1982).

118. West, *Delinquency*, p. 114.

119. David Farrington, "Understanding and Preventing Bullying," in Michael Tonry, ed., *Crime and Justice*, vol. 17 (Chicago: University of Chicago Press, 1993), pp. 381–457.

120. Terence Thornberry, Adrienne Freeman-Gallant, Alan Lizotte, Marvin Krohn, and Carolyn Smith, "Linked Lives: The Intergenerational Transmission of Antisocial Behavior," *Journal of Abnormal Child Psychology* 31:171–185 (2003).

121. David Rowe and David Farrington, "The Familial Transmission of Criminal Convictions," *Criminology* 35:177–201 (1997).

122. Abigail Fagan and Jake Najman, "Sibling Influences on Adolescent Delinquent Behaviour: An Australian Longitudinal Study," *Journal of Adolescence* 26:547–559 (2003).

123. Louise Arseneault, Terrie Moffitt, Avshalom Caspi, Alan Taylor, Fruhling Rijsdijk, Sara Jaffee, Jennifer Ablow, and Jeffrey Measelle, "Strong Genetic Effects on Cross-situational Antisocial Behaviour among 5-year-old Children According to Mothers, Teachers, Examiner-Observers, and Twins' Self-Reports," *Journal of Child Psychology and Psychiatry* 44:832–848 (2003).

124. Laura Baker, Kristen Jacobson, Adrian Raine, Dora Isabel Lozano, and Serena Bezdjian, "Genetic and Environmental Bases of Childhood Antisocial Behavior: A Multi-Informant Twin Study," *Journal of Abnormal Psychology* 116:219–235 (2007).

125. For a general review, see Nancy Segal, *Entwined Lives: Twins and What They Tell Us about Human Behavior* (New York: Dutton, 2000); David Rowe, "Sibling Interaction and Self-Reported Delinquent Behavior: A Study of 265 Twin Pairs," *Criminology* 23:223–240 (1985); Nancy Segal, "Monozygotic and Dizygotic Twins: A Comparative Analysis of Mental Ability Profiles," *Child Development* 56:1051–1058 (1985).

126. Qin, "The Relationship of Suicide Risk to Family History of Suicide and Psychiatric Disorders."

127. Jane Scourfield, Marianne Van den Bree, Neilson Martin, and Peter McGuffin, "Conduct Problems in Children and Adolescents: A Twin Study," *Archives of General Psychiatry* 61:489–496 (2004); Jeanette Taylor, Bryan Loney, Leonardo Bobadilla, William Iacono, and Matt McGue, "Genetic and Environmental Influences on Psychopathy Trait Dimensions in a Community Sample of Male Twins," *Journal of Abnormal Child Psychology* 31:633–645 (2003).

128. Ginette Dionne, Richard Tremblay, Michel Boivin, David Laplante, and Daniel Perusse, "Physical Aggression and Expressive Vocabulary in 19-Month-Old Twins," *Developmental Psychology* 39:261–273 (2003).

129. Sara R. Jaffee, Avshalom Caspi, Terrie Moffitt, Kenneth Dodge, Michael Rutter, Alan Taylor, and Lucy Tully, "Nature ? Nurture: Genetic Vulnerabilities Interact with Physical Maltreatment to Promote Conduct Problems," *Development and Psychopathology* 17:67–84 (2005).

130. Essi Viding, James Blair, Terrie Moffitt, and Robert Plomin, "Evidence for Substantial Genetic Risk for Psychopathy in 7-Year-Olds," *Journal of Child Psychology and Psychiatry* 46:592–597 (2005).

131. Thomas Bouchard, "Genetic and Environmental Influences on Intelligence and Special Mental Abilities," *American Journal of Human Biology* 70:253–275 (1998); some findings from the Minnesota study can be viewed at www.psych.umn.edu/psylabs/mtfs/ (accessed August 27, 2007).

132. Remi Cadoret, Colleen Cain, and Raymond Crowe, "Evidence for a Gene-Environment Interaction in the Development of Adolescent Antisocial Behavior," *Behavior Genetics* 13:301–310 (1983).

133. Rowe, *The Limits of Family Influence*, p. 110.

134. Bernard Hutchings and Sarnoff Mednick, "Criminality in Adoptees and Their Adoptive and Biological Parents: A Pilot Study," in S. A. Mednick and Karl O. Christiansen, eds., *The Biosocial Bases of Criminal Behavior* (New York: Gardner Press, 1977).

135. For similar findings, see William Gabrielli and Sarnoff Mednick, "Urban Environment, Genetics, and Crime," *Criminology* 22:645–653 (1984).

136. Jody Alberts-Corush, Philip Firestone, and John Goodman, "Attention and Impulsivity Characteristics of the Biological and Adoptive Parents of Hyperactive and Normal Control Children," *American Journal of Orthopsychiatry* 56:413–423 (1986).

137. Wilson and Herrnstein, *Crime and Human Nature*, p. 131.

138. Glenn D. Walters, "A Meta-Analysis of the Gene-Crime Relationship," *Criminology* 30:595–614 (1992).

139. Wilson and Herrnstein, *Crime and Human Nature*, p. 108.

140. Lawrence Cohen and Richard Machalek, "A General Theory of Expropriative Crime: An Evolutionary Ecological Approach," *American Journal of Sociology* 94:465–501 (1988).

141. For a general review, see Martin Daly and Margo Wilson, "Crime and Conflict: Homicide in Evolutionary Psychological Theory," in Michael Tonry, ed., *Crime and Justice, An Annual Edition* (Chicago: University of Chicago Press, 1997), pp. 51–100.

142. David Rowe, Alexander Vazsonyi, and Aurelio Jose Figuerdo, "Mating-Effort in Adolescence: A Conditional of Alternative Strategy," *Personal Individual Differences* 23:105–115 (1997).

143. Ibid.

144. Lee Ellis, "The Evolution of Violent Criminal Behavior and Its Nonlegal Equivalent," in Harry Hoffman, ed., *Crime in Biological, Social, and Moral Contexts* (New York: Praeger, 1990), pp. 61–81.

145. Ellis and Walsh, "Gene-Based Evolutionary Theories of Criminology."

146. Byron Roth, "Crime and Child Rearing," *Society* 34:39–45 (1996).

147. For a thorough review of this issue, see David Brandt and S. Jack Zlotnick, *The Psychology and Treatment of the Youthful Offender* (Springfield, IL: Charles C. Thomas, 1988).

148. Spencer Rathus, *Psychology* (New York: Holt, Rinehart and Winston, 1996), pp. 11–21.

149. See Sigmund Freud, *An Outline of Psychoanalysis*, James Strachey, trans. (New York: Norton, 1963).

150. See Erik Erikson, *Identity, Youth, and Crisis* (New York: Norton, 1968).

151. August Aichorn, *Wayward Youth* (New York: Viking Press, 1935).

152. David Abrahamsen, *Crime and Human Mind* (New York: Columbia University Press, 1944), p. 137.

153. See Fritz Redl and Hans Toch, "The Psychoanalytic Perspective," in Hans Toch, ed., *Psychology of Crime and Criminal Justice* (New York: Holt, Rinehart and Winston, 1979), pp. 193–195.

154. Seymour Halleck, *Psychiatry and the Dilemmas of Crime* (Berkeley: University of California Press, 1971).

155. Brandt and Zlotnick, *The Psychology and Treatment of the Youthful Offender*, pp. 72–73.

156. Halleck, *Psychiatry and the Dilemmas of Crime*.

157. Paige Crosby Ouimette, "Psychopathology and Sexual Aggression in Nonincarcerated Men," *Violence and Victimization* 12:389–397 (1997).

158. Minna Ritakallio, Riittakerttu Kaltiala-Heino, Janne Kivivuori, Tiina Luukkaala, and Matti Rimpelä, "Delinquency and the Profile of Offences among Depressed and Non-Depressed Adolescents," *Criminal Behaviour and Mental Health* 16:100–110 (2006); Ellen Kjelsberg, "Gender and Disorder Specific Criminal Career Profiles in Former Adolescent Psychiatric In-Patients," *Journal of Youth and Adolescence* 33:261–270 (2004).

159. Grégoire Zimmermann, "Delinquency in Male Adolescents: The Role of Alexithymia and Family Structure," *Journal of Adolescence* 29:321–332 (2006).

160. Ching-hua Ho, J. B. Kingree, and Martie P. Thompson, "Associations between Juvenile Delinquency and Weight-Related Variables: Analyses from a National Sample of High School Students," *International Journal of Eating Disorders* 39:477–483 (2006).

161. Joyce Akse, Bill Hale, Rutger Engels, Quinten Raaijmakers, and Wim Meeus, "Co-occurrence of Depression and Delinquency in Personality Types," *European Journal of Personality* 21:235–256 (2007).

162. Jennifer Beyers and Rolf Loeber, "Untangling Developmental Relations between Depressed Mood and Delinquency in Male Adolescents," *Journal of Abnormal Child Psychology* 31:247–267 (2003).

163. Dorothy Espelage, Elizabeth Cauffman, Lisa Broidy, Alex Piquero, Paul Mazerolle, and Hans Steiner, "A Cluster-Analytic Investigation of MMPI Profiles of Serious Male and Female Juvenile Offenders," *Journal of the American Academy of Child and Adolescent Psychiatry* 42:770–777 (2003).

164. Brandt and Zlotnick, *The Psychology and Treatment of the Youthful Offender*, pp. 72–73.

165. Eric Silver, "Mental Disorder and Violent Victimization: The Mediating Role of Involvement in Conflicted Social Relationships," *Criminology* 40:191–212 (2002).

166. Ibid.

167. Ronald Simons, Leslie Gordon Simons, Yi-Fu Chen, Gene Brody, and Kuei-Hsiu Lin, "Identifying the Psychological Factors that Mediate the Association between Parenting Practices and Delinquency," *Criminology* 45:481–517 (2007).

168. Stacy De Coster and Karen Heimer, "The Relationship Between Law Violation and Depression: An Interactionist Analysis," *Criminology* 39:799–836 (2001).

169. B. Lögdberg, L-L. Nilsson, M. T. Levander, and S. Levander, "Schizophrenia, Neighbourhood, and Crime," *Acta Psychiatrica Scandinavica* 110:92–97 (2004); DeCoster and Heimer, "The Relationship between Law Violation and Depression: An Interactionist Analysis."

170. Sonja Siennick, "The Timing and Mechanisms of the Offending-Depression Link," *Criminology* 45:583–615 (2007).

171. Courtenay Sellers, Christopher Sullivan, Bonita Veysey, and Jon Shane, "Responding to Persons with Mental Illnesses: Police Perspectives on Specialized and Traditional Practices," *Behavioral Sciences and the Law* 23:647–657 (2005).

172. Paul Hirschfield, Tina Maschi, Helene Raskin White, Leah Goldman Traub, and Rolf Loeber, "Mental Health and Juvenile Arrests: Criminality, Criminalization, or Compassion?" *Criminology* 44:593–630 (2006).

173. See Albert Bandura and Frances Menlove, "Factors Determining Vicarious Extinction of Avoidance Behavior through Symbolic Modeling," *Journal of Personality and Social Psychology* 8:99–108 (1965); Albert Bandura and Richard Walters, *Social Learning and Personality Development* (New York: Holt, Rinehart and Winston, 1963).

174. David Perry, Louise Perry, and Paul Rasmussen, "Cognitive Social Learning Mediators of Aggression," *Child Development* 57:700–711 (1986).

175. Bonnie Carlson, "Children's Beliefs about Punishment," *American Journal of Orthopsychiatry* 56:308–312 (1986).

176. Albert Bandura and Richard Walters, *Adolescent Aggression* (New York: Ronald Press, 1959), p. 32.

177. Victoria Rideout, Elizabeth Vandewater, and Ellen Wartella, *Zero to Six: Electronic Media in the Lives of Infants, Toddlers and Preschoolers* (Menlo Park, CA: Kaiser Family Foundation, 2003).

178. Michael Brody, "Playing with Death," *The Brown University Child and Adolescent Behavior Letter* 16:8 (2000).

179. Nicholas Carnagey, Craig Anderson, and Brad Bushman, "The Effect of Video Game Violence on Physiological Desensitization to Real-Life Violence," *Journal of Experimental Social Psychology* 43:489–496 (2007).

180. UCLA Center for Communication Policy, Television Violence Monitoring Project (Los Angeles, 1995); Associated Press, "Hollywood Is Blamed in Token Booth Attack," *Boston Globe*, 28 November 1995, p. 30.

181. Joyce Sprafkin, Kenneth Gadow, and Monique Dussault, "Reality Perceptions of Television: A Preliminary Comparison of Emotionally Disturbed and Nonhandicapped Children," *American Journal of Orthopsychiatry* 56:147–152 (1986).

182. Wendy Wood, Frank Wong, and J. Gregory Chachere, "Effects of Media Violence on Viewers' Aggression in Unconstrained Social Interaction," *Psychological Bulletin* 109:371–383 (1991); Lynette Friedrich-Cofer and Aletha Huston, "Television Violence and Aggression: The Debate Continues," *Psychological Bulletin* 100:364–371 (1986).

183. American Psychological Association, *Violence on TV*, a social issue release from the Board of Social and Ethical Responsibility for Psychology (Washington, DC: APA, 1985).

184. Dimitri Christakis, Frederick Zimmerman, David DiGiuseppe, and Carolyn McCarty, "Early Television Exposure and Subsequent Attentional Problems in Children," *Pediatrics* 113:708–713 (2004).

185. Brad Bushman and Craig Anderson, "Media Violence and the American Public Revisited," *American Psychologist* 56:448–450 (2002); Jeffrey Johnson, Patricia Cohen, Elizabeth Smailes, Stephanie Kasen, and Judith Brook, "Television Viewing and Aggressive Behavior During Adolescence and Adulthood," *Science* 295:2468–2471 (2002).

186. American Academy of Pediatrics et al., *Joint Statement on the Impact of Entertainment Violence on Children, Congressional Public Health Summit* (July 2000), www.mediafamily.org/facts/facts_vlent.shtml (accessed June 11, 2007).

187. Jonathon Freedman, "Television Violence and Aggression: What the Evidence Shows," in S. Oskamp, ed., *Applied Social Psychology Annual: Television as a Social Issue* (Newbury Park, CA: Sage Publications, 1988), pp. 144–162.

188. Jonathon Freedman, "Effect of Television Violence on Aggressiveness," *Psychological Bulletin* 96:227–246 (1984); Freedman, "Television Violence and Aggression: A Rejoinder," *Psychological Bulletin* 100:372–378 (1986).

189. Steven Messner, "Television Violence and Violent Crime: An Aggregate Analysis," *Social Problems* 33:218–235 (1986).

190. See Jean Piaget, *The Moral Judgment of the Child* (London: Kegan Paul, 1932).

191. Lawrence Kohlberg, *Stages in the Development of Moral Thought and Action* (New York: Holt, Rinehart and Winston, 1969).

192. L. Kohlberg, K. Kauffman, P. Scharf, and J. Hickey, *The Just Community Approach in Corrections: A Manual* (Niantic, CT: Connecticut Department of Corrections, 1973).

193. Scott Henggeler, *Delinquency in Adolescence* (Newbury Park, CA: Sage Publications, 1989), p. 26.

194. Ibid.

195. K. A. Dodge, "A Social Information Processing Model of Social Competence in Children," in M. Perlmutter, ed., *Minnesota Symposium in Child Psychology*, vol. 18 (Hillsdale, NJ: Erlbaum, 1986), pp. 77–125.

196. Adrian Raine, Peter Venables, and Mark Williams, "Better Autonomic Conditioning and Faster Electrodermal Half-Recovery Time at Age 15 Years as Possible Protective Factors against Crime at Age 29 Years," *Developmental Psychology* 32:624–630 (1996).

197. Jean Marie McGloin and Travis Pratt, "Cognitive Ability and Delinquent Behavior among Inner-City Youth: A Life-Course Analysis of Main, Mediating, and Interaction Effects," *International Journal of Offender Therapy and Comparative Criminology* 47:253–271 (2003).

198. L. Huesmann and L. Eron, "Individual Differences and the Trait of Aggression," *European Journal of Personality* 3:95–106 (1989).

199. Judith Baer and Tina Maschi, "Random Acts of Delinquency: Trauma and Self-Destructiveness in Juvenile Offenders," *Child and Adolescent Social Work Journal* 20:85–99 (2003).

200. Rolf Loeber and Dale Hay, "Key Issues in the Development of Aggression and Violence from Childhood to Early Adulthood," *Annual Review of Psychology* 48:371–410 (1997).

201. Tony Ward and Claire Stewart, "The Relationship Between Human Needs and Criminogenic Needs," *Crime and Law* 9:219–225 (2003).

202. J. E. Lochman, "Self and Peer Perceptions and Attributional Biases of Aggressive and Nonaggressive Boys in Dyadic Interactions," *Journal of Consulting and Clinical Psychology* 55:404–410 (1987).

203. Kathleen Cirillo et al., "School Violence: Prevalence and Intervention Strategies for At-Risk Adolescents," *Adolescence* 33:319–331 (1998).

204. Leilani Greening, "Adolescent Stealers' and Nonstealers' Social Problem-Solving Skills," *Adolescence* 32:51–56 (1997).

205. See Walter Mischel, *Introduction to Personality*, 4th ed. (New York: Holt, Rinehart and Winston, 1986).

206. D. A. Andrews and J. Stephen Wormith, "Personality and Crime: Knowledge and Construction in Criminology," *Justice Quarterly* 6:289–310 (1989); Donald Gibbons, "Comment—Personality and Crime: Non-Issues, Real Issues, and a Theory and Research Agenda," *Justice Quarterly* 6:311–324 (1989).

207. Sheldon Glueck and Eleanor Glueck, *Unraveling Juvenile Delinquency* (Cambridge: Harvard University Press, 1950).

208. See Hans Eysenck, *Personality and Crime* (London: Routledge and Kegan Paul, 1977).

209. David Farrington, "Psychobiological Factors in the Explanation and Reduction of Delinquency," *Today's Delinquent* 7:37–51 (1988).

210. Laurie Frost, Terrie Moffitt, and Rob McGee, "Neuropsychological Correlates of Psychopathology in an Unselected Cohort of Young Adolescents," *Journal of Abnormal Psychology* 98:307–313 (1989).

211. Edelyn Verona and Joyce Carbonell, "Female Violence and Personality," *Criminal Justice and Behavior* 27:176–195 (2000).

212. Hans Eysenck and M. W. Eysenck, *Personality and Individual Differences* (New York: Plenum, 1985).

213. Catrien Bijleveld and Jan Hendriks, "Juvenile Sex Offenders: Differences Between Group and Solo Offenders," *Psychology, Crime and Law* 9:237–246 (2003).

214. For a review of this concept, see Ronald Blackburn, "Personality Disorder and Psychopathy: Conceptual and Empirical Integration," *Psychology, Crime and Law* 13:7–18 (2007).

215. Linda Mealey, "The Sociobiology of Sociopathy: An Integrated Evolutionary Model," *Behavioral and Brain Sciences* 18:523–540 (1995).

216. Gisli Gudjonsson, Emil Einarsson, Ólafur Örn Bragason, and Jon Fridrik Sigurdsson, "Personality Predictors of Self-Reported Offending in Icelandic Students," *Psychology, Crime and Law* 12:383–393 (2006).

217. Peter Johansson and Margaret Kerr, "Psychopathy and Intelligence: A Second Look," *Journal of Personality Disorders* 19:357–369 (2005).

218. Hervey Cleckley, "Psychopathic States," in S. Aneti, ed., *American Handbook of Psychiatry* (New York: Basic Books, 1959), pp. 567–569.

219. Lewis Yablonsky, *The Violent Gang* (Baltimore: Penguin, 1971), pp. 195–205.

220. Sue Kellett and Harriet Gross, "Addicted to Joyriding? An Exploration of Young Offenders' Accounts of Their Car Crime," *Psychology, Crime and Law* 12:39–59 (2006).

221. A. Raine, T. Lencz, K. Taylor, J. B. Hellige, S. Bihrle, L. Lacasse, M. Lee, S. Ishikawa, and P. Colletti, "Corpus Callosum Abnormalities in Psychopathic Antisocial Individuals," *Archives of General Psychiatry* 60:1134–1142 (2003).

222. L. M. Terman, "Research on the Diagnosis of Predelinquent Tendencies," *Journal of Delinquency* 9:124–130 (1925); Terman, *Measurement of Intelligence* (Boston: Houghton Mifflin, 1916). For example, see M. G. Caldwell, "The Intelligence of Delinquent Boys Committed to Wisconsin Industrial School," *Journal of Criminal Law and Criminology* 20:421–428 (1929); and C. Murcheson, *Criminal Intelligence* (Worcester, MA: Clark University, 1926), pp. 41–44.

223. Henry Goddard, *Efficiency and Levels of Intelligence* (Princeton, NJ: Princeton University Press, 1920).

224. William Healy and Augusta Bronner, *Delinquency and Criminals: Their Making and Unmaking* (New York: Macmillan, 1926).

225. Joseph Lee Rogers, H. Harrington Cleveland, Edwin van den Oord, and David Rowe, "Resolving the Debate over Birth Order, Family Size, and Intelligence," *American Psychologist* 55:599–612 (2000).

226. Kenneth Eels, *Intelligence and Cultural Differences* (Chicago: University of Chicago Press, 1951), p. 181.

227. Sorel Cahahn and Nora Cohen, "Age versus Schooling Effects on Intelligence Development," *Child Development* 60:1239–1249 (1989).

228. John Slawson, *The Delinquent Boys* (Boston: Budget Press, 1926).

229. Edwin Sutherland, "Mental Deficiency and Crime," in Kimball Young, ed., *Social Attitudes* (New York: Henry Holt, 1973).

230. Travis Hirschi and Michael Hindelang, "Intelligence and Delinquency: A Revisionist Review," *American Sociological Review* 42:471–586 (1977).

231. Terrie Moffitt and Phil Silva, "IQ and Delinquency: A Direct Test of the Differential Detection Hypothesis," *Journal of Abnormal Psychology* 97:1–4 (1988); E. Kandel et al., "IQ as a Protective Factor for Subjects at a High Risk for Antisocial Behavior," *Journal of Consulting and Clinical Psychology* 56:224–226 (1988); Christine Ward and Richard McFall, "Further Validation of the Problem Inventory for Adolescent Girls: Comparing Caucasian and Black Delinquents and Nondelinquents," *Journal of Consulting and Clinical Psychology* 54:732–733 (1986).

232. Wilson and Herrnstein, *Crime and Human Nature*, p. 148.

233. Alex Piquero, "Frequency, Specialization, and Violence in Offending Careers," *Journal of Research in Crime and Delinquency* 37:392–418 (2000).

234. David Farrington, "Juvenile Delinquency," in John C. Coleman, ed., *The School Years* (London: Routledge, 1992), p. 137.

235. H. D. Day, J. M. Franklin, and D. D. Marshall, "Predictors of Aggression in Hospitalized Adolescents," *Journal of Psychology* 132:427–435 (1998).

236. Deborah Denno, "Sociological and Human Developmental Explanations of Crime: Conflict or Consensus," *Criminology* 23:141–174 (1985).

237. Glenn Walters and Thomas White, "Heredity and Crime: Bad Genes or Bad Research," *Justice Quarterly* 27:455–485 (1989), at p. 478.

238. John Cochran, Peter Wood, and Bruce Arneklev, "Is the Religiosity-Delinquency Relationship Spurious? A Test of Arousal and Social Control Theories," *Journal of Research in Crime and Delinquency* 31:92–113 (1994).

239. Lee Ellis, "Genetics and Criminal Behavior," *Criminology* 10:43–66 (1982), at p. 58.

240. Lee Ellis, "The Evolution of the Nonlegal Equivalent of Aggressive Criminal Behavior," *Aggressive Behavior* 12:57–71 (1986).

241. Edwin Schur, *Radical Nonintervention: Rethinking the Delinquency Problem* (Englewood Cliffs, NJ: Prentice Hall, 1973).

Social Structure, Process, Culture, and Delinquency

4

Chapter Outline

Chapter Objectives

1. Be familiar with the association between social conditions and crime
2. Be familiar with the association between social structure and delinquency
3. Describe the principles of social disorganization theory
4. Discuss the work of social ecologists
5. Define the concept of anomie and how it impacts on delinquent behavior
6. Be familiar with recent developments in strain theory
7. Know what is meant by the term "cultural deviance" and be familiar with theories of cultural deviance
8. Discuss the concept of social process and socialization
9. Be familiar with the concept of social learning and social learning theories
10. Discuss the elements of social control theory

© Corbis RF/Alamy

A video that appeared on Internet sites around the nation in June of 2007 showed the brutal attack on a teacher in the hallways of Murphy High School in Mobile, Alabama. The tape revealed in graphic detail 16-year-old Randolph Parker punching his teacher in the face, while his buddy, 17-year-old Dominick Harris, filmed the attack on his cell phone. The teacher, Melinda Rudisill, 61, was rushed to the hospital where she received 20 stitches. Parker appeared to have used brass knuckles during the attack. Police soon concluded that the attack was gang related; there were freshly painted gang symbols outside Parker's home. Charged as adults, the teens could get up to 10 years in prison.[1]

How can this brutal attack on a high school teacher truly be explained? To understand teen violence and antisocial behaviors, many delinquency experts believe it is a mistake to ignore social and environmental factors.[2] According to this view, most delinquents are indigent and desperate, not calculating or evil. They grew up in deteriorated parts of town and lacked the social support and economic resources familiar to more affluent members of society. Their family life may have been dysfunctional, their schools inadequate, and their peer group damaging. Their ties to key elements of socialization—family, school, community—are frayed and damaged. Understanding delinquent behavior, then, requires us to account for the destructive influence these social forces have on human behavior rather than individual characteristics and traits.[3]

Why are social views of delinquency so popular? One reason is the consistent social patterns found in the delinquency rate. We know that youths are more likely to commit crimes if they live in the poorest neighborhoods within large urban areas. It seems unlikely that most kids with physical or mental problems live in a particular section of town that also happens to be indigent and deteriorated. Or that kids in one neighborhood watch violent TV shows and films while those in another focus on the History Channel. The fact that delinquency rates are highest in the poorest neighborhoods seems more than a coincidence.

To see video on the **Murphy High School attack**, go to YouTube via academic.cengage .com/criminaljustice/siegel.

To some delinquency experts, these facts can only mean one thing: The cause of delinquency rests within the dynamics of the social world. They point to cultural norms, social processes, and social institutions as the key elements that shape human behavior. When these elements are strained, delinquency rates increase.[4]

SOCIAL FACTORS AND DELINQUENCY

What are the critical social factors believed to cause or affect delinquent behaviors?

I *Interpersonal interactions.* Social relationships with families, peers, schools, jobs, criminal justice agencies, and the like, may play an important role in shaping behavioral choices.[5] Inappropriate and disrupted social relations have been linked to crime and delinquency.[6]

I *Community conditions.* Crime and delinquency rates are highest in deteriorated inner-city areas. These communities, wracked by poverty, decay, fear, and despair, also maintain high rates of criminal victimization.[7]

I *Exposure to violence.* Kids living in poor neighborhoods are exposed to a constant stream of antisocial behaviors.[8] Even when neighborhood disadvantage and poverty are taken into account, the more often children are exposed to violence within their residential community the more likely they are to become violent themselves.[9]

I *Social change.* Political unrest and mistrust, economic stress, and family disintegration are social changes that have been found to precede sharp increases in delinquency rates.[10]

I *Low socioeconomic status.* Millions of people have scant, if any, resources and suffer socially and economically as a result.[11] People who live in poverty may have the greatest incentive to commit delinquency.

I *Racial disparity.* The consequences of racial disparity take a toll on youth. Poverty rates among minority groups are still significantly higher than that of whites.

All of these social problems and conditions take a toll on American youth and may help turn them toward antisocial behaviors. In this chapter we will review the most prominent social theories of delinquency that are based on the effects of social problems and social relations. They are divided into two main groups:

1. *Social structure theories* hold that delinquency is a function of a person's place in the economic structure.

2. *Social process theories* view delinquency as the result of a person's interaction with critical elements of socialization.

Each of these two independent yet inter-related views of delinquency are discussed below.

SOCIAL STRUCTURE AND DELINQUENCY

stratified society
Grouping society into classes based on the unequal distribution of scarce resources.

People in the United States live in a stratified society. Social strata are created by the unequal distribution of wealth, power, and prestige. Social classes are segments of the population whose members have a relatively similar portion of desirable things and who share attitudes, values, norms, and an identifiable lifestyle. In U.S. society, it is common to identify people as upper-, middle-, and lower-class citizens, with a broad range of economic variations existing within each group. The upper-upper class is reserved for a small number of exceptionally well-to-do families who maintain enormous financial and social resources. In contrast, the indigent have scant, if any, resources and suffer socially and economically as a result. More than 37 million Americans now live in poverty (see Figure 4.1).

FIGURE 4.1

Number in Poverty and Poverty Rate

NOTE: The data points are placed at the midpoints of the respective years.

SOURCE: *Income, Poverty and Health Insurance in the United States: 2005* (P60-231) (Washington, DC: U.S. Census Department, 2006).

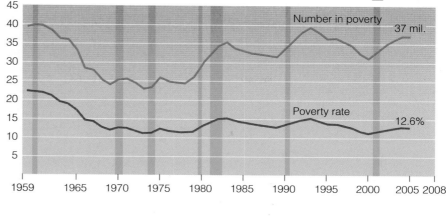

Numbers in millions, rates in percent   ▇ Recession

Those living in poverty are forced to live in neighborhoods that experience inadequate housing and health care, disrupted family lives, underemployment, and despair. Living in poor areas magnifies the effect of personal social and economic problems. Kids whose families are poor are more likely to engage in antisocial behavior if they also reside in a poverty-stricken area than kids from poor families growing up in more affluent areas. The combination of having a poor family living in a disorganized area may be devastating.[12]

Members of the lower class also suffer in other ways. They are more prone to depression, less likely to have achievement motivation, and less likely to put off immediate gratification for future gain. For example, they may be less willing to stay in school because the rewards for educational achievement are in the distant future.

Sociologist Oscar Lewis coined the phrase "**culture of poverty**" to describe this condition.[13] Apathy, cynicism, helplessness, and mistrust of social institutions such as schools, government agencies, and the police mark the culture of poverty. This mistrust prevents members of the lower class from taking advantage of the meager opportunities available to them. Lewis's work was the first of a group that described the plight of **at-risk** children and adults.

Economic disparity will continually haunt members of the **underclass** and their children over the course of their lifespan. Even if they value education and other middle-class norms, their desperate life circumstances (e.g., high unemployment and nontraditional family structures) may prevent them from developing the skills, habits, and lifestyles that lead first to educational success and later to success in the workplace.[14] Their ability to maintain social ties in the neighborhood become weak and attenuated, further weakening a neighborhood's cohesiveness and its ability to regulate the behavior of its citizens.[15]

culture of poverty
View that lower-class people form a separate culture with their own values and norms, which are sometimes in conflict with conventional society.

at-risk youths
Young people who are extremely vulnerable to the negative consequences of school failure, substance abuse, and early sexuality.

underclass
Group of urban poor whose members have little chance of upward mobility or improvement.

Child Poverty

Children are hit especially hard by poverty, and being poor during early childhood may have a more severe impact on behavior than it does during adolescence and adulthood.[16] This is particularly important today because, as Figure 4.2 shows, children have a higher poverty rate, almost 18 percent, than any other age group.

Considering that there are about 70 million juveniles in the United States, this means that more than 12 million are now living below the poverty line. Hundreds of studies have documented the association between family poverty and children's health, achievement, and behavior impairments.[17] Children who grow up in low-income homes are less likely to achieve in school and are less likely to complete their schooling than children with more affluent parents.[18] Poor children are also more likely to suffer from health problems and to receive inadequate health care. The number of U.S. children covered by health insurance is declining and will continue to do so for the foreseeable future.[19] Without health benefits or the means to afford medical

FIGURE 4.2
Poverty Rates by Age

NOTE: The data points are placed at the midpoints of the respective years.

Data for people 18 to 64 and 65 and older are not available from 1960 to 1965.

SOURCE: *Income, Poverty and Health Insurance in the United States: 2005* (P60-231) (Washington, DC: U.S. Census Department, 2006).

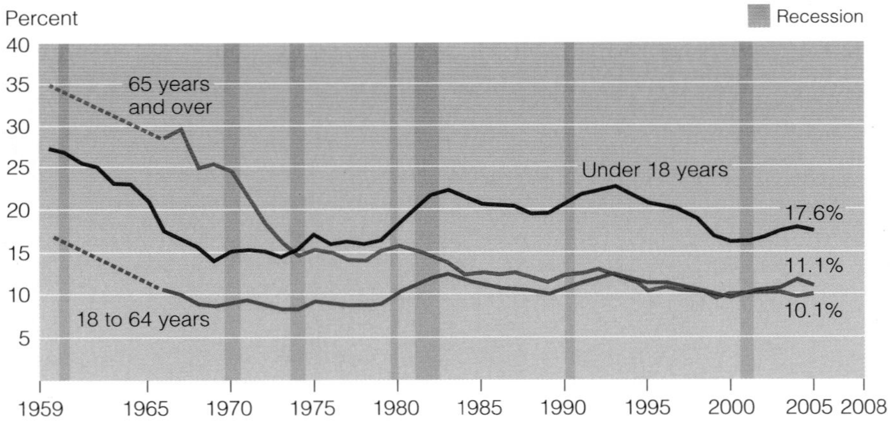

FIGURE 4.2
Poverty Rates by Age

Kids Count, a project of the Annie E. Casey Foundation, is a national and state-by-state effort to track the relative status of children in the United States. Go to their website via academic.cengage.com/criminaljustice/siegel.

care, these children are likely to have health problems that impede their long-term development. Children who live in extreme poverty or who remain poor for multiple years appear to suffer the worst outcomes.

Besides their increased chance of physical illness, poor children are much more likely than wealthy children to suffer various social and physical ills, ranging from low birthweight to a limited chance of earning a college degree. Many live in substandard housing—high-rise, multiple-family dwellings—which can have a negative influence on their long-term psychological health.[20] Adolescents in the worst neighborhoods share the greatest risk of dropping out of school and becoming teenage parents.

Racial Disparity

The rates of child poverty in the United States also vary significantly by race and ethnicity. Latino and African American children are more than twice as likely to be poor as Asian and white children. Minority children are four times less likely to have health insurance as other kids. There are large ethnic disparities in the time preschool-age children spend in structured preschool settings.

truly disadvantaged
According to William Julius Wilson, those people who are left out of the economic mainstream and reduced to living in the most deteriorated inner-city areas.

Clearly, minority children begin life with significant social and educational deficits.[21] They have been referred to as the **truly disadvantaged**.[22] Minority kids are also exposed to race-based disparity such as income inequality and institutional racism.[23] Black delinquency rates, more so than white, seem to be influenced by the shift of high-paid manufacturing jobs overseas and their replacement with lower-paid service sector jobs. African Americans seem less able to prosper in a service economy than whites, and over time the resulting economic disadvantage translates into increased levels of violence. In desperation, some may turn to acts such as joining a gang or committing an armed robbery as a means of economic survival. And when things go awry, as they so often do, the result may be gunplay and death.[24]

SOCIAL STRUCTURE THEORIES

social structure theories
Explain delinquency using socioeconomic conditions and cultural values.

The effects of income inequality, poverty, racism, and despair are viewed by many delinquency experts as key causes of youth crime and drug abuse. Kids growing up poor and living in households that lack economic resources are much more likely to get involved in serious crime than their wealthier peers.[25] To explain this phenomenon, **social structure theories** suggest that social and economic forces operating in deteriorated lower-class areas are the key determinant of delinquent behavior patterns. Social forces begin to affect people while they are relatively young and continue to influence them throughout their lives. Though not all youthful offenders become adult criminals, those who reside in poverty-stricken lower-class areas and become **enculturated** into the values of inner-city neighborhoods are the ones most likely to persist in delinquency. Logically, because delinquency rates are consistently higher in lower-class urban centers than in middle-class suburbs, social forces must be operating in blighted urban areas that influence or control behavior.[26]

How can this association between poverty and delinquency be precisely explained? What are the connections that lead from being poor to becoming a delinquent? There are actually three independent yet overlapping theories that reside within the social structure perspective—social disorganization theory, strain theory, and cultural deviance theory (outlined in Figure 4.3).

Social disorganization theory focuses on the conditions within the urban environment that affect delinquency rates. A disorganized area is one in which institutions of social control—such as the family, commercial establishments, and schools—have broken down and can no longer carry out their expected or stated functions. Indicators of social disorganization include high unemployment, school dropout rates, deteriorated housing, low income levels, and large numbers of single-parent households. Residents in these areas experience conflict and despair, and, as a result, antisocial behavior flourishes.

Strain theory holds that delinquency is a function of the conflict between the goals people have and the means they can use to obtain them legally. Most people in the United States desire wealth, material possessions, power, prestige, and other life comforts. And although these social and economic goals are common to people in all economic strata, strain theorists insist that the ability to obtain these goals is class dependent. Members of the lower class are unable to achieve these symbols of success through conventional means. Consequently, they feel anger, frustration, and resentment, which is referred to as strain. Lower-class citizens can either accept their condition and live out their days as socially responsible, if unrewarded, citizens, or

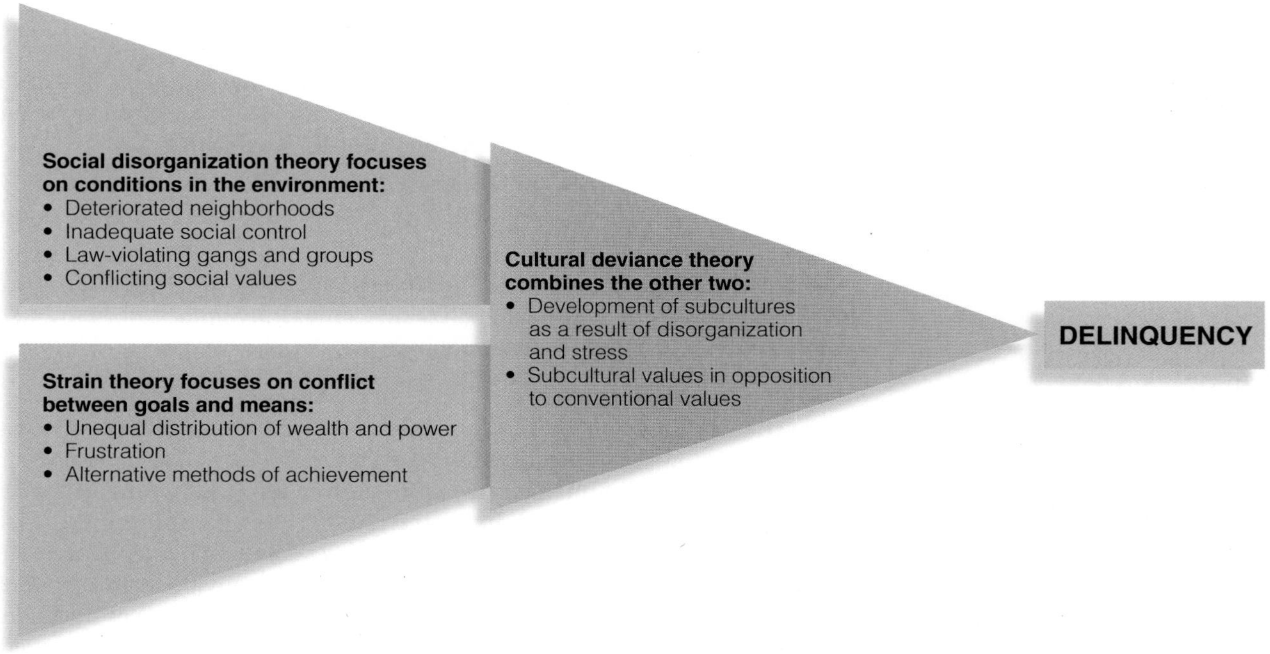

enculturated
The process by which an established culture teaches an individual its norms and values, so that the individual can become an accepted member of the society. Through enculturation, the individual learns what is accepted behavior within that society and his or her particular status within the culture.

social disorganization theory
The inability of a community to exert social control allows youths the freedom to engage in illegal behavior.

strain theory
Links delinquency to the strain of being locked out of the economic mainstream, which creates the anger and frustration that lead to delinquent acts.

Social disorganization theory focuses on conditions in the environment:
• Deteriorated neighborhoods
• Inadequate social control
• Law-violating gangs and groups
• Conflicting social values

Strain theory focuses on conflict between goals and means:
• Unequal distribution of wealth and power
• Frustration
• Alternative methods of achievement

Cultural deviance theory combines the other two:
• Development of subcultures as a result of disorganization and stress
• Subcultural values in opposition to conventional values

DELINQUENCY

FIGURE **4.3**
The Three Branches of Social Structure Theory

they can choose an alternative means of achieving success, such as theft, violence, or drug trafficking.

cultural deviance theory
A unique lower-class culture develops in disorganized neighborhoods whose unique set of values and beliefs puts residents in conflict with conventional social norms.

Cultural deviance theory, the third variation of structural theory, combines elements of both strain and social disorganization. According to this view, because of strain and social isolation, a unique lower-class culture develops in disorganized neighborhoods. These independent subcultures maintain a unique set of values and beliefs that are in conflict with conventional social norms. Criminal behavior is an expression of conformity to lower-class subcultural values and traditions and not a rebellion from conventional society. Subcultural values are handed down from one generation to the next in a process called cultural transmission.

cultural transmission
Cultural norms and values that are passed down from one generation to the next.

Although each of these theories is distinct in critical aspects, each approach has at its core the view that socially isolated people, living in disorganized neighborhoods, are the ones most likely to experience delinquency-producing social forces. Each branch of social structure theory will now be discussed in some detail.

SOCIAL DISORGANIZATION THEORY

Social disorganization theory ties delinquency rates to socioeconomic conditions:

I Long-term, unremitting poverty undermines a community and its residents. Delinquency rates are sensitive to the destructive social forces operating in lower-class urban neighborhoods

I Residents develop a sense of hopelessness and mistrust of conventional society. Residents of such areas are frustrated by their inability to become part of the "American Dream."

I Kids growing up in these disadvantaged areas are at risk for delinquency because they hear from adults that there is little hope of success in the conventional world.

I Poverty undermines the basic stabilizing forces of the community—family, school, peers, and neighbors—rendering them weakened, attenuated, and ineffective.

social control
Ability of social institutions to influence human behavior; the justice system is the primary agency of formal social control.

I The ability of the community to control its inhabitants—to assert informal social control—is damaged and frayed.

I The community has become socially disorganized and its residents free to succumb to the lure of antisocial. Without social controls kids are free to join gangs, violate the law, and engage in uncivil and destructive behaviors.

I Neighborhood kids are constantly exposed to disruption, violence, and incivility factors that increase the likelihood that they themselves will become delinquency involved.[27]

I Neighborhood disintegration and the corresponding erosion of social control are the primary causes of delinquent behavior. Community values, norms, and cohesiveness control behavior choices, not personal decision making and individual traits.

Social disorganization theory was first formulated early in the twentieth century by sociologists Clifford Shaw and Henry McKay. These Chicago-based scholars found that delinquency rates were high in what they called transitional neighborhoods—areas that had changed from affluence to decay. Here, factories and commercial establishments were interspersed with private residences. In such environments, teenage gangs developed as a means of survival, defense, and friendship. Gang leaders recruited younger members, passing on delinquent traditions and ensuring survival of the gang from one generation to the next, a process referred to as *cultural transmission*.

transitional neighborhood
Area undergoing a shift in population and structure, usually from middle-class residential to lower-class mixed use.

While mapping delinquency rates in Chicago, Shaw and McKay noted that distinct ecological areas had developed that could be visualized as a series of concentric zones, each with a stable delinquency rate (see Figure 4.4).[28]

The areas of heaviest delinquency concentration appeared to be the poverty-stricken, transitional, inner-city zones. The zones farthest from the city's center were the least prone to delinquency. Analysis of these data indicated a stable pattern of delinquent activity in the ecological zones over a 65-year period.[29] These patterns persisted as different ethnic or racial groups moved into the zone. Shaw and McKay found that delinquency was tied to neighborhood characteristics rather than the personal characteristics or culture of the residents.

According to their social disorganization view, a healthy, organized community has the ability to regulate itself so that common goals are met.[30] Those neighborhoods that become disorganized are incapable of social control because they are wracked by deterioration and economic failure.[31] Shaw and McKay claimed that areas continually hurt by poverty and long-term unemployment also experience social disorganization.[32]

The Legacy of Shaw and McKay

Social disorganization concepts articulated by Shaw and McKay have remained a prominent fixture of criminological scholarship and thinking for more than 75 years. While cultural and social conditions have changed and American society today is much more heterogeneous and mobile than during Shaw and McKay's time, the most important elements of their findings still hold up.[33]

Despite these noteworthy achievements, the validity of some of Shaw and McKay's positions have been challenged. Some critics have faulted their assumption that neighborhoods are essentially stable, suggesting that there is a great deal more fluidity and transition than assumed by Shaw and McKay.[34] There is also concern about their reliance on police records to calculate neighborhood delinquency rates. Relying on official data means that findings may be more sensitive to the validity of police generated data than they are true interzone delinquency rate differences. Numerous studies indicate that police use extensive discretion when arresting people and that social status is one factor that influences their decisions.[35] It is possible that kids in middle-class neighborhoods commit many delinquent acts that never show up in official statistics, whereas lower-class adolescents face a far greater chance of arrest and court adjudication.[36] The relationship between ecology and delinquency rates, therefore, may reflect police behavior more than criminal behavior.

These criticisms aside, the concept of social disorganization provides a valuable contribution to our understanding of the causes of delinquent behavior. Because they introduced new variables such as social control and the ecology of the city to the study of delinquency, Shaw and McKay's pioneering efforts have had a lasting influence on our understanding of human behaviors.

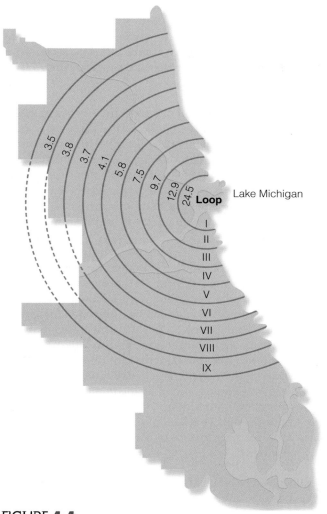

FIGURE 4.4
Concentric Zones Map of Chicago

NOTE: Arabic numbers represent the rate of male delinquency.

SOURCE: Clifford R. Shaw et al., *Delinquency Areas* (Chicago: University of Chicago Press, 1929), p. 99. Used by permission of the publisher.

social ecology
Theory focuses attention on the influence social institutions have on individual behavior and suggests that law-violating behavior is a response to social rather than individual forces operating in an urban environment.

Contemporary Social Ecology Theory

Shaw and McKay's social disorganization views have been updated by contemporary **social ecologists**, whose work emphasizes the association of community deterioration and economic decline to delinquency, but places less emphasis on values and norms and more on community characteristics and their influence on interpersonal relations. According to this more contemporary view, living in deteriorated, crime-ridden neighborhoods exerts a powerful influence over behavior that is strong enough to neutralize the positive effects of a supportive family and close social ties.[37] In the following sections, some of the most important social ecological concepts are discussed in detail.

The concept of **community deterioration and crime** was the subject of a famous *Atlantic Magazine* article titled "Broken Windows." Check it out via academic.cengage.com/criminaljustice/siegel.

Community Disorder Social ecologists have found an association between delinquency rates and community deterioration: disorder, poverty, alienation, disassociation, and fear of delinquency.[38] They find that neighborhoods with a high percentage of deserted houses and apartments experience high delinquency rates; abandoned buildings serve as a "magnet for delinquency."[39] Areas in which houses are in poor repair, boarded up and burned out, and whose owners are best described as "slumlords" are also the location of the highest violence rates and gun crime.[40] These are neighborhoods in which retail establishments often go bankrupt, are abandoned, and deteriorate physically.[41]

Poverty Concentration Poverty becomes "concentrated" in deteriorated areas.[42] As working- and middle-class families flee, elements of the most disadvantaged population are consolidated within inner-city poverty areas. Emigrants take with them their financial and institutional resources and support. Businesses are disinclined to locate in poverty areas; banks become reluctant to lend money for new housing or businesses.[43] Areas of poverty concentration experience significant income and wealth disparities, lack of employment opportunities, inferior housing patterns, and unequal access to health care; not surprisingly, they also experience high rates of delinquency.[44]

Poverty concentration destabilizes households, and unstable families are the ones most likely to produce children who put a premium on violence and aggression as a means of dealing with limited opportunity. This lack of opportunity perpetuates higher delinquency rates, especially when large groups or cohorts of kids of the same age compete for relatively scant resources.[45]

Community Fear People feel safe in neighborhoods that are orderly and in repair.[46] In contrast, those living in neighborhoods that suffer social and physical incivilities—rowdy youth, trash and litter, graffiti, abandoned storefronts, burned-out buildings, strangers, drunks, vagabonds, loiterers, prostitutes, noise, congestion, angry words, dirt, and stench—are much more likely to be fearful. Put another way, disorder breeds fear.[47]

Fear is based on experience. Residents who have already been victimized are more fearful of the future than those who have escaped crime.[48] People become afraid when they are approached by neighborhood kids selling drugs or when they see them hanging out in community parks and playgrounds, or when gangs proliferate in the neighborhood.[49] They may fear that their children will also be approached and seduced into the drug life.[50]

Fear can become contagious. People tell others when they have been victimized, spreading the word that the neighborhood is getting dangerous and that the chances of future victimization are high.[51] They dread leaving their homes at night and withdraw from community life. When people live in areas where the death rates are high and life expectancies are short, they may alter their behavior out of fear. They may feel, "Why plan for the future when there is a significant likelihood that I may never see it?" In such areas, young boys and girls may psychologically adjust by taking risks and discounting the future. Teenage birthrates soar and so do violence rates.[52] For these children, the inevitability of death skews their perspective of how they live their lives.

Siege Mentality The presence of community incivilities, especially when accompanied by relatively high delinquency rates and gang activity, convinces older residents that their neighborhood is dangerous; becoming a crime victim seems inevitable.[53] Eventually they become emotionally numb and indifferent to the suffering of others.[54]

When fear grips a neighborhood, people may seek to flee to safer environments, undermining the area's human capital. A woman walks past graffiti in an alley where residents say gang members congregate in Irvington, New Jersey. State and local police swept through this block, arresting six people and painting over gang graffiti in what they promised would be a sustained crackdown on street gangs in one of New Jersey's deadliest cities.

siege mentality
Residents become so suspicious of authority that they consider the outside world to be the enemy out to destroy the neighborhood.

Some residents become so suspicious of authority that they develop a siege mentality in which the outside world is considered the enemy out to destroy the neighborhood. Government officials seem arrogant and haughty. Residents become self-conscious, worried about garnering any respect, and are particularly attuned to anyone who disrespects them. Considering this feeling of mistrust, when police ignore delinquency in poor areas or, conversely, when they are violent and corrupt, anger flares, and people take to the streets and react in violent ways.[55]

Gangs and Fear Gangs flourish in deteriorated neighborhoods with high levels of poverty, lack of investment, high unemployment rates, and population turnover.[56] Unlike any other delinquency, however, gang activity is frequently undertaken out in the open, on the public ways, and in full view of the rest of the community.[57] Brazen gang activity undermines community solidarity because it signals that the police must be either corrupt or inept. The fact that gangs are willing to openly engage in drug sales and other types of criminal activity shows their confidence that they have silenced or intimidated law-abiding people in their midst. The police and the community alike become hopeless about their ability to restore community stability, producing greater levels of community fear.

Community Change In our postmodern society, urban areas are undergoing rapid structural changes in racial and economic composition. Some may become multiracial, while others become racially homogeneous. Some areas become stable and family oriented, while in others, mobile, never-married people predominate.[58] While changing neighborhoods experience higher delinquency rates, stable neighborhoods have the strength to restrict substance abuse and criminal activity.[59]

As areas decline, residents flee to safer, more stable localities. Those who can move to more affluent neighborhoods find that their lifestyles and life chances improve immediately and continue to do so over their lifespan.[60] Those who cannot leave because they cannot afford to live in more affluent communities face an increased risk of victimization.

High population turnover can have a devastating effect on community culture because it thwarts communication and information flow.[61] In response to this turnover, a culture may develop that dictates standards of dress, language, and behavior to neighborhood youth that are in opposition to those of conventional society.

Collective Efficacy Cohesive communities, whether urban or rural, with high levels of social control and social integration, where people know one another and develop interpersonal ties, may also develop **collective efficacy**: mutual trust, a willingness to intervene in the supervision of children, and the maintenance of public order.[62] It is the cohesion among neighborhood residents combined with shared expectations for informal social control of public space that promotes collective efficacy.[63] Residents in these areas are able to enjoy a better life because the fruits of cohesiveness can be better education, health care, and housing opportunities.[64] Collective efficacy may actually occur as a response to escalating delinquency rates: neighbors may band to fight a common problem.[65]

In contrast, residents of socially disorganized neighborhoods find that efforts at social control are weak and attenuated. People living in economically disadvantaged areas are significantly more likely to perceive their immediate surroundings in more negative terms (i.e., higher levels of incivilities) than those living in areas that maintain collective efficacy.[66] When community social control efforts are blunted, delinquency rates increase, further weakening neighborhood cohesiveness.[67]

There are actually three forms of collective efficacy:

▌ *Informal social control.* Some elements of collective efficacy operate on the primary or private level and involve peers, families, and relatives. These sources exert informal control by either awarding or withholding approval, respect, and admiration. Informal control mechanisms include direct criticism, ridicule, ostracism, desertion, or physical punishment.[68]

The most important wielder of informal social control is the family that may keep at-risk kids in check through such mechanisms as corporal punishment, withholding privileges, or ridiculing lazy or disrespectful behavior. The importance of the family to apply informal social control takes on greater importance in neighborhoods with few social ties among adults and limited collective efficacy. In these areas parents cannot call upon neighborhood resources to take up the burden of controlling children and face the burden of providing adequate supervision.[69]

The family is not the only force of informal social control. In some neighborhoods, people are committed to preserving their immediate environment by confronting destabilizing forces such as teen gangs.[70] By helping neighbors become more resilient and self-confident, adults in these areas provide the external support systems that

Communities that maintain collective efficacy, that can pull together to combat antisocial behavior, are the ones with the lowest rates of delinquency. In these areas, older, respected residents may work with kids to help them resist the temptations of the street. Here, Kenneth Jackson, former semipro football running back, leads a peer-mediation class at Harding High School in Bridgeport, Connecticut, May 2, 2006. Jackson helped create the school's peer-mediation program, designed to reduce fights, arguments, and disputes among students.

---

collective efficacy
The ability of communities to regulate the behavior of their residents through the influence of community institutions, such as the family and school. Residents in these communities share mutual trust and a willingness to intervene in the supervision of children and the maintenance of public order.

enable youth to desist from delinquency. Residents teach one another that they have moral and social obligations to their fellow citizens; children learn to be sensitive to the rights of others and to respect differences.

▌ *Institutional social control.* Social institutions such as schools and churches cannot work effectively in a climate of alienation and mistrust. Unsupervised peer groups and gangs, which flourish in disorganized areas, disrupt the influence of those neighborhood control agents that do exist.[71]

Institutional social control is quite important. Children are at risk for recruitment into gangs and law-violating groups when there is a lack of effective public services. Gangs become an attractive alternative when adolescents have little to do after school and must rely on out-of-home care rather than more structured school-based programs.[72] As a result, delinquency may flourish and neighborhood fear increases, conditions that decrease a community's cohesion and thwart the ability of its institutions to exert social control over its residents.[73]

▌ *Public social control.* Stable neighborhoods are also able to arrange for external sources of social control. If they can draw on outside help and secure external resources—a process referred to as public social control—they are better able to reduce the effects of disorganization and maintain lower levels of delinquency and gang membership.[74]

The level of policing, one of the primary sources of public social control, may vary from neighborhood to neighborhood. The police presence is typically greatest when community organizations and local leaders have sufficient political clout to get funding for additional law enforcement personnel. An effective police presence sends a message that the area will not tolerate deviant behavior. Because they can respond vigorously to delinquency, the police prevent delinquent gangs from gaining a toehold in the neighborhood.[75] In contrast, delinquency rates are highest in areas where police are mistrusted or disliked.[76]

In more disorganized areas, the absence of political powerbrokers limits access to external funding and protection.[77] Without outside funding, a neighborhood may lack the ability to "get back on its feet."[78] In these areas there are fewer police, and those that do patrol the area are less motivated and their resources are stretched tighter. These communities cannot mount an effective social control effort because as neighborhood disadvantage increases, its level of informal social control decreases.[79]

The Effect of Collective Efficacy The ramifications of having adequate controls are critical. In areas where collective efficacy remains high, children are less likely to become involved with deviant peers and engage in problem behaviors.[80] In these more stable areas, kids are able to use their wits to avoid violent confrontations and to feel safe in their own neighborhood, a concept referred to as **street efficacy**.[81] In contrast, adolescents who live in neighborhoods with concentrated disadvantage and low collective efficacy lose confidence in their ability to avoid violence. And as research by sociologist Patrick Sharkey has shown, this is important because adolescents with high levels of street efficacy are less likely to resort to violence themselves or to associate with delinquent peers. [82]

Collective efficacy has other benefits. When residents are satisfied that their neighborhoods are good places to live, they feel a sense of obligation to maintain order and are more willing to work hard to encourage informal social control. In areas where social institutions and processes—such as police protection—are working adequately, residents are willing to intervene personally to help control unruly children and uncivil adults.[83]

According to the social ecology school, then, the quality of community life, including levels of change, fear, incivility, poverty, and deterioration, has a direct influence on an area's delinquency rate. It is not some individual property or trait that causes people to commit delinquency but the quality and ambience of the community in which they reside. Conversely, in areas that have high levels of social control and collective efficacy, delinquency rates have been shown to decrease—no matter what the economic situation.

street efficacy
Using one's wits to avoid violent confrontations and to feel safe.

To read an article showing the association between **collective efficacy and crime**, go to academic .cengage.com/criminaljustice/siegel.

Strain theory suggests that while most people share similar values and goals, such as a good education, a nice home, a great car, and stylish clothes, the ability to achieve these personal goals is stratified by socioeconomic class. While the affluent may live out the "American Dream," the poor are shut out from achieving their goals. Because poor kids can't always get what they want, they begin to feel frustrated and angry, a condition referred to as *strain*.

While some kids can cope with feelings of strain, others who feel economically and socially humiliated want to humiliate others in return.[84] Psychologists warn that under these circumstances kids who consider themselves "losers" begin to fear and envy "winners" who are doing very well at their expense. If they fail to take risky aggressive tactics, they are surely going to lose out in social competition and have little chance of future success.[85] Sharp divisions between the rich and poor create an atmosphere of envy and mistrust that may lead to violence and aggression.[86]

Merton's Theory of Anomie

anomie
Normlessness produced by rapidly shifting moral values; according to Merton, anomie occurs when personal goals cannot be achieved using available means.

French sociologist Émile Durkheim coined the term **anomie** (from the Greek *a nomos*, "without norms") to describe a society is one in which rules of behavior (i.e., values, customs, and norms) have broken down during periods of rapid social change or social crisis. Anomie undermined society's social control function. If a society becomes anomic, it can no longer establish and maintain control. Under these circumstances, the will to obey legal codes is strained, and alternatives, such as crime, become more attractive alternatives.

Durkheim's ideas were applied to the onset of crime and delinquency in contemporary society by sociologist Robert Merton in his theory of anomie.[87] Merton used a modified version of the concept of anomie to fit social, economic, and cultural conditions found in modern U.S. society.[88] He found that two elements of culture interact to produce potentially anomic conditions: the clash of culturally defined goals and socially approved means. Contemporary society stresses the goals of acquiring wealth, success, and power. Socially permissible means include hard work, education, and thrift. If there is a dissonance between goals and means, anomie results.

In the United States, Merton argued, legitimate means to acquire wealth are stratified across class and status lines. Indigent lower-class kids, with insufficient formal education and few economic resources, soon find that they are denied the opportunity to get what they want: money, power, success. While everyone may want the same thing, millions of people are simply unable to get them through legal or legitimate means. Consequently, they may develop criminal or delinquent solutions to the problem of attaining goals.

Social Adaptations Merton argued that each person has his or her own concept of the goals of society and the means at his or her disposal to attain them. Table 4.1 shows Merton's diagram of the hypothetical relationship between social goals, the

TABLE 4.1

Typology of Individual Modes of Adaptation

Modes of Adaptation	Cultural Goals	Institutionalized Means
Conformity	+	+
Innovation	+	−
Ritualism	−	+
Retreatism	−	−
Rebellion	±	±

SOURCE: Robert Merton, "Social Structure and Anomie," in *Social Theory and Social Structure* (Glencoe, Ill.: Free Press, 1957).

means for getting them, and the individual actor. Here is a brief description of each of these modes of adaptation:

- *Conformity.* Conformity occurs when individuals both embrace conventional social goals and also have the means at their disposal to attain them. The conformist desires wealth and success and can obtain them through education and a high-paying job. In a balanced, stable society, this is the most common social adaptation. If a majority of its people did not practice conformity, the society would cease to exist.

- *Innovation.* Innovation occurs when an individual accepts the goals of society but rejects or is incapable of attaining them through legitimate means. Many kids desire material goods and luxuries but lack the financial ability to attain them. The resulting conflict forces them to adopt innovative solutions to their dilemma: they steal, sell drugs, or extort money. Of the five adaptations, innovation is most closely associated with criminal behavior.

- *Ritualism.* Ritualists are less concerned about accumulating wealth and instead gain pleasure from practicing traditional ceremonies regardless of whether they have a real purpose or goal. The strict set of manners and customs in religious orders, clubs, and college fraternities encourage and appeal to ritualists.

- *Retreatism.* Retreatists reject both the goals and the means of society. Merton suggests that people who adjust in this fashion are "in the society but not of it." Included in this category are "psychotics, psychoneurotics, chronic autists, pariahs, outcasts, vagrants, vagabonds, tramps, chronic drunkards, and drug addicts." Because such people are morally or otherwise incapable of using both legitimate and illegitimate means, they attempt to escape their lack of success by withdrawing—either mentally or physically.

- *Rebellion.* Rebellion involves substituting an alternative set of goals and means for conventional ones. Revolutionaries who wish to promote radical change in the existing social structure and who call for alternative lifestyles, goals, and beliefs are engaging in rebellion. Rebellion may be a reaction against a corrupt and hated government or an effort to create alternate opportunities and lifestyles within the existing system.

According to anomie theory, social inequality leads to perceptions of anomie. To resolve the goals/means conflict and relieve their sense of strain, some kids innovate by stealing or extorting money, others retreat into drugs and alcohol, others rebel by joining a gang or group, and still others get involved in ritualistic behavior by joining a religious cult.

Anomie and Immigration Considering the economic stratification of U.S. society, and the general emphasis on economic success above all else, anomie predicts that delinquency rates will be higher in lower-class culture. But there are some exceptions to this rule. You may recall that immigrants, especially those from Latin America, have lower delinquency rates than the general population. How can this finding be explained, considering that this group is one where feelings of anomie might be expected? In *Latino Homicide: Immigration, Violence, and Community*, sociologist Ramiro Martinez attempts to explain why the Latino homicide rate is relatively low despite the fact that many Latinos live in substandard communities. One reason is that Latino expectations for success and wealth are also relatively low, a worldview that helps shield them from the influence of residence in deteriorated communities. Moreover, many Latinos are immigrants who have fled conditions in their homelands that are considerably worse than they find in the United States. Since they are now relatively less deprived, the "strain" of living in poverty has less impact.[89] Martinez's conclusions are supported by research conducted by Grace Kao and Marta Tienda who find that despite hardship and socioeconomic disadvantages, immigrants remain committed to their aspirations of conventional success. They believe they have more opportunities in the United States than were available in their countries of origin. Because immigrants often faced harsher environments in their home countries, they are more creative in inventing solutions to their current predicaments that do not involve criminal activities. Thus, because they are oriented toward conventional achievement, immigrants are less likely to seek innovative methods of dealing with anomie and more likely to embrace conformity.[90]

Institutional Anomie Theory

An important addition to the strain literature is the book *Crime and the American Dream*, by Steven Messner and Richard Rosenfeld.[91] Their macro-level version of anomie theory views antisocial behavior as a function of cultural and institutional influences in U.S. society, a model they refer to as institutional anomie theory. Messner and Rosenfeld agree with Merton's view that the success goal is pervasive in American culture. They refer to this as the "American Dream," a term they employ as both a goal and a process. As a goal, the American Dream involves accumulating material goods and wealth via open individual competition. As a process, it involves both being socialized to pursue material success and believing that prosperity is an achievable goal in American culture. In the United States, the capitalist system encourages innovation in pursuit of monetary rewards. Businesspeople such as Bill Gates, Warren Buffett, and Donald Trump are considered national heroes and leaders. Anomic conditions occur because the desire to succeed at any cost drives people apart, weakens the collective sense of community, fosters ambition, and restricts desires to achieve anything that is not material wealth. Achieving a "good name" and respect is not sufficient. Capitalist culture "exerts pressures toward delinquency by encouraging an anomic cultural environment, an environment in which people are encouraged to adopt an 'anything goes' mentality in the pursuit of personal goals . . . [and] the anomic pressures inherent in the American dream are nourished and sustained by an institutional balance of power dominated by the economy."[92]

What is distinct about American society, according to Messner and Rosenfeld, and what most likely determines the exceedingly high national delinquency rate, is that anomic conditions have been allowed to "develop to such an extraordinary degree."[93] There do not seem to be any alternatives that would serve the same purpose or strive for the same goal.

Impact of the American Dream Culture Why does anomie pervade American culture? According to Messner and Rosenfeld, it is because our materialistic culture promotes intense pressures for economic success at the expense of the family, community, and religion. As a result, the value structure of society is dominated by economic realities that weaken institutional social control. In other words, people are so interested in making money that their behavior cannot be controlled by the needs of family or the restraints of morality.

There are three reasons social institutions have been undermined. First, noneconomic functions and roles have been devalued. Performance in other institutional settings—the family, school, or community—is assigned a lower priority than the goal of financial success. Few kids go to school to study the classics; most want a good job and to make money. Second, economic roles are now dominant. Workplace needs now take priority over those of the home, the school, the community, and other aspects of social life. A parent given the opportunity for a promotion thinks nothing of uprooting his family and moving them to another part of the country.

Third, greed and materialism have developed cultlike status. According to Messner and Rosenfeld, delinquency rates remain high in the United States and gangs are ubiquitous because the American Dream mythology ensures that many kids will develop wishes and desires for material goods that cannot be satisfied by legitimate means. Kids will be willing to do anything to get ahead, from cheating on tests to get higher grades to selling drugs on campus.[94] Those who cannot succeed become willing to risk everything, including a prison sentence.

General Strain Theory

Sociologist Robert Agnew's General Strain Theory (GST) helps identify the micro-level or individual influences of strain. Agnew's theory explains why adolescents who feel stress and strain are more likely to engage in delinquent acts.[95]

Multiple Sources of Stress Agnew suggests that delinquency is the direct result of negative affective states—the anger, frustration, and adverse emotions that kids feel in the wake of negative and destructive social relationships. He finds that negative affective states are produced by a variety of sources of strain:

- *Failure to achieve positively valued goals.* This type of strain occurs when a youth aspires for wealth and fame but lacks the financial and educational resources to achieve their goals.[96]

- *Disjunction of expectations and achievements.* This source of strain is produced by a disjunction between expectations and achievements. When kids compare themselves to peers who seem to be doing a lot better financially or socially they will feel strain. For example, when a high school senior is accepted at a good college but not a "prestige school" like some of her friends, she will feel strain. She believes that she has not been treated fairly because the "playing field" is tilted against her or that "other kids have connections."

- *Removal of positively valued stimuli.* Strain may occur because of the actual or anticipated removal or loss of a positively valued stimulus from the individual.[97] The loss of a girlfriend or boyfriend can produce strain, as can the death of a loved one, moving to a new neighborhood or school, or the divorce or separation of parents.[98] The loss of positive stimuli may lead to delinquency as the adolescent tries to prevent the loss, retrieve what has been lost, obtain substitutes, or seek revenge against those responsible for the loss. A child who experiences parental separation or divorce early in his life may seek out deviant peers to help fill his emotional needs and in so doing increases his chances of criminality.[99]

- *Presentation of negative stimuli.* Negative experiences, such as child abuse and neglect, crime victimization, racism and discrimination, physical punishment, family and peer conflict, school failure, and interaction with stressful life events ranging from family breakup to dissatisfaction with friends, can also produce feelings of strain.[100]

According to Agnew, negative experiences such as child abuse and neglect, crime victimization, racism and discrimination, physical punishment, family and peer conflict, and school failure can also produce feelings of strain that lead to negative affective states and antisocial behaviors. Here, Bruce Jackson (right), 21, looks on as his lawyer, Michael Critchley, gives a statement on February 10, 2006, outside the Camden County Hall of Justice in Camden, New Jersey. As a child, Jackson was so severely malnourished by his adoptive mother that he was forced to look for food in his neighbors' garbage. According to General Strain Theory, such experiences may be a precursor to delinquency unless proper coping mechanisms are discovered.

© AP Images/Jose F. Moreno

General Strain Theory (GST)
According to Agnew, the view that multiple sources of strain interact with an individual's emotional traits and responses to produce criminality.

negative affective states
Anger, depression, disappointment, fear, and other adverse emotions that derive from strain.

The Effects of Strain Each type of strain will increase the likelihood of experiencing such negative emotions as disappointment, depression, fear, and, most important, anger. Anger increases perceptions of being wronged and produces a desire for revenge, energizes individuals to take action, and lowers inhibitions. Violence and aggression seem justified if you have been wronged and are righteously angry. Being exposed to negative stimuli gets kids angry and some react inappropriately: they assault their parents and/or teachers; they run away from home or drop out of school; they seek revenge (e.g., vandalize school property), or self-medicate by using drugs and alcohol.[101]

Kids who feel strain are the ones most likely to engage in antisocial behaviors.[102] Some seek out other angry kids and/or join gangs.[103] Peers may pressure them into even more forms of antisocial behavior, creating even more stress in their lives.[104]

Not all kids who feel strain succumb to deviant behaviors but the ones who do, who can't seem to cope, have had a long history of experience with negative stimuli, including being crime victims themselves.[105] Juveniles who are impulsive, lack self-control and have negative emotions are also likely to react to strain with delinquency and antisocial behaviors.[106] In contrast, those people who can call on others for help and have support from family, friends, and social institutions are better able to cope with strain.[107]

Sometimes delinquency can actually relieve these feelings of anger and rage. Although it may be socially disapproved, delinquency can provide relief and satisfaction for someone living an otherwise stress-filled life. Using violence for self-protection may increase feelings of self-worth among those who feel inadequate or intellectually insecure. Kids may lash out to mitigate the effects of strain. Research shows that children who report that they hit or strike their parents also report that they had been the target of parental violence (hitting, slapping). In this case, assaulting their parents may be viewed as a type of remedy for the strain caused by child abuse.[108]

CULTURAL DEVIANCE THEORIES

The third branch of social structure theory combines the effects of social disorganization and strain to explain how kids living in deteriorated neighborhoods react to social isolation and economic deprivation. Because their lifestyle is draining, frustrating, and dispiriting, members of the lower class create an independent subculture with its own set of rules and values. Middle-class culture stresses hard work, delayed gratification, formal education, and being cautious; the lower-class subculture stresses excitement, toughness, risk taking, fearlessness, immediate gratification, and "street smarts." The lower-class subculture is an attractive alternative because the urban poor find that it is impossible to meet the behavioral demands of middle-class society.

Unfortunately, subcultural norms often clash with conventional values. People who have close personal ties to the neighborhood, especially when they are to deviant networks such as gangs and delinquent groups, may find that community norms interfere with their personal desire for neighborhood improvement. So when the police are trying to solve a gang-related killing, neighbors may find that their loyalty to the gang boy and his family outweighs their desire to create a more stable crime-free community by giving information to the police.[109]

Lower-Class Values and Focal Concerns

In his classic 1958 paper, "Lower-Class Culture as a Generating Milieu of Gang Delinquency," Walter Miller identified the unique value system that defines lower-class culture.[110] Conformance to these **focal concerns** dominates life among the lower class. According to Miller, clinging to lower-class focal concerns promotes illegal or violent behavior. Toughness may mean displaying fighting prowess; street smarts may lead to drug deals; excitement may result in drinking, gambling, or drug abuse. Focal concerns do not necessarily represent a rebellion against middle-class values; rather, these values have evolved specifically to fit conditions in lower-class areas. The major lower-class focal concerns are set out in Exhibit 4.1.[111]

According to Miller, loyalty to lower-class culture is a direct cause of urban delinquency. Lower-class adolescents learn to value toughness and want to show they are courageous in the face of any provocation.[112] A reputation for toughness helps them acquire social power while at the same time insulating them from becoming victims. Violence is also seen as a means to acquire the "bling" kids want (nice clothes, flashy cars, and/or jewelry), control or humiliate another person, defy authority, settle drug-related "business" disputes, attain retribution, satisfy the need for thrills or risk taking, and respond to challenges to one's manhood.[113]

The influence of lower-class focal concerns and culture seems as relevant today as when first identified by Miller almost 50 years ago. The Focus on Delinquency feature entitled "The Code of the Streets" discusses a recent version of the concept of cultural deviance.

focal concerns
The value orientation of lower-class culture that is characterized by a need for excitement, trouble, smartness, fate, and personal autonomy.

EXHIBIT **4.1**

Miller's Lower-Class Focal Concerns

Trouble	∥ In lower-class communities, people are evaluated by their actual or potential involvement in making trouble. Getting into trouble includes such behavior as fighting, drinking, and sexual misconduct. Dealing with trouble can confer prestige—for example, when a man establishes a reputation for being able to handle himself well in a fight. Not being able to handle trouble, and having to pay the consequences, can make a person look foolish and incompetent.
Toughness	∥ Lower-class males want local recognition of their physical and spiritual toughness. They refuse to be sentimental or soft and instead value physical strength, fighting ability, and athletic skill. Those who cannot meet these standards risk getting a reputation for being weak, inept, and effeminate.
Smartness	∥ Members of the lower-class culture want to maintain an image of being streetwise and savvy, using their street smarts, and having the ability to outfox and out-con the opponent. Though formal education is not admired, knowing essential survival techniques, such as gambling, conning, and outsmarting the law, is a requirement.
Excitement	∥ Members of the lower class search for fun and excitement to enliven an otherwise drab existence. The search for excitement may lead to gambling, fighting, getting drunk, and sexual adventures. In between, the lower-class citizen may simply "hang out" and "be cool."
Fate	∥ Lower-class citizens believe their lives are in the hands of strong spiritual forces that guide their destinies. Getting lucky, finding good fortune, and hitting the jackpot are all slum dwellers' daily dreams.
Autonomy	∥ Being independent of authority figures, such as the police, teachers, and parents, is required; losing control is an unacceptable weakness, incompatible with toughness.

SOURCE: Walter Miller, "Lower-Class Culture as a Generating Milieu of Gang Delinquency," *Journal of Social Issues 14* (1958): 5–19.

Theory of Delinquent Subcultures

Albert Cohen first articulated the theory of delinquent subcultures in his classic 1955 wbook, *Delinquent Boys*.[114] Cohen's central position was that delinquent behavior of lower-class youths is actually a protest against the norms and values of middle-class U.S. culture. Because social conditions make them incapable of achieving success legitimately, lower-class youths experience a form of culture conflict that Cohen labels **status frustration**.[115] As a result, many of them join together in gangs and engage in behavior that is "non-utilitarian, malicious, and negativistic."[116]

status frustration
A form of culture conflict experienced by lower-class youths because social conditions prevent them from achieving success as defined by the larger society.

Cohen viewed the delinquent gang as a separate subculture, possessing a value system directly opposed to that of the larger society. He describes the subculture as one that "takes its norms from the larger culture, but turns them upside down. The delinquent's conduct is right by the standards of his subculture precisely because it is wrong by the norms of the larger cultures."[117]

According to Cohen, the development of the delinquent subculture is a consequence of socialization practices found in the lower-class inner-city environment. These children lack the basic skills necessary to achieve social and economic success in the demanding U.S. society. They also lack the proper education and therefore do not have the skills upon which to build a knowledge or socialization foundation. He suggests that lower-class parents are incapable of teaching children the necessary techniques for entering the dominant middle-class culture. The consequences of this deprivation include developmental handicaps, poor speech and communication skills, and inability to delay gratification.

Middle-Class Measuring Rods One significant handicap that lower-class children face is the inability to positively impress authority figures, such as teachers, employers, or supervisors. Cohen calls the standards set by these authority figures **middle-class measuring rods**. The conflict and frustration lower-class youths experience when they fail to meet these standards is a primary cause of delinquency. For example, the fact that a lower-class student is deemed by those in power to be substandard or below the average of what is expected can have an important impact on his or her future life chances. A school record may be reviewed by juvenile court authorities and by the military. Because a military record can influence whether or not someone is qualified for certain jobs, it is quite influential.[118] Negative evaluations become part of a permanent file that follows an individual for the rest of his or her life. When he or she wants to improve, evidence of prior failures is used to discourage advancement.

The Code of the Streets

A widely cited view of the interrelationship of culture and behavior is Elijah Anderson's concept of the "code of the streets." Anderson sees that life circumstances are tough for the "ghetto poor"—lack of jobs that pay a living wage, stigma of race, fallout from rampant drug use and drug trafficking, and alienation and lack of hope for the future. Living in such an environment places young people at special risk of delinquency and deviant behavior.

There are two cultural forces running through the neighborhood that shape their reactions. *Decent values* are taught by families committed to middle-class values and representing mainstream goals and standards of behavior. Though they may be better off financially than some of their street-oriented neighbors, they are generally "working poor." They value hard work and self-reliance and are willing to sacrifice for their children; they harbor hopes for a better future for their children. Most go to church and take a strong interest in education. Some see their difficult situation as a test from God and derive great support from their faith and from the church community.

In opposition, *street values* are born in the despair of inner-city life and are in opposition to those of mainstream society. The street culture has developed what Anderson calls a *code of the streets*, a set of informal rules setting down both proper attitudes and ways to respond if challenged. If the rules are violated, there are penalties and sometimes violent retribution.

At the heart of the code is the issue of respect—loosely defined as being treated "right." The code demands that disrespect be punished or hard-won respect will be lost. With the right amount of respect, a person can avoid "being bothered" in public. If he is bothered, not only may he be in physical danger, but he has been disgraced or "dissed" (disrespected). Some forms of dissing, such as maintaining eye contact for too long, may seem pretty mild. But to street kids who live by the code, these actions become serious indications of the other person's intentions and a warning of imminent physical confrontation.

These two orientations—decent and street—socially organize the community. Their coexistence means that kids who are brought up in decent homes must be able to successfully navigate the demands of the street culture. Even in decent families, parents recognize that the code must be obeyed or at the very least negotiated; it cannot simply be ignored.

THE RESPECT GAME

Young men in poor inner-city neighborhoods build their self-image on the foundation of respect. Having "juice" (as respect is sometimes called on the street) means that they can take care of themselves even if it means resorting to violence. For street youth, losing respect on the street can be damaging and dangerous. Once they have demonstrated that they can be insulted, beaten up, or stolen from, they become an easy target. Kids from decent families may be able to keep their self-respect by getting good grades or a scholarship. Street kids do not have that luxury. With nothing to fall back on, they cannot walk away from an insult. They must retaliate with violence.

One method of preventing attacks is to go on the offensive. Aggressive, violence-prone people are not seen as easy prey. Robbers do not get robbed, and street fighters are not the favorite targets of bullies. A youth who communicates an image of not being afraid to die and not being afraid to kill has given himself a sense of power on the street.

Anderson's work has been well received by the criminological community. A number of researchers have found that the code of the streets does exist and that Anderson's observations are valid. Jeffery Fagan's interviews with 150 young men who had experiences with violent crimes while living in some of New York City's toughest neighborhoods found that many alternated their demeanor between decent and street codes of behavior. Both orientations existed side by side within the same individuals. The street code's rules for getting and maintaining respect through aggressive behavior forced many decent youths to situationally adopt a tough demeanor and perhaps behave violently in order to survive an otherwise hostile and possibly dangerous environment.

Critical Thinking

1. Does the code of the street, as described by Anderson, apply in the neighborhood in which you were raised? Is it universal?

2. Is there a form of "respect game" being played out on college campuses? If so, what is the substitute for violence?

SOURCES: Elijah Anderson, *Code of the Street: Decency, Violence, and the Moral Life of the Inner City* (New York: Norton, 2000); Anderson, "Violence and the Inner-City Street Code," in Joan McCord, ed., *Violence and Children in the Inner City* (New York: Cambridge University Press, 1998), pp. 1–30; Anderson, "The Code of the Streets," *Atlantic Monthly* 273:80–94 (1994); Timothy Brezina, Robert Agnew, Francis T. Cullen, and John Paul Wright, "The Code of the Street: A Quantitative Assessment of Elijah Anderson's Subculture of Violence Thesis and Its Contribution to Youth Violence Research," *Youth Violence and Juvenile Justice* 2:303–328 (2004); Jeffrey Fagan, *Adolescent Violence: A View from the Street*, NIJ Research Preview (Washington, DC: National Institute of Justice, 1998).

The Formation of Deviant Subcultures Cohen believes lower-class boys who suffer rejection by middle-class decision makers usually elect to join one of three existing subcultures: the corner boy, the college boy, or the delinquent boy. The *corner boy* role is the most common response to middle-class rejection. The corner boy is not a chronic delinquent but may be a truant who engages in petty or status offenses, such as precocious sex and recreational drug abuse. His main loyalty is to his peer group, on which he depends for support, motivation, and interest. His values, therefore, are those of the group with which he is in close personal contact. The corner boy, well aware of his failure to achieve the standards of the American Dream, retreats into the comforting world of his lower-class peers and eventually becomes a stable member of his neighborhood, holding a menial job, marrying, and remaining in the community.

The *college boy* embraces the cultural and social values of the middle class. Rather than scorning middle-class measuring rods, he actively strives to be successful by those standards. Cohen views this type of youth as one who is embarking on an almost hopeless path, since he is ill-equipped academically, socially, and linguistically to achieve the rewards of middle-class life.

The *delinquent* boy adopts a set of norms and principles in direct opposition to middle-class values. He engages in short-run hedonism, living for today and letting "tomorrow take care of itself."[119] Delinquent boys strive for group autonomy. They resist efforts by family, school, or other sources of authority to control their behavior. They may join a gang because it is perceived as autonomous, independent, and the focus of "attraction, loyalty, and solidarity."[120] Frustrated by their inability to succeed, these boys resort to a process Cohen calls *reaction formation.* Symptoms of reaction formation include overly intense responses that seem disproportionate to the stimuli that trigger them. For the delinquent boy, this takes the form of irrational, malicious, and unaccountable hostility to the enemy, which in this case is "the norms of respectable middle-class society."[121] Reaction formation causes delinquent boys to overreact to any perceived threat or slight. They sneer at the college boy's attempts at assimilation and scorn the corner boy's passivity. The delinquent boy is willing to take risks, violate the law, and flout middle-class conventions.

Cohen's work helps explain the factors that promote and sustain a delinquent subculture. By introducing the concepts of status frustration and middle-class measuring rods, Cohen makes it clear that social forces and not individual traits promote and sustain a delinquent career. By introducing the corner boy, college boy, delinquent boy triad, he helps explain why many lower-class youth fail to become chronic offenders: There is more than one social path open to indigent youth.[122] His work is a skillful integration of strain and social disorganization theories and has become an enduring element of the criminological literature.

Theory of Differential Opportunity

In their classic work *Delinquency and Opportunity*, written more than 40 years ago, Richard Cloward and Lloyd Ohlin combined strain and social disorganization principles into a portrayal of a gang-sustaining delinquent subculture.[123] Cloward and Ohlin maintain that independent delinquent subcultures exist within society, including a delinquent subculture.[124] Youth gangs are an important part of the delinquent subculture and although not all illegal acts are committed by gang youth, they are the source of the most serious, sustained, and costly delinquent behaviors. Delinquent gangs spring up in disorganized areas where youths lack the opportunity to gain success through conventional means. True to strain theory principles, Cloward and Ohlin portray inner-city kids as individuals who want to conform to middle-class values but lack the means to do so.[125]

The centerpiece of the Cloward and Ohlin theory is the concept of **differential opportunity**: The opportunity *for both* successful conventional and delinquent careers is limited. In stable areas, adolescents may be recruited by professional delinquents, drug traffickers, or organized crime groups. Unstable areas, however, cannot support flourishing delinquent opportunities. In these socially disorganized neighborhoods, adult role models are absent, and young delinquents have few opportunities to join established gangs or to learn the fine points of professional crime. In other words, opportunities for success, both illegal and conventional, are closed for the most "truly disadvantaged" youth.

Because of differential opportunity, kids are likely to join one of three types of gangs:

- *Criminal gangs.* Criminal gangs exist in stable lower-class areas in which close connections among adolescent, young adult, and adult offenders create an

middle-class measuring rods
Standards by which teachers and other representatives of state authority evaluate students' behavior; when lower-class youths cannot meet these standards they are subject to failure, which brings on frustration and anger at conventional society.

differential opportunity
The view that lower-class youths, whose legitimate opportunities are limited, join gangs and pursue criminal careers as alternative means to achieve universal success goals.

environment for successful delinquent enterprise.[126] Youths are recruited into established criminal gangs that provide a training ground for a successful delinquent career.

I *Conflict gangs.* Conflict gangs develop in communities unable to provide either legitimate or illegitimate opportunities. These highly disorganized areas are marked by transient residents and physical deterioration. Delinquency in this area is "individualistic, unorganized, petty, poorly paid, and unprotected."[127] Conflict gang members fight to protect their own and their gang's integrity and honor. By doing so, they acquire a "rep," which provides them with a means for gaining admiration from their peers and consequently helps them develop their own self-image.[128]

I *Retreatist gangs.* Retreatists are double failures, unable to gain success through legitimate means and unwilling to do so through illegal ones. Some retreatists have tried crime or violence but are either too clumsy, weak, or scared to be accepted in delinquent or violent gangs. They then "retreat" into a role on the fringe of society. Members of the retreatist subculture constantly search for ways of getting high—alcohol, pot, heroin, unusual sexual experiences, music.

Social Structure Theory and Public Policy

Social structure theory has significantly influenced public policy. If the cause of delinquency is viewed as a function of poverty and lower-class status, than alternatives to delinquency can be provided by giving inner-city youth opportunities to share in the rewards of conventional society.

One approach is to give indigent people direct financial aid through public assistance or welfare. Although welfare has been curtailed under the Federal Welfare Reform Act of 1996, research shows that crime rates decrease when families receive supplemental income through public assistance payments.[129]

Efforts have also been made to reduce delinquency by improving the community structure in inner-city high-crime areas. Crime prevention efforts based on social structure precepts can be traced back to the Chicago Area Project supervised by Clifford R. Shaw. This program attempted to organize existing community structures to develop social stability in otherwise disorganized slums. Today, Operation Weed and Seed is the federal government's major community initiative that aims to prevent, control, and reduce violent crime, drug abuse, and gang activity in targeted high-crime neighborhoods across the country. The Weed and Seed strategy involves a two-pronged approach. First, law enforcement agencies and prosecutors cooperate in "weeding out" criminals who participate in violent crime, gang activity, drug use, and drug trafficking in targeted neighborhoods. Second, "seeding" brings a variety of human services to the area, restoring it through social and economic revitalization.[130]

SOCIAL PROCESS THEORIES

socialization
The process by which human beings learn to adopt the behavior patterns of the community in which they live, which requires them to develop the skills and knowledge necessary to function within their culture and environment.

To some sociological criminologists, an individual's relationship with critical elements of the social process is the key to understanding the onset and continuation of a delinquent career. How you live, they believe, is more important than where you live. According to this view, delinquency is a function of **socialization**, the interactions people have with various organizations, institutions, and processes of society. Most kids are influenced by their family relationships, peer group associations, educational experiences, and interactions with authority figures, including teachers, employers, and agents of the justice system. If these relationships are positive and supportive, kids can succeed within the rules of society; if these relationships are dysfunctional and destructive, conventional success may be impossible, and delinquent solutions may become a feasible alternative. Taken together, this view is referred to as social process theory.

According to the social process theory, proper socialization is the key to behavior. Troubled kids can turn their lives around if they can develop bonds to social institutions and processes. During the sixth annual "Sentenced to the Arts" gallery showing on May 22, 2007, in Kansas City, Missouri, 15-year-old Christopher Van Bibber displays his talent as he makes a painting of the Eiffel Tower. The program helps troubled youth by offering an outlet to channel their energy and emotions. Program officials claim that exposing the kids to painting, sculpting, filmmaking, and other arts has cut down on recidivism, raised grades, and improved self-esteem.

© AP Images/Ed Zurga

The influence of social process theories has endured because the relationship between social class, social structure, and delinquency is still uncertain. Today, more than 12 million kids are living in poor families, yet relatively few become persistent offenders and most who do become offenders later desist from delinquency despite the continuing pressure of poverty and social decay. Some other force, then, must be at work to explain why the majority of at-risk kids do not become persistent delinquent offenders and to explain why some who have no economic or social reason to commit delinquency do so anyway.

What are the elements of socialization that have been linked to delinquency?

I *Family.* The primary influence on children is the family. When parenting is inadequate, a child's maturational processes will be interrupted and damaged. Although much debate still occurs over which elements of the parent-child relationship are most critical, there is little question that family relationships have a significant influence on behavior. There is now evidence that children who grow up in homes where parents use severe discipline, yet lack warmth and are less involved in their children's lives, are prone to antisocial behavior.[131] In contrast, parents who are supportive and effectively control their children in a noncoercive fashion—*parental efficacy*—are more likely to raise children who refrain from delinquency.[132] Delinquency will be reduced if parents provide the type of structure that integrates children into families while giving them the ability to assert their individuality and regulate their own behavior.[133]

I *School.* The literature linking delinquency to poor school performance and inadequate educational facilities is extensive. Youths who feel that teachers do not care, who consider themselves failures, and who do poorly in school are more likely to become involved in a delinquent way of life than adolescents who are educationally successful. Research findings based on studies done over the past two decades indicate that many school dropouts, especially those who have been expelled, face a significant chance of entering a delinquent career.[134] In contrast, doing well in school and developing attachments to teachers have been linked to delinquency resistance.[135]

I *Peer relations.* The typical adolescent struggles to impress his closest friends and to preserve their social circle.[136] If their quest for social acceptance involves peers who engage in antisocial behavior, youths may learn the attitudes that support delinquency and soon find themselves cut off from conventional associates and institutions.[137] Chronic offenders surround themselves with peers who share their antisocial activities, and these relationships seem to be stable over time. Kids who maintain close relations with antisocial peers will sustain their own delinquent behavior into their adulthood[138]

The Effects of Socialization on Delinquency

To many criminologists, the elements of socialization described up to this point are the chief determinants of delinquent behavior. According to this view, adolescents living in even the most deteriorated urban areas can successfully resist inducements to delinquency if they have a positive self-image, learn moral values, and have the support of their parents, peers, teachers, and neighbors. The girl with a positive self-image who is chosen for a college scholarship has the warm, loving support of her parents and is viewed as someone "going places" by friends and neighbors. She is less likely to adopt a delinquent way of life than another adolescent who is abused at home, lives with criminal parents, and whose bond to her school and peer group is shattered because she is labeled a troublemaker.[139] The boy who has learned delinquent behavior from his parents and siblings and then joins a neighborhood gang is much more likely to become an adult criminal than his next-door neighbor who idolizes his hard-working, deeply religious parents. It is socialization, not the social structure, that determines life chances. The more social problems encountered during the socialization process, the greater the likelihood that youths will encounter difficulties and obstacles as they mature, such as being unemployed or becoming a teenage mother.

Theorists who believe that an individual's socialization determines the likelihood of delinquency adopt the social process approach to human behavior. The social process approach has two independent branches:

social learning theory
Hypothesizes that delinquency is learned through close relationships with others; asserts that children are born "good" and learn to be "bad" from others.

I Social learning theory suggests that adolescents learn the techniques and attitudes of crime from close and intimate relationships with delinquent peers; delinquency is a learned behavior.

social control theory
Posits that delinquency results from a weakened commitment to the major social institutions (family, peers, and school); lack of such commitment allows youths to exercise antisocial behavioral choices.

I Social control theory maintains that everyone has the potential to become a delinquent but that most adolescents are controlled by their bonds to society. Delinquency occurs when the forces that bind adolescents to society are weakened or broken.

Put another way, social learning theory assumes adolescents are born good and learn to be bad; social control theory assumes adolescents are born bad and must be controlled in order to be good. Each of these independent branches will be discussed separately.

SOCIAL LEARNING THEORY

Social learning theorists believe delinquency is a product of learning the norms, values, and behaviors associated with delinquent activity. Social learning can involve the actual techniques of crime—how to hot-wire a car or roll a joint—as well as the psychological aspects of criminality—how to deal with the guilt or shame associated with illegal activities. This section briefly reviews the three most prominent forms of social learning theory: differential association theory, differential reinforcement theory, and neutralization theory.

Differential Association Theory

differential association theory
Asserts that criminal behavior is learned primarily within interpersonal groups and that youths will become delinquent if definitions they have learned favorable to violating the law exceed definitions favorable to obeying the law within that group.

One of the most prominent social learning theories is Edwin H. Sutherland's differential association theory. Often considered the preeminent U.S. criminologist, Sutherland first put forth his theory in his 1939 text, *Principles of Criminology.*[140] The final version of the theory appeared in 1947. When Sutherland died in 1950, Donald Cressey, his long-time associate, continued his work. Cressey was so successful in explaining and popularizing his mentor's efforts that differential association remains one of the most enduring explanations of delinquent behavior.

Sutherland's research on white-collar crime, professional theft, and intelligence led him to dispute the notion that delinquency was a function of the inadequacy of children in the lower classes.[141] To Sutherland, delinquency stemmed neither from individual traits nor from socioeconomic position; instead, he believed it to be a function of a learning process that could affect any individual in any culture. Acquiring a behavior is a social learning process, not a political or legal process. Skills and motives conducive to delinquency are learned as a result of contacts with pro-delinquency values, attitudes, and definitions and other patterns of delinquent behavior.

Principles of Differential Association The basic principles of differential association are explained as follows:[142]

I *Delinquent behavior is learned.* Sutherland believes that the tools for crime and delinquency are acquired in the same manner as any other learned behavior, such as writing, painting, or reading.

I *Learning is a by-product of interaction.* Delinquent behavior is learned as a by-product of interacting with others. Children actively participate in the learning process as they interact with other individuals, even their boyfriends or girlfriends.[143] Thus, delinquency cannot occur without the aid of others; it is a function of socialization.

I *Learning occurs within intimate groups.* Learning delinquent behavior occurs within intimate personal groups. Children's contacts with their most intimate social companions—family, friends, peers—have the greatest influence on their deviant behavior and attitude development. Research shows that children who grow up in homes where parents abuse alcohol are more likely to view drinking as being socially and physically beneficial.[144]

I *Criminal techniques are learned.* Some kids may meet and associate with older criminal "mentors" who teach them how to be successful criminals and gain the greatest benefits from their criminal activities.[145] They learn the proper way to pick a lock, shoplift, and obtain and use narcotics. In addition, novice delinquents learn to use the proper terminology for their acts and then acquire "proper" reactions to law violations. For example, getting high on marijuana and learning the proper way to smoke a joint are behavior patterns usually acquired from more experienced companions. Delinquents must learn how to react properly to their illegal acts, such as when to defend them, rationalize them, or show remorse for them.

I *Perceptions of legal code influence motives and drives.* The reaction to social rules and laws is not uniform across society, and children constantly come into contact with others who maintain different views on the utility of obeying the legal code. Some kids they admire may openly disdain or flout the law or ignore its substance. Kids experience what Sutherland calls culture conflict when they are exposed to different and opposing attitudes toward what is right and wrong, moral and immoral. The conflict of social attitudes and cultural norms is the basis for the concept of differential association.

I *Differential associations may vary in duration, frequency, priority, and intensity.* Whether a person learns to obey the law or to disregard it is influenced by the quality of social interactions. Those of lasting duration have greater influence than those that are brief. Similarly, *frequent* contacts have greater effect than rare and haphazard contacts. Sutherland did not specify what he meant by priority, but Cressey and others have interpreted the term to mean the age of children when they first encounter definitions of criminality. Contacts made early in life probably have a greater and more far-reaching influence than those developed later on. Finally, intensity is generally interpreted to mean the importance and prestige attributed to the individual or groups from whom the definitions are learned. The influence of a father, mother, or trusted friend far outweighs the effect of more socially distant figures.

> *Delinquent behavior is an expression of general needs and values, but it is not excused by those general needs and values because nondelinquent behavior is also an expression of those same needs and values.* What Sutherland means here is that delinquency and nondelinquency cannot have the same cause. For example, delinquency cannot be caused by economic needs because poor kids can also get jobs, save money and so on. It is only the learning of deviant norms through contact with an excess of definitions favorable toward delinquency that produces illegal behavior.

According to Sutherland's theory, adolescents will learn to become law violators when they are in contact with kids, groups, or events that produce an excess of definitions favorable toward delinquency and are isolated from counteracting forces. A definition favorable toward delinquency occurs, for example, when a child is exposed to friends who sneak into a theater to avoid paying for a ticket or talk about the virtues of getting high on drugs. A definition unfavorable toward delinquency occurs when friends or parents demonstrate their disapproval of antisocial acts. Neutral behavior, such as reading a book, is neither positive nor negative with respect to law violation. Cressey argues that neutral behavior is important; for example, when a child is occupied doing something neutral, it prevents him or her from being in contact with those involved in delinquent behaviors.[146]

In sum, differential association theory holds that adolescents learn delinquent attitudes and behavior while in their adolescence from close and trusted friends and/or relatives. A delinquent career develops if learned antisocial values and behaviors are not at least matched or exceeded by conventional attitudes and behaviors. Delinquent behavior, then, is learned in a process that is similar to learning any other human behavior.

Neutralization Theory

Neutralization theory is another type of social learning theory.[147] According to this view, the process of becoming a delinquent is a learning experience in which potential delinquents and criminals master techniques that enable them to counterbalance or neutralize conventional values and drift back and forth between illegitimate and conventional behavior. One reason this is possible is the subterranean value structure of American society. Subterranean values are morally tinged influences that have become entrenched in the culture but are publicly condemned. They exist side by side with conventional values and, while condemned in public, may be admired or practiced in private. Examples include viewing pornographic films, drinking alcohol to excess, and gambling on sporting events. In American culture, it is common to hold both subterranean and conventional values; few kids are "all good" or "all bad."

Even the most committed delinquents are not involved in delinquency all the time; they also attend school, family functions, and religious services. Their behavior can be conceived as falling along a continuum between total freedom and total restraint. This process, which is called **drift**, refers to the movement from one extreme of behavior to another, resulting in behavior that is sometimes unconventional, free, or deviant and at other times constrained and sober.[148]

Techniques of Neutralization To neutralize moral constraints, kids develop a distinct set of justifications for their law-violating behavior. These neutralization techniques enable them to temporarily drift away from the rules of the normative society and participate in subterranean behaviors. These techniques of neutralization include the following patterns:[149]

> *Deny responsibility.* Young offenders sometimes claim their unlawful acts were simply not their fault. Delinquents' acts resulted from forces beyond their control or were accidents.

> *Deny injury.* By denying the wrongfulness of an act, delinquents are able to neutralize illegal behavior. For example, stealing is viewed as borrowing; vandalism is considered mischief that has gotten out of hand. Delinquents may find that

subterranean values
The ability of youthful law violators to repress social norms.

drift
Idea that youths move in and out of delinquency and that their lifestyles can embrace both conventional and deviant values.

neutralization techniques
A set of attitudes or beliefs that allow would-be delinquents to negate any moral apprehension they may have about committing crime so that they may freely engage in antisocial behavior without regret.

their parents and friends support their denial of injury. In fact, they may claim that the behavior was merely a prank, helping affirm the offender's perception that delinquency can be socially acceptable.

▮ *Deny the victim.* Delinquents sometimes neutralize wrongdoing by maintaining that the victim of crime "had it coming." Vandalism may be directed against a disliked teacher or neighbor, or homosexuals may be beaten up by a gang because their behavior is considered offensive. Denying the victim may also take the form of ignoring the rights of an absent or unknown victim: for example, stealing from the unseen owner of a department store. It becomes morally acceptable for the criminal to commit such crimes as vandalism when the victims, because of their absence, cannot be sympathized with or respected.

▮ *Condemn the condemners.* An offender views the world as a corrupt place with a dog-eat-dog code. Because police and judges are on the take, teachers show favoritism, and parents take out their frustrations on their kids, it is ironic and unfair for these authorities to condemn his or her misconduct. By shifting the blame to others, delinquents are able to repress the feeling that their own acts are wrong.

▮ *Appeal to higher loyalties.* Novice delinquents often argue that they are caught in the dilemma of being loyal to their own peer group while at the same time attempting to abide by the rules of the larger society. The needs of the group take precedence over the rules of society because the demands of the former are immediate and localized (Figure 4.5).

In sum, the theory of neutralization presupposes a condition that allows people to neutralize unconventional norms and values by using such slogans as "I didn't mean to do it," "I didn't really hurt anybody," "They had it coming to them," "Everybody's picking on me," and "I didn't do it for myself." These excuses allow people to drift into criminal modes of behavior.

Testing Neutralization Theory Attempts have been made to verify the assumptions of neutralization theory empirically, but the results have been inconclusive.[150] One area of research has been directed at determining whether there really is a need for law violators to neutralize moral constraints. The thinking behind this research is this: If delinquents hold values *in opposition* to accepted social norms, then there is really no need to neutralize. So far, the evidence is mixed. Some studies

FIGURE 4.5
Techniques of Neutralization

show that law violators approve of criminal behavior, such as theft and violence, and still others find evidence that even though they may be active participants themselves, delinquents voice disapproval of illegal behavior.[151] Some studies indicate that law violators approve of social values such as honesty and fairness; others come to the opposite conclusion.[152] For example, recent research by criminologist Volkan Topalli finds that neutralization theory may have ignored the influential street culture that exists in highly disadvantaged neighborhoods. Kids living in disorganized, gang-ridden neighborhoods "disrespect authority, lionize honor and violence, and place individual needs above those of all others." Rather than having to neutralize conventional values in order to engage in deviant ones, these offenders do not experience guilt that requires neutralizations; they are "guilt free." There is no need for them to drift into delinquency, because their allegiance to nonconventional values and lack of guilt perpetually leave them in a state of openness to delinquency. Rather than being contrite or ashamed, the offenders Topalli interviewed took great pride in their criminal activities and abilities.[153]

SOCIAL CONTROL THEORY

Social control theory maintains that all kids have the potential to violate the law and that modern society presents many opportunities for illegal activity. Delinquent activities, such as drug abuse and car theft, are often exciting pastimes that hold the promise of immediate reward and gratification.

Considering the attractions of delinquency, the question control theorists pose is, Why do most people obey the rules of society? A choice theorist would respond that it is the fear of punishment; structural theorists would say that obedience is a function of having access to legitimate opportunities; learning theorists would explain that obedience is acquired through contact with law-abiding parents and peers. In contrast, social control theorists argue that people obey the law because their behavior is controlled by their upbringing and socialization. Because they have been properly socialized, most people have developed a strong moral sense, which renders them incapable of hurting others and violating social norms.[154] Properly socialized people believe that getting caught at criminal activity will hurt a dearly loved parent or jeopardize their chance at a college scholarship, or perhaps they feel that their job will be forfeited if they get in trouble with the law. In other words, adolescent behavior, including delinquent activity, is controlled by their attachment and commitment to conventional institutions, individuals, and processes. On the other hand, those who have not been properly socialized, who lack a commitment to others or themselves, are free to violate the law and engage in deviant behavior. Those who are "uncommitted" are not deterred by the threat of legal punishments because they have little to lose.[155]

Self-Concept and Delinquency

Early versions of control theory speculated that control was a product of social interactions. Maladaptive social relations produced weak self-concept and poor self-esteem, rendering kids at risk to delinquency. In contrast, youths who felt good about themselves and maintained a positive attitude were able to resist the temptations of the streets. As early as 1951, sociologist Albert Reiss described how delinquents had weak egos.[156] Scott Briar and Irving Piliavin noted that youths who believe criminal activity will damage their self-image and their relationships with others will be most likely to conform to social rules; they have a *commitment to conformity*. In contrast, those less concerned about their social standing are free to violate the law.[157] In his containment theory, pioneering control theorist Walter Reckless argued that a strong self-image insulates a youth from the pressures and pulls of criminogenic influences in the environment.[158] In a series of studies conducted within the school setting, Reck-

One of the techniques of neutralization is denial of the victim: It is permissible to harm someone if "they had it coming." Here, Bryant Purvis, a member of the so-called "Jena Six," stands in front of the LaSalle Parish Courthouse in Jena, Louisiana, on September 21, 2007. According to custom at Jena High School, white students would gather under a large shade tree, while African American students would get together on bleachers near the auditorium. On August 31, 2006, a black male freshman casually asked the principal whether he could sit under the "white tree" and was told that students could sit wherever they wanted. When some black students began to gather near the tree, they were soon greeted by several nooses hanging from its limbs. The noose, a symbol of lynching in the South, is highly offensive to African Americans. Though the white teens responsible were suspended and the tree cut down, several fights followed in the coming days and racial tensions mounted. On December 4, 2006, Justin Barker was attacked by six black students after he was overheard commenting on a fight in which a black youth was beaten. Though injured, Barker attended a school function that evening. The six boys who were accused of beating Barker were charged with attempted second-degree murder, prompting a national outcry and rallies in their defense. Can the violence that stems from racial disputes and conflict be a function of neutralization? Is it possible that Purvis and the other members of the Jena Six neutralized any personal disinclination to use violence to settle conflicts because they believed that white students such as Barker were racists and responsible for the racial tension in the school?

less and his colleagues found that nondelinquent youths are able to maintain a positive self-image in the face of environmental pressures toward delinquency.[159]

While these early works are critical, Travis Hirschi's vision of social control, articulated in his highly influential 1969 book *Causes of Delinquency*, is now the dominant version of the theory.[160]

Hirschi's Social Bond Theory

In his insightful work, Hirschi links the onset of delinquency to the weakening of the ties that bind people to society. All kids are potential law violators, but they are kept under control by their relationships with friends, parents, neighbors, teachers, and employers. Without these social ties or bonds, and in the absence of sensitivity to and interest in others, they would be free to commit criminal acts. Hirschi does not view society as containing competing subcultures with unique value systems. Most people are aware of the prevailing moral and legal code. He suggests, however, that in all elements of society people vary in how they respond to conventional social rules and values. Among all ethnic, religious, racial, and social groups, people whose bond to society is weak may fall prey to criminogenic behavior patterns.

social bond
Ties a person to the institutions and processes of society; elements of the bond include attachment, commitment, involvement, and belief.

Elements of the Social Bond Hirschi argues that the social bond a person maintains with society is divided into four main elements: attachment, commitment, involvement, and belief.

▌ *Attachment*. Attachment refers to a person's sensitivity to and interest in others.[161] Without a sense of attachment, psychologists believe a person becomes a psychopath and loses the ability to relate coherently to the world. The acceptance of social norms and the development of a social conscience depend on attachment to and caring for other human beings. Attachment to parents is the most important. Even if a family is shattered by divorce or separation, a child must retain a strong attachment to one or both parents. Without this attachment, it is unlikely that feelings of respect for others in authority will develop.

- *Commitment.* Commitment involves the time, energy, and effort expended in conventional lines of action, such as getting an education and saving money for the future. If people build a strong commitment to conventional society, they will be less likely to engage in acts that will jeopardize their hard-won position. A lack of commitment to conventional values may foreshadow a condition in which risk-taking behavior, such as delinquency, becomes a reasonable behavior alternative. The association may be reciprocal. Kids who drink and engage in deviant behavior are more likely to fail in school; kids who fail in school are more likely to later drink and engage in deviant behavior.[162]

- *Involvement.* Heavy involvement in conventional activities leaves little time or opportunity for illegal behavior. When kids become involved in school, recreation, and family, it insulates them from the potential lure of delinquent behavior, whereas idleness enhances it.

- *Belief.* People who live in the same social setting often share common moral beliefs; they may adhere to such values as sharing, sensitivity to the rights of others, and admiration for the legal code. If these beliefs are absent or weakened, an adolescent is more likely to participate in antisocial or illegal acts.

Hirschi further suggests that the interrelationship of social bond elements controls subsequent behavior. Kids who feel kinship and sensitivity to parents and friends should be more likely to adopt and work toward legitimate goals. Those who reject social relationships are more likely to lack commitment to conventional goals. Similarly, youths who are highly committed to conventional acts and beliefs are more likely to be involved in conventional activities.

Testing Social Bond Theory One of Hirschi's most significant contributions was his attempt to test the principal hypotheses of social bond theory. He administered a detailed self-report survey to a sample of more than 4,000 junior and senior high school students in Contra Costa County, California.[163] In a detailed analysis of the data, Hirschi found considerable evidence to support the control theory model. Among Hirschi's more important findings are the following:

- Youths who were strongly attached to their parents were less likely to commit criminal acts.

- Commitment to conventional values, such as striving to get a good education and refusing to drink alcohol and "cruise around," was indicative of conventional behavior.

- Youths involved in conventional activity, such as homework, were less likely to engage in criminal behavior.

- Youths involved in unconventional behavior, such as smoking and drinking, were more delinquency prone.

- Youths who maintained weak and distant relationships with people tended toward delinquency.

- Those who shunned unconventional acts were attached to their peers.

- Delinquents and nondelinquents shared similar beliefs about society.

Supporting Research Hirschi's data lent important support to the validity of control theory. Even when the statistical significance of his findings was less than he expected, the direction of his research data was notably consistent. Only in very rare instances did his findings contradict the theory's most critical assumptions.

Hirschi's version of social control theory has been corroborated by numerous research studies, in the United States and abroad, showing that delinquent youth often feel detached from society.[164] Their relationships within the family, peer group, and school often appear strained, indicative of a weakened social bond.[165] Associations among indicators of lack of attachment, commitment, involvement, and belief with measures of delinquency have tended to be positive and significant.[166] In contrast, strong positive attachments help control delinquency.[167]

I   *Attachment*. Research indicates that, as Hirschi predicts, kids who are attached to their families, friends, and school are less likely to get involved in a deviant peer group and consequently less likely to engage in criminal activities.[168] Teens who are attached to their parents are also able to develop the social skills that equip them both to maintain harmonious social ties and to escape life stresses such as school failure.[169] In contrast, family detachment—including intrafamily conflict, abuse of children, and lack of affection, supervision, and family pride—are predictive of delinquent conduct.[170] In a recent study of adolescent motherhood, Trina Hope, Esther Wilder, and Toni Terling Watt discovered that adolescent mothers who keep their babies reduce deviant activities such as smoking and marijuana use. The birth of a child serves as a mechanism of social control and reduces the likelihood of delinquent behavior. Attachment to a child, even during difficult circumstances, may produce the behavior change predicted by Hirschi.[171]

   Attachment to education is equally important. Youths who are detached from the educational experience are at risk to criminality; those who are committed to school are less likely to engage in delinquent acts.[172] Youths who fail at school and are detached from the educational experience are at risk of criminality; those who seem attached to school are less likely to engage in delinquent acts.[173]

I   *Commitment*. As predicted by Hirschi, kids who are committed to school and educational achievement are less likely to become involved in delinquent behaviors than those who lack such commitment.[174]

I   *Involvement*. Research shows that youths who are involved in conventional leisure activities, such as supervised social activities and noncompetitive sports, are less likely to engage in delinquency than those who are involved in unconventional leisure activities and unsupervised, peer-oriented social pursuits.[175] One study found that students who engage in a significant amount of extracurricular activities from 8th grade through 12th grade are more likely to experience high academic achievement and prosocial behaviors extending into young adulthood.[176]

I   *Belief*. Other research efforts have shown that holding positive beliefs are inversely related to criminality. Children who are involved in religious activities and hold conventional religious beliefs are less likely to become involved in substance abuse.[177] Kids who live in areas marked by strong religious values and who hold strong religious beliefs themselves are less likely to engage in delinquent activities than adolescents who do not hold such beliefs or who live in less devout communities.[178]

Cross-national surveys have also supported the general findings of Hirschi's control theory.[179] For example, one study of Canadian youth found that perceptions of parental attachment were the strongest predictor of delinquent or law-abiding behavior. Teens who are attached to their parents may develop the social skills that equip them both to maintain harmonious social ties and to escape life stresses such as school failure.[180]

Opposing Views   More than 70 published attempts have been made to corroborate social control theory by replicating Hirschi's original survey techniques.[181] There has been significant empirical support for Hirschi's work, but there are also those who question some or all of its elements. Here are some elements that have come under criticism and need further study:

I   *Friendship*. One significant criticism concerns Hirschi's contention that delinquents are detached loners whose bond to their family and friends has been broken. However, a number of research efforts show that delinquents maintain relationships and that their friendship patterns seem similar to conventional youth.[182] Some maintain friendships with and are influenced by deviant peers.[183]

  I *Deviant peers and parents.* Hirschi's conclusion that any form of social attachment is beneficial, even to deviant peers and parents, has also been disputed. Rather than deterring delinquency, attachment to deviant peers and parents may support and nurture antisocial behavior.[184] A number of research efforts have found that youths attached to drug-abusing parents are more likely to become drug users themselves.[185]

  I *Restricted scope.* There is some question as to whether the theory can explain all modes of delinquency (as Hirschi maintains) or is restricted to particular groups or forms of criminality. Control variables seem better able to explain minor delinquency (such as alcohol and marijuana abuse) than more serious criminal acts and associations (such as the association between child abuse and violence).[186]

  I *Gender specific.* Research efforts have found control variables are more predictive of female than male behavior.[187] Perhaps girls are more deeply influenced by the quality of their bond to society than boys.

  I *Changing bonds.* Social bonds seem to change over time, a phenomenon ignored by Hirschi.[188] It is possible that at one age level weak bonds (to parents) lead to delinquency, while at another strong bonds (to peers) lead to delinquency. It is also possible that Hirschi miscalculated the direction of the relationship between delinquency and a weakened social bond.[189] Social bond theory projects that a weakened bond leads to delinquency, but it is possible the chain of events may flow in the opposite direction: Kids who break the law find that their bond to parents, schools, and society eventually becomes weak and attenuated.[190]

  I *Not all involvement is beneficial.* Hirschi argues that involvement in conventional activities enforces the social bond and therefore may be beneficial. But research indicates that involvement in activities that seem normative on the surface, such as rigorous sports activities, may actually encourage delinquency if they involve assuming a deviant or macho self-image.[191] Recent (2007) research by Kathleen Miller and her associates found that kids who join a sports team are more likely to get involved in antisocial acts, especially if they assume a "jock" identity.[192] It is not surprising, then, that Douglas Hartmann and Michael Massoglia found that although participating on high school sports teams is related to lower incidence of some antisocial behaviors such as shoplifting, it is also correlated with higher levels of status offense type behaviors such as drinking.[193]

To read more about **Hirschi's work**, go to academic.cengage.com/ criminaljustice/siegel.

Although these criticisms need to be addressed with further research, the weight of existing empirical evidence supports control theory, and it has emerged as one of the preeminent theories in criminology. For many criminologists, it is perhaps the most important way of understanding the onset of youthful misbehavior.

PUBLIC POLICY IMPLICATIONS OF SOCIAL THEORIES

Social theories have had a major influence on policymaking since the 1950s. Learning theories have greatly influenced the way criminal offenders are dealt with and treated. The effect of these theories has mainly been felt by young offenders, who are viewed as being more salvageable than "hardened" criminals. If people become criminal by learning definitions and attitudes toward criminality, advocates of the social learning approach argue that they can "unlearn" them by being exposed to definitions toward conventional behavior. It is common today for residential and nonresidential programs to offer treatment programs that teach offenders about the harmfulness of drugs, how to forgo delinquent behavior, and how to stay in school. If learning did not affect behavior, such exercises would be futile.

Homeboy Industries

ave gangs and
k the means to
ed to ease the

, located in Los Angeles, California. It
Father Gregory Boyle, a Jesuit priest,
as that when people are employed,
to lead happy, productive, and con-
many programs reflect this viewpoint.
only receive access to numerous free
counseling, job referrals, and life-skills
work (with pay) in the program's sev-
clude silk-screening, maintenance, and
-food café and bakery).

rmer gang members in the program,
. Receiving a paycheck and developing
as tangible benefits of the program. But
intangibles—altered perspectives and
change their lives. Among the many ser-
rogram are:

es. Homeboy assists at-risk, disadvan-
olved youth to find employment. They
me job developers to assist in job place-
ny of their clients are not obvious choices
se job developers go out into the com-
relationships with local businesses, search
would be willing to work with parolees
mbers, and take the time to overcome
reservations. Because of this extra effort,
e to create a positive work environment.

ough a collaboration with the Cathedral of
eboy offers a special program for young
Is Noble (WIN). Participants are assigned
business in an area in which they have
, and Homeboy covers their salary. The
omen are given the opportunity to work
ests them while developing concrete skills
continue to work in the field. Participating
le to make use of extra help at no extra
not only teaches the young men and

women that there are constructive alternatives to life on the streets, but also gives them real work experience, preferably in a company that may hire them after the program. Further, by being placed in a work environment, young people are surrounded by adults who are living examples of a commitment to earning an honest day's wage, and who can serve as mentors.

I *Counseling*. Many of Homeboy's clients face severe challenges adjusting to life outside the gangs. Many are struggling to overcome abusive or dysfunctional home situations, or are trying to transition to life outside prison or detention camps. Youth on probation are now court-mandated to have mental health counseling. Both male and female counselors are able to offer much-needed counseling services to clients, free of charge.

Homeboy's services are open to the community, and have become a welcome and much-needed resource for clients who wish to successfully overcome the pressures of the workplace, or who want to establish a more stable home life. Additionally, as leaving a gang and/or adjusting to life off the streets is an ongoing process and not a simple, one-time decision, having a staff of full-time counselors has proven to be a significant benefit for kids who want to leave the gang life.

Critical Thinking

1. Are there certain classes of offenders, such as sex offenders, that you would ban from programs such as Homeboy Industries or should all kids be accepted?

2. Could participation in such programs label or stigmatize participants and thereafter lock them into a deviant role rather then help them open doors to a conventional life?

SOURCE: Homeboy Industries, www.homeboy-industries.org (accessed November 4, 2007; "L.A.'s Homeboy Industries Intervenes with Gang-Involved Youth," OJJDP News @ a Glance, www.ncjrs.gov/html/ojjdp/news_at_glance/214739/topstory.html (accessed November 4, 2007).

Control theories have also influenced criminal justice and other public policy. Programs have been developed to increase people's commitment to conventional lines of action. Some work at creating and strengthening bonds early in life before the onset of criminality. The educational system has been the scene of numerous programs designed to improve basic skills and create an atmosphere in which youths will develop a bond to their schools. Control theories have focused on the family and have played a key role in putting into operation programs designed to strengthen the bond between parent and child. Others attempt to repair bonds that have been broken and frayed. Examples of this approach are the career, work furlough, and educational opportunity programs being developed in the nation's prisons. These programs are designed to help inmates maintain a stake in society so they will be less willing to resort to criminal activity on their release. One well-known program, Homeboy Industries, directed at helping former gang boys and girls get meaningful employment, is profiled in the accompanying Policy and Practice feature.

Summary

1. Be familiar with the association between social conditions and crime

- According to sociologists, most delinquents are indigent and desperate, not calculating or evil.

- They grew up in deteriorated parts of town and lacked the social support and economic resources familiar to more affluent members of society.

- Social relationships with families, peers, schools, jobs, criminal justice agencies, and the like may play an important role in shaping behavioral choices.

- Crime and delinquency rates are highest in deteriorated inner-city areas.

- Kids living in poor neighborhoods are exposed to a constant stream of antisocial behaviors.

- Political unrest and mistrust, economic stress, and family disintegration are social changes that have been found to precede sharp increases in delinquency rates.

- Millions of people have scant, if any, resources and suffer socially and economically as a result.

- The consequences of racial disparity take a toll on youth. Poverty rates among minority groups are still significantly higher than that of whites.

2. Be familiar with the association between social structure and delinquency

- People in the United States live in a stratified society.

- Social strata are created by the unequal distribution of wealth, power, and prestige.

- Social classes are segments of the population whose members have a relatively similar portion of desirable things and who share attitudes, values, norms, and an identifiable lifestyle.

- Those living in poverty are forced to live in neighborhoods that experience inadequate housing and health care, disrupted family lives, underemployment, and despair.

- Sociologist Oscar Lewis coined the phrase "culture of poverty" to describe this condition.

- Children are hit especially hard by poverty, and being poor during early childhood may have a more severe impact on behavior than it does during adolescence and adulthood.

- Besides their increased chance of physical illness, poor children are much more likely than wealthy children to suffer various social and physical ills, ranging from low birthweight to a limited chance of earning a college degree.

- Latino and African American children are more than twice as likely to be poor as Asian and white children.

- The effects of income inequality, poverty, racism, and despair are viewed by many delinquency experts as key causes of youth crime and drug abuse.

- Kids growing up poor and living in households that lack economic resources are much more likely to get involved in serious crime than their wealthier peers.

3. Describe the principles of social disorganization theory

- Social disorganization theory focuses on the conditions within the urban environment that affect delinquency rates.

- Social disorganization theory ties delinquency rates to socioeconomic conditions.

- Long-term, unremitting poverty undermines a community and its residents. Delinquency rates are sensitive to the destructive social forces operating in lower-class urban neighborhoods.

- Residents develop a sense of hopelessness and mistrust of conventional society. Residents of such areas are frustrated by their inability to become part of the "American Dream."

- Kids growing up in these disadvantaged areas are at risk for delinquency because they hear from adults that there is little hope of success in the conventional world.

- Poverty undermines the basic stabilizing forces of the community—family, school, peers, and neighbors—rendering them weakened, attenuated, and ineffective.

- The ability of the community to control its inhabitants—to assert informal social control—is damaged and frayed.

- The community has become socially disorganized and its residents free to succumb to the lure of antisocial conduct. Without social controls kids are free to join gangs, violate the law, and engage in uncivil and destructive behaviors.

- Neighborhood kids are constantly exposed to disruption, violence, and incivility factors that increase the likelihood that they themselves will become involved in delinquency.

- Neighborhood disintegration and the corresponding erosion of social control are the primary causes of delinquent behavior. Community values, norms, and cohesiveness control behavior choices, not personal decision making.

- While mapping delinquency rates in Chicago, Shaw and McKay noted that distinct ecological areas had developed that could be visualized as a series of concentric zones, each with a stable delinquency rate.

- Social disorganization concepts articulated by Shaw and McKay have remained a prominent fixture of criminological scholarship and thinking for more than 75 years.

4. Discuss the work of social ecologists

- Social ecologists have found an association between delinquency rates and community deterioration: disorder, poverty, alienation, disassociation, and fear of delinquency.

- Poverty becomes "concentrated" in deteriorated areas. As working- and middle-class families flee, elements of the most disadvantaged population are consolidated within inner-city poverty areas.

- People feel safe in neighborhoods that are orderly and in repair. In contrast, those living in neighborhoods that suffer social and physical incivilities are much more likely to be fearful. Put another way, disorder breeds fear.

- The presence of community incivilities, especially when accompanied by relatively high delinquency rates and gang activity, convinces older residents that their neighborhood is dangerous; becoming a crime victim seems inevitable.

- Gangs flourish in deteriorated neighborhoods with high levels of poverty, lack of investment, high unemployment rates, and frequent population turnover.

- Urban areas are undergoing rapid structural changes in racial and economic composition. Some may become multiracial, while others become racially homogeneous. Some areas become stable and family oriented, while in others, mobile, never-married people predominate.

- As areas decline, residents flee to safer, more stable localities.

- Cohesive communities develop collective efficacy: mutual trust, a willingness to intervene in the supervision of children, and the maintenance of public order.

- According to the social ecology school, the quality of community life, including levels of change, fear, incivility, poverty, and deterioration, has a direct influence on an area's delinquency rate.

5. Define the concept of anomie and how it impacts on delinquent behavior

- Strain theory suggests that while most people share similar values and goals, the ability to achieve these personal goals is stratified by socioeconomic class.

- French sociologist Émile Durkheim coined the term "anomie" to describe a society in which rules of behavior have broken down during periods of rapid social change or social crisis.

- Anomie undermines society's social control function.

- Robert Merton in his theory of anomie used a modified version of the concept of anomie to fit social, economic, and cultural conditions found in modern U.S. society.

- He found that two elements of culture interact to produce potentially anomic conditions: the clash of culturally defined goals and socially approved means.

- Merton argued that each person has his or her own concept of the goals of society and the means at his or her disposal to attain them.

- According to anomie theory, social inequality leads to perceptions of anomie.

6. Be familiar with recent developments in strain theory

- Steven Messner and Richard Rosenfeld view antisocial behavior as a function of cultural and institutional influences in U.S. society, a model they refer to as institutional anomie theory.

- The American Dream involves accumulating material goods and wealth via open individual competition.

- Sociologist Robert Agnew's General Strain Theory helps identify the micro-level or individual influences of strain. Agnew's theory explains why individuals who feel stress and strain are more likely to engage in delinquent acts.

- Agnew suggests that delinquency is the direct result of negative affective states—the anger, frustration, and adverse emotions that kids feel in the wake of negative and destructive social relationships.

7. Know what is meant by the term "cultural deviance" and be familiar with theories of cultural deviance

- Cultural deviance theories combine the effects of social disorganization and strain to explain how kids living in deteriorated neighborhoods react to social isolation and economic deprivation.

- Because their lifestyle is draining, frustrating, and dispiriting, members of the lower class create an independent subculture with its own set of rules and values.

- Walter Miller identified the unique value system that defines lower-class culture. Conformance to these focal concerns dominates life among the lower class.

- It is this adherence to the prevailing cultural demands of lower-class society that causes urban delinquency. Research shows that members of the lower class value toughness and want to show they are courageous in the face of provocation.

- Albert Cohen first articulated the theory of delinquent subcultures in his classic 1955 book, *Delinquent Boys*.

- Cohen's central position was that delinquent behavior of lower-class youths is actually a protest against the norms and values of middle-class U.S. culture.

- Because social conditions make them incapable of achieving success legitimately, lower-class youths experience a form of culture conflict.

- Cohen believes lower-class boys who suffer rejection by middle-class decision makers usually elect to join one of three existing subcultures: the corner boy, the college boy, or the delinquent boy.

- In their classic work *Delinquency and Opportunity*, Richard Cloward and Lloyd Ohlin combined strain and social disorganization principles into a portrayal of a gang-sustaining delinquent subculture.

I Cloward and Ohlin maintain that independent delinquent subcultures exist within society, including a delinquent subculture.

I Youth gangs are an important part of the delinquent subculture and although not all illegal acts are committed by gang youth, they are the source of the most serious, sustained, and costly delinquent behaviors.

I Delinquent gangs spring up in disorganized areas where youths lack the opportunity to gain success through conventional means.

8. Discuss the concept of social process and socialization

I Some sociological criminologists believe that how you live is more important than where you live.

I According to this view, delinquency is a function of socialization, the interactions people have with various organizations, institutions, and processes of society.

I Most kids are influenced by their family relationships, peer group associations, educational experiences, and interactions with authority figures, including teachers, employers, and agents of the justice system.

I If these relationships are positive and supportive, kids can succeed within the rules of society; if these relationships are dysfunctional and destructive, conventional success may be impossible, and delinquent solutions may become a feasible alternative.

9. Be familiar with the concept of social learning and social learning theories

I One of the most prominent social learning theories is Edwin H. Sutherland's differential association theory, which asserts that criminal behavior is learned primarily within interpersonal groups and that youths will become delinquent if definitions they have learned favorable to violating the law exceed definitions favorable to obeying the law within that group.

I A delinquent career develops if learned antisocial values and behaviors are not at least matched or exceeded by conventional attitudes and behaviors.

I Neutralization theory is another type of social learning theory. According to this view, the process of becoming a delinquent is a learning experience in which potential delinquents and criminals master techniques that enable them to counterbalance or neutralize conventional values and drift back and forth between illegitimate and conventional behavior.

10. Discuss the elements of social control theory

I Social control theory maintains that all people have the potential to violate the law and that modern society presents many opportunities for illegal activity.

I Social control theorists argue that people obey the law because behavior and passions are being controlled by internal and external forces.

I Travis Hirschi links the onset of delinquency to the weakening of the ties that bind people to society.

I Hirschi argues that the social bond a person maintains with society is divided into four main elements: attachment, commitment, involvement, and belief.

I Youths who are strongly attached to their parents are less likely to commit criminal acts.

I Youths involved in conventional activity, such as homework, are less likely to engage in criminal behavior.

I Youths who maintain weak and distant relationships with people tend toward delinquency.

Key Terms

stratified society, p. 116
culture of poverty, p. 117
at-risk youth, p. 117
underclass, p. 117
truly disadvantaged, p. 118
social structure theories, p. 118
enculturated, p. 119
social disorganization theory, p. 119
strain theory, p. 119
cultural deviance theory, p. 120
cultural transmission, p. 120

social control, p. 120
transitional neighborhood, p. 120
social ecology, p. 121
siege mentality, p. 123
collective efficacy, p. 124
street efficacy, p. 125
anomie, p. 126
General Strain Theory (GST), p. 129
negative affective states, p. 129
focal concerns, p. 130
status frustration, p. 131

middle-class measuring rods, p. 131
differential opportunity, p. 133
socialization, p. 134
social learning theory, p. 136
social control theory, p. 136
differential association theory, p. 136
subterranean values, p. 138
drift, p. 138
neutralization techniques, p. 138
social bond, p. 141

Viewpoint

You have just been appointed as a presidential adviser on urban problems. The president informs you that he wants to initiate a demonstration project in a major city aimed at showing that government can do something to reduce poverty, crime, and drug abuse. The area he has chosen for development is a large inner-city neighborhood with more than 100,000 residents. The neighborhood suffers from disorganized community structure, poverty, and hopelessness. Predatory delinquent gangs run free and terrorize local merchants and citizens. The school system has failed to provide opportunities and education experiences sufficient to dampen enthusiasm for gang recruitment. Stores, homes, and public buildings are deteriorated and decayed. Commercial enterprise has fled the area, and civil servants are reluctant to enter the neighborhood. There is an uneasy truce among the various ethnic and racial groups that populate the area. Residents feel that little can be done to bring the neighborhood back to life.

You are faced with suggesting an urban redevelopment program that can revitalize the area and eventually bring down the crime rate. You can bring any element of the public and private sector to bear on this rather overwhelming problem—including the military! You can also ask private industry to help in the struggle, promising them tax breaks for their participation.

▌ Do you believe that living in such an area contributes to high delinquency rates? Or is poverty merely an excuse and delinquency a matter of personal choice?

▌ What programs do you feel could break the cycle of urban poverty?

▌ Would reducing the poverty rate produce a lowered delinquency rate?

▌ What role does the family play in creating delinquent behaviors?

Doing Research on the Web

The National Center for Children in Poverty has a great deal of information that can help formulate an answer to these questions. CARE is a leading humanitarian organization fighting global poverty. Its site also has a lot of useful information on child poverty.

To access these websites, visit
academic.cengage.com/criminaljustice/siegel

Questions for Discussion

1. Is there a transitional area in your town or city?

2. Is it possible that a distinct lower-class culture exists? Are lower-class values different from those of the middle class?

3. Have you ever perceived anomie? What causes anomie? Is there more than one cause of strain?

4. How does poverty cause delinquency?

5. Do middle-class youths become delinquent for the same reasons as lower-class youths?

Notes

1. Rena Havner, "DA: Teacher Attack Was Gang-Related," *Mobile Press Register*, 30 May 2007, www.al.com/news/press-register/index.ssf?/base/news/1180516798143650.xml&coll=3 (accessed June 29, 2007).

2. Steven Messner and Richard Rosenfeld, *Crime and the American Dream* (Belmont, CA: Wadsworth, 1994), p. 11.

3. Edwin Lemert, *Human Deviance, Social Problems and Social Control.*

4. Gary LaFree, *Losing Legitimacy: Street Crime and the Decline of Social Institutions in America* (Boulder, CO: Westview, 1998).

5. Lemert, *Human Deviance, Social Problems, and Social Control.*

6. See, generally, Stephen Cernkovich and Peggy Giordano, "Family Relationships and Delinquency," *Criminology* 25:295–321 (1987); Paul Howes and Howard Markman, "Marital Quality and Child Functioning: A Longitudinal Investigation," *Child Development* 60:1044–1051 (1989).

7. Lance Hannon, "Extremely Poor Neighborhoods and Homicide," *Social Science Quarterly* 86:1418–1434 (2005); Geetanjali Dabral Datta, S. V. Subramanian. Graham Colditz, Ichiro Kawachi, Julie Palmer, and Lynn Rosenberg, "Individual, Neighborhood, and State-Level Predictors of Smoking among U.S. Black Women: A Multilevel Analysis," *Social Science and Medicine* 63:1034–1044 (2006).

8. Stacey Nofziger and Don Kurtz, "Violent Lives: A Lifestyle Model Linking Exposure to Violence to Juvenile Violent Offending," *Journal of Research in Crime and Delinquency* 42:3–26 (2005). Joanne Kaufman, "Explaining the Race/Ethnicity–Violence Relationship: Neighborhood Context and Social Psychological Processes," *Justice Quarterly* 22:224–251 (2005).

9. Justin Patchin, Beth Huebner, John McCluskey, Sean Varano, and Timothy Bynum, "Exposure to Community Violence and Childhood Delinquency," *Crime and Delinquency* 52:307–332 (2006).

10. Gary LaFree, *Losing Legitimacy: Street Crime and the Decline of Social Institutions in America* (Boulder, CO: Westview, 1998).

11. Sam Roberts, *Who We Are Now: The Changing Face of America in the Twenty-First Century* (New York: Times Books, Henry Holt, 2004).

12. Carter Hay, Edward Fortson, Dusten Hollist, Irshad Altheimer, and Lonnie Schaible, "Compounded Risk: The Implications for Delinquency of Coming from a Poor Family that Lives in a Poor Community," *Journal of Youth and Adolescence* 36:593–605 (2007).

13. Oscar Lewis, "The Culture of Poverty," *Scientific American* 215:19–25 (1966).

14. James Ainsworth-Darnell and Douglas Downey, "Assessing the Oppositional Culture Explanation for Racial/Ethnic Differences in School Performances," *American Sociological Review* 63:536–553 (1998).

15. Barbara Warner, "The Role of Attenuated Culture in Social Disorganization Theory," *Criminology* 41:73–97 (2003).

16. Jeanne Brooks-Gunn and Greg J. Duncan, "The Effects of Poverty on Children," *Future of Children* 7:34–39 (1997).

17. Ibid.

18. Greg Duncan, W. Jean Yeung, Jeanne Brooks-Gunn, and Judith Smith, "How Much Does Childhood Poverty Affect the Life Chances of Children?" *American Sociological Review* 63:406–423 (1998).

19. Ibid., p. 409.

20. Gary Evans, Nancy Wells, and Annie Moch, "Housing and Mental Health: A Review of the Evidence and a Methodological and Conceptual Critique," *Journal of Social Issues* 59:475–501 (2003).

21. UCLA Center for Health Policy Research, "The Health of Young Children in California: Findings from the 2001 California Health Interview Survey," (Los Angeles: UCLA Center for Health Policy Research, 2003).

22. William Julius Wilson, *The Truly Disadvantaged* (Chicago: University of Chicago Press, 1987).

23. Karen Parker and Matthew Pruitt, "Poverty, Poverty Concentration, and Homicide," *Social Science Quarterly* 81:555–582 (2000).

24. Karen Parker, "Industrial Shift, Polarized Labor Markets, and Urban Violence: Modeling the Dynamics between the Economic Transformation and Disaggregated Homicide," *Criminology* 42:619–645 (2004); Tim Wadsworth and Charis Kubrin, "Structural Factors and Black Interracial Homicide: A New Examination of the Causal Process," *Criminology* 42:647–672 (2004).

25. David Bjerk, "Measuring the Relationship Between Youth Criminal Participation and Household Economic Resources," *Journal of Quantitative Criminology* 23:23–39 (2007).

26. See Charles Tittle and Robert Meier, "Specifying the SES/Delinquency Relationship," *Criminology* 28:271–295 (1990), at 293.

27. Hilary Byrnes, Chen Meng-Jinn, Brenda Miller, and Eugene Maguin, "The Relative Importance of Mothers' and Youths' Neighborhood Perceptions for Youth Alcohol Use and Delinquency," *Journal of Youth and Adolescence* 36:649–659 (2007).

28. Clifford R. Shaw and Henry D. McKay, *Juvenile Delinquency and Urban Areas*, rev. ed. (Chicago: University of Chicago Press, 1972), p. 355.

29. Frederick Thrasher, *The Gang* (Chicago: University of Chicago Press, 1927).

30. Robert Bursik and Harold Grasmick, "The Multiple Layers of Social Disorganization," paper presented at the annual meeting of the American Society of Criminology, New Orleans, November 1992; Robert Bursik and Harold Grasmick, "Longitudinal Neighborhood Profiles in Delinquency: The Decomposition of Change," *Journal of Quantitative Criminology* 8:247–256 (1992).

31. Shaw and McKay, *Juvenile Delinquency and Urban Areas*, rev. ed.

32. Steven Messner, Lawrence Raffalovich, and Richard McMillan, "Economic Deprivation and Changes in Homicide Arrest Rates for White and Black Youths, 1967–1998: A National Time Series—Analysis," *Criminology* 39:591–614 (2001).

33. Claire Valier, "Foreigners, Crime and Changing Mobilities," *British Journal of Criminology* 43:1–21 (2003).

34. For a discussion of these issues, see Robert Bursik, Jr., "Social Disorganization and Theories of Crime and Delinquency: Problems and Prospects," *Criminology* 26:519–552 (1988).

35. Robert Sampson, "Effects of Socioeconomic Context of Official Reaction to Juvenile Delinquency," *American Sociological Review* 51:876–885 (1986).

36. Jeffrey Fagan, Ellen Slaughter, and Eliot Hartstone, "Blind Justice? The Impact of Race on the Juvenile Justice Process," *Crime and Delinquency* 33:224–258 (1987); Merry Morash, "Establishment of a Juvenile Police Record," *Criminology* 22:97–113 (1984).

37. Stacy De Coster, Karen Heimer, and Stacy Wittrock, "Neighborhood Disadvantage, Social Capital, Street Context, and Youth Violence," *Sociological Quarterly* 47:723–753 (2006).

38. See, generally, Bursik, "Social Disorganization and Theories of Crime and Delinquency," pp. 519–552.

39. William Spelman, "Abandoned Buildings: Magnets for Crime?" *Journal of Criminal Justice* 21:481–493 (1993).

40. Keith Harries and Andrea Powell, "Juvenile Gun Crime and Social Stress: Baltimore, 1980–1990," *Urban Geography* 15:45–63 (1994).

41. Ellen Kurtz, Barbara Koons, and Ralph Taylor, "Land Use, Physical Deterioration, Resident-Based Control, and Calls for Service on Urban Streetblocks," *Justice Quarterly* 15:121–149 (1998).

42. Paul Stretesky, Amie Schuck, and Michael Hogan, "Space Matters: An Analysis of Poverty, Poverty Clustering, and Violent Crime," *Justice Quarterly* 21:817–841 (2004).

43. Jeffrey Morenoff, Robert Sampson, and Stephen Raudenbush, "Neighborhood Inequality, Collective Efficacy, and the Spatial Dynamics of Urban Violence," *Criminology* 39:517–560 (2001).

44. Gregory Squires and Charis Kubrin, "Privileged Places: Race, Uneven Development and the Geography of Opportunity in Urban America," *Urban Studies* 42:47–68 (2005).

45. Scott Menard and Delbert Elliott, "Self-Reported Offending, Maturational Reform, and the Easterlin Hypothesis," *Journal of Quantitative Criminology* 6:237–268 (1990).

46. Joseph Schafer, Beth Huebner, and Timothy Bynum, "Fear of Crime and Criminal Victimization: Gender-Based Contrasts," *Journal of Criminal Justice* 34:285–301 (2006).

47. Xu Yili, Mora Fiedler, and Karl Flaming, "Discovering the Impact of Community Policing: The Broken Windows Thesis, Collective Efficacy, and Citizens' Judgment," *Journal of Research in Crime and Delinquency* 42:147–186 (2005).

48. Matthew Lee and Terri Earnest, "Perceived Community Cohesion and Perceived Risk of Victimization: A Cross-National Analysis," *Justice Quarterly* 20:131–158 (2003); Stephanie Greenberg, "Fear and Its Relationship to Crime, Neighborhood Deterioration, and Informal Social Control," in James Byrne and Robert Sampson, eds., *The Social Ecology of Crime* (New York: Springer Verlag, 1985), pp. 47–62.

49. Pamela Wilcox, Neil Quisenberry, and Shayne Jones, "The Built Environment and Community Crime Risk Interpretation," *Journal of Research in Crime and Delinquency* 40:322–345 (2003).

50. C. L. Storr, C.-Y. Chen, and J. C. Anthony, " 'Unequal Opportunity': Neighborhood Disadvantage and the Chance to Buy Illegal Drugs," *Journal of Epidemiology and Community Health* 58:231–238 (2004).

51. Wesley Skogan, "Fear of Crime and Neighborhood Change," in Albert Reiss and Michael Tonry, eds., *Communities and Crime* (Chicago: University of Chicago Press, 1986), pp. 191–232.

52. Margo Wilson and Martin Daly, "Life Expectancy, Economic Inequality, Homicide, and Reproductive Timing in Chicago Neighborhoods," *British Journal of Medicine* 314:1271–1274 (1997).

53. Pamela Wilcox Rountree and Kenneth Land, "Burglary Victimization, Perceptions of Crime Risk, and Routine Activities: A Multilevel Analysis across Seattle Neighborhoods and Census Tracts," *Journal of Research in Crime and Delinquency* 33:147–180 (1996).

54. Tim Phillips and Philip Smith, "Emotional and Behavioural Responses to Everyday Incivility," *Journal of Sociology* 40:378–399 (2004); Catherine E. Ross, John Mirowsky, and Shana Pribesh, "Powerlessness and the Amplification of Threat: Neighborhood Disadvantage, Disorder, and Mistrust," *American Sociological Review* 66:568–580 (2001).

55. William Terrill and Michael Reisig, "Neighborhood Context and Police Use of Force," *Journal of Research in Crime and Delinquency* 40:291–321 (2003).

56. G. David Curry and Irving Spergel, "Gang Homicide, Delinquency, and Community," *Criminology* 26:381–407 (1988).

57. Lawrence Rosenthal, "Gang Loitering and Race," *Journal of Criminal Law and Criminology* 91:99–160 (2000).

58. Finn-Aage Esbensen and David Huizinga, "Community Structure and Drug Use: From a Social Disorganization Perspective," *Justice Quarterly* 7:691–709 (1990).

59. Bridget Freisthler, Elizabeth Lascala, Paul Gruenewald, and Andrew Treno, "An Examination of Drug Activity: Effects of Neighborhood Social Organization on the Development of Drug Distribution Systems," *Substance Use and Misuse* 40:671–686 (2005).

60. Micere Keels, Greg Duncan, Stefanie Deluca, Ruby Mendenhall, and James Rosenbaum, "Fifteen Years Later: Can Residential Mobility Programs Provide a Long-Term Escape from Neighborhood Segregation, Crime, and Poverty?" *Demography* 42:51–72 (2005).

61. Wesley Skogan, *Disorder and Decline: Crime and the Spiral of Decay in American Neighborhoods* (New York: Free Press, 1990), pp. 15–35.

62. Jeffrey Michael Cancino, "The Utility of Social Capital and Collective Efficacy: Social Control Policy in Nonmetropolitan Settings," *Criminal Justice Policy Review* 16:287–318 (2005); Chris Gibson, Jihong Zhao, Nicholas Lovrich, and Michael Gaffney, "Social Integration, Individual Perceptions of Collective Efficacy, and Fear of Crime in Three Cities," *Justice Quarterly* 19:537–564 (2002).

63. Robert J. Sampson and Stephen W. Raudenbush, *Disorder in Urban Neighborhoods Does It Lead to Crime?* (Washington, DC: National Institute of Justice, 2001).

64. Andrea Altschuler, Carol Somkin, and Nancy Adler, "Local Services and Amenities, Neighborhood Social Capital, and Health," *Social Science and Medicine* 59:1219–1230 (2004).

65. Steven Messner, Eric Baumer, and Richard Rosenfeld "Dimensions of Social Capital and Rates of Criminal Homicide," *American Sociological Review* 69:882–905 (2004).

66. Michael Reisig and Jeffrey Michael Cancino, "Incivilities in Nonmetropolitan Communities: The Effects of Structural Constraints, Social Conditions, and Crime," *Journal of Criminal Justice* 32:15–29 (2004).

67. Robert Sampson, Jeffrey Morenoff, and Felton Earls, "Beyond Social Capital: Spatial Dynamics of Collective Efficacy for Children," *American Sociological Review* 64:633–660 (1999).

68. Donald Black, "Social Control as a Dependent Variable," in D. Black, ed., *Toward a General Theory of Social Control* (Orlando: Academic Press, 1990).

69. Jennifer Beyers, John Bates, Gregory Pettit, and Kenneth Dodge, "Neighborhood Structure, Parenting Processes, and the Development of Youths' Externalizing Behaviors: A Multilevel Analysis," *American Journal of Community Psychology* 31:35–53 (2003).

70. Ralph Taylor, "Social Order and Disorder of Street Blocks and Neighborhoods: Ecology, Microecology, and the Systemic Model of Social Disorganization," *Journal of Research in Crime and Delinquency* 34:113–155 (1997).

71. Skogan, *Disorder and Decline.*

72. Jodi Eileen Morris, Rebekah Levine Coley, and Daphne Hernandez, "Out-of-School Care and Problem Behavior Trajectories among Low-Income Adolescents: Individual, Family, and Neighborhood," *Child Development* 75:948–965 (2004).

73. Ruth Triplett, Randy Gainey, and Ivan Sun, "Institutional Strength, Social Control, and Neighborhood Crime Rates," *Theoretical Criminology* 7:439–467 (2003); Fred Markowitz, Paul Bellair, Allen Liska, and Jianhong Liu, "Extending Social Disorganization Theory: Modeling the Relationships between Cohesion, Disorder, and Fear," *Criminology* 39:293–320 (2001).

74. Maria Velez, "The Role of Public Social Control in Urban Neighborhoods: A Multi-Level Analysis of Victimization Risk," *Criminology* 39:837–864 (2001).

75 David Klinger, "Negotiating Order in Patrol Work: An Ecological Theory of Police Response to Deviance," *Criminology* 35:277–306 (1997).

76. Robert Kane, "Compromised Police Legitimacy as a Predictor of Violent Crime in Structurally Disadvantaged Communities," *Criminology* 43:469–498 (2005).

77. Robert Sampson, "Neighborhood and Community," *New Economy* 11:106–113 (2004).

78 Robert Bursik and Harold Grasmick, "Economic Deprivation and Neighborhood Crime Rates, 1960–1980," *Law and Society Review* 27:263–278 (1993).

79. Delbert Elliott, William Julius Wilson, David Huizinga, Robert Sampson, Amanda Elliott, and Bruce Rankin, "The Effects of Neighborhood Disadvantage on Adolescent Development," *Journal of Research in Crime and Delinquency* 33:389–426 (1996).

80. Ibid., p. 414.

81. Patrick Sharkey, "Navigating Dangerous Streets: The Sources and Consequences of Street Efficacy," *American Sociological Review* 71:826–846 (2006).

82. Ibid.

83. Eric Silver and Lisa Miller, "Sources of Informal Social Control in Chicago Neighborhoods," *Criminology* 42:551–585 (2004).

84. John Braithwaite, "Poverty Power, White-Collar Crime, and the Paradoxes of Criminological Theory," *Australian and New Zealand Journal of Criminology* 24:40–58 (1991).

85. Wilson and Daly, "Life Expectancy, Economic Inequality, Homicide, and Reproductive Timing in Chicago Neighborhoods."

86. P. M. Krueger, S. A. Bond Huie, R. G. Rogers, and R. A. Hummer, "Neighborhoods and Homicide Mortality: An Analysis of Race/Ethnic Differences," *Journal of Epidemiology and Community Health* 58:223–230 (2004).

87. Robert Merton, *Social Theory and Social Structure*, enlarged ed. (New York: Free Press, 1968).

88. For an analysis, see Richard Hilbert, "Durkheim and Merton on Anomie: An Unexplored Contrast in Its Derivatives," *Social Problems* 36:242–256 (1989).

89. Ramiro Martinez, Jr., *Latino Homicide: Immigration, Violence, and Community* (New York: Routledge, 2002).

90. Grace Kao and Marta Tienda, "Optimism and Achievement: The Educational Performance of Immigrant Youth," *Social Science Quarterly* 76:1–19 (1995).

91. Messner and Rosenfeld, *Crime and the American Dream.*

92. Ibid., p. 61.

93. Steven Messner and Richard Rosenfeld, "An Institutional-Anomie Theory of the Social Distribution of Crime," paper presented at the annual meeting of the American Society of Criminology, Phoenix, November 1993.

94. Lisa Muftić, "Advancing Institutional Anomie Theory," *International Journal of Offender Therapy and Comparative Criminology* 50:630–653 (2006).

95. Robert Agnew, "Foundation for a General Strain Theory of Crime and Delinquency," *Criminology* 30:47–87 (1992).

96. Stephen Baron, "Street Youth, Strain Theory, and Crime," *Journal of Criminal Justice* 34:209–223 (2006).

97. Agnew, "Foundation for a General Strain Theory of Crime and Delinquency," p. 57.

98. Tami Videon, "The Effects of Parent–Adolescent Relationships and Parental Separation on Adolescent Well-Being," *Journal of Marriage and the Family* 64:489–504 (2002).

99. Cesar Rebellon, "Reconsidering the Broken Homes/Delinquency Relationship and Exploring Its Mediating Mechanism(s)," *Criminology* 40:103–135 (2002).

100. Ronald Simons, Yi Fu Chen, and Eric Stewart, "Incidents of Discrimination and Risk for Delinquency: A Longitudinal Test of Strain Theory with an African American Sample," *Justice Quarterly* 20:827–854 (2003); Robert Agnew and Helene Raskin White, "An Empirical Test of General Strain Theory," *Criminology* 30:475–499 (1992).

101. Sherod Thaxton and Robert Agnew, "The Nonlinear Effects of Parental and Teacher Attachment on Delinquency: Disentangling Strain from Social Control Explanations," *Justice Quarterly* 21:763–791 (2004).

102. Stacy De Coster and Lisa Kort-Butler, "How General Is General Strain Theory?" *Journal of Research in Crime and Delinquency* 43:297–325 (2006).

103. Paul Mazerolle, Velmer Burton, Francis Cullen, T. David Evans, and Gary Payne, "Strain, Anger, and Delinquent Adaptations Specifying General Strain Theory," *Journal of Criminal Justice* 28:89–101 (2000); Paul Mazerolle and Alex Piquero, "Violent Responses to Strain: An Examination of Conditioning Influences," *Violence and Victimization* 12:323–345 (1997).

104. George E. Capowich, Paul Mazerolle, and Alex Piquero, "General Strain Theory, Situational Anger, and Social Networks: An Assessment of Conditioning Influences," *Journal of Criminal Justice* 29:445–461 (2001).
105. Carter Hay and Michelle Evans, "Violent Victimization and Involvement in Delinquency: Examining Predictions from General Strain Theory," *Journal of Criminal Justice* 34:261–274 (2006).
106. Robert Agnew, Timothy Brezina, John Paul Wright, and Francis T. Cullen, "Strain, Personality Traits, and Delinquency: Extending General Strain Theory," *Criminology* 40:43–71 (2002).
107. Wan-Ning Bao, Ain Haas, and Yijun Pi, "Life Strain, Coping, and Delinquency in the People's Republic of China," *International Journal of Offender Therapy and Comparative Criminology* 51:9–24 (2007).
108. Timothy Brezina, "The Functions of Aggression: Violent Adaptations to Interpersonal Violence," paper presented at the annual meeting of the American Society of Criminology, San Diego, 1997.
109. Christopher Browning, Seth Feinberg, and Robert D. Dietz, "The Paradox of Social Organization: Networks, Collective Efficacy, and Violent Crime in Urban Neighborhoods," *Social Forces* 83:503–534 (2004).
110. Walter Miller, "Lower-Class Culture as a Generating Milieu of Gang Delinquency," *Journal of Social Issues* 14:5–19 (1958).
111. Ibid., pp. 14–17.
112. Fred Markowitz and Richard Felson, "Social-Demographic Attitudes and Violence," *Criminology* 36:117–138 (1998).
113. Jeffrey Fagan, *Adolescent Violence: A View from the Street*, NIJ Research Preview (Washington, DC: National Institute of Justice, 1998).
114. Albert Cohen, *Delinquent Boys* (New York: Free Press, 1955).
115. Ibid., p. 25.
116. Ibid., p. 28.
117. Ibid.
118. Clarence Schrag, *Crime and Justice American Style* (Washington, DC: U.S. Government Printing Office, 1971), p. 74.
119. Cohen, *Delinquent Boys*, p. 30.
120. Ibid., p. 31.
121. Ibid., p. 133.
122. J. Johnstone, "Social Class, Social Areas, and Delinquency," *Sociology and Social Research* 63:49–72 (1978); Joseph Harry, "Social Class and Delinquency: One More Time," *Sociological Quarterly* 15:294–301 (1974).
123. Richard Cloward and Lloyd Ohlin, *Delinquency and Opportunity* (New York: Free Press, 1960).
124. Ibid., p. 7.
125. Ibid., p. 85.
126. Ibid., p. 171.
127. Ibid., p. 73.
128. Ibid., p. 24.
129. James DeFronzo, "Welfare and Burglary," *Crime and Delinquency* 42:223–230 (1996).
130. For more on Operation Weed and Seed, see Blaine Bridenball and Paul Jesilow, "Weeding Criminals or Planting Fear: An Evaluation of a Weed and Seed Project," *Criminal Justice Review* 30:64–89 (2005).
131. Ronald Simons, Chyi-In Wu, Kuei-Hsiu Lin, Leslie Gordon, and Rand Conger, "A Cross-Cultural Examination of the Link between Corporal Punishment and Adolescent Antisocial Behavior," *Criminology* 38:47–79 (2000).
132. John Paul Wright and Francis Cullen, "Parental Efficacy and Delinquent Behavior: Do Control and Support Matter?" *Criminology* 39:677–706 (2001).
133. Karol Kumpfer and Rose Alvarado, "Strengthening Approaches for the Prevention of Youth Problem Behaviors," *American Psychologist* 58:457–465 (2003); Carter Hay, "Parenting, Self-Control, and Delinquency: A Test of Self-Control Theory," *Criminology* 39:707–736 (2001).
134. G. Roger Jarjoura, "Does Dropping Out of School Enhance Delinquent Involvement? Results from a Large-Scale National Probability Sample," *Criminology* 31:149–172 (1993); Terence Thornberry, Melaine Moore, and R. L. Christenson, "The Effect of Dropping Out of High School on Subsequent Criminal Behavior," *Criminology* 23:3–18 (1985).
135. Carolyn Smith, Alan Lizotte, Terence Thornberry, and Marvin Krohn, *Resilient Youth: Identifying Factors that Prevent High-Risk Youth from Engaging in Delinquency and Drug Use* (Albany, NY: Rochester Youth Development Study, 1994), pp. 19–21.
136. Danielle Payne and Benjamin Cornwell, "Reconsidering Peer Influences on Delinquency: Do Less Proximate Contacts Matter?" *Journal of Quantitative Criminology* 23:127–149 (2007).
137. Thomas Berndt, "The Features and Effects of Friendship in Early Adolescence," *Child Development* 53:1447–1460 (1982).
138. Isabela Granic and Thomas Dishion, "Deviant Talk in Adolescent Friendships: A Step Toward Measuring a Pathogenic Attractor Process," *Social Development* 12:314–334 (2003).
139. Walter Miller, *Violence by Youth Gangs and Youth Groups as a Crime Problem in Major American Cities* (Washington, DC: U.S. Government Printing Office, 1975).
140. Edwin H. Sutherland, *Principles of Criminology* (Philadelphia: Lippincott, 1939).
141. See, for example, Edwin Sutherland, "White-Collar Criminality," *American Sociological Review* 5:2–10 (1940).
142. See Edwin Sutherland and Donald Cressey, *Criminology*, 8th ed. (Philadelphia: Lippincott, 1970), pp. 77–79.
143. Dana Haynie, Peggy Giordano, Wendy Manning, and Monica Longmore, "Adolescent Romantic Relationships and Delinquency Involvement," *Criminology* 43:177–210 (2005).
144. Sandra Brown, Vicki Creamer, and Barbara Stetson, "Adolescent Alcohol Expectancies in Relation to Personal and Parental Drinking Patterns," *Journal of Abnormal Psychology* 96:117–121 (1987).
145. Carlo Morselli, Pierre Tremblay, and Bill McCarthy, "Mentors and Criminal Achievement," *Criminology* 44:17–43 (2006).
146. Ibid.
147. Gresham Sykes and David Matza, "Techniques of Neutralization: A Theory of Delinquency," *American Sociological Review* 22:664–670 (1957); David Matza, *Delinquency and Drift* (New York: Wiley, 1964).
148. Matza, *Delinquency and Drift*, p. 51.
149. Sykes and Matza, "Techniques of Neutralization," pp. 664–670; see also David Matza, "Subterranean Traditions of Youths," *Annals of the American Academy of Political and Social Science* 378:116 (1961).
150. Ian Shields and George Whitehall, "Neutralization and Delinquency among Teenagers," *Criminal Justice and Behavior* 21:223–235 (1994); Robert A. Ball, "An Empirical Exploration of Neutralization Theory," *Criminologica* 4:22–32 (1966). See also M. William Minor, "The Neutralization of Criminal Offense," *Criminology* 18:103–120 (1980); Robert Gordon, James Short, Desmond Cartwright, and Fred Strodtbeck, "Values and Gang Delinquency: A Study of Street Corner Groups," *American Journal of Sociology* 69:109–128 (1963).
151. Robert Agnew, "The Techniques of Neutralization and Violence," *Criminology* 32:555–580 (1994); Michael Hindelang, "The Commitment of Delinquents to Their Misdeeds: Do Delinquents Drift?" *Social Problems* 17:500–509 (1970); Robert Regoli and Eric Poole, "The Commitment of Delinquents to Their Misdeeds: A Reexamination," *Journal of Criminal Justice* 6:261–269 (1978).
152. Larry Siegel, Spencer Rathus, and Carol Ruppert, "Values and Delinquent Youth: An Empirical Reexamination of Theories of Delinquency," *British Journal of Criminology* 13:237–244 (1973).
153. Volkan Topalli, "When Being Good Is Bad: An Expansion of Neutralization Theory," *Criminology* 43:797–836 (2005).
154. Scott Briar and Irving Piliavin, "Delinquency: Situational Inducements and Commitment to Conformity," *Social Problems* 13:35–45 (1965–1966).
155. Lawrence Sherman and Douglas Smith, with Janell Schmidt and Dennis Rogan, "Crime, Punishment, and Stake in Conformity: Legal and Informal Control of Domestic Violence," *American Sociological Review* 57:680–690 (1992).
156. Albert Reiss, "Delinquency as the Failure of Personal and Social Controls," *American Sociological Review* 16:196–207 (1951).
157. Briar and Piliavin, "Delinquency: Situational Inducements and Commitment to Conformity."
158. Walter Reckless, *The Crime Problem* (New York: Appleton-Century-Crofts, 1967), pp. 469–483.
159. Among the many research reports by Reckless and his colleagues are Frank Scarpitti, Ellen Murray, Simon Dinitz, and Walter Reckless, "The Good Boy in a High Delinquency Area: Four Years Later," *American Sociological Review* 23:555–558 (1960); Walter Reckless, Simon Dinitz, and Ellen Murray, "The Good Boy in a High Delinquency Area," *Journal of Criminal Law, Criminology, and Police Science* 48:12–26 (1957); Reckless, Dinitz, and Murray, "Self-Concept as an Insulator against Delinquency," *American Sociological Review* 21:744–746 (1956); Walter Reckless and Simon Dinitz, "Pioneering with Self-Concept as a Vulnerability Factor in Delinquency," *Journal of Criminal Law, Criminology, and Police Science* 58:515–523 (1967); Walter Reckless, Simon Dinitz, and Barbara Kay, "The Self-Component in Potential Delinquency and Potential Non-Delinquency," *American Sociological Review* 22:566–570 (1957).
160. Travis Hirschi, *Causes of Delinquency* (Berkeley: University of California Press, 1969).
161. Ibid., p. 231.

162. Robert Crosnoe, "The Connection Between Academic Failure and Adolescent Drinking in Secondary School," *Sociology of Education* 79:44–60 (2006).

163. Hirschi, *Causes of Delinquency*, pp. 66–74.

164. Özden Özbay and Yusuf Ziya Özcan, "A Test of Hirschi's Social Bonding Theory," *International Journal of Offender Therapy and Comparative Criminology* 50:711–726 (2006); Michael Wiatrowski, David Griswold, and Mary K. Roberts, "Social Control Theory and Delinquency," *American Sociological Review* 46:525–541 (1981).

165. Patricia Van Voorhis, Francis Cullen, Richard Mathers, and Connie Chenoweth Garner, "The Impact of Family Structure and Quality on Delinquency: A Comparative Assessment of Structural and Functional Factors," *Criminology* 26:235–261 (1988).

166. Marc LeBlanc, "Family Dynamics, Adolescent Delinquency, and Adult Criminality," paper presented at the Society for Life History Research conference, Keystone, Colorado, October 1990, p. 6.

167. Bobbi Jo Anderson, Malcolm Holmes, and Erik Ostresh, "Male and Female Delinquents' Attachments and Effects of Attachments on Severity of Self-Reported Delinquency," *Criminal Justice and Behavior* 26:435–452 (1999).

168. Helen Garnier and Judith Stein, "An 18-Year Model of Family and Peer Effects on Adolescent Drug Use and Delinquency," *Journal of Youth and Adolescence* 31:45–56 (2002).

169. Teresa LaGrange and Robert Silverman, "Perceived Strain and Delinquency Motivation: An Empirical Evaluation of General Strain Theory," paper presented at the annual meeting of the American Society of Criminology, Boston, November 1995.

170. Voorhis, Cullen, Mathers, and Garner, "The Impact of Family Structure and Quality on Delinquency."

171. Trina Hope, Esther Wilder, and Toni Terling Watt, "The Relationships among Adolescent Pregnancy, Pregnancy Resolution, and Juvenile Delinquency," *Sociological Quarterly* 44:555–576 (2003).

172. Thomas Vander Ven, Francis Cullen, Mark Carrozza, and John Paul Wright, "Home Alone: The Impact of Maternal Employment on Delinquency," *Social Problems* 48:236–257 (2001); Patricia Jenkins, "School Delinquency and the School Social Bond," *Journal of Research in Crime and Delinquency* 34:337–367 (1997).

173. Jenkins, "School Delinquency and the School Social Bond."

174. Michael Cretacci, "Religion and Social Control: An Application of a Modified Social Bond of Violence," *Criminal Justice Review* 28:254–277 (2003).

175. Robert Agnew and David Peterson, "Leisure and Delinquency," *Social Problems* 36:332–348 (1989).

176. Jonathan Zaff, Kristin Moore, Angela Romano Papillo, and Stephanie Williams, "Implications of Extracurricular Activity Participation during Adolescence on Positive Outcomes," *Journal of Adolescent Research* 18:599–631 (2003).

177. John Cochran and Ronald Akers, "An Exploration of the Variable Effects of Religiosity on Adolescent Marijuana and Alcohol Use," *Journal of Research in Crime and Delinquency* 26:198–225 (1989).

178. Mark Regnerus and Glen Elder, "Religion and Vulnerability among Low-Risk Adolescents," *Social Science Research* 32:633–658 (2003); Mark Regnerus, "Moral Communities and Adolescent Delinquency: Religious Contexts and Community Social Control," *Sociological Quarterly* 44:523–554 (2003).

179. Marianne Junger and Ineke Haen Marshall, "The Interethnic Generalizability of Social Control Theory: An Empirical Test," *Journal of Research in Crime and Delinquency* 34:79–112 (1997); Josine Junger-Tas, "An Empirical Test of Social Control Theory," *Journal of Quantitative Criminology* 8:18–29 (1992).

180. LaGrange and Silverman, "Perceived Strain and Delinquency Motivation."

181. Kimberly Kempf, "The Empirical Status of Hirschi's Control Theory," in Bill Laufer and Freda Adler, eds., *Advances in Criminological Theory* (New Brunswick, NJ: Transaction Books, 1992).

182. Peggy Giordano, Stephen Cernkovich, and M. D. Pugh, "Friendships and Delinquency," *American Journal of Sociology* 91:1170–1202 (1986).

183. Vander Ven, Cullen, Carrozza, and Wright, "Home Alone: The Impact of Maternal Employment on Delinquency," p. 253.

184. Michael Hindelang, "Causes of Delinquency: A Partial Replication and Extension," *Social Problems* 21:471–487 (1973); Leslie Samuelson, Timothy Hartnagel, and Harvey Krahn, "Crime and Social Control among High School Dropouts," *Journal of Crime and Justice* 18:129–161 (1990).

185. Gary Jensen and David Brownfield, "Parents and Drugs," *Criminology* 21:543–554 (1983). See also M. Wiatrowski, D. Griswold, and M. Roberts, "Social Control Theory and Delinquency," *American Sociological Review* 46:525–541 (1981).

186. Cesar Rebellon and Karen van Gundy, "Can Control Theory Explain the Link between Parental Physical Abuse and Delinquency? A Longitudinal Analysis," *Journal of Research in Crime and Delinquency* 42:247–274 (2005); Marvin Krohn and James Massey, "Social Control and Delinquent Behavior: An Examination of the Elements of the Social Bond," *Sociological Quarterly* 21:529–543 (1980).

187. Jill Leslie Rosenbaum and James Lasley, "School, Community Context, and Delinquency: Rethinking the Gender Gap," *Justice Quarterly* 7:493–513 (1990).

188. Randy LaGrange and Helene Raskin White, "Age Differences in Delinquency: A Test of Theory," *Criminology* 23:19–45 (1985).

189. Robert Agnew, "Social Control Theory and Delinquency: A Longitudinal Test," *Criminology* 23:47–61 (1985).

190. Alan E. Liska and M. D. Reed, "Ties to Conventional Institutions and Delinquency: Estimating Reciprocal Effects," *American Sociological Review* 50:547–560 (1985).

191. Guy Faulkner, Edward Adlaf, Hyacinth Irving, Kenneth Allison, John Dwyer, and Jack Goodman, "The Relationship between Vigorous Physical Activity and Juvenile Delinquency: A Mediating Role for Self-Esteem?" *Journal of Behavioral Medicine* 30:155–163 (2007).

192. Kathleen Miller, Merrill Melnick, Grace Barnes, Don Sabo, and Michael Farrell, "Athletic Involvement and Adolescent Delinquency," *Journal of Youth and Adolescence* 36:711–723 (2007).

193. Douglas Hartmann and Michael Massoglia, "Reassessing the Relationship between High School Sports Participation and Deviance: Evidence of Enduring, Bifurcated Effects," *Sociological Quarterly* 48:485–505 (2007).

5

Social Reaction, Conflict, and Delinquency

Chapter Outline

Chapter Objectives

1. Understand the concept of symbolic interaction and the role symbols play in defining reality
2. Be aware of the impact of the labeling process
3. Define the terms "primary deviance" and "secondary deviance"
4. Identify the four quadrants of Becker's table of deviance and reaction
5. Discuss the unequal application of delinquent labels
6. Be familiar with the long-term effects of labels
7. Analyze the strengths of the social reaction perspective
8. Be familiar with the core elements of social conflict theory
9. Define the basic principles of restorative justice
10. Discuss how restoration can be used to reduce delinquent behaviors

n March of 2002, one boy walked away from a courtroom in Calgary, Canada, free to grow up, enjoy his friends, have a family, and live his life, while another, his victim, was dead and his family living with pain. The accused, a 17-year-old boy from the small Canadian city of Chestermere, had been on trial for killing the victim with a single punch to the head delivered during a prearranged fight in a public park on May 25, 2001. What led the judge in the case to render a verdict that allowed the perpetrator to go free? Judge Gordon Clozza stated in his six-page judgment: "It goes without saying that there never should have been a fight in the first place, but that's not the reality of the situation." Clozza said his decision hinged on whether or not the accused intended to cause serious bodily harm. He concluded that the intent was simply not there. "Both youths were old enough to understand and appreciate the consequences of their decision. Both youths were physically strong enough to cause serious bodily harm to the other. . . . I find the accused did not have the necessary intent to cause bodily harm to the deceased so as to preclude the defense of consent. I therefore find the accused not guilty of manslaughter."

After the trial concluded, defense lawyer Patrick Fagan said: "This time last year, the young man was facing a charge of second-degree murder. He now walks out of this courtroom a young man without a single criminal conviction." But even though a not-guilty verdict was handed down, Fagan felt that his client did not get off scot-free. When asked what the trial has done to his client, Fagan responded: "What hasn't been done to my client? I mean, he's been through hell, the family's been through hell this past year. It will profoundly affect and shape the rest of his life."[1]

he Calgary case illustrates how labeling and stigma shape the contours of our lives and how critical judgments are often based on subjective interpretation. Judge Clozza's finding was based on what he believed the accused boy was thinking at the time he committed the crime. The judge believed that while the boy did in fact intend to strike his victim, and perhaps intended to hurt

155

him severely, he did not want to cause his death. Both boys entered the fight willingly and neither wanted to kill the other. The judge's decision might have been influenced by the fact that the death was caused by a single blow and not a sustained beating. Had he concluded that the boy intended to kill, he would have found him guilty as charged and sentenced him to a long period of confinement. Thereafter, the boy would have been considered a killer or murderer. His friends, neighbors, and teachers might have shunned him and avoided contact. His future would have been tarnished forever. In prison he would have fallen in with a rough crowd and, realizing that his old life was over, might have been convinced to join a gang and enter a life of crime. But all that did not happen because, instead of labeling him a criminal, the judge decided that he was a "good kid who made a bad mistake." Instead of going to prison, the young man is now free to resume a normal life, almost as if nothing had happened. As time passes, the incident may fade and the details be lost: "I was the victim here, the other guy started the fight, I had no choice."

The two theories of delinquency discussed in this chapter—social reaction theory and social conflict theory—reflect the circumstances of this Canadian case: People in power control the law and this power allows them to decide what behavior is illegal and which kids are to be considered delinquent. The decision to label behavior as deviant or delinquent is subjective, based on the attitudes, values, and morals of those who hold power. The law serves the interests of the powerful, and the decision to punish based on whether people are viewed as a threat to the existing social structure. Social reaction theory and social conflict theory differ, however, on the motivation for labeling and social control. While social reaction theory focuses on the beliefs, attitudes, and moral values of those in power, social conflict theory ties their economic and political interests to the cause of delinquency.

SOCIAL REACTION THEORY

labeling theory
Posits that society creates deviance through a system of social control agencies that designate (or label) certain individuals as delinquent, thereby stigmatizing youths and encouraging them to accept this negative personal identity.

Social reaction theory, which is also commonly called labeling theory (the two terms are used interchangeably here), explains how sustained delinquent behavior stems from destructive social interactions and encounters. According to this view, illegal acts, including delinquent behaviors, are defined by the social audience's reaction and not the moral content of the illegal act itself.[2] A boy is considered delinquent not because he did something wrong but because others label him as such; an act is considered delinquent because others view it as immoral or wrong. A death can be viewed as a tragic accident or a murder based on how people interpret what went on. A rape can be a consensual sex act or a brutal violation based on some decision makers' subjective interpretation. The roots of this vision can be found in a branch of sociology known as symbolic interaction.[3]

symbolic interaction
The concept of how people communicate via symbols—gestures, signs, words, or images—that stand for or represent something else.

The Concept of Symbolic Interaction

Symbolic interaction theory holds that people communicate via symbols—gestures, signs, words, or images—that stand for or represent something else. For example, when you see a person with a gold ring on the fourth finger of his left hand you know he is married. The ring is not merely a piece of jewelry but a representation or symbol of the wearer's status. It tells you that he lives a conventional lifestyle, is most likely emotionally stable, ready for commitment, and so on. Similarly, wearing an expensive watch such as a Rolex symbolizes that the owner is successful, wealthy, and confident; this is referred to as a status symbol. Sometimes symbols take the form of a gesture: If a guy asks a girl out on a date and she rolls her eyes, shakes her head, and turns her back, he quickly gets the message: This is not going to work.

The **Society for the Study of Symbolic Interaction (SSSI)** is an international professional organization of social science scholars interested in interactionist research. You can visit their site via academic.cengage.com/criminaljustice/siegel.

status symbol
Something, such as a possession, rank, or activity, by which one's social or economic prestige is measured.

As you can imagine, symbols are subjective. A Rolex may keep no better time than a Timex, yet one conveys an image of wealth and success and the other of thrift and frugality. Similarly, body language is open to interpretation and can be easily misread.

According to social reaction theory, behavior is controlled and shaped by the reactions of others. Dylan, a teen in the foster care system, pauses during an interview at a New Jersey Division of Youth and Family Services (DYFS) office in Trenton, New Jersey. DYFS director Edward Cotton came across Dylan when the teen ended up in a group care center. Cotton was struck by the 17-year-old's intelligence and good attitude despite the troubles he had experienced in his short life. Cotton offered to help and Dylan asked for just one thing: a good foster family, which the DYFS director promised to find. Social reaction theory would predict that this positive feedback will strengthen Dylan's self-image and help others see him as a "good kid" to whom bad things had happened, rather than a "bad kid" who deserved to be punished.

euthanasia
The act or practice of ending the life of an individual suffering from a terminal illness or an incurable condition.

People often interpret symbolic gestures from others and incorporate them in their self-image. Symbols are also used by people to let others know how well they are doing and whether they are liked or appreciated. How people view reality depends on the content of the messages and situations they encounter, the subjective interpretation of these interactions, and how they shape future behavior. There is no objective reality. People interpret the reactions of others, and this interpretation assigns meaning. Because interpretation changes over time, so do the meanings of concepts and symbols.

Interpreting Deviance

Because the definitions of crime and delinquency are purely subjective, they can change from place to place and from year to year. Acts such as abortion, marijuana use, possession of a handgun, and gambling have been legal at some time in history and illegal at others. In some jurisdictions, driving at 35 miles an hour is illegal while in others 70 is just fine!

But what about very serious crimes such as murder, rape, and assault? Surely they are always objectively wrong and evil. According to social reaction theory, even the most serious acts are subject to interpretation. Consider the incident described in the chapter-opening vignette: While most people would agree that killing someone is wrong and evil, there are many times in which taking a life is excusable: in self-defense; in time of war; if it is the product of a mental disease; if it is legally mandated (capital punishment); if it is the result of an accident. And there are gray areas that are subject to debate: Some people consider euthanasia of the sick and elderly justified, whereas others consider it murder; some people are opposed to abortion, whereas others fight to preserve its legalization.

Definitions of crime and delinquency vary between nations and states, creating the anomaly wherein an act that is outlawed in one jurisdiction is perfectly legal in another. Take for instance the crime of rape, which often involves a great deal of interpretation. In some states it is considered rape if, after the sex act begins, a man continues after his partner tells him to stop; in other states the same act is considered legal and justified.[4] Each state defines the age limit for consent differently (for example, in California it is 18, in New Hampshire 16) so that what is defined as the crime of statutory rape in one state is legal in another.

Two famous statements sum up this position. In one, sociologist Kai Erickson argued, "Deviance is not a property inherent in certain forms of behavior, it is a property conferred upon those forms by the audience which directly or indirectly witnesses them."[5] In another, Howard Becker stated:

Social groups create deviance by making rules whose infractions constitute deviance, and by applying those rules to particular people and labeling them as outsiders. From this point of view, deviance is not a quality of the act a person commits, but rather a consequence of the application by others of rules and sanctions to an "offender." The deviant is one to whom the label has successfully been applied; deviant behavior is behavior that people so label.[6]

Becker refers to people who create rules as *moral entrepreneurs*. An example of a moral entrepreneur today might be members of an ultra-orthodox religious group who target the gay lifestyle and mount a campaign to prevent gays from adopting children or conducting same-sex marriages.[7]

Becoming Labeled

Social reaction theory picks up on these concepts of *interaction* and *interpretation*.[8] Throughout their lives, people are given a variety of symbolic labels, some positive ("She's a real go-getter"), others negative ("He is an accident waiting to happen"). These labels help define not just one trait but the whole person. Kids labeled as "at risk" are also assumed to be dangerous, dishonest, unstable, violent, strange, and otherwise unsound. In contrast, an "honor student" is also assumed to be smart, honest, hardworking, and competent. Labels can improve self-image and social standing. Research shows that people who are labeled with one positive trait, such as being physically attractive, are assumed to maintain other traits, such as being intelligent and competent.[9] In contrast, negative labels—including troublemaker, mentally ill, and stupid—help stigmatize the recipients of these labels and reduce their self-image. Those who have accepted these labels are more prone to engage in delinquent behaviors than those whose self-image has not been so tarnished.[10]

stigmatize
To mark someone with disgrace or reproach; to characterize or brand someone as disgraceful or disreputable.

Both positive and negative labels involve subjective interpretation of behavior: A troublemaker is merely a kid whom people label as troublesome. There need not be any objective proof or measure indicating that the person is actually a troublemaker. Just as we assume that a Rolex is a terrific timepiece, we assume that someone labeled a "troublemaker" is a bad apple. Though a label may be a function of rumor, innuendo, or unfounded suspicion, its adverse impact can be immense.

Primary and Secondary Deviance

primary deviance
Norm violations that have very little influence on the actor and can be quickly forgotten and/or overlooked.

Edwin Lemert's concept of primary deviance and secondary deviance has become a standard view of the labeling process.[11] According to Lemert, primary deviance involves norm violations or crimes that have very little influence on the actor and can be quickly forgotten. For example, a college student takes a "five-finger discount" at the campus bookstore. He successfully steals a textbook, uses it to get an A in a course, goes on to graduate, is admitted into law school, and later becomes a famous judge. Because his shoplifting goes unnoticed, it is a relatively unimportant event that has little bearing on his future life.

secondary deviance
Deviant acts that define the actor and create a new identity.

In contrast, secondary deviance occurs when a deviant event comes to the attention of significant others or social control agents who apply a negative label. The newly labeled offender then reorganizes his or her behavior and personality around the consequences of the deviant act. The shoplifting student is caught by a security guard and expelled from college. With his law school dreams dashed and his future cloudy, his options are limited; people who know him say he "lacks character," and he begins to share their opinion. He eventually becomes a drug dealer and winds up in prison.

Florida State University maintains a site that has information on **labeling theory** and links to scholarly articles. You can access it via academic.cengage.com/criminaljustice/siegel.

Secondary deviance involves resocialization into a deviant role. The labeled person is transformed into one who, according to Lemert, "employs his behavior or a role based upon it as a means of defense, attack, or adjustment to the overt and covert problems created by the consequent social reaction to him."[12] Secondary deviance produces a deviance amplification effect. Offenders feel isolated from the mainstream of society and become firmly locked within their deviant role. They may seek out others similarly labeled to form deviant subcultures or groups. Ever more firmly enmeshed in their deviant role, they are locked into an escalating cycle of deviance, apprehension, more powerful labels, and identity transformation. Lemert's concept of secondary deviance expresses the core of social reaction theory: Deviance is a process in which one's identity is transformed. Efforts to control the offenders, whether by treatment or punishment, simply help lock them in their deviant role.

The Secret Deviant and the Falsely Accused In one of the most well-known social reaction concepts, Howard Becker recognized that four possible outcomes develop in the relationship between labeling and delinquent or other deviant behaviors.[13] (See Concept Summary 5.1.)

Concept Summary 5.1

Becker's Fourfold Model of Labeling

	Delinquent	Not Delinquent
Labeled	Pure deviant	Falsely accused
Not Labeled	Secret deviant	Conformist

Those kids who engage in delinquency and also get caught and labeled are called *pure deviants*; their opposite number, *conformists*, are both rule-abiding and free of negative labels. Some kids are *falsely accused* or blamed for something they did not do, while some who continually break rules are able to avoid labeling; these are called *secret deviants*.

Pure deviants are the kids most likely to repeat their antisocial activities, while conformists are the ones most likely to stay straight and never engage in antisocial behaviors. While this outcome is a key to the validity of social reaction theory, what happens to the kids who fall in the other two categories is even more critical. If labeling theory is valid, then the falsely accused will be more likely to become secondary deviants (i.e., chronic offenders) than the secret deviants. While the latter may be more troubled, because they have escaped the labeling process they are not affected by negative stigma. And, according to social reaction theory, negative labels, even false ones, are the critical elements that create secondary deviance and result in a delinquent career. In other words, it is more damaging in the long run to be falsely accused than to be a secret deviant. This is one of the key concepts in labeling theory.

Differential Labeling

Why are some kids labeled while others escape judgment? An important principle of social reaction theory is that labels are differentially applied, benefiting those who hold economic and social power and penalizing the powerless. The probability of being brought under the control of legal authority is a function of a person's social status. While wealthy white-collar criminals are most often punished by a relatively small fine, poor kids who get involved in street crimes, such as burglary or car theft, most often face incarceration and other harsh punishments.[14]

Why is this differential labeling allowed to take place? Although the rule of law should be fair and objective, discretionary decision making controls its operation at every level. From the police officer's decision on whom to arrest, to the prosecutor's decisions on whom to charge and for how many and what kind of charges or whether to treat the offender as a juvenile or prosecute in adult court, to the judge's decision on the length of the sentence, discretion works to the detriment of minorities, including African Americans, Latinos, Asian Americans, and Native Americans.[15] Race bias adversely influences decision making in many critical areas of the justice system.[16] Some juvenile court judges may sympathize with white defendants and help them avoid delinquent labels, especially if they seem to come from "good families," whereas minority youth are not afforded that luxury.[17]

In sum, a major premise of social reaction theory is that racial, age, income, and gender differences in the delinquency rate reflect the fact that the law is differentially constructed and applied. It favors the powerful members of society who direct its content and penalizes people whose actions represent a threat to those in control, such as minority group members and the poor who demand equal rights.[18] If the law was totally unbiased, official data would reflect self-report studies, which show that delinquency is spread equally among racial and class groups.

The Consequences of Labeling

If a devalued status is conferred by a significant other—teacher, police officer, elder, parent, or valued peer—the negative label and resulting stigma may cause permanent harm. Labeled kids may consider themselves social outcasts. The degree to which a person is perceived as a social outcast may affect his or her treatment at home, at work, at school, and in other social situations. Children may find that their parents consider them a bad influence on younger brothers and sisters. School officials may limit them to classes reserved for people with behavioral problems. If they are labeled as a delinquent or druggie, they may find their eligibility for employment severely restricted. Furthermore, if the label is bestowed as the result of adjudication for a delinquent act, the labeled person may be subjected to official sanctions ranging from a mild reprimand to incarceration.

Beyond these immediate results, social reaction theory maintains that, depending on the visibility of the label and the manner and severity with which it is applied, a person who has been negatively labeled will have an increasing commitment to a deviant career.[19] Labeled kids may find themselves turning to others similarly stigmatized for support and companionship. Isolated from conventional society, they may identify themselves as members of an outcast group and become locked into a deviant career.

The Source of Labels The source of labels can be critical. Kids who perceive that they have been negatively labeled by significant others such as peers and teachers are also more likely to self-report delinquent behavior and to adopt a deviant self-concept.[20] They are likely to seek out deviant friends and join gangs, associations that escalate their involvement in criminal activities.[21] Parental labeling is extremely damaging because it may cause adolescents to seek deviant peers whose behavior amplifies the effect of the labeling.[22] Children negatively labeled by their parents routinely suffer a variety of problems, including antisocial behavior and school failure.[23] This process has been observed in the United States and abroad, indicating that the labeling process is universal.[24]

In addition to these informal labels, official labels from the juvenile justice system can also have a devastating effect. An official label increases the risk of their later dropping out of high school. Rather than deterring crime, court intervention increases the likelihood of future criminality.[25] The younger the adolescent, the more powerful influence the negative label can have on their self-image.[26]

Damaged Identity Once stigmatized as troublemakers, adolescents may begin to reassess their self-image.[27] Although labels may not have caused adolescents to initiate delinquent behaviors, once applied they increase the likelihood of persistent offending because kids now have a "damaged identity."[28]

Because negative labeling experiences help create a deviant identity, those exposed to negative sanctions experience both self-rejection and lowered self-image. Self-rejecting attitudes result in both a weakened commitment to conventional values and the acquisition of motives to deviate from social norms.[29] This transformation is amplified by the bonds social outcasts form with peers.[30] Labeled delinquents will seek out others who are similarly stigmatized.[31] Associating with deviant peers helps reinforce conventional society's negative evaluations: "We were right all along about him, look who his friends are!" (See Figure 5.1.)

A damaged identity provokes some adolescents into repeating their antisocial behaviors, creating new labels and amplifying old ones; this creates what is called a cumulative disadvantage.[32] Using longitudinal data obtained from youths ages 13 to 22, Jón Gunnar Bernburg and Marvin Krohn found evidence that, rather than deterring future offending, the "cumulative disadvantage" created by official intervention actually increases the probability that a labeled person will get involved in subsequent involvement in antisocial behavior. A label limits conventional opportunities, such as educational attainment and employment. Kids who were labeled in adolescence were much more likely to engage in crime in early adulthood unless they were able to overcome labels and do well in school and obtain meaningful employment opportunities.[33]

Joining Deviant Cliques When kids are labeled as troublemakers or social problems, they may join up with similarly outcast delinquent peers in a clique or group that facilitates their antisocial behavior.[34] Eventually, antisocial behavior becomes habitual and automatic.[35] The desire to join deviant cliques and groups may stem from a self-rejecting attitude ("at times, I think I am no good at all"), which eventually results in a weakened commitment to conventional values and behaviors. In turn, these children may acquire motives to deviate from social norms. Facilitating

FIGURE 5.1

The Cycle of Deviance Amplification

According to sociologist Edwin Lemert, people who bear negative labels become secondary deviants—their label becomes a master status by which they are defined.

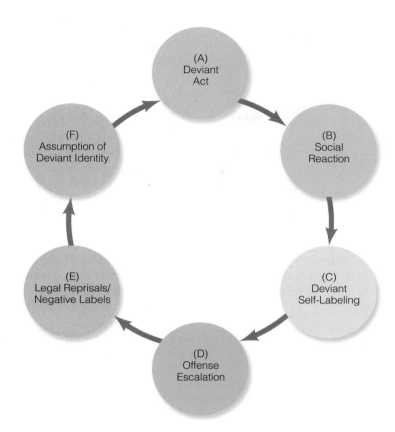

this attitude and value transformation is the bond social outcasts form with similarly labeled peers in the form of a deviant subculture.[36] Delinquent peers then may help labeled youths "reject their rejectors." Teachers are "stupid"; cops are "dishonest"; parents "just don't understand."[37] Group identity enables outcast youths to show contempt for the sources of the labels and to distance themselves. These actions help solidify both the grip of deviant peers and the impact of the labels.[38] Those who have accepted these labels are more prone to engage in delinquent behaviors than those whose self-image has not been so tarnished.[39]

Membership in a deviant subculture often involves conforming to group norms that conflict with those of conventional society. Deviant behaviors that defy conventional values can serve a number of different purposes. Some acts are defiant, designed to show contempt for the source of the negative labels. Other acts are planned to distance the transgressor from further contact with the source of criticism (for example, joining a gang gives kids the social support lacking from absent or overly critical parents).[40]

Retrospective Reading On January 19, 2007, area residents were shocked to learn that John Odgren, a student at upscale Lincoln-Sudbury Regional High School in Massachusetts, had stabbed to death a fellow student whom he barely knew. Within days, the media began to issue reports on Odgren's background in an effort to explain his act—the fact that he had often boasted of violence, kept a gun at home, and had bragged to fellow students that he once tried to kill someone. Odgren asked kids, "How many people have you killed in the virtual world?" and told them "I once tried to kill a person for real." He seemed fascinated by violent books and told friends about part of a book he liked that describes the dripping sound of blood. He visited websites that taught bomb-making skills. After the murder, the public also learned that the teenager had been diagnosed both with Asperger syndrome, a mild form of autism, and a hyperactivity disorder, and had been taking several medications. He had been enrolled in a special education program called Great Opportunities, which

John Odgren dusts for fingerprints during a Basic Crime Scene Investigation summer program, July 27, 2005, at Mount Wachusett Community College in Gardner, Massachusetts. Odgren was charged with first-degree murder in the fatal stabbing of James Alenson, 15, after an early morning fight on January 19, 2007, at Lincoln-Sudbury Regional High School. Though you have never met Odgren, speculate on why he committed an unprovoked murder. What could have driven a kid who takes summer courses on police investigation techniques to become a killer?

"provides a welcoming place for students whose significant emotional and/or psychiatric disabilities have interfered with their ability to access public education without the intensive support provided at GO."[41]

This attempt to mesh Odgren's present behavior with his past characteristics is referred to as a **retrospective reading**: After someone is labeled because of some unusual or inexplicable act, people begin to reconstruct their identity so that the act and the label are correlated, for example, "We always knew there was something wrong with that boy!" It is not unusual for the media to lead the way and interview boyhood friends of an assassin or serial killer. On the 11 o'clock news we can hear them report that the suspect was withdrawn, suspicious, and negativistic as a youth, expressing violent thoughts and ideation, a loner, troubled, and so on. Yet, until now no one was suspicious and nothing was done. Once the label is bestowed, all the prior evidence suddenly makes sense. By conducting a retrospective reading, we can now understand what prompted his current behavior; therefore, the label must be accurate.[42]

retrospective reading
The reassessment of a person's past to fit a current generalized label.

dramatization of evil
The process of social typing that transforms an offender's identity from a doer of evil to an evil person.

Dramatization of Evil Labels become the basis of personal identity. As the negative feedback of law enforcement agencies, parents, friends, teachers, and other figures amplifies the force of the original label, stigmatized offenders may begin to reevaluate their own identities. If they are not really evil or bad, they may ask themselves, why is everyone making such a fuss? Frank Tannenbaum, a social reaction theory pioneer, referred to this process as the **dramatization of evil**. With respect to the consequences of labeling delinquent behavior, Tannenbaum stated:

The process of making the criminal, therefore, is a process of tagging, defining, identifying, making conscious and self-conscious; it becomes a way of stimulating, suggesting and evoking the very traits that are complained of. If the theory of relation of response to stimulus has any meaning, the entire process of dealing with the young delinquent is mischievous insofar as it identifies him to himself or to the environment as a delinquent person. The person becomes the thing he is described as being.[43]

self-fulfilling prophecy
Deviant behavior patterns that are a response to an earlier labeling experience; youths act out these social roles even if they were falsely bestowed.

Self-Fulfilling Prophecy The labeling process helps create a **self-fulfilling prophecy**.[44] If children continually receive negative feedback from parents, teachers, and others whose opinion they take to heart, they will interpret this rejection as accurate. Their behavior will begin to conform to the negative expectations; they will become the person others perceive them to be ("Teachers already think I'm stupid, so why should I bother to study?"). The self-fulfilling prophecy leads to a damaged self-image and an increase in antisocial behaviors.[45] Research shows that adolescents who perceive labels from significant others also report more frequent delinquent involvement; perceptions of negative labels are significant predictors of serious delinquent behaviors.[46]

The Juvenile Justice Process and Labeling

Processing through the juvenile justice system seems to unleash the labeling process and create secondary deviant identities. Here offenders find (perhaps for the first time) that authority figures consider them incorrigible outcasts who must be separated from the right-thinking members of society. To reach that decision, the judge relies on the testimony of witnesses—parents, teachers, police officers, social workers, and psychologists—who may testify that the offender is unfit to be part of conventional society. As the label *juvenile delinquent* is conferred on offenders, their identities may be transformed from kids who have done something bad to "bad kids."[47]

degradation ceremony
Going to court, being scolded by a judge, or being found delinquent after a trial are examples of public ceremonies that can transform youthful offenders by degrading their self-image.

Degradation Ceremonies To drive home the point that the youthful suspect is an outcast who should be shunned by society, the justice system relies on what sociologist Harold Garfinkel called a **degradation ceremony**. During this ritual the public identity of an offender is transformed in a solemn process during which the targeted person is thrust outside the social mainstream.[48] This process may be seen in juvenile court when a youngster goes before the court, is scolded by a judge, has charges read, and is officially labeled a delinquent; this process contains all the conditions for "successful degradation." Recognizing the role stigma plays in developing a delinquent career has prompted some juvenile justice agencies to create programs designed to limit delinquent labels.[49]

There is little question that being initiated into the juvenile justice system with a degradation ceremony may be a life-transforming event. Kids enter the system as people in trouble with the law, but emerge as bearers of criminal histories, which are likely to reinvolve them in criminal activity. Authority figures anticipate that these troublemakers will continue their life of crime and they become perennial suspects.[50] If they are institutionalized the effect is even more damaging. A recent (2007) study by Nadine Lanctôt and her colleagues found that having been institutionalized as an adolescent is predictive of precarious, premature, unstable, and unsatisfied life conditions in adulthood. Formerly institutionalized males and females experienced more socioeconomic difficulties, earlier and premature transitions to adulthood, difficulties at work, instability in romantic relationships, and less emotional well-being. Being institutionalized as a juvenile will hit girls particularly hard. As adults, young women who had been sent away as juveniles had significant difficulty coping with adulthood, were dependent on government assistance, were significantly more likely to have become teen mothers, and suffered from low self-esteem and depression.[51] Because it creates stigma and a damaged self-image, the system designed to reduce delinquency may help produce young criminals.

Is Labeling Theory Valid?

Labeling theory has been the subject of academic debate in criminological circles. Those who criticize it point to its inability to specify the conditions that must exist before an act or individual is labeled deviant—that is, why some people are labeled and others remain "secret deviants."[52] Some critics argued that the crime-controlling effects of punishment more than make up for the crime-producing effects of stigma. In *Beyond Probation*, Charles Murray and Louis Cox found that youths assigned to a program designed to reduce labels were more likely later to commit delinquent acts than a comparison group who were placed in a more punitive state training school. The implication was that the threat of punishment was deterrent and that the crime-producing influence of labels was minimal.[53]

There is also some question about the real cost of being labeled. Some doubt whether negative social reactions and stigma produce delinquency.[54] Many delinquent careers exist without labeling and it is possible that negative labeling often comes after, rather than before, chronic offending. Getting labeled by the justice system and having an enduring delinquent record may have relatively little effect on kids who have been burdened with social and emotional problems since birth.[55]

While these criticisms are telling, there are a number of reasons why social reaction may play an important role in understanding the ebb and flow of a delinquent career:[56]

I   The labeling perspective identifies the role played by social control agents in the process of delinquency causation. Delinquent behavior cannot be fully understood if the agencies and individuals empowered to control and treat it are neglected.

I   Labeling theory recognizes that delinquency is not a disease or pathological behavior. It focuses attention on the social interactions and reactions that shape individual behavior.

I   Labeling theory distinguishes between delinquent acts (primary deviance) and delinquent careers (secondary deviance) and shows that these concepts must be interpreted and treated differently.

Social reaction is also important because of its focus on interaction as well as the situations surrounding the crime. Rather than viewing the delinquent as a robotlike creature whose actions are predetermined, it recognizes that crime is often the result of complex interactions and processes. The decision to commit crime involves actions of a variety of people, including peers, the victim, the police, and other key characters. Labels may expedite crime because they guide the actions of all parties involved in these delinquent interactions. Actions deemed innocent when performed by one person are considered provocative when someone who has been labeled as deviant engages in them. Similarly, labeled people may be quick to judge, take offense, or misinterpret behavior of others because of past experience.

Labeling theory is also supported by research showing that offenders who are placed in treatment programs aimed at reconfiguring their self-image may be able to develop revamped identities and desist from crime. Some are able to go through "redemption rituals" in which they are able to cast off their damaged identities and develop new ones. As a result, they develop an improved "self-concept," which reflects the positive reinforcement they receive while in treatment.[57]

As interest in delinquent careers has escalated, labeling theory has taken on new relevance. Labeling theory may help explain why some youths continue down the path of antisocial behaviors (they are labeled), whereas most are able to desist from crime (they are free of stigma). Kids who are labeled may find themselves shut out of educational and employment opportunities. Those who have been suspended from school or labeled as troublemakers may find that these experiences haunt them a decade later when they seek employment as adults.[58] As a result, these labeled youths are more likely to sustain delinquent careers and persist in their behavior into adulthood.[59] In addition to explaining the continuity of crime, labeling theory may also help us understand why many hardcore offenders desist. Those who receive sufficient positive feedback may be able to transform their self-image and create a new self, helping them to go straight.[60]

Social Reaction Theory and Social Policy

As the dangers of labeling became known, a massive effort was made to limit the interface of youths with the juvenile justice system. One approach was to divert youths from official processing at the time of their initial contact with police. The usual practice was to have police refer children to treatment facilities rather than to the juvenile court. In a similar vein, children who were petitioned to juvenile court might be eligible for alternative programs rather than traditional juvenile justice processing. For example, restitution allowed children to pay back the victims of their crimes for the damage (or inconvenience) they caused instead of receiving an official delinquency label.

If a youth was found delinquent, efforts were made to reduce stigma by using alternative programs such as boot camp or intensive probation monitoring. Alternative community-based sanctions substituted for state training schools, a policy known as **deinstitutionalization**. Whenever possible, anything producing stigma was to be avoided, a philosophy referred to as nonintervention.

While these programs were initially popular, critics claimed that the nonintervention movement created a new class of juvenile offenders who heretofore might have avoided prolonged contact with juvenile justice agencies; they referred to this phenomenon as "widening the net."[61] Evaluation of existing programs did not indicate that they could reduce the recidivism rate of clients.[62] While these criticisms proved damaging, many nonintervention programs still operate.

deinstitutionalization
Removing juveniles from adult jails and placing them in community-based programs to avoid the stigma attached to these facilities.

SOCIAL CONFLICT THEORY

social conflict theory
Asserts that society is in a state of constant internal conflict, and focuses on the role of social and governmental institutions as mechanisms for social control.

According to social conflict theory (also called critical theory, the two terms are interchangeable), those who hold power in contemporary society get to set the rules, control the law, and decide who is a deviant, delinquent, and/or criminal. Their motives are not moral but financial and economic. They care little about the moral content

Social conflict theory links individual behavior to the inter- and intragroup conflict that is common in contemporary society. Here, protesters hold a march and rally on May 1, 2007, denouncing the actions of riot police at a May Day immigrant rights rally at MacArthur Park in Los Angeles, California. Demonstrators, journalists, and police officers were injured at the end of the immigration march when officers in riot gear used batons and fired 146 rounds of foam-rubber bullets to disperse the crowd. Does the social conflict that takes place between police and public, between the haves and have-nots, influence antisocial behaviors? Does conflict create a climate where deviant behavior becomes inevitable?

of the law as long as it protects the interests of capitalist power brokers.

According to this view, society is in a constant state of internal conflict, as different groups strive to impose their will on others. Those with money and power succeed in shaping the law to meet their needs and maintain their interests. They want to make sure that manipulating the system to make enormous profits is legal while shoplifting, pilferage, and theft are severely punished. The law must protect the wealth of those in power while controlling people whose behavior does conform to the needs of the power elite. Those who violate their rules are defined as criminals, delinquents, and status offenders and punished accordingly.

Those in power use the justice system to maintain their status while keeping others subservient: Men use their economic power to subjugate women; members of the majority want to stave off the economic advancement of minorities; capitalists want to reduce the power of workers to ensure they are willing to accept low wages. Conflict theory centers around a view of society in which an elite class uses the law as a means of meeting threats to its status. The ruling class is a self-interested collective whose primary interest is self-gain.[63] For example, conflict theorists observe that while spending has been cut on social programs during the past few years, spending on the prison system has skyrocketed. Draconian criminal laws designed to curb terrorism, such as the USA Patriot Act, have been turned against political dissenters. Critical thinkers believe that they are responsible for informing the public about the dangers of these developments.[64]

Law and Justice

Social conflict theorists view the law and the justice system as vehicles for controlling the have-not members of society. Legal institutions help the powerful and rich to impose their standards of good behavior on the entire society. The law protects the property and physical safety of the haves from attack by the have-nots, and helps control the behavior of those who might otherwise threaten the status quo.[65] The ruling elite draws the lower-middle class into this pattern of control, leading it to believe it has a stake in maintaining the status quo.[66] The poor may or may not commit more crimes than the rich, but they certainly are arrested more often.[67] It is not surprising to conflict theorists that complaints of police brutality are highest in minority neighborhoods, especially those that experience relative deprivation. (African American residents earn significantly less money than the majority and therefore have less political and social power.[68]) Police misbehavior, which is routine in minority neighborhoods, would never be tolerated in affluent white areas. Consequently, a deep-rooted hostility is generated among members of the lower class toward a social order they may neither shape nor share.[69]

Defining Delinquency In our advanced technological society, those with economic and political power control the legal definition of delinquency and the manner in which the law is enforced.[70] Consequently, the only crimes available to poor kids are the severely sanctioned "street crimes": rape, murder, theft, and mugging. Members of the middle class may engage in petty delinquent acts such as smoking marijuana or shoplifting, acts that generate social disapproval but are rarely punished severely.

At the top of the social pyramid are the power elite, extremely wealthy people whose fortunes were created and are now maintained on the backs of the working class. They make millions while paying desperate workers subsistence wages. Moreover, the power elite are involved in acts that should be described as crimes but are not, such as racism, sexism, and profiteering. Although regulatory laws control illegal business activities, these are rarely enforced, and violations are lightly punished.

The Conflict Concept of Delinquency

Conflict theorists view delinquency as a normal response to the conditions created by capitalism.[71] In fact, the creation of a legal category, delinquency, is a function of the class consciousness that occurred around the turn of the twentieth century.[72] In *The Child Savers*, Anthony Platt documented the creation of the delinquency concept and the role played by wealthy child savers in forming the philosophy of the juvenile court. Platt believed the child-saving movement's real goal was to maintain order and control while preserving the existing class system.[73] He and others have concluded that the child savers were powerful citizens who aimed to control the behavior of disenfranchised youths. (See Figure 5.2.)

Critical thinkers still view delinquent behavior as a function of the capitalist system's inherent inequity. They argue that capitalism accelerates the trend toward replacing human labor with machines so that youths are removed from the labor force. From early childhood, the values of capitalism are reinforced. Social control agencies such as schools prepare youths for placement in the capitalist system by presenting them with behavior models that will help them conform to later job expectations. Rewards for good schoolwork correspond to the rewards a manager uses with employees. In fact, most schools are set up to reward youths who show promise in self-discipline and motivation and are therefore judged likely to perform well in the capitalist system. Youths who are judged inferior as potential job prospects become known as losers and punks and wind up in delinquent roles.

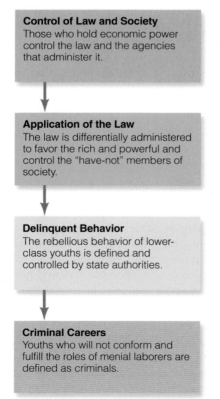

FIGURE 5.2
Social Conflict Theory

Control of Law and Society
Those who hold economic power control the law and the agencies that administer it.

Application of the Law
The law is differentially administered to favor the rich and powerful and control the "have-not" members of society.

Delinquent Behavior
The rebellious behavior of lower-class youths is defined and controlled by state authorities.

Criminal Careers
Youths who will not conform and fulfill the roles of menial laborers are defined as criminals.

Class and Delinquency The capitalist system affects youths differently at each level of the class structure. In the lowest classes, youths form gangs, which can be found in the most desolated ghetto areas. These gangs serve as a means of survival in a system that offers no reasonable alternative. Lower-class youths who live in more stable areas are on the fringe of delinquent activity because the economic system excludes them from meaningful opportunity.

Conflict theory also acknowledges middle-class delinquency. The alienation of individuals from one another, the competitive struggle, and the absence of human feeling, all qualities of capitalism, contribute to middle-class delinquency. Because capitalism is dehumanizing, it is not surprising that even middle-class youths turn to drugs, gambling, and illicit sex to find escape.

Controlling Delinquents Conflict theorists suggest that, rather than inhibiting delinquent behavior, the justice system may help to sustain such behavior. They claim that the capitalist state fails to control delinquents because it is in the state's interest to maintain a large number of outcast deviant youths. These youths can be employed as marginal workers, willing to work for minimum wage in jobs no one else wants. Thus, labeling by the justice system fits within the capitalist managers' need to maintain an underclass of cheap labor.

What the Future Holds

Critical thinkers are deeply concerned about the current state of the American political system and the creation of what they consider to be an American Empire abroad. Their concern stems from recent events such as the war in Iraq and the efforts to penalize immigrants and close the borders.[74] The conservative agenda, they believe, calls for the dismantling of welfare and health programs, lowering of labor costs through union busting, tax cuts that favor the wealthy, ending affirmative action, and reducing environmental control and regulation. Each of these acts will harm poor youth and increase the risk of delinquency.

Racism still pervades the American system and manifests itself in a wide variety of social practices ranging from the administration of criminal justice to the "whitening" of the teaching force because selection of teachers, even in minority communities, rests upon a racially skewed selection process.[75]

Globalization

globalization
The process of creating a global economy through transnational markets and political and legal systems.

The new global economy is a particular vexing development for critical theorists and their use of the concept of surplus value. Globalization, which usually refers to the process of creating transnational markets and political and legal systems, has shifted the focus of critical inquiry to a world perspective.

Globalization began when large companies decided to establish themselves in foreign markets by adapting their products or services to the local culture. The process took off with the fall of the Soviet Union, which opened new European markets. The development of China into a super-industrial power encouraged foreign investors to take advantage of China's huge supply of workers. As the Internet and communication revolution unfolded, companies were able to establish instant communications with their far-flung corporate empires, a technological breakthrough that further aided trade and foreign investments. A series of transnational corporate mergers (such as DaimlerChrysler) and takeovers (such as Ford and Volvo) produced ever-larger transnational corporations.

To read more about **globalization** go to the site maintained by the Levin Institute via academic.cengage.com/criminaljustice/siegel.

Some experts believe globalization can improve the standard of living in third-world nations by providing jobs and training, but critical theorists question the altruism of multinational corporations. Their motives are exploiting natural resources, avoiding regulation, and taking advantage of desperate workers. When these giant corporations set up factories in a developing nation, it is not to help the local population but to get around environmental laws and take advantage of needy workers who may be forced to labor in substandard conditions. Globalization has replaced imperialism and colonization as a new form of economic domination and oppression.

Globalization and Delinquency Globalization may have a profound influence on the future of indigent youth. Workers in the United States may be replaced in high-paying manufacturing jobs not by machines but by foreign workers in overseas factories. Instant communication via the Internet and global communications will speed the effect immeasurably. Government policies that are designed to increase corporate profits tend to aggravate rather than ease the financial stress being placed on ordinary families. Contemporary monetary policy, trade policy, and tax policy are harmful to working-class families. While affluent whites fear corporate downsizing, poor minorities in central cities are shut out of any economic revival. The modern marketplace, with its reliance on sophisticated computer technologies, is continually decreasing demand for low-skilled workers, which impacts African Americans more negatively than other better-educated and more affluent groups.[76]

Minority youth are hit the hardest by the effects of globalization. Sociologist William Julius Wilson has written of the plight of the African American community. He suggests that as difficult as life was in the 1940s and 1950s for African Americans, they at least had a reasonable hope of steady work. Now, because of the globalization of the economy, those opportunities have evaporated. Though in the past racial segregation had limited opportunity, growth in the manufacturing sector fueled upward mobility and provided the foundation of today's African American middle class. Those opportunities no longer exist as manufacturing plants have moved to inaccessible rural and overseas locations where the cost of doing business is lower. With manufacturing opportunities all but obsolete in the United States, service and retail establishments, which depended on blue-collar spending, have similarly disappeared, leaving behind an economy based on welfare and government supports. In less than 20 years, formerly active African American communities have become crime-infested inner-city neighborhoods.

Beyond sustaining inner-city poverty, the absence of employment opportunities has torn at the social fabric of the nation's inner-city neighborhoods. Work helps socialize young people into the wider society, instilling in them such desirable values as hard work, caring, and respect for others. When work becomes scarce, however, the discipline and structure it provides are absent. Community-wide underemployment destroys social cohesion, increasing the presence of neighborhood social problems ranging from drug use to educational failure. Schools in these areas are unable to teach basic skills and because desirable employment is lacking, there are few adults to serve as role models. In contrast to more affluent suburban households where daily life is organized around job and career demands, children in inner-city areas are not socialized in the workings of the mainstream economy. If anything, globalization increases the attractiveness of gangs, and gang membership may provide inner-city youth with a substitute for the now-vanished high paid manufacturing jobs that are located overseas.[77]

Critical Theory and Delinquency Prevention: Restorative Justice

Some critical theorists believe that if conflict is the cause of delinquency, then removing or reducing economic and personal conflict is the key to its control. For some, this goal can only be accomplished by thoroughly reordering society so that capitalism is destroyed and a socialist state is created. Others call for a more "practical" application of conflict principles. Nowhere has this been more successful than in what is known as the restorative justice movement.

There has been an ongoing effort to reduce the conflict created by the application of harsh punishments to offenders, many of whom are powerless social outcasts. Conflict theorists argue that the "old methods" of punishment are a failure and scoff at claims that the crime rate has dropped because we have toughened laws and increased penalties.[78]

Rather than cast troubled kids aside, restorative justice is a method of restoring them back into the community.[79] The next sections discuss the foundation and principles of restorative justice.

The Concept of Restorative Justice The term "restorative justice" is often hard to define because it encompasses a variety of programs and practices that address victims' harms and needs, hold kids accountable for the harm they cause, and involve victims, offenders, and communities in the process of healing. The core value of the restoration process can be translated into respect for all, including those who are different from us and even those who seem to be our enemies. Restorative justice is a set of principles, a philosophy, an alternate set of guiding questions that provide an alternative framework for thinking about wrongdoing.[80] Restorative justice would reject concepts such as "punishment," "deterrence," and "incarceration" and embrace " apology," "rehabilitation," "reparation," "healing," "restoration," and "reintegration."

Restorative justice has grown out of a belief that the traditional justice system has done little to involve the community in the process of dealing with crime and wrongdoing. What has developed is a system of coercive punishments administered by bureaucrats that are inherently harmful to offenders and reduce the likelihood that offenders will ever become productive members of society. This system relies on punishment, stigma, and disgrace. Advocates of restorative justice argue that rather than today's punitive mentality what is needed is a justice policy that repairs the

The restorative justice approach to delinquency prevention would have police officers talk to youngsters about the potential social harm caused by delinquent acts rather than acting as social control agents who rely on punishment and deterrence to control crime.

harm caused by delinquency and that includes all parties who have suffered from that harm: the victim, the community, and the offender.

Reintegrative Shaming One of the key foundations of the restoration movement is contained in John Braithwaite's influential book *Crime, Shame, and Reintegration*.[81] Braithwaite's vision rests on the concept of **shame**: the feeling we get when we don't meet the standards we have set for ourselves or that significant others have set for us. Shame can lead people to believe that they are defective, that there is something wrong with them. Braithwaite notes that countries such as Japan, in which conviction for crimes brings an inordinate amount of shame, have extremely low crime rates. In Japan, criminal prosecution proceeds only when the normal process of public apology, compensation, and the victim's forgiveness breaks down.

> **shame**
> The feeling we get when we don't meet the standards we have set for ourselves or that significant others have set for us.

Shame is a powerful tool of informal social control. Citizens in cultures in which crime is not shameful, such as the United States, do not internalize an abhorrence for crime because when they are punished, they view themselves as mere victims of the justice system. Their punishment comes at the hands of neutral strangers, like police and judges, who are being paid to act. In contrast, shaming relies on the victim's participation.[82]

Braithwaite divides the concept of shame into two distinct types. The most common form of shaming typically involves stigmatization, an ongoing process of degradation in which the offender is branded as an evil person and cast out of society. Shaming can occur at a school disciplinary hearing or a juvenile court trial. Bestowing stigma and degradation may have a general deterrent effect: It makes people afraid of social rejection and public humiliation. As a specific deterrent, stigma is doomed to failure; kids who suffer humiliation at the hands of the juvenile justice system "reject their rejectors" by joining a deviant subculture of like-minded people, such as a juvenile gang, that collectively resists social control. Despite these dangers, there has been an ongoing effort to brand offenders and make their shame both public and permanent. Many states have passed sex offender registry and notification laws that make public the names of those convicted of sex offenses and warn neighbors of their presence in the community.[83]

But the fear of shame can backfire or be neutralized. When shame is managed well, people acknowledge they made mistakes and suffered disappointments, and try to work out what can be done to make things right; this is referred to as shame management. However, in some cases, to avoid the pain of shaming, people engage in improper shame management, a psychological process in which they deny shame by shifting the blame of their actions to their target or to others.[84] They may blame others, get angry, and take out their frustrations on those whom they can dominate. Improper shame management of this sort has been linked to antisocial acts including school yard bullying.[85]

Braithwaite argues that crime control can be better achieved through a policy of reintegrative shaming. Here disapproval is extended to the offenders' evil deeds, while at the same time they are cast as respected people who can be reaccepted by society. A critical element of reintegrative shaming occurs when the offenders begin to understand and recognize their wrongdoing and shame themselves. To be reintegrative, shaming must be brief and controlled and then followed by ceremonies of forgiveness, apology, and repentance.

To prevent delinquency, Braithwaite charges, society must encourage reintegrative shaming.[86] Similarly, parents who use reintegrative shaming techniques in their child-rearing practices may improve parent-child relationships and ultimately reduce the delinquent involvement of their children.[87] Because informal social controls may have a greater impact than legal or formal ones, it may not be surprising that the fear of personal shame can have a greater deterrent effect than the fear of legal sanctions. It may also be applied to produce specific deterrence. Offenders can meet with victims so that delinquents can experience shame. Family members and peers can be present to help the offender reintegrate.[88] Such efforts can humanize a system of justice that today relies on repression rather than forgiveness as the basis of specific deterrence. The Case Profile entitled "Jay's Story" shows how one young offender was restored back into society.

reintegrative shaming
Techniques used to allow offenders to understand and recognize their wrongdoing and shame themselves. To be reintegrative, shaming must be brief and controlled and then followed by ceremonies of forgiveness, apology, and repentance.

Case Profile

Jay's Story

JAY SIMMONS, THE YOUNGEST OF SIX CHILDREN, WAS LIVING WITH HIS FAMILY IN AN IMPOVERISHED COMMUNITY WHEN HE ENTERED THE JUVENILE JUSTICE SYSTEM. Growing up in a tough urban neighborhood took an early toll on Jay and his family. Around the age of 11, his problems were becoming more evident at home and school. He was absent from school on a regular basis, often stayed out all night with friends, and was eventually arrested on retail theft charges. Jay's parents were struggling to find permanent housing and faced being homeless, so Jay was voluntarily placed in foster care. A teacher at his school took a strong interest in Jay and offered to care for him until his parents could again meet his needs. The family continued to have contact with Jay and hoped to have him return home when their situation improved.

A smart young man with many positive attributes, Jay was an engaging person and a talented athlete who excelled in school sports. Many adults could see great potential in him, but Jay's criminal activity continued. His foster parents became increasingly concerned that they could not provide the care and treatment Jay needed. In a short period of time Jay was arrested on two more violations for disorderly conduct and battery while becoming involved in fights at school. He was at risk for being placed in a more secure living environment. In juvenile court for his delinquent behavior, Jay was sentenced to community supervision and probation. After an initial assessment, Jay's probation officer made formal dispositional recommendations to the court.

Although his foster parents had established clear rules for him, Jay felt torn between his old way of life and the new possibilities. Because of his family's issues of poverty, health concerns, unemployment, and homelessness, he had been very independent prior to his involvement with the juvenile justice system, doing what he wanted, staying in different places with different people much of the time. Jay would now struggle with the new rules and expectations. He missed some of his initial appointments with his probation officer and continued to skip school. There were also concerns that Jay was drinking alcohol and becoming involved in gang activities.

Jay's probation officer, family, and foster parents encouraged him to follow the court-ordered recommendations and understand the consequences of his behavior. He developed

(continued)

a very strong relationship with his foster parents, who were direct and honest with Jay about their concerns, often confronting him and contacting his coach, social workers, and parents about his behavior. The Substitute Care Unit at the local human services agency provided valuable support to Jay, his family, and foster parents during these difficult times, making home and school visits, trying to help maintain his placement in the foster home, and encouraging him to make good decisions. The team of professionals, coaches, and parents remained in close contact regarding Jay's behavior, as well as his academic progress. This level of parental involvement and teamwork made a huge impact on Jay and held him more accountable for his choices. He began to see his own potential and the need to make changes in his life.

Accountability was a key ingredient to Jay's success. He attended a retail theft group to address his criminal behavior and to encourage him to take responsibility for his actions. The program brought together eight to ten teenagers who had been involved in retail thefts with volunteers from the community, store security personnel, and a program leader. With fellow group members Jay could discuss the nature of his crimes, why they were wrong, the impact on victims, and how to prevent future delinquent acts by making better choices. The group participants and family members also met with a group facilitator to discuss the juvenile court process and what parents could expect if their children had further delinquencies, providing valuable information to the parents and a forum to ask questions and learn about other resources. Jay was also held accountable by being required to complete a period of community service. He worked with the Youth Restitution Program and was assigned a counselor who would help him locate volunteer opportunities and verify his participation.

Jay's involvement with a variety of programs and the many caring adults in his life made a significant difference for him. He continued to excel in sports and began to work harder in school. Although Jay never returned to his parental home, with the support of his foster parents he did remain in close contact with his family and they regularly attended activities together. With a new vision for his life, Jay started thinking seriously about going to college. He successfully completed his court-ordered programs and stayed out of trouble, eventually graduating from high school and receiving a full athletic scholarship to attend college. ∎

CRITICAL THINKING

Is there a danger that efforts to involve kids in restorative programs may backfire and instead label them as troubled youth who need to be monitored? What can be done to limit stigma and labeling?

The Process of Restoration The restoration process begins by redefining antisocial behavior in terms of a conflict among the offender, the victim, and affected constituencies (families, schools, workplaces, and so forth). Therefore, it is vitally important that the resolution take place within the context in which the conflict originally occurred rather than being transferred to a specialized institution that has no social connection to the community or group from which the conflict originated. In other words, most conflicts are better settled in the community than in a court.

By maintaining "ownership" or jurisdiction over the conflict, the community is able to express its shared outrage about the offense. Shared community outrage is directly communicated to the offender. The victim is also given a chance to voice his or her story, and the offender can directly communicate his or her need for social reintegration and treatment. All restoration programs involve an understanding between all the parties involved in a criminal act: the victim, the offender, and community. Although processes differ in structure and style, they generally include these elements:

▌ The offender is asked to recognize that he or she caused injury to personal and social relations along with a determination and acceptance of responsibility (ideally accompanied by a statement of remorse). Only then can the offender be restored as a productive member of the community.

▌ Restoration involves turning the justice system into a "healing" process rather than being a distributor of retribution and revenge.

■ Reconciliation is a big part of the restorative approach. Most people involved in offender-victim relationships actually know one another or were related in some way before the criminal incident took place. Instead of treating one of the involved parties as a victim deserving of sympathy and the other as a criminal deserving of punishment, it is more productive to address the issues that produced conflict between these people.[89]

■ The effectiveness of justice ultimately depends on the stake a person has in the community (or a particular social group). If a person does not value his or her membership in the group, the person will be unlikely to accept responsibility, show remorse, or repair the injuries caused by his or her actions. In contrast, people who have a stake in the community and its principle institutions, such as work, home, and school, find that their involvement enhances their personal and familial well-being.[90]

■ A commitment to the victim to make both material (monetary) restitution and symbolic reparation (an apology).

■ A determination of community support and assistance for both victim and offender.

 The **restorative justice** site discusses various programs that are ongoing around the world. Access the site via academic.cengage.com/criminaljustice/siegel.

The intended result of the process is to repair injuries suffered by the victim and the community while assuring reintegration of the offender. The basic principles of restorative justice are set out in Exhibit 5.1

Restoration Programs Negotiation, mediation, consensus-building, and peacemaking have been part of the dispute resolution process in European and Asian communities for centuries.[91] Native American and Native Canadian people have long used the type of community participation in the adjudication process (for example, sentencing circles, sentencing panels, elders panels) that restorative justice advocates are now embracing.[92]

In some Native American communities, people accused of breaking the law meet with community members, victims (if any), village elders, and agents of the justice system in a **sentencing circle**. Each member of the circle expresses his or her feelings about the act that was committed and raises questions or concerns. The accused can express regret about his or her actions and a desire to change the harmful behavior. People may suggest ways the offender can make things up to the community and those he or she harmed. A treatment program, such as Alcoholics Anonymous, can be suggested, if appropriate.

Restorative justice is now being embraced on many levels within our society and the justice system:

sentencing circle
A peacemaking technique in which offenders, victims, and other community members are brought together in an effort to formulate a sanction that addresses the needs of all.

EXHIBIT **5.1** -

The Basic Principles of Restorative Justice

■ Crime is an offense against human relationships.

■ Victims and the community are central to justice processes.

■ The first priority of justice processes is to assist victims.

■ The second priority is to restore the community, to the degree possible.

■ The offender has personal responsibility to victims and to the community for crimes committed.

■ The offender will develop improved competency and understanding as a result of the restorative justice experience.

■ Stakeholders share responsibilities for restorative justice through partnerships for action.

SOURCE: Anne Seymour, "Restorative Justice/Community Justice," in *National Victim Assistance Academy Textbook* (Washington, DC: National Victim Assistance Academy, 2001).

Willmar, Minnesota, Judge Donald Spilseth is an advocate of sentencing circles. He believes that this approach to sentencing gives youths time and attention the traditional court system never could. Circle sentencing is a court-approved option for some juvenile offenders, an alternative to the traditional route through the system that often involves a quick session in court, probation, and sometimes time spent at a detention facility. Circle sentencing focuses on restoring justice among offenders, the victims they harmed, and the community.

I *Community.* Communities that isolate people and have few mechanisms for interpersonal interaction encourage and sustain delinquency. Those that implement forms of community dialogue to identify problems and plan tactics for their elimination, guided by restorative justice practices and principles, may create a climate in which violent crime is less likely to occur.[93]

I *Schools.* Some schools have embraced restorative justice practices to deal with students who are involved in drug and alcohol abuse without having to resort to more punitive measures such as expulsion. Schools in Minnesota, Colorado, and elsewhere are now trying to involve students in "relational rehabilitation" programs that strive to improve individuals' relationships with key figures in the community who may have been harmed by their actions.[94]

I *Police.* Restorative justice has also been implemented by police when crime is first encountered. The new community policing models are an attempt to bring restorative concepts into law enforcement. Restorative justice relies on the fact that policy makers need to listen and respond to the needs of those who are to be affected by their actions, and community policing relies on policies established with input and exchanges between officers and citizens.[95]

I *Courts.* Restorative programs in the courts typically involve diverting the formal court process. These programs encourage meeting and reconciling the conflicts between offenders and victims via victim advocacy, mediation programs, and sentencing circles, in which crime victims and their families are brought together with offenders and their families in an effort to formulate a sanction that addresses the needs of each party. Victims are given a chance to voice their stories, and offenders can help compensate them financially or provide some service (for example, fixing damaged property).[96] The goal is to enable offenders to appreciate the damage they have caused, to make amends, and to be reintegrated back into society.

Two other popular restorative justice models are discussed in more detail below.

Family Group Conferencing (FGC) One popular restorative justice initiative, Family Group Conferencing (FGC), involves the group of people most affected by crime and delinquency—the victim and the offender, and the family, friends, and key supporters of both—in deciding the resolution of the delinquent/criminal act. FGC begins when a facilitator contacts the victim and offender to explain the process and invites them to the conference; the facilitator also asks them to identify and invite key members of their support system. Participation is voluntary. In order to participate in the FGC, the offending youth must be willing to admit his or her culpability in the delinquent act. The parties affected are brought together by a trained facilitator to discuss how they and others have been harmed by the offense and how that harm might be repaired.[97]

The conference typically begins with the offender describing the incident, followed by each participant describing the impact of the incident on his or her life. Through these narrations, a youthful offender is faced with the human impact of his or her behavior on the victim, on those close to the victim, and on the offender's own family and friends. The victim has the opportunity to express feelings and ask questions about the offense. After a thorough discussion of the impact of the offense on those present, the victim is asked to identify desired outcomes from the conference and thus helps to shape the obligations that will be placed on the offender. All participants may contribute to the process of determining how the offender might best repair the harm he or she has caused. The session ends with participants signing an agreement outlining their expectations and commitments.

Do FGC programs actually work? In a recent (2007) evaluation, Edmund McGarrell and Natalie Kroovand Hipple used a randomized design in order to test a FGC program in Indianapolis, Indiana. More than 800 first-time-offending youths were randomly assigned to either a family group conference or one of a number of more traditional court-ordered programs. The cases were tracked for 24 months following the initial arrest, and the results indicated a significant difference between the two groups: Kids in the traditional programs experienced much higher failure rates and committed more offenses after arrest than those assigned to FGC. Because this study was so carefully constructed, the findings are an important indicator of the utility of restorative justice measures with delinquent youth.[98]

Balanced and Restorative Justice (BARJ) Gordon Bazemore has argued that restoration programs should focus on the concept of *balance*.[99] According to this approach, the juvenile justice system should give equal weight to:

To read more about **BARJ** and how it is being implemented, go to academic.cengage.com/criminaljustice/siegel.

▌ *Holding offenders accountable to victims.* "Offender accountability" refers specifically to the requirement that offenders make amends for the harm resulting from their crimes by repaying or restoring losses to victims and the community.

▌ *Providing competency development for offenders in the system so they can pursue legitimate endeavors after release.* Competency development, the rehabilitative goal for intervention, requires that people who enter the justice system should exit the system more capable of being productive and responsible in the community.

▌ *Ensuring community safety.* The community protection goal explicitly acknowledges and endorses a long-time public expectation—a safe and secure community.

The balanced approach means that justice policies and priorities should seek to address each of the three goals in each case and that system balance should be pursued. The goal of achieving balance suggests that no one objective can take precedence over any other without creating a system that is "out of balance" and implies that efforts to achieve one goal (e.g., offender accountability) should not hinder efforts to achieve other goals.

BARJ is founded on the belief that justice is best served when the victim, community, and offender are viewed as equal clients of the justice system who will receive fair and balanced attention, be actively involved in the justice process, and gain tangible benefits from their interactions with the justice system. Elements of one program based on the BARJ system that is now being used in Washington County, New York, are set out in Exhibit 5.2.

Research efforts generally show that BARJ programs can effectively reduce offender recidivism rates. In addition to recidivism reduction, restoration, victim and offender satisfaction with the process, and program completion are commonly desired outcomes. Research indicates the following circumstances affect the likelihood of program completion:

▌ When there is a strong focus on restoration, program completion is higher.

▌ The likelihood of completion, particularly for restitution and community service, may be related to level of supervision and time for program completion.[100]

Program satisfaction for the victim and offender may be affected by a number of issues:

▌ Perceived fairness of the process and outcome increases satisfaction.

▌ Satisfaction with mediation activities increases when they are in person and is related to the attitude of the mediator.

▌ Voluntary participation by the victim affects satisfaction with the program.

Though victims' desire to participate in BARJ programs is widespread, a small but substantial proportion prefer for the offender be processed through traditional juvenile justice means. Victim satisfaction with the program decreases when participation is mandatory.[101]

EXHIBIT **5.2**

Juvenile Community Restoration

The mission of the Washington County Juvenile Community Restoration Program is to develop competency and accountability in adjudicated juveniles, age 7 to 15. The program:

▌ Treats each youth as an individual

▌ Identifies risk factors that contribute to the offense or behavior

▌ Develops a case plan targeting those risk factors

▌ Provides intensive supervision of the juvenile for 120 days

▌ May require the juvenile to participate in other competency programs which may include basic life skills, cognitive skills development, anger management

▌ Provides strict rules

▌ Makes referrals to outside services (drug treatment, etc.)

▌ Periodically visits the juvenile's home, school, other family members, and service providers to discuss his/her progress and verify information

▌ Requires each juvenile to participate in community restoration projects

The Balanced Approach Restorative Justice Model

There is an obligation on the part of the juvenile to restore both the victim and the community. Each juvenile will be required to sign a behavior contract, work a minimum of 25 hours of community service, make payment of restitution, and when appropriate, participate in victim/offender mediation. Each component of the Juvenile Community Restoration program must, in some way, promote the three components of the Balanced Approach:

Restorative Justice Model

▌ Community Protection: The public has the right to be safe and secure.

▌ Victim Restoration: The victim, to the degree possible, is to be restored to pre-crime state, giving the victim a chance to become involved in the justice system and protecting the victim from further harm and intimidation.

▌ Competency Building: Juvenile offenders who come within the jurisdiction of the court should leave the system more capable of being productive and responsible to the community.

SOURCE: Washington County Alternative Sentencing Agency, 383 Broadway, Fort Edward, NY 12828, www.co.washington.ny.us/Departments/Alt/jcr.htm (accessed September 30, 2007).

Summary

1. Understand the concept of symbolic interaction and the role symbols play in defining reality

▌ Social reaction or labeling theory holds that criminality is promoted by becoming negatively labeled by significant others.

▌ Social reaction theory is based on the concept of symbolic interaction.

▌ People communicate through symbols that can be gestures, words, or physical products.

▌ According to this view, those in power, moral entrepreneurs, wish to shape the law and justice process according to their own sense of morality.

▌ People are labeled deviant if they fall outside this subjective definition of good.

2. Be aware of the impact of the labeling process

▌ Labels such as delinquent isolate kids from society and lock them into lives of antisocial behaviors.

▌ Labels create expectations that the labeled person will act in a certain way; labeled people are always watched and suspected.

▌ Eventually these people begin to accept their labels as personal identities, locking them further into lives of crime and deviance.

3. Define the terms "primary deviants" and "secondary deviants"

▌ According to Lemert, primary deviants are people who do bad acts but are not defined as deviants by others.

▌ Secondary deviants are people who consider themselves deviants and are viewed by others as such. They accept a deviant identity as a personal role.

▌ Lemert suggests that people who accept labels are involved in secondary deviance, while primary deviants are able to maintain an undamaged identity.

4. Identify the four quadrants of Becker's table of deviance and reaction

▌ Those kids who engage in delinquency and also get caught and labeled are called *pure deviants*.

▌ *Conformists* are both rule-abiding and free of negative labels.

▌ Some kids are *falsely accused* or blamed for something they did not do.

▌ Some kids who continually break rules are able to avoid labeling; these are called *secret deviants*.

5. Discuss the unequal application of delinquent labels

▌ An important principle of social reaction theory is that the law is differentially applied, benefiting those who hold economic and social power and penalizing the powerless.

▌ The probability of being brought under the control of legal authority is a function of a person's race, wealth, gender, and social standing.

▌ The labeling process favors the powerful members of society who direct its content and penalize people whose actions represent a threat to those in control, such as minority group members and the poor who demand equal rights

6. Be familiar with the long-term effects of labels

| If a devalued status is conferred by a significant other—teacher, police officer, elder, parent, or valued peer—the negative label and resulting stigma may cause permanent harm.

| Labeled kids may consider themselves social outcasts.

| If they are labeled as a delinquent they may find their eligibility for employment severely restricted.

| If the label is bestowed as the result of adjudication for a delinquent act, the labeled person may be subjected to official sanctions ranging from a mild reprimand to incarceration.

| Beyond these immediate results, a person who has been negatively labeled will have an increasing commitment to a deviant career.

| Kids who perceive that they have been negatively labeled by significant others such as peers and teachers are also more likely to self-report delinquent behavior and to adopt a deviant self-concept.

| Although labels may not have caused adolescents to initiate delinquent behaviors, once applied they increase the likelihood of persistent offending because kids now have a "damaged identity."

| When kids are labeled as troublemakers or as having social problems, they may join up with similarly outcast delinquent peers in a clique or group that facilitates their antisocial behavior.

| Membership in a deviant subculture often involves conforming to group norms that conflict with those of conventional society.

| After someone is labeled because of some unusual or inexplicable act, people begin to reconstruct their identity so that the act and the label are correlated.

| Labels become the basis of personal identity. As the negative feedback of law enforcement agencies, parents, friends, teachers, and other figures amplifies the force of the original label, stigmatized offenders may begin to reevaluate their own identities.

| Deviant behavior patterns are a response to an earlier labeling experience; youths act out these social roles even if they were falsely bestowed.

7. Analyze the strengths of the social reaction perspective

| Social reaction theory identifies the role played by social control agents in the process of delinquency causation. Delinquent behavior cannot be fully understood if the agencies and individuals empowered to control and treat it are neglected.

| Social reaction theory recognizes that delinquency is not a disease or pathological behavior. It focuses attention on the social interactions and reactions that shape individual behavior.

| Social reaction theory distinguishes between delinquent acts (primary deviance) and delinquent careers (secondary deviance) and shows that these concepts must be interpreted and treated differently.

8. Be familiar with the core elements of social conflict theory

| According to social conflict theory, those who hold power in contemporary society get to set the rules, control the law, and decide who is a deviant, delinquent, and/or criminal.

| Social conflict theory asserts that society is in a state of constant internal conflict, and focuses on the role of social and governmental institutions as mechanisms for social control.

| Social conflict theorists view the law and the justice system as vehicles for controlling the have-not members of society.

| Conflict theorists view delinquency as a normal response to the conditions created by capitalism.

| Conflict theorists suggest that, rather than inhibiting delinquent behavior, the justice system may help to sustain such behavior.

| Globalization, which usually refers to the process of creating transnational markets and political and legal systems, has shifted the focus of critical inquiry to a world perspective.

| Globalization may have a profound influence on the future of indigent youth. Workers in the United States may be replaced in high-paying manufacturing jobs not by machines but by foreign workers in overseas factories.

9. Define the basic principles of restorative justice

| Restorative justice uses humanistic, nonpunitive strategies to right wrongs and restore social harmony.

| Restorative justice grew out of a belief that the traditional justice system has done little to involve the community in the process of dealing with crime and wrongdoing.

| Reintegrative shaming techniques can be used to allow offenders to understand and recognize their wrongdoing and shame themselves. To be reintegrative, shaming must be brief and controlled and then followed by ceremonies of forgiveness, apology, and repentance.

| The restoration process begins by redefining antisocial behavior in terms of a conflict among the offender, the victim, and affected constituencies.

| The offender is asked to recognize that he or she caused injury to personal and social relations along with a determination and acceptance of responsibility.

| Restoration involves turning the justice system into a "healing" process rather than being a distributor of retribution and revenge.

| Reconciliation is a big part of the restorative approach.

- The effectiveness of justice ultimately depends on the stake a person has in the community.
- A commitment to the victim to make both material restitution and symbolic reparation is an important part of restorative justice.

10. Discuss how restoration can be used to reduce delinquent behaviors
- Restoration techniques include negotiation, mediation, consensus-building, sentencing circles, sentencing panels, and elders panels.

- According to restorative justice, rather than punishing, shaming, and excluding those who violate the law, efforts should be made to use humanistic techniques that reintegrate people into society.
- Restorative programs rely on victims, relatives, neighbors, and community institutions rather than courts and prisons.
- Two well-known restorative programs are Family Group Conferencing and the BARJ approach.

Key Terms

labeling theory, p. 156
symbolic interaction, p. 156
status symbol, p. 156
euthanasia, p. 157
stigmatize, p. 158
primary deviance, p. 158

secondary deviance, p. 158
retrospective reading, p. 162
dramatization of evil, p. 162
self-fulfilling prophecy, p. 162
degradation ceremony, p. 163
deinstitutionalization, p. 164

social conflict theory, p. 164
globalization, p. 167
restorative justice, p. 168
shame, p. 169
reintegrative shaming, p. 170
sentencing circle, p. 172

Viewpoint

As an expert on juvenile justice, you have been asked to review and revise a proposed court-based restorative justice program. The administrator sends you the following proposal:

- In cases where an offender has admitted to the act, the judge can, at his or her discretion, offer the adolescent the choice of either the normal course of justice or participation in the community reparation project.
- At this point the court adjourns for approximately 30 minutes while the probation officer explains the project to the offender. If the offender decides to participate in the project, a meeting will be called in the near future.
- This meeting is always attended by the youth, two panel members representing the community, the police officers who have been involved in the case, and the probation officer. If the delinquent acts involve victims, they are also invited to attend the meeting, although their participation is not mandatory.
- At the meeting, offenders are asked to explain the circumstances of the offense, why it happened, how they felt about it then, and how they feel about their actions now. Together, the group decides how the

offender might make reparation to the victim and/or the community for the damage caused by the offense.
- Once agreement is reached about the form of the reparation, a contract is drawn up that sets out treatment courses (for example, treatment for alcoholism, substance abuse, anger management, and so on) the offender will be expected to take. Reparation may include letters of apology to the victim, restitution, and other proportionate and appropriate activities.
- Contracts generally cover a period of approximately six months and are monitored by the probation officer. If the terms of the contract are successfully completed, the record of the offense will be dropped. If the terms are not met, the case will go back to the juvenile court and proceed in the normal manner.

As a delinquency expert, what is your take on the proposed program? How do you think the program should handle kids who fail to complete the restoration bargain? Are there any other approaches you would try with these kids?

Doing Research on the Web

There are numerous restorative justice sites on the web that can help you formulate an answer. Many are internationally based. You might want to look at:
- The Victim-Offender Reconciliation Program (VORP) Information and Resource Center

- Restorative Justice Online
- Australian Institute of Criminology
- Restorative Justice Knowledge Base
  All these websites can be accessed via
  academic.cengage.com/criminaljustice/siegel

Questions for Discussion

1. How would a restorative justice advocate respond to a proposed policy easing the waiver of youth to adult court?

2. Considering recent changes in American culture, how would a critical theorist explain an increase in the juvenile gang population?

3. Is conflict inevitable in all cultures? If not, what can be done to reduce the level of conflict in our own society?

4. One way to reduce stigma and labeling would be to legalize acts that are now considered illegal. If you had the power, what would you legalize and what might be the consequences?

6. Are you familiar with any instances of "retrospective reading" in your home town? Have you ever engaged in it yourself, saying "I always knew he had problems"?

Notes

1. Lynne Koziey, "Teen Found Not Guilty in Fatal Fist Fight," *Calgary Herald*, 10 March 2002.

2. Edwin Schur, *Labeling Deviant Behavior* (New York: Harper & Row, 1972), p. 21.

3. George Herbert Mead, *Mind, Self and Society* (Chicago: University of Chicago Press, 1934); George Herbert Mead, *The Philosophy of the Act* (Chicago: University of Chicago Press, 1938); Charles Horton Cooley, *Human Nature and the Social Order* (New York: Schocken, 1964), originally published in 1902; Herbert Blumer, *Symbolic Interactionism: Perspective and Method* (Englewood Cliffs, NJ: Prentice Hall, 1969).

4. Ernesto Londoño, "Court Says Consensual Sex Can't Become Rape," *Washington Post*, 2 November 2006, www.washingtonpost.com/wp-dyn/content/article/2006/11/01/AR2006110103225.html (accessed August 27, 2007).

5. Kai Erickson, "Notes on the Sociology of Deviance," *Social Problems* 9:397–414 (1962).

6. Howard Becker, *Outsiders, Studies in the Sociology of Deviance* (New York: Macmillan, 1963), p. 9.

7. Laurie Goodstein, "The Architect of the 'Gay Conversion' Campaign," *New York Times*, 13 August 1998, p. A10.

8. Bruce Link, Elmer Streuning, Francis Cullen, Patrick Shrout, and Bruce Dohrenwend, "A Modified Labeling Theory Approach to Mental Disorders: An Empirical Assessment," *American Sociological Review* 54:400–423 (1989).

9. Linda Jackson, John Hunter, and Carole Hodge, "Physical Attractiveness and Intellectual Competence: A Meta-Analytic Review," *Social Psychology Quarterly* 58:108–122 (1995).

10. Mike Adams, Craig Robertson, Phyllis Gray-Ray, and Melvin Ray, "Labeling and Delinquency," *Adolescence* 38:171–186 (2003).

11. Edwin Lemert, *Social Pathology* (New York: McGraw-Hill, 1951).

12. Ibid., p. 75.

13. Howard Becker, *Outsiders*.

14. Roland Chilton and Jim Galvin, "Race, Crime and Criminal Justice," *Crime and Delinquency* 31:3–14 (1985).

15. National Minority Advisory Council on Criminal Justice, *The Inequality of Justice* (Washington, DC: author, 1981), p. 200.

16. Leslie Margolin, "Deviance on Record: Techniques for Labeling Child Abusers in Official Documents," *Social Problems* 39:58–68 (1992).

17. Christina DeJong and Kenneth Jackson, "Putting Race into Context: Race, Juvenile Justice Processing, and Urbanization," *Justice Quarterly* 15:487–504 (1998).

18. Joan Petersilia, "Racial Disparities in the Criminal Justice System: A Summary," *Crime and Delinquency* 31:15–34 (1985).

19. *President's Commission on Law Enforcement and the Administration of Youth Crime, Task Force Report: Juvenile Delinquency and Youth* (Washington, DC: U.S. Government Printing Office, 1967), p. 43.

20. Adams, Robertson, Gray-Ray, and Ray, "Labeling and Delinquency."

21. Jón Gunnar Bernburg, Marvin Krohn, and Craig Rivera, "Official Labeling, Criminal Embeddedness, and Subsequent Delinquency: A Longitudinal Test of Labeling Theory," *Journal of Research in Crime and Delinquency* 43:67–88 (2006).

22. Xiaoru Liu, "The Conditional Effect of Peer Groups on the Relationship between Parental Labeling and Youth Delinquency," *Sociological Perspectives* 43:499–515 (2000).

23. Ruth Triplett, "The Conflict Perspective, Symbolic Interactionism, and the Status Characteristics Hypothesis," *Justice Quarterly* 10:540–558 (1993).

24. Lening Zhang, "Official Offense Status and Self-Esteem among Chinese Youths," *Journal of Criminal Justice* 31:99–105 (2003).

25. Lee Michael Johnson, Ronald Simons, and Rand Conger, "Criminal Justice System Involvement and Continuity of Youth Crime," *Youth and Society* 36:3–29 (2004).

26. Gary Sweeten, "Who Will Graduate? Disruption of High School Education by Arrest and Court Involvement," *Justice Quarterly* 23:462–480 (2006).

27. Suzanne Ageton and Delbert Elliott, *The Effect of Legal Processing on Self-Concept* (Boulder, CO: Institute of Behavioral Science, 1973).

28. Robert Sampson and John Laub, "A Life-Course Theory of Cumulative Disadvantage and the Stability of Delinquency," in Terence Thornberry, ed., *Developmental Theories of Crime and Delinquency* (New Brunswick, NJ: Transaction Press, 1997), pp. 133–161; Douglas Smith and Robert Brame, "On the Initiation and Continuation of Delinquency," *Criminology* 4:607–630 (1994).

29. Howard Kaplan and Hiroshi Fukurai, "Negative Social Sanctions, Self-Rejection, and Drug Use," *Youth and Society* 23:275–298 (1992).

30. Howard Kaplan, *Toward a General Theory of Deviance: Contributions from Perspectives on Deviance and Criminality* (College Station, TX: Texas A&M University, n.d.).

31. M. J. Harris, R. Milich, E. M. Corbitt, D. W. Hoover, and M. Brady, "Self-Fulfilling Effects of Stigmatizing Information on Children's Social Interactions," *Journal of Personality and Social Psychology* 63:41–50 (1992).

32. Sampson and Laub, "A Life-Course Theory of Cumulative Disadvantage and the Stability of Delinquency."

33. Jón Gunnar Bernburg and Marvin Krohn, "Labeling, Life Chances, and Adult Crime: The Direct and Indirect Effects of Official Intervention in Adolescence on Crime in Early Adulthood," *Criminology* 41:1287–1319 (2003).

34. Bernburg, Krohn, and Rivera, "Official Labeling, Criminal Embeddedness, and Subsequent Delinquency: A Longitudinal Test of Labeling Theory."

35. Karen Heimer and Ross L. Matsueda, "Role-Taking, Role-Commitment, and Delinquency," *American Sociological Review* 59:365–390 (1994).

36. See, for example, Kaplan and Fukurai, "Negative Social Sanctions, Self-Rejection, and Drug Use"; Howard Kaplan and Robert Johnson, "Negative Social Sanctions and Juvenile Delinquency: Effects of Labeling in a Model of Deviant Behavior," *Social Science Quarterly* 72:98–122 (1991); Howard Kaplan, Robert Johnson, and Carol Bailey, "Deviant Peers and Deviant Behavior: Further Elaboration of a Model," *Social Psychology Quarterly* 30:277–284 (1987).

37. Kaplan, *Toward a General Theory of Deviance.*

38. Kaplan, Johnson, and Bailey, "Deviant Peers and Deviant Behavior: Further Elaboration of a Model."

39. Adams, Robertson, Gray-Ray, and Ray, "Labeling and Delinquency."

40. Kaplan, *Toward a General Theory of Deviance.*

41. Michael Levenson and Brian R. Ballou, "Teen Reportedly Talked of Trying to Kill," *Boston Globe*, 21 January 2007, p. 1.

42. John Lofland, *Deviance and Identity* (Englewood Cliffs, NJ: Prentice Hall, 1969).

43. Frank Tannenbaum, *Crime and the Community* (New York: Columbia University Press, 1938), pp. 19–20.

44. Charles H. Cooley, *Human Nature and the Social Order* (New York: Scribner's, 1902).

45. Ross Matsueda, "Reflected Appraisals, Parental Labeling, and Delinquency: Specifying a Symbolic Interactionist Theory," *American Journal of Sociology* 97:1577–1611 (1992).

46. Adams, Robertson, Gray-Ray, Ray, "Labeling and Delinquency."
47. Tannenbaum, *Crime and the Community*.
48. Garfinkel, *Conditions of Successful Degradation Ceremonies*, p. 424.
49. Adams, Robertson, Gray-Ray, and Ray, "Labeling and Delinquency," pp. 171–186.
50. Ibid., p. 178.
51. Nadine Lanctôt, Stephen Cernkovich, and Peggy Giordano, "Delinquent Behavior, Official Delinquency, and Gender: Consequences for Adulthood Functioning and Well-Being," *Criminology* 45:131–157 (2007).
52. Jack Gibbs, "Conceptions of Deviant Behavior: The Old and the New," *Pacific Sociological Review* 9:11–13 (1966).
53. Charles A. Murray and Louis Cox, *Beyond Probation* (Beverly Hills: Sage Publications, 1979).
54. Charles Tittle, "Labeling and Crime: An Empirical Evaluation," in Walter Gove, ed., *The Labeling of Deviance: Evaluating a Perspective* (New York: Wiley, 1975), pp. 157–179.
55. Megan Kurlychek, Robert Brame, and Shawn Bushway, "Enduring Risk? Old Criminal Records and Predictions of Future Criminal Involvement," *Crime and Delinquency* 53:64–83 (2007).
56. Raymond Paternoster and Leeann Iovanni, "The Labeling Perspective and Delinquency: An Elaboration of the Theory and an Assessment of the Evidence," *Justice Quarterly* 6:358–394 (1989).
57. Shadd Maruna, Thomas Lebel, Nick Mitchell, and Michelle Naples, "Pygmalion in the Reintegration Process: Desistance from Crime through the Looking Glass," *Psychology, Crime, and Law* 10:271–281 (2004).
58. Scott Davies and Julian Tanner, "The Long Arm of the Law: Effects of Labeling on Employment," *Sociological Quarterly* 44:385–404 (2003).
59. Bernburg and Krohn, "Labeling, Life Chances, and Adult Crime."
60. Maruna, Lebel, Mitchell, and Naples, "Pygmalion in the Reintegration Process."
61. James Austin and Barry Krisberg, "The Unmet Promise of Alternatives to Incarceration," *Crime and Delinquency* 28:3–19 (1982).
62. William Selke, "Diversion and Crime Prevention," *Criminology* 20:395–406 (1982).
63. Robert F. Meier, "The New Criminology: Continuity in Criminological Theory," *The Journal of Criminal Law and Criminology (1973–)* 67:461–469 (1976).
64. Tony Platt and Cecilia O'Leary, "Patriot Acts," *Social Justice* 30:5–21 (2003).
65. Gresham M. Sykes, "The Rise of Critical Criminology," *The Journal of Criminal Law and Criminology (1973–)*, 65:206–213 (1974).
66. Ibid.
67. Matthew Petrocelli, Alex Piquero, and Michael Smith, "Conflict Theory and Racial Profiling: An Empirical Analysis of Police Traffic Stop Data," *Journal of Criminal Justice* 31:1–10 (2003).
68. Malcolm Homes, "Minority Threat and Police Brutality: Determinants of Civil Rights Criminal Complaints in U.S. Municipalities," *Criminology* 38:343–368 (2000).
69. Ibid.
70. Jeffery Reiman, *The Rich Get Richer and the Poor Get Prison* (New York: Wiley, 1984), pp. 43–44.
71. Robert Gordon, "Capitalism, Class, and Crime in America," *Crime and Delinquency* 19:174 (1973).
72. Richard Quinney, *Class, State, and Crime* (New York: Longman, 1977), p. 52.
73. Anthony Platt, "The Triumph of Benevolence: The Origins of the Juvenile Justice System in the United States," in Richard Quinney, ed., *Criminal Justice in America: A Critical Understanding* (Boston: Little, Brown, 1974), p. 367; see also Anthony Platt, *The Child Savers* (Chicago: University of Chicago Press, 1969).
74. Gregg Barak, "Revisionist History, Visionary Criminology, and Needs-Based Justice," *Contemporary Justice Review* 6:217–225 (2003).
75. Kitty Kelley Epstein, "The Whitening of the American Teaching Force: A Problem of Recruitment or a Problem of Racism?" *Social Justice* 32:89–102 (2005).
76. William Julius Wilson, *The Truly Disadvantaged* (Chicago: University of Chicago Press, 1987); *When Work Disappears, The World of the Urban Poor* (New York: Alfred Knopf, 1996); *The Bridge over the Racial Divide: Rising Inequality and Coalition Politics* (Wildavsky Forum Series, 2) (Berkeley: University of California Press, 1999).
77. To read about Wilson's views, go to William Julius Wilson and Richard Taub, *There Goes the Neighborhood: Racial, Ethnic, and Class Tensions in Four Chicago Neighborhoods and Their Meaning for America* (New York: Knopf, 2006); Wilson, *The Truly Disadvantaged; When Work Disappears, The World of the Urban Poor; The Bridge over the Racial Divide: Rising Inequality and Coalition Politics*.
78. Robert DeFina and Thomas Arvanites, "The Weak Effect of Imprisonment on Crime: 1971–1998," *Social Science Quarterly* 83:635–654 (2002).
79. Kathleen Daly and Russ Immarigeon, "The Past, Present and Future of Restorative Justice: Some Critical Reflections," *Contemporary Justice Review* 1:21–45 (1998).
80. Howard Zehr, *The Little Book of Restorative Justice* (Intercourse, PA: Good Books, 2002), pp. 1–10.
81. John Braithwaite, *Crime, Shame, and Reintegration* (Melbourne, Australia: Cambridge University Press, 1989).
82. Ibid., p. 81.
83. Anthony Petrosino and Carolyn Petrosino, "The Public Safety Potential of Megan's Law in Massachusetts: An Assessment from a Sample of Criminal Sexual Psychopaths," *Crime and Delinquency* 45:140–158 (1999).
84. Eliza Ahmed, Nathan Harris, John Braithwaite, and Valerie Braithwaite, *Shame Management through Reintegration* (Cambridge, England: Cambridge University Press, 2001).
85. Eliza Ahmed, "What, Me Ashamed? Shame Management and School Bullying," *Journal of Research in Crime and Delinquency* 41:269–294 (2004).
86. For more on this approach, see Jane Mugford and Stephen Mugford, "Shame and Reintegration in the Punishment and Deterrence of Spouse Assault," paper presented at the annual meeting of the American Society of Criminology, San Francisco, November 1991.
87. Carter Hay, "An Exploratory Test of Braithwaite's Reintegrative Shaming Theory," *Journal of Research in Crime and Delinquency* 38:132–153 (2001).
88. Mugford and Mugford, "Shame and Reintegration in the Punishment and Deterrence of Spouse Assault."
89. Gene Stephens, "The Future of Policing: From a War Model to a Peace Model," in Brendan Maguire and Polly Radosh, eds., *The Past, Present and Future of American Criminal Justice* (Dix Hills, NY: General Hall, 1996), pp. 77–93.
90. Rick Shifley, "The Organization of Work as a Factor in Social Well-Being," *Contemporary Justice Review* 6:105–126 (2003).
91. Kay Pranis, "Peacemaking Circles: Restorative Justice in Practice Allows Victims and Offenders to Begin Repairing the Harm," *Corrections Today* 59:74–78 (1997).
92. Carol LaPrairie, "The 'New' Justice: Some Implications for Aboriginal Communities," *Canadian Journal of Criminology* 40:61–79 (1998).
93. Diane Schaefer, "A Disembodied Community Collaborates in a Homicide: Can Empathy Transform a Failing Justice System?" *Contemporary Justice Review* 6:133–143 (2003).
94. David R. Karp and Beau Breslin, "Restorative Justice in School Communities," *Youth and Society* 33:249–272 (2001).
95. Paul Jesilow and Deborah Parsons, "Community Policing as Peacemaking," *Policing and Society* 10:163–183 (2000).
96. Gordon Bazemore and Curt Taylor Griffiths, "Conferences, Circles, Boards, and Mediations: The 'New Wave' of Community Justice Decision Making," *Federal Probation* 61:25–37 (1997).
97. This section is based on Mark Umbreit, *Family Group Conferencing, Implications for Crime Victims* (Washington, DC: Office for Victims of Crime, 2000) www.ojp.usdoj.gov/ovc/publications/infores/restorative_justice/restorative_justice_ascii_pdf/ncj176347.pdf (accessed June 17, 2007).
98. Edmund McGarrell and Natalie Kroovand, "Hipple Family Group Conferencing and Re-Offending Among First-Time Juvenile Offenders: The Indianapolis Experiment," *Justice Quarterly* 24:221–246 (2007).
99. This section is based on Gordon Bazemore and Mara Schiff, "Paradigm Muddle or Paradigm Paralysis? The Wide and Narrow Roads to Restorative Justice Reform (or, a Little Confusion May Be a Good Thing)," *Contemporary Justice Review* 7:37–57 (2004).
100. Juvenile Justice Evaluation Center online, www.jrsa.org/jjec/programs/barj/state-of-evaluation.html (accessed July 5, 2007).
101. Ibid.

Developmental Theories of Delinquency: Life-Course and Latent Trait

6

Chapter Outline

Creating a Life-Course Theory of Delinquency

Life-Course Fundamentals

Life-Course Concepts

Problem Behavior Syndrome

Pathways to Delinquency

Age of Onset/Continuity of Crime

Continuity and Desistance

FOCUS ON DELINQUENCY: The Path to Delinquency

Adolescent-Limiteds and Life-Course Persisters

Theories of the Delinquent Life Course

Sampson and Laub: Age-Graded Theory

FOCUS ON DELINQUENCY: Shared Beginnings, Divergent Lives

Latent Trait Theories

Crime and Human Nature

General Theory of Crime

Evaluating Developmental Theories

Public Policy Implications of Developmental Theory

POLICY AND PRACTICE: Across Ages

Chapter Objectives

1. Compare and contrast the two forms of developmental theory
2. Trace the history of and influences on developmental theory
3. Know the principles of the life-course approach to developmental theory
4. Be familiar with the concept of problem behavior syndrome
5. Identify the paths and directions of the delinquent life course
6. Distinguish between adolescent-limited and life-course persistent offenders
7. Articulate the principles of Sampson and Laub's age-graded life-course theory
8. Be able to define the concept of the latent trait
9. Know the principles and assumptions of the General Theory of Crime
10. Discuss the strengths and weaknesses of the GTC

On September 4, 1989, investigators in Warwick, Rhode Island, went to the home of Joan Heaton, 39, and her two children, Jennifer, 10, and Melissa, 8, who had been found murdered, victims of an apparent burglary attempt gone awry. Suspicion swiftly fell on Craig Price, a neighborhood kid with a long history of offenses, including breaking and entering, theft, peeping into houses, and using drugs. Craig was also known to have a violent temper, and police had been called to his house on more than one occasion to settle disputes. While investigating the case, they discovered quite a bit of similarity with the July 1987 death of Rebecca Spencer, who had been found in her living room, stabbed repeatedly with a packing knife.

Investigators working on the Heaton case decided it was time to question Craig more thoroughly. They went to Craig's house and asked him to come with his parents to the police station. They later obtained a warrant, and while searching his home found evidence incriminating him in the Heaton case. A trash bag full of incriminating evidence was also found in a shed behind the house. Now under arrest, Craig gave a detailed account of the Heaton murders, confessing that he had only planned a burglary and killed the mother and her daughters when they were awakened. He also confessed to killing Rebecca Spencer under similar circumstances when he was just 13 years old.

Originally sentenced as a juvenile to serve a five-year term, Craig refused to submit to psychiatric examinations and therapy while in the juvenile institution. At a court hearing he was found in civil contempt and had a year added to his incarceration, to be served at the Adult Correctional Institution in Cranston, Rhode Island. He continued to have problems while in prison and had additional years added to his sentence, perhaps because authorities were simply afraid to release him. Today, there is no telling exactly when Craig Price will be released from prison. His projected release date is scheduled for February 2022.[1]

What drives someone such as Craig Price to begin killing at age 13? According to developmental theorists, the roots of delinquency can be traced to an adolescent's childhood. Few kids begin their offending career by getting involved in a murder plot. Most serious offenders have a long history of antisocial activities, beginning early in their childhood and continuing into adolescence and adulthood.

Because serious juvenile offending is rarely a "one shot deal," it has become important to chart the natural history of a delinquent career. We know that most young offenders do not become adult delinquents. Why is it that some kids become delinquents and then abandon the delinquent way of life as they mature, whereas others persist in delinquency into their adulthood? Why do some offenders escalate their delinquent activities while others decrease or limit their law violations? Why do some offenders specialize in a particular delinquency while others become generalists who shoplift, take drugs, engage in violence, steal cars, and so on? Why do some delinquents reduce delinquent activity and then resume it later in life? Research now shows that some offenders begin their delinquent careers at a very early age, whereas others begin later. How can early- and late-onset delinquency be explained?

Focusing attention on these questions has produced what is known as the developmental theory of delinquency, a view that looks at the onset, continuity, and termination of a delinquent career. There are actually two distinct developmental views. The first, referred to as the life-course theory, suggests that delinquent behavior is a dynamic process, influenced by individual characteristics as well as social experiences, and that the factors that cause antisocial behaviors change dramatically over a person's lifespan.

The life-course theory is challenged by another group of scholars who suggest that human development is controlled by a "master" or latent trait that remains stable and unchanging throughout a person's lifetime. As people travel through their life course this trait or propensity is always there, directing their behavior. Because this master latent trait is enduring, the ebb and flow of delinquent behavior is shaped less by personal change and more by the impact of external forces such as delinquent opportunity. Delinquency may increase when an adolescent joins a gang, which provides him with more opportunities to steal, take drugs, and attack others. In other words, the propensity to commit delinquent acts is constant, but the opportunity to commit them is constantly fluctuating. The main points, similarities, and differences of both positions are set out in Concept Summary 6.1.

developmental theory
The view that delinquency is a dynamic process, influenced by social experiences as well as individual characteristics.

life-course theory
Theory that focuses on changes in criminality over the life course; developmental theory.

latent trait
A stable feature, characteristic, property, or condition, such as defective intelligence or impulsive personality, that makes some people delinquency-prone over the life course.

CREATING A LIFE-COURSE THEORY OF DELINQUENCY

The foundation of developmental theory can be traced to the pioneering work of Sheldon and Eleanor Glueck. While at Harvard University in the 1930s, the Gluecks popularized research on the life cycle of delinquent careers. In a series of longitudinal research studies, they followed the careers of known delinquents to determine the social, biological, and psychological characteristics that predicted persistent offending.[2]

Concept Summary 6.1
Latent Trait vs. Life-Course Theories

Latent Trait Theory
- People do not change, delinquent opportunities change; maturity brings fewer opportunities
- People have a master trait: personality, intelligence, genetic makeup
- Early social control and proper parenting can reduce delinquent propensity

Life-Course Theories
- People have multiple traits: social, psychological, economic
- People change over the life course
- Family, job, peers influence behavior

Similarities
- Delinquent careers are a passage
- Personal and structural factors influence crime
- External change affects crime

Differences
- Latent trait: An unchanging master trait controls antisocial behavior
- Life-course: People are constantly evolving

The Gluecks made extensive use of interviews and records in their elaborate comparisons of delinquents and nondelinquents.[3]

The Gluecks' research focused on early onset of delinquency as a harbinger of a delinquent career: "The deeper the roots of childhood maladjustment, the smaller the chance of adult adjustment."[4] They also noted the stability of offending careers: Children who are antisocial early in life are the most likely to continue their offending careers into adulthood.

The Gluecks identified a number of personal and social factors related to persistent offending. The most important of these factors was family relations, considered in terms of quality of discipline and emotional ties with parents. The adolescent raised in a large, single-parent family of limited economic means and educational achievement was the most vulnerable to delinquency.

The Gluecks did not restrict their analysis to social variables. When they measured such biological and psychological traits as body type, intelligence, and personality, they found that physical and mental factors also played a role in determining behavior. Children with low intelligence, a background of mental disease, and a powerful (mesomorph) physique were the most likely to become persistent offenders.

The Philadelphia cohort research by Marvin Wolfgang and his associates was another milestone prompting interest in explaining delinquent career development.[5] As you may recall (Chapter 2), Wolfgang found that while many offenders commit a single delinquent act and desist from crime, a small group of chronic offenders engage in frequent and repeated delinquent activity and continue to do so across their lifespan. Wolfgang's research focused attention on delinquent careers. Criminologists were now asking this fundamental question: What prompts one person to engage in persistent delinquent activity while another, who on the surface suffers the same life circumstances, finds a way to steer clear of delinquency and travel along a more conventional path?

Life-Course Fundamentals

According to the life-course view, even as toddlers people begin relationships and behaviors that will determine their adult life course. At first they must learn to conform to social rules and function effectively in society. Later they are expected to begin to think about careers, leave their parental homes, find permanent relationships, and eventually marry and begin their own families.[6] These transitions are expected to take place in order—beginning with finishing school, then entering the workforce, getting married, and having children.

Some individuals, however, are incapable of maturing in a reasonable and timely fashion because of family, environmental, or personal problems.[7] In some cases, transitions can occur too early—for example, an adolescent girl who engages in precocious sex gets pregnant and is forced to drop out of high school. In other cases, transitions may occur too late—a teenage male falls in with the wrong crowd, goes to prison, and subsequently finds it difficult to break into the job market; he puts off getting married because of his diminished economic circumstances. Sometimes interruption of one trajectory can harm another. A teenager who has family problems may find that her educational and career development is upset or that they suffer from psychological impairments.[8] Because a transition from one stage of life to another can be a bumpy ride, the propensity to commit crimes is neither stable nor constant: It is a developmental process. A positive life experience may help some kids desist from delinquency for a while, whereas a negative one may cause them to resume their activities. Delinquent careers are said to be developmental because people are influenced by the behavior of those around them, and they, in turn, influence others' behavior. A youth's antisocial behavior may turn his more conventional friends against him; their rejection solidifies and escalates his antisocial behavior.[9]

Disruption Promotes Delinquency Disruptions in life's major transitions can be destructive and ultimately can promote delinquency. Those who are already at risk because of socioeconomic problems or family dysfunction are the most susceptible to these awkward transitions. Delinquency, according to this view, cannot be attributed to a single cause, nor does it represent a single underlying tendency.[10] People are influenced by different factors as they mature. Consequently, a factor that may have an important influence at one stage of life (such as delinquent peers) may have little influence later on.[11]

These negative life events can become cumulative: As people acquire more personal deficits, the chances of acquiring additional ones increase.[12] The cumulative impact of these disruptions sustains antisocial behaviors from childhood into adulthood.[13]

Changing Life Influences Life-course theories also recognize that as people mature, the factors that influence their behavior change.[14] As people make important life transitions—from child to adolescent, from adolescent to adult, from unwed to married—the nature of social interactions changes.[15]

At first, family relations may be most influential; it comes as no shock to life-course theorists when research shows that antisocial behavior runs in families and that having criminal relatives is a significant predictor of future misbehaviors.[16] In later adolescence, school and peer relations predominate; in adulthood, vocational achievement and marital relations may be the most critical influences. Some antisocial children who are in trouble throughout their adolescence may manage to find stable work and maintain intact marriages as adults; these life events help them desist from crime. In contrast, less fortunate adolescents who develop arrest records and get involved with the wrong crowd may find themselves limited to menial jobs and at risk for delinquent careers.

LIFE-COURSE CONCEPTS

A view of delinquency is now emerging that incorporates personal change and growth:

▌ The factors that produce delinquency at one point in the life cycle may not be relevant at another.

▌ As people mature, the social, physical, and environmental influences on their behavior are transformed.

▌ People may show a propensity to offend early in their lives, but the nature and frequency of their activities are often affected by the forces that shape their personal development.[17]

Below, some of the more important concepts associated with this newly emerging developmental perspective of delinquency are discussed in some detail.

Problem Behavior Syndrome

problem behavior syndrome (PBS)
A cluster of antisocial behaviors that may include family dysfunction, substance abuse, smoking, precocious sexuality and early pregnancy, educational underachievement, suicide attempts, sensation seeking, and unemployment, as well as delinquency.

Most criminological theories portray delinquency as the outcome of social problems. Learning theorists view a troubled home life and deviant friends as precursors of delinquency; structural theorists maintain that acquiring deviant cultural values leads to delinquency. In contrast, the developmental view is that delinquency may best be understood as one of many social problems faced by at-risk youth, a view called problem behavior syndrome (PBS). According to this view, delinquency is one among a group of interrelated antisocial behaviors that cluster together and typically involve family dysfunction, sexual and physical abuse, substance abuse, smoking, precocious sexuality and early pregnancy, educational underachievement, suicide attempts, sensation seeking, and unemployment.[18] People who suffer from one of these conditions typically exhibit many symptoms of the rest.[19] All varieties of delinquent behavior, including violence, theft, and drug offenses, may be part of a generalized PBS, indicating that all forms of antisocial behavior have similar developmental patterns.[20]

- Adolescents with a history of gang involvement are more likely to have been expelled from school, be a binge drinker, test positively for marijuana, have been in three or more fights in the past six months, have a nonmonogamous partner, and test positive for sexually transmitted diseases.[21]

- Kids who gamble and take risks at an early age also take drugs and commit crimes.[22]

- People who exhibit one of these conditions typically exhibit many of the others.[23]

Those who suffer PBS are prone to more difficulties than the general population.[24] They find themselves with a range of personal dilemmas ranging from drug abuse to being accident prone, to requiring more health care and hospitalization, to becoming teenage parents, to having mental health problems.[25] PBS has been linked to individual-level personality problems (such as impulsiveness, rebelliousness, and low ego), family problems (such as intrafamily conflict and parental mental disorder), substance abuse, and educational failure.[26] Research shows that social problems such as drug abuse, low income, aggression, single parenthood, residence in isolated urban areas, lack of family support or resources, racism, and prolonged exposure to poverty are all interrelated.[27] According to this view, delinquency is a type of social problem rather than the product of other social problems.[28]

Pathways to Delinquency

Some life-course theorists recognize that career delinquents may travel more than a single road: Some may specialize in violence and extortion; some may be involved in theft and fraud; others may engage in a variety of delinquent acts. Some offenders may begin their careers early in life, whereas others are late bloomers who begin committing delinquency when most people desist. Some are frequent offenders while others travel a more moderate path.[29]

Some of the most important research on delinquent paths or trajectories has been conducted by Rolf Loeber and his associates. Using data from a longitudinal study of Pittsburgh youth, Loeber has identified three distinct paths to a delinquent career (Figure 6.1).[30]

authority conflict pathway
Pathway to delinquent deviance that begins at an early age with stubborn behavior and leads to defiance and then to authority avoidance.

covert pathway
Pathway to a delinquent career that begins with minor underhanded behavior, leads to property damage, and eventually escalates to more serious forms of theft and fraud.

overt pathway
Pathway to a delinquent career that begins with minor aggression, leads to physical fighting, and eventually escalates to violent delinquency.

1. The authority conflict pathway begins at an early age with stubborn behavior. This leads to defiance (doing things one's own way, disobedience) and then to authority avoidance (staying out late, truancy, running away).

2. The covert pathway begins with minor, underhanded behavior (lying, shoplifting) that leads to property damage (setting nuisance fires, damaging property). This behavior eventually escalates to more serious forms of delinquency, ranging from joyriding, pocket picking, larceny, and fencing to passing bad checks, using stolen credit cards, stealing cars, dealing drugs, and breaking and entering.

3. The overt pathway escalates to aggressive acts beginning with aggression (annoying others, bullying), leading to physical (and gang) fighting, and then to violence (attacking someone, forced theft).

The Loeber research indicates that each of these paths may lead to a sustained deviant career. Some people enter two and even three paths simultaneously: They are stubborn, lie to teachers and parents, are bullies, and commit petty thefts. These adolescents are the most likely to become persistent offenders as they mature.

Although some persistent offenders may specialize in one type of behavior, others engage in varied delinquent acts and antisocial behaviors as they mature. As adolescents they cheat on tests, bully kids in the school yard, take drugs, commit burglary, steal a car, and then shoplift from a store. Later as adults, some specialize in a particular delinquent activity such as drug trafficking, while others are involved in an assortment of deviant acts—selling drugs, committing robberies, and getting involved in break-ins—when the situation arises and the opportunities are present.[31] There may be a multitude of delinquent career subgroupings (for example, prostitutes, drug dealers) that each have their own distinctive career paths.

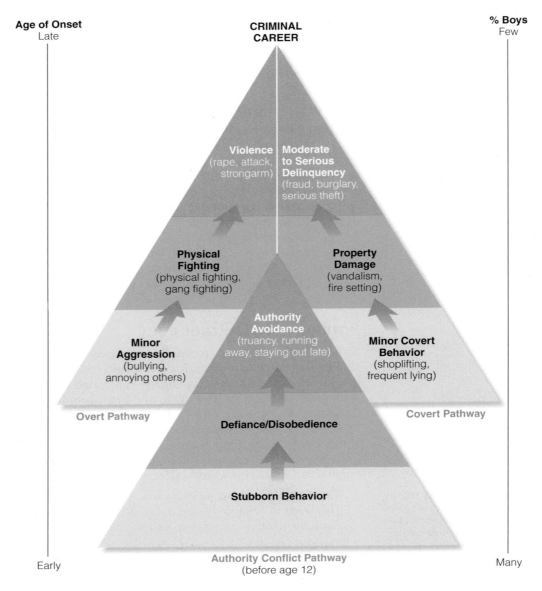

Age of Onset
Late

**CRIMINAL
CAREER**

% Boys
Few

Violence
(rape, attack, strongarm)

**Moderate
to Serious
Delinquency**
(fraud, burglary, serious theft)

**Physical
Fighting**
(physical fighting, gang fighting)

**Property
Damage**
(vandalism, fire setting)

**Authority
Avoidance**
(truancy, running away, staying out late)

**Minor
Aggression**
(bullying, annoying others)

**Minor Covert
Behavior**
(shoplifting, frequent lying)

Overt Pathway

Covert Pathway

Defiance/Disobedience

Stubborn Behavior

Early

Authority Conflict Pathway
(before age 12)

Many

FIGURE 6.1

Loeber's Pathways to Crime

SOURCE: "Serious and Violent Juvenile Offenders," *Juvenile Justice Bulletin*, May 1998.

Age of Onset/Continuity of Crime

Most life-course theories assume that the seeds of a delinquent career are planted early in life and that early onset of deviance strongly predicts later and more serious delinquency.[32] Children who will later become the most serious delinquents begin their deviant careers at a very early (preschool) age, and the earlier the onset of delinquency the more frequent, varied, and sustained the delinquent career.[33] If children are aggressive and antisocial during their public school years, they are much more likely to be troublesome and aggressive in adulthood.[34]

Early-onset delinquents seem to be more involved in aggressive acts ranging from cruelty to animals to peer-directed violence.[35] In contrast, late starters are more likely to be involved in nonviolent crimes such as theft.[36] Recent research by Daniel Nagin and Richard Tremblay shows that late-onset physical aggression is the exception, not the rule, and that the peak frequency of physical aggression occurs during early childhood and generally declines thereafter.[37]

A key element of developmental theory is that kids begin their offending careers early in life. Maribel Cuevas, 11, arrives at juvenile court in Fresno, California, under the charge of assault with a deadly weapon for throwing a rock at a boy during a water balloon fight. The girl's lawyers reached a deal that allowed her to escape jail time.

This finding is quite important because it suggests that the factors that produce long-term violent offending must emerge early in life before environmental influences can have an effect, a finding that contradicts social structure theories. The earlier the onset of crime, the longer its duration.[38] As they emerge into adulthood, persisters report less emotional support, lower job satisfaction, distant peer relationships, and more psychiatric problems than those who desist.[39]

Continuity and Desistance

What causes some kids to begin offending at an early age? Research shows that poor parental discipline and monitoring seem to be keys to the early onset of delinquency and that these influences may follow kids into their adulthood. The psychic scars of childhood are hard to erase.[40]

Children who are improperly socialized by unskilled parents are the most likely to rebel by wandering the streets with deviant peers.[41] Parental influences may be replaced: In middle childhood, social rejection by conventional peers and academic failure sustain antisocial behavior; in later adolescence, commitment to a deviant peer group creates a training ground for crime. While the youngest and most serious offenders may persist in their delinquent activity into late adolescence and even adulthood, others are able to age out of delinquency or desist.

Gender and Desistance As they mature, both males and females who have early experiences with antisocial behavior are the ones most likely to persist throughout their life course. Like boys, early-onset girls continue to experience difficulties—increased drug and alcohol use, poor school adjustment, mental health problems, poor sexual health, psychiatric problems, higher rates of mortality, delinquent behavior, insufficient parenting skills, relationship dysfunction, lower performance in academic and occupational environments, involvement with social service assistance, and adjustment problems—as they enter young adulthood and beyond.[42]

There are also some distinct gender differences. For males, the path runs from early onset in childhood to later problems at work and involvement with substance abuse. For females, the path seems somewhat different: Early antisocial behavior leads to relationship problems, depression, a tendency to commit suicide, and poor health in adulthood.[43] Males seem to be more deeply influenced by an early history

The Path to Delinquency

One of the most important longitudinal studies tracking persistent offenders is the Cambridge Study in Delinquent Development, which has followed the offending careers of 411 London boys born in 1953. This cohort study, directed since 1982 by David Farrington, is one of the most serious attempts to isolate the factors that predict lifelong continuity of delinquent behavior. The study uses self-report data as well as in-depth interviews and psychological testing. The boys have been interviewed eight times over 24 years, beginning at age 8 and continuing to age 32.

The results of the Cambridge study show that many of the same patterns found in the United States are repeated in a cross-national sample: the existence of chronic offenders, the continuity of offending, and early onset of delinquent activity. Each of these patterns leads to persistent delinquency.

Farrington found that the traits present in persistent offenders can be observed as early as age 8. The chronic delinquent begins as a property offender, is born into a large low-income family headed by parents who have delinquent records, and has delinquent older siblings. The future criminal receives poor parental supervision, including the use of harsh or erratic punishment and childrearing techniques; the parents are likely to divorce or separate. The chronic offender tends to associate with friends who are also future criminals. By age 8, the child exhibits antisocial behavior, including dishonesty and aggressiveness; at school the chronic offender tends to have low educational achievement and is restless, troublesome, hyperactive, impulsive, and often truant. After leaving school at age 18, the persistent criminal tends to take a relatively well paid but low-status job and is likely to have an erratic work history and periods of unemployment.

Farrington found that deviant behavior tends to be versatile rather than specialized. That is, the typical offender not only commits property offenses, such as theft and burglary, but also engages in violence, vandalism, drug use, excessive drinking, drunk driving, smoking, reckless driving, and sexual promiscuity—evidence of a generalized problem behavior syndrome. Chronic offenders are more likely to live away from home and have conflicts with their parents. They get tattoos, go out most evenings, and enjoy hanging out with groups of their friends. They are much more likely than nonoffenders to get involved in fights, to carry weapons, and to use them in violent encounters.

The frequency of offending reaches a peak in the teenage years (about 17 or 18) and then declines in the 20s, when offenders marry or live with a significant other.

By the 30s, the former delinquent is likely to be separated or divorced and is an absent parent. His employment record remains spotty, and he moves often between rental units. His life is still characterized by evenings out, heavy drinking, substance abuse, and more violent behavior than his contemporaries.

Because the typical offender provides the same kind of deprived and disrupted family life for his own children that he experienced, the social experiences and conditions that produce delinquency are carried on from one generation to the next. The following list summarizes the specific risk factors that Farrington associates with forming a delinquent career:

Prenatal and perinatal. Early childbearing increases the risk of such undesirable outcomes for children as low school attainment, antisocial behavior, substance use, and early sexual activity. An increased risk of offending among children of teenage mothers is associated with low income, poor housing, absent fathers, and poor childrearing methods.

Personality. Impulsiveness, hyperactivity, restlessness, and limited ability to concentrate are associated with low attainment in school and a poor ability to foresee the consequences of offending.

Intelligence and attainment. Low intelligence and poor performance in school, although important statistical predictors of offending, are difficult to disentangle from each other. One plausible explanation of the link between low intelligence and delinquency is its association with a poor ability to manipulate abstract concepts and to appreciate the feelings of victims.

Parental supervision and discipline. Harsh or erratic parental discipline and cold or rejecting parental attitudes have been linked to delinquency and are associated with children's lack of internal inhibitions against offending. Physical abuse by parents has been associated with an increased risk of the children themselves becoming violent offenders in later life.

Parental conflict and separation. Living in a home affected by separation or divorce is more strongly related to delinquency

of childhood aggression. Males who exhibited chronic physical aggression during the elementary school years exhibit the risk of continued physical violence and delinquency during adolescence. There is less evidence of a linkage between childhood physical aggression and adult aggression among females.[44]

The path kids take to delinquency is further discussed in the accompanying Focus on Delinquency feature.

Adolescent-Limiteds and Life-Course Persisters

Not all persistent offenders begin at an early age. Some are precocious, beginning their delinquent careers early and persisting into adulthood.[45] Others stay out of trouble in adolescence and do not violate the law until their teenage years. Some offenders than when the disruption has been caused by the death of one parent. However, it may not be a "broken home" that creates an increased risk of offending so much as the parental conflict that leads to the separation.

Socioeconomic status. Social and economic deprivation are important predictors of antisocial behavior and crime, but low family income and poor housing are better measurements than the prestige of parents' occupations.

Delinquent friends. Delinquents tend to have delinquent friends. But it is not certain whether membership in a delinquent peer group leads to offending or whether delinquents simply gravitate toward each other's company (or both). Breaking up with delinquent friends often coincides with desisting from crime.

School influences. The prevalence of offending by pupils varies widely between secondary schools. But it is not clear how far schools themselves have an effect on delinquency (for example, by paying insufficient attention to bullying or providing too much punishment and too little praise), or whether it is simply that troublesome children tend to go to high-delinquency-rate schools.

Community influences. The risks of becoming criminally involved are higher for young people raised in disorganized inner-city areas, characterized by physical deterioration, overcrowded households, publicly subsidized renting, and high residential mobility. It is not clear, however, whether this is due to a direct influence on children, or whether environmental stress causes family adversities, which in turn cause delinquency.

NONOFFENDERS AND DESISTERS

Farrington has also identified factors that predict the discontinuity of delinquent offenses. He found that people who exhibit these factors have backgrounds that put them at risk of becoming offenders; however, either they are able to remain nonoffenders or they begin a delinquent career and then later desist. The factors that protected high-risk youths from beginning delinquent careers include having a somewhat shy personality, having few friends (at age 8), having nondeviant families, and being highly regarded by their mothers. Shy children with few friends avoided damaging relationships with other adolescents (members of a high-risk group) and were therefore able to avoid delinquency.

WHAT CAUSED OFFENDERS TO DESIST?

Holding a relatively good job helped reduce delinquent activity. Conversely, unemployment seemed to be related to the escalation of theft offenses; violence and substance abuse were unaffected by unemployment. In a similar vein, getting married also helped diminish delinquent activity. However, finding a spouse who was also involved in delinquent activity and had a delinquent record increased delinquent involvement.

Physical relocation also helped some offenders desist because they were forced to sever ties with co-offenders. For this reason, leaving the city for a rural or suburban area was linked to reduced delinquent activity. Although employment, marriage, and relocation helped potential offenders desist, not all desisters found success. At-risk youths who managed to avoid delinquent convictions were unlikely to avoid other social problems. Rather than becoming prosperous homeowners with flourishing careers, they tended to live in unkempt homes and have large debts and low-paying jobs. They were also more likely to remain single and live alone. Youths who experienced social isolation at age 8 were also found to experience it at age 32.

Farrington suggests that life experiences shape the direction and flow of behavior choices. He finds that while there may be continuity in offending, the factors that predict delinquency at one point in the life course may not be the ones that predict delinquency at another. Although most adult delinquents begin their careers in childhood, life events may help some children forgo delinquency as they mature.

Critical Thinking

Farrington finds that the traits present in persistent offenders can be observed as early as age 8. Should such young children be observed and monitored, even though they have not actually committed crimes? Would such monitoring create a self-fulfilling prophecy?

SOURCES: David Farrington, "Key Results from the First Forty Years of the Cambridge Study in Delinquent Development," in Terence Thornberry and Marvin Krohn, eds., *Taking Stock of Delinquency: An Overview of Findings from Contemporary Longitudinal Studies* (New York: Kluwer, 2002), pp. 137–185; David Farrington, "The Development of Offending and Anti-Social Behavior from Childhood: Key Findings from the Cambridge Study of Delinquent Development," *Journal of Child Psychology and Psychiatry* 36:2–36 (1995); David Farrington, *Understanding and Preventing Youth Crime* (London: Joseph Rowntree Foundation, 1996).

adolescent-limited offenders
Kids who get into minor scrapes as youths but whose misbehavior ends when they enter adulthood.

may peak at an early age, whereas others persist into adulthood. Some youth maximize their offending rates at a relatively early age and then reduce their delinquent activity; others persist into their 20s. Some are high-rate offenders, whereas others offend at relatively low rates.[46]

While some kids begin their deviant life course at an early age, others do not. However, some non–early starters may "catch up" later in their adolescence. According to psychologist Terrie Moffitt, most young offenders follow one of two paths: **adolescent-limited offenders** may be considered "typical teenagers" who get into minor scrapes and engage in what might be considered rebellious teenage behavior with their friends.[47] As they reach their mid-teens, adolescent-limited delinquents begin to mimic the antisocial behavior of more troubled teens, only to reduce the frequency of their offending as they mature to around age 18.[48]

The second path is the one taken by a small group of life-course persisters who begin their offending career at a very early age and continue to offend well into adulthood.[49] Moffit finds that life-course persisters combine family dysfunction with severe neurological problems that predispose them to antisocial behavior patterns. These afflictions can be the result of maternal drug abuse, poor nutrition, or exposure to toxic agents such as lead. It is not surprising then that life-course persisters display social and personal dysfunctions, including lower than average verbal ability, reasoning skills, learning ability, and school achievement.

Research shows that the persistence patterns predicted by Moffitt are valid and accurate.[50] Life-course persisters offend more frequently and engage in a greater variety of antisocial acts than other offenders; they also manifest significantly more mental health problems, including psychiatric pathologies, than adolescent-limited offenders.[51]

There is also evidence, as predicted by Moffitt, that the cause of early-onset/life-course persistent delinquency can be found at the individual level. Life-course persisters are more likely to manifest traits such as low verbal ability and hyperactivity; they display a negative or impulsive personality and seem particularly impaired on spatial and memory functions.[52] Individual traits rather than environment seem to have the greatest influence on life-course persistence.[53]

Some recent research shows that there may even be more than one subset or group of life-course persisters:

▌ One group suffers from ADHD and is persistently disobedient and hard to control.

▌ A second group shows few symptoms of ADHD but, from an early age, is aggressive, underhanded, and in constant opposition to authority.[54]

THEORIES OF THE DELINQUENT LIFE COURSE

A number of systematic theories have been formulated that account for onset, continuance, and desistance from crime. They typically interconnect *personal factors* such as personality and intelligence, *social factors* such as income and neighborhood, *socialization factors* such as marriage and military service, *cognitive factors* such as information processing and attention/perception, and *situational factors* such as delinquent opportunity, effective guardianship, and apprehension risk into complex multifactor explanations of human behavior. In this sense they are integrated theories because they incorporate social, personal, and developmental factors into complex explanations of human behavior. They do not focus on the relatively simple question—why do people commit crime?—but on more complex issues: Why do some offenders persist in delinquent careers while others desist from or alter their delinquent activity as they mature?[55] Why do some people continually escalate their delinquent involvement while others slow down and turn their lives around? Are all delinquents similar in their offending patterns, or are there different types of offenders and paths to offending? Life-course theorists want to know not only why people enter a delinquent way of life but why, once they do, they are able to alter the trajectory of their delinquent involvement. In Exhibit 6.1, two of the more important life-course theories are briefly described, and in the next section, Sampson and Laub's age-graded theory is set out in some detail.

Sampson and Laub: Age-Graded Theory

If there are various pathways to delinquency, are there trails back to conformity? In an important 1993 work, *Crime in the Making*, Robert Sampson and John Laub formulated what they call the age-graded theory of *informal social control* (Figure 6.2). In their

Principal Life-Course Theories

Social Development Model

Principal Theorists J. David Hawkins, Richard Catalano, Joseph Weis

Major Premise Community-level risk factors make some people susceptible to antisocial behaviors. Preexisting risk factors are either reinforced or neutralized by socialization. To control the risk of antisocial behavior, a child must maintain prosocial bonds. Over the life course, involvement in prosocial or antisocial behavior determines the quality of attachments. Commitment and attachment to conventional institutions, activities, and beliefs insulate youths from the criminogenic influences in their environment. The prosocial path inhibits deviance by strengthening bonds to prosocial others and activities. Without the proper level of bonding, adolescents can succumb to the influence of deviant others.

Interactional Theory

Principal Theorists Terence Thornberry and Marvin Krohn, Alan Lizotte, Margaret Farnworth

Major Premise The onset of crime can be traced to a deterioration of the social bond during adolescence, marked by weakened attachment to parents, commitment to school, and belief in conventional values. The cause of delinquency is bidirectional: Weak bonds lead kids to develop friendships with deviant peers and get involved in delinquency. Frequent delinquency involvement further weakens bonds and makes it difficult to reestablish conventional ones. Delinquency-promoting factors tend to reinforce one another and sustain a chronic criminal career. Kids who go through stressful life events such as a family financial crisis are more likely to later get involved in antisocial behaviors and vice versa. Delinquency is a developmental process that takes on different meaning and form as a person matures. During early adolescence, attachment to the family is critical; by mid-adolescence, the influence of the family is replaced by friends, school, and youth culture; by adulthood, a person's behavioral choices are shaped by his or her place in conventional society and his or her own nuclear family. Although delinquency is influenced by these social forces, it also influences these processes and associations. Therefore, delinquency and social processes are interactional.

SOURCES: Terence Thornberry, "Toward an Interactional Theory of Delinquency," *Criminology* 25:863–891 (1987); Richard Catalano and J. David Hawkins, "The Social Development Model: A Theory of Antisocial Behavior," in J. David Hawkins, ed., *Delinquency and Crime: Current Theories* (New York: Cambridge University Press. 1996), pp. 149–197.

pioneering research, Laub and Sampson reanalyzed the data originally collected by the Gluecks. Using modern statistical analysis, Laub and Sampson rely on this data to formulate a life-course/developmental view of crime.[56]

Some of the principles of age-graded theory are listed below:

▮ Individual traits and childhood experiences are important in understanding the onset of delinquent and criminal behavior. But these alone cannot explain the continuity of crime into adulthood.

▮ Experiences in young adulthood and beyond can redirect delinquent trajectories or paths. In some cases people can be turned in a positive direction, while in others negative life experiences can be harmful and injurious.

▮ Repeat negative experiences create a condition called **cumulative disadvantage**. Serious problems in adolescence undermine life chances and reduce employability and social relations. People who increase their cumulative disadvantage risk continued offending.

▮ Positive life experiences and relationships can help people become reattached to society and allow them to knife off from a delinquent career path.

▮ Positive life experiences such as gaining employment, getting married, or joining the military create informal social control mechanisms that limit delinquent behavior opportunities. These then are **turning points** in a delinquent career.

▮ Two critical turning points are marriage and career. A term of military service is quite beneficial. Adolescents who are at risk for delinquency can live conventional lives if they can find good jobs, achieve successful military careers, or enter into a successful marriage. Turning points may be serendipitous and unexpected: Success may hinge on a lucky break—someone takes a chance on them, or they win the lottery.

▮ Another vital feature that helps people desist from delinquency is "human agency" or the purposeful execution of choice and free will. Former delinquents may choose

cumulative disadvantage
A condition whereby serious delinquency in adolescence undermines things such as employability and social relations and helps increase the chances of continued offending in adulthood.

turning points
Positive life experiences such as gaining employment, getting married, or joining the military, which create informal social control mechanisms that limit delinquent behavior opportunities.

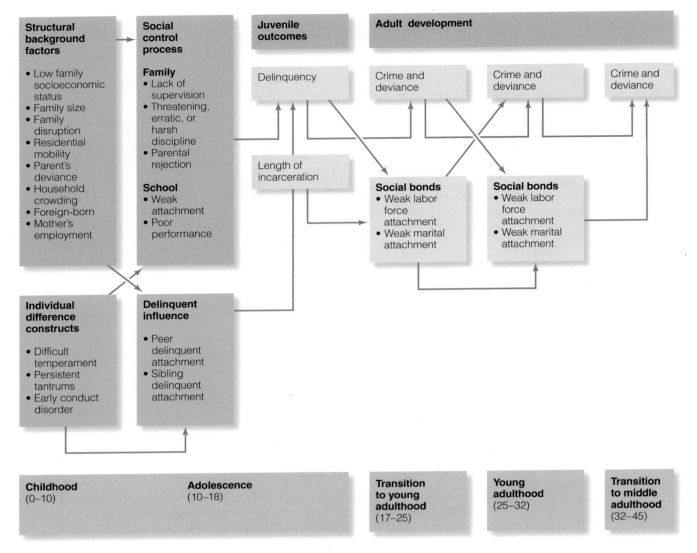

FIGURE 6.2

Sampson and Laub's Age-Graded Theory

SOURCE: Robert Sampson and John Laub, *Crime in the Making: Pathways and Turning Points through Life* (Cambridge, MA: Harvard University Press, 1993), pp. 244–245.

to go straight and develop a new sense of self and an identity. They can choose to desist from delinquency and become family men and hard workers.[57]

| While some kids persist in delinquency simply because they find it lucrative or perhaps because it serves as an outlet for their frustrations, others choose not to participate because as human beings they find other more conventional paths more beneficial and rewarding. Human choice cannot be left out of the equation.

Social Capital Laub and Sampson view the development of social capital as essential for desistance. Social scientists recognize that people build social capital—positive relations with individuals and institutions that are life sustaining. In the same manner that building financial capital improves the chances for personal success, building social capital supports conventional behavior and inhibits deviant behavior. A successful marriage creates social capital when it improves a person's stature, creates feelings of self-worth, and encourages people to trust the individual. A successful career inhibits delinquency by creating a stake in conformity; why commit delinquency when you are doing well at school? The relationship is reciprocal. If kids are chosen by teachers as being a top student, they return the favor by doing the best job in class possible; if they

social capital
Positive relations with individuals and institutions, as in a successful marriage or a successful career, that support conventional behavior and inhibit deviant behavior.

Sampson and Laub's age-graded theory posits that the key influences on behavior change over the life course. At first, families are critical. In adolescence, the peer group is the most important influence on behavior. In adulthood, marriage and work shape people's lives.

are chosen as spouses, they blossom into devoted partners. In contrast, people who fail to accumulate social capital are more prone to commit delinquent acts.[58]

The fact that social capital influences the trajectory of a delinquent career underscores the life-course view that events that occur in later adolescence and adulthood do in fact influence behavior choices. Life events that occur in adulthood can help either terminate or sustain deviant careers.

Testing Age-Graded Theory Empirical research now shows that, as predicted by Sampson and Laub, people change over the life course and the factors that predict antisocial behavior choices evolve over time.[59] Delinquency appears to be (a) dynamic and (b) affected by levels of informal social control. For example, as predicted by Laub and Sampson, kids who accumulate deviant peers in adolescence are the ones most likely to maintain a delinquent career.[60] Deviant peers help neutralize the informal social control wielded by parents and teachers.

As predicted by Laub and Sampson, as levels of *cumulative disadvantage* increase, delinquency-resisting elements of social life are impaired. Adolescents who are convicted of delinquency at an early age are more likely to develop antisocial attitudes later in life. They develop low educational achievement, declining occupational status, and unstable employment records.[61] People who get involved with the justice system as adolescents may find that their career paths are blocked well into adulthood.[62] The relationship is reciprocal: Men who are unemployed or underemployed report higher delinquent participation rates than employed men.[63]

Evidence is also available that confirms Sampson and Laub's suspicion that delinquent career trajectories can be reversed if life conditions improve and they gain social capital.[64] Kids who have long-term exposure to poverty find that their involvement in delinquency escalates. Those, however, whose life circumstances improve because their parents are able to escape poverty and move to more attractive environments find that they can knife off from delinquent trajectories. Relocating may place them in better educational environments where they can have a positive high school experience, facilitated by occupationally oriented course work, small class size, and positive peer climates. Such adolescents are less likely to become incarcerated as adults than those who do not enjoy these social benefits.[65] Research by Ross Macmillan and his colleagues shows that children whose mothers were initially poor but escaped from poverty were no more likely to develop behavior problems than children whose mothers were never poor. Gaining social capital then may help erase some of the damage caused by its absence.[66]

A number of research efforts have supported Sampson and Laub's position that accumulating social capital reduces delinquency rates. Youths who accumulate social

Shared Beginnings, Divergent Lives

Why are some delinquents destined to become persistent criminals as adults? John Laub and Robert Sampson conducted a follow-up to their reanalysis of Sheldon and Eleanor Glueck's study that matched 500 delinquent boys with 500 nondelinquents. The individuals in the original sample were reinterviewed by the Gluecks at ages 25 and 32. Now Sampson and Laub have located the survivors of the delinquent sample—the oldest 70 years old and the youngest 62—and have again interviewed this cohort.

PERSISTENCE AND DESISTANCE

Laub and Sampson find that delinquency and other forms of antisocial conduct in childhood are strongly related to adult delinquency and drug and alcohol abuse. Former delinquents also suffer consequences in other areas of social life, such as school, work, and family life. For example, delinquents are far less likely to finish high school than are nondelinquents and subsequently are more likely to be unemployed, receive welfare, and experience separation or divorce as adults.

In their latest research, Laub and Sampson address one of the key questions posed by life-course theories: Is it possible for former delinquents to turn their lives around as adults? They find that most antisocial children do not remain antisocial as adults. For example, of men in the study cohort who survived to age 50, 24 percent had no arrests for delinquent acts of violence and property after age 17 (6 percent had no arrests for total delinquency); 48 percent had no arrests for these predatory delinquency after age 25 (19 percent for total delinquency); 60 percent had no arrests for predatory delinquency after age 31 (33 percent for total delinquency); and 79 percent had no arrests for predatory delinquency after age 40 (57 percent for total delinquency). They conclude that desistance from delinquency is the norm and that most, if not all, serious delinquents desist from delinquency.

WHY DO DELINQUENTS DESIST?

Laub and Sampson's earlier research indicated that building social capital through marriage and jobs were key components of desistance from delinquency. However, in this latest round of research, Laub and Sampson were able to find out more about long-term desistance by interviewing 52 men as they approached age 70. The follow-up showed a dramatic drop in criminal activity as the men aged: Between the ages of 17 and 24, 84 percent of the subjects had committed violent crimes; in their 30s and 40s, that number dropped to 14 percent; it fell to just 3 percent as the men reached their 60s and 70s. Property crimes and alcohol- and drug-related crimes showed significant decreases. They found that men who desisted from crime were rooted in structural routines and had strong social ties to family and community. Drawing on the men's own words, they found that one important element for "going straight" is the "knifing off" of individuals from their immediate environment and offering the men a new script for the future. Joining the military can provide this knifing-off effect, as does marriage or changing one's residence. One former delinquent (age 69) told them:

I'd say the turning point was, number one, the Army. You get into an outfit, you had a sense of belonging, you made your friends. I think I became a pretty good judge of character. In the Army, you met some good ones, you met some foul balls. Then I met the wife. I'd say probably that would be the turning point. Got married, then naturally, kids come. So now you got to get a better job, you got to make more money. And that's how I got to the Navy Yard and tried to improve myself.

---

capital in childhood by doing well in school or having a tightly knit family are also the most likely to maintain steady work as adults; employment may help insulate them from crime.[67] Delinquents who enter the military, serve overseas, and receive veterans' benefits enhance their occupational status (social capital) while reducing delinquent involvement.[68] Similarly, high-risk adults who are fortunate enough to obtain high-quality jobs are likely to reduce their delinquent activities even if they have a prior history of offending.[69]

While a great deal of research supports age-graded theory, there are still questions left unanswered. To create their vision, Sampson and Laub used the Glueck data that was collected many years ago. Do the same social relations still exist and do they have the same influence on delinquency? When the Gluecks collected their data, the effects of marriage and military service might have been much different. The divorce rate was much lower and marriages more stable. People had served in World War II and were part of the "Greatest Generation." Other influential elements of contemporary society had not yet been invented: computers, the Internet, TV, DVDs, and iPods. Though the Glueck boys and men drank alcohol, their drug use was minimal. Recent research by Ryan Schroeder and his colleagues find that drug use has unique effects and prevents people from desisting from crime. Drug use negates the influence of marriage and other elements of social capital, and is certainly an element of contemporary life that must be explored more fully.[70]

Former delinquents who "went straight" were able to put structure into their lives. Structure often led the men to disassociate from delinquent peers, reducing the opportunity to get into trouble. Getting married, for example, may limit the number of nights men can "hang with the guys." As one wife of a former delinquent said, "It is not how many beers you have, it's who you drink with." Even multiple offenders who did time in prison were able to desist with the help of a stabilizing marriage.

Former delinquents who can turn their life around, who have acquired a degree of maturity by taking on family and work responsibilities, and who have forged new commitments are the ones most likely to make a fresh start and find new direction and meaning in life. It seems that men who desisted changed their identity as well, and this, in turn, affected their outlook and sense of maturity and responsibility. The ability to change did not reflect delinquency "specialty": Violent offenders followed the same path as property offenders.

While many former delinquents desisted from delinquency, they still faced the risk of an early and untimely death. Thirteen percent (N=62) of the delinquent as compared to only 6 percent (N=28) of the nondelinquent subjects died unnatural deaths such as violence, cirrhosis of the liver caused by alcoholism, poor self-care, suicide, and so on. By age 65, 29 percent (N=139) of the delinquent and 21 percent (N=95) of the nondelinquent subjects had died from natural causes. Frequent delinquent involvement in adolescence and alcohol abuse were the strongest predictors of an early and unnatural death. So while many troubled youth are able to reform, their early excesses may haunt them across their lifespan.

POLICY IMPLICATIONS

Laub and Sampson find that youth problems—delinquency, substance abuse, violence, dropping out, teen pregnancy—often share common risk characteristics. Intervention strategies, therefore, should consider a broad array of antisocial, delinquent, and deviant behaviors and not limit the focus to just one subgroup or delinquency type. Because delinquency and other social problems are linked, early prevention efforts that reduce delinquency will probably also reduce alcohol abuse, drunk driving, drug abuse, sexual promiscuity, and family violence. The best way to achieve these goals is through four significant life-changing events: marriage, joining the military, getting a job, and changing one's environment or neighborhood. What appears to be important about these processes is that they all involve, to varying degrees, the following items: a knifing off of the past from the present; new situations that provide both supervision and monitoring as well as new opportunities of social support and growth; and new situations that provide the opportunity for transforming identity. Prevention of delinquency must be a policy at all times and at all stages of life.

Critical Thinking

1. Do you believe that the factors that influenced the men in the original Glueck sample are still relevant for change, for example, a military career?

2. Would it be possible for men such as these to join the military today?

3. Do you believe that some sort of universal service program might be beneficial and help people turn their lives around?

SOURCES: John Laub and Robert Sampson, *Shared Beginnings, Divergent Lives: Delinquent Boys to Age 70* (Cambridge, MA: Harvard University Press, 2003); Laub and Sampson, "Understanding Desistance from Delinquency," in Michael Tonry, ed., *Delinquency and Justice: An Annual Review of Research*, vol. 28 (Chicago: University of Chicago Press, 2001), pp. 1–71; John Laub and George Vaillant, "Delinquency and Mortality: A 50-Year Follow-Up Study of 1,000 Delinquent and Nondelinquent Boys," *American Journal of Psychiatry* 157:96–102 (2000).

To test their theory further, Sampson and Laub have conducted a series of interviews with the survivors of the Glueck survey. Their findings are presented in the Focus on Delinquency feature "Shared Beginnings, Divergent Lives."

LATENT TRAIT THEORIES

In a critical 1990 article, David Rowe, D. Wayne Osgood, and W. Alan Nicewander proposed the concept of latent traits to explain the flow of delinquency over the life cycle. Their model assumes that a number of people in the population have a personal attribute or characteristic that controls their inclination or propensity to commit crimes.[71] This disposition, or latent trait, may be either present at birth or established early in life, and it can remain stable over time. Suspected latent traits include defective intelligence, damaged or impulsive personality, genetic abnormalities, the physical-chemical functioning of the brain, and environmental influences on brain function such as drugs, chemicals, and injuries.[72]

Regardless of gender or environment, those who maintain one of these suspect traits may be at risk to delinquency and in danger of becoming career criminals; those who lack the traits have a much lower risk.[73]

Because latent traits are stable, people who are antisocial during adolescence are the most likely to persist in crime. The positive association between past and future delinquency detected in the cohort studies of career criminals reflects the presence of this underlying criminogenic trait. That is, if low IQ contributes to delinquency in childhood, it should also cause the same people to offend as adults because intelligence is usually stable over the lifespan.

Whereas the propensity to commit delinquency is stable, the opportunity to commit delinquency fluctuates over time. People age out of crime: As they mature and develop, there are simply fewer opportunities to commit crimes and greater inducements to remain "straight." They may marry, have children, and obtain jobs. The former delinquents' newfound adult responsibilities leave them little time to hang with their friends, abuse substances, and get into scrapes with the law.

To understand this concept better, assume that intelligence as measured by IQ tests is a stable latent trait associated with crime. Intelligence remains stable and unchanging over the life course, but delinquency rates decline with age. How can latent trait theory explain this phenomenon? Teenagers have more opportunity to commit delinquency than adults, so at every level of intelligence, adolescent delinquency rates will be higher. As they mature, however, teens with both high and low IQs will commit less delinquency because their adult responsibilities provide them with fewer delinquent opportunities. They may get married and raise a family, get a job and buy a home. And like most people, as they age they lose strength and vigor, qualities necessary to commit crime. Though their IQ remains stable and their propensity to commit delinquency is unchanged, their living environment and biological condition have undergone radical change. Even they wanted to engage in antisocial activities, the former delinquents may lack the opportunity and the energy to engage in delinquent activities.

Crime and Human Nature

Latent trait theorists were encouraged when two prominent social scientists, James Q. Wilson and Richard Herrnstein, published *Crime and Human Nature* in 1985 and suggested that personal traits—such as genetic makeup, intelligence, and body build—may outweigh the importance of social variables as predictors of delinquent activity.[74]

According to Wilson and Herrnstein, all human behavior, including delinquency, is determined by its perceived consequences. A delinquent incident occurs when an individual chooses delinquent over conventional behavior (referred to as *non-crime*) after weighing the potential gains and losses of each: "The larger the ratio of net rewards of crime to the net rewards of non-crime, the greater the tendency to commit the crime."[75]

Wilson and Herrnstein's model assumes that both biological and psychological traits influence the crime–non-crime choice. They see a close link between a person's decision to choose crime and such biosocial factors as low intelligence, mesomorphic body type, genetic influences (parental criminality), and possessing an autonomic nervous system that responds too quickly to stimuli. Psychological traits, such as an impulsive or extroverted personality or generalized hostility, also determine the potential to commit crime.

In their focus on the association between these constitutional and psychological factors and delinquency, Wilson and Herrnstein seem to be suggesting the existence of an elusive latent trait that predisposes people to commit antisocial acts.[76] Their vision helped inspire other social scientists to identify the elusive latent trait that causes delinquent behavior. The most prominent latent trait theory is Gottfredson and Hirschi's General Theory of Crime (GTC).

General Theory of Crime (GTC)
A developmental theory that modifies social control theory by integrating concepts from biosocial, psychological, routine activities, and rational choice theories.

General Theory of Crime

In their important work, *A General Theory of Crime*, Michael Gottfredson and Travis Hirschi modified and redefined some of the principles articulated in Hirschi's original social control theory by adding elements of trait and rational choice theories and shifting the focus from social control to self-control or the tendency to avoid acts whose long-term costs exceed their momentary advantages.[77]

According to Gottfredson and Hirschi, the propensity to commit antisocial acts is tied directly to a person's level of self-control. People with limited self-control tend to be impulsive; they are insensitive to other people's feelings, physical (rather than mental), risk-takers, shortsighted, and nonverbal.[78] They have a here-and-now orientation and refuse to work for distant goals; they lack diligence, tenacity, and persistence. People lacking self-control tend to be adventuresome, active, physical, and self-centered. As they mature, they often have unstable marriages, jobs, and friendships.[79] They are less likely to feel shame if they engage in deviant acts and are more likely to find them pleasurable.[80] They are also more likely to engage in dangerous behaviors such as drinking, smoking, and reckless driving; all of these behaviors are associated with delinquency.[81]

Because those with low self-control enjoy risky, exciting, or thrilling behaviors with immediate gratification, they are more likely to enjoy delinquent acts, which require stealth, agility, speed, and power, than conventional acts, which demand long-term study and cognitive and verbal skills. As Gottfredson and Hirschi put it, they derive satisfaction from "money without work, sex without courtship, revenge without court delays."[82]

Gottfredson and Hirschi suggest that delinquency is not the only outlet for people with an impulsive personality. Even if they do not engage in antisocial behaviors, impulsive people enjoy other risky behaviors such as smoking, drinking, gambling, and illicit sexuality.[83] Although these acts are not illegal, they provide immediate, short-term gratification. It is not surprising then, considering their risky lifestyle, that impulsive people are more prone to be crime victims themselves than their less impulsive peers.[84]

Low self-control develops early in life and remains stable into and through adulthood.[85] Considering the continuity of criminal motivation, Hirschi and Gottfredson have questioned the utility of the juvenile justice system and of giving more lenient treatment to young delinquent offenders. Why separate youthful and adult offenders legally when the source of their antisocial behaviors (for example, impulsivity) is essentially the same?[86]

What Causes Impulsivity? Gottfredson and Hirschi trace the root cause of poor self-control to inadequate childrearing practices that begin soon after birth and can influence neural development. Once experiences are ingrained, the brain establishes a pattern of electrochemical activation that remains for life.[87] Parents who refuse or are unable to monitor a child's behavior, to recognize deviant behavior when it occurs, and to punish that behavior will produce children who lack self-control. Children who are not attached to their parents, who are poorly supervised, and whose parents are delinquent or deviant themselves are the most likely to develop poor self-control. In a sense, lack of self-control occurs naturally when steps are not taken to stop its development.[88]

While Gottfredson and Hirschi believe that parenting and not heredity shapes self-control, some recent research efforts do show that impulsive personality may have physical or social roots, or perhaps both. Children who suffer anoxia (oxygen starvation) during the birthing process are the ones most likely to lack self-control later in life, suggesting that impulsivity may have a biological basis.[89]

Crime Rate Variations If individual differences are stable over the life course, why do delinquency rates vary? Why do people commit less delinquency as they age? Why are some regions or groups more delinquency-prone than others between groups? Does that mean there are differences in self-control between groups? If male delinquency rates are higher than female rates, does that mean men are more impulsive and lacking in self-control? How does the GTC address these issues?

Gottfredson and Hirschi remind us that delinquent propensity and delinquent acts are separate concepts (Figure 6.3). On one hand, delinquent acts, such as robberies or burglaries, are illegal events or deeds that offenders engage in when they perceive

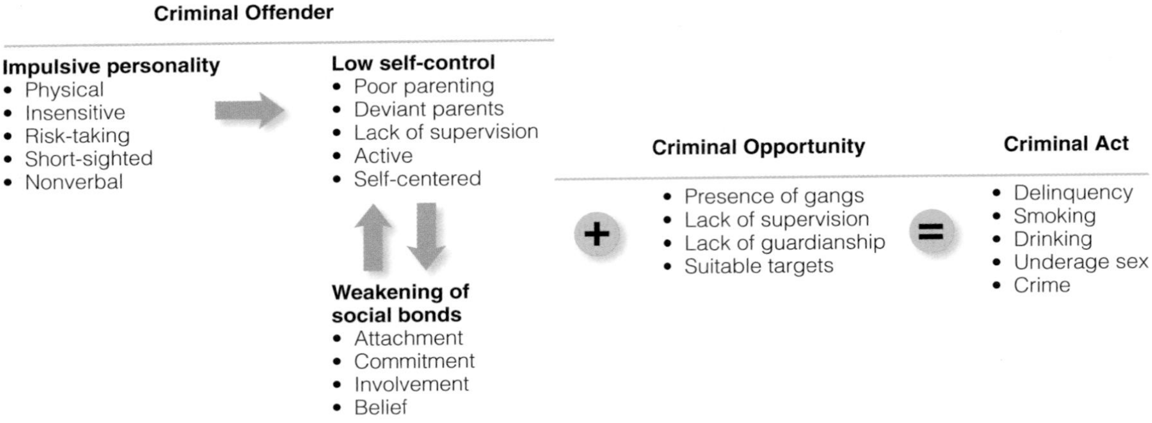

Criminal Offender

Impulsive personality
- Physical
- Insensitive
- Risk-taking
- Short-sighted
- Nonverbal

Low self-control
- Poor parenting
- Deviant parents
- Lack of supervision
- Active
- Self-centered

Weakening of social bonds
- Attachment
- Commitment
- Involvement
- Belief

Criminal Opportunity
- Presence of gangs
- Lack of supervision
- Lack of guardianship
- Suitable targets

+

Criminal Act
- Delinquency
- Smoking
- Drinking
- Underage sex
- Crime

=

FIGURE 6.3
Gottfredson and Hirschi's General Theory of Crime

them to be advantageous. Burglaries are typically committed by young males looking for cash, liquor, and entertainment; delinquency provides "easy, short-term gratification."[90] Delinquency is rational and predictable; kids commit delinquency when it promises rewards with minimal threat of pain; the threat of punishment can deter crime. If targets are well guarded, delinquency rates diminish. Only the truly irrational offender would dare to strike under those circumstances.

On the other hand, delinquent offenders may be predisposed to commit crimes, but they are not robots who commit antisocial acts without restraint; their days are also filled with conventional behaviors, such as going to school, parties, concerts, and church. But given the same set of delinquent opportunities, such as having a lot of free time for mischief and living in a neighborhood with unguarded homes containing valuable merchandise, crime-prone people have a much higher probability of violating the law than do nondelinquents. The propensity to commit crimes remains stable throughout a person's life. Change in the frequency of delinquent activity is purely a function of change in delinquent opportunity.

If we accept this provision of the GTC, then both delinquent propensity and delinquent opportunity must be considered to explain delinquent participation. So if males and females are equally impulsive but their delinquency rates vary, the explanation is that males have more opportunity to commit crime. Young teenage girls may be more closely monitored by their parents and therefore lack the freedom to offend. Girls are also socialized to have more self-control than boys: Although females get angry as often as males, many have been taught to blame themselves for such feelings. Females are socialized to fear that anger will harm relationships; males are encouraged to react with "moral outrage," blaming others for their discomfort.[91]

Opportunity can also be used to explain ecological variation in the delinquency rate. How does the GTC explain the fact that delinquency rates are higher in the summer than the winter? The number of impulsive people lacking in self-control is no higher in August than it is in December. Gottfredson and Hirschi would argue that seasonal differences are explained by opportunity: During the summer, kids are out of school and have more opportunity to commit crime. Similarly, if delinquency rates are higher in Los Angeles than Minneapolis, it is because either there are more delinquent opportunities in the western city or because the fast-paced life of Los Angeles attracts more impulsive people than the laid-back Midwest.

Self-Control and Delinquency Gottfredson and Hirschi claim that their version of self-control theory can explain all varieties of delinquent behavior and all the social and behavioral correlates of crime. That is, such widely disparate crimes as burglary, robbery, embezzlement, drug dealing, murder, rape, and insider trading all stem from a deficiency of self-control. Likewise, gender, racial, and ecological differences

self-control theory
The theory of delinquency that holds that antisocial behavior is caused by a lack of self-control stemming from an impulsive personality.

According to latent trait theories, delinquent propensity varies among people. Walter Stawarz IV is escorted to the courtroom in Beaver, Pennsylvania. Stawarz, 16, was charged as an adult with attempted homicide, reckless endangerment, and aggravated assault for allegedly beating 15-year-old Jeremy Delon alongside the Ohio River. Police accused Stawarz of beating Delon around the time the teenagers attempted to buy some marijuana. On May 18, 2007, a jury found Stawarz guilty of first-degree murder for the beating death of the Hopewell High School student.

in delinquency rates can be explained by discrepancies in self-control. Unlike other theoretical models that explain only narrow segments of delinquent behavior (such as theories of teenage gang formation), Gottfredson and Hirschi argue that self-control applies equally to all crimes, ranging from murder to corporate theft.

Support for the GTC Since the publication of *A General Theory of Crime*, numerous researchers have attempted to test the validity of Gottfredson and Hirschi's theoretical views, and a great many research efforts using a variety of methodologies and subject groups have found empirical support for the basic assumptions of the GTC.[92] Gottfredson and Hirschi's view has become a cornerstone of contemporary criminological theory.

Importantly, the self-control–delinquency association has been found across different cultures, nationalities, and ethnicities, supporting its universal status.[93] When Alexander Vazsonyi and his associates analyzed self-control and deviant behavior with samples drawn from a number of different countries (including Hungary, Switzerland, the Netherlands, the United States, and Japan), they found that low self-control was significantly related to antisocial behavior and that the association can be seen regardless of culture or national settings.[94]

A number of additional empirical findings support the GTC's basic ideas about delinquency:

▮ Adolescents who lack self-control commit a garden variety of delinquent acts.[95]

▮ Kids who take drugs and commit violent crime are impulsive, lack self-control, and enjoy engaging in risky behaviors.[96]

▮ Kids whose problems develop early in life are the most resistant to change.[97]

▮ Parents who manage their children's behavior increase their self-control, which helps reduce their delinquent activities.[98]

▮ Having parents (or guardians) available to control behavior may reduce the opportunity to commit crime.[99]

Analyzing the General Theory of Crime By integrating the concepts of socialization and delinquency, Gottfredson and Hirschi help explain why some people who lack self-control can escape delinquency, and, conversely, why some people who have self-control might not escape delinquency. People who are at risk because they have impulsive personalities may forgo delinquent careers because there are no delinquent opportunities that satisfy their impulsive needs; instead, they may find other outlets for their impulsive personalities. In contrast, if the opportunity is strong enough, even people with relatively strong self-control may be tempted to violate the law; the incentives to commit delinquency may overwhelm self-control.

Integrating delinquent propensity and delinquent opportunity can explain why some children enter into chronic offending while others living in similar environments are able to resist delinquent activity. It can also help us understand why the corporate executive with a spotless record gets caught up in business fraud. Even a successful executive may find self-control inadequate if the potential for illegal gain is large. The driven executive, accustomed to both academic and financial success, may find that the fear of failure can overwhelm self-control. During tough economic times, the impulsive manager who fears dismissal may be tempted to circumvent the law to improve the bottom line.[100]

Although the General Theory seems persuasive, several questions and criticisms remain unanswered. Among the most important are the following:

▌ *Tautological.* Some critics argue that the theory is tautological or involves circular reasoning: How do we know when people are impulsive? When they commit crimes! Are all delinquents impulsive? Of course, or else they would not have broken the law![101] Gottfredson and Hirschi counter by saying that impulsivity is not itself a propensity to commit delinquency but a condition that inhibits people from appreciating the long-term consequences of their behavior. Consequently, if given the opportunity, they are more likely to indulge in delinquent acts than their nonimpulsive counterparts.[102] According to Gottfredson and Hirschi, impulsivity and delinquency are neither identical nor equivalent. Some impulsive people may channel their reckless energies into nondelinquent activity, such as trading on the commodities markets or real estate speculation, and make a legitimate fortune for their efforts.

▌ *Different classes of delinquents.* Terrie Moffitt has identified two classes of criminals— adolescent-limited and life-course persistent.[103] Other researchers have found that there may be different delinquent paths or trajectories. People offend at a different pace, commit different kinds of crimes, and are influenced by different external forces.[104] For example, most delinquents tend to be "generalists" who engage in a garden variety of delinquent acts. However, people who commit violent crimes may be different than nonviolent offenders and maintain a unique set of personality traits and problem behaviors.[105] This would contradict the GTC vision that a single factor causes delinquency and that there is a single class of offender.

▌ *Ecological differences.* The GTC also fails to address individual and ecological patterns in the delinquency rate. For example, if delinquency rates are higher in Los Angeles than in Albany, New York, can it be assumed that residents of Los Angeles are more impulsive than residents of Albany? There is little evidence of regional differences in impulsivity or self-control. Can these differences be explained solely by variation in delinquent opportunity? Few researchers have tried to account for the influence of culture, ecology, economy, and so on. Gottfredson and Hirschi might counter that delinquency rate differences may reflect delinquent opportunity: One area may have more effective law enforcement, more draconian laws, and higher levels of guardianship. In their view, opportunity is controlled by economy and culture.

▌ *Racial and gender differences.* Although distinct gender differences in the delinquency rate exist, there is little evidence that males are more impulsive than females (although females and males differ in many other personality traits).[106] Some research efforts have found gender differences in the association between self-control and crime; the theory predicts no such difference should occur.[107]

Looking at this relationship from another perspective, males who persist in delinquency exhibit characteristics that are different from female persisters. Women seem to be influenced by their place of residence, childhood and recent abuses, living with a delinquent partner, selling drugs, stress, depression, fearfulness, their romantic relationships, their children, and whether they have suicidal thoughts. In contrast, men are more likely to persist because of their delinquent peer associations, carrying weapons, alcohol abuse, and aggressive feelings. Impulsivity alone may not be able to explain why males and females persist or desist.[108]

Similarly, Gottfredson and Hirschi explain racial differences in the delinquency rate as a failure of childrearing practices in the African American community.[109] In so doing, they overlook issues of institutional racism, poverty, and relative deprivation, which have been shown to have a significant impact on delinquency rate differentials.

▍ *Moral beliefs.* The General Theory also ignores the moral concept of right and wrong, or "belief," which Hirschi considered a cornerstone in his earlier writings on the social bond.[110] Does this mean that learning and assimilating moral values has little effect on delinquency? Belief may be the weakest of the bonds associated with crime, and the General Theory reflects this relationship.[111]

▍ *Peer influence.* A number of research efforts show that the quality of peer relations either enhances or controls delinquent behavior and that these influences vary over time.[112] As children mature, peer influence continues to grow.[113] Research shows that kids who lack self-control also have trouble maintaining relationships with law-abiding peers. They may choose (or be forced) to seek out friends who are similarly limited in their ability to maintain self-control. Similarly, as they mature they may seek out romantic relationships with law-violating boyfriends or girlfriends. These entanglements enhance the likelihood that they will get further involved in delinquency (girls seem more deeply influenced by their delinquent boyfriends than boys by their delinquent girlfriends).[114]

This finding contradicts the GTC, which suggests the influence of friends should be stable and unchanging and that a relationship established later in life (for example, making friends) should not influence delinquent propensity. Gottfredson and Hirschi might counter that it should come as no surprise that impulsive kids, lacking in self-control, seek out peers with similar personality characteristics.

▍ *People change.* One of the most important questions raised about the GTC concerns its assumption that delinquent propensity does not change. Is it possible that human personality and behavior patterns remain unaltered over the life course? Research shows that changing life circumstances, such as starting and leaving school, abusing substances and then "getting straight," and starting or ending personal relationships, all influence the frequency of offending.[115] Involvement in organized activities that teach self-discipline and self-regulation, such as karate, has been shown to improve personality traits in at-risk kids, even those diagnosed with oppositional defiance disorder.[116] As people mature, they may be better able to control their impulsive behavior and reduce their delinquent activities.[117]

▍ *Effective parenting.* Gottfredson and Hirschi propose that children either develop self-control by the end of early childhood or fail to develop it at all. Research shows, however, that some kids who are predisposed toward delinquency may find their life circumstances improved and their involvement with antisocial behavior diminished if they are exposed to positive and effective parenting that appears later in life.[118] Effective parenting may be able to influence self-control even in later adolescence.[119]

Some of the most significant research on this topic has been conducted by Ronald Simons and his colleagues. They found that boys who were involved in deviant and oppositional behavior during childhood were able to turn their lives around if they later experienced improved parenting, increased school commitment, and/or reduced involvement with deviant peers. So while early childhood antisocial behavior may increase the chances of later delinquency, even the most difficult children are at no greater risk for delinquency than are their conventional counterparts if they later experience positive changes in their daily lives and increased ties with significant others and institutions.[120]

I *Modest relationship.* Some research results support the proposition that self-control is a causal factor in delinquent and other forms of deviant behavior but that the association is at best quite modest.[121] This would indicate that other forces influence delinquent behavior and that low self-control alone cannot predict the onset of a delinquent or deviant career. Perhaps antisocial behavior is best explained by a condition that either develops subsequent to the development of self-control or is independent of a person's level of impulsivity.[122] This alternative quality, which may be the real stable latent trait, is still unknown.

I *Cross-cultural differences.* There is some evidence that delinquents in other countries do not lack self-control, indicating that the GTC may be culturally limited. For example, Otwin Marenin and Michael Resig actually found equal or higher levels of self-control in Nigerian criminals than in noncriminals.[123] Behavior that may be considered imprudent in one culture may be socially acceptable in another and therefore cannot be viewed as lack of self-control.[124] There is, however, emerging evidence that the GTC may have validity in predicting delinquency abroad.[125]

I *Misreads human nature.* According to Francis Cullen, John Paul Wright, and Mitchell Chamlin, the GTC makes flawed assumptions about human character.[126] It assumes that people are essentially selfish, self-serving, and hedonistic and must therefore be controlled lest they gratify themselves at the expense of others. A more plausible view is that humans are inherently generous and kind; selfish hedonists may be a rare exception.

I *One of many causes.* Research shows that even if lack of self-control is a prerequisite to delinquency, so are other social, neuropsychological, and physiological factors.[127] Social and cultural factors have been found to make an independent contribution to delinquent offending patterns.[128] Among the many psychological characteristics that set delinquents apart from the general population is their lack of self-direction; their behavior has a here-and-now orientation rather than being aimed at providing long-term benefits.[129] Law violators exhibit lower resting heart rate and perform poorly on tasks that trigger cognitive functions.[130]

I *Some delinquents are not impulsive.* Gottfredson and Hirschi assume that delinquents are impatient or "present-oriented." They choose to commit delinquency because the rewards can be enjoyed immediately while the costs or punishments come later or not at all. As long as the gains from delinquency are immediate while the costs of delinquency are delayed, impulsive present-oriented individuals will commit crimes even if they are not obviously lucrative. Not all research efforts support this position. Steven Levitt and Sudhir Alladi Venkatesh found that many young gang boys are willing to wait years to "rise through the ranks" before earning high wages. Their stay in the gang is fueled by the promises of future compensation, a fact that contradicts the GTC. Levitt and Venkatesh conclude that the economic aspects of the decision to join the gang can be viewed as a tournament in which participants vie for large awards that only a small fraction will eventually obtain. Members of the gang accept low wages in the present in the hope that they will advance in the gang and earn well above market wages in the future.[131] Moreover, gang members seem acutely aware that they are making an investment in the future by foregoing present gains. As one noted:

> You think I want to be selling drugs on the street my whole life? No way, but I know these n— [above me] are making more money . . . So you know, I figure I got a chance to move up. But if not, s——, I get me a job doin' something else.[132]

This quotation does not comport with the notion of a super-impulsive young delinquent. Even though few gang recruits will ever become gang leaders, they are willing to take the risk in order to earn a future benefit. Legal economist

Yair Listokin notes that this expectation of future gains is strikingly inconsistent with the notion of present-oriented delinquents and contradicts Gottfredson and Hirschi's vision of an impulsive delinquent who lives for today without worrying about tomorrow. In contrast, the young foot soldiers of the gang are sacrificing present wages for the hope of future gains. Listokin finds that the gang is using the same compensation structure as the one commonly used to characterize law firms where newly hired attorneys work long hours at low pay with the hope of becoming partners. The foot soldiers, he concludes, are filling the role of law associates, a group not known for their impulsiveness.[133]

Self-control may waiver. Gottfredson and Hirschi assume that impulsivity is a singular construct—one is either impulsive or not. However, (a) there may be more than one kind of impulsive personality, and (b) it may waiver over time. Some people may be impulsive because they are sensation seekers who are constantly looking for novel experiences, while others lack deliberation and rarely think through problems. Some may give up easily while others act without thinking. Some people may have the ability to persist in self-control while others "get tired" and eventually succumb to their impulses.[134] Think of it this way: A dieter ogles the cheesecake in the fridge all day but has the self-control not to take a slice. Then he wakes hungry in the middle of the night and makes his way into the kitchen, thinking, "A little piece of cheesecake won't hurt me." His self-control slips, and his diet goes out the window.

Although questions like these remain, the strength of GTC lies in its scope and breadth: It attempts to explain all forms of crime and deviance, from lower-class gang delinquency to sexual harassment in the business community.[135] By integrating concepts of delinquent choice, delinquent opportunity, socialization, and personality, Gottfredson and Hirschi make a plausible argument that all deviant behaviors may originate at the same source. Continued efforts are needed to test the GTC and establish the validity of its core concepts. It remains one of the key developments of modern criminological theory.

A number of other theories have been formulated that pose that a master trait controls human development and the propensity to commit delinquency. Some of the most prominent ones are summarized in Exhibit 6.2.

EVALUATING DEVELOPMENTAL THEORIES

Although the differences among the views presented in this chapter may seem irreconcilable, they in fact share some common ground. They indicate that a delinquent career must be understood as a passage along which people travel, that it has a beginning and an end, and that events and life circumstances influence the journey. The factors that affect a delinquent career may include structural factors, such as income and status; socialization factors, such as family and peer relations; biological factors, such as size and strength; psychological factors, including intelligence and personality; and opportunity factors, such as free time, inadequate police protection, and a supply of easily stolen merchandise.

Life-course theories emphasize the influence of changing interpersonal and structural factors (that is, people change along with the world they live in). Latent trait theories place more emphasis on the fact that behavior is linked less to personal change and more to changes in the surrounding world.

These perspectives differ in their view of human development. Do people constantly change, as life-course theories suggest, or are they stable, constant, and changeless, as the latent trait view indicates? Are the factors that produce delinquency different at each stage of life, as the life-course view suggests? Or does a master trait—for example, control balance, self-control, or coercion—steer the course of human behavior?

EXHIBIT **6.2**

Some Important Latent Trait Theories

Differential Coercion Theory

Principal Theorist Mark Colvin

Latent Trait Perceptions of Coercion

Major Premise Perceptions of coercion begin early in life when children experience punitive forms of discipline, including both physical attacks and psychological coercion such as negative commands, critical remarks, teasing, humiliation, whining, yelling, and threats. Through these destructive family interchanges, coercion becomes ingrained and guides reactions to adverse situations that arise in both family and nonfamily settings.

There are two sources of coercion: interpersonal and impersonal. *Interpersonal coercion* is direct, involving the use or threat of force and intimidation from parents, peers, and significant others. *Impersonal coercion* involves pressures beyond individual control, such as economic and social pressure caused by unemployment, poverty, or competition among businesses or other groups. High levels of coercion produce criminality especially when the episodes of coercive behavior are inconsistent and random because it teaches people that they cannot control their lives. Chronic offenders grew up in homes where parents used erratic control and applied it in an inconsistent fashion.

Control Balance Theory

Principal Theorist Charles Tittle

Latent Trait Control/balance

Major Premise The concept of control has two distinct elements: the amount of control one is subject to by others and the amount of control one can exercise over others. Conformity results when these two elements are in balance; control imbalances produce deviant and criminal behaviors.

Those people who sense a deficit of control turn to three types of behavior to restore balance: (1) *Predation* involves direct forms of physical violence, such as robbery, sexual assault, or other forms of physical violence. (2) *Defiance* challenges control mechanisms but stops short of physical harm—for example, vandalism, curfew violations, and unconventional sex. (3) *Submission* involves passive obedience to the demands of others, such as submitting to physical or sexual abuse without response.

An excess of control can result in crimes of (a) exploitation, which involves using others to commit crimes, such as contract killers or drug runners, (b) *plunder*, which involves using power without regard for others, such as committing a hate crime or polluting the environment, or (c) decadence, which involves spur of the moment, irrational acts such as child molesting.

SOURCES: Charles Tittle, *Control Balance: Toward a General Theory of Deviance* (Boulder, CO: Westview Press, 1995); Mark Colvin, *Crime and Coercion: An Integrated Theory of Chronic Criminality* (New York: Palgrave Press, 2000).

It is also possible that these positions are not mutually exclusive, and each may make a notable contribution to understanding the onset and continuity of a delinquent career. While more research is necessary, there is some indication that there may be an interaction between delinquent propensity and life-course changes. Life-impacting events, marriage, military service, jobs, and so on may have greater and or lesser impact on people depending on their level of self-control and impulsivity.[136] For example, research by Bradley Entner Wright and his associates found evidence supporting both latent trait and life-course theories.[137] Their research, conducted with subjects in New Zealand, indicates that low self-control in childhood predicts disrupted social bonds and delinquent offending later in life, a finding that supports latent trait theory. They also found that maintaining positive social bonds helps reduce delinquency and that maintaining prosocial bonds could even counteract the effect of low self-control. Latent traits are an important influence on crime, but their findings indicate that social relationships that form later in life appear to influence delinquent behavior "above and beyond" individuals' preexisting characteristics.[138] This finding may reflect the fact that there are two classes of delinquents: a less serious group who are influenced by life events, and a more chronic group whose latent traits insulate them from any positive prosocial relationships.[139]

PUBLIC POLICY IMPLICATIONS OF DEVELOPMENTAL THEORY

Developmental theory has served as the basis for a number of delinquency control and prevention efforts. These typically feature multisystemic treatment efforts designed to provide at-risk kids with personal, social, educational, and family services.[140]

Treatment programs based on developmental models are now employing multidimensional strategies and are aimed at targeting children in preschool through the early elementary grades in order to alter the direction of their life course. Many of the most successful programs are aimed at strengthening children's social-emotional competence and positive coping skills and suppressing the development of antisocial, aggressive behavior.[141] Research evaluations indicate that the most promising multi-component delinquency and substance abuse prevention programs for youths, especially those at high risk, are aimed at improving their developmental skills. They may include a school component, an after-school component, and a parent-involvement component. All of these components have the common goal of increasing protective factors and decreasing risk factors in the areas of the family, the community, the school, and the individual.[142] The Boys and Girls Clubs and School Collaborations' Substance Abuse Prevention Program includes a school component called SMART (Skills Mastery and Resistance Training) Teachers, an after-school component called SMART Kids, and a parent-involvement component called SMART Parents. Each component is designed to reduce specific risk factors in the children's school, family, community, and personal environments.[143]

Another successful program, Fast Track, is designed to prevent serious antisocial behavior and related adolescent problems in high-risk children entering first grade. The intervention is guided by a developmental approach that suggests that antisocial behavior is the product of the interaction of multiple social and psychological influences:

- Residence in low-income, high-delinquency communities places stressors and influences on children and families that increase their risk levels. In these areas, families characterized by marital conflict and instability make consistent and effective parenting difficult to achieve, particularly with children who are impulsive and of difficult temperament.

- Children of high-risk families usually enter the education process poorly prepared for its social, emotional, and cognitive demands. Their parents often are unprepared to relate effectively with school staff, and a poor home–school bond often aggravates the child's adjustment problems. They may be grouped with other children who are similarly unprepared. This peer group may be negatively influenced by disruptive classroom contexts and punitive teachers.

- Over time, aggressive and disruptive children are rejected by families and peers and tend to receive less support from teachers. All of these processes increase the risk of antisocial behaviors, in a process that begins in elementary school and lasts throughout adolescence. During this period, peer influences, academic difficulties, and dysfunctional personal identity development can contribute to serious conduct problems and related risky behaviors.[144]

Developmental theory favors programs that use multifaceted approaches to help at-risk kids. None is more well known than Boys Town in Omaha, Nebraska. Begun in 1917 by Father Edward Flanagan, Boys Town soon became one of the most famous institutions in the United States. The first girls enrolled in 1979 and now make up half the population. Boys and Girls Town now houses 500 kids, and boasts a middle school and a high school, two churches, a park and post office, police and fire stations, an athletic facility and fields, and the iconic statue of one boy shouldering the weight of another.

© Landon Nordeman/National Geographic/Getty Images

Across Ages

Across Ages is a drug prevention program for youths ages 9 to 13. The program's goal is to strengthen the bonds between adults and children to provide opportunities for positive community involvement. It is unique and highly effective in its pairing of older adult mentors (age 55 and above) with young adolescents, mainly those entering middle school.

Designed as a school- and community-based demonstration research project, Across Ages was founded in 1991 by the Substance Abuse and Mental Health Services Administration's Center for Substance Abuse Prevention and was replicated in Philadelphia and West Springfield, Massachusetts. Today, there are more than 30 replication sites in 17 states. Specifically, the program aims to

- Increase knowledge of health and substance abuse and foster healthy attitudes, intentions, and behavior toward drug use among targeted youth.
- Improve school bonding, academic performance, school attendance, and behavior and attitudes toward school.
- Strengthen relationships with adults and peers.
- Enhance problem-solving and decision-making skills.

TARGET POPULATION

The project was designed for and tested on African American, Hispanic/Latino, white, and Asian American middle school students living in a large urban setting. The goal was to assess many risk factors faced by urban youth, including no opportunity for positive free-time activities, few positive role models, and stresses caused by living in extended families when parents are incarcerated or substance abusers.

HOW IT WORKS

Program materials are offered in English or Spanish so they can be used cross-culturally. A child is matched up with an older adult and participates in activities and interventions that include:

- Mentoring for a minimum of two hours each week in one-on-one contact
- Community service for one to two hours per week
- Social competence training, which involves the "Social Problem-Solving Module," composed of 26 weekly lessons at 45 minutes each
- Activities for the youth and family members and mentors

BENEFITS AND OUTCOMES

Participating youth learn positive coping skills and have an opportunity to be of service to their community. The program aims to increase prosocial interactions and protective factors and decrease negative ones.

PROTECTIVE FACTORS TO INCREASE

- *Individual.* Relationship with significant adult; engagement in positive free-time activities; problem-solving/conflict resolution skills; bonding to school.
- *Peer.* Association with peers engaged in positive behavior and activities.
- *Family.* Engagement in positive family activities; improved communication between parents and children.
- *School.* Improved school attendance, behavior, and performance.
- *Community.* Useful role in the community; positive feedback from community members.

Compared with children in the control group, children in the intervention group displayed significantly less aggressive behavior at home, in the classroom, and on the playground. By the end of third grade, 37 percent of the intervention group had become free of conduct problems, as compared with 27 percent of the control group. By the end of elementary school, 33 percent of the intervention group had a developmental trajectory of decreasing conduct problems, as compared with 27 percent of the control group. Furthermore, placement in special education by the end of elementary school was about one-fourth lower in the intervention group than in the control group.

Group differences continued through adolescence. Court records indicate that by 8th grade, 38 percent of the intervention group boys had been arrested, in contrast with 42 percent of the control group. Finally, psychiatric interviews after 9th grade indicate that the Fast Track intervention reduced serious conduct disorder by over a third, from 27 percent to 17 percent. These effects generalized across gender and ethnic groups and across the wide range of child and family characteristics measured by Fast Track. The Policy and Practice feature describes another developmental-based program, Across Ages.

RISK FACTORS TO DECREASE

I *Individual*. School failure; identified behavior problems in school; lack of adult role models; poor decision-making and problem-solving skills.

I *Peer*. Engagement in risky behavior.

I *Family*. Substance-abusing parents and siblings; incarcerated family members; little positive interaction between parents and children.

I *School*. Lack of bonding to school.

I *Community*. Residence in communities lacking opportunities for positive recreational activities and with high incidence of drug-related delinquency.

APPLYING ACROSS AGES IN MARYLAND

An important Across Ages program is now being run by Interages, a nonprofit agency whose goal is to address community needs through caring and supportive partnerships between older adults and children and youth. For more than 18 years, Interages has operated the Montgomery County Intergenerational Resource Center, through which it assists professionals and organizations in developing intergenerational programs for their communities. They have run an Across Ages program since 2003 that focuses on helping children develop strong decision-making skills, problem-solving abilities, and community awareness, and helping to build a strong relationship between mentors and children. Mentoring is the cornerstone of the program. The key concepts taught to the children are reinforced by the relationship they have with their mentors. Mentors act as advocates, challengers, nurturers, role models, and—most of all—friends. Through these relationships, the children begin to develop awareness, self-confidence, and the skills needed to overcome overwhelming obstacles. Among the most popular activities are:

I Problem-solving "talk time"

I Creating problem-solving skits

I Group community service activities at local nursing homes

I "Social Problem-Solving Skills" academic lessons

I Self-esteem and team-building activities

I Group discussions

I Family day field trips

I Tree planting and stream clean-up

I Yearly donation of snacks and gifts benefiting local homeless children

I Individual mentor/mentee activities

Results show that participation in the project leads to increased knowledge about the negative effects of drug abuse and decreased use of alcohol and tobacco. Participants improve school attendance, improve grades, and get fewer suspensions. Another positive outcome from the project is seen in the youths' attitudes toward older adults. At the same time, the project helps the older volunteers feel more productive, experience a greater sense of purpose, and regain a central role in their communities.

Critical Thinking

1. Should such issues as early onset and problem behavior syndrome be considered when choosing participants for prevention programs such as Across Ages?

2. Could participation in such programs label or stigmatize participants and thereafter lock them into a deviant role?

SOURCES: U.S. Department of Health and Human Services, Substance Abuse and Mental Health Services Administration, Center for Substance Abuse Prevention, Across Ages, http://modelprograms.samhsa.gov/pdfs/model/ AcrossAges.pdf (accessed July 15, 2007); Interages, Wheaton, Maryland, www. interages.com/programs/acrossages.php (accessed July 12, 2007).

Summary

1. Compare and contrast the two forms of developmental theory

I The developmental theory of delinquency is a view that looks at the onset, continuity, and termination of a delinquent career.

I There are two forms of developmental theory, life-course and latent trait.

I Life-course theory suggests that delinquent behavior is a dynamic process, influenced by individual characteristics as well as social experiences, and that the factors that cause antisocial behaviors change dramatically over a person's lifespan.

I Latent trait theory suggests that a stable feature, characteristic, property, or condition, such as defective intelligence or impulsive personality, makes some people delinquency-prone over the life course.

I Human development is controlled by a "master" or latent trait that remains stable and unchanging throughout a person's lifetime.

I The propensity to commit delinquent acts is constant, but the opportunity to commit them is constantly fluctuating.

I There are similarities between the two approaches: Delinquent careers are a passage; personal and structural factors influence crime; external change affects crime.

2. **Trace the history of and influences on developmental theory**

I The foundation of developmental theory can be traced to the pioneering work of Sheldon and Eleanor Glueck.

I The Gluecks followed the careers of known delinquents to determine the social, biological, and psychological characteristics that predicted persistent offending.

I The most important of these factors was family relations, considered in terms of quality of discipline and emotional ties with parents.

I The Philadelphia cohort research by Marvin Wolfgang and his associates was another milestone in explaining delinquent career development.

3. **Know the principles of the life-course approach to developmental theory**

I According to the life-course view, even as toddlers people begin relationships and behaviors that will determine their adult life course.

I Some individuals are incapable of maturing in a reasonable and timely fashion because of family, environmental, or personal problems.

I Because a transition from one stage of life to another can be a bumpy ride, the propensity to commit crimes is neither stable nor constant: It is a developmental process.

I A positive life experience may help some kids desist from delinquency for a while, whereas a negative one may cause them to resume their activities.

I Disruptions in life's major transitions can be destructive and ultimately can promote delinquency.

I Life-course theories also recognize that as people mature, the factors that influence their behavior change.

I As people make important life transitions—from child to adolescent, from adolescent to adult, from unwed to married—the nature of social interactions changes.

I People may show a propensity to offend early in their lives, but the nature and frequency of their activities are often affected by the forces that shape their personal development.

4. **Be familiar with the concept of problem behavior syndrome**

I The developmental view is that delinquency may best be understood as one of many social problems faced by at-risk youth, a view called problem behavior syndrome (PBS).

I According to this view, delinquency is one of a group of interrelated antisocial behaviors that cluster together.

I PBS typically involves family dysfunction, sexual and physical abuse, substance abuse, smoking, precocious sexuality and early pregnancy, educational underachievement, suicide attempts, sensation seeking, and unemployment.

5. **Identify the paths and directions of the delinquent life course**

I Life-course theorists recognize that career delinquents may travel more than a single road: Some may specialize in violence and extortion; some may be involved in theft and fraud; others may engage in a variety of delinquent acts.

I Some offenders may begin their careers early in life, whereas others are late bloomers who begin committing delinquency when most people desist. Some are frequent offenders, while others travel a more moderate path.

I Most life-course theories assume that the seeds of a delinquent career are planted early in life and that early onset of deviance strongly predicts later and more serious delinquency.

I Children who will later become the most serious delinquents begin their deviant careers at a very early (preschool) age, and the earlier the onset of delinquency the more frequent, varied, and sustained the delinquent career.

6. **Distinguish between adolescent-limited and life-course persistent offenders**

I According to psychologist Terrie Moffitt, adolescent-limited offenders may be considered "typical teenagers" who get into minor scrapes and engage in what might be considered rebellious teenage behavior with their friends.

I They reduce the frequency of their offending as they mature to around age 18.

I In contrast, life-course persisters begin their offending career at a very early age and continue to offend well into adulthood.

I Moffit finds that life-course persisters combine family dysfunction with severe neurological problems that predispose them to antisocial behavior patterns.

7. **Articulate the principles of Sampson and Laub's age-graded life-course theory**

I According to this view, individual traits and childhood experiences are important in understanding the onset of delinquent and criminal behavior. But these alone cannot explain the continuity of crime into adulthood.

I Experiences in young adulthood and beyond can redirect delinquent trajectories or paths. In some cases people can be turned in a positive direction, while in others negative life experiences can be harmful and injurious.

I Repeat negative experiences create a condition called cumulative disadvantage. Serious problems in adolescence undermine life chances and reduce employability and social relations. People who increase their cumulative disadvantage risk continued offending.

- Positive life experiences and relationships can help people become reattached to society and allow them to knife off from a delinquent career path.

- Positive life experiences such as gaining employment, getting married, or joining the military create informal social control mechanisms that limit delinquent behavior opportunities. These then are turning points in a delinquent career.

- Turning points may be serendipitous and unexpected: Success may hinge on a lucky break—someone takes a chance on them, or they win the lottery.

- Another vital feature that helps people desist from delinquency is "human agency" or the purposeful execution of choice and free will.

8. Be able to define the concept of the latent trait

- In a critical 1990 article, David Rowe, D. Wayne Osgood, and W. Alan Nicewander proposed the concept of latent traits to explain the flow of delinquency over the life cycle.

- Their model assumes that a number of people in the population have a personal attribute, or latent trait, that may be either present at birth or established early in life, and it can remain stable over time.

- Suspected latent traits include defective intelligence, damaged or impulsive personality, genetic abnormalities, the physical-chemical functioning of the brain, and environmental influences on brain function such as drugs, chemicals, and injuries.

- Because latent traits are stable, people who are antisocial during adolescence are the most likely to persist in crime.

- James Q. Wilson and Richard Herrnstein suggest that personal traits—such as genetic makeup, intelligence, and body build—may outweigh the importance of social variables as predictors of delinquent activity.

9. Know the principles and assumptions of the General Theory of Crime

- In A *General Theory of Crime*, Michael Gottfredson and Travis Hirschi argue that the propensity to commit antisocial acts is tied directly to a person's level of self-control.

- People with limited self-control tend to be impulsive; they are insensitive to other people's feelings, physical (rather than mental), risk-takers, shortsighted, and nonverbal.

- Because those with low self-control enjoy risky, exciting, or thrilling behaviors with immediate gratification, they are more likely to enjoy delinquent acts, which require stealth, agility, speed, and power, than conventional acts, which demand long-term study and cognitive and verbal skills.

- Low self-control develops early in life and remains stable into and through adulthood.

- Gottfredson and Hirschi trace the root cause of poor self-control to inadequate childrearing practices that begin soon after birth and can influence neural development.

- Children who are not attached to their parents, who are poorly supervised, and whose parents are delinquent or deviant themselves are the most likely to develop poor self-control.

- Gottfredson and Hirschi claim that the principles of self-control theory can explain all varieties of delinquent behavior and all the social and behavioral correlates of crime.

10. Discuss the strengths and weaknesses of the GTC

- By integrating the concepts of socialization and delinquency, Gottfredson and Hirschi help explain why some people who lack self-control can escape delinquency, and, conversely, why some people who have self-control might not escape delinquency.

- Some critics argue that the theory is tautological or involves circular reasoning: How do we know when people are impulsive? When they commit crimes! Are all delinquents impulsive?

- The GTC also fails to address individual and ecological patterns in the delinquency rate.

- Although distinct gender differences in the delinquency rate exist, there is little evidence that males are more impulsive than females.

- A number of research efforts show that the quality of peer relations either enhances or controls delinquent behavior and that these influences vary over time.

- One of the most important questions raised about the GTC concerns its assumption that delinquent propensity does not change.

Key Terms

developmental theory, p. 182
life-course theory, p. 182
latent trait, p. 182
problem behavior syndrome (PBS), p. 184
authority conflict pathway, p. 185

covert pathway, p. 185
overt pathway, p. 185
adolescent-limited offenders, p. 189
life-course persisters, p. 190
integrated theories, p. 190

cumulative disadvantage, p. 191
turning points, p. 191
social capital, p. 192
General Theory of Crime (GTC), p. 196
self-control theory, p. 198

Viewpoint

Luis Francisco is the leader of the Almighty Latin Kings and Queens Nation. He was convicted of murder in 1998 and sentenced to life imprisonment plus 45 years. Luis Francisco's life has been filled with displacement, poverty, and chronic predatory delinquency. The son of a prostitute in Havana, at the age of 9 he was sent to prison for robbery. He had trouble in school, and teachers described him as having attention problems; he dropped out in the seventh grade. On his 19th birthday in 1980, he immigrated to the United States and soon after became a gang member in Chicago, where he joined the Latin Kings. After moving to the Bronx, he shot and killed his girlfriend in 1981. He fled back to Chicago and was not apprehended until 1984. Sentenced to nine years for second-degree manslaughter, Luis Francisco ended up in a New York prison, where he started a New York prison chapter of the Latin Kings. As King Blood, Inka, First Supreme Crown, Francisco ruled the 2,000 Latin Kings in and out of prison. Disciplinary troubles erupted when some Kings were found stealing from the organization. Infuriated, King Blood wrote to his street lieutenants and ordered their termination. Federal authorities, who had been monitoring Francisco's mail, arrested 35 Latin Kings. The other 34 pled guilty; only Francisco insisted on a trial, where he was found guilty of conspiracy to commit murder.

▌ Explain Luis's behavior patterns from a developmental perspective.

▌ How would a latent trait theorist explain his escalating delinquent activities?

Doing Research on the Web

The Seattle Social Development Project uses the social development model as a cornerstone for their treatment programs. The Life History Studies Program at the University of Pittsburgh is a longitudinal study designed to test the principles of life-course theory. You might also want to read some of the highlights of the Rochester Youth Study, another longitudinal study of the delinquent life course. All three websites can be accessed via

academic.cengage.com/criminaljustice/siegel

Questions for Discussion

1. Do you consider yourself to have social capital? If so, what form does it take?

2. Someone you know gets a perfect score on the SAT. What personal, family, and social characteristics do you think this individual has? Another person becomes a serial killer. Without knowing this person, what personal, family, and social characteristics do you think this individual has? If "bad behavior" is explained by multiple problems, is "good behavior" explained by multiple strengths?

3. Do you believe it is a latent trait that makes a kid delinquency prone, or is delinquency a function of environment and socialization?

4. Do you agree with Loeber's multiple pathways model? Do you know people who have traveled down those paths?

5. Do people really change, or do they stay the same but appear to be different because their life circumstances have changed?

Notes

1. Gregg McCrary and Katherine Ramsland, *The Unknown Darkness* (New York: William Morrow/HarperCollins, 2003).

2. See, generally, Sheldon Glueck and Eleanor Glueck, *500 Criminal Careers* (New York: Knopf, 1930); Glueck and Glueck, *One Thousand Juvenile Delinquents* (Cambridge, MA: Harvard University Press, 1934); Glueck and Glueck, *Predicting Delinquency and Crime* (Cambridge, MA: Harvard University Press, 1967), pp. 82–83; Glueck and Glueck, *Unraveling Juvenile Delinquency* (Cambridge, MA: Harvard University Press, 1950).

3. Glueck and Glueck, *Unraveling Juvenile Delinquency*.

4. Ibid., p. 48.

5. Marvin Wolfgang, Robert Figlio, and Thorsten Sellin, *Delinquency in a Birth Cohort* (Chicago: University of Chicago Press, 1972).

6. Marvin Krohn, Alan Lizotte, and Cynthia Perez, "The Interrelationship between Substance Use and Precocious Transitions to Adult Sexuality," *Journal of Health and Social Behavior* 38:87–103, at 88 (1997).

7. Jennifer M. Beyers and Rolf Loeber, "Untangling Developmental Relations between Depressed Mood and Delinquency in Male Adolescents," *Journal of Abnormal Child Psychology* 31:247–266 (2003).

8. Stephanie Milan and Ellen Pinderhughes, "Family Instability and Child Maladjustment Trajectories during Elementary School," *Journal of Abnormal Child Psychology* 34:43–56 (2006).

9. Bradley Entner Wright, Avashalom Caspi, Terrie Moffitt, and Phil Silva, "The Effects of Social Ties on Crime Vary by Criminal Propensity: A Life-Course Model of Interdependence," *Criminology* 39:321–352 (2001).

10. Joan McCord, "Family Relationships, Juvenile Delinquency, and Adult Criminality," *Criminology* 29:397–417 (1991).

11. Paul Mazerolle, "Delinquent Definitions and Participation Age: Assessing the Invariance Hypothesis," *Studies on Crime and Crime Prevention* 6:151–168 (1997).

12. Peggy Giordano, Stephen Cernkovich, and Jennifer Rudolph, "Gender, Delinquency, and Desistance: Toward a Theory of Cognitive Transformation?" *American Journal of Sociology* 107:990–1064 (2002).

13. John Hagan and Holly Foster, "S/He's a Rebel: Toward a Sequential Stress Theory of Delinquency and Gendered Pathways to Disadvantage in Emerging Adulthood," *Social Forces* 82:53–86 (2003).

14. G. R. Patterson, Barbara DeBaryshe, and Elizabeth Ramsey, "A Developmental Perspective on Antisocial Behavior," *American Psychologist* 44:329–335 (1989).

15. Robert Sampson and John Laub, "Crime and Deviance in the Life Course," *American Review of Sociology* 18:63–84 (1992).

16. David Farrington, Darrick Jolliffe, Rolf Loeber, Magda Stouthamer-Loeber, and Larry Kalb, "The Concentration of Offenders in Families, and Family Criminality in the Prediction of Boys' Delinquency," *Journal of Adolescence* 24:579–596 (2001).

17. Raymond Paternoster, Charles Dean, Alex Piquero, Paul Mazerolle, and Robert Brame, "Generality, Continuity, and Change in Offending," *Journal of Quantitative Criminology* 13:231–266 (1997).

18. Magda Stouthamer-Loeber and Evelyn Wei, "The Precursors of Young Fatherhood and Its Effect on Delinquency of Teenage Males," *Journal of Adolescent Health* 22:56–65 (1998); Richard Jessor, John Donovan, and Francis Costa, *Beyond Adolescence: Problem Behavior and Young Adult Development* (New York: Cambridge University Press, 1991); Xavier Coll, Fergus Law, Aurelio Tobias, Keith Hawton, and Joseph Tomas, "Abuse and Deliberate Self-Poisoning in Women: A Matched Case-Control Study," *Child Abuse and Neglect* 25:1291–1293 (2001).

19. Richard Miech, Avshalom Caspi, Terrie Moffitt, Bradley Entner Wright, and Phil Silva, "Low Socioeconomic Status and Mental Disorders: A Longitudinal Study of Selection and Causation during Young Adulthood," *American Journal of Sociology* 104:1096–1131 (1999); Krohn, Lizotte, and Perez, "The Interrelationship between Substance Use and Precocious Transitions to Adult Sexuality," p. 88; Richard Jessor, "Risk Behavior in Adolescence: A Psychosocial Framework for Understanding and Action," in D. E. Rogers and E. Ginzburg, eds., *Adolescents at Risk: Medical and Social Perspectives* (Boulder, CO: Westview Press, 1992).

20. Deborah Capaldi and Gerald Patterson, "Can Violent Offenders Be Distinguished from Frequent Offenders? Prediction from Childhood to Adolescence," *Journal of Research in Crime and Delinquency* 33:206–231 (1996); D. Wayne Osgood, "The Covariation among Adolescent Problem Behaviors," paper presented at the annual meeting of the American Society of Criminology, Baltimore, November 1990.

21. Gina Wingood, Ralph DiClemente, Rick Crosby, Kathy Harrington, Susan Davies, and Edward Hook III, "Gang Involvement and the Health of African American Female Adolescents," *Pediatrics* 110:57 (2002).

22. David Husted, Nathan Shapira, and Martin Lazoritz, "Adolescent Gambling, Substance Use, and Other Delinquent Behavior," *Psychiatric Times* 20:52–55 (2003).

23. Krohn, Lizotte, and Perez, "The Interrelationship between Substance Use and Precocious Transitions to Adult Sexuality," p. 88; Jessor, "Risk Behavior in Adolescence: A Psychosocial Framework for Understanding and Action."

24. Terence Thornberry, Carolyn Smith, and Gregory Howard, "Risk Factors for Teenage Fatherhood," *Journal of Marriage and the Family* 59:505–522 (1997); Todd Miller, Timothy Smith, Charles Turner, Margarita Guijarro, and Amanda Hallet, "A Meta-Analytic Review of Research on Hostility and Physical Health," *Psychological Bulletin* 119:322–348 (1996); Marianne Junger, "Accidents and Crime," in T. Hirschi and M. Gottfredson, eds., *The Generality of Deviance* (New Brunswick, NJ: Transaction Books, 1993).

25. James Marquart, Victoria Brewer, Patricia Simon, and Edward Morse, "Lifestyle Factors among Female Prisoners with Histories of Psychiatric Treatment," *Journal of Criminal Justice* 29:319–328 (2001); Rolf Loeber, David Farrington, Magda Stouthamer-Loeber, Terrie Moffitt, Avshalom Caspi, and Don Lynam, "Male Mental Health Problems, Psychopathy, and Personality Traits: Key Findings from the First 14 Years of the Pittsburgh Youth Study," *Clinical Child and Family Psychology Review* 4:273–297 (2002).

26. Robert Johnson, S. Susan Su, Dean Gerstein, Hee-Choon Shin, and John Hoffman, "Parental Influences on Deviant Behavior in Early Adolescence: A Logistic Response Analysis of Age and Gender-Differentiated Effects," *Journal of Quantitative Criminology* 11:167–192 (1995); Judith Brooks, Martin Whiteman, and Patricia Cohen, "Stage of Drug Use, Aggression, and Theft/Vandalism," in Howard Kaplan, ed., *Drugs, Crime and Other Deviant Adaptations: Longitudinal Studies* (New York: Plenum Press, 1995), pp. 83–96.

27. Helene Raskin White, Peter Tice, Rolf Loeber, and Magda Stouthamer-Loeber, "Illegal Acts Committed by Adolescents under the Influence of Alcohol and Drugs," *Journal of Research in Crime and Delinquency* 39:131–153 (2002).

28. David Fergusson, L. John Horwood, and Elizabeth Ridder, "Show Me the Child at Seven II: Childhood Intelligence and Later Outcomes in Adolescence and Young Adulthood," *Journal of Child Psychology and Psychiatry & Allied Disciplines* 46:850–859 (2005).

29. Margit Wiesner and Ranier Silbereisen, "Trajectories of Delinquent Behaviour in Adolescence and Their Covariates: Relations with Initial and Time-Averaged Factors," *Journal of Adolescence* 26:753–771 (2003).

30. Rolf Loeber, Phen Wung, Kate Keenan, Bruce Giroux, Magda Stouthamer-Loeber, Wemoet Van Kammen, and Barbara Maughan, "Developmental Pathways in Disruptive Behavior," *Development and Psychopathology* 23:12–48 (1993).

31. Sheila Royo Maxwell and Christopher Maxwell, "Examining the 'Criminal Careers' of Prostitutes within the Nexus of Drug Use, Drug Selling, and Other Illicit Activities," *Criminology* 38:787–809 (2000).

32. Alex R. Piquero and He Len Chung, "On the Relationships between Gender, Early Onset, and the Seriousness of Offending," *Journal of Criminal Justice* 29:189–206 (2001).

33. David Nurco, Timothy Kinlock, and Mitchell Balter, "The Severity of Preaddiction Criminal Behavior among Urban, Male Narcotic Addicts and Two Nonaddicted Control Groups," *Journal of Research in Crime and Delinquency* 30:293–316 (1993).

34. Hanno Petras, Nicholas Ialongo, Sharon Lambert, Sandra Barrueco, Cindy Schaeffer, Howard Chilcoat, and Sheppard Kellam, "The Utility of Elementary School TOCA-R Scores in Identifying Later Criminal Court Violence Among Adolescent Females," *Journal of the American Academy of Child and Adolescent Psychiatry* 44:790–797 (2005); Hanno Petras, Howard Chilcoat, Philip Leaf, Nicholas Ialongo, and Sheppard Kellam, "Utility of TOCA-R Scores during the Elementary School Years in Identifying Later Violence among Adolescent Males," *Journal of the American Academy of Child and Adolescent Psychiatry* 43:88–96 (2004).

35. W. Alex Mason, Rick Kosterman, J. David Hawkins, Todd Herrenkohi, Liliana Lengua, and Elizabeth McCauley, "Predicting Depression, Social Phobia, and Violence in Early Adulthood from Childhood Behavior Problems," *Journal of the American Academy of Child and Adolescent Psychiatry* 43:307–315 (2004); Rolf Loeber and David Farrington, "Young Children Who Commit Crime: Epidemiology, Developmental Origins, Risk Factors, Early Interventions, and Policy Implications," *Development and Psychopathology* 12:737–762 (2000); Patrick Lussier, Jean Proulx, and Marc Leblanc, "Criminal Propensity, Deviant Sexual Interests and Criminal Activity of

Sexual Aggressors Against Women: A Comparison of Explanatory Models," *Criminology* 43:249–281 (2005).

36. Dawn Jeglum Bartusch, Donald Lynam, Terrie Moffitt, and Phil Silva, "Is Age Important? Testing a General versus a Developmental Theory of Antisocial Behavior," *Criminology* 35:13–48 (1997).

37. Daniel Nagin and Richard Tremblay, "What Has Been Learned from Group-Based Trajectory Modeling? Examples from Physical Aggression and Other Problem Behaviors," *The Annals of the American Academy of Political and Social Science* 602:82–117 (2005).

38. Mason, Kosterman, Hawkins, Herrenkohi, Lengua, and McCauley, "Predicting Depression, Social Phobia, and Violence in Early Adulthood from Childhood Behavior Problems"; Ronald Prinz and Suzanne Kerns, "Early Substance Use by Juvenile Offenders," *Child Psychiatry and Human Development* 33:263–268 (2003).

39. Glenn Clingempeel and Scott Henggeler, "Aggressive Juvenile Offenders Transitioning into Emerging Adulthood: Factors Discriminating Persistors and Desistors," *American Journal of Orthopsychiatry* 73:310–323 (2003).

40. David Gadd and Stephen Farrall, "Criminal Careers, Desistance and Subjectivity: Interpreting Men's Narratives of Change," *Theoretical Criminology* 8:123–156 (2004).

41. G. R. Patterson, L. Crosby, and S. Vuchinich, "Predicting Risk for Early Police Arrest," *Journal of Quantitative Criminology* 8:335–355 (1992).

42. Holly Hartwig and Jane Myers, "A Different Approach: Applying a Wellness Paradigm to Adolescent Female Delinquents and Offenders," *Journal of Mental Health Counseling* 25:57–76 (2003).

43. Terrie Moffitt, Avshalom Caspi, Michael Rutter, and Phil Silva, *Sex Differences in Antisocial Behavior: Conduct Disorder, Delinquency, and Violence in the Dunedin Longitudinal Study* (London: Cambridge University Press, 2001).

44. Lisa Broidy, Richard Tremblay, Bobby Brame, David Fergusson, John Horwood, Robert Laird, Terrie Moffitt, Daniel Nagin, John Bates, Kenneth Dodge, Rolf Loeber, Donald Lynam, Gregory Pettit, and Frank Vitaro, "Developmental Trajectories of Childhood Disruptive Behaviors and Adolescent Delinquency: A Six-Site, Cross-National Study," *Developmental Psychology* 39:222–245 (2003).

45. Ick-Joong Chung, Karl G. Hill, J. David Hawkins, Lewayne Gilchrist, and Daniel Nagin, "Childhood Predictors of Offense Trajectories," *Journal of Research in Crime and Delinquency* 39:60–91 (2002).

46. Amy D'Unger, Kenneth Land, Patricia McCall, and Daniel Nagin, "How Many Latent Classes of Delinquent/Criminal Careers? Results from Mixed Poisson Regression Analyses," *American Journal of Sociology* 103:1593–1630 (1998).

47. Alex Piquero and Timothy Brezina, "Testing Moffitt's Account of Adolescent-Limited Delinquency," *Criminology* 39:353–370 (2001).

48. Terrie Moffitt, "Adolescence-Limited and Life-Course Persistent Antisocial Behavior: A Developmental Taxonomy," *Psychological Review* 100:674–701 (1993).

49. Terrie Moffitt, "Natural Histories of Delinquency," in Elmar Weitekamp and Hans-Jurgen Kerner, eds., *Cross-National Longitudinal Research on Human Development and Criminal Behavior* (Dordrecht, Netherlands: Kluwer, 1994), pp. 3–65.

50. Andrea Donker, Wilma Smeenk, Peter van der Laan, and Frank Verhulst, "Individual Stability of Antisocial Behavior from Childhood to Adulthood: Testing the Stability Postulate of Moffitt's Developmental Theory," *Criminology* 41:593–609 (2003).

51. Robert Vermeiren, "Psychopathology and Delinquency in Adolescents: A Descriptive and Developmental Perspective," *Clinical Psychology Review* 23:277–318 (2003); Paul Mazerolle, Robert Brame, Ray Paternoster, Alex Piquero, and Charles Dean, "Onset Age, Persistence, and Offending Versatility: Comparisons across Sex," *Criminology* 38:1143–1172 (2000).

52. Adrian Raine, Rolf Loeber, Magda Stouthamer-Loeber, Terrie Moffitt, Avshalom Caspi, and Don Lynam, "Neurocognitive Impairments in Boys on the Life-Course Persistent Antisocial Path," *Journal of Abnormal Psychology* 114:38–49 (2005).

53. Per-Olof Wikstrom and Rolf Loeber, "Do Disadvantaged Neighborhoods Cause Well-Adjusted Children to Become Adolescent Delinquents? A Study of Male Juvenile Serious Offending, Individual Risk and Protective Factors, and Neighborhood Context," *Criminology* 38:1109–1142 (2000).

54. Rolf Loeber and Magda Stouthamer-Loeber, "Development of Juvenile Aggression and Violence," *American Psychologist* 53:242–259 (1998).

55. Stephen Farrall and Benjamin Bowling, "Structuration, Human Development, and Desistance from Crime," *British Journal of Criminology* 39:253–268 (1999).

56. Robert Sampson and John Laub, *Crime in the Making: Pathways and Turning Points through Life* (Cambridge, MA: Harvard University Press, 1993); John

Laub and Robert Sampson, "Turning Points in the Life Course: Why Change Matters to the Study of Crime," paper presented at the annual meeting of the American Society of Criminology, New Orleans, November 1992.

57. Robert Sampson and John Laub, "A Life-Course View of the Development of Crime," *The Annals of the American Academy of Political and Social Science* 602:12–45 (2005).

58. Daniel Nagin and Raymond Paternoster, "Personal Capital and Social Control: The Deterrence Implications of a Theory of Criminal Offending," *Criminology* 32:581–606 (1994).

59. Leonore M. J. Simon, "Social Bond and Criminal Record History of Acquaintance and Stranger Violent Offenders," *Journal of Crime and Justice* 22:131–146 (1999).

60. Raymond Paternoster and Robert Brame, "Multiple Routes to Delinquency? A Test of Developmental and General Theories of Crime," *Criminology* 35:49–84 (1997).

61. Spencer De Li, "Legal Sanctions and Youths' Status Achievement: A Longitudinal Study," *Justice Quarterly* 16:377–401 (1999).

62. Shawn Bushway, "The Impact of an Arrest on the Job Stability of Young White American Men," *Journal of Research on Crime and Delinquency* 35:454–479 (1999).

63. Candace Kruttschnitt, Christopher Uggen, and Kelly Shelton, "Individual Variability in Sex Offending and Its Relationship to Informal and Formal Social Controls," paper presented at the annual meeting of the American Society of Criminology, San Diego, November 1997; Mark Collins and Don Weatherburn, "Unemployment and the Dynamics of Offender Populations," *Journal of Quantitative Criminology* 11:231–245 (1995).

64. Robert Hoge, D. A. Andrews, and Alan Leschied, "An Investigation of Risk and Protective Factors in a Sample of Youthful Offenders," *Journal of Child Psychology and Psychiatry* 37:419–424 (1996).

65. Richard Arum and Irenee Beattie, "High School Experience and the Risk of Adult Incarceration," *Criminology* 37:515–540 (1999).

66. Ross Macmillan, Barbara J. McMorris, and Candace Kruttschnitt, "Linked Lives: Stability and Change in Maternal Circumstances and Trajectories of Antisocial Behavior in Children," *Child Development* 75:205–220 (2004).

67. Avshalom Caspi, Terrie Moffitt, Bradley Entner Wright, and Phil Silva, "Early Failure in the Labor Market: Childhood and Adolescent Predictors of Unemployment in the Transition to Adulthood," *American Sociological Review* 63:424–451 (1998).

68. Robert Sampson and John Laub, "Socioeconomic Achievement in the Life Course of Disadvantaged Men: Military Service as a Turning Point, circa 1940–1965," *American Sociological Review* 61:347–367 (1996).

69. Christopher Uggen, "Ex-Offenders and the Conformist Alternative: A Job Quality Model of Work and Crime," *Social Problems* 46:127–151 (1999).

70. Ryan Schroeder, Peggy Giordano, and Stephen Cernkovich, "Drug Use and Desistance Processes," *Criminology* 45:191–222 (2007).

71. David Rowe, D. Wayne Osgood, and W. Alan Nicewander, "A Latent Trait Approach to Unifying Criminal Careers," *Criminology* 28:237–270 (1990).

72. Lee Ellis, "Neurohormonal Bases of Varying Tendencies to Learn Delinquent and Criminal Behavior," in E. Morris and C. Braukmann, eds., *Behavioral Approaches to Crime and Delinquency* (New York: Plenum, 1988), pp. 499–518.

73. David Rowe, Alexander Vazsonyi, and Daniel Flannery, "Sex Differences in Crime: Do Means and Within-Sex Variation Have Similar Causes?" *Journal of Research in Crime and Delinquency* 32:84–100 (1995).

74. James Q. Wilson and Richard Herrnstein, *Crime and Human Nature* (New York: Simon & Schuster, 1985).

75. Ibid., p. 44.

76. Ibid., p. 171.

77. Travis Hirschi and Michael Gottfredson, eds., *The Generality of Deviance* (New Brunswick, NJ: Transaction, 1994), p. 3.; Michael Gottfredson and Travis Hirschi, *A General Theory of Crime* (Stanford, CA: Stanford University Press, 1990).

78. Gottfredson and Hirschi, *A General Theory of Crime*, p. 90.

79. Ibid., p. 89.

80. Alex Piquero and Stephen Tibbetts, "Specifying the Direct and Indirect Effects of Low Self-Control and Situational Factors in Offenders' Decision Making: Toward a More Complete Model of Rational Offending," *Justice Quarterly* 13:481–508 (1996).

81. David Forde and Leslie Kennedy, "Risky Lifestyles, Routine Activities, and the General Theory of Crime," *Justice Quarterly* 14:265–294 (1997).

82. Gottfredson and Hirschi, *A General Theory of Crime*, p. 112.

83. Ibid.

84. Christopher Schreck, Eric Stewart, and Bonnie Fisher, "Self-Control, Victimization, and Their Influence on Risky Lifestyles: A Longitudinal Analysis Using Panel Data," *Journal of Quantitative Criminology* 22:319–340 (2006).

85. Robert Agnew, "The Contribution of Social-Psychological Strain Theory to the Explanation of Crime and Delinquency," in Freda Adler and William Laufer, eds., *Anomie Theory: Advances in Criminological Theory*, vol. 6 (New Brunswick, NJ: Transaction Books, 1995), pp. 81–96.

86. Travis Hirschi and Michael Gottfredson, "Rethinking the Juvenile Justice System," *Crime and Delinquency* 39:262–271 (1993).

87. Anthony Walsh and Lee Ellis, "Shoring Up the Big Three: Improving Criminological Theories with Biosocial Concepts," paper presented at the annual meeting of the American Society of Criminology, San Diego, November 1997, p. 15.

88. Dennis Giever, "An Empirical Assessment of the Core Elements of Gottfredson and Hirschi's General Theory of Crime," paper presented at the annual meeting of the American Society of Criminology, Boston, November 1995.

89. Kevin Beaver and John Paul Wright, "Evaluating the Effects of Birth Complications on Low Self-Control in a Sample of Twins," *International Journal of Offender Therapy and Comparative Criminology* 49:450–472 (2005).

90. Gottfredson and Hirschi, *A General Theory of Delinquency*, p. 27.

91. For a review of this issue, see Anne Campbell, *Men, Women, and Aggression* (New York: Basic Books, 1993).

92. David Brownfield and Ann Marie Sorenson, "Self-Control and Juvenile Delinquency: Theoretical Issues and an Empirical Assessment of Selected Elements of a General Theory of Crime," *Deviant Behavior* 14:243–264 (1993); Harold Grasmick, Charles Tittle, Robert Bursik, and Bruce Arneklev, "Testing the Core Empirical Implications of Gottfredson and Hirschi's General Theory of Crime," *Journal of Research in Crime and Delinquency* 30:5–29 (1993); John Cochran, Peter Wood, and Bruce Arneklev, "Is the Religiosity–Delinquency Relationship Spurious? A Test of Arousal and Social Control Theories," *Journal of Research in Crime and Delinquency* 31:92–123 (1994); Marc LeBlanc, Marc Ouimet, and Richard Tremblay, "An Integrative Control Theory of Delinquent Behavior: A Validation 1976–1985," *Psychiatry* 51:164–176 (1988).

93. Gregory Morris, Peter Wood, and Gregory Dunaway, "Self-Control, Native Traditionalism, and Native American Substance Use: Testing the Cultural Invariance of a General Theory of Crime," *Crime and Delinquency* 52:572–598 (2006).

94. Alexander Vazsonyi, Janice Clifford Wittekind, Lara Belliston, and Timothy Van Loh, "Extending the General Theory of Crime to 'The East': Low Self-Control in Japanese Late Adolescents." *Journal of Quantitative Criminology* 20:189–216 (2004); Alexander Vazsonyi, Lloyd Pickering, Marianne Junger, and Dick Hessing, "An Empirical Test of a General Theory of Crime: A Four-Nation Comparative Study of Self-Control and the Prediction of Deviance," *Journal of Research in Crime and Delinquency* 38:91–131 (2001).

95. Xiaogang Deng and Lening Zhang, "Correlates of Self-Control: An Empirical Test of Self-Control Theory," *Journal of Crime and Justice* 21:89–103 (1998).

96. Daniel Nagin and Greg Pogarsky, "Time and Punishment: Delayed Consequences and Criminal Behavior," *Journal of Quantitative Criminology* 20:295–317 (2004); Brownfield and Sorenson, "Self-Control and Juvenile Delinquency."

97. Linda Pagani, Richard Tremblay, Frank Vitaro, and Sophie Parent, "Does Preschool Help Prevent Delinquency in Boys with a History of Perinatal Complications?" *Criminology* 36:245–268 (1998).

98. John Gibbs, Dennis Giever, and Jamie Martin, "Parental Management and Self-Control: An Empirical Test of Gottfredson and Hirschi's General Theory," *Journal of Research in Crime and Delinquency* 35:40–70 (1998).

99. Vic Bumphus and James Anderson, "Family Structure and Race in a Sample of Offenders," *Journal of Criminal Justice* 27:309–320 (1999).

100. Michael Benson and Elizabeth Moore, "Are White-Collar and Common Offenders the Same? An Empirical and Theoretical Critique of a Recently Proposed General Theory of Crime," *Journal of Research in Crime and Delinquency* 29:251–272 (1992).

101. Ronald Akers, "Self-Control as a General Theory of Crime," *Journal of Quantitative Criminology* 7:201–211 (1991).

102. Gottfredson and Hirschi, *A General Theory of Crime*, p. 88.

103. Moffitt, "Adolescence-Limited and Life-Course Persistent Antisocial Behaviors."

104. Alex Piquero, Robert Brame, Paul Mazerolle, and Rudy Haapanen, "Crime in Emerging Adulthood," *Criminology* 40:137–170 (2002).

105. Donald Lynam, Alex Piquero, and Terrie Moffitt, "Specialization and the Propensity to Violence: Support from Self-Reports but Not Official Records," *Journal of Contemporary Criminal Justice* 20:215–228 (2004).

106. Alan Feingold, "Gender Differences in Personality: A Meta Analysis," *Psychological Bulletin* 116:429–456 (1994).

107. Charles Tittle, David Ward, and Harold Grasmick, "Gender, Age, and Crime/Deviance: A Challenge to Self-Control Theory," *Journal of Research in Crime and Delinquency* 40:426–453 (2003).

108. Brent Benda, "Gender Differences in Life-Course Theory of Recidivism: A Survival Analysis," *International Journal of Offender Therapy and Comparative Criminology* 49:325–342 (2005).

109. Gottfredson and Hirschi, *A General Theory of Crime*, p. 153.

110. Ann Marie Sorenson and David Brownfield, "Normative Concepts in Social Control," paper presented at the annual meeting of the American Society of Criminology, Phoenix, November 1993.

111. Brent Benda, "An Examination of Reciprocal Relationship between Religiosity and Different Forms of Delinquency within a Theoretical Model," *Journal of Research in Crime and Delinquency* 34:163–186 (1997).

112. Delbert Elliott and Scott Menard, "Delinquent Friends and Delinquent Behavior: Temporal and Developmental Patterns," in J. David Hawkins, ed., *Crime and Delinquency: Current Theories* (Cambridge: Cambridge University Press, 1996).

113. Graham Ousey and David Aday, "The Interaction Hypothesis: A Test Using Social Control Theory and Social Learning Theory," paper presented at the annual meeting of the American Society of Criminology, Boston, November 1995.

114. Dana Haynie, Peggy Giordano, Wendy Manning, and Monica Longmore, "Adolescent Romantic Relationships and Delinquency Involvement," *Criminology* 43:177–210 (2005).

115. Julie Horney, D. Wayne Osgood, and Ineke Haen Marshall, "Criminal Careers in the Short-Term: Intra-Individual Variability in Crime and Its Relations to Local Life Circumstances," *American Sociological Review* 60:655–673 (1995); Martin Daly and Margo Wilson, "Killing the Competition," *Human Nature* 1:83–109 (1990).

116. Mark Palermo, Massimo Di Luigi, Gloria Dal Forno, Cinzia Dominici, David Vicomandi, Augusto Sambucioni, Luca Proietti, and Patrizio Pasqualetti, "Externalizing and Oppositional Behaviors and Karate-do: The Way of Crime Prevention," *International Journal of Offender Therapy and Comparative Criminology* 50:654–660 (2006).

117. Charles R. Tittle and Harold G. Grasmick, "Criminal Behavior and Age: A Test of Three Provocative Hypotheses," *Journal of Criminal Law and Criminology* 88:309–342 (1997).

118. Callie Harbin Burt, Ronald Simons, and Leslie Simons, "A Longitudinal Test of the Effects of Parenting and the Stability of Self-Control: Negative Evidence for the General Theory of Crime," *Criminology* 44:353–396 (2006).

119. Carter Hay and Walter Forrest, "The Development of Self-Control: Examining Self-Control Theory's Stability Thesis," *Criminology* 44:739–774 (2006).

120. Ronald Simons, Christine Johnson, Rand Conger, and Glen Elder, "A Test of Latent Trait versus Life-Course Perspectives on the Stability of Adolescent Antisocial Behavior," *Criminology* 36:217–244 (1998).

121. Carter Hay, "Parenting, Self-Control, and Delinquency: A Test of Self-Control Theory," *Criminology* 39:707–736 (2001); Douglas Longshore, "Self-Control and Criminal Opportunity: A Prospective Test of the General Theory of Crime," *Social Problems* 45:102–114 (1998); Finn-Aage Esbensen and Elizabeth Piper Deschenes, "A Multisite Examination of Youth Gang Membership: Does Gender Matter?" *Criminology* 36:799–828 (1998).

122. Raymond Paternoster and Robert Brame, "The Structural Similarity of Processes Generating Criminal and Analogous Behaviors," *Criminology* 36:633–670 (1998).

123. Otwin Marenin and Michael Resig, "A General Theory of Crime and Patterns of Crime in Nigeria: An Exploration of Methodological Assumptions," *Journal of Criminal Justice* 23:501–518 (1995).

124. Bruce Arneklev, Harold Grasmick, Charles Tittle, and Robert Bursik, "Low Self-Control and Imprudent Behavior," *Journal of Quantitative Criminology* 9:225–246 (1993).

125. Peter Muris and Cor Meesters, "The Validity of Attention Deficit Hyperactivity and Hyperkinetic Disorder Symptom Domains in Nonclinical Dutch Children," *Journal of Clinical Child and Adolescent Psychology* 32:460–466 (2003).

126. Francis Cullen, John Paul Wright, and Mitchell Chamlin, "Social Support and Social Reform: A Progressive Crime Control Agenda," *Crime and Delinquency* 45:188–207 (1999).

127. Alex Piquero, John MacDonald, Adam Dobrin, Leah Daigle, and Francis Cullen, "Self-Control, Violent Offending, and Homicide Victimization: Assessing the General Theory of Crime," *Journal of Quantitative Criminology* 21:55–71 (2005).

128. Ibid.

129. Richard Wiebe, "Reconciling Psychopathy and Low Self-Control," *Justice Quarterly* 20:297–336 (2003).

130. Elizabeth Cauffman, Laurence Steinberg, and Alex Piquero, "Psychological, Neuropsychological and Physiological Correlates of Serious Antisocial Behavior in Adolescence: The Role of Self-Control" *Criminology* 43:133–176 (2005).

131. Steven Levitt and Sudhir Alladi Venkatesh, "An Economic Analysis of a Drug-Selling Gang's Finances," *Quarterly Journal of Economics* 13(4):755–789 (2000).

132. Ibid., p. 773.

133. Yair Listokin, "Future-Oriented Gang Members? Gang Finances and the Theory of Present-Oriented Criminals," *The American Journal of Economics and Sociology* 64:1073–1083 (2005).

134. Mark Muraven, Greg Pogarsky, and Dikla Shmueli, "Self-Control Depletion and the General Theory of Crime," *Journal of Quantitative Criminology* 22:263–277 (2006).

135. Kevin Thompson, "Sexual Harassment and Low Self-Control: An Application of Gottfredson and Hirschi's General Theory of Crime," paper presented at the annual meeting of the American Society of Criminology, Phoenix, November 1993.

136. Graham Ousey and Pamela Wilcox, "The Interaction of Antisocial Propensity and Life-Course Varying Predictors of Delinquent Behavior: Differences by Method of Estimation and Implications for Theory," *Criminology* 45:313–354 (2007).

137. Bradley Entner Wright, Avashalom Caspi, Terrie Moffitt, and Phil Silva, "Low Self-Control, Social Bonds, and Crime: Social Causation, Social Selection, or Both?" *Criminology* 37:479–514 (1999).

138. Ibid., p. 504.

139. Stephen Cernkovich and Peggy Giordano, "Stability and Change in Antisocial Behavior: The Transition from Adolescence to Early Adulthood," *Criminology* 39:371–410 (2001).

140. Heather Lonczk, Robert Abbott, J. David Hawkins, Rick Kosterman, and Richard Catalano, "Effects of the Seattle Social Development Project on Sexual Behavior, Pregnancy, Birth, and Sexually Transmitted Disease Outcomes by Age 21 Years," *Archive of Pediatrics and Adolescent Medicine* 156:438–447 (2002).

141. Kathleen Bodisch Lynch, Susan Rose Geller, and Melinda G. Schmidt, "Multi-Year Evaluation of the Effectiveness of a Resilience-Based Prevention Program for Young Children," *Journal of Primary Prevention* 24:335–353 (2004).

142. This section leans on Thomas Tatchell, Phillip Waite, Renny Tatchell, Lynne Durrant, and Dale Bond, "Substance Abuse Prevention in Sixth Grade: The Effect of a Prevention Program on Adolescents' Risk and Protective Factors," *American Journal of Health Studies* 19:54–61 (2004).

143. Nancy Tobler and Howard Stratton, "Effectiveness of School-Based Drug Prevention Programs: A Meta-Analysis of the Research," *Journal of Primary Prevention* 18:71–128 (1997).

144. Project overview, Fast Track Data Center, www.pubpol.duke.edu/centers/child/fasttrack/ (accessed February 2, 2007).

3

Social, Community, and Environmental Influences on Delinquency

S ocial, community, and environmental relations are thought to exert a powerful influence on an adolescent's involvement in delinquent activities. Kids who fail at home, at school, and in the neighborhood are considered in danger of developing and/or sustaining delinquent careers. Research indicates that chronic, persistent offenders are quite likely to experience educational failure, poor home life, substance abuse, and unsatisfactory peer relations.

Social, community, and environmental relations can also have a positive influence and shield at-risk children from involvement in a delinquent way of life. Consequently, many delinquency prevention efforts focus on improving family relations, supporting educational achievement, and utilizing community resources. Some begin early in childhood, others during the teen years, while a third type of prevention effort is designed to help those who have been involved in antisocial behavior to desist from further activities.

Part Three contains six chapters devoted to the influences critical social forces have on delinquency. Chapter 7 explores gender relations and their relationship to delinquency. Chapter 8 is devoted to the family, and Chapter 9 looks at peer relations, including juvenile groups and gangs. Chapter 10 examines the relationship between education and delinquency, and Chapter 11 concerns substance abuse. Finally, Chapter 12 looks at how the community environment is being used to help youth avoid involvement in delinquent behaviors.

Gender and Delinquency

7

Chapter Outline

Chapter Objectives

1. Be able to discuss the development of interest in female delinquency
2. Be familiar with the gender differences in development
3. Discuss the basis of gender differences
4. Know the trends in gender differences in the delinquency rate
5. Be familiar with early trait explanations of female delinquency
6. Discuss contemporary trait views of female delinquency
7. Discuss the association between socialization and female delinquency
8. Know the feminist view of female delinquency
9. Be able to discuss Hagan's power-control theory
10. Discuss the treatment of girls in the juvenile justice system

On May 18, 2007, six men were indicted on sex trafficking charges stemming from their involvement in a violent Boston-based prostitution ring that forced girls as young as 15 into service and transported them across the country and as far away as Bermuda to work as prostitutes. The alleged conspirators include Darryl "Young Stallion" Tavares, 23; Shaun "Syncere" Leoney, 25; Rueben "Ruby Black" Porcher, 28; Eddie "Young Indian" Jones, 24; Aaron "Breeze" Brooks, 22; and Trueheart "Dwayne" Peeples, 29, who were all charged with conspiracy to transport adults and minors across state lines for prostitution from 2001 to 2005, as well as other prostitution-related offenses. They were also accused of networking with convicted sex traffickers from other states to swap or hand off girls after they grew tired of them; these so-called "toss ups" occurred when pimps traded young prostitutes among themselves.

Members of the ring are accused of transporting the girls within Massachusetts and to New York, New Jersey, Pennsylvania, Maine, New Hampshire, and Florida to engage in prostitution. Some of the sex trafficking involved children who were 15, 16, and 17 years old when they were forced to become prostitutes. Ruby Black Porcher was accused of arranging for a 15-year-old girl to get false identification and then taking her to Bermuda in summer 2002 to work as a prostitute.

The gang used force and intimidation to keep the girls in line. A 17-year-old girl who wanted to get out of the life went back to work for Young Stallion Tavares after he covered her head with a garbage bag and secured it with duct tape; another 17-year-old girl was allegedly raped by Tavares with a hair brush in April 2005 because he suspected she had turned over some of the money she made from prostitution to Young Indian Jones. The following month, the same victim was allegedly kicked in the face by Jones, while he was wearing Timberland boots, for using a cell phone that he gave her to call a man who wasn't a customer. After disfiguring the girl's mouth and kicking out her teeth in the attack, Jones "gave" the girl back to Tavares because he didn't want her working for him anymore.[1]

This terrible Boston case aptly illustrates the numerous social problems faced by young girls in contemporary society. Many are at risk to horrific abuse and violence, while others are involved in substance abuse and gang membership. Yet, early delinquency experts often ignored female offenders, assuming that girls rarely violated the law, or if they did, that their illegal acts were status-type offenses. Female delinquency was viewed as emotional or family-related, and such problems were not an important concern of criminologists. In fact, the few "true" female delinquents were oddities whose criminal activity was a function of having masculine traits and characteristics, a concept referred to today as the **masculinity hypothesis.**[2]

masculinity hypothesis
View that women who commit crimes have biological and psychological traits similar to those of men.

Contemporary interest in the association between gender and delinquency has surged, fueled by observations that although the female delinquency rate is still much lower than the male rate, girls are now getting involved in serious delinquent acts. Australian sociologist Kerry Carrington reports that young women represent the fastest growing population within juvenile justice systems around the world. In Canada, for instance, the number of young women charged with criminal offences has more than tripled during the past two decades. In England, the gender gap has also narrowed, with the ratio of delinquent boys to delinquent girls declining from 7:1 during the 1960s to 5:1 today; a similar pattern of rising adolescent female crime rates is evident in Australia.[3]

The types of delinquent acts that young women engage in today also seem quite similar to those of young men. Larceny and aggravated assault, the crimes for which most young men are arrested, are also the most common offenses for which females are arrested. There is evidence that girls get more heavily involved in gangs and gang violence.[4] And while the young women whose vicious exploitation was described in the opening vignette were involved in a prostitution ring, sex work is no longer the exclusive domain of young women. Research now indicates, ironically, that boys rather than girls are more likely to be arrested for sexually related offenses, such as prostitution. When David Finkelhor and Richard Ormrod analyzed national arrest data, they found that juvenile prostitution offenders known to police were more often male (60 percent) than female (40 percent), a greater disproportion than among adult prostitution offenders (53 percent male and 47 percent female).[5]

Another reason for the interest in gender studies is that conceptions of gender differences have changed. A feminist approach to understanding crime is now firmly established. The result has been an increased effort to conduct research that would adequately explain differences and similarities in male and female offending patterns.

This chapter provides an overview of gender factors in delinquency. We first discuss some of the gender differences in development and how they may relate to the gender differences in offending rates. Then we turn to some explanations for these differences: (1) the trait view, (2) the socialization view, (3) the liberal feminist view, and (4) the critical feminist view.

To find information on the state of adolescent girls and the risks they face, go to the website of the **Commonwealth Fund** via academic.cengage .com/criminaljustice/siegel.

GENDER DIFFERENCES IN DEVELOPMENT

Do gender differences in development, including socialization, cognition, and personality, pave the way for future differences in misbehaving?[6] It is possible that the gender-based traits that produce delinquency may exist as early as infancy, when infant girls show greater control over their emotions, whereas boys are more easily angered and depend more on input from their mothers.[7]

Socialization Differences

Psychologists believe that differences in the way females and males are socialized affect their development. Parents may treat boys and girls differently, encouraging what they consider to be appropriate male and female behavior, respectively. It is not surprising that fathers are more likely to teach their sons about using and maintaining weapons while not sharing this knowledge with their daughters: Self-report studies show that boys are three times as likely to report hunting or shooting with a family member than girls.[8]

Males learn to value independence, whereas females are taught that their self-worth depends on their ability to sustain relationships. Girls, therefore, run the risk of losing themselves in their relationships with others and, because so many relationships go sour, also run the risk of feeling alienated, because of the failure to achieve relational success.[9] It is not surprising that research shows that, given a similar set of provocations such as lack of social support from families and peers, girls react by getting depressed while boys are more likely to engage in delinquent behaviors.[10]

Socialization also influences aggressive behaviors. Although there are few gender differences in aggression during the first few years of life, girls are socialized to be less aggressive than boys and are supervised more closely.[11] Boys are exposed to more risk factors in their development and are given fewer protections. The combination of greater risk and less protections may manifest itself in levels of antisocial behaviors and aggression.[12] Differences in aggression become noticeable between ages 3 and 6, when children are socialized into organized groups, such as the daycare center. Males are more likely to display physical aggression, whereas females display relational aggression—for example, by excluding disliked peers from play groups.[13]

As they mature, girls learn to respond to provocation by feeling anxious, unlike boys, who are encouraged to retaliate.[14] Although females get angry as often as males, many have been taught to blame themselves for such feelings. Females are, therefore, much more likely than males to respond to anger with feelings of depression, anxiety, and shame. Females are socialized to fear that anger will harm relationships; males are encouraged to react with "moral outrage," blaming others for their discomfort.[15] Michael Rutter, Henri Giller, and Ann Hagell have argued that depression and delinquency represent equivalent outcomes for females and males, respectively: Males and females are taught to cope with stress in different ways, with females being socialized to display higher rates of internalizing responses (depression) and males showing higher rates of externalizing responses (delinquency).[16] So while girls will react to a family crisis by becoming depressed, boys are more likely to externalize their pain with aggressive and violent behaviors.[17]

Cognitive Differences

There are also cognitive differences between males and females starting in childhood. The more replicated findings about gender difference in cognitive performance suggest female superiority on visual-motor speed and language ability and male superiority on mechanical and visual-spatial tasks.[18] Put another way, males excel in tasks that assess the ability to manipulate visual images in working memory, whereas females do better in tasks that require retrieval from long-term memory and the acquisition and use of verbal information.[19] Gender group strengths found in the early school years become more established at adolescence and remain stable through adulthood.[20]

Girls learn to speak earlier and faster, and with better pronunciation, most likely because parents talk more to their infant daughters than to their infant sons. A girl's verbal proficiency enables her to develop a skill that may later help her deal with conflict without resorting to violence.[21] When faced with conflict, women might be more likely to attempt to negotiate, rather than to respond passively or resist physically, especially when they perceive increased threat of harm or death.[22]

When girls are aggressive, they are more likely than boys to hide their behavior from adults; girls who "bully" others are less likely than boys to admit their behavior.[23]

Girls are shielded by their moral sense, which directs them to avoid harming others. Their moral sensitivity may counterbalance the effects of family problems.[24] Females display more self-control than males, a factor that has been related to criminality.[25]

In most cases cognitive differences are small, narrowing, and usually attributed to cultural expectations. When given training, girls can increase their visual-spatial skills. However, differences still exert a penalty on young girls. For example, performance on the mathematics portion of the Scholastic Aptitude Test (SAT) still favors males: Twice as many boys as girls attain scores over 500, and 13 times as many boys as girls attain scores over 700.[26]

Personality Differences

Girls are often stereotyped as talkative, but research shows that in many situations boys spend more time talking than girls do. Females are more willing to reveal their feelings and more likely to express concern for others. Females are more concerned about finding the "meaning of life" and less interested in competing for material success.[27] Males are more likely to introduce new topics and to interrupt conversations.

Adolescent females use different knowledge than males and have different ways of interpreting their interactions with others. These gender differences may have an impact on self-esteem and self-concept. Research shows that, as adolescents develop, male self-esteem and self-concept rise, whereas female self-confidence is lowered.[28] One reason is that girls are more likely to stress about their weight and be more dissatisfied with the size and shape of their bodies.[29] Young girls are regularly confronted with unrealistically high standards of slimness that make them extremely unhappy with their own bodies; it is not surprising that the incidence of eating disorders, such as *anorexia* and *bulimia*, has increased markedly in recent years. Psychologist Carol Gilligan uncovered an alternative explanation for this decline in female self-esteem: As girls move into adolescence, they become aware of the conflict between the positive way they see themselves and the negative way society views females. Many girls respond by "losing their voices"—that is, submerging their own feelings and accepting the negative view of women conveyed by adult authorities.[30]

Concept Summary 7.1 discusses these various gender differences.

What Causes Gender Differences? Biology or Socialization?

Why do these gender differences occur? Some experts suggest that gender differences may have a biological origin: Males and females are essentially different. They have somewhat different brain organizations; females are more left brain–oriented

Concept Summary 7.1

Gender Differences

	Females	Males
Socialization	Sustain relationships Are less aggressive Blame self	Are independent Are aggressive Externalize anger
Cognitive	Have superior verbal ability Speak earlier Have better pronunciation Read better	Have superior visual/spatial ability Are better at math
Personality	Have lower self-esteem Are self-aware Have better attention span	Have higher self-esteem Are materialistic Have lower attention span

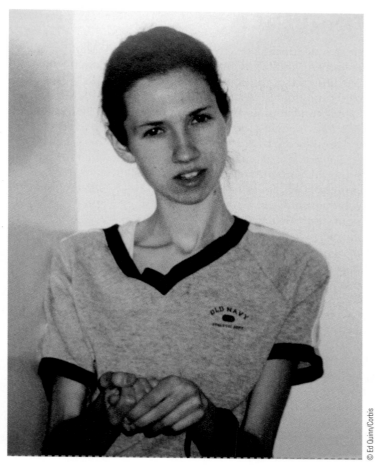

Girls learn to respond to provocation by feeling anxious and depressed. Their anxiety may lead to psychological turmoil manifested in eating conditions such as anorexia and bulimia. Jennifer Shortis, a young Massachusetts girl, developed anorexia and wasted away from 124 pounds to 70. After more than $100,000 in anorexia-related treatment costs, she is on the road to recovery.

and males more right brain–oriented. (The left brain is believed to control language; the right, spatial relations.)[31] Others point to the hormonal differences between the sexes as the key to understanding their behavior.

A second view is that gender differences are developed over the life course and reflect different treatment of males and females. In her book *The Two Sexes: Growing up Apart, Coming Together*, psychologist Eleanor Maccoby argues that gender differences are not a matter of individual personality or biological difference but the way kids socialize and how their relationships are structured.[32] Despite the best efforts of parents who want to break down gender boundaries, kids still segregate themselves by gender in their playgroups. Thus a "boy culture" and a "girl culture" develop side by side. Kids also take on different roles depending on whom they are with and who is being exposed to the behavior. A boy will be all macho bravado when he is with his peers but may be a tender, loving big brother when asked to baby-sit his little sister. Take for instance the macho male jock culture, which encourages its members to become risk takers and engage in status type offenses such as drinking.[33]

Little girls aren't "passive" as a result of some ingrained quality; they have learned to be passive only when boys are present. According to Maccoby, gender separation has partly biological and partly social causes. Though biological and cognitive differences do impact on behavior, Maccoby claims that gender distinctions arise mainly in social interactions and that peer groups are highly influential in greatly enhancing gender. Nonetheless, biological and social factors are so intertwined that it is erroneous to think of gender differences as having an independent social or physical origin.

Another view is that gender differences are a result of the interaction of socialization, learning, and enculturation. Boys and girls may behave differently, because they have been exposed to different styles of socialization, learned different values, and had different cultural experiences.[34] According to psychologist Sandra Bem's **gender-schema theory**, our culture polarizes males and females by forcing them to obey mutually exclusive gender roles, or "scripts." Girls are expected to be "feminine," exhibiting sympathetic and gentle traits. In contrast, boys are expected to be "masculine," exhibiting assertiveness and dominance.

gender-schema theory
A theory of development that holds that children internalize gender scripts that reflect the gender-related social practices of the culture. Once internalized, these gender scripts predispose the kids to construct a self-identity that is consistent with them.

Children internalize these scripts and accept gender polarization as normal. Children's self-esteem becomes wrapped up in how closely their behavior conforms to the proper sex role stereotype. When children begin to perceive themselves as either boys or girls (which occurs at about age 3), they search for information to help them define their role; they begin to learn what behavior is appropriate for their sex.[35] Girls are expected to behave according to the appropriate script and to seek approval of their behavior: Are they acting as girls should at that age? Masculine behavior is to be avoided. In contrast, males look for cues from their peers to define their masculinity; aggressive behavior may be rewarded with peer approval, whereas sensitivity is viewed as unmasculine.[36]

Regardless of their origin, gender distinctions may partly explain the significant gender differences in the delinquency rate. Research conducted in the United States and abroad has found that the factors that direct the trajectories of male delinquency are quite different from those that influence female delinquency. Among males, early offending is highly correlated with later misbehavior, whereas females take on a more haphazard criminal career path. Females are more likely to be influenced by current levels of social support than they are by their early history of antisocial behavior.[37] Males seem more aggressive and less likely to form attachments to others, which are factors that might help them maintain their crime rates over their lifespan. Males view aggression as an appropriate means to gain status. Boys are also more likely than girls to socialize with deviant peers, and when they do, they display personality traits that make them more susceptible to delinquency.

This pattern fits within the two cultures view, which suggests that girls and boys differ in their social behavior largely because their sex-segregated peer groups demand behaviors, such as aggression, that may not be characteristic of them in other social situations.[38] What is typically assumed to be an inherent difference in antisocial behavior tendencies may actually be a function of peer socialization differences. The fact that young boys perceive their roles as being more dominant than young girls may be a function of peer pressure. Male perceptions of power, their ability to have freedom and hang with their friends, help explain gender differences in personality.[39] It follows, then, that if members of both sexes were equally exposed to the factors that produce delinquency, their delinquency rates would be equivalent.

While socialization may be a strong force, inherent gender differences in cognition, personality, and biology still seem to play a role in shaping interpersonal interactions, including aggression, and cannot be totally discounted.[40] Cognitive and personality differences are magnified when children internalize gender-specific behaviors. Boys who aren't tough are labeled sissies. Girls are expected to form closer bonds with their friends and to share feelings.

The mission of the **National Council for Research on Women** is to enhance the connections among research, policy analysis, advocacy, and innovative programming on behalf of women and girls. Check them out via academic.cengage.com/criminaljustice/siegel.

Gender Patterns in Delinquency

At about 5:30 A.M. on July 6, 2007, abductors broke into the house of a 1-year-old Oklahoma boy, Brandon Wells, and took him while his mother, Sheila Wells, was sleeping. They left behind a ransom note that said:

If you want to see your son again then you won't call police and report him missing and you will leave $200,000 on the sofa tonight and we will return your son back safe.

It was signed "the kidnappers." The plan began to unravel when the kidnappers brought the child back to their home and told their mother they had found the boy on the corner. Realizing that the jig was up, one of the kidnappers returned to the scene of the crime and told Sheila Wells her son was safe. Wells immediately retrieved her child and called the police, who arrested the kidnappers—a 12-year-old neighbor girl and her 10-year-old sister, who may have been the ringleader in the plot.[41]

As we noted in Chapter 2, males, both adults and juveniles, are arrested far more often than females, but females are now committing the same type of offense as males, even kidnapping. Today males account for about 76 percent of the total number of arrests and 82 percent of all serious violent crime arrests. Yet, as Figure 7.1 shows, for certain delinquent offenses—aggravated assault, burglary—the percentage of delinquency arrests involving female offenders has been climbing steadily for more than 20 years. Did young females become more violent during this period? The data suggest otherwise, increasing for assault but remaining constant for robbery and murder. It is possible that the increase in assault arrests was a function of police behavior: Police are more willing to make arrests in domestic violence cases, and domestic assaults represent a larger proportion of female violence than male violence.[42]

FIGURE 7.1

Trends in Violent Delinquency
by Gender

SOURCE: Howard Snyder and
Melissa Sickmund, *Juvenile Offenders
and Victims: 2006 National Report*
(Washington, DC: Office of Juvenile
Justice, 2006), www.ojjdp.ncjrs.gov/
ojstatbb/nr2006/downloads/NR2006
.pdf (accessed November 18, 2007).

Violent crime

Percentage of delinquency arrests of female offenders

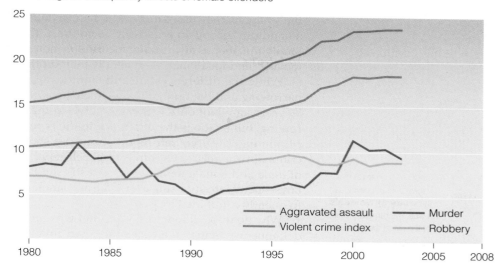

Property crime

Percentage of delinquency arrests of female offenders

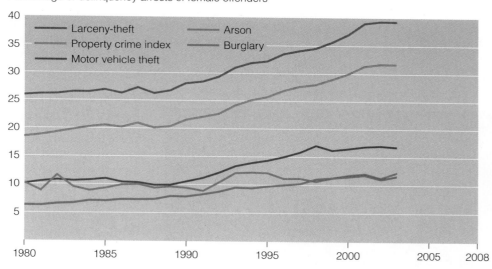

Darrell Steffensmeier and his associates recently conducted research using a variety of self-report and official data sources and found that the rise in girls' violence over the past one to two decades may be more a matter of how and why police are now making arrests than actual behavior changes. Several policy shifts have may have escalated girls' arrest-proneness:

I The definition of "violent crime" may have expanded so that minor incidents that girls, in relative terms, are more likely to commit are now included in the arrest data.

I Police are more likely to make arrests in private settings (e.g., home and school) where girls' violence is more widespread.

I Family and societal attitudes toward juvenile females are less tolerant now. These developments reflect both a growing intolerance of violence in the law and among the citizenry and an expanded application of preventive punishment and risk management strategies that emphasize early identification and enhanced formal control of problem individuals or groups, particularly problem youth.[43]

For the most violent crimes the differences are even more striking: Arrest for murder is typically 10:1 in favor of males. One reason for the gender disparity in lethal violence is that males and females display differences in the victims they target and the weapons they use. The typical male juvenile kills a friend or acquaintance with a handgun during an argument. In contrast, the typical female is as likely to kill a family member as an acquaintance and is more likely to use a knife. Both males and females tend to kill males—generally their brothers, fathers, or friends.

While the differences are still significant, over time the gender gap has been narrowing and the ratio of male-female juvenile arrests is much smaller today than 30 years ago. Not only is the gap between the ratio of male-to-female arrests narrowing, but so too is the difference in the type and pattern of delinquent acts. The *Monitoring the Future* self-report study also shows that patterns of male and female criminality appear to be converging. Self-report data indicate that the rank-ordering of male and female deviant behaviors is similar. The illegal acts most common for boys—petty larceny, using a false ID, and smoking marijuana—are also the ones most frequently committed by girls.[44]

Why do these differences occur, and why are girls increasing their involvement in delinquent activities at a faster pace than boys? The wide range of opinions on these questions will be presented in the remaining sections of this chapter.

A number of institutes at major universities are devoted to the **study of women's issues**. You can visit the site of the one at the University of Michigan via academic.cengage.com/criminaljustice/siegel.

ARE FEMALE DELINQUENTS BORN THAT WAY?

There is a long tradition of tracing gender differences in delinquency to traits that are uniquely male or female. The argument that biological and psychological differences between males and females can explain differences in crime rates is not a new one. The earliest criminologists focused on physical characteristics believed to be precursors of crime.

While girls violate the law far less often than boys, the pattern of their delinquency is quite similar. In this image taken from amateur video evidence released by the Suffolk County Police Department, a 13-year-old girl is beaten by one of the three teenage girls who attacked her in a North Babylon, New York, school yard. The victim, who thought she was meeting another teen to resolve a love triangle, was instead dragged by her hair, beaten, and kicked repeatedly in the head. The video of the attack was posted online and broadcast nationwide, resulting in the arrest of three attackers on January 16, 2007, on delinquency charges stemming from the assault.

© AP Images/Suffolk County Police Department

Early Biological Explanations

With the publication in 1895 of *The Female Offender*, Lombroso (with William Ferrero) extended his work on criminality to females.[45] Lombroso maintained that women were lower on the evolutionary scale than men, more childlike and less intelligent.[46] Women who committed crimes could be distinguished from "normal" women by physical characteristics—excessive body hair, wrinkles, and an abnormal cranium, for example.[47] In appearance, delinquent females appeared closer to men than to other women. The masculinity hypothesis suggested that delinquent girls had excessive male characteristics.[48]

Lombrosian thought had a significant influence for much of the twentieth century. Delinquency rate differentials were explained in terms of gender-based differences. For example, in 1925, Cyril Burt linked female delinquency to menstruation.[49] Similarly, William Healy and Augusta Bronner suggested that males' physical superiority enhanced their criminality. Their research showed that about 70 percent of the delinquent girls they studied had abnormal weight and size, a finding that supported the "masculinity hypothesis."[50]

So-called experts suggested that female delinquency goes unrecorded, because the female is the instigator rather than the perpetrator.[51] Females first use their sexual charms to instigate crime and then beguile males in the justice system to obtain deferential treatment. This

chivalry hypothesis (also known as paternalism hypothesis) The view that low female crime and delinquency rates are a reflection of the leniency with which police treat female offenders.

observation, referred to as the chivalry hypothesis, holds that gender differences in the delinquency rate can be explained by the fact that female criminality is overlooked or forgiven by male agents of the justice system. Those who believe in the chivalry hypothesis point to data showing that even though women make up about 20 percent of arrestees, they account for less than 5 percent of inmates. Police and other justice system personnel may be less willing to penalize female offenders than male offenders.[52]

Early Psychological Explanations

Psychologists also viewed the physical differences between males and females as a basis for their behavior differentials. Sigmund Freud maintained that girls interpret their lack of a penis as a sign that they have been punished. Boys fear that they can be punished by having their penises cut off, and thus learn to fear women. From this conflict comes *penis envy*, which often produces an inferiority complex in girls, forcing them to make an effort to compensate for their "defect." One way to compensate is to identify with their mothers and accept a maternal role. Also, girls may attempt to compensate for their lack of a penis by dressing well and beautifying themselves.[53] Freud also claimed that "if a little girl persists in her first wish—to grow into a boy—in extreme cases she will end as a manifest homosexual, and otherwise she will exhibit markedly masculine traits in the conduct of her later life, will choose a masculine vocation, and so on."[54]

At mid-century, psychodynamic theorists suggested that girls are socialized to be passive, which helps explain their low crime rate. However, this condition also makes some females susceptible to being manipulated by men; hence, their participation in sex-related crimes, such as prostitution. A girl's wayward behavior, psychoanalysts suggested, was restricted to neurotic theft (kleptomania) and overt sexual acts, which were symptoms of personality maladaption.[55]

According to these early versions of the psychoanalytic approach, gender differences in the delinquency rate can be traced to differences in psychological orientation. Male delinquency reflects aggressive traits, whereas female delinquency is a function of repressed sexuality, gender conflict, and abnormal socialization.

Contemporary Trait Views

Contemporary biosocial and psychological theorists have continued the tradition of attributing gender differences in delinquency to physical and emotional traits. These theorists recognize that it is the interaction of biological and psychological traits with the social environment that produces delinquency.

precocious sexuality Sexual experimentation in early adolescence.

Early Puberty/Precocious Sexuality Early theorists linked female delinquency to early puberty and precocious sexuality. According to this view, girls who experience an early onset of physical maturity are most likely to engage in antisocial behavior.[56] Female delinquents were believed to be promiscuous and more sophisticated than male delinquents.[57] Linking female delinquency to sexuality was responsible, in part, for the view that female delinquency is symptomatic of maladjustment.[58]

Equating female delinquency purely with sexual activity is no longer taken seriously, but early sexual maturity has been linked to other problems, such as a higher risk of teen pregnancy and sexually transmitted diseases.[59] Empirical evidence suggests that girls who reach puberty at an early age are at the highest risk for delinquency.[60] One reason is that "early bloomers" may be more attractive to older adolescent boys, and increased contact with this high-risk group places the girls in jeopardy for antisocial behavior. Research shows that young girls who date boys three or more years older are more likely to engage in precocious sex, feel pressured into having sex, and engage in sex while under the influence of drugs and/or alcohol than girls who date more age-appropriate boys.[61]

Girls who are more sexually developed relative to their peers are more likely to socialize at an early age and to get involved in deviant behaviors, especially "party deviance," such as drinking, smoking, and substance abuse. Early puberty is most likely to encourage delinquent activities that occur in the context of socializing with peers and having romantic relationships with boys.[62] The delinquency gap between early and late bloomers narrows when the latter group reaches sexual maturity and increases in exposure to boys.[63] Biological and social factors seem to interact to postpone or accelerate female delinquent activity.

Early Puberty and Victimization If reaching puberty at an early age increases the likelihood of delinquent behavior, does it also increase victimization risk? Recent research by Dana Haynie and Alex Piquero found that both boys and girls who reached puberty at an early age increase their chances of victimization. The association was gendered: Boys were less likely to become victims if their friendship network contained girls; in contrast, girls' victimization was not moderated by the sexual makeup of their peer group.[64]

Why does peer group makeup influence boys' victimization more than girls'? It is possible that females are much less likely to be involved in serious, violent delinquency, and therefore having a higher concentration of them in a male's peer network reduces their exposure to more violent boys. In contrast, boys who associate mostly with male peers may feel compelled to engage in risky behaviors; for example, in order to keep up with their friends they have to drink, drive fast, and get involved in brawls. Girls may feel less peer pressure to engage in risky behavior; their male friends may protect them rather than put them in danger.

In sum, although early puberty and sexual development may put girls at risk for juvenile delinquency and substance abuse, it may also help shield them from victimization risk.

Why Do Some Girls Mature Early? Why do some girls mature early and place themselves at risk for delinquency? Psychologist Jay Belsky proposed an explanation for the finding that girls whose fathers abandon them tend to reach puberty early and to exhibit increased promiscuity. Belsky suggested that some girls exposed to high levels of stress, particularly due to paternal absence in early childhood, may often respond by becoming depressed and insecure, gaining weight and then experiencing accelerated puberty as a result of hormonal changes precipitated by the weight gain, and becoming sexually active with multiple partners and unstable relationships, often resulting in early childbearing.

New research, however, suggests a different explanation for the link between paternal absence and both early puberty and promiscuity in girls. David Comings and colleagues tested male and female subjects and found a particular gene pattern with a short AR allele was associated with assaultive behavior, impulsiveness, sexual compulsiveness and increased number of sexual partners, and feelings of reduced internal control in the male subjects. In females, the presence of the short AR pattern was associated with parental divorce, paternal absence during childhood, and early puberty. Their conclusion: The link between paternal abandonment and early puberty in girls is genetic. Fathers who have the suspect gene pattern engage in marital conflict and abandonment. Their daughters, who inherit the gene, are more likely to reach puberty at an early age and engage in risky behaviors such as precocious sexual activity, childbearing, and disruptive personal relationships. The cause of these mutually dysfunctional behaviors is not stress or learning, but due to shared genes passed from the fathers to their daughters. Their findings also explain why girls whose fathers die do not experience the same changes in behavior and timing of puberty onset as girls whose fathers abandon them: Fathers who die early would be no more likely to carry the short AR gene than are fathers in the general population.[65]

Hormonal Effects As you may recall from Chapter 3, some biosocial theorists link antisocial behavior to hormonal influences.[66] One view is that hormonal imbalance may influence aggressive behavior in young girls. For example, cortisol, responsible for controlling inflammation and suppressing the immune response, is the primary hormone released during long periods of stress or physical trauma. It has also been linked to aggressive behavior in young women. When Kathleen Pajer and her colleagues studied 47 adolescent girls with conduct disorder (CD) and 37 control girls, taking three separate measurements of cortisol, they found that girls with conduct disorder had significantly lower cortisol levels than girls in the normal control group at all three sampling times. They conclude that antisocial girls may suffer from "dysregulation of the hypothalamic-pituitary-adrenal axis," which regulates cortisol levels.[67]

Another view is that excessive amounts of male hormones (androgens) are related to delinquency. The androgen most often related to antisocial behavior is testosterone.[68] In general, females who test higher for testosterone are more likely to engage in stereotypical male behaviors.[69] Females who have low androgen levels are less aggressive than males, whereas those who have elevated levels will take on characteristically male traits, including aggression.[70]

Some females who are overexposed to male hormones in utero may become "constitutionally masculinized." They may develop abnormal hair growth, large musculature, low voice, irregular menstrual cycle, and hyperaggressive behavior. Females exposed to male hormones in utero are more likely to engage in aggressive behavior later in life.[71]

Premenstrual Syndrome Early biotheorists suspected that premenstrual syndrome (PMS) was a direct cause of the relatively rare instances of female violence: "For several days prior to and during menstruation, the stereotype has been that 'raging hormones' doom women to irritability and poor judgment—two facets of premenstrual syndrome."[72] The link between PMS and delinquency was popularized by Katharina Dalton, whose studies of Englishwomen led her to conclude that females are more likely to commit suicide and be aggressive and otherwise antisocial before or during menstruation.[73]

Today there is conflicting evidence on the relationship between PMS and female delinquency. Research shows that a significant number of incarcerated females committed their crimes during the premenstrual phase, and also that a small percentage of women appear vulnerable to cyclical hormonal changes that make them more prone to anxiety and hostility.[74] Although this evidence is persuasive, the true relationship between crime and the female menstrual cycle still remains unknown. There is a causal dilemma: While it is possible that the stress associated with menstruation produces crime, it is also possible that the stress of antisocial behavior produces early menstruation.[75]

Aggression According to some biosocial theorists, gender differences in the delinquency rate can be explained by inborn differences in aggression.[76] Some psychologists believe that males are inherently more aggressive, a condition that appears very early in life, before socialization can influence behavior.

Gender-based differences in aggression have been developing for millions of years and reflect the dissimilarities in the male and female reproductive systems. Males are more aggressive, because they wish to possess as many sex partners as possible to increase their chances of producing offspring. Females have learned to control their aggressive impulses, because having multiple mates does not increase their chances of conception. Instead, females concentrate on acquiring things that will help them rear their offspring, such as a reliable mate who will supply material resources.[77]

Contemporary Psychological Views

Because girls are socialized to be less aggressive than boys, it is possible that the young women who get involved in antisocial and violent behavior are suffering from some form of mental anguish or abnormality. Girls are also more likely than boys to be involved in status offenses, such as running away and truancy, behaviors that suggest underlying psychological distress.

Research indicates that antisocial adolescent girls do suffer a wide variety of psychiatric problems and have dysfunctional and violent relationships.[78] Incarcerated adolescent female offenders have more acute mental health symptoms and psychological disturbances than male offenders.[79] Female delinquents score high on psychological tests measuring such traits as psychopathic deviation, schizophrenia, paranoia, and psychasthenia (a psychological disorder characterized by phobias, obsessions, compulsions, or excessive anxiety).[80] Clinical interviews indicate that female delinquents are significantly more likely than males to suffer from mood disorders, including any disruptive disorder, major depressive disorder, and separation anxiety disorder.[81] For example, serious female delinquents have been found to have a relatively high incidence of callous-unemotional (CU) traits, an affective disorder described by a lack of remorse or shame, poor judgment, failure to learn by experience, and chronic lying.[82] In sum, there are some experts who believe that female delinquents suffer from psychological deficits ranging from lack of self-control to serious impairments.[83]

SOCIALIZATION VIEWS

Socialization views are based on the idea that a child's social development may be the key to understanding delinquent behavior. If a child experiences impairment, family disruption, and so on, the child will be more susceptible to delinquent associations and criminality.

Linking crime rate variations to gender differences in socialization is not a recent phenomenon. In a 1928 work, *The Unadjusted Girl*, W. I. Thomas suggested that some girls who have not been socialized under middle-class family controls can become impulsive thrill seekers. According to Thomas, female delinquency is linked to the "wish" for luxury and excitement.[84] Inequities in social class condemn poor girls from demoralized families to using sex as a means to gain amusement, pretty clothes, and other luxuries. Precocious sexuality makes these girls vulnerable to older men, who lead them down the path to decadence.[85]

Socialization and Delinquency

Scholars concerned with gender differences in crime are interested in the distinction between the lifestyles of males and females. Girls may be supervised more closely than boys. If girls behave in a socially disapproved fashion, their parents may be more likely to notice. Adults may be more tolerant of deviant behavior in boys and expect boys to act tough and take risks.[86] Closer supervision restricts the opportunity for crime and the time available to mingle with delinquent peers. It follows, then, that the adolescent girl who is growing up in a troubled home and lacks supervision may be more prone to delinquency.[87]

Focus on Socialization In the 1950s, a number of researchers began to focus on gender-specific socialization patterns. They made three assumptions about gender differences in socialization: families exert a more powerful influence on girls than on boys; girls do not form close same-sex friendships, but compete with their peers; and female criminals are primarily sexual offenders. First, parents are stricter with girls because they perceive them as needing control. In some families, adolescent girls rebel against strict controls. In others, where parents are absent or unavailable, girls may turn to the streets for companionship. Second, girls rarely form close relationships with female peers, because they view them as rivals for males who would make eligible marriage partners.[88] Instead, girls enter into affairs with older men who exploit them, involve them in sexual deviance, and father their illegitimate children.[89] The result is prostitution, drug abuse, and marginal lives. Their daughters repeat this pattern in a never-ending cycle of exploitation.

Broken Homes/Fallen Women A number of experts share emphasis on the family as a primary influence on delinquent behavior. Male delinquents were portrayed as rebels who esteemed toughness, excitement, and other lower-class values. Males succumbed to the lure of delinquency when they perceived few legitimate opportunities. In contrast, female delinquents were portrayed as troubled adolescents who suffered inadequate home lives, and more often than not, were victims of sexual and physical abuse. Ruth Morris described delinquent girls as unattractive youths who

According to early socialization views, a child's social development may be the key to understanding delinquent behavior. Children will be more susceptible to delinquent associations if they experience impairment or family disruption. Improper socialization is likely to have an even more damaging effect on females than on males because girls are less likely than boys to have close-knit peer associations and are therefore in need of close parental relationships to retain emotional stability. In fact, girls may become sexually involved with boys to receive support from them, a practice that tends to magnify their problem.

reside in homes marked by family tensions.[90] In *The Delinquent Girl* (1970), Clyde Vedder and Dora Somerville suggest that female delinquency is usually a problem of adjustment to family pressure; an estimated 75 percent of institutionalized girls have family problems.[91] They also suggest that girls have serious problems in a male-dominated culture with rigid and sometimes unfair social practices.

Other early efforts linked rebellious behavior to sexual conflicts in the home.[92] Broken or disrupted homes were found to predict female delinquency.[93] Females petitioned to juvenile court were more likely than males to be charged with ungovernable behavior and sex offenses. They also were more likely to reside in single-parent homes.[94] Studies of incarcerated juveniles found that most of the male delinquents were incarcerated for burglary and other theft-related offenses, but female delinquents tended to be involved in incorrigibility and sex offenses. The conclusion: Boys became delinquent to demonstrate their masculinity; girls were delinquent as a result of hostility toward parents and a consequent need to obtain attention from others.[95]

Contemporary Socialization Views

Investigators continue to support the view that female delinquents have more dysfunctional home lives than male offenders.[96] One focus is the effects of abuse on behavior. Girls seem to be more deeply affected than boys by child abuse, and the link between abuse and female delinquency seems stronger than it is for male delinquency.[97] These experiences take a toll on their behavior choices: Research shows that girls who are the victims of child sexual abuse and physical abuse are the ones most likely to engage in violent and nonviolent criminal behavior.[98] Their predicament has long-term consequences. Some are placed outside the home early in childhood, because of family breakdown and their own conduct problems. Institutionalization does little to help matters. Those sent away are much more likely to develop criminal records as adults than similarly troubled girls who manage to stay with their families throughout their childhood.[99]

Girls may be forced into a life of sexual promiscuity, because their sexual desirability makes them a valuable commodity for families living on the edge. There are cases of young women being "lent out" to drug dealers so their parents or partners can get high. Girls on the streets are encouraged to sell their bodies, because they have little else of value to trade.[100] Meda Chesney-Lind, a prominent feminist scholar, has described this association: "Young women on the run from homes characterized by sexual abuse and parental neglect are forced, by the very statutes designed to protect them, into the life of an escaped convict."[101] Many of these girls may find themselves pregnant at a very young age. Physical and sexual abuse and the toll it takes on young girls is not unique to any one culture. As the accompanying Focus on Delinquency feature shows, girls in developing nations may become the victims of one particularly vile form of exploitation: human trafficking and sexual exploitation.

Human Trafficking and the Sexual Exploitation of Children

Human trafficking includes all forms of transportation of women and girls (as well as young boys) through the use of force, abduction, fraud, and coercion for the purpose of sexual and/or commercial exploitation. Trafficking activities include recruiting individuals, transporting and transferring them from their home country or region to other transshipment points and to destination countries, receiving such trafficked persons, and keeping them in custody or housing them.

Many forms of trafficking exist. Young girls and women are common targets of commercial sexual exploitation. They may be forced into prostitution and other sexual activities such as the production of pornography. There are accounts of women being forced to service 30 men a day and children trapped in pornography rings. Others become human containers in the transportation of drugs through forced ingestion of condoms or other containers of illegal substances. Labor servitude can be found in nearly every area of industry. Young girls have been forced to work in sweatshops, factories, agricultural fields, and fisheries. Victims may work long hours in unpleasant, unsanitary, or dangerous conditions for low wages, sometimes unable to take breaks or leave the facility. In some instances debts may be passed on to other family members or even entire villages from generation to generation, creating a constant supply of indentured servants for traffickers.

How common is the practice? While data are unreliable, estimates of the amount of people trafficked internationally each year range from 600,000 men, women, and children to 1.2 million children alone. The United States is not immune: The CIA issued a report in 2000 estimating that 45,000 to 50,000 individuals were trafficked into the United States annually. Despite the differences in these numbers, it is undeniable that a huge amount of trafficking in humans occurs around the globe.

CONTRIBUTING FACTORS

Human trafficking is facilitated by the global economy and relaxation of corporate boundaries. The young female victims are often poor and aspire to a better life. They may be forced, coerced, deceived, and psychologically manipulated into industrial or agricultural work, marriage, domestic servitude, organ donation, or sexual exploitation. Although victims often come from poorer countries, the market for labor and sex is found in wealthier countries or in countries that, while economically poor, cater to the needs of citizens from wealthy countries, of corporations, or of tourists.

While some individuals are trafficked directly for purposes of prostitution or commercial sexual exploitation, other trafficked persons and even those trafficked for legitimate work may become victims of interpersonal violence. Women trafficked for domestic work in wealthy countries or laborers trafficked for construction, logging, factory or farm work are vulnerable to exploitation by their employers. Individuals trafficked for the labor purposes are usually unfamiliar with their new location and the language spoken there. They often lack formal education and do not know about the human and legal resources that could help them. For these reasons, individuals are vulnerable to the violence of exploitation.

SEX TOURISM

Sex tourism is a booming business, and many men from wealthy nations engage in sexual activities with trafficked individuals by travelling to destinations where women and children are prostituted. One area of particular concern is child prostitution that flourishes along the German-Czech border. Girls (and boys) hang out near petrol stations, bus stops, and restaurants on the connecting roads between the two nations. Within towns, they are found in parks, in front of supermarkets and the entrances of gambling halls and houses, and at the railway station. In some areas, the children wait for tourists in cars or by windows. Small babies and children up to 6 years of age are usually offered to tourists by women.

Socialization and Gangs There is a significant body of literature linking abusive home lives to gang participation and crime. Joan Moore's analysis of gang girls in East Los Angeles found that many came from troubled homes. Sixty-eight percent of the girls she interviewed were afraid of their fathers, and 55 percent reported fear of their mothers.[102] Many of the girls reported that their parents were overly strict and controlling, despite the fact that they engaged in criminality themselves. Moore also details accounts of sexual abuse; about 30 percent of the girls reported that family members had made sexual advances.[103] Emily Gaarder and Joanne Belknap's interviews with young women sent to adult prisons indicated that most had endured prolonged sexual abuse and violence. One of their subjects, Lisa, a young European American woman, was serving time for attempted murder. Lisa had used drugs and alcohol, and joined gangs to escape the pain and troubles of her home life. Her mother was an alcoholic and her father a convicted rapist. She had been sexually and physically abused by her stepfather from the ages of 9 to 11. Soon after, Lisa began skipping school, started using alcohol, and took acid. She joined a gang when

Children older than 7 years are usually accompanied by a male adolescent or an adult. Small children can be seen addressing German men asking if they want sex or begging for money or food. Many of the children get inside the cars of German tourists and drive away with them. Older children from 8 years on negotiate prices and sexual services. The men usually drive with their victim to a place they are familiar with and where they will not be observed. These places may be on the outskirts of a town, in nearby forests, near parks, in isolated garages or empty side-streets, or the abusers go with their victims—sometimes accompanied by a pimp—to a nearby flat.

Many of the children were raped or sexually abused before they became involved in commercial sexual exploitation. Poverty, sexual abuse, and family obligation are the main reasons given by children for entering into prostitution. The children usually receive between 5 and 25 euros in payment. Sometimes they just receive sweets. Some sex tourists take the children for a meal or give financial support to their families.

CAN SEX TRAFFICKING BE CONTROLLED?

Controlling human trafficking and sex tourism has proven to be difficult. Some countries have recently written laws to prevent their citizens from engaging in sexual activities with minors while travelling outside of their own country. These laws try to deter sex tourism, making travellers reconsider their actions as a result of the consequences. However, enforcement of these laws may prove challenging due to jurisdiction and proof, so that the practice continues unabated in many parts of the world. The United States passed the Trafficking Victims Protection Act of 2003 and then strengthened it with a 2005 revision. Included in the bills was a $360 million funding package for an expansion of the Operation Innocence Lost program, a nationwide initiative that helps law enforcement agents pursue sex traffickers and child prostitution rings. The federal laws created several new crimes, including human trafficking, sex

trafficking, forced labor, and document servitude, which involves the withholding or destruction of identity or travel documents as a means of controlling young women. They outlawed psychological manipulation, which means that traffickers can be prosecuted if they cause victims to believe that they would be harmed if they resist. Provisions of the 2005 Act provide state and local law enforcement with new tools to target demand and investigate and prosecute sex trafficking. Whether or not these measures will prove sufficient to reduce the sexual exploitation of children remains to be seen.

Critical Thinking

1. How would you reduce the incidence of human trafficking? Would you punish the sex tourists as felons? Can anything be done to protect young girls from sexual predators?
2. Does pornography on the Internet increase interest in sex with underage females and should there be greater controls placed on Internet viewing?

SOURCES: Linda Williams and Jennifer Ngo, "Human Trafficking," in Claire M. Renzetti and Jeffrey I. Edelson, eds., *Encyclopedia of Interpersonal Violence* (Thousand Oaks, CA: Sage Publications, 2007); "Remedying the Injustices of Human Trafficking Through Tort Law," *Harvard Law Review* 119:2574–2595 (2006); Cathrin Schauer, *Children in Street Prostitution—Report from the German-Czech Border*, publication by ECPAT Germany, UNICEF Germany, Horlemann Editors, Bad Honnef, 2003, available at www.childcentre.info/projects/exploitation/germany/dbaFile11447.doc (accessed October 11, 2007); International Office of Migration (IOM), *Journeys of Jeopardy: A Review of Research on Trafficking on Women and Children in Europe* (Publication No. 11, 2002), www.iom.int/documents/publication/en/mrs%5F11%5F2002.pdf and www.iom.int/jahia/Jahia/pid/8/Servlet SearchPublication?event=detail&id=5112 (accessed October 11, 2007); U.S. Department of State. *Trafficking in Persons Report* (Washington, DC: U.S. Department of State, 2005), www.state.goWv/g/tip/rls/tiprpt/2005/ (accessed October 11, 2007); United Nations Population Fund (UNFPA), *Trafficking in Human Misery*, www.unfpa.org/gender/violence1.htm (accessed October 12, 2007); UNESCO Trafficking Project, www.unescobkk.org/culture/trafficking (accessed October 11, 2007).

she was 12. "They were like a family to me," she told Gaarder and Belknap. "But I became involved in a lot of stuff. . . . I got high a lot, I robbed people, burglarized homes, stabbed people, and was involved in drive-bys." At age 15, she stabbed a woman in a fight. She is serving seven to fifteen years for the crime. Lisa made this statement:

> I had just gotten out of this group home. The lady I stabbed had been messing with my sister's fiancé. This woman [had] a bunch of my sister's stuff, like her stereo and VCR, so me, my sister, her fiancé, and my boyfriend went over to pick up the stuff. We were all getting high beforehand. When we got to the house, my sister and I went in. . . . They [her sister and the victim] started fighting over him, and I started stabbing her with a knife. I always carried a knife with me because I was in a gang.[104]

In summary, the socialization approach holds that family interaction is the key to understanding female delinquency. If a girl grows up in an atmosphere of sexual tension, where hostility exists between her parents, or where her parents are absent,

Laticia's Story

LATICIA, A 15-YEAR-OLD FEMALE OF AFRICAN DESCENT, WAS REFERRED TO THE TEEN CENTER FOR HER INVOLVEMENT IN A GANG-RELATED PHYSICAL ASSAULT. ACCORDING to Laticia, she "beat the girl down" because she had publicly disrespected Laticia's gang and friends. Laticia had been fighting and having significant behavioral issues in school. When she was referred to the program by the juvenile court, she had not been attending school for several months and had little positive direction in her life. Standing nearly six feet tall and weighing close to 300 pounds, she was aggressive and intimidating to many people in her life. Even some school personnel felt intimidated by Laticia, and for many reasons were glad she had dropped out. Laticia had threatened a number of teachers and was often suspended. Difficult to get to know and seeming hostile most of the time, she would be a challenge for teen counselors. They would have to work hard to engage her in the program and build trust.

Upon referral to the teen drop-in program, Laticia resisted involvement. One counselor in particular, who had significant experience with similar situations, made it his mission to assist her. Looking beyond her exterior and striving to make a positive connection with her, he engaged Laticia in the program by focusing on her positive attributes as well as standing firm on the code of conduct at the center. He discovered that Laticia's mother worked three jobs to support the family and that her father was not in her life. Despite her mother's hard work, the children were neglected in many ways and their basic needs were rarely met. It was also suspected that their mother was physically abusive to the children. Laticia was generally responsible for taking care of her many siblings, which she resented, and she often acted out because she herself was not receiving the attention she needed. Because of her larger size, she also felt rejected by males her own age, reporting that they would "sleep" with her, but never want to date her on a longer-term basis. Laticia's counselor tried to help her understand that she needed to focus on respecting herself and that her negative behaviors were not the way to get her needs met. He spent a lot of time with her trying to help her gain insight, to deconstruct her negative belief system, and to address her negative self-image.

The program provided groups to address Laticia's anger management issues, concerns about relationships and her unhealthy sexual activity, and criminal and gang involvement. In addition, Laticia participated in a group to complete her court-ordered requirement for community services. Lastly, the program coordinated a field trip to a maximum security female prison, which made a significant impression on Laticia. It helped her face the reality of where her behavior could lead if she did not make some major changes in her life choices.

Laticia continued attending the center even after she had completed the requirements of the juvenile court. It was a significant advantage of this particular program because the center is open to all teens in the community. The relationship Laticia established with her primary counselor continued for many years. They often visited with each other and he became somewhat of a parental figure in her life. Laticia returned to school and achieved a level of success that surprised many adults involved. She tried to make better relationship decisions and had no further delinquency referrals. Laticia graduated from high school and was able to continue her education at the local community college. ■

CRITICAL THINKING

1. Laticia is described as being very big and strong. How does her size and strength jibe with the masculinity hypothesis?
2. Did Laticia's social achievement, illustrated by her educational success, help turn her life around?
3. Laticia got in trouble when she beat a girl because she had publicly disrespected Laticia's gang and friends. Did her perceptions of disrespect lead to the fight? Is this a good example of how cognition influences delinquency?
4. Laticia's counselor became a highly significant figure in her life. Does such a relationship provide an adequate substitute for parental relations?

she is likely to turn to outside sources for support. In contrast, a strong bond to parents may help insulate girls from social forces that produce delinquency.[105]

Girls are expected to follow narrowly defined behavioral patterns. In contrast, it is not unusual for boys to stay out late, drive around with friends, or get involved in other unstructured behaviors linked to delinquency. If in reaction to loneliness and parental hostility, girls engage in the same "routine activities" as boys (staying out late, partying, and riding around with friends), they run the risk of engaging in similar types of delinquent behavior.[106]

The socialization approach holds that a poor home life is likely to have an even more damaging effect on females than on males. Because girls are less likely than boys to have close-knit peer associations, they are more likely to need close parental relationships to retain emotional stability. In fact, girls may become sexually involved with boys to receive support from them, a practice that tends to magnify their problems. The Case Profile entitled "Laticia's Story" illustrates the problems faced by a young woman whose home life could not provide the support she so desperately needed.

LIBERAL FEMINIST VIEWS

The feminist movement has, from its origins, fought to help women break away from their traditional roles and gain economic, educational, and social advancement. There is little question that the women's movement has revised the way women perceive their roles in society, and it has altered the relationships of women to many social institutions.

liberal feminism
Asserts that females are less delinquent than males, because their social roles provide them with fewer opportunities to commit crimes; as the roles of girls and women become more similar to those of boys and men, so too will their crime patterns.

Liberal feminism has influenced thinking about delinquency. According to liberal feminists, females are less delinquent than males, because their social roles provide fewer opportunities to commit crime. As the roles of women become more similar to those of men, so will their crime patterns. Female criminality is motivated by the same influences as male criminality. According to Freda Adler's *Sisters in Crime* (1975), by striving for independence women have begun to alter the institutions that had protected males in their traditional positions of power.[107] Adler argued that female delinquency would be affected by the changing role of women. As females entered new occupations and participated in sports, politics, and other traditionally male endeavors, they would also become involved in crimes that had heretofore been male-oriented; delinquency rates would then converge. She noted that girls were becoming increasingly involved in traditionally masculine crimes such as gang activity and fighting.

Adler predicted that the women's movement would produce steeper increases in the rate of female delinquency, because it created an environment in which the roles of girls and boys converge. She predicted that the changing female role would produce female criminals who are similar to their male counterparts.[108]

Support for Liberal Feminism

A number of studies support the feminist view of gender differences in delinquency.[109] More than 20 years ago, Rita James Simon explained how the increase in female criminality is a function of the changing role of women. She claimed that as women were empowered economically and socially, they would be less likely to feel dependent and oppressed. Consequently, they would be less likely to attack their traditional targets: their husbands, their lovers, or even their own children.[110] Instead, their new role as breadwinner might encourage women to engage in traditional male crimes, such as larceny and car theft.

Simon's view has been supported in part by research showing a significant correlation between the women's rights movement and the female crime rate.[111] If 1966 is used as a jumping-off point (because the National Organization for Women was

According to liberal feminist views, as gender role differences erode so too will gender differences in the nature and extent of delinquency. Teenager Jessica M. Reid, shown here, was charged with participating in a double murder in 2006 after she and her boyfriend, Gregory Fester, admitted to breaking into the rural Nebraska home of Wayne and Sharmon Stocks and shooting them in the head at close range with a shotgun. Reid and Fester were already in custody on car theft and other charges when charged with the murders. For killing the Stocks, Fester and Reid were each sentenced to two terms of life in prison, to be served consecutively.

founded in that year), there are indications that patterns of serious female crime (robbery and auto theft) correlate with indicators of female emancipation (the divorce rate and participation in the labor force). Although this research does not prove that female crime is related to social change, it identifies behavior patterns that support that hypothesis.

In addition to these efforts, self-report studies support the liberal feminist view by showing that gender differences in delinquency are fading—that is, the delinquent acts committed most and least often by girls are nearly identical to those reported most and least often by boys.[112] The pattern of female delinquency, if not the extent, is now similar to that of male delinquency, and with few exceptions the factors that seem to motivate both male and female criminality seem similar.[113]

As the sex roles of males and females have become less distinct, their offending patterns have become more similar. Girls may be committing crimes to gain economic advancement and not because they lack parental support. Both of these patterns were predicted by liberal feminists.

CRITICAL FEMINIST VIEWS

A number of writers take a more critical view of gender differences in crime. These **critical feminists** believe gender inequality stems from the unequal power of men and women in society and the exploitation of females by fathers and husbands; in a patriarchal society women are a "commodity" like land or money.[114] Female delinquency originates with the onset of male supremacy (*patriarchy*), the subordination of women, male aggression, and the efforts of men to control females sexually (see the Focus on Delinquency box "The Honor Killing of Girls").[115] Women's victimization rates decline as they are empowered socially, economically and legally.[116]

critical feminists
Hold that gender inequality stems from the unequal power of men and women and the subsequent exploitation of women by men; the cause of female delinquency originates with the onset of male supremacy and the efforts of males to control females' sexuality.

Critical feminists focus on the social forces that shape girls' lives.[117] They attempt to show how the sexual victimization of girls is often a function of male socialization and that young males learn to be exploitive of women. James Messerschmidt, an influential feminist scholar, has formulated a theoretical model to show how misguided concepts of "masculinity" flow from the inequities built into "patriarchal capitalism." Men dominate business in capitalist societies, and males who cannot function well within its parameters are at risk for crime. Women are inherently powerless in such a society, and their crimes reflect their limited access to both legitimate and illegitimate opportunity.[118] It is not surprising that research surveys have found that 90 percent of adolescent girls are sexually harassed in school, with almost 30 percent reporting having been psychologically pressured to "do something sexual," and 10 percent physically forced into sexual behaviors.[119]

According to the critical feminist view, male exploitation acts as a trigger for female delinquent behavior. Female delinquents recount being so severely harassed at school that they were forced to carry knives. Some reported that boyfriends—men sometimes in their 30s—who "knew how to treat a girl" would draw them into

© AP Images/Dodge County Detention Center

The Honor Killing of Girls

On July 9, 2007, a Jordanian court sentenced a man to six months in prison for suffocating his pregnant sister with a pillow. This "honor killing," the defendant claimed, was necessary to uphold his family's reputation. The court concluded that the lenient sentence was justified by the man's "state of fury" that led to the woman's slaying.

What brought about this rage? The victim had told her brother she was five months pregnant with her former husband's child. The judge concluded that the woman's "shameful behavior" deviated from the traditions of Jordanian society and harmed her family's honor. This case is not that unusual: In Jordan, an average of 20 women are killed in "honor killings" by male relatives each year. Men have the final say in all family matters and many consider sex out of wedlock an unbearable stain on a family's reputation. International human rights organizations have condemned honor killings in Jordan and appealed to the country's ruler, King Abdullah II, to put an end to the practice.

Honor killing and honor crime involve violence against women and girls, including such acts as beating, battering, or killing, by a family member or relative. The attacks are provoked by the belief or perception that an individual's or family's honor has been threatened because of the actual or perceived sexual misconduct of the female. Honor killings are most common in traditional societies in the Middle East, Southwest Asia, India, China, and Latin America.

Honor killing of a woman or girl by her father, brother, or other male relative may occur because of a suspicion that she engaged in sexual activities before or outside marriage and thus has dishonored the family. Even rape of a woman or girl may be seen as violation of the honor of the family for which the female must be killed. Wives' adultery and daughters' premarital "sexual activity," including rape, are seen as extreme violations of the codes of behavior and thus may result in the death of the female through this so-called honor killing. Honor killing/crime is based on the shame that a loss of control of the woman or girl brings to the family and to the male heads of the family.

According to sociologist Linda Williams, men consider honor killings culturally necessary because any suspicion of sexual activity or suspicion that a girl or woman has been touched by another in a sexual manner is enough to raise questions about the family's honor. Consequently, strict control of women and girls within the home and outside the home is justified. Women are restricted in their activities in the community, religion, and politics. These institutions, in turn, support the control of females. Williams believes that the existence of honor killing is designed for maintaining male dominance. Submissiveness may be seen as a sign of sexual purity and a woman's or girl's attempts to assert her rights can be seen as a violation of the family's honor that needs to be redressed. Rules of honor and threats against females who "violate" such rules reinforce the control of women and have a powerful impact on their lives. Honor killings/crimes serve to keep women and girls from "stepping out of line." The manner in which such behaviors silence women and kill their spirit have led some to label honor killings/crimes more broadly as "femicide."

Critical Thinking

While we may scoff at honor killings, are there elements of American culture and life that you consider harmful to women yet are still tolerated? What can be done to change them?

SOURCES: Shafika Mattar, "Man Gets 6 Months for Killing Sister," *Boston Globe*, 9 July 2007, p. 3, www.boston.com/news/world/middleeast/articles/2007/07/09/man_gets_6_months_for_killing_sister/ (accessed September 21, 2007); Linda M. Williams, "Honor Killings," in Claire M. Renzetti and Jeffrey I. Edelson, eds., *Encyclopedia of Interpersonal Violence* (Thousand Oaks, CA: Sage Publications, 2007); Dan Bilefsky, "How to Avoid Honor Killing in Turkey? Honor Suicide," *New York Times*, 16 July 2006; Nadera Shalhoub-Kevorkian, "Reexamining Femicide: Breaking the Silence and Crossing 'Scientific' Borders," *Signs* 28:581–608 (2003).

---

criminal activity, such as drug trafficking, which eventually entangled them in the justice system.[120]

When female adolescents run away and use drugs, they may be reacting to abuse at home or at school. Their attempts at survival are then labeled delinquent.[121] Research shows that a significant number of girls who are victims of sexual and other forms of abuse will later engage in delinquency.[122] All too often, school officials ignore complaints made by female students. Young girls therefore may feel trapped and desperate.

Delinquency and Patriarchy

A number of theoretical models have attempted to use a critical or Marxist feminist perspective to explain gender differences in delinquency. In *Capitalism, Patriarchy, and Crime*, James Messerschmidt argues that capitalist society is marked by both patriarchy and class conflict. Capitalists control workers, and men control women, both

Power, Gender, and Adolescent Dating Violence

Research on domestic violence among adults most often concludes that females are the primary targets of violence and when they fight back it is most often in self-defense. However, studies of adolescent dating violence often find equal or higher rates of female-perpetrated physical violence than male violence. How can this discrepancy be explained?

To find out, sociologists Jody Miller and Norman White conducted in-depth interviews with 70 African American youths, aged 12 to 19, in north St. Louis, Missouri. Rather than take a "gender-neutral" approach and treat gender simply as a category, either male or female, the researchers considered gender, and the conflict and power relationships it creates, as an important factor that shaped the direction and content of adolescent personal relationships.

Miller and White find significant differences in dating violence structured by gender relationships. Girls achieve status by having boyfriends but get less emotional support than might be imagined. Boys actually get more from relationships but must disguise their stake in order to conform to cultural norms. To gain status among their friends, they must take the role of being a "playa" (player)—guys who use girls for sex and have multiple sexual partners and conquests. Playas have little emotional attachment to their sexual partners, and adopt a detached, uninvolved "cool" attitude and demeanor. They bestow derogatory sexual labels on the girls they are with (e.g., "hood rats" or "ho's") especially if they "give in" too easily. This attitude seems to correspond with the fact that the boys are given strong messages from their male peers that "love equals softness"). Consequently, to avoid being labeled soft by their friends, they engage in aggressive behavior during their relationships. They are much more likely to cheat on their girlfriends, whereas girls are more likely to be loyal to their boyfriends. In addition, boys are more willing to share sexual details with their peers, mistreat their girlfriends openly in front of friends, and downplay the meaningfulness of their relationships.

Miller and White found significant differences in the motivation for domestic dating violence. Girls' violence is attributed to their emotionality, especially the anger they experience when they suspect their boyfriend is cheating. Though jealousy is considered emotional instability, its basis is tied to reality: Girls are much more likely to have been the actual victim of infidelity than boys. If confronted by a jealous mate, boys are more likely to react to their accusations with a "cool" response,

walking away or minimizing the damage caused by their infidelity. The cool response only makes girls angrier and more willing to cause a confrontation. Ironically, some girls attack their boyfriends to get an emotional response from them, to drive them out of their cool state, even if it means being struck back harder in return. Some are willing to interpret the violent response as an indicator that the boy actually likes them; any response is favorable, even if it is violent.

In contrast, boys are taught not to use violence against girls, who are considered weaker; hitting them is unmanly: "If a boy hits a girl they a punk." However, violence against girlfriends is justifiable in retaliation for female-perpetrated violence: The boy cheats, the girl slaps him, and he slaps her back.

Though most dating violence is of the retaliatory type, some boys describe using violence to control a girlfriend or put her in her place. Some describe girls as deserving male violence when they are "runnin' they mouth" or "get all up in my face." Miller and White find that there are significant differences in the dynamics of dating violence. Girls' violence may actually be more frequent in incidence, but it is not considered dangerous. Its motives are the girls' desire to exercise control in their relationships—to keep their boyfriends from flirting, chatting, or showing off with other girls. When their anger escalates they become the target for retaliation because they typically lack the power to achieve these goals. Consequently, boys describe girls' violence as resulting from girls being emotionally "out of control" and they do not view it as posing a serious threat. This dynamic reveals the substantial gender-based inequalities in dating relationships.

Critical Thinking

1. Do you think that the description of girls' violence as "emotional" undermines their ability to challenge the inequality in their relationships? How can this inequality be addressed?

2. Are the relationships found by Miller and White normative? Do they exist in your own peer network? Are they universal or limited to the group they studied?

SOURCE: Jody Miller and Norman White, "Gender and Adolescent Relationship Violence: A Contextual Examination," *Criminology* 41:1207–1248 (2003).

economically and biologically.[123] This "double marginality" explains why females in a capitalist society commit fewer crimes than males. They are isolated in the family and have fewer opportunities to engage in elite deviance (white-collar and economic crimes); they are also denied access to male-dominated street crimes. Because capitalism renders women powerless, they are forced to commit less serious crimes such as abusing drugs. The Focus on Delinquency box entitled "Power, Gender, and Adolescent Dating Violence" explores how gender inequality shapes dating violence among adolescents.

Power-Control Theory

John Hagan and his associates have speculated that gender differences in delinquency are a function of class differences that influence family life. Hagan, who calls his view **power-control theory**, suggests that class influences delinquency by controlling the quality of family life.[124] In paternalistic families, fathers assume the role of breadwinners, and mothers have menial jobs or remain at home. Mothers are expected to control the behavior of their daughters while granting greater freedom to sons. The parent-daughter relationship can be viewed as a preparation for the "cult of domesticity," which makes daughters' involvement in delinquency unlikely. Hence, males exhibit a higher degree of delinquent behavior than their sisters.

In **egalitarian families**—in which the husband and wife share similar positions of power at home and in the workplace—daughters gain a kind of freedom that reflects reduced parental control. These families produce daughters whose law-violating behaviors mirror those of their brothers. Ironically, these kinds of relationships also occur in households with absent fathers. Similarly, Hagan and his associates found that when both fathers and mothers hold equally valued managerial positions, the similarity between the rates of their daughters' and sons' delinquency is greatest. Therefore, middle-class girls are most likely to violate the law because they are less closely controlled than lower-class girls.

Research conducted by Hagan and his colleagues has tended to support the core relationship between family structure and gender differences in delinquency.[125] Other social scientists have produced tests of the theory, which have generally supported its hypothesis. For example, Brenda Sims Blackwell and Mark Reed found that the gap between brother-sister delinquency is greatest in patriarchal families and least in egalitarian families, a finding consistent with the core premise of power-control theory.[126]

However, some of the basic premises of power-control theory, such as the relationship between social class and delinquency, have been challenged. For example, some critics have questioned the assumption that upper-class youths may engage in more petty delinquency than lower-class youths because they are brought up to be "risk takers" who do not fear the consequences of their misdeeds.[127]

Power-control theory encourages a new approach to the study of delinquency, one that addresses gender differences, class position, and family structure. It also helps explain the relative increase in female delinquency by stressing the significance of changing feminine roles. With the increase in single-parent homes, the patterns

According to power-control theory, as more families become egalitarian, with both parents sharing equal roles and having equal authority, children's roles will become more homogenous. Because sons and daughters are treated equally, their behavior will take on similar patterns. Some, like Alice Blair, shown here listening to coach Russ Wilson during a huddle in Paint Creek, Texas, will take on what has been considered a traditional male role. Blair plays defense on the school's six-person football team.

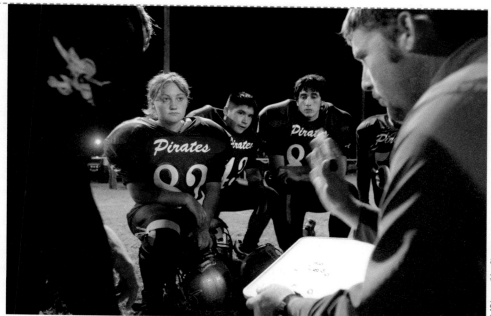

© AP Images/Matt Slocum

Hagan has identified may change. The decline of the patriarchal family may produce looser family ties on girls, changing sex roles, and increased delinquency. Ironically, this raises an interesting dilemma: The daughters of successful and powerful mothers are more at risk for delinquency than the daughters of stay-at-home moms! However, as sociologist Christopher Uggen points out, there may be a bright side to this dilemma. Not only are they more likely to commit delinquent acts, the daughters of independent working mothers may also be encouraged to take prosocial risks such as engaging in athletic competition and breaking into traditional male-dominated occupations, such as policing and the military.[128]

GENDER AND THE JUVENILE JUSTICE SYSTEM

Gender differences not only have an effect on crime patterns, but also may have a significant impact on the way children are treated by the juvenile justice system. As a general rule males who are involved in the justice system are sanctioned more severely than females:

I Males are much more likely (ratio 10:6) to be ordered placed in a residential facility if they commit a crime against another person (for example, assault or robbery).

I The male-female difference in residential placement rates in cases involving attacks on people reflects the fact that male cases are more likely to be petitioned; if petitioned, are more likely to be adjudicated; and finally, if adjudicated, are more likely to receive residential placement as a sanction.

I About 40 percent of juvenile court offenses-against-people cases involving males result in some sort of court-ordered sanction (residential placement, formal probation, restitution, community service, etc.) following adjudication; in comparison, about 30 percent of girls receive similar sanctions.

I Cases involving males are more likely to be waived to criminal court (10 in 1,000) than are cases involving females (1 in 1,000).[129]

While these data suggest that boys are treated more harshly than girls by the juvenile justice authorities, they do not take into account such factors as offense seriousness or a prior record that might result in harsher dispositions. If these factors were controlled, gender differences in case outcome might disappear. In fact, some feminist scholars contend that in many ways girls receive harsher and more punitive treatment than boys, especially in cases involving sexual matters or offenses. More than 30 years ago Meda Chesney-Lind's now classic research first identified the fact that police are more likely to arrest female adolescents for sexual activity and to ignore the same behavior among male delinquents. Girls were more likely than boys to be picked up by police for status offenses and are more likely to be kept in detention for such offenses.[130]

Some critics believe that girls, more than boys, are still disadvantaged if their behavior is viewed as morally incorrect by government officials or if they are considered beyond parental control.[131] Research conducted by John MacDonald and Meda Chesney-Lind found that the juvenile justice system categorizes female offenders into two distinct groups: girls who momentarily strayed from the "good girl" path and are therefore deserving of solicitous, humanitarian treatment, and dangerously wayward girls who have serious problems and must therefore be kept under strict control lest they stray further.[132]

Girls may still be subject to harsh punishments if they are considered dangerously immoral. Girls are significantly more likely to be arrested on status offense charges than boys.[133] However, the arrest rates for girls show that girls are charged with status offenses more often than boys, because some of the behaviors they are participating in are considered negative when perpetrated by a female, but would not gain official attention if engaged in by a male.[134] There still appears to be an association between male standards of beauty and sexual behavior: Criminal justice professionals may look on attractive girls who engage in sexual behavior more harshly, overlooking some of the same behaviors in less attractive girls. In some jurisdictions, girls are still being incarcerated for status offenses, because their behavior does not measure up to concepts of "proper" female behavior.[135] Even though girls are still less likely to be arrested than boys, those who fail to measure up to stereotypes of proper female behavior are more likely to be sanctioned than male offenders.[136] For status-offending girls, formal processing in the juvenile justice system is a substitute when parents fail to provide control, are absent, or are ambivalent. Parents or guardians act as informal agents of control until a breakdown in family solidarity prompts reliance on more formal measures of control such as the juvenile justice system.[137]

Why do these differences persist? The reason may be because correctional authorities continue to subscribe to stereotyped beliefs about the needs of young girls. Even gender-specific programming, designed to mesh with the needs of young women, may be used to pigeonhole them into what is considered "appropriate" behavior for young ladies.[138]

Writing with Randall Shelden, Meda Chesney-Lind found that court officials and policy makers still show a lack of concern about girls' victimization and instead are more concerned with controlling their behavior than addressing the factors that brought them to the attention of the juvenile justice system in the first place.[139]

The Downside of Reform

Girls may also be suffering because states have toughened their juvenile codes and increased sanctions. Girls more so than boys may be feeling the brunt of the more punitive policies now being used in the juvenile justice system. When Chesney-Lind and Vickie Paramore analyzed data from the city and county of Honolulu they found that tougher juvenile justice standards meant that more cases were being handled formally in the juvenile justice system.[140] While girls are actually committing fewer violent crimes, they are more likely to become enmeshed in the grasp of the juvenile justice system. Once in the system, they may receive fewer benefits and services than their male counterparts. Institutionalized girls report that they are given fewer privileges and less space, equipment, programs, and treatment than institutionalized boys.[141]

This effect is not confined to the United States. In nations such as Australia, England, and Canada, the rate of female delinquency has been rising at a faster rate than that for boys. One reason may be changes in governmental policy that resulted in more equal treatment for girls and boys. As a result, more girls are being processed as delinquents instead of having their misbehavior viewed as being sexual in nature and involving them with the welfare or social service departments. This policy change has had the effect of closing the gender gap between those males and females officially designated as delinquent.[142]

Summary

1. Be able to discuss the development of interest in female delinquency

❚ Early delinquency experts often ignored female offenders, assuming that girls rarely violated the law, or if they did, that their illegal acts were status offenses.

❚ Female delinquency was viewed as emotional or family-related, and such problems were not an important concern of criminologists.

❚ The few "true" female delinquents were oddities whose criminal activity was a function of having masculine traits and characteristics, a concept referred to today as the masculinity hypothesis.

❚ Contemporary interest in the association between gender and delinquency has surged, because girls are now getting involved in serious delinquent acts that are quite similar to those of young men.

❚ Another reason for the interest in gender studies is that conceptions of gender differences have changed.

❚ A feminist approach to understanding crime is now firmly established.

- The result has been an increased effort to conduct research that would adequately explain differences and similarities in male and female offending patterns.

2. Be familiar with the gender differences in development

- There are gender differences in development, including socialization, cognition, and personality.
- Psychologists believe that differences in the way females and males are socialized affect their development.
- Parents may treat boys and girls differently, encouraging what they consider to be appropriate male and female behavior.
- Socialization also influences aggressive behaviors.
- Although there are few gender differences in aggression during the first few years of life, girls are socialized to be less aggressive than boys and are supervised more closely.
- As they mature, girls learn to respond to provocation by feeling anxious, unlike boys, who are encouraged to retaliate.
- There are also cognitive differences between males and females starting in childhood.
- Findings about gender difference in cognitive performance suggest female superiority on visual-motor speed and language ability and male superiority on mechanical and visual-spatial tasks.
- Girls learn to speak earlier and faster, and with better pronunciation, most likely because parents talk more to their infant daughters than to their infant sons.
- In most cases cognitive differences are small, narrowing, and usually attributed to cultural expectations.

3. Discuss the basis of gender differences

- Some experts suggest that gender differences may have a biological origin: Males and females are essentially different.
- They have somewhat different brain organizations; females are more left brain–oriented and males more right brain–oriented.
- A second view is that gender differences are developed over the life course and reflect different treatment of males and females.
- Another view is that gender differences are a result of the interaction of socialization, learning, and enculturation.
- Sandra Bem's gender-schema theory suggests that our culture polarizes males and females by forcing them to obey mutually exclusive gender roles, or "scripts."
- While socialization may be a strong force, inherent gender differences in cognition, personality, and biology still seem to play a role in shaping interpersonal interactions.

4. Know the trends in gender differences in the delinquency rate

- Gender differences in the delinquency rates have narrowed.
- Boys still account for about 76 percent of the total number of arrests and 82 percent of all serious violent crime arrests.
- Gender patterns in delinquency have become similar.

5. Be familiar with early trait explanations of female delinquency

- Lombroso maintained that women were lower on the evolutionary scale than men, more childlike, and less intelligent.
- Women who committed crimes could be distinguished from "normal" women by physical characteristics—excessive body hair, wrinkles, and an abnormal cranium, for example.
- In appearance, delinquent females appeared closer to men than to other women. The masculinity hypothesis suggested that delinquent girls had excessive male characteristics.
- So-called experts suggested that female delinquency goes unrecorded, because the female is the instigator rather than the perpetrator.
- The chivalry hypothesis holds that gender differences in the delinquency rate can be explained by the fact that female criminality is overlooked or forgiven by male agents of the justice system.
- Psychologists also viewed the physical differences between males and females as a basis for their behavior differentials.
- Sigmund Freud maintained that girls interpret their lack of a penis as a sign that they have been punished.
- Psychodynamic theorists suggested that girls are socialized to be passive, which helps explain their low crime rate.
- According to these early versions of the psychoanalytic approach, gender differences in the delinquency rate can be traced to differences in psychological orientation.
- Male delinquency reflects aggressive traits, whereas female delinquency is a function of repressed sexuality, gender conflict, and abnormal socialization.
- Contemporary biosocial and psychological theorists have continued the tradition of attributing gender differences in delinquency to physical and emotional traits.
- Early theorists linked female delinquency to early puberty and precocious sexuality.

6. Discuss contemporary trait views of female delinquency

- Equating female delinquency purely with sexual activity is no longer taken seriously, but early sexual maturity has been linked to other problems, such as a higher risk of teen pregnancy and sexually transmitted diseases.

- Empirical evidence suggests that girls who reach puberty at an early age are at the highest risk for delinquency.

- One reason is that "early bloomers" may be more attractive to older adolescent boys, and increased contact with this high-risk group places the girls in jeopardy for antisocial behavior.

- Recent research found that both boys and girls who reached puberty at an early age increase their chances of victimization.

- One view is that hormonal imbalance may influence aggressive behavior in young girls.

- Another view is that excessive amounts of male hormones (androgens) are related to delinquency.

- Today there is conflicting evidence on the relationship between PMS and female delinquency.

- Some psychologists believe that males are inherently more aggressive, a condition that appears very early in life, before socialization can influence behavior.

- Because girls are socialized to be less aggressive than boys, it is possible that the young women who get involved in antisocial and violent behavior are suffering from some form of mental anguish or abnormality.

- Girls are also more likely than boys to be involved in status offenses, such as running away and truancy, behaviors that suggest underlying psychological distress.

- Clinical interviews indicate that female delinquents are significantly more likely than males to suffer from mood disorders.

7. Discuss the association between socialization and female delinquency

- Socialization views are based on the idea that a child's social development may be the key to understanding delinquent behavior.

- If a child experiences impairment, family disruption, and so on, the child will be more susceptible to delinquent associations and criminality.

- Girls may be supervised more closely than boys. If girls behave in a socially disapproved fashion, their parents may be more likely to notice.

- Parents are stricter with girls because they perceive them as needing control. In some families, adolescent girls rebel against strict controls.

- Girls seem to be more deeply affected than boys by child abuse, and the link between abuse and female delinquency seems stronger than it is for male delinquency.

- Girls may be forced into a life of sexual promiscuity, because their sexual desirability makes them a valuable commodity for families living on the edge.

- There is a significant body of literature linking abusive home lives to gang participation and crime.

- The socialization approach holds that family interaction is the key to understanding female delinquency.

- Girls are expected to follow narrowly defined behavioral patterns.

8. Know the feminist view of female delinquency

- Liberal feminism has influenced thinking about delinquency.

- According to liberal feminists, females are less delinquent than males, because their social roles provide fewer opportunities to commit crime.

- Critical feminists hold that gender inequality stems from the unequal power of men and women and the subsequent exploitation of women by men.

- The cause of female delinquency originates with the onset of male supremacy and the efforts of males to control females' sexuality.

- In a patriarchal society, women are a "commodity" like land or money.

- Critical feminists focus on the social forces that shape girls' lives. They attempt to show how the sexual victimization of girls is often a function of male socialization and that young males learn to be exploitive of women.

9. Be able to discuss Hagan's power-control theory

- John Hagan and his associates have speculated that gender differences in delinquency are a function of class differences that influence family life.

- His power-control theory suggests that class influences delinquency by controlling the quality of family life.

- In paternalistic families, fathers assume the role of breadwinners, and mothers have menial jobs or remain at home.

- In egalitarian families—in which the husband and wife share similar positions of power at home and in the workplace—daughters gain a kind of freedom that reflects reduced parental control.

- These families produce daughters whose law-violating behaviors mirror those of their brothers.

- Power-control theory helps explain the relative increase in female delinquency by stressing the significance of changing feminine roles.

- The decline of the patriarchal family may produce looser family ties on girls, changing sex roles, and increased delinquency.

10. Discuss the treatment of girls in the juvenile justice system

- Gender differences not only have an effect on crime patterns, but also may have a significant impact on the way children are treated by the juvenile justice system.

- As a general rule males who are involved in the justice system are sanctioned more severely than females.
- Some critics believe that girls, more than boys, are still disadvantaged if their behavior is viewed as morally incorrect by government officials or if they are considered beyond parental control.
- Girls may still be subject to harsh punishments if they are considered dangerously immoral.

Key Terms

masculinity hypothesis, p. 218
gender-schema theory, p. 221
chivalry hypothesis, p. 225

precocious sexuality, p. 225
liberal feminism, p. 233
critical feminists, p. 234

power-control theory, p. 237
egalitarian families, p. 237

Viewpoint

As the principal of a northeastern junior high school, you get a call from a parent who is disturbed because he heard a rumor that the student literary digest plans to publish a story with a sexual theme. The work is written by a junior high school girl who became pregnant during the year and underwent an abortion. You ask for and receive a copy of the narrative.

The girl's story is actually a cautionary tale of young love that results in an unwanted pregnancy. The author details the abusive home life that led her to engage in an intimate relationship with another student, her pregnancy, her conflict with her parents, her decision to abort, and the emotional turmoil that the incident created. She tells students to use contraception if they are sexually active and recommends appropriate types of birth control. There is nothing provocative or sexually explicit in the work.

Some teachers argue that girls should not be allowed to read this material, because it has sexual content from which they must be protected, and that in a sense it advocates defiance of parents. Also, some parents may object to a story about precocious sexuality because they fear it

may encourage their children to "experiment." Such behavior is linked to delinquency and drug abuse. Those who advocate publication believe that girls have a right to read about such important issues and decide on their own course of action.

- Should you force the story's deletion, because its theme is essentially sexual and controversial?
- Should you allow publication, because it deals with the subject matter in a mature fashion?
- Do you think reading and learning about sexual matters encourages or discourages experimentation in sexuality?
- Should young girls be protected from such material? Would it cause them damage?
- Inequalities still exist in the way boys and girls are socialized by their parents and treated by social institutions. Do these gender differences also manifest themselves in the delinquency rate? What effect do gender roles have on behavior choices?

Doing Research on the Web

To help you answer these questions and to find more information on the gender of status offenders, go to the website

academic.cengage.com/criminaljustice/siegel

Once there, go to the website for *Hazelwood School District et al. v. Kuhlmeier et al.* and other landmark cases. Go also to the National Scholastic Press Association and the high school journalism websites to read more about school news and censorship issues.

Questions for Discussion

1. Are girls delinquent for different reasons than boys? Do girls have a unique set of problems?
2. As sex roles become more homogenous, do you believe female delinquency will become identical to male delinquency in rate and type?
3. Does the sexual double standard still exist?
4. Are lower-class girls more strictly supervised than upper- and middle-class girls? Is control stratified across class lines?
5. Are girls the victims of unfairness at the hands of the justice system, or do they benefit from "chivalry"?

Notes

1. Shelley Murphy, "6 Face Charges in Sex Ring Said to Force Girls into Prostitution," *Boston Globe*, 18 May 2007, www.boston.com/news/local/articles/2007/05/18/6_face_charges_in_sex_ring/ (accessed September 21, 2007).

2. Cesare Lombroso and William Ferrero, *The Female Offender* (New York: Philosophical Library, 1895).

3. Kerry Carrington, "Does Feminism Spoil Girls? Explanations for Official Rises in Female Delinquency," *Australian and New Zealand Journal of Criminology* 39:34–53 (2006).

4. Cheryl Maxson and Monica Whitlock, "Joining the Gang: Gender Differences in Risk Factors for Gang Membership," in C. Ronald Huff, ed., *Gangs in America III* (Thousand Oaks, CA: Sage, 2002), pp. 19–35.

5. David Finkelhor and Richard Ormrod, "Prostitution of Juveniles: Patterns from NIBRS," *Juvenile Justice Bulletin,* June 2004 (Washington, DC: The Office of Juvenile Justice and Delinquency Prevention, 2004), available at www.ncjrs.org/html/ojjdp/203946/contents.html (accessed October 10, 2007).

6. This section relies on Spencer Rathus, *Psychology in the New Millennium* (Fort Worth, TX: Harcourt, Brace, 1996); see also Darcy Miller, Catherine Trapani, Kathy Fejes-Mendoza, Carolyn Eggleston, and Donna Dwiggins, "Adolescent Female Offenders: Unique Considerations," *Adolescence* 30:429–435 (1995).

7. Rolf Loeber and Dale Hay, "Key Issues in the Development of Aggression and Violence from Childhood to Early Adulthood," *Annual Review of Psychology* 48:371–410 (1997).

8. Philip Cook and Susan Sorenson, "The Gender Gap among Teen Survey Respondents: Why Are Boys More Likely to Report a Gun in the Home than Girls?" *Journal of Quantitative Criminology* 22:61–76 (2006).

9. Allison Morris, *Women, Crime, and Criminal Justice* (Oxford, England: Basil Blackwell, 1987).

10. Sarah Meadows, "Evidence of Parallel Pathways: Gender Similarity in the Impact of Social Support on Adolescent Depression and Delinquency," *Social Forces* 85:1143–1167 (2007).

11. Dennis Giever, "An Empirical Assessment of the Core Elements of Gottfredson and Hirschi's General Theory of Crime," paper presented at the annual meeting of the American Society of Criminology, Boston, November 1995.

12. Abigail A. Fagan, M. Lee Van Horn, J. David Hawkins, and Michael W. Arthur, "Gender Similarities and Differences in the Association Between Risk and Protective Factors and Self-Reported Serious Delinquency," *Prevention Science* 8:115–124 (2007).

13. Loeber and Hay, "Key Issues in the Development of Aggression and Violence," p. 378.

14. John Mirowsky and Catherine Ross, "Sex Differences in Distress: Real or Artifact?" *American Sociological Review* 60:449–468 (1995).

15. For a review of this issue, see Anne Campbell, *Men, Women, and Aggression* (New York: Basic Books, 1993).

16. Michael Rutter, Henri Giller, and Ann Hagell, *Antisocial Behavior by Young People* (London: Cambridge University Press, 1998).

17. Sarah Meadows, "Evidence of Parallel Pathways: Gender Similarity in the Impact of Social Support on Adolescent Depression and Delinquency," *Social Forces* 85:1143–1167 (2007).

18. Thomas Parsons, Albert Rizzo, Cheryl Van Der Zaag, Jocelyn McGee, and J. Galen Buckwalter, "Gender Differences and Cognition Among Older Adults," *Aging, Neuropsychology and Cognition* 12:78–88 (2005).

19. Diane Halpern and Mary LaMay, "The Smarter Sex: A Critical Review of Sex Differences in Intelligence," *Educational Psychology Review* 12:229–246 (2000).

20. Parsons, Rizzo, Van Der Zaag, McGee, and Buckwalter, "Gender Differences and Cognition Among Older Adults."

21. James Messerschmidt, *Masculinities and Crime: Critique and Reconceptualization of Theory* (Lanham, MD: Rowman and Littlefield, 1993).

22. Debra Kaysen, Miranda Morris, Shireen Rizvi, and Patricia Resick, "Peritraumatic Responses and Their Relationship to Perceptions of Threat in Female Crime Victims," *Violence Against Women* 11:1515–1535 (2005).

23. D. J. Pepler and W. M. Craig, "A Peek Behind the Fence: Naturalistic Observations of Aggressive Children with Remote Audiovisual Recording," *Developmental Psychology* 31:548–553 (1995).

24. Daniel Mears, Matthew Ploeger, and Mark Warr, "Explaining the Gender Gap in Delinquency: Peer Influence and Moral Evaluations of Behavior," *Journal of Research in Crime and Delinquency* 35:251–266 (1998).

25. John Gibbs, Dennis Giever, and Jamie Martin, "Parental Management and Self-Control: An Empirical Test of Gottfredson and Hirschi's General Theory," *Journal of Research in Crime and Delinquency* 35:40–70 (1998); Velmer Burton, Francis Cullen, T. David Evans, Leanne Fiftal Alarid, and R. Gregory Dunaway, "Gender, Self-Control, and Crime," *Journal of Research in Crime and Delinquency* 35:123–147 (1998).

26. Camilla Benbow, David Lubinski, Daniel Shea, and Hossain Eftekhari-Sanjani, "Sex Differences in Mathematical Reasoning Ability at Age 13: Their Status 20 Years Later," *Psychological Science* 11:474–480 (2000).

27. Ann Beutel and Margaret Mooney Marini, "Gender and Values," *American Sociological Review* 60:436–448 (1995).

28. American Association of University Women, *Shortchanging Girls, Shortchanging America: Executive Summary* (Washington, DC: American Association of University Women, 1991).

29. Spencer Rathus, *Voyages in Childhood* (Belmont, CA: Wadsworth, 2004).

30. Carol Gilligan, *In a Different Voice* (Cambridge, MA: Harvard University Press, 1982).

31. David Roalf, Natasha Lowery, and Bruce Turetsky, "Behavioral and Physiological Findings of Gender Differences in Global-Local Visual Processing," *Brain and Cognition* 60:32–42 (2006).

32. Eleanor Maccoby, *The Two Sexes: Growing Up Apart, Coming Together* (Cambridge, MA: Belknap Press, 1999).

33. Kathleen Miller, Merrill Melnick, Grace Barnes, Don Sabo, and Michael Farrell, "Athletic Involvement and Adolescent Delinquency," *Journal of Youth and Adolescence* 36:711–723 (2007).

34. David Rowe, Alexander Vazsonyi, and Daniel Flannery, "Sex Differences in Crime: Do Means and Within-Sex Variation Have Similar Causes?" *Journal of Research in Crime and Delinquency* 32:84–100 (1995).

35. Sandra Bem, *The Lenses of Gender* (New Haven: Yale University Press, 1993).

36. Walter DeKeseredy and Martin Schwartz, "Male Peer Support and Woman Abuse," *Sociological Spectrum* 13:393–413 (1993).

37. Johannes Landsheer and Cor van Dijkum, "Male and Female Delinquency Trajectories from Pre through Middle Adolescence and Their Continuation in Late Adolescence," *Adolescence* 40:729–748 (2005).

38. Eleanor Maccoby, "Gender and Group Process: A Developmental Perspective," *Current Directions in Psychological Science* 11:54–58 (2002).

39. Jean Bottcher, "Social Practices of Gender: How Gender Relates to Delinquency in the Everyday Lives of High-Risk Youths," *Criminology* 39:893–932 (2001).

40. Audrey Zakriski, Jack Wright, and Marion Underwood, "Gender Similarities and Differences in Children's Social Behavior: Finding Personality in Contextualized Patterns of Adaptation," *Journal of Personality and Social Psychology* 88:844–855 (2005).

41. Associated Press, "Girls, Ages 10 and 12, Kidnap Baby and Demand Ransom," *New York Daily News*, 6 July 2007, www.nydailynews.com/news/crime_file/2007/07/06/2007–07–06_girls_ages_10_and_12_kinap_baby_and_dema.html (accessed October 10, 2007).

42. Howard Snyder and Melissa Sickmund, *Juvenile Offenders and Victims: 2006 National Report* (Washington, DC: Office of Juvenile Justice, 2006), p. 129.

43. Darrell Steffensmeier, Jennifer Schwartz, Hua Zhong, and Jeff Ackerman, "An Assessment of Recent Trends in Girls' Violence Using Diverse Longitudinal Sources: Is the Gender Gap Closing?" *Criminology* 43:355–406 (2005).

44. *Monitoring the Future, 2005* (Ann Arbor, MI: Institute for Social Research, 2006).

45. Lombroso and Ferrero, *The Female Offender*.

46. Ibid., p. 122.

47. Ibid., pp. 51–52.

48. For a review, see Anne Campbell, *Girl Delinquents* (Oxford, England: Basil Blackwell, 1981), pp. 41–48.

49. Cyril Burt, *The Young Delinquent* (New York: Appleton, 1925); see also Warren Middleton, "Is There a Relation Between Kleptomania and Female Periodicity in Neurotic Individuals?" *Psychology Clinic* (December 1933), pp. 232–247.

50. William Healy and Augusta Bronner, *Delinquents and Criminals: Their Making and Unmaking* (New York: Macmillan, 1926).

51. Ibid., p. 10.

52. Miriam Sealock and Sally Simpson, "Unraveling Bias in Arrest Decisions: The Role of Juvenile Offender Typescripts," *Justice Quarterly* 15:427–457 (1998).

53. Sigmund Freud, *An Outline of Psychoanalysis*, trans. James Strachey (New York: Norton, 1949), p. 278.

54. Dorie Klein, "The Etiology of Female Crime: A Review of the Literature," in Freda Adler and Rita Simon, eds., *The Criminology of Deviant Women* (Boston: Houghton Mifflin, 1979), pp. 69–71.

55. Peter Blos, "Pre-Oedipal Factors in the Etiology of Female Delinquency," *Psychoanalytic Studies of the Child* 12:229–242 (1957).

56. Sheldon Glueck and Eleanor Glueck, *Five Hundred Delinquent Women* (New York: Knopf, 1934).

57. John Cowie, Valerie Cowie, and Eliot Slater, *Delinquency in Girls* (London: Heinemann, 1968).

58. Anne Campbell, "On the Invisibility of the Female Delinquent Peer Group," *Women and Criminal Justice* 2:41–62 (1990).

59. Carolyn Smith, "Factors Associated with Early Sexual Activity Among Urban Adolescents," *Social Work* 42:334–346 (1997).

60. For a review, see Christy Miller Buchanan, Jacquelynne Eccles, and Jill Becker, "Are Adolescents the Victims of Raging Hormones? Evidence for Activational Effects of Hormones on Moods and Behavior at Adolescence," *Psychological Bulletin* 111:63–107 (1992).

61. L. Kris Gowen, S. Shirley Feldman, Rafael Diaz, and Donnovan Somera Yisrael, "A Comparison of the Sexual Behaviors and Attitudes of Adolescent Girls with Older vs. Similar-Aged Boyfriends," *Journal of Youth and Adolescence* 33:167–176 (2004).

62. Dana Haynie, "Contexts of Risk? Explaining the Link Between Girls' Pubertal Development and Their Delinquency Involvement," *Social Forces* 82:355–397 (2003).

63. Avshalom Caspi, Donald Lyman, Terrie Moffitt, and Phil Silva, "Unraveling Girls' Delinquency: Biological, Dispositional, and Contextual Contributions to Adolescent Misbehavior," *Developmental Psychology* 29:283–289 (1993).

64. Dana Haynie and Alex Piquero, "Pubertal Development and Physical Victimization in Adolescence," *Journal of Research in Crime and Delinquency* 43:3–35 (2006).

65. David Comings, Donn Muhleman, James Johnson, and James MacMurray, "Parent-Daughter Transmission of the Androgen Receptor Gene as an Explanation of the Effect of Father Absence on Age of Menarche," *Child Development* 73:1046–1051 (2002).

66. Eleanor Maccoby and Carol Jacklin, *The Psychology of Sex Differences* (Stanford, CA: Stanford University Press, 1974).

67. Kathleen Pajer, William Gardner, Robert Rubin, James Perel, and Stephen Neal, "Decreased Cortisol Levels in Adolescent Girls with Conduct Disorder," *Archives of General Psychiatry* 58:297–302 (2001).

68. Alan Booth and D. Wayne Osgood, "The Influence of Testosterone on Deviance in Adulthood: Assessing and Explaining the Relationship," *Criminology* 31:93–118 (1993).

69. D. H. Baucom, P. K. Besch, and S. Callahan, "Relationship Between Testosterone Concentration, Sex Role Identity, and Personality Among Females," *Journal of Personality and Social Psychology* 48:1218–1226 (1985).

70. Lee Ellis, "Evidence of Neuroandrogenic Etiology of Sex Roles from a Combined Analysis of Human, Nonhuman Primate, and Nonprimate Mammalian Studies," *Personality and Individual Differences* 7:519–552 (1986).

71. Diana Fishbein, "The Psychobiology of Female Aggression," *Criminal Justice and Behavior* 19:99–126 (1992).

72. Spencer Rathus, *Psychology*, 3rd ed. (New York: Holt, Rinehart & Winston, 1987), p. 88.

73. See, generally, Katharina Dalton, *The Premenstrual Syndrome* (Springfield, IL: Charles C Thomas, 1971).

74. Diana Fishbein, "Selected Studies on the Biology of Antisocial Behavior," in John Conklin, ed., *New Perspectives in Criminology* (Needham Heights, MA: Allyn and Bacon, 1996), pp. 26–38.

75. Julie Horney, "Menstrual Cycles and Criminal Responsibility," *Law and Human Nature* 2:25–36 (1978).

76. Lee Ellis, "The Victimful-Victimless Crime Distinction and Seven Universal Demographic Correlates of Victimful Criminal Behavior," *Personality and Individual Differences* 9:525–548 (1988).

77. Lee Ellis, "Evolutionary and Neurochemical Causes of Sex Differences in Victimizing Behavior: Toward a Unified Theory of Criminal Behavior and Social Stratification," *Social Science Information* 28:605–636 (1989).

78. Kathleen Pajer, "What Happens to 'Bad' Girls? A Review of the Adult Outcomes of Antisocial Adolescent Girls," *American Journal of Psychiatry* 155:862–870 (1998).

79. Jan ter Laak, Martijn de Goede, Liesbeth Aleva, Gerard Brugman, Miranda van Leuven, and Judith Hussmann, "Incarcerated Adolescent Girls: Personality, Social Competence, and Delinquency," *Adolescence* 38:251–265 (2003).

80. Dorothy Espelage, Elizabeth Cauffman, Lisa Broidy, Alex Piquero, Paul Mazerolle, and Hans Steiner, "A Cluster-Analytic Investigation of MMPI Profiles of Serious Male and Female Juvenile Offenders," *Journal of the American Academy of Child and Adolescent Psychiatry* 42:770–777 (2003).

81. Kristen McCabe, Amy Lansing, Ann Garland, and Richard Hough, "Gender Differences in Psychopathology, Functional Impairment, and Familial Risk Factors Among Adjudicated Delinquents," *Journal of the American Academy of Child and Adolescent Psychiatry* 41:860–867 (2002).

82. Paul Frick, Amy Cornell, Christopher Barry, Doug Bodin, and Heather Dane, "Callous-Unemotional Traits and Conduct Problems in the Prediction of Conduct Problem Severity, Aggression, and Self-Report of Delinquency," *Journal of Abnormal Child Psychology* 31:457–470 (2003).

83. Alex Mason and Michael Windle, "Gender, Self-Control, and Informal Social Control in Adolescence: A Test of Three Models of the Continuity of Delinquent Behavior," *Youth and Society* 33:479–514 (2002).

84. William I. Thomas, *The Unadjusted Girl with Cases and Standpoint for Behavior Analysis* (Boston: Little Brown and Company, 1923).

85. Ibid., p. 109.

86. David Farrington, "Juvenile Delinquency," in John Coleman, ed., *The School Years* (London: Routledge, 1992), p. 133.

87. Ibid.

88. Ruth Morris, "Female Delinquents and Relational Problems," *Social Forces* 43:82–89 (1964).

89. Cowie, Cowie, and Slater, *Delinquency in Girls*, p. 27.

90. Morris, "Female Delinquency and Relational Problems."

91. Clyde Vedder and Dora Somerville, *The Delinquent Girl* (Springfield, IL: Charles C Thomas, 1970).

92. Ames Robey, Richard Rosenwal, John Small, and Ruth Lee, "The Runaway Girl: A Reaction to Family Stress," *American Journal of Orthopsychiatry* 34:763–767 (1964).

93. William Wattenberg and Frank Saunders, "Sex Differences Among Juvenile Court Offenders," *Sociology and Social Research* 39:24–31 (1954).

94. Don Gibbons and Manzer Griswold, "Sex Differences Among Juvenile Court Referrals," *Sociology and Social Research* 42:106–110 (1957).

95. Gordon Barker and William Adams, "Comparison of the Delinquencies of Boys and Girls," *Journal of Criminal Law, Criminology, and Police Science* 53:470–475 (1962).

96. George Calhoun, Janelle Jurgens, and Fengling Chen, "The Neophyte Female Delinquent: A Review of the Literature," *Adolescence* 28:461–471 (1993).

97. Angela Dixon, Pauline Howie, and Jean Starling, "Trauma Exposure, Posttraumatic Stress, and Psychiatric Comorbidity in Female Juvenile Offenders," *Journal of the American Academy of Child and Adolescent Psychiatry* 44:798–806 (2005).

98. Veronica Herrera and Laura Ann McCloskey, "Sexual Abuse, Family Violence, and Female Delinquency: Findings from a Longitudinal Study," *Violence and Victims* 18:319–334 (2003).

99. Julie Messer, Barbara Maughan, and David Quinton, "Precursors and Correlates of Criminal Behaviour in Women," *Criminal Behaviour and Mental Health* 14:82–107 (2004).

100. Emily Gaarder and Joanne Belknap, "Tenuous Borders: Girls Transferred to Adult Court," *Criminology* 40:481–518 (2002).

101. Ibid., p. 20.

102. Joan Moore, *Going Down to the Barrio: Homeboys and Homegirls in Change* (Philadelphia: Temple University Press, 1991), p. 93.

103. Ibid., p. 101.

104. Gaarder and Belknap, "Tenuous Borders."

105. Jennifer Kerpelman and Sondra Smith-Adcock, "Female Adolescents' Delinquent Activity: The Intersection of Bonds to Parents and Reputation Enhancement," *Youth and Society* 37:176–200 (2005).

106. D. Wayne Osgood, Janet Wilson, Patrick O'Malley, Jerald Bachman, and Lloyd Johnston, "Routine Activities and Individual Deviant Behaviors," *American Sociological Review* 61:635–655 (1996).

107. Freda Adler, *Sisters in Crime* (New York: McGraw-Hill, 1975).

108. Ibid., pp. 10–11.

109. Rita James Simon, "Women and Crime Revisited," *Social Science Quarterly* 56:658–663 (1976).

110. Ibid., pp. 660–661.

111. Roy Austin, "Women's Liberation and Increase in Minor, Major, and Occupational Offenses," *Criminology* 20:407–430 (1982).

112. "Delinquency Involvements," *Social Forces* 14:525–534 (1971).

113. Darrell Steffensmeier and Dana Haynie, "Gender, Structural Disadvantage, and Urban Crime: Do Macrosocial Variables Also Explain Female Offending Rates?" *Criminology* 38:403–438 (2000); Beth Bjerregaard and Carolyn Smith, "Gender Differences in Gang Participation and Delinquency," *Journal of Quantitative Criminology* 9:329–350 (1993).

114. Julia Schwendinger and Herman Schwendinger, *Rape and Inequality* (Beverly Hills, CA: Sage, 1983).

115. For a review of feminist theory, see Sally Simpson, "Feminist Theory, Crime and Justice," *Criminology* 27:605–632 (1989).

116. Victoria Titterington, "A Retrospective Investigation of Gender Inequality and Female Homicide Victimization," *Sociological Spectrum* 26:205–236 (2006).

117. Simpson, "Feminist Theory, Crime and Justice," p. 611.

118. Messerschmidt, *Masculinities and Crime.*

119. Center for Research on Women, *Secrets in Public: Sexual Harassment in Our Schools* (Wellesley, MA: Wellesley College, 1993).

120. Joanne Belknap, Kristi Holsinger, and Melissa Dunn, "Understanding Incarcerated Girls: The Results of a Focus Group Study," *Prison Journal* 77:381–405 (1997)

121. Kathleen Daly and Meda Chesney-Lind, "Feminism and Criminology," *Justice Quarterly* 5:497–538 (1988).

122. Jane Siegel and Linda Williams, "The Relationship Between Child Sexual Abuse and Female Delinquency and Crime: A Prospective Study," *Journal of Research in Crime and Delinquency* 40:71–94 (2003).

123. James Messerschmidt, *Capitalism, Patriarchy and Crime* (Totowa, NJ: Rowman and Littlefield, 1986); for a critique of this work, see Herman Schwendinger and Julia Schwendinger, "The World According to James Messerschmidt," *Social Justice* 15:123–145 (1988).

124. John Hagan, A. R. Gillis, and John Simpson, "The Class Structure and Delinquency: Toward a Power-Control Theory of Common Delinquent Behavior," *American Journal of Sociology* 90:1151–1178 (1985); John Hagan, John Simpson, and A. R. Gillis, "Class in the Household: A Power-Control Theory of Gender and Delinquency," *American Journal of Sociology* 92:788–816 (1987).

125. John Hagan, A. R. Gillis, and John Simpson, "Clarifying and Extending Power-Control Theory," *American Journal of Sociology* 95:1024–1037 (1990).

126. Brenda Sims Blackwell and Mark Reed, "Power-Control as a Between and Within-Family Model: Reconsidering the Unit of Analysis," *Journal of Youth and Adolescence* 32:385–400 (2003).

127. Gary Jensen and Kevin Thompson, "What's Class Got to Do with It? A Further Examination of Power-Control Theory," *American Journal of Sociology* 95:1009–1023 (1990); Kevin Thompson, "Gender and Adolescent Drinking Problems: The Effects of Occupational Structure," *Social Problems* 36:30–44 (1989); for some critical research, see Simon Singer and Murray Levine, "Power-Control Theory, Gender and Delinquency: A Partial Replication with Additional Evidence on the Effects of Peers," *Criminology* 26:627–648 (1988).

128. Christopher Uggen, "Class, Gender, and Arrest: An Intergenerational Analysis of Workplace Power and Control," *Criminology* 38:835–862 (2001).

129. Snyder and Sickmund, *Juvenile Offenders and Victims: 2006 National Report.*

130. Thomas J. Gamble, Sherrie Sonnenberg, John Haltigan, and Amy Cuzzola-Kern, "Detention Screening: Prospects for Population Management and the Examination of Disproportionality by Race, Age, and Gender," *Criminal Justice Policy Review* 13:380–395 (2002); Kimberly Kempf-Leonard and Lisa Sample, "Disparity Based on Sex: Is Gender-Specific Treatment Warranted?" *Justice Quarterly* 17:89–128 (2000).

131. Meda Chesney-Lind and Randall Shelden, *Girls, Delinquency, and Juvenile Justice* (Belmont, CA: West/Wadsworth, 1998).

132. John MacDonald and Meda Chesney-Lind, "Gender Bias and Juvenile Justice Revisited: A Multiyear Analysis," *Crime and Delinquency* 47: 173–195 (2001).

133. Holly Hartwig and Jane Myers, "A Different Approach: Applying a Wellness Paradigm to Adolescent Female Delinquents and Offenders," *Journal of Mental Health Counseling* 25:57–75 (2003).

134. Ibid.

135. Jill Leslie Rosenbaum and Meda Chesney-Lind, "Appearance and Delinquency: A Research Note," *Crime and Delinquency* 40:250–261 (1994).

136. Sealock and Simpson, "Unraveling Bias in Arrest Decisions."

137. Carla Davis, "At-Risk Girls and Delinquency," *Crime and Delinquency* 53:408–435 (2007).

138. Sara Goodkind and Diane Lynn Miller, "A Widening of the Net of Social Control? 'Gender-Specific' Treatment for Young Women in the U.S. Juvenile Justice System," *Journal of Progressive Human Services* 17:45–70 (2006).

139. Chesney-Lind and Shelden, *Girls, Delinquency, and Juvenile Justice,* p. 243.

140. Meda Chesney-Lind and Vickie Paramore, "Are Girls Getting More Violent? Exploring Juvenile Robbery Trends," *Journal of Contemporary Criminal Justice* 17:142–166 (2001).

141. Belknap, Holsinger, and Dunn, "Understanding Incarcerated Girls."

142. Carrington, "Does Feminism Spoil Girls?"

The Family and Delinquency

8

Chapter Outline

Chapter Objectives

1. Be familiar with the link between family relationships and juvenile delinquency
2. Chart the changes American families are now undergoing
3. Understand the complex association between family breakup and delinquent behavior
4. Understand why families in conflict produce more delinquents than those that function harmoniously
5. Compare and contrast the effects of good and bad parenting on delinquency
6. Discuss whether having deviant parents affects a child's behavioral choices
7. Know about sibling influence on delinquency
8. Discuss the nature and extent of child abuse
9. List the assumed causes of child abuse
10. Be familiar with the child protection system and the stages in the child protection process
11. Know how courts have protected child witnesses
12. Know the various positions in the delinquency–child maltreatment debate

In 2006, in one of New York City's most notorious child abuse cases in history, a 7-year-old Brooklyn girl, Nixzmary Brown, was horribly tortured and abused before being killed by a severe blow to the head. The suspects in the case: Nixzaliz Santiago, her mother, and Cesar Rodriguez, her stepfather. At the time of her death, Nixzmary weighed only 36 pounds, and had been tied to a chair and forced to use a litter box for a toilet. According to a statement given by her mother, Rodriguez, who beat the girl regularly for stealing food or hitting her siblings, pushed her head under the running bathtub faucet after stripping her naked, beat her, and tied her to a stool. Then he listened to music in another room. Some time later, the mother got up the nerve to go to her daughter and found that the little girl's body was cold. Law enforcement agents said that the abuse the 7-year-old experienced was among the worst they had ever witnessed. Autopsy reports revealed she had cuts and bruises all over her body, two black eyes, and a skull that was hit so hard her brain bled.

In the aftermath of this terrible crime, New York Mayor Michael Blumberg told the press, "How can anybody fathom what these parents did to this young, 7-year-old girl? It sort of defies description." Tragically, Nixzmary's situation was known to authorities for some time before her death. The city's Administration for Children's Services had received two complaints about the family; the first, in 2004, was found to be unsubstantiated, and the second occurred on December 1, 2005, when the young girl showed up at school with a black eye. Yet little was done to help her or remove her from her brutal home. When asked why they did not get a court order, child welfare authorities blamed the parents for being uncooperative, ignoring repeated phone calls from caseworkers and turning them away at the door. Still, the head of New York's welfare system couldn't explain why caseworkers didn't get a warrant to enter the house. Nor did they attempt to take Nixzmary from home and place her in foster care.[1] While tragic, Nixzmary's case was not unique—it was the fourth homicide that year involving a family monitored by the city's Administration for Children's Services, renewing concerns about the agency's ability to protect abused children. Due to public outcry, top-level administrators within the massive child welfare system bureaucracy were reassigned and two top officials were also demoted. The city promised to add 30 new managers and 575 child protection workers; managers' caseloads were to be reduced from 240 down to 165.

T he Nixzmary Brown case aptly illustrates the risk many children find in their own homes. There is little question that family dysfunction is a key ingredient in the development of the emotional deficits that eventually lead to long-term social problems.[2] Interactions between parents and children, and between siblings, provide opportunities for children to acquire or inhibit antisocial behavior patterns.[3] Even kids who are predisposed toward delinquency because of personality traits, such as low self-control and impulsive personality, may find their life circumstances improved and their involvement with antisocial behavior diminished if they are exposed to positive and effective parenting.[4] Families may be more important than peer groups as an influence on adolescent misbehavior.[5] It comes as no surprise that recent (2007) research shows that, as young adults, people who maintain positive lifestyles report having had warm relationships with their parents, while those who perceived a lack of parental warmth and support were later much more likely to get involved in antisocial behaviors.[6]

Good parenting lowers the risk of delinquency for children living in high-crime areas. Research shows kids are able to resist the temptation of the streets if they receive fair discipline and support from parents who provide them with positive role models.[7]

The existence of warm and supportive relationships with parents provides an environment for adolescents where they are able to adapt to environmentally derived stress and strain in a healthy manner. The existence of positive relationships with parents promotes prosocial behavior regardless of whether or not adolescents are exposed to damaging life events or chronic strains.[8]

However, children in affluent families who are being raised in a household characterized by abuse and conflict, or whose parents are absent or separated, will still be at risk for delinquency.[9] Nor is the relationship between family life and delinquency unique to U.S. culture; cross-national data support a significant association between family variables and delinquency.[10]

The assumed relationship between delinquency and family life is critical today, because the American family is changing. Extended families, once common, are now for the most part anachronisms. In their place is the nuclear family, described as a "dangerous hothouse of emotions," because of the close contact between parents and children; in these families, problems are unrelieved by contact with other kin living nearby.[11]

And now the nuclear family is showing signs of breakdown. About half of all marriages may one day end in divorce.[12] Much of the responsibility for childrearing is delegated to television and day care providers. Despite these changes, some families are able to continue functioning as healthy units, producing well-adjusted children. Others have crumbled under the stress, severely damaging their children.[13] This is particularly true when child abuse and neglect become part of family life.

Because these issues are critical for understanding delinquency, this chapter is devoted to an analysis of the family's role in producing or inhibiting delinquency. We first cover the changing face of the American family. We will review the way family structure and function influences delinquent behavior. The relationship between child abuse, neglect, and delinquency is covered in some depth.

A great deal of information on families and children can be found at the website of the **David and Lucile Packard Foundation** by going to academic.cengage.com/criminaljustice/siegel.

nuclear family
A family unit composed of parents and their children; this smaller family structure is subject to great stress due to the intense, close contact between parents and children.

THE CHANGING AMERICAN FAMILY

The so-called traditional family—with a male breadwinner and a female who cares for the home—is largely a thing of the past. No longer can this family structure be considered the norm. Changing sex roles have created a family where women play a much greater role in the economic process; this has created a more egalitarian family structure. About three-quarters of all mothers of school-age children are employed, up from 50 percent in 1970 and 40 percent in 1960. The changing economic structure may be reflected in shifting sex roles. Fathers are now spending more time with their children on workdays than they did 20 years ago, and mothers are spending somewhat less time.[14]

Family Makeup

There are now about 70 million children living in America ages 0 to 17. As Figure 8.1 shows, children today live in a profusion of family living arrangements. Seventy percent of them live with two parents, 26 percent live with one parent, and about 4 percent

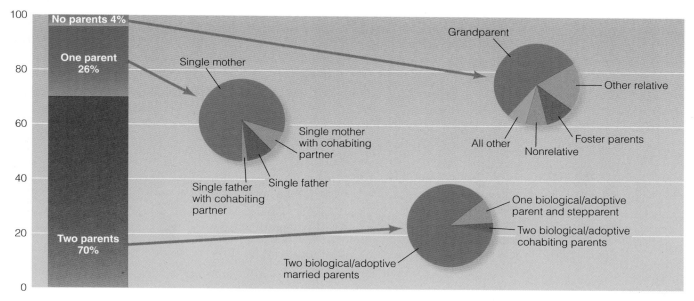

FIGURE 8.1

Various Family Arrangements

SOURCE: U.S. Census Bureau, Survey of Income and Program Participation, www.childstats.gov/americaschildren/famsoc1.asp (accessed October 18, 2007).

live in households without parents. Of these, more than half (56 percent or 1.6 million kids) live with their grandparents, 19 percent live with other relatives, and 25 percent live with nonrelatives. Of children in nonrelatives' homes, more than 300,000 live with foster parents.

There are still significant racial differences in family makeup. About one-third of all African American children live in families that have two parents compared to about three-quarters of European American children.[15] By age 16, 40 percent of European American children and 75 percent of African American children will experience parental separation or divorce and some will experience multiple family disruptions.[16] Though there has been a sharp decline in teen pregnancies, more than 1.3 million children are still being born to unmarried women annually; in 2006, the teen pregnancy rate rose 3 percent, the first increase in more than 15 years.[17]

Child Care

Charged with caring for children is a day care system whose workers are often paid minimum wage. Of special concern are "family day care homes," in which a single provider takes care of three to nine children. Today, about 12 million children receive some form of child care on a regular basis from persons other than their parents. As Figure 8.2 shows, kids living in poverty are much more likely to be in nonparental care than more affluent kids. Several states neither license nor monitor these private providers. Even in states that mandate registration and inspection of day care providers, it is estimated that 90 percent or more of the facilities operate "underground." It is not uncommon for one adult to care for eight infants, an impossible task regardless of training or feelings of concern.

Children from working poor families are most likely to suffer from inadequate child care; these children often spend time in makeshift arrangements that allow their parents to work, but lack the stimulating environment children need to thrive.[18] About 3.5 million children under age 13 spend some time at home alone each week while their parents are at work.

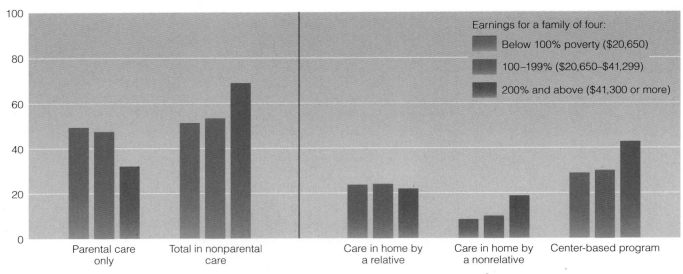

Percent

Earnings for a family of four:

Below 100% poverty ($20,650)

100–199% ($20,650–$41,299)

200% and above ($41,300 or more)

Parental care only | Total in nonparental care | Care in home by a relative | Care in home by a nonrelative | Center-based program

FIGURE 8.2

Percentage of Children Ages 0–6 Not Yet in Kindergarten, by Type of Care Arrangement

SOURCE: U.S. Department of Education, National Center for Education Statistics, National Household Education Surveys Program (NHES), www.childstats.gov/americaschildren/famsoc3.asp (accessed October 18, 2007).

Economic Stress

The family is also undergoing economic stress. Nearly 20 percent of all children live in poverty and about 8 percent live in extreme poverty—at least 50 percent below the poverty line. About 33 percent of all children live in families where no parent has full-time, year-round employment.[19] The majority of indigent families live in substandard housing without adequate health care, nutrition, or child care. Those whose incomes place them above the poverty line are deprived of government assistance. Recent political trends suggest that the social "safety net" is under attack and that poor families can expect less government aid in the coming years.

Will this economic pressure be reduced in the future? The number of senior citizens is on the rise. As people retire, there will be fewer workers to cover the costs of Social Security, medical care, and nursing home care. These costs will put greater economic stress on families. Voter sentiment has an impact on the allocation of public funds, and there is concern that an older generation, worried about health care costs, may be reluctant to spend tax dollars on at-risk kids.

THE FAMILY'S INFLUENCE ON DELINQUENCY

The effect of these family stressors can have a significant impact on children's behavior. The family is the primary unit in which children learn the values and attitudes that guide their actions throughout their lives. Family disruption or change can have a long-lasting impact on children. In contrast, effective parenting can help neutralize the effect of both individual (e.g., emotional problems) and social (e.g., delinquent peers) forces, which promote delinquent behaviors.[20]

Four categories of family dysfunction seem to promote delinquent behavior: families disrupted by spousal conflict or breakup, families involved in interpersonal conflict, ineffective parents who lack proper parenting skills, and families that contain deviant parents who may transmit their behavior to their children (see Figure 8.3 on page 253).[21] These factors may interact with one another: Drug-abusing parents may be more likely

Many American families are undergoing economic stress. Though the economy has been robust, more than 37 million people are living below the poverty line. The family shown in this photo relocated to Grandview, Washington, from Texas because Grandview offers support for education, housing, clothing, and food.

to experience family conflict, child neglect, and marital breakup. We now turn to the specific types of family problems that have been linked to delinquent behavior.

Family Breakup

One of the most enduring controversies in the study of delinquency is the relationship between a parent absent from the home and the onset of delinquent behavior. Parents or guardians act as informal agents of control, and when a breakdown in family occurs children are more apt to get involved in antisocial behaviors.[22]

Research indicates that parents whose marriage is secure produce children who are in turn assured and independent.[23] In contrast, research conducted both in the United States and abroad shows that children raised in homes with one or both parents absent may be prone to antisocial behavior.[24] A number of experts contend that a **broken home** is a strong determinant of a child's law-violating behavior. The connection seems self-evident, because a child is first socialized at home. Any disjunction in an orderly family structure could be expected to have a negative impact on the child.

The suspected broken home–delinquency relationship is important, because, if current trends continue, less than half of all children born today will live continuously with their biological mother and father throughout childhood. And because stepfamilies, or so-called **blended families**, are less stable than families consisting of two biological parents, an increasing number of children will experience family breakup two or even three times during childhood.[25]

Children who have experienced family breakup are more likely to demonstrate behavior problems and hyperactivity than children in intact families.[26] Family breakup is often associated with conflict, hostility, and aggression; children of divorce are suspected of having lax supervision, weakened attachment, and greater susceptibility to peer pressure.[27] One study of more than 4,000 youths in Denver, Pittsburgh, and Rochester, New York, found that the more often children are forced to go through family transitions the more likely they are to engage in delinquent activity.[28]

The Effects of Divorce The relationship between broken homes and delinquency has been controversial, to say the least. It was established in early research, which suggested that a significant association existed between parental absence and youthful misconduct.[29] For many years the link was clear: Children growing up in broken homes were much more likely to fall prey to delinquency than those who lived in two-parent households.[30]

Beginning in the late 1950s, some researchers began to question the link between broken homes and delinquency. Early studies, they claimed, used the records of police, courts, and correctional institutions.[31] This research may have been tainted by sampling bias: Youths from broken homes may get arrested more often than youths from intact families, but this does not necessarily mean they engage in more frequent and serious delinquent behavior. Official statistics may reflect the fact that agents of the justice system treat children from disrupted households more severely, because they cannot call on parents for support. The *parens patriae*

broken home
Home in which one or both parents are absent due to divorce or separation; children in such an environment may be prone to antisocial behavior.

blended families
Nuclear families that are the product of divorce and remarriage, blending one parent from each of two families and their combined children into one family unit.

For Better or for Worse: Does Divorce Matter?

Does divorce matter? Are the children of divorced couples more at risk for antisocial behavior than those who reside in intact homes? Two well-received books reach startlingly opposite conclusions on this important matter.

In their classic book, *The Unexpected Legacy of Divorce*, Judith Wallerstein, Julia M. Lewis, and Sandra Blakeslee reported on the findings of a longitudinal study, begun in the early 1970s, with 131 children whose parents divorced during their adolescence. Wallerstein and her associates checked in with 93 of the original 131 children and extensively profiled 5 children who most embody the common life experiences of the larger group. They followed their lives in detail through adolescence, delving into their love affairs, their marital successes and failures, and the parenting of their own children.

The researchers found that the effects of divorce on children are not short-term and transient but long lasting and cumulative. Children of divorce develop lingering fears about their own ability to develop long-term relationships; these fears often impede their ability to marry and raise families. While most spouses are able to reduce their emotional pain and get on with their lives a few years after they divorce, this is not true of their children, whose emotional turmoil may last for decades. The children often find it emotionally draining to spend time with their noncustodial parents and resent the disruption for years afterward. Some of the children in the study felt they had been an "inconvenience" and that their parents fit them in around their schedules. Considering their emotional turmoil, it is not surprising that these kids exhibit high levels of drug and alcohol abuse and, for girls, precocious sexuality. Consequently, only 40 percent of the kids followed in the study, many in their late 20s to early 30s, have ever married (compared to 81 percent of men and 87 percent of women in the general population). Some subjects told the researchers that marriage seemed impossible because their traumatic home life gave them no clue what a loving relationship was actually like.

In some cases, the parents' intense love/hate relationship that developed during marriage never ends, and parents continue to battle for years after separating; some collapse emotionally and physically. The authors document how some kids cope with long-term psychological turmoil by taking on the job of family caregiver. They become nurse, analyst, mentor, and confidant to their parents. One told them how, at 10 years old, she would spend time with her insomniac mother watching television and drinking beer at midnight. She frequently stayed home from school to make sure that her mother would not become depressed and suicidal or take the car out when she was drinking. Such personal burdens compromise the child's ability to develop friendships and personal interests. Such children may feel both trapped and guilty when they put their own needs ahead of the needy parent.

Wallerstein and her associates found that adolescents who grew up in homes where they experienced divorce are now struggling with the fear that their relationships will fail like those of their parents. Lacking guidance and experience, they must invent their own codes of behavior in a culture that offers few guidelines on how to become successful, protective parents themselves. This development has serious consequences, considering the theoretical importance placed on the development of positive family relationships as an inhibitor of delinquency and adult criminality.

DOES DIVORCE MATTER?

Award-winning psychologist E. Mavis Hetherington and writing partner John Kelly collected data from a study conducted over a 30-year period of more than 1,400 families and 2,500 children. Rather than the tumultuous event described by Wallerstein, Hetherington sees divorce as part of a series of a life transitions that can be destructive in the short term but actually have positive benefits in the long run. Divorce creates an opportunity for long-term personal growth. If the ex-partners can bring a sense of maturity to the dissolution of their relationship and have enough material and personal strength to become autonomous, they will be able to weather the short-term upheaval of separation. Within five or six years of separating they stand a good chance of becoming much happier than they were while married. Of course, those ex-partners whose personalities render them impulsive and antisocial have a diminished chance of turning their lives around.

Hetherington found that children of divorce may undergo some trauma, but for the most part they are much better off than those Wallerstein encountered. While children in single-parent families and stepfamilies have more psychological problems than those in intact families, more than 75 percent ultimately do as well as children from intact families. Though divorce is a painful experience, most go on to establish careers, create intimate relationships, and build meaningful lives.

Although Hetherington's picture of the aftermath of divorce is somewhat rosier than Wallerstein's, she too finds peril in family breakup. After six years, about one-quarter of her sample had contact with their noncustodial father once a year or less. Many women report anxiety six years after the breakup, and stepfathers often find it difficult to connect with the kids in their blended families; many stop trying after a few years of frustration.

Critical Thinking

1. Considering the long-term effects of divorce, should we make it more difficult to dissolve marriages—for example, by doing away with the concept of no-fault divorce and requiring stringent reasons for obtaining a separation?

2. Should it be more difficult to get married? Should couples be forced to go through counseling and education programs before being granted a marriage license? We do it for driving, why not marriage?

3. Which researcher, Wallerstein or Hetherington, paints a more accurate picture of the aftermath of family dissolution?

SOURCES: Judith S. Wallerstein, Julia M. Lewis, and Sandra Blakeslee, *The Unexpected Legacy of Divorce* (New York: Hyperion, 2000); E. Mavis Hetherington and John Kelly, *For Better or for Worse: Divorce Reconsidered* (New York: W. W. Norton, 2002).

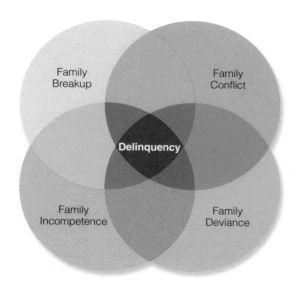

FIGURE 8.3
Family Influences on Behavior

Each of these four factors has been linked to antisocial behavior and delinquency. Interaction between these factors may escalate delinquent activity.

philosophy of the juvenile courts calls for official intervention when parental supervision is considered inadequate.[32] A number of subsequent studies, using self-report data, have failed to establish any clear-cut relationship between broken homes and delinquent behavior.[33] Boys and girls from intact families seem as likely to self-report delinquency as those whose parents are divorced or separated. Researchers concluded that the absence of parents has a greater effect on agents of the justice system than it does on the behavior of children.[34]

Divorce Reconsidered Although some researchers still question the divorce-delinquency link, there is growing sentiment that family breakup is traumatic and most likely has a direct influence on factors related to adolescent misbehavior.[35]

In her study of the effects of parental absence on children, sociologist Sara McLanahan found that children who grow up apart from their biological fathers typically do less well than children who grow up with both biological parents. They are less likely to finish high school and attend college, less likely to find and keep a steady job, and more likely to become teen mothers. Although most children who grow up with a single parent do quite well, differences between children in one- and two-parent families are significant, and there is fairly good evidence that father absence per se is responsible for some social problems.[36]

The McLanahan research has been supported by other studies showing that divorce is in fact related to delinquency and status offending, especially if a child had a close relationship with the parent who is forced to leave the home.[37] The effects of divorce seem gender-specific:

- Boys seem to be more affected by the post-divorce absence of the father. In post-divorce situations, fathers seem less likely to be around to solve problems, to discuss standards of conduct, or to enforce discipline. A divorced father who remains actively involved in his child's life reduces his son's chances of delinquency.

- Girls are more affected by both the quality of the mother's parenting and post-divorce parental conflict. It is possible that extreme levels of parental conflict may serve as a model to young girls coping with the aftermath of their parents' separation.[38]

- There are distinct racial and ethnic differences in the impact of divorce/separation on youth. Some groups (i.e., Hispanics, Asians) have been raised in cultures where divorce is rare and parents have less experience in developing childrearing practices that buffer the effects of family breakup on adolescent problem behavior.[39]

Divorce and Parental Deviance Divorce may influence children's misbehavior through its effect on parental misbehavior. As you may recall (Chapter 7) developmental/life-course theorists, such as Robert Sampson and John Laub, believe that a good marriage helps men "knife off" from misbehavior. If marriage helps subdue antisocial behavior, then it stands to reason that divorce may encourage *parental deviance*. Anger and rage that may have precipitated the dissolution of marriage may not be alleviated by separation. Research shows that domestic violence that may have been present in stress-filled marriages does not abate after separation but merely shifts to ex-partners who are targeted in the aftermath of divorce.[40] Parents who are in postdivorce turmoil may influence their children to misbehave.

When Sara Jaffee and her associates studied the quality of marriage they found that the less time fathers lived with their children, the more conduct problems their children had. However, when fathers engaged in high levels of antisocial behavior

EXHIBIT 8.1

The Family Structure–Delinquency Link

I Children growing up in families disrupted by parental death are better adjusted than children of divorce. Parental absence is not per se a cause of antisocial behavior.

I Remarriage does not lessen the effects of divorce on youth: Children living with a stepparent exhibit (a) as many problems as youths in divorce situations and (b) considerably more problems than do children living with both biological parents.

I Continued contact with the noncustodial parent has little effect on a child's well-being.

I Evidence that the behavior of children of divorce improves over time is inconclusive.

I Postdivorce conflict between parents is related to child maladjustment.

I Parental divorce raises the likelihood of teenage marriage.

SOURCES: Nicholas Wolfinger, "Parental Divorce and Offspring Marriage: Early or Late?" *Social Forces* 82: 337–354 (2003); Paul Amato and Bruce Keith, "Parental Divorce and the Well-Being of Children: A Meta-Analysis," *Psychological Bulletin* 110:26–46 (1991).

themselves, the more time they spent with their children, the more conduct problems their children had. Staying married, Jaffee concludes, may not be the answer to the problems faced by children living in single-parent families unless parents can refrain from deviant behaviors and become reliable sources of emotional and economic support.[41] The Focus on Delinquency feature entitled "For Better or for Worse: Does Divorce Matter?" examines the issue of divorce more closely. See Exhibit 8.1 for key findings on divorce.

Family Conflict

Not all unhappy marriages end in divorce; some continue in an atmosphere of conflict. Intrafamily conflict is a common experience in many American families.[42] The link between parental conflict and delinquency was established more than 50 years ago when F. Ivan Nye found that a child's perception of his or her parents' marital happiness was a significant predictor of delinquency.[43] Contemporary studies support these early findings that children who grow up in maladapted homes and witness discord or violence later exhibit emotional disturbance and behavior problems. Research efforts have consistently supported the relationship between family conflict, hostility, and delinquency.[44] There seems to be little difference between the behavior of children who merely *witness* **intrafamily violence** and those who are its *victims*.[45] In fact, some research efforts show that observing family conflict is a more significant determinant of delinquency than being its target.[46]

intrafamily violence
An environment of discord and conflict within the family; children who grow up in dysfunctional homes often exhibit delinquent behaviors, having learned at a young age that aggression pays off.

Although damaged parent-child relationships are associated with delinquency, it is difficult to assess the relationship. It is often assumed that preexisting family problems cause delinquency, but it may also be true that children who act out put enormous stress on a family. Kids who are conflict prone may actually help to destabilize households. To avoid escalation of a child's aggression, these parents may give in to their children's demands. The children learn that aggression pays off.[47] Parents may feel overwhelmed and shut their child out of their lives. Adolescent misbehavior may be a precursor of family conflict; strife leads to more adolescent misconduct, producing an endless cycle of family stress and delinquency.[48]

Which is worse, growing up in a home marked by conflict or growing up in a broken home? Research shows that children in both broken homes and high-conflict intact homes were worse off than children in low-conflict, intact families.[49] However, even when parents are divorced, kids who maintain attachments to their parents are less likely to engage in delinquency than those who are alienated and detached.[50]

Family Competence

Children raised by parents who lack proper parenting skills are more at risk than those whose parents are supportive and effectively control their children in a noncoercive fashion.[51] While some parents are effective authority figures, others are overly permissive and indulgent, while still others are repressive and strict. Permissive and disengaged parenting and punitive parenting have been associated with negative behavioral outcomes.[52] The quality of parenting becomes more acute when kids lack other forms of social support. Research findings have shown that the impact of uninvolved and permissive parenting for problematic youth outcomes is greater in higher risk neighborhoods. In other words, parental competence is required if a youngster hopes to escape the carnage wrought by residence in a disorganized lower-class neighborhood.[53]

Parents of beyond-control youngsters have been found to be inconsistent rule-setters, to be less likely to show interest in their children, and to display high levels of hostile detachment. Children who feel inhibited with their parents and refuse to discuss important issues with them are more likely to engage in deviant activities. Kids who report having troubled home lives also exhibit lower levels of self-esteem and are more prone to antisocial behaviors.[54]

One reason for child-parent conflict is discipline style. Parents who rely solely on authoritarian disciplinary practices may be less successful than parents who are firm and consistent yet nurturing with their children. Holding a "my way or the highway" orientation and telling kids that "as long as you live in my house you will obey my rules" does little to improve communications and may instead produce kids who are rebellious and crime prone.[55]

Parental Efficacy If bad or incompetent parenting can produce antisocial children, can competent parenting produce an opposite result? Studies show that delinquency will be reduced if both or at least one parent can provide the type of structure that integrates children into families, while giving them the ability to assert their individuality and regulate their own behavior.[56] This phenomenon is referred to as **parental efficacy**.[57] In some cultures emotional support from the mother is critical, whereas in others the father's support remains the key factor.[58] Adolescents whose parents maintain close relationships with them report less delinquent behavior and substance use regardless of the type of family structure—that is, blended families, same-sex parents, and so on. This finding suggests that the quality of parent-adolescent relationships better predicts adolescent outcomes than family type.[59]

The importance of close relations with the family may diminish as children reach late adolescence and develop stronger peer-group relations, but most experts believe family influence remains considerable throughout life.[60] While the consensus of opinion is that family relations is a key factor in antisocial behavior, the Focus on Delinquency feature entitled "The Chicken or the Egg?" shows that not all experts agree on the direction of this association.

Inconsistent Discipline Studies show that the parents of delinquent youths tend to be inconsistent disciplinarians, either overly harsh or extremely lenient.[61] But what conclusions can we draw from this observation?

The link between discipline and deviant behavior is uncertain. Most Americans still support the use of corporal punishment in disciplining children. The use of physical punishment cuts across racial, ethnic, and religious groups.[62] However, despite this public support, there is growing evidence of a "violence begetting violence" cycle. Children who are subject to even minimal amounts of physical punishment may be more likely to use violence themselves; the effect seems greatest among Caucasian children and less among African American and Latino children.[63]

Sociologist Murray Straus reviewed the concept of discipline in a series of surveys and found a powerful relationship between exposure to physical punishment and later aggression.[64]

parental efficacy
Families in which parents are able to integrate their children into the household unit while at the same time helping assert their individuality and regulate their own behavior.

The Chicken or the Egg?

Which comes first, bad parents or bad kids? Does poor parenting cause delinquency or do delinquents undermine their parents' supervisory abilities? In a recent survey, David Huh and colleagues surveyed almost 500 adolescent girls from eight different schools to determine their perceived parental support and control and whether they engage in problem behaviors such as lying, stealing, running away, or substance abuse. Huh and his colleagues found little evidence that poor parenting is a direct cause of children's misbehavior problems or that it escalates misbehavior. Rather, their results suggested that children's problem behaviors undermine parenting effectiveness. *Increases* in adolescent behavior problems, such as substance abuse, resulted in *decreases* in parental control and support. Low parental control played a small role in escalating behavior problems. Huh suggests it is possible that the parents of adolescents who consistently misbehave may become more tolerant of their behavior and give up on attempts at control. As their kids' behaviors become increasingly threatening, parents may detach and reject adolescents exhibiting problem behavior.

Huh is not alone. In her provocative book *The Nurture Assumption*, psychologist Judith Rich Harris questions the cherished belief that parents play an important role in a child's upbringing. Instead of family influence, Harris claims that genetics and environment determine, to a large extent, how a child turns out. Children's own temperament and peer relations shape their behavior and modify the characteristics they were born with; their interpersonal relations determine the kind of people they will be when they mature.

Harris reasons that parenting skills may be irrelevant to children's future success. Most parents don't have a single child-rearing style, and they may treat each child in the family independently. They are more permissive with their mild-mannered kids and more strict and punitive with those who are temperamental or defiant. Even if every child were treated the same in a family, this would not explain why siblings raised in the same family under relatively similar conditions turn out so differently. Those sent to day care are quite similar to those who remain at home; having working parents seems to have little long-term effect. Family structure also does not seem to matter: Adults who grew up in one-parent homes are as likely to be successful as those who were raised in two-parent households.

In addition to genetics, the child's total social environment is the other key influence that shapes behavior. Kids who act one way at home may be totally different at school or with their peers. Some who are mild-mannered around the house are hell-raisers in the school yard, whereas others who bully their siblings are docile with friends. Children may conform to parental expectations at home, but leave those expectations behind in their own social environment. Children develop their own culture with unique traditions, words, rules, and activities, which often conflict with parental and adult values.

GENETICS RATHER THAN PARENTING

Is it the chicken or the egg? Most theories of delinquency assume that factors related to parenting—discipline, socialization, learning—influence children. However, it is also possible that key traits associated with delinquent behaviors, such as low self-control, are inherited and not learned. Although Gottfredson and Hirschi, in their General Theory of Crime (see Chapter 6), claim that low self-control is a function of inadequate parenting, John Paul Wright and Kevin Beaver disagree. They counter that a large body of research shows that impulsivity and attention deficit/hyperactivity disorder—both of which are aspects of low self-control—are inherited. Therefore, what appears to be the effect of bad parenting is actually caused by "bad genes." Because of this genetic effect, the role of parenting may be more complicated than is typically assumed. Parents may help neutralize the effect of inherited traits, or the traits of parents may interact in unique ways with the traits of each of their children. It is possible the genetically determined traits of a child are likely to influence how a parent treats the child and not vice versa.

Critical Thinking

1. Some studies now show that a given parenting style can have different effects on children with different temperaments. The result is that parenting can function to make children in the same family different rather than alike. From your own experiences, do parents treat all siblings in the family in a similar fashion, or are there clear intersibling differences? How might parenting style influence children's behavior within a family?

2. Can teen rebellion be linked to poor parenting? After all, what parents would encourage their children to pierce their bodies or get tattoos?

SOURCES: David Huh, Jennifer Tristan, Emily Wade, and Eric Stice, "Does Problem Behavior Elicit Poor Parenting? A Prospective Study of Adolescent Girls," *Journal of Adolescent Research* 21:185–204 (2006); John Paul Wright and Kevin Beaver, "Do Parents Matter in Creating Self-Control in Their Children? A Genetically Informed Test of Gottfredson and Hirschi's Theory of Low Self-Control," *Criminology* 43:1169–1202 (2005); Judith Rich Harris, *The Nurture Assumption, Why Children Turn Out the Way They Do* (New York: Free Press, 1998).

Nonviolent societies are also ones in which parents rarely punish their children physically; there is a link between corporal punishment, delinquency, spousal abuse, and adult crime.[65] Research conducted in 10 European countries shows that the degree to which parents and teachers approve of corporal punishment is related to the homicide rate.[66]

Physical punishment weakens the bond between parents and children, lowers the children's self-esteem, and undermines their faith in justice. It is not surprising, then, that Straus finds a high correlation between physical discipline and street crime. It is possible that physical punishment encourages children to become more secretive and dishonest.[67] Overly strict discipline may have an even more insidious link to antisocial behaviors: abused children have a higher risk of neurological dysfunction than the nonabused, and brain abnormalities have been linked to violent crime.[68]

Inconsistent and Ineffective Supervision Evidence also exists that inconsistent supervision can promote delinquency. Early research by F. Ivan Nye found that mothers who threatened discipline but failed to carry it out were more likely to have delinquent children than those who were consistent in their discipline.[69]

Nye's early efforts have been supported by research showing a strong association between ineffective or negligent supervision and a child's involvement in delinquency.[70] The data show that youths who believe their parents care little about their activities are more likely to engage in criminal acts than those who believe their actions will be closely monitored.[71] Kids who are not closely supervised spend more time out in the community with their friends and are more likely to get into trouble. Poorly supervised kids may be more prone to acting impulsively and are therefore less able to employ self-control to restrain their activities.[72]

In contrast, children who are properly supervised, especially in disorganized areas, are less likely to succumb to the temptations of the streets. The ability of a family to provide parental supervision seems even more important for children growing up in poor neighborhoods with fewer social ties among adults. In these areas parents cannot call upon neighborhood resources to take up the burden of controlling children; there is, therefore, a greater burden placed on families to provide adequate supervision.[73]

Mother's Employment Parents who closely supervise their children, and have close ties with them, help reduce the likelihood of adolescent delinquent behavior.[74] When life circumstances prevent or interfere with adequate supervision, delinquent opportunities may increase. Some critics have suggested that even in intact homes, a working mother who is unable to adequately supervise her children provides the opportunity for delinquency. This phenomenon may be inflated by economic factors: In poor neighborhoods that lack collective efficacy, parents cannot call upon neighborhood resources to take up the burden of controlling children.[75]

While the suggestion that working mothers produce delinquent kids is troubling, the association is far from certain. There is also research that finds that a mother's employment may have little effect on youthful misbehavior.[76] So the true relationship between mother's employment and child misbehavior remains to be established.

Resource Dilution Parents may find it hard to control their children, because they have such large families that their resources, such as time, are spread too thin (**resource dilution**). It is also possible that the relationship is indirect, caused by the connection of family size to some external factor; resource dilution has been linked to educational underachievement, long considered a correlate of delinquency.[77] Middle children may suffer, because they are most likely to be home when large numbers of siblings are also at home and economic resources are most stretched.[78] Larger families are more likely to produce delinquents than smaller ones, and middle children are more likely to engage in delinquent acts than first- or last-born children.

Resource dilution may force some mothers into the workforce in order to support their young children. Critics have suggested that these working mothers are unable to adequately supervise their children, leaving them prone to delinquency. However, recent research by Thomas Vander Ven and his associates found that having a mother who is employed has little if any effect on youthful misbehavior, especially if the children are adequately supervised.[79]

resource dilution
A condition that occurs when parents have such large families that their resources, such as time and money, are spread too thin, causing lack of familial support and control.

Family Deviance

A number of studies have found that parental deviance has a powerful influence on delinquent behavior.[80] The effects can be both devastating and long term: The children of deviant parents produce delinquent children themselves.[81] Some of the most important data on the influence of parental deviance were gathered by British criminologist David Farrington, whose research involves longitudinal data he and his colleagues have obtained from a number of ongoing projects, including the Cambridge Youth Survey and the Cambridge Study in Delinquent Development (CSDD). Some of the most important results include:

▌ A significant number of delinquent youths have criminal fathers. About 8 percent of the sons of noncriminal fathers became chronic offenders, compared to 37 percent of youths with criminal fathers.[82]

▌ School yard bullying may be both inter- and intragenerational. Bullies have children who bully others, and these "second-generation bullies" grow up to become the fathers of children who are also bullies (see Chapter 10 for more on bullying in the school yard).[83] Thus, one family may have a grandfather, father, and son who are or were school yard bullies.[84]

▌ Kids whose parents go to prison are much more likely to be at risk to delinquency than children of nonincarcerated parents. While it is possible that parental separation caused by incarceration is the key factor, kids who suffer parental separation due to illness, death, or divorce are less likely to become delinquents. Separation caused by parental imprisonment predicted antisocial behaviors up to age 32, signaling the long-term consequences of parental deviance.[85]

The cause of intergenerational deviance is uncertain. A number of factors may play a role:

▌ *Inheritance/genetic factors.* The link between parental deviance and child misbehavior may be genetic.[86] Parents of delinquent youth have been found to suffer neurological conditions linked to antisocial behaviors, and these conditions may be inherited genetically.[87] It is possible that childhood misbehavior is strongly genetically influenced, with little or no environmental or experiential effect.[88] If children behave like their parents, it's because they share the same genes and not because they have learned to be bad or live in an environment that causes both parental and child misbehaviors.

There is a strong association between parental and children's deviance. In this photo from surveillance videotape in a Bedford, New Hampshire, store, a woman with her daughter (behind the counter) and her son (at left) are shown in the process of stealing more than $2,000 worth of jewelry. The woman turned herself in after Bedford police made the video public.

- *Substance abuse.* Children of drug-abusing parents are more likely to get involved in drug abuse and delinquency than the children of nonabusers.[89] This link might have a biological basis: Parental substance abuse can produce children with neurological impairments that are related to delinquency.[90]
- *Parenting ability.* The link between parental deviance and child delinquency may be shaped by parenting ability: Deviant parents are the ones least likely to have close relationships with their offspring. They are more likely to use overly harsh and inconsistent discipline, a parenting style that has consistently been linked to the onset of delinquent behavior.[91] Parents who themselves have been involved in crime exhibit lower levels of effective parenting and greater association with factors that can impede their parenting abilities (e.g., substance abuse and mental illness). Their children are more likely to have experienced such negative effects of ineffective parenting as abuse and out-of-home placement, factors highly associated with delinquency.[92]
- *Stigma.* The association between parental deviance and children's delinquency may be related to labeling and stigma. Social control agents may be quick to fix a delinquent label on the children of known law violators, increasing the likelihood that they will pick up an "official" delinquent label.[93] The resulting stigma increases the chances they may fall into a delinquent career.

Sibling Deviance   Some evidence also exists that siblings may influence behavior too; research shows that if one sibling is a delinquent there is a significant likelihood that his brother or sister will engage in delinquent behaviors.[94] Not surprisingly, siblings who maintain a warm relationship and feel close to one another are also likely to behave in a similar fashion. If one of these siblings takes drugs and engages in delinquent behavior, so too will his brother or sister.[95] A number of interpretations of these data are possible:

- Siblings who live in the same environment are influenced by similar social and economic factors; it is not surprising that their behavior is similar.
- Deviance is genetically determined, and the traits that cause one sibling to engage in delinquency are shared by his or her brother or sister.
- Deviant siblings grow closer because of shared interests. It is possible that the relationship is due to personal interactions: Older siblings are imitated by younger siblings.

FOSTER CARE

foster care
Placing a child in the temporary care of a family other than its own as a result of state intervention into problems that are taking place within the birth family; can be used as a temporary shelter while a permanent adoption effort is being completed.

Every year, more than 250,000 children are removed from their homes due to parental absence, deviance, conflict, or incompetence.[96] In the 1960s, the number of children in **foster care** increased from 200,000 to 600,000, then fell back to about 200,000 by 1980 before beginning to increase once again, so that today there are more than 500,000 children in out-of-home placements. Many of these kids have already experienced multiple threats to their healthy development and safety. And to make matters worse, these vulnerable children then enter a fragmented foster care system that lacks the necessary resources, technical proficiency, and interagency coordination to provide families with needed services and supports. Various aspects of the current foster care population are noteworthy:

- African American children comprise the largest proportion of children in care.
- Over one-quarter of all children in care are under age 5.
- Most children are placed in nonrelative foster homes, but substantial numbers are also placed with relatives or in group homes or institutions.
- Of those children exiting care, most are reunited with their birth parents or primary caretakers, or are adopted.

While some kids find it a haven from a troubled home life, others have trouble in foster care. Vermonter Kellie Coakley, 23, fled her foster family at age 17, and months later got pregnant. Coakley says her life may have taken a different turn if she had the possibility of staying in foster care after her 18th birthday. Vermont officials are hoping a change in state law, which allows kids to remain in foster care until they're 22, will help make the road to adulthood less bumpy.

I A child is more likely to enter care due to neglect than due to physical, sexual, and psychological abuse combined.[97]

Living within the foster care system can be a trying and emotionally traumatic experience for children. It is estimated that somewhere between 30 to 80 percent of children in foster care exhibit emotional and/or behavioral problems. Many are traumatized by their experiences before entering foster care, while others are troubled by the foster care experience itself. Within three months of placement, many children exhibit signs of depression, aggression, or withdrawal. Children in foster care are often forced to change schools, placing them at risk educationally. It comes as no surprise that many youths leaving foster care end up in jail or on public assistance.[98]

Are kids better off being taken from a conflict-ridden or otherwise troubled home care situation and placed in foster care? A recent study using the advanced analytic tools of applied economics shows that children faced with two options—being allowed to stay at home or being placed into foster care—have generally better life outcomes when they remain with their families. Economist Joseph Doyle used a randomized design and found that children on the margin of foster care placement have better employment, delinquency, and teen motherhood outcomes when they remain at home. Among the findings:[99]

I Only 14 percent of young adults were arrested at least once when staying at home and 44 percent were arrested when going to foster care.

I Only 33 percent became teen mothers when staying at home and 56 percent became mothers when going to foster care.

I At least 33 percent held a job for at least three months when staying at home and only 20 percent held a job for at least three months when going to foster care.

This outcome is significant considering the number of kids in foster care today: Doyle's research suggests that keeping families intact will produce better results and therefore a greater portion of the social welfare budget should be spent on family preservation.

CHILD ABUSE AND NEGLECT

Concern about the quality of family life has increased because of reports that many children are physically abused or neglected by their parents and that this treatment has serious consequences for their behavior over the life course. Because of this topic's importance, the remainder of this chapter is devoted to the issue of child abuse and neglect and its relationship with delinquent behavior.

Historical Foundation

Parental abuse and neglect are not modern phenomena. Maltreatment of children has occurred throughout history. Some concern for the negative effects of such maltreatment was voiced in the eighteenth century in the United States, but concerted efforts to deal with the problem did not begin until 1874.

In that year, residents of a New York City apartment building reported to public health nurse Etta Wheeler that a child in one of the apartments was being abused by her stepmother. The nurse found a young child named Mary Ellen Wilson who had been repeatedly beaten and was malnourished from a diet of bread and water. Even though the child was seriously ill, the police agreed that the law entitled the parents to raise Mary Ellen as they saw fit. The New York City Department of Charities claimed it had no custody rights over Mary Ellen.

According to legend, Mary Ellen's removal from her parents had to be arranged through the Society for the Prevention of Cruelty to Animals (SPCA) on the ground that she was a member of the animal kingdom. The truth, however, is less sensational: Mary Ellen's case was heard by a judge. Because the child needed protection, she was placed in an orphanage.[100] The SPCA was actually founded the following year.[101]

Little research into the problems of maltreated children occurred before that of C. Henry Kempe, of the University of Colorado. In 1962, Kempe reported the results of a survey of medical and law-enforcement agencies that indicated the child abuse rate was much higher than had been thought. He coined a term, **battered child syndrome**, which he applied to cases of nonaccidental injury of children by their parents or guardians.[102]

Defining Abuse and Neglect

Kempe's pioneering work has been expanded in a more generic expression of **child abuse** that includes neglect as well as physical abuse. Specifically, it describes any physical or emotional trauma to a child for which no reasonable explanation, such as an accident, can be found. Child abuse is generally seen as a pattern of behavior rather than a single act. The effects of a pattern of behavior are cumulative. That is, the longer the abuse continues, the more severe the effect will be.[103]

Although the terms "child abuse" and "neglect" are sometimes used interchangeably, they represent different forms of maltreatment. **Neglect** refers to deprivations children suffer at the hands of their parents (lack of food, shelter, health care, love). Abuse is a more overt form of aggression against the child, one that often requires medical attention. The distinction between the terms is often unclear because, in many cases, both abuse and neglect occur simultaneously. What are the forms that abuse and neglect may take?

- *Physical abuse* includes throwing, shooting, stabbing, burning, drowning, suffocating, biting, or deliberately disfiguring a child. Included within this category is shaken-baby syndrome (SBS), a form of child abuse affecting between 1,200 and 1,600 children every year. SBS is a collection of signs and symptoms resulting from violently shaking an infant or child.[104]

- *Physical neglect* results from parents' failure to provide adequate food, shelter, or medical care for their children, as well as failure to protect them from physical danger.

- *Emotional abuse* or neglect is manifested by constant criticism and rejection of the child.[105] Those who suffer emotional abuse have significantly lower self-esteem as adults.[106]

- *Emotional neglect* includes inadequate nurturing, inattention to a child's emotional development, and lack of concern about maladaptive behavior.

- *Abandonment* refers to the situation in which parents leave their children with the intention of severing the parent-child relationship.[107]

- *Sexual abuse* refers to the exploitation of children through rape, incest, and molestation by parents, family members, friends, or legal guardians. Sexual abuse can vary from rewarding children for sexual behavior that is inappropriate for their level of development to using force or the threat of force for the purposes of sex. It can involve children who are aware of the sexual content of their actions and others too young to have any idea what their actions mean.

battered child syndrome
Nonaccidental physical injury of children by their parents or guardians.

child abuse
Any physical, emotional, or sexual trauma to a child, including neglecting to give proper care and attention, for which no reasonable explanation can be found.

neglect
Passive neglect by a parent or guardian, depriving children of food, shelter, health care, and love.

abandonment
Parents physically leave their children with the intention of completely severing the parent-child relationship.

The Effects of Abuse

Regardless of how it is defined, the effects of abuse can be devastating. Mental health and delinquency experts have found that abused kids experience mental and social problems across their lifespan, ranging from substance abuse to possession of a damaged personality.[108] Children who have experienced some form of maltreatment possess mental representations characterized by a devalued sense of self, mistrust of others, a tendency to perceive hostility in others in situations where the intentions of others are ambiguous, and a tendency to generate antagonistic solutions to social conflicts. Victims of abuse are prone to suffer mental illness, such as dissociative identity disorder (DID) (sometimes known as multiple personality disorder [MPD]); research shows that child abuse is present in the histories of the vast majority of DID subjects.[109] Children who experience maltreatment are at increased risk for adverse health effects and behaviors across the life course, including smoking, alcoholism, drug abuse, eating disorders, severe obesity, depression, suicide, sexual promiscuity, and certain chronic diseases.[110] Maltreatment during infancy or early childhood can cause brain impairment, leading to physical, mental, and emotional problems such as sleep disturbances, panic disorder, and attention deficit/hyperactivity disorder. Brain dysfunction is particularly common among victims of shaken baby syndrome: About 25 to 30 percent of infant victims with SBS die from their injuries; nonfatal consequences of SBS include varying degrees of visual impairment (e.g., blindness), motor impairment (e.g., cerebral palsy) and cognitive impairments.[111]

Psychologists suggest that maltreatment encourages children to use aggression as a means of solving problems and prevents them from feeling empathy for others. It diminishes their ability to cope with stress and makes them vulnerable to the violence in the culture. Abused children have fewer positive interactions with peers, are less well liked, and are more likely to have disturbed social interactions.[112]

Sexual Abuse Adolescent victims of sexual abuse are particularly at risk to stress and anxiety.[113] Kids who have undergone traumatic sexual experiences have been later found to suffer psychological deficits.[114] Many run away to escape their environment, which puts them at risk for juvenile arrest and involvement with the justice system.[115] Others suffer post-traumatic mental problems, including acute stress disorders, depression, eating disorders, nightmares, anxiety, suicidal ideation, and other psychological problems.[116] Stress, however, does not end in childhood. Children who are psychologically, sexually, or physically abused are more likely to suffer low self-esteem and be more suicidal as adults.[117] They are also placed at greater risk to be reabused as adults than those who escaped childhood victimization.[118] The reabused carry higher risks for psychological and physical problems, ranging from sexual promiscuity to increased HIV infection rates.[119] Abuse as a child may lead to despair, depression, and even homelessness as adults. One study of homeless women found that they were much more likely than other women to report childhood physical abuse, childhood sexual abuse, adult physical assault, previous sexual assault in adulthood, and a history of mental health problems.[120]

The Extent of Child Abuse

It is almost impossible to estimate the extent of child abuse. Many victims are so young that they have not learned to communicate. Some are too embarrassed or afraid to do so. Many incidents occur behind closed doors, and even when another adult witnesses inappropriate or criminal behavior, the adult may not want to get involved in a "family matter." Some indications of the severity of the problem came from a groundbreaking 1980 survey conducted by sociologists Richard Gelles and Murray Straus.[121] Gelles and Straus estimated that between 1.4 and 1.9 million children in the United States were subject to physical abuse from their parents. This abuse was rarely a onetime act. The average number of assaults per year was 10.5, and the median was 4.5. Gelles and Straus also found that 16 percent of the couples in their sample reported spousal abuse; 50 percent of the multichild families reported attacks between siblings; 20 percent of the families reported incidents in which children attacked parents.[122]

The Gelles and Straus survey was a milestone in identifying child abuse as a national phenomenon. Subsequent surveys conducted in 1985 and 1992 indicated that the incidence of severe violence toward children had declined.[123] One reason was that parental approval of corporal punishment, which stood at 94 percent in 1968, decreased to 68 percent by 1994.[124] Recognition of the problem may have helped moderate cultural values and awakened parents to the dangers of physically disciplining children. Nonetheless, more than 1 million children were still being subjected to severe violence annually. If the definition of "severe abuse" used in the survey had included hitting with objects such as a stick or a belt, the number of child victims would have been closer to 7 million per year.

Monitoring Abuse Since the pioneering efforts by Gelles and Straus, the Department of Health and Human Services has been monitoring the extent of child maltreatment through its annual survey of Child Protective Services (CPS). The most recent survey available finds that:

- Approximately 3.3 million allegations of child abuse and neglect including 6 million children were made to CPS agencies. About 62 percent of those allegations reached the report stage and either were investigated or received an alternative response. Nearly 30 percent (28.5 percent) of the investigations that reached the report stage determined that at least one child was a victim of child abuse or neglect.

- An estimated 899,000 children in the 50 states, the District of Columbia, and Puerto Rico were determined to be victims of abuse or neglect.

- Since 2001, the rate and number of children who received an investigation have been increasing. For 2001, the rate was 43 children per 1,000 children, resulting in an estimated 3,136,000 children who received an investigation; today, the rate is 48, resulting in an estimated 3,598,000 investigations.

- Of kids who were found to be abused, about 63 percent of child victims experienced neglect, 17 percent were physically abused, 9 percent were sexually abused, and 7 percent were emotionally or psychologically maltreated.

- About 1,500 children die of abuse or neglect each year.[125]

Who are the victims of abuse? There is a direct association between age and abuse: Victimization rates are higher for younger children than their older brothers and sisters (Figure 8.4). There are also racial differences in the abuse rate: African American children, Pacific Islander children, and American Indian or Alaska Native children suffer child abuse rates (per 1,000 children) far higher than European American children, Hispanic children, and Asian children.

Sexual Abuse Attempts to determine the extent of sexual abuse indicate that perhaps 1 in 10 boys and 1 in 3 girls have been the victims of some form of sexual exploitation. Richard J. Estes and Neil Alan Weiner, two researchers at the School of Social Welfare at the University of Pennsylvania, found that the problem of child sexual abuse is much more widespread than was previously believed or documented. Their research indicated that each year in the United States 325,000 children are subjected to some form of sexual exploitation, which includes sexual abuse, prostitution, use in pornography, and molestation by adults. Most are European American and middle-class. Equal numbers of boys and girls are involved, but the activities of boys generally receive less attention from authorities. Many of these kids are runaways (more than 120,000) whereas others have fled mental hospitals and foster homes. More than 50,000 are thrown out of their home by a parent or guardian.[126]

Preventing child abuse before it occurs is the aim of **Prevent Child Abuse America**. Checkout their website via academic.cengage.com/criminaljustice/siegel.

Age group

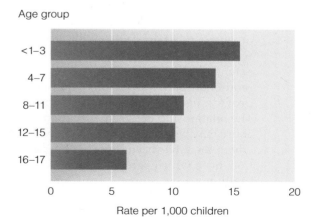

FIGURE 8.4
Victimization Rates by Age Group

SOURCE: Department of Health and Human Services, *Child Maltreatment, 2005*, www.acf.hhs.gov/programs/cb/pubs/cm05/cm05.pdf (accessed October 18, 2007).

Although sexual abuse is still quite prevalent, the number of reported cases has been in significant decline.[127] These data may either mean that the actual number of cases is truly in decline or that social service professionals are failing to recognize abuse cases because of overwork and understaffing.

Who Commits Abuse?

The most recent child maltreatment survey found that nearly 84 percent of victims were abused by a parent acting alone or with another person. Most victims of child abuse (40 percent) were maltreated by their mothers acting alone, another 18 percent were maltreated by their fathers acting alone, and 17 percent were abused by both parents. As Figure 8.5 shows, about 11 percent of maltreatment victims were abused by a nonparent such as a foster parent, child day care staff, unmarried partner of parent, legal guardian, or residential facility staff.

Causes of Child Abuse and Neglect

Why do these people abuse and hurt children? Maltreatment of children is a complex problem with neither a single cause nor a single solution. It cuts across racial, ethnic, religious, and socioeconomic lines. Abusive parents cannot be categorized by sex, age, or educational level.

Of all factors associated with child abuse, three are discussed most often: (1) parents who themselves suffered abuse tend to abuse their own children; (2) the presence of an unrelated adult increases the risk of abuse; and (3) isolated and alienated families tend to become abusive. A cyclical pattern of violence seems to be perpetuated from one generation to another. Evidence indicates that a large number of abused and neglected children grow into adulthood with a tendency to engage in violent behavior. The behavior of abusive parents can often be traced to negative experiences in their own childhood—physical abuse, emotional neglect, and incest. These parents become unable to separate their own childhood traumas from their relationships with their children. Abusive parents often have unrealistic perceptions of normal development. When their children are unable to act appropriately—when they cry or strike their parents—the parents may react in an abusive manner.[128]

Parents may also become abusive if they are isolated from friends, neighbors, or relatives. Many abusive parents describe themselves as alienated from their extended families, and they lack close relationships with persons who could provide help in stressful situations.[129] The relationship between alienation and abuse may be particularly acute in homes where there has been divorce or separation, or in which parents have never actually married; abusive punishment in single-parent homes has been found to be twice that of two-parent families.[130] Parents who are unable to cope with stressful events—divorce, financial stress, recurring mental illness, drug addiction—are most at risk.[131]

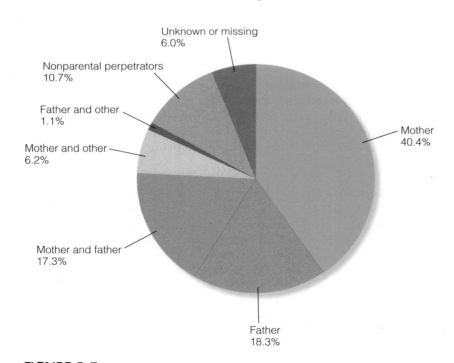

Unknown or missing
6.0%

Nonparental perpetrators
10.7%

Father and other
1.1%

Mother and other
6.2%

Mother and father
17.3%

Father
18.3%

Mother
40.4%

FIGURE 8.5

Abuse Victims by Perpetrator Relationship

SOURCE: Department of Health and Human Services, *Child Maltreatment, 2005*, www.acf.hhs.gov/programs/cb/pubs/cm05/cm05.pdf (accessed October 18, 2007).

Despite a decline in rate, child abuse and neglect remain all too common national phenomena. Jeffrey Caudill (left) pleaded guilty to child endangering charges in the Franklin County Court of Common Pleas in Columbus, Ohio, on June 20, 2006, for torturing his two stepchildren by firing a BB gun at them and locking them in containers partially filled with water. He was sentenced to 10 years in prison. His wife, Shelly Caudill, pleaded guilty to three counts of permitting child abuse.

Substance Abuse and Child Abuse Abusive families suffer from severe stress, and it is therefore not surprising that they frequently harbor members who turn to drugs and alcohol. Studies have found a strong association between child abuse and parental alcoholism.[132] In addition, evidence exists of a significant relationship between cocaine and heroin abuse and neglect and abuse of children. Because this relationship is so important, it is explored further in the Focus on Delinquency feature, "Relationship between Substance Abuse and Child Maltreatment."

Stepparents and Abuse Research indicates that stepchildren share a greater risk for abuse than do biological offspring.[133] Stepparents may have less emotional attachment to the children of another. Often the biological parent has to choose between the new mate and the child, sometimes even becoming an accomplice in the abuse.[134]

Stepchildren are overrepresented in cases of **familicide**, mass murders in which a spouse and one or more children are slain. It is also more common for fathers who kill their biological children to commit suicide than those who kill stepchildren, an indication that the latter act is motivated by hostility and not despair.[135]

familicide
Mass murders in which a spouse and one or more children are slain.

Social Class and Abuse Surveys indicate a high rate of reported abuse and neglect among people in lower economic classes. Children from families with a household income of less than $15,000 per year experience more abuse than children living in more affluent homes. Child care workers indicate that most of their clients either live in poverty or face increased financial stress because of unemployment and economic recession. These findings suggest that parental maltreatment of children is predominantly a lower-class problem. Is this conclusion valid?

One view is that low-income families, especially those headed by a single parent, are often subject to greater environmental stress and have fewer resources to deal with such stress than families with higher incomes.[136] A relationship seems to exist between the burdens of raising a child without adequate resources and the use of excessive force. Self-report surveys do show that indigent parents are more likely than affluent parents to hold attitudes that condone physical chastisement of children.[137]

Relationship between Substance Abuse and Child Maltreatment

The relationship between parental alcohol or other drug problems and child maltreatment is becoming increasingly evident. It is a serious problem because substance abuse is so widespread: An estimated 14 million adult Americans abuse alcohol, and there may be more than 12 million illicit drug users. With more than 6 million children under the age of 18 living in alcoholic households, and an additional number living in households where parents have problems with illicit drugs, it is evident that a significant number of children in this country are being raised by addicted parents.

DO PARENTAL ALCOHOL OR OTHER DRUG PROBLEMS CAUSE CHILD MALTREATMENT?

Research clearly indicates a connection between substance abuse and child abuse. Among confirmed cases of child maltreatment, 40 percent involve the use of alcohol or other drugs. This suggests that, of the 900,000 confirmed victims of child maltreatment each year, an estimated 360,000 children are mistreated by a caretaker with alcohol or other drug problems. In addition, research suggests that alcohol and other drug problems are factors in a majority of cases of emotional abuse and neglect. In fact, neglect is the main reason why children are removed from a home in which parents have alcohol or other drug problems. Children in these homes suffer from a variety of physical, mental, and emotional health problems at a greater rate than do children in the general population. Children of alcoholics suffer more injuries and poisonings than do children in the general population. Alcohol and other substances may act as disinhibitors, lessening impulse control and allowing parents to behave abusively. Children in this environment often demonstrate behavioral problems and are diagnosed as having conduct disorders. This may result in provocative behavior. Increased stress resulting from preoccupation with drugs on the part of the parent combined with behavioral problems exhibited by the child increases the likelihood of maltreatment. Frequently, these parents suffer from depression, anxiety, and low self-esteem. They live in an atmosphere of stress and family conflict. Children raised in such households are themselves more likely to have problems with alcohol and other drugs.

IN WHAT WAYS ARE CHILDREN AFFECTED?

Children of alcoholics are more likely than children in the general population to suffer a variety of physical, mental, and emotional health problems. They often have feelings of low self-esteem and failure and suffer from depression and anxiety.

It is thought that exposure to violence in both alcohol-abusing and child-maltreating households increases the likelihood that the children will commit, and be recipients of, acts of violence. The effects don't end when these children reach adulthood; they may have difficulty coping with and establishing healthy relationships as adults. In addition to suffering from all the effects of living in a household where alcohol or child-maltreatment problems exist, children whose parents abuse illicit drugs live with the knowledge that their parents' actions are illegal. Although the research is in its infancy, clinical evidence shows that children of parents who have problems with illicit drug use may suffer from an inability to trust legitimate authority because of fear of discovery of a parent's illegal habits.

As they mature, many fall victim to the same patterns exhibited by their parents. Those who have been severely physically abused often have symptoms of post-traumatic stress disorder and dissociation. Individuals suffering from mental health disorders may use alcohol and illicit drugs to decrease or mitigate their psychological distress. Research suggests that adults who were abused as children may be more likely to abuse their own children than adults who were not abused as children.

Can child maltreatment, when alcohol or other drugs are a problem, be successfully treated? Research has shown that when families exhibit both of these behaviors, the problems must be treated simultaneously in order to ensure a child's safety. Although ending the drug dependency does not automatically end child maltreatment, very little can be done to improve parenting skills until this step is taken. The withdrawal experienced by parents who cease using alcohol or other drugs presents specific risks. The effects of withdrawal often cause a parent to experience intense emotions, which may increase the likelihood of child maltreatment. During this time, lasting as long as two years, it is especially important that resources be available to the family.

Critical Thinking

1. Considering the substance abuse–child abuse association, should the government be proactive in removing kids from homes where parents are known substance abusers?

2. Does the substance abuse–child abuse link support or contradict the view that delinquent behavior is inherited?

SOURCE: *The Relationship Between Parental Alcohol or Other Drug Problems and Child Maltreatment* (Chicago: Prevent Child Abuse America, 2000).

Higher rates of maltreatment in low-income families reflect the stress caused by the limited resources that lower-class parents have to help them raise their children; in contrast, middle-class parents devote a smaller percentage of their total resources to raising a family.[138] This burden becomes especially onerous in families with emotionally and physically handicapped children. Stressed-out parents may consider special-needs children a drain on the families' finances with little potential for future success; research finds that children with disabilities are maltreated at a rate almost double that of other children.[139]

THE CHILD PROTECTION SYSTEM: PHILOSOPHY AND PRACTICE

For most of our nation's history, courts have assumed that parents have the right to bring up their children as they see fit. In the 2000 case, *Troxel v. Granville*, the Supreme Court ruled that the due process clause of the Constitution protects against government interference with certain fundamental rights and liberty interests, including parents' fundamental right to make decisions concerning the care, custody, and control of their children.[140] If the care a child receives falls below reasonable standards, the state may take action to remove the child from the home and place her or him in a less threatening environment. In these extreme circumstances, the rights of both parents and children are constitutionally protected. In the cases of *Lassiter v. Department of Social Services* and *Santosky v. Kramer*, the U.S. Supreme Court recognized the child's right to be free from parental abuse and set down guidelines for a termination-of-custody hearing, including the right to legal representation.[141] States provide a guardian *ad litem* (a lawyer appointed by the court to look after the interests of those who do not have the capacity to assert their own rights). States also ensure confidentiality of reporting.[142]

Although child protection agencies have been dealing with abuse and neglect since the late nineteenth century, recent awareness of the problem has prompted judicial authorities to take increasingly bold steps to ensure the safety of children.[143] The assumption that the parent-child relationship is inviolate has been challenged. In 1974, Congress passed the Child Abuse Prevention and Treatment Act (CAPTA), which provides funds to states to bolster their services for maltreated children and their parents.[144] The act provides federal funding to states in support of prevention, investigation, and treatment. It also provides grants to public agencies and nonprofit organizations for demonstration programs.

The Child Abuse Prevention and Treatment Act has been the impetus for the states to improve the legal frameworks of their child protection systems. Abusive parents are subject to prosecution under statutes against assault, battery, and homicide.

Investigating and Reporting Abuse

Maltreatment of children can easily be hidden from public view. Although state laws require doctors, teachers, and others who work with children to report suspected cases to child protection agencies, many maltreated children are out of the law's reach, because they are too young for school or because their parents do not take them to a doctor or a hospital. Parents abuse their children in private, and even when confronted, often accuse their children of lying or blame the children's medical problems on accidents. Social service agencies must find more effective ways to locate abused children and handle such cases once found.

All states have statutes requiring that persons suspected of abuse and neglect be reported. Many have made failure to report child abuse a criminal offense. Though such statutes are rarely enforced, teachers and nurses have been criminally charged for failing to report abuse or neglect cases.[145]

Once reported to a child protection agency, the case is screened by an intake worker and then turned over to an investigative caseworker. In some jurisdictions, if CPS substantiates a report, the case will likely be referred to a law enforcement agency that will have the responsibility of investigating the case, collecting evidence that can later be used in court proceedings. If the caseworker determines that the child is in imminent danger of severe harm, the caseworker may immediately remove the child from the home. A court hearing must be held shortly after to approve custody. Stories abound of children erroneously taken from their homes, but it is much more likely that these "gatekeepers" will consider cases unfounded and take no action. Among the most common reasons for screening out cases is that the reporting party is involved in a child custody case, despite the research showing that the risk of abuse increases significantly in the aftermath of divorce.[146] One of the success stories is discussed in the Case Profile entitled "Joey's Story."

The Children's Bureau (CB), the oldest federal agency for children, is located in the U.S. Department of Health and Human Services' Administration for Children and Families, Administration on Children, Youth and Families. It is responsible for assisting states in the delivery of child welfare services, services designed to protect children and strengthen families. Check out their website via academic.cengage.com/criminaljustice/siegel.

Joey's Story

JOEY WILLIAMS ENTERED THE CHILD WELFARE SYSTEM AT THE AGE OF 9, WHEN IT WAS DISCOVERED THAT HE AND HIS YOUNGER SISTER AND BROTHER WERE BEING sexually abused by their stepfather. The children had also been experiencing neglect due to a lack of sufficient resources in the family; they often went without food or proper clothing. Joey's mother struggled to provide structure for the children, but she was also facing many personal problems of her own. All three of the children were acting out and having difficulties in school. When Joey's stepfather was incarcerated, the child welfare system placed the children in separate foster homes and began to provide services for the family with the goal of returning the children to their mother's home. Joey had a difficult time adjusting to foster care and being separated from his family.

At the age of 12, he was charged with sexual assault and labeled a "sexual offender." According to reports, Joey and another child about the same age, engaged in "consensual" sexual contact in the foster home. Joey was ordered to complete treatment for sexual offenders, was removed from the foster home, and entered a series of placements where he continued to have a very difficult time adjusting and maintaining positive behavior.

Joey spent several years in residential treatment centers and mental health hospitals, trying to get the help he needed. Professionals were concerned that he was a threat to the community, and therefore he could not be placed in a community setting. During this time, Joey completed all the required sexual offender treatment and never "reoffended"; however, he did continue to have significant behavior issues and to struggle with school. It was recommended by the court that Joey's mother participate in therapy and enter some programs that would assist the family and eventually facilitate Joey's return to his family, but she did not comply with those recommendations.

As Joey approached his 17th birthday, the professionals involved in his case began to prepare for him to exit the juvenile system. He had not committed any more law violations. His siblings had been able to return home to their mother, and it was decided that Joey, with significant family supports and interventions, would also be able to return home. The family entered intensive therapy, which utilized a "wrap-around" approach that focused on family strengths and on the positive aspects of their situation. The wrap-around service model shifts the focus away from pathologies and weaknesses, and works with the family to build on their assets, skills, and resources.

In Joey's family, there were many things going well. They needed some assistance getting a few items to meet the children's basic needs, but overall, they were doing much better in the areas of employment and housing. Joey received the correct combination of medications, appropriate therapy, and support to enable him to live at home again. Because he always had a passion for music, as part of his reintegration into the family home, wrap-around funds were utilized to purchase guitar lessons for him, providing structure and a positive and creative outlet. Joey, his family, and the team of professionals involved with his case worked together very closely for a period of six months. The transition home was difficult at times, but ultimately successful. Joey studied for his GED and worked hard to accomplish his educational goals. The younger siblings also began to show signs of improvement and Joey became a role model in his family. Joey is doing well today, has a full-time job, and has not had any further problems with the law. ■

CRITICAL THINKING

1. What is the responsibility of parents when their child is removed from their home?
2. What should happen in situations where parents are not following the juvenile court–ordered recommendations?

Even when there is compelling evidence of abuse, most social service agencies will try to involve the family in voluntary treatment. Post-investigation services are offered on a voluntary basis by child welfare agencies to ensure the safety of children. These services address the safety of the child and are usually based on an assessment of the family's strengths, weaknesses, and needs. Examples of post-investigation services include individual counseling, case management, family-based services (services provided to the entire family, such as counseling or family support), in-home services, foster care services, and court services. Each year more than 60 percent of victims received post-investigation services; and an estimated 317,000 children received foster care services as a result of an investigation.[147]

Case managers will do periodic follow-ups to determine if treatment plans are being followed. If parents are uncooperative, or if the danger to the children is so great that they must be removed from the home, a complaint will be filed in the criminal, family, or juvenile court system. To protect the child, the court could then issue temporary orders placing the child in shelter care during investigation, ordering services, or ordering suspected abusers to have no contact with the child.

The Process of State Intervention

Although procedures vary from state to state, most follow a similar legal process once a social service agency files a court petition alleging abuse or neglect.[148] Figure 8.6 diagrams this process.

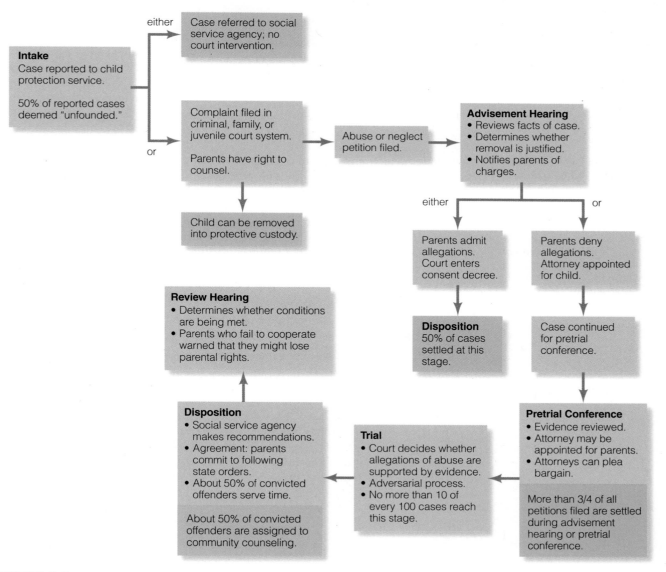

FIGURE 8.6
The Process of State Intervention in Cases of Abuse and Neglect

Usually no more than 10 out of every 100 abuse cases actually reach the trial stage. During this adversarial hearing, witnesses testify in order to prove the state's allegations. Here, Judge Timothy L. Cardwell listens to testimony from social worker Jo Johnson in Huron County Juvenile Court in Norwalk, Ohio, in a case involving abuse of adopted special-needs children. Johnson testified that some of the 11 adoptive special-needs children of Michael and Sharen Gravelle were found sleeping in cages.

If the allegation of abuse is confirmed, the child may be placed in protective custody. Most state statutes require that the court be notified "promptly" or "immediately" if the child is removed; some states, including Arkansas, North Carolina, and Pennsylvania, have gone as far as requiring that no more than 12 hours elapse before official action is taken. If the child has not been removed from the home, state authorities are given more time to notify the court of suspected abuse. Some states set a limit of 30 days to take action, whereas others mandate that state action take no more than 20 days once the case has been investigated.

When an abuse or neglect petition is prosecuted, an **advisement hearing** (also called a *preliminary protective hearing* or *emergency custody hearing*) is held. The court will review the facts of the case, determine whether permanent removal of the child is justified, and notify the parents of the charges against them. Parents have the right to counsel in all cases of abuse and neglect, and many states require the court to appoint an attorney for the child as well. If the parents admit the allegations, the court enters a consent decree, and the case is continued for disposition. Approximately one-half of all cases are settled by admission at the advisement hearing. If the parents deny the petition, an attorney is appointed for the child and the case is continued for a **pretrial conference**.

advisement hearing
A preliminary protective or temporary custody hearing in which the court will review the facts and determine whether removal of the child is justified and notify parents of the charges against them.

At the pretrial conference, the attorney for the social service agency presents an overview of the case and the evidence. Such matters as admissibility of photos and written reports are settled. At this point the attorneys can negotiate a settlement of the case, in which the parents accept a treatment plan detailing:

pretrial conference
The attorney for the social services agency presents an overview of the case, and a plea bargain or negotiated settlement can be agreed to in a consent decree.

▌ The types of services that the child and the child's family will receive, such as parenting classes, mental health or substance abuse treatment, and family counseling

▌ Reunification goals, including visitation schedules and a target date for a child's return home

▌ Concurrent plans for alternative permanent placement options should reunification goals not be met

About three-fourths of the cases that go to pretrial conference are settled by a consent decree. About 85 out of every 100 petitions filed are settled at either the advisement hearing or the pretrial conference. Of the 15 remaining cases, 5 are generally settled before trial. Usually no more than 10 cases out of every 100 actually reach the trial stage of the process. This is an adversarial hearing designed to prove the state's allegations.

disposition hearing
The social service agency presents its case plan and recommendations for care of the child and treatment of the parents, including incarceration and counseling or other treatment.

Disposition

The most crucial part of an abuse or neglect proceeding is the **disposition hearing**. The social service agency presents its case plan, which includes recommendations such as conditions for returning the child to the parents, or a visitation plan if the child is to be taken permanently from the parents. An agreement is reached by which the parents commit themselves to following the state orders. Between one-half and two-thirds of all convicted parents will be required to serve time in incarceration; almost half will be assigned to a form of treatment. As far as the children are concerned, some may be placed in temporary care; in other cases, parental rights are terminated and the child is placed in the custody of the child protective service. Legal custody can then be assigned to a relative or some other person.

In making their decisions, courts are guided by three interests: the role of the parents, protection for the child, and the responsibility of the state. Frequently, these interests conflict with each other. In fact, at times even the interests of the two parents are not in harmony. The state attempts to balance the parents' natural right to control their child's upbringing with the child's right to grow into adulthood free from harm. This is referred to as the **balancing-of-the-interests approach**.

Periodically, **review hearings** are held to determine if the conditions of the case plan are being met. Parents who fail to cooperate are warned that they may lose their parental rights. Most abuse and neglect cases are concluded within a year. Either the parents lose their rights and the child is given a permanent placement, or the child is returned to the parents and the court's jurisdiction ends.

The Abused Child in Court

One of the most significant problems associated with abuse cases is the trauma a child must go through in a court hearing. Children get confused and frightened and may change their testimony. Much controversy has arisen over the accuracy of children's reports of physical and sexual abuse, resulting in hung juries. Prosecutors and experts have been accused of misleading children or eliciting incriminating testimony. In probably what is the most well-known case, the McMartin Day Care case in California, children told not only of being sexually abused but also of being forced to participate in bizarre satanic rituals during which the McMartins mutilated animals and forced the children to touch corpses in hidden underground passageways. Prosecutors decided not to press forward after two trials ended in deadlock. Some jurors, when interviewed after the verdict, said that although they believed that children had been abused, the interviewing techniques used by prosecutors had been so suggestive that they had not been able to discern what really happened.[149]

State jurisdictions have instituted procedures to minimize the trauma to the child. Most have enacted legislation allowing videotaped statements or interviews with child witnesses taken at a preliminary hearing or at a formal deposition to be admissible in court. Videotaped testimony spares child witnesses the trauma of testifying in open court. States that allow videotaped testimony usually put some restrictions on its use: Some prohibit the government from calling the child to testify at trial if the videotape is used; some states require a finding that the child is "medically unavailable" because of the trauma of the case before videotaping can be used; some require that the defendant be present during the videotaping; a few specify that the child not be able to see or hear the defendant.

Most of the states now allow a child's testimony to be given on closed-circuit television (CCTV). The child is able to view the judge and attorneys, and the courtroom participants are able to observe the child. The standards for CCTV testimony vary widely. Some states, such as New Hampshire, assume that any child witness under age 12 would benefit from not having to appear in court. Others require an independent examination by a mental health professional to determine whether there is a "compelling need" for CCTV testimony.

In addition to innovative methods of testimony, children in sexual abuse cases have been allowed to use anatomically correct dolls to demonstrate happenings that they cannot describe verbally. The Victims of Child Abuse Act of 1990 allows children to use these dolls when testifying in federal courts; at least eight states have passed similar legislation.[150] Similarly, states have relaxed their laws of evidence to allow

balancing-of-the-interests approach
Efforts of the courts to balance the parents' natural right to raise a child with the child's right to grow into adulthood free from physical abuse or emotional harm.

review hearings
Periodic meetings to determine whether the conditions of the case plan for an abused child are being met by the parents or guardians of the child.

hearsay

Out-of-court statements made by one person and recounted in court by another; such statements are generally not allowed as evidence except in child abuse cases wherein a child's statements to social workers, teachers, or police may be admissible.

out-of-court statements by the child to a social worker, teacher, or police officer to be used as evidence (such statements would otherwise be considered hearsay). Typically, corroboration is required to support these statements if the child does not also testify.

The prevalence of sexual abuse cases has created new problems for the justice system. Often accusations are made in conjunction with marital disputes. The fear is growing that children may become pawns in custody battles; the mere suggestion of sexual abuse is enough to affect the outcome of a divorce action. The justice system must develop techniques that can get at the truth without creating a lifelong scar on the child's psyche.

Legal Issues A number of cases have been brought before the Supreme Court testing the right of children to present evidence at trial using nontraditional methods. Two issues stand out. One is the ability of physicians and mental health professionals to testify about statements made to them by children, especially when the children are incapable of testifying. The second concerns the way children testify in court.

In a 1992 case, *White v. Illinois,* the Supreme Court ruled that the state's attorney is not required to produce young victims at trial or to demonstrate the reason why they were unavailable to serve as witnesses.[151] *White* involved statements given by the child to the child's baby-sitter and mother, a doctor, a nurse, and a police officer concerning the alleged assailant in a sexual assault case. The prosecutor twice tried to call the child to testify, but both times the 4-year-old experienced emotional difficulty and could not appear in court. The outcome hinged solely on the testimony of the five witnesses.

By allowing others to testify as to what the child said, *White* removed the requirement that prosecutors produce child victims in court. This facilitates the prosecution of child abusers in cases where a court appearance by a victim would prove too disturbing or where the victim is too young to understand the court process.[152] The Court noted that statements made to doctors during medical examinations or those made when a victim is upset carry more weight than ones made after careful reflection. The Court ruled that such statements can be repeated during trial, because the circumstances in which they were made could not be duplicated simply by having the child testify to them in court.

In-Court Statements Children who are victims of sexual or physical abuse often make poor witnesses. Yet their testimony may be crucial. In a 1988 case, *Coy v. Iowa,* the Supreme Court placed limitations on efforts to protect child witnesses in court. During a sexual assault case, a "one-way" glass screen was set up so that the child victims would not be able to view the defendant (the defendant, however, could view the witnesses).[153] The Iowa statute that allowed the protective screen assumed that children would be traumatized by their courtroom experience. The court ruled that unless there is a finding that the child witness needs special protection, the Sixth Amendment of the Constitution grants defendants "face-to-face" confrontation with their accusers. In her dissenting opinion, Justice Sandra Day O'Connor suggested that if courts found it necessary, it would be appropriate to allow children to testify via CCTV or videotape.

Justice O'Connor's views became law in *Maryland v. Craig.*[154] In this case a day care operator was convicted of sexually abusing a 6-year-old child; one-way CCTV testimony was used during the trial. The decision was overturned in the Maryland Court of Appeals on the grounds that the procedures used were insufficient to show that the child could only testify in this manner, because a trial appearance would be too traumatic. On appeal, the court ruled that the Maryland statute that allows CCTV testimony is sufficient because it requires a determination that the child will suffer distress if forced to testify. The court noted that CCTV could serve as the equivalent of in-court testimony and would not interfere with the defendant's right to confront witnesses.

Disposition of Abuse and Neglect Cases

There is considerable controversy over what forms of intervention are helpful in abuse and neglect cases. Today, social service agents avoid removing children from the home whenever possible and instead try to employ techniques to control abusive relationships. In serious cases, the state may remove children from their parents and place them in shelter care or foster homes. Placement of children in foster care is intended to be temporary, but it is not uncommon for children to remain in foster care for three years or more.

Ultimately, the court has the power to terminate the rights of parents over their children, but because the effects of destroying the family unit are far-reaching, the court does so only in the most severe cases. Judicial hesitancy is illustrated in a Virginia appellate case in which grandparents contested a father's being awarded custody of his children. Even though he had a history of alcohol abuse, had already been found to be an unfit parent, and was awaiting appeal of his conviction for killing the children's mother, the trial court claimed that he had turned his life around and granted him custody.[155]

Despite such occurrences, efforts have been ongoing to improve the child protection system. Jurisdictions have expedited case processing, instituted procedures designed not to frighten child witnesses, coordinated investigations between social service and law enforcement agencies, and assigned an advocate or guardian *ad litem* to children in need of protection.

ABUSE, NEGLECT, AND DELINQUENCY

Experts fear that maltreated youth will later engage in violent and criminal acts. This assumed link between maltreatment and delinquency is supported by a number of theories of delinquency:

- *Social control theory.* By disrupting normal relationships and impeding socialization, maltreatment reduces the social bond and frees individuals to become involved in deviance.
- *Social learning theory.* Maltreatment leads to delinquency, because it teaches children that aggression and violence are justifiable forms of behavior.
- *General Strain Theory.* Maltreatment creates the "negative affective states" that are related to strain, anger, and aggression.
- *Trait theory.* Maltreated youth will develop symptoms of psychological abnormality, such as depression or psychosis, that have been linked to antisocial behaviors.

A significant amount of literature suggests that being the target of abuse is associated with subsequent episodes of delinquency and violence.[156] The effects of abuse appear to be long term: Exposure to abuse in early life provides a foundation for violent and antisocial behavior in late adolescence and adulthood.[157] Delinquency researchers have used a number of techniques to gauge the association between abuse and antisocial behavior. A number of prominent forms are described below.

Clinical Histories

Studies of juvenile offenders have confirmed that between 70 and 80 percent may have had abusive backgrounds. Many of these juveniles report serious injury, including bruises, lacerations, fractures, and being knocked unconscious by a parent or guardian.[158] Likewise, several studies reveal an association between homicide and maltreatment in early childhood.[159] Among children who kill or who attempt murder, the most common factor is a child's tendency to identify with aggressive parents and imitate their behavior.[160] One study of murder and murderous assault by juveniles indicated that in all cases "one or both parents had fostered and condoned murderous assault."[161]

Cohort Studies

These findings do not necessarily prove that maltreatment causes delinquency. It is possible that child abuse is a reaction to misbehavior and not vice versa. In other words, it is possible that angry parents attack their delinquent and drug-abusing children and that child abuse is a *result* of delinquency, not its cause.

One way of solving this dilemma is to follow a cohort of youths who have been reported as victims of abuse and compare them with a similar cohort of nonabused youths. A classic study conducted by Jose Alfaro in New York found that about half of all children reported to area hospitals as abused children later acquired arrest records. Conversely, a significant number of boys (21 percent) and girls (29 percent) petitioned to juvenile court had prior histories as abuse cases. Children treated for abuse were disproportionately involved in violent offenses.[162]

Cathy Spatz Widom followed the offending careers of 908 youths reported as abused from 1967 to 1971 and compared them with a control group of 667 nonabused youths. Widom found that the abuse involved a variety of perpetrators, including parents, relatives, strangers, and even grandparents. Twenty-six percent of the abused sample had juvenile arrests, compared with 17 percent of the comparison group; 29 percent of those who were abused had adult criminal records, compared with 21 percent of the control group. Race, gender, and age also affected the probability that abuse would lead to delinquency. The highest risk group was composed of older African American males who had suffered abuse; about 67 percent of this group went on to become adult criminals. In contrast, only 4 percent of young, European American, nonabused females became adult offenders.[163] Her conclusion: Being abused increases the likelihood of arrest both as a juvenile and as an adult.[164]

Widom also tested the hypothesis that victims of childhood violence resort to violence themselves as they mature. The children in her sample who suffered from physical abuse were the most likely to get arrested for violent crimes; their violent crime arrest rate was double that of the control group. More surprising was the discovery that neglected children maintained higher rates of violence than children in the comparison group. Clearly, family trauma of all kinds may influence violence.

Child Victims and Persistent Offending Widom also interviewed 500 subjects 20 years after their childhood victimization. Preliminary analysis of this sample indicates that the long-term consequences of childhood victimization continue throughout life. Potential problems include mental health concerns, educational problems, health problems, and occupational difficulties. In a more recent analysis, Widom and Michael Maxfield found that by the time they reached age 32, the abused children had a higher frequency of adult offending than the nonabused. People who began their offending careers as adults were also more likely to have been abused as children. Widom and Maxfield conclude that early intervention may be necessary to stop this cycle of violence.[165]

Sexual Abuse Cohort research shows that sexually abused youths are much more likely to suffer an arrest than nonabused children. The risk is greatest if the abuse took place when the child was less than seven years of age and the offense was committed by a male.[166] Sexually abused girls share a significant risk of becoming violent over the life course. There is also evidence that sexual abuse victims are more likely to abuse others, especially if they were exposed to other forms of family violence.[167] Self-report studies also confirm that child maltreatment increases the likelihood of delinquency. The most severely abused youths are at the greatest risk for long-term serious delinquency.[168]

The Abuse-Delinquency Link

Many questions remain to be answered about the abuse-delinquency linkage. Even though an association has been found, it does not necessarily mean that most abused children become delinquent. Many do not, and many delinquent youths come from what appear to be model homes. Though Widom found that more abused than nonabused children in her cohort became involved in delinquency, the majority of *both* groups did not engage in antisocial behavior.[169] And, although many studies have found an abuse-delinquency link, there are others that find the association is either nonsignificant or inconsistent (e.g., applying to girls and not to boys).[170]

Beyond the difficulty of showing a clear-cut link between abuse and delinquency, it is also difficult to assess the temporal order of the linkage: Does early abuse lead to later delinquency? Or conversely, are antisocial kids subject to overly harsh parental discipline and abuse? It is also possible that a third explanation exists: Some external factor, such as environmental deprivation, causes both abuse and delinquency. That is, kids in lower-class areas are the ones most likely to be abused and kids living in lower-class areas are also more likely to become delinquent. Hence, the observed association between abuse and delinquency may in fact be spurious.[171]

Research also shows that the timing and extent of abuse may shape its impact. Kids who are maltreated solely during early childhood may be less likely to engage in chronic delinquency than those whose abuse was lasting and persisted into later adolescence.[172] Timothy Ireland speculates that adolescents who have experienced persistent and long-term maltreatment are more likely to have families suffering an array of other social deficits, including poverty, parental mental illness, and domestic violence, which may make children more likely to engage in antisocial behavior. Persistent maltreatment also gives the victims little opportunity to cope or deal with their ongoing victimization.[173]

Finally, abuse may impact on some groups of adolescents more than it does others. When Kristi Holsinger and Alexander Holsinger surveyed incarcerated adolescent girls they found distinct racial differences in the way the girls reacted to abuse experiences. For European American girls, they found a strong link between a history of abuse and indicators of poor mental health (e.g., suicide attempts and self-injurious behaviors); African American girls who suffered abuse are more likely to externalize their anger and violence. Holsinger and Holsinger speculate that because African American girls are socialized to be self-reliant and independent, they may be more likely to act in a stronger, more assertive manner. They have a higher self-esteem and fewer mental health issues. Conversely, because European American girls are raised to be dependent and accepting of feminine gender roles, when they experience abuse they tend to internalize their problems—a reaction that produces lower self-esteem and more mental health issues.[174]

THE FAMILY AND DELINQUENCY CONTROL POLICY

Since the family is believed to play such an important role in the production of youth crime, it follows that improving family functioning can help prevent delinquency. Counselors commonly work with the families of antisocial youths as part of a court-ordered treatment strategy. Family counseling and therapy are almost mandatory when the child's acting-out behavior is suspected to be the result of family-related problems such as child abuse or neglect.[175] Some jurisdictions have integrated family counseling services into the juvenile court.[176]

Another approach to involving the family in delinquency prevention is to attack the problem before it occurs. Early childhood prevention programs that target at-risk youths can relieve some of the symptoms associated with delinquency.[177] Frequent home visits by trained nurses and social service personnel help reduce child abuse and other injuries to infants.[178] Evidence suggests that early intervention may be the most effective method and that the later the intervention, the more difficult the change process.[179]

Because the family plays such an important role in delinquency prevention and control policies, it is one of the focus areas in Chapter 12's discussion of delinquency prevention strategies. Since it is suspected that child abuse leads to a cycle of violence, there are also programs designed to help abusive parents refrain from repeating their violent episodes. One of these is discussed in the Policy and Practice box entitled "Fathering After Violence."

Fathering After Violence

The Family Violence Prevention Fund (FVPF) has created the Fathering After Violence Project (FAV) aimed at encouraging abusive men to become better father figures for their children. Developed in Boston with Dorchester Community Roundtable, the Child Witness to Violence Project, EMERGE, Roxbury Comprehensive Community Health Services, and Common Purpose, FAV targets men who have used violence and children who have witnessed violence. Materials are being developed that include:

▌ Exercises that could be incorporated into typical sessions in any batterers' intervention program

▌ Tools and homework for program participants to use with their children outside the program

▌ Outreach materials about fathering for men who have used violence

▌ Policy and practice recommendations that support the objectives of the project

▌ A monograph on considerations in working with fathers for child mental health practitioners

▌ A list of resources for batterers' intervention programs

▌ A safety and accountability guide for doing this work

The program asks abusive men to evaluate their own violent past and become aware of the long-term effects their violent behavior can have on their children. Abusers are taught to realize the importance of engaging in positive behaviors so children will have appropriate role models. The program uses an eight-point system designed to achieve nonviolent relationships in the home:

1. *Changing abusive behavior.* Violence must end immediately. Men must also realize that establishing a better relationship with their children may be an arduous procedure; patience by the abuser is critical.

2. *Modeling constructive behavior.* Children need role models. With the termination of abusive behavior, men must learn to adopt more positive actions. In addition, fathers must realize they can no longer disrespect the child's mother, since that would constitute negative behavior.

3. *Stopping denial, blaming, and justification.* Abusers must learn what happens to a child who witness violence, is blamed for violent actions, and who feels responsible for their father's actions.

4. *Being fully accountable.* Abusers must accept the consequences of their behavior. They must confront the fact that their children may not forgive or accept their attempts at rebuilding their relationship.

5. *Acknowledging damage.* Abusers must not only understand the effects of violence on their children, but they must also communicate to their child that they are aware of the damage they have caused.

6. *Not forcing the process.* Every child will react differently when an abusive father decides he wants to improve his relationship with his son/daughter; thus, it is important that the abuser be patient and not force unwanted contact with the child.

7. *Not trying to turn the page.* Abusers must be willing to revisit their violent past as often as necessary.

8. *Listening and validating.* Abusers must be ready to accept that their children may be angry, scared, sad, and/or rejecting.

The hope is that through these eight components men who have been abusive toward their families will be able to improve their family relations. In addition, the program is designed to send the message to abused children that using violence against others is wrong.

FAV has been implemented within various batterer intervention programs. The program is now being used with batterer's intervention programs (BIPs) and supervised visitation centers (SVCs) across the country. In the last four years, dozens of training sessions have been conducted around the nation, reaching over 1,000 practitioners across the country in various fields, including child welfare, batterer's intervention, supervised visitation, criminal and civil justice, home visitation, healthy marriage, child and adult mental health, and parenting and fatherhood programs. More than 1,500 copies of the FAV Guidelines and Tools have also been distributed nationally and internationally. For the future, the Family Violence Prevention Fund is proposing a National Institute on Fatherhood and Domestic Violence (NIFDV), building on the past five years of work on the Fathering After Violence initiative. The National Institute would adapt and expand the FAV work for use in new and different practice fields and support the next generation of leaders in helping fathers to renounce their violence, create healthier relationships with their children, and be more supportive parenting partners. This project would be developed in partnership with other national organizations, such as the Center for Family Policy and Practice (CFFPP).

Critical Thinking

Could a program such as Fathering After Violence help break the cycle of violence? Or are more severe measures needed, such as mandatory sentences for child abusers?

SOURCES: Fathering After Violence Project, www.endabuse.org/programs/display.php3?DocID=197 (accessed September 22, 2007); Juan Carlos Arean, "The Fathering After Violence Project: Dealing with a Complex and Unavoidable Issue," Family Violence Prevention Fund (2003), pp. 1–5, www.endabuse.org (accessed October 19, 2007); Family Violence Prevention Fund, "New Program Promotes Healthy Parenting for Fathers While Addressing Past Violence," pp. 1–2, http://library.adoption.com/Violence-and-Violence-Prevention/ New-Program-Promotes-Healthy-Parenting-for-Fathers-While-Addressing-Past-Violence/article/8335/1.html (accessed July 20, 2007). Updated with information provided by Lonna Davis Director, Children's Program Family Violence Prevention Fund, July 20, 2007.

Summary

1. **Be familiar with the link between family relationships and juvenile delinquency**

- There is little question that family dysfunction can lead to long-term social problems.
- Interactions between parents and children provide opportunities for children to acquire or inhibit antisocial behavior patterns.
- Families may be more important than peer groups as an influence on adolescent misbehavior.
- People who maintain positive lifestyles report having had warm relationships with their parents.
- People who perceived a lack of parental warmth and support were later much more likely to get involved in antisocial behaviors.
- Good parenting lowers the risk of delinquency for children living in high-crime areas.

2. **Chart the changes American families are now undergoing**

- The nuclear family is showing signs of breakdown. About half of all marriages may one day end in divorce.
- The so-called traditional family—with a male breadwinner and a female who cares for the home—is largely a thing of the past.
- There are now about 70 million children living in America ages 0 to 17.
- Children today live in a profusion of family living arrangements.
- About one-third of all African American children live in families that have two parents compared to about three-quarters of European American children.
- Though there has been a sharp decline in teen pregnancies over the past decade, more than 1.3 million children are still being born to unmarried women annually.
- Charged with caring for children is a day care system whose workers are often paid minimum wage.
- Of special concern are "family day care homes," in which a single provider takes care of three to nine children.
- Children from working poor families are most likely to suffer from inadequate child care.
- The family is also undergoing economic stress. Nearly 20 percent of all children live in poverty and about 8 percent live in extreme poverty—at least 50 percent below the poverty line.

3. **Understand the complex association between family breakup and delinquent behavior**

- The family is the primary unit in which children learn the values and attitudes that guide their actions throughout their lives.
- One of the most enduring controversies in the study of delinquency is the relationship between a parent absent from the home and the onset of delinquent behavior.
- Research indicates that parents whose marriage is secure produce children who are secure and independent.
- Children who have experienced family breakup are more likely to demonstrate behavior problems and hyperactivity than children in intact families.
- The relationship between broken homes and delinquency has been controversial.
- Children growing up in broken homes are much more likely to fall prey to delinquency than those who live in two-parent households.
- There is growing sentiment that family breakup is traumatic and most likely has a direct influence on factors related to adolescent misbehavior.
- Divorce may influence children's misbehavior through its effect on parental misbehavior.
- Judith Wallerstein, Julia M. Lewis, and Sandra Blakeslee found that the effects of divorce on children are not short-term and transient but long-lasting and cumulative.
- Children of divorce develop lingering fears about their own ability to develop long-term relationships; these fears often impede their ability to marry and raise families.
- Children growing up in families disrupted by parental death are better adjusted than children of divorce. Remarriage does not lessen the effects of divorce on youth.
- Continued contact with the noncustodial parent has little effect on a child's well-being.
- Evidence that the behavior of children of divorce improves over time is inconclusive.
- Post-divorce conflict between parents is related to child maladjustment.
- Parental divorce raises the likelihood of teenage marriage.

4. **Understand why families in conflict produce more delinquents than those that function harmoniously**

- The link between parental conflict and delinquency was established more than 50 years ago.
- Some research efforts show that observing family conflict is a more significant determinant of delinquency than being its target.
- Children who grow up in dysfunctional homes often exhibit delinquent behaviors, having learned at a young age that aggression pays off.

I Kids who are conflict prone may actually help to destabilize households.

5. Compare and contrast the effects of good and bad parenting on delinquency

I Children raised by parents who lack proper parenting skills are more at risk than those whose parents are supportive and effectively control their children.

I Parents of beyond-control youngsters have been found to be inconsistent rule-setters.

I Children who feel inhibited with their parents and refuse to discuss important issues with them are more likely to engage in deviant activities.

I Delinquency will be reduced if both or at least one parent can provide the type of structure that integrates children into families, while giving them the ability to assert their individuality and regulate their own behavior.

I The importance of close relations with the family may diminish as children reach late adolescence and develop stronger peer-group relations.

I Studies show that the parents of delinquent youths tend to be inconsistent disciplinarians, either overly harsh or extremely lenient.

I Nonviolent societies are also ones in which parents rarely punish their children physically.

I Physical punishment weakens the bond between parents and children, lowers the children's self-esteem, and undermines their faith in justice.

I Evidence also exists that inconsistent supervision can promote delinquency.

I Parents who closely supervise their children, and have close ties with them, help reduce the likelihood of adolescent delinquent behavior.

I Parents may find it hard to control their children, because they have such large families that their resources, such as time, are spread too thin.

I Resource dilution may force some mothers into the workforce in order to support their young children.

6. Discuss whether having deviant parents affects a child's behavioral choices

I A number of studies have found that parental deviance has a powerful influence on delinquent behavior.

I A significant number of delinquent youths have criminal fathers.

I School yard bullying may be both inter- and intragenerational.

I Kids whose parents go to prison are much more likely to be at risk for delinquency than children of nonincarcerated parents.

I The link between parental deviance and child misbehavior may be genetic.

I Children of drug-abusing parents are more likely to get involved in drug abuse and delinquency than the children of nonabusers.

I The link between parental deviance and child delinquency may be shaped by parenting ability.

I The association between parental deviance and children's delinquency may also be related to labeling and stigma.

7. Know about sibling influence on delinquency

I Some evidence exists that siblings may influence behavior.

I Siblings who live in the same environment are influenced by similar social and economic factors; it is not surprising that their behavior is similar.

I Deviance is genetically determined, and the traits that cause one sibling to engage in delinquency are shared by his or her brother or sister.

I Deviant siblings grow closer because of shared interests. It is possible that the relationship is due to personal interactions: Older siblings are imitated by younger siblings.

8. Discuss the nature and extent of child abuse

I Many children are physically abused or neglected by their parents.

I Parental abuse and neglect are not modern phenomena. Maltreatment of children has occurred throughout history.

I Child abuse includes neglect as well as physical abuse.

I Physical abuse includes throwing, shooting, stabbing, burning, drowning, suffocating, and biting.

I Physical neglect results from parents' failure to provide adequate food, shelter, or medical care for their children.

I Emotional abuse or neglect is manifested by constant criticism and rejection of the child.

I Emotional neglect includes inadequate nurturing or inattention to a child's emotional development.

I Abandonment refers to the situation in which parents leave their children with the intention of severing the parent-child relationship.

I Sexual abuse refers to the exploitation of children through rape, incest, and molestation by parents, family members, friends, or legal guardians.

I Victims of abuse are prone to suffer mental illness; adolescent victims of sexual abuse are particularly at risk for stress and anxiety.

- Gelles and Straus estimated that between 1.4 and 1.9 million children in the United States were subject to physical abuse from their parents.
- Approximately 3.3 million allegations of child abuse and neglect including 6 million children were made to CPS agencies.

9. List the assumed causes of child abuse

- Abusive families suffer from severe stress, and it is therefore not surprising that they frequently harbor members who turn to drugs and alcohol.
- Research indicates that stepchildren share a greater risk for abuse than do biological offspring. Stepchildren are overrepresented in cases of familicide, mass murders in which a spouse and one or more children are slain.
- For most of our nation's history, courts have assumed that parents have the right to bring up their children as they see fit.
- If the care a child receives falls below reasonable standards, the state may take action to remove the child from the home and place her or him in a less threatening environment.

10. Be familiar with the child protection system and the stages in the child protection process

- Child protection agencies have been dealing with abuse and neglect since the late nineteenth century.
- The Child Abuse Prevention and Treatment Act has been the impetus for the states to improve the legal frameworks of their child protection systems.
- All states have statutes requiring that persons suspected of abuse and neglect be reported.
- Once reported to a child protection agency, the case is screened by an intake worker and then turned over to an investigative caseworker.
- Even when there is compelling evidence of abuse, most social service agencies will try to involve the family in voluntary treatment.
- Post-investigation services are offered on a voluntary basis by child welfare agencies to ensure the safety of children.
- Case managers will do periodic follow-ups to determine if treatment plans are being followed.
- Although procedures vary from state to state, most follow a similar legal process once a social service agency files a court petition alleging abuse or neglect.
- If the allegation of abuse is confirmed, the child may be placed in protective custody.
- When an abuse or neglect petition is prosecuted, an advisement hearing (also called a preliminary protective hearing or emergency custody hearing) is held.

- The most crucial part of an abuse or neglect proceeding is the disposition hearing.
- In making their decisions, courts are guided by three interests: the role of the parents, protection for the child, and the responsibility of the state.

11. Know how courts have protected child witnesses

- One of the most significant problems associated with abuse cases is the trauma a child must go through in a court hearing.
- Children get confused and frightened and may change their testimony.
- State jurisdictions have instituted procedures to minimize the trauma to the child.
- Most of the states now allow a child's testimony to be given on closed-circuit television (CCTV).
- In addition to innovative methods of testimony, children in sexual abuse cases have been allowed to use anatomically correct dolls to demonstrate happenings that they cannot describe verbally.
- A number of cases have been brought before the Supreme Court testing the right of children to present evidence at trial using nontraditional methods.
- In a 1992 case, *White v. Illinois*, the Supreme Court ruled that the state's attorney is not required to produce young victims at trial or to demonstrate the reason why they were unavailable to serve as witnesses.
- In *Maryland v. Craig*, the Court ruled that the Maryland statute that allows CCTV testimony is sufficient because it requires a determination that the child will suffer distress if forced to testify.
- There is considerable controversy over what forms of intervention are helpful in abuse and neglect cases.

12. Know the various positions in the delinquency–child maltreatment debate

- Experts fear that maltreated youth will later engage in violent and criminal acts.
- This assumed link between maltreatment and delinquency is supported by a number of criminological theories.
- A significant amount of literature suggests that being the target of abuse is associated with subsequent episodes of delinquency and violence.
- Studies of juvenile offenders have confirmed that between 70 and 80 percent may have had abusive backgrounds.
- Cohort research shows that sexually abused youths are much more likely to suffer an arrest than nonabused children.

- It is difficult to assess the temporal order of the linkage: Does early abuse lead to later delinquency? Or conversely, are antisocial kids subject to overly harsh parental discipline and abuse?
- It is also possible that some external factor, such as environmental deprivation, causes both abuse and delinquency.

- Since the family is believed to play such an important role in the production of youth crime, it follows that improving family functioning can help prevent delinquency.

Key Terms

nuclear family, p. 248
broken home, p. 251
blended families, p. 251
intrafamily violence, p. 254
parental efficacy, p. 255
resource dilution, p. 258
foster care, p. 259

battered child syndrome, p. 261
child abuse, p. 261
neglect, p. 261
abandonment, p. 261
familicide, p. 265
advisement hearing, p. 270

pretrial conference, p. 270
disposition hearing, p. 270
balancing-of-the-interests approach, p. 271
review hearings, p. 271
hearsay, p. 272

Viewpoint

You are an investigator with the county bureau of social services. A case has been referred to you by a middle school's head guidance counselor. It seems that a young girl, Emily M., has been showing up to school in a dazed and listless condition. She has had a hard time concentrating in class and seems withdrawn and uncommunicative. The 13-year-old has missed more than her normal share of school days and has often been late to class. Last week, she seemed so lethargic that her homeroom teacher sent her to the school nurse. A physical examination revealed that she was malnourished and in poor physical health. She also had evidence of bruising that could only come from a severe beating. Emily told the nurse that she had been punished by her parents for doing poorly at school and failing to do her chores at home.

When her parents were called to school to meet with the principal and guidance counselor, they claimed to be members of a religious order that believes children should be punished severely for their misdeeds. Emily had been placed on a restricted diet as well as beaten with a belt to correct her misbehavior. When the guidance counselor asked them if they would be willing to go into family therapy, they were furious and told her to "mind her own business." It's a sad day, they said, when "God-fearing

American citizens cannot bring up their children according to their religious beliefs." The girl was in no immediate danger, they believed, because her punishment had not been life threatening.

The case is then referred to your office. When you go to see the parents at home, they refuse to make any change in their behavior, claiming that they are in the right and you represent all that is wrong with society. The "lax" discipline you suggest leads to drugs, sex, and other teenage problems.

- Would you get a court order removing Emily from her house, placing her in foster care, and requiring the parents to go into counseling?
- Would you report the case to the district attorney's office so it could take criminal action against her parents under the state's child protection act?
- Would you take no further action, reasoning that Emily's parents have the right to discipline their child as they see fit?
- Would you talk with Emily and see what she wants to happen?

Doing Research on the Web

The Child Welfare Information Gateway provides resources about child maltreatment, including definitions, signs and symptoms, statistics and prevalence, types of child abuse and neglect, risk and protective

factors, the impact on individuals and society, and child fatalities.

Access their website via
academic.cengage.com/criminaljustice/siegel

Questions for Discussion

1. What are the meanings of the terms "child abuse" and "child neglect"?

2. Discuss the association between child abuse and delinquency. Give two different explanations for the positive relationship between abuse and antisocial behavior.

3. What causes parents to abuse their children?

4. What is meant by the phrase "child protection system"? Do courts act in the best interest of the child when they allow an abused child to remain with the family?

5. Should children be allowed to testify in court via CCTV? Does this approach prevent defendants in child abuse cases from confronting their accusers?

6. Is corporal punishment ever permissible as a disciplinary method?

Notes

1. CBS News, "Outrage Over Abuse, Death of NYC Girl," 13 January 2006, www.cbsnews.com/stories/2006/01/13/earlyshow/main1206722.shtml (accessed September 22, 2007); Associated Press, MSNBC, "Girl's Death Hastens Review of NYC Abuse Cases," 13 January 2006, www.msnbc. msn.com/id/10835619/ (accessed October 12, 2007); Pablo Guzmán, WCBSTV, "Nixzmary Brown's Mother Blows Up in Court," 5 December 2006, http://wcbstv.com/topstories/local_story_339202149.html (accessed October 12, 2007).

2. Tracy Harachi, Charles Fleming, Helene White, Margaret Ensminger, Robert Abbott, Richard Catalano, and Kevin Haggerty, "Aggressive Behavior among Girls and Boys During Middle Childhood: Predictors and Sequelae of Trajectory Group Membership," *Aggressive Behavior* 32:279–293 (2006).

3. Rolf Loeber and Magda Stouthamer-Loeber, "Development of Juvenile Aggression and Violence," *American Psychologist* 53:250 (1998).

4. Callie Harbin Burt, Ronald Simons, and Leslie Simons, "A Longitudinal Test of the Effects of Parenting and the Stability of Self-Control: Negative Evidence for the General Theory of Crime," *Criminology* 44:353–396 (2006).

5. Dana Haynie and D. Wayne Osgood, "Reconsidering Peers and Delinquency: How Do Peers Matter?" *Social Forces* 84:1110–1130 (2005).

6. Emma Palmer and Kirsty Gough, "Childhood Experiences of Parenting and Causal Attributions for Criminal Behavior among Young Offenders and Non-Offenders," *Journal of Applied Social Psychology* 37:790–806 (2007).

7. Joan McCord, "Family Relationships, Juvenile Delinquency, and Adult Criminality," *Criminology* 29:397–417 (1991); Scott Henggeler, ed., *Delinquency and Adolescent Psychopathology: A Family Ecological Systems Approach* (Littleton, MA: Wright–PSG, 1982).

8. Sarah O. Meadows, "Evidence of Parallel Pathways: Gender Similarity in the Impact of Social Support on Adolescent Depression and Delinquency," *Social Forces* 85:1143–1167 (2007).

9. For a general review of the relationship between families and delinquency, see Alan Jay Lincoln and Murray Straus, *Crime and the Family* (Springfield, IL: Charles C Thomas, 1985); Rolf Loeber and Magda Stouthamer-Loeber, "Family Factors as Correlates and Predictors of Juvenile Conduct Problems and Delinquency," in Michael Tonry and Norval Morris, eds., *Crime and Justice*, vol. 7 (Chicago: University of Chicago Press, 1986), pp. 29–151.

10. David Farrington, "Juvenile Delinquency," in John Coleman, ed., *The School Years* (London: Routledge, 1992), pp. 139–140.

11. Ruth Inglis, *Sins of the Fathers: A Study of the Physical and Emotional Abuse of Children* (New York: St. Martin's Press, 1978), p. 131.

12. National Vital Statistics Report, *Births, Marriages, Divorces, and Deaths: Provisional Data for 2005*, vol. 54, no. 20, July 21, 2006, www.cdc.gov/ nchs/data/nvsr/nvsr54/nvsr54_20.pdf (accessed October 12, 2007).

13. See Joseph J. Costa and Gordon K. Nelson, *Child Abuse and Neglect: Legislation, Reporting, and Prevention* (Lexington, MA: Heath, 1978), p. xiii.

14. Tamar Lewin, "Men Assuming Bigger Role at Home, New Survey Shows," *New York Times*, 15 April 1998, p. A18.

15. U.S. Census Bureau, *Children's Living Arrangements and Characteristics 2006*, www.census.gov/population/www/socdemo/hh-fam.html (accessed July 10, 2007).

16. Terence P. Thornberry, Carolyn A. Smith, Craig Rivera, David Huizinga, and Magda Stouthamer-Loeber, *Family Disruption and Delinquency, Juvenile Justice Bulletin* (Washington, DC: Office of Juvenile Justice and Delinquency Prevention, September 1999).

17. *U.S. Pregnancy Rate Down from Peak; Births and Abortions on the Decline*, press release (Washington, DC: Department of Health and Human Services, October 31, 2003); *HHS Report Shows Teen Birth Rate Falls to New Record Low in 2001*, press release (Washington, DC: Department of Health and Human Services, June 6, 2002).

18. *Kids Count Survey 2006* (Baltimore: Annie E. Casey Foundation, 2006), www.aecf.org/kidscount/sld/index.jsp (accessed July 25, 2007).

19. Ibid.

20. Christopher Sullivan, "Early Adolescent Delinquency: Assessing the Role of Childhood Problems, Family Environment, and Peer Pressure," *Youth Violence and Juvenile Justice* 4:291–313 (2006).

21. Loeber and Stouthamer-Loeber, "Family Factors," pp. 39–41.

22. Carla Davis, "At-Risk Girls and Delinquency," *Crime and Delinquency* 53:408–435 (2007).

23. Paul Howes and Howard Markman, "Marital Quality and Child Functioning: A Longitudinal Investigation," *Child Development* 60: 1044–1051 (1989).

24. Andre Sourander, Henrik Elonheimo, Solja Niemelä, Art-Matti Nuutila, Hans Helenius, Lauri Sillanmäki, Jorma Piha, Tuulk Tamminen, Kirsti Kumpulkinen, Irma Moilanen, and Frederik Almovist, "Childhood Predictors of Male Criminality: A Prospective Population-Based Follow-up Study from Age 8 to Late Adolescence," *Journal of the American Academy of Child and Adolescent Psychiatry* 45:578–586 (2006).

25. Barbara Dafoe Whitehead, "Dan Quayle Was Right," *Atlantic Monthly* 271:47–84 (1993).

26. C. Patrick Brady, James Bray, and Linda Zeeb, "Behavior Problems of Clinic Children: Relation to Parental Marital Status, Age, and Sex of Child," *American Journal of Orthopsychiatry* 56:399–412 (1986).

27. Scott Henggeler, *Delinquency in Adolescence* (Newbury Park, CA: Sage, 1989), p. 48.

28. Thornberry, Smith, Rivera, Huizinga, and Stouthamer-Loeber, *Family Disruption and Delinquency*.

29. Sheldon Glueck and Eleanor Glueck, *Unraveling Juvenile Delinquency* (Cambridge, MA: Harvard University Press, 1950); Ashley Weeks, "Predicting Juvenile Delinquency," *American Sociological Review* 8:40–46 (1943).

30. Jackson Toby, "The Differential Impact of Family Disorganization," *American Sociological Review* 22:505–512 (1957); Ruth Morris, "Female Delinquency and Relation Problems," *Social Forces* 43:82–89 (1964); Roland Chilton and Gerald Markle, "Family Disruption, Delinquent Conduct, and the Effects of Sub-classification," *American Sociological Review* 37:93–99 (1972).

31. For a review of these early studies, see Thomas Monahan, "Family Status and the Delinquent Child: A Reappraisal and Some New Findings," *Social Forces* 35:250–258 (1957).

32. Clifford Shaw and Henry McKay, *Report on the Causes of Crime: Social Factors in Juvenile Delinquency*, vol. 2 (Washington, DC: U.S. Government Printing Office, 1931), p. 392.

33. John Laub and Robert Sampson, "Unraveling Families and Delinquency: A Reanalysis of the Gluecks' Data," *Criminology* 26:355–380 (1988); Lawrence Rosen, "The Broken Home and Male Delinquency," in M. Wolfgang, L. Savitz, and N. Johnston, eds., *The Sociology of Crime and Delinquency* (New York: Wiley, 1970), pp. 489–495.

34. Christina DeJong and Kenneth Jackson, "Putting Race into Context: Race, Juvenile Justice Processing, and Urbanization," *Justice Quarterly* 15:487–504 (1998).

35. Robert Johnson, John Hoffman, and Dean Gerstein, *The Relationship between Family Structure and Adolescent Substance Abuse* (Washington, DC: Office of Applied Studies, Substance Abuse and Mental Health Services Administration, 1996).

36. Sara McLanahan, "Father Absence and the Welfare of Children," working paper (Chicago: John D. and Catherine T. MacArthur Research Foundation, 1998).

37. Cesar Rebellon, "Reconsidering the Broken Homes/Delinquency Relationship and Exploring Its Mediating Mechanism(s)," *Criminology* 40:103–135 (2002).

38. Ronald Simons, Kuei-Hsiu Lin, Leslie Gordon, Rand Conger, and Frederick Lorenz, "Explaining the Higher Incidence of Adjustment Problems among Children of Divorce Compared with Those in Two-Parent Families," *Journal of Marriage and the Family* 61:131–148 (1999).

39. En-Ling Pan and Michael Farrell, "Ethnic Differences in the Effects of Intergenerational Relations on Adolescent Problem Behavior in U.S. Single-Mother Families," *Journal of Family Issues* 27:1137–1158 (2006).

40. Lisa Stolzenberg and Stewart D'Alessio, "The Effect of Divorce on Domestic Crime," *Crime and Delinquency* 53:281–302 (2007).

41. Sara Jaffee, Terrie Moffitt, Avshalom Caspi, and Alan Taylor, "Life with (or without) Father: The Benefits of Living with Two Biological Parents Depend on the Father's Antisocial Behavior," *Child Development* 74:109–117 (2003).

42. Judith Smetena, "Adolescents' and Parents' Reasoning About Actual Family Conflict," *Child Development* 60:1052–1067 (1989).

43. F. Ivan Nye, "Child Adjustment in Broken and Unhappy Unbroken Homes," *Marriage and Family* 19:356–361 (1957); Nye, *Family Relationships and Delinquent Behavior* (New York: Wiley, 1958).

44. Diana Formoso, Nancy Gonzales, and Leona Aiken, "Family Conflict and Children's Internalizing and Externalizing Behavior: Protective Factors," *American Journal of Community Psychology* 28:175–199 (2000).

45. Peter Jaffe, David Wolfe, Susan Wilson, and Lydia Zak, "Similarities in Behavior and Social Maladjustment among Child Victims and Witnesses to Family Violence," *American Journal of Orthopsychiatry* 56:142–146 (1986).

46. Veronica Herrera, "Equals in Risk? The Differential Impact of Family Violence on Male and Female Delinquency," paper presented at the annual meeting of the American Society of Criminology, San Diego, November 1997.

47. Loeber and Stouthamer-Loeber, "Development of Juvenile Aggression and Violence," p. 251.

48. Carolyn Smith, Sung Joon Jang, and Susan Stern, "The Effect of Delinquency on Families," *Family and Corrections Network Report* 13:1–11 (1997).

49. Paul Amato and Bruce Keith, "Parental Divorce and the Well-Being of Children: A Meta-Analysis," *Psychological Bulletin* 110:26–46 (1991).

50. Christopher Kierkus and Douglas Baer, "A Social Control Explanation of the Relationship between Family Structure and Delinquent Behaviour," *Canadian Journal of Criminology*, 44:425–458 (2002).

51. John Paul Wright and Francis Cullen, "Parental Efficacy and Delinquent Behavior: Do Control and Support Matter?" *Criminology* 39:677–706 (2001).

52. Kathleen Roche, Margaret Ensminger, and Andrew Cherlin, "Variations in Parenting and Adolescent Outcomes among African American and Latino Families Living in Low-Income, Urban Areas," *Journal of Family Issues* 28:882–909 (2007).

53. Ibid.

54. Roslyn Caldwell, Jenna Silverman, Noelle Lefforge, and Clayton Silver, "Adjudicated Mexican-American Adolescents: The Effects of Familial Emotional Support on Self-Esteem, Emotional Well-Being, and Delinquency," *American Journal of Family Therapy* 32:55–69 (2004);

Robert Vermeiren, Jef Bogaerts, Vladislav Ruchkin, Dirk Deboutte, and Mary Schwab-Stone, "Subtypes of Self-Esteem and Self-Concept in Adolescent Violent and Property Offenders," *Journal of Child Psychology and Psychiatry* 45:405–411 (2004).

55. Jacinta Bronte-Tinkew, Kristin Moore, and Jennifer Carrano, "The Father-Child Relationship, Parenting Styles, and Adolescent Risk Behaviors in Intact Families," *Journal of Family Issues* 27:850–881 (2006).

56. Leslie Gordon Simons and Rand Conger, "Linking Mother-Father Differences in Parenting to a Typology of Family Parenting Styles and Adolescent Outcomes," *Journal of Family Issues* 28:212–241 (2007).

57. Carter Hay, "Parenting, Self-Control, and Delinquency: A Test of Self-Control Theory," *Criminology* 39:707–736 (2001).

58. Sonia Cota-Robles and Wendy Gamble, "Parent-Adolescent Processes and Reduced Risk for Delinquency: The Effect of Gender for Mexican American Adolescents," *Youth and Society* 37:375–392 (2006).

59. Jennifer Wainright and Charlotte Patterson, "Delinquency, Victimization, and Substance Use among Adolescents with Female Same-Sex Parents," *Journal of Family Psychology* 20:526–530 (2006).

60. Sung Joon Jang and Carolyn Smith, "A Test of Reciprocal Causal Relationships among Parental Supervision, Affective Ties, and Delinquency," *Journal of Research in Crime and Delinquency* 34:307–336 (1997).

61. Gerald Patterson and Magda Stouthamer-Loeber, "The Correlation of Family Management Practices and Delinquency," *Child Development* 55:1299–1307 (1984); Gerald R. Patterson, *A Social Learning Approach: Coercive Family Process*, vol. 3 (Eugene, OR: Castalia, 1982).

62. Christopher Ellison and Darren Sherkat, "Conservative Protestantism and Support for Corporal Punishment," *American Sociological Review* 58:131–144 (1993).

63. Eric Slade and Lawrence Wissow, "Spanking in Early Childhood and Later Behavior Problems: A Prospective Study of Infants and Young Toddlers," *Pediatrics* 113:1321–1330 (2004).

64. Murray Straus, "Discipline and Deviance: Physical Punishment of Children and Violence and Other Crime in Adulthood," *Social Problems* 38:101–123 (1991).

65. Murray A. Straus, "Spanking and the Making of a Violent Society: The Short- and Long-Term Consequences of Corporal Punishment," *Pediatrics* 98:837–843 (1996).

66. Ibid.

67. Loeber and Stouthamer-Loeber, "Development of Juvenile Aggression and Violence," p. 251.

68. Nathaniel Pallone and James Hennessy, "Brain Dysfunction and Criminal Violence," *Society* 35:21–27 (1998).

69. Nye, *Family Relationships and Delinquent Behavior.*

70. Laurence Steinberg, Ilana Blatt-Eisengart, and Elizabeth Cauffman, "Patterns of Competence and Adjustment among Adolescents from Authoritative, Authoritarian, Indulgent, and Neglectful Homes: A Replication in a Sample of Serious Juvenile Offenders," *Journal of Research on Adolescence* 26:47–58 (2006).

71. Lisa Broidy, "Direct Supervision and Delinquency: Assessing the Adequacy of Structural Proxies," *Journal of Criminal Justice* 23:541–554 (1995).

72. James Unnever, Francis Cullen, and Robert Agnew, "Why Is 'Bad' Parenting Criminogenic? Implications from Rival Theories," *Youth Violence and Juvenile Justice* 4:3–33 (2006).

73. Jennifer Beyers, John Bates, Gregory Pettit, and Kenneth Dodge, "Neighborhood Structure, Parenting Processes, and the Development of Youths' Externalizing Behaviors: A Multilevel Analysis," *American Journal of Community Psychology* 31:35–53 (2003).

74. Jang and Smith, "A Test of Reciprocal Causal Relationships among Parental Supervision, Affective Ties, and Delinquency"; Linda Waite and Lee Lillard, "Children and Marital Disruption," *American Journal of Sociology* 96:930–953 (1991).

75. Beyers, Bates, Pettit, and Dodge, "Neighborhood Structure, Parenting Processes, and the Development of Youths' Externalizing Behaviors."

76. Thomas Vander Ven and Francis Cullen, "The Impact of Maternal Employment on Serious Youth Crime: Does the Quality of Working Conditions Matter?" *Crime and Delinquency* 50:272–292 (2004); Thomas Vander Ven, Francis Cullen, Mark Carrozza, and John Paul Wright, "Home Alone: The Impact of Maternal Employment on Delinquency," *Social Problems* 48:236–257 (2001).

77. Douglas Downey, "Number of Siblings and Intellectual Development," *American Psychologist* 56:497–504 (2001); Downey, "When Bigger Is Not Better: Family Size, Parental Resources, and Children's Educational Performance," *American Sociological Review* 60:746–761 (1995).

78. G. Rahav, "Birth Order and Delinquency," *British Journal of Criminology* 20:385–395 (1980); D. Viles and D. Challinger, "Family Size and Birth Order of Young Offenders," *International Journal of Offender Therapy and Comparative Criminology* 25:60–66 (1981).

79. Vander Ven, Cullen, Carrozza, and Wright, "Home Alone: The Impact of Maternal Employment on Delinquency."

80. For an early review, see Barbara Wooton, *Social Science and Social Pathology* (London: Allen and Unwin, 1959).

81. Daniel Shaw, "Advancing Our Understanding of Intergenerational Continuity in Antisocial Behavior," *Journal of Abnormal Child Psychology* 31:193–199 (2003).

82. Donald J. West and David P. Farrington, eds., "Who Becomes Delinquent?" in *The Delinquent Way of Life* (London: Heinemann, 1977); Donald J. West, *Delinquency: Its Roots, Careers, and Prospects* (Cambridge, MA: Harvard University Press, 1982).

83. David Farrington, "Understanding and Preventing Bullying," in Michael Tonry, ed., *Crime and Justice*, vol. 17 (Chicago: University of Chicago Press, 1993), pp. 381–457.

84. Carolyn Smith and David Farrington, "Continuities in Antisocial Behavior and Parenting Across Three Generations," *Journal of Child Psychology and Psychiatry* 45:230–247 (2004).

85. Joseph Murray and David Farrington, "Parental Imprisonment: Effects on Boys' Antisocial Behaviour and Delinquency Through the Life-Course," *Journal of Child Psychology and Psychiatry* 46:1269–1278 (2005).

86. John Paul Wright and Kevin Beaver, "Do Parents Matter in Creating Self-Control in Their Children? A Genetically Informed Test of Gottfredson and Hirschi's Theory of Low Self-Control," *Criminology* 43:1169–1202 (2005).

87. Leonore Simon, "Does Criminal Offender Treatment Work?" *Applied and Preventive Psychology* Summer:1–22 (1998).

88. Laura Baker, Kristen Jacobson, Adrian Raine, Dora Isabel Lozano, and Serena Bezdjian, "Genetic and Environmental Bases of Childhood Antisocial Behavior: A Multi-Informant Twin Study," *Journal of Abnormal Psychology* 116:219–235 (2007).

89. Nancy Day, Lidush Goldschmidt, and Carrie Thomas, "Prenatal Marijuana Exposure Contributes to the Prediction of Marijuana Use at Age 14," *Addiction* 101:1313–1322 (2006).

90. Philip Harden and Robert Pihl, "Cognitive Function, Cardiovascular Reactivity, and Behavior in Boys at High Risk for Alcoholism," *Journal of Abnormal Psychology* 104:94–103 (1995).

91. Laub and Sampson, "Unraveling Families and Delinquency," p. 370.

92. Anne Dannerbeck, "Differences in Parenting Attributes, Experiences, and Behaviors of Delinquent Youth with and without a Parental History of Incarceration," *Youth Violence and Juvenile Justice* 3:199–213 (2005).

93. David P. Farrington, Gwen Gundry, and Donald J. West, "The Familial Transmission of Criminality," in Alan Lincoln and Murray Straus, eds., *Crime and the Family* (Springfield, IL: Charles C Thomas, 1985), pp. 193–206.

94. Abigail Fagan and Jake Najman, "Sibling Influences on Adolescent Delinquent Behaviour: An Australian Longitudinal Study," *Journal of Adolescence* 26:546–558 (2003).

95. David Rowe and Bill Gulley, "Sibling Effects on Substance Use and Delinquency," *Criminology* 30:217–232 (1992); see also David Rowe, Joseph Rogers, and Sylvia Meseck-Bushey, "Sibling Delinquency and the Family Environment: Shared and Unshared Influences," *Child Development* 63:59–67 (1992).

96. *The Future of Children*, a publication of the Woodrow Wilson School of Public and International Affairs at Princeton University and the Brookings Institution, www.futureofchildren.org/information3862/information_show.htm?doc_id=211282 (accessed July 25, 2007).

97. Ibid.

98. Ibid.

99. Joseph Doyle, "Child Protection and Child Outcomes: Measuring the Effects of Foster Care" *American Economic Review* (forthcoming, 2008), www.mit.edu/~jjdoyle/doyle_fosterlt_march07_aer.pdf (accessed July 25, 2007).

100. Richard Gelles and Claire Pedrick Cornell, *Intimate Violence in Families*, 2nd ed. (Newbury Park, CA: Sage, 1990), p. 33.

101. Lois Hochhauser, "Child Abuse and the Law: A Mandate for Change," *Harvard Law Journal* 18:200 (1973); see also Douglas J. Besharov, "The Legal Aspects of Reporting Known and Suspected Child Abuse and Neglect," *Villanova Law Review* 23:458 (1978).

102. C. Henry Kempe, F. N. Silverman, B. F. Steele, W. Droegemueller, and H. K. Silver, "The Battered-Child Syndrome," *Journal of the American Medical Association* 181:17–24 (1962).

103. Brian G. Fraser, "A Glance at the Past, a Gaze at the Present, a Glimpse at the Future: A Critical Analysis of the Development of Child Abuse Reporting Statutes," *Chicago-Kent Law Review* 54:643 (1977–1978).

104. National Center for Injury Prevention and Control, www.cdc.gov/ncipc/factsheets/cmfacts.htm (accessed September 22, 2007).

105. See, especially, Inglis, *Sins of the Fathers*, ch. 8.

106. William Downs and Brenda Miller, "Relationships between Experiences of Parental Violence During Childhood and Women's Self-Esteem," *Violence and Victims* 13:63–78 (1998).

107. Ruth S. Kempe and C. Henry Kempe, *Child Abuse* (Cambridge, MA: Harvard University Press, 1978), pp. 6–7.

108. Fred Rogosch and Dante Cicchetti, "Child Maltreatment and Emergent Personality Organization: Perspectives from the Five-Factor Model," *Journal of Abnormal Child Psychology* 32:123–145 (2004).

109. Wendy Fisk, "Childhood Trauma and Dissociative Identity Disorder," *Child and Adolescent Psychiatric Clinics of North America* 5:431–447 (1996).

110. National Center for Injury Prevention and Control, www.cdc.gov/ncipc/factsheets/cmfacts.htm (accessed September 22, 2007).

111. National Center for Shaken Baby Syndrome, www.dontshake.com (accessed September 22, 2007).

112. Mary Haskett and Janet Kistner, "Social Interactions and Peer Perceptions of Young Physically Abused Children," *Child Development* 62:679–690 (1991).

113. Catherine Grus, "Child Abuse: Correlations with Hostile Attributions," *Journal of Developmental and Behavioral Pediatrics* 24:296–298 (2006).

114. Kim Logio, "Gender, Race, Childhood Abuse, and Body Image among Adolescents," *Violence Against Women* 9:931–955 (2003).

115. Jeanne Kaufman and Cathy Spatz Widom, "Childhood Victimization, Running Away, and Delinquency," *Journal of Research in Crime and Delinquency* 36:347–370 (1999).

116. N. N. Sarkar and Rina Sarkar, "Sexual Assault on Woman: Its Impact on Her Life and Living in Society," *Sexual and Relationship Therapy* 20:407–419 (2005).

117. Michael Wiederman, Randy Sansone, and Lori Sansone, "History of Trauma and Attempted Suicide among Women in a Primary Care Setting," *Violence and Victims* 13:3–11 (1998); Susan Leslie Bryant and Lillian Range, "Suicidality in College Women Who Were Sexually and Physically Abused and Physically Punished by Parents," *Violence and Victims* 10:195–215 (1995); William Downs and Brenda Miller, "Relationships between Experiences of Parental Violence During Childhood and Women's Self-Esteem," *Violence and Victims* 13:63–78 (1998); Sally Davies-Netley, Michael Hurlburt, and Richard Hough, "Childhood Abuse as a Precursor to Homelessness for Homeless Women with Severe Mental Illness," *Violence and Victims* 11:129–142 (1996).

118. Jane Siegel and Linda Williams, "Risk Factors for Sexual Victimization of Women," *Violence Against Women* 9:902–930 (2003).

119. Michael Miner, Jill Klotz Flitter, and Beatrice Robinson, "Association of Sexual Revictimization with Sexuality and Psychological Function," *Journal of Interpersonal Violence* 21:503–524 (2006).

120. Lana Stermac and Emily Paradis, "Homeless Women and Victimization: Abuse and Mental Health History among Homeless Rape Survivors," *Resources for Feminist Research* 28:65–81 (2001).

121. Murray Straus, Richard Gelles, and Suzanne Steinmentz, *Behind Closed Doors: Violence in the American Family* (Garden City, NY: Anchor Books, 1980); Richard Gelles and Murray Straus, "Violence in the American Family," *Journal of Social Issues* 35:15–39 (1979).

122. Gelles and Straus, "Violence in the American Family," p. 24.

123. Richard Gelles and Murray Straus, *The Causes and Consequences of Abuse in the American Family* (New York: Simon & Schuster, 1988); see also Murray A. Straus and Glenda Kaufman Kantor, "Trends in Physical

Abuse by Parents from 1975 to 1992: A Comparison of Three National Surveys," paper presented at the annual meeting of the American Society of Criminology, Boston, November 1995.

124. Murray A. Straus and Anita K. Mathur, "Social Change and Trends in Approval of Corporal Punishment by Parents from 1968 to 1994," in D. Frehsee, W. Horn, and K. Bussman, eds., *Violence Against Children* (New York: Aldine de Gruyter, 1996), pp. 91–105.

125. Department of Health and Human Services, *Child Maltreatment, 2005* (Washington, DC: Department of Health and Human Services, 2007), www.acf.hhs.gov/programs/cb/pubs/cm05/cm05.pdf (accessed September 22, 2007).

126. Richard Estes and Neil Alan Weiner, *The Commercial Sexual Exploitation of Children in the U.S., Canada and Mexico* (Philadelphia: University of Pennsylvania, 2001).

127. Lisa Jones and David Finkelhor, *The Decline in Child Sexual Abuse Cases* (Washington, DC: Office of Juvenile Justice and Delinquency Prevention, 2001).

128. Carolyn Webster-Stratton, "Comparison of Abusive and Nonabusive Families with Conduct-Disordered Children," *American Journal of Orthopsychiatry* 55:59–69 (1985); Brandt F. Steele and Carl B. Pollock, "A Psychiatric Study of Parents Who Abuse Infants and Small Children," in Ray Helfer and C. Henry Kempe, eds., *The Battered Child* (Chicago: University of Chicago Press, 1968), pp. 103–145.

129. Brandt F. Steele, "Violence within the Family," in Ray E. Helfer and C. Henry Kempe, eds., *Child Abuse and Neglect: The Family and the Community* (Cambridge, MA: Ballinger, 1976), p. 13.

130. William Sack, Robert Mason, and James Higgins, "The Single-Parent Family and Abusive Punishment," *American Journal of Orthopsychiatry* 55:252–259 (1985).

131. Blair Justice and Rita Justice, *The Abusing Family* (New York: Human Sciences Press, 1976); Nanette Dembitz, "Preventing Youth Crime by Preventing Child Neglect," *American Bar Association Journal* 65:920–923 (1979).

132. Douglas Ruben, *Treating Adult Children of Alcoholics: A Behavioral Approach* (New York: Academic Press, 2000).

133. Martin Daly and Margo Wilson, "Violence Against Stepchildren," *Current Directions in Psychological Science* 5:77–81 (1996).

134. Ibid.

135. Margo Wilson, Martin Daly, and Antonietta Daniele, "Familicide: The Killing of Spouse and Children," *Aggressive Behavior* 21:275–291 (1995).

136. Richard Gelles, "Child Abuse and Violence in Single-Parent Families: Parent Absence and Economic Deprivation," *American Journal of Orthopsychiatry* 59:492–501 (1989).

137. Susan Napier and Mitchell Silverman, "Family Violence as a Function of Occupation Status, Socioeconomic Class, and Other Variables," paper presented at the annual meeting of the American Society of Criminology, Boston, November 1995.

138. Robert Burgess and Patricia Draper, "The Explanation of Family Violence," in Lloyd Ohlin and Michael Tonry, eds., *Family Violence* (Chicago: University of Chicago Press, 1989), pp. 59–117.

139. Ibid., pp. 103–104.

140. *Troxel et vir. v. Granville* No. 99-138 (June 5, 2000).

141. 452 U.S. 18, 101 S.Ct. 2153 (1981); 455 U.S. 745, 102 S.Ct. 1388 (1982).

142. For a survey of each state's reporting requirements, abuse and neglect legislation, and available programs and agencies, see Costa and Nelson, *Child Abuse and Neglect.*

143. Linda Gordon, "Incest and Resistance: Patterns of Father-Daughter Incest, 1880–1930," *Social Problems* 33:253–267 (1986).

144. P.L. 93B247 (1974); P.L. 104B235 (1996).

145. Barbara Ryan, "Do You Suspect Child Abuse? The Story of 2-Year-Old Dominic James Made Headlines Not Only Because of His Tragic Death, but Because Criminal Charges Were Lodged Against a Nurse for Failing to Report His Suspicious Injuries. A Cautionary Tale," *RN* 66:73–76 (2003).

146. Robin Fretwell Wilson, "Children at Risk: The Sexual Exploitation of Female Children After Divorce," *Cornell Law Review* 86:251–327 (2001).

147. Department of Health and Human Services, Child Maltreatment, 2005 (Washington, DC: Department of Health and Human Services, 2007), www.acf.hhs.gov/programs/cb/pubs/cm05/cm05.pdf (accessed September 22, 2007).

148. Sue Badeau and Sarah Gesiriech, *A Child's Journey Through the Child Welfare System* (Washington, DC: The Pew Commission on Children in Foster Care, December 13, 2003).

149. PBS Frontline, "Innocence Lost the Plea," www.pbs.org/wgbh/pages/frontline/shows/innocence/etc/other.html (accessed September 22, 2007). For an analysis of the accuracy of children's recollections of abuse, see Candace Kruttschnitt and Maude Dornfeld, "Will They Tell? Assessing Preadolescents' Reports of Family Violence," *Journal of Research in Crime and Delinquency* 29:136–147 (1992).

150. Debra Whitcomb, *When the Victim Is a Child* (Washington, DC: National Institute of Justice, 1992), p. 33.

151. *White v. Illinois*, 502 U.S. 346; 112 S.Ct. 736 (1992).

152. Myrna Raeder, "*White's* Effect on the Right to Confront One's Accuser," *Criminal Justice*, Winter 2–7 (1993).

153. *Coy v. Iowa*, 487 U.S. 1012 (1988).

154. *Maryland v. Craig*, 110 S.Ct. 3157 (1990).

155. *Walker v. Fagg*, 400 S.E. 2d 708 (Va. App. 1991).

156. Cesar Rebellon and Karen Van Gundy, "Can Control Theory Explain the Link between Parental Physical Abuse and Delinquency? A Longitudinal Analysis," *Journal of Research in Crime and Delinquency* 42:247–274 (2005).

157. Gelles and Straus, "Violence in the American Family."

158. National Center on Child Abuse and Neglect, Department of Health, Education, and Welfare, *1977 Analysis of Child Abuse and Neglect Research* (Washington, DC: U.S. Government Printing Office, 1978), p. 29.

159. Steele, "Violence within the Family," p. 22.

160. L. Bender and F. J. Curran, "Children and Adolescents Who Kill," *Journal of Criminal Psychopathology* 1:297 (1940), cited in Steele, "Violence within the Family," p. 21.

161. W. M. Easson and R. M. Steinhilber, "Murderous Aggression by Children and Adolescents," *Archives of General Psychiatry* 4:1–11 (1961), cited in Steele, "Violence within the Family," p. 22; see also J. Duncan and G. Duncan, "Murder in the Family: A Study of Some Homicidal Adolescents," *American Journal of Psychiatry* 127:1498–1502 (1971); C. King, "The Ego and Integration of Violence in Homicidal Youth," *American Journal of Orthopsychiatry* 45:134–145 (1975); James Sorrells, "Kids Who Kill," *Crime and Delinquency* 23:312–326 (1977).

162. Jose Alfaro, "Report of the Relationship between Child Abuse and Neglect and Later Socially Deviant Behavior." Unpublished paper (Albany, NY: New York State Government, n.d.), pp. 175–219.

163. Cathy Spatz Widom, "Child Abuse, Neglect, and Violent Criminal Behavior," *Criminology* 27:251–271 (1989).

164. Cathy Spatz Widom, "The Cycle of Violence." *Science* 244:160–166 (1989).

165. Michael Maxfield and Cathy Spatz Widom, "Childhood Victimization and Patterns of Offending Through the Life Cycle: Early Onset and Continuation," paper presented at the annual meeting of the American Society of Criminology, Boston, November 1995.

166. Jane Siegel and Linda Meyer Williams, "Violent Behavior among Men Abused as Children," paper presented at the annual meeting of the American Society of Criminology, Boston, November 1995; Jane Siegel and Linda Meyer Williams, "Aggressive Behavior among Women Sexually Abused as Children," paper presented at the annual meeting of the American Society of Criminology meeting, Phoenix, November 1993 (rev. version).

167. David Skuse, Arnon Bentovim, Jill Hodges, Jim Stevenson, Chriso Andreou, Monica Lanyado, Michelle New, Bryn Williams, and Dean McMillan, "Risk Factors for Development of Sexually Abusive Behaviour in Sexually Victimised Adolescent Boys: Cross Sectional Study," *British Medical Journal* 317:175–180 (1998).

168. Carolyn Smith and Terence Thornberry, "The Relationship between Childhood Maltreatment and Adolescent Involvement in Delinquency," *Criminology* 33:451–477 (1995).

169. Widom, "Child Abuse, Neglect, and Violent Criminal Behavior," p. 267.

170. Bruce Rind, Philip Tromovitch, and Robert Bauserman, "A Meta-Analytic Examination of Assumed Properties of Child Sexual Abuse Using College Samples," *Psychological Bulletin* 124:22–53 (1998).

171. Matthew Zingraff, "Child Maltreatment and Youthful Problem Behavior," *Criminology* 31:173–202 (1993).

172. Timothy Ireland, Carolyn Smith, and Terence Thornberry, "Developmental Issues in the Impact of Child Maltreatment on Later Delinquency and Drug Use," *Criminology* 40:359–401 (2002).

173. Ibid.

174. Kristi Holsinger and Alexander Holsinger, "Differential Pathways to Violence and Self-Injurious Behavior: African American and White Girls in the Juvenile Justice System," *Journal of Research in Crime and Delinquency* 42:211–242 (2005).

175. Leonard Edwards and Inger Sagatun, "Dealing with Parent and Child in Serious Abuse Cases," *Juvenile and Family Court Journal* 34:9–14 (1983).

176. Susan McPherson, Lance McDonald, and Charles Ryer, "Intensive Counseling with Families of Juvenile Offenders," *Juvenile and Family Court Journal* 34:27–34 (1983).

177. The programs in this section are described in Edward Zigler, Cara Taussig, and Kathryn Black, "Early Childhood Intervention, a Promising Preventative for Juvenile Delinquency," *American Psychologist* 47:997–1006 (1992).

178. Lawrence W. Sherman, Denise C. Gottfredson, Doris L. MacKenzie, John Eck, Peter Reuter, and Shawn D. Bushway, *Preventing Crime: What Works, What Doesn't, What's Promising* (Washington, DC: National Institute of Justice, 1998).

179. Zigler, Taussig, and Black, "Early Childhood Intervention: A Promising Preventative for Juvenile Delinquency," pp. 1000–1004.

9

Peers and Delinquency: Juvenile Gangs and Groups

Chapter Outline

Chapter Objectives

1. Be familiar with the influence of peers on delinquency
2. Compare and contrast the different views of the association between peers and delinquency
3. Understand the problem of lumping troubled kids together in the same programs
4. Know the various definitions used to describe gangs
5. Discuss the history of gangs
6. Be familiar with the extent and location of the gang problem
7. Discuss the various forms contemporary gangs take
8. Describe the makeup of gangs
9. Describe gang criminality
10. Compare the various theories of gang formation
11. Describe the various forms of gang-control efforts that are in use today

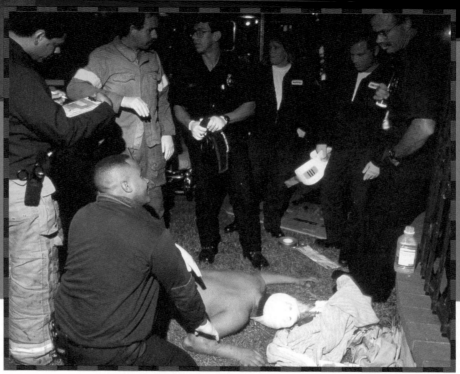

In June 2007, gang investigator Greg Ross faced a dilemma. He had been led to believe that a local gang kid named Squiggy, currently locked up in the Gwinnett County, Georgia, jail, was in store for a "beat-down" by a rival.[1] Before he could do something to prevent that from happening, Ross had to figure out what gang Squiggy belonged to, who was after Squiggy, and Squiggy's real name. Ross specializes in gathering intelligence on gang members who are currently serving time in jail. In order for Ross to keep the peace and maintain security in the county jail, he has to know which prisoners are gang members, which gangs are feuding, and who belongs to which group. He tries to prevent members of feuding gangs such as the Bloods and Crips from being housed together in the same cell. He knows that members of the Folk Nation use a six-pointed star as an identifying symbol while People Nation members use a five-pointed star in their tattoos and graffiti. The difference is important because if you house members of the different gangs together they are apt to kill one another. Even though it is located in a rural county, rougly 10 percent of Gwinnett County Jail's 2,400 inmates have gang affiliations, and they belong to 30 to 40 different gangs. Ross gets his information from a variety of sources, including inmates' letters about who's joining which gang and where they are meeting. He watches to see who comes in with similar markings, and he listens to inmates who are gang members. Without his vigilance, people like Squiggy might not live long enough to complete their sentence.

Few issues in the study of delinquency are more important today than the problems presented by law-violating gangs and groups.[2] Although some gangs are made up of only a few loosely organized neighborhood youths, others have thousands of members who cooperate in complex illegal enterprises. A significant portion of all drug distribution in the nation's inner cities is believed to be gang-controlled; gang violence accounts for more than 1,000 homicides each year. There has been an outcry from politicians to increase punishment for the "little monsters" and to save the "fallen angels," or the victimized youths who are innocent.[3]

The problem of gang control is a difficult one. Many gangs flourish in inner-city areas that offer lower-class youths few conventional opportunities, and members are resistant to offers of help that cannot deliver legitimate economic hope. Although

For a general overview of **gangs in America**, go to the Know Gangs website via academic.cengage.com/criminaljustice/siegel.

gang members may be subject to arrest, prosecution, and incarceration, a new crop of young recruits is always ready to take the place of their fallen comrades. Those sent to prison find that, upon release, their former gangs are only too willing to have them return to action.

We begin this chapter with a discussion of peer relations, showing how they influence delinquent behavior. Then we explore the definition, nature, and structure of delinquent gangs. Finally, the chapter presents theories of gang formation, the extent of gang activity, and gang-control efforts.

ADOLESCENT PEER RELATIONS

Although parents are the primary source of influence and attention in children's early years, between ages 8 and 14 children seek out a stable peer group, and both the number and the variety of friendships increase as children go through adolescence. Friends soon begin to have a greater influence over decision making than parents.

cliques
Small groups of friends who share intimate knowledge and confidences.

As they go through adolescence, children form cliques, small groups of friends who share activities and confidences.[4] They also belong to crowds, loosely organized groups of children who share interests and activities such as sports, religion, or hobbies. Intimate friends play an important role in social development, but adolescents are also deeply influenced by this wider circle of friends. Adolescent self-image is in part formed by perceptions of one's place in their social world.[5] Kids not only are influenced by their close intimates but also model their behavior on that displayed by others they are less familiar with or do not associate with as long as it can impress their immediate group. In mid-adolescence, kids strive for peer approval and to impress their closest friends.[6]

crowds
Loosely organized groups who share interests and activities.

In later adolescence, acceptance by peers continues to have a major impact on socialization. By their teens, children report that their friends give them emotional support when they are feeling bad and that they can confide intimate feelings to peers without worrying about their confidences being betrayed. Poor peer relations such as negative interactions with best friends has been found to be related to high social anxiety while, in contrast, close affiliation with a high-status peer crowd seems to afford protection against depression and other negative adolescent psychological symptoms.[7] Some kids may seek out others with similar tastes, fears, and anxieties. They may feed off each other emotionally. Girls may seek peers with similar body image problems and together get involved in diet and extreme weight loss activities that can be physically and emotionally harmful.[8]

Popular youths do well in school and are socially astute. In contrast, children who are rejected by their peers are more likely to display aggressive behavior and to disrupt group activities by bickering or behaving antisocially. Another group of kids—controversial status youth—are aggressive kids who are either highly liked or intensely disliked by their peers. These controversial youths are the ones most likely to become engaged in antisocial behavior. When they find themselves in leadership positions among their peers they get them involved in delinquent and problem behaviors.[9]

controversial status youth
Aggressive kids who are either highly liked or intensely disliked by their peers and who are the ones most likely to become engaged in antisocial behavior.

It is clear that peer status during childhood is an important contributor to a child's social and emotional development that follows the child across the life course. Girls who engage in aggressive behavior with childhood peers later have more conflict-ridden relationships with their romantic partners.[10] Boys who are highly aggressive and are therefore rejected by their peers in childhood are also more likely to engage in criminality and delinquency from adolescence into young adulthood.[11] Peer relations, then, are a significant aspect of maturation. Peer influence may be more important than parental nurturance in the development of long-term behavior.[12] Recent research by Marvella Bowman and her associates found that at least among one group, young African American males, peer influence was able to neutralize the positive effects of maternal monitoring and control on deviant behaviors.[13] Peers guide each other and help each other learn to share and cooperate, to cope with aggressive impulses, and to discuss feelings they would not dare bring up at home. Youths can compare their own experiences with peers and learn that others have similar concerns and problems.[14]

Peer Relations and Delinquency

Youths who report inadequate or strained peer relations are the ones most likely to become delinquent.[15] Adolescents who maintain delinquent friends are more likely to engage in antisocial behavior and drug abuse.[16] In fact, kids who abstain from delinquency are widely considered to be socially isolated and deviant since engaging in antisocial activities such as drinking, smoking pot, and shoplifting is the norm in adolescence.[17]

Research shows that peer group relationships are closely tied to delinquent behaviors: Delinquent acts tend to be committed in small groups rather than alone, a process referred to as *co-offending*.[18] Many kids are initiated into deviant activities such as smoking marijuana by their friends, and their friends prodeviant attitudes are then used to help support continued involvement in antisocial and or illegal acts.[19] Some kids are particularly susceptible to peer influence. A number of research efforts have found that boys who go through puberty at an early age were more likely to later engage in violence, property crimes, drug use, and precocious sexual behavior.[20] The boys who matured early were the most likely to develop strong attachments to delinquent friends and to be influenced by peer pressure.[21] The conclusion: The earlier youngsters develop relationships with delinquent peers and the closer those relationships get, the more likely they will become delinquent. It is not surprising that delinquent girls are significantly more likely than nondelinquent girls to identify males as their closest friends.[22] For girls, hanging out with males, who are at a higher risk for delinquency than female peers, may be a precursor to antisocial behavior choices.

Peer relations, in all cultures, have been linked to adolescent behavior choices, including substance abuse and delinquency.

© Janine Wiedel/Photolibrary/Alamy

Impact of Peer Relations

Does having antisocial peers cause delinquency, or are delinquents antisocial youths who seek out like-minded companions because they can be useful in committing crimes? There are actually five independent viewpoints on this question:

I   *Alienation.* According to the control theory approach articulated by Travis Hirschi (Chapter 5), delinquents are as detached from their peers as they are from other elements of society.[23] Although they appear to have close friends, delinquents actually lack the social skills to make their peer relations rewarding or fulfilling.[24] Antisocial adolescents seek out like-minded peers for criminal associations. If delinquency is committed in groups, it is because "birds of a feather flock together."

I   *Peer influence.* Delinquent friends cause law-abiding youth to get in trouble. Kids who fall in with a bad crowd are at risk for delinquency. Youths who maintain friendships with antisocial peers are more likely to become delinquent regardless of their own personality or the type of supervision they receive at home.[25] Even previously law-abiding youths are more likely to get involved in delinquency if they become associated with friends who initiate them into delinquent careers.[26]

I   *Peer selection.* Antisocial youths join up with like-minded friends; deviant peers sustain and amplify delinquent careers.[27] Deviant peers do not cause straight kids to go bad, but they amplify the likelihood of a troubled kid getting further involved in antisocial behaviors.[28] As children move through the life course, antisocial friends help them maintain delinquent careers and obstruct the aging-out process.[29] In contrast, nondelinquent friends moderate delinquency.[30] If adulthood brings close and sustaining ties to conventional friends, and marriage and family, the level of deviant behavior will decline.[31]

I   *Conspirators.* Troubled kids choose delinquent peers out of necessity rather than desire. Delinquent kids come from distressed homes, maintain emotional problems, and do poorly in school. These social factors, and not peer influence, are the true cause of their delinquent behaviors.[32] Why do delinquent kids have delinquent friends? The social baggage they cart around prevents them from developing associations with conventional peers. Because they are impulsive, they may hook up with friends who are of similar temperaments in order to sell drugs and commit crimes.[33]

I   *Outsiders.* Kids who display emotional or behavioral problems early in childhood are labeled "strange" or "weird" by other kids, labels that stick into mid-adolescence. Stigma leads to estrangement and feelings of isolation and loneliness. Alienated kids are susceptible to depression and psychological deficits that some-day may lead to antisocial behavior and substance abuse.[34]

Although each of these scenarios has its advocates, the weight of the empirical evidence clearly indicates that delinquent peers have a significant influence on behavior: youths who are loyal to delinquent friends, belong to gangs, and have "bad companions" are the ones most likely to commit crimes and engage in violence.[35] It is also possible that there is an interactive effect: Kids who are outsiders select delinquent friends who then have an important influence on their behavior. For example, kids who smoke may choose other smokers as their friends; hanging out with smokers supports and accelerates their smoking activity.[36]

It is also possible that the friendship patterns of delinquents may not be dissimilar from those of nondelinquents; delinquent youths report that their peer relations contain elements of caring and trust and that they can be open and intimate with their friends.[37] Warm intergroup associations contradict the control theory model, which holds that delinquents are loners, and support the cultural deviance view that delinquents form close-knit groups that sustain their behavior.

Public Policy and Peer Influence

Ironically, even though the prevailing wisdom is that delinquency is strongly influenced by interaction and involvement with older and/or more experienced peers, most correctional programs in school and the juvenile justice system continue to organize deviant peers into groups and isolate them from conventional law-abiding kids. In their important 2006 book, *Deviant Peer Influences in Programs for Youth: Problems and Solutions*, Kenneth A. Dodge, Thomas Dishion, and Jennifer Lansford find that public policy is often based on the need to remove deviant youth from the mainstream and segregate them, together, in groups.[38]

This policy takes place on many different levels. Schools place children who display conduct problems in special education for diagnosis as "seriously emotionally disturbed" (SED) or "behaviorally or emotionally handicapped" (BEH). Once in these groups, students are treated in self-contained classrooms for almost the whole day. The effects of this aggregation include both the possibility of deviant peer influence and the loss of opportunities for positive influence from well-adjusted peers. Several studies indicate that students receiving special education services are more likely to be suffer suspension and expulsion than non–special education students. There is evidence that special education for children with conduct problems may actually increase problem behavior.

Problem kids are also lumped together in the juvenile justice system. Delinquents are placed in residential settings such as detention centers, training schools, reform schools, prisons, boot camps, and wilderness camps that are populated exclusively by other offending youth. In all of these settings, youth interact primarily with other deviant youth under circumstances of limited adult supervision.

While we might suspect that programs in the juvenile justice system are forced to aggregate at-risk kids, Dodge, Dishion, and Lansford find that community programs employ the same policy. A variety of programs that are designed to keep at-risk youth off the streets offer little structure or adult supervision and simply provide a place for youth to hang out. These programs may have the unintended effect of increasing behavior problems by increasing the aggregation of at-risk youth.

Foster care programs may also lead to the aggregation of deviant youth. Sometimes vulnerable children and adolescents who are removed from the homes of their biological parents risk increased exposure to negative peer influences through experiences in group foster care.

In sum, while the influence of peers on youth behavior is well known and well documented, our national policy in the school, community, and justice system has been to isolate at-risk kids, lump them together, and exacerbate the negative effects of peer influence.

YOUTH GANGS

gang
Group of youths who collectively engage in delinquent behaviors.

As youths move through adolescence, they gravitate toward cliques that provide them with support, assurance, protection, and direction. In some instances the peer group provides the social and emotional basis for antisocial activity. When this happens, the clique is transformed into a **gang**.

Today, such a powerful mystique has grown up around gangs that mere mention of the word evokes images of black-jacketed youths roaming the streets in groups bearing such names as the MS-13, Latin Kings, Crips, and Bloods. Films, television shows, novels, and even Broadway musicals (e.g., *West Side Story, Grease*), have popularized the youth gang.[39]

Considering the suspected role gangs play in violent crime and drug activity, it is not surprising that gangs have recently become the target of a great deal of research interest.[40] Important attempts have been made to gauge their size, location, makeup, and activities.

What Are Gangs?

Gangs are groups of youths who engage in delinquent behaviors. Yet gang delinquency differs from group delinquency. Whereas group delinquency consists of a short-lived alliance created to commit a particular crime or violent act, gang delinquency involves

EXHIBIT 9.1
Definitions of Teen Gangs

Frederick Thrasher

An interstitial group originally formed spontaneously and then integrated through conflict. It is characterized by the following types of behavior: meeting face to face, milling, movement through space as a unit, conflict, and planning. The result of this collective behavior is the development of tradition, unreflective internal structure, esprit de corps, solidarity, morale, group awareness, and attachment to local territory.

Malcolm Klein

Any denotable adolescent group of youngsters who (a) are generally perceived as a distinct aggregation by others in their neighborhood; (b) recognize themselves as a denotable group (almost invariably with a group name); and (c) have been involved in a sufficient number of delinquent incidents to call forth a consistent negative response from neighborhood residents and/or law enforcement agencies.

Desmond Cartwright

An interstitial and integrated group of people who meet face to face more or less regularly and whose existence and activities are considered an actual or potential threat to the prevailing social order.

Walter Miller

A self-formed association of peers, bound together by mutual interests, with identifiable leadership, well-developed lines of authority, and other organizational features, who act in concert to achieve a specific purpose or purposes, which generally include the conduct of illegal activity and control over a particular territory, facility, or type of enterprise.

G. David Curry and Irving Spergel

Groups containing law-violating juveniles and adults that are complexly organized, although sometimes diffuse, and sometimes cohesive, with established leadership and membership rules. The gang also engages in a range of crime (but with significantly more violence) within a framework of norms and values in respect to mutual support, conflict relations with other gangs, and a tradition of turf, colors, signs, and symbols. Subgroups of the gang may be deferentially committed to various delinquent or criminal patterns, such as drug trafficking, gang fighting, or burglary.

James Short

Gangs are groups of young people whose members meet together with some regularity, over time, on the basis of group-defined criteria of membership and group-defined organizational characteristics. In the simplest terms, gangs are unsupervised (by adults), self-determining groups that demonstrate continuity over time.

National Youth Gang Center

A youth gang is commonly thought of as a self-formed association of peers having the following characteristics: three or more members, generally ages 12 to 24; a name and some sense of identity, generally indicated by such symbols as style of clothing, graffiti, and hand signs; some degree of permanence and organization; and an elevated level of involvement in delinquent or criminal activity.

SOURCES: Frederick Thrasher, *The Gang* (Chicago: University of Chicago Press, 1927), p. 57; Malcolm Klein, *Street Gangs and Street Workers* (Englewood Cliffs, NJ: Prentice Hall, 1971), p. 13; Desmond Cartwright, Barbara Tomson, and Hersey Schwarts, eds., *Gang Delinquency* (Pacific Grove, CA: Brooks/Cole, 1975), pp. 149–150; Walter Miller, "Gangs, Groups, and Serious Youth Crime," in David Schicor and Delos Kelly, eds., *Critical Issues in Juvenile Delinquency* (Lexington, MA: Lexington Books, 1980); G. David Curry and Irving Spergel, "Gang Homicide, Delinquency, and Community," *Criminology* 26:382; James Short, Jr., and Fred Strodtbeck, *Group Process and Gang Delinquency* (Chicago: University of Chicago Press, 1965); National Youth Gang Center, www.iir.com/nygc/faq.htm#q1 (accessed July 20, 2007).

long-lived institutions that have a distinct structure and organization, including identifiable leadership, division of labor, rules, rituals, and possessions.

Delinquency experts are often at odds over the precise definition of a gang. The term is sometimes used broadly to describe any congregation of youths who have joined together to engage in delinquent acts. However, police departments often use it only to refer to cohesive groups that hold and defend territory, or turf.[41]

Academic experts have also created a variety of definitions (see Exhibit 9.1). The core elements in the concept of the gang are that it is an **interstitial group**— one falling within the cracks and crevices of society—and that it maintains standard group processes, such as recruiting new members, setting goals, assigning roles, and developing status.[42]

interstitial group
Delinquent group that fills a crack in the social fabric and maintains standard group practices.

Malcolm Klein argues that two factors stand out in all of these definitions:

1. Members have self-recognition of their gang status and use special vocabulary, clothing, signs, colors, graffiti, and names. Members set themselves apart from the community and are viewed as a separate entity by others. Once they get the label of gang, members eventually accept and take pride in their status.

2. There is a commitment to criminal activity, although even the most criminal gang members spend the bulk of their time in noncriminal activities.[43]

How Did Gangs Develop?

The youth gang is sometimes viewed as uniquely American, but gangs have also been reported in several other nations.[44] Nor are gangs a recent phenomenon. In the 1600s, London was terrorized by organized gangs that called themselves Hectors, Bugles,

Dead Boys, and other colorful names. In the seventeenth and eighteenth centuries, English gang members wore distinctive belts and pins marked with serpents, animals, stars, and the like.[45] The first mention of youth gangs in America occurred in the late 1780s, when prison reformers noted the presence of gangs of young people hanging out on Philadelphia's street corners. By the 1820s, New York's Bowery and Five Points districts, Boston's North End and Fort Hill, and the outlying Southwark and Moya-mensing sections of Philadelphia were the locales of youth gangs with colorful names like the Roach Guards, Chichesters, the Plug Uglies, and the Dead Rabbits.[46]

In the 1920s, Frederick Thrasher initiated the study of the modern gang in his analysis of more than 1,300 youth groups in Chicago.[47] He found that the social, economic, and ecological processes that affect the structure of cities create cracks in the normal fabric of society—weak family controls, poverty, and social disorganization— and referred to this as an *interstitial area*. According to Thrasher, groups of youths develop to meet such needs as play, fun, and adventure—activities that sometimes lead to delinquent acts. Impoverished areas present many opportunities for conflict between groups of youths and adult authority. If this conflict continues, the groups become more solidified and their activities become primarily illegal, and the groups develop into gangs.

According to Thrasher, adult society does not meet the needs of lower-class youths, and the gang solves the problem by offering excitement, fun, and opportunity. The gang is not a haven for disturbed youths but an alternative lifestyle for normal boys. Thrasher's work has had an important influence. Recent studies of delinquent gang behavior also view the gang as a means for lower-class boys to achieve advancement and opportunity as well as to defend themselves and to attack rivals.[48]

To view current examples of **gang graffiti and learn to interpret what they mean**, visit gangwar.com via academic.cengage.com/criminaljustice/siegel.

Gangs in the 1950s and 1960s In the 1950s and early 1960s, the threat of gangs and gang violence swept the public consciousness. Rarely did a week go by without a major city newspaper featuring a story on the violent behavior of fighting gangs and their colorful leaders and names—the Egyptian Kings, the Vice Lords, the Blackstone Rangers. Social service and law enforcement agencies directed major efforts to either rehabilitate or destroy the gangs. Movies, such as *The Wild Ones* and *Blackboard Jungle*, were made about gangs, and the Broadway musical *West Side Story* romanticized violent gangs.

In his classic 1967 work, *Juvenile Gangs in Context*, Malcolm Klein summarized existing knowledge about gangs.[49] He concluded that gang membership was a way for individual boys to satisfy certain personal needs that were related to the development of youths caught up in the emotional turmoil typical of the period between adolescence and adulthood. A natural inclination to form gangs is reinforced by the perception that the gang represents a substitute for unattainable middle-class rewards.

The experience of being a member of a gang will dominate a youngster's perceptions, values, expectations, and behavior. Finally, the gang is self-reinforcing: It is within the gang more than anywhere else that a youngster may find forms of acceptance for delinquent behavior—rewards instead of negative sanctions. And as the gang strives for internal cohesion, the negative sanctions of the "outside world" become interpreted as threats to cohesion, thus providing secondary reinforcement for the values central to the legitimization of gang behavior.[50]

By the mid-1960s, the gang menace seemed to have disappeared. Some experts attribute the decline of gang activity to successful gang-control programs.[51] They believed that gangs were eliminated because police gang-control units infiltrated gangs, arrested leaders, and constantly harassed members.[52] Gang boys were more likely to be sanctioned by the juvenile justice system and receive more severe sentences than nongang youths.[53] Another explanation for the decline in gang activity was the increase in political awareness that developed during the 1960s. Many gang leaders became involved in the social or political activities of ethnic pride, civil rights, and antiwar groups. In addition, many gang members were drafted. Still another explanation is that gang activity diminished during the 1960s because many gang members became active users of heroin and other drugs, which curtailed their group-related criminal activity.[54]

Members of the New York youth gang the Savage Skulls fighting in the street in 1972. The trademark of the gang was a sleeveless denim jacket with a skull and crossbones design on the back. Based around Fox Street in the South Bronx, the gang fought battles with rival gangs such as the Seven Immortals and Savage Nomads. By 1975, there were 275 police-verified gangs with a total of 11,000 members.

© JP Laffont/Sygma/Corbis

Gangs Reemerge Interest in gang activity began anew in the early 1970s. Bearing such names as Savage Skulls and Black Assassins, gangs began to form in New York's South Bronx neighborhoods in the spring of 1971 and quickly spread to other parts of the city. By 1975, there were 275 police-verified gangs, with 11,000 members.[55]

Gang activity also reemerged in other major cities, such as Chicago and Los Angeles. The Crips gang was created in Los Angeles in 1969 by teens Raymond Washington and Stanley "Tookie" Williams. Initially called the Baby Avenues, they evolved to Avenue Cribs, and then Cribs. According to legend, the gang name evolved into Crips because some of its members used canes to attack victims; it is also possible it was a simple spelling mistake in newspaper articles about the gang.

As the Crips gained power, other rival gangs feared their growing dominance. By late 1971, L.A. Brims, Piru Street Boys, the Bishops, Athens Park Boys, and other gang boys met to discuss how to combat Crip intimidation. The gangs merged and called themselves the Bloods, known for wearing a red bandana and slashing victims to draw their blood as part of the gang initiation rights. Eventually both these gangs sent representatives to organize chapters in distant areas or to take over existing gangs.

Why Did Gangs Reemerge? One reason for the increase in gang activity may be involvement in the sale of illegal drugs.[56] Early gangs relied on group loyalty to encourage membership, but modern gang members are lured by the quest for drug profits. In some areas, gangs replaced organized crime families as the dominant suppliers of cocaine and crack. The traditional weapons of gangs—chains, knives, and homemade guns—were replaced by automatic weapons.

Gang formation was also the natural consequence of the economic and social dislocation that occurred when the economy shifted from a relatively high-paying manufacturing to low-wage service economy.[57] Some U.S. cities that required a large population base for their manufacturing plants now face economic stress as these plants shut down. In this uneasy economic climate, gangs flourish, while the influence of successful adult role models and stable families declines. The presence of gangs in areas unaccustomed to delinquent group activity can have a devastating effect on community life.

While this social dislocation was occurring, the media fell in love with gang images, which appeared in films and music videos. Gangsta rap became a national phenomenon. Because there has been a diffusion of the gang culture through the popular media, in which gang boys are made to appear as successful heroes, urban kids may find the lure of gangs and law-violating peer groups irresistible.

CONTEMPORARY GANGS

The gang cannot be viewed as a uniform or homogeneous social concept. Gangs vary by activity, makeup, location, leadership style, and age. The next sections describe some of the most salient features of contemporary gangs.

Extent

The federal government sponsors the National Youth Gang Survey (NYGS) to measure gang activity around the United States. The most recent NYGS found that a significant majority of urban areas report the presence of gangs and that gangs exist in all levels of the social strata, from rural counties to metropolitan areas. However, as Figure 9.1 shows, gang activity has declined during the past decade.[58] While the national survey shows that there are actually fewer gang members today than in the past, there is still an enormous number of gang kids. At recent count an estimated 760,000 gang members and 24,000 gangs were active in more than 2,900 jurisdictions around the United States.

Location

Traditionally, gangs have operated in large urban areas experiencing rapid population change. In these transitional neighborhoods, diverse ethnic and racial groups find themselves in competition with one another.[59] Intergang conflict and homicide rates are high in these areas, which house the urban "underclass."[60] However, these neighborhoods eventually evolve into permanently **disorganized neighborhoods**, where population shifts slow down, permitting patterns of behavior and traditions to develop over a number of years. Most typical are the poverty-stricken areas of New York and Chicago and the Mexican American barrios of the southwestern states and

disorganized neighborhood
Inner-city areas of extreme poverty where the critical social control mechanisms have broken down.

FIGURE 9.1
Estimated Total Gang Membership

SOURCE: National Youth Gang Survey Analysis, www.iir.com/NYGC/nygsa/ measuring_the_extent_of_gang_ problems.htm#numberofgangs (accessed October 20, 2007).

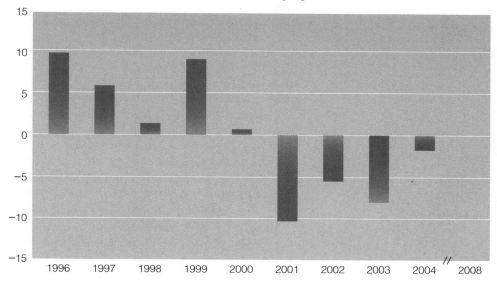

Percent difference from 9-year average: The number of gang members is in decline

California. These areas contain large, structured gang clusters that are resistant to change or control by law enforcement agencies.

While some people think of gangs as a purely urban phenomenon, an estimated 15,000 gangs with 300,000 members are located in small cities, suburban counties, and even rural areas. The growth of gangs in suburban and rural areas has been attributed to a restructuring of the population. There has been a massive movement of people out of the central city to outlying communities and suburbs. In some cities, once-fashionable neighborhoods have declined, while in others downtown areas have undergone extensive renewal. Previously impoverished inner-city districts of major cities such as New York and Chicago are now quite fashionable and expensive, devoted to finance, retail stores, high-priced condos, and entertainment. Two aspects of this development inhibit urban gang formation: (1) there are few residential areas and thus few adolescent recruits, and (2) there is intensive police patrol.

Migration

Because of redevelopment, gangs in some areas have relocated or migrated; gang members have organized new chapters when they relocate to new areas. The most recent NYGS found many jurisdictions have experienced gang migration and in a few areas more than half of all gang members had come from other areas.

Why do gang members migrate? While the prevailing wisdom is that gang members move for criminal purposes (e.g., to sell drugs to new customers at higher prices), the NYGS found that most did so for social reasons (e.g., members moving with families, pursuit of legitimate employment opportunities). Others sought new drug market opportunities or wanted to avoid law enforcement crackdowns in their home towns. In all, less than 20 percent moved to a new location solely in order to participate in illegal ventures in a new area that may have less gang competition.[61]

Read more about **gang migration**, from the Office of Juvenile Justice and Delinquency Prevention, via academic.cengage.com/criminaljustice/siegel.

Most migrators are African American or Hispanic males who maintain close ties with members of their original gangs "back home."[62] Some migrants join local gangs, shedding old ties and gaining new affiliations. Although some experts fear the outcome of migration, it appears the number of migrants is relatively small in proportion to the overall gang population, supporting the contention that most gangs actually are "homegrown."[63]

International Migration and Development

The gang problem is not unique to the United States. John Hagedorn, a noted gang expert, finds that a global criminal economy, especially the illegal distribution of drugs, involves gangs as both major and bit players. Numerous gangs operate in distressed areas such as the townships of South Africa where they rule politically and control the underground economy. Chinese Triads operate all across the globe but are especially active in South Asia and the United States. In eastern Europe, the turmoil caused by the move to a market economy and the loss of social safety nets has strengthened gangs and drug organizations. In Albania, one-quarter of all young males are involved in the drug economy.[64]

Hagedorn finds that gangs are now being exported from one nation to another. There are Jamaican posses in Kansas; San Diego's Calle Trente gang had a past relationship to Mexico's Arellano brothers cartel; the Russian "mafiya" now operates in Chicago; female Muslim gangs are active in Oslo, Norway; and L.A.'s MS-13 and 18th Street gangs are now the largest gangs in Honduras and El Salvador (more on these gangs follows).[65] Hagedorn finds that changing social and economic conditions in our post-globalization world supports the spread of gang activity:

▎ Worldwide urbanization and the concentration of population in crowded, poor, and disorganized cities has created fertile conditions for the growth of gangs, particularly in Latin America, Asia, and Africa.

- In the global era, the state has retreated from its role of providing social welfare and an economic safety net. Gangs and other groups of armed young men occupy the vacuum created by the retreat of the social welfare policies of the state.

- Kids who fear being marginalized in a technological economy that is growing more sophisticated by the day seek alternatives to conventional society. In some nations they may join fundamentalist religious groups or extremely nationalistic political parties. Others have embraced the hip-hop or gangsta culture that provides them with a new identity in opposition to the conventional mainstream culture from which they have been excluded.

- Globalization has created a flourishing underground economy that can be exploited by internationally connected enterprises run by gangs, cartels, and similar groups who can easily export black market items ranging from guns to pirated films and CDs.

- The wealth of the global economy has led to the redivision of space in cities all across the globe. "Economic development," "making the city safe," and "ethnic cleansing" has meant clearing out undesirables from urban spaces coveted by dominant ethnic or religious majorities. In America, this often means displacing African American youth from city centers so they can be gentrified and rebuilt. This upheaval has increased the attractiveness of gangs for the displaced youths now living in ring-cities or nearby suburbs.

- Some gangs institutionalize and become permanent social actors in communities, cities, and nations rather than fading away after a generation. These gangs often replace or rival demoralized political groups and play important social, economic, and political roles in cities around the world.

Types

Gangs have been categorized by their dominant activity: Some are devoted to violence and to protecting neighborhood boundaries or turf; others are devoted to theft; some specialize in drug trafficking; still others are concerned with recreation rather than crime.[66] Jeffrey Fagan found that most gangs fall into one of these four categories:

- *Social gang.* Involved in few delinquent activities and little drug use other than alcohol and marijuana. Members are more interested in social activities.

- *Party gang.* Concentrates on drug use and sales but forgoes most delinquent behavior. Drug sales are designed to finance members' personal drug use.

- *Serious delinquent gang.* Engages in serious delinquent behavior while avoiding drug dealing and usage. Drugs are used only on social occasions.

- *Organized gang.* Heavily involved in criminality. Drug use and sales are related to other criminal acts. Gang violence is used to establish control over drug sale territories. This gang is on the verge of becoming a formal criminal organization.[67]

The format and structure of gangs may be changing. They are now commonly described as having a "hybrid gang culture," meaning they do not follow a single code of rules or method of operation. Today's gangs do have several common characteristics:

- A mixture of racial/ethnic groups
- A mixture of symbols and graffiti associated with different gangs
- Wearing colors traditionally associated with a rival gang
- Less concern over turf or territory
- Members who sometimes switch from one gang to another[68]

The Focus on Delinquency feature entitled "Getting High and Getting By" presents research showing that not only are there different types of gangs, but there may also be different types of gang boys.

Getting High and Getting By: Drug Dealing Gangs and Gang Boys in Southwest Texas

Avelardo Valdez and Stephen J. Sifaneck, two gang experts, have studied the role that Mexican American gangs and gang members play in drug markets, and the relationship between gang member drug use and drug-selling behaviors. Using an innovative research design that involved identifying and observing gang members creating focus groups (essentially group interviews, relying on in-group interaction, designed to obtain perceptions on a defined area of interest), and life history interviews, they gained in-depth knowledge of the lives of 160 males in 26 different Hispanic gangs operating in southwest Texas.

GANG CATEGORIES

Valdez and Sifaneck found that gangs could be divided into two separate categories according to their involvement in drug-dealing criminal enterprise. One grouping, made up of 19 of the 26 gangs they identified, shun drug dealing and are organized as traditional, territory-based gangs. They engage in gang rituals such as identification with distinct colors, hand signs, and gang "placas" (symbols) and are involved in a variety of criminal acts, including auto theft, burglary, robbery, vandalism, criminal mischief, and petty crime; some members deal drugs on their own. Members of these types of gangs tend to act as individuals. Their violence is personal and random rather than collective and organized. Gang membership offers protection from rivals, other gang boys, or people in the community who threaten them; protection is extended to those members who are involved in drug selling and dealing activities.

The second group was made up of the remaining seven gangs that were organized into criminal drug-dealing enterprises. These have a more clearly defined leadership that takes a share of the profits generated from all gang members involved in the business. These gangs are not concerned with territorial issues or "turf violations," and do not engage in random acts of violence such as drive-by shootings. Violence among these gangs tends to be more organized and related to drug distribution (though some members may be involved in other criminal enterprises such as auto theft and fencing stolen goods).

THE GANG MEMBER'S ROLE

The second dimension discovered by Valdez and Sifaneck was an individual gang member's role in selling and dealing drugs within

the gang. The one extreme of this dimension is the user-seller who is primarily buying drugs for personal consumption, and selling a portion of the drugs to offset the costs associated with his own personal drug use. The other extreme of this dimension includes the dealers, gang members who deal drugs (marijuana, cocaine, and heroin) for their own profit. The cross-classification of drug style with gang type is illustrated in Figure 9-A.

Homeboys

Homeboys are gang members who belong to a street gang whose criminal behavior tends to be more individual, less organized, and less gang-directed. Most of their violence is centered on interpersonal fights and random situational acts of violence often associated with male bravado. Most of these user-sellers usually buy just what they are going to use to get high and sell small remaining quantities to reduce the costs associated with their own consumption. These members usually score small amounts for themselves, friends, and other associates.

Hustlers: Drug Dealers in Nondealing Gangs

In this category gang members identified as hustlers are dealing drugs for profit within a street gang that is not

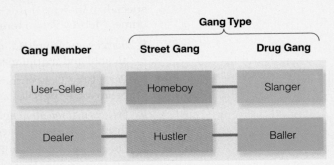

FIGURE 9.A

A Typology of Drug Dealers and User-Sellers in Street and Drug Gangs

---

Cohesion

near-groups
Clusters of youth who, outwardly, seem unified but actually have limited cohesion, impermanence, minimal consensus of norms, shifting membership, disturbed leadership, and limited definitions of membership expectations.

The standard definition of a gang implies that it is a cohesive group. However, some experts refer to gangs as **near-groups**, which have limited cohesion, impermanence, minimal consensus of norms, shifting membership, disturbed leadership, and limited definitions of membership expectations.[69] Gangs maintain a small core of committed members, who work constantly to keep the gang going, and a much larger group of affiliated youths, who participate in gang activity only when the mood suits them.

characterized as a drug-dealing organization. However, it does provide protection to hustlers within the territory controlled by the gang. Protection is extended to those persons because they are members of the organization rather than because of their drug-selling activities. Profits generated by these hustlers are their own and are not used to support the collective activities of the street gang.

Slanger: Drug User/Sellers in Drug-Dealing Gangs

Gang members in this category are characterized as user/sellers in gangs that are organized as drug-dealing enterprises. Slangers are members who either choose not to participate in the higher levels of the gang's organized drug-dealing activities or who are excluded from those circles for various reasons. However, the slangers continue to use and sell drugs at an individual level, mostly to help offset costs associated with their drug use and to support themselves economically. In the vernacular of the gangs, these members are dealing to "get high and get by." The slangers stand in contrast to the hard-core dealer members in the drug gang who are heavily involved in the gang's higher level organized drug distribution activities.

Ballers: Drug Dealers/Drug-Dealing Gangs

Ballers are the individuals who control the drug distribution business in hard-core drug gangs. Ballers sit atop the gang's hierarchy and comprise a leadership structure that provides protection to members against rival gangs and predatory adult criminals. Among these gang members, heroin use was generally discouraged, although as the gangs began to deal heroin, many ballers began shabanging (noninjection) and or picando (injecting), and some subsequently became addicted. One of the distinctions of ballers from seller-dealers, slangers, and homeboys is their generally lower visibility and the higher volume of drugs they deal. Furthermore, they avoid ostentatious aggressive behavior that attracts law enforcement, such as drive-by shootings. Violence among ballers is also more purposeful and revolved around business transactions.

Gangs in Context

Valdez and Sifaneck found that gangs must be evaluated within the context of the community environment. Juvenile gang members' involvement in selling and dealing is influenced by the presence of adult criminals in the community. Many of these adult criminals were former juvenile gang members and later joined prison gangs. Their presence was a stabilizing force, giving the gang an intergenerational gang presence that made it more cohesive.

An important part of gang membership is protection it can give members in exchange for their commitment and obligation to the gang. Protection may often be misperceived by police as evidence that a gang is a drug-dealing enterprise when in reality members may be operating independently from the gang as an organization. Often law enforcement personnel indiscriminately extend this perception to all Mexican American youth living in these neighborhoods, resulting in continual harassment, shakedowns, and detainment of many innocent youth.

A serious consequence of this perception is very often drug law enforcement indiscriminately arrests and prosecutes offenders without distinguishing the differences that constitute the four distinct types of gang members. Consequently, when homeboys are arrested for minor violations of drug laws, such as possession of small amounts of marijuana, they are often treated like ballers, the big-time dealers. If gangs and gang members are to be dealt with in a realistic fashion, these distinctions must be recognized by law enforcement agents engaged in anti-gang activities.

Critical Thinking

1. Of the four types of gang boys identified by Valdez and Sifaneck, which do you believe might be the easiest to wean away from the gang?
2. Is it realistic to believe that a government program could convince ballers to give up drug profits for some low-paying, albeit legitimate, job?

SOURCE: Avelardo Valdez and Stephen J. Sifaneck, "Getting High and Getting By: Dimensions of Drug Selling Behaviors Among U.S. Mexican Gang Members in South Texas," *Journal of Research in Crime and Delinquency* 41:82–105 (2004).

barrio
A Spanish word meaning "district."

James Diego Vigil found that boys in Latino **barrio** gangs (Hispanic neighborhood gangs) could be separated into regular members and those he describes as "peripheral," "temporary," and "situational."[70]

Current research indicates that, although some gangs remain near-groups, others become quite organized and stable. These gangs resemble traditional organized crime families more than temporary youth groups. Some, such as Chicago's Latin Kings and Gangster Disciples, have members who pay regular dues, are expected to attend gang meetings regularly, and carry out political activities to further gang ambitions.

Age

The ages of gang members range widely, perhaps from as young as 8 to as old as 55.[71] Traditionally, most members of offending groups were usually no more than a few years apart in age, with a leader who may be a few years older than most other members.[72] However, because members are staying in gangs longer than in the past, the age spread between gang members has widened considerably.

Research indicates that youths first hear about gangs at around 9 years of age, get involved in violence at 10 or 11, and join their first gang at 12. By age 13, most members have (a) fired a pistol, (b) seen someone killed or seriously injured, (c) gotten a gang tattoo, and (d) been arrested.[73] Gang experts believe the average age of gang members has been increasing yearly, a phenomenon explained in part by the changing structure of the U.S. economy.[74]

Why Are Gang Members Aging? Gang members are getting older and the majority are now legal adults. As noted earlier, relatively high-paid, low-skilled factory jobs that would entice older gang members to leave the gang have been lost to overseas competition. A transformed U.S. economy now prioritizes information and services over heavy industry. This shift in emphasis undermines labor unions that might have attracted former gang boys. Equally damaging has been the embrace of social policies that stress security and the needs of the wealthy while weakening the economic safety net for the poor (e.g., reducing welfare eligibility). William Julius Wilson found that the inability of inner-city males to obtain adequate jobs means that they cannot afford to marry and raise families. Criminal records acquired at an early age quickly lock these youths out of the job market so that remaining in a gang becomes an economic necessity.[75] In the wake of reduced opportunity for unskilled labor, gangs have become an important ghetto employer that offers low-level drug-dealing opportunities that are certainly not available in the nongang world.[76]

Gender

Traditionally, gangs were considered a male-dominated enterprise. Of the more than 1,000 groups included in Thrasher's original survey, only half a dozen were female gangs. Females were involved in gangs in three ways: as auxiliaries (or branches) of male gangs, as part of sexually mixed gangs, or as autonomous gangs. Auxiliaries are a feminized version of the male gang name, such as the Lady Disciples rather than the Devil's Disciples.

Today the number of female gang members and female gangs is rapidly increasing and some jurisdictions report that 25 percent or more of all gang members are female.[77] However, national data indicate that (Figure 9.2) less than 10 percent of gang members are female; smaller cities and rural counties report a higher percentage of female gang membership compared to urban areas.[78]

Girls in the Gang Why do girls join gangs? There are a variety of reasons, including but not limited to financial opportunity, identity and status, peer pressure, family dysfunction, and protection.[79] Some admit that they join because they are bored and look to gangs for a social life; they are seeking fun and excitement and a means to find parties and meet boys. Still, others join simply because gangs are there in the neighborhood and are viewed as part of their way of life. And some are the children of gang members and are just following in their parents' footsteps.[80]

What benefits does gang membership offer to females? According to the "liberation" view, ganging can provide girls with a sense of sisterhood, independence, and solidarity, as well as a chance to earn profit through illegal activities.

Mark Fleisher and Jessie Krienert's research in Illinois found that girls from tough inner-city neighborhoods drift into gangs to escape the turmoil of their home lives, characterized by abuse, parental crime, and fatherless homes. Their affiliation begins when they hang around the street with gang boys, signaling their gang affiliation and

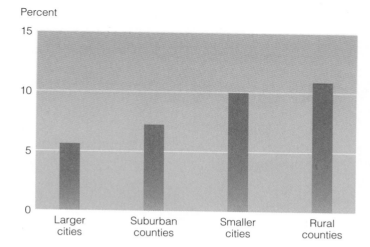

Percent

FIGURE 9.2

Percentage of Gang Members Who Are Female, by Area

SOURCE: National Young Gang Analysis, www.iir.com/NYGC/nygsa/demographics
.htm#anchorgender (accessed October 20, 2007).

symbolizing a lifestyle shift away from their home and school and into the street culture. The shift causes rifts with parents leading to more time on the street and closer gang ties.[81] These young girls, typically aged 14 to 15, are targets for sexual and criminal exploitation.

Although initial female gang participation may be forged by links to male gang members, once in gangs girls form close ties with other female members and engage in group criminal activity.[82] In contrast, the "social injury" view suggests that female members are still sexually exploited by male gang boys and are sometimes forced to exploit other females.

Girls who are members of male gang auxiliaries report that males control them by determining the arenas within which they can operate (i.e., the extent to which they may become involved in intergang violence). Males also play a divisive role in the girls' relationships with each other; this manipulation is absent for girls in independent gangs.[83] When criminologist Jody Miller studied female gangs in St. Louis, Missouri, and Columbus, Ohio, she found that girls in mixed gangs expressed little evidence of sisterhood and solidarity with other female gang members.[84] Rather, female gang members expressed hostility to other women in the gang, believing, for example, that those who suffered sexual assault by males in the same gang actually deserved what they got. Instead of trying to create a sense of sisterhood, female gang members tried to identify with males and viewed themselves as thereby becoming "one of the guys" in the gang.

Why then do girls join gangs if they are exploitive and provide little opportunities for sisterhood? Miller found that even though being a gang member is not a walk in the park, most girls join gangs in an effort to cope with their turbulent personal lives, which may provide them with an even harsher reality; they see the gang as an institution that can increase their status and improve their lifestyle. The gang provides them with an alternative to a tough urban lifestyle filled with the risk of violence and victimization. Many of the girl gang members had early exposure to neighborhood violence, had encounters with girl gangs while growing up, had experienced severe family problems (violence or abuse), and had close family members who were gang-involved.[85] Did they experience life benefits after they joined the gang? The evidence is mixed. Miller found that female gang members increased their delinquent activities and increased their risk of becoming a crime victim; they were more likely to suffer physical injury than girls who shunned gang membership. The risk of being sexually assaulted by male members of their own gang was also not insignificant. However, female gang membership did have some benefits: It protected female gang members from sexual assault by nongang neighborhood men, which they viewed as a more dangerous and deadly risk.

Why do girls leave the gang? One not so surprising answer is that female gang members begin to drift away from gangs when they become young mothers. Fleisher and Krienert found that a majority of the Illinois gang girls they studied became inactive members soon after getting pregnant. Pregnancy leads to a disinterest in hanging around the streets and an interest in the safety of the fetus. Other girls became inactive after they decided to settle down and raise a family. But pregnancy seemed to be the primary motivating factor for leaving the gang life.[86]

Formation

Gang formation involves a sense of territoriality. Most gang members live in close proximity to one another, and their sense of belonging extends only to their small area of the city. At first, a gang may form when members of an ethnic minority

The number and extent of girl gangs are increasing. Here, a female gang member in the Grape Street area of Los Angeles is about to kick another young woman. This is not a random or spontaneous attack, but part of the "court in" ceremony in which new members are initiated into the gang.

© Nancy Siesel

join together for self-preservation. As the group gains domination over an area, it may view the area as its own territory, or turf, which needs to be defended from outsiders.

Once formed, gangs grow when youths who admire the older gang members "apply" and are accepted for membership. Sometimes the new members will be given a special identity that reflects their apprenticeship status. Joan Moore and her associates found that *klikas*, or youth cliques, in Hispanic gangs remain together as unique groups with separate names, identities, and experiences; they also have more intimate relationships among themselves than among the general gang membership.[87] She likens *klikas* to a particular class in a university, such as the class of '05.

Moore also found that gangs can expand by including members' kin, even if they do not live in the neighborhood, and rival gang members who wish to join because they admire the gang's way of doing things. Adding outsiders gives the gang the ability to take over new territory. However, it also brings with it new problems because it usually results in greater conflicts with rival gangs.

klikas
Subgroups of same-aged youths in Hispanic gangs that remain together and have separate names and a unique identity in the gang.

Leadership

Delinquent gangs tend to be small and transitory.[88] Youths often belong to more than a single group or clique and develop an extensive network of delinquent associates. Group roles can vary, and an adolescent who assumes a leadership role in one group may be a follower in another.

Those who assume leadership roles are described as "cool characters" who have earned their position by demonstrating fighting prowess, verbal quickness, or athletic distinction. They emphasize that leadership is held by one person and varies with particular activities, such as fighting, sex, and negotiations. In fact, in some gangs each age level has its own leaders. Older members are not necessarily considered leaders by younger members. In his analysis of Los Angeles gangs, Malcolm Klein observed that many gang leaders deny leadership. He overheard one gang boy claim, "We got no leaders, man. Everybody's a leader, and nobody can talk for nobody else."[89] The most plausible explanation of this ambivalence is the boy's fear that his decisions will conflict with those of other leaders.

There appear, then, to be diverse concepts of leadership, depending on the structure of the gang. Less-organized gangs are marked by diffuse and shifting leadership. More organized gangs have a clear chain of command and leaders who are supposed to plan activities and control members' behavior.[90]

Communications

graffiti
Inscriptions or drawings made on a wall or structure and used by delinquents for gang messages and turf definition.

Gangs seek recognition, both from their rivals and from the community. Image and reputation depend on the ability to communicate to the rest of the world. One major source of communication is graffiti (see Figure 9.3). These wall writings are especially elaborate among Latino gangs, who call them *placasos* or *placa*, meaning "sign" or "plaque." Latino graffiti usually contain the writer's street name and the name of the gang. Strength or power is asserted through the terms *rifa*, which means to rule, and *controllo*, indicating that the gang controls the area. Another common inscription is "p/v," for *por vida*; this refers to the fact that the gang expects to control the area "for life." The numeral 13 signifies that the gang is *loco*, or wild. Crossed-out graffiti indicate that a territory is contested by a rival gang.

Gangs also communicate by means of a secret vocabulary. Members may refer to their crew, posse, troop, or tribe. Within larger gangs are "sets" who hang in particular neighborhoods, and "tips," small groups formed for particular purposes. Other slang terms are contained in Exhibit 9.2.

In some areas, gang members communicate their membership by wearing jackets with the name of their gang on the back. In Boston neighborhoods, certain articles of clothing (for example, sneakers) are worn to identify gang membership. In Los Angeles, the Crips are identified with the color blue and will wear some article of blue clothing to communicate their allegiance; their rivals, the Bloods, identify with the color red.

Hand Signs Several years ago, a young woman was at a dance concert in Milwaukee, Wisconsin, when she was so carried away by the music that she jumped on stage and started to dance with the band. While dancing she used sign language to convey the message, "I love you," over and over. What she did not realize was that her gestures were almost identical to the Latin King hand sign, a turn of events that enraged several Latin King members who were on the dance floor; they perceived her hand signing as a blatant disrespect to the Latin King and Queen Nation. Her innocent gestures cost the woman her life, as the FBI found out subsequently during a gang conspiracy investigation of the Latin Kings.[91]

Gang hand signs are quickly displayed with the fingers, hands, and body, and have very specific meanings to gang members. Hand signs are a powerful nonverbal form of communication because a quick flash of the hand can be used to announce gang affiliation or to issue a challenge or insult to a rival. They have been used by gangs for quite some time, beginning with Chinese Triads, which were later picked up by black gangs when they formed in Los Angeles in the mid-1950s.[92]

FIGURE 9.3
Gang Symbols Used in Graffiti
SOURCE: Polk County Florida Sheriffs Office, 2006, http://polksheriff.org/library/gangs/identifying.html (accessed October 21, 2007).

National symbols of the Folk Nation gang

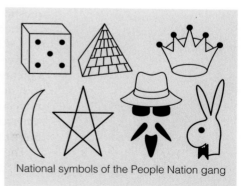
National symbols of the People Nation gang

EXHIBIT 9.2

Common Gang Slang

13, XIII, X3, trece	▌	Thirteenth letter in the alphabet (M), which symbolizes or identifies gang affiliation of Mexican heritage. Also may refer to allegiance to Southern California gangs.
14, XIV, X4	▌	Fourteenth letter of the alphabet (N); refers to allegiance to Northern California or *Norte Califas* gangs.
8-ball	▌	A reference to a quantity of cocaine.
5-O	▌	The police.
AK	▌	Used to denote a semi-automatic assault rifle, such as AK47 or SKS rifles.
PV	▌	*Por vida*; Spanish for "for life," "always."

SOURCE: Gangs OR Us, www.gangsorus.com (accessed November 21, 2007).

posting
A system of positions, facial expressions, and body language used by gang members to convey a message.

Similar to signing, posting is a system of positions, facial expressions, and body language to convey a message. Gang boys may hold their chin up to display their feeling of defiance and arrogance or they may cross their arms and intently stare at someone to show their feeling of disapproval or as a challenge.[93]

representing
Tossing or flashing gang signs in the presence of rivals, often escalating into a verbal or physical confrontation.

Flashing or tossing gang signs in the presence of rivals often escalates into a verbal or physical confrontation. Chicago gangs call this representing. Gang members will proclaim their affiliation and ask victims "Who do you ride?" or "What do you be about?" An incorrect response will provoke an attack. False representing can be used to misinform witnesses and victims.

Tattoos Gang tattoos are used to communicate an individual's membership in a gang. Many tattoos are messages, such as "outlaw," "thug life," "1%er," among others, and serve as expressions of gang mentality and do not specify any particular gang. While the meaning of a tattoo is often subjective, police and prosecutors consider having symbolic tattoos as evidence of gang membership.

Ethnic and Racial Composition

According to the national youth gang survey, African American/black and/or Hispanic/Latino youth predominate among documented gang members: About half are Latino, one-third African American and about 10 percent Caucasian, with the rest being other races (e.g., Asian). This association applies to all types of environments except rural counties, where black gang members predominate. While the view that gangs are predominantly a minority problem predominates, a recent report by the Justice Policy Institute finds evidence that whites make up a greater percentage of gang membership than is generally believed. However, their evidence is collected from self-report studies rather than police records. Nonetheless, this research raises a question about the actual racial composition of gangs.[94]

There is an association between gang membership size, gang-problem onset, and race/ethnicity characteristics: Areas with smaller numbers of gang members or a relatively new emergence of gang problems are significantly more likely to report a greater percentage of Caucasian/white gang members (Figure 9.4). Larger cities with newer gang problems are more than twice as likely to report greater variation in racial/ethnic composition of gang members (that is, proportionally fewer African American/black and/or Hispanic/Latino gang members) than larger cities with long-standing gang problems.[95]

The ethnic distribution of gangs corresponds to their geographic location; the racial/ethnic composition of gangs is an extension of the characteristics of the larger

Gang signs and graffiti are important methods of communication among gang members. Flashing the wrong sign at the wrong time can lead to violent confrontations. Here, a Cambodian teen gang member, Boney, flashes a gang sign outside Long Beach, California.

community.[96] In Philadelphia and Detroit the overwhelming majority of gang members are African American. In New York and Los Angeles, Latino gangs predominate. Newly emerging immigrant groups are making their presence felt in gangs. Authorities in Buffalo, New York, estimate that 10 percent of their gang population is Jamaican. A significant portion of Honolulu's gangs are Filipino.

African American Gangs The first black youth gangs were organized in the early 1920s.[97] Since they had few rival organizations, they were able to concentrate on criminal activity rather than defending their turf. By the 1930s, the expanding number of rival gangs spawned inner-city gang warfare.

In Los Angeles, the first black youth gang formed in the 1920s was the Boozies. This gang virtually ran the inner city until the 1930s. In the next 20 years, a number of black gangs, including the Businessmen, Home Street, Slauson, and Neighborhood, emerged and met with varying degrees of criminal success. In the 1970s, the dominant Crips gang was formed. Other gangs merged into the Crips or affiliated with it by adding "Crips" to their name, so that the Main Street gang became the Main Street Crips. The dominance of the Crips has since been challenged by its archrivals, the Bloods. Both of these groups, whose total membership exceeds 25,000 youths, are heavily involved in drug trafficking.

In Chicago, the Blackstone Rangers dominated illicit activities for almost 25 years, beginning in the 1960s and lasting into the early 1990s, when its leader, Jeff Fort, and many of his associates were indicted and imprisoned.[98] The Rangers, who later evolved into the El Rukn gang, worked with "legitimate" businessmen to import and sell heroin. Earning millions in profits, they established businesses that helped them launder drug money. Though many of the convictions were later overturned, the power of El Rukn was ended.

One of the Rangers' chief rivals, the Black Gangster Disciples, morphed into the dominant gang in Chicago. They have a structure, activities, and relationships similar to traditional organized crime. Members are actively involved in politics through the formation of the "Growth and Development" movement. Gangster Disciples registered voters from the inner city and then "encouraged" the newly registered voters to vote for candidates loyal to their cause. While incarcerated, the Black Gangster Disciples will unite with allied gangs under the guise of the Brothers of Struggle (BOS). The gang continues to be involved in large-scale drug trafficking, murders, and white-collar crime.[99] They also have extensive ownership of "legitimate" private businesses. They offer protection against rival gangs and supply stolen merchandise to customers and employees.[100]

African American gang members have some unique characteristics. They frequently use nicknames. "Little 45" might be used by someone whose favorite weapon

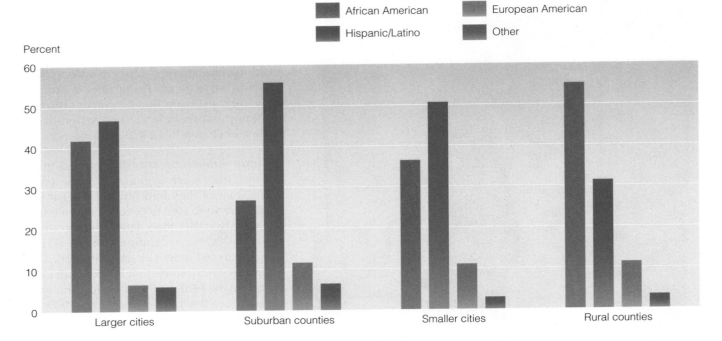

FIGURE 9.4

Racial Makeup of Gangs by Area Type

SOURCE: National Youth Gang Survey Analysis, www.iir.com/NYGC/nygsa/demographics.htm#anchorregmat (accessed October 20, 2007).

is a large handgun. Although TV shows portray gangs as wearing distinctive attire, members usually favor nondescript attire to reduce police scrutiny. However, gang members frequently have distinctive hairstyles, such as shaving or braids that are designed to look like their leaders'. Tattooing is popular, and members often wear colored scarves or "rags" to identify their gang affiliation. It is also common for black gang members to mark their territory with distinctive graffiti: drawings of guns, dollar signs, proclamations of individual power, and profanity.

Hispanic Gangs The popularity of gangs and gang culture is relatively high among youth of Hispanic background, explaining in part their disproportionate participation in gang membership.[101] Take for instance the feared MS-13 gang, begun in Los Angeles by Salvadorans fleeing a civil war. When they first arrived in L.A., they were preyed upon by preexisting Mexican gangs. The MS-13 gang was formed as a means of self-protection. The name refers to a *mara*, Spanish slang for "posse" or gang. *Salvatruchas* is local slang for being alert and ready to take action; the "13" is a reference to their beginnings on 13th street in Los Angeles.

Over time, the gang's ranks grew and members entered a variety of rackets, from extortion to drug trafficking. When law enforcement cracked down and deported members, the deportees quickly created outposts in El Salvador and throughout Central America. The Salvadoran government has responded by criminalizing gang membership and arresting thousands. But government efforts have not stemmed the tide of recruitment and the gangs appear to be more popular than ever.[102]

Developing alongside the MS-13 were their main rivals, the 18th Street Gang. This group began as an offshoot of a preexisting Los Angeles gang, the Clanton 14 (named after a street in the gang's home neighborhood). The Clanton gang had been active in Los Angeles for decades and had also become quite choosy in its membership, rejecting recent Mexican immigrants and Chicanos. Those rejected formed their own gang and named it the 18th Street Gang. Today, 18th Street Gang members can be identified by their tattoos, most common the number 18, which is usually represented in Roman numerals (XVIII). Although 18th Street maintains a stronghold in several Southern California cities, members have migrated throughout the nation.[103]

Latino gangs such as MS-13 and the 18th Street Gang have continued to grow and now constitute the largest number of gangs and gang memberships. Some experts believe that the 10,000-member MS-13 is now the nation's most dangerous gang, while others claim that the 18th Street Gang, with over 20,000 members, is the largest.

Hispanic gangs are made up of youths whose ethnic ancestry can be traced to one of several Spanish-speaking cultures. They are known for their fierce loyalty to their "home" gang. Admission to the gang usually involves an initiation ritual in which boys are required to prove their *machismo*. The most common test requires novices to fight several established members or to commit some crime, such as a robbery. The code of conduct associated with membership means never ratting on a brother or even a rival.

In some areas, Latino gangs have a fixed leadership hierarchy. However, in Southern California, which has the largest concentration of Hispanic youth gangs, leadership is fluid. During times of crisis those with particular skills will assume command.[104] One boy will lead in combat while another negotiates drug deals.

Latino gang members are known for their dress codes. Some wear dark-colored caps pulled down over the ears with a small roll at the bottom. Others wear a folded bandana over the forehead and tied in back. Another popular headpiece is the "stingy brim" fedora or a baseball cap with the wearer's nickname and gang affiliation written on the bill. Members favor tank-style T-shirts that give them quick access to weapons.

Members also mark off territory with colorful and intricate graffiti ("tagging"). Hispanic gang graffiti has very stylized lettering and frequently uses three-dimensional designs.

Latino gangs have a strong sense of turf, and a great deal of gang violence is directed at warding off any threat to their control. Slights by rivals, including putdowns, stare-downs ("mad-dogging"), defacing gang insignia, and territorial intrusions, can set off a violent confrontation, often with high-powered automatic weapons. The Case Profile entitled "Luis's Story" examines one Latino gang member who was able to turn his life around.

Asian Gangs Asian gangs are prominent in New York, Los Angeles, San Francisco, Seattle, and Houston. The earliest gangs, the Wah Ching, were formed in the nineteenth century by Chinese youths affiliated with adult crime groups (*tongs*). In the 1960s, two other gangs formed in San Francisco, the Joe Boys and Yu Li, and they now operate, along with the Wah Ching, in many major U.S. cities. National attention focused on the activities of these Chinese gangs in 1977 when a shootout in the Golden Dragon restaurant in San Francisco left five dead and eleven wounded.

In addition to Chinese gangs, Samoan gangs have operated on the West Coast, as have Vietnamese gangs. The formation of Vietnamese gangs can be tied to external factors, including racism and economic problems, and to internal problems, including family stress and failure to achieve the success enjoyed by other Asians. Vietnamese gangs are formed when youths feel they need their *ahns*, or brothers, for protection.[105]

Asian gangs are unique and do not share many qualities with other ethnically centered groups. They tend to victimize members of their own ethnic group. They are more organized, have recognizable leaders, and are far more secretive than black or Hispanic groups. They tend to be far less territorial and less openly visible. Asian gangs are also known for the strict control gang elders have over younger members. Elders, some of whom may be in their 30s and 40s, are no longer engaged in street crime and violence but may instead be involved in other forms of illegal activities such as running gambling parlors. They use the younger gang members to protect their business interests and to collect any unpaid gambling debts. In some jurisdictions, police can pressure the elders to control the violent tendencies of the younger members by threatening to crack down on their illegitimate business enterprises (i.e., having patrol cars parked in front of suspected gambling locations).[106]

Luis's Story

LUIS IS A 16-YEAR-OLD LATINO MALE WHO IDENTIFIED HIMSELF AS GANG-INVOLVED. HE WAS CHARGED WITH SUBSTANTIAL BATTERY AND RESISTING ARREST, DUE TO A FIGHT at a party with a rival gang member. Luis already had a history of truancy and a police record for several thefts, vandalism, truancy, underage drinking, and curfew violations. He was smoking marijuana on a daily basis, not attending school, and had experienced little success in the educational environment outside of sports. Luis also exhibited significant anger management concerns and was viewed as a threat to the community.

His family was supportive yet apprehensive about his behavior. Luis's mother was very involved in his life and was doing her best to raise her four children without any assistance or involvement from their father. Luis had felt like "the man of the family" from an early age. Within their family culture, Luis, being the oldest male, felt responsible for caring for his mother and younger siblings. He had joined a gang around the age of 11 in hopes that it would provide additional protection for his family. Despite numerous concerns from his family and the juvenile court, following his arrest Luis was allowed to return home until the next juvenile court proceeding. He was referred for electronic monitoring and an intensive home supervision program.

Luis arrived at his initial juvenile court plea hearing intoxicated and belligerent. His family was concerned that Luis was using drugs and alcohol and felt that he needed treatment. The prosecuting attorney did not agree and petitioned for him to be sent directly to a juvenile correctional facility. While the next court hearing was pending, Luis participated in an alcohol and drug assessment, and it was recommended that he enter a residential treatment facility for his drug use and alcohol issues, anger management problems, and gang involvement issues. During the wait between court proceedings, he was involved in an intensive supervision program where he received individual counseling, group treatment, intensive monitoring of his whereabouts and school activities, family and individual crisis intervention, and significant redirection regarding his choices. He was also referred to an alternative school program where his chances for success would be better. Luis's mother was hopeful that the services would assist him and that Luis would start to turn his life around.

At the dispositional hearing, there was disagreement regarding the best plan for Luis, and a contested hearing took place. The prosecuting attorney again wanted him sent directly to a juvenile correctional facility. The defense attorney argued that Luis needed alcohol and drug treatment, as well as other services, and that he should be sent to an inpatient treatment facility that had already agreed to take him. Luis's probation officer and his family all advocated for him to get treatment, over the correctional placement. He had been doing better in the community setting with the additional services and supports. The judge listened to all of the testimony and expressed concerns regarding Luis's juvenile court involvement record and the safety of the community. At the same time, she wanted to give him a chance to be successful in drug treatment. In the end, the judge ordered Luis to the juvenile correctional facility, but "stayed" the order, permitting Luis to enter treatment. This "stay" meant that if Luis left the treatment facility, or if he was terminated from the program, he would automatically go to juvenile corrections. If he was successful in treatment, he would most likely return to the community with the needed supports and services. If at any time Luis decided not to cooperate with the community aftercare plans, or if he had any further law violations, he could also be immediately sent to juvenile corrections. Luis and his family seemed to understand the seriousness of the situation and Luis agreed to treatment.

Luis entered the voluntary 90-day alcohol and drug treatment program and began to work on his sobriety, anger issues, gang involvement, and criminal thinking concerns. Though it was difficult to coordinate given her work schedule and responsibility for the other children in the household, Luis's mother came to visit on a regular basis and participated in family sessions. The involved professionals assisted with coordinating child care and arranging transportation so she could be there for Luis, who struggled at first and was having a hard time adjusting to the rules of the facility. His mother and the team encouraged him to remain in treatment and

(continued)

try to focus on a positive future, and they reminded him of the "stayed" correctional order. Luis ultimately decided to engage in treatment and he completed the 90-day program.

The team of professionals, along with Luis and his mother, created an aftercare plan that initially included ongoing drug counseling and support, individual counseling, intensive supervision and monitoring, group supports, and placement in an alternative educational setting. Through the alternative school, Luis got involved in a program that offers troubled youth the experience of building homes for underprivileged families. Luis was able to gain valuable work skills, as well as time to focus on positive activities. Though he still struggled with school, with his past gang involvement, and with making good choices, he was able to significantly decrease his police contacts and he had no further arrests as a juvenile. Luis remained living at home with his mother and siblings and was eventually released from the juvenile court–ordered services. The "stayed" correctional order remained in place until the juvenile court closed the case upon Luis's 18th birthday. ■

CRITICAL THINKING

1. Unlike Luis, many kids are not helped and remain in gangs longer than ever before. Do you see a way, considering the global information economy, to wean kids out of gangs? Are there any alternatives? What about easing the entry requirements for the military? After all, Laub and Sampson argue that a military career can help people "knife off" from crime (see Chapter 6).
2. Luis's mother was very involved in his life and says she was doing her best to raise her four children without any assistance or involvement from their father. Could this family situation have been a pivotal factor in Luis's decision to join a gang? What can be done to help kids in this situation?

Anglo Gangs The first American youth gangs were made up of white ethnic youths of European ancestry. During the 1950s, they competed with African American and Hispanic gangs in the nation's largest cities. Today, Anglo gang activity is not uncommon, especially in smaller towns.[107] Many are derivatives of the English punk and skinhead movement of the 1970s. These youths, generally children of lower-class parents, sported wildly dyed hair often shaved into "mohawks," military clothes, and iron-cross earrings. Their creed was antiestablishment, and their anger was directed toward foreigners, who they believed were taking their jobs.

skinhead
Member of a white supremacist gang, identified by a shaved skull and Nazi or Ku Klux Klan markings.

Today, white gang members are often alienated middle-class youths rather than poor lower-class youths. They include "punkers," "stoners," "goths," and others, who dress in heavy-metal fashions and engage in drug- and violence-related activities. Some espouse religious beliefs involving the occult and satanic worship. Some are obsessed with occult themes, suicide, ritual killings, and animal mutilations. They get involved in devil worship, tattoo themselves with occult symbols, and gouge their bodies to draw blood for satanic rituals.[108] Some skinhead groups are devoted to white supremacist activities and are being actively recruited by adult hate groups.

A recent survey of almost 6,000 youths found that about 25 percent of youths who claimed to be gang members were white, a far higher number than that found in national surveys.[109]

Criminality and Violence

Regardless of their type, gang members typically commit more crimes than any other youths in the social environment.[110] Members self-report significantly more crime than nonmembers, and the more enmeshed a youth is in a gang the more likely he is to report criminal behavior, to have an official record, and to get sent to juvenile court. The gang membership–crime relationship begins as early as middle school.[111]

While the association between gang membership and delinquency is unquestioned, there are actually three different explanations for the relationship:

▮ *Selection hypothesis.* Kids with a history of crime and violence join gangs and maintain their persistent delinquency once they become members.

- *Facilitation hypothesis.* Gang membership facilitates deviant behavior because it provides the structure and group support for antisocial activities.
- *Enhancement hypothesis.* Selection and facilitation work interactively, increasing the likelihood of enhanced criminality.[112]

Gang criminality has numerous patterns.[113] Some gangs specialize in drug dealing. But not all gangs are major players in drug trafficking, and those that are tend to distribute small amounts of drugs at the street level. The world of major dealing belongs to adults, not to gang youths.[114] Other gangs engage in a wide variety of criminal activity, ranging from felony assaults to drug dealing.[115] Gang members are most commonly involved in such crimes as larceny/theft, aggravated assault, and burglary/breaking and entering; a significant portion are involved in street drug sales to generate profits for the gang.[116] Drug use is quite common. Geoffrey Hunt and his associates found that 82 percent of the female gang members they surveyed were multiple-drug users, using drugs such as cocaine, crack, LSD, PCP, methamphetamine, heroin, glue/inhalants, MDMA, and quaaludes.[117]

Do gang kids increase their involvement in criminal activity after they join gangs or do gangs recruit kids who are already high rate offenders? Data from the Rochester Youth Development Study (RYDS), a longitudinal cohort study of 1,000 youths in upstate New York, supports the gang membership–crime association theory. Although only 30 percent of the youths in the sample report being gang members, they account for 65 percent of all reported delinquent acts. The RYDS data show that gang members account for 86 percent of all serious crimes, 63 percent of the alcohol use, and 61 percent of the drug abuse.[118] Gang members ratchet up their criminal activities. In the RYDS study, two-thirds (66 percent) of the chronic violent offenders were gang members.[119]

Gang Violence Not surprisingly, research shows that gang members are more violent than nonmembers. One reason is that kids who join gangs are also more likely to carry weapons than nonmembers.[120] Thornberry and his associates found that young gang members in Rochester, New York, were about 10 times more likely to carry handguns than nongang juvenile offenders, and gun-toting gang members committed about 10 times more violent crimes than nonmembers.[121]

It is not surprising, then, that youth gangs are responsible for a disproportionate number of homicides. In two cities, Los Angeles and Chicago—considered the most gang-populated cities in the United States—over half of the annual homicides are attributed to gangs. Nationally, approximately one-fourth of all homicides are considered gang-related and the numbers are increasing.[122]

Research indicates that gang violence is impulsive and therefore comes in spurts. It usually involves defense of the gang and gang members' reputations.[123] Once the threat ends, the level of violence may recede, but it remains at a level higher than it was previously. Peaks in gang homicides tend to correspond to a series of escalating confrontations, usually over control of gang turf or a drug market.[124] The most dangerous areas are

Ashley Benton, 17, and defense attorney Rick DeToto dramatize an incident for the jurors during Benton's murder trial on June 26, 2007. Benton was accused of the murder of Gabriel Granillo, a member of MS-13, during a gang fight at Chew Park in Houston, Texas. She claimed she stabbed Granillo in self-defense after he attacked her with a bat: "I closed my eyes, and I just stabbed him." The prosecutor disputed this claim: "In a gang conflict, they don't beat up girls, they beat up other boys" who are rival gang members. The case ended in a hung jury.

© AP Images/Houston Chronicle/Mayra Beltran

along disputed boundaries where a drug hot spot intersects with a turf hot spot. There are also "marauder" patterns in which members of rival gangs travel to their enemy's territory in search of victims.[125]

Violence is a core fact of gang formation and life.[126] Gang members feel threatened by other gangs and are wary of encroachments on their turf. It is not surprising that gangs try to recruit youths who are already gun owners; new members are likely to increase gun ownership and possession.[127] Gang members face a far greater chance of death at an early age than do nonmembers.[128]

Revenge, Honor, Courage, and Prestige When criminologist Scott Decker interviewed gang boys he found that violence is essential to the transformation of a peer group into a gang. When asked why he calls the group he belongs to a gang, one member replied: "There is more violence than a family. With a gang it's like fighting all the time, killing, shooting."[129]

When joining the gang, members may be forced to partake in violent rituals to prove their reliability. Gang members are ready to fight when others attack them or when they believe their territory or turf is being encroached upon. Violence may be directed against rival gang members accused of insults or against those involved in personal disputes. Gang members also expect to fight when they go to certain locations that are "off-limits" or attend events where violence is routine. A girl gang member may fight when she senses that a member of a rival gang is trying to hook up with her boyfriend. Gini Sykes spent two years hanging with girl gangs in New York City in order to develop an understanding of their lives and lifestyle. One girl, Tiny, told her how ferociousness made up for her lack of stature:

> Tiny fixed me with a cold stare that wiped away any earlier impression of childish cuteness. "See, we smaller girls, we go for your weak spot." Her gaze moved across my features. "Your face. Your throat. Your eyes, so we can blind you. I don't care if you have more weight on me. I'll still try to kill you because, you know, I have a bad temper...."[130]

Tiny related the story of how she attacked a rival whom she caught in a sexual encounter with her boyfriend:

> "She was crying and begging, but she'd disrespected me in front of everybody. We started fighting and she pulled that blade out—." Tiny shrugged. "I just wasn't prepared. You can't tell when someone's got a razor in their mouth."

After she was cut, Tiny went into a defensive rage, and

> ...frantically felt for the wound, blood seeping between her fingers. Suddenly, in self-preservation, she grabbed the girl's neck, and blinded by her own blood, began smashing her rival's head into the concrete until Isabel, hearing a siren, dragged her away. The girl had slashed Tiny's face eleven times.

Gang members are sensitive to any rivals who question their honor. Once an insult is perceived, the gang's honor cannot be restored until the "debt" is repaid. Police efforts to cool down gang disputes only delay the revenge, which can be a beating or a drive-by shooting. Random acts of revenge have become so common that physicians now consider them a significant health problem—a major contributor to early morbidity and mortality among adolescents and children in major gang cities.[131]

Violence is also used to maintain the gang's internal discipline. If subordinates disobey orders, perhaps by using rather than selling drugs, they may be subject to disciplinary action by other gang members.

Another common gang crime is extortion, called "turf tax," which involves forcing people to pay the gang to be protected from dangerous neighborhood youths. **Prestige crimes** occur when a gang member steals or assaults someone to gain prestige in the gang. These crimes may be part of an initiation rite or an effort to establish a special reputation, a position of responsibility, or a leadership role; to prevail in an internal power struggle; or to respond to a challenge from a rival.

prestige crimes
Stealing or assaulting someone to gain prestige in the neighborhood; often part of gang initiation rites.

Organized Crime and Gangs While the general public may associate gangs with violent acts such as drive-by shootings, some also equate gangs with organized crime such as large-scale drug dealing. There is no question that in particular communities in certain cities, youth gangs are very active in drug trafficking. However, the common stereotypes of the relationships among youth gangs, drug trafficking, and violence are often overblown. Youth gang expert Malcolm Klein finds distinctions between youth gangs and organized criminal cartels. To remain in business, he argues, organized crime groups must have strong leadership, codes of behavior which are enforced by the threat of severe sanctions, and a membership with a level of expertise and sophistication that enables them to accumulate and invest the proceeds of illegal activity. They can safely import narcotics and launder the proceeds of drug deals.[132] In contrast, his studies show that most street gangs are only loosely structured, with transient leadership and membership, easily transcended codes of loyalty, and informal rather than formal roles for the members.[133] As a result, very few youth gangs meet the essential criteria for classification as "organized crime." Youth gang involvement in the drug trade is mainly in street-level distribution rather than large-scale importation and distribution, activities that are managed by adult drug cartels or syndicates, traditional narcotic importers, and other adult criminal organizations. However, while they may not fit the classic definition of organized crime syndicates, youth gangs can become integrally involved in existing, adult-based distribution systems. Where drug-related violence occurs, it mainly stems from drug use and dealing by individual gang members and from gang member involvement in adult criminal drug distribution networks more than from drug-trafficking activities of the youth gang as an organized entity.

WHY DO YOUTHS JOIN GANGS?

Though gangs flourish in inner-city areas, gang membership cannot be assumed to be solely a function of lower-class identity. Many lower-class youths do not join gangs, and middle-class youths are found in suburban skinhead groups. Let's look at some of the suspected causes of gang delinquency.

The Anthropological View

In the 1950s, Herbert Block and Arthur Niederhoffer suggested that gangs appeal to adolescents' longing for the tribal process that sustained their ancestors.[134] They found that gang processes do seem similar to the puberty rites of some tribal cultures; gang rituals help the child bridge the gap between childhood and adulthood. For example, tattoos and other identifying marks are an integral part of gang culture. Gang initiation ceremonies are similar to the activities of young men in Pacific Island cultures. Many gangs put new members through a hazing to make sure they have "heart," a feature similar to tribal rites. In tribal societies, initiation into a cult is viewed as the death of childhood. By analogy, boys in lower-class urban areas yearn to join the gang and "really start to live." Membership in the gang "means the youth gives up his life as a child and assumes a new way of life."[135] Gang names are suggestive of "totemic ancestors" because they usually are symbolic (Cobras, Jaguars, and Kings, for example).

The Gang Prevention and Intervention Survey found that fully two-thirds of gang members reported having members in their gang whose parents are also active members. These data indicate that ganging is passed on as a rite of passage from one generation to the next.[136] James Diego Vigil has described the rituals of gang initiation, which include pummeling to show that the boy is ready to leave his matricentric (mother-dominated) household; this is reminiscent of tribal initiation rites.[137] These rituals become an important part of gang activities. Hand signs and graffiti have a tribal flavor. Gang members adopt nicknames that reflect personality or physical traits: the more volatile are called "Crazy," "Loco," or "Psycho," and those who wear glasses are dubbed "Professor."[138]

The Social Disorganization/Sociocultural View

Sociologists have commonly viewed the destructive sociocultural forces in poor inner-city areas as the major cause of gang formation. Thrasher introduced this concept, and it is found in the classic studies of Richard Cloward and Lloyd Ohlin and of Albert Cohen.[139] Irving Spergel's study *Racketville, Slumtown, and Haulburg* found that Slumtown—the area with the lowest income and the largest population—had the highest number of violent gangs.[140] According to Spergel, the gang gives lower-class youths a means of attaining status. Malcolm Klein's research of the late 1960s and 1970s also found that typical gang members came from dysfunctional and destitute families and lacked adequate role models.[141]

The social disorganization/sociocultural view retains its prominent position today. In *Barrio Gangs*,[142] Vigil shows that gang members are pushed into membership because of poverty and minority status. Those who join gangs are the most marginal youths in their neighborhoods and families. Vigil finds that barrio dwellers experience psychological, economic, and social "stressors." Gang members usually have more than one of these problems, causing them to suffer from "multiple marginality." Barrio youths join gangs seeking a sense of belonging.[143]

Overall, the sociocultural view assumes that gangs are a natural response to lower-class life and a status-generating medium for boys whose aspirations cannot be realized by legitimate means. Youths who join gangs may hold conventional goals but are either unwilling or unable to accomplish them through conventional means.[144] Gangs are not solely made up of youths who seek deviant peers to compensate for parental brutality or incompetence. They recruit youths from many different kinds of families. The gang thus is a coalition of troubled youths who are socialized mainly by the streets rather than by conventional institutions.[145]

The Anomie/Alienation View

According to this view, conditions of anomie/alienation encourage gang formation on both a cultural and individual level. On a cultural level, youths are encouraged to join gangs during periods of social, economic, and cultural turmoil.[146] Immigration or emigration, rapidly expanding or contracting populations, and the incursion of different racial/ethnic groups, or even different segments or generations of the same racial/ethnic population, can create fragmented communities and gang problems.[147]

Historically, gangs formed during the Russian Revolution of 1917 and after the crumbling of the Soviet Union in the early 1990s. The rise of right-wing youth gangs in Germany is associated with the unification of East and West Germany. Skinhead groups have formed in Germany in response to immigration from Turkey and North Africa. In the United States, gangs have formed in areas where rapid change has unsettled communities. The gangs and militia groups in present-day Iraq may have formed as a response to the upheaval in that society.

On an individual level, gang membership has appeal to adolescents who are alienated from the mainstream of society. It is not surprising that (a) kids who have had problems with the law and suffer juvenile justice processing are more likely to join gangs than nonstigmatized kids and (b) joining gangs further involves them in criminal activities.[148]

The Psychological View

Some believe that gangs serve as an outlet for disturbed youths who suffer a multitude of personal problems and deficits. Gang expert Lewis Yablonsky found that violent gangs recruit their members from among the more sociopathic youths living in poverty-stricken communities.[149] Yablonsky views the sociopathic youth as one who "has not been trained to have human feelings or compassion or responsibility for another."[150]

Malcolm Klein's analysis of Los Angeles gang members also found that many suffer from a variety of personal deficits, including low self-concept, social deficits, poor impulse control, and limited life skills.[151] In their in-depth study of Rochester youth, Thornberry and his colleagues found that those who joined gangs suffered from a multitude of social problems, including early involvement in delinquency, violence, and drug abuse, dysfunctional family relations, educational deficits, and involvement with deviant peers.[152]

The Rational Choice View

Some youths may make a rational choice to join a gang. Members of the underclass turn to gangs as a method of obtaining desired goods and services, either directly, through theft and extortion, or indirectly, through drug dealing and weapons sales. In this case, joining a gang can be viewed as an "employment decision." Mercer Sullivan's study of Brooklyn gangs found that members call success at crime "getting paid." Gang boys also refer to the rewards of crime as "getting over," which refers to their pride at "beating the system" even though they are far from the economic mainstream.[153] According to this view, the gang boy has long been involved in criminal activity *prior* to his gang membership, and he joins the gang as a means of improving his illegal "productivity."[154]

Gang membership is *not* a necessary precondition for delinquency. Felix Padilla found this when he studied the Diamonds, a Latino gang in Chicago.[155] The decision to join the gang was made after an assessment of legitimate opportunities. The Diamonds made collective business decisions, and individuals who made their own deals were penalized. The gang maintained a distinct structure and carried out other functions similar to those of legitimate enterprises, including recruiting personnel and financing business ventures.

Drug use is a big part of the gang experience and drug users may join gangs to enhance availability of drugs and support for their usage.[156] Terence Thornberry and his colleagues at the Rochester Youth Development Study found that before youths join gangs, their substance abuse and delinquency rates are no higher than those of nongang members. When they are in the gang, their crime and drug abuse rates increase, only to decrease when they leave the gang. Thornberry concludes that gangs facilitate criminality rather than provide a haven for youths who are disturbed or already highly delinquent. This research is important because it lends support to the life course model: Events that take place during the life cycle, such as joining a gang, have a significant impact on criminal behavior and drug abuse.[157]

Personal Safety According to Spergel, some adolescents choose to join gangs from a "rational calculation" to achieve safety.[158] Youths who are new to a community may believe they will be harassed or attacked if they remain "unaffiliated." Girls also join gangs for protection. Though they may be exploited by male gang members, they are protected from assaults by nongang males in the neighborhood.[159]

Motivation may have its roots in interrace or interethnic rivalry; youths who reside in an area dominated by a different racial or ethnic group may be persuaded that gang membership is a means of protection. Ironically, gang members are more likely to be attacked than nonmembers.

Fun and Support Some youths join gangs simply to have fun.[160] They enjoy hanging out with others like themselves and want to get involved in exciting experiences. There is evidence that youths learn pro-gang attitudes from their peers and that these attitudes direct them to join gangs.[161]

Some experts suggest that youths join gangs in an effort to obtain a family-like atmosphere. Many gang members report that they have limited contact with their parents, many of whom are unemployed and have substance abuse problems.[162] Those members who have strained family relations are also the ones most likely to be involved in the most serious and frequent criminal activity.[163] Kids may join gangs to compensate for the lack of a family life they have experienced at home.

The Thug Lifestyle Some kids enter the gang life because they want to enhance a "thug" lifestyle. They choose ganging because it celebrates deviance and criminality, values they have already embraced.[164] Where does the "thug" style come from? In some instances, kids see older boys in the neighborhood acting tough and getting respect. Sometimes, the thug style emulates the dress, swagger, and lingo of media gangster's such as Tony Montana from the cult movie *Scarface*. Set in 1980s Miami, the film's protagonist, Tony (played by Al Pacino), is a determined Cuban immigrant who uses street smarts, toughness, and callous brutality to take over a drug empire, becoming enormously rich and powerful before succumbing to greed and his own psychological demons. Tony's analysis of how the American system works symbolizes the thug lifestyle:

> In this country, you gotta make the money first. Then when you get the money, you get the power. Then when you get the power, then you get the women.

Young gang boys want to embrace the movie gangster lifestyle and fatalism. They are ready to shoot it out with rival gang members and with the cops. In this "outlaw' world, gang boys can make their own rules, do what they want and take what they wish without worrying about the consequences. It is a lifestyle where respect is demanded and power rules. Thugs enjoy their ability to use violence to gain vengeance against their enemies or to demonstrate their criminal skills. And like Tony Montana, their prowess is envied and rewarded with respect and financial gain. Just as a doctor, lawyer, or police officer identifies with his profession and gains self-worth from his professional calling and successes, self-esteem for many who choose to join a gang becomes dependent on their "thug" exploits. These views are summarized in Concept Summary 9.1.

CONTROLLING GANG ACTIVITY

The presence of gangs instills fear in community residents, and fear of gang intimidation, vandalism, graffiti, and drugs is very great in the most gang-infested communities. One study in Orange County, California, found that, not surprisingly, fear of crime and gangs was an "immediate" daily experience for people who lived in

Concept Summary 9.1
Views of Gang Formation

View	Premise	Evidence
Anthropological	Gangs appeal to kids' tribal instincts	Use of totems, signs, secret languages, and symbols
Sociocultural	Gangs form because of destructive sociocultural forces in disorganized inner-city areas	Concentration of gangs in inner-city areas
Anomie/Alienation	Alienated kids join gangs; anomic, social, and economic conditions encourage gang activity	Upswing in gang activities after market force creates anomic situations Gangs activity increases with globalization
Psychological	Kids with personality problems form gangs and become leaders	Antisocial, destructive behavior patterns Increase in violence
Rational choice	Kids join gangs for protection, fun, survival, and to enhance their lifestyle	Presence of party gangs, gang members protect one another

lower-income neighborhoods where gangs were most common. But there was also a spillover effect: Fear of gangs and gang violence was present even if gangs were not an immediate danger or fixture in the neighborhood.[165] In the most gang-ridden areas, intimidation of other youths, adults, and business owners was common. Gang boys also intimidated witnesses or potential witnesses to their crimes, a crime that is particularly serious because it undermines the justice process.

Because gangs are now a national threat, there has been a concerted effort to control gang activity. A number of approaches have been tried, some involving efforts to control or deter gang activity through tough legal sanctions backed up by effective law enforcement. Another approach involves social service efforts designed to provide alternatives to gang membership. Both of these methods will be discussed in the next sections.

Legal Controls

A number of states have created laws specifically designed to control gang activity. One approach has been to create enhanced penalties for behaviors typically associated with gang members. Take for example drive-by shootings, a form of retaliation popular with gangs. A number of states have passed legislation increasing penalties for such behavior and adding sanctions to control its reoccurrence (e.g., the driver loses his license). Arizona's drive-by shooting law is set out below in Exhibit 9.3.

Other jurisdictions have made it a crime to recruit gang members, to engage in organized gang activity, and to loiter for the purpose of carrying out gang business. Some cities have gone as far as passing anti-graffiti measures to curb the proliferation of written gang messages and threats. Exhibit 9.4 shows Denver's anti-graffiti statute.

Legal Injunctions

Some jurisdictions such as Fort Worth, Texas, and San Francisco, California, have filed lawsuits against gangs and gang members, asking courts for injunctions barring them from hanging out together on street corners, in cars, or in particular areas. The injunctions are aimed at disrupting gang activity before it can escalate into violence. If successful, these injunctions give police legal reasons to stop and question gang members, who often are found with drugs or weapons. The injunctions prohibit gang members from associating with each other, carrying weapons, possessing drugs, committing crimes, and displaying gang symbols in a safety zone—neighborhoods where suspected gang members live and are most active. Some injunctions set curfews for members and ban them from possessing alcohol in public areas—even if they're of legal drinking age.

Those who disobey the order face a misdemeanor charge and up to a year in jail. In some cases, such injunctions don't allow gang members to even talk to people passing in cars or to carry spray paint.[166] Some libertarian organizations consider these restrictions as overreaching and violating civil rights and appellate courts have restricted the scope of gang injunctions. In one case, *People v. Englebrecht*, the California Court of Appeal ruled that prosecutors must first prove through clear and convincing evidence that a person is a gang member before using an anti-gang injunction to restrict his or her right to engage in everyday activities. The case involved David Englebrecht, a 26-year-old father of three who despite not being a gang member was placed under a civil injunction designed to combat a local gang. Under the injunction, Englebrecht was prohibited from making loud noises, whistling, wearing certain clothing, using certain words or hand gestures, or being seen in public with other alleged gang members within an approximately one-square-mile area of Oceanside, California. Recognizing that the case involved a mistake of fact (i.e., Englebrecht was not a gang member), the court's decision means that all nongang members will have

EXHIBIT **9.3**

Drive-By Shooting Statute: Arizona

Arizona 13-1209. Drive-by shooting; driver's license revocation; classification; definitions

A. A person commits drive-by shooting by intentionally discharging a weapon from a motor vehicle at a person, another occupied motor vehicle, or an occupied structure.

B. Motor vehicles that are used in violation of this section are subject to seizure for forfeiture in the manner provided for in chapter 39 of this title.

C. Notwithstanding title 28, chapter 4, the judge shall order the surrender to the judge of any driver's license of the convicted person

and, on surrender of the license, shall invalidate or destroy the license and forward the abstract of conviction to the department of transportation with an order of the court revoking the driving privilege of the person for a period of at least one year but not more than five years. On receipt of the abstract of conviction and order, the department of transportation shall revoke the driving privilege of the person for the period of time ordered by the judge.

D. Drive-by shooting is a class 2 felony.

SOURCE: Arizona State Legislature, www.azleg.state.az.us/ars/13/01209.htm (accessed September 22, 2007).

EXHIBIT **9.4**

Anti-Graffiti Statute: Denver, Colorado

Sec. 34-66. Possession of graffiti materials by minors prohibited

(a) It shall be unlawful for any person under the age of eighteen (18) years to possess any can of spray paint, broad tipped marker pen, glass cutting tool, or glass etching tool or instrument.

(b) A broad tipped marker pen is one with a tip that exceeds one-quarter (1/4) inch in width.

(c) It shall be an affirmative defense to charges under this section that the person possessing the materials was:
(1) Within their home;
(2) At their place of employment; or
(3) Upon real property with permission from the owner, occupant, or person having lawful control of such property, to possess such materials. (Ord. No. 424-95, § 1, 6-12-95)

SOURCE: Denver website, www.denvergov.org/web/ccbills/CB0807-02.pdf (accessed September 22, 2007).

---

greater protection against being wrongfully and arbitrarily subjected to court restrictions on their ordinary daily activities.[167]

Law Enforcement Efforts

As gangs have spread from the central city to ring city, suburban, and even rural areas, police departments have responded by creating specialized gang-control units. As Figure 9.5 shows, the number of gang units in less populated areas is growing while their counterparts in urban areas have declined.

Gang control takes three basic forms:

I *Youth services programs*, in which traditional police personnel, usually from the youth unit, are given responsibility for gang control

I *Gang details*, in which one or more police officers, usually from youth or detective units, are assigned exclusively to gang-control work

I *Gang units*, established solely to deal with gang problems, to which one or more officers are assigned exclusively to gang-control work.

Today, about one in four law enforcement agencies with a gang problem operates a gang unit, including more than half of larger cities. Across all area types, agencies with long-standing gang problems and/or higher numbers of documented gang members are more likely to report operating a gang unit.[168] Some programs rely on intelligence gathering, aggressive enforcement, and "gang-breaking" activities. They attempt to arrest, prosecute, convict, and incarcerate gang leaders. The Chicago Police Department's gang crime section maintains intelligence on gang problems and trains its more than 400 officers to deal with gang problems. Officers identify street gang members and enter their names in a computer bank that is programmed to alert the unit if the youths are picked up or arrested.

FIGURE 9.5

Police Departments That Have
Created Gang Units, by Area

SOURCE: National Youth Gang Center,
National Youth Gang Survey Analysis,
2006, www.iir.com/nygc/nygsa/
(accessed October 21, 2007).

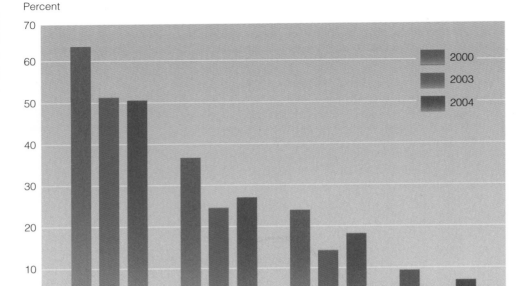

Other departments take a more prevention/treatment-oriented approach. Take for instance the Gang Intervention through Curfew Enforcement program that is used in Akron, Ohio.[169] A small detail of gang unit officers are assigned to conduct neighborhood sweeps in high-crime and gang neighborhoods to take the juveniles off the street who are at highest risk of gang membership, gang violence, or gang victimization. When juveniles are arrested for violation of the curfew ordinance, they are transported to a rehabilitative program center known as the Oriana House. Here the juveniles receive counseling and are advised on how to stay out of street gangs. Parents or guardians are notified to pick up their child and upon arrival at the program site they are given educational materials designed to help them prevent their kids from becoming involved in gangs. A follow-up call is made by gang unit officers to the parents or guardians of the suspected gang members to further reinforce the educational materials provided the Oriana House. Target sites are determined by locating gang parties, suspected gang fight locations, and known drug trafficking spots used by gang members to "post up" and sell drugs.

Many large police departments maintain gang units that engage in **gang sweeps**, a method of enforcement in which police, armed with arrest and search warrants, enter a neighborhood in force in an operation to make as many arrests as possible. Each department has its own method of sweeping up known gang members. In Las Vegas, gang unit officers split into teams, each assigned to its own squad car. One pair of officers will patrol down a "hot street"—a street or area where gang members are known to hang out and conduct drug sales. Two other pairs in squad cars patrol the two streets immediately parallel to the hot street, keeping pace with the lead car. The fourth squad car remains out of sight at the end of the street, slowly patrolling toward the other three. This tactic squeezes gang members toward the center of the targeted area and allows easy pursuit if a suspect tries to flee.[170]

Gang sweeps and other traditional police tactics may not work on today's drug gangs. It might be more appropriate to view gangs as organized criminal enterprises and deal with them as traditional organized crime families. It might be useful to (a) develop informants through criminal prosecutions, payments, and witness protection programs; (b) rely heavily on electronic surveillance and long-term

gang sweep
A method of enforcement in which police, armed with arrest and search warrants, enter a neighborhood in force in an operation to make as many arrests as possible.

undercover investigations; and (c) use special statutes that create criminal liabilities for conspiracy, extortion, or engaging in criminal enterprises.[171] Of course, such policies are expensive and difficult to implement because they may be needed only against the most sophisticated gangs. However, the gangs that present the greatest threat to urban life may be suitable targets for more intensive police efforts. In addition, as new community-policing strategies are implemented in which police officers are assigned to keep the peace in local neighborhoods (see Chapter 14 for more on community policing), it may be possible to garner sufficient local support and information to counteract gang influences. The Policy and Practice box entitled "Boston's Youth Violence Strike Force" describes one of the more successful police-sponsored gang-control efforts.

Operation Ceasefire One oft-cited and controversial gang reduction program begun by the Youth Violence Strike Force in Boston was Operation Ceasefire, a problem-oriented policing approach that focused police attention on specific places that were known for gang activity and gun violence. The program involved stepped-up law enforcement combined with cooperation between police, prosecutors, probation authorities, and community groups to form partnerships aimed at reducing gun violence in the community. The concept was that each agency and community group brings specialized expertise to the problem that agencies working independently could not muster. The program proved so successful that it was implemented by other departments around the country.

Los Angeles adopted the Ceasefire approach in an effort to reduce gang-related gun violence in local neighborhoods such Hollenbeck, an area east of downtown Los Angeles made up of neighborhoods (such as El Sereno, Lincoln Heights, and Boyle Heights) that were known to have a great deal of gang and gun violence and disputes over turf and respect. Operation Ceasefire in L.A. used several approaches:

▌ Using police records so that after a violent incident by a given gang, all members, regardless of who committed the act, were given the highest priority in terms of probation, parole, and warrant enforcement. This policy is known as "collective accountability"—each member of the group is as guilty as the next.

▌ Increasing police patrols, in both the area of the offender's gang and the victim's gang.

▌ Stricter enforcement of public housing residency requirements for properties used by gang members, including prohibitions of drugs, firearms, and other contraband.

▌ Dynamic and rapid application of these and other intervention elements after violent acts to ensure that perpetrators and victims understand that there are consequences to supporting violence.

At the same time that Ceasefire was in operation the community attempted to reach out with a variety of supportive services for gang members, including job training and development, tattoo removal, and substance abuse treatment.

A recent evaluation of Ceasefire by the Rand Corporation found that results were somewhat mixed. While violent and gun- and gang-related crime in general dropped throughout the area during the intervention, the effects decreased over time, particularly when resources were not directly applied; there was little residual deterrent effect on gang behaviors.[172]

detached street workers
Social workers who go out into the community and establish close relationships with juvenile gangs with the goal of modifying gang behavior to conform to conventional behaviors and help gang members get jobs and educational opportunities.

Community Control Efforts

During the late nineteenth century, social workers of the YMCA worked with youths in Chicago gangs.[173] During the 1950s, the detached street worker program was developed in major centers of gang activity. Social workers went into the community to work with gangs on their own turf. They participated in gang activities and tried

Boston's Youth Violence Strike Force (YVSF)

At about 1:45 A.M., on July 13, 2007, officers from the Youth Violence Strike Force received a radio call about a crowd gathering in front of the Boston Medical Center. The group gathered at the hospital told officers they were there to check on the condition of two individuals shot in the area of Franklin Hill and Shandon Streets. While officers were monitoring the crowd, they observed four individuals quickly enter a motor vehicle and flee the scene. The officers knew the individuals—in fact, all four were known to be closely associated with the shooting victims.

Following the individuals, the officers observed their motor vehicle fail to stop for a red light. The officers activated their siren and pulled the car over. As they approached the vehicle, the officers observed the occupants moving in such a way as to suggest they were in the process of attempting to hide weapons and/or drugs. As a result, the officers asked all four occupants to exit the motor vehicle. Searching the car, officers recovered a loaded semi-automatic firearm and a large amount of crack cocaine.

The Youth Violence Strike Force (YVSF) is one of the primary enforcement strategies that Boston is pursuing to combat youth gang violence. The YVSF is a multi-agency coordinated task force made up of 45 to 50 full-time Boston police officers and 15 officers from outside agencies. The membership of the YVSF includes the Massachusetts State Police, the Department of Treasury's Bureau of Alcohol, Tobacco, Firearms, and Explosives (ATF), police departments from neighboring jurisdictions, Massachusetts Corrections, Probation, Parole, and Division of Youth Service (juvenile corrections) officers, and other agencies as appropriate. It works closely with the Suffolk County District Attorney's and state Attorney General's offices, and participates in the Department of Justice's Anti-Violent Crime Initiative (AVCI) led locally by the United States Attorney. The YVSF investigates youth crimes, arrests those responsible, and breaks up the environment for crime. One important accomplishment of the YVSF was the creation of a comprehensive computer database, which has allowed tough enforcement efforts against the leaders of gangs, and positive intervention in the lives of those who are at risk of becoming hard-core gang members.

In addition, the Youth Violence Strike Force, in cooperation with the city of Boston and the Department of Justice, has used criminal and civil forfeiture laws to help secure the safety of the community by taking over drug dens and renovating them as new homes. Drug dens have been closed through joint federal-state-local cooperation. Some former drug houses have been renovated in order to provide low-income elderly housing.

The Youth Violence Strike Force takes tough action every day against gangs and gang members across Boston. Yet many of the strike force officers view their work in prevention as equally important, and many of these officers help to sponsor numerous prevention activities in the community. For example, members of the YVSF work in partnership with law enforcement, social service, and private institutions to raise funds for a series of "Kids at Risk" programs, including camping programs, membership at the Boys and Girls Clubs and YMCAs, and attendance at basketball camp or the Boston Police's Teen Summer Academy.

Another program, Operation Night Light, puts the YVSF together with concerned clergy members, youth outreach workers, and social service professionals to prevent youth and gang violence of probationers by regularly visiting their homes. Operation Night Light pairs one probation officer with two police officers to make surprise visits to the homes, schools, and worksites of high-risk youth probationers during the nontraditional hours of 7 P.M. to midnight.

Critical Thinking

Is it possible to reduce gang membership without providing youth with a reasonable legitimate alternative, including first-rate schools and job opportunities?

SOURCES: Boston Police Department News, "Youth Violence Strike Force Recovers Semi-Automatic Firearm, Arrests Four," www.bpdnews.com/2007/07/post_9.html (accessed July 20, 2007); Office of Juvenile Justice and Delinquency Prevention, Operation Night Light, http://ojjdp.ncjrs.org/pubs/gun_violence/profile33.html (accessed July 20, 2007); *Youth Violence: A Community-based Response: One City's Success Story* (Washington, DC: Office of the Attorney General, 1996).

---

to get to know their members. The purpose was to act as advocates for the youths, to provide them with positive role models, and to treat individual problems.

Detached street worker programs are sometimes credited with curbing gang activities in the 1950s and 1960s, although some critics claimed that they turned delinquent groups into legitimate neighborhood organizations.[174] Others believe they helped maintain group solidarity, and as a result, new members were drawn to gangs.

Today, there are numerous community-level programs designed to limit gang activity. Some employ recreation areas open in the evening hours that provide supervised activities.[175] In some areas, citywide coordinating groups help orient gang-control efforts. In Los Angeles County, the Gang Alternative Prevention Program (GAPP) provides prevention services to juveniles before they become

EXHIBIT **9.5**

The Elements of Spergel's Community Gang-Control Program

1. Community mobilization, including citizens, youth, community groups, and agencies.
2. Provision of academic, economic, and social opportunities. Special school training and job programs are especially critical for older gang members who are not in school but may be ready to leave the gang or decrease participation in criminal gang activity for many reasons, including maturation and the need to provide for family.
3. Social intervention, using street outreach workers to engage gang-involved youth.

4. Gang suppression, including formal and informal social control procedures of the juvenile and criminal justice systems and community agencies and groups. Community-based agencies and local groups must collaborate with juvenile and criminal justice agencies in the surveillance and sharing of information under conditions that protect the community and the civil liberties of youths.
5. Organizational change and development—that is, the appropriate organization and integration of the preceding strategies and potential reallocation of resources.

SOURCES: Irving Spergel and Candice Kane, *Community-Based Youth Agency Model* (Washington, DC: Office of Juvenile Justice and Delinquency Prevention, 1990); Jim Burch and Candice Kane, *Implementing the OJJDP Comprehensive Gang Model* (Washington, DC: Office of Juvenile Justice and Delinquency Prevention, 1999).

entrenched in gangs, including (a) individual and group counseling, (b) bicultural and bilingual services to adolescents and their parents, and (c) special programs such as tutoring, parent training, job development, and recreational and educational experiences.[176] Some police departments also sponsor prevention programs such as school-based lectures, police-school liaisons, recreation programs, and street worker programs that offer counseling, assistance to parents, and other services. The Stockton, California, police department sponsors a gang intervention called Operation Peacekeeper.[177] It puts outreach workers, former gang members themselves, onto the street to support kids who want to leave gangs. The program includes monthly forums at which known gang members are offered information about available programs as well as a warning that they are being watched. Operation Peacekeeper has been credited with a drop in gang-related homicides and has been praised because outreach workers are able to form bonds with youths unavailable to uniformed officers.

Still another approach has been to involve schools in gang-control programs. Some invite law enforcement agents to lecture students on the dangers of gang involvement and teach them gang-resistance techniques. Others provide resources that can help parents prevent their children from joining gangs, or if they already are members, get them out. As the Policy and Practice feature entitled "Gang-Control Efforts in the City of Miami" shows, some jurisdictions have used both enforcement and community efforts to reduce gang activity.

Sociologist Irving Spergel, a leading expert on gangs, has developed a model for helping communities deal with gang-involved youth that has become the basis for gang-control efforts around the nation. His model includes the five distinct strategies, contained in Exhibit 9.5.

Evaluating Gang-Control Efforts

Gang control can be difficult to attain. While aggressive police tactics can work, they also run the risk of becoming overzealous and alienating the community. Take for instance Los Angeles's anti-gang unit, the Community Resources Against Street Hoodlums (CRASH), which at its peak contained 200 sworn officers. The unit conducted aggressive anti-gang actions, including Operation Hammer, which involved the unit moving through some of the city's toughest neighborhoods, arresting gang members for the slightest infractions, including wearing colors, flashing signs, jaywalking, and curfew violations. By making 25,000 arrests per year, the unit significantly reduced gang activity. But problems began to emerge. Unit members developed a warlike mentality and CRASH officers began resisting supervision and flagrantly ignoring policies and procedures. This subculture eventually gave rise to the Rampart Scandal, in which Rampart CRASH unit officers in Los Angeles were found to be engaging in hard-core criminal activity. Officers admitted to attacking known gang members and falsely accusing them of crimes they had not committed. As a consequence, approximately 10 years after it had been fully staffed and promoted as the ideal in anti-gang enforcement, LAPD's gang unit was shut down because of corruption, the use of excessive force, and civil rights violations; and the city had paid out about $70 million to settle lawsuits related to the scandal.[178] The Rampart Scandal serves as a cautionary tale for police departments attempting to control gang activity.

A recent report by Judith Greene and Kevin Pranis of the Justice Policy Institute, a Washington, D.C.–based think-tank, takes the law enforcement strategy to task. According to the report, police, prisons, and punitive measures haven't stopped the cycle of gang violence in major cities such as Los Angeles. Greene and Pranis find that one problem is overkill: While gangs do commit a lot of crime, they are responsible for a relatively small share of the total numbers of crimes in the community. Nonetheless, their share of the crime problem has remained relatively stable. Despite decades of aggressive gang enforcement—including mass arrests and surveillance, huge gang databases, and increased prison sentences for gang crimes—gang violence has not been reduced.

Ironically, these heavy-handed suppression tactics can increase gang cohesion while failing to reduce violence, and keep kids in gangs who would have quit if left to their own devices. In Chicago, a cycle of police suppression and incarceration combined to *sustain* unacceptably high levels of gang violence. Results from Dallas, Detroit, and St. Louis show no evidence of a positive impact on target neighborhoods. Most young people who enter gangs will leave the gang within a year. But law enforcement practices can target former gang members long after their active participation in the gang has ended, and may dissuade employers from offering jobs to former gang members or youth who merely look like gang members.

Because gangs represent only a small part of the crime rate, aggressive suppression tactics simply make the situation worse by alienating local residents and trapping youth in the criminal justice system. More often than not, minority youth are the target of anti-gang efforts, and their suppression gives people the impression that police are targeting minority kids. The Greene/Pranis review found no evidence that gang enforcement strategies have achieved meaningful reductions in violence.

In contrast to suppression tactics, cities that adopted treatment alternatives fared far better. New York City has not embraced the aggressive tactics used in Los Angeles even when gang crime was on the rise, and has consequently experienced far less gang violence. When gang violence became a serious problem, the city established a system of well-trained street workers and gang intervention programs, grounded in effective social work practices and independent of law enforcement. Gang experts conclude that the city's serious problem with street gang violence had largely faded away by the 1980s. Crime is at an historic low in New York.

The Problems of Reform Social and economic solutions seem equally challenging. Experts suggest that to reduce the gang problem, hundreds of thousands of high-paying jobs are needed. Economic opportunities might prove to be particularly effective, because surveys reveal that many gang members might leave gangs if such opportunities existed.[179] This solution does not, however, seem practical. Many of the jobs for which undereducated gang boys can qualify are now being shipped overseas. Highly paid manufacturing jobs are particularly hard to obtain. It is unlikely that a boy who has five years as a Crip on his résumé will be in demand for legitimate work opportunities. The more embedded youths become in criminal enterprise, the less likely they are to find meaningful adult work. It is unlikely that gang members can suddenly be transformed into highly paid professionals.

Gang-Control Efforts in the City of Miami

The city of Miami has employed several programs to target at-risk youth to either prevent them from joining gangs or to help them leave the gang life. Some are based on providing alternatives to gang life while others are traditional law enforcement models aimed at identifying gang crime, apprehending perpetrators, and handing them over for prosecution.

ALTERNATIVE MEASURES

G.R.E.A.T. (Gang Resistance Education and Training)

Miami officers go through a strict training regimen and obtain a federal certification to teach this middle school curriculum to public school children. This program provides the children with alternatives to gang membership and helps build their self-esteem. Miami officers teach a minimum of two classes per school year and are challenged to graduate a minimum of 60 students. In addition, every instructor must participate in the summer program component. (There is more on the G.R.E.A.T. program in Chapter 12.)

G.R.A.S.P. (Gang Reduction Activities and Sports Program)

The Miami Gang Detail unit developed this program in 1997. Each officer is committed to sponsor at-risk youth and track their progress through their stay in the program. The initial contact with the youth entails a meeting with the parents and school officials. A file is then built tracking the youth's development as he or she progresses throughout the term of the program. The program itself has multiple phases. Self-esteem building programs are implemented in order to build rapport with the youth.

Examples of these programs include ROPES course (similar to those used by corporations to build camaraderie among employees), and programs in which Miami officers take youths sailing with an area group called Shake-a-leg. (These are disabled individuals who may seem incapacitated yet are able to master the complexity of sailing.) The youth learn that seemingly impossible situations do have possible solutions. They are also rewarded for positive progress with excursions to local area attractions.

S.A.V.E. (Stop Active Vandalism Everywhere)

In this program officers take youth who have been involved in graffiti or gang activity throughout the city to paint over existing graffiti. Youth who have committed crimes and have been sentenced to community service time are also recruited for this learning venture. Officers lecture the youth on the dangers of being involved in gang activity, as well as the impact graffiti has on the community. The officers are also challenged to build rapport with the participating youth.

ENFORCEMENT MEASURES

The Miami gang detail keeps a database on documented gang members and their associates who reside or loiter within the jurisdiction of the city. This provides information in tracking gang-related incidents and serves as a fount of information for support to other investigative units. (i.e., homicide, burglary, robbery, etc.). The unit also proactively engages in gang sweeps throughout the city, documenting and enforcing criminal activity. Furthermore, the gang detail conducts long- and short-term investigations involving gang members and their associates. The unit is also an active participant in the Multi-Agency Gang Task Force. This task force provides networking within the different police departments and an exchange of intelligence between agencies relating to gang activity. The participating agencies meet once a month and proactively engage in gang sweeps throughout the Dade County area (the common jurisdictional geographic).

Critical Thinking

If you were a police chief in a city similar to Miami, would you adopt the police department's gang-control process or would you employ a different strategy?

SOURCE: "Gang Control Efforts in the City of Miami," the United States Conference of Mayors, *Best Practices of Community Policing in Gang Intervention and Gang Violence Prevention, 2006*, www.usmayors.org/uscm/best_practices/community_policing_2006/gangBP_2006.pdf (accessed September 22, 2007).

Although social solutions to the gang problem seem elusive, the evidence shows that gang involvement is a socioecological phenomenon and must be treated as such. Youths who live in areas where their needs cannot be met by existing institutions join gangs when gang members are there to recruit them.[180] Social causes demand social solutions. Programs that enhance the lives of adolescents are the key to reducing gang delinquency. A more effective alternative would be to devote more resources to the most deteriorated urban areas, even if it requires pulling funds from other groups that receive government aid, such as the elderly.[181] A recent report of the Justice Policy Institute, a Washington-based think tank, suggests the following changes:

▌ *Expand the use of evidence-based practice to reduce youth crime.* Instead of devoting more resources to the already heavily funded and ineffective gang enforcement tactics, policy makers should expand the use of "evidence-based" interventions that are scientifically proven to reduce juvenile recidivism.

▌ *Promote jobs, education, and healthy communities, and lower barriers to the reintegration into society of former gang members.* Gang researchers observe that employment and family formation help draw youth away from gangs. Creating positive opportunities through which gang members can leave their past, as opposed to ineffective policies that lock people into gangs or strengthen their attachments, can help to improve public safety.

▌ *Redirect resources from failed gang enforcement efforts to proven public safety strategies.* Gang injunctions, gang sweeps, and various ineffective enforcement initiatives reinforce negative images of whole communities and run counter to best practices in youth development. JPI suggests that, instead, localities should end practices that can make the youth violence problem worse, and refocus funds on effective public safety strategies.[182]

Summary

1. Be familiar with the influence of peers on delinquency

▌ In adolescence, friends begin to have a greater influence over decision making than parents.

▌ As they go through adolescence, children form cliques, small groups of friends who share activities and confidences.

▌ In mid-adolescence, kids strive for peer approval and to impress their closest friends.

▌ Acceptance by peers has a major impact on socialization.

▌ Popular youths do well in school and are socially astute.

▌ Peer status during childhood is an important contributor to children's social and emotional development that follows them across the life course.

▌ Youths who report inadequate or strained peer relations are the ones most likely to become delinquent.

▌ Adolescents who maintain delinquent friends are more likely to engage in antisocial behavior and drug abuse.

▌ Delinquent acts tend to be committed in small groups rather than alone, a process referred to as co-offending.

2. Compare and contrast the different views of the association between peers and delinquency

▌ There are actually five independent views on the association between friendship and delinquency.

▌ According to the control theory approach, delinquents are as detached from their peers as they are from other elements of society.

▌ Delinquent friends cause law-abiding youth to get in trouble.

▌ Antisocial youths join up with like-minded friends; deviant peers sustain and amplify delinquent careers.

▌ Troubled kids choose delinquent peers out of necessity rather than desire.

▌ Kids who display emotional or behavioral problems early in childhood are labeled "strange" or "weird" by other kids; labeling causes delinquency.

▌ Delinquent peers have a significant influence on behavior: youths who are loyal to delinquent friends, belong to gangs, and have "bad companions."

3. Understand the problem of lumping troubled kids together in the same programs

▌ Most correctional programs in school and the juvenile justice system continue to organize deviant peers into groups and isolate them from conventional law-abiding kids.

▌ A variety of programs that are designed to keep at-risk youth off the streets offer little structure or adult supervision and simply provide a place for youth to hang out.

4. Know the various definitions used to describe gangs

▌ As youths move through adolescence, they gravitate toward cliques that provide them with support, assurance, protection, and direction.

▌ Gangs are groups of youths who engage in delinquent behaviors.

▌ Gangs are an interstitial group—one falling within the cracks and crevices of society.

▌ Members have self-recognition of their gang status and use special vocabulary, clothing, signs, colors, graffiti, and names.

▌ There is a commitment to criminal activity, although even the most criminal gang members spend the bulk of their time in noncriminal activities.

5. Discuss the history of gangs

▌ The youth gang is sometimes viewed as uniquely American, but gangs have also been reported in several other nations.

▌ In the 1600s, London was terrorized by organized gangs that called themselves Hectors, Bugles, Dead Boys, and other colorful names.

▌ In the 1920s, Frederick Thrasher initiated the study of the modern gang in his analysis of more than 1,300 youth groups in Chicago.

▌ According to Thrasher, gangs form because society does not meet the needs of lower-class youths.

▌ In the 1950s and early 1960s, the threat of gangs and gang violence swept the public consciousness.

▌ By the mid-1960s, the gang menace seemed to have disappeared.

▌ Some experts attribute the decline of gang activity to successful gang-control programs.

▌ Interest in gang activity began anew in the early 1970s.

▌ Bearing such names as Savage Skulls and Black Assassins, gangs began to form in New York's South Bronx.

▌ One reason for the increase in gang activity may be involvement in the sale of illegal drugs.

▌ Gang formation was also the natural consequence of the economic and social dislocation that occurred when the economy shifted from a relatively high-paying manufacturing to low-wage service economy.

6. Be familiar with the extent and location of the gang problem

▌ At recent count an estimated 760,000 gang members and 24,000 gangs were active in more than 2,900 jurisdictions around the United States.

▌ Traditionally, gangs have operated in large urban areas experiencing rapid population change.

▌ While some people think of gangs as a purely urban phenomenon, an estimated 15,000 gangs with 300,000 members are located in small cities, suburban counties, and even rural areas.

▌ Because of redevelopment, gangs in some areas have relocated or migrated; gang members have organized new chapters when they relocate to new areas.

▌ The gang problem is not unique to the United States.

▌ Worldwide urbanization and the concentration of population in crowded, poor, and disorganized cities has created fertile conditions for the growth of gangs, particularly in Latin America, Asia, and Africa.

▌ Globalization has created a flourishing underground economy that can be exploited by internationally connected enterprises run by gangs.

7. Discuss the various forms contemporary gangs take

▌ There are different types of gangs, including the social gang, party gang, serious delinquent gang, and organized gang.

▌ Gangs are near-groups, which have limited cohesion, impermanence, minimal consensus of norms, shifting membership, disturbed leadership, and limited definitions of membership expectations.

8. Describe the makeup of gangs

▌ The ages of gang members range widely, but members are staying in gangs longer than in the past so that the average age of gang members is increasing.

▌ A transformed U.S. economy now prioritizes information and services over heavy industry.

▌ Traditionally, gangs were considered a male-dominated enterprise.

▌ Today the number of female gang members and female gangs is rapidly increasing

▌ There are a variety of reasons why girls join gangs, including but not limited to financial opportunity, identity and status, peer pressure, family dysfunction, and protection.

▌ Ganging can provide girls with a sense of sisterhood, independence, and solidarity, as well as a chance to earn profit through illegal activities.

▌ Once in gangs, girls form close ties with other female members and engage in group criminal activity.

▌ Many girls join gangs in an effort to cope with their turbulent personal lives

▌ Female gang members begin to drift away from gangs when they become young mothers.

- Gang formation involves a sense of territoriality.
- Delinquent gangs tend to be small and transitory.
- Those who assume leadership roles are described as "cool characters" who have earned their position by demonstrating fighting prowess, verbal quickness, or athletic distinction.
- Gangs seek recognition, both from their rivals and from the community.
- Image and reputation depend on the ability to communicate to the rest of the world.
- One major source of communication is graffiti.
- Gang hand signs are quickly displayed with the fingers, hands, and body, and have very specific meanings to gang members.
- The ethnic distribution of gangs corresponds to their geographic location.
- The first black youth gangs were organized in the early 1920s.
- Latino gangs such as MS-13 and the 18th Street Gang have continued to grow and now constitute the largest number of gangs and gang memberships.
- Today, white gang members are often alienated middle-class youths rather than poor lower-class youths.
- Skinheads are members of a white supremacist gang, identified by a shaved skull and Nazi or Ku Klux Klan markings.
- Regardless of their type, gang members typically commit more crimes than any other youths in the social environment.

9. Describe gang criminality

- While the association between gang membership and delinquency is unquestioned, there are actually different explanations for the relationship.
- Some gangs specialize in drug dealing.
- Not all gangs are major players in drug trafficking, and those that are tend to distribute small amounts of drugs at the street level.
- It is not surprising that youth gangs are responsible for a disproportionate number of homicides.
- Research indicates that gang violence is impulsive and therefore comes in spurts.
- Violence is a core fact of gang formation and life.

10. Compare the various theories of gang formation

- There are a number of theories of gang formation.
- The anthropological view is that gangs appeal to adolescents' longing for the tribal process that sustained

their ancestors. Hand signs and graffiti have a tribal flavor.
- Sociologists have commonly viewed the destructive sociocultural forces in poor inner-city areas as the major cause of gang formation.
- According to this view, conditions of anomie/alienation encourage gang formation on both a cultural and individual level.
- Some believe that gangs serve as an outlet for disturbed youths who suffer a multitude of personal problems and deficits.
- Some youths may make a rational choice to join a gang.
- According to Spergel, some adolescents choose to join gangs from a "rational calculation" to achieve safety.
- Some youths join gangs simply to have fun.
- Some kids enter the gang life because they want to enhance a chosen "thug" lifestyle.

11. Describe the various forms of gang-control efforts that are in use today

- A number of states have created laws specifically designed to control gang activity.
- One approach has been to create enhanced penalties for behaviors typically associated with gang members.
- Some jurisdictions have filed lawsuits against gangs and gang members, asking courts for injunctions barring them from hanging out together on street corners, in cars, or in particular areas.
- As gangs have spread from the central city to ring city, suburban, and even rural areas, police departments have responded by creating specialized gang-control units.
- Today, about one in four law enforcement agencies with a gang problem operates a gang unit, including more than half of larger cities.
- Gang sweeps are a method of enforcement in which police, armed with arrest and search warrants, enter a neighborhood in force in an operation to make as many arrests as possible.
- Detached street workers are social workers who go out into the community and establish close relationships with juvenile gangs with the goal of modifying gang behavior.
- Still another approach has been to involve schools in gang-control programs.
- Social and economic solutions seem equally challenging.

Key Terms

cliques, p. 288
crowds, p. 288
controversial status youth, p. 288
gang, p. 291
interstitial group, p. 292
disorganized neighborhood, p. 295

near-groups, p. 298
barrio, p. 299
klikas, p. 302
graffiti, p. 303
posting, p. 304

representing, p. 304
skinhead, p. 309
prestige crimes, p. 311
gang sweep, p. 318
detached street workers, p. 319

Viewpoint

You are a professor at a local state university who teaches courses on delinquent behavior. One day you are approached by the director of the president's National Task Force on Gangs (NTFG). This group has been formed to pool resources from a variety of federal agencies, ranging from the FBI to Health and Human Services, in order to provide local jurisdictions with a comprehensive plan to fight gangs. The director claims that the gang problem is big and becoming bigger. Thousands of gangs are operating around the country, with hundreds of thousands of members. Government sources, he claims, indicate that there has been a significant growth in gang membership over the past 20 years. So far, the government has not been able to do anything at either a state or national level to stem this growing tide of organized criminal activity. The NTFG would like you to be part of the team that provides state and local jurisdictions with a gang-control activity model, which, if implemented, would provide a cost-effective means of reducing both gang membership and gang activity.

▌ Would you recommend that police employ anti-gang units that use tactics developed in the fight against organized crime families?

▌ Would you recommend the redevelopment of deteriorated neighborhoods in which gangs flourish?

▌ Would you try to educate kids about the dangers of gang membership?

▌ Would you tell the director that gangs have always existed and there is probably not much the government can do to reduce their numbers?

Doing Research on the Web

The National Gang Center (NGC) is a collaborative effort between the Office of Justice Programs' (OJP) Bureau of Justice Assistance (BJA) and the Office of Juvenile Justice and Delinquency Prevention (OJJDP). The May 2006 issue of the *United States Attorneys' Bulletin* on gangs has a number of articles covering prevention, investigation, and prosecution of gang crime.

You can access both of these resources via

academic.cengage.com/criminaljustice/siegel

Questions for Discussion

1. Do gangs serve a purpose? Differentiate between a gang and a fraternity.

2. Discuss the differences between violent, criminal, and drug-oriented gangs.

3. How do gangs in suburban areas differ from inner-city gangs?

4. Do delinquents have cold and distant relationships with their peers?

5. Can gangs be controlled without changing the economic opportunity structure of society? Are there any truly meaningful alternatives to gangs today for lower-class youths?

6. Can you think of other rituals in society that reflect an affinity or longing for more tribal times? (Hint: Have you ever pledged a fraternity or sorority, gone to a wedding, or attended a football game?) Do TV shows like *Survivor* show a longing for more tribal times? After all, they even use tribal names for the competing teams.

Notes

1. George Chidi, "Gwinnett Targets Jailhouse Gangs," *Atlanta Journal-Constitution*, 12 June 2007.

2. For a general review, see Scott Cummings and Daniel Monti, *Gangs: The Origin and Impact of Contemporary Youth Gangs in the United States* (Albany: SUNY Press, 1993); this chapter also makes extensive use of George Knox et al., *Gang Prevention and Intervention: Preliminary Results from the 1995 Gang Research Task Force* (Chicago: National Gang Crime Research Center, 1995).

3. Paul Perrone and Meda Chesney-Lind, "Representations of Gangs and Delinquency: Wild in the Streets?" *Social Justice* 24:96–117 (1997).

4. Spencer Rathus, *Understanding Child Development* (New York: Holt, Rinehart & Winston, 1988), p. 462.

5. Peggy Giordano, "The Wider Circle of Friends in Adolescence," *American Journal of Sociology* 101:661–697 (1995).

6. Danielle Payne and Benjamin Cornwell, "Reconsidering Peer Influences on Delinquency: Do Less Proximate Contacts Matter?" *Journal of Quantitative Criminology* 23:127–149 (2007).

7. Annette La Greca and Hannah Moore Harrison, "Adolescent Peer Relations, Friendships, and Romantic Relationships: Do They Predict Social Anxiety and Depression?" *Journal of Clinical Child and Adolescent Psychology* 34:49–61 (2005).

8. Delyse Hutchinson and Ronald Rapee, "Do Friends Share Similar Body Image and Eating Problems? The Role of Social Networks and Peer Influences in Early Adolescence," *Behaviour Research and Therapy* 45:1557–1577 (2007).

9. Shari Miller-Johnson, Philip Costanzo, John Coie, Mary Rose, Dorothy Browne, and Courtney Johnson, "Peer Social Structure and Risk-Taking Behaviors among African American Early Adolescents," *Journal of Youth and Adolescence* 32:375–384 (2003).

10. John Coie and Shari Miller-Johnson, "Peer Factors in Early Offending Behavior," in Rolf Loeber and David Farrington, eds., *Child Delinquents* (Thousand Oaks, CA: Sage, 2001), pp. 191–210.

11. Ibid.

12. Judith Rich Harris, *The Nurture Assumption: Why Children Turn Out the Way They Do* (New York: Free Press, 1998).

13. Marvella Bowman, Hazel Prelow, and Scott Weaver, "Parenting Behaviors, Association with Deviant Peers, and Delinquency in African American Adolescents: A Mediated-Moderation Model," *Journal of Youth and Adolescence* 36:517–527 (2007).

14. Harris, *The Nurture Assumption*, p. 463.

15. Robert Agnew and Timothy Brezina, "Relational Problems with Peers, Gender, and Delinquency," *Youth and Society* 29:84–111 (1997).

16. Maury Nation and Craig Anne Heflinger, "Risk Factors for Serious Alcohol and Drug Use: The Role of Psychosocial Variables in Predicting the Frequency of Substance Use among Adolescents," *American Journal of Drug and Alcohol Abuse* 32:415–433 (2006).

17. Timothy Brezina and Alex Piquero, "Moral Beliefs, Isolation from Peers, and Abstention from Delinquency," *Deviant Behavior* 28:433–465 (2007).

18. Albert Reiss, "Co-Offending and Criminal Careers," in Michael Tonry and Norval Morris, eds., *Crime and Justice*, vol. 10 (Chicago: University of Chicago Press, 1988).

19. Arpana Agrawal, Michael Lynskey, Kathleen Bucholz, Pamela Madden, and Andrew Heath, "Correlates of Cannabis Initiation in a Longitudinal Sample of Young Women: The Importance of Peer Influences," *Preventive Medicine* 45:31–34 (2007).

20. Kevin Beaver and John Paul Wright, "Biosocial Development and Delinquent Involvement," *Youth Violence and Juvenile Justice* 3:168–192 (2005).

21. Richard Felson and Dana Haynie, "Pubertal Development, Social Factors, and Delinquency among Adolescent Boys," *Criminology* 40:967–989 (2002).

22. Brett Johnson Solomon, "Other-Sex Friendship Involvement among Delinquent Adolescent Females," *Youth Violence and Juvenile Justice* 4:75–96 (2006).

23. See Travis Hirschi, *Causes of Delinquency* (Berkeley: University of California Press, 1969).

24. James Short and Fred Strodtbeck, *Group Process and Gang Delinquency* (Chicago: Aldine de Gruyter, 1965).

25. Kate Keenan, Rolf Loeber, Quanwu Zhang, Magda Stouthamer-Loeber, and Welmoet Van Kammen, "The Influence of Deviant Peers on the Development of Boys' Disruptive and Delinquent Behavior: A Temporal Analysis," *Development and Psychopathology* 7:715–726 (1995).

26. John Cole, Robert Terry, Shari-Miller Johnson, and John Lochman, "Longitudinal Effects of Deviant Peer Groups on Criminal Offending in Late Adolescence," paper presented at the annual meeting of the American Society of Criminology, Boston, November 1995.

27. Terence Thornberry and Marvin Krohn, "Peers, Drug Use, and Delinquency," in David Stoff, James Breiling, and Jack Maser, eds., *Handbook of Antisocial Behavior* (New York: Wiley, 1997), pp. 218–233; Thomas Dishion, Deborah Capaldi, Kathleen Spracklen, and Fuzhong Li, "Peer Ecology of Male Adolescent Drug Use," *Development and Psychopathology* 7:803–824 (1995).

28. Daneen Deptula and Robert Cohen, "Aggressive, Rejected, and Delinquent Children and Adolescents: A Comparison of Their Friendships," *Aggression and Violent Behavior* 9:75–104 (2004).

29. Mark Warr, "Age, Peers, and Delinquency," *Criminology* 31:17–40 (1993).

30. Sara Battin, Karl Hill, Robert Abbott, Richard Catalano, and J. David Hawkins, "The Contribution of Gang Membership to Delinquency Beyond Delinquent Friends," *Criminology* 36:93–116 (1998).

31. Mark Warr, "Life-Course Transitions and Desistance from Crime," *Criminology* 36:502–536 (1998).

32. Dana Haynie and D. Wayne Osgood, "Reconsidering Peers and Delinquency: How Do Peers Matter?" *Social Forces* 84:1110–1130 (2005).

33. Stephen W. Baron, "Self-Control, Social Consequences, and Criminal Behavior: Street Youth and the General Theory of Crime," *Journal of Research in Crime and Delinquency* 40:403–425 (2003).

34. Sara Pedersen, Frank Vitaro, Edward Barker, and Anne Borge, "The Timing of Middle-Childhood Peer Rejection and Friendship: Linking Early Behavior to Early-Adolescent Adjustment," *Child Development* 78:1037–1051 (2007).

35. David Farrington and Rolf Loeber, "Epidemiology of Juvenile Violence," *Child and Adolescent Psychiatric Clinics of North America* 9:733–748 (2000).

36. Beth Hoffman, Peter Monge, Chih-Ping Chou, and Thomas Valente, "Perceived Peer Influence and Peer Selection on Adolescent Smoking," *Addictive Behaviors* 32:1546–1554 (2007).

37. Peggy Giordano, Stephen Cernkovich, and M. D. Pugh, "Friendships and Delinquency," *American Journal of Sociology* 91:1170–1202 (1986).

38. Kenneth A. Dodge, Jennifer E. Lansford, and Thomas J. Dishion, "The Problem of Deviant Peer Influences in Intervention Programs" in Kenneth Dodge, Thomas Dishion, and Jennifer Lansford, eds., *Deviant Peer Influences in Programs for Youth: Problems and Solutions* (New York: Guilford Press, 2006), pp. 3–13.

39. Well-known movie representations of gangs include *The Wild Ones* and *Hell's Angels on Wheels*, which depict motorcycle gangs, and *Saturday Night Fever*, which focused on neighborhood street toughs; see also David Dawley, *A Nation of Lords* (Garden City, NY: Anchor, 1973).

40. For a review of gang research, see James Howell, "Recent Gang Research: Program and Policy Implications," *Crime and Delinquency* 40:495–515 (1994).

41. Walter Miller, *Violence by Youth Gangs and Youth Groups as a Crime Problem in Major American Cities* (Washington, DC: U.S. Government Printing Office, 1975).

42. Ibid., p. 20.

43. Malcolm Klein, *The American Street Gang: Its Nature, Prevalence, and Control* (New York: Oxford University Press, 1995), p. 30.

44. Irving Spergel, *The Youth Gang Problem: A Community Approach* (New York: Oxford University Press, 1995).

45. Ibid., p. 3.

46. Christopher Adamson, "Defensive Localism in White and Black: A Comparative History of European-American and African American Youth Gangs," *Ethnic and Racial Studies* 23:272–298 (2000).

47. Frederick Thrasher, *The Gang* (Chicago: University of Chicago Press, 1927).

48. National Youth Gang Center, 2003, www.iir.com/nygc/faq.htm#q1 (accessed October 21, 2007).

49. Malcolm Klein, ed., *Juvenile Gangs in Context* (Englewood Cliffs, NJ: Prentice Hall, 1967), pp. 1–12.

50. Ibid., p. 6.

51. Irving Spergel, *Street Gang Work: Theory and Practice* (Reading, MA: Addison-Wesley, 1966).

52. Miller, *Violence by Youth Gangs*, p. 2.

53. Marjorie Zatz, "*Los Cholos*: Legal Processing of Chicago Gang Members," *Social Problems* 33:13–30 (1985).

54. Miller, *Violence by Youth Gangs*, pp. 1–2.

55. Ibid.

56. Felix Padilla, *The Gang as an American Enterprise* (New Brunswick, NJ: Rutgers University Press, 1992), p. 3.

57. Pamela Irving Jackson, "Crime, Youth Gangs, and Urban Transition: The Social Dislocations of Postindustrial Economic Development," *Justice Quarterly* 8:379–397 (1991); Joan Moore, *Going Down to the Barrio: Homeboys and Homegirls in Change* (Philadelphia: Temple University Press, 1991), pp. 89–101.

58. Arlen Egley, Jr., and Christina E. Ritz, *Highlights of the 2004 National Youth Gang Survey* (Washington, DC: Office of Juvenile Justice and Delinquency Prevention, 2006).

59. William Julius Wilson, *The Truly Disadvantaged* (Chicago: University of Chicago Press, 1987).

60. Ibid.

61. Egley and Ritz, *Highlights of the 2004 National Youth Gang Survey*.

62. Cheryl Maxson, *Gang Members on the Move*, bulletin, Youth Gang Series (Washington, DC: Office of Juvenile Justice and Delinquency Prevention, 1998).

63. Ibid.

64. John Hagedorn, "Gangs," in Karen Christianson and David Levinson, eds., *The Encyclopedia of Community* (Thousand Oaks, CA: Sage Publications, 2003), pp. 517–522.

65. John M. Hagedorn, "The Global Impact of Gangs," *Journal of Contemporary Criminal Justice* 21:153–169 (2005).

66. Jeffrey Fagan, "The Social Organization of Drug Use and Drug Dealing among Urban Gangs," *Criminology* 27:633–669 (1989).

67. Ibid.

68. National Youth Gang Center, "Are Today's Youth Gangs Different from Gangs in the Past?" www.iir.com/nygc/faq.htm (accessed October 21, 2007).

69. Lewis Yablonsky, *The Violent Gang* (Baltimore: Penguin, 1966), p. 109.

70. James Diego Vigil, *Barrio Gangs* (Austin: Texas University Press, 1988), pp. 11–19.

71. Mark Warr, "Organization and Instigation in Delinquent Groups," *Criminology* 34:11–37 (1996).

72. Knox et al., *Gang Prevention and Intervention*, p. vii.

73. Ibid.

74. Wilson, *The Truly Disadvantaged*.

75. Ibid.

76. Hagedorn, "The Global Impact of Gangs."

77. Finn-Aage Esbensen and David Huizinga, "Gangs, Drugs and Delinquency in a Survey of Urban Youth," *Criminology* 31:565–587 (1993); Finn-Aage Esbensen, "Race and Gender Differences between Gang and Nongang Youths: Results from a Multisite Survey," *Justice Quarterly* 15:504–525 (1998).

78. Cheryl Maxson and Monica Whitlock, "Joining the Gang: Gender Differences in Risk Factors for Gang Membership," in C. Ronald Huff, ed., *Gangs in America III* (Thousand Oaks, CA: Sage, 2002), pp. 19–35.

79. Mars Eghigian and Katherine Kirby, "Girls in Gangs: On the Rise in America," *Corrections Today* 68:48–50 (2006).

80. Ibid.

81. Mark Fleisher and Jessie Krienert, "Life-Course Events, Social Networks, and the Emergence of Violence among Female Gang Members," *Journal of Community Psychology* 32:607–622 (2004).

82. Karen Joe Laidler and Geoffrey Hunt, "Violence and Social Organization in Female Gangs," *Social Justice* 24:148–187 (1997); Moore, *Going Down to the Barrio*; Anne Campbell, *The Girls in the Gang* (Cambridge, MA: Basil Blackwell, 1984).

83. Karen Joe Laidler and Meda Chesney-Lind, "'Just Every Mother's Angel': An Analysis of Gender and Ethnic Variations in Youth Gang Membership," *Gender and Society* 9:408–430 (1995).

84. Jody Miller, *One of the Guys: Girls, Gangs, and Gender* (New York: Oxford University Press, 2001).

85. Ibid.

86. Fleisher and Krienert, "Life-Course Events, Social Networks, and the Emergence of Violence among Female Gang Members."

87. Joan Moore, James Diego Vigil, and Robert Garcia, "Residence and Territoriality in Chicano Gangs," *Social Problems* 31:182–194 (1983).

88. Mark Warr, "Organization and Instigation in Delinquent Groups," *Criminology* 34:11–37 (1996).

89. Malcolm Klein, "Impressions of Juvenile Gang Members," *Adolescence* 3:59 (1968).

90. Scott Decker, Tim Bynum, and Deborah Weisel, "A Tale of Two Cities: Gangs and Organized Crime Groups," *Justice Quarterly* 15:395–425 (1998).

91. Donald Lyddane, "Understanding Gangs and Gang Mentality: Acquiring Evidence of the Gang Conspiracy," *United States Attorneys' Bulletin* 54: 1–15 (2006), www.usdoj.gov/usao/eousa/foia_reading_room/usab5403.pdf (accessed September 22, 2007).

92. Know Hand Signs, http://knowgangs.com/gang_resources/handsigns/menu_001.htm (accessed September 22, 2007).

93. Ibid.

94. Judith Greene and Kevin Pranis, *Gang Wars: The Failure of Enforcement Tactics and the Need for Effective Public Safety Strategies* (Washington, DC: Justice Policy Institute, 2007), www.justicepolicy.org/images/upload/07-07_EXS_GangWars_GC-PS-AC-JJ.pdf (accessed September 22, 2007).

95. National Youth Gang Survey data, www.iir.com/NYGC/faq.htm#q12 (accessed July 20, 2007).

96. Data provided by the National Youth Gang Center, 2003, www.iir.com/nygc/faq.htm#q6 (accessed September 22, 2007).

97. The following description of ethnic gangs leans heavily on the material developed in National School Safety Center, *Gangs in Schools*, pp. 11–23.

98. Spergel, *The Youth Gang Problem*, pp. 136–137.

99. Know Gangs, www.knowgangs.com/gang_resources/black_gangster_disciples/bgd_001.htm (accessed September 22, 2007).

100. Decker, Bynum, and Weisel, "A Tale of Two Cities."

101. Thomas Winfree, Jr., Frances Bernat, and Finn-Aage Esbensen, "Hispanic and Anglo Gang Membership in Two Southwestern Cities," *Social Science Journal* 38:105–118 (2001).

102. Arian Campo-Flores, "The Most Dangerous Gang in the United States," *Newsweek*, 28 March 2006; Ricardo Pollack, "Gang Life Tempts Salvador Teens," BBC News, http://news.bbc.co.uk/1/hi/world/americas/4201183.stm (accessed September 22, 2007).

103. Knowgangs.com, "18th Street Gang," www.knowgangs.com/gang_resources/profiles/18th/ (accessed July 30, 2007).

104. Los Angeles County Sheriff's Department, *Street Gangs of Los Angeles County*.

105. James Diego Vigil and Steve Chong Yun, "Vietnamese Youth Gangs in Southern California," in C. Ronald Huff, ed., *Gangs in America* (Newbury Park, CA: Sage, 1990), pp. 146–163.

106. Anthony Braga, Jack McDevitt, and Glenn Pierce, "Understanding and Preventing Gang Violence: Problem Analysis and Response Development in Lowell, Massachusetts," *Police Quarterly* 9:20–46 (2006).

107. See Glazier, "Small Town Delinquent Gangs."

108. For a review, see Lawrence Trostle, *The Stoners, Drugs, Demons and Delinquency* (New York: Garland, 1992).

109. Esbensen, "Race and Gender Differences Between Gang and Nongang Youths."

110. Darlene Wright and Kevin Fitzpatrick, "Violence and Minority Youth: The Effects of Risk and Asset Factors on Fighting among African American Children and Adolescents," *Adolescence* 41:251–262 (2006); Terence Thornberry and James H. Burch, *Gang Members and Delinquent Behavior* (Washington, DC: Office of Juvenile Justice and Delinquency Prevention, 1997).

111. G. David Curry, Scott Decker, and Arlen Egley, Jr., "Gang Involvement and Delinquency in a Middle School Population," *Justice Quarterly* 19:275–292 (2002).

112. Uberto Gatti, Richard Tremblay, Frank Vitaro, and Pierre McDuff, "Youth Gangs, Delinquency and Drug Use: A Test of the Selection, Facilitation, and Enhancement Hypotheses," *Journal of Child Psychology and Psychiatry* 46:1178–1190 (2005).

113. Malcolm Klein, Cheryl Maxson, and Lea Cunningham, "Crack, Street Gangs, and Violence," *Criminology* 4:623–650 (1991); Mel Wallace, "The Gang-Drug Debate Revisited," paper presented at the annual meeting of the American Society of Criminology, New Orleans, November 1992.

114. Kevin Thompson, David Brownfield, and Ann Marie Sorenson, "Specialization Patterns of Gang and Nongang Offending: A Latent Structure Analysis," *Journal of Gang Research* 3:25–35 (1996).

115. Sara Battin, Karl Hill, Robert Abbott, Richard Catalano, and J. David Hawkins, "The Contribution of Gang Membership to Delinquency Beyond Delinquent Friends," *Criminology* 36:93–116 (1998).

116. National Youth Gang Survey, 2001.

117. Geoffrey Hunt, Karen Joe Laidler, and Kristy Evans, "The Meaning and Gendered Culture of Getting High: Gang Girls and Drug Use Issues," *Contemporary Drug Problems* 29:375 (2002).

118. Terence P. Thornberry and James H. Burch, *Gang Members and Delinquent Behavior;* James C. Howell, "Youth Gang Drug Trafficking and Homicide: Policy and Program Implications," *Juvenile Justice Journal* 4:3–5 (1997).

119. Terence Thornberry, Marvin Krohn, Alan Lizotte, Carolyn Smith, and Kimberly Tobin, *Gangs and Delinquency in Developmental Perspective* (New York: Cambridge University Press, 2003).

120. Michael Vaughn, Matthew Howard, and Lisa Harper-Chang, "Do Prior Trauma and Victimization Predict Weapon Carrying among Delinquent Youth?" *Youth Violence and Juvenile Justice* 4:314–327 (2006).

121. Terence Thornberry, Marvin Krohn, Alan Lizotte, Carolyn Smith, and Kimberly Tobin, *Gangs and Delinquency in Developmental Perspective* (New York: Cambridge University Press, 2003).

122. James C. Howell, The Impact of Gangs on Communities, OJJDP, *NYGC Bulletin #2 Aug. 2006, p. 3.

123. Ibid.

124. Ibid.

125. Howell, "Youth Gang Drug Trafficking and Homicide."

126. Beth Bjerregaard and Alan Lizotte, "Gun Ownership and Gang Membership," *Journal of Criminal Law and Criminology* 86:37–53 (1995).

127. Ibid.

128. Pamela Lattimore, Richard Linster, and John MacDonald, "Risk of Death among Serious Young Offenders," *Journal of Research in Crime and Delinquency* 34:187–209 (1997).

129. Scott Decker, "Collective and Normative Features of Gang Violence," *Justice Quarterly* 13:243–264 (1996).

130. Gini Sykes, *8 Ball Chicks: A Year in the Violent World of Girl Gangsters* (New York: Doubleday, 1998), pp. 2–11.

131. H. Range Hutson, Deirdre Anglin, and Michael Pratts, Jr., "Adolescents and Children Injured or Killed in Drive-By Shootings in Los Angeles," *New England Journal of Medicine* 330:324–327 (1994). Miller, *Violence by Youth Gangs*, pp. 2–26.

132. Malcolm Klein, *Gang Cop: The Words and Ways of Officer Paco Domingo* (Walnut Creek, CA: Alta Mira Press, 2004).

133. Ibid., p. 59.

134. Herbert Block and Arthur Niederhoffer, *The Gang: A Study in Adolescent Behavior* (New York: Philosophical Library, 1958).

135. Ibid., p. 113.

136. Knox et al., *Gang Prevention and Intervention*, p. 44.

137. James Diego Vigil, "Group Processes and Street Identity: Adolescent Chicano Gang Members," *Ethos* 16:421–445 (1988).

138. James Diego Vigil and John Long, "Emic and Etic Perspectives on Gang Culture: The Chicano Case," in C. Ronald Huff, ed., *Gangs in America* (Newbury Park, CA: Sage, 1990), p. 66.

139. Albert Cohen, *Delinquent Boys* (New York: Free Press, 1955), pp. 1–19.

140. Irving Spergel, *Racketville, Slumtown, and Haulburg: An Exploratory Study of Delinquent Subcultures* (Chicago: University of Chicago Press, 1964).

141. Malcolm Klein, *Street Gangs and Street Workers* (Englewood Cliffs, NJ: Prentice Hall, 1971), pp. 12–15.

142. Vigil, *Barrio Gangs*.

143. Vigil and Long, "Emic and Etic Perspectives on Gang Culture," p. 61.

144. David Brownfield, Kevin Thompson, and Ann Marie Sorenson, "Correlates of Gang Membership: A Test of Strain, Social Learning, and Social Control," *Journal of Gang Research* 4:11–22 (1997).

145. John Hagedorn, Jose Torres, and Greg Giglio, "Cocaine, Kicks, and Strain: Patterns of Substance Use in Milwaukee Gangs," *Contemporary Drug Problems* 25:113–145 (1998).

146. Spergel, *The Youth Gang Problem*, pp. 4–5.

147. Ibid.

148. Jon Gunnar Bernburg, Marvin Krohn, and Craig Rivera, "Official Labeling, Criminal Embeddedness, and Subsequent Delinquency: A Longitudinal Test of Labeling Theory," *Journal of Research in Crime and Delinquency* 43:67–88 (2006).

149. Yablonsky, *The Violent Gang*, p. 237.

150. Ibid., pp. 239–241.

151. Klein, *The American Street Gang*.

152. Thornberry, Krohn, Lizotte, Smith, and Tobin, *Gangs and Delinquency in Developmental Perspective*.

153. Mercer Sullivan, *Getting Paid: Youth Crime and Work in the Inner City* (Ithaca, NY: Cornell University Press, 1989), pp. 244–245.

154. Finn-Aage Esbensen and David Huizinga, "Gangs, Drugs, and Delinquency in a Survey of Urban Youth," *Criminology* 31:565–587 (1993); G. David Curry and Irving Spergel, "Gang Involvement and Delinquency among Hispanic and African American Adolescent Males," *Journal of Research in Crime and Delinquency* 29:273–291 (1992).

155. Padilla, *The Gang as an American Enterprise*, p. 103.

156. Kathleen MacKenzie, Geoffrey Hunt, and Karen Joe Laidler, "Youth Gangs and Drugs: The Case of Marijuana" *Journal of Ethnicity in Substance Abuse* 4:99–134 (2005).

157. Terence Thornberry, Marvin Krohn, Alan Lizotte, and Deborah Chard-Wierschem, "The Role of Juvenile Gangs in Facilitating Delinquent Behavior," *Journal of Research in Crime and Delinquency* 30:55–87 (1993).

158. Spergel, *The Youth Gang Problem*, pp. 93–94.

159. Miller, *One of the Guys*.

160. Ibid., p. 93.

161. L. Thomas Winfree, Jr., Teresa Vigil Backstrom, and G. Larry Mays, "Social Learning Theory, Self-Reported Delinquency, and Youth Gangs: A New Twist on a General Theory of Crime and Delinquency," *Youth and Society* 26:147–177 (1994).

162. Karen Joe Laidler and Geoffrey Hunt, "Violence and Social Organization in Female Gangs," *Social Justice* 24:148–187 (1997).

163. Chanequa Walker-Barnes and Craig A. Mason, "Delinquency and Substance Use among Gang-Involved Youth: The Moderating Role of Parenting Practices," *American Journal of Community Psychology* 34:235–250 (2004).

164. Lyddane, "Understanding Gangs and Gang Mentality."

165. Jodi Lane and James Meeker, "Subcultural Diversity and the Fear of Crime and Gangs," *Crime and Delinquency* 46:497–521 (2000).

166. Angela K. Brown, "Cities Sue Gangs in Bid to Stop Violence," *USA Today*, www.usatoday.com/news/topstories/2007-07-29-3155555107_x.htm (accessed September 22, 2007).

167. *People v. Englebrecht* (2001) May 09 CA1/4 D033527, www.courtinfo.ca.gov/opinions/archive/D033527.PDF (accessed October 21, 2007).

168. National Youth Gang Center, *National Youth Gang Survey Analysis* (2006), www.iir.com/nygc/nygsa/ (accessed September 22, 2007).

169. The United States Conference of Mayors, "Gang Control Efforts in the City of Akron, Ohio," *Best Practices of Community Policing in Gang Intervention and Gang Violence Prevention, 2006*, www.usmayors.org/uscm/best_practices/community_policing_2006/gangBP_2006.pdf (accessed September 22, 2007).

170. Charles Katz and Vincent J. Webb, *Police Response to Gangs: A Multi-Site Study* (Washington, DC: U.S. Department of Justice, 2004).

171. Mark Moore and Mark A. R. Kleiman, *The Police and Drugs* (Washington, DC: National Institute of Justice, 1989), p. 8.

172. Rand Corporation News Release, "Agency Collaboration, Community Participation Vital to Cut Violent Gang-Related Neighborhood Crime," November 12, 2003, www.rand.org/news/press.03/11.12.html (accessed July 20, 2007).

173. Barry Krisberg, "Preventing and Controlling Violent Youth Crime: The State of the Art," in Ira Schwartz, ed., *Violent Juvenile Crime* (Minneapolis: University of Minnesota, Hubert Humphrey Institute of Public Affairs, n.d.).

174. For a revisionist view of gang delinquency, see Hedy Bookin-Weiner and Ruth Horowitz, "The End of the Youth Gang," *Criminology* 21:585–602 (1983).

175. Quint Thurman, Andrew Giacomazzi, Michael Reisig, and David Mueller, "Community-Based Gang Prevention and Intervention: An Evaluation of the Neutral Zone," *Crime and Delinquency* 42:279–296 (1996).

176. Michael Agopian, "Evaluation of the Gang Alternative Prevention Program," paper presented at the annual meeting of the American Society of Criminology, Boston, November 1995.

177. Ellen Thompson, "Intervention Effective to Cut Gang Crime, Study Says," *Stockton Record*, July 19, 2007, www.recordnet.com/apps/pbcs.dll/article?AID=/20070719/A_NEWS/707190323/-1/A_COMM01 (accessed September 22, 2007).

178. Charles Katz and Vincent Webb, *Policing Gangs in America* (New York: Cambridge University Press, 2006).

179. James Houston, "What Works: The Search for Excellence in Gang Intervention Programs," paper presented at the annual meeting of the American Society of Criminology, Boston, November 1995.

180. Curry and Spergel, "Gang Involvement and Delinquency among Hispanic and African American Adolescent Males."

181. Hagedorn, "Gangs, Neighborhoods, and Public Policy."

182. Judith Greene and Kevin Pranis, *Gang Wars: The Failure of Enforcement Tactics and the Need for Effective Public Safety Strategies* (Washington, DC: Justice Policy Institute, 2007), www.justicepolicy.org/images/upload/07-07_EXS_GangWars_GC-PS-AC-JJ.pdf (accessed September 22, 2007).

Schools and Delinquency

10

Chapter Outline

The School in Modern American Society

CASE PROFILE: Ciara's Story

Academic Performance and Delinquency

Delinquency in the School

FOCUS ON DELINQUENCY: Bullying in School

The Role of the School in Delinquency Prevention

POLICY AND PRACTICE: Safe Harbor: A School-Based Victim Assistance and Violence Prevention Program

Legal Rights in the School

POLICY AND PRACTICE: *Board of Education of Independent School District No. 92 of Pottawatomie County et al. v. Earls et al.*

Chapter Objectives

1. Discuss the role the educational experience plays in human development over the life course
2. Be familiar with the problems facing the educational system in the United States
3. Understand the hazards faced by children if they are truants or dropouts
4. Describe the association between school failure and delinquency
5. List the personal and social factors that have been related to school failure
6. Know about the nature and extent of school crime
7. Discuss the factors that contribute to delinquency in schools
8. Be familiar with the efforts school systems are making to reduce crime on campus
9. Understand what is being done to improve school climate and increase educational standards
10. Be familiar with the legal rights of students

On September 29, 2006, Eric Hainstock, 15, shot and killed principal John Klang of the Weston Schools in Cazenovia, Wisconsin. After the shooting, he told police that he carried out the attack because he was upset with a reprimand Klang had given him and because he felt teachers didn't intervene when he had been harassed by other students. Faced with a suspension for getting caught by Klang with tobacco, Hainstock pried open his family's gun cabinet, took out a shotgun, retrieved the key to his parents' locked bedroom, and took their .22-caliber revolver. He then entered the school with the shotgun before classes began and pointed the gun at a social studies teacher, but had it wrested away. When Klang went into the hallway and confronted Hainstock, the boy pulled the handgun and shot him three times. Klang, already wounded, wrestled the shooter to the ground and swept away the gun before collapsing. Klang was shot in the head, chest, and leg, and died hours later at a hospital in Madison, Wisconsin. After the attack Hainstock was described as a "normal teenager," but one who often bragged about getting into trouble.[1]

The Cazenovia shooting is not unique; school violence has been called "pervasive."[2] Violence and other serious social problems, ranging from drug use to vandalism, have become commonplace on school grounds. School officials must make daily decisions on discipline and crime prevention, something they may not have thought much about when they decided on a career in education!

The school environment has been found to have a significant effect on a child's emotional well-being. Some research efforts suggest that its effect may be even greater than the home environment.[3] Because so much of an adolescent's time is spent in school, it would seem logical that some relationship exists between delinquent behavior and what is happening—or not happening—in classrooms. Yet while the school experience is so important, the nation's educational system has been rocked in recent years with scandals and problems ranging from school shootings to educational failures, from budget cuts to the embarrassing revelation that teachers are having sexual affairs with underage minors. In one notorious case, Rachel Holt, 35, a sixth-grade science teacher, pleaded guilty, on March 18, 2007, to having sex with one of her 13-year-old students and received a very harsh 10-year prison sentence. Clearly, judicial authorities believe that an example had to be made in order to reduce teacher-student contacts.[4]

333

academic.cengage.com/criminaljustice/siegel.

academic achievement
Being successful in a school environment.

In addition to these issues, numerous studies have confirmed that delinquency is related to **academic achievement**. Experts have concluded that many of the underlying problems of delinquency, as well as their prevention and control, are intimately connected with the nature and quality of the school experience.[5] Although there are differences of opinion, most theorists agree that problems associated with the educational system bear some responsibility for the relatively high rate of juvenile crime.

In this chapter, we first explore how educational achievement and delinquency are related and what factors in the school experience appear to contribute to delinquent behavior. Next, we turn to delinquency in the school setting—vandalism, theft, violence, and so on. Finally, we look at the attempts made by schools to prevent delinquency.

THE SCHOOL IN MODERN AMERICAN SOCIETY

The school plays a significant role in shaping the values of children.[6] In contrast to earlier periods, when formal education was a privilege of the upper classes, the U.S. system of compulsory public education has made schooling a legal obligation. Today, more than 90 percent of school-age children attend school, compared with only 7 percent in 1890.[7]

In contrast to the earlier, agrarian days of U.S. history, when most adolescents shared in the work of the family, today's young people spend most of their time in school. The school has become the primary instrument of socialization, the "basic conduit through which the community and adult influences enter into the lives of adolescents."[8]

Because young people spend a longer time in school, their adolescence is prolonged. As long as students are still dependent on their families and have not entered the work world, they are not considered adults. The responsibilities of adulthood come later to modern-day youths than to those in earlier generations, and some experts see this prolonged childhood as one factor contributing to the irresponsible and often irrational behavior of many juveniles who commit delinquent acts.

The **U.S. Department of Education** seeks to ensure equal access to education and promote educational excellence for all Americans. View its website via academic.cengage.com/criminaljustice/siegel.

Socialization and Status

Another significant aspect of the educational experience is that children spend their school hours with their peers, and most of their activities after school take place with school friends. Young people rely increasingly on school friends and become less interested in adult role models. The norms of the peer culture are often at odds with those of adult society, and a pseudoculture with a distinct social system develops. Law-abiding behavior may not be among the values promoted in such an atmosphere. Kids enmeshed in this youth culture may admire bravery, defiance, and having fun much more than adults do.

The school has become a primary determinant of economic and social status. In this technological age, education is the key to a job that will mark its holder as "successful." No longer can parents ensure the status of their children through social class alone. Educational achievement has become of equal, if not greater, importance as a determinant of economic success. This emphasis on the value of education is fostered by parents, the media, and the schools themselves. Regardless of their social or economic background, most children grow up believing education is the key to success. However, many youths do not meet acceptable standards of school achievement. Whether failure is measured by test scores, not being promoted, or dropping out, the incidence of school failure continues to be a major problem for U.S. society. A single school failure often leads to a pattern of chronic failure. The links between school failure and delinquency will be explored more fully in the next sections.

The school itself has become an engine of social change and improvement. School desegregation efforts have heralded a new age of improved race relations which in the long run may help reduce crime rates. African American youth educated in states where a higher proportion of their classmates are white experience significantly lower incarceration rates later as adults. The constructive effects of racial inclusiveness in the school setting have grown stronger over time, highlighting the need for further educational integration.[9]

Educational Trends

The role schools play in adolescent development is underscored by the problems faced by the U.S. education system. There has been some improvement in reading, math, and science achievement during the past decade, but in some cases improvements have been minimal. Take for instance reading scores. As Figure 10.1 shows, there has been improvement in grades 4 and 8 since 1992, but scores in grade 12 have declined. This could mean that scores will be trending upward as the super-smart current fourth-graders enter their senior year of high school eight years from now, or that scores will continue to trend downward because once entering high school these good readers give up their books for video games and reading levels decline.

Cross-national surveys that compare academic achievement show that the United States trails in critical academic areas. As Table 10.1 shows, 15-year-olds in the United States still lag behind students in some less-affluent nations (Poland, Slovakia) in math achievement.

High school students in the United States are consistently outperformed by those from Asian and some European countries on international assessments of mathematics and science. In contrast, fourth-graders score as well or better than most of their international peers. Does this mean that kids in the United States fall further as their education progresses?[10] One reason may be that many secondary school math and science teachers did not major in the subjects they teach.

Another reason is that the United States, the richest country in the world, devotes less of its resources to education than do many other nations. Spending on elementary and secondary education (as a percentage of the U.S. gross domestic product) is less than that of other nations. And budget cutting has reduced educational resources in many communities and curtailed state support for local school systems. As Figure 10.2 shows, kids who are poor (as indicated by their eligibility for free or reduced-price lunches) do less well on math achievement tests than their more well-to-do peers. Poverty and economic marginality may have a direct impact on learning and the child's future chances of success.

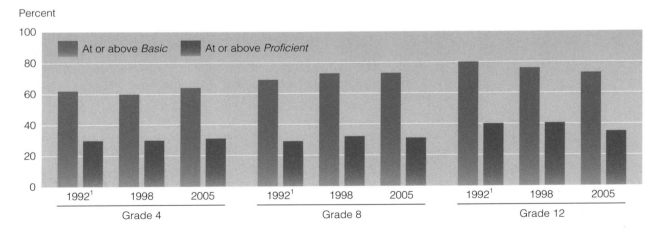

FIGURE 10.1

Reading Performance: Average Reading Scores for 4th, 8th, and 12th Graders

[1] Testing accommodations (e.g., extended time, small group testing) for children with disabilities and limited-English-proficient students were not permitted.

NOTE: Percentage of students performing at or above *Basic* and at or above *Proficient* in reading, by grade: 1992, 1998, and 2005.

SOURCE: U.S. Department of Education, National Center for Education Statistics, National Assessment of Educational Progress (NAEP), 1992, 1998, and 2005 Reading Assessments, NAEP Data Explorer.

TABLE **10.1**

Average Mathematics Literacy Scores of 15-Year-Olds, by Country

Average Score Relative to the United States	Country and Score						
Significantly higher	Hong Kong-China	550	Switzerland	527	Sweden	509
	Finland	544	Macao-China	527	Austria	506
	Korea	542	Australia	524	Germany	503
	Netherlands	538	New Zealand	523	Ireland	503
	Liechtenstein	536	Czech Republic	516	*Average Score*	*500*
	Japan	534	Iceland	515	Slovak Republic	498
	Canada	532	Denmark	514	Norway	495
	Belgium	529	France	511	Luxembourg	493
Not significantly different	Poland	490	Spain	485	Latvia	483
	Hungary	490	**United States**	**483**		
Significantly lower	Russian Federation	468	Serbia and Montenegro	437	Mexico	385
	Portugal	466	Turkey	423	Indonesia	360
	Italy	466	Uruguay	422	Tunisia	359
	Greece	445	Thailand	417		

SOURCE: U.S. Department of Education, National Center for Education Statistics (2004). *International Outcomes of Learning in Mathematics Literacy and Problem Solving: PISA 2003 Results from the U.S. Perspective* (NCES 2005-003), table 2. Data from Organization for Economic Cooperation and Development (OECD), Program for International Student Assessment (PISA), 2003.

Educational Problems

These data highlight the fact that many children are at risk for educational problems, school failure, and delinquency. It is now estimated that one of every five children are unprepared when they first enter school at kindergarten. These disadvantaged children enter school lagging behind their more advantaged peers in terms of the knowledge and social competencies that are widely recognized as enabling children to perform at even the most basic level.[11] They face substantial gaps in measures of reading and mathematics proficiency, in prosocial behaviors and behavior problems, and in readiness to learn. About 18 percent of children overall are not familiar with basic rules of print or writing (e.g., knowing that English is read from left to right and top to bottom, or where a story ends); that fraction is 32 percent for children whose mothers have less than a high school education but only 8 percent for children whose mothers have a college degree or higher. Many children from disadvantaged backgrounds fail to meet grade-level expectations on core subjects. As a consequence they face higher rates of special education placement and grade repetition.[12] These disadvantages may increase their risk of leaving school early and becoming dropouts.

Dropping Out

truant
Being out of school without permission.

dropping out
To leave school before completing the required program of education.

Every day, hundreds of thousands of youth are absent from school; many are absent without an excuse and deemed truant. Some large cities report that unexcused absences can number in the thousands on certain days. Truancy can lead to school failure and dropping out.

Dropping out of high school can have devastating long-term effects. People (ages 18 to 65) who left high school early have an average current income of about $20,000 per year; in comparison, the average income of persons ages 18 to 65 who finish high school or obtain a General Educational Development (GED) certificate is about $30,000.[13] Dropouts are also less likely to be in the labor force than those with a high school credential or higher and are more likely to be unemployed if they are

FIGURE 10.2

Poverty and Achievement

Average mathematics scores of public school 4th-graders, by whether the student was eligible for free or reduced-price lunch and the percentage of students in the school eligible for free or reduced-price lunch.

SOURCE: U.S. Department of Education, National Center for Education Statistics, National Assessment of Educational Progress (NAEP), 2005 Mathematics Assessment, previously unpublished tabulation (October 2005).

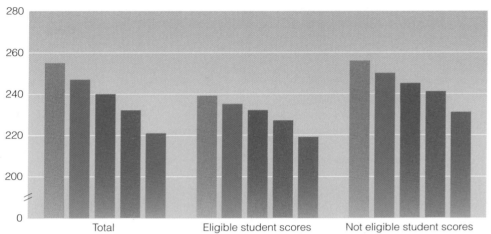

Percentage of students in the school eligible for free or reduced-price lunch

| 10 or less | 11–25 | 26–50 | 51–75 | More than 75 |

in the labor force. In terms of health, dropouts older than age 24 tend to report being in worse health than adults who are not dropouts, regardless of income. Dropouts also make up disproportionately higher percentages of the nation's prison and death row inmates.

While dropout rates remain too high, they have been in decline for quite some time. Figure 10.3 shows the current status dropout rate, which is the percentage of an age group that is not enrolled in school and has not earned a high school credential (i.e., diploma or equivalent, such as a GED certificate). According to this measure, slightly less than 10 percent of 16- to 24-year-olds were out of school without a high school credential in 2005, a significant decline from the 15 percent who did not complete high school in 1972. The status dropout rate declined for this age group between 1972 and 2005, including the more recent period since 1990. Status dropout rates and changes in these rates over time differ by race/ethnicity. Since 1972, status dropout rates for white, black, and Hispanic young adults have declined, with rates remaining lowest for whites and highest for Hispanics. However, the relative decline for racial and ethnic minorities was greater than that achieved by whites. As Figure 10.3 shows, the African American dropout rate has declined from more than 20 percent in 1972 to about 10 percent today.

The school system in the United States is faced with many challenges, ranging from educational deficiencies to security issues. This photo shows the front lobby of English High School in Boston's Jamaica Plain section on April 26, 2007. English was chartered after a town meeting at Boston's Faneuil Hall and became the country's first public high school in 1821. Today it is one of the most diverse in the city and one of its lowest performing. America's oldest high school is suffering, along with many other newer schools, with some of the newest problems in urban education.

Why Do Kids Drop Out? When surveyed, most dropouts say they left either because they did not like school or because they wanted to get a job. Other risk factors include low academic achievement, poor problem-solving ability, low self-esteem, difficulty getting along with teachers, dissatisfaction with school, substance abuse, and being too old for their grade level.[14] Some dropouts could not get along

Percent

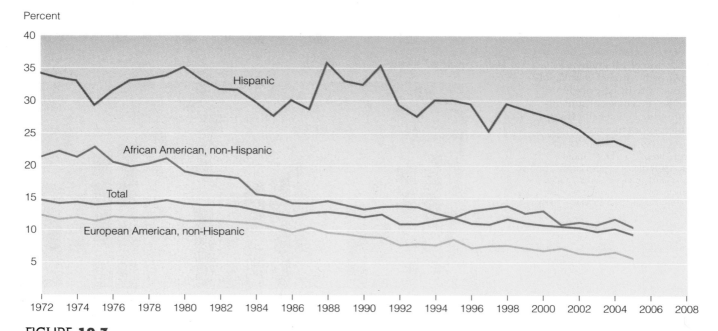

FIGURE 10.3

Status Dropout Rates for Whites, Blacks, and Hispanics Ages 16–24

SOURCE: National Center for Education Statistics, http://nces.ed.gov/pubs2007/dropout05/figures/figure_02.asp (accessed October 22, 2007).

with teachers, had been expelled, or were under suspension. Almost half of all female dropouts left school because they were pregnant or had already given birth.

Poverty and family dysfunction increase the chances of dropping out among all racial and ethnic groups. Dropouts are more likely than graduates to have lived in single-parent families headed by parents who were educational underachievers themselves. As Figure 10.4 shows, wealthier kids residing with high-income parents have a much greater chance of completing high school than their indigent peers. Each year, students living in low-income families are approximately six times more likely to drop out than their peers from high-income families (8.9 percent compared with 1.5 percent).

Some youths have no choice but to drop out. They are pushed out of school because they lack attention or have poor attendance records. Teachers label them troublemakers, and school administrators use suspensions, transfers, and other means to "convince" them that leaving school is their only option. Because minority students often come from circumstances that interfere with their attendance, they are more likely to be labeled "disobedient." Race-based disciplinary practices may help sustain high minority dropout rates. Although the African American dropout rate has declined faster than the white dropout rate over the past three decades, minority students still drop out at a higher rate than white students.

In his thoughtful book *Creating the Dropout*, Sherman Dorn shows that graduation rates slowly but steadily rose during the twentieth century while regional, racial, and ethnic differences in graduation rates declined.[15] Nonetheless, Dorn argues that the relatively high dropout rate among minorities is the legacy of disciplinary policies instituted more than 40 years ago when educational administrators opposed to school desegregation employed a policy of race-based suspension and expulsion directed at convincing minority students to leave previously all-white high school districts. This legacy still affects contemporary school districts. Dorn believes that the dropout problem is a function of inequality of educational opportunity rather than the failure of individual students. The proportion of blacks who fail to graduate from high school remains high compared with the proportion of whites who fail to graduate

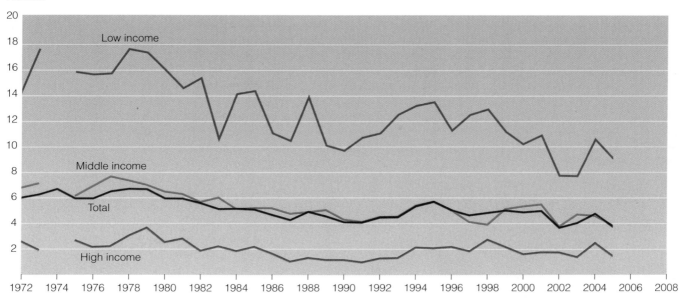

Percent

FIGURE 10.4

Dropout Rates of 15- through 24-Year-Olds Who Dropped Out of Grades 10–12, by Family Income

SOURCE: National Center for Education Statistics, http://nces.ed.gov/pubs2007/dropout05/figures/figure_01.asp (accessed October 22, 2007).

because the educational system still fails to provide minority group members with the services and support they need.

Though the dropout rate has declined, it remains a significant social problem with consequences that extend into adulthood and beyond. Estimates indicate that a high school dropout costs society $243,000 to $388,000 in present-value dollars over his or her lifetime, and if they turn to crime, they cost society $1.3 to $1.5 million in present-value dollars.[16] Of course, not all kids drop out, and some are able to defy the odds and stay in school as attested to by the Case Profile entitled "Ciara's Story."

ACADEMIC PERFORMANCE AND DELINQUENCY

underachievers
Those who fail to meet expected levels of school achievement.

Whether they drop out or not, kids who do poorly in school are at risk for delinquent behavior; students who are chronic underachievers in school are among the most likely to be delinquent.[17] In fact, researchers find that school failure is a stronger predictor of delinquency than variables such as economic class membership, racial or ethnic background, or peer-group relations. Studies that compare the academic records of delinquents and nondelinquents—including their scores on standardized tests, failure rate, and other academic measures—have found that delinquents are often academically deficient, a condition that may lead to their leaving school and becoming involved in antisocial activities.[18] Children who report that they do not like school and do not do well in school are most likely to self-report delinquent acts.[19] In contrast, at-risk youths who do well in school are often able to avoid delinquent involvement.[20]

An association between academic failure and delinquency is commonly found among chronic offenders. Those leaving school without a diploma were more likely to become involved in chronic delinquency than high school graduates.[21] Only 9 percent of the chronic offenders in Marvin Wolfgang's Philadelphia *Delinquency in a Birth Cohort* study graduated from high school, compared with 74 percent of nonoffenders.[22] Chronic offenders also had more disciplinary actions than nonoffenders.[23]

The relationship between school achievement and persistent offending is supported by surveys that indicate that less than 40 percent of incarcerated felons

Ciara's Story

CIARA LIVES IN THE EAST HARLEM BOROUGH OF NEW YORK CITY WITH HER MOTHER AND THREE SIBLINGS. HER FATHER IS NOT INVOLVED WITH THE FAMILY, SO THEY struggle to make ends meet and rely on Ciara's grandmother to provide much of the children's care. From an early age Ciara had problems in school, both behaviorally and academically. Significantly behind her grade level in reading, regularly challenging her teachers and other adults, and being disruptive in class, Ciara was at great risk for dropping out of school and becoming involved in further delinquent behavior. The group of older troubled teens whom she considered to be her only friends set poor examples for behavior, causing more problems for Ciara. The one area where she seemed confident and happy was on the basketball court, where Ciara exhibited talent and a love for the game.

When her school started a mandatory after-school program, Ciara began attending Drum Power, a youth leadership program that provides young people with an opportunity to learn the techniques and cultural/historical significance of West African traditional, Afro-Cuban, and Afro-Brazilian drumming. The goal of the program is to build self-esteem and self-confidence through discovering the rewards of discipline, teamwork, creativity, responsibility, and self-respect. Ciara was drawn to both the power of drums and the rhythms of African drumming. The process of learning traditional hand drumming requires discipline, commitment, and practice, and students learn that they can achieve their goals by employing their own positive energy and self-determination.

Ciara thrived in the program. Although she still posed many challenges to school staff and was at risk due to her living and community environment, she showed great interest, motivation, and success in the Drum Power program. She loved the drums and music, and was able to connect with her youth counselors running the program. Because Drum Power was based at the school, the program counselors could communicate on a daily basis with Ciara's teachers and the school staff regarding her progress, and they were able to discuss any ongoing concerns. This provided immediate resolution when there were problems and ongoing accountability for Ciara. The program counselors also remained in close contact with her mother.

Participating in Drum Power for several years allowed Ciara to establish excellent relationships with her program counselors, who in turn provided great encouragement to Ciara, having a positive impact on her decisions and choices. Drumming was good for Ciara, and her interest in African music grew, but it was her relationships with the program counselors that made the most difference for her. She started to understand how her behavior and bad choices were affecting her life. Ciara learned the importance of self-control and setting priorities for herself daily. Seeing what a difference these things made for her, she could also begin to have a more positive vision for her life. Ciara's mother became more involved with school and also became involved with the Drum Power professionals when requested. The support of the professionals at school and at the Drum Power program was helpful to Ciara's mother, who had been struggling with her own set of issues, and now she was better able to encourage her daughter to be successful.

Ciara eventually graduated from the program. She continued with her education and hopes to attend college upon graduation from high school. She stayed out of the juvenile justice system and was able to make significant changes in her life with the support of the counselors at Drum Power. ■

CRITICAL THINKING

1. Did the program Ciara attended shield her from the problems that she may have encountered in school? Can you think of other types of nonstigmatizing alternatives?
2. Do you think kids benefit from special education programs or do such programs have hidden drawbacks? Is it possible the program may cause long-term problems?

had 12 or more years of education, compared with about 80 percent of the general population.[24] In sum, the school experience can be a significant factor in shaping the direction of an adolescent's life course.

School Failure and Delinquency

Although there is general agreement that school failure and delinquency are related, some questions remain concerning the nature and direction of this relationship. There are actually three independent views on the association:

1. School failure is a direct cause of delinquent behavior. Children who fail at school soon feel frustrated and rejected. Believing they will never achieve success through conventional means, they seek out like-minded companions and together engage in antisocial behaviors. Educational failure evokes negative responses from important people in the child's life, including teachers, parents, and prospective employers. These reactions help solidify feelings of inadequacy, and in some cases, lead to a pattern of chronic delinquency.

2. School failure leads to emotional and psychological problems that are the actual cause of antisocial behavior. Academic failure reduces self-esteem, and reduced self-esteem is the actual cause of delinquency. Studies using a variety of measures of academic competence and self-esteem demonstrate that good students have a better attitude about themselves than poor students; low self-esteem has been found to contribute to delinquent behavior.[25] The association then runs from school failure to low self-concept to delinquency. Schools may mediate these effects by taking steps to improve the self-image of academically challenged children.

3. School failure and delinquency share a common cause such as poverty or family disruption. Both are caused by external conditions so that while it appears that school failure precedes and causes delinquency the association is actually false and spurious.

Correlates of School Failure

Despite disagreement over the direction the relationship takes, there is little argument that delinquent behavior is influenced by educational experiences. A number of factors have been linked to school failure; the most prominent are discussed in the next sections

Personal Problems Some kids have personal problems that they bring with them to school. Because of their deprived background and ragged socialization, some kids lack the verbal skills that are a prerequisite of educational success.[26] Others live in a dysfunctional family; a turbulent family life has been linked to academic underachievement.

Still others suffer psychological abnormality. The adolescent who both fails at school and engages in delinquency may be experiencing depression and other mental deficits that are associated both with their school failure and involvement in antisocial activities.[27] Personality structure may also be a key factor. Kids who have low self-control are more likely to engage in delinquent behavior *and* fail in school. An impulsive personality can cause both school failure and delinquency.[28]

School failure may also be linked to learning disabilities or reading disabilities that might actually be treatable if the proper resources were available.[29]

To get more educational data, go to the **National Center for Education Statistics (NCES)** website via academic .cengage.com/criminaljustice/siegel.

Social Class During the 1950s, research by Albert Cohen indicated that delinquency was a phenomenon of working-class students who were poorly equipped to function in middle-class schools. Cohen referred to this phenomenon as a failure to live up to "middle-class measuring rods."[30] Jackson Toby reinforced this concept, contending that the disadvantages lower-class children have in school (for example, lack of verbal skills) are a result of their position in the social structure and that these disadvantages foster delinquency.[31] These views have been supported by the higher-than-average dropout rates among lower-class children.

One reason why lower-class children may do poorly in school is that economic problems require them to take part-time jobs. Working while in school seems to lower commitment to educational achievement and is associated with higher levels of delinquent behavior.[32]

Not all experts agree with the social class–school failure–delinquency hypothesis. There is evidence that boys who do poorly in school, regardless of their socioeconomic background, are more likely to be delinquent than those who perform well.[33] Affluent students may be equally affected by school failure as lower-class youths, and that middle-class youths who do poorly in school are even more likely to become delinquent than their lower-class peers who also have academic performance problems.[34] Since expectations are so much higher for affluent youth, their failure to achieve in school may have a more profound effect on their behavior and well-being than it does on lower-class youth, who face so many other social problems. Middle-class kids who are involved in antisocial behaviors may be even more likely to experience school failure than lower-class youth who experience similar social problems.[35]

Tracking Most researchers have looked at academic tracking—dividing students into groups according to ability and achievement level—as a contributor to school failure. Placement in a non-college track means consignment to educational oblivion without apparent purpose. Studies indicate that non-college–track students experience greater academic failure and progressive deterioration of achievement, participate less in extracurricular activities, have an increased tendency to drop out, and commit more delinquent acts.

Some school officials begin tracking students in the lowest grade levels. Educators separate youths into groups that have innocuous names ("special enrichment program"), but may carry the taint of academic incompetence. High school students may be tracked within individual subjects based on ability. Classes may be labeled in descending order: advanced placement, academically enriched, average, basic, and remedial. It is common for students to have all their courses in only one or two tracks.[36]

The effects of school labels accumulate over time. If students fail academically, they are often destined to fail again. Repeated instances of failure can help produce the career of the "misfit" or "dropout." Using a tracking system keeps certain students from having any hope of achieving academic success, thereby causing lack of motivation, which may foster delinquent behavior.[37]

Alienation Student alienation has also been identified as a link between school failure and delinquency (see Exhibit 10.1). Students who report they neither like school nor care about their teachers' opinions are more likely to exhibit delinquent behaviors.[38] Alienation may be a function of students' inability to see the relevance of what they are taught. The gap between their education and the real world leads some students to feel that the school experience is a waste of time.[39]

Many students, particularly those from low-income families, believe schooling has no payoff. Because this legitimate channel appears to be meaningless, delinquent acts become increasingly more attractive. This middle- and upper-class bias is evident in the preeminent role of the college preparatory curriculum in many school systems. Furthermore, both methods of instruction and curriculum materials reflect middle-class language and customs that have little meaning for the disadvantaged child.

In contrast, kids who form a bond to school also find that this commitment helps them resist delinquency-producing factors in the environment (e.g., antisocial peers).[40] Youths who report liking school and being involved in school activities are also less likely to engage in delinquent behaviors.[41] Involvement is especially beneficial in schools where students are treated fairly and where rules are laid out clearly.[42] Schools might lower delinquency rates if they can develop programs that counteract student alienation.

EXHIBIT **10.1**

Sources of Student Alienation

- *School size.* Schools are getting larger because smaller school districts have been consolidated into multijurisdictional district schools. In 1900, there were 150,000 school districts; today there are approximately 16,000. Larger schools are often impersonal, and relatively few students can find avenues for meaningful participation. Teachers and other school personnel do not have the opportunity to deal with early indications of academic or behavior problems and thus act to prevent delinquency.

- *Irrelevant curriculum.* Some students may be unable to see the relevance or significance of what they are taught in school. The gap between their education and the real world leads them to feel that the school experience is little more than a waste of time.

- *Lack of payoff.* Many students, particularly those from low-income families, believe that school has no payoff in terms of their future. Because the legitimate channel of education appears to be meaningless, illegitimate alternatives become increasingly more attractive for students who did not plan to attend college or to use their high school educations directly in their careers.

- *Middle- and upper-class bias.* The preeminent role of the college preparatory curriculum and the second-class position of vocational and technical programs in many school systems alienates some lower-class students. Furthermore, methods of instruction as well as curriculum materials reflect middle-class mores, language, and customs and have little meaning for the disadvantaged child.

DELINQUENCY IN THE SCHOOL

In its pioneering study of school crime, *Violent Schools–Safe Schools* (1977),[43] the federal government found that, although teenagers spend only 25 percent of their time in school, 40 percent of the robberies and 36 percent of the physical attacks involving this age group occur there.

Since the Safe Schools study was published, crime has continued to be a significant problem in the nation's schools.[44] At last count, an estimated 55 million students were enrolled in pre-kindergarten through grade 12. According to the last data available, the students most likely to be victimized, those ages 12 to 18, suffered about 1.4 million nonfatal crimes at school in a single year, including about 863,000 thefts and 583,000 violent crimes such as simple assault. Of the violent crimes, about 107,000 were very serious, including rape, sexual assault, robbery, and aggravated assault. These figures represent victimization rates of 33 thefts and 22 violent crimes per 1,000 students. While these data indicate the seriousness of the school crime problem, school crime, like delinquency in the streets, has been in decline. The victimization rate of students ages 12 to 18 at school declined from 73 victimizations per 1,000 students in 2003 to 55 victimizations in 2004 (see Figure 10.5). However, other aspects of crime have not improved. The number of homicides of school-age youth ages 5 to 18 at school was higher in 2004–05 than in 2000–01 (21 vs. 11 homicides). One aspect of school crime that is considered particularly serious is bullying, and that is the subject of the Focus on Delinquency feature "Bullying in School."

Teacher Attacks

Students are not the only victims of intimidation or violence in schools.[45] Teachers are also subject to threats and physical attacks from students and school intruders. Surveys indicate that about 7 percent of teachers have been the victim of crimes. However, like student victimization, teachers are much less likely to be attacked today than a decade ago (see Figure 10.6). Teachers in central city schools are consistently more likely to be threatened with injury or physically attacked than teachers in urban fringe or rural schools.

School Shootings

Though incidents of school-based crime and violence are not uncommon, it is the highly publicized incidents of fatal school shootings that have helped focus attention on school crime. Upward of 10 percent of students report bringing weapons to school on a regular basis and knowing this, many of their peers report being afraid of school-based gun violence.[46]

FIGURE 10.5

Rate of Student-Reported Nonfatal Crimes Against Students Ages 12–18 per 1,000 Students, by Type of Crime and Location

SOURCE: U.S. Department of Justice, Bureau of Justice Statistics, *National Crime Victimization Survey (NCVS)*, *1992–2004*, http://nces.ed.gov/programs/crimeindicators/figure_02_1.asp (accessed October 22, 2007).

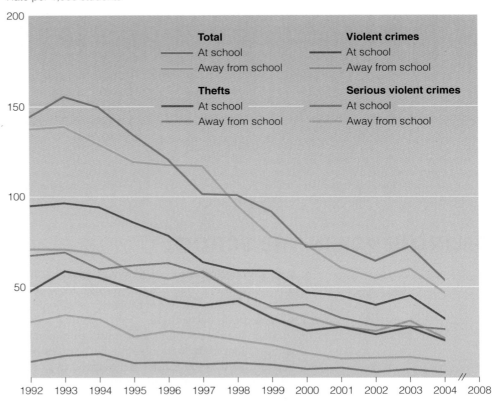

Rate per 1,000 students

Who brings guns to schools? Many of these kids have a history of being abused and bullied; many perceive a lack of support from peers, parents, and teachers.[47] Kids who have been the victims of crime themselves and who hang with peers who carry weapons are the ones most likely to bring guns to school.[48] A troubled kid who has little social support but carries deadly weapons makes for an explosive situation.

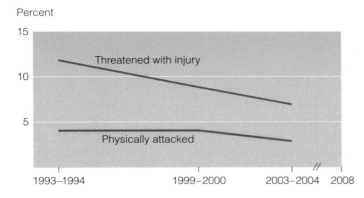

Percent

FIGURE 10.6

Percentage of Public and Private School Teachers Who Reported That They Were Threatened with Injury or That They Were Physically Attacked by a Student from School during the Previous 12 Months

SOURCE: U.S. Department of Education, National Center for Education Statistics, Schools and Staffing Survey (SASS), "Public School Teacher Questionnaire," 1993–94, 1999–2000, and 2003–04; "Private School Teacher Questionnaire," 1993–94, 1999–2000, and 2003–04; "Charter School Questionnaire," 1999–2000; and "Bureau of Indian Affairs Teacher Questionnaire," 1999–2000 and 2003–04, http://nces.ed.gov/programs/crimeindicators/figure_05_1.asp?referrer=report (accessed November 21, 2007).

Nature and Extent of Shootings Social scientists are now conducting studies of these events in order to determine their trends and patterns. One study examined all 220 school-related shootings occurring between July 1, 1994, and June 30, 1999.[49] Of the 220 shooting incidents, 172 were homicides, 30 were suicides, 11 were homicide-suicides, 5 were caused by law enforcement agents responding to calls, and 2 were unintentional firearm-related deaths. Although highly publicized in the media, this amounted to 0.068 per 100,000 students being affected by these shootings.

The research discovered that most shooting incidents occur around the start of the school day, the lunch period, or the end of the school day. In most of the shootings (55 percent), a note, threat, or other action indicating risk for violence occurred prior to the event. Shooters were also likely to have expressed some form of suicidal behavior prior to the event and to report having been bullied by their peers. These patterns may help school officials one day to identify potential risk factors and respond in a timely fashion.

Bullying in School

Experts define bullying among children as repeated, negative acts committed by one or more children against another. These negative acts may be physical or verbal in nature—for example, hitting or kicking, teasing or taunting—or they may involve indirect actions such as manipulating friendships or purposely excluding other children from activities. Implicit in this definition is an imbalance in real or perceived power between the bully and victim. It may come as no surprise that 30 to 50 percent of gay, lesbian, and bisexual young people, a group not known for its ability for violent retaliation, experience harassment in an educational setting.

Studies of bullying suggest that there are short- and long-term consequences for both the perpetrators and the victims of bullying. Students who are chronic victims of bullying experience more physical and psychological problems than their peers who are not harassed by other children, and they tend not to grow out of the role of victim. Young people mistreated by peers may not want to be in school and may thereby miss out on the benefits of school connectedness as well as educational advancement. Longitudinal studies have found that victims of bullying in early grades also reported being bullied several years later. Studies also suggest that chronically victimized students may, as adults, be at increased risk for depression, poor self-esteem, and other mental health problems, including schizophrenia.

It is not only victims who are at risk for short- and long-term problems; bullies too are at increased risk for negative outcomes. One researcher found that those elementary students who were bullies attended school less frequently and were more likely to drop out than other students. Several studies suggest that bullying in early childhood may be a critical risk factor in the development of future problems with violence and delinquency. Bullies are more likely to carry weapons in and out of school and get involved with substance abuse. Research conducted in Scandinavia found that, in addition to threatening other children, bullies were several times more likely than their nonbullying peers to commit antisocial acts, including vandalism, fighting, theft, drunkenness, and truancy, and to have an arrest by young adulthood. Another study of more than 500 children found that aggressive behavior at the age of 8 was a powerful predictor of criminality and violent behavior at the age of 30.

CAN BULLYING BE PREVENTED?

The first and best-known intervention to reduce bullying among schoolchildren was launched by Dan Olweus in Norway and Sweden in the early 1980s. Prompted by the suicides of several severely victimized children, Norway supported the development and implementation of a comprehensive program to address bullying among children in school. The program involved interventions at multiple levels:

▌ *Schoolwide interventions.* A survey of bullying problems at each school, increased supervision, schoolwide assemblies, and teacher in-service training to raise the awareness of children and school staff regarding bullying.

▌ *Classroom-level interventions.* The establishment of classroom rules against bullying, regular class meetings to discuss bullying at school, and meetings with all parents.

▌ *Individual-level interventions.* Discussions with students to identify bullies and victims.

The program was found to be highly effective in reducing bullying and other antisocial behavior among students in primary and junior high schools. Within two years of implementation, both boys' and girls' self-reports indicated that bullying had decreased by half. These changes in behavior were more pronounced the longer the program was in effect. Moreover, students reported significant decreases in rates of truancy, vandalism, and theft, and indicated that their school's climate was significantly more positive as a result of the program. Not surprisingly, those schools that had implemented more of the program's components experienced the most marked changes in behavior. The core components of the Olweus antibullying program have been adapted for use in several other cultures, including Canada, England, and the United States and the results have been similar: Schools that were more active in implementing the program observed the most marked changes in reported behaviors.

While these results are encouraging, bullying still remains a major social problem. And some critics such as Ronald Jacobson warn that typical antibullying strategies may train bullies to be better at bullying. Because they know they are being watched, bullies may learn to terrorize their victims more covertly, more expertly, so as to inflict the same devastation without adult detection.

Critical Thinking

Should school yard bullies be expelled from school? Would such a measure make a bad situation worse? For example, might expelled bullies shift their aggressive behavior from the school yard to the community?

SOURCES: Ronald Jacobson, "A Lost Horizon: The Experience of an Other and School Bullying," *Studies in Philosophy and Education* 26:297–317 (2007); Kate Gross, "Homophobic Bullying and Schools—Responding to the Challenge," *Youth Studies Australia* 25:60 (2006); T. Joscelyne and S. Holttum, "Children's Explanations of Aggressive Incidents at School within an Attribution Framework," *Child and Adolescent Mental Health* 11:104–110 (2006); Dan Olweus, "A Useful Evaluation Design, and Effects of the Olweus Bullying Prevention Program," *Psychology, Crime and Law* 11:389–402 (2005); Jane Ireland and Rachel Monaghan, "Behaviours Indicative of Bullying among Young and Juvenile Male Offenders: A Study of Perpetrator and Victim Characteristics," *Aggressive Behavior* 32:172–180 (2006); Marla Eisenberg, Dianne Neumark-Sztainer, and Cheryl Perry, "Peer Harassment, School Connectedness, and Academic Achievement," *Journal of School Health* 73:311–316 (2003); Michael Reiff, "Bullying and Violence," *Journal of Developmental and Behavioral Pediatrics* 24:296–297 (2003); Susan Limber and Maury Nation, "Bullying among Children and Youth," in June Arnette and Marjorie Walsleben, eds., *Combating Fear and Restoring Safety in Schools* (Washington, DC: Office of Juvenile Justice and Delinquency Prevention, 1998); Dan Olweus, "Victimization by Peers: Antecedents and Long-Term Outcomes," in K. H. Rubin and J. B. Asendorf, eds., *Social Withdrawal, Inhibitions, and Shyness* (Hillsdale, NJ: Erlbaum, 1993), pp. 315–341.

Who Is the School Shooter? The United States Secret Service has developed a profile of school shootings and shooters after evaluating 41 school shooters who participated in 37 incidents.[50] They found that most attacks were neither spontaneous nor impulsive. Shooters typically developed a plan of attack well in advance; more than half had considered the attack for at least two weeks and had a plan for at least two days.

The attackers' mental anguish was well known, and these kids had come to the attention of someone (school officials, police, fellow students) because of their bizarre and disturbing behavior prior to the attack taking place. One student told more than 20 friends beforehand about his plans, which included killing students and planting bombs. Threats were communicated in more than three-fourths of the cases, and in more than half the incidents the attacker told more than one person. Some people knew detailed information, while others knew "something spectacular" was going to happen on a particular date. In less than one-fourth of the cases did the attacker make a direct threat to the target.

The Secret Service found that the shooters came from such a wide variety of backgrounds that no accurate or useful profile of at-risk kids could be developed. They ranged in age from 11 to 21 and came from a wide variety of ethnic and racial backgrounds; about 25 percent of the shooters were minority-group members. Some lived in intact families with strong ties to the community, while others were reared in foster homes with histories of neglect. Some were excellent students, while others were poor academic performers. Shooters could not be characterized as isolated and alienated; some had many friends and were considered popular. There was no evidence that shootings were a result of the onset of mental disorder. Drugs and alcohol seemed to have little involvement in school violence.

What the Secret Service did find, however, was that many of the shooters had a history of feeling extremely depressed or desperate because they had been picked on or bullied. About three-fourths either threatened to kill themselves, made suicidal gestures, or tried to kill themselves before the attack; six of the students studied killed themselves during the incident. The most frequent motivation was revenge. More than three-fourths were known to hold a grievance, real or imagined, against the target or others. In most cases, this was the first violent act against the target. Two-thirds of the attackers described feeling persecuted, and in more than three-fourths of the incidents the attackers had difficulty coping with a major change in a significant relationship or a loss of status, such as a lost love or a humiliating failure. Not surprisingly, most shooters had experience with guns and weapons and had access to them at home. Some of the most important factors linked to extreme incidents of school violence are contained in Exhibit 10.2.

The Causes of School Crime

What are the suspected causes of school violence? Research indicates that they may be found at the individual, school, and community levels.

School shootings have become a routine event on many school grounds. Here, two students watch police investigate a shooting at Martin Luther King Jr. High School in New York City. The incident involved a teenager who opened fire, seriously wounding two students.

© Spencer Platt/Getty Image

EXHIBIT **10.2**

Factors Linked to Children Who Engage in Serious School Violence

I *Social withdrawal.* In some situations, gradual and eventually complete withdrawal from social contacts occurs. The withdrawal often stems from feelings of depression, rejection, persecution, unworthiness, and lack of confidence.

I *Excessive feelings of isolation and being alone.* Research indicates that in some cases feelings of isolation and not having friends are associated with children who behave aggressively and violently.

I *Excessive feelings of rejection.* Children who are troubled often are isolated from their mentally healthy peers. Some aggressive children who are rejected by nonaggressive peers seek out aggressive friends who, in turn, reinforce their violent tendencies.

I *Being a victim of violence.* Children who are victims of violence, including physical or sexual abuse in the community, at school, or at home, are sometimes at risk of becoming violent toward themselves or others.

I *Feelings of being picked on and persecuted.* The youth who feels constantly picked on, teased, bullied, singled out for ridicule, and humiliated at home or at school may initially withdraw socially.

I *Low school interest and poor academic performance.* In some situations—such as when the low achiever feels frustrated, unworthy, chastised, and denigrated—acting out and aggressive behaviors may occur.

I *Expression of violence in writings and drawings.* An overrepresentation of violence in writings and drawings that is consistently directed at specific individuals (family members, peers, other adults) over time may signal emotional problems and the potential for violence.

I *Uncontrolled anger.* Patterns of impulsive and chronic hitting, intimidating, and bullying behaviors, if left unattended, may later escalate into more serious behaviors.

I *History of discipline problems.* Chronic behavior and disciplinary problems, both in school and at home, may suggest that underlying emotional needs are not being met.

I *History of violent and aggressive behavior.* Unless provided with support and counseling, a youth who has a history of aggressive or violent behavior is likely to repeat those behaviors. Similarly, youths who engage in overt behaviors such as bullying, generalized aggression, and defiance, and covert behaviors such as stealing, vandalism, lying, cheating, and fire setting also are at risk for more serious aggressive behavior.

I *Membership in hate groups.* Belonging to a hate group and also the willingness to victimize individuals with disabilities or health problems are seen as precursors to violence.

I *Drug use and alcohol use.* Apart from being unhealthy behaviors, drug use and alcohol use reduce self-control and expose children and youth to violence, either as perpetrators or victims or both.

I *Inappropriate access to, possession of, and use of firearms.* Children and youth who inappropriately possess or have access to firearms can have an increased risk for violence or other emotional problems.

I *Serious threats of violence.* Recent incidents across the country clearly indicate that threats to commit violence against oneself or others should be taken very seriously. Steps must be taken to understand the nature of these threats and to prevent them from being carried out.

SOURCE: Kevin Dwyer, *Early Warning, Timely Response: A Guide to Safe Schools* (Washington, DC: U.S. Department of Education, 1998), sec. 3.

Individual-Level Causes Schools with high-achieving students, a drug-free environment, strong discipline, and involved parents have fewer behavioral problems in the student body.[51] Conversely, schools whose student body contains large numbers of students with emotional and psychological problems also have high rates of crime and violence.

Kids who feel isolated and alone with little parental attention may be the most prone to alienation and substance abuse.[52] The level of student drinking and substance abuse may increase violent crime rates. As substance abuse increases among the student body, so too may school violence rates.[53] Because heavy drinking reduces cognitive ability, information processing skills, and the ability to process and react to verbal and nonverbal behavior, a student argument may quickly turn into a full-scale battle.[54]

School-Level Causes Research shows that the school climate is one of the most important predictors of campus crime and violence. Schools with a high proportion of students behind grade level in reading, with many students from families on welfare, and located in a community with high unemployment, crime, and poverty rates, are also at risk for delinquency. When Rami Benbenishty and Ron Avi Astor compared violence rates in schools located in California with those in Israel, they found that the forms and patterns of school crime and victimization were extremely similar in both school systems. They also found that in both cultures victimization was less dependent on individual factors than on school climate. School policy, teachers' relationships with students, and peer group support explain violence levels better than community or family influences.[55]

EXHIBIT 10.3
Security Measures Being Used to Reduce School Crime

Outsiders on Campus

I Posted signs regarding penalties for trespassing
I Enclosed campus (fencing)
I Guard at main entry gate to campus
I Greeters in strategic locations
I Vehicle parking stickers
I Uniforms or dress codes
I Exterior doors locked from the outside
I A challenge procedure for anyone out of class
I Cameras in remote locations
I School laid out so all visitors must pass through front office
I Temporary "fading" badges issued to all visitors
I Designating one main door entry to school, equipping exits with push bars, and locking all other doors to outside entry
I Installing bulletproof windows
I Equipping the school with closed-circuit video surveillance systems to reduce property crime such as break-ins, theft, vandalism, and assaults
I Designing landscaping to create an inviting appearance without offering a hiding place for trespassers or criminals
I Installing motion-sensitive lights to illuminate dark corners in hallways or on campus
I Mounting convex mirrors to monitor blind spots in school hallways
I Requiring photo identification badges for students, teachers, and staff and identification cards for visitors on campus

Fights on Campus

I Cameras
I Duress alarms
I Whistles

Vandalism

I Graffiti-resistant sealers
I Glass-break sensors
I Aesthetically pleasing wall murals (these usually are not hit by graffiti)
I Law enforcement officers living on campus
I Eight-foot fencing
I Well-lit campus

Theft

I Interior intrusion detection sensors
I Property marking (including microdots) to deter theft
I Bars on windows
I Reinforced doors
I Elimination of access points up to rooftops
I Cameras
I Doors with hinge pins on secure side
I Bolting down computers and TVs
I Locating high-value assets in interior rooms
I Key control
I Biometric entry into rooms with high-value assets
I Law enforcement officer living on campus

Drugs

I Drug detection swipes
I Hair analysis kits for drug use detection (intended for parental application)
I Drug dogs
I Removal of lockers
I Random searches
I Vapor detection of drugs

Alcohol

I No open campus at lunch
I Breathalyzer test equipment
I No access to vehicles
I No lockers
I Clear or open mesh backpacks
I Saliva test kits

Weapons

I Walk-through metal detectors
I Handheld metal detectors
I Vapor detection of gunpowder
I Crime stopper hotline with rewards for information
I Gunpowder detection swipes

In general, researchers find that several characteristics make schools more conducive to violent student behavior:

I Violence is more prevalent in large schools as compared to smaller ones. Eighty-nine percent of the large schools surveyed admitted to one or more criminal incidents in a year compared to only 38 percent of the smaller schools. Given a larger student population, exposure to violent acts on the school campus is greater, thereby leading to a larger number of incidents.

I Schools located in a city are more likely to experience criminal behaviors and violence than rural schools.

I The physical condition of the school building can influence students' motivation, attitude, and behavior. Buildings that have uncomfortable temperatures, are polluted, have a large amount of graffiti, and are in need of repairs have higher incidences of fighting and other forms of violence. The physical learning atmosphere affects daily conduct.[56]

Neighborhood-Level Causes A number of researchers have observed that school crime is a function of the community in which the school is located. In other words, crime in schools does not occur in isolation from crime in the community.[57]

- Random locker, backpack, and vehicle searches
- X-ray inspection of book bags and purses

Malicious Acts
- Distancing school buildings from vehicle areas
- Inaccessibility of air intake and water source
- All adults on campus required to wear badges
- Vehicle barriers near main entries and student gathering areas

Parking Lot Problems
- Cameras
- Parking decals
- Fencing
- Card identification systems for parking lot entry
- Parking lots sectioned off for different student schedules
- Sensors in parking areas that should have no access during school day
- Roving guards
- Bike patrol

False Fire Alarms
- Sophisticated alarm systems that allow assessment of alarms (and cancellation if false) before they become audible
- Boxes installed over alarm pulls that alarm locally (screamer boxes)

Bomb Threats
- Caller I.D. on phone system
- Crime stopper program with big rewards for information
- Recording all phone calls, with a message regarding this at the beginning of each incoming call
- All incoming calls routed through a district office
- Phone company support
- No pay phones on campus
- Policy to extend the school year when plagued with bomb threats and subsequent evacuations

Bus Problems
- School bus drivers tested for drug and alcohol use
- Video cameras and recorders within enclosures on buses
- Identification required to ride school buses
- Security aides on buses
- Smaller buses
- Duress alarm system or radios for bus drivers

Teacher Safety
- Duress alarms
- Roving patrols
- Classroom doors left open during class
- Cameras in black boxes in classrooms
- Controlled access to classroom areas
- Equipping classrooms with intercom systems connected to the central school office
- Issuing two-way radios to security patrols or campus staff members
- Purchasing cellular phones for use in crises or emergency situations

Campus Safety
- Establishing neighborhood watch programs in areas near schools
- Recruiting parents to provide safe houses along school routes and to monitor "safe corridors" or walkways to and from school
- Enlisting parent volunteers to monitor hallways, cafeterias, playgrounds, and school walkways in order to increase visibility of responsible adults
- Creating block safety watch programs carried out by area residents at school bus stops as a crime deterrent for schoolchildren and area residents
- Fencing school grounds to secure campus perimeters
- Replacing bathroom doors with zigzag entrances to make it easier to monitor sounds, and installing roll-down doors to secure bathrooms after hours

SOURCE: Adapted from Mary W. Green, *The Appropriate and Effective Use of Security Technologies in U.S. Schools* (Washington, DC: National Institute of Justice, 1999).

Schools experiencing crime and drug abuse are most likely to be found in socially disorganized neighborhoods with a high proportion of students behind grade level in reading, with many students from families on welfare, and with high unemployment and poverty rates.[58] Neighborhoods with high population density and transient populations also have problem-prone schools.[59] In contrast, schools located in more stable areas, with high-achieving students, drug-free environments, and involved parents have fewer behavioral problems within the student body.[60]

When Wayne Welsh, Robert Stokes, and Jack Greene studied community influences on school crime, they found that community influences may undermine school stability and climate.[61] Poverty in a school's surrounding area influences the social characteristics of students. They may lack the readiness and interest to learn when compared with students from more affluent neighborhoods. Poor areas may find it difficult to hire and retain the most qualified faculty and/or provide students with the most up-to-date equipment and books. Because poor communities have lower tax bases, they are handcuffed when they want to provide remedial programs for students with learning issues, or conversely, enrichment programs for the gifted. Finally, parents and other students have neither the time nor resources to become involved in school activities or participate in governance. These factors may eventually undermine school climate and destabilize the educational environment, which leads to school crime and disorder.

Cross-national research efforts confirm the community influences on school crime. One study of violent crimes in the schools of Stockholm, Sweden, found that, although only one-fifth of schools were located in areas of social instability and disorganization, almost a third of school crime happened in these schools.[62]

There is also evidence that crime in schools reflects the patterns of antisocial behavior that exist in the surrounding neighborhood.[63] Schools in high-crime areas experience more crime than schools in safer areas. Students who report being afraid in school are actually more afraid of being in city parks, streets, or subway. Because of this fear, students in high-crime areas may carry weapons for self-protection as they go from their homes to school.[64]

Research also shows that many perpetrators of school crime have been victims of delinquency themselves.[65] It is possible that school-based crimes have "survival value"—striking back against a weaker victim is a method of regaining lost possessions or self-respect.[66] This would imply that areas with high crime rates produce a large pool of student victims who will also manifest high rates of school crime. It may be futile to attempt to eliminate school crime without considering the impact of communities. The Welsh research found that schools that are stable and have a positive climate manifest lower rates of criminal activity on school grounds.

Reducing School Crime

Schools around the country have mounted a campaign to reduce the incidence of delinquency on campus. Nearly all states have developed some sort of crime-free, weapon-free, or safe-school zone statute.[67] Most have defined these zones to include school transportation and school-sponsored functions. Schools are also cooperating with court officials and probation officers to share information and monitor students who have criminal records. School districts are formulating crisis prevention and intervention policies and are directing individual schools to develop safe-school plans.

Some schools have instituted strict controls over student activity—for example, making locker searches, preventing students from having lunch off campus, and using patrols to monitor drug use. According to one national survey, a majority of schools have adopted a **zero tolerance policy** that mandates predetermined punishments for specific offenses, most often possession of drugs, weapons, and tobacco, and also for engaging in violent behaviors.[68]

School Security Efforts Almost every school attempts to restrict entry of dangerous persons by having visitors sign in before entering, and most close the campus for lunch (see Exhibit 10.3 on pages 348–349). Schools have attempted to ensure the physical safety of students and staff by using mechanical security devices such as surveillance cameras, metal detectors, and electronic barriers to keep out intruders, and have also employed roving security guards (Figure 10.7).[69] Security measures include the following:

I *Access control.* Most schools control access to school buildings by locking or monitoring doors. About one-third of schools control access to school grounds with locked or monitored gates.

I *Lighting.* Some administrators keep buildings dark at night, believing that brightly illuminated schools give the buildings too high a profile and attract vandals who might have not bothered with the facility, or even noticed it, if the premises were not illuminated.[70]

I *Picture IDs.* Almost half of all schools require faculty or staff to wear picture IDs; about 6 percent of schools require students to wear similar identification.

I *Book bags.* About 6 percent of schools require transparent book bags or ban book bags altogether.

I *Random checks.* About 6 percent of schools use random metal detector checks, 20 percent use random dog sniffs, and an additional 13 percent use random sweeps for contraband.

zero tolerance policy
Mandating specific consequences or punishments for delinquent acts and not allowing anyone to avoid these consequences.

FIGURE 10.7

School Safety Measure by School Level

‡ Reporting standards not met.

SOURCE: National Center for Education Statistics, http://nces.ed.gov/ programs/crimeindicators/ figure_19_1.asp?referrer=report (accessed October 22, 2007).

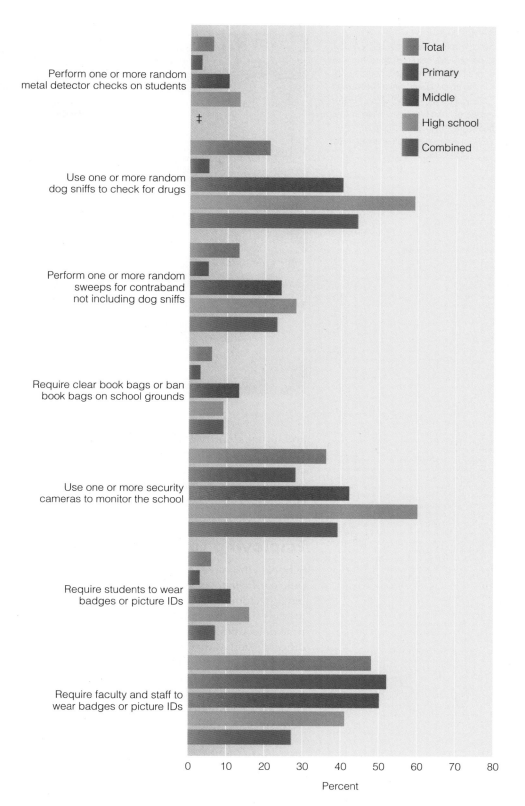

■ *Security cameras.* About 28 percent of primary schools, 42 percent of middle schools, and 60 percent of secondary schools used one or more security cameras to monitor the school.[71]

While these measures seem extreme, they are by no means unique to the United States. School districts in Australia report that local schools are installing spy cameras

Some schools now employ safety and/or school resource officers to patrol hallways in an effort to increase school security. In this image taken from a Greenwood (Mississippi) High School security videotape, police officer Casey Wiggins, four months into his job, is seen holding a gun on an unarmed teen.

© AP Images

and hiring security guards. Security is warranted because of arson, assaults or threats against school staff and students, repeated burglaries, theft and criminal damage of computers, gang fights spilling onto school grounds, student violence over teenage relationships, and stress claims by teachers, partly due to clashes with parents and students.[72]

Employing Law Enforcement

Schools who have experienced behavioral problems are now employing uniformed police officers on school grounds, typically called school resource officers. The system developed by the village of Hempstead in New York is not dissimilar from other models. In Hempstead, the school resource officer (SRO) program places two full-time detectives within the local high school. Before entering the school system, these officers receive advanced training and earn an SRO certification from the state of New York Police Juvenile Officers Association, which requires at least 40 hours of training. The detectives regularly participate in criminal investigations and gang violence intervention, and develop and share information with other police units.

The close interaction, both during school and at after-school activities, allows the detectives to build close relationships with students. This close proximity with the students also allows the detectives to see whom the students are hanging out with and notify their parents, if necessary. The Hempstead SRO detectives work closely with the vice principal of the school to reduce gang violence by having the students (including rival gang members) participate in activities such as rap sessions. Classroom presentations are also given by the detectives on topics such as peer pressure, law and police matters, and gang resistance.[73]

Some districts have gone so far as to infiltrate undercover detectives on school grounds. These detectives attend classes, mingle with students, contact drug dealers, make buys, and arrest campus dealers.[74] New York City recently instituted a program that focuses on reducing crime in the city's 12 most dangerous schools. Though these schools constitute less than 1 percent of the city's enrollment, they account for

13 percent of all serious crimes and 11 percent of the total safety incidents. To reduce delinquency, the NYPD doubled the number of officers assigned to each school site and formed a 150-member task force of officers to focus on danger zones such as hallways and cafeterias. The police also monitored the perimeters of the schools and organized truancy sweeps. Each school received frequent visits from school-safety teams made up of police officers, community workers, and educators. Evaluations showed that criminal incidents in schools receiving the extra enforcement declined almost 10 percent.[75]

Improving the School Climate

Some critics complain that even when security methods are effective, they reduce staff and student morale. Tighter security may reduce acts of crime and violence in school, only to displace them to the community. Similarly, expelling or suspending troublemakers puts them on the street with nothing to do so that, in the end, lowering the level of crime in schools may not reduce the total amount of crime committed by young people. A more realistic approach might involve early identification of at-risk students and exposing them to prosocial skills rather than threaten them with consequence-based punishments.[76]

Another approach to improving the school climate is to increase educational standards. Programs have been designed to improve the standards of the teaching staff and administrators and the educational climate in the school, increase the relevance of the curriculum, and provide law-related education classes. The Policy and Practice box entitled "Safe Harbor" discusses one such program.

Efforts to improve school climate should be encouraged. Recent research efforts have found preliminary support for the linkage between climate and delinquency. Schools that encourage order, organization, and student bonding may also experience a decline in disorder and crime.[77]

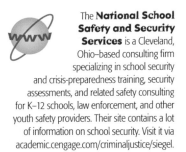

The **National School Safety and Security Services** is a Cleveland, Ohio–based consulting firm specializing in school security and crisis-preparedness training, security assessments, and related safety consulting for K–12 schools, law enforcement, and other youth safety providers. Their site contains a lot of information on school security. Visit it via academic.cengage.com/criminaljustice/siegel.

Social Programs Controlling school crime is ultimately linked to the community and family conditions. When communities undergo such changes as increases in unemployment and the number of single-parent households, both school disruption and community crime rates may rise.[78] The school environment can be made safer only if community issues are addressed—for example, by taking steps to keep intruders out of school buildings, putting pressure on local police to develop community safety programs, increasing correctional services, strengthening laws on school safety, and making parents bear greater responsibility for their children's behavior.[79]

Schools must also use the resources of the community when controlling school crime. Most school districts refer problem students to social services outside the school. About 70 percent of public schools provide outside referrals for students with substance abuse problems, while 90 percent offer drug education within the school.[80]

THE ROLE OF THE SCHOOL IN DELINQUENCY PREVENTION

Numerous organizations and groups have called for reforming the educational system to make it more responsive to the needs of students. Educational leaders now recognize that children undergo enormous pressures while in school that can lead to emotional and social problems. At one extreme are the pressures to succeed academically; at the other are the crime and substance abuse students face on school grounds. It is difficult to talk of achieving academic excellence in a deteriorated school dominated by gang members.

One way of improving schools and reducing delinquency is through sponsored educational reform. The cornerstone of the Bush administration's policy has been the No Child Left Behind (NCLB) Act of 2001 (Public Law 107-110). This act authorizes federal programs aimed at improving America's primary and secondary schools by

Safe Harbor: A School-Based Victim Assistance and Violence Prevention Program

All too many school officials have witnessed students being drawn into a cycle of violence. First, they are victimized by other students. They then retaliate against weaker or younger peers, only to be victimized once again. To help remedy this troubling situation, Safe Harbor, a violence prevention and victim assistance program for schools, was developed. This multifaceted program attempts to prevent school crime and victimization while providing assistance to curb future victimization.

The Safe Harbor program has five core components:

1. A 10-lesson violence prevention and victim assistance curriculum.

2. Individual and group counseling with social workers and school counselors for victims.

3. Prevention workshops in parenting and stress management to strengthen relationships with children and/or students in order to help parents and teachers understand what students are facing in today's society.

4. Group activities (art, physical, and relaxation programs) and discussion groups for students. These are aimed at helping them understand and discuss current issues and also learn how to resolve conflict with their peers in a nonviolent fashion.

5. Poster campaigns, school assemblies, and/or arts and crafts projects that are all geared toward a schoolwide antiviolence stand. These activities provide students with opportunities for leadership in their community without violence.

So far Safe Harbor seems very successful. Preliminary evaluations show that students enrolled in the program improve their conflict resolution skills and change their attitudes about violence.

Critical Thinking

1. If you were called upon to design a school-based delinquency prevention program, what activities would you suggest?

2. Do you think that school bullies and troublemakers would make themselves available for help in a school-based program? If not, why?

SOURCE: U.S. Department of Justice, Office for Victims of Crime, "Safe Harbor: A School Based Victim Assistance/Violence Prevention Program," *OVC Bulletin*, January 2003.

increasing the accountability for states, school districts, and schools and also providing parents more flexibility in choosing which schools their children will attend.[81] The NCLB increases focus on reading and relies on outcome-based education or the belief that high expectations and setting of goals will result in success for all students.[82] The NCLB has proven quite controversial and it remains to be seen whether it will be retained.

School-Based Prevention Programs

Education officials have instituted numerous programs to make schools more effective instruments of delinquency prevention. Some of the most prevalent strategies are as follows:

I *Cognitive.* Increase students' awareness about the dangers of drug abuse and delinquency.

I *Affective.* Improve students' psychological assets and self-image to give them the resources to resist antisocial behavior.

I *Behavioral.* Train students in techniques to resist peer pressure.

I *Environmental.* Establish school management and disciplinary programs that deter crime, such as locker searches.

I *Therapeutic.* Treat youths who have already manifested problems.

More specific suggestions include creating special classes or schools with individualized programs that foster success for nonadjusting students. Efforts can be made to help students deal constructively with academic failure when it does occur.

More personalized student-teacher relationships have been recommended. This effort to provide young people with a caring, accepting adult role model will, it is hoped, strengthen the controls against delinquency. Counselors acting as liaisons between the family and the school might also be effective in preventing delinquency.

Schools have taken a leadership role in delinquency prevention efforts. Here, former journalist Colman McCarthy addresses students in his "Alternatives to Violence" class on April 5, 2006, at the School Without Walls in Washington, D.C. McCarthy has been teaching the class for more than 20 years with the theme that nonviolent force is always stronger than violent force. McCarthy says students are thirsty to know alternatives to violence of all types—from armed violence and family violence to capital punishment.

These counselors try to ensure cooperation between the parents and the school and to secure needed services for troubled students. Some programs that help families and schools develop conflict avoidance skills have proven effective in reducing violence levels and helping restrict disciplinary measures such as suspensions and expulsions.[83]

Experiments have been proposed to integrate job training and experience with classroom instruction, allowing students to see education as a relevant prelude to their careers. Job training programs emphasize public service, encouraging students to gain a sense of attachment to their communities.

Because three out of four mothers with school-age children are employed, and two-thirds of them work full time, there is a growing need for after-school programs. Today, after-school options include child-care centers, tutoring programs at school, dance groups, basketball leagues, and drop-in clubs. State and federal budgets for education, public safety, crime prevention, and child care provide some funding for after-school programs. Research shows that younger children (ages 5 to 9) and those in low-income neighborhoods gain the most from after-school programs, showing improved work habits, behavior with peers and adults, and performance in school. Young teens who attend after-school activities achieve higher grades in school and engage in less risky behavior. These findings must be interpreted with caution. Because after-school programs are voluntary, participants may be the more motivated youngsters in a given population and the least likely to engage in antisocial behavior.[84]

LEGAL RIGHTS IN THE SCHOOL

The actions of education officials often run into opposition from the courts, which are concerned with maintaining the legal rights of minors. The U.S. Supreme Court has sought to balance the civil liberties of students with the school's mandate to provide a safe environment. Three of the main issues involved are privacy, free speech in school, and school discipline.

The Right to Personal Privacy

One major issue is the right of school officials to search students and their possessions on school grounds. Drug abuse, theft, assault and battery, and racial conflicts in schools have increased the need to take action against troublemakers. School administrators have questioned students about their illegal activities, conducted searches of students' persons and possessions, and reported suspicious behavior to the police.

In 1984, in *New Jersey v. T.L.O.*, the Supreme Court helped clarify a vexing problem: whether the Fourth Amendment's prohibition against unreasonable searches and seizures applies to school officials as well as to police officers.[85] In this case, the Court found that students are in fact constitutionally protected from illegal searches but that school officials are not bound by the same restrictions as law enforcement agents. Police need "probable cause" before they can conduct a search, but educators can legally search students when there are reasonable grounds to believe the students have violated the law or broken school rules. In creating this distinction, the Court recognized the needs of school officials to preserve an environment conducive to education and to secure the safety of students.

One question left unanswered by *New Jersey v. T.L.O.* is whether teachers and other school officials can search lockers and desks. Here, the law has been controlled by state decisions, and each jurisdiction may create its own standards. Some allow teachers a free hand in opening lockers and desks.[86]

Drug Testing Another critical issue involving privacy is the drug testing of students. In 1995, the Supreme Court extended schools' authority to search by legalizing a random drug-testing policy for student athletes. The Supreme Court's decision in *Vernonia School District 47J v. Acton* expanded the power of educators to ensure safe learning environments.[87] In this case, the Supreme Court extended one step further the schools' authority to search, despite court-imposed constitutional safeguards for children. Underlying this decision, like that of *New Jersey v. T.L.O.*, is a recognition that the use of drugs is a serious threat to public safety and to the rights of children to receive a decent and safe education. In a subsequent case, *Board of Education of Independent School District No. 92 of Pottawatomie County et al. v. Earls et al.*, the court extended the right to test for drugs to all students. Because of its importance, *Pottawatomie County* is set out in the accompanying Policy and Practice feature.

Academic Privacy Students have the right to expect that their records will be kept private. Although state laws govern the disclosure of information from juvenile court records, a 1974 federal law—the Family Educational Rights and Privacy Act (FERPA)—restricts disclosure of information from a student's education records without parental consent.[88] The act defines an education record to include all records, files, and other materials, such as photographs, containing information related to a student that an education agency maintains. In 1994, Congress passed the Improving America's Schools Act, which allowed educational systems to disclose education records under these circumstances: (1) state law authorizes the disclosure, (2) the disclosure is to a juvenile justice agency, (3) the disclosure relates to the justice system's ability to provide preadjudication services to a student, and (4) state or local officials certify in writing that the institution or individual receiving the information has agreed not to disclose it to a third party other than another juvenile justice system agency.[89]

passive speech
A form of expression protected by the First Amendment but not associated with actually speaking words; examples include wearing symbols or protest messages on buttons or signs.

Free Speech

Freedom of speech is guaranteed in the First Amendment to the U.S. Constitution. This right has been divided into two categories as it affects children in schools: passive speech and active speech. **Passive speech** is a form of expression not associated

The Tecumseh, Oklahoma, school district adopted a student activities drug-testing policy that required all middle and high school students to consent to urinalysis testing for drugs in order to participate in any extracurricular activity. The policy was a response to increased perceptions of student drug use by faculty and administrators. Teachers saw students who appeared to be under the influence of drugs and heard students speaking openly about using drugs. A drug dog found marijuana near the school parking lot. Police found drugs or drug paraphernalia in a car driven by an extracurricular club member. And the school board president reported that people in the community were calling the board to discuss the "drug situation."

In practice, the policy was applied only to competitive extracurricular activities sanctioned by the Oklahoma Secondary Schools Activities Association (OSSAA). A group of students and their parents filed suit against the policy, arguing that it infringed on a student's right to personal privacy. The Tenth Circuit Court of Appeals agreed and held that before imposing a suspicionless drug-testing program a school must demonstrate some identifiable drug abuse problem among a sufficient number of students such that testing that group will redress its drug problem. The federal court held that the school district had failed to demonstrate such a problem among Tecumseh students participating in competitive extracurricular activities. However, the Supreme Court reversed its decision and ruled that the policy is a reasonable means of furthering the school district's important interest in preventing and deterring drug use among its schoolchildren and does not violate the students' rights to privacy or their due process rights.

The Court ruled that, so as not to violate due process, drug-testing policies had to be "reasonable." However, in contrast to searches for criminal evidence, students could be searched by school authorities (to determine whether they used drugs) without probable cause because the need for that level of evidence interferes with maintaining swift and informal disciplinary procedures that are needed to maintain order in a public school. Because the schools' responsibility for children cannot be disregarded, it would not be unreasonable to search students for drug usage even if no single student was suspected of abusing drugs.

The Court also ruled that within this context, students have a limited expectation of privacy. In their complaint, the students argued that children participating in nonathletic extracurricular activities have a stronger expectation of privacy than athletes who regularly undergo physicals as part of their participation in sports. However, the Court disagreed, maintaining that students who participate in competitive extracurricular activities voluntarily subject themselves to many of the same intrusions on their privacy as do athletes. Some of these clubs and activities require off-campus travel and communal undress, and all of them have their own rules and requirements that do not

Board of Education of Independent School District No. 92 of Pottawatomie County et al. v. Earls et al.

apply to the student body as a whole. Each of them must abide by OSSAA rules, and a faculty sponsor monitors students for compliance with the various rules dictated by the clubs and activities. Such regulation diminishes the student's expectation of privacy.

Finally, the Court concluded that the means used to enforce the drug policy was not overly invasive or an intrusion on the students' privacy. Under the policy, a faculty monitor would wait outside a closed restroom stall for the student to produce a sample and must listen for the normal sounds of urination to guard against tampered specimens and ensure an accurate chain of custody. This procedure is virtually identical to the "negligible" intrusion concept which was approved in an earlier case, *Vernonia v. Acton*, which applied to student athletes. The policy requires that test results be kept in confidential files separate from a student's other records and released to school personnel only on a "need to know" basis. Moreover, the test results are not turned over to any law enforcement authority. Nor do the test results lead to the imposition of discipline or have any academic consequences. Rather, the only consequence of a failed drug test is to limit the student's privilege of participating in extracurricular activities.

SIGNIFICANCE

In *Pottawatomie County*, the Court concluded that a drug-testing policy effectively serves a school district's interest in protecting its students' safety and health. It reasoned that preventing drug use by schoolchildren is an important governmental concern. School districts need not show that kids participating in a particular activity have a drug problem in order to test them for usage. The need to prevent and deter the substantial harm of childhood drug use itself provides the necessary immediacy for a school testing policy. Given what it considers a "nationwide epidemic of drug use," it was entirely reasonable for the school district to enact a drug-testing policy.

Critical Thinking

Pottawatomie County extends the drug testing allowed in the *Vernonia* case from athletes to all students who participate in any form of school activity. Do you believe this is a reasonable exercise of state authority or a violation of due process? After all, the students being tested have not shown any evidence of drug abuse. Furthermore, nonathletic school activities do not provide the same degree of danger as an athletic activity, during the course of which an impaired participant may suffer serious injury.

SOURCE: *Board of Education of Independent School District No. 92 of Pottawatomie County et al. v. Earls et al.*, 01.332 (2002).

In an important case, *Morse v. Frederick*, the Supreme Court of the United States held that a school principal may restrict passive student speech at a school event when that speech is reasonably viewed as promoting illegal drug use. The case involved 18-year-old Joseph Frederick, who was suspended from high school in 2002 after he displayed a banner reading "BONG HiTS 4 JESUS" across the street from his Juneau, Alaska, high school during the Winter Olympics torch relay. The "Bong Hits 4 Jesus" case is important because it shows that the Supreme Court under Chief Justice Roberts is willing to encourage control and security at the expense of students' rights. This is the banner that caused the uproar. Is it really so different from the armbands worn by the Tinker Twins, a means of expression allowed by the Court? Does this sign really advocate drug use or is it merely a student prank aimed at tweaking the principal and other school authorities?.

with actually speaking words; examples include wearing armbands or political protest buttons. The most important U.S. Supreme Court decision concerning a student's right to passive speech was in 1969 in the case of *Tinker v. Des Moines Independent Community School District*.[90] This case involved the right to wear black armbands to protest the war in Vietnam. Three high school students, ages 15, 16, and 13, were suspended for wearing the armbands in school. This decision is significant because it recognizes the child's right to free speech in a public school system. Justice Abe Fortas stated in his majority opinion, "Young people do not shed their constitutional rights at the schoolhouse door."[91] *Tinker* established two things: (1) a child is entitled to free speech in school under the First Amendment of the U.S. Constitution, and (2) the test used to determine whether the child has gone beyond proper speech is whether he or she materially and substantially interferes with the requirements of appropriate discipline in the operation of the school.

The concept of free speech was at issue again in the 1986 case *Bethel School District No. 403 v. Fraser*.[92] This case upheld a school system's right to suspend or otherwise discipline a student who uses obscene or profane

active speech
Speech involving actual language, expression, or gesture.

language and gestures, legally known as **active speech**. Matthew Fraser, a Bethel high school student, used sexual metaphors in making a speech nominating a friend for student office. His statement included these remarks:

I know a man who is firm—he's firm in his pants, he's firm in his shirt, his character is firm—but most . . . of all, his belief in you, the students of Bethel, is firm.

Jeff Kuhlman is a man who takes his point and pounds it in. If necessary, he'll take an issue and nail it to the wall. He doesn't attack things in spurts—he drives hard, pushing and pushing until finally—he succeeds.

Jeff is a man who will go to the very end—even the climax—for each and every one of you.

So vote for Jeff for A.S.B. vice-president—he'll never come between you and the best our high school can be.

The Court found that a school has the right to control lewd and offensive speech that undermines the educational mission. The Court drew a distinction between thesexual content of Fraser's remarks and the political nature of Tinker's armband. It ruled that the pervasive sexual innuendo of the speech interfered with the school's mission to implant "the shared values of a civilized social order" in the student body.

In a 1988 case, *Hazelwood School District v. Kuhlmeier*, the Court extended the right of school officials to censor "active speech" when it ruled that the principal could censor articles in a student publication.[93] In this case, students had written about their personal experiences with pregnancy and parental divorce. The majority ruled that censorship was justified in this case because school-sponsored publications, activities, and productions were part of the curriculum and therefore designed to impart knowledge. Control over such school-supported activities could be differentiated from the action the Tinkers initiated on their own accord. In a dissent, Justice William J. Brennan accused school officials of favoring "thought control." While the Court has dealt with speech on campus, it may now be asked to address off-campus speech issues. Students have been suspended for posting messages on their Internet web pages that school officials consider defamatory.[94] In the future, the Court may be asked to rule whether schools can control such forms of speech or whether they are shielded by the First Amendment.

School Prayer One of the most divisive issues involving free speech is school prayer. While some religious-minded administrators, parents, and students want to have prayer sessions in schools or have religious convocations, others view the practice both as a violation of the principle of separation of church and state and as an infringement on the First Amendment caution against creating a state-approved religion. The 2000 case of *Santa Fe Independent School District, Petitioner v. Jane Doe* helps clarify the issue.[95]

Prior to 1995, the Santa Fe High School student who occupied the school's elective office of student council chaplain delivered a prayer over the public address system before each varsity football game for the entire season. After the practice was challenged in federal district court, the school district adopted a different policy that permitted, but did not require, prayer initiated and led by a student at all home games. The district court entered an order modifying that policy to permit only nonsectarian, nonproselytizing prayer. However, a federal appellate court held that, even as modified, the football prayer policy was invalid. This decision was appealed to the United States Supreme Court, which ruled that prayers led by an elected student undermine the protection of minority viewpoints. Such a system encourages divisiveness along religious lines and threatens the students not desiring to participate in a religious exercise.

Though the Santa Fe case severely limits school-sanctioned prayer at public events, the Court has not totally ruled out the role of religion in schools. In its ruling in *Good News Club v. Milford Central School* (2001), the Supreme Court required an upstate New York school district to provide space for an after-school Bible club for elementary students.[96] The Court ruled that it was a violation of the First Amendment's free speech clause to deny the club access to the school's space on the ground that the club was religious in nature; the school routinely let secular groups use its space. The Court reasoned that because the club's meetings were to be held after school hours, not sponsored by the school, and open to any student who obtained parental consent, it could not be perceived that the school was endorsing the club or that students might feel coerced to participate in its activities. In 2001, the Court let stand a Virginia statute that mandates that each school division in the state establish in its classrooms a "minute of silence" so that "each pupil may, in the exercise of his or her individual choice, meditate, pray, or engage in any other silent activity which does not interfere with, distract, or impede other pupils in the like exercise of individual choice."[97] The Court refused to hear an appeal filed by several Virginia students and their parents, which contended that a "moment of silence" establishes religion in violation of the First Amendment.[98] In its most recent statement on the separation of church and state, the Court refused to hear a case brought by a California father contesting the recital of the Pledge of Allegiance because it contains the phrase "under God."[99] Though the Court dismissed the case on a technical issue, some of the justices felt the issue should have been dealt with and dismissed. Chief Justice Rehnquist wrote in his opinion:

> To give the parent of such a child a sort of "heckler's veto" over a patriotic ceremony willingly participated in by other students, simply because the Pledge of Allegiance contains the descriptive phrase "under God," is an unwarranted extension of the establishment clause, an extension which would have the unfortunate effect of prohibiting a commendable patriotic observance.[100]

School Discipline

in loco parentis
In the place of the parent; rights given to schools that allow them to assume parental duties in disciplining students.

Most states have statutes permitting teachers to use corporal punishment to discipline students in public school systems. Under the concept of *in loco parentis*, discipline is one of the assumed parental duties given to the school system. In two decisions, the Supreme Court upheld the school's right to use corporal punishment. In the 1975 case of *Baker v. Owen*, the Court stated:

> *We hold that the Fourteenth Amendment embraces the right of parents generally to control the means and discipline of their children, but that the state has a countervailing interest in the maintenance of order in the schools . . . sufficient to sustain the right of teachers, and school officials must accord to students minimal due process in the course of inflicting such punishment.*[101]

In 1977, the Supreme Court again spoke on the issue of corporal punishment in school systems in the case of *Ingraham v. Wright*, which upheld the right of teachers to use corporal punishment.[102] In this case, students James Ingraham and Roosevelt Andrews sustained injuries as a result of paddling in the Charles Drew Junior High School in Dade County, Florida. The legal problems raised in the case were (a) whether corporal punishment by teachers was a violation in this case of the Eighth Amendment against cruel and unusual punishment and (b) whether the due process clause of the Fourteenth Amendment required that the students receive proper notice and a hearing prior to receiving corporal punishment. The Court held that neither the Eighth Amendment nor the Fourteenth Amendment was violated in this case. Even though Ingraham suffered hematomas on his buttocks as a result of 20 blows with a wooden paddle and Andrews was hurt in the arm, the Supreme Court ruled that such punishment was not a constitutional violation. The Court established the standard that only reasonable discipline is allowed in school systems, but it accepted the degree of punishment administered in this case. The key principle in *Ingraham* is that the reasonableness standard that the Court articulated represents the judicial attitude that the scope of the school's right to discipline a child is by no means more restrictive than the rights of the child's own parents to impose corporal punishment. Today 24 states still use physical punishment in schools.

Other issues involving the legal rights of students include their due process rights when interrogated, if corporal punishment is to be imposed, and when suspension and expulsion are threatened. When students are questioned by school personnel, no warning as to their legal rights to remain silent or right to counsel need be given. However, when school security guards, on-campus police officials, and public police officers question students, such constitutional warnings are required. In the area of corporal punishment, procedural due process established with the case of *Baker v. Owen* requires that students at least be forewarned about the possibility of corporal punishment as a discipline. In addition, the *Baker* case requires that there be a witness to the administration of corporal punishment and allows the student and the parent to elicit reasons for the punishment.

With regard to suspension and expulsion, the Supreme Court ruled in 1976 in the case of *Goss v. Lopez* that any time a student is to be suspended for up to a period of 10 days, he or she is entitled to a hearing.[103] The hearing would not include a right to counsel or a right to confront or cross-examine witnesses. The Court went on to state in *Goss* that the extent of the procedural due process requirements would be established on a case-by-case basis. That is, each case would represent its own facts and have its own procedural due process elements.

In sum, schools have the right to discipline students, but students are protected from unreasonable, excessive, and arbitrary discipline.

Summary

1. **Discuss the role the educational experience plays in human development over the life course**

   I The school environment has been found to have a significant effect on a child's emotional well-being.

   I The school plays an important role in shaping the values of children.

   I Because young people spend a longer time in school in contrast to the earlier, agrarian days of U.S. history, their adolescence is prolonged.

   I Young people rely increasingly on school friends and become less interested in adult role models.

   I The school has become a primary determinant of economic and social status.

   I The school itself has become an engine of social change and improvement.

2. **Be familiar with the problems facing the educational system in the United States**

   I The role schools play in adolescent development is underscored by the problems faced by the U.S. education system.

   I Cross-national surveys that compare academic achievement show that the United States trails in critical academic areas.

   I High school students in the United States are consistently outperformed by those from Asian and some European countries on international assessments of mathematics and science.

   I Many children are at risk for educational problems, school failure, and delinquency.

3. **Understand the hazards faced by children if they are truants or dropouts**

   I Every day, hundreds of thousands of youth are absent from school; many are absent without an excuse and deemed truant.

   I Truancy can lead to school failure and dropping out.

   I Dropout rates remain high but have been in decline.

   I Most dropouts say they left either because they did not like school or because they wanted to get a job.

   I Other risk factors include low academic achievement, poor problem-solving ability, low self-esteem, difficulty getting along with teachers, dissatisfaction with school, substance abuse, and being too old for their grade level.

   I Poverty and family dysfunction increase the chances of dropping out among all racial and ethnic groups.

   I Dropouts are more likely than graduates to have lived in single-parent families headed by parents who were educational underachievers themselves.

   I Some youths are pushed out of school because they lack attention or have poor attendance records.

   I Though the dropout rate has declined, it remains a significant social problem with consequences that extend into adulthood and beyond.

4. **Describe the association between school failure and delinquency**

   I Kids who do poorly in school are at risk for delinquent behavior.

   I School failure is a stronger predictor of delinquency than variables such as economic class membership, racial or ethnic background, or peer-group relations.

   I An association between academic failure and delinquency is commonly found among chronic offenders.

   I Academic failure reduces self-esteem, and reduced self-esteem is the actual cause of delinquency.

   I School failure and delinquency share a common cause.

5. **List the personal and social factors that have been related to school failure**

   I Some kids have personal problems that they bring with them to school.

   I School failure may also be linked to learning disabilities or reading disabilities that might actually be treatable if the proper resources were available.

   I There is evidence that boys who do poorly in school, regardless of their socioeconomic background, are more likely to be delinquent than those who perform well.

   I Most researchers have looked at academic tracking—dividing students into groups according to ability and achievement level—as a contributor to school failure.

   I The effects of school labels accumulate over time.

   I Using a tracking system keeps certain students from having any hope of achieving academic success, thereby causing lack of motivation, which may foster delinquent behavior.

   I Student alienation has also been identified as a link between school failure and delinquency.

   I Students who report they neither like school nor care about their teachers' opinions are more likely to exhibit delinquent behaviors.

   I Schools are getting larger because smaller school districts have been consolidated into multijurisdictional district schools.

   I Some students may be unable to see the relevance or significance of what they are taught in school.

   I Many students, particularly those from low-income families, believe that school has no payoff in terms of their future.

- College preparatory curriculum alienates some lower-class students.

6. Know about the nature and extent of school crime

- In its pioneering study of school crime, *Violent Schools–Safe Schools* (1977), the federal government found that there was a significant amount of delinquency in schools.
- Teachers are subject to threats and physical attacks from students and school intruders.
- About 10 percent of students report bringing weapons to school on a regular basis.
- Shooting incidents occur around the start of the school day, the lunch period, or the end of the school day.
- Most attacks are neither spontaneous nor impulsive. Shooters typically develop a plan of attack well in advance.
- Many of the shooters had a history of feeling extremely depressed or desperate because they had been picked on or bullied.

7. Discuss the factors that contribute to delinquency in schools

- Kids who feel isolated and alone with little parental attention may be the most prone to alienation and substance abuse.
- The level of student drinking and substance abuse may increase violent crime rates. Climate is one of the most important predictors of campus crime and violence.
- Violence is more prevalent in large schools as compared to smaller ones.
- Schools located in a city are more likely to experience criminal behaviors and violence than rural schools.
- The physical condition of the school building can influence students' motivation, attitude, and behavior.
- School crime is a function of the community in which the school is located.
- Schools experiencing crime and drug abuse are most likely to be found in socially disorganized neighborhoods.
- There is also evidence that crime in schools reflects the patterns of antisocial behavior that exist in the surrounding neighborhood.
- Perpetrators of school crime have been victims of delinquency themselves.

8. Be familiar with the efforts school systems are making to reduce crime on campus

- Schools around the country have mounted a campaign to reduce the incidence of delinquency on campus.
- Nearly all states have developed some sort of crime-free, weapon-free, or safe-school zone statute.

- A majority of schools have adopted a zero tolerance policy that mandates predetermined punishments for specific offenses.
- Almost every school attempts to restrict entry of dangerous persons by having visitors sign in before entering, and most close the campus for lunch.
- Most schools control access to school buildings by locking or monitoring doors.
- Schools use random metal detector checks and one or more security cameras to monitor the school.
- Schools who have experienced behavioral problems are now employing uniformed police officers on school grounds, typically called school resource officers.
- Some districts have gone so far as to infiltrate undercover detectives on school grounds.

9. Understand what is being done to improve school climate and increase educational standards

- Numerous organizations and groups have called for reforming the educational system to make it more responsive to the needs of students.
- The No Child Left Behind (NCLB) Act of 2001 (Public Law 107-110) authorizes federal programs aimed at improving America's primary and secondary schools.
- Students' awareness about the dangers of drug abuse and delinquency is being improved.
- Students are being trained in techniques to resist peer pressure.
- School management and disciplinary programs are being set up that deter crime, such as locker searches.

10. Be familiar with the legal rights of students

- The U.S. Supreme Court has sought to balance the civil liberties of students with the school's mandate to provide a safe environment.
- Educators can legally search students when there are reasonable grounds to believe the students have violated the law or broken school rules.
- The Supreme Court's decision in *Vernonia School District 47J v. Acton* expanded the power of educators to ensure safe learning environments through drug testing of student athletes
- In *Board of Education of Independent School District No. 92 of Pottawatomie County et al. v. Earls et al.*, the Court extended the right to test for drugs to all students.
- *Tinker v. Des Moines Independent Community School District* established (1) a child is entitled to free speech in school under the First Amendment of the U.S. Constitution, and (2) the test used to determine whether the child has gone beyond proper speech is whether he or she materially and substantially interferes with the requirements of appropriate discipline in the operation of the school.

- *Bethel School District No. 403 v. Fraser* upheld a school system's right to suspend or otherwise discipline a student who uses obscene or profane language and gestures.

- In *Hazelwood School District v. Kuhlmeier*, the Court ruled that the principal could censor articles in a student publication.

- In *Santa Fe Independent School District, Petitioner v. Jane*, the Court ruled that prayers led by an elected student undermine the protection of minority viewpoints.

- In *Good News Club v. Milford Central School*, the Supreme Court required an upstate New York school district to provide space for an after-school Bible club for elementary students.

- Most states have statutes permitting teachers to use corporal punishment to discipline students in public school systems.

- *Ingraham v. Wright* upheld the right of teachers to use corporal punishment.

- Today 24 states still use physical punishment in schools.

- *Baker v. Owen* requires that students at least be forewarned about the possibility of corporal punishment as a discipline.

- *Goss v. Lopez* determined that any time a student is to be suspended for up to a period of 10 days, he or she is entitled to a hearing.

Key Terms

academic achievement, p. 334
truant, p. 336
dropping out, p. 336
underachievers, p. 339

school failure, p. 341
tracking, p. 342
zero tolerance policy, p. 350

passive speech, p. 356
active speech, p. 358
in loco parentis, p. 360

Viewpoint

You are the principal of a suburban high school. It seems that one of your students, Steve Jones, has had a long-running feud with Mr. Metcalf, an English teacher whom he blames for unfairly giving him a low grade and for being too strict with other students. Steve set up a home-based website that posted insulting images of Metcalf and contained messages describing him in unflattering terms ("a slob who doesn't bathe often enough," for example). He posted a photo of the teacher with the caption "Public Enemy Number One." Word of the website has gotten around school, and although students think it's funny and "cool," the faculty is outraged. You bring Steve into your office and ask him to take down the site, explaining that its existence has had a negative effect on school discipline and morale. He refuses, arguing that the site is home-based and you have no right to ask for its removal. Besides, he claims, it is just in fun and not really hurting anyone.

School administrators are asked to make these kinds of decisions every day, and the wrong choice can prove costly. You are aware that a case very similar to this one resulted in a $30,000 settlement in a damage claim against a school system when the principal did suspend a student for posting an insulting website and the student later sued for violating his right to free speech.

- Would you suspend Steve if he refuses your request to take down the site?

- Would you allow him to leave it posted and try to placate Mr. Metcalf?

- What would you do if Mr. Metcalf had posted a site ridiculing students and making fun of their academic abilities?

Doing Research on the Web

There are a number of important resources for educational law on the Internet. Check out the Education Law Association site, the Educational Resource Information Center, and Edlaw via

academic.cengage.com/criminaljustice/siegel

Questions for Discussion

1. Was there a delinquency problem in your high school? If so, how was it dealt with?

2. Should disobedient youths be suspended from school? Does this solution hurt or help?

3. What can be done to improve the delinquency prevention capabilities of schools?

4. Is school failure responsible for delinquency, or are delinquents simply school failures?

Notes

1. Associated Press, "Details Emerge about Teen Held in Wisconsin Murder; Neighbor: Boy Charged in Principal's Death Bragged about Getting in Trouble," MSNBC Online, October 1, 2006, www.msnbc.msn.com/id/15060698/ (accessed October 22, 2007).

2. Kristin Eisenbraun, "Violence in Schools: Prevalence, Prediction, and Prevention," *Aggression and Violent Behavior* 12:459–469 (2007).

3. Roslyn Caldwell, Susan Sturges, and Clayton Silver, "Home versus School Environments and their Influences on the Affective and Behavioral States of African American, Hispanic, and Caucasian Juvenile Offenders," *Journal of Child and Family Studies* 16:119–132 (2007).

4. CNN, "Teacher Charged with Raping Student 28 Times," April 6, 2006, http://edition.cnn.com/2006/LAW/04/04/teacher.sex/ (accessed October 29, 2007).

5. Alexander Vazsonyi and Lloyd Pickering, "The Importance of Family and School Domains in Adolescent Deviance: African American and Caucasian Youth," *Journal of Youth and Adolescence* 32:115–129 (2003).

6. See, generally, Richard Lawrence, *School Crime and Juveniles* (New York: Oxford University Press, 1998).

7. U.S. Office of Education, *Digest of Educational Statistics* (Washington, DC: U.S. Government Printing Office, 1969), p. 25.

8. Kenneth Polk and Walter E. Schafer, eds., *Schools and Delinquency* (Englewood Cliffs, NJ: Prentice Hall, 1972), p. 13.

9. Gary LaFree and Richard Arum, "The Impact of Racially Inclusive Schooling on Adult Incarceration Rates among U.S. Cohorts of African Americans and Whites Since 1930," *Criminology* 44:73–103 (2006).

10. Andrea Livingston, *The Condition of Education 2006 in Brief* (Washington, DC: National Center for Education Statistics, 2006).

11. Lynn Karoly, M. Rebecca Kilburn, and Jill Cannon, *Early Childhood Interventions: Proven Results, Future Promise* (Santa Monica, CA: Rand Corporation, 2005).

12. Ibid.

13. Data in this section come from the National Center for Education Statistics, National Event Dropout Rates, http://nces.ed.gov/pubs2007/dropout05/ (accessed October 22, 2007).

14. Spencer Rathus, *Voyages in Childhood* (Belmont, CA: Wadsworth, 2004).

15. Sherman Dorn, *Creating the Dropout* (New York: Praeger, 1996).

16. Karoly, Kilburn, and Cannon, *Early Childhood Interventions: Proven Results, Future Promise*.

17. For reviews, see Bruce Wolford and LaDonna Koebel, "Kentucky Model for Youths at Risk," *Criminal Justice* 9:5–55 (1995); J. David Hawkins, Richard Catalano, Diane Morrison, Julie O'Donnell, Robert Abbott, and L. Edward Day, "The Seattle Social Development Project," in Joan McCord and Richard Tremblay, eds., *The Prevention of Antisocial Behavior in Children* (New York: Guilford Press, 1992), pp. 139–160.

18. Eugene Maguin and Rolf Loeber, "Academic Performance and Delinquency," in Michael Tonry, ed., *Crime and Justice: A Review of Research*, vol. 20 (Chicago: University of Chicago Press, 1995), pp. 145–264.

19. Terence Thornberry, Alan Lizotte, Marvin Krohn, Margaret Farnworth, and Sung Joon Jang, "Testing Interactional Theory: An Examination of Reciprocal Causal Relationships among Family, School, and Delinquency," *Journal of Criminal Law and Criminology* 82:3–35 (1991).

20. Carolyn Smith, Alan Lizotte, Terence Thornberry, and Marvin Krohn, "Resilience to Delinquency," *Prevention Researcher* 4:4–7 (1997); Matthew Zingraff, Jeffrey Leiter, Matthew Johnsen, and Kristen Myers, "The Mediating Effect of Good School Performance on the Maltreatment–Delinquency Relationship," *Journal of Research in Crime and Delinquency* 31:62–91 (1994).

21. Lyle Shannon, *Assessing the Relationship of Adult Criminal Careers to Juvenile Careers: A Summary* (Washington, DC: U.S. Government Printing Office, 1982).

22. Marvin Wolfgang, Robert Figlio, and Thorsten Sellin, *Delinquency in a Birth Cohort* (Chicago: University of Chicago Press, 1972).

23. Ibid., p. 94.

24. Caroline Wolf Harlow, *Education and Correctional Populations* (Washington, DC: Bureau of Justice Statistics, 2003).

25. Martin Gold, "School Experiences, Self-Esteem, and Delinquent Behavior: A Theory for Alternative Schools," *Crime and Delinquency* 24:294–295 (1978).

26. Paul Bellair and Thomas McNulty, "Beyond the Bell Curve: Community Disadvantage and the Explanation of Black-White Differences in Adolescent Violence," *Criminology* 43:1135–1168 (2005).

27. Michael Gottfredson and Travis Hirschi, *A General Theory of Crime* (Stanford, CA: Stanford University Press, 1990); J. D. McKinney, "Longitudinal Research on the Behavioral Characteristics of Children with Learning Disabilities," *Journal of Learning Disabilities* 22:141–150 (1990).

28. Richard Felson and Jeremy Staff, "Explaining the Academic Performance–Delinquency Relationship," *Criminology* 44:299–320 (2006).

29. John Shelley-Tremblay, Natalie O'Brien, and Jennifer Langhinrichsen-Rohling, "Reading Disability in Adjudicated Youth: Prevalence Rates, Current Models, Traditional and Innovative Treatments," *Aggression and Violent Behavior* 12:376–392 (2007).

30. Albert K. Cohen, *Delinquent Boys* (New York: Free Press, 1955); see also Kenneth Polk, Dean Frease, and F. Lynn Richmond, "Social Class, School Experience, and Delinquency," *Criminology* 12:84–95 (1974).

31. Jackson Toby, "Orientation to Education as a Factor in the School Maladjustment of Lower-Class Children," *Social Forces* 35:259–266 (1957).

32. John Paul Wright, Francis Cullen, and Nicolas Williams, "Working While in School and Delinquent Involvement: Implications for Social Policy," *Crime and Delinquency* 43:203–221 (1997).

33. Polk, Frease, and Richmond, "Social Class, School Experience, and Delinquency," p. 92.

34. Delos Kelly and Robert Balch, "Social Origins and School Failure," *Pacific Sociological Review* 14:413–430 (1971).

35. Lance Hannon, "Poverty, Delinquency, and Educational Attainment: Cumulative Disadvantage or Disadvantage Saturation?" *Sociological Inquiry* 73:575–595 (2003).

36. Jeannie Oakes, *Keeping Track: How Schools Structure Inequality* (New Haven, CT: Yale University Press, 1985), p. 48.

37. Delos Kelly, *Creating School Failure, Youth Crime, and Deviance* (Los Angeles: Trident Shop, 1982), p. 11.

38. Travis Hirschi, *Causes of Delinquency* (Berkeley: University of California Press, 1969), pp. 113–124, 132.

39. *Learning into the 21st Century, Report of Forum 5* (Washington, DC: White House Conference on Children, 1970).

40. Jane Sprott, Jennifer Jenkins, and Anthony Doob, "The Importance of School: Protecting At-Risk Youth from Early Offending," *Youth Violence and Juvenile Justice* 3:59–77 (2005); Patricia Jenkins, "School Delinquency and the School Social Bond," *Journal of Research in Crime and Delinquency* 34:337–367 (1997).

41. Richard Lawrence, "Parents, Peers, School and Delinquency," paper presented at the annual meeting of the American Society of Criminology, Boston, November 1995.

42. Gary Gottfredson, Denise Gottfredson, Allison Payne, and Nisha Gottfredson, "School Climate Predictors of School Disorder: Results from a National Study of Delinquency Prevention in Schools," *Journal of Research in Crime and Delinquency* 42:412–444 (2005).

43. National Institute of Education, U.S. Department of Health, Education and Welfare, *Violent Schools–Safe Schools: The Safe Schools Study Report to the Congress*, vol. 1 (Washington, DC: U.S. Government Printing Office, 1977).

44. Data in these sections provided by National Center for Education Statistics, *Indicators of School Crime and Safety, 2006*, http://nces.ed.gov/programs/crimeindicators/ind_02.asp (accessed July 20, 2007).

45. Ibid.

46. Ben Brown and William Reed Benedict, "Bullets, Blades, and Being Afraid in Hispanic High Schools: An Exploratory Study of the Presence of Weapons and Fear of Weapon-Associated Victimization among High School Students in a Border Town," *Crime and Delinquency* 50:372–395 (2004).

47. Christine Kerres Malecki and Michelle Kilpatrick Demaray, "Carrying a Weapon to School and Perceptions of Social Support in an Urban Middle School," *Journal of Emotional and Behavioral Disorders* 11:169–178 (2003).

48. Pamela Wilcox and Richard Clayton, "A Multilevel Analysis of School-Based Weapon Possession," *Justice Quarterly* 18:509–542 (2001).

49. Mark Anderson, Joanne Kaufman, Thomas Simon, Lisa Barrios, Len Paulozzi, George Ryan, Rodney Hammond, William Modzeleski, Thomas Feucht, Lloyd Potter, and the School-Associated Violent Deaths Study Group, "School-Associated Violent Deaths in the United States, 1994–1999," *Journal of the American Medical Association* 286:2695–2702 (2001).

50. Bryan Vossekuil, Marisa Reddy, Robert Fein, Randy Borum, and William Modzeleski, *Safe School Initiative: An Interim Report on the Prevention of Targeted Violence in Schools* (Washington, DC: United States Secret Service, 2000).

51. Nancy Weishew and Samuel Peng, "Variables Predicting Students' Problem Behaviors," *Journal of Educational Research* 87:5–17 (1993).

52. Lisa Hutchinson Wallace and David May, "The Impact of Parental Attachment and Feelings of Isolation on Adolescent Fear of Crime at School," *Adolescence* 40:457–474 (2005).

53. Robert Brewer and Monica Swahn, "Binge Drinking and Violence," *JAMA: Journal of the American Medical Association* 294:16–20 (2005).

54. Tomika Stevens, Kenneth Ruggiero, Dean Kilpatrick, Heidi Resnick, and Benjamin Saunders, "Variables Differentiating Singly and Multiply Victimized Youth: Results from the National Survey of Adolescents and Implications for Secondary Prevention," *Child Maltreatment* 10:211–223 (2005); James Collins and Pamela Messerschmidt, "Epidemiology of Alcohol-Related Violence," *Alcohol Health and Research World* 17:93–100 (1993).

55. Rami Benbenishty and Ron Avi Astor, *School Violence in Context: Culture, Neighborhood, Family, School and Gender* (New York: Oxford University Press, 2005).

56. Eisenbraun, "Violence in Schools: Prevalence, Prediction, and Prevention."

57. James Q. Wilson, "Crime in Society and Schools," in J. M. McPartland and E. L. McDill, eds., *Violence in Schools: Perspective, Programs and Positions* (Lexington, MA: D.C. Heath, 1977), p. 48.

58. Gary Gottfredson and Denise Gottfredson, *Victimization in Schools* (New York: Plenum Press, 1985), p. 18.

59. Daryl Hellman and Susan Beaton, "The Pattern of Violence in Urban Public Schools: The Influence of School and Community," *Journal of Research in Crime and Delinquency* 23:102–127 (1986).

60. Nancy Weishew and Samuel Peng, "Variables Predicting Students' Problem Behaviors," *Journal of Educational Research* 87:5–17 (1993).

61. Wayne Welsh, Robert Stokes, and Jack Greene, "A Macro-Level Model of School Disorder," *Journal of Research in Crime and Delinquency* 37:243–283 (2000).

62. Peter Lindstrom, "Patterns of School Crime: A Replication and Empirical Extension," *British Journal of Criminology* 37:121–131 (1997).

63. Richard Lawrence, *School Crime and Juvenile Justice* (New York: Oxford University Press, 1998).

64. Wayne Welsh, Robert Stokes, and Jack Greene, "A Macro-Level Model of School Disorder," p. 270.

65. Joan McDermott, "Crime in the School and in the Community: Offenders, Victims, and Fearful Youth," *Crime and Delinquency* 29:270–283 (1983).

66. Ibid.

67. June L. Arnette and Marjorie C. Walsleben, *Combating Fear and Restoring Safety in Schools* (Washington, DC: Office of Juvenile Justice and Delinquency Prevention, 1998).

68. Sheila Heaviside, Cassandra Rowand, Catrina Williams, Elizabeth Burns, Shelley Burns, and Edith McArthur, *Violence and Discipline Problems in U.S. Public Schools: 1996–97* (Washington, DC: United States Government Printing Office, 1998).

69. Crystal A. Garcia, "School Safety Technology in America: Current Use and Perceived Effectiveness," *Criminal Justice Policy Review* 14:30–54 (2003).

70. Mike Kennedy, "Fighting Crime by Design," *American School and University* 73:46–47 (2001).

71. National Center for Education Statistics, *Indicators of School Crime and Safety 2006*, http://nces.ed.gov/programs/crimeindicators/ (accessed October 22, 2007).

72. Robyn Colman and Adrian Colman, "School Crime," *Youth Studies Australia* 23:6–7 (2004).

73. The United States Conference of Mayors, *Best Practices of Community Policing in Gang Intervention and Gang Violence Prevention: Village of Hempstead*, www.usmayors.org/uscm/best_practices/community_policing_2006/gangBP_2006.pdf (accessed October 22, 2007).

74. Bruce Jacobs, "Anticipatory Undercover Targeting in High Schools," *Journal of Criminal Justice* 22:445–457 (1994).

75. Darcia Harris Bowman, "Curbing Crime," *Education Week* 23:30 (2004).

76. Stuart Tremlow, "Preventing Violence in Schools," *Psychiatric Times* 21:61–65 (2004).

77. Allison Ann Payne, Denise Gottfredson, and Gary Gottfredson, "Schools as Communities: The Relationships among Communal School Organization, Student Bonding, and School Disorder," *Criminology* 41:749–777 (2003).

78. Hellman and Beaton, "The Pattern of Violence in Urban Public Schools," pp. 122–123.

79. Julius Menacker, Ward Weldon, and Emanuel Hurwitz, "Community Influences on School Crime and Violence," *Urban Education* 25:68–80 (1990).

80. Wendy Mansfield and Elizabeth Farris, *Public School Principal Survey on Safe, Disciplined, and Drug-Free Schools. Contractor Report. E.D. TABS* (Washington, DC: U.S. Government Printing Office, Superintendent of Documents, 1992), p. iii.

81. Glenn Cook, "Education Debates Return to the Headlines as Midterms Near," *American School Board Journal* 193:6–7 (2006).

82. Stuart Yeh, "Reforming Federal Testing Policy to Support Teaching and Learning." *Educational Policy* 20:495–524 (2006).

83. Douglas Breunlin, Rocco Cimmarusti, Joshua Hetherington, and Jayne Kinsman, "Making the Smart Choice: A Systemic Response to School-Based Violence," *Journal of Family Therapy* 28:246–266 (2006).

84. "When School Is Out," *The Future of Children*, vol. 9 (Los Altos, CA: David and Lucile Packard Foundation, Fall 1999).

85. *New Jersey v. T.L.O.*, 469 U.S. 325, 105 S.Ct. 733 (1985).

86. *People v. Overton*, 24 N.Y.2d 522, 301 N.Y.S.2d 479, 249 N.E.2d 366 (1969); Brenda Walts, "*New Jersey v. T.L.O.*: Questions the Court Did Not Answer about School Searches," *Law and Education Journal* 14:421 (1985).

87. *Vernonia School District 47J v. Acton*, 115 S.Ct. 2394 (1995); Bernard James and Jonathan Pyatt, "Supreme Court Extends School's Authority to Search," *National School Safety Center News Journal* 26:29 (1995).

88. Michael Medaris, *A Guide to the Family Educational Rights and Privacy Act* (Washington, DC: Office of Juvenile Justice and Delinquency Prevention, 1998).

89. Ibid.

90. 393 U.S. 503, 89 S.Ct. 733 (1969).

91. Ibid., p. 741.

92. *Bethel School District No. 403 v. Fraser*, 478 U.S. 675, 106 S.Ct. 3159, 92 L.Ed.2d 549 (1986).

93. *Hazelwood School District v. Kuhlmeier*, 484 U.S. 260, 108 S.Ct. 562, 98 L.Ed.2d 592 (1988).

94. Terry McManus, "Home Web Sites Thrust Students into Censorship Disputes," *New York Times*, 13 August 1998, p. E9.

95. *Santa Fe Independent School District, Petitioner v. Jane Doe*, individually and as next friend for her minor children, Jane and John Doe, et al., No. 99-62 (June 19, 2000).

96. *Good News Club et al. v. Milford Central School* No. 99-2036 (2001).

97. Va. Code Ann. S 22.1-203 (Michie 2000).

98. *Brown v. Gilmore*, 01-384 (case heard on October 29, 2001).

99. *Elk Grove Unified School District v. Newdow*, No. 02-1624 (2004).

100. Ibid.

101. 423 U.S. 907, 96 S.Ct. 210, 46 L.Ed.2d 137 (1975).

102. 430 U.S. 651, 97 S.Ct. 1401 (1977).

103. 419 U.S. 565, 95 S.Ct. 729 (1976).

Drug Use and Delinquency

11

Chapter Outline

Chapter Objectives

1. Know which drugs are most frequently abused by American youth

2. Understand the extent of the drug problem among American youth today

3. Be able to discuss how teenage drug use in this country has changed over time

4. Know the main explanations for why youths take drugs

5. Recognize the different behavior patterns of drug-involved youths

6. Understand the relationship between drug use and delinquency

7. Be familiar with the major drug-control strategies

8. Be able to argue the pros and cons of government use of different drug-control strategies

On her way home from high school, after celebrating the last day of classes by drinking alcohol and smoking marijuana with friends, Carla Wagner lost control of her car and hit Helen Marie Witty, age 16. Helen Marie was rollerblading on the sidewalk. The impact of the collision instantly killed the young victim. Wagner was convicted of manslaughter while driving under the influence and was sentenced to six years at a women's prison in Florida. As part of her sentence she is required to speak to high school students about the dangers of drinking and driving and the lifelong consequences that this criminal action can cause to victims and their families, as well as offenders. The victim's parents, Helen and John Witty, also speak to the same high school students to tell the story of their tragic loss. These educational campaigns have become more widespread in recent years, along with teen-focused antidrug workshops, which help youths learn more about what works and how they can play a role in preventing drug use in the community.

substance abuse
Using drugs or alcohol in such a way as to cause physical, emotional and/or psychological harm to yourself.

The Lindesmith Center is one of the leading independent drug policy institutes in the United States. View its website via academic.cengage.com/ criminaljustice/siegel.

T here is little question that adolescent substance abuse and its association with delinquency are vexing problems. Almost every town, village, and city in the United States has confronted some type of teenage substance abuse problem. Self-report surveys indicate that just under half of high school seniors have tried drugs and almost three-quarters have used alcohol.[1] Adolescents at high risk for drug abuse often come from the most impoverished communities and experience a multitude of problems, including school failure and family conflict.[2] Equally troubling is the association between drug use and crime.[3] Research indicates that between 5 and 8 percent of all juvenile male arrestees in some cities test positive for cocaine.[4] Self-report surveys show that drug abusers are more likely to become delinquents than are nonabusers.[5] The pattern of drug use and crime makes teenage substance abuse a key national concern.

This chapter addresses some important issues involving teenage substance abuse, beginning with a review of the kinds of drugs children and adolescents are using and how often they are using them. Then we discuss who uses drugs and what causes substance abuse. After describing the association between drug abuse and delinquent behavior, the chapter concludes with a review of efforts to control the use of drugs in the United States.

FREQUENTLY ABUSED DRUGS

A wide variety of substances referred to as "drugs" are used by teenagers. Some are addicting, others not. Some create hallucinations, others cause a depressed stupor, and a few give an immediate uplift. This section identifies the most widely used substances and discusses their effects. All of these drugs can be abused, and because of the danger they present, many have been banned from private use. Others are available legally only with a physician's supervision, and a few are available to adults but prohibited for children.

Marijuana and Hashish

hashish
A concentrated form of cannabis made from unadulterated resin from the female cannabis plant.

marijuana
The dried leaves of the cannabis plant.

Commonly called "pot" or "grass," marijuana is produced from the leaves of *Cannabis sativa*. **Hashish** (hash) is a concentrated form of cannabis made from unadulterated resin from the female plant. The main active ingredient in both marijuana and hashish is tetrahydrocannabinol (THC), a mild hallucinogen. **Marijuana** is the drug most commonly used by teenagers.

Smoking large amounts of pot or hash can cause distortions in auditory and visual perception, even producing hallucinatory effects. Small doses produce an early excitement ("high") that gives way to drowsiness. Pot use is also related to decreased activity, overestimation of time and space, and increased food consumption. When the user is alone, marijuana produces a dreamy state. In a group, users become giddy and lose perspective.

Marijuana is not physically addicting, but its long-term effects have been the subject of much debate. During the 1970s, it was reported that smoking pot caused a variety of physical and mental problems, including brain damage and mental illness. Although the dangers of pot and hash may have been overstated, use of these drugs does present some health risks, including an increased risk of lung cancer, chronic bronchitis, and other diseases. Marijuana smoking should be avoided by prospective parents because it lowers sperm count in male users, and females experience disrupted ovulation and a greater chance of miscarriage.[6]

Cocaine

cocaine
A powerful natural stimulant derived from the coca plant.

Cocaine is an alkaloid derivative of the coca plant. When first isolated in 1860, it was considered a medicinal breakthrough that could relieve fatigue, depression, and other symptoms, and it quickly became a staple of patent medicines. When its addictive qualities and dangerous side effects became apparent, its use was controlled by the Pure Food and Drug Act of 1906.

Cocaine is the most powerful natural stimulant. Its use produces euphoria, restlessness, and excitement. Overdoses can cause delirium, violent manic behavior, and possible respiratory failure. The drug can be sniffed, or "snorted," into the nostrils, or it can be injected. The immediate feeling of euphoria, or "rush," is short-lived, and heavy users may snort coke as often as every 10 minutes. Another dangerous practice is "speedballing"—injecting a mixture of cocaine and heroin.

crack
A highly addictive crystalline form of cocaine containing remnants of hydrochloride and sodium bicarbonate, which emits a crackling sound when smoked.

Crack is processed street cocaine. Its manufacture involves using ammonia or baking soda (sodium bicarbonate) to remove the hydrochlorides and create a crystalline form of cocaine that can be smoked. In fact, crack gets its name from the fact that the sodium bicarbonate often emits a crackling sound when the substance is smoked. Also referred to as "rock," "gravel," and "roxanne," crack gained popularity in the mid-1980s.

It is relatively inexpensive, can provide a powerful high, and is highly addictive psychologically. Crack cocaine use has been in decline in recent years. Heavy criminal penalties, tight enforcement, and social disapproval have helped to lower crack use.

Heroin

Narcotic drugs have the ability to produce insensibility to pain and to free the mind of anxiety and emotion. Users experience relief from fear and apprehension, release of tension, and elevation of spirits. This short period of euphoria is followed by a period of apathy, during which users become drowsy and may nod off. Heroin, the most commonly used narcotic in the United States, is produced from opium, a drug derived from the opium poppy flower. Dealers cut the drug with neutral substances (sugar or lactose), and street heroin is often only 1 to 4 percent pure.

Heroin is probably the most dangerous commonly used drug. Users rapidly build up a tolerance for it, fueling the need for increased doses to obtain the desired effect. At first heroin is usually sniffed or snorted; as tolerance builds, it is "skin popped" (shot into skin, but not into a vein), and finally it is injected into a vein, or "mainlined."[7] Through this progressive use, the user becomes an addict—a person with an overpowering physical and psychological need to continue taking a particular substance by any means possible. If addicts cannot get enough heroin to satisfy their habit, they will suffer withdrawal symptoms, which include irritability, depression, extreme nervousness, and nausea.

Alcohol

The drug of choice for most teenagers continues to be alcohol. Two-thirds of high school seniors reported using alcohol in the past year, and almost three-quarters (73 percent) say they have tried it at some time during their lifetime; by the 12th grade 56 percent of American youth report that they have "been drunk."[8] More than 20 million Americans are estimated to be problem drinkers, and at least half of these are alcoholics.

Alcohol may be a factor in nearly half of all murders, suicides, and accidental deaths.[9] Alcohol-related deaths number 100,000 a year, far more than all other illegal drugs combined. Just under 1.4 million drivers are arrested each year for driving under the influence (including 13,000 teens), and around 1.2 million more are arrested for other alcohol-related violations.[10] The economic cost is staggering. An estimated $185 billion is lost each year, including $36 billion from premature deaths, $88 billion in reduced work effort, and $19 billion arising from short- and long-term medical problems.[11]

Considering these problems, why do so many youths drink to excess? Youths who use alcohol report that it reduces tension, enhances pleasure, improves social skills, and transforms experiences for the better.[12] Although these reactions may result from limited use of alcohol, alcohol in higher doses acts as a depressant. Long-term use has been linked with depression and physical ailments ranging from heart disease to cirrhosis of the liver. Many teens also think drinking stirs their romantic urges, but scientific evidence indicates that alcohol decreases sexual response.[13]

Other Drug Categories

Other drug categories include anesthetic drugs, inhalants, sedatives and barbiturates, tranquilizers, hallucinogens, stimulants, steroids, designer drugs, and cigarettes.

Anesthetic Drugs Anesthetic drugs are central nervous system (CNS) depressants. Local anesthetics block nervous system transmissions; general anesthetics act on the brain to produce loss of sensation, stupor, or unconsciousness. The most widely abused anesthetic drug is phencyclidine (PCP), known as "angel dust." Angel dust can be sprayed on marijuana or other leaves and smoked, drunk, or injected. Originally

© Jupiterimages/BananaStock/Alamy

developed as an animal tranquilizer, PCP creates hallucinations and a spaced-out feeling that causes heavy users to engage in violent acts. The effects of PCP can last up to two days, and the danger of overdose is high.

Inhalants Some youths inhale vapors from lighter fluid, paint thinner, cleaning fluid, or model airplane glue to reach a drowsy, dizzy state that is sometimes accompanied by hallucinations. **Inhalants** produce a short-term euphoria followed by a period of disorientation, slurred speech, and drowsiness. Amyl nitrite ("poppers") is a commonly used volatile liquid packaged in capsule form, which is inhaled when the capsule is broken open.

inhalants
Volatile liquids that give off a vapor, which is inhaled, producing short-term excitement and euphoria followed by a period of disorientation.

Sedatives and Barbiturates **Sedatives**, the most commonly used drugs of the barbiturate family, depress the central nervous system into a sleeplike condition. On the illegal market, sedatives are called "goofballs" or "downers" and are often known by the color of the capsules: "reds" (Seconal), "blue devils" (Amytal), and "rainbows" (Tuinal).

sedatives
Drugs of the barbiturate family that depress the central nervous system into a sleeplike condition.

Sedatives can be prescribed by doctors as sleeping pills. Illegal users employ them to create relaxed, sociable feelings; overdoses can cause irritability, repellent behavior, and unconsciousness. Barbiturates are the major cause of drug-overdose deaths.

Tranquilizers **Tranquilizers** reduce anxiety and promote relaxation. Legally prescribed tranquilizers, such as Ampazine, Thorazine, Pacatal, and Sparine, were originally designed to control the behavior of people suffering from psychoses, aggressiveness, and agitation. Less powerful tranquilizers, such as Valium, Librium, Miltown, and Equanil, are used to combat anxiety, tension, fast heart rate, and headaches. The use of illegally obtained tranquilizers can lead to addiction, and withdrawal can be painful and hazardous.

tranquilizers
Drugs that reduce anxiety and promote relaxation.

Hallucinogens **Hallucinogens**, either natural or synthetic, produce vivid distortions of the senses without greatly disturbing the viewer's consciousness. Some produce hallucinations, and others cause psychotic behavior in otherwise normal people.

hallucinogens
Natural or synthetic substances that produce vivid distortions of the senses without greatly disturbing consciousness.

One common hallucinogen is mescaline, named after the Mescalero Apaches, who first discovered its potent effect. Mescaline occurs naturally in peyote, a small cactus that grows in Mexico and the southwestern United States. After initial discomfort, mescaline produces vivid hallucinations and out-of-body sensations.

A second group of hallucinogens are synthetic alkaloid compounds. These can be transformed into lysergic acid diethylamide, commonly called LSD. This powerful substance stimulates cerebral sensory centers to produce visual hallucinations, intensify hearing, and increase sensitivity. Users often report a scrambling of sensations; they may "hear colors" and "smell music." Users also report feeling euphoric and mentally superior, although to an observer they appear disoriented. Anxiety and panic may occur, and overdoses can produce psychotic episodes, flashbacks, and even death.

stimulants
Synthetic substances that produce an intense physical reaction by stimulating the central nervous system.

Stimulants Stimulants ("uppers," "speed," "pep pills," "crystal") are synthetic drugs that stimulate action in the central nervous system. They produce increased blood pressure, breathing rate, and bodily activity, and mood elevation. One widely used amphetamine produces psychological effects such as increased confidence, euphoria, impulsive behavior, and loss of appetite. Commonly used stimulants include Benzedrine ("bennies"), Dexedrine ("dex"), Dexamyl, Bephetamine ("whites"), and Methedrine ("meth," "speed," "crystal meth"). Methedrine is probably the most widely used and most dangerous amphetamine. Some people swallow it; heavy users inject it. Long-term heavy use can result in exhaustion, anxiety, prolonged depression, and hallucinations.

A more recent form of methamphetamine is a crystallized substance with the street name of "ice" or "crystal." Ice methamphetamine looks similar to shards of ice or chunks of rock salt and is highly pure and extremely addictive.[14] Smoking this ice or crystal causes weight loss, kidney damage, heart and respiratory problems, and paranoia.[15]

Methamphetamine in general, whether in its three main forms of powder, ice, or tablets, have become an increasingly important priority of United States law enforcement authorities. Although its use among secondary school students has shown a downward trend in the eight years it has been investigated (1999 to 2006),[16] authorities are concerned because it has spread from its origins in the rural West to other parts of the country and into urban and suburban areas. According to the U.S. Department of Justice's National Drug Intelligence Center, methamphetamine availability is highest in the Pacific Region, followed by the West, Southwest, Southeast, Midwest, and Northeast Regions.[17] Other problems arise from the majority of it being produced domestically, either in "Mom and Pop" laboratories or superlabs, which are mostly found in the Central Valley and southern areas of California. It can be made with many household products that are difficult or not feasible to regulate, and its production presents many dangers to people and the environment.[18] A number of states, such as Oklahoma and Iowa, have banned over-the-counter cold medicines like Sudafed that contain pseudoephedrine, an essential ingredient of methamphetamines, making them only available by prescription.[19]

anabolic steroids
Drugs used by athletes and bodybuilders to gain muscle bulk and strength.

Steroids Teenagers use highly dangerous anabolic steroids to gain muscle bulk and strength.[20] Black-market sales of these drugs approach $1 billion annually. Although not physically addicting, steroids can become an "obsession" among teens who desire athletic success. Long-term users may spend up to $400 a week on steroids and may support their habit by dealing the drug.

Steroids are dangerous because of the health problems associated with their long-term use: liver ailments, tumors, kidney problems, sexual dysfunction, hypertension, and mental problems such as depression. Steroid use runs in cycles, and other drugs—Clomid, Teslac, and Halotestin, for example—that carry their own dangerous side effects are often used to curb the need for high dosages of steroids. Finally, steroid users often share needles, which puts them at high risk for contracting HIV, the virus that causes AIDS.

designer drugs
Lab-made drugs designed to
avoid existing drug laws.

Designer Drugs Designer drugs are lab-created synthetics that are designed to get around existing drug laws, at least temporarily. The most widely used designer drug is "ecstasy," which is derived from speed and methamphetamine. After being swallowed, snorted, injected, or smoked, it acts simultaneously as a stimulant and a hallucinogen, producing mood swings, disturbing sleeping and eating habits, altering thinking processes, creating aggressive behavior, interfering with sexual function, and affecting sensitivity to pain. The drug can also increase blood pressure and heart rate. Teenage users taking ecstasy at raves have died from heat stroke because the drug can cause dehydration.

Cigarettes Many countries around the world have established laws to prohibit the sale of cigarettes to minors. The reality, however, is that in many countries children and adolescents have easy access to tobacco products.[21] In the United States, the Synar Amendment, enacted in 1992, requires states to enact and enforce laws restricting the sale of tobacco products to youths under the age of 18. States are required to reduce illegal sales rates to minors to no more than 20 percent within several years. The FDA rules require age verification for anyone under the age of 27 who is purchasing tobacco products. The FDA has also banned cigarette vending machines and self-service displays except in adult-only facilities. The signing of the Master Tobacco Settlement Agreement between 46 states and the tobacco industry in 1998 placed further restrictions on the advertising and marketing of cigarettes to young people and allocated substantial sums to antismoking campaigns.[22] Some efforts to enforce compliance with these restrictions and educate tobacco retailers about the new laws have produced promising results.[23] Despite all of these measures, almost one out of every two high school seniors in America (47 percent) report having smoked cigarettes over their lifetime. However, in recent years cigarette use by high school students has been on the decline.[24]

TRENDS IN TEENAGE DRUG USE

Has America's decades-long War on Drugs paid off? Has drug use declined, or is it on the upswing? A number of national surveys conduct annual reviews of teen drug use by interviewing samples of teens around the nation. What do national surveys tell us about the extent of drug use, and what have been the recent trends in teen usage?

The Monitoring the Future (MTF) Survey

One of the most important and influential surveys of teen substance abuse is the annual Monitoring the Future survey conducted by the Institute for Social Research at the University of Michigan. In all, about 45,000 students located in 433 secondary schools participate in the study.

The most recent MTF survey in 2006 indicates that, with a few exceptions, drug use among American adolescents continued to decline from the peak levels reached in 1996 and 1997. Annual drug use was down by more than one-third (37 percent) for 8th-graders during this time period, while reductions have been somewhat lower for those in the 10th (25 percent) and 12th (14 percent) grades.[25] As Figure 11.1 shows, drug use peaked in the late 1970s and early 1980s and then began a decade-long decline until showing an uptick in the mid-1990s; usage for most drugs has been stable or in decline since then. Especially encouraging has been a significant drop in the use of alcohol by the youngest kids in the survey—a 13 percent drop in annual rates in the last five years (from 38.7 percent in 2002 to 33.6 percent in 2006) and a 26 percent drop in the last 10 years (from 45.5 percent in 1997). There has also been a continuing decline in cigarette smoking, as well as the use of smokeless tobacco products. More troubling is the use of ecstasy, which, because of its popularity at dance clubs and raves, rose among older teens (10th- and 12th-graders) for much of the late 1990s and up to 2001, but has

Percent

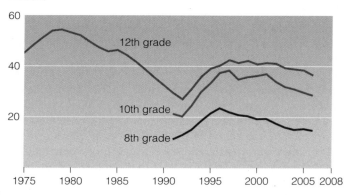

FIGURE 11.1

Trends in Annual Prevalence of an Illicit Drug Use Index

SOURCE: Lloyd D. Johnston, Patrick M. O'Malley, Jerald G. Bachman, and John E. Schulenberg, *Teen Drug Use Continues Down in 2006, Particularly Among Older Teens; But Use of Prescription-Type Drugs Remains High* (Ann Arbor, MI: University of Michigan News and Information Services, December 21, 2006), table 2.

since dropped sharply. In 2006, less than 3 percent (2.8 percent) of 10th-graders reported some use of ecstasy during the previous 12 months (down from 4.9 percent in 2002); 4.1 percent of the 12th-graders also reported some use (down from 7.4 percent in 2002). On the other hand, study authors drew particular attention to the relatively high usage rates of prescription-type drugs such as narcotics, tranquilizers, and sedatives. Annual use of OxyContin, a prescription painkiller narcotic, was down for the first time in the last five years among 12th-graders (from 5.5 percent in 2005 to 4.3 percent in 2006), but reached its highest level among younger students: 2.6 percent for 8th-graders and 3.8 percent for 10th-graders.[26] This may be part of a larger trend in the abuse of prescription drugs on the part of youths and young adults.[27]

The PRIDE Survey

A second source of information on teen drug and alcohol abuse is the National Parents' Resource Institute for Drug Education (PRIDE) survey, which is also conducted annually.[28] Typically, findings from the PRIDE survey correlate highly with the MTF drug survey. The most recent PRIDE survey (for the 2004–05 school year) indicates little to no change in drug activity over the previous school year, but substantial decreases over the last 10 years. For example, just over 22 percent of students in grades 6 to 12 claimed to have used drugs during the past year, down from about 30 percent in the 1995–96 school year (see Table 11.1). Cigarette smoking and alcohol use are also down from 10 years ago. The fact that two surveys generate roughly the same pattern in drug abuse helps bolster their validity and give support to a decline in teenage substance abuse.

The National Survey on Drug Use and Health

Sponsored by the U.S. Department of Health and Human Services' Substance Abuse and Mental Health Services Administration, the National Survey on Drug Use and Health (NSDUH, formerly called the National Household Survey on Drug Abuse) interviews approximately 70,000 people at home each year.[29] Like the MTF and PRIDE surveys, the latest NSDUH survey shows that drug and alcohol use, although still a problem, has stabilized or declined.

Although overall illicit drug use by youth aged 12 to 17 has declined somewhat in recent years (a significant 8.6 percent reduction between 2002 and 2004),[30] it still remains a significant problem. For example, *heavy drinking* (defined as having five or more alcoholic drinks on the same occasion on at least five different days in the past 30 days) was reported by about 7 percent of the population aged 12 and older, or just

TABLE 11.1

Drug Use, 1995–96 Versus 2004–05, Grades 6–12

	1995–96 (%)	2004–05 (%)	Rate of Decrease (%)
Cigarettes	40.5	24.3	40.0
Any alcohol	58.8	47.2	19.7
Any illicit drug	29.5	22.3	24.4

SOURCE: PRIDE Surveys, *PRIDE Questionnaire Report for Grades 6 thru 12: 2004–05 National Summary* (Bowling Green, KY: Author, August 17, 2006), tables 2.9, 2.10.

under 17 million people. Among youths aged 12 to 17, about 3 percent were heavy drinkers and 11 percent engaged in *binge drinking*, defined as having five or more alcoholic beverages on the same occasion at least once in the past 30 days.[31]

The latest NSDUH results also showed that—for the first time in the survey's decades-long history—overall illicit drug use in the past month by adolescent girls was identical to that of adolescent boys (10.6 percent for both). Girls continued to have a higher rate than boys in the misuse of prescription drugs when asked about lifetime (14.4 percent versus 12.5 percent), past year (10.1 percent versus 7.6 percent), and past month (4.1 percent versus 3.2 percent) usage.[32] The survey also found that adolescent girls are closing the gap with their male counterparts in terms of usage of marijuana, alcohol, and cigarettes. In each of the last three years (2002 to 2004), more girls than boys started using marijuana, and in the latest survey more girls than boys started using alcohol (1.5 million compared to 1.3 million) and cigarettes (730,000 compared to 565,000). Some of this might be explained by teen girls having higher rates of depression and anxiety and greater concerns about weight and appearance and being more susceptible to pressure from friends when it comes to drinking.[33]

Are the Survey Results Accurate?

Student drug surveys must be interpreted with caution. First, it may be overly optimistic to expect that heavy users are going to cooperate with a drug-use survey, especially one conducted by a government agency. Even if willing, these students are likely to be absent from school during testing periods. Also, drug abusers are more likely to be forgetful and to give inaccurate accounts of their substance abuse.

Another problem is the likelihood that the most drug-dependent portion of the adolescent population is omitted from the sample. In some cities, almost half of all youths arrested dropped out of school before the 12th grade, and more than half of these arrestees are drug users.[34] Juvenile detainees (those arrested and held in a lockup) test positively for cocaine at a rate many times higher than those reporting recent use in the MTF and PRIDE surveys.[35] The inclusion of eighth-graders in the MTF sample is one way of getting around the dropout problem. Nonetheless, high school surveys may be excluding some of the most drug-prone young people in the population.

There is evidence that the accuracy of reporting may be affected by social and personal traits: Girls are more willing than boys to admit taking drugs; kids from two-parent homes are less willing to admit taking drugs than kids growing up in single-parent homes. Julia Yun Soo Kim, Michael Fendrich, and Joseph Wislar speculate that it is culturally unacceptable for some subgroups in the population, such as Hispanic females, to use drugs, and therefore, in self-report surveys, they may underrepresent their involvement.[36]

Although these problems are serious, they are consistent over time and therefore do not hinder the *measurement of change* or trends in drug usage. That is, prior surveys also omitted dropouts and other high-risk individuals and were biased because of cultural issues. However, because these problems are built into every wave of the surveys, any change recorded in the annual substance abuse rate is probably genuine. So, although the validity of these surveys may be questioned, they are probably reliable indicators of trends in substance abuse.

WHY DO YOUTHS TAKE DRUGS?

Why do youths engage in an activity that is sure to bring them overwhelming problems? It is hard to imagine that even the youngest drug users are unaware of the problems associated with substance abuse. Although it is easy to understand dealers' desires for quick profits, how can we explain users' disregard for long- and short-term consequences? Concept Summary 11.1 reviews some of the most likely reasons.

Concept Summary 11.1

Key Reasons Why Youths Take Drugs

Social Disorganization	Poverty; growing up in disorganized urban environment
Peer Pressure	Associating with youths who take drugs
Family Factors	Poor family life, including harsh punishment, neglect
Genetic Factors	Parents abuse drugs
Emotional Problems	Feelings of inadequacy; blame others for failures
Problem Behavior Syndrome	Drug use is one of many problem behaviors
Rational Choice	Perceived benefits, including relaxation, greater creativity

Social Disorganization

One explanation ties drug abuse to poverty, social disorganization, and hopelessness. Drug use by young minority group members has been tied to factors such as racial prejudice, low self-esteem, poor socioeconomic status, and the stress of living in a harsh urban environment.[37] The association among drug use, race, and poverty has been linked to the high level of mistrust and defiance found in lower socioeconomic areas.[38] Despite the long-documented association between social disorganization and drug use, the empirical data on the relationship between class and crime has been inconclusive. For example, the National Youth Survey (NYS), a longitudinal study of delinquent behavior conducted by Delbert Elliott and his associates, found little if any association between drug use and social class. The NYS found that drug use is higher among urban youths, but there was little evidence that minority youths or members of the lower class were more likely to abuse drugs than white youths and the more affluent.[39] Research by the Rand Corporation indicates that many drug-dealing youths had legitimate jobs at the time they were arrested for drug trafficking.[40] Therefore, it would be difficult to describe drug abusers simply as unemployed dropouts.

Peer Pressure

Research shows that adolescent drug abuse is highly correlated with the behavior of best friends, especially when parental supervision is weak.[41] Youths in inner-city areas where feelings of alienation run high often come in contact with drug users who teach them that drugs provide an answer to their feelings of inadequacy and stress.[42] Perhaps they join with peers to learn the techniques of drug use; their friendships with other drug-dependent youths give them social support for their habit. Empirical research efforts show that a youth's association with friends who are substance abusers increases the probability of drug use.[43] The relationship is reciprocal: Adolescent substance abusers seek friends who engage in these behaviors, and associating with drug abusers leads to increased levels of drug abuse.

Peer networks may be the most significant influence on long-term substance abuse. Shared feelings and a sense of intimacy lead youths to become enmeshed in what has been described as the "drug-use subculture."[44] Research indicates that drug users do in fact have warm relationships with substance-abusing peers who help support their behaviors.[45] This lifestyle provides users with a clear role, activities they enjoy, and an opportunity for attaining status among their peers.[46] One reason it is so difficult to treat hard-core users is that quitting drugs means leaving the "fast life" of the streets.

Young people may take drugs for many reasons, including peer pressure, growing up in a rough neighborhood, poor family life, living with parents who abuse drugs, or to escape reality. This teen is one of a number who were interviewed and photographed for Jim Goldberg's book *Raised by Wolves*, a gritty and sobering account of life on the streets of Los Angeles and San Francisco.

© Jim Goldberg/Magnum Photos

Family Factors

Poor family life is also offered as an explanation for drug use. Studies have found that the majority of drug users have had an unhappy childhood, which included harsh punishment and parental neglect.[47] The drug abuse and family quality association may involve both racial and gender differences: Females and whites who were abused as children are more likely to have alcohol and drug arrests as adults; abuse was less likely to affect drug use in males and African Americans.[48] It is also common to find substance abusers within large families and where parents are divorced, separated, or absent.[49]

Social psychologists suggest that drug abuse patterns may also result from observation of parental drug use.[50] Youths who learn that drugs provide pleasurable sensations may be most likely to experiment with illegal substances; a habit may develop if the user experiences lower anxiety and fear.[51] Research shows, for example, that gang members raised in families with a history of drug use were more likely than other gang members to use cocaine and to use it seriously. And even among gang members, parental abuse was found to be a key factor in the onset of adolescent drug use.[52] Observing drug abuse may be a more important cause of drug abuse than other family-related problems.

Other family factors associated with teen drug abuse include parental conflict over childrearing practices, failure to set rules, and unrealistic demands followed by harsh punishments. Low parental attachment, rejection, and excessive family conflict have all been linked to adolescent substance abuse.[53] The Case Profile entitled "Fernando's Story" tells how one young person worked to deal with family problems that contributed to his drug use and criminal activity.

To read more about the **concept of addiction**, go to the Psychedelic Library via academic.cengage.com/criminaljustice/siegel.

Genetic Factors

The association between parental drug abuse and adolescent behavior may have a genetic basis. Research has shown that biological children of alcoholics reared by nonalcoholic adoptive parents develop alcohol problems more often than the natural

Fernando's Story

FERNANDO ELLIS WAS A 15-YEAR-OLD YOUNG MAN OF LATINO HERITAGE WHO WAS REFERRED TO THE LOCAL MENTAL HEALTH/SUBSTANCE ABUSE AGENCY AFTER he attempted to jump out of his father's moving vehicle during a verbal argument. Fernando had been using and was high on drugs at the time. He was skipping school, using marijuana on a daily basis, and had numerous drug-related police contacts and charges. He was also on probation for selling drugs on school grounds.

Fernando's father worked long hours and drank to excess when he was at home. He introduced his son to alcohol and drugs at an early age, and offered little supervision or guidance. Fernando's mother was killed in an accident when Fernando was 12 years old, leaving his father to care for him and his three older siblings. In addition, Fernando was born with a birth defect that had often resulted in teasing by other children. At times, it was difficult to understand his speech and he walked with a significant limp. It appeared Fernando was trying to fit in, "be cool," and gain acceptance by engaging in criminal activity.

At the juvenile court hearing, Fernando was ordered to complete community service and individual counseling, and was referred to the community mental health center for an alcohol and drug assessment, as well as a suicide risk assessment. He reluctantly cooperated with the order to avoid a more serious disposition.

Fernando's assessments indicated that although he did try to jump out of a moving car, he did not appear to be a suicide risk. He was under the influence at the time and in a very heated argument with his father. There was concern about his daily use of drugs and alcohol, and Fernando was referred to an outpatient drug treatment program at the center. In addition, Fernando met weekly with his counselor for individual counseling. They worked on his drug and alcohol issues, changing his behavior and habits, and on the grief and loss issues related to the sudden death of his mother. This loss was a significant turning point for Fernando. Up to that time, he had been a good student who was not involved with drugs. Everything changed when his mother was killed.

Over the course of his work with his counselor, Fernando began to process this significant loss, as well as make positive changes in his life. A team of professionals including his teachers, probation officer, drug and alcohol counselor, and a mentor provided by the school all worked with Fernando to help him realize his goals. He began to attend school on a more regular basis, and worked to improve his relationships with his father and siblings and to reduce his criminal activity and drug and alcohol use. Fernando continued to occasionally use alcohol, but eliminated his drug use. He also struggled with his home situation and sometimes ran away from home to stay with friends. Overall, Fernando significantly reduced his criminal activity, although he remained on probation for the duration of the court order. ∎

CRITICAL THINKING

1. Based on the information you read in this chapter, list the reasons why Fernando may have abused alcohol and drugs. What were the significant family factors that may have played a role?

2. Although there was progress in the case, involved team members continued to have concerns for Fernando and his siblings. What could have been done to address these concerns? Do you think Fernando should have been removed from his parental home? How would this have impacted his situation?

3. If you were going to use a multisystemic treatment approach with Fernando, whom would you involve and what issues would you plan to address? Do you think this approach could be successful in the case? Why or why not?

children of the adoptive parents.[54] A number of studies comparing alcoholism among identical and fraternal twins have found that the degree of concordance (both siblings behaving identically) is twice as high among the identical twin groups.[55]

A genetic basis for drug abuse is also supported by evidence showing that future substance abuse problems can be predicted by behavior exhibited as early as 6 years of age. The traits predicting future abuse are independent from peer relations and environmental influences.[56]

Emotional Problems

As we have seen, not all drug-abusing youths reside in lower-class urban areas. To explain drug abuse across social classes, some experts have linked drug use to emotional problems that can strike youths in any economic class. Psychodynamic explanations of substance abuse suggest that drugs help youths control or express unconscious needs. Some psychoanalysts believe adolescents who internalize their problems may use drugs to reduce their feelings of inadequacy. Introverted people may use drugs as an escape from real or imagined feelings of inferiority.[57] Another view is that adolescents who externalize their problems and blame others for their perceived failures are likely to engage in antisocial behaviors, including substance abuse. Research exists to support each of these positions.[58]

Drug abusers are also believed to exhibit psychopathic or sociopathic behavior characteristics, forming what is called an **addiction-prone personality**.[59] Drinking alcohol may reflect a teen's need to remain dependent on an overprotective mother or an effort to reduce the emotional turmoil of adolescence.[60]

Research on the psychological characteristics of narcotics abusers does, in fact, reveal the presence of a significant degree of pathology. Personality testing of users suggests that a significant percentage suffer from psychotic disorders. Studies have found that addicts suffer personality disorders characterized by a weak ego, a low frustration tolerance, and fantasies of omnipotence. Up to half of all drug abusers may also be diagnosed with antisocial personality disorder (ASPD), which is defined as a pervasive pattern of disregard for the rights of others.[61]

Problem Behavior Syndrome

For some adolescents, substance abuse is one of many problem behaviors that begin early in life and remain throughout the life course.[62] Longitudinal studies show that youths who abuse drugs are maladjusted, emotionally distressed, and have many social problems.[63] Having a deviant lifestyle means associating with delinquent peers, living in a family in which parents and siblings abuse drugs, being alienated from the dominant values of society, and engaging in delinquent behaviors at an early age.[64]

Youths who abuse drugs lack commitment to religious values, disdain education, and spend most of their time in peer activities.[65] Youths who take drugs do poorly in school, have high dropout rates, and maintain their drug use after they leave school.[66] This view of adolescent drug taking is discussed in the Focus on Delinquency box entitled "Problem Behaviors and Substance Abuse."

Rational Choice

Youths may choose to use drugs because they want to get high, relax, improve their creativity, escape reality, or increase their sexual responsiveness. Research indicates that adolescent alcohol abusers believe getting high will increase their sexual performance and facilitate their social behavior; they care little about negative consequences.[67] Substance abuse, then, may be a function of the rational, albeit mistaken, belief that substance abuse benefits the user.

PATHWAYS TO DRUG ABUSE

gateway drug
A substance that leads to use of more serious drugs; alcohol use has long been thought to lead to more serious drug abuse.

There is no single path to becoming a drug abuser, but it is generally believed that most users start at a young age using alcohol as a **gateway drug** to harder substances. That is, drug involvement begins with drinking alcohol at an early age, which progresses to experimentation with marijuana, and finally, to using cocaine and even heroin. Research on adolescent drug users in Miami found that youths who began their substance abuse careers early—by experimenting with alcohol at age 7, getting drunk at age 8, having alcohol with an adult present by age 9, and becoming regular drinkers by the time they were 11 years old—later became crack users.[68] Drinking with an adult present was a significant precursor of substance abuse and delinquency.[69]

Although the gateway concept is still being debated, there is little disagreement that serious drug users begin their involvement with alcohol.[70] Though most recreational users do not progress to "hard stuff," most addicts first experiment with recreational alcohol and recreational drugs before progressing to narcotics. By implication, if teen drinking could be reduced, the gateway to hard drugs would be narrowed.

What are the patterns of teenage drug use? Are all abusers similar, or are there different types of drug involvement? Research indicates that drug-involved youths do take on different roles, lifestyles, and behavior patterns, some of which are described in the next sections.[71]

Adolescents Who Distribute Small Amounts of Drugs

Many adolescents who use and distribute small amounts of drugs do not commit any other serious delinquent acts. They occasionally sell marijuana, "crystal," and PCP to support their own drug use. Their customers include friends, relatives, and acquaintances. Deals are arranged over the phone, in school, or at public meeting places; however, the actual distribution takes place in more private arenas, such as at home or in cars.

Petty dealers do not consider themselves "seriously" involved in drugs. One girl commented, "I don't consider it dealing. I'll sell hits of speed to my friends, and joints and nickel bags [of marijuana] to my friends, but that's not dealing." Petty dealers are insulated from the justice system because their activities rarely result in apprehension. In fact, few adults notice their activities because these adolescents are able to maintain a relatively conventional lifestyle. In several jurisdictions, however, agents of the justice system are cooperating in the development of educational programs to provide nonusers with the skills to resist the "sales pitch" of petty dealers.

According to the gateway model of drug abuse, drug involvement begins with drinking alcohol at an early age, which progresses to experimentation with recreational drugs such as marijuana, and, finally, to using hard drugs such as cocaine and even heroin. Although most recreational users do not progress to addictive drugs, few addicts begin their drug involvement with narcotics.

© Joel Gordon

Problem Behaviors and Substance Abuse

According to the problem behavior syndrome model, substance abuse may be one of a constellation of social problems experienced by at-risk youth. There is significant evidence to substantiate the view that kids who abuse substances are also more likely to experience an array of social problems. For example, a recent study examined the relationship among adolescent illicit-drug use, physical abuse, and sexual abuse with a sample of Mexican American and non-Hispanic white youths living in the southwestern United States. The research found that youths who report physical and/or sexual abuse are significantly more likely to report illicit drug use than those who have never been abused. About 40 percent of youths who have experienced physical abuse report using marijuana in the previous month, while only 28 percent of youths who have never been abused report using the drug within that time. These findings were independent of factors such as academic achievement and family structure, and they suggest that treatment directed at abused adolescents should include drug-use prevention, intervention, and education components (see Figure 11-A).

Kids who abuse drugs and alcohol are also more likely to have educational problems. A recent study of substance use

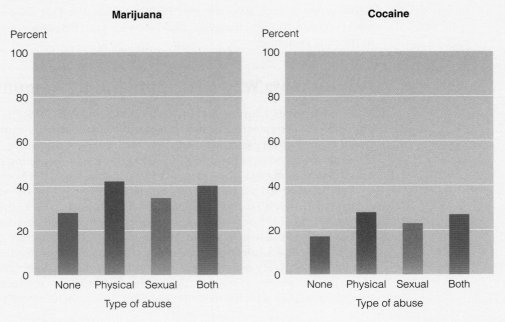

FIGURE 11-A

Percentage of Youths Reporting Past-Month Marijuana or Past-Year Cocaine Use, by Type of Abuse Suffered (N = 2,468)

NOTE: These analyses were based on data collected between 1988 and 1992 for the Mexican-American Drug Use and Dropout Survey, a yearly survey of Mexican American and non-Hispanic white school dropouts and a comparison group of enrolled students from one school district in each of three communities in the southwestern United States.

SOURCE: Deanna Pérez, "The Relationship between Physical Abuse, Sexual Victimization, and Adolescent Illicit Drug Use," *Journal of Drug Issues* 30:641–662 (2000).

Adolescents Who Frequently Sell Drugs

A small number of adolescents are high-rate dealers who bridge the gap between adult drug distributors and the adolescent user. Though many are daily users, they take part in many normal activities, including going to school and socializing with friends.

Frequent dealers often have adults who "front" for them—that is, sell them drugs for cash. The teenagers then distribute the drugs to friends and acquaintances. They among Texas students in grades 7 through 12 found that those who were absent 10 or more days during the previous school year were more likely to report alcohol, tobacco, and other drug use. For example, twice as many students with high absentee rates reported using marijuana in the previous month (29 percent vs. 14 percent, respectively) than students who did not miss school.

There is also a connection between substance abuse and serious behavioral and emotional problems. One national study found that behaviorally troubled youth are seven times more likely than those with less serious problems to report that they were dependent on alcohol or illicit drugs (17.1 percent vs. 2.3 percent). In addition, youths with serious emotional problems were nearly four times more likely to report dependence (13.2 percent vs. 3.4 percent) (see Figure 11-B).

Critical Thinking

These studies provide dramatic evidence that drug abuse is highly associated with other social problems—abuse, school failure, and emotional disorders. They imply that getting kids off drugs may take a lot more effort than relying on some simple solution like "Just Say No." What would it take to get kids to refrain from using drugs?

SOURCES: Deanna Pérez, "The Relationship between Physical Abuse, Sexual Victimization, and Adolescent Illicit Drug Use," *Journal of Drug Issues* 30:641–662 (2000); Texas Commission on Alcohol and Drug Abuse, "Substance Use among Youths at High Risk of Dropping Out: Grades 7–12 in Texas, 1998," Texas Commission on Alcohol and Drug Abuse Research Brief, June 2000; Substance Abuse and Mental Health Services Administration, Office of Applied Studies, "The Relationship between Mental Health and Substance Abuse among Adolescents," Analytic Series: A-9, 1999. Data and tables supplied by the Center for Substance Abuse Research, University of Maryland, College Park (2001).

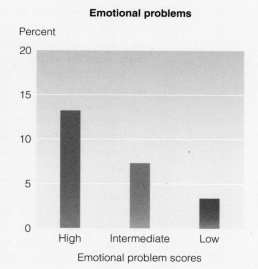

FIGURE 11-B

Percentage of Youths Ages 12 to 17 Reporting Dependence on Alcohol or Illicit Drugs, by Behavioral and Emotional Problem Scores, 1994–1996

NOTE: Severity levels (high, intermediate, and low) for the behavioral and emotional problem scale were determined using values set in the Youth Self-Report (YSR), an instrument extensively used in adolescent studies to assess psychological difficulties.

SOURCE: Substance Abuse and Mental Health Services Administration, Office of Applied Studies, "The Relationship between Mental Health and Substance Abuse among Adolescents," Analytic Series A-9, 1999.

return most of the proceeds to the supplier, keeping a commission for themselves. They may also keep drugs for their personal use, and, in fact, some consider their drug dealing as a way of "getting high for free." One young user, Winston, age 17, told investigators, "I sell the cracks for money and for cracks. The man, he give me this *much*. I sell most of it and I get the rest for me. I like this much. Every day I do this."[72] James Inciardi and his associates found that about 80 percent of the youths who dealt crack regularly were daily users.[73]

Frequent dealers are more likely to sell drugs in parks, schools, or other public places. Deals occur irregularly, so the chance of apprehension is not significant. This irregularity combined with having to pay off others means the amount earned by drug dealers can be rather meager. Research on the earnings of drug dealers is discussed in the Focus on Delinquency box entitled "Does Drug Dealing Pay?"

Teenage Drug Dealers Who Commit Other Delinquent Acts

A more serious type of drug-involved youth is the one who distributes multiple substances and commits both property and violent crimes; many are gang members.[74] These youngsters make up about 2 percent of the teenage population, but they may commit up to 40 percent of robberies and assaults and about 60 percent of all teenage felony thefts and drug sales. Few gender or racial differences exist among these youths: Girls are as likely as boys to become persistent drug-involved offenders, white youths as likely as black youths, and middle-class adolescents raised outside cities as likely as lower-class city children.[75]

In cities, these youths frequently are hired by older dealers to act as street-level drug runners. Each member of a crew of 3 to 12 youths will handle small quantities of drugs; the supplier receives 50 to 70 percent of the drug's street value. The crew members also act as lookouts, recruiters, and guards. Although they may be recreational drug users themselves, crew members refrain from using addictive drugs such as heroin. Between drug sales, the young dealers commit robberies, burglaries, and other thefts.[76]

Most youngsters in the street drug trade either terminate their dealing or become drug dependent. A few, however, develop entrepreneurial skills. Those who are rarely apprehended by police advance in the drug business. They develop their own crews and may handle more than half a million dollars a year.

In many instances, these drug dealer–delinquents are members of teenage gangs. The gangs maintain "rock houses," or "stash houses," that receive drug shipments arranged by members who have the overseas connections and financial backing needed to wholesale drugs. The wholesalers pay the gang for permission to deal in their territory. Lower-echelon gang members help transport the drugs and work the houses, retailing cocaine and other drugs to neighborhood youths. Each member makes a profit for every ounce of rock sold. Police estimate that youths who work in rock houses will earn $700 and up for a 12-hour shift.[77]

Some experts question whether gangs are responsible for as much drug dealing as the media would have us believe. Some believe that the tightly organized "super" gangs are being replaced with loosely organized neighborhood groups. The turbulent environment of drug dealing is better handled by flexible organizations than by rigid, vertically organized gangs with a leader who is far removed from the action.[78]

Losers and Burnouts

Some drug-involved youths do not have the savvy to join gangs or groups and instead begin committing unplanned crimes that increase their chances of arrest. Their heavy drug use increases their risk of apprehension and decreases their value for organized drug distribution networks.

Drug-involved "losers" can earn a living by steering customers to a seller in a "copping" area, touting drug availability for a dealer, or acting as a lookout. However, they are not considered trustworthy or deft enough to handle drugs or money. Though these offenders get involved in drugs at an early age, they receive little attention from the justice system until they have developed an extensive arrest record. By then they are approaching the end of their minority and will either desist or become so entrapped in the drug-crime subculture that little can be done to deter their illegal activities.

Does Drug Dealing Pay?

In one of the first studies to investigate if drug dealing pays, economists Robert MacCoun and Peter Reuter found that drug dealers in Washington, D.C., make about $30 per hour when they are working and clear on average about $2,000 per month. These amounts are greater than most dealers could hope to have earned in legitimate jobs, but they are not enough to afford a steady stream of luxuries. It was also found that most small-time dealers also hold conventional jobs.

Two more recent studies offer differing views on the economics of drug dealing. In an analysis of the financial activities of a drug-selling street gang in Chicago, economist Steven Levitt and sociologist Sudhir Venkatesh found that the average hourly wage of drug dealers or "foot soldiers" was between $2.50 and $7.10 (see Table 11-A). The results are based on a four-year period in which the gang was active. As an average wage per month, this comes to $140 to $470. In a typical month, drug dealers worked just over 50 hours. As shown in the table, the hourly wage of drug dealers is substantially lower than the average wage for all gang members and the gang leader. This finding suggests that, at least for drug dealers, factors other than income may explain participation in this activity.

In contrast, psychologists Michelle Little and Laurence Steinberg found that drug dealers derive a substantial income from selling drugs. Based on a large sample of serious male juvenile offenders in Philadelphia who reported incomes from drug sales, it was found that their average weekly wage was about $1,693, or more than $6,700 per month. Based on Levitt and Venkatesh's finding that drug dealers worked a little over 50 hours per week, the average hourly wage for this group of drug dealers comes to $135. Drug dealers who also held conventional jobs reported that their income from dealing was on average 41 times greater than what they made in the legal economy. It was also found that more than half the sample reported that they were involved in dealing drugs for more than a year. The authors speculated that income from drug sales served as an important incentive for continued involvement in illicit activities and may have acted as a disincentive for investment in conventional goals.

Critical Thinking

Many are of the opinion that drug dealers make a great deal of money, which contributes to the public's view that dealers should be subject to more punitive dispositions. Does this research change your opinion of how society should treat drug dealers? Explain. How might this research be used to deter juveniles from dealing drugs?

SOURCES: Steven D. Levitt and Sudhir A. Venkatesh, "An Economic Analysis of a Drug-Selling Gang's Finances," *Quarterly Journal of Economics* 115:755–789 (2000); Michelle Little and Laurence Steinberg, "Psychosocial Correlates of Adolescent Drug Dealing in the Inner City: Potential Roles of Opportunity, Conventional Commitments, and Maturity," *Journal of Research in Crime and Delinquency* 43:357–386 (2006); Robert MacCoun and Peter Reuter, "Are the Wages of Sin $30 an Hour? Economic Aspects of Street-Level Drug Dealing," *Crime and Delinquency* 38:477–491 (1992).

TABLE 11-A ESTIMATED HOURLY WAGES OF MEMBERS IN A DRUG-SELLING GANG

	Drug Dealers	All Gang Members	Gang Leader
Year 1	$2.50	$5.90	$32.50
Year 2	$3.70	$7.40	$47.50
Year 3	$3.30	$7.10	$65.90
Year 4	$7.10	$11.10	$97.20

NOTE: Estimated hourly wages include both official and unofficial income sources. All wages are in 1995 dollars.
SOURCE: Adapted from Steven D. Levitt and Sudhir A. Venkatesh, "An Economic Analysis of a Drug-Selling Gang's Finances," *Quarterly Journal of Economics* 115:755–789 (2000), Table III.

Persistent Offenders

About two-thirds of substance-abusing youths continue to use drugs in adulthood, but about half desist from other criminal activities. Those who persist in both substance abuse and crime maintain these characteristics:

I They come from poor families.

I Other criminals are members of their families.

I They do poorly in school.

I They started using drugs and committing other delinquent acts at an early age.

I They use multiple types of drugs and commit crimes frequently.

I They have few opportunities in late adolescence to participate in legitimate and rewarding adult activities.[79]

Some evidence exists that these drug-using persisters have low nonverbal IQs and poor physical coordination. Nonetheless, there is little evidence to explain why some drug-abusing youths drop out of crime while others remain active.

DRUG USE AND DELINQUENCY

An association between drug use and delinquency has been established, and this connection can take a number of forms. Crime may be an instrument of the drug trade: Violence erupts when rival gangs use weapons to settle differences and establish territorial monopolies. In New York City, authorities report that crack gangs will burn down their rivals' headquarters. It is estimated that between 35 and 40 percent of New York's homicides are drug related.[80]

Drug users may also commit crimes to pay for their habits.[81] One study conducted in Miami found that 573 narcotics users *annually* committed more than 200,000 crimes to obtain cash. Similar research with a sample of 356 addicts accounted for 118,000 crimes annually.[82] If such proportions hold true, then the nation's estimated 700,000 heroin addicts alone may be committing more than 100 million crimes each year.

Drug users may be more willing to take risks because their inhibitions are lowered by substance abuse. Cities with high rates of cocaine abuse are also more likely to experience higher levels of armed robbery. It is possible that crack and cocaine users are more willing to engage in a risky armed robbery to get immediate cash than a burglary, which requires more planning and effort.[83]

The relationship between alcohol and drug abuse and delinquency has been substantiated by a number of studies. Some have found that youths who abuse alcohol are most likely to engage in violence; as adults, those with long histories of drinking are more likely to report violent offending patterns.[84]

The National Institute of Justice's Arrestee Drug Abuse Monitoring (ADAM) program tracked trends in drug use among arrestees in urban areas. Some, but not all, of its 36 sites collect data on juveniles. Due to a lack of funding, the Department of Justice ended this program in 2004.[85] The most recent report (2002) found that, among juvenile detainees, almost 60 percent of juvenile males and 30 percent of juvenile females tested positive for marijuana, the most commonly used drug, and its prevalence was ten and six times higher than cocaine use for juvenile males and females, respectively.[86] With the exception of methamphetamines, male detainees were more likely to test positive for the use of any drug than were female detainees. While males and minority-group members have somewhat higher positive test rates than females and Caucasians, drug use is prevalent among juvenile arrestees, reaffirming the close association between substance abuse and criminality.

There is evidence that incarcerated youths are much more likely to be involved in substance abuse than adolescents in the general population. For example, research by David Cantor on incarcerated youths in Washington, D.C., found their drug involvement more than double that of nonincarcerated area youths.[87]

Drugs and Chronic Offending

It is possible that most delinquents are not drug users, but that police are more likely to apprehend muddle-headed substance abusers than clear-thinking abstainers. A second, more plausible, interpretation of the existing data is that the drug abuse–crime connection is so powerful because many delinquents are in fact substance abusers. Research by Bruce Johnson and his associates confirms this suspicion. Using data from a national self-report survey, these researchers found that less than 2 percent of the youths who responded to the survey (a) report using cocaine or heroin, and (b) commit two or more index crimes each year. However, these drug-abusing adolescents accounted for 40 to 60 percent of all the index crimes reported in the sample. Less than one-quarter of these delinquents committed crimes solely to support a drug habit. These data suggest that a small core of substance-abusing adolescents commits a significant proportion of all serious crimes. It is also evident that a behavior—drug abuse—that develops late in adolescence influences the extent of delinquent activity through the life course.[88]

The relationship between drug abuse and chronic offending is illustrated by Inciardi, Horowitz, and Pottieger's interviews with crack-involved youths in Miami. The 254 kids in their sample reported committing 223,439 criminal offenses during the 12 months prior to their interviews. It is not surprising that 87 percent of the sample had been arrested. The greater the involvement in the crack business, the greater the likelihood of committing violent crime. About 74 percent of the dealers committed robbery, and 17 percent engaged in assault. Only 12 percent of the nondealers committed robbery, and 4 percent engaged in assault.[89]

Explaining Drug Use and Delinquency

The association between delinquency and drug use has been established in a variety of cultures.[90] It is far from certain, however, whether (a) drug use *causes* delinquency, (b) delinquency *leads* youths to engage in substance abuse, or (c) both drug abuse and delinquency are *functions* of some other factor.[91]

Some of the most sophisticated research on this topic has been conducted by Delbert Elliott and his associates at the Institute of Behavioral Science at the University of Colorado.[92] Using data from the National Youth Survey, a longitudinal study of self-reported delinquency and drug use, Elliott and his colleagues David Huizinga and Scott Menard found a strong association between delinquency and drug use.[93] However, the direction of the relationship is unclear. As a general rule, drug abuse appears to be a *type* of delinquent behavior and not a *cause* of delinquency. Most youths become involved in delinquent acts *before* they are initiated into drugs; it is difficult therefore to conclude that drug use causes crime.

In other research involving the National Youth Survey, Jason Ford found that there is a reciprocal and ongoing relationship between alcohol use and delinquency during adolescence, and that part of the reason for this reciprocal relationship is that both behaviors have the effect of weakening youths' bonds with society, thereby promoting continued alcohol use and delinquency.[94]

According to the Elliott research, both drug use and delinquency seem to reflect developmental problems; they are both part of a disturbed lifestyle. This research reveals some important associations between substance abuse and delinquency:

1. Alcohol abuse seems to be a cause of marijuana and other drug abuse because most drug users started with alcohol, and youths who abstain from alcohol almost never take drugs.

2. Marijuana use is a cause of multiple-drug use: About 95 percent of youths who use more serious drugs started on pot; only 5 percent of serious drug users never smoked pot.

3. Youths who commit felonies started off with minor delinquent acts. Few delinquents (1 percent) report committing only felonies.

The Elliott research has been supported by other studies also indicating that delinquency and substance abuse are part of a general pattern of deviance or problem behavior syndrome, such as association with an antisocial peer group and educational failure.[95] There seems to be a pattern in which troubled youths start by committing petty crimes and drinking alcohol and proceed to harder drugs and more serious crimes. Kids who drink at an early age later go on to engage in violent acts in their adolescence; violent adolescents increase their alcohol abuse as they mature.[96] Both their drug abuse

Concept Summary 11.2

Key Drug Control Strategies

Law Enforcement	Preventing drugs from entering the country; destroying crops used to make drugs; arresting members of drug cartels and street-level dealers
Education	Informing children about the dangers of drug use; teaching children to resist peer pressure
Community-Based	Community organizations and residents taking action to deter drug dealing; engaging youth in prosocial activities
Treatment	Intervening with drug users, including counseling and experiential activities
Harm Reduction	Minimizing the harmful effects caused by drug use and some of the more punitive responses to drug use

and the delinquency are part of an urban underclass lifestyle involving limited education, few job skills, unstable families, few social skills, and patterns of law violations.[97]

DRUG CONTROL STRATEGIES

Billions of dollars are being spent each year to reduce the importation of drugs, deter drug dealers, and treat users. Yet although the overall incidence of drug use has declined, drug use has concentrated in the nation's poorest neighborhoods, with a consequent association between substance abuse and crime.

A number of drug-control strategies have been tried. Some are designed to deter drug use by stopping the flow of drugs into the country, apprehending dealers, and cracking down on street-level drug deals. Another approach is to prevent drug use by educating would-be users and convincing them to "say no" to drugs. A third approach is to treat users so that they can terminate their addictions. These and other drug control strategies efforts are discussed in the following sections. Concept Summary 11.2 reviews the key strategies.

Law Enforcement Efforts

Law enforcement strategies are aimed at reducing the supply of drugs and, at the same time, deterring would-be users from drug abuse.

Source Control One approach to drug control is to deter the sale of drugs through apprehension of large-volume drug dealers, coupled with enforcement of drug laws that carry heavy penalties. This approach is designed to punish known dealers and users and to deter those who are considering entering the drug trade.

A major effort has been made to cut off supplies of drugs by destroying overseas crops and arresting members of drug cartels; this approach is known as *source control*. The federal government has been encouraging exporting nations to step up efforts to destroy drug crops and to prosecute dealers. Other less aggressive source control approaches, such as crop substitution and alternative development programs for the largely poor farmers in other countries, have also been tried, and a recent review of international efforts suggests that "some success can be achieved in reduction of narcotic crop production."[98] Three South American nations—Peru, Bolivia, and Colombia—have agreed to coordinate control efforts with the United States. However, translating words into deeds is a formidable task. Drug lords fight back through intimidation, violence, and corruption. The United States was forced to invade Panama with 20,000 troops in 1989 to stop its leader, General Manuel Noriega, from trafficking in cocaine.

Even when efforts are successful in one area, production may shift to another. For example, enforcement efforts in Peru and Bolivia were so successful that they altered cocaine cultivation patterns. As a consequence, Colombia became the premier coca-cultivating country when the local drug cartels encouraged growers to cultivate coca plants. When the Colombian government mounted an effective eradication campaign

Crop eradication is one form of source control that the U.S. government continues to support in an effort to prevent drugs from entering the country. Here, Afghan police destroy opium poppies as part of a drug eradication operation in Tarin Kowt in Urugzan, a southern province of Afghanistan.

in the traditional growing areas, the cartel linked up with rebel groups in remote parts of the country for their drug supply.[99] Leaders in neighboring countries expressed fear when the United States announced that they would provide billions in military aid—under the program known as "Plan Colombia"—to fight Colombia's rural drug dealers/rebels, assuming that success would drive traffickers over the border.[100] Another unintended effect of this campaign has been a recent shift by drug cartels to exploit new crops, from a traditional emphasis on coca to opium poppy, the plant used to make heroin. It is estimated that Latin American countries, including Mexico, now supply upwards of 80 percent of the heroin consumed in the United States.[101]

On the other side of the world, Afghanistan has since reclaimed its position as the world leader in opium production, accounting for 92 percent of the global market.[102] This has come about after the fall of the Taliban government in 2001, which had banned poppy growing. Now, almost all of the heroin sold in Russia and three-quarters of that sold in Europe comes from Afghanistan. This has occurred despite new laws against poppy growing, law enforcement efforts, and crop substitution efforts on the part of agricultural aid organizations. Breaking with religious beliefs, Taliban forces are now promoting the growing of poppies—in some areas distributing leaflets that order farmers to grow the crop—and providing protection to drug smugglers, all in an effort to finance their operations against the United States military and Coalition forces in the country.[103]

To find out more about the **federal government's drug control strategies**, go to the White House website via academic.cengage.com/criminaljustice/siegel.

Border Control Law enforcement efforts have also been directed at interdicting drug supplies as they enter the country. Border patrols and military personnel have been involved in massive interdiction efforts, and many billion-dollar seizures have been made. It is estimated that between one-quarter and one-third of the annual cocaine supply shipped to the United States is seized by drug enforcement agencies. Yet U.S. borders are so vast and unprotected that meaningful interdiction is impossible. In 2005 (most recent data available), U.S. federal law enforcement agencies seized 382,000 pounds of cocaine and almost 4,000 pounds of heroin.[104] Global rates of interception of heroin and cocaine indicate that only 26 percent and 42 percent of all imports are being seized by law enforcement.[105]

In recent years, another form of border control to interdict drugs entering the country has emerged: targeting Internet drug traffickers in foreign countries. With the increasing popularity of the Internet, some offenders are now turning to this source to obtain designer-type drugs. In Buffalo, New York, U.S. customs agents discovered that a steady flow of packages containing the drug gamma-butyrolactone or GBL, an ingredient of GBH (gamma hydroxybutyrate)—the date-rape drug—were entering the country from Canada; the drug was disguised as a cleaning product. Operation Webslinger, a joint investigation of federal law enforcement agencies in the United States and Canada, was put in place to track down the suppliers. Within a year, Operation Webslinger had shut down four Internet drug rings operating in the United States and Canada, made 115 arrests in 84 cities, and seized the equivalent of 25 million doses of GBH and other related drugs.[106] Shortly following this, another federal task force, known as Operation Gray Lord and involving the Food and Drug Administration (FDA) and the Drug Enforcement Administration (DEA), was set up to combat illegal sales of narcotics on the Internet.[107]

If all importation were ended, homegrown marijuana and lab-made drugs such as ecstasy could become the drugs of choice. Even now, their easy availability and relatively low cost are increasing their popularity; they are a $10 billion business in the United States today. But there have been some signs of success. In 2005 (most recent data available), 5,846 illegal methamphetamine laboratories were seized by authorities across the United States. This is down considerably from the peak in 2003 when more than 10,000 labs were seized nationwide. The DEA attributes this success to state restrictions on retail sales of ephedrine and pseudoephedrine products.[108] Many of these labs are operated out of homes, putting children—3,300 children were found in 8,000 of these labs over the years—at grave risk of being burned or injured, not to mention exposing them to illegal drugs.[109]

Targeting Dealers Law enforcement agencies have also made a concerted effort to focus on drug trafficking. Efforts have been made to bust large-scale drug rings. The long-term consequence has been to decentralize drug dealing and to encourage teenage gangs to become major suppliers. Ironically, it has proven easier for federal agents to infiltrate traditional organized crime groups than to take on drug-dealing gangs.

Police can also intimidate and arrest street-level dealers and users in an effort to make drug use so much of a hassle that consumption is cut back. Some street-level enforcement efforts have had success, but others are considered failures. "Drug sweeps" have clogged correctional facilities with petty offenders while proving a drain on police resources. These sweeps are also suspected of creating a displacement effect: Stepped-up efforts to curb drug dealing in one area or city may encourage dealers to seek friendlier territory.[110] People arrested on drug-related charges are the fastest growing segment of both the juvenile and adult justice systems. National surveys have found that juvenile court judges are prone to use a get-tough approach on drug-involved offenders. They are more likely to be processed formally by the court and to be detained between referral to court and disposition than other categories of delinquent offenders, including those who commit violent crimes.[111] Despite these efforts, juvenile drug use continues, indicating that a get-tough policy is not sufficient to deter drug use.

Education Strategies

For a web-based **antidrug education campaign**, see Freevibe via academic.cengage.com/criminaljustice/siegel.

Another approach to reducing teenage substance abuse relies on educational programs. Drug education now begins in kindergarten and extends through the 12th grade. An overwhelming majority of public school districts across the United States have implemented drug education programs with various components, including teaching students about the causes and effects of alcohol, drug, and tobacco use; teaching students to resist peer pressure; and referring students for counseling and treatment.[112] In a Texas survey of drug use among secondary school students that found drug use in rural school districts to be fast approaching usage rates in urban schools, the researchers speculate that funding cutbacks for drug education programs in the rural schools may be partly to blame.[113] Education programs, such as Project ALERT that now operates in all 50 states, have been shown to be successful in training middle-school youths to avoid recreational drugs and to resist peer pressure to

To go to the official site of **D.A.R.E.**, check out academic .cengage.com/criminaljustice/ siegel.

use cigarettes and alcohol.[114] Drug Abuse Resistance Education (D.A.R.E.) is an elementary school course designed to give students the skills for resisting peer pressure to experiment with tobacco, drugs, and alcohol. It is unique because it employs uniformed police officers to carry the antidrug message to the students before they enter junior high school. Critics question whether the program is actually as effective as advertised. Because of its importance, D.A.R.E. is discussed in the accompanying Policy and Practice box.

Two recent large-scale studies demonstrate the effectiveness of antidrug messages targeted at youth. An evaluation of the National Youth Anti-Drug Media Campaign, which features ads showing the dangers of marijuana use, reported that 41 percent of students in grades 7 to 12 "agree a lot" that the ads made them less likely to try or use drugs. Importantly, the study also reported that past-year marijuana use among the students was down 6 percent.[115] The second study, the National Survey on Drug Use and Health, which asked young people ages 12 to 17 about antidrug messages they had heard or seen outside of school hours, reported that past-month drug use by those exposed to the messages was 13 percent lower than those who had not been exposed to the messages.[116] These are encouraging findings given the limited effectiveness of D.A.R.E.

Community Strategies

Another type of drug-control effort relies on local community groups. Representatives of local government agencies, churches, civic organizations, and similar institutions are being brought together to create drug-prevention programs. Their activities include drug-free school zones, which encourage police to keep drug dealers away from schools; Neighborhood Watch programs, which are geared to reporting drug dealers; citizen patrols, which frighten dealers away from public-housing projects; and community centers, which provide an alternative to the street culture.

Community-based programs reach out to some of the highest-risk youths, who are often missed by the well-known education programs that take place in schools.[117] These programs try to get youths involved in after-school programs offering counseling, delivering clothing, food, and medical care when needed, and encouraging school achievement. Community programs also sponsor drug-free activities involving the arts, clubs, and athletics. In many respects, evaluations of community programs have shown that they may encourage antidrug attitudes and help insulate participating youths from an environment that encourages drugs.[118]

The Drug Abuse Resistance Education (D.A.R.E.) program is an elementary school course designed to give students the skills for resisting peer pressure to experiment with tobacco, drugs, and alcohol. It employs uniformed police officers to deliver the antidrug message to students before they enter junior high school. While reviews have been mixed, the program continues to be used around the nation.

© Michael Newman/PhotoEdit

Drug Abuse Resistance Education (D.A.R.E.)

The most widely known drug education program, Drug Abuse Resistance Education (D.A.R.E.), is an elementary school course designed to give students the skills they need to resist peer pressure to try tobacco, drugs, and alcohol. It is unique because it employs uniformed police officers to carry the antidrug message to the children before they enter junior high school. The program focuses on five major areas:

1. Providing accurate information about tobacco, alcohol, and drugs
2. Teaching students techniques to resist peer pressure
3. Teaching students to respect the law and law enforcers
4. Giving students ideas for alternatives to drug use
5. Building the self-esteem of students

The D.A.R.E. program is based on the concept that the young students need specific analytical and social skills to resist peer pressure and say no to drugs. Instructors work with children to raise their self-esteem, provide them with decision-making tools, and help them identify positive alternatives to substance abuse.

The D.A.R.E. approach has been adopted widely since it was founded in 1983. D.A.R.E. America indicates that the program is now taught in almost 80 percent of school districts nationwide and in 54 other countries. It is also claimed that 26 million children in the United States and 10 million children in other countries participated in the program. More than 40 percent of all school districts incorporate assistance from local law enforcement agencies in their drug-prevention programming.

DOES D.A.R.E. WORK?

Although D.A.R.E. is popular with both schools and police agencies, a number of evaluations have not found it to have an impact on student drug usage. For example, in a highly sophisticated evaluation of the program, Donald Lynam and his colleagues found the program to be ineffective over the short and long term. They followed a cohort of sixth-grade children who attended a total of 31 schools. Twenty-three of the schools were randomly assigned to receive D.A.R.E. in the sixth grade, while the other eight received whatever drug education was routinely provided in their classes. The research team assessed the participants yearly through the tenth grade and then recontacted them when they were 20 years old. They found that D.A.R.E. had no effect on students' drug use at any time through tenth grade. The 10-year follow-up failed to find any hidden or "sleeper" effects that were delayed in developing. At age 20, there were no differences between those who received D.A.R.E. and those who did not in their use of cigarettes, alcohol, marijuana, or other drugs; the only difference was that those who had participated in D.A.R.E. reported slightly lower levels of self-esteem at age 20, an effect that proponents were not aiming for. In the most rigorous and comprehensive review so far on the effectiveness

Treatment Strategies

Each year more than 150,000 youths ages 12 to 17 are admitted to treatment facilities in the United States, with just over half (52 percent) being referred through the juvenile justice system. Almost two-thirds (64 percent) of all admissions involve marijuana as the primary drug of abuse.[119]

Many approaches are available to treat users.[120] Some efforts stem from the perspective that users have low self-esteem, and they use various techniques to build up the user's sense of self. Some use psychological counseling, and others, such as the **multisystemic therapy (MST)** technique developed by Scott Henggeler, direct attention to family, peer, and psychological problems by focusing on problem solving and communication skills.[121] In a long-term evaluation of MST, Henggeler found that adolescent substance abusers who went through the program were significantly less likely to recidivate than youths who received traditional counseling services. However, mixed treatment effects were reported for future substance abuse by those who received MST compared with those who did not.[122]

multisystemic therapy (MST)
Addresses a variety of family, peer, and psychological problems by focusing on problem-solving and communication skills training.

Another approach is to involve users in outdoor activities, wilderness training, and after-school community programs.[123] More intensive efforts use group therapy, in which leaders try to give users the skills and support that can help them reject the social pressure to use drugs. These programs are based on the Alcoholics Anonymous philosophy that users must find the strength to stay clean and that support from those who understand their experiences can be a successful way to achieve a drug-free life.

of D.A.R.E, the General Accountability Office (GAO, formerly the General Accounting Office), the research arm of Congress, found that the program neither prevents student drug use nor changes student attitudes toward drugs.

CHANGING THE D.A.R.E. CURRICULUM

Although national evaluations and independent reviews have questioned the validity of D.A.R.E. and many communities have discontinued its use—due in part to the program not meeting U.S. Department of Education effectiveness standards—it is still widely employed in school districts around the country. To meet criticism head-on, D.A.R.E. began testing a new curriculum for middle and high school programs, known as "Take Charge of Your Life." The new program is aimed at older students and relies more on having them question their assumptions about drug use than on listening to lectures on the subject. The new program will work largely on changing social norms, teaching students to question whether they really have to use drugs to fit in with their peers. Emphasis will shift from fifth-grade students to those in the seventh grade and a booster program will be added in ninth grade, when kids are more likely to experiment with drugs. Police officers will now serve more as coaches than as lecturers, encouraging students to challenge the social norm of drug use in discussion groups. Students also will do more role-playing in an effort to learn decision-making skills. There will also be an emphasis on the role of media and advertising in shaping behavior. The new curricula is undergoing tests in a total of 83 high schools and 122 middle schools in six large cities—half the schools will continue using the curriculum they do now, and the other half will use the new D.A.R.E. program—so that the new curriculum may be scientifically evaluated. Early study results suggest that the new curriculum is being delivered as designed and reaching the highest-risk youth.

Critical Thinking

1. Do you believe that an education program such as D.A.R.E. can turn kids away from drugs, or are the reasons for teenage drug use so complex that a single school-based program is doomed to fail?

2. If you ran D.A.R.E., what experiences would you give to the children? Do you think it would be effective to have current or former addicts address classes about how drugs influenced their lives?

SOURCES: Carnevale Associates, *A Longitudinal Evaluation of the New Curricula for the D.A.R.E. Middle (7th Grade) and High School (9th Grade) Programs: Take Charge of Your Life. Year Four Progress Report* (Washington, DC: Author, 2006); D.A.R.E. America (2006), www.dare.com (accessed October 25, 2007); Carol Hirschon Weiss, Erin Murphy-Graham, and Sarah Birkeland, "An Alternative Route to Policy Influence: How Evaluations Affect D.A.R.E.," *American Journal of Evaluation* 26:12–30 (2005); Anthony Petrosino, "D.A.R.E. and Scientific Evidence: A 20 Year History," *Japanese Journal of Sociological Criminology* 30:72–88 (2005); *Youth Illicit Drug Use Prevention: D.A.R.E. Long-Term Evaluations and Federal Efforts to Identify Effective Programs* (Washington, DC: U.S. General Accountability Office, 2003), p. 2; Brian Vastag, "GAO: D.A.R.E. Does Not Work," *Journal of the American Medical Association* 289:539 (2003); Donald R. Lynam, Rick Milich, Rick Zimmerman, Scott Novak, T. K. Logan, Catherine Martin, Carl Leukefeld, and Richard Clayton, "Project D.A.R.E.: No Effects at 10-Year Follow-Up," *Journal of Consulting and Clinical Psychology* 67:590–593 (1999).

Residential programs are used with more heavily involved drug abusers. Some are detoxification units that use medical procedures to wean patients from the more addicting drugs. Others are therapeutic communities that attempt to deal with the psychological causes of drug use. Hypnosis, aversion therapy (getting users to associate drugs with unpleasant sensations, such as nausea), counseling, biofeedback, and other techniques are often used.

There is little evidence that these residential programs can effectively reduce teenage substance abuse.[124] Many are restricted to families whose health insurance will pay for short-term residential care; when the coverage ends, the children are released. Adolescents do not often enter these programs voluntarily, and most have little motivation to change.[125] A stay can stigmatize residents as "addicts," even though they never used hard drugs; while in treatment, they may be introduced to hard-core users with whom they will associate upon release. One residential program that holds promise for reducing teenage substance abuse is UCLA's Comprehensive Residential Education, Arts, and Substance Abuse Treatment (CREASAT) program, which integrates "enhanced substance abuse services" (group therapy, education, vocational skills) and visual and performing arts programming.[126]

Balanced and Restorative Justice Model Another approach to treating drug-involved juveniles is referred to as the *balanced and restorative justice* (BARJ) method. This model integrates the traditional rehabilitative philosophy of the juvenile court with increasing societal concern about victims' rights and community safety.[127]

BARJ programs attempt to make offenders more accountable by having them make amends to the victim and community, while at the same time improving their competency development by changing their behaviors and improving functional skills. BARJ programs also focus on community safety and stress protecting the community by carefully monitoring the juvenile's behavior. BARJ has become the guiding philosophy in juvenile justice system change in a number of states. An important aspect of the BARJ philosophy is a system of graduated sanctions that hold juveniles accountable for their actions and reward them for positive progress toward rehabilitation. Good behavior results in increased freedom or other rewards, while negative behavior results in more severe restrictions or a more intensive therapeutic environment. If the offender lapses into alcohol or drug (AOD) use and/or delinquent behavior at any point in the treatment process, graduated sanctions involving placing the juvenile in a higher-security, more intense therapeutic environment are applied. This approach may be applied in a specialized juvenile drug court, where the juvenile's progress is generally monitored by a judge who relies on a variety of professionals in assessing needs, recommending services, monitoring behaviors, and applying sanctions when a lack of improvement is evident.

Harm Reduction

A harm reduction approach involves lessening the harms caused to youths by drug use and by some of the more punitive responses to drug use. Harm reduction encapsulates some of the efforts advanced under the community and treatment strategies noted above, but maintains as its primary focus efforts to minimize the harmful effects of drug use. This approach includes the following components:

1. The availability of drug treatment facilities so that all addicts who wish to do so can overcome their habits and lead drug-free lives.

2. The use of health professionals to administer drugs to addicts as part of a treatment and detoxification program.

3. Needle exchange programs that will slow the transmission of HIV and educate drug users about how HIV is contracted and spread.

4. Special drug courts or pretrial diversion programs that compel drug treatment.[128] (Juvenile drug courts are discussed in Chapter 13.)

Needle exchange programs—providing drug users with clean needles in exchange for used ones—have been shown to maintain the low prevalence of HIV transmission among drug users and lower rates of hepatitis C. Methadone maintenance clinics in which heroin users receive doctor-prescribed methadone (a nonaddictive substance that satisfies the cravings caused by heroin) have been shown to reduce illegal heroin use and criminal activity.[129]

Critics of the harm reduction approach warn that it condones or promotes drug use, "encouraging people either to continue using drugs or to start using drugs, without recognizing the dangers of their addiction."[130] Advocates, on the other hand, refer to harm reduction as a valuable interim measure in dealing with drug use: "There are safer ways of using drugs, and harm reduction for patients is a valuable interim measure to help them make informed choices and improve their overall health."[131] Advocates also call for this approach to replace the War on Drugs, and claim that this change in drug policy will go a long way toward solving two key problems caused by punitive responses. First, it will reduce the number of offenders, both juvenile and adult, being sent to already overcrowded institutionalized settings for what amounts to less serious offenses. Second, it will discourage police crackdowns in minority neighborhoods that result in racial minorities being arrested and formally processed at much higher rates for drug offenses.[132]

The War on Drugs has been a major source of the racial discrimination that occurs in the juvenile justice system. (For more on racial discrimination in the juvenile justice system, see Chapters 13, 14, and 15.) The latest data show that African Americans make up 16 percent of the juvenile population, but account for 21 percent (40,570)

To learn more about the **harm reduction** approach to teenage drug use, check out the Harm Reduction Coalition via academic.cengage.com/criminaljustice/siegel.

of all drug law violations referred to juvenile court. This is down from 44 percent in 1990 and 33 percent in 1995. African American juveniles involved in drug offense cases are also more likely to be detained (held in a detention facility or in shelter care to await court appearances) than white juveniles.[133]

WHAT DOES THE FUTURE HOLD?

The United States appears willing to go to great lengths to fight the drug war.[134] Law enforcement efforts, along with prevention programs and treatment projects, have been stepped up. Yet all drug-control strategies are doomed to fail as long as youths want to take drugs and drugs remain widely available and accessible. Prevention, deterrence, and treatment strategies ignore the core reasons for the drug problem: poverty, alienation, and family disruption. As the gap between rich and poor widens and the opportunities for legitimate advancement decrease, it should come as no surprise that adolescent drug use continues.

Despite all efforts, drug control is difficult because there can be a great deal of money to be made in drug trafficking. For example, the profits involved in the sale of a single drug such as ecstasy are enormous. Ecstasy, or MDMA, is manufactured clandestinely in western Europe, primarily in the Netherlands and Belgium. A typical clandestine laboratory is capable of producing 70,000 to 100,000 tablets per day; one laboratory raided by Dutch police was producing 350,000 tablets per day. The cost of producing a tablet runs as little as 50 cents, and they sell for up to about $2, giving the lab owners a potential profit of between $100,000 and $150,000 per day. Once the MDMA reaches the United States, a domestic cell distributor will charge from $6 to $8 per tablet. The MDMA retailer will, in turn, distribute the MDMA for $25 to $40 per tablet.[135]

legalization of drugs
Decriminalizing drug use to reduce the association between drug use and crime.

Some commentators have called for the legalization of drugs. This approach can have the short-term effect of reducing the association between drug use and crime (because, presumably, the cost of drugs would decrease), but it may have grave consequences. Drug use would most certainly increase, creating an overflow of unproductive people who must be cared for by the rest of society. The problems of teenage alcoholism should serve as a warning of what can happen when controlled substances are made readily available. However, the implications of decriminalization should be further studied: What effect would a policy of partial decriminalization (for example, legalizing small amounts of marijuana) have on drug-use rates? Does a get-tough policy on drugs "widen the net"? Are there alternatives to the criminalization of drugs that could help reduce their use?[136]

The studies of drug dealing in Philadelphia and Washington, D.C., suggests that law enforcement efforts may have little influence on drug-abuse rates as long as dealers can earn more than the minimal salaries they might earn in the legitimate world. Only by giving youths legitimate future alternatives can hard-core users be made to forgo drug use willingly.[137]

Summary

1. Know which drugs are most frequently abused by American youth

- Alcohol is the drug most frequently abused by American teens.

- Other popular drugs include marijuana; cocaine and its derivative, crack; and designer drugs such as ecstasy.

2. Understand the extent of the drug problem among American youth today

- Self-report surveys indicate that just under half of all high school seniors have tried drugs.

- Surveys of arrestees indicate that a significant proportion of teenagers are drug users and many are high school dropouts.

- The number of drug users may be even higher than surveys suggest, because surveys of teen abusers may be missing the most delinquent youths.

3. Be able to discuss how teenage drug use in this country has changed over time

▮ Although the national survey conducted by PRIDE shows that teenage drug use increased slightly in the past year, this survey, the Monitoring the Future survey, and the National Survey on Drug Use and Health (both also national) report that drug and alcohol use are much lower today than 5 and 10 years ago.

4. Know the main explanations for why youths take drugs

▮ The main explanations for why youths take drugs include:

— Growing up in disorganized areas in which there is a high degree of hopelessness, poverty, and despair

— Peer pressure

— Parental substance abuse

— Emotional problems

— Suffering from general problem behavior syndrome

5. Recognize the different behavior patterns of drug-involved youths

▮ Some youths are occasional users who might sell to friends.

▮ Others are seriously involved in both drug abuse and delinquency; many of these are gang members.

▮ There are also "losers," who filter in and out of the juvenile justice system.

▮ A small percentage of teenage users remain involved with drugs into adulthood.

6. Understand the relationship between drug use and delinquency

▮ It is not certain whether drug abuse causes delinquency.

▮ Some experts believe there is a common cause for both delinquency and drug abuse—perhaps alienation and rage.

7. Be familiar with the major drug-control strategies

▮ Many attempts have been made to control the drug trade.

▮ Some try to inhibit the importation of drugs, others to close down major drug rings, and a few to stop street-level dealing.

▮ There are also attempts to treat users through rehabilitation programs, reduce juvenile use by educational efforts, and implement harm reduction measures.

▮ Some communities have mounted grassroots drives.

▮ These efforts have not been totally successful, although overall use of drugs may have declined somewhat.

8. Be able to argue the pros and cons of government use of different drug-control strategies

▮ It is difficult to eradicate drug abuse because there is so much profit to be made from the sale of drugs.

▮ One suggestion: legalize drugs. But critics warn that such a step may produce greater numbers of substance abusers. Supporters of legalization argue that it would greatly reduce the violence and other criminal activity associated with drug dealing.

Key Terms

Viewpoint

You are a state legislator who is a member of the subcommittee on juvenile justice. Your committee has been asked to redesign the state's juvenile code because of public outrage over serious juvenile crime. At an open hearing, a professor from the local university testifies that she has devised a surefire test to predict violence-prone delinquents. The procedure involves brain scans, DNA testing, and blood analysis. Used with samples of incarcerated adolescents, her procedure has been able to distinguish with 90 percent accuracy between youths with a history of violence and those who are exclusively property offenders. The professor testifies that if each juvenile offender was tested with her techniques, the violence-prone career offender could easily be identified and given special treatment.

Opponents argue that this type of testing is unconstitutional because it violates the Fifth Amendment protection against self-incrimination and can unjustly label nonviolent offenders. Any attempt to base policy on biosocial makeup seems inherently wrong and unfair.

Those who favor the professor's approach maintain that it is not uncommon to single out the insane or mentally incompetent for special treatment and that these conditions often have a biological basis. It is better that a few delinquents be unfairly labeled than seriously violent offenders be ignored until it is too late.

I Is it possible that some kids are born to be delinquents? Or do kids "choose" crime?

I Is it fair to test kids to see if they have biological traits related to crime, even if they have never committed a single offense?

I Should special laws be created to deal with the potentially dangerous offender?

I Should offenders be typed on the basis of their biological characteristics?

Doing Research on the Web

The following organizations provide more information on different approaches to reducing teenage drug use. Before you answer the questions above, check out their websites via **academic.cengage.com/criminaljustice/siegel**

The Open Society Institute

Centers for Disease Control and Prevention Health Programs

National Institute on Drug Abuse

National Center on Addiction and Substance Abuse at Columbia University

Partnership for a Drug-Free America

The U.S. Bureau of Customs and Border Protection

Questions for Discussion

1. Discuss the differences among the various categories and types of substances of abuse. Is the term "drugs" too broad to have real meaning?

2. Why do you think youths take drugs? Do you know anyone with an addiction-prone personality?

3. What policy might be the best strategy to reduce teenage drug use: Source control? Reliance on treatment? National education efforts? Community-level enforcement? Harm reduction measures?

4. Under what circumstances, if any, might the legalization or decriminalization of drugs be beneficial to society?

5. Do you consider alcohol a drug? Should greater controls be placed on the sale of alcohol?

6. Do TV shows and films glorify drug usage and encourage youths to enter the drug trade? Should all images of drinking and smoking be banned from TV? What about advertisements that try to convince youths how much fun it is to drink beer or smoke cigarettes?

Notes

1. Lloyd D. Johnston, Patrick M. O'Malley, Jerald G. Bachman, and John E. Schulenberg, *Teen Drug Use Continues Down in 2006, Particularly among Older Teens; But Use of Prescription-Type Drugs Remains High* (Ann Arbor, MI: University of Michigan News and Information Services, December 21, 2006), table 1.

2. Peter Greenwood, "Substance Abuse Problems among High-Risk Youth and Potential Interventions," *Crime and Delinquency* 38:444–458 (1992).

3. Office of Applied Studies, Substance Abuse and Mental Health Services Administration, "Youth Violence and Illicit Drug Use," *The NSDUH Report* 5 (Washington, DC: Author, 2006).

4. Gary M. McClelland, Linda A. Teplin, and Karen M. Abram, *Detection and Prevalence of Substance Use among Juvenile Detainees* (Washington, DC: Office of Juvenile Justice and Delinquency Prevention, 2006), pp. 4, 6.

5. Jonathan G. Tubman, Andrés G. Gil, and Eric F. Wagner, "Co-Occurring Substance Use and Delinquent Behavior during Early Adolescence: Emerging Relations and Implications for Intervention Strategies," *Criminal Justice and Behavior* 31:463–488 (2004).

6. Dennis Coon, *Introduction to Psychology* (St. Paul, MN: West, 1992), p. 178.

7. Alan Neaigus, Aylin Atillasoy, Samuel Friedman, Xavier Andrade, Maureen Miller, Gilbert Ildefonso, and Don Des Jarlais, "Trends in the Noninjected Use of Heroin and Factors Associated with the Transition to Injecting," in James Inciardi and Lana Harrison, eds., *Heroin in the Age of Crack-Cocaine* (Thousand Oaks, CA: Sage Publications, 1998), pp. 108–130.

8. Johnston, O'Malley, Bachman, and Schulenberg, *Teen Drug Use Continues Down in 2006, Particularly among Older Teens; But Use of Prescription-Type Drugs Remains High*, tables 1, 2.

9. Special Issue, "Drugs—The American Family in Crisis," *Juvenile and Family Court* 39:45–46 (1988).

10. Federal Bureau of Investigation, *Crime in the United States, 2005* (Washington, DC: U.S. Government Printing Office, 2006), tables 29, 38.

11. Henrick J. Harwood, *Updating Estimates of the Economic Costs of Alcohol Abuse in the United States: Estimates, Update Methods, and Data,* report prepared by the Lewin Group for the National Institute of Alcohol Abuse

and Alcoholism (Rockville, MD: U.S. Department of Health and Human Services, 2000), table 3.

12. D. J. Rohsenow, "Drinking Habits and Expectancies about Alcohol's Effects for Self versus Others," *Journal of Consulting and Clinical Psychology* 51:75–76 (1983).

13. Spencer Rathus, *Psychology*, 4th ed. (New York: Holt, Rinehart & Winston, 1990), p. 161.

14. National Drug Intelligence Center, *Methamphetamine Drug Threat Assessment* (Johnstown, PA: Author, 2005), p. 10.

15. Mary Tabor, "'Ice' in an Island Paradise," *Boston Globe*, 8 December 1989, p. 3.

16. Johnston, O'Malley, Bachman, and Schulenberg, *Teen Drug Use Continues Down in 2006, Particularly among Older Teens; But Use of Prescription-Type Drugs Remains High*, table 2.

17. National Drug Intelligence Center, *Methamphetamine Drug Threat Assessment*, p. 8.

18. Dana Hunt, Sarah Kuck, and Linda Truitt, *Methamphetamine Use: Lessons Learned* (Cambridge, MA: Abt Associates Inc., 2005), pp. iv, v.

19. Fox Butterfield, "Fighting an Illegal Drug Through Its Legal Source," *New York Times*, 30 January 2005, p. A18; Kate Zernike, "Potent Mexican Meth Floods In as States Curb Domestic Variety," *New York Times*, 23 January 2006.

20. Paul Goldstein, "Anabolic Steroids: An Ethnographic Approach," unpublished paper (Narcotics and Drug Research, Inc., March 1989).

21. Centers for Disease Control and Prevention, "Use of Cigarettes and Other Tobacco Products among Students Aged 13–15 Years—Worldwide, 1999–2005," *Morbidity and Mortality Weekly Report* 55:553–556 (2006).

22. Joe Nocera, "If It's Good for Philip Morris, Can It Also Be Good for Public Health?," *New York Times Magazine*, 18 June 2006, pp. 46–53, 70, 76–78.

23. Clete Snell and Laura Bailey, "Operation Storefront: Observations of Tobacco Retailer Advertising Compliance with Tobacco Laws," *Youth Violence and Juvenile Justice* 3:78–90 (2005).

24. Johnston, O'Malley, Bachman, and Schulenberg, *Teen Drug Use Continues Down in 2006, Particularly among Older Teens; But Use of Prescription-Type Drugs Remains High*, table 1.

25. Ibid., table 2.

26. Ibid., p. 4.

27. Steven P. Kurtz, James A. Inciardi, Hilary L. Surratt, and Linda Cottler, "Prescription Drug Abuse among Ecstasy Users in Miami," *Journal of Addictive Diseases* 24:1–16 (2005); Ronnie Garrett, "Legal Highs: When the Drug Is Legal, What Can Law Enforcement Do?" *Law Enforcement Technology* 32(5):34–39, 42–44, 46 (2005).

28. *PRIDE Questionnaire Report for Grades 6 thru 12: 2004–05 National Summary* (Bowling Green, KY: PRIDE Surveys, August 17, 2006), tables 2.9, 2.10.

29. Department of Health and Human Services, *Results from the 2004 National Survey on Drug Use and Health: National Findings* (Rockville, MD: Department of Health and Human Services, Substance Abuse and Mental Health Services Administration, Office of Applied Studies, 2005).

30. Ibid., p. 14.

31. Ibid., pp. 23–24.

32. Ibid., p. 17; Office of National Drug Control Policy, *Girls and Drugs: A New Analysis: Recent Trends, Risk Factors, and Consequences* (Washington, DC: Office of National Drug Control Policy, Executive Office of the President, 2006), fig. 3.

33. Office of National Drug Control Policy, *Girls and Drugs: A New Analysis: Recent Trends, Risk Factors, and Consequences*, pp. 1–3.

34. Diana C. Noone, "Drug Use among Juvenile Detainees," in National Institute of Justice, *Arrestee Drug Abuse Monitoring: 2000 Annual Report* (Washington, DC: National Institute of Justice, 2003), p. 135.

35. McClelland, Teplin, and Abram, *Detection and Prevalence of Substance Use among Juvenile Detainees*.

36. Julia Yun Soo Kim, Michael Fendrich, and Joseph Wislar, "The Validity of Juvenile Arrestees' Drug Use Reporting: A Gender Comparison," *Journal of Research in Crime and Delinquency* 37:419–432 (2000).

37. G. E. Vallant, "Parent-Child Disparity and Drug Addiction," *Journal of Nervous and Mental Disease* 142:534–539 (1966).

38. Charles Winick, "Epidemiology of Narcotics Use," in D. Wilner and G. Kassenbaum, eds., *Narcotics* (New York: McGraw-Hill, 1965), pp. 3–18.

39. Delbert Elliott, David Huizinga, and Scott Menard, *Multiple Problem Youth: Delinquency, Substance Abuse and Mental Health Problems* (New York: Springer-Verlag, 1989).

40. Peter Reuter, Robert MacCoun, and Patrick Murphy, *Money from Crime: A Study of the Economics of Drug Dealing in Washington, D.C.* (Santa Monica: Rand, 1990).

41. Thomas Dishion, Deborah Capaldi, Kathleen Spracklen, and Fuzhong Li, "Peer Ecology of Male Adolescent Drug Use," *Development and Psychopathology* 7:803–824 (1995).

42. C. Bowden, "Determinants of Initial Use of Opioids," *Comprehensive Psychiatry* 12:136–140 (1971).

43. Terence Thornberry and Marvin Krohn, "Peers, Drug Use and Delinquency," in David Stoff, James Breiling, and Jack Maser, eds., *Handbook of Antisocial Behavior* (New York: Wiley, 1997), pp. 218–233.

44. Richard Cloward and Lloyd Ohlin, *Delinquency and Opportunity: A Theory of Delinquent Gangs* (Glencoe, IL: Free Press, 1960).

45. Denise Kandel and Mark Davies, "Friendship Networks, Intimacy and Illicit Drug Use in Young Adulthood: A Comparison of Two Competing Theories," *Criminology* 29:441–471 (1991).

46. James Inciardi, Ruth Horowitz, and Anne Pottieger, *Street Kids, Street Drugs, Street Crime: An Examination of Drug Use and Serious Delinquency in Miami* (Belmont, CA: Wadsworth, 1993), p. 43.

47. D. Baer and J. Corrado, "Heroin Addict Relationships with Parents during Childhood and Early Adolescent Years," *Journal of Genetic Psychology* 124:99–103 (1974).

48. Timothy Ireland and Cathy Spatz Widom, *Childhood Victimization and Risk for Alcohol and Drug Arrests* (Washington, DC: National Institute of Justice, 1995).

49. See S. F. Bucky, "The Relationship between Background and Extent of Heroin Use," *American Journal of Psychiatry* 130:709–710 (1973); I. Chien, D. L. Gerard, R. Lee, and E. Rosenfield, *The Road to H: Narcotics Delinquency and Social Policy* (New York: Basic Books, 1964).

50. J. S. Mio, G. Nanjundappa, D. E. Verlur, and M. D. DeRios, "Drug Abuse and the Adolescent Sex Offender: A Preliminary Analysis," *Journal of Psychoactive Drugs* 18:65–72 (1986).

51. G. T. Wilson, "Cognitive Studies in Alcoholism," *Journal of Consulting and Clinical Psychology* 55:325–331 (1987).

52. John Hagedorn, Jose Torres, and Greg Giglio, "Cocaine, Kicks, and Strain: Patterns of Substance Use in Milwaukee Gangs," *Contemporary Drug Problems* 25:113–145 (1998).

53. For a thorough review, see Karol Kumpfer, "Impact of Maternal Characteristics and Parenting Processes on Children of Drug Abusers," paper presented at the annual meeting of the American Society of Criminology, Boston, November 1995.

54. D. W. Goodwin, "Alcoholism and Genetics," *Archives of General Psychiatry* 42:171–174 (1985).

55. Ibid.

56. Patricia Dobkin, Richard Tremblay, Louise Masse, and Frank Vitaro, "Individual and Peer Characteristics in Predicting Boys' Early Onset of Substance Abuse: A Seven-Year Longitudinal Study," *Child Development* 66:1198–1214 (1995).

57. Ric Steele, Rex Forehand, Lisa Armistead, and Gene Brody, "Predicting Alcohol and Drug Use in Early Adulthood: The Role of Internalizing and Externalizing Behavior Problems in Early Adolescence," *American Journal of Orthopsychiatry* 65:380–387 (1995).

58. Ibid., pp. 380–381.

59. Jerome Platt and Christina Platt, *Heroin Addiction* (New York: Wiley, 1976), p. 127.

60. Rathus, *Psychology*, p. 158.

61. Eric Strain, "Antisocial Personality Disorder, Misbehavior and Drug Abuse," *Journal of Nervous and Mental Disease* 163:162–165 (1995).

62. Dobkin, Tremblay, Masse, and Vitaro, "Individual and Peer Characteristics in Predicting Boys' Early Onset of Substance Abuse."

63. J. Shedler and J. Block, "Adolescent Drug Use and Psychological Health: A Longitudinal Inquiry," *American Psychologist* 45:612–630 (1990).

64. Greenwood, "Substance Abuse Problems among High-Risk Youth and Potential Interventions," p. 448.

65. John Wallace and Jerald Bachman, "Explaining Racial/Ethnic Differences in Adolescent Drug Use: The Impact of Background and Lifestyle," *Social Problems* 38:333–357 (1991).

66. Marvin Krohn, Terence Thornberry, Lori Collins-Hall, and Alan Lizotte, "School Dropout, Delinquent Behavior, and Drug Use," in Howard Kaplan, ed., *Drugs, Crime and Other Deviant Adaptations: Longitudinal Studies* (New York: Plenum Press, 1995), pp. 163–183.

67. B. A. Christiansen, G. T. Smith, P. V. Roehling, and M. S. Goldman, "Using Alcohol Expectancies to Predict Adolescent Drinking Behavior after One Year," *Journal of Counseling and Clinical Psychology* 57:93–99 (1989).

68. Inciardi, Horowitz, and Pottieger, *Street Kids, Street Drugs, Street Crime*, p. 135.

69. Ibid., p. 136.

70. Mary Ellen Mackesy-Amiti, Michael Fendrich, and Paul Goldstein, "Sequence of Drug Use among Serious Drug Users: Typical vs. Atypical Progression," *Drug and Alcohol Dependence* 45:185–196 (1997).

71. The following sections lean heavily on Marcia Chaiken and Bruce Johnson, *Characteristics of Different Types of Drug-Involved Youth* (Washington, DC: National Institute of Justice, 1988).

72. Ibid., p. 100.

73. Inciardi, Horowitz, and Pottieger, *Street Kids, Street Drugs, Street Crime*.

74. Lening Zhang, John Welte, and William Wieczorek, "Youth Gangs, Drug Use and Delinquency," *Journal of Criminal Justice* 27:101–109 (1999).

75. Chaiken and Johnson, *Characteristics of Different Types of Drug-Involved Youth*, p. 12.

76. Carolyn Rebecca Block, Antigone Christakos, Ayad Jacob, and Roger Przybylski, *Street Gangs and Crime* (Chicago: Illinois Criminal Justice Information Authority, 1996).

77. Rick Graves and Ed Allen, *Narcotics and Black Gangs* (Los Angeles: Los Angeles County Sheriff's Department, n.d.).

78. John Hagedorn, "Neighborhoods, Markets, and Gang Drug Organization," *Journal of Research in Crime and Delinquency* 31:264–294 (1994).

79. Chaiken and Johnson, *Characteristics of Different Types of Drug-Involved Youth*, p. 14.

80. Eric Baumer, Janet Lauritsen, Richard Rosenfeld, and Richard Wright, "The Influence of Crack Cocaine on Robbery, Burglary, and Homicide Rates: A Cross-City, Longitudinal Analysis," *Journal of Research in Crime and Delinquency* 35:316–340 (1998).

81. Ibid.

82. James Inciardi, "Heroin Use and Street Crime," *Crime and Delinquency* 25:335–346 (1979); James Inciardi, *The War on Drugs* (Palo Alto, CA: Mayfield, 1986); see also W. McGlothlin, M. Anglin, and B. Wilson, "Narcotic Addiction and Crime," *Criminology* 16:293–311 (1978); George Speckart and M. Douglas Anglin, "Narcotics Use and Crime: An Overview of Recent Research Advances," *Contemporary Drug Problems* 13:741–769 (1986); Charles Faupel and Carl Klockars, "Drugs-Crime Connections: Elaborations from the Life Histories of Hard-Core Heroin Addicts," *Social Problems* 34:54–68 (1987).

83. Eric Baumer, "Poverty, Crack and Crime: A Cross-City Analysis," *Journal of Research in Crime and Delinquency* 31:311–327 (1994).

84. Marvin Dawkins, "Drug Use and Violent Crime among Adolescents," *Adolescence* 32:395–406 (1997); Robert Peralta, "The Relationship between Alcohol and Violence in an Adolescent Population: An Analysis of the Monitoring the Future Survey," paper presented at the annual meeting

of the Society of Criminology, San Diego, November 1997; Helene Raskin White and Stephen Hansell, "The Moderating Effects of Gender and Hostility on the Alcohol-Aggression Relationship," *Journal of Research in Crime and Delinquency* 33:450–470 (1996); D. Wayne Osgood, "Drugs, Alcohol, and Adolescent Violence," paper presented at the annual meeting of the American Society of Criminology, Miami, November 1994.

85. Fox Butterfield, "Justice Department Ends Testing of Criminals for Drug Use," *New York Times*, 28 January 2004.

86. Arrestee Drug Abuse Monitoring [ADAM] Program, *Preliminary Data on Drug Use and Related Matters among Adult Arrestees and Juvenile Detainees, 2002* (Washington, DC: National Institute of Justice) tables 2 and 3.

87. David Cantor, "Drug Involvement and Offending of Incarcerated Youth," paper presented at the annual meeting of the American Society of Criminology, Boston, November 1995.

88. B. D. Johnson, E. Wish, J. Schmeidler, and D. Huizinga, "Concentration of Delinquent Offending: Serious Drug Involvement and High Delinquency Rates," *Journal of Drug Issues* 21:205–229 (1991).

89. Inciardi, Horowitz, and Pottieger, *Street Kids, Street Drugs, Street Crime.*

90. W. David Watts and Lloyd Wright, "The Relationship of Alcohol, Tobacco, Marijuana, and Other Illegal Drug Use to Delinquency among Mexican-American, Black, and White Adolescent Males," *Adolescence* 25:38–54 (1990).

91. For a general review of this issue, see Helene Raskin White, "The Drug Use–Delinquency Connection in Adolescence," in Ralph Weisheit, ed., *Drugs, Crime and Criminal Justice* (Cincinnati: Anderson, 1990), pp. 215–256; Speckart and Anglin, "Narcotics Use and Crime"; Faupel and Klockars, "Drugs-Crime Connections."

92. Delbert Elliott, David Huizinga, and Susan Ageton, *Explaining Delinquency and Drug Abuse* (Beverly Hills: Sage Publications, 1985).

93. David Huizinga, Scott Menard, and Delbert Elliott, "Delinquency and Drug Use: Temporal and Developmental Patterns," *Justice Quarterly* 6:419–455 (1989).

94. Jason A. Ford, "The Connection Between Heavy Drinking and Juvenile Delinquency during Adolescence," *Sociological Spectrum* 25:629–650 (2005).

95. Helene Raskin White, Robert Padina, and Randy LaGrange, "Longitudinal Predictors of Serious Substance Use and Delinquency," *Criminology* 25:715–740 (1987).

96. Bu Huang, Helene White, Rick Kosterman, Richard Catalano, and J. David Hawkins, "Developmental Associations between Alcohol and Interpersonal Aggression during Adolescence," *Journal of Research in Crime and Delinquency* 38:64–83 (2001).

97. Eric Wish, "U.S. Drug Policy in the 1990s: Insights from New Data from Arrestees," *International Journal of the Addictions* 25:1–15 (1990).

98. Graham Farrell, "Drugs and Drug Control," in Graeme Newman, ed., *Global Report on Crime and Justice* (New York: Oxford University Press, 1999), p. 177.

99. U.S. Department of State, 1998 International Narcotics Control Strategy Report, February 1999.

100. Clifford Krauss, "Neighbors Worry about Colombian Aid," *New York Times*, 25 August 2000, p. A3; see also Juan Forero, "Colombia's Coca Survives U.S. Plan to Uproot It," *New York Times*, 19 August 2006.

101. Juan Forero with Tim Weiner, "Latin America Poppy Fields Undermine U.S. Drug Battle," *New York Times*, 8 August 2003, p. A1.

102. United Nations, *2007 World Drug Report* (Vienna, Austria: Office on Drugs and Crime, United Nations, 2007).

103. Carlotta Gall, "Another Year of Drug War, and the Poppy Crop Flourishes," *New York Times*, 17 February 2006.

104. U.S. Drug Enforcement Administration, *National Drug Threat Assessment 2007* (Washington, DC: National Drug Intelligence Center, U.S. Drug Enforcement Administration, 2006), app. B, table 3.

105. United Nations, *2007 World Drug Report*, p. 8.

106. "Operation Webslinger Targets Illegal Internet Trafficking of Date-Rape Drug," *U.S. Customs Today* 38 (2002).

107. Gardiner Harris, "Two Agencies to Fight Online Narcotics Sales," *New York Times*, 18 October 2003.

108. U.S. Drug Enforcement Administration, *National Drug Threat Assessment 2007*, fig. 1.

109. Fox Butterfield, "Home Drug-Making Laboratories Expose Children to Toxic Fallout," *New York Times*, 23 February 2004.

110. Mark Moore, *Drug Trafficking* (Washington, DC: National Institute of Justice, 1988).

111. Howard Snyder and Melissa Sickmund, *Juvenile Offenders and Victims: 2006 National Report* (Pittsburgh, PA: National Center for Juvenile Justice, 2006), pp. 168, 178–182.

112. Christopher L. Ringwalt, Susan Ennett, Amy Vincus, Judy Thorne, Louise Ann Rohrbach, and Ashley Simons-Rudolph, "The Prevalence of Effective Substance Use Prevention in U.S. Middle Schools," *Prevention Science* 3:257–265.

113. Jane Carlisle Maxwell, Melissa Tackett-Gibson, and James Dyer, "Substance Use in Urban and Rural Texas School Districts," *Drugs: Education, Prevention and Policy* 13:327–339 (2006).

114. Denise C. Gottfredson, David B. Wilson, and Stacy S. Najaka, "School-Based Crime Prevention," in Lawrence W. Sherman, David P. Farrington, Brandon C. Welsh, and Doris Layton MacKenzie, eds., *Evidence-Based Crime Prevention* (New York: Routledge, 2006, rev. ed.), table 4.9; see also Phyllis Ellickson, Robert Bell, and K. McGuigan, "Preventing Adolescent Drug Use: Long-Term Results of a Junior High Program," *American Journal of Public Health* 83:856–861 (1993).

115. *Partnership Attitude Tracking Study: Teens, 2004* (Washington, DC: Office of National Drug Control Policy, 2005), pp. 12, 24.

116. Department of Health and Human Services, *Results from the 2004 National Survey on Drug Use and Health: National Findings*, p. 65.

117. Lori K. Holleran, Margaret A. Taylor-Seehafer, Elizabeth C. Pomeroy, and James Alan Neff, "Substance Abuse Prevention for High-Risk Youth: Exploring Culture and Alcohol and Drug Use," *Alcoholism Treatment Quarterly* 23:165–184 (2005).

118. Brandon C. Welsh and Akemi Hoshi, "Communities and Crime Prevention," in Sherman, Farrington, Welsh, and MacKenzie, eds., *Evidence-Based Crime Prevention*, pp. 184–186.

119. Substance Abuse and Mental Health Services Administration, Office of Applied Studies, *Treatment Episode Data Sets (TEDS). Highlights—2004* (Rockville, MD: National Admissions to Substance Abuse Treatment Services, DASIS Series: S-31, DHHS Publication No. (SMA) 06-4140, 2006).

120. Andrew R. Morral, Daniel F. McCaffrey, Greg Ridgeway, Arnab Mukherji, and Christopher Beighley, *The Relative Effectiveness of 10 Adolescent Substance Abuse Treatment Programs in the United States* (Arlington, VA: Drug Policy Research Center, RAND Corporation, 2006).

121. Scott W. Henggeler, Sonja K. Schoenwald, Charles M. Borduin, Melisa D. Rowland, and Phillippe B. Cunningham, *Multisystemic Treatment of Antisocial Behavior in Children and Adolescents* (New York: Guilford, 1998).

122. Scott W. Henggeler, W. Glenn Clingempeel, Michael J. Brondino, and Susan G. Pickrel, "Four-Year Follow-Up of Multisystemic Therapy with Substance-Abusing and Substance-Dependent Juvenile Offenders," *Journal of the American Academy of Child and Adolescent Psychiatry* 41:868–874 (2002).

123. Eli Ginzberg, Howard Berliner, and Miriam Ostrow, *Young People at Risk: Is Prevention Possible?* (Boulder: Westview Press, 1988), p. 99.

124. James C. Howell, *Preventing and Reducing Juvenile Delinquency: A Comprehensive Framework* (Thousand Oaks, CA: Sage Publications, 2003), p. 139; see also Morral, McCaffrey, Ridgeway, Mukherji, and Beighley, *The Relative Effectiveness of 10 Adolescent Substance Abuse Treatment Programs in the United States.*

125. Ginzberg, Berliner, and Ostrow, *Young People at Risk: Is Prevention Possible?*

126. Donnie W. Watson, Lorrie Bisesi, Susie Tanamly, and Noemi Mai, "Comprehensive Residential Education, Arts, and Substance Abuse Treatment (CREASAT): A Model Treatment Program for Juvenile Offenders," *Youth Violence and Juvenile Justice* 1:388–401 (2003).

127. The following section is adapted from Curtis J. Vander Waal, Duane C. McBride, Yvonne M. Terry-McElrath, and Holly Van Buren, *Breaking the Juvenile Drug-Crime Cycle* (Washington, DC: National Institute of Justice, 2001).

128. Steven R. Donziger, ed., *The Real War on Crime: The Report of the National Criminal Justice Commission* (New York: HarperPerennial, 1996), pp. 201–202.

129. Charlotte Allan and Nat Wright, "Harm Reduction: The Least Worst Treatment of All; Tackling Drug Addiction Has Few Easy Solutions," *Student British Medical Journal* 12:92–93 (2004), p. 92.

130. Ibid.

131. Ibid.; see also Erik K. Laursen and Paul Brasler, "Is Harm Reduction a Viable Choice for Kids Enchanted with Drugs?" *Reclaiming Children and Youth* 11:181–183 (2002).

132. Donziger, *The Real War on Crime*, p. 201.

133. Snyder and Sickmund, *Juvenile Offenders and Victims: 2006 National Report*, pp. 163, 169.

134. Eric L. Jensen, Jurg Gerber, and Clayton Mosher, "Social Consequences of the War on Drugs: The Legacy of Failed Policy," *Criminal Justice Policy Review* 15:100–121 (2004).

135. Donnie R. Marshall, DEA congressional testimony, Senate Caucus on International Narcotics Control, March 21, 2001.

136. Kathryn Ann Farr, "Revitalizing the Drug Decriminalization Debate," *Crime and Delinquency* 36:223–237 (1990).

137. Reuter, MacCoun, and Murphy, *Money from Crime*, pp. 165–168.

12

Delinquency Prevention: Social and Developmental Perspectives

Chapter Outline

Chapter Objectives

1. Know the difference between delinquency prevention and delinquency control
2. Have an understanding of the magnitude of cost to society caused by juvenile crime and violence
3. Be able to identify some of the major historical events that gave rise to the present focus on delinquency prevention
4. Be familiar with different approaches to classifying delinquency prevention programs
5. Know the key features of the developmental perspective of delinquency prevention
6. Have an understanding of the many different types of effective delinquency prevention programs for children and teens
7. Be able to identify some of the key factors of effective programs
8. Be able to discuss some of the other benefits that are produced by delinquency prevention programs
9. Be able to identify and comment on pressing issues facing the future of delinquency prevention

For Michelle, a British citizen, age 16 and pregnant with her first child, violence came early in life and at the hands of her mother, her unborn child's grandmother. Living in poverty, with no family other than her distant mother, and having already experienced violence at the hands of a loved one, Michelle (her last name withheld to protect her identity) is confronted with many of the obstacles in life that put her and her baby at increased risk for a wide range of health and social problems. Some of these problems include abuse of drugs and alcohol, unemployment, and reliance on social services, and for the child, low birth weight, neglect and abuse, behavioral problems, and later involvement in delinquent and criminal activities.

In April 2007, the British government set out to help improve the life chances of Michelle and her baby along with hundreds of other similar young mothers and their newborns by providing specially trained nurses to visit them at their homes during the final months of pregnancy and up to the child's second birthday. The nurses visit every week in the beginning and then every other week. Each visit lasts about two hours. During these visits mothers get advice about care of the child, infant development, and the importance of proper nutrition and avoiding smoking and drinking during pregnancy. The home visits also serve to improve the well-being of the mothers, linking them to community resources to help with employment, education, or addiction recovery. In the words of the early intervention expert Deanna Gomby and her colleagues, "Home visitors can see the environments in which families live, gain a better understanding of the families' needs, and therefore tailor services to meet those needs. The relationships forged between home visitors and parents can break through loneliness and isolation and serve as the first step in linking families to their communities."

In the United States, this program, known as the Nurse-Family Partnership and developed by David Olds at the University of Colorado, has proven tremendously successful. Through three large-scale trials in Elmira (New York), Memphis, and Denver, it has been found to improve women's prenatal health, increase the spacing among subsequent pregnancies, reduce child abuse, neglect, and injuries, improve children's school readiness, and reduce adolescent crime and substance use. Today, the Nurse-Family Partnership is operating in 280 counties in 22 states across the country, serving 13,000 families each year.

It was this success that caught the attention of the British government. (The program has already been implemented in 10 cities and towns across Britain.) For Michelle and hundreds of other teenage mothers like her, the government sees this scientifically proven program as the best chance of saving these children from the cycle of violence, poverty, and despair to which their young mothers fell victim.[1]

Public officials faced with the problem of juvenile delinquency in their cities have many options. For some, it will be a clear choice of getting tough on juvenile delinquency and implementing punitive or justice-oriented measures. For others, it will be a matter of getting tough on the causes of juvenile delinquency and implementing prevention programs to ward off delinquency before it takes place. Still others will combine justice and nonjustice measures to combat the problem. Ideally, decisions about which approach or which combination of measures to use will be based on the needs of the community and the highest quality available evidence on what works best in preventing juvenile delinquency.

This chapter begins with a discussion of key features of delinquency prevention, which include the differences between prevention and other approaches to tackle delinquent behavior, the financial costs that delinquency imposes on society, and efforts to make sense of the many different types of prevention programs and measures. The history of delinquency prevention in the United States is also discussed. Next, we review the effectiveness of delinquency prevention programs that are provided in the childhood years. Day care, preschool, and primary school programs are among the different types of prevention programs covered. This is followed by a review of the effectiveness of a wide range of delinquency prevention programs implemented in the teenage years, including school-based, after-school, and job training programs. The chapter concludes with a look at key issues to be faced in the ongoing efforts to prevent delinquency.

THE MANY FACES OF DELINQUENCY PREVENTION

delinquency control or delinquency repression
Involves any justice program or policy designed to prevent the occurrence of a future delinquent act.

delinquency prevention
Involves any nonjustice program or policy designed to prevent the occurrence of a future delinquent act.

Preventing juvenile delinquency means many different things to many different people. Programs or policies designed to prevent juvenile delinquency can include the police making an arrest as part of an operation to address gang problems, a juvenile court sanction to a secure correctional facility, or, in the extreme case, a death penalty sentence. These measures are often referred to as **delinquency control** or **delinquency repression**. More often, though, **delinquency prevention** refers to intervening in young people's lives before they engage in delinquency in the first place—that is, preventing the first delinquent act. Both forms of delinquency prevention have a common goal of trying to prevent the occurrence of a future delinquent act, but what distinguishes delinquency prevention from delinquency control is that prevention typically does not involve the juvenile justice system. Instead, programs or policies designed to prevent delinquency involve day care providers, nurses, teachers, social workers, recreation staff at the YMCA, counselors at Boys and Girls Clubs of America, other young people in school, and parents. This form of delinquency prevention is sometimes referred to as nonjustice delinquency prevention or alternative delinquency prevention. Exhibit 12.1 lists examples of programs to prevent and control delinquency.

EXHIBIT **12.1**

Delinquency Prevention vs. Control

Prevention		Control
Home visitation	▮	Antigang police task force
Preschool	▮	Boot camps
Child skills training	▮	Wilderness programs
Mentoring	▮	Probation
After-school recreation	▮	Electronic monitoring
Job training	▮	Secure confinement

Delinquency prevention programs are not designed with the intention of excluding juvenile justice personnel. Many types of delinquency prevention programs, especially those that focus on adolescents, involve juvenile justice personnel such as the police. In these cases, the juvenile justice personnel work in close collaboration with those from such areas as education, health care, recreation, and social services. In this chapter, we focus on delinquency prevention programs that are driven or led by these non–juvenile justice agencies.

An important issue facing delinquency prevention is cost: Programs cost money to run. Expenses include staff salaries, equipment, and sometimes rent for the facilities in which programs take place. Though prevention programs can be costly, they are beneficial because they save money that would otherwise be spent in the justice system.

Costs of Delinquency: A Justification for Prevention

The impacts of juvenile delinquency on society, which include such things as damaged property, pain and suffering to victims, and the involvement of police and other agencies of the juvenile justice system, can be converted into dollars and cents. The damaged property will need to be repaired or replaced, and it is the victim who will often have to pay for this, as many crime victims do not have insurance. The pain and suffering inflicted on an individual from an assault or robbery can result not only in immediate costs of medical care and lost wages from missing work, but also in reduced quality of life from debilitating injuries or fear of being victimized again, which can result in not being able to go to work, long-term medical care, and counseling.

Here again it is the crime victim and also the victim's family, employer, and many services, such as Medicaid, welfare, and mental health, that incur the dollar costs associated with these services. Victim costs resulting from an assault are as high as $9,400, and are even higher for rape and arson (see Figure 12.1). The average murder costs around $3 million.[2] Another study puts the total cost of a murder, which includes victim costs plus costs to the justice system, at just under $10 million.[3] Then there is the cost of the involvement of the police, courts, and corrections agencies. While some of the costs incurred by the juvenile justice system go toward addressing the needs of victims, such as follow-up interviews by police and court-based victim assistance programs, the majority of the costs are directed at the processing of offenders. Police arrest, public defender costs, court appearances, serving a sentence—whether it be probation or incarceration—and aftercare programs upon release into the community are all costly steps in the justice system. There are also costs incurred by society in efforts to prevent juvenile delinquency, through different types of prevention programs.

Economist Mark Cohen estimates that the typical criminal career over the juvenile (ages 14 to 17) and adult (ages 18 to 23) years costs society between $1.3 and $1.5 million.[4] Adding the costs of drug use and dropping out of high school brings the total cost to $1.7 to $2.3 million. Just focusing on juveniles, it has been estimated that a typical juvenile

Costs to crime victims (dollars)

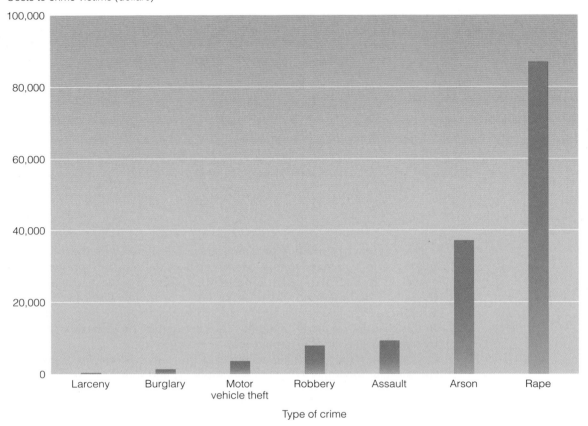

FIGURE 12.1
Costs to Crime Victims

SOURCE: Adapted from Ted R. Miller, Mark A. Cohen, and Brian Wiersema, *Victim Costs and Consequences: A New Look* (Washington, DC: National Institute of Justice, U.S. Department of Justice, 1996), p. 9, table 2.

criminal career imposes costs on society in the range of $80,000 to $325,000. A similar estimate of the cost of a criminal career—for the adult years only—was reported by criminologists Matt Delisi and Jewel Gatling. Based on a sample of 500 career criminals, the authors found that the average criminal career costs society more than $1.1 million.[5] Another study of 500 urban boys between the ages of 7 and 17—based on the youngest sample of the Pittsburgh Youth Study—estimated that those who were chronic offenders caused as much as eight times higher average costs to victims than other juvenile offenders, with costs approaching $1 million for the chronic offenders.[6]

Studies have also looked at the costs of juvenile delinquency to different states and the nation as a whole.

State Costs Ted Miller and his associates examined the costs of juvenile violence in the state of Pennsylvania.[7] The study was based on the violent offenses of murder, rape, robbery, assault, and physical and sexual abuse. Violence by juveniles was estimated to cost $2.6 billion in victim costs and $46 million in perpetrator costs per year. Juvenile perpetrator costs were made up of costs to the juvenile and adult justice systems, which included costs from probation, detention, juvenile treatment programs, and incarceration in adult prisons. Interestingly, this study also reported on the costs of violence against juveniles that was committed by adults and other juveniles. Compared to the victim costs of violence committed by juveniles, the victim costs of violence committed against juveniles was much higher: $4.5 billion versus $2.6 billion. The main reason for this difference was because juveniles suffered more sexual abuse—a very costly offense—at the hands of adults, but there was very little sexual abuse by juveniles against adults.

National Costs The only national estimate of the costs of juvenile delinquency focuses on juvenile violence. Violent crime by juveniles costs the United States $158 billion each year.[8] This estimate includes some of the costs incurred by federal, state, and local governments to assist victims of juvenile violence, such as medical treatment for injuries and services for victims. These tangible, or out-of-pocket, victim costs of juvenile violence came to $30 billion. But the majority of the costs of juvenile violence, the remaining $128 billion, were due to losses suffered by victims, such as lost wages, pain, suffering, and reduced quality of life. Missing from this $158 billion price tag of juvenile violence are the costs from society's response to juvenile violence, which include early prevention programs, services for juveniles, and the juvenile justice system. These costs are unknown.

To read more about the **costs of juvenile violence in the United States**, go to the Children's Safety Network Economics and Data Analysis Resource Center via academic.cengage.com/ criminaljustice/siegel.

Considering these costs, it is not surprising that there has been a long-standing effort to prevent juvenile delinquency.

A Brief History of Delinquency Prevention

The history of the prevention of juvenile delinquency in the United States is closely tied to the history of juvenile justice in this country. From the founding of the House of Refuge, which opened in New York in 1825, to more contemporary events, such as amendments to the federal Juvenile Justice and Delinquency Prevention Act of 1974, child-saving organizations and lawmakers have had an interest in both the prevention and control of delinquency. However, many social scientists have noted that efforts to prevent juveniles from engaging in delinquency in the first place were secondary to and often overlooked in favor of interventions with juveniles who had already committed delinquent acts.[9] This imbalance between prevention and control of juvenile delinquency remains in place to this day.

Chicago Area Project One of the earliest juvenile delinquency prevention programs was the Chicago Area Project, which was started in 1933 by Clifford Shaw and Henry McKay.[10] This project was designed to produce social change in communities that suffered from high delinquency rates and gang activity. As part of the project, qualified local leaders coordinated social service centers that promoted community solidarity and counteracted social disorganization. More than 20 different programs were developed, featuring discussion groups, counseling services, hobby groups, school-related activities, and recreation. There is still some question of whether these programs had a positive influence on the delinquency rate. Some evaluations

After identifying that the highest delinquency rates in early 1930s Chicago were in the poverty-stricken, transitional, inner-city zones, sociologists Clifford Shaw and Henry McKay set out to design and implement a program to target key community-level determinants of the delinquency problem. The result was the Chicago Area Project, an early innovative model of delinquency prevention. Shown here are youths of the Boy Scout Troop at Camp Reinberg in 1946, one of the programs offered by the Chicago Area Project.

Courtesy of Chicago Area Project

indicated positive results, but others showed that the Chicago Area Project efforts did little to reduce juvenile delinquency.[11]

Cambridge-Somerville Youth Study Another well-known delinquency prevention program that was implemented around the same time as the Chicago project was the Cambridge-Somerville (Massachusetts) Youth Study.[12] The focus of this program was more on improving individuals than their surroundings. One interesting feature of this program is that it was one of the first delinquency prevention programs to be evaluated using a randomized experimental design. Prior to the start of the program, 650 boys (325 matched pairs) were assigned to receive the program (the experimental group) or not to receive the program (the control group). The experimental group boys received regular friendly attention from counselors for an average of five years and whatever medical and educational services were needed. The counselors talked to the boys, took them on trips and to recreational activities, tutored them in reading and arithmetic, played games with them at the project's center, encouraged them to attend church, and visited their families to give advice and general support. The program was to have continued for 10 years, but when America became involved in World War II, many of the adult counselors were drafted.[13] An evaluation of the program 30 years after it ended, when the men were 45 years old, found that those in the experimental group committed more crime than those in the control group.[14] One possible reason for this negative result was that the program was done in groups instead of one on one. The group format was thought to have resulted in minor delinquents being influenced by more involved or serious delinquents.[15]

Detached Street Workers In the 1950s, a major focus of delinquency prevention programs was to reach out to youths who were unlikely to use community centers. Instead of having troubled youths come to them, detached street workers were sent into inner-city neighborhoods, creating close relationships with juvenile gangs and groups in their own milieu.[16] The best-known detached street worker program was Boston's Mid-City Project, which dispatched trained social workers to seek out and meet with youth gangs three to four times a week on the gangs' own turf. Their goal was to modify the organization of the gang and allow gang members a chance to engage in more conventional behaviors. The detached street workers tried to help gang members get jobs and educational opportunities. They acted as go-betweens for gang members with agents of the power structure—lawyers, judges, parole officers, and the like. Despite these efforts, an evaluation of the program by Walter Miller failed to show that it resulted in a significant reduction in criminal activity.[17]

Federally Funded Programs The 1960s ushered in a tremendous interest in the prevention of delinquency. Much of this interest was in programs based on social structure theory. This approach seemed quite compatible with the rehabilitative policies of the Kennedy (New Frontier) and Johnson (Great Society/War on Poverty) administrations. Delinquency prevention programs received a great deal of federal funding. The most ambitious of these was the New York City–based Mobilization for Youth (MOBY). Funded by more than $50 million, MOBY attempted an integrated approach to community development. Based on Cloward and Ohlin's concept of providing opportunities for legitimate success, MOBY created employment opportunities in the community, coordinated social services, and sponsored social action groups such as tenants' committees, legal action services, and voter registration. But MOBY ended for lack of funding amid questions about its utility and use of funds.

Improving the socialization of lower-class youths to reduce their potential for future delinquency was also an important focus of other federally funded programs during the 1960s. The largest and best known of these programs was Head Start, a national program for preschoolers that continues to this day. (See the accompanying Policy and Practice box.)

Contemporary Preventive Approaches The emphasis on large-scale federally funded programs aimed at the prevention of delinquency continued into the 1970s

randomized experimental design
Considered the "gold standard" of evaluation designs to measure the effect of a program on delinquency or other outcomes. Involves randomly assigning subjects either to receive the program (the experimental group) or not receive it (the control group).

experimental group
The group of subjects that receives the program.

control group
The comparison group of subjects that does not receive the program.

To read more about **Head Start**, go to academic.cengage.com/criminaljustice/siegel.

POLICY AND PRACTICE

Head Start

Head Start is probably the best-known effort to help lower-class youths achieve proper socialization and, in so doing, reduce their potential for future criminality. Head Start programs were instituted in the 1960s as part of President Lyndon Johnson's War on Poverty. In the beginning, Head Start was a two-month summer program for children who were about to enter a school that was aimed at embracing the "whole child." In embracing the whole child, the school offered comprehensive programming that helped improve physical health, enhance mental processes, and improve social and emotional development, self-image, and interpersonal relationships. Preschoolers were provided with an enriched educational environment to develop their learning and cognitive skills. They were given the opportunity to use pegs and pegboards, puzzles, toy animals, dolls, letters and numbers, and other materials that middle-class children take for granted. These opportunities provided the children a leg up in the educational process.

Today, with annual funding approaching $7 billion and an enrollment of close to 1 million children, the Head Start program is administered by the Head Start Bureau, the Administration on Children, Youth, and Families (ACYF), the Administration for Children and Families (ACF), and the Department of Health and Human Services (DHHS). Head Start teachers strive to provide a variety of learning experiences appropriate to the child's age and development. These experiences encourage the child to read books, to understand cultural diversity, to express feelings, and to play with and relate to peers in an appropriate fashion. Students are guided in developing gross and fine motor skills and self-confidence. Health care is also an issue, and most children enrolled in the program receive comprehensive health screening, physical and dental examinations, and appropriate follow-up. Many programs provide meals, and in so doing help children receive proper nourishment.

Head Start programs now serve parents in addition to their preschoolers. Some programs allow parents to enroll in classes, which cover parenting, literacy, nutrition/weight loss, domestic violence prevention, and other social issues; social services, health, nutrition, and educational services are also available.

Considerable controversy has surrounded the success of the Head Start program. In 1970, the Westinghouse Learning Corporation issued a definitive evaluation of the Head Start effort and concluded that there was no evidence of lasting cognitive gains on the part of the participating children. Initial gains seemed to fade away during the elementary school years, and by the third grade, the performance of the Head Start children was no different than their peers.

While disappointing, this evaluation focused on IQ levels and gave short shrift to improvement in social competence and other survival skills. More recent research has produced dramatically different results. One report found that by age 5, children who experienced the enriched day care offered by Head Start averaged more than 10 points higher on their IQ scores than their peers who did not participate in the program. Other research that carefully compared Head Start children to similar youngsters who did not attend the program found that the former made significant intellectual gains. Head Start children were less likely to have been retained in a grade or placed in classes for slow learners; they outperformed peers on achievement tests; and they were more likely to graduate from high school.

Head Start kids also made strides in nonacademic areas: They appear to have better health, immunization rates, nutrition, and enhanced emotional characteristics after leaving the program. Research also shows that the Head Start program can have important psychological benefits for the mothers of participants, such as decreasing depression and anxiety and increasing feelings of life satisfaction. While findings in some areas may be tentative, they are all in the same direction: Head Start enhances school readiness and has enduring effects on social competence.

If, as many experts believe, there are close links among school performance, family life, and crime, programs such as Head Start can help some potentially criminal youths avoid coming into conflict with the law. A large-scale study of the long-term effects of Head Start by economists Eliana Garces, Duncan Thomas, and Janet Currie provides some support for this view. Based on a national panel survey of households, the authors found that children who attended Head Start (at ages 3 to 5) were significantly less likely to report being arrested or referred to court for a crime by ages 18 to 30, compared to their siblings who did not attend the program.

Head Start has also been shown to be a worthwhile investment of taxpayer dollars. One cost-benefit analysis found that the program's short- and medium-term benefits could offset between 40 and 60 percent of its costs, and the addition of a small fraction of long-term benefits (like reductions in juvenile crime) could make it pay for itself. Another cost-benefit analysis by the Washington State Institute for Public Policy found that for every dollar spent on Head Start and early education programs in general, $2.36 was saved to the public in the long run.

Despite these views and the research findings, Head Start faces challenges on a number of fronts. Some proposals for change include turning the program over to state control, focusing more narrowly on improving children's literacy, and mandating more qualified teachers but not providing the necessary resources to improve their low pay. Experts and advocates alike argue that these measures threaten to "water down" one of the most successful national programs for children and families in need.

Critical Thinking

1. Head Start reaches almost one-half of all children and families in need. In addition to spending more money, what does the U.S. government need to do to expand Head Start's reach?
2. What changes could be made to Head Start to make it more effective in improving the lives of children and families?

SOURCES: Edward Zigler, Walter S. Gilliam, and Stephanie M. Jones, eds., *A Vision for Universal Preschool Education* (New York: Cambridge University Press, 2006); Steve Aos, Roxanne Lieb, Jim Mayfield, Marna Miller, and Annie Pennucci, *Benefits and Costs of Prevention and Early Intervention Programs for Youth* (Olympia, WA: Washington State Institute for Public Policy, 2004); Carol H. Ripple and Edward Zigler, "Research, Policy, and the Federal Role in Prevention Initiatives for Children," *American Psychologist* 58:482–490 (2003); Eliana Garces, Duncan Thomas, and Janet Currie, "Longer-Term Effects of Head Start," *American Economic Review* 92:999–1012 (2002); Janet Currie, "Early Childhood Education Programs," *Journal of Economic Perspectives* 15:213–238 (2001); Nancy Kassebaum, "Head Start, Only the Best for America's Children," *American Psychologist* 49:123–126 (1994); Faith Lamb Parker, Chaya Piorkowski, and Lenore Peay, "Head Start as Social Support for Mothers: The Psychological Benefits of Involvement," *American Journal of Orthopsychiatry* 57:220–233 (1987).

and 1980s, and these types of programs are still important today. But in recent years the focus of delinquency prevention efforts has shifted from neighborhood reclamation projects of the 1960s to more individualized, family-centered treatments.[18]

Classifying Delinquency Prevention

Just as there are a number of different ways to define delinquency prevention and very little agreement on the best way to do so,[19] the organization or classification of delinquency prevention is equally diverse, and there is very little agreement on the most effective way to do this.

Public Health Approach One of the first efforts to classify the many different types of delinquency prevention activities drew upon the public health approach to preventing diseases and injuries.[20] This method divided delinquency prevention activities into three categories: primary prevention, secondary prevention, and tertiary prevention. Primary prevention focuses on improving the general well-being of individuals through such measures as access to health care services and general prevention education, and modifying conditions in the physical environment that are conducive to delinquency through such measures as removing abandoned vehicles and improving the appearance of buildings. Secondary prevention focuses on intervening with children and young people who are potentially at risk for becoming offenders, as well as the provision of neighborhood programs to deter known delinquent activity. Tertiary prevention focuses on intervening with adjudicated juvenile offenders through such measures as substance abuse treatment and imprisonment. Here, the goal is to reduce repeat offending or recidivism.[21]

risk factor
A negative prior factor in an individual's life that increases the risk of occurrence of a future delinquent act.

protective factor
A positive prior factor in an individual's life that decreases the risk of occurrence of a future delinquent act.

Developmental Perspective Another popular approach to classifying delinquency prevention activities is the developmental perspective. Developmental prevention refers to interventions, especially those targeting risk and protective factors, designed to prevent the development of criminal potential in individuals.[22] Developmental prevention of juvenile delinquency is informed generally by motivational or human development theories on juvenile delinquency, and specifically by longitudinal studies that follow samples of young persons from their early childhood experiences to the peak of their involvement with delinquency in their teens and crime in their 20s.[23] The developmental perspective claims that delinquency in adolescence (and later criminal offending in adulthood) is influenced by "behavioral and attitudinal patterns that have been learned during an individual's development."[24] Concept Summary 12.1 lists key features of the developmental perspective. From this perspective, prevention activities are organized around different stages of the life course. We divide our discussion of developmental prevention of juvenile delinquency into two stages: childhood and adolescence.

For the most part, we have adopted the developmental perspective in discussing the effectiveness of different types of delinquency prevention programs in the rest of this chapter. This approach has several advantages: It allows for assessing the success of programs at different life-course stages; its coverage of the types of delinquency prevention programs that have been implemented is vast; and it is a well-recognized approach that has been used by other social scientists in reviews of the effectiveness of delinquency prevention.[25]

Concept Summary 12.1

Developmental Perspective on Delinquency Prevention

- Informed by human development theories and longitudinal studies
- Designed to prevent the development of criminal potential in individuals
- Targeted at-risk factors for delinquency and protective factors against delinquency
- Provided to children and families
- Implemented at different stages over the life course: childhood, early school years, adolescence, and transition to work

In the effort to address juvenile delinquency, early childhood interventions—initiated before delinquency occurs—have received much interest and have come to be seen as an important part of an overall strategy to reduce the harm caused by juvenile delinquency. Recent research shows that the general public is highly supportive of delinquency prevention programs and is even willing to pay more in taxes for these programs compared to more punitive options like military-style boot camps and prison. (This is discussed in the Focus on Delinquency box entitled "Public Support for Delinquency Prevention.") Early childhood delinquency prevention programs aim at positively influencing the early risk factors or "root causes" of delinquency and criminal offending that may continue into the adult years. These early risk factors are many, some of which include growing up in poverty, a high level of hyperactivity or impulsiveness, inadequate parental supervision, and harsh or inconsistent discipline. Early childhood interventions are often multidimensional, targeted at more than one risk factor, because they take a variety of different forms, including cognitive development, child skills training, and family support. The following sections examine early childhood delinquency prevention programs that have been implemented in the four most influential settings: home, day care, preschool, and the school. Most of the programs have been carried out in the United States.

Home-Based Programs

In a supportive and loving home environment, parents care for their children's health and general well-being, help instill in their children positive values such as honesty and respect for others, and nurture prosocial behaviors. One of the most important types of home-based programs to prevent juvenile delinquency involves the provision of support for families. Support for families in their homes can take many different forms. A popular and effective form of family support is home visitation.[26]

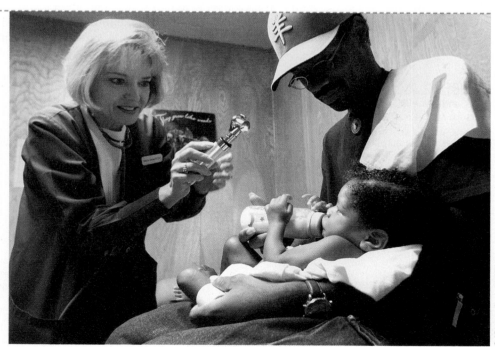

Early prevention programs that stress family support can reduce child abuse and neglect and juvenile delinquency. The most effective early family support programs provide infants with regular pediatrician checkups and provide parents with advice about care for the child, infant development, and local services. Here, Arlington, Texas, nurse practitioner Marilyn Graham gives 3-month-old Donovan Washington a checkup, as his father, Guy Washington, holds him.

Home Visitation The best-known home visitation program is the Nurse-Family Partnership (formerly Prenatal/Early Infancy Project) that was started in Elmira, New York.[27] This program was designed with three broad objectives:

1. To improve the outcomes of pregnancy
2. To improve the quality of care that parents provide to their children (and their children's subsequent health and development)
3. To improve women's own personal life-course development (completing their education, finding work, and planning future pregnancies)[28]

The program targeted first-time mothers-to-be who were under 19 years of age, unmarried, or poor. In all, 400 women were enrolled in the program. The mothers-to-be received home visits from nurses during pregnancy and during the first two years of the child's life. Each home visit lasted about one and one-quarter hours, and the mothers were visited on average every two weeks. The home visitors gave advice to the mothers about care of the child, infant development, and the importance of proper nutrition and avoiding smoking and drinking during pregnancy. Fifteen years after the program started, children of the mothers who received home visits had half as many arrests as children of mothers who received no home visits (the control group).[29] It was also found that these children, compared to those in the control group, had fewer convictions and violations of probation, were less likely to run away from home, and were less likely to drink alcohol. In addition to the program's success in preventing juvenile crime and other delinquent activities, it also produced a number of improvements in the lives of the mothers, such as lower rates of child abuse and neglect, crime in general, and substance abuse, as well as less reliance on welfare and social services.[30] A Rand study found that the program's desirable effects, for both the children and the mothers, translated into substantial financial benefits for government and taxpayers, and that the total amount of these benefits was more than four times the cost of the program (see Figure 12.2).[31]

Two other experiments of the Nurse-Family Partnership (NFP) program in Memphis, Tennessee, and Denver, Colorado, have produced similar benefits for the mothers and their children, including a reduction in child abuse and neglect. The success of the program has resulted in its use in almost 300 counties in 22 states across the country, serving 13,000 families each year.[32] In Colorado, the program was established in law, and in its first year of operation served almost 1,400 families in 49 of the state's 64 counties.[33] It is also now being replicated throughout England.[34] The use of nurses instead of para-professionals, its intensity (a minimum of two years), and its targeted nature (for first time, disadvantaged mothers only) are critical features that distinguish it from other, less effective home visitation programs such as Hawaii Healthy Start.[35]

FIGURE 12.2

Costs and Benefits of Home Visits for High-Risk Families

SOURCE: Adapted from Peter W. Greenwood et al., "Estimating the Costs and Benefits of Early Childhood Interventions: Nurse Home Visits and the Perry Preschool," in Brandon C. Welsh, David P. Farrington, and Lawrence W. Sherman, eds., *Costs and Benefits of Preventing Crime* (Boulder, CO: Westview Press, 2001), table 4.3.

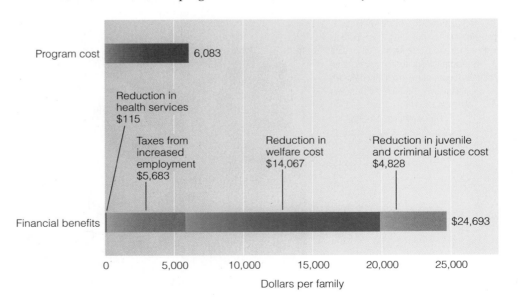

Public Support for Delinquency Prevention

Politicians who support "get tough" responses to juvenile offenders have long claimed to have the full backing of the general public, and that it is indeed the public that demands tougher dispositions (or sentences) such as military-style boot camps and longer terms in institutions to hold them accountable for their transgressions. To be sure, there is public support for "get tough" responses to juvenile delinquency, especially violent acts. But this support is not at the levels often claimed and, more importantly, not as high when compared to alternatives such as rehabilitation or treatment for juvenile offenders or early childhood or youth prevention programs. This overestimate of the punitiveness of the general public on the part of politicians and others has become known as the "mythical punitive public."

New, cutting-edge research provides more evidence to substantiate the mythical punitive public—that is, that citizens are highly supportive of delinquency prevention and are even willing to pay more in taxes to support these programs compared to other responses. In a review of the public opinion literature, criminologist Frank Cullen and his colleagues found that the American public is generally supportive of delinquency prevention programs, especially for at-risk children and youth. They also found that public opinion is no longer a barrier—as it once was perceived to be—to the implementation of delinquency prevention programs in communities across the country.

In a study of public preferences of responses to juvenile offending, criminologist Daniel Nagin and his colleagues found that the public values early prevention and offender rehabilitation or treatment more than increased incarceration. As shown in Table 12-A, households were willing to pay an average of $125.71 in additional taxes on nurse home visitation programs to prevent delinquency compared to $80.97 on longer sentences, a difference of $44.74 per year. Support for paying more in taxes for rehabilitation was also higher than for longer sentences: $98.10 versus $80.97. At the state level, public support for the prevention option translated into $601 million that hypothetically could be used to prevent delinquency compared to $387 million for longer sentences for juvenile offenders.

This study was based on a large sample of residents in Pennsylvania and used a highly rigorous methodology of public opinion polling known as contingent valuation (CV), which has many advantages over conventional polling methods. The contingent valuation approach allows for the "comparison of respondents' willingness to pay for competing policy alternatives."

In another innovative study to gauge the public's preferences for a range of alternative responses to crime, Mark Cohen, Ronald Rust, and Sara Steen found the public overwhelmingly supported increased spending of tax dollars on youth prevention programs compared to building more prisons. Public support for spending more taxes on drug treatment for nonviolent offenders as well as police also ranked higher than support for building more prisons, but not as high as for youth prevention programs.

While the mythical punitive public appears to be just that, there is no denying that the general public do see some value in "get tough" policies to tackle juvenile crime. But this new crop of public opinion research reveals—even more convincingly than past research—that there is a growing demand for early prevention programs and little demand for increased use of incarceration.

Critical Thinking

1. If you were a politician, would these research findings influence your decision on the policy positions you take on juvenile crime? Explain.

2. Public opinion is one important consideration in implementing delinquency prevention programs. What are some other key factors?

TABLE 12-A PUBLIC WILLINGNESS TO PAY FOR DELINQUENCY PREVENTION VERSUS OTHER MEASURES

Program	Average WTP per Household per Year	Statewide WTP per Year
Longer Sentence	$80.97	$387 million
Rehabilitation	$98.10	$468 million
Nurse Visitation	$125.71	$601 million

NOTE: WTP = willingness to pay.

SOURCE: Adapted from Daniel S. Nagin, Alex R. Piquero, Elizabeth S. Scott, and Laurence Steinberg, "Public Preferences for Rehabilitation versus Incarceration of Juvenile Offenders: Evidence from a Contingent Valuation Survey," *Criminology and Public Policy* 5:627–652 (2006), table 2.

SOURCES: Francis T. Cullen, Brenda A. Vose, Cheryl N. Lero, and James D. Unnever, "Public Support for Early Intervention: Is Child Saving a 'Habit of the Heart'?" *Victims and Offenders* 2:108–124 (2007); Mark A. Cohen, Ronald T. Rust, and Sara Steen, "Prevention, Crime Control or Cash? Public Preferences Toward Criminal Justice Spending Priorities," *Justice Quarterly* 23:317–335 (2006); Daniel S. Nagin, Alex R. Piquero, Elizabeth S. Scott, and Laurence Steinberg, "Public Preferences for Rehabilitation versus Incarceration of Juvenile Offenders: Evidence from a Contingent Valuation Survey," *Criminology and Public Policy* 5:627–652 (2006); Julian V. Roberts, "Public Opinion and Youth Justice," in Michael Tonry and Anthony N. Doob, eds., *Youth Crime and Youth Justice: Comparative and Cross-National Perspectives. Crime and Justice: A Review of Research*, vol. 31 (Chicago: University of Chicago Press, 2004).

Improving Parenting Skills

Another form of family support that has shown some success in preventing juvenile delinquency is improving parenting skills. Although the main focus of parent training programs is on the parents, many of these programs also involve children with the aim of improving the parent-child bond.

Oregon Social Learning Center The most widely cited parenting skills program is one created at the Oregon Social Learning Center (OSLC) by Gerald Patterson and his colleagues.[36] Patterson's research convinced him that poor parenting skills were associated with antisocial behavior in the home and at school. Family disruption and coercive exchanges between parents and children led to increased family tension, poor academic performance, and negative peer relations. The primary cause of the problem seemed to be that parents did not know how to deal effectively with their children. Parents sometimes ignored their children's behavior, but at other times the same actions would trigger explosive rage. Some parents would discipline their children for reasons that had little to do with the children's behavior, instead reflecting their own frustrations.

The children reacted in a regular progression, from learning to be noncompliant to learning to be assaultive. Their "coercive behavior," which included whining, yelling, and temper tantrums, would sometimes be acquired by other family members. Eventually family conflict would flow out of the home and into the school and social environment.

The OSLC program uses behavior modification techniques to help parents acquire proper disciplinary methods. Parents are asked to select several behaviors for change and to count the frequency of their occurrence. OSLC personnel teach social skills to reinforce positive behaviors, and constructive disciplinary methods to discourage negative ones. Incentive programs are initiated in which a child can earn points for desirable behaviors. Points can be exchanged for allowance, prizes, or privileges. Parents are also taught disciplinary techniques that stress firmness and consistency rather than "nattering" (low-intensity behaviors, such as scowling or scolding) or explosive discipline, such as hitting or screaming. One important technique is the "time out," in which the child is removed for brief isolation in a quiet room. Parents are taught the importance of setting rules and sticking to them. A number of evaluation studies carried out by Patterson and his colleagues showed that improving parenting skills can lead to reductions in juvenile delinquency.[37]

To read more about the **OSLC parenting skills program**, go to academic.cengage.com/criminaljustice/siegel.

The parent training method used by the OSLC may be the most cost-effective method of early intervention. A Rand study found that parent training costs about one-twentieth what a home visit program costs and is more effective in preventing serious crimes. The study estimates that 501 serious crimes could be prevented for every million dollars spent on parent training (or $2,000 per crime), a far cheaper solution than long-term incarceration, which would cost about $16,000 to prevent a single crime.[38]

Day Care Programs

Day care services are available to children as young as 6 weeks old in the United States and other Western countries.[39] In addition to allowing parents to return to work, day care serves to provide children with a number of important benefits, including social interaction with other children and stimulation of their cognitive, sensory, and motor control skills. The effectiveness of early childhood intervention has been studied in two programs described here—one in Syracuse, New York, and one in Houston, Texas.

Among the best-known of early childhood intervention programs that provide high-quality day care services is the Syracuse University Family Development Research Program. This program involved high-risk women during the later stages of their pregnancies. After the women gave birth, paraprofessionals were assigned to work with them, encouraging sound parent-child relationships, providing nutrition

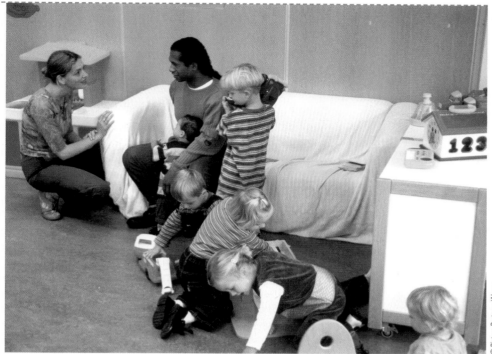

Day care programs serve largely as an organized form of child care to allow parents to return to work. But they also provide children with a number of important benefits, including social interaction with other children, and stimulation of their cognitive, sensory, and motor control skills. A number of day care programs have been effective in preventing delinquency.

information, and helping them establish relationships with social service agencies. In addition, the children received free full-time day care, designed to develop their intellectual abilities, up to age 5. A 10-year follow-up compared children involved in the program with a control group and found that those who received the intervention were less likely to be referred to the juvenile court for delinquency offenses, more likely to express positive feelings about themselves, and able to take a more active role in dealing with personal problems. Girls seemed especially to benefit, doing better in school; parents were more likely to express prosocial attitudes.[40]

Another high-quality day care program was that of the Houston Parent-Child Development Center. Like the Syracuse University program, both mothers and their children received services. In the first year of the program, the mothers received home visits from social service professionals, for the purpose of informing them about child development and parenting skills and helping them to develop prosocial bonds with their children. In the second year of the program, the mothers and their children attended a child development center four mornings a week. Here, children were provided with day care services to foster cognitive skills and encourage positive interactions with other children. Mothers participated in classes on family communication and child management. Eight years after the program ended, children who received the program were less involved in fighting and other delinquent activities when compared to a control group.[41]

The success of these programs rests in their targeting of important individual- and family-level risk factors for delinquency, such as low intelligence, impulsiveness, and inconsistent and poor parenting. Social scientists point to a package of child- and parent-centered interventions targeted at multiple risk factors as a core ingredient of successful delinquency prevention programs.[42]

Preschool

Preschool programs differ from day care programs in that preschool is geared more toward preparing children for school. Preschool is typically provided to children ages 3 to 5 years. These are the formative years of brain development; more learning takes place during this developmental stage than at any other stage over the life course. Low intelligence and school failure are important risk factors for juvenile delinquency.[43] (See Chapter 6 for why these are risk factors for juvenile delinquency.) For these reasons, highly structured, cognitive-based preschool programs give young children a positive start in life. Some of the key features of preschool programs include the provision of:

▌ Developmentally appropriate learning curricula

▌ A wide array of cognitive-based enriching activities

▌ Activities for parents, usually of a less intensive nature, so that they may be able to support the school experience at home[44]

A preschool in Michigan, a program in Chicago, and Head Start centers in Washington provide some positive findings on the benefits of early intervention.

Started in the mid-1960s, the Perry Preschool in Ypsilanti, Michigan, provided disadvantaged children with a program of educational enrichment supplemented with weekly home visits. The main hypothesis of the program was that "good preschool programs can help children in poverty make a better start in their transition from home to community and thereby set more of them on paths to becoming economically self-sufficient, socially responsible adults."[45] The main intervention was high-quality, active-learning preschool programming administered by professional teachers for two years. Preschool sessions were half a day long and were provided five days a week for the duration of the 30-week school year. The educational approach focused on supporting the development of the children's cognitive and social skills through individualized teaching and learning.

A number of assessments were made of the program at important stages of development. The first assessment of juvenile delinquency, when the participants were age 15, found that those who received the program reported one-third fewer offenses than a control group.[46] By the age of 27, program participants had accumulated half the arrests of the control group. The researchers also found that the preschoolers had achieved many other significant benefits compared to their control group counterparts, including higher monthly earnings, higher percentages of home ownership and second car ownership, a higher level of schooling completed, and a lower percentage receiving welfare benefits.[47] All of these benefits translated into substantial dollar cost savings. It was estimated that for each dollar it cost to run and administer the program, more than $7 was saved to taxpayers, potential crime victims, and program participants.[48] An independent study by Rand also found that Perry Preschool was a very worthwhile investment.[49]

The most recent assessment of the effectiveness of Perry Preschool—when the subjects were age 40—found that it continues to make an important difference in the lives of those who were enrolled in the program. Compared to the control group, program group members had achieved many significant benefits, including

▌ Fewer lifetime arrests for violent crimes (32 percent vs. 48 percent), property crimes (36 percent vs. 58 percent), and drug crimes (14 percent vs. 34 percent)

▌ Higher levels of schooling completed (77 percent vs. 60 percent graduated from high school)

▌ Higher annual earnings (57 percent vs. 43 percent had earnings in the top half of the sample)[50]

An assessment of the costs and benefits at age 40 found that for every dollar spent on the program, more than $17 was returned to society—in the form of savings in crime, education, welfare, and increased tax revenue.

The Child-Parent Center (CPC) program in Chicago, like Perry Preschool, provided disadvantaged children, ages 3 to 4 years, with high-quality, active-learning preschool supplemented with family support. However, unlike Perry, CPC continued to provide the children with the educational enrichment component into elementary school, up to the age of 9 years. Just focusing on the effect of the preschool, it was found that, compared to a control group, those who received the program were less likely to be arrested for nonviolent offenses (17 percent vs. 25 percent) and violent offenses (9 percent vs. 15 percent) by the time they were 18. Preschool participants, compared to a control group, were also less likely to be arrested more than once (10 percent vs. 13 percent). Other significant benefits realized by the preschool participants compared to the control group included

I   A higher rate of high school completion (50 percent vs. 39 percent)

I   More years of completed education (11 vs. 10)

I   A lower rate of dropping out of school (47 percent vs. 55 percent)[51]

The success of the CPC program in preventing juvenile delinquency and improving other life-course outcomes produced substantial cost savings. For each dollar spent on the program, $7.14 was saved to taxpayers, potential crime victims, and program participants.[52]

Another early intervention that closely resembles these preschool programs is Head Start. (See the Policy and Practice box earlier in the chapter.) Head Start provides children with, among other things, an enriched educational environment to develop their learning and cognitive skills. One study of Head Start centers in Seattle, Washington, found that very young children who were enrolled in the program were less likely to misbehave than children in the control group.[53]

Overall, high-quality, intensive preschool programs show strong support for preventing delinquency and improving the lives of young people.[54] The provision of family support services combined with preschool programming likely adds to the strength of the Perry and CPC programs in preventing delinquency, but it is clear that preschool was the most important element. The intellectual enrichment component of preschool helps prepare children for the academic challenges of elementary and later grades; reducing the chances of school failure is a significant factor in reducing delinquency. Another notable point about the positive findings of Perry and CPC is that these two programs were implemented many years apart, yet the CPC, as a semi-replication of Perry, demonstrates that preschool programs today can still be effective in preventing delinquency.

School Programs in the Primary Grades

Schools are a critical social context for delinquency prevention efforts, from the early to later grades.[55] (See Chapter 10.) All schools work to produce vibrant and productive members of society. The school's role in preventing delinquency in general, which is the focus of this section, differs from measures taken to make the school a safer place. In this case, a school may adopt a greater security orientation and implement such measures as metal detectors, police in school, and closed-circuit television cameras. A number of experimental programs have attempted to prevent or reduce delinquency by manipulating factors in the learning environment; two are discussed here.

The Seattle Social Development Project (SSDP) used a method in which teachers learn techniques that reward appropriate student behavior and minimize disruptive behavior. The program started in first grade and continued through sixth grade. Students were taught in small groups. Students were also provided with skills training to help them master problem solving, communication, and conflict resolution skills. Family training classes were offered, teaching parents how to reward and encourage desirable behavior and provide negative consequences for undesirable behavior in a consistent fashion. Other parent training focused on improving their children's academic performance while reducing at-risk behaviors such as drug abuse. In short, the program was extremely comprehensive, targeting an array of important risk factors for delinquency.

A long-term evaluation of the Seattle program—at age 21—found that children who received the program reported more commitment and attachment to school, better academic achievement, fewer delinquent acts, and fewer instances of selling

To read more about **SSDP**, go to academic.cengage.com/criminaljustice/siegel.

EXHIBIT **12.2**

School-Based Delinquency Prevention Programs

What Works?

▌ Programs aimed at building school capacity to initiate and sustain innovation

▌ Programs aimed at clarifying and communicating norms about behaviors by establishing school rules, improving the consistency of their enforcement (particularly when they emphasize positive reinforcement of appropriate behavior), or communicating norms through schoolwide campaigns (for example, antibullying campaigns) or ceremonies

▌ Comprehensive instructional programs that focus on a range of social competency skills (such as developing self-control and skills in stress management, responsible decision making, social problem solving, and communication) and that are delivered over a long period of time to continually reinforce skills

What Does Not Work?

▌ Instructional programs that do not focus on social competency skills or do not make use of cognitive-behavioral teaching methods

What Is Promising?

▌ Programs that group youths into smaller "schools within schools" to create smaller units, more supportive interactions, or greater flexibility in instruction

▌ Classroom or instructional management

SOURCE: Denise C. Gottfredson, David B. Wilson, and Stacy Skroban Najaka, "School-Based Crime Prevention," in Lawrence W. Sherman, David P. Farrington, Brandon C. Welsh, and Doris Layton MacKenzie, eds., *Evidence-Based Crime Prevention* (New York: Routledge, 2006, rev. ed.).

drugs compared to a control group. Program participants were also less likely than their control counterparts to have received an official court charge in their lifetime.[56] One study found that the program's success in preventing delinquency alone—not including the other important successes—produced cost savings to the criminal justice system and victims of crime that outweighed the costs of running the program by more than 300 percent. In other words, for each dollar spent on the program, more than $3 was saved to the government and crime victims.[57]

In Montreal, child psychologist Richard Tremblay set up an experiment to investigate the effects of an early preventive intervention program for 6-year-old boys who were aggressive and hyperactive and from poor neighborhoods. Known as the Montreal Longitudinal-Experimental Study, the program lasted for two years and had two components: school-based social skills training and home-based parent training. Social skills training for the children focused predominantly on improving social interactions with peers. The parent-training component was based on the social learning principles of Gerald Patterson and involved training parents in how to provide positive reinforcement for desirable behavior, use nonpunitive and consistent discipline practices, and develop family crisis management techniques. The program was successful in reducing delinquency. By age 12, boys in the experimental group compared to those in the control group committed less burglary and theft and were less likely to be involved in fights. At every age from 10 to 15, self-reported delinquency was lower for the boys in the experimental group compared to those in the control group.[58]

Schools may not be able to reduce delinquency single-handedly, but a number of viable alternatives to their present operations could aid a communitywide effort to reduce the problem of juvenile crime. A recent review of school-based programs was conducted by Denise Gottfredson and her colleagues as part of a study to determine the best methods of delinquency prevention. Some of their findings are contained in Exhibit 12.2. The main difference between the programs that work and those that do not is that successful programs target an array of important risk factors. Often it is not enough to improve only the school environment or only the family environment; for example, a youth who has a troubled family life may find it more difficult to do well at school, regardless of the improvements made at school. Some effective early school-based delinquency prevention programs also show that greater gains are made with those who are at the highest risk for future delinquency. An evaluation of Peace-Builders, a school-based violence prevention program for kindergarteners to fifth graders, found that decreases in aggression and improvements in social competence were larger for the highest-risk kids compared to those at medium and low levels of risk.[59] Another important ingredient of successful school-based programs is that they be intensive; two or three sessions a semester often does not cut it.

PREVENTION OF DELINQUENCY IN THE TEENAGE YEARS

Like early childhood interventions, delinquency prevention programs started in the teenage years also play an important role in an overall strategy to reduce juvenile delinquency. A wide range of non–juvenile justice delinquency prevention programs attempt to address such risk factors as parental conflict and separation, poor housing, dropping out of high school, and antisocial peers. The following sections examine the five main delinquency prevention approaches targeted at teenagers: mentoring, school-based programs, after-school programs, job training, and comprehensive community-based programs.

Mentoring

Mentoring programs usually involve nonprofessional volunteers spending time with young people at risk for delinquency, dropping out of school, school failure, and other social problems. Mentors behave in a supportive, nonjudgmental manner while acting as role models.[60] In recent years, there has been a large increase in the number of mentoring programs, many of which are aimed at preventing delinquency.[61]

Federal Mentoring Programs The Office of Juvenile Justice and Delinquency Prevention (OJJDP) has supported mentoring for many years in all parts of the United States, most notably through the Juvenile Mentoring Program (JUMP), now called the Mentoring Initiative for System Involved Youth (MISIY). The new initiative provides funding to faith- and community-based agencies to mentor youth involved in the

Mentoring is one of many types of interventions that have been used with teens considered to be at high risk for engaging in delinquent acts. These two juniors at North High School in Evansville, Indiana, are part of a mentor program to help incoming freshmen.

juvenile justice system, foster care, and reentry programs.[62] Under JUMP, thousands of at-risk youths were provided with mentors. The mentors were responsible and caring adults who volunteered their time to work with young people exposed to one or more risk factors, including delinquency, dropping out of school, and problems in school.

The most common areas of increased risk, based on a large number of male and female youths enrolled in the program, are school and social/family domains. (See Table 12.1.) Mentors work one-on-one with young people.[63] Research has shown that mentoring and other types of delinquency prevention programs offered in group settings, particularly for high-risk youths, may end up causing more harm than good. By participating in these types of programs in groups, young people who are more chronically involved in delinquency may negatively affect those who are marginally involved in delinquency.[64] An evaluation of the program found significant reductions in risk in three critical areas: aggressive behavior/delinquency, peer relationships, and mental health.[65]

Quantum Opportunities Program One of the most successful mentoring programs in preventing juvenile delinquency was the Quantum Opportunities Program (QOP). QOP was implemented in five sites across the country: Milwaukee, Oklahoma City, Philadelphia, Saginaw (Michigan), and San Antonio. At each of the five sites, 25 young people received the program, while another 25 young people served as the comparison group. The main goal of the program was to improve the life-course opportunities of disadvantaged, at-risk youths during the high school years. The program ran for four years or up to grade 12, and was designed around the provision of three "quantum opportunities":

▌ Educational activities (peer tutoring, computer-based instruction, homework assistance)

▌ Service activities (volunteering with community projects)

▌ Development activities (curricula focused on life and family skills, and college and career planning)

Incentives in the form of cash and college scholarships were also offered to students for work carried out in these three areas. These incentives served to provide

TABLE 12.1

Risk Factors of Young People in the Juvenile Mentoring Program (JUMP)

Risk Domain	Percentage of Enrolled Youth*	
	Male (n = 3,592)	Female (n = 3,807)
School problems	74.6%	63.0%
School behavior	39.5	23.5
Poor grades	53.6	45.9
Truancy	10.4	9.1
Social/family problems	51.7	56.4
Delinquency	17.5	8.5
Fighting	12.8	6.3
Property crime	2.8	0.5
Gang activity	3.0	1.0
Weapons	1.1	0.4
Alcohol use	3.2	1.5
Drug use	4.0	1.8
Tobacco use	2.3	1.9
Pregnancy/early parenting	0.2	1.5

* Percentage of total JUMP enrollment for each gender. For 23 youths, no gender was reported in the database.

SOURCE: Laurence C. Novotney, Elizabeth Mertinko, James Lange, and Tara Kelly Baker, *Juvenile Mentoring Program: A Progress Review* (Washington, DC: OJJDP *Juvenile Justice Bulletin*, 2000), p. 5.

short-run motivation for school completion and future academic and social achievement. Staff also received cash incentives and bonuses for keeping youths involved in the program.[66]

An evaluation of the program six months after it ended found that those who received the program were less likely to be arrested compared to the control group (17 percent vs. 58 percent). A number of other significant effects were observed. For example, compared to the control group, QOP group members were

▌ More likely to have graduated from high school (63 percent vs. 42 percent)

▌ More likely to be enrolled in some form of postsecondary education (42 percent vs. 16 percent)

▌ Less likely to have dropped out of high school (23 percent vs. 50 percent)[67]

Big Brothers Big Sisters Program Another effective mentoring program is offered by Big Brothers Big Sisters (BBBS) of America, a national youth mentoring organization, founded in 1904 and committed to improving the life chances of at-risk children and teens. The BBBS program brings together unrelated pairs of adult volunteers and youths, ages 6 to 18. Rather than trying to address particular problems facing a youth, the program focuses on providing a youth with an adult friend. The premise behind this is that "[t]he friendship forged with a youth by the Big Brother or Big Sister creates the framework through which the mentor can support and aid the youth."[68] The program also stresses that this friendship needs to be long lasting. To this end, mentors meet with youths on average three or four times a month (for three to four hours each time) for at least one year. An evaluation of the program took place at eight sites across the country and involved randomly assigning more than 1,100 youths to a program group that received mentoring or to a control group that did not. Eighteen months after the start of the program, it was found that those youths who received the program, compared to their control counterparts, were significantly less likely to have hit someone, initiated illegal drug use, or been truant from school. The program group members were also more likely than the controls to do better in school and have better relationships with their parents and peers.[69]

Despite the findings of these three mentoring programs, the overall evidence of the impact of mentoring on delinquency remains mixed.[70] Furthermore, other mentoring programs have not had success in other areas, such as academic achievement, school attendance, school dropout, and employment.[71] So, why do some mentoring programs work and not others? The biggest issue has to do with what the mentors actually do and how they do it. In all three of the profiled programs, mentors are a source of support and guidance to help young people deal with a broad range of issues that have to do with their family, school, and future career. They work one-on-one with young people, in many cases forming strong bonds. Care is taken in matching the mentor and young person. Other research on effective mentoring relationships between adults and teens points to the need for the mentors to display empathy, pay particular attention to and nurture the strengths of the young person, and treat them "as a person of equal worth and value."[72] For future mentoring programs to be successful they should follow the approaches adopted by these programs and the research findings on effective mentoring relationships.

To learn more about **Big Brothers Big Sisters of America**, go to academic.cengage.com/criminaljustice/siegel.

School Programs for Teens

Safety of students in middle schools and high schools takes on a much higher profile than in the early grades because of a larger number of school shootings and other violent incidents. However, the role of schools in the prevention of delinquency in the wider community remains prominent. A wide range of programs to deal with juvenile delinquency in the community have been set up in middle schools and high schools across the United States and in other countries. We review just a couple of the most influential school-based delinquency prevention programs.

Project PATHE Positive Action Through Holistic Education (PATHE) is a comprehensive program used in secondary schools that reduces school disorder and aims to improve the school environment. The goal is to enhance students' experiences and attitudes about school by increasing their bonds to the school, enhancing their self-esteem, and improving educational and occupational attainment. These improvements will help reduce juvenile delinquency.

PATHE was initially operated in four middle schools and three high schools in South Carolina. It focused on four elements: strengthening students' commitment to school, providing successful school experiences, encouraging attachment to the educational community, and increasing participation in school activities. By increasing students' sense of belonging and usefulness, the project sought to promote a positive school experience. The PATHE program has undergone extensive evaluation by sociologist Denise Gottfredson, who found that the schools in which it was used experienced a moderate reduction in delinquency. Replications of the project are currently under development.[73]

Violence Prevention Curriculum for Adolescents Violence prevention curricula as part of health education classes is one type of school-based prevention program that has received much attention in recent years in the United States.[74] However, few rigorous evaluations of these programs or other instructional-based violence prevention programs in schools have assessed effects on juvenile violence.[75] One of these evaluations assessed the impact of this type of program on high school students in a number of locations across the country. The curriculum was designed to do five main things in the following order:

1. Provide statistical information on adolescent violence and homicide

2. Present anger as a normal, potentially constructive emotion

3. Create a need in the students for alternatives to fighting by discussing the potential gains and losses from fighting

4. Have students analyze the precursors to a fight and practice avoiding fights using role-play and videotape

5. Create a classroom ethos that is nonviolent and values violence prevention behavior[76]

The curriculum was administered in 10 sessions. The sessions were very interactive between the teacher and the students, relying on many different techniques, including brainstorming and role-playing. Like many school-based delinquency prevention programs, the violence prevention curriculum was concerned with reducing delinquency, specifically fighting, in schools and in the larger community. An evaluation of the program in four major urban areas showed that fighting had been significantly reduced among the young people who attended the sessions compared to a control group that did not receive the curriculum.[77]

The review of what works in preventing delinquency in schools by Denise Gottfredson and her colleagues (see Exhibit 12.2) is not limited to the early grades, but also includes programs in middle schools and high schools. And the conclusion on the effectiveness of school-based delinquency prevention programs in the later grades is the same as for the early grades: Some programs work and some programs do not work. But what are the key features of successful school-based delinquency prevention programs? As with the successful school programs in the early grades, successful programs in the later grades are those that target a number of important risk factors. For the two programs described here, this meant a focus on reducing school disorder and improving the school environment. Two additional components of successful school-based delinquency prevention programs in the later grades are improving the family environment by engaging parents in helping the student to learn, and reducing negative peer influences through information about the downsides of gun carrying, drug use, and gang involvement.

After-School Programs

More than two-thirds of all married couples with school-age children (ages 6 to 17) have both parents working outside the home, and the proportion of single parents with school-age children working outside the home is even higher.[78] This leaves many unsupervised young people in communities during the after-school hours (2:00 P.M. to 6:00 P.M.), which is believed to be the main reason for the elevated rates of delinquency during this period of time.[79] After-school programs have become a popular response to this problem in recent years. While recreation is just one form of after-school programs—other options include child-care centers, tutoring programs at schools, dance groups, and drop-in clubs—it plays an important role in young people's lives, especially for a large number who do not have access to organized sport and other recreational opportunities. State and federal budgets for education, public safety, delinquency prevention, and child care provide some funding for after-school programs.

In a large-scale study of after-school programs in the state of Maryland, Denise Gottfredson and her colleagues found that participation in the programs reduced delinquent behavior among children in middle school but not elementary school. The researchers found that increasing intentions not to use drugs as well as positive peer associations were the key reasons for the favorable effects on delinquency among the older children. Interestingly, decreasing the time spent unsupervised or increasing the involvement in constructive activities was found to play no significant role.[80]

Boys and Girls Clubs of America One of the most successful after-school programs in preventing delinquency (and substance abuse) is provided by the Boys and Girls Clubs of America. Founded in 1902, the Boys and Girls Clubs of America is a nonprofit organization with a membership today of more than 1.3 million boys and girls nationwide. Boys and Girls Clubs (BGCs) provide programs in six main areas:

I Cultural enrichment

I Health and physical education

I Social recreation

I Personal and educational development

I Citizenship and leadership development

I Environmental education[81]

One study examined the effectiveness of BGCs for high-risk youths in public housing developments at five sites across the country. The usual services of BGCs, which include reading classes, sports, and homework assistance, were offered, as well as a program to prevent substance abuse, known as SMART Moves (Self-Management and Resistance Training). This program targets the specific pressures that young people face to try drugs and alcohol. It also provides education to parents and the community at large to assist young people in learning about the dangers of substance abuse and strategies for resisting the pressures to use drugs and alcohol.[82] Evaluation results showed that housing developments with BGCs, with and without SMART Moves, had fewer damaged units and less delinquency in general than housing developments without the clubs. There was also an overall reduction in substance abuse, drug trafficking, and other drug-related delinquency activity.[83]

Participate and Learn Skills A Canadian program implemented in a public housing development in the nation's capital, Ottawa, recruited low-income young people to participate in after-school activities, such as sports (ice hockey), music, dance, and scouting. Known as Participate and Learn Skills (PALS), the program ran for almost three years and aimed to advance young people toward higher skill levels in the activities they chose and to integrate them into activities in the wider

To learn more about the **Boys and Girls Clubs of America**, go to academic.cengage.com/criminaljustice/siegel.

community. PALS was based on the belief that skill development in sports, music, dance, and so on, could affect other areas of young people's lives, such as prosocial attitudes and behaviors, which in turn could help them avoid engaging in delinquent activities.

At the end of the program, it was found that those who participated in the after-school activities were much better off than their control counterparts on a range of measures. The strongest impact of the program was found for juvenile delinquency, with an 80 percent reduction in police arrests. This positive effect was diminished somewhat in the 16 months after the program ended. The researchers speculated that the effects of the program may wear off. Substantial gains were also observed in skill acquisition, as measured by the number of levels advanced in an activity, and in integration in the wider community. These benefits translated into impressive cost savings. For every dollar that was spent on the program, more than $2.50 was saved to the juvenile justice system (fewer arrests), the housing development (less need for private security services), and the city government.[84]

Overall, after-school recreation represents a promising approach to preventing juvenile delinquency. This is because it engages young people in productive, fun, and rewarding activities. For some young people, this is enough to keep them occupied and out of trouble. These programs are also successful in reducing delinquency because they instill in young people important messages about the downsides of drug use and gang membership.

Although the evidence shows that after-school programs can be successful, there is a need for further evaluation.[85] The fact that some (but not all) types of delinquency are elevated during the after-school hours underscores the importance of high-quality after-school programs.[86]

Job Training

The effects of having an after-school job can be problematic (see Chapter 3). Some research indicates that it may be associated with delinquency and substance abuse. However, helping kids to prepare for the adult workforce is an important aspect of delinquency prevention. Job training programs play an important role in improving the chances of young people obtaining jobs in the legal economy and thereby may reduce delinquency.[87] The developmental stage of transition to work is difficult for many young people. Coming from a disadvantaged background, having poor grades in school or perhaps dropping out of school, and having some involvement in delinquency can all pose difficulties in securing a steady, well-paying job in early adulthood. Programs like the two described here are concerned not only with providing young people with employable skills, but also with helping them overcome some of these immediate obstacles.

Job Corps The best-known and largest job training program in the United States is Job Corps, which was established in 1964 as a federal training program for disadvantaged, unemployed youths. The designers of the national program, the Department of Labor, were hopeful that spin-off benefits in the form of reduced dependence on social assistance and a reduction in delinquency would occur as a result of empowering at-risk youth to achieve stable, long-term employment opportunities. The program is still active today, operating out of 119 centers across the nation, and each year provides services to more than 60,000 new young people at a cost of over $1 billion.[88]

The main goal of Job Corps is to improve the employability of participants by offering a comprehensive set of services that largely includes vocational skills training, basic education (the ability to obtain graduate equivalent degrees), and health care. Job Corps is provided to young people between the ages of 16 and 24 years. Most of the young people enrolled in the program are at high risk for delinquency, substance abuse, and social assistance dependency. Two out of five youths come from families on social assistance, four out of five have dropped out of school, and the average

Job Corps is a national program serving more than 60,000 at-risk young people each year. It seeks to help them improve their vocational skills and education, find sustainable jobs, serve their communities, and avoid lives of crime. Pictured here are teen Job Corps students removing graffiti from the Tatum Waterway near Biscayne Bay, Florida.

© Jeff Greenberg/Alamy

family income is $6,000 per year.[89] Almost all of the Job Corps centers require the participants to live there while taking the program.

A large-scale evaluation of Job Corps, involving almost 12,000 young people, found that the program was successful in reducing delinquency. Arrest rates were 16 percent lower for those who received the program compared to a comparison group. Program group members were less likely to be convicted and serve jail time upon conviction. Also, there were higher employment rates and greater earnings for those who received the program.[90] An earlier evaluation of Job Corps found it to be a worthwhile investment of public resources: For each dollar that was spent on the program, $1.45 was saved to government or taxpayers, crime victims, and program participants.[91] A more recent analysis of the program's costs and benefits also found it to be a worthwhile investment of public resources, saving society at large $2 for each dollar spent on the program.[92]

To read more about **Job Corps**, go to academic.cengage.com/criminaljustice/siegel.

YouthBuild U.S.A. Another job training program for disadvantaged, unemployed youths is YouthBuild U.S.A. Started in 1978 by a group of young people in New York City, YouthBuild has become a national program, each year serving more than 7,000 youths between the ages of 16 and 24 years in the 225 programs across the country.[93] The program's focus is on building or renovating affordable housing, and through this young people learn skills in carpentry and construction. YouthBuild also provides educational services—for example, to achieve a high school diploma or prepare for college—and promotes the development of leadership skills. The program's impact on delinquency varies from site to site, with some sites reporting reductions as high as 40 percent among youths enrolled in the program compared to similar youths who did not receive the program.[94] The program has also proven tremendously successful in helping a large percentage of participants find work in the construction industry and get into college.[95]

Comprehensive Community-Based Programs

Experimentation with comprehensive community-based delinquency prevention programs began as early as the 1930s, with Shaw and McKay's Chicago Area Project. The Mobilization for Youth program of the 1960s is another example of this type of initiative to prevent juvenile delinquency. Neither of these programs was found to be overly successful in reducing delinquency, but few of these types of programs have been evaluated. Typically implemented in neighborhoods with high delinquency and crime rates, they are made up of a range of different types of interventions and usually involve an equally diverse group of community and government agencies that are concerned with the problem of juvenile delinquency, such as the YM/YWCA, Boys and Girls Clubs of America, and social and health services. The three programs discussed here rely on a systematic approach or comprehensive planning model to develop preventive interventions. This includes analyzing the delinquency problem, identifying available resources in the community, developing priority delinquency problems, and identifying successful programs in other communities and tailoring them to local conditions and needs.[96] Not all comprehensive community-based prevention programs follow this model, but there is evidence to suggest that this approach will produce the greatest reductions in juvenile delinquency.[97] One of the main drawbacks to this approach is the difficulty in sustaining the level of resources and the cooperation between agencies that are necessary to lower the rates of juvenile delinquency across a large geographical area such as a city.[98]

CASASTART One contemporary example of a comprehensive community-based delinquency prevention program that has been evaluated is the Children At Risk (CAR) program, which is now undergoing further experimentation and is known as CASASTART or the Center on Addiction and Substance Abuse's Striving Together to Achieve Rewarding Tomorrows.[99] The program was set up to help improve the lives of young people at high risk for delinquency, gang involvement, substance abuse, and other problem behaviors. It was delivered to a large number of young people in poor and high-crime neighborhoods in five cities across the country. It involved a wide range of preventive measures, including case management and family counseling, family skills training, tutoring, mentoring, after-school activities, and community policing. The program was different in each neighborhood. A study of all five cities showed that one year after the program ended the young people who received the program, compared to a control group, were less likely to have committed violent delinquent acts and to have used or sold drugs. Some of the other beneficial results for those in the program included less association with delinquent peers, less peer pressure to engage in delinquency, and more positive peer support.[100]

Communities That Care and SafeFutures Initiative Other large-scale comprehensive community-based delinquency prevention programs include Communities That Care (CTC)[101] and the SafeFutures Initiative.[102] Both programs received start-up funding by OJJDP and are now sustained by local governments and communities. The CTC strategy emphasizes the reduction of risk factors for delinquency and the enhancement of protective factors against delinquency for different developmental stages from birth through adolescence.[103] CTC follows a rigorous, multilevel planning process that includes drawing upon interventions that have previously demonstrated success and tailoring them to the needs of the community.[104] Two recent case studies of CTC demonstrate its ability to help mobilize communities to plan and implement delinquency prevention programs based on the highest quality research evidence on what works best.[105]

The SafeFutures Initiative operates much like CTC; for example, by emphasizing the reduction of risk factors for delinquency and protective factors against delinquency, using what works, and following a rigorous planning model to implement different interventions. It also works to build or strengthen existing collaborations among the many community groups and government departments working to prevent delinquency. Unlike CTC, the SafeFutures Initiative is only targeted at youths who are both at high risk for delinquency and adjudicated offenders. (See Exhibit 12.3.)

EXHIBIT 12.3

SafeFutures Program to Reduce Juvenile Delinquency and Youth Violence

SafeFutures is made up of nine program areas:

▎ After-school programs

▎ Juvenile mentoring programs (JUMP)

▎ Family strengthening and support services

▎ Mental health services for at-risk and adjudicated youth

▎ Delinquency prevention programs in general

▎ Comprehensive communitywide approaches to gang-free schools and communities

▎ Community-based day treatment programs

▎ Continuum-of-care services for at-risk and delinquent girls

▎ Serious, violent, and chronic juvenile offender programs (with an emphasis on enhancing graduated sanctions)

SOURCE: Elaine Morley, Shelli B. Rossman, Mary Kopczynski, Janeen Buck, and Caterina Gouvis, *Comprehensive Responses to Youth at Risk: Interim Findings from the SafeFutures Initiative* (Washington, DC: Office of Juvenile Justice and Delinquency Prevention, 2000).

FUTURE OF DELINQUENCY PREVENTION

To learn more about the **Blueprints for Violence Prevention** initiative, go to academic.cengage.com/criminaljustice/siegel.

The success of delinquency prevention is shown by evaluations of individual programs (as described throughout this chapter) and larger efforts to assess what works, such as the Blueprints for Violence Prevention initiative, discussed in the accompanying Policy and Practice box. Despite the success of many different types of delinquency prevention programs—from preschool to mentoring—these programs receive a fraction of what is spent on the juvenile justice system to deal with young people once they have broken the law.[106] This is also true in the adult criminal justice system.[107] To many juvenile justice officials, policy makers, and politicians, prevention is tantamount to being soft on crime, and delinquency prevention programs are often referred to as "pork," otherwise known as pork barrel, or wasteful, spending.[108] Aside from these views, delinquency prevention programs face a number of very real obstacles, including

▎ *Ethical concerns about early intervention.*[109] Is it right to intervene in the lives of children and young people using methods that may or may not be successful?

▎ *Labeling and stigmatization associated with programs that target high-risk populations.*[110] Children and families receiving support may be called hurtful names and/or looked down upon by fellow community members.

▎ *Long delay before early childhood programs can have an impact on delinquency.*[111] While the saying "pay now, save later" is true for early childhood delinquency prevention programs, the length of time for this benefit to be felt can act as a deterrent. In a society and political system that demand immediate results, the building of a juvenile corrections facility is often seen as a more tangible measure than the building of a preschool.

The future of delinquency prevention programs depends on educating the public and key decision makers about the value of preventing delinquency. One example of this is discussing the success of prevention programs in financial terms.[112] For the handful of programs that have measured costs and benefits, some of which are discussed in this chapter, the savings are substantial.[113] The costs of running prevention programs are low relative to the costly nature of delinquency. Notwithstanding these important issues, the future of delinquency prevention is likely to be bright. With many local efforts, state initiatives, and a growing list of national programs showing positive results, the prevention of delinquency is proving its worth.

Blueprints for Violence Prevention

In 1996, the Center for the Study and Prevention of Violence (CSPV) at the University of Colorado at Boulder launched the Blueprints for Violence Prevention initiative. The principal aim of the Blueprints initiative is to "identify and replicate effective youth violence prevention programs across the nation." For programs to be labeled as effective, they must adhere to a set of strict scientific standards. The key standards include

- Statistical evidence of effectiveness in reducing violent behavior
- Evaluations using the most rigorous designs (for example, randomized experiment)
- Large sample size to allow for any changes to be detected
- Low attrition of subjects
- Use of reliable and accepted instruments to assess impact on violence
- Sustained reductions in violence for at least one year after the end of the program
- Replication: implementation of the program in at least two different sites

More than 600 programs have been reviewed. There are 11 model programs, or Blueprints, that have proven to be effective in reducing juvenile violence or risk factors for juvenile violence. Another 23 programs have been designated as promising. Not all of the model programs are designed to prevent violence before it takes place; some are designed for offenders and involve the juvenile justice system. The 11 model programs are

1. Prenatal and infancy home visitation by nurses
2. Promotion of social competence and reduction of child conduct problems
3. Promotion of alternative thinking strategies
4. Prevention of bullying
5. Big Brothers Big Sisters of America
6. Life skills training
7. Comprehensive substance abuse prevention
8. Functional family therapy: brings together families and juvenile offenders to address family problems and unlearn aggressive behavior
9. Multisystemic therapy: multiple component treatment for chronic and violent juvenile offenders, which may involve individual, family, peer, school, and community interventions
10. Multidimensional treatment foster care: an alternative to incarceration that matches juvenile offenders with trained foster families
11. Project Toward No Drug Abuse

These model programs are distributed to communities and serve as a prevention menu, allowing communities to select proven programs that are best suited to their needs. An OJJDP survey of state juvenile justice specialists found that 40 states have implemented one or more of these model programs, with the most widely implemented programs being multisystemic therapy (30 states), functional family therapy (21 states), Big Brothers Big Sisters of America (15 states), and the prevention of bullying (12 states).

Critical Thinking

1. What is the importance of replicating delinquency prevention programs in multiple sites?
2. How is the Blueprints initiative helpful to communities faced with a delinquency problem?

SOURCES: Peter W. Greenwood, *Changing Lives: Delinquency Prevention as Crime-Control Policy* (Chicago: University of Chicago Press, 2006); Sharon F. Mihalic, Abigail Fagan, Katherine Irwin, Diane Ballard, and Delbert Elliott, *Blueprints for Violence Prevention* (Washington, DC: OJJDP Report, 2004); Sharon F. Mihalic and Katherine Irwin, "Blueprints for Violence Prevention: From Research to Real-World Settings—Factors Influencing the Successful Replication of Model Programs," *Youth Violence and Juvenile Justice* 1:307–329 (2003); *OJJDP News @ A Glance*, "Implementing Blueprints for Violence Prevention" (Washington, DC: Office of Juvenile Justice and Delinquency Prevention, U.S. Department of Justice, 2003), p. 4.

Summary

1. **Know the difference between delinquency prevention and delinquency control**

- Prevention is distinguished from control or repression in that prevention seeks to reduce the risk factors for delinquency before antisocial behavior or delinquency becomes a problem.
- Delinquency control programs, which involve the juvenile justice system, intervene in the lives of juvenile offenders with the aim of preventing the occurrence of future delinquent acts.

2. **Have an understanding of the magnitude of cost to society caused by juvenile crime and violence**

- The costs of juvenile delinquency are considerable.
- These costs include the responses of the juvenile justice system, losses to victims of delinquent acts, and the financial impact on offenders and their families.
- One approach to reducing these costs that has garnered a great deal of attention in recent years is prevention.

3. **Be able to identify some of the major historical events that gave rise to the present focus on delinquency prevention**

I The history of the prevention of juvenile delinquency in the United States is closely tied to the history of the juvenile justice system in this country.

I A number of key events, including the Chicago Area Project and federally funded initiatives, helped shape the development of delinquency prevention today.

4. **Be familiar with different approaches to classifying delinquency prevention programs**

I There are a number of different ways to classify or organize delinquency prevention programs, including the public health approach and the developmental perspective.

5. **Know the key features of the developmental perspective of delinquency prevention**

I Key features of the developmental perspective of delinquency prevention include:

— The targeting of risk factors and the promotion of protective factors

— The provision of services to children and families

— Programs provided over the life course

6. **Have an understanding of the many different types of effective delinquency prevention programs for children and teens**

I Some of the most effective delinquency prevention programs for children and teens include:

— Home visits for new mothers

— Parent training

— Enriched preschool programs

— School-based programs that are intensive, cognitive-oriented, and targeted on high-risk kids

— Job training programs

7. **Be able to identify some of the key factors of effective programs**

I Key factors of effective delinquency prevention programs include:

— Theory-driven

— Target multiple risk factors for delinquency

— Intensive

— Successful implementation

8. **Be able to discuss some of the other benefits that are produced by delinquency prevention programs**

I Delinquency prevention programs have also been shown to lead to improvements in other areas of life, such as educational achievement, health, and employment.

I These benefits often translate into substantial cost savings.

9. **Be able to identify and comment on pressing issues facing the future of delinquency prevention**

I More attention needs to be paid to understanding what works in preventing delinquency and addressing some of the concerns with prevention programs.

I Intervening in the lives of children, young people, and their families to prevent delinquency before it takes place is a key component of an overall strategy to address the problem of juvenile delinquency.

Key Terms

delinquency control or delinquency repression, p. 400

delinquency prevention, p. 400

randomized experimental design, p. 404

experimental group, p. 404

control group, p. 404

risk factor, p. 406

protective factor, p. 406

Viewpoint

You are the mayor of a medium-sized city. Juvenile delinquency is on the rise, and there have been disturbing reports of increased gang activity. The police chief informs you that some urban gangs, seeking to migrate to your city, have sent members to recruit local youth. Their appeal appears to be working, and several local chapters of the Crips, Bloods, and Latin Kings have now been formed. Street shootings, thefts of cars, and other serious delinquency problems have risen in recent weeks, and all have been linked to this new gang activity. The police, business groups in the downtown core of the city, and the public are all calling for you to take immediate action to deal with these problems.

When you meet with local community leaders, they inform you that the gangs appeal to many local kids who come from troubled homes and have no real hope of success in the conventional world. Some are doing poorly in school and receive little educational support. Others who have left school have trouble finding jobs. The gangs also appeal to kids with emotional and developmental problems.

The police chief says that you cannot coddle these hoodlums. He tells you to put more police on the streets and hire more police officers. He also argues that you should lobby the governor and legislature to pass new laws making it mandatory that kids involved in gang violence are transferred to the adult court for trial.

In contrast, community advocates ask you to spend more money on disadvantaged families so they have access to child care and health care. They suggest you beef up the educational budget to reduce class sizes, reduce dropout rates, and improve attendance rates.

I Would you spend more money on community-based services for young people, or would you order the chief to crack down on the gangs?

I If you choose to spend money on prevention, which programs would you support?

I When should prevention begin? Should kids be given special help even before they get in trouble with the law?

Doing Research on the Web

The following organizations provide more information on different approaches to preventing juvenile delinquency:

The American Youth Policy Forum
Fight Crime: Invest in Kids
The National Crime Prevention Council

The Child Welfare League of America
The Office of Juvenile Justice and Delinquency Prevention

Access these websites via
academic.cengage.com/criminaljustice/siegel

Questions for Discussion

1. Prevention and control are the two broad-based approaches that can be used to reduce delinquency. How do these approaches differ?

2. The costs of juvenile delinquency are wide-ranging and substantial. Do you think these costs justify spending money on delinquency prevention programs?

3. What are some of the benefits of implementing prevention programs in childhood compared to adolescence?

4. In addition to reducing delinquency, many prevention programs also have a positive impact on other

social problems. Identify four of these problems, and give an example of a program that was successful in reducing each of them.

5. What are comprehensive community-based delinquency prevention programs?

6. Many programs have been successful in preventing delinquency, but many have not been successful. What are some of the reasons why a program may fail to reduce delinquency?

Notes

1. Helen Rumbelow and Alice Miles, "How to Save this Child from a Life of Poverty, Violence and Despair," *The Times*, 9 June 2007; Deanna S. Gomby, Patti L. Culross, and Richard E. Behrman, "Home Visiting: Recent Program Evaluations—Analysis and Recommendations," *The Future of Children* 9(1):4–26 (1999), p. 5.

2. Ted R. Miller, Mark A. Cohen, and Brian Wiersema, *Victim Costs and Consequences: A New Look* (Washington, DC: NIJ, 1996), p. 9, table 2.

3. Mark A. Cohen, Roland T. Rust, Sara Steen, and Simon T. Tidd, "Willingness-to-Pay for Crime Control Programs," *Criminology* 42: 89–109 (2004), p. 98, table 2.

4. Mark A. Cohen, "The Monetary Value of Saving a High-Risk Youth," *Journal of Quantitative Criminology* 14:5–33 (1998).

5. Matt Delisi and Jewel M. Gatling, "Who Pays for a Life of Crime? An Empirical Assessment of the Assorted Victimization Costs Posed by Career Criminals," *Criminal Justice Studies* 16:283–293 (2003).

6. Brandon C. Welsh, Rolf Loeber, Bradley R. Stevens, Magda Stouthamer-Loeber, Mark A. Cohen, and David P. Farrington, "Costs of Juvenile Crime in Urban Areas: A Longitudinal Perspective," *Youth Violence and Juvenile Justice* 6:3–27 (2008).

7. Ted R. Miller, Deborah A. Fisher, and Mark A. Cohen, "Costs of Juvenile Violence: Policy Implications," *Pediatrics* 107(1):1–7 (2001), http://pediatrics .aappublications.org (accessed October 28, 2007); see also Joint State Government Commission, General Assembly of the Commonwealth of Pennsylvania, *The Cost of Juvenile Violence in Pennsylvania*, staff report to the Task Force to Study the Issues Surrounding Violence as a Public Health Concern (Harrisburg, PA: Author, January 1995).

8. Children's Safety Network, "State Costs of Violence Perpetrated by Youth," July 12, 2000, www.edarc.org/pubs/tables/youth-viol.htm (accessed October 28, 2007).

9. Barry Krisberg and James Austin, *The Children of Ishmael: Critical Perspectives on Juvenile Justice* (Palo Alto, CA: Mayfield, 1978), pp. 7–45; Joseph G. Weis and J. David Hawkins, *Preventing Delinquency*

(Washington, DC: Office of Juvenile Justice and Delinquency Prevention, 1981), pp. 1–6; Richard J. Lundam, *Prevention and Control of Juvenile Delinquency*, 3rd ed. (New York: Oxford University Press, 2001), pp. 23, 25.

10. Clifford R. Shaw and Henry D. McKay, *Juvenile Delinquency and Urban Areas: A Study of Rates of Delinquents in Relation to Differential Characteristics of Local Communities in American Cities* (Chicago: University of Chicago Press, 1942).

11. For an intensive look at the Chicago Area Project, see Steven Schlossman and Michael Sedlack, "The Chicago Area Project Revisited," *Crime and Delinquency* 29:398–462 (1983).

12. Joan McCord and William McCord, "A Follow-Up Report on the Cambridge-Somerville Youth Study," *Annals of the American Academy of Political and Social Science* 322:89–96 (1959).

13. Richard J. Lundman, *Prevention and Control of Juvenile Delinquency*, 3rd ed. (New York: Oxford University Press, 2001), p. 50.

14. Joan McCord, "A Thirty-Year Follow-Up of Treatment Effects," *American Psychologist* 33:284–289 (1978).

15. Thomas J. Dishion, Joan McCord, and François Poulin, "When Interventions Harm: Peer Groups and Problem Behavior," *American Psychologist* 54:755–764 (1999). See also Joan McCord, "Counterproductive Juvenile Justice," *Australian and New Zealand Journal of Criminology* 35:230–237 (2002); Joan McCord, "Cures that Harm: Unanticipated Outcomes of Crime Prevention Programs," *Annals of the American Academy of Political and Social Science* 587:16–30 (2003).

16. See New York City Youth Board, *Reaching the Fighting Gang* (New York: New York City Youth Board, 1960).

17. Walter Miller, "The Impact of a 'Total Community' Delinquency Control Project," *Social Problems* 10:168–191 (1962).

18. See Karol L. Kumpfer and Rose Alvarado, "Family-Strengthening Approaches for the Prevention of Youth Problem Behaviors," *American Psychologist* 58:457–465 (2003).

19. Trevor Bennett, "Crime Prevention," in Michael Tonry, ed., *The Handbook of Crime and Punishment* (New York: Oxford University Press, 1998).

20. Paul J. Brantingham and Frederick L. Faust, "A Conceptual Model of Crime Prevention," *Crime and Delinquency* 22:284–296 (1976).

21. See Brandon C. Welsh, "Public Health and the Prevention of Juvenile Criminal Violence," *Youth Violence and Juvenile Justice* 3:23–40 (2005).

22. David P. Farrington, "Early Developmental Prevention of Juvenile Delinquency," *Criminal Behaviour and Mental Health* 4:209–227 (1994).

23. David P. Farrington, "The Development of Offending and Antisocial Behaviour from Childhood: Key Findings from the Cambridge Study in Delinquent Development," *Journal of Child Psychology and Psychiatry* 36:929–964 (1995).

24. Richard E. Tremblay and Wendy M. Craig, "Developmental Crime Prevention," in Michael Tonry and David P. Farrington, eds., *Building a Safer Society: Strategic Approaches to Crime Prevention. Crime and Justice: A Review of Research*, vol. 19 (Chicago: University of Chicago Press, 1995), p. 151.

25. Tremblay and Craig, "Developmental Crime Prevention"; Gail A. Wasserman and Laurie S. Miller, "The Prevention of Serious and Violent Juvenile Offending," in Rolf Loeber and David P. Farrington, eds., *Serious and Violent Juvenile Offenders: Risk Factors and Successful Interventions* (Thousand Oaks, CA: Sage Publications, 1998); Joan McCord, Cathy Spatz Widom, and Nancy A. Crowell, eds., *Juvenile Crime, Juvenile Justice*, panel on Juvenile Crime: Prevention, Treatment, and Control (Washington, DC: National Academy Press, 2001); Patrick Tolan, "Crime Prevention: Focus on Youth," in James Q. Wilson and Joan Petersilia, eds., *Crime: Public Policies for Crime Control* (Oakland, CA: Institute for Contemporary Studies, 2002).

26. Deanna S. Gomby, Patti L. Culross, and Richard E. Behrman, "Home Visiting: Recent Program Evaluations—Analysis and Recommendations," *The Future of Children* 9(1):4–26 (1999).

27. David L. Olds, Charles R. Henderson, Robert Chamberlin, and Robert Tatelbaum, "Preventing Child Abuse and Neglect: A Randomized Trial of Nurse Home Visitation," *Pediatrics* 78:65–78 (1986).

28. David L. Olds, Charles R. Henderson, Charles Phelps, Harriet Kitzman, and Carole Hanks, "Effects of Prenatal and Infancy Nurse Home Visitation on Government Spending," *Medical Care* 31:155–174 (1993).

29. David L. Olds et al., "Long-Term Effects of Nurse Home Visitation on Children's Criminal and Antisocial Behavior: 15-Year Follow-Up of a Randomized Controlled Trial," *Journal of the American Medical Association* 280:1238–1244 (1998).

30. David L. Olds et al., "Long-Term Effects of Home Visitation on Maternal Life Course and Child Abuse and Neglect: Fifteen-Year Follow-Up of a Randomized Trial," *Journal of the American Medical Association* 278:637–643 (1997).

31. Peter W. Greenwood, Lynn A. Karoly, Susan S. Everingham, Jill Houbè, M. Rebecca Kilburn, C. Peter Rydell, Matthew Sanders, and James Chiesa, "Estimating the Costs and Benefits of Early Childhood Interventions: Nurse Home Visits and the Perry Preschool," in Brandon C. Welsh, David P. Farrington, and Lawrence W. Sherman, eds., *Costs and Benefits of Preventing Crime* (Boulder, CO: Westview Press, 2001), p. 133.

32. David L. Olds, "Preventing Crime with Prenatal and Infancy Support of Parents: The Nurse-Family Partnership," *Victims and Offenders* 2:205–225 (2007).

33. Ned Calonge, "Community Interventions to Prevent Violence: Translation into Public Health Practice," *American Journal of Preventive Medicine* 28(2S1):4–5 (2005).

34. Rumbelow and Miles, "How to Save this Child from a Life of Poverty, Violence and Despair."

35. Anne K. Duggan et al., "Evaluation of Hawaii's Healthy Start Program," *The Future of Children* 9(1):66–90 (1999); Anne K. Duggan, Amy Windham, Elizabeth McFarlane, Loretta Fuddy, Charles Rohde, Sharon Buchbinder, and Calvin Sia, "Hawaii's Healthy Start Program of Home Visiting for At-Risk Families: Evaluation of Family Identification, Family Engagement, and Service Delivery," *Pediatrics* 105:250–259 (2000).

36. See Gerald R. Patterson, "Performance Models for Antisocial Boys," *American Psychologist* 41:432–444 (1986); Gerald R. Patterson, *Coercive Family Process* (Eugene, OR: Castalia, 1982).

37. Gerald R. Patterson, Patricia Chamberlain, and John B. Reid, "A Comparative Evaluation of a Parent-Training Program," *Behavior Therapy* 13:638–650 (1982); Gerald R. Patterson, John B. Reid, and Thomas J. Dishion, *Antisocial Boys* (Eugene, OR: Castalia, 1992).

38. Peter W. Greenwood, Karyn E. Model, C. Peter Rydell, and James Chiesa, *Diverting Children from a Life of Crime: Measuring Costs and Benefits* (Santa Monica: Rand, 1996).

39. Sonya Michel, *Children's Interests/Mother's Rights: The Shaping of America's Child Care Policy* (New Haven, CT: Yale University Press, 1999).

40. J. Ronald Lally, Peter L. Mangione, and Alice S. Honig, "The Syracuse University Family Development Research Program: Long-Range Impact of an Early Intervention with Low-Income Children and their Families," in D. R. Powell, ed., *Parent Education as Early Childhood Intervention: Emerging Directions in Theory, Research and Practice* (Norwood, NJ: Ablex, 1988).

41. Dale L. Johnson and Todd Walker, "Primary Prevention of Behavior Problems in Mexican-American Children," *American Journal of Community Psychology* 15:375–385 (1987).

42. Tremblay and Craig, "Developmental Crime Prevention."

43. Farrington, "Early Developmental Prevention of Juvenile Delinquency," pp. 216–217.

44. Greg J. Duncan and Katherine Magnuson, "Individual and Parent-Based Intervention Strategies for Promoting Human Capital and Positive Behavior," *Human Development Across Lives and Generations: The Potential for Change*, edited by P. Lindsay Chase-Lansdale, Kathleen Kiernan, and Ruth J. Friedman (New York: Cambridge University Press, 2004).

45. Lawrence J. Schweinhart, Helen V. Barnes, and David P. Weikart, *Significant Benefits: The High/Scope Perry Preschool Study through Age 27* (Ypsilanti, MI: High/Scope Press, 1993), p. 3.

46. Lawrence J. Schweinhart and David P. Weikart, *Young Children Grow Up: The Effects of the Perry Preschool Program through Age 15* (Ypsilanti, MI: High/Scope Press, 1980).

47. Schweinhart, Barnes, and Weikart, *Significant Benefits: The High/Scope Perry Preschool Study through Age 27*, p. xv.

48. W. Steven Barnett, *Lives in the Balance: Age 27 Benefit-Cost Analysis of the High/Scope Perry Preschool Program* (Ypsilanti, MI: High/Scope Press, 1996); W. Steven Barnett, "Cost-Benefit Analysis," in Schweinhart, Barnes, and Weikart, *Significant Benefits: The High/Scope Perry Preschool Study through Age 27* (Ypsilanti, MI: High/Scope Press, 1993).

49. Greenwood et al., "Estimating the Costs and Benefits of Early Childhood Interventions: Nurse Home Visits and the Perry Preschool."

50. Lawrence J. Schweinhart, "Crime Prevention by the High/Scope Perry Preschool Program," *Victims and Offenders* 2:141–160 (2007); Lawrence J. Schweinhart, Jeanne Montie, Xiang Zongping, W. Steven Barnett, Clive R. Belfield, and Milagros Nores, *Lifetime Effects: The High/Scope Perry Preschool Study through Age 40* (Ypsilanti, MI: High/Scope Press, 2005).

51. Arthur J. Reynolds, Judy A. Temple, Dylan L. Robertson, and Emily A. Mann, "Long-Term Effects of an Early Childhood Intervention on Educational Achievement and Juvenile Arrest: A 15-Year Follow-up of Low-Income Children in Public Schools," *Journal of the American Medical Association* 285:2339–2346 (2001).

52. Arthur J. Reynolds, Judy A. Temple, and Suh-Ruu Ou, "School-Based Early Intervention and Child Well-Being in the Chicago Longitudinal Study," *Child Welfare* 82:633–656 (2003).

53. Carolyn Webster-Stratton, "Preventing Conduct Problems in Head Start Children: Strengthening Parenting Competencies," *Journal of Consulting and Clinical Psychology* 66:715–730 (1998).

54. Edward Zigler and Sally J. Styfco, "Extended Childhood Intervention Prepares Children for School and Beyond," *Journal of the American Medical Association* 285:2378–2380 (2001).

55. Delbert S. Elliott, Beatrix Hamburg, and Kirk R. Williams, "Violence in American Schools: An Overview," in Delbert S. Elliott, Beatrix Hamburg, and Kirk R. Williams, eds., *Violence in American Schools: A New Perspective* (New York: Cambridge University Press, 1998), p. 16.

56. J. David Hawkins, Brian H. Smith, Karl G. Smith, Rick Kosterman, and Richard F. Catalano, "Promoting Social Development and Preventing Health and Behavior Problems during the Elementary Grades: Results from the Seattle Social Development Project," *Victims and Offenders* 2:161–181 (2007).

57. Steve Aos, Roxanne Lieb, Jim Mayfield, Marna Miller, and Annie Pennucci, *Benefits and Costs of Prevention and Early Intervention Programs for Youth* (Olympia, WA: Washington State Institute for Public Policy, 2004). Available at www.wsipp.wa.gov/rptfiles/04-07-3901.pdf.

58. Richard E. Tremblay et al., "Parent and Child Training to Prevent Early Onset of Delinquency: The Montrèal Longitudinal-Experimental Study," in Joan McCord and Richard E. Tremblay, eds., *Preventing Antisocial Behavior: Interventions from Birth through Adolescence* (New York: Guilford, 1992); Richard E. Tremblay, Linda Pagani-Kurtz, Louise C. Mâsse, Frank Vitaro, and Robert O. Pihl, "A Bimodal Preventive Intervention for Disruptive Kindergarten Boys: Its Impact through Mid-Adolescence," *Journal of Consulting and Clinical Psychology* 63:560–568 (1995); Richard E. Tremblay, Louise C. Mâsse, Linda Pagani-Kurtz, and Frank Vitaro, "From Childhood Physical Aggression to Adolescent Maladjustment: The Montreal Prevention Experiment," in R. DeV. Peters and R. J. McMahon, eds., *Preventing Childhood Disorders, Substance Abuse, and Delinquency* (Thousand Oaks, CA: Sage Publications, 1996).

59. Alexander T. Vazsonyi, Lara B. Belliston, and Daniel J. Flannery, "Evaluation of a School-Based, Universal Violence Prevention Program: Low-, Medium-, and High-Risk Children," *Youth Violence and Juvenile Justice* 2:185–206 (2004).

60. James C. Howell, ed., *Guide for Implementing the Comprehensive Strategy for Serious, Violent, and Chronic Juvenile Offenders* (Washington, DC: Office of Juvenile Justice and Delinquency Prevention, U.S. Department of Justice, 1995), p. 90.

61. MENTOR United States, *Mentoring in America, 2005* (Alexandria, VA: Author, 2006); Joan McCord, Cathy Spatz Widom, and Nancy A. Crowell, eds., *Juvenile Crime, Juvenile Justice*, panel on Juvenile Crime: Prevention, Treatment, and Control (Washington, DC: National Academy Press, 2001), p. 147.

62. Edith Fairman Cooper, *Mentoring Programs Funded by the Federal Government Dedicated to Disadvantaged Youth: Issues and Activities. CRS Report for Congress* (Washington, DC: Congressional Research Service, The Library of Congress, March 20, 2006), p. 15.

63. Laurence C. Novotney, Elizabeth Mertinko, James Lange, and Tara Kelly Baker, *Juvenile Mentoring Program: A Progress Review* (Washington, DC: OJJDP Juvenile Justice Bulletin, 2000).

64. Thomas J. Dishion, Joan McCord, and François Poulin, "When Interventions Harm: Peer Groups and Problem Behavior," *American Psychologist* 54:755–764 (1999).

65. Information Technology International, *Jump Annual Report, 2003* (Alexandria, VA: Author, 2003).

66. Andrew Hahn, "Extending the Time of Learning," in Douglas J. Besharov, ed., *America's Disconnected Youth: Toward a Preventive Strategy* (Washington, DC: Child Welfare League of America Press, 1999).

67. Andrew Hahn, *Evaluation of the Quantum Opportunities Program (QOP): Did the Program Work?* (Waltham, MA: Brandeis University, 1994).

68. Jean Baldwin Grossman and Joseph P. Tierney, "Does Mentoring Work? An Impact Study of the Big Brothers Big Sisters Program," *Evaluation Review* 22:403–426 (1998), p. 405.

69. Ibid., p. 422.

70. David L. DuBois, Bruce E. Holloway, Jeffrey C. Valentine, and Harris Cooper, "Effectiveness of Mentoring Programs for Youth: A Meta-Analytic Review," *American Journal of Community Psychology* 30:157–197 (2002); Brandon C. Welsh and Akemi Hoshi, "Communities and Crime Prevention," in Lawrence W. Sherman, David P. Farrington, Brandon C. Welsh, and Doris Layton MacKenzie, eds., *Evidence-Based Crime Prevention* (New York: Routledge, 2006, rev. ed.); Joan McCord, Cathy Spatz Widom, and Nancy A. Crowell, eds., *Juvenile Crime, Juvenile Justice*.

71. McCord, Widom, and Crowell, eds., *Juvenile Crime, Juvenile Justice*, p. 147.

72. Renée Spencer, "Understanding the Mentoring Process between Adolescents and Adults," *Youth and Society* 37:287–315 (2006), pp. 309–311.

73. Denise C. Gottfredson, "An Empirical Test of School-Based Environmental and Individual Interventions to Reduce the Risk of Delinquent Behavior," *Criminology* 24:705–731 (1986); Denise C. Gottfredson, "Changing School Structures to Benefit High-Risk Youth," in Peter Leone, ed., *Understanding Troubled and Troubling Youth* (Newbury Park, CA: Sage Publications, 1990); Denise C. Gottfredson, *Schools and Delinquency* (New York: Cambridge University Press, 2001).

74. Debra Galant, "Violence Offers Its Own Lessons," *New York Times*, 15 June 2003.

75. Gottfredson et al., "School-Based Crime Prevention."

76. James Larson, "Violence Prevention in the Schools: A Review of Selected Programs and Procedures," *School Psychology Review* 23:151–164 (1994).

77. Ibid., p. 153.

78. Denise C. Gottfredson, Gary D. Gottfredson, and Stephanie A. Weisman, "The Timing of Delinquent Behavior and Its Implications for After-School Programs," *Criminology and Public Policy* 1:61–86 (2001), p. 61.

79. Ibid., p. 63.

80. Denise C. Gottfredson, Stephanie A. Gerstenblith, David A. Soulé, Shannon C. Womer, and Shaoli Lu, "Do After School Programs Reduce Delinquency?" *Prevention Science* 5:253–266 (2004), pp. 263–264.

81. Steven P. Schinke, Mario A. Orlandi, and Kristin C. Cole, "Boys and Girls Clubs in Public Housing Developments: Prevention Services for Youth at Risk," *Journal of Community Psychology, Office of Substance Abuse Prevention* Special Issue:118–128 (1992).

82. Ibid., p. 120.

83. Ibid., pp. 125–127.

84. Marshall B. Jones and David R. Offord, "Reduction of Anti-Social Behaviour in Poor Children by Nonschool Skill Development," *Journal of Child Psychology and Psychiatry* 30:737–750 (1989).

85. Gottfredson, Gerstenblith, Soulé, Womer, and Shaoli, "Do After School Programs Reduce Delinquency?"; Welsh and Hoshi, "Communities and Crime Prevention."

86. Denise C. Gottfredson and David A. Soulé, "The Timing of Property Crime, Violent Crime, and Substance Abuse among Juveniles," *Journal of Research in Crime and Delinquency* 42:110–120 (2005).

87. McCord, Widom, and Crowell, eds., *Juvenile Crime, Juvenile Justice*, pp. 150–151.

88. Peter Z. Schochet, John Burghardt, and Steven Glazerman, *National Job Corps Study: The Impacts of Job Corps on Participants' Employment and Related Outcomes* (Washington, DC: Employment and Training Administration, U.S. Department of Labor, 2001), p. xxv.

89. Lynn A. Curtis, *The State of Families: Family, Employment and Reconstruction: Policy Based on What Works* (Milwaukee, WI: Families International, 1995).

90. Schochet, Burghardt, and Glazerman, *National Job Corps Study*.

91. David A. Long, Charles D. Mallar, and Craig V. D. Thornton, "Evaluating the Benefits and Costs of the Job Corps," *Journal of Policy Analysis and Management* 1:55–76 (1981).

92. Sheena McConnell and Steven Glazerman, *National Job Corps Study: The Benefits and Costs of Job Corps* (Washington, DC: Employment and Training Administration, U.S. Department of Labor, 2001).

93. Tim Cross and Daryl Wright, "What Works with At-Risk Youths," *Corrections Today* 66:64–68 (2004), p. 64.

94. Ibid., p. 65.

95. Rudy Hernandez, *YouthBuild U.S.A.* (Washington, DC: OJJDP Youth in Action Fact Sheet, 2001).

96. J. David Hawkins, Richard F. Catalano, and Associates, *Communities That Care: Action for Drug Abuse* (San Francisco: Jossey-Bass, 1992).

97. Richard F. Catalano, Michael W. Arthur, J. David Hawkins, Lisa Berglund, and Jeffrey J. Olson, "Comprehensive Community- and School-Based Interventions to Prevent Antisocial Behavior," in Rolf Loeber and David P. Farrington, eds., *Serious and Violent Juvenile Offenders: Risk Factors and Successful Interventions* (Thousand Oaks, CA: Sage Publications, 1998), p. 281.

98. Abraham Wandersman and Paul Florin, "Community Interventions and Effective Prevention," *American Psychologist* 58:441–448 (2003).

99. Lawrence F. Murray and Steven Belenko, "CASASTART: A Community-Based, School-Centered Intervention for High-Risk Youth," *Substance Use and Misuse* 40:913–933 (2005); National Center on Addiction and Substance Abuse, *CASASTART* (New York: Columbia University, 2007).

100. Adele V. Harrell, Shannon E. Cavanagh, and Sanjeev Sridharan, *Evaluation of the Children At Risk Program: Results 1 Year after the End of the Program* (Washington, DC: NIJ Research in Brief, 1999).

101. Hawkins, Catalano, and Associates, *Communities That Care: Action for Drug Abuse Prevention*.

102. Elaine Morley, Shelli B. Rossman, Mary Kopczynski, Janeen Buck, and Caterina Gouvis, *Comprehensive Responses to Youth at Risk: Interim Findings from the Safe Futures Initiative* (Washington, DC: Office of Juvenile Justice and Delinquency Prevention, 2000).

103. Catalano, Arthur, Hawkins, Berglund, and Olson, "Comprehensive Community- and School-Based Interventions to Prevent Antisocial Behavior."

104. James C. Howell and J. David Hawkins, "Prevention of Youth Violence," in Michael Tonry and Mark H. Moore, eds., *Youth Violence: Crime and Justice: A Review of Research*, vol. 24 (Chicago: University of Chicago Press, 1998), pp. 303–304.

105. Tracy W. Harachi, J. David Hawkins, Richard F. Catalano, Andrea M. Lafazia, Brian H. Smith, and Michael W. Arthur, "Evidence-Based Community Decision Making for Prevention: Two Case Studies of Communities That Care," *Japanese Journal of Sociological Criminology* 28:26–38 (2003).

106. Bryan J. Vila, "Human Nature and Crime Control: Improving the Feasibility of Nurturant Strategies," *Politics and the Life Sciences* 16:3–21 (1997).

107. Irvin Waller and Brandon C. Welsh, "International Trends in Crime Prevention: Cost-Effective Ways to Reduce Victimization," in Graeme Newman, ed., *Global Report on Crime and Justice* (New York: Oxford University Press, 1999).

108. Richard A. Mendel, *Prevention or Pork? A Hard-Headed Look at Youth-Oriented Anti-Crime Programs* (Washington, DC: American Youth Policy Forum, 1995), p. 1.

109. McCord, "Cures that Harm: Unanticipated Outcomes of Crime Prevention Programs." See also Thomas Gabor, "Prevention into the Twenty-First Century: Some Final Remarks," *Canadian Journal of Criminology* 32:197–212 (1990).

110. David R. Offord, Helena Chmura Kraemer, Alan E. Kazdin, Peter S. Jensen, and Richard Harrington, "Lowering the Burden of Suffering from Child Psychiatric Disorder: Trade-Offs among Clinical, Targeted, and Universal Interventions," *Journal of the American Academy of Child and Adolescent Psychiatry* 37:686–694 (1998).

111. David P. Farrington and Brandon C. Welsh, *Saving Children from a Life of Crime: Early Risk Factors and Effective Interventions* (New York: Oxford University Press, 2007).

112. National Crime Prevention Council, "Saving Money While Stopping Crime," *Topics in Crime Prevention* (Washington, DC: NCPC, Fall 1999).

113. Brandon C. Welsh, "Economic Costs and Benefits of Early Developmental Prevention," in Rolf Loeber and David P. Farrington, eds., *Child Delinquents: Development, Intervention, and Service Needs* (Thousand Oaks, CA: Sage Publications, 2001); Brandon C. Welsh, David P. Farrington, and Lawrence W. Sherman, eds., *Costs and Benefits of Preventing Crime* (Boulder: Westview Press, 2001).

PART

4

The Juvenile Justice System

Since 1900, a separate juvenile justice system has been developed that features its own rules, institutions, laws, and processes. The separation of juvenile and adult offenders reflects society's concern for the plight of children. Ideally, care, protection, and treatment are the bywords of the juvenile justice system. However, because of public fear of violent youth, there have been efforts to "toughen up" the juvenile justice system and treat some delinquents much more like adult offenders. Because of these concerns, the treatment of delinquents has become an American dilemma. Severe punishment seems to have little deterrent effect on teenagers—if anything, it may prepare them for a life of adult criminality. Many incarcerated adult felons report that they were institutionalized as youths. The juvenile justice system is caught between the futility of punishing juveniles and the public's demand that something be done about serious juvenile crime. Yet, the rehabilitative ideal of the juvenile justice system has not been totally lost. Even though the nation seems to be in a punishment cycle, juvenile justice experts continue to press for judicial fairness, rehabilitation, and innovative programs for juvenile offenders.

Part Four provides a general overview of the juvenile justice system, including its process, history, and legal rules. Chapter 13 reviews the history and development of juvenile justice and provides an overview of its major components, processes, goals, and institutions. Chapter 14 deals with police handling of delinquent and status offenders. It contains information on the police role, the organization of police services, legal rights of minors in police custody, and prevention efforts. Chapter 15 is concerned with the juvenile court process. It describes such issues and programs as diversion; the transfer of youths to adult courts; legal rights during trial; the roles of the prosecutor, the juvenile court judge, and the defense attorney; and the sentencing of juvenile offenders.

Chapter 16 discusses efforts to treat juveniles who have been found to be delinquent. It reviews the history and practices of probation, community corrections, and juvenile institutions. Finally, Chapter 17 reviews international efforts to treat delinquent offenders. It compares how other nations organize their juvenile justice systems and treat juvenile offenders with methods used in the United States.

13

Juvenile Justice: Then and Now

Chapter Outline

Chapter Objectives

1. Understand the major social changes leading to the creation of the first modern juvenile court in Chicago in 1899

2. Be familiar with some of the landmark Supreme Court decisions that have influenced present-day juvenile justice procedures

3. Know how children are processed by the juvenile justice system, beginning with arrest and concluding with reentry into society

4. Understand the conflicting values in contemporary juvenile justice

5. Recognize key similarities and differences between the adult and juvenile justice systems

6. Be able to argue the pros and cons of the juvenile justice system's goal to treat rather than punish and assess if this goal is being met today

7. Understand the need for and be aware of the key elements of a comprehensive juvenile justice strategy to deal with juvenile delinquency

8. See the difference between prevention and intervention efforts to reduce juvenile delinquency

9. Be able to identify and comment on pressing issues in the future of juvenile justice

According to the Miami, Florida, state attorney's office, Michael Hernandez, age 14, acted alone and with premeditation in slashing the throat of his friend and classmate, Jaime Gough, also 14, in a bathroom at the Southwood Middle School. Hernandez then returned to class in his blood-soaked clothes. The knife used in the killing, along with a bloody latex glove, was later found in the accused's book bag.

Hernandez has never disputed these events or his role in the killing, although the motive remains a mystery. Hernandez's taped confession to Miami-Dade police detective Salvatore Garofalo, taken just hours after the killing, is revealing of his intentions on that day:

> Garolfalo: "Why did you suggest to Jaime to go inside the school today?"
> Hernandez: "I planned to murder him."
> Garolfalo: "Do you know why you were going to do this?"
> Hernandez: "No, I don't."

Michael Hernandez's waiver to adult court was never in question. Nor will be his sentence if he is convicted of first-degree murder: life without parole. In Florida and in many other states across the country this is a mandatory sentence that the judge must impose. But although this sentence has the support of many, there is growing opposition to its severity for juveniles who are so young and who may benefit from early treatment.

One proposal is that juvenile killers under the age of 16 with clean records be eligible for aftercare (parole in the juvenile justice system) after serving a minimum of eight years in a secure juvenile institution. Advocates of this and similar proposals argue that this is in keeping with the juvenile justice system's treatment philosophy and the need to separate juveniles from adult offenders.

Society has struggled with cases like that of Michael Hernandez ever since the creation of the first modern juvenile court in Chicago in 1899. This chapter begins with a discussion of the major social changes leading up to this milestone event. We then cover the reform efforts of the twentieth century, including the movement to grant children the procedural rights typically given to adult offenders. This discussion includes descriptions of some landmark Supreme Court decisions that have influenced present-day juvenile justice procedures.

The second part of this chapter presents an overview of the contemporary juvenile justice system and the various philosophies, processes, organizations, and legal constraints that dominate its operations. The chapter describes the process that takes a youthful offender through a series of steps, beginning with arrest and concluding with reentry into society. What happens to young people who violate the law? Do they have legal rights? How are they helped? How are they punished? Should juvenile killers be released from custody prior to their 18th birthday? Should the goal of the system be rehabilitation or punishment?

To help address such questions, we have included a discussion of the similarities and differences between the adult and juvenile justice systems. This discussion draws attention to the principle that children are treated separately. By segregating delinquent children from adult offenders, society has placed greater importance on the delinquent being a *child* rather than being a *criminal*. Consequently, rehabilitation rather than punishment has traditionally been the goal. Today, with children committing more serious crimes, the juvenile justice system is having great difficulty handling these offenders.

In the final section, we discuss the need for a comprehensive juvenile justice strategy and the role of the federal government in juvenile justice reform—the key element in funding state juvenile justice and delinquency prevention efforts.

JUVENILE JUSTICE IN THE NINETEENTH CENTURY

At the beginning of the nineteenth century, delinquent, neglected, and runaway children in the United States were treated the same as adult criminal offenders.[1] Like children in England, when convicted of crimes they received harsh sentences similar to those imposed on adults. The adult criminal code applied to children, and no juvenile court existed.

During the early nineteenth century, various pieces of legislation were introduced to humanize criminal procedures for children. The concept of probation, introduced in Massachusetts in 1841, was geared toward helping young people avoid imprisonment. Many books and reports written during this time heightened public interest in juvenile care.

Despite this interest, no special facilities existed for the care of youths in trouble with the law, nor were there separate laws or courts to control their behavior. Youths who committed petty crimes, such as stealing or vandalism, were viewed as wayward children or victims of neglect and were placed in community asylums or homes. Youths who were involved in more serious crimes were subject to the same punishments as adults—imprisonment, whipping, or death.

Several events led to reforms and nourished the eventual development of the juvenile justice system: (a) urbanization, (b) the child saving movement and growing interest in the concept of *parens patriae*, and (c) development of institutions for the care of delinquent and neglected children.

Urbanization

Especially during the first half of the nineteenth century, the United States experienced rapid population growth, primarily due to an increased birthrate and expanding immigration. The rural poor and immigrant groups were attracted to urban commercial centers that promised jobs in manufacturing. In 1790, 5 percent of the population lived in cities. By 1850, the share of the urban population had increased to 15 percent; it jumped to 40 percent in 1900, and 51 percent in 1920.[2] New York had more than quadrupled its population in the 30-year stretch between 1825 and 1855—from 166,000 in 1825 to 630,000 in 1855.[3]

Urbanization gave rise to increased numbers of young people at risk, who overwhelmed the existing system of work and training. To accommodate destitute youths, local jurisdictions developed poorhouses (almshouses) and workhouses. The poor, the insane, the diseased, and vagrant and destitute children were housed there in crowded and unhealthy conditions.

By the late eighteenth century, the family's ability to exert control over children began to be questioned. Villages developed into urban commercial centers, and work began to center around factories, not the home. Children of destitute families left home or were cast loose to make out as best they could; wealthy families could no longer absorb vagrant youth as apprentices or servants.[4] Chronic poverty became an American dilemma. The affluent began to voice concern over the increase in the number of people in what they considered the "dangerous classes"—the poor, single, criminal, mentally ill, and unemployed.

Urbanization and industrialization also generated the belief that certain segments of the population (youths in urban areas, immigrants) were susceptible to the influences of their decaying environment. The children of these classes were considered a group that might be "saved" by a combination of state and community intervention.[5] Intervention in the lives of these so-called dangerous classes became acceptable for wealthy, civic-minded citizens. Such efforts included *settlement houses*, a term used around the turn of the twentieth century to describe shelters or nonsecure residential facilities for vagrant children.

To learn more about the **early urbanization movement in America**, go to the Library of Congress web page devoted to American history via academic.cengage.com/criminaljustice/siegel.

The Child Saving Movement

The problems generated by urban growth sparked interest in the welfare of the "new" Americans, whose arrival fueled this expansion. In 1816, prominent New Yorkers formed the Society for the Prevention of Pauperism. Although they concerned themselves with shutting down taverns, brothels, and gambling parlors, they also were concerned that the moral training of children of the dangerous classes was inadequate. Soon other groups concerned with the plight of poor children began to form. Their focus was on extending government control over youthful activities (drinking, vagrancy, and delinquency) that had previously been left to private or family control.

To read more about the **child savers**, go to academic.cengage.com/criminaljustice/siegel.

These activists became known as *child savers*. Prominent among them were penologist Enoch Wines, Judge Richard Tuthill, Lucy Flowers, of the Chicago Women's Association, Sara Cooper, of the National Conference of Charities and Corrections, and Sophia Minton, of the New York Committee on Children.[6] Poor children could become a financial burden, and the child savers believed these children presented a threat to the moral fabric of society. Child saving organizations influenced state legislatures to enact laws giving courts the power to commit children who were runaways or criminal offenders to specialized institutions.

House of Refuge

House of Refuge
A care facility developed by the child savers to protect potential criminal youths by taking them off the street and providing a family-like environment.

The most prominent of the care facilities developed by child savers was the House of Refuge.[7] Its creation was effected by prominent Quakers and influential political leaders, such as Cadwallader Colden and Stephen Allen. In 1816, they formed the Society for the Prevention of Pauperism, which was devoted to the concept of protecting indigent youths who were at risk to crime by taking them off the streets and reforming them in a family-like environment.

The first House of Refuge, constructed in New York City, was the product of their reform efforts. Though the house was privately managed, the state legislature began providing funds, partly through a head tax on arriving transatlantic passengers and seamen, plus the proceeds from license fees for New York City's taverns, theaters, and circuses. These revenue sources were deemed appropriate, since supporters blamed immigration, intemperance, and commercial entertainment for juvenile crime!

The reformatory opened January 1, 1825, with only six boys and three girls, but within the first decade of its operation 1,678 inmates were admitted. Most kids were

sent because of vagrancy and petty crimes and were sentenced or committed indefinitely until they reached adulthood. Originally, the institution accepted inmates from across the state of New York, but when a Western House of Refuge was opened in Rochester, New York, in 1849, residents came mostly from the New York City environs.

Once a resident, the adolescent's daily schedule was devoted for the most part to supervised labor, which was regarded as beneficial to education and discipline. Inmate labor also supported operating expenses for the reformatory. Male inmates worked in shops that produced brushes, cane chairs, brass nails, and shoes. The female inmates sewed uniforms, did laundry, and carried out other domestic work. A badge system was used to segregate inmates according to their behavior. Although students received rudimentary educational skills, greater emphasis was placed on evangelical religious instruction; non-Protestant clergy were excluded. The reformatory had the authority to bind out inmates through indenture agreements to private employers; most males were farm workers and females were domestic laborers.

The Refuge Movement Spreads When the House of Refuge opened, the majority of children admitted were status offenders placed there because of vagrancy or neglect. Children were placed in the institution by court order, sometimes over parents' objections. Their length of stay depended on need, age, and skill. Critics complained that the institution was run like a prison, with strict discipline and absolute separation of the sexes. Such a harsh program drove many children to run away, and the House of Refuge was forced to take a more lenient approach. Despite criticism, the concept enjoyed expanding popularity. In 1826, the Boston City Council founded the House of Reformation for juvenile offenders.[8] The courts committed children found guilty of criminal violations, or found to be beyond the control of their parents, to these schools. Because the child savers considered parents of delinquent children to be as guilty as convicted offenders, they sought to have the reform schools establish control over the children. Refuge managers believed they were preventing poverty and crime by separating destitute and delinquent children from their parents and placing them in an institution.[9]

The earliest institutions resembled the New York House of Refuge and housed a small number of children in relatively small buildings. But by the 1850s, the number of incarcerated children began to climb, resulting in the construction of larger institutions removed from the urban environment. For example, in New York the number of youthful residents expanded from 9 at the outset to more than 1,000 housed on Randall's Island in the East River in an institution indistinguishable from an adult prison.[10] Despite ongoing criticism and scandal, the Houses of Refuge hung on for more than 100 years. After the Civil War, the urban Refuge began to be replaced by state institutions located in rural areas. In 1935, the institution on Randall's Island closed forever.

Were They Really Child Savers?

Debate continues over the true objectives of the early child savers. Some historians conclude that they were what they seemed—concerned citizens motivated by humanitarian ideals.[11] Modern scholars, however, have reappraised the child saving movement. In *The Child Savers*, Anthony Platt paints a picture of representatives of the ruling class who were galvanized by immigrants and the urban poor to take action to preserve their own way of life.[12] He claims

> The child savers should not be considered humanists: (1) their reforms did not herald a new system of justice but rather expedited traditional policies which had been informally developed during the nineteenth century; (2) they implicitly assumed the natural dependence of adolescents and created a special court to impose sanctions on premature independence and behavior unbecoming to youth; (3) their attitudes toward delinquent youth were largely paternalistic and romantic but their commands were backed up by force; (4) they promoted correctional programs requiring longer terms of imprisonment, longer hours of labor, and militaristic discipline, and the inculcation of middle class values and lower class skills.[13]

Other critical thinkers followed Platt in finding that child saving was motivated more by self-interest than by benevolence. For example, Randall Shelden and Lynn Osborne traced the child saving movement in Memphis, Tennessee, and found that its leaders were a small group of upper-class citizens who desired to control the behavior and lifestyles of lower-class youth. The outcome was ominous. Most cases petitioned to the juvenile court (which opened in 1910) were for petty crimes and status offenses, yet 25 percent of the youths were committed to some form of incarceration; more than 96 percent of the actions with which females were charged were status offenses.[14]

In summary, these scholars believe that the reformers applied the concept of *parens patriae* for their own purposes, including the continuance of middle- and upper-class values and the furtherance of a child labor system consisting of marginal and lower-class skilled workers.

In the course of "saving children" by turning them over to houses of refuge, the basic legal rights of children were violated: Children were simply not granted the same constitutional protections as adults.

Development of Juvenile Institutions

State intervention in the lives of children continued well into the twentieth century. The child savers influenced state and local governments to create special institutions, called *reform schools*, which would house delinquent youths who would have otherwise been sent to adult prisons. The first institutions opened in Westboro, Massachusetts, in 1848 and in Rochester, New York, in 1849.[15] Institutional programs began in Ohio in 1850 and in Maine, Rhode Island, and Michigan in 1906. The Houses of Refuge began to be replaced by rural facilities, which used cottages to house residents rather than large prisonlike facilities. In New York, for example, the legislature authorized a State Training School for Boys at Warwick for inmates under 16, and the State Vocational School at Coxsackie for those 16 to 19.[16]

Children spent their days working in the institution, learning a trade where possible, and receiving some basic education. They were racially and sexually segregated, discipline was harsh, and their physical care was poor. Some were labeled as criminal, but were in reality abused and neglected. They too were subject to harsh working conditions, strict discipline, and intensive labor.[17] Although some people viewed reform schools as humanitarian answers to poorhouses and prisons, many were opposed to such programs.

Children's Aid Society

Children's Aid Society
Child saving organization that took children from the streets of large cities and placed them with farm families on the prairie.

orphan trains
The name for trains in which urban youths were sent west by the Children's Aid Society for adoption with local farm couples.

To read more about **the life of Charles Loring Brace**, go to academic.cengage.com/criminaljustice/siegel.

As an alternative to secure correctional facilities, New York philanthropist Charles Loring Brace helped develop the Children's Aid Society in 1853.[18] Brace's formula for dealing with delinquent youths was to rescue them from the harsh environment of the city and provide them with temporary shelter.

Deciding there were simply too many needy children to care for in New York City, and believing the urban environment was injurious to children, Brace devised what he called his *placing-out plan* to send these children to western farms where they could be cared for and find a home. They were placed on what became known as orphan trains, which made preannounced stops in western farming communities. Families wishing to take in children would meet the train, be briefly introduced to the passengers, and leave with one of the children. Brace's plan was activated in 1854 and very soon copied by other child care organizations. Though the majority of the children benefited from the plan and did find a new life, others were less successful, and some were exploited and harmed by the experience. By 1930, political opposition to Brace's plan, coupled with the negative effects of the economic depression, spelled the end of the orphan trains, but not before 150,000 children were placed in rural homesteads. Concept Summary 13.1 describes those first juvenile institutions and organizations.

Society for the Prevention of Cruelty to Children

Society for the Prevention of Cruelty to Children
First established in 1874, these organizations protected children subjected to cruelty and neglect at home or at school.

In 1874, the first Society for the Prevention of Cruelty to Children (SPCC) was established in New York. Agents of the society were granted power to remove children from their homes and arrest anyone who interfered with their work; they also assisted the court in making placement decisions.[19] By 1890, the society controlled the intake and disposition of an annual average of 15,000 poor and neglected children. By 1900, there were 300 such societies in the United States.[20]

Leaders of the SPCCs were concerned that abused boys would become lower-class criminals and that mistreated young girls might become sexually promiscuous women. A growing crime rate and concern about a rapidly changing population served to swell SPCC membership. In addition, these organizations protected children who had been subjected to cruelty and neglect at home and at school.

SPCC groups influenced state legislatures to pass statutes protecting children from parents who did not provide them with adequate food and clothing or made them beg or work in places where liquor was sold.[21] Criminal penalties were created

Concept Summary 13.1

The First Juvenile Institutions and Organizations

Reform Schools	Devoted to the care of vagrant and delinquent youths
Children's Aid Society	Designed to protect delinquent youths from the city's dangers through the provision of temporary shelter
Orphan Trains	The practice of using trains to place delinquent urban youths with families in western farming communities
Society for the Prevention of Cruelty to Children	Designed to protect abused and neglected children by placing them with other families and advocating for criminal penalties for negligent parents

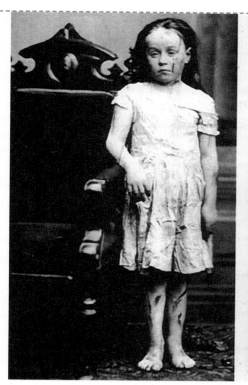

In 1874, Henry Bugh and Etta Angell Wheeler persuaded a New York court to take a child, Mary Ellen, away from her stepmother on the grounds of child abuse. This is the first recorded case in which a court was used to protect a child. Mary Ellen is shown at age 9 (left) when she appeared in court showing bruises from a whipping and several gashes from a pair of scissors. The second photograph shows her a year later.

for negligent parents, and provisions were established for removing children from the home. In some states, agents of the SPCC could actually arrest abusive parents; in others, they would inform the police about suspected abuse cases and accompany officers when they made an arrest.[22]

The organization and control of SPCCs varied widely. For example, the New York City SPCC was a city agency supported by municipal funds. It conducted investigations of delinquent and neglected children for the court. In contrast, the Boston SPCC emphasized delinquency prevention and worked with social welfare groups; the Philadelphia SPCC emphasized family unity and was involved with other charities.[23]

A CENTURY OF JUVENILE JUSTICE

Although reform groups continued to lobby for government control over children, the committing of children under the doctrine of *parens patriae* without due process of law began to be questioned. Could the state incarcerate children who had not violated the criminal law? Should children be held in the same facilities that housed adults? Serious problems challenged the effectiveness of the existing system. Institutional deficiencies, the absence of due process for poor, ignorant, and noncriminal delinquents, and the treatment of these children by inadequate private organizations all spurred the argument that a juvenile court should be established.

Increasing delinquency rates also hastened the development of a juvenile court. Theodore Ferdinand's analysis of the Boston juvenile court found that in the 1820s and 1830s very few juveniles were charged with serious offenses. By 1850, juvenile delinquency was the fastest growing component of the local crime problem.[24] Ferdinand concluded that the flow of juvenile cases strengthened the argument that juveniles needed their own court.

The Illinois Juvenile Court Act and Its Legacy

The child saving movement culminated in passage of the Illinois Juvenile Court Act of 1899, which established the nation's first independent juvenile court. Interpretations of its intentions differ, but unquestionably the Illinois Juvenile Court Act established juvenile delinquency as a legal concept. For the first time the distinction was made between children who were neglected and those who were delinquent. Delinquent children were those under the age of 16 who violated the law. Most important, the act established a court and a probation program specifically for children. In addition, the legislation allowed children to be committed to institutions and reform programs under the control of the state. The key provisions of the act were these:

- A separate court was established for delinquent and neglected children.
- Special procedures were developed to govern the adjudication of juvenile matters.
- Children were to be separated from adults in courts and in institutional programs.
- Probation programs were to be developed to assist the court in making decisions in the best interests of the state and the child.

Following passage of the Illinois Juvenile Court Act, similar legislation was enacted throughout the nation. The special courts these laws created maintained jurisdiction over predelinquent (neglected and dependent) and delinquent children. Juvenile court jurisdiction was based primarily on a child's noncriminal actions and status, not strictly on a violation of criminal law. The *parens patriae* philosophy predominated, ushering in a form of personalized justice that still did not provide juvenile offenders with the full array of constitutional protections available to adult criminal offenders. The court's process was paternalistic rather than adversarial. Attorneys were not required, and hearsay evidence, inadmissible in criminal trials, was admissible in the adjudication of juvenile offenders. Verdicts were based on a *preponderance of the evidence* instead of the stricter standard used by criminal courts, *beyond a reasonable doubt*, and children were often not granted any right to appeal their convictions.

The principles motivating the Illinois reformers were these:

- Children should not be held as accountable as adult transgressors.
- The objective of the juvenile justice system is to treat and rehabilitate rather than punish.
- Disposition should be predicated on analysis of the youth's special circumstances and needs.
- The system should avoid the trappings of the adult criminal process with all its confusing rules and procedures.

This was a major event in the juvenile justice movement. Its significance was such that by 1917, juvenile courts had been established in all but three states.

The Legacy of Illinois Just what were the ramifications of passage of the Illinois Juvenile Court Act? The traditional interpretation is that the reformers were genuinely motivated to pass legislation that would serve the best interests of the child. U.S. Supreme Court Justice Abe Fortas took this position in the landmark 1967 *In re Gault* case:

> The early reformers were appalled by adult procedures and penalties and by the fact that children could be given long prison sentences and mixed in jails with hardened criminals. They were profoundly convinced that society's duty to the child could not be confined by the concept of justice alone. . . . The child—essentially good, as they saw it—was to be made to feel that he was the object of the state's care and solicitude, not that he was under arrest or on trial. . . . The idea of crime and punishment was to be abandoned. The child was to be treated and rehabilitated and the procedures from apprehension through institutionalization were to be clinical rather than punitive.[25]

The child savers believed that children were influenced by their environments. Society was to be concerned with what their problems were and how these problems could be handled in the interests of the children and the state.

Nowhere can this procedural informality be seen more fully than in the Denver Juvenile Court presided over by Judge Benjamin Lindsey.[26] He viewed the children who came before him as "his boys" who were fundamentally good human beings led astray by their social and psychological environment. While Lindsey had no specific statutory authority to do so, he adopted a social worker–friend approach to the children who had been petitioned to court. The need for formal adjudication of the charges was unimportant compared to an effort to treat and rehabilitate these wayward youth. He condemned the criminal justice system, which he saw operating as a "medieval torture chamber" that victimized children.[27]

The Early Juvenile Court The major functions of the juvenile justice system were to prevent juvenile crime and to rehabilitate juvenile offenders. The roles of the judge and the probation staff were to diagnose the child's condition and prescribe programs to alleviate it; judgments about children's actions and consideration for their constitutional rights were secondary.

By the 1920s, noncriminal behavior in the form of incorrigibility and truancy from school was added to the jurisdiction of many juvenile court systems. Of particular interest was the sexual behavior of young girls, and the juvenile court enforced a strict moral code on working-class girls, not hesitating to incarcerate those who were sexually active.[28] Programs of all kinds, including individualized counseling and institutional care, were used to *cure* juvenile criminality.

By 1925, juvenile courts existed in virtually every jurisdiction in every state. Although the juvenile court concept expanded rapidly, it cannot be said that each state implemented it thoroughly. Some jurisdictions established elaborate juvenile court systems, whereas others passed legislation but provided no services. Some courts had trained juvenile court judges; others had nonlawyers sitting in juvenile cases. Some courts had extensive probation departments; others had untrained probation personnel. In 1920, a U.S. Children's Bureau survey found that only 16 percent of these new juvenile courts held separate calendars or hearings for children's cases or had an officially established probation service, and recorded social information about the children coming through the court. In 1926, it was reported that five out of six of these courts in the United States failed to meet the minimum standards of the Children's Bureau.[29]

Great diversity also marked juvenile institutions. Some maintained a lenient orientation, but others relied on harsh punishments, including beatings, straitjacket restraints, immersion in cold water, and solitary confinement with a diet of bread and water.

These conditions were exacerbated by the rapid growth in the juvenile institutional population. Between 1890 and 1920, the number of institutionalized youths jumped 112 percent, a rise that far exceeded the increase in the total number of adolescents in the United States.[30] Although social workers and court personnel deplored the increased institutionalization of youth, the growth was due in part to the successful efforts by reformers to close poorhouses, thereby creating a need for institutions to house their displaced populations. In addition, the lack of a coherent national policy on needy children allowed private entrepreneurs to fill the void.[31] Although the increase in institutionalization seemed contrary to the goal of rehabilitation, such an approach was preferable to the poorhouse and the streets.

Reforming the System

Reform of this system was slow in coming. In 1912, the U.S. Children's Bureau was formed as the first federal child welfare agency. By the 1930s, the bureau began to investigate the state of juvenile institutions and tried to expose some of their more repressive aspects.[32] After World War II, critics such as Paul Tappan and Francis Allen began to identify problems in the juvenile justice system, among which were the neglect of procedural rights and the warehousing of youth in ineffective institutions. Status offenders commonly were housed with delinquents and given sentences that were more punitive than those given to delinquents.[33]

From its origin, the juvenile court system denied children procedural rights normally available to adult offenders. Due process rights, such as representation by counsel, a jury trial, freedom from self-incrimination, and freedom from unreasonable search and seizure, were not considered essential for the juvenile court system because its primary purpose was not punishment but rehabilitation. However, the dream of trying to rehabilitate children was not achieved. Individual treatment approaches failed, and delinquency rates soared.

Reform efforts, begun in earnest in the 1960s, changed the face of the juvenile justice system. In 1962, New York passed legislation creating a family court system.[34] The new court assumed responsibility for all matters involving family life, with emphasis on delinquent and neglected children. In addition, the legislation established the PINS classification (person in need of supervision). This category included individuals involved in such actions as truancy and incorrigibility. By using labels like PINS and CHINS (children in need of supervision) to establish jurisdiction over children, juvenile courts expanded their role as social agencies. Because noncriminal children were now involved in the juvenile court system to a greater degree, many juvenile courts had to improve their social services. Efforts were made to personalize the system of justice for children. These reforms were soon followed by a due process revolution, which ushered in an era of procedural rights for court-adjudicated youth.

In the 1960s and 1970s, the U.S. Supreme Court radically altered the juvenile justice system when it issued a series of decisions that established the right of juveniles to receive due process of law.[35] The Court established that juveniles had the same rights as adults in important areas of trial process, including the right to confront witnesses, notice of charges, and the right to counsel. Exhibit 13.1 illustrates some of the most important legal cases bringing procedural due process to the juvenile justice process.

Federal Commissions In addition to the legal revolution brought about by the Supreme Court, a series of national commissions sponsored by the federal government helped change the shape of juvenile justice. In 1967, the President's Commission on Law Enforcement and the Administration of Justice, organized by President Lyndon Johnson, suggested that the juvenile justice system must provide underprivileged youths with opportunities for success, including jobs and education. The commission also recognized the need to develop effective law enforcement procedures to control hard-core offenders, while at the same time granting them due process. The commission's report acted as a catalyst for passage of the federal Juvenile Delinquency Prevention and Control (JDP) Act of 1968. This law created a Youth Development and Delinquency Prevention Administration, which concentrated on helping states develop new juvenile justice programs, particularly those involving diversion of youth, decriminalization, and decarceration. In 1968, Congress also passed the Omnibus Safe Streets and Crime Control Act.[36] Title I of this law established the Law Enforcement Assistance Administration (LEAA) to provide federal funds for improving the adult and juvenile justice systems. In 1972, Congress amended the JDP Act to allow the LEAA to focus its funding on juvenile justice and delinquency prevention programs. State and local governments were required to develop and adopt comprehensive plans to obtain federal assistance.

Because crime continued to receive much publicity, a second effort called the National Advisory Commission on Criminal Justice Standards and Goals was established in 1973 by the Nixon administration.[37] Its report identified such strategies as (a) preventing delinquent behavior, (b) developing diversion activities, (c) establishing dispositional alternatives, (d) providing due process for all juveniles, and (e) controlling violent and chronic delinquents. This commission's recommendations formed the basis for the Juvenile Justice and Delinquency Prevention Act of 1974.[38] This act eliminated the Youth Development and Delinquency Prevention Administration and replaced it with the Office of Juvenile Justice and Delinquency

EXHIBIT **13.1**

Leading Constitutional Cases in Juvenile Justice

Kent v. United States (1965) Determined that a child has due process rights, such as having an attorney present at waiver hearings.

In re Gault (1967) Ruled that a minor has basic due process rights, including (a) notice of the charges with respect to their timeliness and specificity, (b) right to counsel, (c) right to confrontation and cross-examination, (d) privilege against self-incrimination, (e) right to a transcript of the trial record, and (f) right to appellate review.

McKeiver v. Pennsylvania (1971) Held that trial by jury in a juvenile court's adjudicative stage is not a constitutional requirement.

Breed v. Jones (1975) Ruled that a child has the protection of the double-jeopardy clause of the Fifth Amendment and cannot be tried twice for the same crime.

Fare v. Michael C. (1979) Held that a child's request to see his probation officer at the time of interrogation did not operate to invoke his Fifth Amendment right to remain silent. According to the Court, the probation officer cannot be expected to offer the type of advice that an accused would expect from an attorney. The landmark *Miranda v. Arizona* case ruled that a request for a lawyer is an immediate revocation of a person's right to silence, but this rule is not applicable for a request to see the probation officer.

Eddings v. Oklahoma (1982) Ruled that a defendant's age should be a mitigating factor in deciding whether to apply the death penalty.

Schall v. Martin (1984) Upheld a statute allowing for the placement of children in preventive detention before their adjudication. The Court concluded that it was not unreasonable to detain juveniles for their own protection.

New Jersey v. T.L.O. (1985) Determined that the Fourth Amendment applies to school searches. The Court adopted a "reasonable suspicion" standard, as opposed to the stricter standard of "probable cause," to evaluate the legality of searches and seizures in a school setting.

Thompson v. Oklahoma (1988) Ruled that imposing capital punishment on a juvenile murderer who was 15 years old at the time of the offense violated the Eighth Amendment's constitutional prohibition against cruel and unusual punishment.

Stanford v. Kentucky and Wilkins v. Missouri (1989) Concluded that the imposition of the death penalty on a juvenile who committed a crime between the ages of 16 and 18 was not unconstitutional and that the Eighth Amendment's cruel and unusual punishment clause did not prohibit capital punishment.

Vernonia School District v. Acton (1995) Held that the Fourth Amendment's guarantee against unreasonable searches is not violated by the suspicionless drug testing of all students choosing to participate in interscholastic athletics. The Supreme Court expanded power of public educators to ensure safe learning environments in schools.

United States v. Lopez (1995) Ruled that Congress exceeded its authority under the Commerce Clause when it passed the Gun-Free School Zone Act, which made it a federal crime to possess a firearm within 1,000 feet of a school.

SOURCES: *Kent v. United States*, 383 U.S. 541, 86 S.Ct. 1045, 16 L.Ed.2d 84 (1966); *In re Gault*, 387 U.S. 1; 87 S.Ct. 1248 (1967); *McKeiver v. Pennsylvania*, 403 U.S. 528, 91 S.Ct. 1976 (1971); *Breed v. Jones*, 421 U.S. 519, 95 S.Ct. 1779 (1975); *Fare v. Michael C.*, 442 U.S. 707, 99 S.Ct. 2560 (1979); *Eddings v. Oklahoma*, 455 U.S. 104, 102 S.Ct. 869, 71 L.Ed.2d 1 (1982); *Schall v. Martin*, 467 U.S. 253, 104 S.Ct. 2403 (1984); *New Jersey v. T.L.O.*, 469 U.S. 325, 105 S.Ct. 733 (1985); *Thompson v. Oklahoma*, 487 U.S. 815, 108 S.Ct. 2687, 101 L.Ed.2d 702 (1988); *Stanford v. Kentucky*, 492 U.S. 361, 109 S.Ct. 2969 (1989); *Wilkins v. Missouri*, 492 U.S. 361, 109 S.Ct. 2969 (1989); *Vernonia School District v. Acton*, 515 U.S. 646, 115 S.Ct. 2386, 132 L.Ed.2d 564 (1995); *United States v. Lopez*, 115 S.Ct. 1624 (1995).

To read about the **Juvenile Justice and Delinquency Prevention Act of 1974**, go to academic.cengage.com/criminaljustice/siegel.

Prevention (OJJDP) within the LEAA. In 1980, the LEAA was phased out, and the OJJDP became an independent agency in the Department of Justice. Throughout the 1970s, its two most important goals were (1) removing juveniles from detention in adult jails, and (2) eliminating the incarceration together of delinquents and status offenders. During this period, the OJJDP stressed the creation of formal diversion and restitution programs.

The latest effort was the Violent Crime Control and Law Enforcement Act of 1994.[39] The largest piece of crime legislation in the history of the United States, it provided 100,000 new police officers and billions of dollars for prisons and prevention programs for both adult and juvenile offenders. A revitalized juvenile justice system would need both a comprehensive strategy to prevent and control delinquency and a consistent program of federal funding.[40]

JUVENILE JUSTICE TODAY

Today the juvenile justice system exercises jurisdiction over two distinct categories of offenders—delinquents and status offenders.[41] *Delinquent children* are those who fall under a jurisdictional age limit, which varies from state to state, and who commit an act in violation of the penal code. *Status offenders* are commonly characterized in state statutes as persons or children in need of supervision (PINS or CHINS). Most states distinguish such behavior from delinquent conduct to reduce the effect of any stigma on children as a result of their involvement with the juvenile court. In addition, juvenile courts generally have jurisdiction over situations involving conduct directed at (rather than committed by) juveniles, such as parental neglect, deprivation, abandonment, and abuse.

The states have also set different maximum ages below which children fall under the jurisdiction of the juvenile court. Most states (and the District of Columbia) include all children under 18, others set the upper limit at 17, and still others include children under 16 (see Table 13.1).

Some states exclude certain classes of offenders or offenses from the juvenile justice system. For example, youths who commit serious violent offenses such as rape and/or murder may be automatically excluded from the juvenile justice system and treated as adults, on the premise that they stand little chance of rehabilitation within the confines of the juvenile system. Juvenile court judges may also transfer, or *waive*, repeat offenders whom they deem untreatable by the juvenile authorities.

Today's juvenile justice system exists in all states by statute. Each jurisdiction has a juvenile code and a special court structure to accommodate children in trouble. Nationwide, the juvenile justice system consists of thousands of public and private agencies, with a total budget amounting to hundreds of millions of dollars. Most of the nation's police agencies have juvenile components, and there are more than 3,000 juvenile courts and about an equal number of juvenile correctional facilities.

Figure 13.1 depicts the numbers of juvenile offenders removed at various stages of the juvenile justice process. These data do not take into account the large number of children who are referred to community diversion and mental health programs. There are thousands of these programs throughout the nation. This multitude of agencies and people dealing with juvenile delinquency has led to the development of what professionals view as an incredibly expansive and complex system.

The Juvenile Justice Process

juvenile justice process
Under the paternal (*parens patriae*) philosophy, juvenile justice procedures are informal and nonadversarial, invoked for the juvenile offender rather than against him or her; a petition instead of a complaint is filed; courts make findings of involvement or adjudication of delinquency instead of convictions; and juvenile offenders receive dispositions instead of sentences.

How are children processed by the juvenile justice system?[42] Most children come into the justice system as a result of contact with a police officer. When a juvenile commits a serious crime, the police are empowered to make an arrest. Less serious offenses may also require police action, but in these instances, instead of being arrested, the child may be warned or a referral may be made to a social service program. A little more than 70 percent of all children arrested are referred to the juvenile court.[43] Figure 13.2 outlines the juvenile justice process, and a detailed analysis of this process is presented in the next sections.

Police Investigation When youths commit a crime, police have the authority to investigate the incident and decide whether to release the youths or commit them to the juvenile court. This is often a discretionary decision, based not only on the nature of the offense but also on conditions existing at the time of the arrest. Such factors as the seriousness of the offense, the child's past contacts with the police, and whether the child denies committing the crime determine whether a petition is filed. Juveniles

TABLE 13.1

Oldest Age for Juvenile Court Jurisdiction in Delinquency Cases

Age	State (Total Number)
15	Connecticut, New York, North Carolina (3)
16	Georgia, Illinois, Louisiana, Massachusetts, Michigan, Missouri, New Hampshire, South Carolina, Texas, Wisconsin (10)
17	Alabama, Alaska, Arizona, Arkansas, California, Colorado, Delaware, Florida, Hawaii, Idaho, Indiana, Iowa, Kansas, Kentucky, Maine, Maryland, Minnesota, Mississippi, Montana, Nebraska, Nevada, New Jersey, New Mexico, North Dakota, Ohio, Oklahoma, Oregon, Pennsylvania, Rhode Island, South Dakota, Tennessee, Utah, Vermont, Virginia, Washington, West Virginia, Wyoming (37 and the District of Columbia)

SOURCE: Howard N. Snyder and Melissa Sickmund, *Juvenile Offenders and Victims: 2006 National Report* (Pittsburgh, PA: National Center for Juvenile Justice, 2006), p. 103.

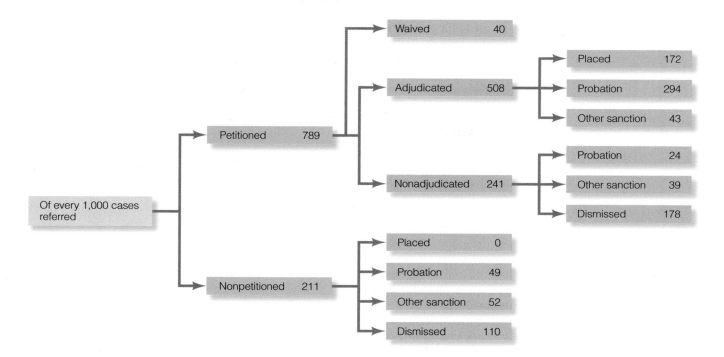

FIGURE 13.1

Case Processing of Typical Violent Crime in the Juvenile Justice System

NOTE: Cases are categorized by their most severe or restrictive sanction. Detail may not add to totals because of rounding.

SOURCE: Office of Juvenile Justice and Delinquency Prevention, *OJJDP Statistical Briefing Book*, released on March 19, 2007, available at: http://ojjdp.ncjrs.gov/ojstatbb/ (accessed July 24, 2007).

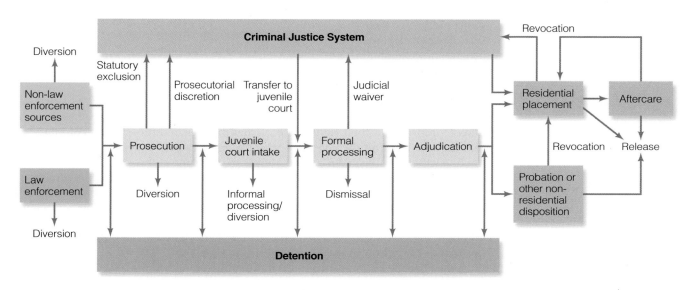

FIGURE 13.2

Case Flow through the Juvenile Justice Process

SOURCE: Office of Juvenile Justice and Delinquency Prevention, www.ojjdp.ncjrs.org (accessed November 26, 2007).

in custody have constitutional rights similar to those of adult offenders. Children are protected against unreasonable search and seizure under the Fourth and Fourteenth Amendments of the Constitution. The Fifth Amendment places limitations on police interrogation procedures.

Detention If the police decide to file a petition, the child is referred to juvenile court. The primary decision at this point is whether the child should remain in the community or be placed in a detention facility or shelter home. In the past, children were routinely held in detention facilities to await court appearances. Normally, a detention hearing is held to determine whether to remand the child to a shelter. At this point, the child has a right to counsel and other procedural safeguards. A child who is not detained is usually released to a parent or guardian. Most state juvenile-court acts provide for a child to return home to await further court action, except when it is necessary to protect the child, when the child presents a serious danger to the public, or when it is not certain that the child will return to court. In many cases the police will refer the child to a community service program instead of filing a formal charge.

detention hearing
A hearing by a judicial officer of a juvenile court to determine whether a juvenile is to be detained or released while juvenile proceedings are pending in the case.

Many critical decisions are made before the juvenile trial begins, including whether to detain youths or release them to the community and whether to waive them to the adult court or retain them in the juvenile justice system. Here, Stephen Blake, Lorain County Domestic Relations Magistrate, explains Daniel Petric's rights during his initial hearing in juvenile court on October 22, 2007, in Elyria, Ohio. Petric, the 16-year-old son of a preacher, is accused of shooting his mother to death and critically wounding his father by shooting him in the face.

Pretrial Procedures In most jurisdictions, the adjudication process begins with some sort of hearing. At this hearing, juvenile court rules normally require that juveniles be informed of their right to a trial, that the plea or admission be voluntary, and that they understand the charges and consequences of the plea. The case will often not be further adjudicated if a child admits to the crime at the initial hearing.

In some cases, youths may be detained at this stage pending a trial. Juveniles who are detained are eligible for bail in a handful of jurisdictions. Plea bargaining may also occur at any stage of the proceedings. A plea bargain is an agreement between the prosecution and the defense by which the juvenile agrees to plead guilty for certain considerations, such as a lenient sentence. This issue is explored more thoroughly in Chapter 15, which discusses pretrial procedures.

If the child denies the allegation of delinquency, an adjudicatory hearing or trial is scheduled. Under extraordinary circumstances, a juvenile who commits a serious crime may be transferred or waived to an adult court. Today, most jurisdictions have laws providing for such transfers. Whether such a transfer occurs depends on the type of offense, the youth's prior record, the availability of treatment services, and the likelihood that the youth will be rehabilitated in the juvenile court system.

adjudicatory hearing
The fact-finding process wherein the juvenile court determines whether there is sufficient evidence to sustain the allegations in a petition.

Adjudication Adjudication is the trial stage of the juvenile court process. If the child does not admit guilt at the initial hearing and is not transferred to an adult court, an adjudication hearing is held to determine the facts of the case. The court hears evidence on the allegations in the delinquency petition. This is a trial on the merits (dealing with issues of law and facts), and rules of evidence similar to those of criminal proceedings generally apply. At this stage, the juvenile offender is entitled to many of the procedural guarantees given adult offenders. These include the right to counsel, freedom from self-incrimination, the right to confront and cross-examine witnesses, and, in certain instances, the right to a jury trial. In addition, many states have their own procedures concerning rules of evidence, competence of witnesses, pleadings, and pretrial motions. At the end of the adjudicatory hearing, the court enters a judgment against the juvenile.

Disposition If the adjudication process finds the child delinquent, the court must decide what should be done to treat the child. Most juvenile court acts require a dispositional hearing separate from the adjudication. This two-stage decision is often referred to as a **bifurcated process**. The dispositional hearing is less formal than adjudication. Here, the judge imposes a **disposition** on the offender in light of the offense, the youth's prior record, and his or her family background. The judge can prescribe a wide range of dispositions, ranging from a reprimand to probation to institutional commitment. In theory, the judge's decision serves the best interests of the child, the family, and the community.

Treatment After disposition in juvenile court, delinquent offenders may be placed in some form of correctional treatment. Probation is the most commonly used formal sentence for juvenile offenders, and many states require that a youth fail on probation before being sent to an institution (unless the criminal act is extremely serious). Probation involves placing the child under the supervision of the juvenile probation department for the purpose of community treatment. The most severe of the statutory dispositions available to the juvenile court involves commitment of the child to an institution. The committed child may be sent to a state training school or a private residential treatment facility. These are usually minimum-security facilities with small populations and an emphasis on treatment and education. Some states, however, maintain facilities with populations of over 1,000 youths. Currently there are more than 100,000 youths in some form of correctional institution.

Some jurisdictions allow for a program of juvenile aftercare or parole. A youth can be paroled from an institution and placed under the supervision of a parole officer. This means that he or she will complete the period of confinement in the community and receive assistance from the parole officer in the form of counseling, school referral, and vocational training.

Juveniles who are committed to programs of treatment and control have a legal right to treatment. States are required to provide suitable rehabilitation programs that

bifurcated process
The procedure of separating adjudicatory and dispositionary hearings so different levels of evidence can be heard at each.

disposition
For juvenile offenders, the equivalent of sentencing for adult offenders; however, juvenile dispositions should be more rehabilitative than retributive.

Although juvenile offenders have a legal right to treatment, is correctional treatment more rhetoric than reality? Many experts argue that there is more punishment than rehabilitation in juvenile treatment programs. Shown here is one type of juvenile treatment, the Juvenile Justice Alternative Education Program in Denton County, Texas. Students expelled from regular school attend daily course instruction in math, English, and social studies, as well as receiving psychological counseling and transition services.

Courtesy of Juvenile Justice Alternative Education Program, Denton County, Texas

EXHIBIT **13.2**

Time Line of Juvenile Justice Ideology

Prior to 1899 Juveniles treated similarly to adult offenders. No distinction by age or capacity to commit criminal acts.

1899 to 1950s Children treated differently, beginning with the Illinois Juvenile Court Act of 1899. By 1925 juvenile court acts are established in virtually every state.

1950s to 1970s Recognition by experts that the rehabilitation model and the protective nature of *parens patriae* have failed to prevent delinquency.

1960s to 1970s Constitutional due process is introduced into the juvenile justice system. The concept of punishing children or protecting them under *parens patriae* is under attack by the courts.

1970s to 1980s Failure of rehabilitation and due process protections to control delinquency leads to a shift to a crime control and

punishment philosophy similar to that of the adult criminal justice system.

Early 1990s Mixed constitutional protections with some treatment. Uncertain goals and programs; the juvenile justice system relies on punishment and deterrence.

Mid-1990s to present Attention given to strategy that focuses on reducing the threat of juvenile crime and expanding options for handling juvenile offenders. Emphasis is placed on "what works" and implementing the best intervention and control programs. Effort is made to utilize the restorative justice model, which involves balancing the needs of the victim, the community, and the juvenile.

include counseling, education, and vocational services. Appellate courts have ruled that if such minimum treatment is not provided, individuals must be released from confinement.

Conflicting Values in Juvenile Justice

This overview of the juvenile justice process hints at the often-conflicting values at the heart of the system. Efforts to ensure that juveniles are given appropriate treatment are consistent with the doctrine of *parens patriae* that predominated in the first half of the twentieth century. (See Exhibit 13.2 for a time line of ideologies of juvenile justice during the twentieth century.)

Over the past century, the juvenile court struggled to provide treatment for juvenile offenders while guaranteeing them constitutional due process. But the system has been so overwhelmed by the increase in violent juvenile crime and family breakdown that some judges and politicians have suggested abolishing the juvenile system. Even those experts who want to retain an independent juvenile court have called for its restructuring. Crime control advocates want to reduce the court's jurisdiction over juveniles charged with serious crimes and liberalize the prosecutor's ability to try them in adult courts. In contrast, child advocates suggest that the court scale back its judicial role and transfer its functions to community groups and social service agencies.[44]

Criminal Justice vs. Juvenile Justice

The components of the adult and juvenile criminal processes are similar. However, the juvenile system has a separate organizational structure. In many communities, juvenile justice is administered by people who bring special skills to the task. Also, more kinds of facilities and services are available to juveniles than to adults.

One concern of the juvenile court reform movement was to make certain that the stigma attached to a convicted offender would not be affixed to young people in juvenile proceedings. Thus, even the language used in the juvenile court differs from that used in the adult criminal court (see Exhibit 13.3). Juveniles are not indicted for a crime; they have a **petition** filed against them. Secure pretrial holding facilities are called *detention centers* rather than jails. Similarly, the criminal trial is called a *hearing* in the juvenile justice system. (See the Focus on Delinquency box entitled "Similarities and Differences between Juvenile and Adult Justice Systems.")

petition
Document filed in juvenile court alleging that a juvenile is a delinquent, a status offender, or a dependent and asking that the court assume jurisdiction over the juvenile.

EXHIBIT 13.3

Comparison of Terms Used in Adult and Juvenile Justice Systems

	Juvenile Terms	Adult Terms
The Person and the Act	Delinquent child Delinquent act	Criminal Crime
Preadjudicatory Stage	Take into custody Petition Agree to a finding Deny the petition Adjustment Detention facility; child care shelter	Arrest Indictment Plead guilty Plead not guilty Plea bargain Jail
Adjudicatory Stage	Substitution Adjudication or fact-finding hearing Adjudication	Reduction of charges Trial Conviction
Postadjudicatory Stage	Dispositional hearing Disposition Commitment Youth development center; treatment; training school Residential child care facility Aftercare	Sentencing hearing Sentence Incarceration Prison Halfway house Parole

A COMPREHENSIVE JUVENILE JUSTICE STRATEGY

At a time when much attention is focused on serious juvenile offenders, a comprehensive strategy has been called for to deal with all aspects of juvenile crime. This strategy focuses on delinquency prevention and expanding options for handling juvenile offenders. It addresses the links among crime and poverty, child abuse, drugs, weapons, and school behavior. Programs are based on a continuum of care that begins in early childhood and progresses through late adolescence. The components of this strategy include (a) prevention in early childhood, (b) intervention for at-risk teenage youths, (c) graduated sanctions to hold juvenile offenders accountable for crimes, (d) proper utilization of detention and confinement, and (e) placement of serious juvenile offenders in adult courts.[45] There are many expected benefits from the use of this comprehensive strategy (see Exhibit 13.4). Proponents of this strategy have called for an expanded framework that focuses on youth facing a wider range of problem behaviors, including mental health, school, and drug use problems, and a greater integration of services across juvenile justice, child welfare, and other youth-serving agencies.[46]

Prevention

Research has identified an array of early risk factors that may suggest future delinquency. For young children, some of the most important risk factors include low intelligence and attainment, impulsiveness, poor parental supervision, parental conflict, and living in crime-ridden and deprived neighborhoods.[47] A number of early childhood programs have been shown to be effective in tackling these risk factors and preventing delinquency and later criminal offending, including preschool intellectual enrichment, child skills training, parent management training, and parent education programs such as home visiting.[48] Some of these programs can pay back program costs and produce substantial monetary benefits for the government and taxpayers.[49] There are a number of promising federal early childhood programs. Head Start provides children in poverty with, among other things, an enriched educational environment to develop learning and cognitive skills to be better prepared for the early

Since its creation, the juvenile justice system has sought to maintain its independence from the adult justice system. Yet there are a number of similarities that characterize the institutions, processes, and law of the two systems.

Similarities and Differences between Juvenile and Adult Justice Systems

SIMILARITIES

▌ Police officers, judges, and correctional personnel use discretion in decision making in both the adult and the juvenile systems.

▌ The right to receive *Miranda* warnings applies to juveniles as well as to adults.

▌ Juveniles and adults are protected from prejudicial lineups or other identification procedures.

▌ Similar procedural safeguards protect juveniles and adults when they make an admission of guilt.

▌ Prosecutors and defense attorneys play equally critical roles in juvenile and adult advocacy.

▌ Juveniles and adults have the right to counsel at most key stages of the court process.

▌ Pretrial motions are available in juvenile and criminal court proceedings.

▌ Negotiations and plea bargaining exist for juvenile and adult offenders.

▌ Juveniles and adults have a right to a hearing and an appeal.

▌ The standard of evidence in juvenile delinquency adjudications, as in adult criminal trials, is proof beyond a reasonable doubt.

▌ Juveniles and adults can be placed on probation by the court.

▌ Both juveniles and adults can be placed in pretrial detention facilities.

▌ Juveniles and adults can be kept in detention without bail if they are considered dangerous.

▌ After trial, both can be placed in community treatment programs.

▌ Juveniles and adults can be required to undergo drug testing.

▌ Boot camp correctional facilities are now being used for both juveniles and adults.

DIFFERENCES

▌ The primary purposes of juvenile procedures are protection and treatment. With adults, the aim is to punish the guilty. Age determines the jurisdiction of the juvenile court. The nature of the offense determines jurisdiction in the adult system. Juveniles can be ordered to the criminal court for trial as adults.

▌ Juveniles can be apprehended for acts that would not be criminal if committed by an adult (status offenses).

▌ Juvenile proceedings are not considered criminal; adult proceedings are.

▌ Juvenile court procedures are generally informal and private. Those of adult courts are more formal and are open to the public.

▌ Courts cannot release identifying information about a juvenile to the press, but they must release information about an adult.

▌ Parents are highly involved in the juvenile process but not in the adult process.

▌ The standard of arrest is more stringent for adults than for juveniles.

▌ Juveniles are released into parental custody. Adults are generally given the opportunity for bail.

▌ Juveniles have no constitutional right to a jury trial. Adults have this right. Some state statutes provide juveniles with a jury trial.

▌ Juveniles can be searched in school without probable cause or a warrant.

▌ A juvenile's record is generally sealed when the age of majority is reached. The record of an adult is permanent.

▌ A juvenile court cannot sentence juveniles to county jails or state prisons; these are reserved for adults.

▌ The U.S. Supreme Court has declared that the Eighth Amendment does not prohibit the death penalty for crimes committed by juveniles ages 16 and 17, but it is not a sentence given to children under age 16.

Critical Thinking

1. What are some of the key principles of the juvenile justice system that distinguish it from the adult justice system and that have come under increased scrutiny of late?

2. What can be done to ensure that these key principles are protected so that the juvenile justice system remains distinct from the adult system?

school years. One study found that children who attended Head Start at ages 3 to 5 were significantly less likely to report being arrested or referred to court for a crime by ages 18 to 30 compared to their siblings who did not attend the program.[50] Smart Start is designed to make certain children are healthy before starting school. State-funded home-visiting programs like those in Hawaii and Colorado are especially concerned with reducing child abuse and neglect and bettering the lives of at-risk families and their children.[51] Chapter 12 discusses some of these programs in greater detail.

EXHIBIT **13.4**

Benefits of Using the Comprehensive Strategy

I Increased prevention of delinquency (and thus fewer young people enter the juvenile justice system)
I Enhanced responsiveness from the juvenile justice system
I Greater accountability on the part of youth
I Decreased costs of juvenile corrections
I A more responsible juvenile justice system

I More effective juvenile justice programs
I Less delinquency
I Fewer delinquents become serious, violent, and chronic offenders
I Fewer delinquents become adult offenders

SOURCE: James C. Howell, *Preventing and Reducing Juvenile Delinquency: A Comprehensive Framework* (Thousand Oaks, CA: Sage Publications, 2003), p. 245.

Intervention

Intervention programs are focused on teenage youths considered to be at higher risk for engaging in petty delinquent acts, using drugs or alcohol, or associating with antisocial peers.[52] Interventions at this stage are designed to ward off involvement in more serious delinquency. Many jurisdictions are developing new intervention programs for teenage youths. An example is the Big Brother Big Sister program, which matches an adult volunteer with a youngster.[53] Similarly, in the Office of Juvenile Justice and Delinquency Prevention's Mentoring Initiative for System Involved Youth (MISIY), responsible and caring adults volunteer their time as mentors to youths at risk for delinquency and dropping out of school, as well as youths involved in the juvenile justice system, foster care, and reentry programs. The mentors work one-on-one with the youths, offering support and guidance.[54] Job training, through the likes of Job Corps and YouthBuild U.S.A., is another important intervention that receives government funding. These programs improve the chances of young people obtaining jobs in the legal economy and thereby may reduce delinquency. Efforts are also being made to deter them from becoming involved with gangs, because gang members ordinarily have higher rates of serious violent behavior. Chapter 12 discusses some of these programs in greater detail.

Graduated Sanctions

Graduated sanction programs for juveniles are another solution being explored by states across the country. Types of graduated sanctions include immediate sanctions for nonviolent offenders (these consist of community-based diversion and day treatment); intermediate sanctions such as probation and electronic monitoring, which target repeat minor offenders and first-time serious offenders; and secure institutional care, which is reserved for repeat serious offenders and violent offenders. The philosophy behind this approach is to limit the most restrictive sanctions to the most dangerous offenders, while increasing restrictions and intensity of treatment services as offenders move from minor to serious offenses.[55]

Institutional Programs

Another key to a comprehensive strategy is improving institutional programs. Many experts believe juvenile incarceration is overused, particularly for nonviolent offenders. That is why the concept of deinstitutionalization—removing as many youths from secure confinement as possible—was established by the Juvenile Justice and Delinquency Prevention Act of 1974. Considerable research supports the fact that warehousing juveniles without proper treatment does little to deter criminal behavior.

Teen Courts

To relieve overcrowding and provide an alternative to traditional forms of juvenile courts, jurisdictions across the country are now experimenting with teen courts, also called youth courts. These differ from other juvenile justice programs, because young people rather than adults determine the disposition in a case. Cases handled in these courts typically involve young juveniles (ages 10 to 15) with no prior arrest records who are being charged with minor law violations, such as shoplifting, vandalism, and disorderly conduct. Usually, young offenders are asked to volunteer to have their case heard in a teen court instead of the more formal court of the traditional juvenile justice system.

As in a regular juvenile court, teen court defendants may go through an intake process, a preliminary review of charges, a court hearing, and disposition. In a teen court, however, other young people are responsible for much of the process. Charges may be presented to the court by a 15-year-old "prosecutor." Defendants may be represented by a 16-year-old "defense attorney." Other youth may serve as jurors, court clerks, and bailiffs. In some teen courts, a youth "judge" (or panel of youth judges) may choose the best disposition or sanction for each case. In a few teen courts, teens even determine whether the facts in a case have been proven by the prosecutor (similar to a finding of guilt). Offenders are often ordered to pay restitution or perform community service. Some teen courts require offenders to write formal apologies to their victims; others require offenders to serve on a subsequent teen court jury. Many courts use other innovative dispositions, such as requiring offenders to attend classes designed to improve their decision-making skills, enhance their awareness of victims, and deter them from future theft.

Although decisions are made by juveniles, adults are also involved in teen courts. They often administer the programs, and they are usually responsible for essential functions, such as budgeting, planning, and personnel. In many programs, adults supervise the courtroom activities, and they often coordinate the community service placements where the young offenders work to fulfill the terms of their dispositions. In some programs, adults act as the judges while teens serve as attorneys and jurors.

Proponents of teen court argue that the process takes advantage of one of the most powerful forces in the life of an adolescent—the desire for peer approval and the reaction to peer pressure. According to this argument, youth respond better to prosocial peers than to adult authority figures. Thus, teen courts are seen as a potentially effective alternative to traditional juvenile courts that are staffed with paid professionals, such as lawyers, judges, and probation officers. Teen courts advocates also point out that the benefits extend beyond defendants. Teen courts may benefit the volunteer youth attorneys and judges, who probably learn more about the legal system than they ever could in a classroom. The presence of a teen court may also encourage the entire community to take a more active role in responding to juvenile crime. In sum, teen courts offer at least four potential benefits:

▌ *Accountability.* Teen courts may help to ensure that young offenders are held accountable for their illegal behavior, even when their offenses are relatively minor and would not likely result in sanctions from the traditional juvenile justice system.

▌ *Timeliness.* An effective teen court can move young offenders from arrest to sanctions within a matter of days rather than the months that may pass with traditional juvenile courts. This rapid response may increase

---

The most effective secure corrections programs are those that provide individual services for a small number of participants.[56]

Alternative Courts

New venues of juvenile justice that provide special services to youth while helping to alleviate the case flow problems that plague overcrowded juvenile courts are being implemented across the United States. For example, as of 2006, there were 411 juvenile drug courts (another 127 are in the planning process) operating in 47 states and the District of Columbia, Guam, Northern Mariana Islands, and Puerto Rico.[57] These special courts have jurisdiction over the burgeoning number of cases involving substance abuse and trafficking. Although juvenile drug courts operate under a number of different frameworks, the aim is to place nonviolent first offenders into intensive treatment programs rather than placing them in a custodial institution.[58]

drug courts
Courts whose focus is providing treatment for youths accused of drug-related acts.

the positive impact of court sanctions, regardless of their severity.

▌ *Cost savings.* Teen courts usually depend heavily on youth and adult volunteers. If managed properly, they may handle a substantial number of offenders at relatively little cost to the community.

▌ *Community cohesion.* A well-structured and expansive teen court program may affect the entire community by increasing public appreciation of the legal system, enhancing community-court relationships, encouraging greater respect for the law among youth, and promoting volunteerism among both adults and youth.

The teen court movement is one of the fastest growing delinquency intervention programs in the country, with more than 1,000 of these courts in operation in 48 states and the District of Columbia, serving an estimated 110,000 to 125,000 young offenders each year; another 100,000 youth benefit from their participation as volunteers. Some recent evaluations (but not all) of teen courts have found that they did not "widen the net" of justice by handling cases that in the absence of the teen court would have been subject to a lesser level of processing. Also, in the OJJDP Evaluation of Teen Courts Project, which covered four states—Alaska, Arizona, Maryland, and Missouri—and compared 500 first-time offending youths referred to teen court with 500 similar youths handled by the regular juvenile justice system, it was found that six-month recidivism rates were lower for those who went through the teen court program in three of the four jurisdictions. Importantly, in these three teen courts, the six-month recidivism rates were under 10 percent. Similar findings were reported in a rigorous evaluation of a teen court in Florida, and in one for repeat offenders in Washington State. However, other recent evaluations of teen courts in Kentucky, New Mexico, and Delaware indicate that short-term recidivism rates range from 25 to 30 percent. The

conclusions from the OJJDP teen court evaluation may be the best guide for future experimentation with teen courts:

Teen courts and youth courts may be preferable to the normal juvenile justice process in jurisdictions that do not, or cannot, provide meaningful sanctions for all young, first-time juvenile offenders. In jurisdictions that do not provide meaningful sanctions and services for these offenders, youth court may still perform just as well as a more traditional, adult-run program.

Critical Thinking

1. Could teen courts be used to try serious criminal acts, such as burglary and robbery?

2. Is a conflict of interest created when teens judge the behavior of other teens? Does the fact that they themselves may one day become defendants in a teen court influence decision making?

SOURCES: Deborah Kirby Forgays and Lisa DeMilio, "Is Teen Court Effective for Repeat Offenders? A Test of the Restorative Justice Approach," *International Journal of Offender Therapy and Comparative Criminology* 49:107–118 (2005); Sarah S. Pearson and Sonia Jurich, *Youth Court: A Community Solution for Embracing At-Risk Youth: A National Update* (Washington, DC: American Youth Policy Forum, 2005); Andrew Rasmussen, "Teen Court Referral, Sentencing, and Subsequent Recidivism: Two Proportional Hazards Models and a Little Speculation," *Crime and Delinquency* 50:615–635 (2004); Jeffrey A. Butts and Janeen Buck, "Teen Courts: A Focus on Research," *Juvenile Justice Bulletin October 2000* (Washington, DC: Office of Juvenile Justice and Delinquency Prevention, 2000); Jeffrey A. Butts, "Encouraging Findings from the OJJDP Evaluation," *In Session: Newsletter of the National Youth Court Center* 2(3):1, 7 (Summer 2002); Kevin Minor, James Wells, Irinia Soderstrom, Rachel Bingham, and Deborah Williamson, "Sentence Completion and Recidivism Among Juveniles Referred to Teen Courts," *Crime and Delinquency* 45:467–480 (1999); Paige Harrison, James R. Maupin, and G. Larry Mays, "Teen Court: An Examination of Processes and Outcomes," *Crime and Delinquency* 47:243–264 (2001); Arthur H. Garrison, "An Evaluation of a Delaware Teen Court," *Juvenile and Family Court Journal* 52:11–21 (2001); Anthony P. Logalbo and Charlene M. Callahan, "An Evaluation of a Teen Court as a Juvenile Crime Diversion Program," *Juvenile and Family Court Journal* 52:1–11 (2001).

systematic review
A type of review that uses rigorous methods for locating, appraising, and synthesizing evidence from prior evaluation studies.

meta-analysis
A statistical analysis technique that synthesizes results from prior evaluation studies.

To read more about **juvenile drug courts**, go to academic.cengage.com/criminaljustice/siegel.

teen courts
Courts that make use of peer juries to decide nonserious delinquency cases.

In a systematic review and meta-analysis of the effects of drug courts, David Wilson and his colleagues found that drug courts are an effective alternative crime control measure to reducing recidivism rates among drug-involved offenders. Of the 55 evaluations included in the review, only six were of juvenile drug courts. This is explained, in part, by the relatively recent interest of juvenile justice agencies in experimenting with drug courts. The findings of the six juvenile drug court evaluations were mixed. On the one hand, their overall effectiveness was fairly large (but not significant) for all offenses measured. On the other hand, they were no more effective in reducing drug offenses than traditional juvenile court processing.[59]

Teen courts, also called youth courts, are another alternative to traditional forms of juvenile court that have received increased attention of late in an effort to relieve overcrowding and provide a more effective response to reducing recidivism. The Policy and Practice box entitled "Teen Courts" discusses this alternative, and it is the subject of the Case Profile entitled "Jennifer's Story."

In teen courts, which are increasingly being used across the country as alternatives to traditional forms of juvenile courts, young people rather than adults determine the disposition of a case. Shown here is the swearing-in ceremony for participants at Onslow County's Teen Court annual training session in Jacksonville, North Carolina.

© AP Images/*The Daily News*/Randy Davey

FUTURE OF JUVENILE JUSTICE

The National Research Council and Institute of Medicine's Panel on Juvenile Crime expressed alarm over an increasingly punitive juvenile justice system and called for a number of changes to uphold the importance of treatment for juveniles. One of their recommendations is particularly noteworthy:

> The federal government should assist the states through federal funding and incentives to reduce the use of secure detention and secure confinement, by developing community-based alternatives. The effectiveness of such programs both for the protection of the community and the benefit of the youth in their charge should be monitored.[60]

Although calling for reforms to the juvenile justice system was a key element of the national panel's final report, panel members were equally or more concerned with the need to prevent delinquency before it occurs and intervene with at-risk children and adolescents. Importantly, there is growing public support for prevention and intervention programs designed to reduce delinquency,[61] not to mention a high level of public disapproval for abolishing the juvenile justice system in favor of a harsher, criminal justice system response.[62] The panel also called attention to the need for more rigorous experimentation with prevention and intervention programs with demonstrated success in reducing risk factors associated with delinquency.[63] Some states, such as Washington, have begun to incorporate a research-based approach to guide juvenile justice programming and policy.[64]

It should be noted that there is some, albeit limited, evidence that points to a slow-down of sorts in recent years in this get-tough approach toward juvenile offenders. In an analysis of state juvenile transfer laws, Howard Snyder and Melissa Sickmund report that there has been a considerable reduction in the number of states that have expanded their transfer provisions. From 2003 through 2004, only two states enacted further provisions to make it easier to waive juveniles to adult courts.[65] However, it is important to note that very few states have reversed their restrictive transfer laws.

Those who support the juvenile justice concept believe that it is too soon to write off the rehabilitative ideal that has always underpinned the separate treatment of juvenile offenders. They note that fears of a juvenile crime wave are misplaced and that the actions of a few violent children should not mask the needs of millions who can benefit from solicitous treatment rather than harsh punishments. Authors Alida Merlo, Peter Benekos, and William Cook note that a child is more likely to be hit by

Case Profile

Jennifer's Story

JENNIFER, A BRIGHT YOUNG CAUCASIAN FEMALE, LIVED IN A FAST-PACED URBAN COMMUNITY WITH HER PARENTS AND TWO YOUNGER BROTHERS. AT 16 YEARS OLD, she was in trouble. Jennifer went to a party one night and found out that her boyfriend, Sam, whom she had dated for several months and with whom she felt she had a serious relationship, had been cheating on her with a classmate. She was irate. Although Sam was not at the party, the other girl was there. She and Jennifer had words and threw a few punches at each other. Both were asked to leave, but Jennifer refused and the police were called to the party. Jennifer received a ticket for disorderly conduct.

At Jennifer's initial hearing on the matter, she was told about youth court. If she would agree to plead guilty to the charge and attend and cooperate with youth court recommendations, her record would be cleared. Jennifer agreed to the youth court diversion program and the referral was made. Facing a jury of her peers, she explained what happened the night she received the ticket. The youth court encourages family involvement, so Jennifer's mother accompanied her for support. Jennifer explained that she had recently lost a close relative and that she had been under a lot of stress when the fight occurred. She was sorry for her behavior and wanted things to be better.

The jury "sentenced" Jennifer to attend counseling and a drug and alcohol pre-assessment, as well as to write a paper on how to better handle her anger. Defendants in the court are also required to serve on two future juries themselves and given 90 days to comply or the case is returned to juvenile court for disposition. Jennifer cooperated with the requirements and her record was cleared. She completed her jury duty and has chosen to continue as a regular volunteer. According to the program director, Jennifer is an "excellent volunteer with great leadership potential." She avoided any further delinquent behavior, graduated from high school, and is now pursuing a degree in computer science. ∎

CRITICAL THINKING

1. Some might argue that Jennifer's referral to youth court was too lenient. Do you think this was an appropriate treatment consistent with *parens patriae*? Explain.
2. What types of juvenile delinquent behavior/charges would not be appropriate for a teen court? What are the most appropriate types of cases for this intervention and why?
3. If you were the program director of a teen court, what would you do if the jury was being too punitive with a peer? It is important to respect the jury's decisions, but there are times when an adult may need to step in. What would be the best process for this?

lightning than shot in a school.[66] And although a get-tough approach may be able to reduce the incidence of some crimes, economic analysis indicates that the costs incurred by placing children in more punitive secure facilities outweigh the benefits accrued in crime reduction.[67]

Summary

1. **Understand the major social changes leading to creation of the first modern juvenile court in Chicago in 1899**

   ▌ Urbanization created a growing number of at-risk youth in the nation's cities.

   ▌ Reformers known as child savers sought to create an independent category of delinquent offender and keep their treatment separate from adults.

2. **Be familiar with some of the landmark Supreme Court decisions that have influenced present-day juvenile justice procedures**

   ▌ Over the past four decades, the U.S. Supreme Court and lower courts have granted procedural safeguards and the protection of due process in juvenile courts.

   ▌ Major court decisions have laid down the constitutional requirements for juvenile court proceedings.

- In years past, the protections currently afforded to both adults and children were not available to children.

3. **Know how children are processed by the juvenile justice system, beginning with arrest and concluding with reentry into society**

- The juvenile justice process consists of a series of steps:
  1. Police investigation
  2. Intake procedure in the juvenile court
  3. Pretrial procedures used for juvenile offenders
  4. Adjudication, disposition, and postdispositional procedures

4. **Understand the conflicting values in contemporary juvenile justice**

- Some experts want to get tough with young criminals, while others want to focus on rehabilitation.

- Crime control advocates want to reduce the court's jurisdiction over juveniles charged with serious crimes and liberalize the prosecutor's ability to try them in adult courts.

- Child advocates suggest that the court scale back its judicial role and transfer its functions to community groups and social service agencies.

5. **Recognize key similarities and differences between the adult and juvenile justice systems**

- One of the similarities is the right to receive *Miranda* warnings; this applies to juveniles as well as adults.

- One of the differences is that juvenile proceedings are not considered criminal, while adult proceedings are.

6. **Be able to argue the pros and cons of the juvenile justice system's goal to treat rather than punish and assess if this goal is being met today**

- There has been a movement to toughen the juvenile justice system, and because of this many view the importance of treatment as having been greatly diminished.

- Proponents of treatment argue that it is best suited to the developmental needs of juveniles.

- Critics contend that treatment simply serves to mollycoddle juveniles and reduces the deterrent value of the juvenile court.

7. **Understand the need for and be aware of the key elements of a comprehensive juvenile justice strategy to deal with juvenile delinquency**

- A comprehensive juvenile justice strategy has been developed to preserve the need for treatment services for juveniles while at the same time using appropriate sanctions to hold juveniles accountable for their actions.

- Elements of this strategy include delinquency prevention, intervention programs, graduated sanctions, improvement of institutional programs, and treating juveniles like adults.

- New courts, such as drug courts and teen courts, are now in place.

8. **See the difference between prevention and intervention efforts to reduce juvenile delinquency**

- Prevention efforts are targeted at children and teens in an effort to prevent the onset of delinquency.

- Intervention efforts are targeted at children and teens considered at higher risk for delinquency and are designed to ward off involvement in more serious delinquent behavior.

9. **Be able to identify and comment on pressing issues in the future of juvenile justice**

- The future of the juvenile justice system continues to be debated.

- A number of state jurisdictions, although fewer today than in the 1990s, are revising their juvenile codes to restrict eligibility in the juvenile justice system, and to remove the most serious offenders.

- At the same time, there are some promising signs, such as juvenile crime rates being lower than in decades past, public support for prevention and intervention programs, and some states beginning to incorporate research-based initiatives to guide juvenile justice programming and policy.

Key Terms

Fourteen-year-old Daphne, a product of New York City's best private schools, lives with her wealthy family in a luxury condo in a fashionable neighborhood. Her father is an executive at a local financial services conglomerate and earns close to a million dollars per year. Daphne is always in trouble at school, and teachers report she is impulsive and has poor self-control. At times she can be kind and warm, but on other occasions she is obnoxious, unpredictable, insecure, and demanding of attention. She is overly self-conscious about her body and has a drinking problem.

Despite repeated promises to get her life together, Daphne likes to hang out at night in a local park, drinking with neighborhood kids. On more than one occasion she has gone to the park with her friend and confidant Chris, a quiet boy with his own personal problems. His parents have separated and he is prone to suffer severe anxiety attacks. He has been suspended from school and diagnosed with depression, for which he takes two drugs—an antidepressant and a sedative.

One night, the two met up with Michael, a 44-year-old man with a long history of alcoholism. After a night of drinking, a fight broke out and Michael was stabbed, his throat cut, and his body dumped in a pond. Soon after the attack, Daphne called 911, telling police that a friend "jumped in the lake and didn't come out." Police searched the area and found Michael's slashed and stabbed body in the water; the body had been disemboweled in an attempt to sink it. When the authorities traced the call, Daphne was arrested, and she confessed to police that she had helped Chris murder the victim.

During an interview with court psychiatrists, Daphne admitted she participated in the killing but could not articulate what caused her to get involved. She had been drinking and remembers little of the events. She said she was flirting with Michael and Chris stabbed him in a jealous rage. She spoke in a flat, hollow voice and showed little remorse for her actions. It was a spur-of-the-moment thing, she claimed, and, after all, it was Chris who had the knife and not she. Later, Chris claimed that Daphne instigated the fight, egged him on, taunting him that he was too scared to kill someone. Chris said that Daphne, while drunk, often talked of killing an adult because she hates older people, especially her parents.

If Daphne is tried as a juvenile she can be kept in institutions until she is 17; the sentence could be expanded to age 21, but only if she has behavior problems in custody and demonstrates conclusive need for further secure treatment.

▌ Should the case of Daphne be dealt with in the juvenile court, even though the maximum possible sentence she can receive is two to six years? If not, over what kind of cases should the juvenile court have jurisdiction?

▌ How does the concept of *parens patriae* apply in cases such as that of Daphne?

▌ If you believe that the juvenile court is not equipped to handle cases of extremely violent youth, then should it be abolished?

▌ What reforms must be made in the juvenile justice system to rehabilitate adolescents like Daphne? Or should it even try?

Doing Research on the Web

Before you answer these questions, you may want to learn more about this topic by checking out the following websites, all of which can be accessed via

academic.cengage.com/criminaljustice/siegel

National Center for Juvenile Justice
Office of Juvenile Justice and Delinquency Prevention
Office of the Surgeon General
Urban Institute
Washington State Institute for Public Policy

Questions for Discussion

1. What factors precipitated the development of the Illinois Juvenile Court Act of 1899?

2. One of the most significant reforms in dealing with the juvenile offender was the opening of the New York House of Refuge in 1825. What were the social and judicial consequences of this reform on the juvenile justice system?

3. The child savers have been accused of wanting to control the lives of poor and immigrant children for their own benefit. Are there any parallels to the child saving movement in modern-day America?

4. Should there be a juvenile justice system, or should juveniles who commit serious crimes be treated as adults, while the others be handled by social welfare agencies?

5. The Supreme Court has made a number of major decisions in the area of juvenile justice. What are these decisions? What is their impact on the juvenile justice system?

6. What is the meaning of the term *procedural due process of law*? Explain why and how procedural due process has had an impact on juvenile justice.

7. The formal components of the criminal justice system are often considered to be the police, the court, and the correctional agency. How do these components relate to the major areas of the juvenile justice system? Is the operation of justice similar in the juvenile and adult systems?

8. What role has the federal government played in the juvenile justice system over the last 25 years?

Notes

1. Robert M. Mennel, "Origins of the Juvenile Court: Changing Perspectives on the Legal Rights of Juvenile Delinquents," *Crime and Delinquency* 18:68–78 (1972).

2. Anthony Salerno, "The Child Saving Movement: Altruism or Conspiracy," *Juvenile and Family Court Journal* 42:37 (1991).

3. Frank J. Coppa and Philip C. Dolce, *Cities in Transition: From the Ancient World to Urban America* (Chicago: Nelson Hall, 1974), p. 220.

4. Robert Mennel, "Attitudes and Policies toward Juvenile Delinquency," *Crime and Justice*, vol. 5 (Chicago: University of Chicago Press, 1983), p. 198.

5. Anthony M. Platt, *The Child Savers: The Invention of Delinquency* (Chicago: University of Chicago Press, 1969).

6. See Anne Meis Knupfer, *Reform and Resistance: Gender, Delinquency, and America's First Juvenile Court* (London: Routledge, 2001).

7. This section is based on material from the New York State Archives, *The Greatest Reform School in the World: A Guide to the Records of the New York House of Refuge: A Brief History 1824–1857* (Albany, NY, 2001); Sanford J. Fox, "Juvenile Justice Reform: A Historical Perspective," *Stanford Law Review* 22:1187–1229 (1970).

8. Robert S. Pickett, *House of Refuge—Origins of Juvenile Reform in New York State, 1815–1857* (Syracuse, NY: Syracuse University Press, 1969).

9. Mennel, "Origins of the Juvenile Court," pp. 69–70.

10. Sanford Fox, "The Early History of the Court" from *The Future of Children* (Los Altos, CA: David and Lucille Packard Foundation, 1996).

11. Salerno, "The Child Saving Movement," p. 37.

12. Platt, *The Child Savers*.

13. Ibid., p. 116.

14. Randall Shelden and Lynn Osborne, "'For Their Own Good': Class Interests and the Child Saving Movement in Memphis, Tennessee, 1900–1917," *Criminology* 27:747–767 (1989).

15. U.S. Department of Justice, Juvenile Justice and Delinquency Prevention, *Two Hundred Years of American Criminal Justice: An LEAA Bicentennial Study* (Washington, DC: LEAA, 1976).

16. New York State Law Ch. 412, Laws of 1929; Ch. 538, Laws of 1932.

17. Beverly Smith, "Female Admissions and Paroles of the Western House of Refuge in the 1880s: An Historical Example of Community Corrections," *Journal of Research in Crime and Delinquency* 26:36–66 (1989).

18. Fox, "Juvenile Justice Reform," p. 1229.

19. Fox, "The Early History of the Court."

20. Elizabeth Pleck, "Criminal Approaches to Family Violence, 1640–1980," in Lloyd Ohlin and Michael Tonry, eds., *Family Violence* (Chicago: University of Chicago Press, 1989), pp. 19–58.

21. Elizabeth Pleck, *Domestic Tyranny: The Making of Social Policy against Family Violence from Colonial Times to the Present* (New York: Oxford University Press, 1987), pp. 28–30.

22. Linda Gordon, *Family Violence and Social Control* (New York: Viking, 1988).

23. Kathleen Block and Donna Hale, "Turf Wars in the Progressive Era of Juvenile Justice: The Relationship of Private and Public Child Care Agencies," *Crime and Delinquency* 37:225–241 (1991).

24. Theodore Ferdinand, "Juvenile Delinquency or Juvenile Justice: Which Came First?" *Criminology* 27:79–106 (1989).

25. *In re Gault*, 387 U.S. 1, 87 S.Ct. 1428, 18 L.Ed.2d 527 (1967).

26. Fox, "The Early History of the Court," p. 4.

27. Ibid.

28. Mary Odem and Steven Schlossman, "Guardians of Virtue: The Juvenile Court and Female Delinquency in Early 20th-Century Los Angeles," *Crime and Delinquency* 37:186–203 (1991).

29. Fox, "The Early History of the Court," p. 4.

30. John Sutton, "Bureaucrats and Entrepreneurs: Institutional Responses to Deviant Children in the United States, 1890–1920," *American Journal of Sociology* 95:1367–1400 (1990).

31. Ibid., p. 1383.

32. Marguerite Rosenthal, "Reforming the Juvenile Correctional Institution: Efforts of the U.S. Children's Bureau in the 1930s," *Journal of Sociology and Social Welfare* 14:47–74 (1987); see also David Steinhart, "Status Offenses," The Center for the Future of Children, The Juvenile Court (Los Altos, CA: David and Lucille Packard Foundation, 1996).

33. For an overview of these developments, see Theodore Ferdinand, "History Overtakes the Juvenile Justice System," *Crime and Delinquency* 37:204–224 (1991).

34. N.Y. Fam.Ct. Act, Art. 7, Sec. 712 (Consol. 1962).

35. *Kent v. United States*, 383 U.S. 541, 86 S.Ct. 1045, 16 L.Ed.2d 84 (1966); *In re Gault*, 387 U.S. 1, 87 S.Ct. 1428, 18 L.Ed.2d 527 (1967): Juveniles have the right to notice, counsel, confrontation, and cross-examination, and to the privileges against self-incrimination in juvenile court proceedings. *In re Winship*, 397 U.S. 358, 90 S.Ct. 1068, 25 L.Ed.2d 368 (1970): Proof beyond a reasonable doubt is necessary for conviction in juvenile proceedings. *Breed v. Jones*, 421 U.S. 519, 95 S.Ct. 1779, 44 L.Ed.2d 346 (1975): Jeopardy attaches in a juvenile court adjudicatory hearing, thus barring subsequent prosecution for the same offense as an adult.

36. Public Law 90-351, Title I—Omnibus Safe Streets and Crime Control Act of 1968, 90th Congress, June 1968.

37. National Advisory Commission on Criminal Justice Standards and Goals, *A National Strategy to Reduce Crime* (Washington, DC: U.S. Government Printing Office, 1973).

38. Juvenile Justice and Delinquency Prevention Act of 1974, Public Law 93-415 (1974). For a critique of this legislation, see Ira Schwartz, *Justice for Juveniles—Rethinking the Best Interests of the Child* (Lexington, MA: D.C. Heath, 1989), p. 175.

39. For an extensive summary of the Violent Crime Control and Law Enforcement Act of 1994, see *Criminal Law Reporter* 55:2305–2430 (1994).

40. Shay Bilchik, "A Juvenile Justice System for the 21st Century," *Crime and Delinquency* 44:89 (1998).

41. For a comprehensive view of juvenile law, see Joseph J. Senna and Larry J. Siegel, *Juvenile Law: Cases and Comments*, 2nd ed. (St. Paul, MN: West, 1992).

42. For an excellent review of the juvenile process, see Adrienne Volenik, *Checklists for Use in Juvenile Delinquency Proceedings* (Washington, DC: American Bar Association, 1985); see also Jeffrey Butts and Gregory Halemba, *Waiting for Justice—Moving Young Offenders through the Juvenile Court Process* (Pittsburgh: National Center for Juvenile Justice, 1996).

43. Howard N. Snyder and Melissa Sickmund, *Juvenile Offenders and Victims: 2006 National Report* (Pittsburgh, PA: National Center for Juvenile Justice, 2006), p. 152.

44. Fox Butterfield, "Justice Besieged," *New York Times*, 21 July 1997, p. A16.

45. National Conference of State Legislatures, *A Legislator's Guide to Comprehensive Juvenile Justice, Juvenile Detention, and Corrections* (Denver: National Conference of State Legislators, 1996).

46. James C. Howell, Marion R. Kelly, James Palmer, and Ronald L. Mangum, "Integrating Child Welfare, Juvenile Justice, and Other Agencies in a Continuum of Services," *Child Welfare* 83:143–156 (2004).

47. David P. Farrington and Brandon C. Welsh, *Saving Children from a Life of Crime: Early Risk Factors and Effective Interventions* (New York: Oxford University Press, 2007).

48. Ibid.

49. Ibid.; see also Peter W. Greenwood, *Changing Lives: Delinquency Prevention as Crime-Control Policy* (Chicago: University of Chicago Press, 2006); Steve Aos, Roxanne Lieb, Jim Mayfield, Marna Miller, and Annie Pennucci, *Benefits and Costs of Prevention and Early Intervention Programs for Youth* (Olympia, WA: Washington State Institute for Public Policy, 2004).

50. Eliana Garces, Duncan Thomas, and Janet Currie, "Longer-Term Effects of Head Start," *American Economic Review* 92:999–1012 (2002).

51. Anne K. Duggan, Amy Windham, Elizabeth McFarlane, Loretta Fuddy, Charles Rohde, Sharon Buchbinder, and Calvin Sia, "Hawaii's Health Start Program of Home Visitation for At-Risk Families: Evaluation of Family Identification, Family Engagement, and Service Delivery," *Pediatrics* 105:250–259 (2000); Ned Calonge, "Community Interventions to Prevent Violence: Translation into Public Health Practice," *American Journal of Preventive Medicine* 28(2S1):4–5 (2005).

52. *Youth Violence: A Report of the Surgeon General* (Rockville, MD: U.S. Department of Health and Human Services, 2001).

53. Jean Baldwin Grossman and Joseph P. Tierney, "Does Mentoring Work? An Impact Study of the Big Brothers Big Sisters Program," *Evaluation Review* 22:403–426 (1998).

54. Edith Fairman Cooper, *Mentoring Programs Funded by the Federal Government Dedicated to Disadvantaged Youth: Issues and Activities. CRS Report for Congress* (Washington, DC: Congressional Research Service, The Library of Congress, March 20, 2006), p. 15.

55. James C. Howell, *Preventing and Reducing Juvenile Delinquency: A Comprehensive Framework* (Thousand Oaks, CA: Sage Publications, 2003), p. 248; see also Shelley Zavlek, *Planning Community-Based Facilities for Violent Juvenile Offenders as Part of a System of Graduated Sanctions* (Washington, DC: OJJDP Juvenile Justice Bulletin, 2005).

56. Peter W. Greenwood, "Juvenile Crime and Juvenile Justice," in James Q. Wilson and Joan Petersilia, eds., *Crime: Public Policies for Crime Control* (Oakland, CA: Institute for Contemporary Studies, 2002), pp. 90–91.

57. "Drug Court Activity Update: Composite Summary Information" (Washington, DC: Bureau of Justice Assistance Drug Court Clearinghouse at American University, June 15, 2006); "Summary of Juvenile/Family Drug Court Activity by State and County" (Washington, DC: Bureau of Justice Assistance Drug Court Clearinghouse at American University, July 10, 2006).

58. *Juvenile Drug Courts: Strategies in Practice* (Washington, DC: Bureau of Justice Assistance, 2003).

59. David B. Wilson, Ojmarrh Mitchell, and Doris Layton MacKenzie, "A Systematic Review of Drug Court Effects on Recidivism," *Journal of Experimental Criminology* 2:459–487 (2006), p. 476, table 8.

60. Joan McCord, Cathy Spatz Widom, and Nancy A. Crowell, *Juvenile Crime, Juvenile Justice*, panel on Juvenile Crime: Prevention, Treatment, and Control (Washington, DC: National Academy Press) p. 224.

61. Francis T. Cullen, Brenda A. Vose, Cheryl N. Lero, and James D. Unnever, "Public Support for Early Intervention: Is Child Saving a 'Habit of the Heart'?" *Victims and Offenders* 2:108–124 (2007).

62. Daniel P. Mears, Carter Hay, Marc Gertz, and Christina Mancini, "Public Opinion and the Foundation of the Juvenile Court," *Criminology* 45: 223–258 (2007), p. 246.

63. Joan McCord, Cathy Spatz Widom, and Nancy A. Crowell, *Juvenile Crime, Juvenile Justice*, p. 152.

64. Greenwood, *Changing Lives*.

65. Snyder and Sickmund, *Juvenile Offenders and Victims: 2006 National Report*, p. 113.

66. Alida Merlo, Peter Benekos, and William Cook, "The Juvenile Court at 100 Years: Celebration or Wake?" *Juvenile and Family Court Journal* 50:1–9 at 7 (1999).

67. Simon M. Fass and Chung-Ron Pi, "Getting Tough on Juvenile Crime: An Analysis of Costs and Benefits," *Journal of Research in Crime and Delinquency* 39:363–399 (2002).

Police Work with Juveniles

Chapter Outline

Chapter Objectives

1. Be able to identify key historical events that have shaped juvenile policing in America today
2. Understand key roles and responsibilities of the police in responding to juvenile offenders
3. Be able to comment on the organization and management of police services for juveniles
4. Be aware of major court cases that have influenced police practices
5. Understand key legal aspects of police work, including search and seizure and custodial interrogation, and how they apply to juveniles
6. Be able to describe police use of discretion and factors that influence discretion
7. Understand the importance of police use of discretion with juveniles and some of the associated problems
8. Be familiar with the major policing strategies to prevent delinquency
9. See the pros and cons of police using different delinquency prevention strategies

© Alex Webb/Magnum Photos

In the early evening of March 31, 2006, six gunshots rang out in the Wilson-Haverstick housing project in Trenton, New Jersey. One of these shots—from a .45 caliber handgun—struck 7-year-old Tajahnique Lee as she was riding her bicycle to her grandmother's apartment. The bullet passed in one cheek and out the other, knocking out two molars and clipping the tip of her tongue. Tajahnique was rushed to the emergency room at the local Trenton hospital. She survived.

As shocking as this near tragedy was, the events that have since transpired have become even more troubling for the police. Trenton police believe that the stray bullet that struck Tajahnique was intended for a gang member affiliated with the Gangsta Killer Bloods who was driving through the housing complex. The police also believe that the bullet, along with the five others that were shot, came from the gun of a member of the local, rival gang known as Sex Money Murder, part of the larger Bloods gang. The police interviewed more than 100 residents and rounded up an equal number of suspected gang members in the days following the shooting. This led to the arrest of two members of Sex Money Murder.

But this would be as far as the police would get. The one eyewitness to the shooting changed his story, others who had cooperated earlier in the investigation refused to talk further with police, and even the shooting victim's grandmother and other family members were not willing to talk with police. One neighbor—who wished to remain anonymous—said of the little girl who was shot: "What are you going to do, testify so they can come back and get the rest of your family?" Faced with little information and no witness willing to testify in court, prosecutors were forced to release the two suspects three weeks later. The case remains unsolved.

This case, just one of many across the country, is at the center of a growing concern to police that juvenile and criminal violence, particularly by gangs, is increasingly being perpetrated with near immunity because of witness intimidation. Threats of reprisals against witnesses willing to testify in court or come forward to the police with information have significantly hampered police efforts to solve juvenile gang killings and other violent crimes, and, in the words of one reporter, "allowed gangs to tyrannize entire communities."[1] While certainly in the extreme, this case highlights an important obstacle facing police work in juvenile justice today. How the police respond to juvenile offenders is the focus of this chapter.

The chapter first takes a brief look at the history of policing juveniles, from the time of the Norman conquest of England up to today. Community policing in modern times is the focus of the next section. Here the relationship between police and community efforts to prevent crime is explored. We then look at the roles and responsibilities of the police and the organization and management of police-juvenile operations. Legal aspects of police work, including the arrest procedure, search and seizure, and custodial interrogation, are reviewed. We also examine the concept of police discretion in light of the broad authority that police have in dealing with juveniles. The chapter ends with a review of police work and delinquency prevention. A wide range of police techniques in preventing delinquency are discussed, including those that rely on the deterrent powers of police and those that engage schools and the community.

HISTORY OF JUVENILE POLICING

Providing specialized police services for juveniles is a relatively recent phenomenon. At one time citizens were responsible for protecting themselves and maintaining order.

pledge system
Early English system in which neighbors protected each other from thieves and warring groups.

watch system
Replaced the pledge system in England; watchmen patrolled urban areas at night to provide protection from harm.

 To access a comprehensive history of the **London Metropolitan Police** from 1829 to present day, go academic.cengage.com/criminaljustice/siegel.

The origin of police agencies can be traced to early English society.[2] Before the Norman conquest of England, the pledge system assumed that neighbors would protect each other from thieves and warring groups. Individuals were entrusted with policing themselves and resolving minor problems. By the thirteenth century, however, the watch system was created to police larger communities. Men were organized in church parishes to patrol areas at night and guard against disturbances and breaches of the peace. This was followed by establishment of the constable, who was responsible for dealing with more serious crimes. By the seventeenth century, the constable, the justice of the peace, and the night watchman formed the nucleus of the police system in England.

When the Industrial Revolution brought thousands of people from the countryside to work in factories, the need for police protection increased. As a result, the first organized police force was established in London in 1829. The British "bobbies" (so-called after their founder, Sir Robert Peel) were not successful at stopping crime and were influenced by the wealthy for personal and political gain.[3]

In the American colonies, the local sheriff became the most important police official. By the mid-1800s, city police departments had formed in Boston, New York, and Philadelphia. Officers patrolled on foot, and conflicts often arose between untrained officers and the public.

By this time, children began to be treated as a distinguishable group (see Chapter 1). When children violated the law they were often treated the same as adult offenders. But even at this stage a belief existed that the enforcement of criminal law should be applied differently to children.

During the late nineteenth century and into the twentieth, the problems associated with growing numbers of unemployed and homeless youths increased. Groups such as the Wickersham Commission of 1931 and the International Association of Chiefs of Police became the leading voices for police reform.[4] Their efforts resulted in creation of specialized police units, known as delinquency control squads.

The most famous police reformer of the 1930s was August Vollmer. As the police chief of Berkeley, California, Vollmer instituted numerous reforms, including university training, modern management techniques, prevention programs, and juvenile aid bureaus.[5] These bureaus were the first organized police services for juvenile offenders.

In the 1960s, policing entered a turbulent period.[6] The U.S. Supreme Court handed down decisions designed to restrict police operations and discretion. Civil unrest produced growing tensions between police and the public. Urban police departments were unable to handle the growing crime rate. Federal funding from the Law Enforcement Assistance Administration (LEAA), an agency set up to fund justice-related programs, was a catalyst for developing hundreds of new police programs and enhancement of police services for children. By the 1980s, most urban police departments recognized that the problem of juvenile delinquency required special attention.

Today, the role of the juvenile police officer—an officer assigned to juvenile work—has taken on added importance, particularly with the increase in violent juvenile crime. Most of the nation's urban law enforcement agencies now have specialized juvenile police programs. Typically, such programs involve prevention (police athletic leagues, D.A.R.E. programs, community outreach) and law enforcement work (juvenile court, school policing, gang control). Other concerns of the programs include child abuse, domestic violence, and missing children.

COMMUNITY POLICING IN THE NEW MILLENNIUM

community policing
Police strategy that emphasizes reducing fear, organizing the community, and maintaining order rather than fighting crime.

In the minds of most citizens, the primary responsibility of the police is to protect the public. While the image depicted in films, books, and TV shows is one of crime fighters who always get their man, since the 1960s, the public has become increasingly aware that the reality of police work is substantially different from its fictional glorification. When police departments failed to bring the crime rate down despite massive government subsidies, when citizens complained of civil rights violations, and when tales of police corruption became widespread, it was evident that a crisis was imminent in American policing.

Over the last two decades, a new view of policing has emerged. Discarding the image of crime fighters who track down serious criminals or stop armed robberies in progress, many police departments have adopted the concept that the police role should be to maintain order and be a visible and accessible component of the community. The argument is that police efforts can be successful only when conducted in partnership with concerned citizens. This movement is referred to as community policing.[7]

Interest in community policing does not mean that the crime control model of law enforcement is history. An ongoing effort is being made to improve the crime-fighting capability of police agencies and there are some indications that the effort is paying off.[8] Some research suggests that police innovation in crime-fighting techniques contributed to the substantial reduction in crime rates during the 1990s, whereas other research suggests that the reduction simply had more to do with cities hiring more police.[9]

Working with juvenile offenders may be especially challenging for police officers, because the desire to help young people and to steer them away from crime seems

One of the main functions of the police is to deter juvenile crime. But in the last couple of decades policing has taken on many new functions, including being a visible and accessible component of the community and working with youths and other community members to address delinquency problems. This has come to be known as community policing.

to conflict with the traditional police duties of crime prevention and maintenance of order. In addition, the police are faced with a nationwide adolescent drug problem and renewed gang activity. Although the need to help troubled youths may conflict with traditional police roles, it fits nicely with the newly emerging community policing models. Improving these relationships is critical because many juveniles do not have a high regard for the police; minority teens are especially critical of police performance.[10]

One large-scale study carried out to investigate juveniles' attitudes toward police confirmed this long-held finding. While African American teens rated the police less favorably than all other racial groups for all questions asked (for example, "Are police friendly?" "Are police courteous?"), the most striking racial differences pertained to the question about police honesty: Only 15 percent of African American youths said the police were honest. In contrast, 57 percent of whites, 51 percent of Asians, 31 percent of Hispanics, and 30 percent of Native Americans said they were.[11] Another study focusing solely on the attitudes of female juveniles toward the police found similar results. Of the more than 400 female high school students interviewed, African Americans compared to their white counterparts were significantly more likely to report having an overall negative attitude toward police. When asked about police honesty ("In general, I trust the police"), the difference was even greater: Only 22 percent of African American female juveniles either agreed or strongly agreed with the statement compared to 56 percent of white female juveniles.[12] In addition to the importance these results hold for improving police relations with juveniles, especially minorities, in order to prevent crime, the results may also hold special significance for the reporting of crimes to the police to address juvenile victimization. Research shows that juvenile crime victims are much less likely than adult victims to contact the police. This disparity in reporting crimes to the police holds true even after taking account of a number of important factors, such as crime severity, school victimization, and reporting crimes to officials other than police.[13]

The Community Policing Model

The premise of the community policing model of crime prevention is that the police can carry out their duties more effectively by gaining the trust and assistance of concerned citizens. Under this model, the main police role is to increase feelings of community safety and encourage area residents to cooperate with their local police agencies.[14] Advocates of community policing regard the approach as useful in juvenile justice for a number of reasons:

▌ Direct engagement with a community gives police more immediate information about problems unique to a neighborhood and better insight into their solutions.

▌ Freeing officers from the emergency response system permits them to engage more directly in proactive crime prevention.

▌ Making police operations more visible increases police accountability to the public.

▌ Decentralizing operations allows officers to develop greater familiarity with the needs of various constituencies in the community and to adapt procedures to accommodate those needs.

▌ Encouraging officers to view citizens as partners improves relations between police and the public.

▌ Moving decision making to patrol officers places more authority in the hands of the people who best know the community's problems and expectations.[15]

The community policing model has been translated into a number of policy initiatives. It has encouraged police departments to get officers out of patrol cars, where they were insulated from the community, and into the streets via foot patrol.[16] The official survey of policing in the United States—the Law Enforcement Management and Administrative Statistics (LEMAS) survey—reports that 58 percent of local police departments, employing 82 percent of all officers, had full-time community policing officers. Across the country, local police departments employ about 55,000 community policing officers.[17] However, the use of community policing officers has decreased in recent years. Between 2000 and 2003 (the most recent data available), the percentage of local police departments using community policing officers was lower, sometimes substantially, in all sizes of cities, from rural to large urban.[18] The main reason for this has been a reduction in federal funding.

One community policing program, the Youth Firearms Violence Initiative (YFVI) of the federal Office of Community Oriented Policing Services (COPS), which is running in 10 cities across the United States, aims to reduce juvenile gun violence. Each city was provided with up to $1 million to pay for interventions that incorporated community policing strategies.[19] The strategies include:

▌ Working in partnership with other city agencies to promote education, prevention, and intervention programs related to handguns and their safety

To learn more about **COPS**, go to academic.cengage.com/criminaljustice/siegel.

▌ Developing community-based programs focused on youth handgun violence

▌ Developing programs involving and assisting families in addressing youth handgun problems[20]

The YFVI programs also include some traditional law enforcement measures, such as the setup of new enforcement units within the police department and standard surveillance and intelligence-gathering techniques. An evaluation of the YFVI was conducted in all ten cities, but program effectiveness in reducing gun violence was measured in only five cities (Baltimore; Cleveland; Inglewood, California; Salinas, California; and San Antonio). Police-reported gun crimes were reduced in each of the five cities and in every target area of the cities, with the exception of Cherry Hill in Baltimore. (See Table 14.1 for the impact of the program on gun crimes.) The evaluation also examined the percentage change of gun crimes involving young people in the before and after periods. The results were not as encouraging. Only San Antonio demonstrated a significant reduction in the percentage of gun crimes involving youths, from 57 percent to 55 percent.

TABLE 14.1

Impact of YFVI Programs on Gun Crimes

	Number of Gun Crimes in 12-Month Period before YFVI Began	Number of Gun Crimes in 12-Month Period after YFVI Began	Change (%)
Baltimore, MD	8,764	8,581	−2
Cherry Hill	104	105	0
Park Heights	643	594	−8
Cleveland, OH	3,149	2,672	−15
Three RAPP houses*	26	16	−38
Inglewood, CA	945	730	−23
Darby-Dixon	43	22	−49
Salinas, CA, citywide	552	490	−11
San Antonio, TX	2,895	1,716	−41
Four target areas	523	328	−37

* RAPP = Residential Area Policing Program

SOURCE: Adapted from Terence Dunworth, *National Evaluation of the Youth Firearms Violence Initiative* (Washington, DC: NIJ Research in Brief, 2000), p. 8, exhibit 6.

The Office of Community Oriented Policing Services is also involved in other initiatives to reduce gun violence by serious juvenile offenders.[21] One of these initiatives is Project Safe Neighborhoods, which brings together federal, state, and local law enforcement, prosecutors, and community leaders to deter and punish gun crime.[22]

Efforts are being made by police departments to involve citizens in delinquency control. Community policing is a philosophy that promotes community, government, and police partnerships that address juvenile crime, as well as adult crime.[23] Although there is not a great deal of evidence that these efforts can lower crime rates,[24] they do seem to be effective methods of improving perceptions of community safety and the quality of community life,[25] and involving citizens in the juvenile justice network. Under the community policing philosophy, prevention programs may become more effective crime control measures. Programs that combine the reintegration of youths into the community after institutionalization with police surveillance and increased communication are vital for improving police effectiveness with juveniles.[26]

THE POLICE AND JUVENILE OFFENDERS

The alarming increase in serious juvenile crime in recent decades has made it obvious that the police can no longer neglect youthful antisocial behavior. Departments need to assign resources to the problem and have the proper organization for coping with it. The theory and practice of police organization have undergone many changes, and as a result, police departments are giving greater emphasis to the juvenile function. The organization of juvenile work depends on the size of the police department, the kind of community in which the department is located, and the amount and quality of resources available in the community.

Police Services

Police who work with juvenile offenders usually have skills and talents that go beyond those generally associated with regular police work. In large urban police departments, juvenile services are often established through a special unit. Ordinarily this unit is the responsibility of a command-level police officer, who assigns officers to deal with juvenile problems throughout the police department's jurisdiction. Police departments with very few officers have little need for an internal division with special functions. Most small departments make one officer responsible for handling juvenile matters for the entire community. A large proportion of justice agencies have written policy directives for handling juvenile offenders. Figure 14.1 illustrates the major elements of a police department organization dealing with juvenile offenders. However, in both large and small departments, officers assigned to work

Prevention programs

- Community Relations
- Police Athletic League (PAL)
- D.A.R.E. programs (drug prevention)
- Officer Friendly

Juvenile crimes

- Detective Bureau
- Juvenile Court Processing
- School Liaison
- Gang Control Unit

FIGURE 14.1
Typical Urban Police Department Organization with Juvenile Justice Component

with juveniles will not necessarily be the only ones involved in handling juvenile offenses. When officers on patrol encounter a youngster committing a crime, they are responsible for dealing with the problem initially; they generally refer the case to the juvenile unit or to a juvenile police officer for follow-up.

Police Roles

juvenile officers
Police officers who specialize in dealing with juvenile offenders; they may operate alone or as part of a juvenile police unit within the department.

Juvenile officers operate either as specialists within a police department or as part of the juvenile unit of a police department. Their role is similar to that of officers working with adult offenders: to intervene if the actions of a citizen produce public danger or disorder. Most juvenile officers are appointed after having had some general patrol experience. A desire to work with juveniles as well as an aptitude for the work are considered essential for the job. Officers must also have a thorough knowledge of the law, especially the constitutional protections available to juveniles. Some officers undergo special training in the handling of aggressive or potentially aggressive juveniles.[27]

Most officers regard the violations of juveniles as nonserious unless they are committed by chronic troublemakers or involve significant damage to persons or property. Police encounters with juveniles are generally the result of reports made by citizens, and the bulk of such encounters pertain to matters of minor legal consequence.[28] Of course, police must also deal with serious juvenile offenders whose criminal acts are similar to those of adults; these are a minority of the offender population. Thus, police who deal with delinquency must concentrate on being peacekeepers and crime preventers.[29]

role conflicts
Conflicts police officers face that revolve around the requirement to perform their primary duty of law enforcement and a desire to aid in rehabilitating youthful offenders.

Handling juvenile offenders can produce major role conflicts for police. They may experience a tension between their desire to perform what they consider their primary duty, law enforcement, and the need to aid in the rehabilitation of youthful offenders. Police officers' actions in cases involving adults are usually controlled by the law and their own judgment or discretion. (The concept of discretion is discussed later in this chapter.) In contrast, a case involving a juvenile often demands that the officer consider the "best interests of the child" and how the officer's actions will influence the child's future well-being. However, in recent years police have become more likely to refer juvenile offenders to courts. It is estimated that 71 percent of all juvenile arrests are referred to juvenile court, while 20 percent of all juvenile arrests are handled informally within the police department or are referred to a community-service agency (see Figure 14.2). These informal dispositions are the result of the police officer's discretionary authority.

Police intervention in situations involving juveniles can be difficult and emotional. The officer often encounters hostile behavior from the juvenile offender, as well as agitated witnesses. Overreaction by the officer can result in a violent incident. Even if the officer succeeds in quieting or dispersing the witnesses, they will probably reappear the next day, often in the same place.[30]

Role conflicts are common, because most police-juvenile encounters are brought about by loitering and rowdiness rather than by serious law violations. Public concern has risen about out-of-control youth. Yet, because of legal constraints and family interference, the police are often limited in the ways they can respond to such offenders.[31]

informant
A person who has access to criminal networks and shares information with authorities in exchange for money or special treatment under conditions of anonymity.

Another role conflict arises in the use of juveniles as police informants. Informants are individuals who have access to criminal networks and who, under conditions of anonymity, provide information to authorities in exchange for money or special treatment.[32] Police rely on informants, both adult and juvenile, to obtain evidence to make arrests in serious cases that the police may otherwise not be able to solve, such as gun and drug trafficking. Juvenile informants are also used in less serious cases where age is important to the crime—for example, when retailers sell cigarettes or alcohol to minors. Police must balance the need to obtain evidence and the vulnerabilities of (and extra safeguards that are needed for) juveniles in these cases.

500
Juvenile arrests

354
Referred to
juvenile court

101
Informally
handled
and
released

37
Referred
to criminal
court

7
Referred
to other
police
departments

2
Referred
to welfare

FIGURE 14.2

Police Response to Juvenile Crime

To understand how police deal with juvenile crime, picture a funnel, with the result shown here. For every 500 juveniles taken into custody, a little more than 70 percent are sent to juvenile court, and around 20 percent are released.

SOURCE: FBI, *Crime in the United States*, 2005 (Washington, DC: U.S. Government Printing Office, 2006), table 68.

problem-oriented policing
Law enforcement that focuses on addressing the problems underlying incidents of juvenile delinquency rather than the incidents only.

As criminologist Mary Dodge notes, there is a need for a higher degree of scrutiny in the use of juvenile police informants and this practice should not be warranted in all circumstances.[33]

What role should the police play in mediating problems with youths—law enforcer or delinquency prevention worker? The answer may lie somewhere in between. Most police departments operate juvenile programs that combine law enforcement and delinquency prevention roles, and the police work with the juvenile court to determine a role most suitable for their community.[34] Police officers may even act as prosecutors in some rural courts when attorneys are not available. Thus, the police-juvenile role extends from the on-the-street encounter to the station house to the court. For juvenile matters involving minor criminal conduct or incorrigible behavior, the police ordinarily select the least restrictive alternative, which includes such measures as temporary assistance or referral to community agencies. In contrast, violent juvenile crime requires that the police arrest youths while providing constitutional safeguards similar to those available to adult offenders.

Police and Violent Juvenile Crime

Violent juvenile offenders are defined as those adjudicated delinquent for crimes of homicide, rape, robbery, aggravated assault, and kidnapping. Juveniles account for nearly 16 percent of all violent crime arrests.[35] Since the mid-1990s, the juvenile violence rate has declined rather substantially, leveling off in more recent years. Many experts predicted a surge of violence as children of baby boomers entered their "prime crime" years, whereas others predicted that juvenile arrests for violent crime would double by the year 2010.[36] (See Chapter 2 for more on juvenile crime rates.)

As a result of these predictions, police and other justice agencies are experimenting with different methods of controlling violent youth. Some of these methods, such as placing more officers on the beat, have existed for decades; others rely on state-of-the-art technology to pinpoint the locations of violent crimes and develop immediate countermeasures. Research shows that there are a number of effective policing practices, including increased directed patrols in street-corner hot spots of crime, proactive arrests of serious repeat offenders, and **problem-oriented policing**.[37] (See Exhibit 14.1 for a complete list of policing practices that work, do not work, or are promising.) These strategies address problems of community disorganization and can be effective deterrents when combined with other laws and policies, such as targeting illegal gun carrying.[38] Although many of these policing strategies are not new, implementing them as one element of an overall police plan may have an impact on preventing juvenile violence.

Finally, one key component of any innovative police program dealing with violent juvenile crime is improved communications between the police and the community.

EXHIBIT **14.1**

Policing Programs

What Works
- Increased directed patrols in street-corner hot spots of crime
- Proactive arrests of serious repeat offenders
- Proactive arrests of drunk drivers
- Arrests of employed suspects for domestic assault
- Problem-oriented policing

What Does Not Work
- Neighborhood block watch
- Arrests of some juveniles for minor offenses
- Arrests of unemployed suspects for domestic assault

- Drug market arrests
- Community policing that is not targeted at risk factors
- Adding extra police to cities with no regard to assignment or activity

What Is Promising
- Police traffic enforcement patrols targeting illegally carried handguns
- Community policing when the community is involved in setting priorities
- Community policing focused on improving police legitimacy
- Warrants for arrest of suspect absent when police respond to domestic violence

SOURCE: Lawrence W. Sherman and John E. Eck, "Policing for Crime Prevention," in Lawrence W. Sherman, David P. Farrington, Brandon C. Welsh, and Doris Layton MacKenzie, eds., *Evidence-Based Crime Prevention* (New York: Routledge, 2006, rev. ed.), pp. 321–322.

POLICE AND THE RULE OF LAW

When police are involved with criminal activity of juvenile offenders, their actions are controlled by statute, constitutional case law, and judicial review. Police methods of investigation and control include (a) the arrest procedure, (b) search and seizure, and (c) custodial interrogation.

The Arrest Procedure

When a juvenile is apprehended, the police must decide whether to release the youngster or make a referral to the juvenile court. Cases involving serious crimes against property or persons are often referred to court. Less serious cases, such as disputes between juveniles, petty shoplifting, runaways, and assaults of minors, are often diverted from court action.

arrest
Taking a person into the custody of the law to restrain the accused until he or she can be held accountable for the offense in court proceedings.

Most states require that the law of **arrest** be the same for both adults and juveniles. To make a legal arrest, an officer must have probable cause to believe that an offense took place and that the suspect is the guilty party. **Probable cause** is usually defined as falling somewhere between mere suspicion and absolute certainty. In misdemeanor cases the police officer must personally observe the crime in order to place a suspect in custody. For a felony, the police officer may make the arrest without having observed the crime if the officer has probable cause to believe the crime occurred and the person being arrested committed it. A felony is a serious offense; a misdemeanor is a minor or petty crime. Crimes such as murder, rape, and robbery are felonies; crimes such as petty larceny and disturbing the peace are misdemeanors.

probable cause
Reasonable grounds to believe that an offense was committed and that the accused committed that offense.

The main difference between arrests of adult and juvenile offenders is the broader latitude police have to control youthful behavior. Most juvenile codes, for instance, provide broad authority for the police to take juveniles into custody.[39] Such statutes are designed to give the police the authority to act *in loco parentis* (Latin for "in place of the parent"). Accordingly, the broad power granted to police is consistent with the notion that a juvenile is not arrested but taken into custody, which implies a protective rather than a punitive form of detention.[40] Once a juvenile is arrested, however, the constitutional safeguards of the Fourth and Fifth Amendments available to adults apply to the juvenile as well.

Section 13 of the Uniform Juvenile Court Act is an example of the provisions used in state codes regarding juvenile arrest procedures (see Exhibit 14.2). There is currently a trend toward treating juvenile offenders more like adults. Related to this trend are efforts by the police to provide a more legalistic and less informal approach to the arrest process, and a more balanced approach to case disposition.[41]

EXHIBIT 14.2

Uniform Juvenile Court Act, Section 13 (Taking into Custody)

a. A child may be taken into custody:

1. pursuant to an order of the court under this Act;
2. pursuant to the laws of arrest;
3. by a law enforcement officer (or duly authorized officer of the court) if there are reasonable grounds to believe that the child is suffering from illness or injury or is in immediate danger from his surroundings, and that his removal is necessary; or
4. by a law enforcement officer (or duly authorized officer of the court) if there are reasonable grounds to believe that the child has run away from his parents, guardian, or other custodian.

b. The taking of a child into custody is not an arrest, except for the purpose of determining its validity under the constitution of this State or of the United States.

SOURCE: National Conference of Commissioners on Uniform State Laws, *Uniform Juvenile Court Act* (Chicago: National Conference on Uniform State Laws, 1968), Sect. 13.

Search and Seizure

search and seizure
The U.S. Constitution protects citizens from any search and seizure by police without a lawfully obtained search warrant; such warrants are issued when there is probable cause to believe that an offense has been committed.

Do juveniles have the same right to be free from unreasonable search and seizure as adults? In general, a citizen's privacy is protected by the Fourth Amendment of the Constitution, which states

The right of the people to be secure in their persons, houses, papers, and effects, against unreasonable searches and seizures, shall not be violated, and no warrants shall issue, but upon probable cause, supported by oaths or affirmation, and particularly describing the place to be searched, and the persons or things to be seized.[42]

Most courts have held that the Fourth Amendment ban against unreasonable search and seizure applies to juveniles and that illegally seized evidence is inadmissible in a juvenile trial. To exclude incriminating evidence, a juvenile's attorney makes a pretrial motion to suppress the evidence, the same procedure that is used in the adult criminal process.

A full discussion of search and seizure is beyond the scope of this book, but it is important to note that the Supreme Court has ruled that police may stop a suspect and search for evidence without a warrant under certain circumstances. A person may be searched after a legal arrest, but then only in the immediate area of the suspect's control. For example, after an arrest for possession of drugs, the pockets of a suspect's jacket may be searched;[43] an automobile may be searched if there is probable cause to believe a crime has taken place;[44] a suspect's outer garments may be frisked if police are suspicious of his or her activities;[45] and a search may be conducted if a person volunteers for the search.[46] These rules are usually applied to juveniles as well as to adults. Concept Summary 14.1 reviews when warrantless searches are allowed.

Concept Summary 14.1

Warrantless Searches

Action	Scope of Search
Stop-and-frisk	Pat-down of a suspect's outer garments.
Search incident to arrest	Full body search after a legal arrest.
Automobile search	If probable cause exists, full search of car, including driver, passengers, and closed containers found in trunk. Search must be reasonable.
Consent search	Warrantless search of person or place is justified if suspect knowingly and voluntarily consents to search.
Plain view	Suspicious objects seen in plain view can be seized without a warrant.
Electronic surveillance	Material can be seized electronically without a warrant if suspect has no expectation of privacy.

Navajo Nation police officers search students for weapons at the high school near Ganado, Arizona, on September 6, 2006, after a student reported seeing weapons at the school. The Supreme Court allows police officers and security agents greater latitude in searching students on school premises than they have with other citizens, on the grounds that campuses must be safe and crime-free environments.

© AP Images/Donovan Quintero

Custodial Interrogation

custodial interrogation
Questions posed by the police to a suspect held in custody in the prejudicial stage of the juvenile justice process; juveniles have the same rights against self-incrimination as adults do when being questioned.

In years past, police often questioned juveniles without their parents or even an attorney present. Any incriminating statements arising from such custodial interrogation could be used at trial. However, in the 1966 *Miranda v. Arizona* case, the Supreme Court placed constitutional limitations on police interrogation procedures with adult offenders. *Miranda* held that persons in police custody must be told the following:

▌ They have the right to remain silent.

▌ Any statements they make can be used against them.

▌ They have the right to counsel.

▌ If they cannot afford counsel, it will be furnished at public expense.[47]

Miranda warning
Supreme Court decisions require police officers to inform individuals under arrest of their constitutional rights; warning must also be given when suspicion begins to focus on an individual in the accusatory stage.

The *Miranda* warning has been made applicable to juveniles taken into custody. The Supreme Court case of *In re Gault* stated that constitutional privileges against self-incrimination apply in juvenile as well as adult cases. Because *In re Gault* implies that *Miranda* applies to custodial interrogation in criminal procedures, state court jurisdictions apply the requirements of *Miranda* to juvenile proceedings as well. Since the *Gault* decision in 1967, virtually all courts that have ruled on the question of the *Miranda* warning have concluded that the warning does apply to the juvenile process.

One problem associated with custodial interrogation of juveniles has to do with waiver of *Miranda* rights: Under what circumstances can juveniles knowingly and willingly waive the rights given them by *Miranda v. Arizona*? Does a youngster, acting alone, have sufficient maturity to appreciate the right to remain silent? Most courts have concluded that parents or attorneys need not be present for juveniles effectively to waive their rights.[48] In a frequently cited California case, *People v. Lara*, the court said that the question of a juvenile's waiver is to be determined by the totality of the circumstances doctrine.[49] This means that the validity of a waiver rests not only on the age of the youth but also on a combination of other factors, including the child's education, the child's knowledge of the charge, whether the child was allowed to consult with family or friends, and the method of interrogation.[50] The general rule is that juveniles can waive their rights to protection from self-incrimination, but that the validity of this waiver is determined by the circumstances of each case.

Research by University of Minnesota law professor Barry Feld suggests that older juveniles—16- and 17-year-olds—sufficiently understand their *Miranda* rights, but

To read more about the *Miranda* **decision**, go to academic.cengage.com/criminaljustice/siegel.

younger ones do not. He argues that mandating recordings of all police interrogations would go some way toward ensuring that juveniles of all ages do in fact understand their rights and minimize the risk of false confessions, which is especially problematic among younger juveniles.[51]

The waiver of *Miranda* rights by a juvenile is one of the most controversial legal issues addressed in the state courts. It has also been the subject of federal constitutional review. In two cases, *Fare v. Michael C.* and *California v. Prysock*, the Supreme Court has attempted to clarify children's rights when they are interrogated by the police. In *Fare v. Michael C.*, the Court ruled that a child's asking to speak to his probation officer was not the equivalent of asking for an attorney; consequently, statements he made to the police absent legal counsel were admissible in court.[52] In *California v. Prysock*, the Court was asked to rule on the adequacy of a *Miranda* warning given to Randall Prysock, a youthful murder suspect.[53] After reviewing the taped exchange between the police interrogator and the boy, the Court upheld Prysock's conviction when it ruled that even though the *Miranda* warning was given in slightly different language and out of exact context, its meaning was easily understandable, even to a juvenile.

Taken together, *Fare* and *Prysock* make it seem indisputable that juveniles are at least entitled to receive the same *Miranda* rights as adults. *Miranda v. Arizona* is a historic decision that continues to protect the rights of all suspects placed in custody.[54]

DISCRETIONARY JUSTICE

discretion
Use of personal decision making and choice in carrying out operations in the criminal justice system, such as deciding whether to make an arrest or when to accept a plea bargain.

To read about **trends in juvenile arrests**, go to academic.cengage.com/criminaljustice/siegel.

Today, juvenile offenders receive nearly as much procedural protection as adult offenders. However, the police have broader authority in dealing with juveniles than with adults. Granting such discretion to juvenile officers raises some important questions: Under what circumstances should an officer arrest status offenders? Should a summons be used in lieu of arrest? Under what conditions should a juvenile be taken into protective custody?

When police confront a case involving a juvenile offender, they rely on their discretion to choose an appropriate course of action. Police discretion is selective enforcement of the law by authorized police agents. Discretion gives officers a choice among possible courses of action within the limits on their power.[55] It is a prime example of *low-visibility decision making*—a public official making decisions that the public is not in a position to regulate or criticize.[56]

Discretion exists not only in the police function but also in prosecutorial decision making, judicial judgments, and corrections. Discretion results in the law being applied differently in similar situations. For example, two teenagers are caught in a stolen automobile; one is arrested, the other released. Two youths are drunk and disorderly; one is sent home, the other to juvenile court. A group of youngsters is involved in a gang fight; only a few are arrested, the others are released.

Much discretion is exercised in juvenile work because of the informality that has been built into the system in an attempt to individualize justice.[57] Furthermore, officials in the juvenile justice system make decisions that are often without oversight or review. The daily procedures of juvenile personnel are rarely subject to judicial review, except when they clearly violate a youth's constitutional rights. As a result, discretion sometimes deteriorates into discrimination and other abuses on the part of the police.

The real danger in discretion is that it allows the law to discriminate against precisely those elements in the population—the poor, the ignorant, the unpopular—who are least able to draw attention to their plight.[58]

The problem of discretion in juvenile justice is one of extremes. Too little discretion provides insufficient flexibility to treat juvenile offenders as individuals. Too much discretion can lead to injustice. Guidelines and controls are needed to structure the use of discretion.

Generally, the first contact a youth has with the juvenile justice system is with the police. Research indicates that most police decisions arising from this initial contact involve discretion.[59] These studies show that many juvenile offenders are never referred to juvenile court.

In a classic 1963 study, Nathan Goldman examined the arrest records of more than 1,000 juveniles from four communities in Pennsylvania.[60] He concluded that more than 64 percent of police contacts with juveniles were handled informally. Subsequent research offered additional evidence of informal disposition of juvenile cases.[61] For example, in the 1970s, Paul Strasburg found that about 50 percent of all children who come in contact with the police do not get past the initial stage of the juvenile justice process.[62]

A recent study analyzed juvenile data collected as part of the Project on Policing Neighborhoods—a comprehensive study of police patrols in Indianapolis, Indiana, and St. Petersburg, Florida. This study indicated that police still use discretion.[63] It found that 13 percent of police encounters with juveniles resulted in arrest.[64] As shown in Table 14.2, the most likely disposition of police encounters with juveniles is a command or threat to arrest (38 percent), and the second most likely is search or interrogation of the suspects (24 percent).

After arrest, the most current data show an increase in the number of cases referred to the juvenile court. The FBI estimates that 7 out of every 10 juvenile arrests (71 percent) are referred to juvenile court.[65] Despite the variations between the estimates, these studies indicate that the police use significant discretion in their decisions regarding juvenile offenders. Research shows that differential decision making goes on without clear guidance.

If all police officers acted in a fair and just manner, the seriousness of the crime, the situation in which it occurred, and the legal record of the juvenile would be the factors that affect decision making. Research does show that police are much more likely to take formal action if the crime is serious and has been reported by a victim who is a respected member of the community, and if the offender is well known to them.[66] However, there are other factors that are believed to shape police discretion; they are discussed next.

Environmental Factors

How does a police officer decide what to do with a juvenile offender? The norms of the community are a factor in the decision. Some officers work in communities that tolerate a fair amount of personal freedom. In liberal environments, the police may be inclined to release juveniles rather than arrest them. Other officers work in conservative communities that expect a no-nonsense approach to police enforcement. Here, police may be more inclined to arrest a juvenile.

Police officers may be influenced by their perception of community alternatives to police intervention. Some officers may use arrest because they believe nothing else can be done.[67] Others may favor referring juveniles to social service agencies, particularly if they believe a community has a variety of good resources. These referrals save time and effort; records do not have to be filled out, and court appearances can be avoided. The availability of such options allows for greater latitude in police decision making.[68]

TABLE 14.2

Disposition of Police Encounters with Juveniles

Disposition	Juveniles (%)
Release	14
Advise	11
Search/interrogate	24
Command/threaten	38
Arrest	13

SOURCE: Robert E. Worden and Stephanie M. Myers, *Police Encounters with Juvenile Suspects* (Albany, NY: Hindelang Criminal Justice Research Center and School of Criminal Justice, University at Albany, SUNY, 2001), table 3.

Police Policy

The policies and customs of the local police department also influence decisions. Juvenile officers may be pressured to make more arrests or to refrain from making arrests under certain circumstances. Directives instruct officers to be alert to certain types of juvenile violations. The chief of police might initiate policies governing the arrest practices of the juvenile department. For example, if local merchants complain that youths congregating in a shopping center parking lot are inhibiting business, police may be called on to make arrests. Under other circumstances, an informal warning might be given. Similarly, a rash of deaths caused by teenage drunk driving may galvanize the local media to demand police action. The mayor and the police chief, sensitive to possible voter dissatisfaction, may then demand that formal police action be taken in cases of drunk driving.

Another source of influence is pressure from supervisors. Some supervising officers may believe it is important to curtail disorderly conduct or drug use. In addition, officers may be influenced by the discretionary decisions made by their peers.

procedural justice
An evaluation of the fairness of the manner in which an offender's problem or dispute was handled by police.

Justice in Policing A growing body of research shows that by police exercising a greater degree of fairness or procedural justice in making arrests and handling offenders after arrest they can better gain offenders' cooperation as well as deter them from further involvement in criminal activity.[69] One of the first studies to assess the effect of police fairness on criminal offending was carried out by criminologist Ray Paternoster and his colleagues. As part of the Milwaukee domestic assault experiment, they found that men who were arrested for assaulting their female spouses were much less likely—by almost 40 percent—to commit another act of assault against their spouses if they were handled by police in a fair and just manner compared to a similar group of men who were not handled in a fair way.[70] While it is difficult to know if this research is leading police departments to implement policies on procedural fairness and train their officers appropriately, police scholars have called for more research on the subject to better understand the mechanisms that result in crime control effectiveness.[71]

Situational Factors

In addition to the environment, a variety of situational factors affect a police officer's decisions. Situational factors are those attached to a particular crime, such as specific traits of offenders. Traditionally, it was believed that police officers rely heavily on the demeanor and appearance of the juvenile in making decisions. Some research shows that the decision to arrest is often based on factors such as dress, demeanor, speech, and level of hostility toward the police.[72] Kids who display "attitude" were believed to be the ones more likely to be arrested than those who are respectful and contrite.[73] However, more recent research has challenged the influence of demeanor on police decision making, suggesting that it is delinquent behavior and actions that occur during police detention that influence the police decision to take formal action.[74] For example, a person who struggles or touches police during a confrontation is a likely candidate for arrest, but those who merely sport a bad attitude or negative demeanor are as likely to suffer an arrest as the polite and contrite.[75] It is possible that the earlier research reflected a time when police officers demanded absolute respect and were quick to take action when their authority was challenged. The more recent research may indicate that police, through training or experience, are now less sensitive to slights and confrontational behavior and view them as part of the job. Most studies conclude that the following variables are important in the police discretionary process:[76]

I   The attitude of the complainant

I   The type and seriousness of the offense

I   The race, sex, and age of the offender

- The attitude of the offender

- The offender's prior contacts with the police

- The perceived willingness of the parents to assist in solving the problem (in the case of a child)

- The setting or location in which the incident occurs

- Whether the offender denies the actions or insists on a court hearing (in the case of a child)

- The likelihood that a child can be served by an agency in the community

Bias and Police Discretion

Do police allow bias to affect their decisions on whether to arrest youths? Do they routinely use "racial profiling" when they decide to make an arrest? A great deal of debate has been generated over this issue. Some experts believe that police decision making is deeply influenced by the offender's personal characteristics, whereas others maintain that crime-related variables are more significant.

Racial Bias It has long been charged that police are more likely to act formally with African American suspects and use their discretion to benefit whites.[77] In the context of traffic stops by police, the phrase "driving while black" has been coined to refer to the repeated findings of many studies that African American drivers are disproportionately stopped by police and that race is the primary reason for this practice.[78] As Table 14.3 shows, African American youths are arrested at a rate disproportionate to their representation in the population. Research on this issue has yielded mixed conclusions. One view is that although discrimination may have existed in the past, there is no longer a need to worry about racial discrimination because minorities now possess sufficient political status to protect them within the justice system.[79] As Harvard University law professor Randall Kennedy forcefully argues, even if a law enforcement policy exists that disproportionately affects African American suspects, it might be justified as a "public good" because law-abiding African Americans are statistically more often victims of crimes committed by other African Americans.[80]

In contrast to these views, several research efforts do show evidence of police discrimination against African American youths.[81] Donna Bishop and Charles Frazier found that race can have a direct effect on decisions made at several junctures of the juvenile justice process.[82] According to Bishop and Frazier, African Americans are more likely than whites to be recommended for formal processing, referred to court,

TABLE 14.3

African American Representation in Arrest Statistics

Most Serious Offense	African American Juvenile Arrests in 2005 (%)
Murder	54
Forcible rape	34
Robbery	68
Aggravated assault	42
Burglary	31
Larceny/theft	28
Motor vehicle theft	43
Weapons	37
Drug abuse violations	29
Curfew and loitering	36
Runaways	23

NOTE: Percentage is of all juvenile arrests.

SOURCE: FBI, *Crime in the United States, 2005* (Washington, DC: U.S. Government Printing Office, 2006), table 43b.

When a juvenile commits a crime, police have the authority to investigate the incident and decide whether to release the child or place him or her under arrest. This is often a discretionary decision based not only on the nature of the offense and the behavior of the juvenile during his or her interaction with the police, but also on such factors as the seriousness of the crime, the child's past record, and whether the victim wishes to press charges.

© Jeff Greenberg/PhotoEdit

adjudicated delinquent, and given harsher dispositions for comparable offenses. In the arrest category, specifically, being African American increases the probability of formal police action.[83]

In summary, studies of bias in police decision making have revealed the following:

- Some researchers have concluded that the police discriminate against minority youths.

- Other researchers do not find evidence of discrimination.

- Racial disparity is most often seen at the arrest stage but probably exists at other stages.

- The higher arrest rates of minorities are related to interpersonal, family, community, and organizational differences. Other influences may include police discretion, street crime visibility, and high crime rates within a particular group. Such factors, however, may also be linked to general societal discrimination.

For further information on racial bias in police decisions, see the Focus on Delinquency box entitled "Juvenile Race, Gender, and Ethnicity in Police Decision Making." Further research is needed to better understand and document what appears to be findings of disproportional arrests of minority juvenile offenders.[84]

Gender Bias Is there a difference between police treatment of male and female offenders? Some experts favor the *chivalry hypothesis*, which holds that police are likely to act paternally toward young girls and not arrest them. Others believe that police may be more likely to arrest female offenders because their actions violate officers' stereotypes of the female.

There is some research support for various forms of gender bias. The nature of this bias may vary according to the seriousness of the offense and the age of the offender. Studies offer a variety of conclusions, but there seems to be general agreement that police are less likely to process females for delinquent acts and that they discriminate against them by arresting them for status offenses. Examples of the conclusions reached by some of these studies follow:

- Police tend to be more lenient toward females than males with regard to acts of delinquency. Merry Morash found that boys who engage in "typical male" delinquent activities are much more likely to develop police records than females.[85]

Juvenile Race, Gender, and Ethnicity in Police Decision Making

Does police discretion work against the young, males, the poor, and minority group members, or does it favor special interest groups? Current research has uncovered information supporting both sides.

Although the police are involved in at least some discrimination against racial minorities who are juveniles, the frequency and scope of such discrimination may be less than anticipated. Some of today's literature shows that the police are likely to interfere with or arrest poor African American youths. The police frequently stop and question youths of color walking down the streets of their neighborhoods or hanging around street corners. If this is the case, then race plays a role in police discretion.

In contrast to these findings, data from other studies indicate that racial bias does not influence the decision to arrest and move a youngster through the juvenile justice system. The attitude of the youth, prior record, seriousness of crime, setting or location of the crime, and other variables control police discretion, not race, ethnicity, or gender. Another problem in determining the impact of race or gender on police discretion is that the victim's race, not the juvenile offender's, may be the key to racial bias. Police officers may take different action when the victim is white rather than when the victim is a minority group member.

Police bias may also be a result of organizational and administrative directions as opposed to bias by an individual officer "on the beat" or in a cruiser. For example, the police departments have been found to use racial profiles for stopping and questioning suspects.

Obviously, not all officers operate unfairly or with a racial bias. Quite possibly the impact of juvenile race on police discretion varies from jurisdiction to jurisdiction and from one group of juveniles to another. Many African American youngsters, for example, view their gang affiliation as a means of survival. Teenage gang members and their families often feel frustrated about the lack of opportunities and their experiences as being targets of discrimination.

Despite all the research findings, uncertainty about the extent and degree of racial bias continues to plague the juvenile justice system. Unfortunately, minority youths are involved in a disproportionate percentage of all juvenile arrests. This often gives the impression that racial, gender, and ethnic bias exists in urban police departments.

Critical Thinking

What do you think? Do the police take race into account when making decisions to arrest juveniles suspected of violating the law?

SOURCES: For a review of recent research on police discretion (adult and juvenile), see Wesley G. Skogan and Kathleen Frydl, eds., *Fairness and Effectiveness in Policing: The Evidence* (Washington, DC: National Academy Press, Committee to Review Research on Police Policy and Practices, 2004); also National Council on Crime and Delinquency, *And Justice for Some: Differential Treatment of Youth of Color in the Justice System* (San Francisco, CA: Author, 2007); Carl E. Pope and Howard N. Snyder, *Race as a Factor in Juvenile Arrests* (Washington, DC: OJJDP Juvenile Justice Bulletin, 2003); William Brown, "The Fight for Survival: African American Gang Members and Their Families in a Segregated Society," *Juvenile and Family Court Journal* 49:1–15 (1998); Bohsui Wu, "The Effect of Race on Juvenile Justice Processing," *Juvenile and Family Court Journal* 48:43–53 (1997); Richard Sutphen, David Kurtz, and Martha Giddings, "The Influence of Juveniles' Race on Police Decision-Making: An Exploratory Study," *Juvenile and Family Court Journal* 44:69–78 (1997).

- Females who have committed minor or status offenses seem to be referred to juvenile court more often than males. Meda Chesney-Lind has found that adolescent female status offenders are arrested for less-serious offenses than boys.[86]

- Recent evidence has confirmed earlier studies showing that the police, and most likely the courts, apply a double standard in dealing with male and female juvenile offenders. Bishop and Frazier found that both female status offenders and male delinquents are differently disadvantaged in the juvenile justice system in that, for status offenses, females are more likely to be arrested, and for other offenses, males are more likely to be arrested.[87] Chesney-Lind and Shelden report that in many other countries female teens are also more likely than male teens to be arrested for status offenses and referred to juvenile court for status offenses.[88]

Organizational Bias The policies of some police departments may result in biased practices. Research has found that police departments can be characterized by their professionalism (skills and knowledge) and bureaucratization.[89] Departments that are highly bureaucratized (high emphasis on rules and regulations) and at the same time unprofessional are most likely to be insulated from the communities they serve.

Organizational policy may be influenced by the perceptions of police decision makers. A number of experts have found that law-enforcement administrators have a stereotyped view of the urban poor as troublemakers who must be kept under control.[90] Consequently, lower-class neighborhoods experience much greater police scrutiny than middle-class areas, and their residents face a proportionately greater chance of arrest. For example, there is a significant body of literature that shows that police are more likely to "hassle" or arrest African American males in poor neighborhoods than white males in middle-class neighborhoods.[91] It is therefore not surprising, as Harvard criminologist Robert Sampson has found, that teenage residents of neighborhoods in low socioeconomic areas have a significantly greater chance of acquiring police records than youths living in higher socioeconomic areas, regardless of the actual crime rates in these areas.[92] Sampson's research indicates that although police officers may not discriminate on an individual level, departmental policy that focuses on lower-class areas may result in class and racial bias in the police processing of delinquent youth.

Not all experts believe there is rampant police organizational bias. For example, when Ronald Weitzer surveyed people in three Washington, D.C., neighborhoods, he found that residents in primarily African American neighborhoods value racially integrated police services.[93] Similarly, Thomas Priest and Deborah Brown Carter have found that the African American community is supportive of the local police, especially when they respond quickly to calls for service. It is unlikely that African Americans would appreciate rapid service, or the presence of white officers, if police routinely practiced racial discrimination.[94]

One reason for these contrasting views is that racial influences on police decision making are often quite subtle and hard to detect. Data suggest that, to be valid, any study of police discretion must take into account both victim and offender characteristics.

In summary, the policies, practices, and customs of the local police department influence discretion. Conditions vary from department to department and depend on the judgment of the chief and others in the organizational hierarchy. Because the police retain a large degree of discretionary power, the ideal of nondiscrimination is often difficult to achieve in practice. However, policies to limit police discretion can help eliminate bias.

Limiting Police Discretion

A number of leading organizations have suggested the use of guidelines to limit police discretion. The American Bar Association (ABA) states, "Since individual police officers may make important decisions affecting police operations without discretion, with limited accountability and without any uniformity within a department, police discretion should be structured and controlled."[95] There is an almost unanimous opinion that steps must be taken to provide better control and guidance over police discretion in street and station house adjustments of juvenile cases.

One leading exponent of police discretion is Kenneth Culp Davis, who has done much to raise the consciousness of criminal justice practitioners about discretionary decision making. Davis recommends controlling administrative discretion through (a) the use of more narrowly defined laws, (b) the development of written policies, and (c) the recording of decisions by criminal justice personnel.[96] Narrowing the scope of juvenile codes, for example, would limit and redefine the broad authority police officers currently have to take youths into custody for criminal and noncriminal behavior. Such practices would provide fair criteria for arrests, adjustment, and police referral of juvenile offenders and would help eliminate largely personal judgments based on race, attitude, or demeanor of the juvenile.[97] Discretionary decision making in juvenile police work can be better understood by examining Figure 14.3.

To read about **what is being done to reduce racial profiling**, go to academic.cengage.com/criminaljustice/siegel.

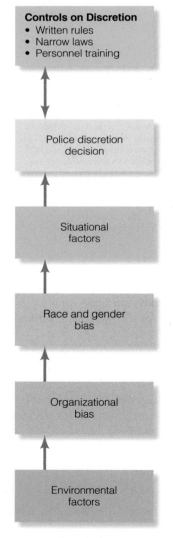

FIGURE 14.3
Discretionary Justice with Juveniles

POLICE WORK AND DELINQUENCY PREVENTION

Police have taken the lead in delinquency prevention. They have used a number of strategies: Some rely on their deterrent powers; others rely on their relationship with schools, the community, and other juvenile justice agencies; and still others rely on a problem-solving model. Concept Summary 14.2 lists the main police strategies to prevent delinquency.

Aggressive Law Enforcement

One method of contemporary delinquency prevention relies on aggressive patrolling targeted at specific patterns of delinquency. Police departments in Chicago and Los Angeles have at one time used saturation patrols, targeting gang areas and arresting members for any law violations. These tactics have not proven to be effective against gangs.

This is a finding of a large-scale review of law enforcement and other responses to the country's gang problems.[98] Conducted by the Justice Policy Institute, the review also found that "heavy-handed suppression efforts" result in increased rather than decreased cohesion among gang members and further exacerbates the sometimes-fragile relations that exist between the police and some communities.[99]

Police in Schools

One of the most important institutions playing a role in delinquency prevention is the school (see Chapter 10). In schools across the country, there are more than 14,000 full-time police working as school resource officers. In addition to helping make the school environment safe for students and teachers, school resource officers work closely with staff and administrators in developing delinquency prevention programs.[100] For example, these officers and liaison officers from schools and police departments have played a leadership role in developing recreational programs for juveniles. In some instances, police have actually operated such programs. In others, they have encouraged community support for recreational activities, including Little League baseball, athletic clubs, camping outings, and police athletic and scouting programs. In short, these officers can make a great deal of difference in the lives of many youth, and this is the subject of the Case Profile entitled "Rico's Story."

The Gang Resistance Education and Training (G.R.E.A.T.) program is one example of a police and school partnership to reduce delinquency. Modeled after D.A.R.E. (Drug Abuse and Resistance Education; see Chapter 11), G.R.E.A.T. was developed among a number of Arizona police departments in an effort to reduce adolescent involvement in criminal behavior. Today the program is in school curricula in all 50 states and the District of Columbia.[101] The program's primary objective is the prevention of delinquency and gang involvement. Trained police officers administer the program in school classrooms about once a week. The program consists of four components: a 13-week middle school curriculum (see Exhibit 14.3 for its 13 lessons), a 6-week elementary school curriculum, a summer program, and family training.

You can visit the **G.R.E.A.T.** website via academic.cengage.com/criminaljustice/siegel.

Concept Summary 14.2

Police Strategies to Prevent Delinquency

Strategy	Scope
Aggressive law enforcement	High visibility; making arrests for minor and serious infractions
Police in schools	Collaborate with school staff to create a safer school environment and develop programs
Problem-oriented policing	Focus on problems underlying criminal incidents; often engage community and other juvenile justice agencies
Community-based policing services and community policing	Engage citizens and community-based organizations

Rico's Story

Rico grew up in Harlem, one of 12 children raised primarily by their mother, a strong and determined African American woman who struggled daily to provide for the basic needs and safety of her family. Rico's father, a man of Puerto Rican descent, was heavily involved in criminal activity and drifted in and out of their lives for brief periods of time.

Rico attended a large New York public high school where there were approximately 8,000 students. Violence and gang activity were common in both his community and the school setting; sexual assaults took place in school stairwells, fights occurred on a daily basis, young drug dealers did business in the hallways, and there had been murders in school. Rico found it difficult to focus on academics with such chaos and fear all around him. The school, like many in the area, enlisted the assistance of the New York City Police Department in an effort to create a safer learning environment. Eight full-time uniformed and armed police officers patrolled the school daily. They had the capability and discretion to arrest on site and to intervene as needed, and they worked in collaboration with the educators and administrators to reduce violence and crime on school grounds. In the lunchroom, halls, and school auditorium, police officers were dressed in full uniform and acted clearly as authority figures. The officers also worked hard to be approachable and friendly to the students. They made efforts to have relationships with the students so that they could be a resource during challenging times.

Rico was a brilliant and gifted young man who, despite being in some trouble during his younger years, aspired to go to college and make a better life for himself. Several of his teachers encouraged him in his studies and although he was thriving academically, he needed a safer environment where he could focus on his education.

During his freshman year, Rico and some other students were playing cards in front of the school during a lunch break when another student threw a glass bottle at Rico's head and threatened his life. Rico went after the young man and a fight ensued. The police at the school intervened to stop the fight and address the young men's behavior. Although both teens could have been arrested for disorderly conduct or battery, Rico explained to them that he was defending himself, and the officers agreed. Knowing he was an excellent student who did not typically engage in this type of conduct, the officers chose to talk with Rico and try to encourage him in a more positive direction, rather than arresting him.

After graduating from high school, Rico attended the University of Cincinnati on a full athletic scholarship for football and track, and he also became a member of the U.S. boxing team. Upon completing his undergraduate degree, Rico attended medical school. Today he is Dr. Richard Larkin, assistant professor at a community college in Illinois. He is currently teaching and working on his Ph.D. in biochemistry. In addition to crediting the New York City Police Department and his teachers for their efforts, he credits his mother's hard work, strict discipline, and tremendous drive for his success. ∎

CRITICAL THINKING

1. In Rico's case, he did not receive any serious consequences for his actions. Do you agree with what the officers did? Explain. Why do you think he wasn't charged?

2. Do you agree that police officers should have the right to use their discretion in school settings? What are the benefits of this approach?

Evaluations of G.R.E.A.T. when it was just an eight-week program for middle school students showed mixed results in reducing delinquency and gang involvement. One evaluation found that students who completed the curriculum developed more prosocial attitudes and had lower rates of gang membership and delinquency than those in a comparison group who were not exposed to G.R.E.A.T.[102] Another evaluation of the program, four years after students completed the curriculum, did not find any significant differences for gang membership or delinquency compared

EXHIBIT 14.3

Lessons of the Middle School G.R.E.A.T. Program

1. **Welcome to G.R.E.A.T.** Students get acquainted with the program.
2. **What's the Real Deal?** Students learn facts and myths about gangs and violence.
3. **It's about Us.** Students learn about their roles and responsibilities to their community and what they can do about gangs.
4. **Where Do We Go from Here?** Students are taught how to set realistic and achievable goals.
5. **Decisions, Decisions, Decisions.** Students learn the impact of decisions on goals.
6. **Do You Hear What I Am Saying?** Students are taught effective communication skills.
7. **Walk in Someone Else's Shoes.** Students learn about expressing empathy for others.

8. **Say It Like You Mean It.** Students learn about self-expression.
9. **Getting Along without Going Along.** Students become acquainted with negative influences and peer pressure and how to resist them.
10. **Keeping Your Cool.** Students are taught techniques to control anger.
11. **Keeping It Together.** Students are taught techniques to recognize anger in others and how to diffuse that anger.
12. **Working It Out.** Students learn about resolving interpersonal conflict and where to go for help.
13. **Looking Back.** Students review what they have learned and think about how to make their school safe.

SOURCE: Bureau of Justice Assistance, Gang Resistance Education and Training (Washington, DC: Office of Justice Programs, Bureau of Justice Assistance, 2007). Available at www.great-online.org (accessed August 1, 2007).

Increased youth gang and violence problems have given rise to many innovative police-led delinquency prevention programs. One of these is the Gang Resistance Education and Training (G.R.E.A.T.) program, which aims to reduce gang activity. Partnering with schools across the country, trained police officers instruct middle school students on conflict resolution, social responsibility, and the dangers of gang life.

Bureau of Justice Assistance, U. S. Department of Justice

to a control group. The evaluation did find that those who took the program held more prosocial attitudes than those who were not in the program.[103] These evaluations contributed to the new and more comprehensive program, which was implemented on a national scale in 2003. Future evaluations will tell if these changes improve G.R.E.A.T.'s impact on delinquency, youth violence, and gang involvement.

Another example of police working in close collaboration with schools is the Community Outreach Through Police in Schools Program. This program brings together Yale University's Child Study Center and the New Haven Police Department to address the mental health and emotional needs of middle school students who have been exposed to violence in the community. Specifically, the program aims to help these students:

▌ Better understand the way their feelings affect their behavior

▌ Develop constructive means of responding to violence and trauma

▌ Change their attitudes toward police and learn how to seek help in their community[104]

An evaluation of the program found that students benefited from it in a number of ways, including improved emotional and psychological functioning (for example, feeling less nervous, having fewer thoughts of death), as well as improved attitudes toward and relationships with the police.[105]

Community-Based Policing Services

Some police departments are now replacing more aggressive measures with cooperative community-based efforts. Because police officers are responsible for the care of juveniles taken into custody, it is essential that they work closely with social service groups day by day. In addition, the police are assuming a leadership role in identifying the needs of children in the community and helping the community meet those needs. In helping to develop delinquency prevention programs, the police are working closely with youth service bureaus, schools, recreational facilities, welfare agencies, and employment programs.

Using community services for juveniles has many advantages. Such services allow young people to avoid the stigma of being processed by a police agency. They also improve the community's awareness of the needs of young people and make it possible to restrict court referral to cases involving serious crime. These are some of the goals of Police Working with Youth, a Connecticut program designed to increase positive youth development and positive police interactions with youth. An evaluation of the program found that participating youths with low levels of social and emotional competencies showed a range of improvements in these areas compared to a similar group of youths who did not participate in the program.[106]

Curfews represent another form of community-based policing service. Curfew laws vary with respect to the locale affected, the time frame, and the sanctions. Most restrict minors to their homes or property between the hours of 11:00 p.m. and 6:00 a.m. Sanctions for curfew violations by youths range from fines to being charged with a misdemeanor violation, and may include participation in diversion programs or, in some jurisdictions, jail time for parents.

Curfew enforcement activities are implemented through regular law enforcement and special policing units. High-quality evaluation studies of the impact of juvenile curfew ordinances are limited, but a recent assessment of the empirical evidence, including an evaluation of a curfew law in Charlotte, North Carolina, suggests that on their own, curfews are not effective in managing juveniles or reducing juvenile delinquency.[107] A recent systematic review of the existing empirical research on juvenile curfew laws reached the same conclusion.[108] The review also found that juvenile curfew laws had no lasting impact on reducing juvenile victimization, an important community justification for these laws.

Problem-Oriented Policing

Also referred to as problem-solving policing, problem-oriented policing involves a systematic analysis and response to the problems or conditions underlying criminal incidents rather than the incidents themselves.[109] The theory is that by attending to the underlying problems that cause criminal incidents, the police will have a greater chance of preventing the crimes from reoccurring—the main problem with reactive or "incident-driven policing."[110] However, as noted by Harvard criminologist Mark Moore, "This is not the same as seeking out the root causes of the crime problem in general. It is a much shallower, more situational approach."[111]

To learn about other **problem-oriented policing programs**, go to academic .cengage.com/criminaljustice/siegel.

The systematic nature of problem-oriented policing is characterized by its adherence to a four-step model, often referred to as S.A.R.A., which stands for Scanning, Analysis, Response, and Assessment. The four steps are as follows:

1. Scanning involves identifying a specific crime problem through various data sources (for example, victim surveys, 911 calls).

2. Analysis involves carrying out an in-depth analysis of the crime problem and its underlying causes.

3. Response brings together the police and other partners to develop and implement a response to the problem based on the results produced in the analysis stage.

4. Assessment is the stage in which the response to the problem is evaluated.[112]

Like community policing, problem-oriented policing is viewed as a proactive delinquency prevention strategy. Unlike community policing, however, the engagement of the community in problem-oriented policing is not imperative, but more often than not these operations involve close collaborations with the community. Collaborations with other juvenile justice agencies, such as probation,[113] are also common in problem-oriented policing operations.

As you may recall, problem-oriented policing has been shown to be effective in reducing juvenile delinquency in some circumstances. One of the most successful applications of this policing strategy is Boston's Operation Ceasefire,[114] which is the subject of the accompanying Policy and Practice box.

Following on the success of the Boston program, the Office of Juvenile Justice and Delinquency Prevention (OJJDP) launched a comprehensive initiative to reduce juvenile gun violence in four other cities (Baton Rouge and Shreveport, Louisiana; Oakland, California; and Syracuse, New York). Called the Partnerships to Reduce Juvenile Gun Violence Program, problem-oriented policing strategies are at the center of the program, but other intervention strategies are also important. These include specific delinquency prevention strategies (job training and mentoring), juvenile justice sanctions, and a public information campaign designed to communicate the dangers and consequences of gun violence to juveniles, families, and community residents.[115] An evaluation of the implementation of the program found that three of the four cities were successful in developing comprehensive strategies.[116] With successful implementation and inclusion of many of the components of the Boston program, this program offers promise.

Around the same time in the late-1990s, the federal COPS Office initiated a national Problem-Solving Partnerships (PSP) program with the objective of assisting police agencies to "solve recurrent crime and disorder problems by helping them form community partnerships and engage in problem-solving activities."[117] Various case studies to emerge out of a national evaluation of this program by the Police Executive Research Forum identify a wide range of successful efforts to reduce delinquency.[118] Closely related, the COPS office also initiated a series of guides to aid police in addressing specific crime problems, with one focusing on underage drinking.[119]

Today, many experts consider delinquency prevention efforts to be crucial to the development of a comprehensive approach to youth crime. Although such efforts cut across the entire juvenile justice system, police programs have become increasingly popular.

FUTURE OF JUVENILE POLICING

Many challenges confront the police response to juvenile offending today and will continue to do so in the years to come. Witness intimidation, charges of racial profiling, and poor relations with some communities and groups of young people who are distrustful of the police are some of the key challenges. The police are making progress in dealing with many of these and other challenges, and in the years ahead it will be even more important that the police implement greater transparency in their operations, be more accountable to those they serve, especially young people, and exercise a greater degree of fairness or procedural justice in arresting juvenile offenders and handling them after arrest. It is very likely that future success in controlling as well as preventing juvenile offending will come to depend even more on these factors.

The integration of "soft" and "hard" technologies into police work with juveniles will also become more important in the years to come. Soft technology involves information

Boston's Operation Ceasefire

One of the most successful examples of problem-oriented policing focused on reducing juvenile crime and violence is the program known as Operation Ceasefire. Implemented in Boston, this program aims to reduce youth homicide victimization and youth gun violence. Although it is a police-led program, Operation Ceasefire involves many other juvenile and criminal justice and social agencies, including probation and parole, the Bureau of Alcohol, Tobacco, Firearms, and Explosives (ATF), gang outreach and prevention street workers, and the Drug Enforcement Administration (DEA). This group of agencies has become known as the Ceasefire Working Group.

The program has two main elements:

1. A direct law enforcement focus on illicit gun traffickers who supply youth with guns
2. An attempt to generate a strong deterrent to gang violence

A wide range of measures have been used to reduce the flow of guns to youth, including pooling the resources of local, state, and federal justice authorities to track and seize illegal guns and targeting traffickers of the types of guns most used by gang members. The response to gang violence has been to pull every deterrence "lever" available, including shutting down drug markets, serving warrants, enforcing probation restrictions, and making disorder arrests. The Ceasefire Working Group delivered its message clearly to gang members: "We're ready, we're watching, we're waiting: Who wants to be next?" An example of how the Working Group communicated this message to gang members is shown by the following poster, which was displayed throughout known gang areas in the city.

FREDDIE CARDOZA

Problem:
Violent Gang Member

"Given his extensive criminal record, if there was a Federal law against jaywalking, we'd indict him for that."

—Don Stern, U.S. Attorney

Solution:
Armed Career Criminal Conviction

Arrested with one bullet
Sentence: 19 years, 7 months
No possibility of parole

Address:

Otisville Federal Correctional Institute
Maximum Security Facility, New York

An evaluation from before the program started to the time it ended showed a 63 percent reduction in the mean monthly number of youth homicide victims across the city. The program was also associated with significant decreases in the mean monthly number of gun assaults and overall gang violence across the city. In a comparison with other New England cities and large cities across the United States, most of which also experienced a reduction in youth homicides over the same period, it was found that the significant reduction in youth homicides in Boston was due to Operation Ceasefire.

Maintaining the level of intensity of this program and cooperation of the many agencies involved, which are essential ingredients of its success, has not been easy. In recent years, there have been cutbacks in local policing, fewer federal criminal justice resources made available to the program, and a perception that the deterrence strategy is no longer focused on the most dangerous suspects. Recent research suggests that in order for the program to maintain its success it will also have to adapt to changes in the nature of gang and youth violence across the city.

Although the city of Boston works to improve its program, similar problem-oriented policing programs have been established in cities across the country, including Oakland, California, and Atlanta. An evaluation of Operation Ceasefire in the Hollenbeck area of Los Angeles, which suffers from exceptionally high rates of gang-related gun violence, showed promising results.

Critical Thinking

1. What is the importance of having a multidisciplinary team as part of the program?
2. With comprehensive programs it is often difficult to assess the independent effects of the different program elements. In your opinion, what is the most important element of this program? Why?

SOURCES: Arthur L. Kellerman, Dawna Fuqua-Whitley, and Constance S. Parramore, *Reducing Gun Violence: Community Problem Solving in Atlanta* (Washington, DC: National Institute of Justice, 2006); George E. Tita, K. Jack Riley, Greg Ridgeway, and Peter W. Greenwood, *Reducing Gun Violence: Operation Ceasefire in Los Angeles* (Washington, DC: National Institute of Justice, 2005); Jack McDevitt, Anthony A. Braga, Dana Nurge, and Michael Buerger, "Boston's Youth Violence Prevention Program: A Comprehensive Community-Wide Approach," in Scott H. Decker, ed., *Policing Gangs and Youth Violence* (Belmont, CA: Wadsworth, 2003); Fox Butterfield, "Killing of Girl, 10, and Increase in Homicides Challenge Boston's Crime-Fighting Model," *New York Times*, 14 July 2002; Anthony A. Braga, David M. Kennedy, Elin J. Waring, and Anne Morrison Piehl, "Problem-Oriented Policing Deterrence, and Youth Violence: An Evaluation of Boston's Operation Ceasefire," *Journal of Research in Crime and Delinquency* 38:195–225 (2001); David M. Kennedy, "Pulling Levers: Getting Deterrence Right," *National Institute of Justice Journal* (July):2–8 (1998), p. 6; David M. Kennedy, "Pulling Levers: Chronic Offenders, High-Crime Settings, and a Theory of Prevention," *Valparaiso University Law Review* 31:449–484 (1997).

Increasingly, the police are turning to surveillance technology to deter juvenile and other crime in various places, including schools. Closed-circuit television (CCTV) cameras are one example. Here, in a video camera image released by the Goose Creek Police Department, an officer with a dog passes by students sitting on the floor during a drug raid at Stratford High School in Charleston, South Carolina. According to Lieutenant Dave Aarons, the raid was initiated after his officers viewed video from cameras positioned throughout the school that showed "consistent, organized drug activity" over several days.

© AP Images/Goose Creek Police Department via *The Post and Courier*

technology (IT) systems to enhance police operational and administrative decision making, such as in analyses of city crime patterns and deployment of resources to the most crime-prone areas.[120] Hard technology involves nonlethal weapons, such as the Taser or stun gun, and other alternative weapons systems used by police.[121] Increasingly, the police are also turning to various forms of surveillance technology, such as closed-circuit television (CCTV), to deter juvenile and other crime in public places. Although evaluations have shown CCTV systems to be rather ineffective in reducing crime, "real-time" communication links between police and CCTV operators and their use in high crime areas, may improve effectiveness.[122]

Some new approaches to policing juvenile delinquency show promising results in reducing serious offenses, such as gang activity and gun crimes. These include community-based policing services, police in schools, and problem-oriented policing. One of the most successful approaches—problem-oriented policing—has involved the police working closely with other juvenile justice agencies and the community. Operation Ceasefire in Boston, which brought together a broad range of juvenile justice and social agencies and community groups, produced substantial reductions in youth homicide victims, youth gun assaults, and gang violence throughout the city. Versions of this successful program are now being replicated in other cities across the country. With the research evidence demonstrating that targeted problem-solving policing strategies of this type are the most effective in reducing serious urban crime problems,[123] continued use of these strategies holds much promise in maintaining record low rates of juvenile violence.

Summary

1. Be able to identify key historical events that have shaped juvenile policing in America today

▌ Modern policing developed in England at the beginning of the nineteenth century.

▌ The Industrial Revolution, recognition of the need to treat children as a distinguishable group, and growing numbers of unemployed and homeless youths were among the key events that helped shape juvenile policing in America.

2. Understand key roles and responsibilities of the police in responding to juvenile offenders

▌ The role of juvenile officers is similar to that of officers working with adult offenders: to intervene if the actions of a citizen produce public danger or disorder.

I Juvenile officers must also have a thorough knowledge of the law, especially the constitutional protections available to juveniles.

3. Be able to comment on the organization and management of police services for juveniles

I Juvenile officers operate either as specialists in a police department or as part of the juvenile unit of a police department.

I The organization of juvenile work depends on the size of the police department, the kind of community in which the department is located, and the amount and quality of resources available in the community.

4. Be aware of major court cases that have influenced police practices

I Through the *Terry v. Ohio* decision, along with others, the U.S. Supreme Court established that police may stop a suspect and search for evidence without a warrant under certain circumstances.

I Through the *Miranda v. Arizona* decision, the U.S. Supreme Court established a clearly defined procedure for custodial interrogation.

5. Understand key legal aspects of police work, including search and seizure and custodial interrogation, and how they apply to juveniles

I Most courts have held that the Fourth Amendment ban against unreasonable search and seizure applies to juveniles and that illegally seized evidence is inadmissible in a juvenile trial.

I Most courts have concluded that parents or attorneys need not be present for children effectively to waive their right to remain silent.

6. Be able to describe police use of discretion and factors that influence discretion

I Discretion is a low-visibility decision made in the administration of adult and juvenile justice.

I Discretionary decisions are made without guidelines from the police administrator.

I Numerous factors influence the decisions police make about juvenile offenders, including the seriousness of the offense, the harm inflicted on the victim, and the likelihood that the juvenile will break the law again.

7. Understand the importance of police use of discretion with juveniles and some of the associated problems

I Discretion is essential in providing individualized justice.

I Problems with discretion include discrimination, unfairness, and bias toward particular groups of juveniles.

8. Be familiar with the major policing strategies to prevent delinquency

I The major policing strategies to prevent delinquency include:

— Aggressive law enforcement

— Police in schools

— Community-based and community policing

— Problem-oriented policing

9. See the pros and cons of police using different delinquency prevention strategies

I Innovation in policing strategies can address the ever-changing nature of juvenile delinquency.

I Tailoring policing activities to local conditions and engaging the community and other stakeholders shows promise in reducing delinquency.

I Saturation patrols that include targeting gang areas and arresting members for any law violations have not proven to be effective against gangs.

I Maintaining the level of intensity and cooperation of the many agencies involved in problem-oriented policing strategies, which are essential to their success, is not easy and requires sustainable funding.

Key Terms

pledge system, p. 460
watch system, p. 460
community policing, p. 461
juvenile officers, p. 465
role conflicts, p. 465

informant, p. 465
problem-oriented policing, p. 466
arrest, p. 467
probable cause, p. 467
search and seizure, p. 468

custodial interrogation, p. 469
Miranda warning, p. 469
discretion, p. 470
procedural justice, p. 472

Viewpoint

You are a newly appointed police officer assigned to a juvenile unit of a medium-sized urban police department. Wayne is an 18-year-old white male who was caught shoplifting with two male friends of the same age. He attempted to leave a large department store with a $25 shirt and was apprehended by a police officer in front of the store.

Wayne seemed quite remorseful about the offense. He said several times that he didn't know why he did it and that he had not planned to do it. He seemed upset and scared, and while admitting the offense, did not want to go to court. Wayne had three previous contacts with the police as a juvenile: one for malicious mischief when he destroyed some property, another involving a minor assault on a boy, and a third involving another shoplifting charge. In all three cases, Wayne promised to refrain from ever committing such acts again, and as a result was not required to go to court. The other shoplifting incident involved a baseball worth only $3.

Wayne appeared at the police department with his mother. His parents are divorced. The mother did not seem overly concerned about the case and felt that her son was not really to blame. She argued that he was always getting in trouble and she was not sure how to control him. She blamed most of his troubles with the law on his being in the wrong crowd. Besides, a $25 shirt was "no big deal" and she offered to pay back the store. The store has left matters in the hands of the police and would support any decision you make.

Deciding what to do in a case like Wayne's is a routine activity for most police officers. When dealing with juveniles, they must consider not only the nature of the offense but also the needs of the juvenile. Police officers realize that actions they take can have a long-term effect on an adolescent's future.

▌ Would you submit Wayne's case for prosecution, release him with a warning, or use some other tactic?

▌ Should police officers be forced to act as counselors for troubled youth?

Doing Research on the Web

Before you answer, you may want to learn more about this topic by checking out the following websites, all of which can be accessed via

academic.cengage.com/criminaljustice/siegel

International Association of Chiefs of Police
Police Foundation
Police Executive Research Forum
Office of Community-Oriented Policing Services

Questions for Discussion

1. The term "discretion" is often defined as selective decision making by police and others in the juvenile justice system who are faced with alternative modes of action. Discuss some of the factors affecting the discretion of the police when dealing with juvenile offenders.

2. What role should police organizations play in delinquency prevention and control? Is it feasible to expect police departments to provide social services to children and families? How should police departments be better organized to provide for the control of juvenile delinquency?

3. What qualities should a juvenile police officer have? Should a college education be a requirement?

4. In light of the traditional and protective roles assumed by law enforcement personnel in juvenile justice, is there any reason to have a *Miranda* warning for youths taken into custody?

5. Can the police and community be truly effective in forming a partnership to reduce juvenile delinquency? Discuss the role of the juvenile police officer in preventing and investigating juvenile crime.

6. The experience of Boston's successful Operation Ceasefire program suggests that it may be difficult to sustain the intensity and problem-solving partnerships needed to keep violent juvenile crime under control over the long term. What other innovative problem-oriented policing measures could be employed to achieve this?

Notes

1. David Kocieniewski, "A Little Girl Shot, and a Crowd that Didn't See," *New York Times*, 9 July 2007.

2. This section relies on sources such as Malcolm Sparrow, Mark Moore, and David Kennedy, *Beyond 911, A New Era for Policing* (New York: Basic Books, 1990); Daniel Devlin, *Police Procedure, Administration, and Organization* (London: Butterworth, 1966); Robert Fogelson, *Big City Police* (Cambridge: Harvard University Press, 1977); Roger Lane, *Policing the City, Boston 1822–1885* (Cambridge: Harvard University Press, 1967); Roger Lane, "Urban Police and Crime in Nineteenth-Century America," in Norval Morris and Michael Tonry, eds., *Crime and Justice*, vol. 2 (Chicago: University of Chicago Press, 1980), pp. 1–45; J. J. Tobias, *Crime and Industrial Society in the Nineteenth Century* (New York: Schocken, 1967); Samuel Walker, *A Critical History of Police Reform: The Emergence of Professionalism* (Lexington, MA: Lexington Books, 1977); Samuel Walker, *Popular Justice* (New York: Oxford University Press, 1980); President's Commission on Law Enforcement and the Administration of Justice, *Task Force Report: The Police* (Washington, DC: U.S. Government Printing Office, 1967), pp. 1–9.

3. See Walker, *Popular Justice*, p. 61.

4. Law Enforcement Assistance Administration, *Two Hundred Years of American Criminal Justice* (Washington, DC: U.S. Government Printing Office, 1976).

5. August Vollmer, *The Police and Modern Society* (Berkeley: University of California Press, 1936).

6. O. W. Wilson, *Police Administration*, 2nd ed. (New York: McGraw-Hill, 1963).

7. Wesley G. Skogan, *Police and Community in Chicago: A Tale of Three Cities* (New York: Oxford University Press, 2006); see also Herman Goldstein, "Toward Community-Oriented Policing: Potential Basic Requirements and Threshold Questions," *Crime and Delinquency* 33:630 (1987); Janet Reno, "Taking America Back for Our Children," *Crime and Delinquency* 44:75 (1998).

8. See Wesley G. Skogan and Kathleen Frydl, eds., *Fairness and Effectiveness in Policing: The Evidence* (Washington, DC: The National Academies Press, 2004); David Weisburd and Anthony A. Braga, eds., *Police Innovation: Contrasting Perspectives* (New York: Cambridge University Press, 2006).

9. Skogan and Frydl, *Fairness and Effectiveness in Policing*; Joel Wallman and Alfred Blumstein, "After the Crime Drop," in Alfred Blumstein and Joel Wallman, eds. *The Crime Drop in America*, 2nd ed. (New York: Cambridge University Press, 2006); Lawrence W. Sherman, "Fair and Effective Policing," in James Q. Wilson and Joan Petersilia, eds., *Crime: Public Policies for Crime Control* (Oakland, CA: Institute for Contemporary Studies, 2002); Steven D. Levitt, "Understanding Why Crime Fell in the 1990s: Four Factors that Explain the Decline and Six that Do Not," *Journal of Economic Perspectives* 18:163–190 (2004).

10. Yolander Hurst, James Frank, and Sandra Lee Browning, "The Attitudes of Juveniles toward the Police: A Comparison of Black and White Youth," *Policing* 23:37–53 (2000).

11. Terrance J. Taylor, K. B. Turner, Finn-Aage Esbensen, and L. Thomas Winfree, Jr., "Coppin' an Attitude: Attitudinal Differences among Juveniles Toward Police," *Journal of Criminal Justice* 29:295–305 (2001), p. 300.

12. Yolander G. Hurst, M. Joan McDermott, and Deborah L. Thomas, "The Attitudes of Girls Toward the Police: Differences by Race," *Policing* 28:578–593 (2005), pp. 585–586.

13. Adam M. Watkins, "Examining the Disparity between Juvenile and Adult Victims in Notifying the Police: A Study of Mediating Variables," *Journal of Research in Crime and Delinquency* 42:333–353 (2005).

14. For an analysis of this position, see George Kelling and James Q. Wilson, "Broken Windows: The Police and Neighborhood Safety," *Atlantic Monthly* 249:29–38 (1982).

15. U.S. Department of Justice, "Community Policing," *National Institute of Justice Journal* 225:1–32 (1992).

16. Robert Trojanowicz and Hazel Harden, *The Status of Contemporary Community Policing Programs* (East Lansing, MI: Michigan State University Neighborhood Foot Patrol Center, 1985).

17. Matthew J. Hickman and Brian A. Reaves, *Local Police Departments, 2003* (Washington, DC: Bureau of Justice Statistics, 2006), p. 20.

18. Ibid.

19. Terence Dunworth, *National Evaluation of the Youth Firearms Violence Initiative* (Washington, DC: NIJ Research in Brief, 2000), p. 1.

20. Ibid.

21. See Anthony A. Braga, *Gun Violence Among Serious Young Offenders* (Washington, DC: Office of Community Oriented Policing Services, U.S. Department of Justice, 2004).

22. *Project Safe Neighborhoods: America's Network Against Gun Violence* (Washington, DC: Bureau of Justice Assistance Program Brief, 2004).

23. Susan Guarino-Ghezzi, "Reintegrative Police Surveillance of Juvenile Offenders: Forging an Urban Model," *Crime and Delinquency* 40:131–153 (1994).

24. See David Weisburd and John E. Eck, "What Can Police Do to Reduce Crime, Disorder, and Fear?" *Annals of the American Academy of Political and Social Science* 593:42–65 (2004), p. 57, Table 1.

25. Michael D. Reisig and Roger B. Parks, "Community Policing and Quality of Life," in Wesley G. Skogan, ed., *Community Policing: Can It Work?* (Belmont, CA: Wadsworth, 2004).

26. The President's Crime Prevention Council, *Preventing Crime and Promoting Responsibility: 50 Programs that Help Communities Help Their Youth* (Washington, DC: U.S. Government Printing Office, 1995).

27. Denise C. Herz, "Improving Police Encounters with Juveniles: Does Training Make a Difference?" *Justice Research and Policy* 3:57–77 (2001).

28. Donald Black and Albert J. Reiss, Jr., "Police Control of Juveniles," *American Sociological Review* 35:63 (1970); Richard Lundman, Richard Sykes, and John Clark, "Police Control of Juveniles: A Replication," *Journal of Research on Crime and Delinquency* 15:74 (1978).

29. American Bar Association, *Standards Relating to Police Handling of Juvenile Problems* (Cambridge, MA: Ballinger, 1977), p. 1.

30. Samuel Walker, *The Police of America* (New York: McGraw-Hill, 1983), p. 133.

31. Karen A. Joe, "The Dynamics of Running Away, Deinstitutionalization Policies and the Police," *Juvenile Family Court Journal* 46:43–45 (1995).

32. Mary Dodge, "Juvenile Police Informants: Friendship, Persuasion, and Pretense," *Youth Violence and Juvenile Justice* 4:234–246 (2006), p. 234.

33. Ibid., p. 244.

34. Richard J. Lundman, *Prevention and Control of Delinquency*, 3rd ed. (New York: Oxford University Press, 2001), p. 23.

35. FBI, *Crime in the United States, 2005* (Washington, DC: U.S. Government Printing Office, 2006), table 38.

36. See Franklin E. Zimring, *American Juvenile Justice* (New York: Oxford University Press, 2005), ch. 8.

37. Lawrence W. Sherman and John E. Eck, "Policing for Crime Prevention," in Lawrence W. Sherman, David P. Farrington, Brandon C. Welsh, and Doris Layton MacKenzie, eds., *Evidence-Based Crime Prevention* (New York: Routledge, 2002), p. 321; for "hot spots" policing, see also Wesley G. Skogan and Kathleen Frydl, eds., *Fairness and Effectiveness in Policing: The Evidence* (Washington, DC: National Academy Press, Committee to Review Research on Police Policy and Practices, 2004); Anthony A. Braga, "The Effects of Hot Spots Policing on Crime," *Annals of the American Academy of Political and Social Science* 578:104–125 (2001).

38. Christopher S. Koper and Evan Mayo-Wilson, "Police Crackdowns on Illegal Gun Carrying: A Systematic Review of Their Impact on Gun Crime," *Journal of Experimental Criminology* 2:227–261 (2006).

39. Linda Szymanski, *Summary of Juvenile Code Purpose Clauses* (Pittsburgh: National Center for Juvenile Justice, 1988); see also, for example, GA Code Ann. 15; Iowa Code Ann. 232.2; Mass. Gen. Laws, ch. 119, 56.

40. Samuel M. Davis, *Rights of Juveniles—The Juvenile Justice System* (New York: Clark-Boardmen, rev. June 1989), sec. 3.3.

41. National Council of Juvenile and Family Court Judges, *Juvenile and Family Law Digest* 29:1–2 (1997).

42. See Fourth Amendment, U.S. Constitution.

43. *Chimel v. Cal.*, 395 U.S. 752, 89 S.Ct. 2034 (1969).

44. *United States v. Ross*, 456 U.S. 798, 102 S.Ct. 2157 (1982).

45. *Terry v. Ohio*, 392 U.S.1, 88 S.Ct. 1868 (1968).

46. *Bumper v. North Carolina*, 391 U.S. 543, 88 S.Ct. 1788 (1968).

47. *Miranda v. Arizona*, 384 U.S. 436, 86 S.Ct. 1602 (1966).

48. *Commonwealth v. Gaskins*, 471 Pa. 238, 369 A.2d 1285 (1977); *In re E.T.C.*, 141 Vt. 375, 449 A.2d 937 (1982).

49. *People v. Lara*, 67 Cal.2d 365, 62 Cal.Rptr. 586, 432 P.2d 202 (1967).

50. *West v. United States*, 399 F.2d 467 (5th Cir. 1968).

51. Barry C. Feld, "Police Interrogation of Juveniles: An Empirical Study of Policy and Practice," *Journal of Criminal Law and Criminology* 97:219–316 (2006); Feld, "Juveniles' Competence to Exercise *Miranda* Rights: An Empirical Study of Policy and Practice," *Minnesota Law Review* 91:26–100 (2006).

52. *Fare v. Michael C.*, 442 U.S. 707, 99 S.Ct. 2560 (1979).

53. *California v. Prysock*, 453 U.S. 355, 101 S.Ct. 2806 (1981).

54. See, for example, Larry Holtz, "*Miranda* in a Juvenile Setting—A Child's Right to Silence," *Journal of Criminal Law and Criminology* 79:534–556 (1987).

55. Kenneth C. Davis, *Discretionary Justice: A Preliminary Inquiry* (Baton Rouge: Louisiana State University Press, 1969); H. Ted Rubin, *Juvenile Justice: Police, Practice and Law* (Santa Monica, CA: Goodyear, 1979).

56. Joseph Goldstein, "Police Discretion Not to Invoke the Criminal Process: Low-Visibility Decisions in the Administration of Justice," *Yale Law Journal* 69:544 (1960).

57. Victor Streib, *Juvenile Justice in America* (Port Washington, NY: Kennikat, 1978).

58. He rbert Packer, *The Limits of the Criminal Sanction* (Palo Alto, CA: Stanford University Press, 1968).

59. Black and Reiss, "Police Control of Juveniles"; Richard J. Lundman, "Routine Police Arrest Practices," *Social Problems* 22:127–141 (1974); Robert E. Worden and Stephanie M. Myers, *Police Encounters with Juvenile Suspects* (Albany, NY: Hindelang Criminal Justice Research Center and School of Criminal Justice, University at Albany, SUNY, 2001).

60. Nathan Goldman, *The Differential Selection of Juvenile Offenders for Court Appearance* (Washington, DC: National Council on Crime and Delinquency, 1963).

61. Irving Piliavin and Scott Briar, "Police Encounters with Juveniles," *American Journal of Sociology* 70:206–214 (1964); Theodore Ferdinand and Elmer Luchterhand, "Inner-City Youth, the Police, Juvenile Court, and Justice," *Social Problems* 8:510–526 (1970).

62. Paul Strasburg, *Violent Delinquents: Report to Ford Foundation from Vera Institute of Justice* (New York: Monarch, 1978), p. 11; Robert Terry, "The Screening of Juvenile Offenders," *Journal of Criminal Law, Criminology, and Police Science* 58:173–181 (1967).

63. Joan McCord, Cathy Spatz Widom, and Nancy A. Crowell, eds., *Juvenile Crime, Juvenile Justice*, Panel on Juvenile Crime: Prevention, Treatment, and Control (Washington, DC: National Academy Press, 2001), p. 163.

64. Worden and Myers, *Police Encounters with Juvenile Suspects*.

65. FBI, *Crime in the United States, 2005*, table 68.

66. Douglas Smith and Christy Visher, "Street-Level Justice: Situational Determinants of Police Arrest Decisions," *Social Problems* 29:167–178 (1981).

67. Douglas Smith and Jody Klein, "Police Control of Interpersonal Disputes," *Social Problems* 31:468–481 (1984).

68. Goldman, *The Differential Selection of Juvenile Offenders for Court Appearance*, p. 25; Norman Werner and Charles Willie, "Decisions of Juvenile Officers," *American Journal of Sociology* 77:199–214 (1971).

69. Skogan and Frydl, *Fairness and Effectiveness in Policing*, pp. 301–303; Sherman, "Fair and Effective Policing," pp. 404–405.

70. Raymond Paternoster, Ronet Bachman, Robert Brame and Lawrence W. Sherman, "Do Fair Procedures Matter? The Effect of Procedural Justice on Spouse Assault," *Law and Society Review* 31:163–204 (1997).

71. Skogan and Frydl, *Fairness and Effectiveness in Policing*, p. 7.

72. Aaron Cicourel, *The Social Organization of Juvenile Justice* (New York: Wiley, 1968).

73. Piliavin and Briar, "Police Encounters with Juveniles," p. 214.

74. David Klinger, "Demeanor or Crime? Why 'Hostile' Citizens Are More Likely to Be Arrested," *Criminology* 32:475–493 (1994).

75. Richard Lundman, "Demeanor or Crime? The Midwest City Police-Citizen Encounters Study," *Criminology* 32:631–653 (1994); Robert Worden and Robin Shepard, "On the Meaning, Measurement, and Estimated Effects of Suspects' Demeanor toward the Police," paper presented at the annual meeting of the American Society of Criminology, Miami, November 1994.

76. James Fyfe, David Klinger, and Jeanne Flaving, "Differential Police Treatment of Male-on-Female Spousal Violence," *Criminology* 35:455–473 (1997).

77. Dale Dannefer and Russel Schutt, "Race and Juvenile Justice Processing in Police and Court Agencies," *American Journal of Sociology* 87:1113–1132 (1982); Smith and Visher, "Street-Level Justice: Situational Determinants of Police Arrest Decisions"; also, Ronald Weitzer, "Racial Discrimination in the Criminal Justice System: Findings and Problems in the Literature," *Journal of Criminal Justice* 24:309–322 (1996); Ronald Weitzer and Steven A. Tuch, "Perceptions of Racial Profiling: Race, Class, and Personal Experience," *Criminology* 40:435–456 (2002).

78. Patricia Warren, Donald Tomaskovic-Devey, William Smith, Matthew Zingraff, and Marcinda Mason, "Driving While Black: Bias Processes and Racial Disparity in Police Stops," *Criminology* 44:709–738 (2006); Richard J. Lundman and Robert L. Kaufman, "Driving While Black: Effects of Race, Ethnicity, and Gender on Citizen Self-Reports of Traffic Stops and Police Actions," *Criminology* 41:195–220 (2003).

79. Dan M. Kahan and Tracey L. Meares, "The Coming Crisis of Criminal Procedure," *Georgetown Law Journal* 86:1153–1184 (2000).

80. Randall Kennedy, *Race, Crime and the Law* (New York: Vintage, 1998).

81. Terence Thornberry, "Race, Socioeconomic Status, and Sentencing in the Juvenile Justice System," *Journal of Criminal Law and Criminology* 70:164–171 (1979); Dannefer and Schutt, "Race and Juvenile Justice Processing in Police and Court Agencies"; Jeffrey Fagan, Ellen Slaughter, and Eliot Hartstone, "Blind Justice? The Impact of Race on the Juvenile Justice Process," *Crime and Delinquency* 33:224–258 (1987).

82. Donna M. Bishop and Charles E. Frazier, "The Influence of Race in Juvenile Justice Processing," *Journal of Research in Crime and Delinquency* 25:242–261 (1988).

83. Ibid., p. 258; see also Howard N. Snyder and Melissa Sickmund, *Juvenile Offenders and Victims: 2006 National Report* (Pittsburgh: National Center for Juvenile Justice, 2006), p. 163.

84. See Samuel Walker, Cassie Spohn, and Miriam DeLone, *The Color of Justice: Race, Ethnicity, and Crime in America* (Belmont, CA: Wadsworth, 1996).

85. Merry Morash, "Establishment of a Juvenile Record: The Influence of Individual and Peer Group Characteristics," *Criminology* 22:97–112 (1984).

86. Meda Chesney-Lind, "Judicial Enforcement of the Female Sex Role: The Family Court and Female Delinquency Issues," *Criminology* 8:51–71 (1973); Chesney-Lind, "Young Women in the Arms of Law," in L. Bowker, ed., *Women, Crime, and the Criminal Justice System*, 2nd ed. (Lexington, MA: Lexington Books, 1978).

87. Donna Bishop and Charles Frazier, "Gender Bias in Juvenile Justice Processing: Implications of the JJDP Act," *Journal of Criminal Law and Criminology* 82:1162–1186 (1992).

88. Meda Chesney-Lind and Randall G. Shelden, *Girls, Delinquency, and Juvenile Justice*, 3rd ed. (Belmont, CA: Wadsworth, 2004), p. 35.

89. Douglas Smith, "The Organizational Context of Legal Control," *Criminology* 22:19–38 (1984); see also Stephen Mastrofski and Richard Ritti, "Police Training and the Effects of Organization on Drunk Driving Enforcement," *Justice Quarterly* 13:291–320 (1996).

90. John Irwin, *The Jail: Managing the Underclass in American Society* (Berkeley: University of California Press, 1985).

91. Darlene Conley, "Adding Color to a Black and White Picture: Using Qualitative Data to Explain Racial Disproportionality in the Juvenile Justice System," *Journal of Research in Crime and Delinquency* 31:135–148 (1994).

92. Robert Sampson, "Effects of Socioeconomic Context of Official Reaction to Juvenile Delinquency," *American Sociological Review* 51:876–885 (1986).

93. Ronald Weitzer, "White, Black, or Blue Cops? Race and Citizen Assessments of Police Officers," *Journal of Criminal Justice* 28:313–324 (2000).

94. Thomas Priest and Deborah Brown Carter, "Evaluations of Police Performance in an African American Sample," *Journal of Criminal Justice* 27: 457–465 (1999); see also Matt De Lisi and Bob Regoli, "Race, Conventional Crime, and Criminal Justice: The Declining Importance of Skin Color," *Journal of Criminal Justice* 27:549–557 (1999).

95. American Bar Association, *Standards of Criminal Justice: Standards Relating to Urban Police Function* (New York: Institute of Judicial Administration, 1972), Standard 4.2, p. 121.

96. Kenneth C. Davis, *Police Discretion* (St. Paul, MN: West, 1975).

97. Robert Shepard, Jr., ed., *Juvenile Justice Standards Annotated—A Balanced Approach* (Chicago: ABA, 1996).

98. Judith Greene and Kevin Pranis, *Gang Wars: The Failure of Enforcement Tactics and the Need for Effective Public Safety Strategies* (Washington, DC: Justice Policy Institute, 2007).

99. Ibid., p. 5.

100. Matthew J. Hickman and Brian A. Reaves, *Local Police Departments, 2003* (Washington, DC: Bureau of Justice Statistics, 2006), p. 20.

101. Finn-Aage Esbensen, D. Wayne Osgood, Terrance J. Taylor, Dana Peterson, and Adrienne Freng, "How Great Is G.R.E.A.T.? Results from a Longitudinal Quasi-Experimental Design," *Criminology and Public Policy* 1:87–118 (2001), p. 88.

102. Finn-Aage Esbensen and D. Wayne Osgood, "Gang Resistance Education and Training (G.R.E.A.T.): Results from the National Evaluation," *Journal of Research in Crime and Delinquency* 36:194–225 (1999).

103. Esbensen, Osgood, Taylor, Peterson, and Freng, "How Great Is G.R.E.A.T.?"

104. Yale University Child Study Center, *Community Outreach Through Police in Schools* (Washington, DC: Office for Victims of Crime Bulletin, 2003), p. 2.

105. Ibid., p. 3.

106. Stephen A. Anderson, Ronald M. Sabatelli, and Jennifer Trachtenberg, "Community Police and Youth Programs as a Context for Positive Youth Development," *Police Quarterly* 10:23–40 (2007).

107. J. David Hirschel, Charles W. Dean, and Doris Dumond, "Juvenile Curfews and Race: A Cautionary Note," *Criminal Justice Policy Review* 12:197–214 (2001), p. 209; see also McCord, Spatz Widom, and Crowell, eds., *Juvenile Crime, Juvenile Justice*, p. 145.

108. Kenneth Adams, "The Effectiveness of Juvenile Curfews at Crime Prevention," *Annals of the American Academy of Political and Social Science* 587:136–159 (2003).

109. Mark H. Moore, "Problem-Solving and Community Policing," in Michael Tonry and Norval Morris, eds., *Modern Policing. Crime and Justice: A Review of Research*, vol. 15 (Chicago: University of Chicago Press, 1992), p. 99.

110. Anthony A. Braga, *Problem-Oriented Policing and Crime Prevention* (Monsey, NY: Criminal Justice Press, 2002), p. 10.

111. Moore, "Problem-Solving and Community Policing," p. 120.

112. Debra Cohen, *Problem-Solving Partnerships: Including the Community for a Change* (Washington, DC: Office of Community Oriented Policing Services, 2001), p. 2.

113. See John L. Worrall and Larry K. Gaines, "The Effect of Police-Probation Partnerships on Juvenile Arrests," *Journal of Criminal Justice* 34:579–589 (2006).

114. Anthony A. Braga, David M. Kennedy, Elin J. Waring, and Anne Morrison Piehl, "Problem-Oriented Policing Deterrence, and Youth Violence: An Evaluation of Boston's Operation Ceasefire," *Journal of Research in Crime and Delinquency* 38:195–225 (2001).

115. David Sheppard, Heath Grant, Wendy Rowe, and Nancy Jacobs, *Fighting Juvenile Gun Violence* (Washington, DC: OJJDP Juvenile Justice Bulletin, 2000), p. 2.

116. Ibid., p. 10.

117. Cohen, *Problem-Solving Partnerships: Including the Community for a Change*, p. 2.

118. Ibid., pp. 5–7.

119. Kelly Dedel Johnson, *Underage Drinking. Problem-Specific Guides Series*, No. 27 (Washington, DC: Office of Community Oriented Policing Services, 2004).

120. Christopher J. Harris, "Police and Soft Technology: How Information Technology Contributes to Police Decision Making," in James M. Byrne and Donald J. Rebovich, eds., *The New Technology of Crime, Law and Social Control* (Monsey, NY: Criminal Justice Press, 2007).

121. Don Hummer, "Policing and 'Hard' Technology," in Byrne and Rebovich, eds., *The New Technology of Crime, Law and Social Control*.

122. Brandon C. Welsh and David P. Farrington, *Making Public Places Safer: Surveillance and Crime Prevention* (New York: Oxford University Press, forthcoming).

123. David Weisburd and John E. Eck, "What Can Police Do to Reduce Crime, Disorder, and Fear?" *Annals of the American Academy of Political and Social Science* 593:42–65 (2004); Wesley G. Skogan and Kathleen Frydl, eds., *Fairness and Effectiveness in Policing: The Evidence*, Committee to Review Research on Police Policy and Practices (Washington, DC: National Academy Press, 2004).

Juvenile Court Process: Pretrial, Trial, and Sentencing

15

Chapter Outline

Chapter Objectives

1. Understand the roles and responsibilities of the main players in the juvenile court
2. Be able to discuss key issues of the preadjudicatory stage of juvenile justice, including detention, intake, diversion, pretrial release, plea bargaining, and waiver
3. Be able to argue the pros and cons of transferring youths to adult court
4. Understand key issues of the trial stage of juvenile justice, including constitutional rights of youths and disposition
5. Be familiar with major U.S. Supreme Court decisions that have influenced the handling of juveniles at the preadjudicatory and trial stages
6. Know the most common dispositions for juvenile offenders
7. Be able to argue the pros and cons of confidentiality in juvenile proceedings and privacy of juvenile records

Warren Messner

Christopher Scamahorn

Bumfights, a website depicting homeless men and women fighting one another as well as performing dangerous and humiliating acts, and other "bum-rushing" video sites that show people causing harm to homeless people, influenced their decision to do it. This was the response of one of four teens, all of whom were found guilty in the gruesome beating death of Michael Roberts, 53, a frail homeless man who slept in woods not far from downtown Daytona Beach, Florida. The teens also said they did it "for fun" and because they had nothing better to do. The teens stumbled upon Roberts in the woods as they were searching for a place to smoke some marijuana.

In three separate attacks over the course of two hours, the four teenagers—a fifth teen alleged to have participated in the attack is awaiting trial—used their fists, feet, sticks, and logs to kill Michael Roberts as he begged for his life. As reported in the *Daytona Beach News-Journal* online, Roberts died of "blunt force trauma to the head, suffered broken ribs, and was found covered in a rug with defensive wounds on his arms. But the medical examiner couldn't say for sure which was the fatal blow."

On April 24, 2006, Daytona Beach Circuit Court Judge Joseph Will sentenced the four teens to a total of 120 years in prison: 35 years for both Jeffery Spurgeon, 19, and Christopher Scamahorn, 15; 28 years for Justin Stearns, 18; and 22 years for Warren Messner, 16. The two youngest, Scamahorn and Messner, were placed in a secure juvenile facility where they will remain until they turn 18 and then be transferred to an adult prison; the other two were placed in an adult prison. All four will be eligible for release upon serving 85 percent of their sentence and then will remain on supervised probation for life. Prior to sentencing the juveniles, Judge Will, a veteran of the juvenile and criminal courts, commented that he had never presided over a case involving such a savage murder.

Cases like these draw the ire of many and rekindle the debate over whether the juvenile court should be abolished. Because of the heinous nature of this crime, these juveniles were transferred to adult court. Some argue that this case shows exactly how the juvenile court should operate: reserve punishment for the most serious violent juvenile offenders through transfer to the adult system and provide specialized treatment for the rest. It may be that striking the right balance between treatment and punishment is becoming more important than calling for further "get tough" measures.

Because the judicial process is one of the most critical points in the juvenile justice process, it is covered here in some detail. We begin with a discussion of the juvenile court and its jurisdiction. We then turn to issues involving the preadjudicatory stage of juvenile justice: detention, intake, diversion, pretrial release, plea bargaining, and waiver. The trial stage is examined next, looking at the rights of the child at trial—particularly those rights dealing with counsel and trial by jury—through a detailed analysis of U.S. Supreme Court decisions. Procedural rules that govern the adjudicatory and dispositional hearings are also reviewed. We conclude with a discussion of dispositional alternatives and trends in sentencing.

THE JUVENILE COURT AND ITS JURISDICTION

Today's juvenile delinquency cases are sometimes handled as part of a criminal trial court jurisdiction or even within the probate court. Also called surrogate court in some states, probate court is a court of special jurisdiction that handles wills, administration of estates, and guardianship of minors and incompetents. However, in most jurisdictions juvenile cases are treated in the structure of a family court or an independent juvenile court (14 states use more than one method to process juvenile cases).[1] The independent juvenile court is a specialized court for children, designed to promote rehabilitation of youths within a framework of procedural due process. It is concerned with acting both in the best interest of the child and in the best interest of public protection, two often-incompatible goals. Family courts, in contrast, have broad jurisdiction over a wide range of personal and household problems, including delinquency, paternity, child support, and custody issues. The major advantages of such a system are that it can serve sparsely populated areas, it permits judicial personnel and others to deal exclusively with children's matters, and it can obtain legislative funding more readily than other court systems.

Court Case Flow

In 2004 (the latest data available), a little more than 1.6 million delinquency cases were referred to juvenile court. This represents a 9 percent decrease in court case flow from the peak year in 1997 and 7 percent decrease in the last decade (1995 to 2004). This recent decline comes after a steady increase or upward trend in court case flow that began in the mid-1980s.[2]

There were distinct gender- and race-based differences in the juvenile court population. In 2004, 73 percent of delinquency cases involved a male and 27 percent a female. However, the number of females processed by juvenile courts has increased from 1990, when less than 20 percent of the cases involved females. Similarly, 31 percent of the juvenile court population was comprised of African American youth, although African Americans make up only about 16 percent of the general population.[3]

The Actors in the Juvenile Courtroom

The key players in the juvenile court are prosecutors, judges, and defense attorneys.

The Defense Attorney As a result of a series of Supreme Court decisions, the right of a delinquent youth to have counsel at state trials has become a fundamental part of the juvenile justice system.[4] Today, courts must provide counsel to indigent defendants who face the possibility of incarceration. Over the past three decades, the rules of juvenile justice administration have become extremely complex. Preparation of a case for juvenile court often involves detailed investigation of a crime, knowledge of court procedures, use of rules of evidence, and skills in trial advocacy. The right to counsel is essential if children are to have a fair chance of presenting their cases in court.[5]

In many respects, the role of juvenile defense attorney is similar to that in the criminal and civil areas. Defense attorneys representing children in the juvenile court play an active and important part in virtually all stages of the proceedings. For example, the defense attorney helps to clarify jurisdictional problems and to decide whether there is sufficient evidence to warrant filing a formal petition. The defense attorney helps outline the child's position regarding detention hearings and bail, and explores the opportunities for informal adjustment of the case. If no adjustment or diversion occurs, the defense attorney represents the child at adjudication, presenting evidence and cross-examining witnesses to see that the child's position is made clear to the court. Defense attorneys also play a critical role in the dispositional hearing. They present evidence bearing on the treatment decision and help the court formulate alternative plans for the child's care. Finally, defense attorneys pursue any appeals from the trial, represent the child in probation revocation proceedings, and generally protect the child's right to treatment.

Important to these roles is the attorney-juvenile relationship and the competence of the attorney. Some studies report that many juvenile offenders do not trust their attorney,[6] but juvenile offenders represented by private attorneys are more trusting in their attorney than those represented by court-appointed attorneys.[7] One possible reason for this difference may be the belief among juveniles that because court-appointed attorneys work for the "system" they might share information with the judge, police, or others.[8] Another important dimension of the attorney-juvenile relationship is effective participation of the juvenile as a defendant, which "requires a personally relevant understanding of the lawyer's advocacy role and the confidential nature of the attorney-client relationship."[9] A recent study investigating effective participation among juvenile and adult defendants concluded that juveniles are in need of extra procedural safeguards, such as training for lawyers on how to be more effective counselors.[10] There may also be a need to improve the competency of juvenile defense attorneys, as well as to overcome some of the time constraints they face in case preparation. In a study of legal representation of juveniles charged with felonies in three juvenile courts in Missouri, it was found that they were more likely to receive an out-of-home placement disposition (instead of a less punitive disposition) if they had an attorney, even after controlling for other legal and individual factors.[11] Another study found that youth not represented by an attorney were more likely to have the charges dismissed than similar youth represented by an attorney, with the effect being more pronounced for minorities.[12] (See the following section for other problems specific to public defenders.)

In some cases, a guardian *ad litem* may be appointed by the court.[13] The guardian *ad litem*—ordinarily seen in abuse, neglect, and dependency cases—may be appointed in delinquency cases where there is a question of a need for a particular treatment (for example, placement in a mental health center), and offenders and their attorneys resist placement. The guardian *ad litem* may advocate for the commitment on the basis that it is in the child's best interests. This individual fulfills many roles, ranging from legal advocate to concerned individual, who works with parents and human service professionals in developing a proper treatment plan that best serves the interests of the minor child.[14]

Court Appointed Special Advocates (CASA) Court Appointed Special Advocates (CASA) employ volunteers who advise the juvenile court about child placement. The CASA programs (*casa* is Spanish for "home") have demonstrated that volunteers can investigate the needs of children and provide a vital link among the judge, the attorneys, and the child in protecting the juvenile's right to a safe placement.[15]

Public Defender Services for Children To satisfy the requirement that indigent children be provided with counsel, the federal government and the states have expanded public defender services. Three alternatives exist for providing children with legal counsel: (1) an all–public defender program, (2) an appointed private-counsel system, and (3) a combination system of public defenders and appointed private attorneys.

The public defender program is a statewide program established by legislation and funded by the state government to provide counsel to children at public expense. This program allows access to the expertise of lawyers, who spend a considerable amount of time representing juvenile offenders every day. Defender programs generally provide separate office space for juvenile court personnel, as well as support staff, and training programs for new lawyers.

In many rural areas, where individual public defender programs are not available, defense services are offered through appointed private counsel. Private lawyers are assigned to individual juvenile court cases, and they receive compensation for the time and services they provide. When private attorneys are used in large urban areas, they are generally selected from a list established by the court, and they often operate in conjunction with a public defender program. The weaknesses of a system of assigned private counsel include assignment to cases for which the lawyers are unqualified, inadequate compensation, and lack of supportive or supervisory services.

Although efforts have been made to supply juveniles with adequate legal representation, many juveniles still go to court unrepresented or with an overworked lawyer who provides inadequate representation. Many juvenile court defense lawyers work on more than 500 cases per year, and more than half leave their jobs in under two years.[16] Other problems facing public defenders include (a) lack of resources for independent evaluations, expert witnesses, and investigatory support; (b) lack of computers, telephones, files, and adequate office space; (c) juvenile public defenders' inexperience, lack of training, low morale, and salaries lower than those of their counterparts who defend adults or serve as prosecutors; and (d) inability to keep up with rapidly changing juvenile codes.[17] In a six-state study of access to counsel and quality of legal representation for indigent juveniles, the American Bar Association found these and many other problems,[18] as shown in Exhibit 15.1. With juvenile offenders facing the prospect of much longer sentences, mandatory minimum sentences, and time in adult prisons, the need for quality defense attorneys for juveniles has never been greater.

juvenile prosecutor
Government attorney responsible for representing the interests of the state and bringing the case against the accused juvenile.

The Prosecutor The juvenile prosecutor is the attorney responsible for bringing the state's case against the accused juvenile. Depending on the level of government and the jurisdiction, the prosecutor can be called a district attorney, a county attorney, a state attorney, or a United States attorney. Prosecutors are members of the bar selected for their positions by political appointment or popular election.

Juvenile defense attorneys play an active role and an important part in virtually all stages of juvenile court proceedings, ranging from representing youths in juvenile court hearings to filing their final appeals.

© Joel Gordon

Ordinarily, the juvenile prosecutor is a staff member of the prosecuting attorney's office. If the office of the district attorney is of sufficient size, the juvenile prosecutor may work exclusively on juvenile and other family law matters. If the caseload of juvenile offenders is small, the juvenile prosecutor may also have criminal prosecution responsibilities.

For the first 60 years of its existence, the juvenile court did not include a prosecutor, because the concept of an adversary process was seen as inconsistent with the philosophy of treatment. The court followed a social service helping model, and informal proceedings were believed to be in the best interests of the child. Today, in a more legalistic juvenile court, almost all jurisdictions require by law that a prosecutor be present in the juvenile court.

A number of states have passed legislation giving prosecutors control over intake and waiver decisions. Some have passed concurrent-jurisdiction laws that allow prosecutors to decide in which court to bring serious juvenile cases. In some jurisdictions, it is the prosecutor and not the juvenile court judge who is entrusted with the decision of whether to transfer a case to adult court. Consequently, the role of juvenile court prosecutor is now critical in the juvenile justice process. Including a prosecutor in juvenile court balances the interests of the state, the defense attorney, the child, and the judge, preserving the independence of each party's functions and responsibilities.

The prosecutor has the power either to initiate or to discontinue delinquency or status offense allegations. Like police officers, prosecutors have broad discretion in the exercise of their duties. Because due process rights have been extended to juveniles, the prosecutor's role in the juvenile court has in some ways become similar to the prosecutor's role in the adult court.

Because children are committing more serious crimes today and because the courts have granted juveniles constitutional safeguards, the prosecutor is likely to play an increasingly significant role in the juvenile court system. According to authors James Shine and Dwight Price, the prosecutor's involvement will promote a due process model that should result in a fairer, more just system for all parties. But they also

To read more about the **players in the court system**, go to the website of the **American Judicature Society**, a nonpartisan organization with a membership of judges, lawyers, and other citizens interested in the administration of justice. You can access this site via academic.cengage.com/criminaljustice/siegel.

EXHIBIT 15.1

Selected Problems in Public Defender Services for Indigent Juveniles in Six States

Maine

▮ Juvenile defenders are paid $50 per hour, with a cap of $315; therefore, defenders are expected to spend only a little over six hours on each case.

▮ In 2002, only two hours of juvenile justice–related training were available to defenders.

Maryland

▮ In one jurisdiction, juvenile public defenders handle about 360 cases each year; this is almost double the ABA standard's recommended maximum of 200.

▮ In 10 of the jurisdictions studied, more than a third of juveniles waived their right to counsel.

Montana

▮ Nearly all of the interviewed youth revealed that their attorneys had done no investigation into their cases.

▮ There are no minimum requirements for attorneys seeking appointment to defend children and youth in the justice system.

North Carolina

▮ Some 44 percent of juvenile defense attorneys surveyed reported that they rarely or never see the police report or other investigative material prior to their first meeting with a client.

▮ Some 44 percent also said they had no or inadequate access to investigators.

Pennsylvania

▮ About 94 percent of juvenile defense attorneys do not have access to independent investigators or social workers.

▮ Of the 40 public defender offices that confirmed representing youth at dispositional reviews, only 9 percent usually interview the youth before hearings.

Washington

▮ In some counties, up to 30 percent of children appear without counsel.

▮ Juvenile defenders working full-time reported that they are assigned an average of nearly 400 cases annually.

SOURCES: Adapted from American Bar Association, *Statistics: Juvenile Indigent Defense Reports by the Numbers* (Chicago: Juvenile Justice Center, 2003); American Bar Association, *Montana: An Assessment of Access to Counsel and Quality of Representation in Delinquency Proceedings* (Chicago: American Bar Association, 2003), p. 5.

point out that, to meet current and future challenges, prosecutors need more information on such issues as (a) how to identify repeat offenders, (b) how to determine which programs are most effective, (c) how early-childhood experiences relate to delinquency, and (d) what measures can be used in place of secure placements without reducing public safety.[19]

Today, prosecutors are addressing the problems associated with juvenile crime. A balanced approach has been recommended—one that emphasizes enforcement, prosecution, and detention of serious offenders and the use of proven prevention and intervention programs.[20]

The Juvenile Court Judge Even with the elevation of the prosecutor's role, the juvenile court judge is still the central character in a court of juvenile or family law. Her or his responsibilities have become far more extensive and complex in recent years. Juvenile or family court judges perform the functions listed in Exhibit 15.2.

In addition, judges often have extensive influence over other agencies of the court: probation, the court clerk, the law enforcement officer, and the office of the juvenile prosecutor. Juvenile court judges exercise considerable leadership in developing solutions to juvenile justice problems. In this role they must respond to the pressures the community places on juvenile court resources. According to the *parens patriae* philosophy, the juvenile judge must ensure that the necessary community resources are available so that the children and families who come before the court can receive the proper care and help.[21] This may be the most untraditional role for the juvenile court judge, but it may also be the most important.

In some jurisdictions juvenile court judges handle family-related cases exclusively. In others they preside over criminal and civil cases as well. Traditionally, juvenile court judges have been relegated to a lower status than other judges. The National Council of Juvenile and Family Court Judges, as part of a larger effort to improve juvenile courts, recently took up this issue by recommending that "Juvenile delinquency court judges should have the same status as the highest level of trial court in the state and should have multiple year or permanent assignments."[22] Furthermore, judges assigned to juvenile courts have not ordinarily been chosen from the highest levels of the legal profession. Such groups as the American Judicature Society have noted that the field of juvenile justice has often been shortchanged by the appointment of unqualified judges. In some jurisdictions, particularly major urban areas, juvenile court judges may be of the highest caliber, but many courts continue to function with mediocre judges.

Inducing the best-trained individuals to accept juvenile court judgeships is a very important goal. Where the juvenile court is part of the highest general court of trial jurisdiction, the problem of securing qualified personnel is not as great. However, if the juvenile court is of limited or specialized jurisdiction and has the authority to try only minor cases, it may attract only poorly trained personnel. Lawyers

juvenile court judge
A judge elected or appointed to preside over juvenile cases and whose decisions can only be reviewed by a judge of a higher court.

The National Council of Juvenile and Family Court Judges is dedicated to serving the nation's children and families by improving the courts of juvenile and family jurisdictions. Their website can be accessed via academic.cengage.com/criminaljustice/siegel.

EXHIBIT 15.2

Duties of the Juvenile Court Judge

I Rule on pretrial motions involving such legal issues as arrest, search and seizure, interrogation, and lineup identification

I Make decisions about the continued detention of children prior to trial

I Make decisions about plea bargaining agreements and the informal adjustment of juvenile cases

I Handle trials, rule on the appropriateness of conduct, settle questions of evidence and procedure, and guide the questioning of witnesses

I Assume responsibility for holding dispositional hearings and deciding on the treatment accorded the child

I Handle waiver proceedings

I Handle appeals where allowed by statute

and judges who practice in juvenile court receive little respect. The juvenile court has a negative image, because even though what it does is of great importance to parents, children, and society in general, it has been placed at the lowest level of the judicial hierarchy.

JUVENILE COURT PROCESS

Now that we have briefly described the setting of the juvenile court and the major players who control its operations, we turn to a discussion of the procedures that shape the contours of juvenile justice—the pretrial process and the juvenile trial and disposition. Many critical decisions are made at this stage in the juvenile justice system: whether to detain a youth or release the youth to the community; whether to waive youths to the adult court or retain them in the juvenile justice system; whether to treat them in the community or send them to a secure treatment center. Each of these can have a profound influence on the child, with effects lasting throughout the life course. What are these critical stages, and how are decisions made within them?

Release or Detain?

After a child has been taken into custody and a decision is made to treat the case formally (that is, with a juvenile court hearing), a decision must be made either to release the child into the custody of parents or to detain the child in the temporary care of the state, in physically restrictive facilities pending court disposition or transfer to another agency.[23] Nationally, about 70 percent of all states have **detention** centers administered at the county level; about 34 percent have state-level facilities, 16 percent have court-administered facilities, and 11 percent contract with private vendors to operate facilities.[24]

detention
Temporary care of a child alleged to be delinquent who requires secure custody in physically restricting facilities pending court disposition or execution of a court order.

Detention can be a traumatic experience because many facilities are prisonlike, with locked doors and barred windows. Consequently, most experts in juvenile justice advocate that detention be limited to alleged offenders who require secure custody for the protection of themselves and others. However, children who are neglected and dependent, runaways, and those who are homeless may under some circumstances be placed in secure detention facilities along with violent and dangerous youths until more suitable placements can be found.[25] Others have had a trial but have not been sentenced, or are awaiting the imposition of their sentence. Some may have violated probation and are awaiting a hearing while being kept alongside a severely mentally ill adolescent for whom no appropriate placement can be found. Another group are adjudicated delinquents awaiting admittance to a correctional training school.[26] Consequently, it is possible for nonviolent status offenders to be housed in the same facility with delinquents who have committed felony-type offenses. A recent study of child detention centers in New Jersey found that one out of every four youths in the centers (about 2,500 out of 10,000) were placed there inappropriately and should have instead been placed in hospitals, foster care homes, or other noncustodial settings. Because of the inappropriate placement in detention facilities, many of these youths were preyed upon by violent youth, did not receive much needed medical or mental care, and resorted to self-harm or suicide attempts as a way to cope or escape from the dangerous and chaotic setting.[27]

shelter care
A place for temporary care of children in physically unrestricting facilities.

To remedy these situations, an ongoing effort has been made to remove status offenders and neglected or abused children from detention facilities that also house juvenile delinquents. In addition, alternatives to detention centers—temporary foster homes, detention boarding homes, and programs of neighborhood supervision—have been developed. These alternatives, referred to as **shelter care**, enable youths to live in a more homelike setting while the courts dispose of their cases.

Project Confirm in New York City is one example of an effort to reduce the detention of foster care youths who have been arrested. Very often these youths who otherwise would have been released are placed in detention facilities because their guardians fail to appear in court, a result of a breakdown in communication between (and within) the child welfare and juvenile justice systems. The project involved two main strategies to overcome this problem: notifying project staff upon a youth's arrest to allow for a search of child welfare databases, and court conferencing among child welfare and juvenile justice authorities. An evaluation of the project found that disparity in detention experienced by foster care youths compared to a similar group of non–foster care youths was reduced among those charged with minor offenses and with no prior detentions but increased among those charged with more serious offenses and prior police contact. The authors speculate that the improved quality of information provided by the project to the court, especially prior detentions, coupled with court officials' preconceived notions of the likelihood of these youths to commit another crime or fail to appear in court, resulted in more serious cases being detained.[28]

National Detention Trends Despite an ongoing effort to limit detention, juveniles are still being detained in one out of every five delinquency cases (21 percent), with some variation across the major offense categories: violent (28 percent), property (19 percent), drugs (22 percent), and public order (30 percent). Although the detention rate for delinquency cases is slightly down in recent years, over the last 10 years (1995 to 2004), the total number of juveniles held in short-term detention facilities increased 40 percent, from 292,300 to 408,400.[29]

The typical delinquent detainee is male, over 16 years of age, and charged with a violent crime,[30] whereas the typical status offenses detainee is female, under 16 years of age, and a runaway.[31] Racial minorities are heavily overrepresented in detention (see Figure 15.1), especially those who are indigent and whose families may be receiving public assistance. Minority overrepresentation is particularly vexing, considering that detention may increase the risk of a youth being adjudicated and eventually confined.[32]

Why Is Detention Increasing? The recent increase in detention use among juvenile offenders may result from the steady growth in the number of offenders. However, some things about juvenile detention have not changed: There remains a serious problem of overrepresentation of minorities in secure detention.[33] In a study of the extent of racial discrimination and disparity among male juvenile property offenders in six Missouri counties at four stages of juvenile justice (decision to file a petition, pretrial detention, adjudication, and disposition), it was found that African American youth were more likely than white youth to be detained prior to adjudication (40 percent compared to 22 percent).[34] The study also found that African American youth were more likely to be formally referred and white youth were more likely to be adjudicated. The authors speculate that a "correction of biases" may be one of the reasons for white youth being more likely than African American youth to be adjudicated; that is, "judges may dismiss black youths because they feel that a detained youth has been punished enough already."[35]

The Decision to Detain Most children taken into custody by the police are released to their parents or guardians. Some are held overnight until their parents can be notified of the arrest. Police officers normally take a child to a place of detention only after other alternatives have been exhausted. Many juvenile courts in urban areas have staff members, such as intake probation officers, on duty 24 hours a day to screen detention admissions.

Ordinarily, delinquent children are detained if the police believe they are inclined to run away while awaiting trial, or if they are likely to commit an offense dangerous to the parent. There is evidence that some decision makers are more likely to detain minority youth, especially if they live in dangerous, lower-class areas.[36]

Generally, children should not be held in a detention facility or shelter care unit for more than 24 hours without a formal petition (a written request to the court) being filed to extend the detention period. To detain a juvenile, there must be clear evidence of probable cause that the child has committed the offense and that he or she will flee if not detained. Although the requirements for detention hearings vary,

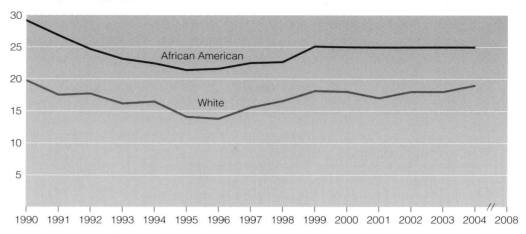

Percent of cases detained

FIGURE 15.1
Cases Involving Detention of African American Juveniles vs. White Juveniles

SOURCE: Office of Juvenile Justice and Delinquency Prevention, *OJJDP Statistical Briefing Book.* Released on March 19, 2007. Available at http://ojjdp.ncjrs.gov/ojstatbb/ (accessed July 27, 2007).

most jurisdictions require that they occur almost immediately after the child's admission to a detention facility and provide the youth with notice and counsel.

New Approaches to Detention Efforts have been ongoing to improve the process and conditions of detention. Experts maintain that detention facilities should provide youth with education, visitation, private communications, counseling, continuous supervision, medical and health care, nutrition, recreation, and reading. Detention should also include, or provide, a system for clinical observation and diagnosis that complements the wide range of helpful services.[37]

The consensus today is that juvenile detention centers should be reserved for youths who present a clear threat to the community. In some states, nonsecure facilities are being used to service juveniles for a limited period. Alternatives to secure detention include in-home monitoring, home detention, day-center electronic monitoring, high-intensity community supervision, and comprehensive case management programs. The successful Detention Diversion Advocacy Program (DDAP) relies on a case management strategy. Because this is an important development, it is covered in more detail in the accompanying Policy and Practice feature.

Undoubtedly, juveniles pose special detention problems, but some efforts are being made to improve programs and to reduce pretrial detention use, especially in secure settings. Of all the problems associated with detention, however, none is as critical as the issue of placing youths in adult jails.

Restricting Detention in Adult Jails A significant problem in juvenile justice is placing youths in adult jails. This is usually done in rural areas where no other facility exists. Almost all experts agree that placing children under the age of 18 in any type of jail facility should be prohibited because youngsters can easily be victimized by other inmates and staff, be forced to live in squalid conditions, and be subject to physical and sexual abuse.

Until a few years ago, placing juveniles in adult facilities was common, but efforts have been made to change this situation. In 1989, the Juvenile Justice and Delinquency Prevention Act (JJDPA) of 1974 was amended to require that the states remove all juveniles from adult jails and lockups. According to federal guidelines, all juveniles in state custody must be separated from adult offenders, or the state could lose federal juvenile justice funds. The OJJDP defines separation as the condition in which juvenile detainees have either totally independent facilities or shared facilities that are designed so that juveniles and adults neither have contact nor share programs or staff.[38]

The Detention Diversion Advocacy Program

The concept behind the Detention Diversion Advocacy Program (DDAP) approach is case advocacy employing the efforts of a staff of laypersons or non–legal experts acting on behalf of youthful offenders at disposition hearings. It relies on a case management strategy that involves coordination of human services, opportunities, or benefits. Case management efforts are designed to integrate services within a cluster of organizations, to ensure continuity of care, and to facilitate development of client skills (for example, job interviewing or reading and writing skills) by involving a variety of social networks and service providers (social agencies that provide specific services to youth, such as drug counseling and crisis intervention).

Detention advocacy involves identifying youths likely to be detained pending their adjudication. Detention Diversion Advocacy Program clients are identified primarily through referrals from the public defender's office, the probation department, community agencies, and parents. Admission to DDAP is restricted to youths currently held, or likely to be held, in secure detention. Once a potential client is identified, DDAP case managers present a release plan to the judge that includes a list of appropriate community services (tutoring, drug counseling, family counseling) that will be made available on the youth's behalf. Additionally, the plan includes specified objectives (improved grades, victim restitution, drug-free status) as a means of evaluating the youth's progress in the program. Emphasis is placed on allowing the youth to live at home while going through the program. If home placement is not a viable option, program staff will identify and secure a suitable alternative. If the judge deems the release plan acceptable, the youth is released to DDAP supervision.

The DDAP case management model provides frequent and consistent support and supervision to youths and their families. Case managers link youths to community-based services and closely monitor their progress. The DDAP program requires the case manager to have daily contact with the youth, the family,

and significant others, including a minimum of three in-person meetings a week with the youth. The youth's family members, particularly parents and guardians, are provided with additional services that typically include assistance in securing employment, daycare, drug treatment services, and income support (for example, food stamps).

Evaluations of the DDAP program have indicated that it is very successful:

- The overall recidivism rate of the DDAP group is 34 percent, compared with 60 percent for the comparison group.
- Fourteen percent of the DDAP group have two or more subsequent referrals, compared with 50 percent of the comparison group.
- Nine percent of the DDAP group return to court on a violent crime charge, compared with 25 percent of the comparison group.
- Five percent of the DDAP group have two or more subsequent petitions, compared with 22 percent of the comparison group.

Critical Thinking

1. Should adolescents be detained for nonviolent offenses such as substance abuse and/or theft?

2. Do you believe that the decision to detain a child is based on an evaluation of the child's behavior or his/her parent's behavior and ability to provide care and supervision? If the latter, is that a violation of due process? In other words, why should children be punished for the shortcomings of their parents?

SOURCE: Randall G. Shelden, "Detention Diversion Advocacy: An Evaluation," *Juvenile Justice Bulletin* (Washington, DC: Office of Juvenile Justice and Delinquency Prevention, 1999).

Much debate has arisen over whether the initiative to remove juveniles from adult jails has succeeded. Most indications are that the number of youths being held in adult facilities has declined significantly from the almost 500,000 a year recorded in 1979.[39]

Removing Status Offenders Along with removing all juveniles from adult jails, the OJJDP has made deinstitutionalization of status offenders a cornerstone of its policy. The Juvenile Justice and Delinquency Prevention Act of 1974 prohibits the placement of status offenders in secure detention facilities.

Removing status offenders from secure facilities serves two purposes: (1) It reduces interaction with serious offenders, and (2) it insulates status offenders from the stigma associated with being a detainee in a locked facility. Efforts appear to be working, and the number of status offenders being held in some sort of secure confinement has been on a two-decade decline. Nonetheless, the debate over the most effective way to handle juvenile status offenders continues, and some critics have argued that if the juvenile court is unable to take effective action in status offender cases, it should be stripped of jurisdiction over these youths. Most judges would prefer to retain jurisdiction so they can help children and families resolve problems that cause runaways, truancy, and other status offense behaviors.[40]

Bail for Children

One critical pretrial issue is whether juveniles can be released on bail. Adults retain the right, via the Eighth Amendment to the Constitution, to reasonable bail in noncapital cases. Most states, however, refuse juveniles the right to bail. They argue that juvenile proceedings are civil, not criminal, and that detention is rehabilitative, not punitive. In addition, they argue that juveniles do not need a constitutional right to bail because statutory provisions allow children to be released into parental custody.

State juvenile bail statutes fall into three categories: (1) those guaranteeing the right to bail, (2) those that grant the court discretion to give bail, and (3) those that deny a juvenile the right to bail.[41] This disparity may be a function of the lack of legal guidance on the matter. The U.S. Supreme Court has never decided the issue of juvenile bail. Some courts have stated that bail provisions do not apply to juveniles. Others rely on the Eighth Amendment against cruel and unusual punishment, or on state constitutional provisions or statutes, and conclude that juveniles do have a right to bail.

Preventive Detention Although the U.S. Supreme Court has not yet decided whether juveniles have a right to traditional money bail, they have concluded that the state has a right to detain dangerous youths until their trial, a practice called preventive detention. On June 4, 1984, the U.S. Supreme Court dealt with this issue in *Schall v. Martin*, when it upheld the state of New York's preventive detention statute.[42] However, the case also established a due process standard for detention hearings that includes notice and a statement of substantial reasons for the detention. Despite these measures, opponents hold that preventive detention deprives offenders of their freedom because guilt has not been proven. It is also unfair, they claim, to punish people for what judicial authorities believe they may do in the future, as it is impossible to predict who will be a danger to the community. Moreover, because judges are able to use discretion in their detention decisions, an offender could unfairly be deprived of freedom without legal recourse. Today, most states allow "dangerous" youths to be held indefinitely before trial. Because preventive detention may attach a stigma of guilt to a child presumed innocent, the practice remains a highly controversial one, and the efficacy of such laws remains unknown.[43]

The Intake Process

The term intake refers to the screening of cases by the juvenile court system. The child and his or her family are screened by intake officers to determine whether the services of the juvenile court are needed. Intake officers may (a) send the youth home with no further action, (b) divert the youth to a social agency, (c) petition the youth to the juvenile court, or (d) file a petition and hold the youth in detention. The intake process reduces demands on court resources, screens out cases that are not within the court's jurisdiction, and enables assistance to be obtained from community agencies without court intervention. Juvenile court intake is provided for by statute in almost all of the states.

After reviewing the case, justice system authorities decide whether to dismiss, informally handle, or formally process the case by taking the matter before a judge. About 17 percent (281,700) of all delinquency cases in 2004 were dismissed at intake, often because they were not legally sufficient. Another 26 percent (438,200) were processed informally, with the juvenile voluntarily agreeing to the recommended disposition (for example, voluntary treatment).[44]

Intake screening allows juvenile courts to enter into consent decrees with juveniles without filing petitions and without formal adjudication. The consent decree is a court order authorizing disposition of the case without a formal label of delinquency. It is based on an agreement between the intake department of the court and the juvenile who is the subject of the complaint.

But intake also suffers from some problems. Although almost all state juvenile court systems provide intake and diversion programs, there are few formal criteria for selecting children for such alternatives. There are also legal problems associated

The intake process involves the screening of cases by the juvenile court system. Intake officers, who are often probation staff members, determine whether the services of the juvenile court are needed. Here, juvenile offenders beginning the intake process are searched by a correctional officer at the Department of Youth Services Detention Center in Rathbone, Ohio.

with the intake process. Among them are whether the child has a right to counsel, whether the child is protected against self-incrimination, and to what degree the child needs to consent to nonjudicial disposition as recommended by the intake officer. Finally, intake dispositions are often determined by the prior record rather than by the seriousness of the offense or the social background of the child. This practice departs from the philosophy of *parens patriae*.[45]

Diversion

One of the most important alternatives chosen at intake is nonjudicial disposition or, as it is variously called, nonjudicial adjustment, handling or processing, informal disposition, adjustment, or (most commonly) **diversion**. Juvenile diversion is the process of placing youths suspected of law-violating behavior into treatment-oriented programs prior to formal trial and disposition in order to minimize their penetration into the justice system and thereby avoid stigma and labeling.

diversion
Official halting or suspending of a formal criminal or juvenile justice proceeding at any legally prescribed processing point after a recorded justice system entry, and referral of that person to a treatment or care program or a recommendation that the person be released.

Diversion implies more than simply screening out cases for which no additional treatment is needed. Screening involves abandoning efforts to apply coercive measures to a defendant. In contrast, diversion encourages an individual to participate in some specific program or activity to avoid further prosecution.

Most court-based diversion programs employ a particular formula for choosing youths for diversion. Criteria such as being a first offender, a nonviolent offender, or a status offender, or being drug or alcohol dependent, are used to select clients. In some programs, youths will be asked to partake of services voluntarily in lieu of a court appearance. In other programs, prosecutors will agree to defer, and then dismiss, a case once a youth has completed a treatment program. Finally, some programs can be initiated by the juvenile court judge after an initial hearing. Concept Summary 15.1 lists the factors considered in diversion decisions.

Concept Summary 15.1
Who Gets Diversion?

Factors Considered	Criteria for Eligibility
Past criminal record	It is the juvenile's first offense.
Type of offense	It is a nonviolent or status offense.
Other circumstances	The juvenile abuses drugs or alcohol.

In sum, diversion programs have been created to remove nonserious offenders from the justice system, provide them with nonpunitive treatment services, and help them avoid the stigma of a delinquent label.

Issues in Diversion: Widening the Net Diversion has been viewed as a promising alternative to official procedures, but over the years its basic premises have been questioned.[46] The most damaging criticism has been that diversion programs are involving children in the juvenile justice system who previously would have been released without official notice. This is referred to as widening the net. Various studies indicate that police and court personnel are likely to use diversion programs for youths who ordinarily would have been turned loose at the intake or arrest stage.[47] Why does net-widening occur? One explanation is that police and prosecutors find diversion a more attractive alternative than both official processing and outright release—diversion helps them resolve the conflict between doing too much and doing too little.

Diversion has also been criticized as ineffective; that is, youths being diverted make no better adjustment in the community than those who go through official channels. However, not all experts are critical of diversion. Some challenge the net-widening concept as naive: How do we know that diverted youths would have had less interface with the justice system if diversion didn't exist?[48] Even if juveniles escaped official labels for their current offense, might they not eventually fall into the hands of the police? The rehabilitative potential of diversion should not be overlooked.[49] There is some evidence that diversion with a treatment component for juveniles suffering from mental health problems can delay or prevent further delinquent activity.[50]

Some experts even argue that diversion has been the centerpiece or at least a core element of the juvenile justice system's success in limiting the growth of juvenile incarceration rates over the last three decades, which were dwarfed by the dramatic increase in incarceration rates among young adult offenders (ages 18 to 24) over the same period of time.[51] In the words of legal scholar Franklin Zimring,

> the angry assaults on juvenile courts throughout the 1990s are a tribute to the efficacy of juvenile justice in protecting delinquents from the incarcerative explosion that had happened everywhere else.[52]

The Petition

A complaint is the report made by the police or some other agency to the court to initiate the intake process. Once the agency makes a decision that judicial disposition is required, a petition is filed. The petition is the formal complaint that initiates judicial action against a juvenile charged with delinquency or a status offense. The petition includes basic information such as the name, age, and residence of the child; the parents' names; and the facts alleging the child's delinquency. The police officer, a family member, or a social service agency can file a petition.

If after being given the right to counsel, the child admits the allegation in the petition, an initial hearing is scheduled for the child to make the admission before the court, and information is gathered to develop a treatment plan. If the child does not admit to any of the facts in the petition, a date is set for a hearing on the petition. This hearing, whose purpose is to determine the merits of the petition, is similar to the adult trial. Once a hearing date has been set, the probation department is normally asked to prepare a social study report. This predisposition report contains relevant information about the child, along with recommendations for treatment and service.

When a date has been set for the hearing on the petition, parents or guardians and other persons associated with the petition (witnesses, the arresting police officer, and victims) are notified. On occasion, the court may issue a summons—a court order requiring the juvenile or others involved in the case to appear for the hearing. The statutes in a given jurisdiction govern the contents of the petition. Some jurisdictions,

widening the net
Phenomenon that occurs when programs created to divert youths from the justice system actually involve them more deeply in the official process.

complaint
Report made by the police or some other agency to the court that initiates the intake process.

for instance, allow for a petition to be filed based on the information of the complainant alone. Others require that the petition be filed under oath or that an affidavit accompany the petition. Some jurisdictions authorize only one official, such as a probation officer or prosecutor, to file the petition. Others allow numerous officials, including family and social service agencies, to set forth facts in the petition.

The Plea and Plea Bargaining

In the adult criminal justice system, the defendant normally enters a plea of guilty or not guilty. More than 90 percent of all adult defendants plead guilty. A large proportion of those pleas involve **plea bargaining**, the exchange of prosecutorial and judicial concessions for guilty pleas.[53] Plea bargaining permits a defendant to plead guilty to a less-serious charge in exchange for an agreement by the prosecutor to recommend a reduced sentence to the court. In the case of juvenile justice, it involves a discussion between the child's attorney and the prosecutor by which the child agrees to plead guilty to obtain a reduced charge or a lenient sentence.

Few juvenile codes require a guilty or not-guilty plea when a petition is filed against a child. In most jurisdictions an initial hearing is held at which the child either submits to a finding of the facts or denies the petition.[54] If the child admits to the facts, the court determines an appropriate disposition. If the child denies the allegations, the case normally proceeds to trial. When a child enters no plea, the court ordinarily imposes a denial of the charges. This may occur where a juvenile doesn't understand the nature of the complaint or isn't represented by an attorney.

A high percentage of juvenile offenders enter guilty pleas; that is, they admit to the facts of the petition. How many of these pleas involve plea bargaining is unknown. In the past it was believed that plea bargaining was unnecessary in the juvenile justice system because there was little incentive to bargain in a system that does not have jury trials or long sentences. In addition, because the court must dispose of cases in the best interests of the child, plea negotiation seemed unnecessary. Consequently, there has long been a debate over the appropriateness of plea bargaining in juvenile justice. The arguments in favor of plea bargaining include lower court costs and efficiency. Counterarguments hold that plea bargaining with juveniles is an unregulated and unethical process. When used, experts believe the process requires the highest standards of good faith by the prosecutor.[55]

Plea bargaining negotiations generally involve one or more of the following: (a) reduction of a charge, (b) change in the proceedings from that of delinquency to a status offense, (c) elimination of possible waiver to the criminal court, and (d) agreements regarding dispositional programs for the child. In states where youths are subject to long mandatory sentences, reduction of the charges may have a significant impact on the outcome of the case. In states where youths may be waived to the adult court for committing certain serious crimes, a plea reduction may result in the juvenile courts maintaining jurisdiction.

There is little clear evidence on how much plea bargaining there is in the juvenile justice system, but it is apparent that such negotiations do take place and seem to be increasing. Joseph Sanborn found that about 20 percent of the cases processed in Philadelphia resulted in a negotiated plea. Most were for reduced sentences, typically probation in lieu of incarceration. Sanborn found that plea bargaining was a complex process, depending in large measure on the philosophy of the judge and the court staff. In general, he found it to have greater benefit for the defendants than for the court.[56]

In summary, the majority of juvenile cases that are not adjudicated seem to be the result of admissions to the facts rather than actual plea bargaining. Plea bargaining is less common in juvenile courts than in adult courts because incentives such as dropping multiple charges or substituting a misdemeanor for a felony are unlikely. Nonetheless, plea bargaining is firmly entrenched in the juvenile process. Any plea bargain, however, must be entered into voluntarily and knowingly; otherwise, the conviction may be overturned on appeal.

---

plea bargaining
The exchange of prosecutorial and judicial concessions for a guilty plea by the accused; plea bargaining usually results in a reduced charge or a more lenient sentence.

TRANSFER TO THE ADULT COURT

transfer process
Transfer of a juvenile offender from the jurisdiction of juvenile court to adult criminal court.

One of the most significant actions that can occur in the early court processing of a juvenile offender is the transfer process. Otherwise known as waiver, bindover, or removal, this process involves transferring a juvenile from the juvenile court to the adult criminal court. Virtually all state statutes allow for this kind of transfer.

The number of delinquency cases judicially waived to criminal court peaked in 1994 with 13,100 cases, an increase of 82 percent over the number of cases waived in 1985 (7,200). From 1994 to 2004 (the latest data available), however, the number of cases waived to criminal court has actually declined 29 percent to 9,300 cases, representing less than 1 percent of the formally processed delinquency caseload. Between 1985 and 2004, person offense cases were the most likely to be waived to criminal court.[57] Figure 15.2 shows numbers of delinquency cases waived to criminal court from 1990 to the present day.

Some youths who commit the most serious crimes are routinely waived to adult court, despite the fact that there has been a long-standing debate over the transfer of juveniles to adult court. Most juvenile justice experts oppose waiver because it clashes with the rehabilitative ideal. Those in favor of it cite the need for public protection. Here, a youth is held in an adult prison cell after having been adjudicated as an adult.

© Joel Gordon

Waiver Procedures

Today, all states allow juveniles to be tried as adults in criminal courts in one of three ways:

▌ *Concurrent jurisdiction.* In 15 states and the District of Columbia, the prosecutor has the discretion of filing charges for certain offenses in either juvenile or criminal court.

▌ *Statutory exclusion policies.* In 29 states, certain offenses are automatically excluded from juvenile court. These offenses can be minor, such as traffic violations, or serious, such as murder or rape. Statutory exclusion accounts for the largest number of juveniles tried as adults.

▌ *Judicial waiver.* In the waiver (or bindover or removal) of juvenile cases to criminal court, a hearing is held before a juvenile court judge, who then decides whether jurisdiction should be waived and the case transferred to criminal court. Forty-five states and the District of Columbia (not Massachusetts, Montana, Nebraska, New Mexico, or New York) offer provisions for juvenile waivers.[58]

Due Process in Transfer Proceedings

The standards for transfer procedures are set by state statute. Some jurisdictions allow for transfer between the ages of 14 and 17. Others restrict waiver

Cases judicially waived to criminal court

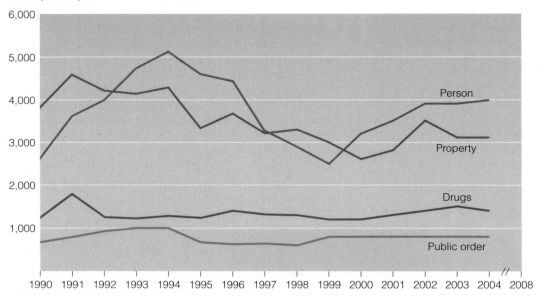

FIGURE 15.2

Delinquency Cases Waived to Criminal Court, by Type of Offense

SOURCE: Office of Juvenile Justice and Delinquency Prevention, *OJJDP Statistical Briefing Book.* Released on March 19, 2007. Available at http://ojjdp.ncjrs.gov/ojstatbb/ (accessed July 27, 2007).

proceedings to mature juveniles and specify particular offenses. In a few jurisdictions, any child can be transferred to the criminal court system, regardless of age.

Those states that have amended their waiver policies with statutory exclusion policies now exclude certain serious offenses from juvenile court jurisdiction. For example, Indiana excludes cases involving 16- and 17-year-olds charged with murder, drug and weapons offenses, and certain felonies and other person offenses. In Illinois, youths ages 13 and older who are charged with murder and youths ages 15 and older who are charged with drug and weapons offenses and certain felonies and other person offenses are automatically sent to criminal court. In Nevada and Pennsylvania, any child accused of murder, regardless of age, is tried before the criminal court.[59] Other jurisdictions use exclusion to remove traffic offenses and public-ordinance violations.

The trend toward excluding serious violent offenses from juvenile court jurisdictions is growing in response to the demand to get tough on crime. In addition, large numbers of youth under age 18 are tried as adults in states where the upper age of juvenile court jurisdiction is 15 or 16.

In a small number of states, statutes allow prosecutors to file particularly serious cases in either the juvenile court or the adult court.[60] Prosecutor discretion may occasionally be a more effective transfer mechanism than the waiver process, because the prosecutor can file a petition in criminal or juvenile court without judicial approval.

Since 1966, the U.S. Supreme Court and other federal and state courts have attempted to ensure fairness in the judicial waiver process by handing down decisions that spell out the need for due process. Two Supreme Court decisions, *Kent v. United States* (1966) and *Breed v. Jones* (1975), are relevant.[61] The *Kent* case declared a District of Columbia transfer statute unconstitutional and attacked the subsequent conviction of the child by granting him the specific due process rights of having an attorney present at the hearing and access to the evidence that would be used in the case.

The *Kent* case was significant because it examined for the first time the substantial degree of discretion associated with a transfer proceeding. Thus, the Supreme Court significantly limited its holding to the statute involved but justified its reference to constitutional principles relating to due process and the assistance of counsel. In addition, it said that the juvenile court waiver hearings need to measure up to the essentials of due process and fair treatment. Furthermore, in an appendix to its opinion, the Court set up criteria concerning waiver of the jurisdictions. These are

- The seriousness of the alleged offense to the community
- Whether the alleged offense was committed in an aggressive, violent, or willful manner
- Whether the alleged offense was committed against persons or against property
- The prosecutive merit of the complaint
- The sophistication and maturity of the juvenile
- The record and previous history of the juvenile
- Prospects for adequate protection of the public and the likelihood of reasonable rehabilitation

In *Breed v. Jones*, the U.S. Supreme Court declared that the child was to be granted the protection of the double jeopardy clause of the Fifth Amendment after he was tried as a delinquent in the juvenile court: Once found to be a delinquent, the youth can no longer be tried as an adult. The *Breed* case provided answers on several important transfer issues: (a) it prohibits trying a child in an adult court when there has been a prior adjudicatory juvenile proceeding; (b) probable cause may exist at a transfer hearing, and this does not violate subsequent jeopardy if the child is transferred to the adult court; and (c) because the same evidence is often used in both the transfer hearing and subsequent trial in either the juvenile or adult court, a different judge is often required for each hearing.

transfer hearing
Preadjudicatory hearing in juvenile court for the purpose of determining whether juvenile court should be retained over a juvenile or waived and the juvenile transferred to adult court for prosecution.

Today, as a result of *Kent* and *Breed*, states that have transfer hearings provide (a) a legitimate transfer hearing, (b) sufficient notice to the child's family and defense attorney, (c) the right to counsel, and (d) a statement of the reason for the court order regarding transfer. These procedures recognize that the transfer process is critical in determining the statutory rights of the juvenile offender.

Should Youths Be Transferred to Adult Court?

Most juvenile justice experts oppose waiver because it clashes with the rehabilitative ideal. Basing waiver decisions on type and seriousness of offense rather than on the rehabilitative needs of the child has advanced the *criminalization* of the juvenile court and interfered with its traditional mission of treatment and rehabilitation.[62] And despite this sacrifice, there is little evidence that strict waiver policies can lower crime rates.[63] This particularly important issue is the subject of the Focus on Delinquency feature entitled "Are Transfers to Adult Court Effective in Reducing Violence?"

Some experts also question whether juveniles waived to adult court, particularly younger ones, are competent to be tried as adults. Adjudicative competency pertains to the mental capacity or cognitive skills of the youth to understand the nature and object of the proceedings against him or her.[64] Two recent studies found that the mental competency of youths under the age of 16 to stand trial is far below that of similarly charged adults, with one study comparing the competency of young juvenile offenders to that of severely mentally impaired adults.[65]

Waiver can also create long-term harm. Waived children may be stigmatized by a conviction in the criminal court. Labeling children as adult offenders early in life may seriously impair their future educational, employment, and other opportunities. Youthful offenders convicted in adult courts are more likely to be incarcerated and to receive longer sentences than had they remained in the juvenile court. In one study in New York and New Jersey, juveniles transferred to criminal court were almost three times more likely to receive sentences of incarceration than juvenile court defendants (36 percent versus 14 percent).[66] In another study in Pennsylvania, the average sentence length for juvenile offenders sentenced in adult court was found to be significantly longer than for a similar group of young adult offenders (18 months compared to 6 months).[67] And these children may be incarcerated under conditions so extreme,

Are Transfers to Adult Court Effective in Reducing Violence?

In all the debate surrounding transfers of juvenile offenders to adult or criminal court, one of the most important issues—for some it is the bottom line on this matter—concerns whether or not transfers are effective in reducing crime rates. One of the pressing questions is: Are juveniles who are transferred to and convicted in adult court less likely to recidivate than similar youths who are convicted in juvenile court? This pertains to a specific or individual deterrent effect of transfers. Another key question, which pertains to a general deterrent effect, can be framed as such: Do transfers decrease crime rates in the juvenile population as a whole? This could be for a city or state, for example. In recent years, a number of high-quality studies have investigated the effectiveness of transfers on these two fronts.

The Task Force on Community Preventive Services, an independent group that receives support from the U.S. Department of Health and Human Services and the Centers for Disease Control and Prevention, conducted the first comprehensive, methodologically rigorous review of the literature—known as a systematic review—on the effects of transfer laws and policies on crime rates. The review identified six high-quality evaluation studies (each had experimental and comparable control groups) that measured the specific deterrent effect of transfers on violent crime rates. As shown in Figure 15-A, not one of the studies found that transfers produced lower violent crime rates.

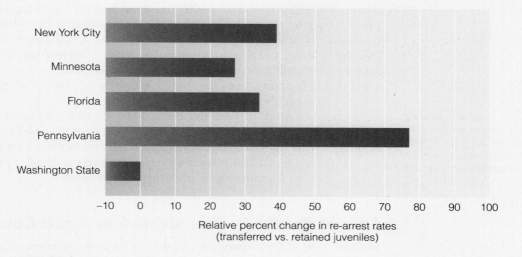

FIGURE 15-A

Effects of Transfer on Rearrests of Transferred Juveniles

SOURCE: Adapted from Angela McGowan et al., "Effects on Violence of Laws and Policies Facilitating the Transfer of Juveniles from the Juvenile Justice System to the Adult Justice System: A Systematic Review," *American Journal of Preventive Medicine* 32(4S):7–28 (2007), fig. 1.

and in institutions where they may be physically and sexually exploited, that they will become permanently damaged.[68] In a small-scale study of female youths transferred to criminal court and subsequently placed in a prison for adult women, it was found that the prison was severely limited in its ability to care for and provide needed treatment services for these youths compared with the adults.[69]

Waivers do not always support the goal of increased public protection. Because juveniles may only serve a fraction of the prison sentence imposed by the criminal court, the actual treatment of delinquents in adult court is similar to what they might have received had they remained in the custody of juvenile authorities.[70] Also, transferred juveniles convicted of felonies are not more likely to be sentenced to prison than similarly charged felons who are under the age of 18 but considered adults by the state.[71] This has prompted some critics to ask: Why bother transferring these children?

Sometimes waiver can add an undue burden to youthful offenders. Studies have found that although transfer to criminal court was intended for the most serious juvenile offenders, many transferred juveniles were not violent offenders but repeat property

In fact, four of the studies found a harmful effect, meaning that juveniles transferred to adult court had higher violent rearrest rates than their counterparts who were retained in juvenile court. For these four studies, rearrest rates for the transferred juveniles were between 27 percent and 77 percent higher than the nontransferred juveniles. The authors of the review also reported that these studies found harmful effects for total crime rates as well. (The sixth study, which also found similar harmful effects for violent crime but favorable effects for property crime, could not be presented in the figure because the review authors could not calculate a comparable effect size.) The Washington State study found that transfers to adult court made no difference: Violent crime rearrest rates were neither higher nor lower for transferred juveniles compared to retained juveniles 18 months after release from prison.

On the matter of a general deterrent effect of transfers, less could be said. The review identified three high-quality evaluation studies that measured whether transfer laws deter juveniles in the general population from violent crime. Inconsistent results were found across the studies: One study reported no effect, one reported mixed effects, and one reported harmful effects. Based on these inconsistent results, the task force concluded that there was insufficient evidence at present to make a determination on the effectiveness of transfer laws and policies in reducing juvenile violence generally.

A more recent study on the general deterrent effects of transfer, the largest and perhaps most rigorous one yet to investigate this question, may shed some light on these inconsistent results. (This study was not included in the systematic review because it was outside of the review's publication date cutoff.) Criminologists Benjamin Steiner, Craig Hemmens, and Valerie Bell examined 22 states that enacted statutory exclusion or automatic transfer laws after 1979. The study found no reduction in arrest rates for violent juvenile crime in 21 of the 22 states over a period of five years following the introduction of the transfer law. Only Maine experienced a reduction in its juvenile arrest rate for violent crime, a reduction that was both immediate and permanent, and thus could be said to provide support for a general deterrent effect of the transfer law.

Based on the overall findings, the Task Force on Community Preventive Services concluded that transferring juvenile offenders to the adult system is "counterproductive for the purpose of reducing juvenile violence and enhancing public safety." The task force did not go so far as to recommend that states repeal their transfer laws and discontinue the practice of transfers altogether, possibly because of the inconsistent results found for general deterrent effects. Legal scholar Michael Tonry, in commenting on the task force's report, says it is time that some of these changes to take place. He also calls for more individualized treatment for juvenile offenders, noting that, "One-size-fits-all policies inevitably produce anomalies, injustices, and unwanted side effects (including increased violent re-offending)."

Critical Thinking

1. Based on this research evidence, what would you recommend to your state legislator? Should the practice of transferring juvenile offenders to adult court be ceased altogether or should transfers be used only in isolated cases involving extreme violence? Or do you remain unconvinced by this research and feel transfers should continue as they are? Explain.

2. While the effects of transfers on crime rates is important, what are some other key issues that need to be considered? Discuss.

SOURCES: Angela McGowan, Robert Hahn, Akiva Liberman, Alex Crosby, Mindy Fullilove, Robert Johnson, Eve Mosciki, LeShawndra Price, Susan Snyder, Farris Tuma, Jessica Lowy, Peter Briss, Stella Cory, Glenda Stone, and the Task Force on Community Preventive Services, "Effects on Violence of Laws and Policies Facilitating the Transfer of Juveniles from the Juvenile Justice System to the Adult Justice System: A Systematic Review," *American Journal of Preventive Medicine* 32(4S):7–28 (2007); Michael Tonry, "Treating Juveniles as Adult Criminals: An Iatrogenic Violence Prevention Strategy if Ever There Was One," *American Journal of Preventive Medicine* 32(4S):3–4 (2007); Benjamin Steiner, Craig Hemmens, and Valerie Bell, "Legislative Waiver Reconsidered: General Deterrent Effects of Statutory Exclusion Laws Enacted Post-1979," *Justice Quarterly* 23:34–59 (2006).

offenders.[72] Cases involving waiver take significantly longer than comparable juvenile court cases, during which time the waived youth is more likely to be held in a detention center. This finding is vexing, considering that some research shows that many waived youths were no more dangerous than youths who remain in juvenile courts.[73]

Transfer decisions are not always carried out fairly or equitably, and there is evidence that minorities are waived at a rate that is greater than their representation in the population.[74] Just over two-fifths (42 percent) of all waived youth are African Americans, even though they represent 31 percent of the juvenile court population.[75] A federal study of transfer in the nation's 40 largest counties found that 62 percent of waived youth were African American.[76] Between the peak year of 1994 and 2004, the number of judicially waived cases involving African American youth decreased 31 percent (from 5,336 to 3,670). A similar decrease (30 percent) was reported for white youth during the same time period (from 6,742 to 4,738).[77] Transfer decisions are also susceptible to overzealous district attorneys. This happened in the "Jena Six" case, when Mychall Bell, age 16, was transferred to adult court (see Chapter 4).

In Support of Waiver Not all experts challenge the waiver concept. Waiver is attractive to conservatives because it jibes with the get-tough policy currently popular. Some have argued that the increased use of waiver can help get violent offenders off the streets and should be mandatory for juveniles committing serious violent crimes.[78] Others point to studies that show that, for the most part, transfer is reserved for the most serious cases and the most serious juvenile offenders. Kids are most likely to be transferred to criminal court if they have injured someone with a weapon or if they have a long juvenile court record.[79] The most recent federal study of waiver found that 27 percent of juveniles tried in criminal court were sent to prison. This outcome might be expected because those waived to criminal court were more likely (64 percent) than adults (24 percent) to be charged with a violent felony. These juvenile defendants were generally regarded as serious offenders, because 52 percent did not receive pretrial release, 63 percent were convicted of a felony, and 43 percent of those convicted received a prison sentence.[80] In an analysis of a Virginia statute that grants prosecutors the authority to certify a juvenile offender to criminal court at intake, it was found that serious offenders were more likely to be waived to criminal court.[81] Clearly, many waived juveniles might be considered serious offenders.

Franklin Zimring argues that, despite its faults, waiver is superior to alternative methods for handling the most serious juvenile offenders.[82] Some cases involving serious offenses, he argues, require a minimum criminal penalty greater than that available to the juvenile court. It is also possible that some juveniles take advantage of decisions to transfer them to the adult court. Although the charge against a child may be considered serious in the juvenile court, the adult criminal court will not find it so; consequently, a child may have a better chance for dismissal of the charges or acquittal after a jury trial.

In sum, though the use of waiver has been in decline, it is still an important strategy for attacking serious youth crime.[83] Its continued use can be attributed to the get-tough attitude toward the serious juvenile offender.

JUVENILE COURT TRIAL

To get **information on juvenile courts**, go to the website of the **National Center for State Courts** via academic.cengage.com/ criminaljustice/siegel.

If the case cannot be decided during the pretrial stage, it will be brought forth for a trial in the juvenile court. An adjudication hearing is held to determine the merits of the petition claiming that a child is either a delinquent youth or in need of court supervision. The judge is required to make a finding based on the evidence and arrive at a judgment. Adjudication is comparable to an adult trial. Rules of evidence in adult criminal proceedings are generally applicable in juvenile court, and the standard of proof used—*beyond a reasonable doubt*—similar to that used in adult trials.

State juvenile codes vary with regard to the basic requirements of due process and fairness. Most juvenile courts have bifurcated hearings—that is, separate hearings for adjudication and disposition (sentencing). At disposition hearings, evidence can be submitted that reflects nonlegal factors such as the child's home life.

Most state juvenile codes provide specific rules of procedure, which have several purposes: They require that a written petition be submitted to the court, ensure the right of a child to have an attorney, provide that the adjudication proceedings be recorded, allow the petition to be amended, and provide that a child's plea be accepted. Where the child admits to the facts of the petition, the court generally seeks assurance that the plea is voluntary. If plea bargaining is used, prosecutors, defense counsel, and trial judges take steps to ensure the fairness of such negotiations.

At the end of the adjudication hearing, most juvenile court statutes require the judge to make a factual finding on the legal issues and evidence. In the criminal court, this finding is normally a prelude to reaching a verdict. In the juvenile court, however, the finding itself is the verdict—the case is resolved in one of three ways:

▌ The juvenile court judge makes a finding of fact that the child or juvenile is not delinquent or in need of supervision.

- The juvenile court judge makes a finding of fact that the juvenile is delinquent or in need of supervision.

- The juvenile court judge dismisses the case because of insufficient or faulty evidence.

In some jurisdictions, informal alternatives are used, such as filing the case with no further consequences or continuing the case without a finding for a period of time, such as six months. If the juvenile does not get into further difficulty during that time, the case is dismissed. These alternatives involve no determination of delinquency or noncriminal behavior. Because of the philosophy of the juvenile court that emphasizes rehabilitation over punishment, a delinquency finding is not the same thing as a criminal conviction. The disabilities associated with conviction, such as disqualifications for employment or being barred from military service, do not apply in an adjudication of delinquency.

There are other differences between adult and juvenile proceedings. For instance, while adults are entitled to public trials by a jury of their peers, these rights are not extended to juveniles.[84] Because juvenile courts are treating some defendants similar to adult criminals, an argument can be made that the courts should extend to these youths the Sixth Amendment right to a public jury trial.[85] For the most part, however, state juvenile courts operate without recognizing a juvenile's constitutional right to a jury trial.

Constitutional Rights at Trial

In addition to mandating state juvenile code requirements, the U.S. Supreme Court has mandated the application of constitutional due process standards to the juvenile trial. **Due process** is addressed in the Fifth and Fourteenth Amendments to the U.S. Constitution. It refers to the need for rules and procedures that protect individual rights. Having the right to due process means that no person can be deprived of life, liberty, or property without such protections as legal counsel, an open and fair hearing, and an opportunity to confront those making accusations against him or her.

For many years, children were deprived of their due process rights because the *parens patriae* philosophy governed their relationship to the juvenile justice system. Such rights as having counsel and confronting one's accusers were deemed unnecessary. After all, why should children need protection from the state when the state was seen as acting in their interest? As we have seen, this view changed in the 1960s, when the U.S. Supreme Court began to grant due process rights and procedures to minors. The key case was that of Gerald Gault; it articulated the basic requirements of due process that must be satisfied in juvenile court proceedings.[86]

The *Gault* decision was significant not only because of the procedural reforms it initiated but also because of its far-reaching impact throughout the entire juvenile justice system. *In re Gault* instilled in juvenile proceedings the development of due process standards at the pretrial, trial, and posttrial stages of the juvenile process. While recognizing the history and development of the juvenile court, it sought to accommodate the motives of rehabilitation and treatment with children's rights. It recognized the principle of fundamental fairness of the law for children as well as for adults. Judged in the context of today's juvenile justice system, *In re Gault* redefined the relationships among juveniles, their parents, and the state. It remains the single most significant constitutional case in the area of juvenile justice.

The *Gault* decision reshaped the constitutional and philosophical nature of the juvenile court system and, with the addition of legal representation, made it more similar to the adult system.[87] Following the *Gault* case, the U.S. Supreme Court decided in *In re Winship* that the amount of proof required in juvenile delinquency adjudications is "beyond a reasonable doubt," a level equal to the requirements in the adult system.[88]

due process
Basic constitutional principle based on the concept of the primacy of the individual and the complementary concept of limitation on governmental power; safeguards the individual from unfair state procedures in judicial or administrative proceedings. Due process rights have been extended to juvenile trials.

For a review of **due process issues in juvenile justice**, go to academic.cengage.com/criminaljustice/siegel.

The appeal of Gerald Gault (center) heralded in the due process revolution in juvenile justice. The case *In re Gault* redefined the relationships among juveniles, their parents, and the state. It remains the single most significant constitutional case in the area of juvenile justice.

Although the ways in which the juvenile court operates were altered by *In re Gault* and *In re Winship*, the trend toward increased rights for juveniles was somewhat curtailed by the U.S. Supreme Court's decision in *McKeiver v. Pennsylvania* (1971), which held that trial by jury in a juvenile court's adjudicative stage is not a constitutional requirement.[89] This decision does not prevent states from giving the juvenile a trial by jury, but in the majority of states a child has no such right.

Once an adjudicatory hearing has been completed, the court is normally required to enter a judgment or finding against the child. This may take the form of declaring the child delinquent, adjudging the child to be a ward of the court, or possibly even suspending judgment so as to avoid the stigma of a juvenile record. After a judgment has been entered, the court can begin its determination of possible dispositions.

Disposition

The sentencing step of the juvenile justice process is called disposition. At this point the court orders treatment for the juvenile.[90] According to prevailing juvenile justice philosophy, dispositions should be in the *best interest of the child*, which in this context means providing the help necessary to resolve or meet the adolescent's personal needs, while at the same time meeting society's needs for protection.

As already mentioned, in most jurisdictions, adjudication and disposition hearings are separated, or bifurcated, so that evidence that could not be entered during the juvenile trial can be considered at the dispositional hearing. At the hearing, the defense counsel represents the child, helps the parents understand the court's decision, and influences the direction of the disposition. Others involved at the dispositional stage include representatives of social service agencies, psychologists, social workers, and probation personnel.

The Predisposition Report After the child has admitted to the allegations, or the allegations have been proved in a trial, the judge normally orders the probation department to complete a predisposition report. The predisposition report, which is similar to the presentence report of the adult justice system, has a number of purposes:

I It helps the judge decide which disposition is best for the child.

I It aids the juvenile probation officer in developing treatment programs if the child is in need of counseling or community supervision.

I It helps the court develop a body of knowledge about the child that can aid others in treating the child.[91]

Sources of dispositional data include family members, school officials, and statements from the juvenile offenders themselves. The results of psychological testing, psychiatric evaluations, and intelligence testing may be relevant. Furthermore, the probation officer might include information about the juvenile's feelings concerning his or her case.

Some state statutes make the predisposition report mandatory. Other jurisdictions require the report only when there is a probability that the child will be institutionalized. Some appellate courts have reversed orders institutionalizing children where the juvenile court did not use a predisposition report in reaching its decision. Access to predisposition reports is an important legal issue.

In the final section of the predisposition report, the probation department recommends a disposition to the presiding judge. This is a critical aspect of the report because it has been estimated that the court follows more than 90 percent of all probation department recommendations.

Juvenile Court Dispositions Historically, the juvenile court has had broad discretionary power to make dispositional decisions. The major categories of dispositional choices are (a) community release, (b) out-of-home placements, (c) fines or restitution, (d) community service, and (e) institutionalization. A more detailed list of the dispositions open to the juvenile court judge appears in Exhibit 15.3.[92]

Most state statutes allow the juvenile court judge to select whatever disposition seems best suited to the child's needs, including institutionalization. In some states the court determines commitment to a specific institution; in other states the youth corrections agency determines where the child will be placed. In addition to the dispositions in Exhibit 15.3, some states grant the court the power to order parents into treatment or to suspend a youth's driver's license. The Case Profile entitled "Cliff's Story" highlights the need for innovative dispositions to address the multifaceted needs of young people who come in conflict with the law.

Today it is common for juvenile court judges to employ a graduated sanction program for juveniles: (1) immediate sanctions for nonviolent offenders, which consist of community-based diversion and day treatment imposed on first-time, nonviolent offenders; (2) intermediate sanctions, which target repeat minor offenders and first-time serious offenders; and (3) secure care, which is reserved for repeat serious offenders and violent offenders.[93]

In 2004, juveniles were adjudicated delinquent in two-thirds (67 percent) of the 940,800 cases brought before a judge. Once adjudicated, the majority of these juveniles (63 percent or 393,100 cases) were placed on formal probation, just over one-fifth (22 percent or 140,700 cases) were placed in a residential facility, and 15 percent (or 94,900 cases) were given another disposition, such as referral to an outside agency, community service, or restitution.[94]

Although the juvenile court has been under pressure to get tough on youth crime, these figures show that probation is the disposition of choice, even in the most serious cases,[95] and its use has grown in recent years. Between 1985 and 2004, the number of cases in which the court ordered an adjudicated delinquent to be placed on formal probation increased 109 percent (from 188,400 to 393,100), while the number of cases involving placement in a residential facility increased 34 percent (from 105,200 to 140,700).[96] Figure 15.3 on page 515 shows recent changes in juvenile court placement of adjudicated youths for different crime types.

Cliff's Story

CLIFF IS A 16-YEAR-OLD CAUCASIAN YOUTH BEING RAISED BY HIS GRANDPARENTS IN A SMALL RURAL COMMUNITY. HE AND HIS YOUNGER SISTERS WERE REMOVED FROM their parental home when Cliff was 7 due to domestic violence and parental drug abuse. Although Cliff was well cared for by his grandparents, he engaged in several delinquent behaviors. He was charged with disorderly conduct for breaking windows in the family home and for threatening to physically assault his grandfather. Cliff was doing poorly in school; his grades dropped dramatically, and concerned family members were worried that he was using drugs.

Cliff began dating a girl he met at school, but her parents did not approve and they refused to allow her go out with him. Upset about the situation, Cliff reacted by taking his anger out on his family and by threatening suicide. He was hospitalized for an evaluation and diagnosed with bipolar disorder. He was at risk for being removed from the family home and placed in detention. Fortunately for Cliff, he received juvenile probation and was ordered by the court to receive a mental health assessment and treatment. Cliff also received medications and a referral for the Functional Family Therapy (FFT) intervention.

The FFT program has three phases that target juvenile delinquents and their families. During FFT intervention, other services to the family are stopped in order for the family to focus on the FFT process and plan. During the first phase of the program, attempts are made to engage and motivate all family members to participate in the process. Also during this initial phase, the family therapists focus on redefining the problem (Cliff's problematic behavior and mental health concerns) as a family issue, and encouraging family members to view the issues in a new light. Everyone has a part in the problem and thus in the solution. In the second phase the therapists work to help the family change their behaviors. They create real and obtainable goals and provide assistance to increase the family's problem-solving skills. This again takes the focus off the adolescent and distributes the responsibility among all family members. In the last phase, the therapists worked with Cliff's family to generalize their new skills to many different situations.

The FFT therapists worked with Cliff's family for 4 months, and then did follow-up calls at 6 and 12 months. They saw a reduction in Cliff's problematic behavior and criminal activity, as well as fewer calls to the police over the course of the intervention. ■

CRITICAL THINKING

1. How do you think this case may have ended if Cliff was initially placed in detention?

2. How should the juvenile justice system handle cases where adolescents are suffering from significant mental health issues and committing crimes? How might a teen's mental health issues affect his behavior and his ability to understand the consequences of this behavior? Should mental health treatment be court ordered? Should juvenile probation officers be required to have a solid understanding of mental health issues?

3. The Functional Family Therapy (FFT) approach takes the focus of the intervention off the adolescent and places responsibility on the entire family to create solutions. Why do you think it works for many juveniles involved in the justice system? What are your concerns about this approach? Do you think there are some situations where this type of intervention may not be appropriate or successful? Why?

Juvenile Sentencing Structures

For most of the juvenile court's history, disposition was based on the presumed needs of the child. Although critics have challenged the motivations of early reformers in championing rehabilitation, there is little question that the rhetoric of the juvenile court has promoted that ideal.[97] For example, in their classic work *Beyond the Best Interest of the Child*, Joseph Goldstein, Anna Freud, and Albert Solnit say that placement of children should be based on the least detrimental alternative available in

least detrimental alternative Choice of a program for the child that will best foster the child's growth and development.

EXHIBIT **15.3**

Common Juvenile Dispositions

Disposition		Action Taken
Informal consent decree	▮	In minor or first offenses, an informal hearing is held, and the judge will ask the youth and his or her guardian to agree to a treatment program, such as counseling. No formal trial or disposition hearing is held.
Probation	▮	A youth is placed under the control of the county probation department and is required to obey a set of probation rules and participate in a treatment program.
Home detention	▮	A child is restricted to his or her home in lieu of a secure placement. Rules include regular school attendance, curfew observance, avoidance of alcohol and drugs, and notification of parents and the youth worker of the child's whereabouts.
Court-ordered school attendance	▮	If truancy was the problem that brought the youth to court, a judge may order mandatory school attendance. Some courts have established court-operated day schools and court-based tutorial programs staffed by community volunteers.
Financial restitution	▮	A judge can order the juvenile offender to make financial restitution to the victim. In most jurisdictions, restitution is part of probation (see Chapter 15), but in a few states, such as Maryland, restitution can be a sole order.
Fines	▮	Some states allow fines to be levied against juveniles age 16 and over.
Community service	▮	Courts in many jurisdictions require juveniles to spend time in the community working off their debt to society. Community service orders are usually reserved for victimless crimes, such as possession of drugs, or crimes against public order, such as vandalism of school property. Community service orders are usually carried out in schools, hospitals, or nursing homes.
Outpatient psychotherapy	▮	Youths who are diagnosed with psychological disorders may be required to undergo therapy at a local mental health clinic.
Drug and alcohol treatment	▮	Youths with drug- or alcohol-related problems may be allowed to remain in the community if they agree to undergo drug or alcohol therapy.
Commitment to secure treatment	▮	In the most serious cases a judge may order an offender admitted to a long-term treatment center, such as a training school, camp, ranch, or group home. These may be either state or privately run institutions, usually located in remote regions. Training schools provide educational, vocational, and rehabilitation programs in a secure environment (see Chapter 16).
Commitment to a residential community program	▮	Youths who commit crimes of a less serious nature but who still need to be removed from their homes can be placed in community-based group homes or halfway houses. They attend school or work during the day and live in a controlled, therapeutic environment at night.
Foster home placement	▮	Foster homes are usually used for dependent or neglected children and status offenders. Judges place delinquents with insurmountable problems at home in state-licensed foster care homes.

order to foster the child's development.[98] Most states have adopted this ideal in their sentencing efforts, and state courts usually insist that the purpose of disposition must be rehabilitation and not punishment.[99] Consequently, it is common for state courts to require judges to justify their sentencing decisions if it means that juveniles are to be incarcerated in a residential treatment center: They must set forth in writing the reasons for the placement, address the danger the child poses to society, and explain why a less-restrictive alternative has not been used.[100]

Traditionally, states have used the **indeterminate sentence** in juvenile court. In about half of the states, this means having the judge place the offender with the state department of juvenile corrections until correctional authorities consider the youth ready to return to society or until the youth reaches legal majority. A preponderance of states consider 18 to be the age of release; others peg the termination age at 19; a few can retain minority status until their 21st birthday. In practice, few youths remain in custody for the entire statutory period; juveniles are usually released if their rehabilitation has been judged to have progressed satisfactorily. This practice is referred to as the **individualized treatment model**.

indeterminate sentence
Does not specify the length of time the juvenile must be held; rather, correctional authorities decide when the juvenile is ready to return to society.

individualized treatment model
Each sentence must be tailored to the individual needs of the child.

When making disposition decisions, juvenile court judges may select programs that will enhance life skills and help youths form a positive bond with society. Here, Timothy Shanks, Jr., 15, is shown with his parents during his disposition hearing on April 19, 2006, in Columbus, Ohio. The juvenile court judge sentenced Shanks to at least six months in a juvenile institution for driving his girlfriend's car without a license during the crash that killed her.

determinate sentence
Specifies a fixed term of detention that must be served.

mandatory sentence
Defined by a statutory requirement that states the penalty to be set for all cases of a specific offense.

Another form of the indeterminate sentence allows judges to specify a maximum term. Under this form of sentencing, youths may be released if the corrections department considers them to be rehabilitated or they reach the automatic age of termination (usually 18 or 21). In states that stipulate a maximum sentence, the court may extend the sentence, depending on the youth's progress in the institutional facility.

A number of states have changed from an indeterminate to a determinate sentence. This means sentencing juvenile offenders to a fixed term of incarceration that must be served in its entirety. Other states have passed laws creating mandatory sentences for serious juvenile offenders. Juveniles receiving mandatory sentences are usually institutionalized for the full sentence and are not eligible for early parole. The difference between mandatory and determinate sentences is that the mandatory sentence carries a statutory requirement that a certain penalty be set in all cases on conviction for a specified offense.

Sentencing Reform

During the past decade there have been a number of attempts to create rational sentencing within juvenile justice. In some instances the goal has been to reduce judicial discretion, in others to toughen sentencing practices and create mandatory periods of incarceration for juveniles who commit serious crimes. However, not all statutory changes have had the desired effect. For instance, New York State has implemented a juvenile offender law requiring that juveniles accused of violent offenses be tried in criminal court as a get-tough-on-crime measure. Evaluations found many youths ended up receiving lighter sentences than they would have in the family court.[101]

Probably the best-known effort to reform sentencing in the juvenile court is the state of Washington's Juvenile Justice Reform Act of 1977. This act created a mandatory sentencing policy requiring juveniles ages 8 to 17 who are adjudicated delinquent to be confined in an institution for a minimum time.[102] The intent of the act was to make juveniles accountable for criminal behavior and to provide for punishment commensurate with the (a) age, (b) crime, and (c) prior history of the offender. Washington's approach is based on the principle of *proportionality*. How much time a youth must spend in confinement is established by the Juvenile Dispositions Standards

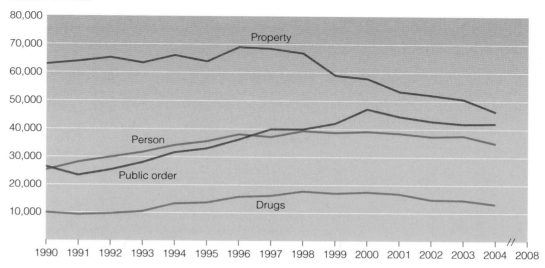

Number of cases

FIGURE 15.3
Juvenile Court Placement of Adjudicated Youths, by Type of Offense

NOTES: In 2004, a little more than one in five (22 percent) adjudicated delinquency cases resulted in out-of-home placement (i.e., placement in a residential treatment center, juvenile corrections facility, foster home, or group home); 63 percent resulted in an order of probation; and 15 percent resulted in some other disposition, such as restitution, fines, community service, or referral to other treatment agencies. Placement cases decreased 7 percent between 1995 and 2004.

SOURCE: Anne L. Stahl, T. Finnegan, and W. Kang, *Easy Access to Juvenile Court Statistics: 1985–2004.* Released in 2007. Available at http://ojjdp/ncjrs.gov/ojstatbb/ezajcs/ (accessed July 28, 2007).

Commission, based on the three stated criteria. The introduction of such mandatory-sentencing procedures reduces disparity in the length of sentences, according to advocates of a more punitive juvenile justice system.

Blended Sentences State sentencing trends indicate that punishment and accountability, in addition to rehabilitation, have become equally important in juvenile justice policy. As a result, many states have created blended sentencing structures for cases involving serious offenders. Blended sentencing allows the imposition of juvenile and adult sanctions for juvenile offenders adjudicated in juvenile court or convicted in criminal court. In other words, this expanded sentencing authority allows criminal and juvenile courts to impose either a juvenile or an adult sentence, or both, in cases involving juvenile offenders. When both sentences are imposed simultaneously, the court suspends the adult sanction. If the youth follows the conditions of the juvenile sentence and commits no further violation, the adult sentence is revoked. Blended sentences of one type or another exist in 26 states.[103]

The Death Penalty for Juveniles

On March 1, 2005, the U.S. Supreme Court, in the case of *Roper v. Simmons*, put an end to the practice of the death penalty for juveniles in the United States. At issue was the minimum age that juveniles who were under the age of 18 when they committed their crimes could be eligible for the death penalty.[104] At the time, 16- and 17-year-olds were eligible for the death penalty, and 21 states permitted the death penalty for juveniles,[105] with a total of 72 juvenile offenders on death row.[106] In a 5–4 decision, the Court ruled that the juvenile death penalty was in violation of the Eighth Amendment's ban on cruel and unusual punishment.[107]

The execution of minor children has not been uncommon in our nation's history; at least 366 juvenile offenders have been executed since 1642.[108] This represents about 2 percent of the total of more than 18,000 executions carried out since colonial times.

Between the reinstatement of the death penalty in 1976 and the last execution of a juvenile in 2003, 22 juvenile offenders had been executed in seven states. Texas accounted for 13 of these 22 executions. All 22 of the executed juvenile offenders were male, 21 committed their crimes at age 17, and just over half (13 of them) were minorities.[109]

Past Legal Issues In *Thompson v. Oklahoma* (1988), the U.S. Supreme Court prohibited the execution of persons under age 16, but left open the age at which execution would be legally appropriate.[110] They then answered this question in two 1989 cases, *Wilkins v. Missouri* and *Stanford v. Kentucky*, in which they ruled that states were free to impose the death penalty for murderers who committed their crimes after they reached age 16 or 17.[111] According to the majority opinion, society at that time had not formed a consensus that the execution of such minors constitutes a cruel and unusual punishment.

Those who oppose the death penalty for children find that it has little deterrent effect on youngsters who are impulsive and do not have a realistic view of the destructiveness of their misdeeds or their consequences. Victor Streib, the leading critic of the death penalty for children, argues that such a practice is cruel and unusual punishment because (a) the condemnation of children makes no measurable contribution to the legitimate goals of punishment; (b) condemning any minor to death violates contemporary standards of decency; (c) the capacity of the young for change, growth, and rehabilitation makes the death penalty particularly harsh and inappropriate; and (d) both legislative attitudes and public opinion reject juvenile executions.[112] Those who oppose the death penalty for children also refer to a growing body of research that shows that the brain continues to develop through the late teen years, as well as important mental functions, such as planning, judgment, and emotional control.[113] Opposition to the juvenile death penalty is also backed up by declining public support in the United States (at least for the execution of juveniles) and world opinion.[114] Supporters of the death penalty hold that, regardless of their age, people can form criminal intent and therefore should be responsible for their actions. If the death penalty is legal for adults, they assert, then it can also be used for children who commit serious crimes.

The Child's Right to Appeal

Regardless of the sentence imposed, juveniles may want to appeal the decision made by the juvenile court judge. Juvenile court statutes normally restrict appeals to cases where the juvenile seeks review of a **final order**, one that ends the litigation between two parties by determining all their rights and disposing of all the issues.[115] The **appellate process** gives the juvenile the opportunity to have the case brought before a reviewing court after it has been heard in the juvenile or family court. Today, the law does not recognize a federal constitutional right of appeal. In other words, the U.S. Constitution does not require any state to furnish an appeal to a juvenile charged and found to be delinquent in a juvenile or family court. Consequently, appellate review of a juvenile case is a matter of statutory right in each jurisdiction. However, the majority of states do provide juveniles with some method of statutory appeal.

The appeal process was not always part of the juvenile law system. In 1965, few states extended the right of appeal to juveniles.[116] Even in the *Gault* case in 1967, the U.S. Supreme Court refused to review the Arizona juvenile code, which provided no appellate review in juvenile matters. It further rejected the right of a juvenile to a transcript of the original trial record.[117] Today, however, most jurisdictions that provide a child with some form of appeal also provide for counsel and for securing a record and transcript, which are crucial to the success of any appeal.

Because juvenile appellate review is defined by individual statutes, each jurisdiction determines for itself what method of review will be used. There are two basic methods of appeal: the direct appeal and the collateral attack.

The *direct appeal* normally involves an appellate court review to determine whether, based on the evidence presented at the trial, the rulings of law and the judgment of

final order
Order that ends litigation between two parties by determining all their rights and disposing of all the issues.

appellate process
Allows the juvenile an opportunity to have the case brought before a reviewing court after it has been heard in juvenile or family court.

the court were correct. The second major area of review involves the collateral attack of a case. The term "collateral" implies a secondary or indirect method of attacking a final judgment. Instead of appealing the juvenile trial because of errors, prejudice, or lack of evidence, *collateral review* uses extraordinary legal writs to challenge the lower-court position. One such procedural device is the writ of habeas corpus. Known as the *Great Writ*, the writ of habeas corpus refers to a procedure for determining the validity of a person's custody. In the context of the juvenile court, it is used to challenge the custody of a child in detention or in an institution. This writ is often the method by which the Supreme Court exercises its discretionary authority to hear cases regarding constitutional issues. Even though there is no constitutional right to appeal a juvenile case and each jurisdiction provides for appeals differently, juveniles have a far greater opportunity for appellate review today than in years past.

writ of habeas corpus
Judicial order requesting that a person detaining another produce the body of the prisoner and give reasons for his or her capture and detention.

Confidentiality in Juvenile Proceedings

Along with the rights of juveniles at adjudication and disposition, the issue of confidentiality in juvenile proceedings has also received attention in recent years. The debate on confidentiality in the juvenile court deals with two areas: (1) open versus closed hearings, and (2) privacy of juvenile records. Confidentiality has become moot in some respects, as many legislatures have broadened access to juvenile records.

confidentiality
Restriction of information in juvenile court proceedings in the interest of protecting the privacy of the juvenile.

Open vs. Closed Hearings Generally, juvenile trials are closed to the public and the press, and the names of the offenders are kept secret. The U.S. Supreme Court has ruled on the issue of privacy in three important decisions. In *Davis v. Alaska*, the Court concluded that any injury resulting from the disclosure of a juvenile's record is outweighed by the right to completely cross-examine an adverse witness.[118] The *Davis* case involved an effort to obtain testimony from a juvenile probationer who was a witness in a criminal trial. The Supreme Court held that a juvenile's interest in confidentiality was secondary to the constitutional right to confront adverse witnesses.

The decisions in two subsequent cases, *Oklahoma Publishing Co. v. District Court* and *Smith v. Daily Mail Publishing Co.*, sought to balance juvenile privacy with freedom of the press. In the *Oklahoma* case, the Supreme Court ruled that a state court was not allowed to prohibit the publication of information obtained in an open juvenile proceeding.[119] The case involved an 11-year-old boy suspected of homicide, who appeared at a detention hearing where photographs were taken and published in local newspapers. When the local district court prohibited further disclosure, the publishing company claimed that the court order was a restraint in violation of the First Amendment, and the Supreme Court agreed.

The *Smith* case involved the discovery and publication of the identity of a juvenile suspect in violation of a state statute prohibiting publication. The Supreme Court, however, declared the statute unconstitutional because the Court believed the state's interest in protecting the child's identity was not of such a magnitude as to justify the use of such a statute.[120] Therefore, if newspapers lawfully obtain pictures or names of juveniles, they may publish them. Based on these decisions, it appears that the Supreme Court favors the constitutional rights of the press over the right to privacy of the juvenile offender.

None of the decisions, however, give the press or public access to juvenile trials. Some jurisdictions still bar the press from juvenile proceedings unless they show at a hearing that their presence will not harm the youth. However, the trend has been to make it easier for the press and the public to have open access to juvenile trials. For example, Georgia amended its juvenile code to allow the public access to juvenile hearings in cases in which a juvenile is charged with certain designated felonies, such as kidnapping and attempted murder. Missouri also passed legislation that "removes the veil of secrecy that once kept juvenile court proceedings private—in the hope that allowing names and photos in newspapers will discourage teen crime and alert school officials." Michigan has granted public access to court proceedings and documents in cases involving delinquents, truants, runaways, and abuse victims. In recent years many jurisdictions have amended their laws to provide for greater openness in juvenile courts.[121]

Privacy of Juvenile Records For most of the twentieth century, juvenile records were kept confidential.[122] Today, however, the record itself, or information contained in it, can be opened by court order in many jurisdictions on the basis of statutory exception. The following groups can ordinarily gain access to juvenile records: (a) law enforcement personnel, (b) the child's attorney, (c) the parents or guardians, (d) military personnel, and (e) public agencies such as schools, court-related organizations, and correctional institutions.

Many states have enacted laws authorizing a central repository for juvenile arrest records. About 30 states have enacted provisions to allow open hearings in at least some juvenile cases. Forty-two states have enacted legislation authorizing the release and publication of the names and addresses of juvenile offenders in some cases. States also began to allow more juveniles to be fingerprinted and photographed. Nearly all states now allow juvenile fingerprints to be included in criminal history records, and nearly all states authorize juveniles to be photographed for later identification.[123] Some states allow a juvenile adjudication for a criminal act to be used as evidence in an adult criminal proceeding for the same act, to show predisposition or criminal nature.

Today, most states recognize the importance of juvenile records in sentencing. Many first-time adult offenders committed numerous crimes as juveniles, and evidence of these crimes may not be available to sentencing for the adult offenses unless states pass statutes allowing access. Knowledge of a defendant's juvenile record may help prosecutors and judges determine appropriate sentencing for offenders ages 18 to 24, the age group most likely to be involved in violent crime.

According to experts such as Ira Schwartz, the need for confidentiality to protect juveniles is far less than the need to open up the courts to public scrutiny.[124] The problem of maintaining confidentiality of juvenile records will become more acute in the future as electronic information storage makes these records both more durable and more accessible.

In conclusion, virtually every state provides prosecutors and judges with access to the juvenile records of adult offenders. There is great diversity, however, regarding provisions for the collection and retention of juvenile records.[125]

FUTURE OF THE JUVENILE COURT

The future of the juvenile court is subject to wide-ranging and sometimes contentious debate. Some experts, including legal scholar Barry Feld, believe that over the years the juvenile justice system has taken on more of the characteristics of the adult courts, which he refers to as the "criminalizing" of the juvenile court,[126] or in a more stern admonition: "Despite juvenile courts' persisting rehabilitative rhetoric, the reality of *treating* juveniles closely resembles *punishing* adult criminals."[127] Robert Dawson suggests that because the legal differences between the juvenile and criminal systems are narrower than they ever have been, it may be time to abolish the juvenile court.[128] This value conflict has led some experts to advocate the actual abolition of the juvenile court, a topic discussed in the accompanying Policy and Practice box.

Other experts, such as Peter Greenwood, contend that despite these and other limitations the treatment programs that the modern juvenile court currently provides play a central role in society's response to the most serious delinquents.[129] Greenwood argues that this comes with a number of specific responsibilities that juvenile courts must take on so as to ensure that these programs are indeed effective, including awareness of the most up-to-date scientific evidence on the effectiveness of court-based programs, diversion of cases that can be handled informally outside of the system, disposition of cases to appropriate programs, and quality control.[130]

The above concerns reflect the changes that have been ongoing in the juvenile justice system. During the 1990s, there was a nationwide effort to modify the system in response to the public's perceived fear of predatory juvenile offenders and the reaction to high-profile cases such as the Columbine tragedy. As a result, states have begun to institute policies that critics believe undermine the true purpose of the juvenile court movement.[131] Between 1992 and 1995, 40 states and the District of Columbia changed their transfer statutes to make it easier to waive juveniles to adult courts, and since 1992, only one state—Nebraska—has not changed its transfer statutes for this purpose.[132] By the end of the 2004 legislative session (the most recent data available), there were 23 states (and the District of Columbia) where no minimum age is specified to transfer a juvenile to adult court (Table 15.1).

Getting tough on juvenile crime is the primary motivation for moving cases to the adult criminal justice system.[133] Some commentators argue that waiving juveniles is a statement that juvenile crime is taken seriously by society; others believe the fear of being transferred serves as a deterrent.[134] Some states, such as Arizona, have initiated legislation that significantly restricts eligibility for juvenile justice processing and criminalizing acts that heretofore would have fallen under the jurisdiction of the juvenile court. For example, the Arizona legislation provides for the statutory exclusion for 15-, 16-, or 17-year-olds charged with violent crimes or if they had two prior felony adjudications and were charged with any third felony. It also added the provision, "once an adult, always an adult," where, if a juvenile was previously tried and convicted in criminal court, any future offenses involving that juvenile will be tried in adult court.[135] Thirty-two other states and the District of Columbia also have the once an adult, always an adult provision.[136] Although there is no mistaking the intention of this provision—to get tough on juvenile crime—some experts point out that inconsistencies that it created between the two justice systems may have inadvertently also produced a number of legal loopholes.[137]

These changes concern juvenile justice advocates such as Hunter Hurst, director of the National Center for Juvenile Justice, who warns:

> How could the wholesale criminalization of children possibly be a wise thing? If their vulnerability to predation in jails and prisons does not destroy them, won't the so-called taint of criminality that they carry with them for the rest of their lives be an impossible social burden for them and us? . . . Have our standards of decency devolved to the point where protection of children is no longer a compelling state interest? In many ways the answer is yes.[138]

Part of the answer to avoiding this state of affairs, argue criminologists Daniel Mears, Carter Hay, Marc Gertz, and Christina Mancini, is that the juvenile court and

TABLE 15.1

Minimum Age Specified in Statute for Transferring Juveniles to Adult Court

Age	State (Total Number)
None	Alaska, Arizona, Delaware, Florida, Georgia, Hawaii, Idaho, Indiana, Maine, Maryland, Montana, Nebraska, Nevada, Oklahoma, Oregon, Pennsylvania, Rhode Island, South Carolina, South Dakota, Tennessee, Washington, West Virginia, Wisconsin (23 and the District of Columbia)
10	Kansas, Vermont (2)
12	Colorado, Missouri (2)
13	Illinois, Mississippi, New Hampshire, New York, North Carolina, Wyoming (6)
14	Alabama, Arkansas, California, Connecticut, Iowa, Kentucky, Louisiana, Massachusetts, Michigan, Minnesota, New Jersey, North Dakota, Ohio, Texas, Utah, Virginia (16)
15	New Mexico (1)

SOURCES: Patrick Griffin, "Montana Transfer Provisions," in *State Juvenile Justice Profiles* (Pittsburgh, PA: National Center for Juvenile Justice, 2005); Howard N. Snyder and Melissa Sickmund, *Juvenile Offenders and Victims: 2006 National Report* (Pittsburgh, PA: National Center for Juvenile Justice, 2006), p. 114.

Should the Juvenile Court Be Abolished?

In an important work, *Bad Kids: Race and the Transformation of the Juvenile Court*, legal expert Barry Feld makes the rather controversial suggestion that the juvenile court system should be discontinued and/or replaced by an alternative method of justice. He suggests that the current structure makes it almost impossible for the system to fulfill or achieve the purpose for which it was originally intended.

Feld maintains that the juvenile court was developed in an effort to create a more lenient atmosphere and process than the one used against adult criminals. Although a worthwhile goal, the juvenile court system was doomed to failure even from the beginning, because it was thrown into the role of providing child welfare at the same time that it was an instrument of law enforcement. These two missions are often at cross-purposes. During its history, various legal developments have further undermined its purpose—most notably the *In re Gault* ruling, which ultimately led to juveniles receiving similar legal protections as adults and to children being treated like adults in all respects. The juvenile court's vision of leniency was further undercut by the fear and consequent racism created by postwar migration and economic trends that led to the development of large enclaves of poor and underemployed African Americans living in northern cities. Then in the 1980s, the sudden rise in gang membership, gun violence, and homicide committed by juveniles further undermined the juvenile court mission and resulted in legislation that created mandatory sentences for juvenile offenders and mandatory waiver to the adult court. As a result, the focus of the court has been on dealing with the offense rather than treating the offender. In Feld's words, the juvenile court has become a "deficient second-rate criminal court." The welfare and rehabilitative purposes of the juvenile court have been subordinated to its role of law enforcement agent.

Can juvenile courts be reformed? Feld maintains that it is impossible because of their conflicting purposes and shifting priorities. The money spent on serving the court and its large staff would be better spent on child welfare, which would target a larger audience and prevent children's antisocial acts before they occur. In lieu of juvenile court, youths who violate the law should receive full procedural protections in the criminal court system. The special protections given youths in the juvenile court could be provided by altering the criminal law and recognizing age as a factor in the creation of criminal liability. Because youths have had a limited opportunity to develop self-control, their criminal liability should also be curtailed or restricted.

Is Feld's rather dour assessment of the juvenile court valid, and should the court in fact be abolished? Not so, according to John Johnson Kerbs, who suggests that Feld makes assumptions that may not be wedded to the reality of the American legal system. First, Kerbs finds that it is naïve to assume the criminal courts can provide the same or greater substantive and procedural protections as the juvenile court. Many juvenile court defendants are indigent, especially those coming from the minority community, and it may be impossible for them to obtain adequate legal defense in the adult system. Second, Feld's assumption that criminal courts will take a defendant's age into close consideration may be illusory. In this get-tough era, it is likely that criminal courts will provide harsher sentences, and the brunt of these draconian sentences will fall squarely on the shoulders of minority youth. Research efforts routinely show that African American adults are unduly punished in adult courts. Sending juvenile offenders to these venues will most likely further enmesh them in an already unfair system. Finally, Kerbs finds that the treatment benefits of the juvenile courts should not be overlooked or abandoned. There is ample research, he maintains, that shows that juvenile courts can create lower recidivism rates than criminal courts. Though the juvenile court is far from perfect and should be improved, it would be foolish to abandon a system aimed at helping kids find alternatives to crime. The alternative is one that produces higher recidivism rates, lowers their future prospects, and has a less than stellar record of providing due process and equal protection for the nation's most needy citizens.

Critical Thinking

1. What's your take on this issue? Should the juvenile court be abolished?

2. Since the trend has been to transfer the most serious criminal cases to the adult court, is there still a purpose for an independent juvenile court? Should the juvenile court be reserved for nonserious first offenders?

SOURCES: Barry C. Feld, *Bad Kids: Race and the Transformation of the Juvenile Court* (New York: Oxford University Press, 1999); John Johnson Kerbs, "(Un)equal Justice: Juvenile Court Abolition and African Americans," *Annals of the American Academy of Political and Social Science* 564:109–125 (1999).

the juvenile justice system in general needs to be guided by a core set of rational and science-based principles such as "systematic assessments of culpability and treatment needs and a consistent balancing of punishment and treatment."[139] These become the overriding considerations in how the juvenile court can best serve society, a course of action that the public find to be much more appealing than the wholesale criminalization of children.[140]

Summary

1. **Understand the roles and responsibilities of the main players in the juvenile court**

I Prosecutors, judges, and defense attorneys are the key players in the juvenile court.

I The juvenile prosecutor is the attorney responsible for bringing the state's case against the accused juvenile.

I The juvenile judge must ensure that the children and families who come before the court receive the proper help.

I Defense attorneys representing children in the juvenile court play an active and important part in virtually all stages of the proceedings.

2. **Be able to discuss key issues of the preadjudicatory stage of juvenile justice, including detention, intake, diversion, pretrial release, plea bargaining, and waiver**

I Many decisions about what happens to a child may occur prior to adjudication.

I Due to personnel limitations, the juvenile justice system is not able to try every child accused of a crime or status offense. Therefore, diversion programs seem to hold greater hope for the control of delinquency.

I As a result, such subsystems as statutory intake proceedings, plea bargaining, and other informal adjustments are essential ingredients in the administration of the juvenile justice system.

3. **Be able to argue the pros and cons of transferring youths to adult court**

I Each year, thousands of youths are transferred to adult courts because of the seriousness of their crimes.

I This process, known as waiver, is an effort to remove serious offenders from the juvenile process and into the more punitive adult system.

I Most juvenile experts oppose waiver because it clashes with the rehabilitative ideal.

I Supporters argue that its increased use can help get violent juvenile offenders off the street, and they point to studies that show that, for the most part, transfer is reserved for the most serious cases and the most serious juvenile offenders.

4. **Understand key issues of the trial stage of juvenile justice, including constitutional rights of youths and disposition**

I Most jurisdictions have a bifurcated juvenile code system that separates the adjudication hearing from the dispositional hearing.

I Juveniles alleged to be delinquent have virtually all the constitutional rights given a criminal defendant at trial—except possibly the right to a trial by jury.

I Juvenile proceedings are generally closed to the public.

5. **Be familiar with major U.S. Supreme Court decisions that have influenced the handling of juveniles at the preadjudicatory and trial stages**

I *In re Gault* is the key legal case that set out the basic requirements of due process that must be satisfied in juvenile court proceedings.

I In *Roper v. Simmons*, the U.S. Supreme Court ruled that the death penalty for juveniles is prohibited, because it constitutes cruel and unusual punishment.

6. **Know the most common dispositions for juvenile offenders**

I The major categories of dispositional choice in juvenile cases are community release, out-of-home placements, fines or restitution, community service, and institutionalization.

I Although the traditional notion of rehabilitation and treatment as the proper goals for disposition is being questioned, many juvenile codes do require that the court consider the least-restrictive alternative.

7. **Be able to argue the pros and cons of confidentiality in juvenile proceedings and privacy of juvenile records**

I Many state statutes require that juvenile hearings be closed and that the privacy of juvenile records be maintained.

I This is done to protect the child from public scrutiny and to provide a greater opportunity for rehabilitation.

I This approach may be inconsistent with the public's interest in taking a closer look at the juvenile justice system.

Key Terms

Viewpoint

As an experienced family court judge, you are often faced with difficult decisions, but few are more difficult than the case of John, arrested at age 14 for robbery and rape. His victim, a young neighborhood girl, was badly injured in the attack and needed extensive hospitalization; she is now in counseling. Even though the charges are serious, because of his age John can still be subject to the jurisdiction of the juvenile division of the state family court. However, the prosecutor has filed a petition to waive jurisdiction to the adult court. Under existing state law, a hearing must be held to determine whether there is sufficient evidence that John cannot be successfully treated in the juvenile justice system and therefore warrants transfer to the adult system; the final decision on the matter is yours alone.

At the waiver hearing, you discover that John is the oldest of three siblings living in a single-parent home. He has had no contact with his father for more than 10 years. His psychological evaluation showed hostility, anger toward females, and great feelings of frustration. His intelligence is below average, and his behavioral and academic records are poor. In addition, he seems to be involved with a local youth gang, although he denies any association with them. This is his first formal involvement with the juvenile court. Previous contact was limited to a complaint for disorderly conduct at age 13, which was dismissed by the court's intake department. During the hearing, John verbalizes what you interpret to be superficial remorse for his offenses.

To the prosecutor, John seems to be a youth with poor controls who is likely to commit future crimes. The defense attorney argues that there are effective treatment opportunities within the juvenile justice system that can meet John's needs. Her views are supported by an evaluation of the case conducted by the court's probation staff, which concludes that the case can be dealt with in the confines of juvenile corrections.

If the case remains in the juvenile court, John can be kept in custody in a juvenile facility until age 18; if transferred to felony court, he could be sentenced to up to 20 years in a maximum-security prison. As the judge, you recognize the seriousness of the crimes committed by John and realize that it is very difficult to predict or assess his future behavior and potential dangerousness.

▌ Would you authorize a waiver to adult court or keep the case in the juvenile justice system?

▌ Can 14-year-olds truly understand the seriousness of their behavior?

▌ Should a juvenile court judge consider the victim in making a disposition decision?

Doing Research on the Web

To get further information on this topic, go to the following websites via

academic.cengage.com/criminaljustice/siegel

The American Bar Association Juvenile Justice Center

OJJDP Statistical Briefing Book

American Youth Policy Forum on Juvenile Justice

The Juvenile Justice Division of the Child Welfare League of America

The National Council on Crime and Delinquency and Children's Research Center

Questions for Discussion

1. Discuss and identify the major participants in the juvenile adjudication process. What are each person's roles and responsibilities in the course of a juvenile trial?

2. The criminal justice system in the United States is based on the adversarial process. Does the same adversary principle apply in the juvenile justice system?

3. Children have certain constitutional rights at adjudication, such as the right to an attorney and the right to confront and cross-examine witnesses. But they do not have the right to a trial by jury. Should juvenile offenders have a constitutional right to a jury trial? Should each state make that determination? Discuss the legal decision that addresses this issue.

4. What is the point of obtaining a predisposition report in the juvenile court? Is it of any value in cases where the child is released to the community? Does it have a significant value in serious juvenile crime cases?

5. The standard of proof in juvenile adjudication is to show that the child is guilty beyond a reasonable doubt. Explain the meaning of this standard of proof in the U.S. judicial system.

6. Should states adopt get-tough sentences in juvenile justice or adhere to the individualized treatment model?

7. What are blended sentences?

8. Do you agree with the Supreme Court's 2005 ruling that prohibits the death penalty for juvenile offenders?

Notes

1. Kelly Dedel, "National Profile of the Organization of State Juvenile Corrections Systems," *Crime and Delinquency* 44:507–525 (1998). Hereinafter cited as National Profile.

2. Office of Juvenile Justice and Delinquency Prevention, *OJJDP Statistical Briefing Book*. Released on March 19, 2007. Available at http://ojjdp.ncjrs.gov/ojstatbb/ (accessed July 26, 2007).

3. Ibid.

4. *Powell v. Alabama*, 287 U.S. 45, 53 S.Ct. 55, 77, L.Ed.2d 158 (1932); *Gideon v. Wainwright*, 372 U.S. 335, 83 S.Ct. 792, 9 L.Ed.2d 799 (1963); *Argersinger v. Hamlin*, 407 U.S. 25, 92 S.Ct. 2006, 32 L.Ed.2d 530 (1972).

5. See Judith B. Jones, *Access to Counsel* (Washington, DC: Office of Juvenile Justice and Delinquency Prevention, 2004).

6. For a review of these studies, see T. Grisso, "The Competence of Adolescents as Trial Defendants," *Psychology, Public Policy, and Law* 3:3–32 (1997).

7. Christine Schnyder Pierce and Stanley L. Brodsky, "Trust and Understanding in the Attorney-Juvenile Relationship," *Behavioral Sciences and the Law* 20:89–107 (2002), p. 102.

8. Ibid.

9. Melinda G. Schmidt, N. Dickon Reppucci, and Jennifer L. Woolard, "Effectiveness of Participation as a Defendant: The Attorney-Juvenile Client Relationship," *Behavioral Sciences and the Law* 21:175–198 (2003), p. 177.

10. Ibid., p. 193.

11. George W. Burruss, Jr., and Kimberly Kempf-Leonard, "The Questionable Advantage of Defense Counsel in Juvenile Court," *Justice Quarterly* 19:37–67 (2002), pp. 60–61.

12. Lori Guevara, Cassia Spohn, and Denise Herz, "Race, Legal Representation, and Juvenile Justice: Issues and Concerns," *Crime and Delinquency* 50:344–371 (2004), pp. 362–364.

13. Howard Davidson, "The Guardian *ad Litem:* An Important Approach to the Protection of Children," *Children Today* 10:23 (1981); Daniel Golden, "Who Guards the Children?" *Boston Globe Magazine*, 27 December 1992, p. 12.

14. Chester Harhut, "An Expanded Role for the Guardian *ad Litem*," *Juvenile and Family Court Journal* 51:31–35 (2000).

15. Steve Riddell, "CASA, Child's Voice in Court," *Juvenile and Family Justice Today* 7:13–14 (1998).

16. American Bar Association, *A Call for Justice: An Assessment of Access to Counsel and Quality of Representation in Delinquency Proceedings* (Washington, DC: ABA Juvenile Justice Center, 1995).

17. Douglas C. Dodge, *Due Process Advocacy* (Washington, DC: Office of Juvenile Justice and Delinquency Prevention, 1997).

18. American Bar Association, "News Release: ABA President Says New Report Shows 'Conveyor Belt Justice' Hurting Children and Undermining Public Safety," Washington, DC, October 21, 2003.

19. James Shine and Dwight Price, "Prosecutor and Juvenile Justice: New Roles and Perspectives," in Ira Schwartz, ed., *Juvenile Justice and Public Policy* (New York: Lexington Books, 1992), pp. 101–133.

20. James Backstrom and Gary Walker, "A Balanced Approach to Juvenile Justice: The Work of the Juvenile Justice Advisory Committee," *The Prosecutor* 32:37–39 (1988); see also *Prosecutors' Policy Recommendations on Serious, Violent, and Habitual Youthful Offenders* (Alexandria, VA: American Prosecutors' Institute, 1997).

21. Leonard P. Edwards, "The Juvenile Court and the Role of the Juvenile Court Judge," *Juvenile and Family Court Journal* 43:3–45 (1992); Lois Haight, "Why I Choose to Be a Juvenile Court Judge," *Juvenile and Family Justice Today* 7:7 (1998).

22. National Council of Juvenile and Family Court Judges, *Juvenile Delinquency Guidelines: Improving Court Practice in Juvenile Delinquency Cases* (Reno, NV: Author, 2005), p. 24.

23. American Correctional Association, *Standards for Juvenile Detention Facilities* (Laurel, MD: ACA, 1991).

24. National Profile, p. 514.

25. Madeline Wordes and Sharon Jones, "Trends in Juvenile Detention and Steps Toward Reform," *Crime and Delinquency* 44:544–560 (1998).

26. Robert Shepard, *Juvenile Justice Standards Annotated: A Balanced Approach* (Chicago: ABA, 1997).

27. Leslie Kaufman, "Child Detention Centers Criticized in New Jersey," *New York Times*, 23 November 2004.

28. Dylan Conger and Timothy Ross, "Project Confirm: An Outcome Evaluation of a Program for Children in the Child Welfare and Juvenile Justice Systems," *Youth Violence and Juvenile Justice* 4:97–115 (2006).

29. Office of Juvenile Justice and Delinquency Prevention, *OJJDP Statistical Briefing Book*. Released on March 19, 2007. Available at http://ojjdp.ncjrs.gov/ojstatbb/ (accessed July 26, 2007).

30. Howard N. Snyder and Melissa Sickmund, *Juvenile Offenders and Victims: 2006 National Report* (Pittsburgh, PA: National Center for Juvenile Justice, 2006), pp. 169–170, 191.

31. Paul Harms, *Detention in Delinquency Cases, 1989–1998* (Washington, DC: Office of Juvenile Justice and Delinquency Prevention, 2002).

32. Bohsiu Wu and Angel Ilarraza Fuentes, "The Entangled Effects of Race and Urban Poverty," *Juvenile and Family Court Journal* 49:41–51 (1998).

33. National Council on Crime and Delinquency, *And Justice for Some: Differential Treatment of Youth of Color in the Justice System* (San Francisco, CA: Author, 2007), pp. 11–12.

34. Katherine E. Brown and Leanne Fiftal Alarid, "Examining Racial Disparity of Male Property Offenders in the Missouri Juvenile Justice System," *Youth Violence and Juvenile Justice* 2:107–128 (2004), p. 116.

35. Ibid., p. 119.

36. James Maupin and Lis Bond-Maupin, "Detention Decision-Making in a Predominantly Hispanic Region: Rural and Non-Rural Differences," *Juvenile and Family Court Journal* 50:11–21 (1999).

37. Earl Dunlap and David Roush, "Juvenile Detention as Process and Place," *Juvenile and Family Court Journal* 46:1–16 (1995).

38. "OJJDP Helps States Remove Juveniles from Jails," *Juvenile Justice Bulletin* (Washington, DC: U.S. Department of Justice, 1990).

39. Community Research Associates, *The Jail Removal Initiative: A Summary Report* (Champaign, IL: Community Research Associates, 1987).

40. David Steinhart, "Status Offenders," *The Future of Children: The Juvenile Court*, vol. 6 (Los Altos, CA: David and Lucile Packard Foundation, 1996), pp. 86–96.

41. Mark Soler, James Bell, Elizabeth Jameson, Carole Shauffer, Alice Shotton, and Loren Warboys, *Representing the Child Client* (New York: Matthew Bender, 1989), sec. 5.03b.

42. *Schall v. Martin*, 467 U.S. 253 (1984).

43. Jeffrey Fagan and Martin Guggenheim, "Preventive Detention for Juveniles: A Natural Experiment," *Journal of Criminal Law and Criminology* 86:415–428 (1996).

44. Office of Juvenile Justice and Delinquency Prevention, *OJJDP Statistical Briefing Book*.

45. Leona Lee, "Factors Influencing Intake Disposition in a Juvenile Court," *Juvenile and Family Court Journal* 46:43–62 (1995).

46. Deborah A. Chapin and Patricia A. Griffin, "Juvenile Diversion," in Kirk Heilbrun, Naomi E. Sevin Goldstein, and Richard E. Redding, eds., *Juvenile Delinquency: Prevention, Assessment, and Intervention* (New York: Oxford University Press, 2005); see also Edwin E. Lemert, "Diversion in Juvenile Justice: What Hath Been Wrought?" *Journal of Research in Crime and Delinquency* 18:34–46 (1981).

47. Don C. Gibbons and Gerald F. Blake, "Evaluating the Impact of Juvenile Diversion Programs," *Crime and Delinquency Journal* 22:411–419 (1976); Richard J. Lundman, "Will Diversion Reduce Recidivism?" *Crime and Delinquency Journal* 22:428–437 (1976); B. Bullington, J. Sprowls, D. Katkin, and M. Phillips, "A Critique of Diversionary Juvenile Justice," *Crime and Delinquency* 24:59–71 (1978); Thomas Blomberg, "Diversion and Accelerated Social Control," *Journal of Criminal Law and Criminology* 68:274–282 (1977); Sharla Rausch and Charles Logan, "Diversion from Juvenile Court: Panacea or Pandora's Box," in J. Klugel, ed., *Evaluating Juvenile Justice* (Beverly Hills: Sage Publications, 1983), pp. 19–30.

48. Arnold Binder and Gilbert Geis, "Ad Populum Argumentation in Criminology: Juvenile Diversion as Rhetoric," *Criminology* 30:309–333 (1984).

49. Mark Ezell, "Juvenile Diversion: The Ongoing Search for Alternatives," in Ira M. Schwartz, ed., *Juvenile Justice and Public Policy* (New York: Lexington Books, 1992), pp. 45–59.

50. Alison Evans Cuellar, Larkin S. McReynolds, and Gail A. Wasserman, "A Cure for Crime: Can Mental Health Treatment Diversion Reduce Crime among Youth?" *Journal of Policy Analysis and Management* 25:197–214 (2006).

51. Peter W. Greenwood, *Changing Lives: Delinquency Prevention as Crime-Control Policy* (Chicago: University of Chicago Press, 2006), ch. 8; Franklin E. Zimring, *American Juvenile Justice* (New York: Oxford University Press, 2005), ch. 4.

52. Zimring, *American Juvenile Justice*, p. 47.

53. Albert W. Alschuler, "The Prosecutor's Role in Plea Bargaining," *University of Chicago Law Review* 36:50–112 (1968); Joyce Dougherty, "A Comparison of Adult Plea Bargaining and Juvenile Intake," *Federal Probation* June:72–79 (1988).

54. Sanford Fox, *Juvenile Courts in a Nutshell* (St. Paul, MN: West, 1985), pp. 154–156.

55. See Darlene Ewing, "Juvenile Plea Bargaining: A Case Study," *American Journal of Criminal Law* 6:167 (1978); Adrienne Volenik, *Checklists for Use in Juvenile Delinquency Proceedings* (Chicago: American Bar Association, 1985); Bruce Green, "Package Plea Bargaining and the Prosecutor's Duty of Good Faith," *Criminal Law Bulletin* 25:507–550 (1989).

56. Joseph Sanborn, *Plea Negotiations in Juvenile Court* (Ph.D. thesis, State University of New York at Albany, 1984); Joseph Sanborn, "Philosophical, Legal, and Systematic Aspects of Juvenile Court Plea Bargaining," *Crime and Delinquency* 39:509–527 (1993).

57. Office of Juvenile Justice and Delinquency Prevention, *OJJDP Statistical Briefing Book.*

58. Patrick Griffin, *Trying and Sentencing Juveniles as Adults: An Analysis of State Transfer and Blended Sentencing Laws* (Pittsburgh, PA: National Center for Juvenile Justice, 2003), pp. 2–3, table 1.

59. Ibid., p. 8, table 5.

60. Ibid., p. 10, table 6.

61. *Kent v. United States*, 383 U.S. 541, 86 S.Ct. 1045, 16 L.Ed.2d 84 (1966); *Breed v. Jones*, 421 U.S. 519, 95 S.Ct. 1179, 44 L.Ed.2d 346 (1975).

62. Barry Feld, "The Juvenile Court Meets the Principle of the Offense: Legislative Changes in Juvenile Waiver Statutes," *Journal of Criminal Law and Criminology* 78:471–534 (1987); Paul Marcotte, "Criminal Kids," *American Bar Association Journal* 76:60–66 (1990); Dale Parent et al., *Transferring Serious Juvenile Offenders to Adult Courts* (Washington, DC: U.S. Department of Justice, National Institute of Justice, 1997).

63. See Craig A. Mason, Derek A. Chapman, Chang Shau, and Julie Simons, "Impacting Re-Arrest Rates Among Youth Sentenced in Adult Court: An Epidemiology Examination of the Juvenile Sentencing Advocacy Project," *Journal of Clinical Child and Adolescent Psychology* 32:205–214 (2003); David L. Myers, "The Recidivism of Violent Youths in Juvenile and Adult Court: A Consideration of Selection Bias," *Youth Violence and Juvenile Justice* 1:79–101 (2003); Richard Redding, "Juvenile Offenders in Criminal Court and Adult Prison: Legal, Psychological and Behavioral Outcomes," *Juvenile and Family Court Journal* 50:1–15 (1999).

64. Griffin, *Trying and Sentencing Juveniles as Adults*, p. 9.

65. Thomas Grisso, Laurence Steinberg, Jennifer Woolard, Elizabeth Cauffman, Elizabeth Scott, Sandra Graham, Fran Lexcon, N. Dickon Repucci, and Robert Schwartz, "Juveniles' Competence to Stand Trial: A Comparison of Adolescents' and Adults' Capacities as Trial Defendants," *Law and Human Behavior* 27:333–363 (2003); Darla M. Burnett, Charles D. Noblin, and Vicki Prosser, "Adjudicative Competency in a Juvenile Population," *Criminal Justice and Behavior* 31:438–462 (2004).

66. Aaron Kupchik, "The Decision to Incarcerate in Juvenile and Criminal Courts," *Criminal Justice Review* 31:309–336 (2006), pp. 321–322.

67. Megan C. Kurlychek and Brian D. Johnson, "The Juvenile Penalty: A Comparison of Juvenile and Young Adult Sentencing Outcomes in Criminal Court," *Criminology* 42:485–517 (2004), p. 498.

68. Redding, "Juvenile Offenders in Criminal Court and Adult Prison: Legal, Psychological and Behavioral Outcomes," p. 11; see also Richard E. Redding, "The Effects of Adjudicating and Sentencing Juveniles as Adults: Research and Policy Implications," *Youth Violence and Juvenile Justice* 1:128–155 (2003).

69. Emily Gaarder and Joanne Belknap, "Tenuous Borders: Girls Transferred to Adult Court," *Criminology* 40:481–518 (2002), p. 508.

70. Redding, "Juvenile Offenders in Criminal Court and Adult Prison."

71. Howard N. Snyder and Melissa Sickmund, *Juvenile Offenders and Victims: 1999 National Report* (Washington, DC: U.S. Department of Justice, Office of Juvenile Justice and Delinquency Prevention, 1999), p. 177.

72. James Howell, "Juvenile Transfers to the Criminal Justice System: State of the Art," *Law and Policy* 18:17–60 (1996).

73. M. A. Bortner, "Traditional Rhetoric, Organizational Realities: Remand of Juveniles to Adult Court," *Crime and Delinquency* 32:53–73 (1986).

74. Snyder and Sickmund, *Juvenile Offenders and Victims*, pp. 186–187; Jeffrey Fagan, Martin Forst, and T. Scott Vivona, "Racial Determinants of the Judicial Transfer Decision: Prosecuting Violent Youth in Criminal Court," *Crime and Delinquency* 33:359–386 (1987); J. Fagan, E. Slaughter, and E. Hartstone, "Blind Justice: The Impact of Race on the Juvenile Justice Process," *Crime and Delinquency* 53:224–258 (1987); J. Fagan and E. P. Deschenes, "Determinants of Judicial Waiver Decisions for Violent Juvenile

Offenders," *Journal of Criminal Law and Criminology* 81:314–347 (1990); see also James Howell, "Juvenile Transfers to Criminal Court," *Juvenile and Family Justice Journal* 6:12–14 (1997).

75. Anne L. Stahl, T. Finnegan, and W. Kang, *Easy Access to Juvenile Court Statistics: 1985–2004*. Released in 2007. Available at http://ojjdp/ncjrs.gov/ojstatbb/ezajcs/ (accessed July 28, 2007).

76. Gerald Rainville and Steven K. Smith, *Juvenile Felony Defendants in Criminal Courts: Survey of 40 Counties, 1998* (Washington, DC: U.S. Department of Justice, Office of Juvenile Justice and Delinquency Prevention, 2003).

77. Stahl, Finnegan, and Kang, *Easy Access to Juvenile Court Statistics: 1985–2004.*

78. Barry Feld, "Delinquent Careers and Criminal Policy," *Criminology* 21:195–212 (1983).

79. Howard N. Snyder, Melissa Sickmund, and Eileen Poe-Yamagata, *Juvenile Transfers to Criminal Court in the 1990s: Lessons Learned from Four Studies* (Washington, DC: Office of Juvenile Justice and Delinquency Prevention, 2000).

80. Rainville and Smith, *Juvenile Felony Defendants in Criminal Courts.*

81. Sanjeev Sridharan, Lynette Greenfield, and Baron Blakley, "A Study of Prosecutorial Certification Practice in Virginia," *Criminology and Public Policy* 3:605–632 (2004).

82. Franklin E. Zimring, "Treatment of Hard Cases in American Juvenile Justice: In Defense of the Discretionary Waiver," *Notre Dame Journal of Law, Ethics and Policy* 5:267–280 (1991); Lawrence Winner, Lonn Kaduce, Donna Bishop, and Charles Frazier, "The Transfer of Juveniles to Criminal Courts: Reexamining Recidivism over the Long Term," *Crime and Delinquency* 43:548–564 (1997).

83. Rainville and Smith, *Juvenile Felony Defendants in Criminal Courts.*

84. Institute of Judicial Administration, American Bar Association Joint Commission on Juvenile Justice Standards, *Standards Relating to Adjudication* (Cambridge, MA: Ballinger, 1980).

85. Joseph B. Sanborn, Jr., "The Right to a Public Jury Trial—A Need for Today's Juvenile Court," *Judicature* 76:230–238 (1993). In the context of delinquency convictions to enhance criminal sentences, see Barry C. Feld, "The Constitutional Tension Between *Apprendi* and *McKeiver*: Sentence Enhancement Based on Delinquency Convictions and the Quality of Justice in Juvenile Courts," *Wake Forest Law Review* 38:1111–1224 (2003).

86. *In re Gault*, 387 U.S. 1; 87 S.Ct. 1248 (1967).

87. Linda Szymanski, *Juvenile Delinquents' Right to Counsel* (Pittsburgh: National Center for Juvenile Justice, 1988).

88. *In re Winship*, 397 U.S. 358, 90 S.Ct. 1068 (1970).

89. *McKeiver v. Pennsylvania*, 403 U.S. 528, 91 S.Ct. 1976 (1971).

90. See, generally, R. T. Powell, "Disposition Concepts," *Juvenile and Family Court Journal* 34:7–18 (1983).

91. Sanford Fox, *Juvenile Courts in a Nutshell* (St. Paul, MN: West, 1984), p. 221.

92. This section is adapted from Jack Haynes and Eugene Moore, "Particular Dispositions," *Juvenile and Family Court Journal* 34:41–48 (1983); see also Grant Grissom, "Dispositional Authority and the Future of the Juvenile Justice System," *Juvenile and Family Court Journal* 42:25–34 (1991).

93. Barry Krisberg, Elliot Currie, and David Onek, "What Works with Juvenile Offenders," *American Bar Association Journal on Criminal Justice* 10:20–24 (1995).

94. Office of Juvenile Justice and Delinquency Prevention, *OJJDP Statistical Briefing Book.*

95. Snyder and Sickmund, *Juvenile Offenders and Victims: 2006 National Report*, p. 177.

96. Office of Juvenile Justice and Delinquency Prevention, *OJJDP Statistical . Briefing Book.*

97. Anthony Platt, *The Child Savers: The Invention of Delinquency* (Chicago: University of Chicago Press, 1969); David Rothman, *Conscience and Convenience: The Asylum and the Alternative in Progressive America* (Boston: Little, Brown, 1980).

98. Joseph Goldstein, Anna Freud, and Albert Solnit, *Beyond the Best Interests of the Child* (New York: Free Press, 1973).

99. See, for example, *in Interest on M.P.* 697 N.E.2d 1153 (Il. App. 1998); *Matter of Welfare of CAW* 579 N.W.2d 494 (MN. App. 1998).

100. See, for example, *Matter of Willis Alvin M.* 479 S.E.2d. 871 (WV 1996).

101. Simon Singer and David McDowall, "Criminalizing Delinquency: The Deterrent Effects of NYJO Law," *Law and Society Review* 22:21–37 (1988).

102. Juvenile Justice Reform Act of 1977, Chap. 291; Wash. Rev.Code Ann. Title 9A, Sec. 1–91 (1977).

103. Griffin, *Trying and Sentencing Juveniles as Adults*, p. 3, table 1.

104. *Roper v. Simmons*, 125 S.Ct. 1183 (2005).

105. Erica Goode, "Young Killer: Bad Seed or Work in Progress?" *New York Times*, 25 November 2003.

106. Adam Liptak, "Court Takes Another Step in Reshaping Capital Punishment," *New York Times*, 2 March 2005.

107. *Roper v. Simmons*, 125 S.Ct. 1183 (2005).

108. Victor L. Streib, *The Juvenile Death Penalty Today: Death Sentences and Executions for Juvenile Crimes, January 1, 1973–September 30, 2003* (Ada, OH: The Claude W. Pettit College of Law, Ohio Northern University, October 6, 2003), p. 3.

109. Victor L. Streib, *The Juvenile Death Penalty Today: Death Sentences and Executions for Juvenile Crimes, January 1, 1973–September 30, 2003*; see also Snyder and Sickmund, *Juvenile Offenders and Victims: 2006 National Report*, p. 239.

110. Steven Gerstein, "The Constitutionality of Executing Juvenile Offenders, *Thompson v. Oklahoma*," *Criminal Law Bulletin* 24:91–98 (1988); *Thompson v. Oklahoma*, 108 S.Ct. 2687 (1988).

111. 109 S.Ct. 2969 (1989); for a recent analysis of the *Wilkins* and *Stanford* cases, see the note in "*Stanford v. Kentucky* and *Wilkins v. Missouri*: Juveniles, Capital Crime, and Death Penalty," *Criminal Justice Journal* 11:240–266 (1989).

112. Victor Streib, "Excluding Juveniles from New York's Impendent Death Penalty," *Albany Law Review* 54:625–679 (1990).

113. Goode, "Young Killer: Bad Seed or Work in Progress?"

114. Peter J. Benekos and Alida V. Merlo, "Juvenile Offenders and the Death Penalty: How Far have Standards of Decency Evolved?" *Youth Violence and Juvenile Justice* 3:316–333 (2006), p. 324.

115. Paul Piersma, Jeanette Ganousis, Adrienne E. Volenik, Harry F. Swanger, and Patricia Connell, *Law and Tactics in Juvenile Cases* (Philadelphia: American Law Institute, American Bar Association, Committee on Continuing Education, 1977), p. 397.

116. J. Addison Bowman, "Appeals from Juvenile Courts," *Crime and Delinquency Journal* 11:63–77 (1965).

117. *In re Gault*, 387 U.S. 1 87 S.Ct. 1428 (1967).

118. *Davis v. Alaska*, 415 U.S. 308 (1974); 94 S.Ct. 1105.

119. *Oklahoma Publishing Co. v. District Court*, 430 U.S. 97 (1977); 97 S.Ct. 1045.

120. *Smith v. Daily Mail Publishing Co.*, 443 U.S. 97, 99 S.Ct. 2667, 61 L.Ed.2d 399 (1979).

121. Thomas Hughes, "Opening the Doors to Juvenile Court: Is There an Emerging Right of Public Access?" *Communications and the Law* 19:1–50 (1997).

122. Linda Szymanski, *Confidentiality of Juvenile Court Records* (Pittsburgh: National Center for Juvenile Justice, 1989).

123. Jeffrey A. Butts, *Can We Do Without Juvenile Justice?* (Washington, DC: Urban Institute, 2000).

124. Ira M. Schwartz, *Justice for Juveniles: Rethinking the Best Interests of the Child* (Lexington, MA: D. C. Heath, 1989), p. 172.

125. Richard E. Redding, "Use of Juvenile Records in Criminal Court," *Juvenile Justice Fact Sheet* (Charlottesville, VA: Institute of Law, Psychiatry, and Public Policy, University of Virginia, 2000).

126. Barry Feld, "Criminology and the Juvenile Court: A Research Agenda for the 1990s," in Ira M. Schwartz, *Juvenile Justice and Public Policy—Toward a National Agenda* (New York: Lexington Books, 1992), p. 59.

127. Barry C. Feld, "Juvenile and Criminal Justice Systems' Responses to Youth Violence," in Michael Tonry and Mark H. Moore, eds., *Youth Violence: Crime and Justice: A Review of Research. Vol. 24* (Chicago: University of Chicago Press, 1998), p. 222.

128. Robert O. Dawson, "The Future of Juvenile Justice: Is It Time to Abolish the System?" *Journal of Criminal Law and Criminology* 81:136–155 (1990); see also Leonard P. Edwards, "The Future of the Juvenile Court: Promising New Directions," *The Future of Children: The Juvenile Court* (Los Altos, CA: David and Lucille Packard Foundation, 1996).

129. Peter W. Greenwood, *Changing Lives: Delinquency Prevention as Crime-Control Policy* (Chicago: University of Chicago Press, 2006), p. 183.

130. Ibid., pp. 193–194.

131. Hunter Hurst, "Juvenile Court: As We Enter the Millennium," *Juvenile and Family Court Journal* 50:21–27 (1999).

132. Snyder and Sickmund, *Juvenile Offenders and Victims: 2006 National Report*, p. 113.

133. Franklin E. Zimring, *American Youth Violence* (New York: Oxford University Press, 1998); Zimring, *American Juvenile Justice*.

134. Shay Bilchik, "A Juvenile Justice System for the 21st Century," *Crime and Delinquency* 44:89 (1998).

135. Patricia Torbet and Linda Szymanski, *State Legislative Responses to Violent Crime: 1996–97 Update* (Washington, DC: Office of Juvenile Justice and Delinquency Prevention, 1998).

136. Snyder and Sickmund, *Juvenile Offenders and Victims: 2006 National Report*, p. 111.

137. Stacy C. Moak and Lisa Hutchinson Wallace, "Legal Changes in Juvenile Justice: Then and Now," *Youth Violence and Juvenile Justice* 1:289–299 (2003), p. 292.

138. Hurst, "Juvenile Court: As We Enter the Millennium," p. 25.

139. Daniel P. Mears, Carter Hay, Marc Gertz, and Christina Mancini, "Public Opinion and the Foundation of the Juvenile Court," *Criminology* 45:223–258 (2007), p. 250.

140. Ibid., p. 246.

16 Juvenile Corrections: Probation, Community Treatment, and Institutionalization

Chapter Outline

Chapter Objectives

1. Be able to distinguish between community treatment and institutional treatment for juvenile offenders

2. Be familiar with the disposition of probation, including how it is administered and by whom and recent trends in its use

3. Be aware of new approaches for providing probation services to juvenile offenders and comment on their effectiveness in reducing recidivism

4. Understand key historical developments of secure juvenile corrections in this country, including the principle of *least restrictive alternative*

5. Be familiar with recent trends in the use of juvenile institutions for juvenile offenders and how their use differs across states

6. Understand key issues facing the institutionalized juvenile offender

7. Be able to identify the various juvenile correctional treatment approaches that are in use today and comment on their effectiveness in reducing recidivism

8. Understand juvenile offenders' legal right to treatment

9. Know the nature of aftercare for juvenile offenders and comment on recent innovations in juvenile aftercare and reentry programs

Memory

Deon Whitfield

On August 31, 2005, Joseph Daniel Maldonado, age 18, was found dead in his cell at the N. A. Chaderjian Youth Correctional Facility, also known as "Chad," in Stockton, California. He had committed suicide. Corrections officers found his limp body on the lower bunk with sheets wrapped around his neck and tied to the upper bunk. The officers were alerted to a potential problem upon discovering that the inmate's cell window was covered with paper, preventing anyone from seeing into the cell. A medical team was dispatched, but they were unable to revive Joseph. He was pronounced dead one hour later.

This was not an isolated event. Joseph's suicide was one of five suicide deaths inside the California juvenile correctional system over a period of 18 months. The other four inmates who committed suicide were Dyron Brewer, 24; Deon Whitfield, 17; Durrell Feaster, 18; and Roberto Lombana, 18.

Some of the circumstances leading up to Joseph's suicide are still in dispute. The Maldonado family claims that Joseph asked for psychological counseling on four separate occasions and it was denied each time. Joseph had sought counseling because he was depressed and troubled over his recent transfer to Chad, considered by many to be the "worst of the worst" of California's juvenile correctional institutions. The family has since filed a wrongful-death lawsuit against state correctional authorities in federal court in Sacramento. Not in dispute, however, are other events that contributed to Joseph's death. Chief among them was the inability of his family to visit or get in touch with him for a lengthy period of time. When Joseph was transferred to Chad, his visitors' list (a list of family members and others who can offer support) was not sent with him. An eight-week lockdown of Pajaro Hall, the ward Joseph resided in, due to gang violence further blocked any contact with family members. In its official report on the suicide, the California Inspector General ruled that Joseph Maldonado's death may have been entirely preventable.

Out of these tragedies has come some good. In October 2007, the Family Connection and Young Offender Rehabilitation Act was signed into law. The act mandates that the California Department of Corrections and Rehabilitation's Division of Juvenile Justice ensure that inmates are able to "communicate with family members, clergy, and others, and to participate in programs that will facilitate his or her education, rehabilitation, and accountability to victims." The act also requires that a number of practical steps be taken to improve contact between family members and inmates, such as establishing a toll-free number for families to confirm visiting times, as well as taking into consideration the proximity of family when placing a juvenile offender in an institution.[1]

This case highlights the importance of correctional treatment for juvenile offenders. There is a wide choice of correctional treatments available for juveniles, which can be subdivided into two major categories: community treatment and institutional treatment. **Community treatment** refers to efforts to provide care, protection, and treatment for juveniles in need. These efforts include probation, treatment services (such as individual and group counseling), restitution, and other programs. Community treatment also refers to the use of privately maintained residences, such as foster homes, small-group homes, and boarding schools, which are located in the community. Nonresidential programs, where youths remain in their own homes but are required to receive counseling, vocational training, and other services, also fall under the rubric of community treatment.

Institutional treatment facilities are correctional centers operated by federal, state, and county governments; these facilities restrict the movement of residents through staff monitoring, locked exits, and interior fence controls. A variety of functions within juvenile corrections are served by these facilities, including (a) reception centers that screen juveniles and assign them to an appropriate facility, (b) specialized facilities that provide specific types of care, such as drug treatment, (c) training schools or reformatories for youths needing a long-term secure setting, (d) ranch or forestry camps that provide long-term residential care, and (e) boot camps, which seek to rehabilitate youths through the application of rigorous physical training.

Choosing the proper mode of juvenile corrections can be difficult. Some experts believe that any hope for rehabilitating juvenile offenders and resolving the problems of juvenile crime lies in community treatment programs. Such programs are smaller than secure facilities for juveniles, operate in a community setting, and offer creative approaches to treating the offender. In contrast, institutionalizing young offenders may do more harm than good. It exposes them to prisonlike conditions and to more-experienced delinquents without giving them the benefit of constructive treatment programs.

Those who favor secure treatment are concerned about the threat that violent young offenders present to the community and believe that a stay in a juvenile institution may have a long-term deterrent effect. They point to the findings of Charles Murray and Louis B. Cox, who uncovered what they call a **suppression effect**—a reduction in the number of arrests per year following release from a secure facility— which is not achieved when juveniles are placed in less-punitive programs.[2] Murray and Cox concluded that the justice system must choose which outcome its programs are aimed at achieving: prevention of delinquency, or the care and protection of needy youths. If the former is a proper goal, institutionalization or the threat of institutionalization is desirable. Not surprisingly, secure treatment is still being used extensively, and the populations of these facilities continue to grow as state legislators pass more stringent and punitive sentencing packages aimed at repeat juvenile offenders.

community treatment
Using nonsecure and noninstitutional residences, counseling services, victim restitution programs, and other community services to treat juveniles in their own communities.

suppression effect
A reduction in the number of arrests per year for youths who have been incarcerated or otherwise punished.

We begin this chapter with a detailed discussion of community treatment, examining both traditional probation and new approaches for providing probation services to juvenile offenders. Next, we trace the development of alternatives to incarceration, including community-based, nonsecure treatment programs and graduated sanctions (programs that provide community-based options while reserving secure care for violent offenders). The current state of secure juvenile corrections is then reviewed, beginning with some historical background, followed by a discussion of life in institutions, treatment issues, legal rights, and aftercare and reentry programs.

JUVENILE PROBATION

probation
Nonpunitive, legal disposition for juveniles emphasizing community treatment in which the juvenile is closely supervised by an officer of the court and must adhere to a strict set of rules to avoid incarceration.

Probation and other forms of community treatment generally refer to nonpunitive legal dispositions for delinquent youths, emphasizing treatment without incarceration. Probation is the primary form of community treatment used by the juvenile justice system. A juvenile who is on probation is maintained in the community under the supervision of an officer of the court. Probation also encompasses a set of rules and conditions that must be met for the offender to remain in the community. Juveniles on probation may be placed in a wide variety of community-based treatment programs that provide services ranging from group counseling to drug treatment.

Community treatment is based on the idea that the juvenile offender is not a danger to the community and has a better chance of being rehabilitated within the community. It provides offenders with the opportunity to be supervised by trained personnel who can help them reestablish forms of acceptable behavior in a community setting. When applied correctly, community treatment (a) maximizes the liberty of the individual while vindicating the authority of the law and protecting the public, (b) promotes rehabilitation by maintaining normal community contacts, (c) avoids the negative effects of confinement, which often severely complicate the reintegration of the offender into the community, and (d) greatly reduces the financial cost to the public.[3]

Historical Development

Although the major developments in community treatment have occurred in the twentieth century, its roots go back much farther. In England specialized procedures for dealing with youthful offenders were recorded as early as 1820, when the magistrates of the Warwickshire quarter sessions (periodic court hearings held in a county, or shire, of England) adopted the practice of sentencing youthful criminals to prison terms of one day, then releasing them conditionally under the supervision of their parents or masters.[4]

In the United States, juvenile probation developed as part of the wave of social reform characterizing the latter half of the nineteenth century. Massachusetts took the first step. Under an act passed in 1869, an agent of the state board of charities was authorized to appear in criminal trials involving juveniles, to find them suitable homes, and to visit them periodically. These services were soon broadened, so that by 1890 probation had become a mandatory part of the court structure.[5]

Probation was a cornerstone in the development of the juvenile court system. In fact, in some states, supporters of the juvenile court movement viewed probation as the first step toward achieving the benefits that the new court was intended to provide. The rapid spread of juvenile courts during the first decades of the twentieth century encouraged the further development of probation. The two were closely related and, to a large degree, both sprang from the conviction that the young could be rehabilitated and that the public was responsible for protecting them.

Expanding Community Treatment

By the mid-1960s, juvenile probation had become a complex institution that touched the lives of an enormous number of children. To many experts, institutionalization of even the most serious delinquent youths is a mistake. Reformers believed that confinement in a high-security institution could not solve the problems that brought a youth into a delinquent way of life, and that the experience could actually help amplify delinquency once the youth returned to the community.[6] Surveys indicating that 30 to 40 percent of adult prison inmates had prior experience with the juvenile court, and that many had been institutionalized as youths, gave little support to the argument that an institutional experience can be beneficial or reduce recidivism.[7]

The Massachusetts Experience The expansion of community programs was energized by correctional reform in the state of Massachusetts. Since the early 1970s, Massachusetts has led the movement to keep juvenile offenders in the community. After decades of documenting the failures of the youth correctional system, Massachusetts, led by its juvenile correctional commissioner Jerome Miller, closed most of its secure juvenile facilities.[8] Today, 30 years later, the Massachusetts Department of Youth Services still operates a community-based correctional system. The majority of youths are serviced in nonsecure community settings, and only a few dangerous or unmanageable youths are placed in some type of secure facilities.

Many of the early programs suffered from residential isolation and limited services. Over time, however, many of the group homes and unlocked structured residential settings were relocated in residential community environments and became highly successful in addressing the needs of juveniles, while presenting little or no security risk to themselves or others. For example, the Roxbury Youthworks is an inner-city program in Boston that aims to control delinquency through a comprehensive range of resources that include (a) evaluation and counseling at a local court clinic, (b) employment and training, (c) detention diversion, and (d) outreach and tracking to help youths reenter the community. Contracting with the state, Roxbury Youthworks provides intensive community supervision for almost 90 percent of the youths under its jurisdiction.[9]

Though the efforts to turn juvenile corrections into a purely community-based system has not been adopted elsewhere, the Massachusetts model encouraged development of nonpunitive programs, which have proliferated across the nation. The concept of probation has been expanded, and new programs have been created.

Contemporary Juvenile Probation

Traditional probation is still the backbone of community-based corrections. As Figure 16.1 shows, almost 385,400 juveniles were placed on formal probation in 2002, which amounts to more than 62 percent of all juvenile dispositions. The use of probation has increased significantly since 1993, when around 224,500 adjudicated youths were placed on probation.[10] These figures show that regardless of public sentiment, probation continues to be a popular dispositional alternative for judges. Here are the arguments in favor of probation:

I For youths who can be supervised in the community, probation represents an appropriate disposition.

I Probation allows the court to tailor a program to each juvenile offender, including those involved in person-oriented offenses. Recent research, however, raises questions about the adequacy of the present system to attend to the specific needs of female youths on probation.[11]

I The justice system continues to have confidence in rehabilitation, while accommodating demands for legal controls and public protection, even when caseloads may include many more serious offenders than in the past.

I Probation is often the disposition of choice, particularly for status offenders.[12]

FIGURE 16.1

Probation and Correctional Population Trends

NOTE: There was a substantial increase between 1993 and 2002 in the number of cases in which adjudicated juveniles were placed on probation.

SOURCE: Howard N. Snyder and Melissa Sickmund, *Juvenile Offenders and Victims: 2006 National Report* (Pittsburgh, PA: National Center for Juvenile Justice, 2006), pp. 174–175. Available at www.ojjdp.ncjrs/ojstatbb/nr2006/downloads/chapter6.xls (accessed September 3, 2007).

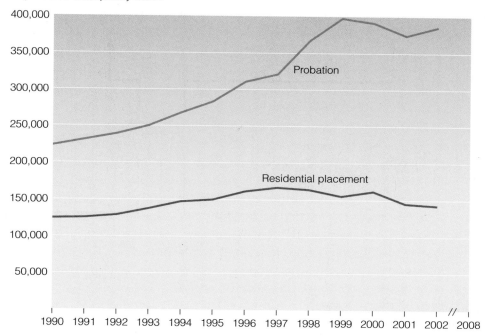

Adjudicated delinquency cases

The Nature of Probation In most jurisdictions, probation is a direct judicial order that allows a youth who is found to be a delinquent or status offender to remain in the community under court-ordered supervision. A probation sentence implies a contract between the court and the juvenile. The court promises to hold a period of institutionalization in abeyance; the juvenile promises to adhere to a set of rules mandated by the court. If the rules are violated—and especially if the juvenile commits another offense—the probation may be revoked. In that case, the contract is terminated and the original commitment order may be enforced. The rules of probation vary, but they typically involve conditions such as attending school or work, keeping regular hours, remaining in the jurisdiction, and staying out of trouble.

In the juvenile court, probation is often ordered for an indefinite period. Depending on the statutes of the jurisdiction, the seriousness of the offense, and the juvenile's adjustment on probation, youths can remain under supervision until the court no longer has jurisdiction over them (that is, when they reach the age of majority). State statutes determine whether a judge can specify how long a juvenile may be placed under an order of probation. In most jurisdictions, the status of probation is reviewed regularly to ensure that a juvenile is not kept on probation needlessly. Generally, discretion lies with the probation officer to discharge youths who are adjusting to the treatment plan.

conditions of probation
The rules and regulations mandating that a juvenile on probation behave in a particular way.

Conditions of Probation Conditions of probation are rules mandating that a juvenile on probation behave in a particular way. They can include restitution or reparation, intensive supervision, intensive counseling, participation in a therapeutic program, or participation in an educational or vocational training program. In addition to these specific conditions, state statutes generally allow courts to insist that probationers lead law-abiding lives, maintain a residence in a family setting, refrain from associating with certain types of people, and remain in a particular area unless they have permission to leave. (See Figure 16.2 for different probation options.)

Although probation conditions vary, they are never supposed to be capricious, cruel, or beyond the capacity of the juvenile to satisfy. Furthermore, conditions of probation should relate to the crime that was committed and to the conduct of the youth. Courts have invalidated probation conditions that were harmful or that violated the juvenile's due process rights. Restricting a young person's movement, insisting on

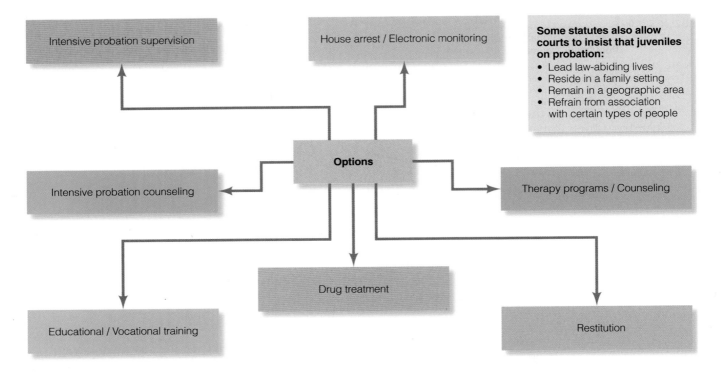

FIGURE 16.2
Conditions of Probation

a mandatory program of treatment, ordering indefinite terms of probation, and demanding financial reparation where this is impossible are all grounds for appellate court review. For example, it would not be appropriate for a probation order to bar a youth from visiting his girlfriend (unless he had threatened or harmed her) merely because her parents objected to the relationship.[13] However, courts have ruled that it is permissible to bar juveniles from such sources of danger as a "known gang area" in order to protect them from harm.[14]

If a youth violates the conditions of probation—and especially if the juvenile commits another offense—the court can revoke probation. In this case, the contract is terminated and the original commitment order may be enforced. The juvenile court ordinarily handles a decision to revoke probation upon recommendation of the probation officer. Today, as a result of Supreme Court decisions dealing with the rights of adult probationers, a juvenile is normally entitled to legal representation and a hearing when a violation of probation occurs.[15]

Organization and Administration

Probation services are administered by the local juvenile court, or by the state administrative office of courts, in 23 states and the District of Columbia. In another 14 states, juvenile probation services are split, with the juvenile court having control in urban counties and a state executive serving in smaller counties. About 10 states have a statewide office of juvenile probation located in the executive branch. In 3 states, county executives administer probation.[16] These agencies employ an estimated 18,000 juvenile probation officers throughout the United States.

In the typical juvenile probation department, the chief probation officer is central to its effective operation. In addition, large probation departments include one or more assistant chiefs, each of whom is responsible for one aspect of probation service. One assistant chief might oversee training, another might supervise special offender groups, and still another might act as liaison with police or community-service agencies.

Although juvenile probation services continue to be predominantly organized under the judiciary, recent legislative activity has been in the direction of transferring those services from the local juvenile court judge to a state court administrative office. Whether local juvenile courts or state agencies should administer juvenile probation services is debatable. In years past, the organization of probation services depended primarily on the size of the program and the number of juveniles under its supervision. Because of this momentum to develop unified court systems, many juvenile court services are being consolidated into state court systems.

Duties of Juvenile Probation Officers

juvenile probation officer
Officer of the court involved in all four stages of the court process—intake, predisposition, postadjudication, and postdisposition—who assists the court and supervises juveniles placed on probation.

The juvenile probation officer plays an important role in the justice process, beginning with intake and continuing throughout the period in which a juvenile is under court supervision. Probation officers are involved at four stages of the court process. At *intake*, they screen complaints by deciding to adjust the matter, refer the juvenile to an agency for service, or refer the case to the court for judicial action. During the *predisposition* stage, they participate in release or detention decisions. At the *postadjudication* stage, they assist the court in reaching its dispositional decision. During *postdisposition*, they supervise juveniles placed on probation.

At intake, the probation staff has preliminary discussions with the juvenile and the family to determine whether court intervention is necessary or whether the matter can be better resolved by some form of social service. If the juvenile is placed in a detention facility, the probation officer helps the court decide whether the juvenile should continue to be held or released pending the adjudication and disposition of the case.

social investigation report, predisposition report
Developed by the juvenile probation officer, this report consists of a clinical diagnosis of the juvenile and his or her need for court assistance, relevant environmental and personality factors, and any other information that would assist the court in developing a treatment plan for the juvenile.

The probation officer exercises tremendous influence over the youth and the family by developing a social investigation report (also called a predisposition report) and submitting it to the court. This report is a clinical diagnosis of the youth's problems and of the need for court assistance based on an evaluation of social functioning, personality, and environmental issues. The report includes an analysis of the child's feelings about the violations and his or her capacity for change. It also examines the influence of family members, peers, and other environmental influences in producing and possibly resolving the problems. All of this information is brought

Juvenile probation officers provide supervision and treatment in the community. The treatment plan is a product of the intake, diagnostic, and investigative aspects of probation. Treatment plans vary in terms of approach and structure. Some juveniles simply report to the probation officer and follow the conditions of probation. In other cases, juvenile probation officers will supervise young people more intensely, monitor their daily activities, and work with them in directed treatment programs. Here, a juvenile probation officer and police officer talk with Crips gang members in California.

© A. Ramey/PhotoEdit

together in a complex but meaningful picture of the offender's personality, problems, and environment.

Juvenile probation officers also provide the youth with supervision and treatment in the community. Treatment plans vary in terms of approach and structure. Some juveniles simply report to the probation officer and follow the conditions of probation. In other cases, the probation officer may need to provide extensive counseling to the youth and family or, more typically, refer them to other social service agencies, such as a drug treatment center. Figure 16.3 provides an overview of the juvenile probation officer's sphere of influence. Exhibit 16.1 summarizes the probation officer's role. Performance of such a broad range of functions requires thorough training. Today, juvenile probation officers have legal or social work backgrounds or special counseling skills.

PROBATION INNOVATIONS

Community corrections have traditionally emphasized offender rehabilitation. The probation officer has been viewed as a caseworker or counselor, whose primary job is to help the offender adjust to society. Offender surveillance and control have seemed more appropriate for law enforcement, jails, and prisons than for community corrections.[17] Since 1980, a more conservative justice system has reoriented toward social control. While the rehabilitative ideals of probation have not been abandoned, new programs have been developed that add a control dimension to community corrections. In some cases this has involved the use of police officers, working in

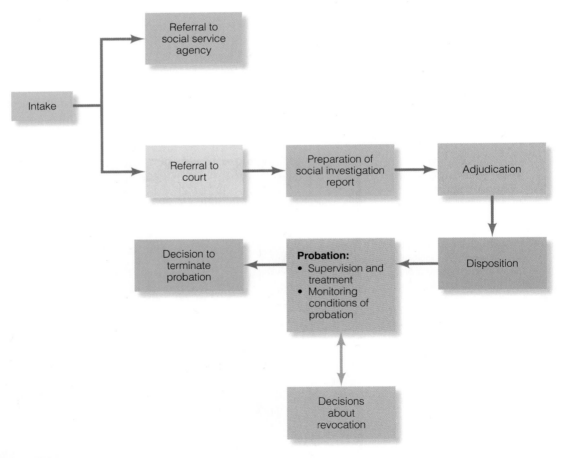

FIGURE 16.3
The Juvenile Probation Officer's Influence

EXHIBIT 16.1

Duties of the Juvenile Probation Officer

I Provide direct counseling and casework services

I Interview and collect social service data

I Make diagnostic recommendations

I Maintain working relationships with law enforcement agencies

I Use community resources and services

I Direct volunteer case aides

I Write predisposition or social investigation reports

I Work with families of children under supervision

I Provide specialized services, such as group therapy

I Supervise specialized caseloads involving children with special problems

I Make decisions about the revocation of probation and its termination

collaboration with probation officers, to enhance the supervision of juvenile probationers.[18] These programs can be viewed as "probation plus," since they add restrictive penalties and conditions to community-service orders. More punitive than probation, intermediate sanctions can be politically attractive to conservatives, while still appealing to liberals as alternatives to incarceration. What are some of these new alternative sanctions? (See Concept Summary 16.1.)

Intensive Supervision

juvenile intensive probation supervision (JIPS)
A true alternative to incarceration that involves almost daily supervision of the juvenile by the probation officer assigned to the case.

Juvenile intensive probation supervision (JIPS) involves treating offenders who would normally have been sent to a secure treatment facility as part of a very small probation caseload that receives almost daily scrutiny.[19] The primary goal of JIPS is *decarceration*; without intensive supervision, youngsters would normally be sent to secure juvenile facilities that are already overcrowded. The second goal is control; high-risk juvenile offenders can be maintained in the community under much closer security than traditional probation efforts can provide. A third goal is maintaining community ties and reintegration. Offenders can remain in the community and complete their education while avoiding the pains of imprisonment.

Intensive probation programs get mixed reviews. Some jurisdictions find that they are more successful than traditional probation supervision and come at a much

Concept Summary 16.1

Community-Based Corrections

Although correctional treatment in the community generally refers to nonpunitive legal dispositions, in most cases there are still restrictions designed to protect the public and hold juvenile offenders accountable for their actions.

Type	Main Restrictions
Probation	I Regular supervision by a probation officer; youth must adhere to conditions such as attend school or work, stay out of trouble.
Intensive supervision	I Almost daily supervision by a probation officer; adhere to similar conditions as regular probation.
House arrest	I Remain at home during specified periods; often there is monitoring through random phone calls, visits, or electronic devices.
Restorative justice	I Restrictions may be prescribed by community members to help repair harm done to victim.
Balanced probation	I Restrictions are tailored to the risk the juvenile offender presents to the community.
Residential programs	I Placement in a residential, nonsecure facility such as group home or foster home; adhere to conditions; close monitoring.
Nonresidential programs	I Remain in own home; comply with treatment regime.

cheaper cost than incarceration.[20] However, some studies indicate that the failure rate is high and that younger offenders who commit petty crimes are the most likely to fail when placed in intensive supervision programs.[21] It is not surprising that intensive probation clients fail more often because, after all, they are more serious offenders who might otherwise have been incarcerated and are now being watched and supervised more closely than other probationers. In one experimental study of intensive probation supervision plus a coordinated team approach for high-risk juveniles, known as the Los Angeles County Repeat Offender Prevention Program (ROPP), mixed results were found for those who received the program compared to a similar group of youths who received regular probation only. Recidivism was reduced in the short term but not over the long term, school performance was increased, and there was no difference in probation technical violations.[22] In another recent California experiment of juvenile intensive probation supervision, no significant differences were observed in recidivism rates among those youths who received intensive probation compared to a similar group of youths who received regular probation.[23]

An innovative experiment in three Mississippi counties examined the differential effects on juvenile justice costs for intensive supervision and monitoring, regular probation, and cognitive behavioral treatment, which involved sessions on problem solving, social skills, negotiation skills, the management of emotion, and values enhancement, to improve the thinking and reasoning ability of juvenile offenders. After one year of the program the intensive supervision treatment was found to be less cost effective than the other two treatments, with the cognitive behavioral treatment imposing the fewest costs on the juvenile justice system.[24]

Despite its poor showing in a number of evaluations, juvenile intensive probation supervision continues to be used across the country. When used in combination with other probation innovations and tailored to the needs of the juvenile, it can produce promising results. The Case Profile entitled "Karen's Story" highlights one such success.

Electronic Monitoring

Another program that has been used with adult offenders and is finding its way into the juvenile justice system is **house arrest**, which is often coupled with **electronic monitoring**. This program allows offenders sentenced to probation to remain in the community on condition that they stay at home during specific periods

house arrest
An offender is required to stay at home during specified periods of time; monitoring is done by random phone calls and visits or by electronic devices.

electronic monitoring
Active monitoring systems consist of a radio transmitter worn by the offender that sends a continuous signal to the probation department computer, alerting officials if the offender leaves his or her place of confinement. Passive systems employ computer-generated random phone calls that must be responded to in a certain period of time from a particular phone or other device.

A number of probation innovations have been experimented with to keep juvenile offenders from being sent to secure juvenile facilities. One of these is electronic monitoring, which, in addition to requiring juveniles to follow regular conditions of probation, monitors their movements to keep them confined to specified areas such as home, work, or school. Pictured here is Steven Wesley, regional manager for Delaware Juvenile Probation and Aftercare, holding a global positioning systems transmitter that is used to track the movements of juvenile delinquents placed on house arrest. The transmitter can be worn on the wrist or ankle.

© AP Images/Suchat Pederson

Karen's Story

KAREN GILLIGAN, 16, WAS THE OLDEST OF FOUR CHILDREN LIVING WITH THEIR PARENTS IN A SMALL RURAL COMMUNITY. HER MOTHER WORKED TWO JOBS, HER father was unemployed, and both parents drank heavily. Karen's high school attendance was sporadic. She had started to experiment with alcohol and vandalized local businesses. After being arrested in a stolen car on several occasions, Karen was referred to juvenile court and was put on community supervision and probation. An initial assessment was provided by her probation officer, and formal dispositional recommendations were made to the court. She was to remain at home on house arrest for 60 days, attend school regularly and maintain at least a C average, follow an alcohol and drug assessment program, and participate in weekly family therapy with her parents. Karen was also ordered to cooperate with the juvenile restitution program, pay her restitution in full within six months, and participate in the Community Adolescent Intensive Supervision Program, as arranged by her probation officer.

Not used to being accountable to anyone, Karen struggled initially with all the new rules and expectations. She missed some of her initial appointments and skipped some classes at school. Karen's probation officer began making unannounced visits to her at school, trying to help her understand the consequences of her behavior. Through the intensive supervision program, Karen was required to meet every day after school at a local community center where she received tutoring, group counseling with other offenders, and the guidance of many counselors. The group sessions focused on changing negative thinking, offering alternatives to aggression, and avoiding criminal behavior, gang involvement, and drugs and alcohol.

It was clear to her probation officer that Karen possessed many strengths and positive attributes. She enjoyed dancing and singing, and even liked school at times. The team of professionals encouraged her to focus on these qualities. With help, Karen began to understand her destructive behavior and seek ways to turn her life around. She spoke with her probation officer about creating life goals and making plans for achieving them.

In addition to Karen's individual counseling, her family participated in weekly family therapy to talk about their issues and to address how to best support the children. Initially, the sessions were very challenging and stressful for the entire family. They blamed each other for their difficulties, and Karen seemed to be the target of much of the anger expressed by her parents. The therapist worked with them to reduce the conflict and help them establish goals for their therapy that could improve their family life.

During the many months of intensive supervision, treatment, and family therapy, Karen was able to stop her delinquent behavior, pay her restitution, attend school regularly, and improve her communication with her parents. Through therapy, Karen's mother also acknowledged that she needed some assistance with her drinking and entered treatment. Karen's probation officer provided the court with regular monthly progress reports showing significant improvement in her behavior and lifestyle choices. Karen has proven her success and continues to live with her parents and siblings. She plans to attend a local college after graduation to prepare for a career in the medical field. ■

CRITICAL THINKING

1. Do you agree or disagree with the probation officer's recommendations to the court? What would you have done differently? Can you think of additional programs or services that would have been helpful in this situation?

2. Initially, Karen struggled with rules and expectations. Her probation officer worked with her to help her accomplish the goals. What could you say to a juvenile who is in this situation? How would you try to motivate a teen in trouble with the law?

3. Do you think it was a good idea to put Karen on house arrest in her parental home? What problems could have come of this? If Karen had continued to break the law, should she have been removed? When should a juvenile delinquent be removed from her parents' home due to her criminal behavior? What crimes do you think would justify an automatic removal and what would need to be accomplished for the child to return?

(for example, after school or work, on weekends, and in the evenings). Offenders may be monitored through random phone calls, visits, or, in some jurisdictions, electronic devices.

Two types of electronic systems are used: active and passive. *Active systems* monitor the offender by continuously sending a signal back to the central office. If an offender leaves home at an unauthorized time, the signal is broken and the failure recorded. In some cases, the control officer is automatically notified through a beeper. In contrast, *passive systems* usually involve random phone calls generated by computers to which the juvenile offender must respond within a particular time (for example, 30 seconds). Some passive systems require the offender to place the monitoring device in a verifier box that sends a signal back to the control computer; another approach is to have the arrestee repeat words that are analyzed by a voice verifier and compared with tapes of the juvenile's voice.

Most systems employ radio transmitters that receive a signal from a device worn by the offender and relay it back to the computer via telephone lines. Probationers are fitted with an unremovable monitoring device that alerts the probation department's computers if they leave their place of confinement.[25]

Joseph B. Vaughn conducted one of the first surveys of juvenile electronic monitoring in 1989, examining eight programs in five different probation departments.[26] Vaughn found that all the programs adopted electronic monitoring to reduce institutional overcrowding and that most agencies reported success in reducing the number of days juveniles spent in detention. In addition, the programs allowed the youths, who would otherwise be detained, to remain in the home and participate in counseling, educational, or vocational activities. Of particular benefit to pretrial detainees was the opportunity to remain in a home environment with supervision. This experience provided the court with a much clearer picture of how the juvenile would eventually reintegrate into society. However, Vaughn found that none of the benefits of the treatment objective in the programs had been empirically validated. The potential for behavior modification and the lasting effects of any personal changes remain unknown.

Currently, there is widespread belief that electronic monitoring can be effective, with some evaluations showing that recidivism rates are no higher than in traditional programs, costs are lower, and institutional overcrowding is reduced. Some studies also reveal that electronic monitoring seems to work better with some individuals than others: serious felony offenders, substance abusers, repeat offenders, and people serving the longest sentences are the most likely to fail.[27] However, in a recent evidence-based review on the effects of electronic monitoring on recidivism, criminologists Marc Renzema and Evan Mayo-Wilson find that the results do not support the claim that it works at the present time. This conclusion was largely based on there being too few high-quality studies available and a difficulty in isolating the independent effects of programs that combine electronic monitoring with other interventions. The researchers do not call for an end to the use of electronic monitoring, but call for new and better experiments.[28]

Restorative Justice

Restorative justice is a nonpunitive strategy for delinquency control that attempts to address the issues that produce conflict between two parties (offender and victim) and, hence, reconcile the parties. Restoration rather than retribution or punishment is at the heart of the restorative justice approach. (See Chapter 5 for more details on restorative justice.)

Researchers Heather Strang and Lawrence Sherman carried out a systematic review and meta-analysis of the effects of restorative justice on juvenile reoffending and victim satisfaction. The review involved two studies from Australia and one from the United States that evaluated the restorative justice practice of face-to-face conferences. (The main reason for the small number of studies is that the authors used only those studies that employed the highest quality evaluation design—randomized controlled experiments—to assess program effects.) The conferences proceeded as follows:

> *Any victims (or their representatives) present have the opportunity to describe the full extent of the harm a crime has caused, offenders are required to listen to the victims and to understand the consequences of their own actions, and all participants are invited to deliberate about what actions the offender could take to repair them. The precondition of such a conference is that the offender does not dispute the fact that he is responsible for the harm caused, and the conference cannot and will not become a trial to determine what happened.*[29]

The review found evidence that this form of restorative justice can be an effective strategy in reducing repeat offending by juveniles who have committed violent crimes. The type of violence includes minor offenses of battery to middle-level offenses of assault and aggravated assault. The review also found that face-to-face conferences can be effective in preventing victims from committing crimes of retaliation against their perpetrators. Perhaps not surprisingly, across all studies victim satisfaction levels strongly favored restorative justice compared to traditional juvenile justice proceedings.[30] Successful results have also been demonstrated in other restorative justice programs for juvenile offenders.[31]

Balanced Probation

To learn more about the **Australian restorative justice experiments**, go to academic.cengage.com/criminaljustice/siegel.

balanced probation
Programs that integrate community protection, accountability of the juvenile offender, competency, and individualized attention to the juvenile offender; based on the principle that juvenile offenders must accept responsibility for their behavior.

In recent years some jurisdictions have turned to a balanced probation approach in an effort to enhance the success of probation.[32] Balanced probation systems build on the principles of restorative justice, by integrating community protection, the accountability of the juvenile offender, and individualized attention to the offender (see Figure 16.4). These programs are based on the view that juveniles are responsible for their actions and have an obligation to society whenever they commit an offense. The probation officer establishes a program tailored to the offender while helping the offender accept responsibility for his or her actions. The balanced approach is promising because it specifies a distinctive role for the juvenile probation system.[33] The balanced approach has been implemented with some success, as these examples demonstrate:

- In Pittsburgh, probationers in an intensive day treatment program solicit suggestions from community organizations about service projects they would like to see completed. They work with community residents on projects such as home repair and gardening for the elderly, voter registration, painting homes and public buildings, and cultivating community gardens.

- In Florida, in a program sponsored by the Florida Department of Juvenile Justice and supervised by The 100 Black Men of Palm Beach County, Inc., offenders create shelters for abused, abandoned, and HIV-positive infants. Victims' rights advocates also train juvenile justice staff on sensitivity in their interaction with victims and help prepare victim awareness curriculums for youths in residential programs.

- In cities and towns in Pennsylvania, Montana, and Minnesota, family members and other citizens acquainted with a juvenile offender, or the victim of a juvenile crime, gather to determine the best response to the offense. Held in schools, churches, or other community facilities, these conferences ensure that offenders hear community disapproval of their behavior. Participants develop an agreement for repairing the damage to the victim and the community and define a plan for reintegrating the offender.[34]

FIGURE 16.4
Balanced Approach Mission

SOURCE: Gordon Bazemore and Mark Umbreit, *Balanced and Restorative Justice for Juveniles—A Framework for Juvenile Justice in the 21st Century* (Washington, DC: Office of Juvenile Justice and Delinquency Prevention, 1997), p. 14.

Another promising program that adheres to a balanced probation approach is the California 8% Solution, which is run by the Orange County Probation Department. The "8%" refers to the percentage of juvenile offenders who are responsible for the majority of crime: In the case of Orange County, 8 percent of first-time offenders were responsible for 55 percent of repeat cases over a three-year period. This 8 percent problem has become the 8 percent solution, by the Probation Department initiating a comprehensive, multiagency program targeting this group of offenders.[35]

Once the probation officer identifies an offender for the program—the 8% Early Intervention Program—the youth is referred to the Youth and Family Resource Center. Here the youth's needs are assessed and an appropriate treatment plan is developed. Some of the services provided to youths include

I   An outside school for students in junior and senior high school

I   Transportation to and from home

I   Counseling for drug and alcohol abuse

I   Employment preparation and job placement services

I   At-home, intensive family counseling[36]

Although balanced probation programs are still in their infancy and their effectiveness remains to be tested, they have generated great interest because of their potential for relieving overcrowded correctional facilities and reducing the pain and stigma of incarceration. There seems to be little question that the use of these innovations, and juvenile probation in general, will increase in the years ahead. Given the $40,000 cost of a year's commitment to a typical residential facility, it should not be a great burden to develop additional probation services.

Restitution

Victim restitution is another widely used method of community treatment. In most jurisdictions, restitution is part of a probationary sentence and is administered by the county probation staff. In many jurisdictions, independent restitution programs have been set up by local governments; in others, restitution is administered by a private nonprofit organization.[37]

Restitution can take several forms. A juvenile can reimburse the victim of the crime or donate money to a charity or public cause; this is referred to as **monetary restitution**. In other instances, a juvenile may be required to provide some service directly to the victim (**victim service restitution**) or to assist a community organization (**community service restitution**).

monetary restitution
A requirement that juvenile offenders compensate crime victims for out-of-pocket losses caused by the crime, including property damage, lost wages, and medical expenses.

victim service restitution
The juvenile offender is required to provide some service directly to the crime victim.

community service restitution
The juvenile offender is required to assist some worthwhile community organization for a period of time.

Requiring youths to reimburse the victims of their crimes is the most widely used method of restitution in the United States. Less widely used, but more common in Europe, is restitution to a charity. In the past few years numerous programs have been set up for the juvenile offender to provide service to the victim or to participate in community programs—for example, working in schools for children with developmental delays. In some cases, juveniles are required to contribute both money and community service. Other programs emphasize employment.[38]

Restitution programs can be employed at various stages of the juvenile justice process. They can be part of a diversion program prior to conviction, a method of informal adjustment at intake, or a condition of probation. Restitution has a number of advantages: It provides alternative sentencing options; it offers monetary compensation or service to crime victims; it allows the juvenile the opportunity to compensate the victim and take a step toward becoming a productive member of society; it helps relieve overcrowded juvenile courts, probation caseloads, and detention facilities. Finally, like other alternatives to incarceration, restitution has the potential for allowing vast savings in the operation of the juvenile justice system. Monetary restitution programs in particular may improve the public's attitude toward juvenile justice by offering equity to the victims of crime and ensuring that offenders take responsibility for their actions.

Despite its many advantages, some believe restitution supports retribution rather than rehabilitation because it emphasizes justice for the victim and criminal responsibility for illegal acts. There is some concern that restitution creates penalties for juvenile offenders where none existed before.

The use of restitution is increasing. In 1977 there were fewer than 15 formal restitution programs around the United States. By 1985, formal programs existed in 400 jurisdictions, and 35 states had statutory provisions that gave courts the authority to order juvenile restitution.[39] Today, all 50 states, as well as the District of Columbia, have statutory restitution programs.

Does Restitution Work? How successful is restitution as a treatment alternative? Most evaluations have shown that it is reasonably effective and should be expanded.[40] In an analysis of restitution programs across the country, Peter Schneider and Matthew Finkelstein found that between 73 percent and 74 percent of youths who received restitution as a condition of probation successfully completed their orders. The researchers also found that juvenile restitution programs that reported a reduction in recidivism rates were the ones with high successful completion rates.[41]

Anne Schneider conducted a thorough analysis of restitution programs in four different states and found that participants had lower recidivism rates than youths in control groups (regular probation caseloads).[42] Although Schneider's data indicate that restitution may reduce recidivism, the number of youths who had subsequent involvement in the justice system still seemed high. In short, there is evidence that most restitution orders are successfully completed and that youths who make restitution are less likely to become recidivists. However, the number of repeat offenses committed by juveniles who made restitution suggests that, by itself, restitution is not the answer to the delinquency problem.

Restitution programs may be difficult to implement in some circumstances. Offenders may find it difficult to make monetary restitution without securing new employment, which can be difficult during periods of high unemployment. Problems also arise when offenders who need jobs suffer from drug abuse or emotional problems. Public and private agencies are likely sites for community service restitution, but their directors are sometimes reluctant to allow delinquent youths access to their organizations. Beyond these problems, some juvenile probation officers view restitution programs as a threat to their authority and to the autonomy of their organizations.

Another criticism of restitution programs is that they foster involuntary servitude. Indigent clients may be unfairly punished when they are unable to make restitution payments or face probation violations. To avoid such bias, probation officers should first determine why payment has stopped and then suggest appropriate action, rather than simply treating nonpayment as a matter of law enforcement.

Finally, restitution orders are subject to the same abuses as traditional sentencing methods. Restitution orders given to one delinquent offender may be quite different from those given another in a comparable case. To remedy this situation, a number of jurisdictions have been using guidelines to encourage standardization of orders.

Restitution programs may be an important alternative to incarceration, benefiting the child, the victim, and the juvenile justice system. H. Ted Rubin, a leading juvenile justice expert, even advocates that courts placing juveniles in day treatment and community-based residential programs also include restitution requirements in their orders and expect that these requirements be fulfilled during placement.[43] However, all restitution programs should be evaluated carefully to answer these questions:

I What type of offenders would be most likely to benefit from restitution?

I When is monetary restitution more desirable than community service?

I What is the best point in the juvenile justice process to impose restitution?

I What is the effect of restitution on the juvenile justice system?

I How successful are restitution programs?

Residential Community Treatment

As noted earlier, many experts believe that institutionalization of even the most serious delinquent youths is a mistake. Confinement in a high-security institution usually cannot solve the problems that brought a youth into a delinquent way of life, and the experience may actually amplify delinquency once the youth returns to the community. Many agree that warehousing juveniles without attention to their treatment needs does little to prevent their return to criminal behavior. Research has shown that the most effective secure-corrections programs provided individualized services for a small number of participants. Large training schools have not proved to be effective.[44] This realization has produced a wide variety of residential community treatment programs to service youths who need a more secure environment than can be provided by probation services, but who do not require placement in a state-run juvenile correctional facility.

How are community corrections implemented? In some cases, youths are placed under probation supervision, and the probation department maintains a residential treatment facility. Placement can also be made to the department of social services or juvenile corrections with the direction that the youth be placed in a residential facility. **Residential programs** are typically divided into four major categories: (1) group homes, including boarding schools and apartment-type settings, (2) foster homes, (3) family group homes, and (4) rural programs.

Group homes are nonsecure residences that provide counseling, education, job training, and family living. They are staffed by a small number of qualified persons, and generally house 12 to 15 youngsters. The institutional quality of the environment is minimized, and youths are given the opportunity to build a close relationship with the staff. Youths reside in the home, attend public schools, and participate in community activities in the area.

Foster care programs involve one or two juveniles who live with a family—usually a husband and wife who serve as surrogate parents. The juveniles enter into a close relationship with the foster parents and receive the attention and care they did not receive at home. The quality of the foster home experience depends on the foster parents. Foster care for adjudicated juvenile offenders has not been extensive in the United States. Welfare departments generally handle foster placements, and funding of this treatment option has been a problem for the juvenile justice system. However, foster home services have expanded as a community treatment approach.

One example of a successful foster care program is the multidimensional treatment foster care (MTFC) program, developed by social scientists at the Oregon Social Learning Center. Designed for the most serious and chronic male young offenders, this program combines individual therapy such as skill building in problem solving for the youths, and family therapy for the biological or adoptive parents. The foster

residential programs
Placement of a juvenile offender in a residential, nonsecure facility such as a group home, foster home, family group home, or rural home where the juvenile can be closely monitored and develop close relationships with staff members.

group homes
Nonsecured, structured residences that provide counseling, education, job training, and family living.

foster care programs
Juveniles who are orphans or whose parents cannot care for them are placed with families who provide the attention, guidance, and care they did not receive at home.

Residential community treatment serves as an important alternative to the placement of youths in juvenile institutions. Residential programs are nonsecure facilities such as group homes, foster homes, family group homes, or rural homes where the juvenile can be closely monitored and develop close relationships with staff members. Here, a group home mother instructs a juvenile offender on how to clean the kitchen in a residential program for delinquent boys in Riverhead, New York.

© Richard Lord/The Image Works

care families receive training by program staff so they can provide the young people with close supervision, fair and consistent limits and consequences, and a supportive relationship with an adult.[45] Foster care families also receive close supervision and are consulted regularly on the progress of the youth by program staff. An experiment of MTFC found that one year after the completion of the program, participating youths were significantly less likely to be arrested than a control group.[46]

family group homes combine elements of foster care and group home placements. Juveniles are placed in a group home that is run by a family rather than by a professional staff. Troubled youths have an opportunity to learn to get along in a family-like situation, and at the same time the state avoids the startup costs and neighborhood opposition often associated with establishing a public institution.

Rural programs include forestry camps, ranches, and farms that provide recreational activities or work for juveniles. Programs typically handle from 30 to 50 youths. Such programs have the disadvantage of isolating juveniles from the community, but reintegration can be achieved if the youth's stay is short and if family and friends are allowed to visit.

Most residential programs use group counseling as the major treatment tool. Although group facilities have been used less often than institutional placements, there is a trend toward developing community-based residential facilities.

Nonresidential Community Treatment

In **nonresidential programs** youths remain in their homes and receive counseling, education, employment, diagnostic, and casework services. A counselor or probation officer gives innovative and intensive support to help the youth remain at home. Family therapy, educational tutoring, and job placement may all be part of the program.

Nonresidential programs are often modeled on the Provo experiment, begun in 1959 in Utah, and on the Essexfields Rehabilitation Project, started in the early 1960s in Essex County, New Jersey.[47] Today, one of the best-known approaches is multisystemic therapy (MST), which has been replicated at a number of sites around the United States. MST and two other innovative programs are the subject of the Policy and Practice box entitled "Three Model Nonresidential Programs."

Pros and Cons of Residential Community Treatment The community treatment approach has limitations. The public may have a negative impression of community treatment, especially when it is offered to juvenile offenders who pose a threat to society. Institutionalization may be the only answer for violent, chronic offenders. Even if the juvenile crime problem abates, society may be unwilling to accept the outcomes of reform-minded policies and practices. For example, it is not uncommon for neighborhood groups to oppose the location of corrections programs in their community. But is their fear realistic?

Much of the early criticism of community treatment was based on poor delivery of services, shabby operation, and haphazard management, follow-up, and planning. In the early 1970s, when Massachusetts deinstitutionalized its juvenile corrections system, a torrent of reports revealed the inadequate operation of community treatment programs, based in part on the absence of uniform policies and procedures and the lack of accountability. The development of needed programs was hampered, and available resources were misplaced. Today's community treatment programs have generally overcome their early deficiencies and operate more efficiently than in the past.

Despite such criticisms, community-based programs continue to present the most promising alternative to the poor results of reform schools for these reasons:

▌ Some states have found that residential and nonresidential settings produce comparable or lower recidivism rates. Some researchers have found that youths in nonsecure settings are less likely to become recidivists than those placed in more secure settings (although this has not been proven conclusively).

Three Model Nonresidential Programs

MULTISYSTEMIC THERAPY

Multisystemic therapy (MST), a nonresidential delinquency treatment program developed by Dr. Scott Henggeler of the Medical University of South Carolina, views individuals as being "nested" within a complex of interconnected systems, including the family, community, school, and peers. The MST treatment team may target problems in any of these systems for change and use the individual's strengths in these systems to effect that change. Treatment teams, which usually include three counselors, provide services over a four-month period for about 50 families per year.

In one evaluation of the effectiveness of MST in Missouri, 176 high-risk juvenile offenders were randomly assigned either to MST or to a control group that received individual therapy that focused on personal, family, and academic issues. Four years later, only 29 percent of the MST offenders had been rearrested, compared with 74 percent of the control group. Significant reductions were also found in the severity of offenses for the MST group compared to the control group. Meta-analyses that include many evaluations of MST also provide evidence of its effectiveness in treating juvenile offenders. In one of the meta-analyses, MST was found to have reduced recidivism by about 20 percent. This corresponds approximately to a decrease in recidivism from 50 percent in the control group to 30 percent in the MST group. Cost-benefit analyses of MST show that it produces substantial financial savings to the juvenile justice system.

PROJECT NEW PRIDE

Begun in 1973 in Denver, Colorado, Project New Pride has been a model for similar programs around the country. The target group for Project New Pride is serious or violent youthful offenders from 14 to 17 years of age who have at least two prior convictions for serious misdemeanors or felonies and are formally charged or convicted of another offense when they are referred to New Pride. The only youths not eligible for participation are those who have committed forcible rape or are diagnosed as severely psychotic. New Pride believes this restriction is necessary in the interest of the safety of the community and of the youths themselves. The project's specific goals are to steer these hard-core offenders back into the mainstream of their communities and to reduce the number of rearrests. Generally, reintegration into the community means enrolling in school, getting a job, or both.

Each participant in New Pride has six months of intensive involvement and a six-month follow-up period during which the youth slowly reintegrates into the community. During the follow-up period, the youth continues to receive as many services as necessary, such as schooling and job placement, and works closely with counselors.

THE BETHESDA DAY TREATMENT CENTER PROGRAM

The Bethesda Day Treatment Center Program in West Milton, Pennsylvania, is another model day-treatment program. The center's services include intensive supervision, counseling, and coordination of a range of services necessary for youths to develop skills to function effectively in the community. The program provides delinquent and dependent youths, ages 10 to 17, with up to 55 hours of services a week without removing them from their homes. A unique program feature requires work experience for all working-age clients, with 75 percent of their paychecks directed toward payment of fines, court costs, and restitution. A preliminary study revealed recidivism rates far lower than state and national norms.

Critical Thinking

1. What are some of the differences between residential and nonresidential treatment programs for juvenile offenders?

2. What are the features that are characteristic of all three of these successful nonresidential treatment programs?

SOURCES: Shay Bilchik, *A Juvenile Justice System for the 21st Century* (Washington, DC: OJJDP, 1998); Charles M. Borduin et al., "Multisystemic Treatment of Serious Juvenile Offenders: Long-Term Prevention of Criminality and Violence," *Journal of Consulting and Clinical Psychology* 63:569–587 (1995); David P. Farrington and Brandon C. Welsh, "Family-Based Prevention of Offending: A Meta-Analysis," *Australian and New Zealand Journal of Criminology* 36:127–151 (2003); Scott W. Henggeler et al., *Multisystemic Treatment of Antisocial Behavior in Children and Adolescents* (New York: Guilford Press, 1998); Project New Pride (Washington, DC: U.S. Government Printing Office, 1985); Susan R. Woolfenden, K. Williams, and J. K. Peat, "Family and Parenting Interventions for Conduct Disorder and Delinquency: A Meta-Analysis of Randomized Controlled Trials," *Archives of Disease in Childhood* 86:251–256 (2002).

I Community-based programs have lower costs and are especially appropriate for large numbers of nonviolent juveniles and those guilty of lesser offenses.

I Public opinion of community corrections remains positive. Many citizens prefer community-based programs for all but the most serious juvenile offenders.[48]

As jurisdictions continue to face high rates of violent juvenile crime and ever-increasing costs for juvenile justice services, community-based programs will play an important role in providing rehabilitation of juvenile offenders and ensuring public safety.

Experts have confirmed the decline of rehabilitation in juvenile justice throughout much of the United States over the last 25 years.[49] But several recent meta-analysis studies have refuted the claim that "nothing works" with juvenile offenders and have given support to community rehabilitation.[50] According to Barry Krisberg and his associates, the most successful community-based programs seem to share at least some of these characteristics: (a) comprehensiveness, dealing with many aspects of youths' lives, (b) intensivity, involving multiple contacts, (c) operation outside the justice system, (d) foundation upon youths' strengths, and (e) adoption of a socially grounded approach to understanding a juvenile's situation rather than an individual-level (medical or therapeutic) approach.[51]

SECURE CORRECTIONS

When the court determines that community treatment cannot meet the special needs of a delinquent youth, a judge may refer the juvenile to a secure treatment program. Today, correctional institutions operated by federal, state, and county governments are generally classified as either secure or open facilities. Secure facilities restrict the movement of residents through staff monitoring, locked exits, and interior fence controls. Open institutions generally do not restrict the movement of the residents and allow much greater freedom of access to the facility.[52] In the following sections, we analyze the state of secure juvenile corrections, beginning with some historical background. This is followed by a discussion of life in institutions, the juvenile client, treatment issues, legal rights, and aftercare and reentry programs.

History of Juvenile Institutions

Until the early 1800s, juvenile offenders, as well as neglected and dependent children, were confined in adult prisons. The inhumane conditions in these institutions were among the factors that led social reformers to create a separate children's court system in 1899.[53] Early juvenile institutions were industrial schools modeled after adult prisons but designed to protect children from the evil influences in adult facilities. The first was the New York House of Refuge, established in 1825. Not long after this, states began to establish **reform schools** for juveniles. Massachusetts was the first, opening the Lyman School for Boys in Westborough in 1846. New York opened the State Agricultural and Industrial School in 1849, and Maine opened the Maine Boys' Training School in 1853. By 1900, 36 states had reform schools.[54] Although it is difficult to determine exact populations of these institutions, by 1880 there were approximately 11,000 youths in correctional facilities, a number that more than quadrupled by 1980.[55] Early reform schools were generally punitive in nature and were based on the concept of rehabilitation (or reform) through hard work and discipline.

In the second half of the nineteenth century, emphasis shifted to the **cottage system**. Juvenile offenders were housed in compounds of cottages, each of which could accommodate 20 to 40 children. A set of parents ran each cottage, creating a homelike atmosphere. This setup was believed to be more conducive to rehabilitation.

The first cottage system was established in Massachusetts in 1855, the second in Ohio in 1858.[56] The system was held to be a great improvement over training schools. The belief was that by moving away from punishment and toward rehabilitation, not only could offenders be rehabilitated, but also crime among unruly children could be prevented.[57]

Twentieth-Century Developments The early twentieth century witnessed important changes in juvenile corrections. Because of the influence of World War I, reform schools began to adopt a militaristic style. Living units became barracks; cottage groups became companies; house fathers became captains; and superintendents became majors or colonels. Military-style uniforms were standard wear. In addition, the establishment of the first juvenile court in 1899 reflected the expanded use of confinement for delinquent children. As the number of juvenile offenders increased, the forms of juvenile institutions varied to include forestry camps, ranches, and

reform schools
Institutions in which educational and psychological services are used in an effort to improve the conduct of juveniles who are forcibly detained.

cottage system
Housing juveniles in a compound containing a series of cottages, each of which accommodates 20 to 40 children and is run by a set of cottage parents who create a homelike atmosphere.

vocational schools. Beginning in the 1930s, camps modeled after those run by the Civilian Conservation Corps became a part of the juvenile correctional system. These camps centered on conservation activities and work as a means of rehabilitation.

Los Angeles County was the first to use camps during this period.[58] Southern California was experiencing problems with transient youths who came to California with no money and then got into trouble with the law. Rather than filling up the jails, the county placed these offenders in conservation camps, paid them low wages, and released them when they had earned enough money to return home. The camps proved more rehabilitative than training schools, and by 1935 California had established a network of forestry camps for delinquent boys. The idea soon spread to other states.[59]

Also during the 1930s, the U.S. Children's Bureau sought to reform juvenile corrections. The bureau conducted studies to determine the effectiveness of the training school concept. Little was learned from these programs because of limited funding and bureaucratic ineptitude, and the Children's Bureau failed to achieve any significant change. But such efforts recognized the important role of positive institutional care.[60]

Another innovation came in the 1940s with passage of the American Law Institute's Model Youth Correction Authority Act. This act emphasized reception/classification centers. California was the first to try out this idea, opening the Northern Reception Center and Clinic in Sacramento in 1947. Today, there are many such centers scattered around the United States.

Since the 1970s, a major change in institutionalization has been the effort to remove status offenders from institutions housing juvenile delinquents. This includes removing status offenders from detention centers and removing all juveniles from contact with adults in jails. This *decarceration* policy mandates that courts use the **least restrictive alternative** in providing services for status offenders. A noncriminal youth should not be put in a secure facility if a community-based program is available. In addition, the federal government prohibits states from placing status offenders in separate facilities that are similar in form and function to those used for delinquent offenders. This is to prevent states from merely shifting their institutionalized population around so that one training school houses all delinquents and another houses all status offenders, but actual conditions remain the same.

Throughout the 1980s and into the 1990s, admissions to juvenile correctional facilities grew substantially.[61] Capacities of juvenile facilities also increased, but not enough to avoid overcrowding. Training schools became seriously overcrowded in some states, causing private facilities to play an increased role in juvenile corrections. Reliance on incarceration became costly to states: Inflation-controlled juvenile corrections expenditures for public facilities grew to more than $2 billion in 1995, an increase of 20 percent from 1982.[62] A 1994 report issued by the OJJDP said that crowding, inadequate health care, lack of security, and poor control of suicidal behavior was widespread in juvenile corrections facilities. Despite new construction, crowding persisted in more than half the states.[63]

least restrictive alternative
Choosing a program with the least restrictive or secure setting that will best benefit the child.

JUVENILE INSTITUTIONS TODAY: PUBLIC AND PRIVATE

Most juveniles are housed in public institutions administered by state agencies: child and youth services, health and social services, corrections, or child welfare.[64] In some states these institutions fall under a centralized system that covers adults as well as juveniles. Recently, a number of states have removed juvenile corrections from an existing adult corrections department or mental health agency. However, the majority of states still place responsibility for the administration of juvenile corrections within social service departments.

Supplementing publicly funded institutions are private facilities that are maintained and operated by private agencies funded or chartered by state authorities. The majority of today's private institutions are relatively small facilities holding fewer than 30 youths. Many have a specific mission or focus (for example, treating females who display serious emotional problems). Although about 80 percent of public institutions can be characterized as secure, only 20 percent of private institutions are high-security facilities.

Population Trends

Whereas most delinquents are held in public facilities, most status offenders are held in private facilities. At last count, there were slightly less than 97,000 juvenile offenders being held in public (69 percent) and private (31 percent) facilities in the United States. Between 1991 and 1999, the number of juveniles held in custody increased 41 percent, followed by a 10 percent drop from 1999 to 2003. Over this full period of time (1991 to 2003), the number of juveniles held in custody increased 27 percent.[65] The juvenile custody rate varies widely among states: Wyoming makes the greatest use of custodial treatment, incarcerating 606 delinquents in juvenile facilities per 100,000 juveniles in the population, whereas Vermont and Hawaii have the lowest juvenile custody rates (72 and 97, respectively). Although not a state, the District of Columbia actually has the highest juvenile custody rate in the nation, at 625 per 100,000 juveniles. This is more than twice the national average (see Table 16.1).[66] Some states rely heavily on privately run facilities, while others place many youths in out-of-state facilities.

This wide variation in state-level juvenile custody rates has been the subject of much speculation but little empirical research. In an important study, criminologist Daniel Mears found that there are three main explanations for why some states incarcerate juveniles at a much higher rate than others: (1) they have high rates of juvenile property crime and adult violent crime; (2) they have higher adult custody rates; and (3) there is a "cultural acceptance of punitive policies" in some parts of the country. Interestingly, Mears found that western and midwestern states were more likely to have higher juvenile incarceration rates than southern states, thus calling into question the widely held view that the South is disproportionately punitive.[67]

Although the number of institutionalized youths appears to have stabilized in the last few years, the data may reveal only the tip of the iceberg. The data do not include many minors who are incarcerated after they are waived to adult courts or who have been tried as adults because of exclusion statutes. Most states place underage juveniles convicted of adult charges in youth centers until they reach the age of majority, whereupon they are transferred to an adult facility. In addition, there may be a hidden, or subterranean, correctional system that places wayward youths in private mental hospitals and substance abuse clinics for behaviors that might otherwise have brought them a stay in a correctional facility or community-based program.[68] These data suggest that the number of institutionalized children may be far greater than reported in the official statistics.[69] Studies also show that large numbers of youths are improperly incarcerated because of a lack of appropriate facilities. A nationwide survey carried out by congressional investigators as part of the House Committee on Government Reform found that 15,000 children with psychiatric disorders who were awaiting mental health services were improperly incarcerated in secure juvenile detention facilities in 2003.[70] In New Jersey, investigations into the state's child welfare system found that large numbers of teenage foster children were being held in secure juvenile detention facilities. Other states resort to similar practices, citing a lack of appropriate noncorrectional facilities.[71]

Physical Conditions

The physical plants of juvenile institutions vary in size and quality. Many older training schools still place all offenders in a single building, regardless of the offense. More acceptable structures include a reception unit with an infirmary, a security unit, and

TABLE 16.1

State Comparison of Numbers and Rates of Juvenile Offenders in Custody, 2003

State of Offense	Number	Rate
U.S. total	*96,655*	*307*
Upper age 17		
Alabama	1,794	351
Alaska	336	370
Arizona	1,890	284
Arkansas	675	217
California	16,782	392
Colorado	1,776	344
Delaware	333	364
District of Columbia	285	625
Florida	8,208	452
Hawaii	129	97
Idaho	489	287
Indiana	3,045	415
Iowa	975	299
Kansas	1,071	336
Kentucky	837	185
Maine	222	153
Maryland	1,167	181
Minnesota	1,527	259
Mississippi	528	152
Montana	261	245
Nebraska	672	331
Nevada	921	362
New Jersey	1,941	199
New Mexico	606	258
North Dakota	246	347
Ohio	4,176	318
Oklahoma	1,059	265
Oregon	1,275	323
Pennsylvania	4,341	317
Rhode Island	342	295
South Dakota	522	564
Tennessee	1,434	226
Utah	954	307
Vermont	51	72
Virginia	2,376	289
Washington	1,656	236
West Virginia	498	269
Wyoming	357	606
Upper age 16		
Georgia	2,451	273
Illinois	2,715	212
Louisiana	1,821	387
Massachusetts	1,302	216
Michigan	2,706	257
Missouri	1,413	246
New Hampshire	198	150
South Carolina	1,443	346
Texas	7,662	318
Wisconsin	1,524	274

(Continued)

State of Offense	Number	Rate
Upper age 15		
Connecticut	627	210
New York	4,308	272
North Carolina	1,203	169

SOURCE: Howard H. Snyder and Melissa Sickmund, *Juvenile Offenders and Victims: 2006 National Report* (Pittsburgh, PA: National Center for Juvenile Justice, 2006), p. 201.

NOTE: The rate is the number of juvenile offenders in residential placement in 2003 per 100,000 juveniles ages 10 through the upper age of original juvenile court jurisdiction in each state. The U.S. totals include 1,398 juvenile offenders in private facilities for whom state of offense was not reported and 124 juvenile offenders in tribal facilities.

dormitory units or cottages. Planners have concluded that the most effective design for training schools is to have facilities located around a community square. The facilities generally include a dining hall and kitchen area, a storage warehouse, academic and vocational training rooms, a library, an auditorium, a gymnasium, an administration building, and other basic facilities.

The individual living areas also vary, depending on the type of facility and the progressiveness of its administration. Most traditional training school conditions were appalling. Today, however, most institutions provide toilet and bath facilities, beds, desks, lamps, and tables. New facilities usually provide a single room for each individual. However, the Juvenile Residential Facility Census, which collects information about the facilities in which juvenile offenders are held, found that 36 percent of the 2,964 facilities that reported information were overcrowded—that is, they had more residents than available standard beds.[72] Some states, like Massachusetts and Rhode Island, report that upwards of 70 percent of all their facilities for juvenile offenders are overcrowded.[73]

Most experts recommend that juvenile facilities have leisure areas, libraries, education spaces, chapels, facilities where youths can meet with their visitors, windows in all sleeping accommodations, and fire-safety equipment and procedures. Because institutions for delinquent youths vary in purpose, it is not necessary that they meet identical standards. Security measures used in some closed institutions, for instance, may not be required in a residential program.

The physical conditions of secure facilities for juveniles have come a long way from the training schools of the turn of the century. However, many administrators realize that more modernization is necessary to comply with national standards for juvenile institutions.[74] Although some improvements have been made, there are still enormous problems to overcome.

THE INSTITUTIONALIZED JUVENILE

To read about **life in a secure Canadian facility**, go to the website maintained by the Prince George Youth Custody Center in British Columbia, which provides a range of programs to allow youths to make maximal constructive use of their time while in custody. You can access this site via academic .cengage.com/criminaljustice/siegel.

The typical resident of a juvenile facility is a 17-year-old white male incarcerated for an average stay of 3.5 months in a public facility or 4 months in a private facility. Private facilities tend to house younger children, while public institutions provide custodial care for older children, including a small percentage of youths between 18 and 21 years of age. Most incarcerated youths are person, property, or drug offenders.[75]

Mental health needs are particularly acute among institutionalized juveniles. Research suggests that as much as 65 percent of youths in the juvenile justice system suffer from mental health problems, and a large proportion of these youths enter the system without previously having been diagnosed or receiving treatment.[76] Incarcerated youths suffering from mental health problems may find it harder to adjust to their new environment, which may in turn lead to acting out behaviors, disciplinary problems, and problems in participating in treatment programs. All of these problems increase the risk of recidivism upon release to the community.[77] Even with a diagnosis, treatment services can be scarce in the juvenile justice system. One study found that only one out of four (23 percent) juvenile offenders diagnosed with a mental disorder received any treatment.[78] Contributing to the problem is that there is little information on what treatment works best for these juveniles.[79] Wraparound-service planning, which involves a number of social and juvenile justice agencies providing coordinated service delivery for children and families with complex needs, has shown some success in reducing recidivism among juvenile offenders with mental health needs.[80] Columbia University's Center for the Promotion of Mental Health in Juvenile Justice is leading a national effort to improve this state of affairs, as well as the need for improved mental health assessments at intake.

Minority youths are incarcerated at a rate two to four times that of white youths. The difference is greatest for African American youths, with a custody rate of 754 per 100,000 juveniles; for white youths the rate is 190.[81] In a number of states, such as New Jersey, South Dakota, and Wisconsin, the difference in custody rates between African American and white youths is considerably greater (see Table 16.2). Research has found that this overrepresentation is not a result of differentials in arrest rates, but often stems from disparity at early stages of case processing.[82] Of equal importance, minorities are more likely to be confined in secure public facilities rather than in open private facilities that might provide more costly and effective treatment,[83] and among minority groups African American youths are more likely to receive punitive treatment—throughout the juvenile justice system—compared with others.[84]

Learn more about **Columbia University's Center for the Promotion of Mental Health in Juvenile Justice** via academic.cengage .com/criminaljustice/siegel.

Minority youths accused of delinquent acts are less likely than white youths to be diverted from the court system into informal sanctions and are more likely to receive sentences involving incarceration. Today, more than six in ten juveniles in custody belong to racial or ethnic minorities, and seven in ten youths held in custody for a violent crime are minorities.[85] Racial disparity in juvenile disposition is a growing problem that demands immediate public scrutiny.[86] In response, many jurisdictions have initiated studies of racial disproportion in their juvenile justice systems, along with federal requirements to reduce disproportionate minority confinement (DMC), as contained in the Juvenile Justice and Delinquency Prevention Act of 2002.[87] The most recent federal government report on state compliance to reduce DMC demonstrates that some progress has been made but that many challenges remain, including the basic need to identify factors that contribute to DMC (at least 18 states have yet to initiate this process), incomplete and inconsistent data systems, and the need for ongoing evaluation of focused interventions and system-wide efforts to reduce DMC.[88] Some promising practices in reducing DMC, such as cultural competency training and increasing community-based detention alternatives, are beginning to emerge.[89]

For more than two decades, shocking exposés, sometimes resulting from investigations by the U.S. Department of Justice's civil rights division, continue to focus public attention on the problems of juvenile corrections.[90] Today, more so than in past years, some critics believe public scrutiny has improved conditions in training schools. There is greater professionalism among the staff, and staff brutality seems to have diminished. Status offenders and delinquents are, for the most part, held in separate facilities. Confinement length is shorter, and rehabilitative programming has increased. However, there are significant differences in the experiences of male and female delinquents within the institution.

Male Inmates

Males make up the great bulk of institutionalized youth, accounting for six out of every seven juvenile offenders in residential placement,[91] and most programs are directed toward their needs. In many ways their experiences mirror those of adult offenders. In an important paper, Clement Bartollas and his associates identified an inmate value system that they believed was common in juvenile institutions:

▍ Exploit whomever you can.

▍ Don't play up to staff.

TABLE 16.2

State Comparison of Custody Rates Between White and African American Juvenile Offenders, 2003

State of Offense	White	African American
U.S average	*190*	*754*
Alabama	235	586
Alaska	177	339
Arizona	223	579
Arkansas	142	468
California	217	1,246
Colorado	268	1,150
Connecticut	105	669
Delaware	128	1,029
District of Columbia	347	683
Florida	355	973
Georgia	142	500
Hawaii	62	199
Idaho	250	725
Illinois	120	589
Indiana	316	1,188
Iowa	242	1,337
Kansas	213	1,320
Kentucky	133	653
Louisiana	202	663
Maine	149	182
Maryland	98	319
Massachusetts	111	811
Michigan	169	602
Minnesota	156	1,149
Mississippi	75	246
Missouri	159	690
Montana	188	418
Nebraska	214	1,529
Nevada	289	958
New Hampshire	144	579
New Jersey	51	795
New Mexico	153	823
New York	138	712
North Carolina	106	332
North Dakota	235	1,384
Ohio	207	916
Oklahoma	196	673
Oregon	291	1,075
Pennsylvania	139	1,207
Rhode Island	192	1,425
South Carolina	201	567
South Dakota	310	3,199
Tennessee	143	507
Texas	194	771
Utah	258	951
Vermont	71	0

(Continued)

State of Offense	White	African American
Virginia	143	715
Washington	200	770
West Virginia	229	953
Wisconsin	143	1,389
Wyoming	507	3,035

NOTE: The custody rate is the number of juvenile offenders in residential placement on October 22, 2003, per 100,000 juveniles age 10 through the upper age of original juvenile court jurisdiction in each state. The U.S. total includes 1,398 juvenile offenders in private facilities for whom state of offense was not reported and 124 juvenile offenders in tribal facilities.

SOURCE: Howard N. Snyder and Melissa Sickmund, *Juvenile Offenders and Victims: 2006 National Report* (Pittsburgh, PA: National Center for Juvenile Justice, 2006), p. 213.

▌ Don't rat on your peers.

▌ Don't give in to others.[92]

In addition to these general rules, the researchers found that there were separate norms for African American inmates ("exploit whites; no forcing sex on blacks; defend your brother") and for whites ("don't trust anyone; everybody for himself").

Other research efforts confirm the notion that residents do in fact form cohesive groups and adhere to an informal inmate culture.[93] The more serious the youth's record and the more secure the institution, the greater the adherence to the inmate social code. Male delinquents are more likely to form allegiances with members of their own racial group and to attempt to exploit those outside the group. They also scheme to manipulate staff and take advantage of weaker peers. However, in institutions that are treatment oriented, and where staff-inmate relationships are more intimate, residents are less likely to adhere to a negativistic inmate code.

Female Inmates

Between 1991 and 2003, the number of female juvenile offenders in custody increased by more than half (52 percent), from 9,600 to 14,590. Over this same period of time, the proportion of female juvenile offenders of the total number of offenders in custody increased 15 percent, from 13 percent in 1991 to 15 percent in 2003.[94]

The growing involvement of female youths in criminal behavior and the influence of the feminist movement have drawn more attention to the female juvenile offender. This attention has revealed a double standard of justice. For example, girls are more likely than boys to be incarcerated for status offenses. Institutions for girls are generally more restrictive than those for boys, and they have fewer educational and vocational programs and fewer services. Institutions for girls also do a less-than-adequate job of rehabilitation. It has been suggested that this double standard operates because of a male-dominated justice system that seeks to "protect" young girls from their own sexuality.[95]

A female juvenile inmate speaks with a correction officer in a juvenile facility in Florida. Although the trend has been to remove female juvenile inmates from closed institutions and place them in private or community-based facilities, female inmates continue to face numerous obstacles, including being placed in institutions far from family members and receiving inadequate educational and recreational services.

© Joel Gordon

Over the years, the number of females held in public institutions has declined, albeit less so in the past few years. This represents the continuation of a long-term trend to remove girls, many of whom are nonserious offenders, from closed institutions and place them in private or community-based facilities. In 2003, 36 percent of all female youths in residential placement were held in private facilities; for male youths it was 31 percent.[96]

The same double standard that brings a girl into an institution continues to exist once she is in custody. Females tend to be incarcerated for longer terms than males. In addition, institutional programs for girls tend to be oriented toward reinforcing traditional roles for women. Most of these programs also fail to take account of the different needs of African American and Caucasian females, as in the case of coping with past abuse.[97] How well these programs rehabilitate girls is questionable.

Many of the characteristics of juvenile female offenders are similar to those of their male counterparts, including poor social skills and low self-esteem. Other problems are more specific to the female juvenile offender (sexual abuse issues, victimization histories, lack of placement options).[98] In addition, there have been numerous allegations of emotional and sexual abuse by correctional workers, who either exploit vulnerable young women or callously disregard their emotional needs. An interview survey conducted by the National Council on Crime and Delinquency uncovered numerous incidents of abuse, and bitter resentment by the young women over the brutality of their custodial treatment.[99]

Although there are more coed institutions for juveniles than in the past, most girls remain incarcerated in single-sex institutions that are isolated in rural areas and rarely offer adequate rehabilitative services. Several factors account for the different treatment of girls. One is sexual stereotyping by administrators, who believe that teaching girls "appropriate" sex roles will help them function effectively in society. These beliefs are often held by the staff as well, many of whom hold highly sexist ideas of what is appropriate behavior for adolescent girls. Another factor that accounts for the different treatment of girls is that staff members often are not adequately trained to understand and address the unique needs of this population.[100] Girls' institutions tend to be smaller than boys' institutions and lack the resources to offer as many programs and services as do the larger male institutions.[101]

It appears that although society is more concerned about protecting girls who act out, it is less concerned about rehabilitating them because the crimes they commit are not serious. These attitudes translate into fewer staff, older facilities, and poorer educational and recreational programs than those found in boys' institutions.[102] To help address these and other problems facing female juveniles in institutions, the American Bar Association and the National Bar Association recommend a number of important changes, including these:

- Identify, promote, and support effective gender-specific, developmentally sound, culturally sensitive practices with girls.

- Promote an integrated system of care for at-risk and delinquent girls and their families based on their competencies and needs.

- Assess the adequacy of services to meet the needs of at-risk or delinquent girls and address gaps in service.

- Collect and review state and local practices to assess the gender impact of decision making and system structure.[103]

CORRECTIONAL TREATMENT FOR JUVENILES

Nearly all juvenile institutions implement some form of treatment program: counseling, vocational and educational training, recreational programs, or religious counseling. In addition, most institutions provide medical programs as well as occasional legal service programs. Generally, the larger the institution, the greater the number of programs and services offered.

The purpose of these programs is to rehabilitate youths to become well-adjusted individuals and send them back into the community to be productive citizens. Despite good intentions, however, the goal of rehabilitation is rarely attained, due in large part to poor implementation of the programs.[104] A significant number of juvenile offenders commit more crimes after release[105] and some experts believe that correctional treatment has little effect on recidivism.[106] However, a large-scale empirical review of institutional treatment programs found that serious juvenile offenders who receive treatment have recidivism rates about 10 percent lower than similar untreated juveniles, and that the best programs reduced recidivism by as much as 40 percent.[107] The most successful of these institutional treatment programs provide training to improve interpersonal skills and family-style teaching to improve behavioral skills (see Exhibit 16.2).

What are the drawbacks to correctional rehabilitation? One of the most common problems in efforts to rehabilitate juveniles is a lack of well-trained staff members. Budgetary limitations are a primary concern. It costs a substantial amount of money per year to keep a child in an institution, which explains why institutions generally do not employ large professional staffs.

However, some correctional programs are highly cost-efficient, producing monetary benefits that outweigh the costs of running the program.[108] In a recent study with the provocative title, "Are Violent Delinquents Worth Treating?" researchers Michael Caldwell, Michael Vitacco, and Gregory Van Rybroek found that an institutional treatment program for violent juvenile offenders that was effective in reducing recidivism rates produced cost savings to taxpayers that were seven times greater than what it cost to run the program. These findings can be particularly influential on policy makers and government funding agencies.[109]

The most glaring problem with treatment programs is that they are not administered as intended. Although the official goals of many institutions may be treatment and rehabilitation, the actual programs may center around security and punishment. The next sections describe some treatment approaches that aim to rehabilitate offenders.

Learn more about **improving the conditions for children in custody** via academic.cengage.com/criminaljustice/siegel.

EXHIBIT 16.2

Effectiveness of Institutional Treatment Programs for Serious Juvenile Offenders

Positive Effects, Consistent Evidence
- Interpersonal skills
- Family-style group home

Positive Effects, Less Consistent Evidence
- Behavioral programs
- Community residential
- Multiple services

Mixed but Generally Positive Effects, Inconsistent Evidence
- Individual counseling
- Guided group
- Group counseling

Weak or No Effects, Inconsistent Evidence
- Employment related
- Drug abstinence
- Wilderness/challenge

Weak or No Effects, Consistent Evidence
- Milieu therapy

SOURCE: Mark W. Lipsey and David B. Wilson, "Effective Intervention for Serious Juvenile Offenders: A Synthesis of Research," in Rolf Loeber and David P. Farrington, eds., *Serious and Violent Juvenile Offenders: Risk Factors and Successful Interventions* (Thousand Oaks, CA: Sage, 1998), p. 332, table 13.8.

Individual Treatment Techniques: Past and Present

In general, effective individual treatment programs are built around combinations of psychotherapy, reality therapy, and behavior modification. **Individual counseling** is one of the most common treatment approaches, and virtually all juvenile institutions use it to some extent. This is not surprising, as psychological problems such as depression are prevalent in juvenile institutions.[110] Individual counseling does not attempt to change a youth's personality. Rather, it attempts to help individuals understand and solve their current adjustment problems. Some institutions employ counselors who are not professionally qualified, which subjects offenders to a superficial form of counseling.

Professional counseling may be based on **psychotherapy**, which requires extensive analysis of the individual's childhood experiences. A skilled therapist attempts to help the individual make a more positive adjustment to society by altering negative behavior patterns learned in childhood. Another frequently used treatment is reality therapy.[111] This approach, developed by William Glasser during the 1970s, emphasizes current, rather than past, behavior by stressing that offenders are completely responsible for their own actions. The object of reality therapy is to make individuals more responsible people. This is accomplished by giving youths confidence through developing their ability to follow a set of expectations as closely as possible. The success of reality therapy depends greatly on the warmth and concern of the counselor. Many institutions rely heavily on this type of therapy because they believe trained professionals aren't needed to administer it. Actually, a skilled therapist is essential to the success of this form of treatment.

Behavior modification is used in many institutions.[112] It is based on the theory that all behavior is learned and that current behavior can be shaped through rewards and punishments. This type of program is easily used in an institutional setting that offers privileges as rewards for behaviors such as work, study, or the development of skills. It is reasonably effective, especially when a contract is formed with the youth to modify certain behaviors. When youths know what is expected of them, they plan their actions to meet these expectations and then experience the anticipated consequences. In this way, youths can be motivated to change. Behavior modification is effective in controlled settings where a counselor can manipulate the situation, but once the youth is back in the real world it becomes difficult to use.

Group Treatment Techniques

Group therapy is more economical than individual therapy because one therapist can counsel more than one individual at a time. Also, the support of the group is often valuable to individuals in the group, and individuals derive hope from other members of the group who have survived similar experiences. Another advantage of group therapy is that a group can often solve a problem more effectively than an individual.

One disadvantage of group therapy is that it provides little individual attention. Everyone is different, and some group members may need more individualized treatment. Others may be afraid to speak up in the group and thus fail to receive the benefits of the group experience. Conversely, some individuals may dominate group interaction, making it difficult for the leader to conduct an effective session. In addition, group condemnation may seriously hurt a participant. Finally, there is also the concern that by providing therapy in a group format, those who are more chronically involved in delinquency may negatively affect those who are marginally involved.[113] This can also happen with non–juvenile justice delinquency prevention programs (see Chapter 12).

More than any other group treatment technique, group psychotherapy probes into an individual's personality and attempts to restructure it. Relationships in these groups tend to be intense. The group is used to facilitate expression of feelings, solve problems, and teach members to empathize with one another.

Unfortunately, the ingredients for an effective group session—interaction, cooperation, and tolerance—are in conflict with the antisocial and antagonistic orientation of delinquents. This technique can be effective when the members of the group are in attendance voluntarily, but such is not the case with institutionalized delinquents. Consequently, the effectiveness of these programs is questionable.

Guided group interaction (GGI) is a fairly common method of group treatment. It is based on the theory that through group interactions, a delinquent can acknowledge and solve personal problems. A leader facilitates interaction, and a group culture develops. Individual members can be mutually supportive and can reinforce acceptable behavior. In the 1980s, a version of GGI called positive peer culture (PPC) became popular. These programs used groups in which peer leaders encourage other youths to conform to conventional behaviors. The rationale is that if negative peer influence can encourage youths to engage in delinquent behavior, then positive peer influence can help them conform.[114] Though research results are inconclusive, there is evidence that PPC may facilitate communication ability for incarcerated youth.[115]

Another common group treatment approach, milieu therapy, seeks to make all aspects of the inmates' environment part of their treatment and to minimize differences between custodial staff and treatment personnel. Based on psychoanalytic theory, milieu therapy was developed during the late 1940s and early 1950s by Bruno Bettelheim.[116] This therapy attempted to create a conscience, or superego, in delinquent youths by getting them to depend on their therapists to a great extent and then threatening them with loss of the caring relationship if they failed to control their behavior. Today, milieu therapy more often makes use of peer interactions and attempts to create an environment that encourages meaningful change, growth, and satisfactory adjustment. This is often accomplished through peer pressure to conform to group norms.

Today, group counseling often focuses on drug and alcohol issues, self-esteem development, or role-model support. In addition, because greater numbers of violent juveniles are entering the system than in years past, group sessions often deal with appropriate expressions of anger and methods for controlling such behavior.

Educational, Vocational, and Recreational Programs

Because educational programs are an important part of social development and have therapeutic as well as instructional value, they are an essential part of most treatment programs. What takes place through education is related to all other aspects of the institutional program—work activities, cottage life, recreation, and clinical services.

Educational programs are probably the best-staffed programs in training schools, but even at their best, most are inadequate. Training programs must contend with a myriad of problems. Many of the youths coming into these institutions are mentally challenged, have learning disabilities, and are far behind their grade levels in basic academics. Most have become frustrated with the educational experience, dislike school, and become bored with any type of educational program. Their sense of frustration often leads to disciplinary problems.

Ideally, institutions should allow the inmates to attend a school in the community or offer programs that lead to a high school diploma or GED. Unfortunately, not all institutions offer these types of programs. Secure institutions, because of their large size, are more likely than group homes or day treatment centers to offer programs such as remedial reading, physical education, and tutoring. Some offer computer-based learning and programmed learning modules.

Vocational training has long been used as a treatment technique for juveniles. Early institutions were even referred to as "industrial schools." Today, vocational programs in institutions include auto repair, printing, woodworking, mechanical drawing, food service, cosmetology, secretarial training, and data processing. A common drawback of vocational training programs is sex-typing. The recent trend has been to allow equal access to all programs offered in institutions that house girls and boys.

Sex-typing is more difficult to avoid in single-sex institutions, because funds are not usually available for all types of training.

These programs alone are not panaceas. Youths need to acquire the kinds of skills that will give them hope for advancement. The Ventura School for Female Juvenile Offenders, established under the California Youth Authority, has been a pioneer in the work placement concept. Private industry contracts with the Youth Authority to establish businesses on the institution's grounds. The businesses hire, train, and pay for work. Wages are divided into a victim's restitution fund, room and board fees, and forced savings, with a portion given to the juvenile to purchase canteen items.[117] A study by the National Youth Employment Coalition (NYEC) finds that employment- and career-focused programs can do a great deal to prepare youths involved in the juvenile justice system for a successful transition to the workforce as long as they are comprehensive, last for a relatively long time, and are connected to further education or long-term career opportunities.[118]

Recreational activity is also an important way to help relieve adolescent aggressions, as evidenced by the many programs that focus on recreation as the primary treatment technique.

In summary, treatment programs that seem to be most effective for rehabilitating juvenile offenders are those that use a combination of techniques. Programs that are comprehensive, build on a juvenile's strengths, and adopt a socially grounded position have a much greater chance for success. Successful programs address issues relating to school, peers, work, and community.

Wilderness Programs

wilderness probation
Programs involving outdoor expeditions that provide opportunities for juveniles to confront the difficulties of their lives while achieving positive personal satisfaction.

Wilderness probation programs involve troubled youths in outdoor activities as a mechanism to improve their social skills, self-concept, and self-control. Typically, wilderness programs maintain exposure to a wholesome environment; where the concepts of education and the work ethic are taught and embodied in adult role models, troubled youth can regain a measure of self-worth.

A number of wilderness programs for juvenile offenders have been evaluated for their effects on recidivism. In a detailed review of the effects of wilderness programs—those emphasizing physical activity over more therapeutic goals—on recidivism, Doris MacKenzie concludes that these programs do not work.[119] Although some of the programs show success, such as the Spectrum Wilderness Program in Illinois,[120] others had negative effects; that is, the group that received the program had higher arrest rates than the comparison group that did not receive the program. Taken together, the programs suffered from

▐ Poor implementation

▐ Weak evaluation designs or problems with too few subjects or large dropout rates

▐ Failure to adhere to principles of successful rehabilitation, such as targeting high-risk youths and lasting for a moderate period of time[121]

However, wilderness programs that include a therapeutic component have been shown to be effective in reducing juvenile offending. Sandra Wilson and Mark Lipsey found that, on average, these programs produced a 20 percent reduction in recidivism rates, with the most successful ones offering more intensive physical activity or therapeutic services.[122]

Juvenile Boot Camps

boot camps
Juvenile programs that combine get-tough elements from adult programs with education, substance abuse treatment, and social skills training.

Correctional **boot camps** were designed with the idea of combining the get-tough elements of adult programs with education, substance abuse treatment, and social skills training. In theory, a successful boot camp program should rehabilitate juvenile offenders, reduce the number of beds needed in secure institutional programs, and thus reduce the overall cost of care. The Alabama boot camp program for youthful offenders estimated savings of $1 million annually when compared with traditional institutional sentences.[123] However, no one seems convinced that participants in these programs have lower recidivism rates than those who serve normal sentences. Ronald Corbett and Joan Petersilia do note, however, that boot camp participants seem to be less antisocial upon returning to society.[124]

Other successes of juvenile boot camps were revealed in a national study comparing the environments of boot camps with more traditional secure correctional facilities for juveniles. Some of the main findings include these:

▌ Boot camp youths report more positive attitudes to their environment.

▌ Initial levels of depression are lower for boot camp youths but initial levels of anxiety are higher; both of these declined over time for youths in both traditional and boot camp facilities.

▌ Staff at boot camps report more favorable working conditions, such as less stress and better communication among staff.[125]

To read more about **boot camps**, go to academic.cengage.com/criminaljustice/siegel.

However, the bottom line for juvenile boot camps, like other correctional sanctions, is whether or not they reduce recidivism. A recent meta-analysis of the effects of juvenile boot camps on recidivism found this to be an ineffective correctional approach to reducing recidivism; from the 17 different program samples, the control groups had, on average, lower recidivism rates than the treatment groups (boot camps).[126] Interestingly, when compared to the effects of 26 program samples of boot camps for adults, the juvenile boot camps had a higher average recidivism rate, although the difference was not significant.[127]

Why do boot camps for juveniles fail to reduce future offending? The main reason is that they provide little in the way of therapy or treatment to correct offending behavior.[128] Also, few are linked to services to help juvenile offenders transition back to the community. One juvenile boot camp program in Quehanna, Pennsylvania, which included a mandatory residential aftercare component, showed a reduction in recidivism rates two years post-release.[129] Experts have also suggested that part of the reason for not finding differences in recidivism between boot camps and other correctional alternatives (the control groups) may be due to juveniles in the control groups receiving enhanced treatment while juveniles in the boot camps are spending more time on physical activities.[130]

The general ineffectiveness of boot camps to reduce reoffending in the community by juvenile offenders (and adult offenders) appears to have resulted in this approach falling into disfavor with some correctional administrators. At the height of its popularity in the mid-1990s, more than 75 state-run boot camps were in operation in more than 30 states across the country; today, 51 remain.[131] Despite this, boot camps appear to still have a place among the array of sentencing options, if for no other reason than to appease the public with the promise of tougher sentences and lower costs.[132] If boot camps are to become a viable alternative for juvenile corrections, they must be seen not as a panacea that provides an easy solution to the problems of delinquency, but as part of a comprehensive approach to juvenile care that is appropriate to a select group of adolescents.[133]

THE LEGAL RIGHT TO TREATMENT

The primary goal of placing juveniles in institutions is to help them reenter the community successfully. Therefore, lawyers claim that children in state-run institutions have a legal right to treatment.

right to treatment
Philosophy espoused by many courts that juvenile offenders have a statutory right to treatment while under the jurisdiction of the courts.

The concept of a **right to treatment** was introduced to the mental health field in 1960 by Morton Birnbaum, who argued that individuals deprived of their liberty because of a mental illness are entitled to treatment to correct that condition.[134] The right to treatment has expanded to include the juvenile justice system, an expansion bolstered by court rulings that mandate that rehabilitation and not punishment or retribution be the basis of juvenile court dispositions.[135] It stands to reason then, that if incarcerated, juveniles are entitled to the appropriate social services that will promote their rehabilitation.

One of the first cases to highlight this issue was *Inmates of the Boys' Training School v. Affleck* in 1972.[136] In its decision, a federal court argued that rehabilitation is the true purpose of the juvenile court and that without that goal, due process guarantees are violated. It condemned such devices as solitary confinement, strip cells, and lack of educational opportunities, and held that juveniles have a statutory right to treatment. The court also established the following minimum standards for all juveniles confined in training schools:

▌ A room equipped with lighting sufficient for an inmate to read until 10:00 P.M.

▌ Sufficient clothing to meet seasonal needs

▌ Bedding, including blankets, sheets, pillows, pillowcases, and mattresses, to be changed once a week

▌ Personal hygiene supplies, including soap, toothpaste, towels, toilet paper, and toothbrush

▌ A change of undergarments and socks every day

▌ Minimum writing materials: pen, pencil, paper, and envelopes

▌ Prescription eyeglasses, if needed

▌ Equal access to all books, periodicals, and other reading materials located in the training school

▌ Daily showers

▌ Daily access to medical facilities, including provision of a 24-hour nursing service

▌ General correspondence privileges[137]

In 1974, in the case of *Nelson v. Heyne*, the First Federal Appellate Court affirmed that juveniles have a right to treatment and condemned the use of corporal punishment in juvenile institutions.[138] In *Morales v. Turman*, the court held that all juveniles confined in training schools in Texas have a right to treatment, including development of education skills, delivery of vocational education, medical and psychiatric treatment, and adequate living conditions.[139] In a more recent case, *Pena v. New York State Division for Youth*, the court held that the use of isolation, hand restraints, and tranquilizing drugs at Goshen Annex Center violated the Fourteenth Amendment right to due process and the Eighth Amendment right to protection against cruel and unusual punishment.[140]

To learn more about **the right to treatment**, read "Meeting the Needs of the Mentally Ill—A Case Study of the 'Right to Treatment' as Legal Rights Discourse in the USA," by Michael McCubbin and David N. Weisstub, available online via academic .cengage.com/criminaljustice/siegel.

The right to treatment has also been limited. For example, in *Ralston v. Robinson*, the Supreme Court rejected a youth's claim that he should continue to be given treatment after he was sentenced to a consecutive term in an adult prison for crimes committed while in a juvenile institution.[141] In the *Ralston* case, the offender's proven dangerousness outweighed the possible effects of rehabilitation. Similarly, in *Santana v. Callazo*, the U.S. First Circuit Court of Appeals rejected a suit brought by residents at the Maricao Juvenile Camp in Puerto Rico on the ground that the administration had failed to provide them with an individualized rehabilitation plan or adequate treatment. The circuit court concluded that it was a legitimate exercise of state authority to incarcerate juveniles solely to protect society if they are dangerous.

The Struggle for Basic Civil Rights

Several court cases have led federal, state, and private groups—for example, the American Bar Association, the American Correctional Association, and the National Council on Crime and Delinquency—to develop standards for the juvenile justice system. These standards provide guidelines for conditions and practices in juvenile institutions and call on administrators to maintain a safe and healthy environment for incarcerated youths.

For the most part, state-sponsored brutality has been outlawed, although the use of restraints, solitary confinement, and even medication for unruly residents has not been eliminated. The courts have ruled that corporal punishment in any form violates standards of decency and human dignity.

There are a number of mechanisms for enforcing these standards. For example, the federal government's Civil Rights of Institutionalized Persons Act (CRIPA) gives the Civil Rights Division of the U.S. Department of Justice (DOJ) the power to bring actions against state or local governments for violating the civil rights of persons institutionalized in publicly operated facilities.[142] CRIPA does not create any new substantive rights; it simply confers power on the U.S. Attorney General to bring action to enforce previously established constitutional or statutory rights of institutionalized persons; about 25 percent of cases involve juvenile detention and correctional facilities. There are many examples in which CRIPA-based litigation has helped ensure that incarcerated adolescents obtain their basic civil rights. For example, in November 1995, a federal court in Kentucky ordered state officials to remedy serious deficiencies in Kentucky's 13 juvenile treatment facilities. The decree required the state to take a number of steps to protect juveniles from abuse, mistreatment, and injury; to ensure adequate medical and mental health care; and to provide adequate educational, vocational, and aftercare services. Another CRIPA consent decree, ordered by a federal court in Puerto Rico in October 1994, addressed life-threatening conditions at eight juvenile detention and correction facilities. These dire conditions included juveniles committing and attempting suicide without staff intervention or treatment, widespread infection-control problems caused by rats and other vermin, and defective plumbing that forced juveniles to drink from their toilet bowls.

What provisions does the juvenile justice system make to help institutionalized offenders return to society? The remainder of this chapter is devoted to this topic.

JUVENILE AFTERCARE AND REENTRY

aftercare
Transitional assistance to juveniles, equivalent to adult parole, to help youths adjust to community life.

Aftercare in the juvenile justice system is the equivalent of parole in the adult criminal justice system. When juveniles are released from an institution, they may be placed in an aftercare program of some kind, so that youths who have been institutionalized are not simply returned to the community without some transitional assistance. Whether individuals who are in aftercare as part of an indeterminate sentence remain in the community or return to the institution for further rehabilitation depends on their actions during the aftercare period. Aftercare is an extremely important stage in the juvenile justice process because few juveniles age out of custody.[143]

reentry
The process and experience of returning to society upon release from a custody facility postadjudication.

Reentry involves aftercare services, but includes preparation for release from confinement, also called prerelease planning.[144] Reentry is further distinguished from aftercare in that reentry is seen as the whole process and experience of the transition of juveniles from "juvenile and adult correctional settings back into schools, families, communities, and society at large."[145] The concept of reentry, which is also the term given to it in the adult criminal justice system, is by no means new.[146] Recently, however, it has come to characterize the larger numbers of juvenile and adult offenders returning to communities each year and the increased needs these offenders exhibit with respect to employment, education, and mental health and substance abuse problems.[147] For juvenile offenders, reentry goes beyond the all-too-common practice of juveniles being placed in aftercare programs that are the same as adult parole programs, which "fail to take account of their unique needs and the challenges they face."[148] (See Exhibit 16.3 for a profile of juvenile offenders returning to the community.) Through the Serious and Violent Offender Reentry Initiative (SVORI), the federal government has invested $150 million on reentry programs for adult and juvenile offenders in all 50 states, the District of Columbia, and the Virgin Islands.[149]

For more information on **SVORI programs for juvenile offenders**, go to academic.cengage.com/criminaljustice/siegel.

EXHIBIT **16.3**

The latest data indicate that about 100,000 juvenile offenders each year are released from custody facilities following adjudication (or conviction in the adult system) and return to the communities from which they came. Reentry services play an important role in their successful reintegration to society. A profile of these juveniles shows that:

▌ 86 percent are male.

▌ 12 percent are age 14 or younger and 44 percent are age 17 or older.

▌ 40 percent are white, 38 percent are black, and 18 percent are Hispanic.

▌ 34 percent are committed for a violent offense, 32 percent for a property offense, 10 percent for a drug offense, 10 percent for public order offense, 10 percent for a technical violation of probation or parole, and 5 percent for a status offense.

SOURCE: Howard N. Snyder and Melissa Sickmund, *Juvenile Offenders and Victims: 2006 National Report* (Pittsburgh, PA: National Center for Juvenile Justice, 2006), p. 232.

parole guidelines
Recommended length of confinement and kinds of aftercare assistance most effective for a juvenile who committed a specific offense.

In a number of jurisdictions, a paroling authority, which may be an independent body or part of the corrections department or some other branch of state services, makes the release decision. Juvenile aftercare authorities, like adult parole officers, review the youth's adjustment within the institution, whether there is chemical dependence, what the crime was, and other specifics of the case. Some juvenile authorities are even making use of **parole guidelines** first developed with adult parolees. Each youth who enters a secure facility is given a recommended length of confinement that is explained at the initial interview with parole authorities. The stay is computed on the basis of the offense record, influenced by aggravating and mitigating factors. The parole authority is not required to follow the recommended sentence but uses it as a tool in making parole decisions.[150] Whatever approach is used, several primary factors are considered by virtually all jurisdictions when recommending a juvenile for release: (a) institutional adjustment, (b) length of stay and general attitude, and (c) likelihood of success in the community.

Risk classifications have also been designed to help parole officers make decisions about which juveniles should receive aftercare services.[151] The risk-based system uses an empirically derived risk scale to classify youths. Juveniles are identified as most likely or least likely to commit a new offense based on factors such as prior record, type of offense, and degree of institutional adjustment.

Supervision

One purpose of aftercare and reentry is to provide support during the readjustment period following release. First, individuals whose activities have been regimented for some time may not find it easy to make independent decisions. Second, offenders may perceive themselves as scapegoats, cast out by society. Finally, the community may view the returning minor with a good deal of prejudice; adjustment problems may reinforce a preexisting need to engage in deviant behavior.

Juveniles in aftercare programs are supervised by parole caseworkers or counselors whose job is to maintain contact with the juvenile, make sure that a corrections plan is followed, and show interest and caring. The counselor also keeps the youth informed of services that may assist in reintegration and counsels the youth and his or her family. Unfortunately, aftercare caseworkers, like probation officers, often carry such large caseloads that their jobs are next to impossible to do adequately.

Intensive Aftercare Program (IAP)
A balanced, highly structured, comprehensive continuum of intervention for serious and violent juvenile offenders returning to the community.

The Intensive Aftercare Program (IAP) Model New models of aftercare and reentry have been aimed at the chronic and/or violent offender. The **Intensive Aftercare Program (IAP)** model, developed by David Altschuler and Troy Armstrong, offers a continuum of intervention for serious juvenile offenders returning to the community following placement.[152] The IAP model begins by drawing attention to five basic principles, which collectively establish a set of fundamental operational goals:

1. Preparing youth for progressively increased responsibility and freedom in the community

2. Facilitating youth-community interaction and involvement

3. Working with both the offender and targeted community support systems (families, peers, schools, employers) on qualities needed for constructive interaction and the youth's successful community adjustment

4. Developing new resources and supports where needed

5. Monitoring and testing the youth and the community on their ability to deal with each other productively

These basic goals are then translated into practice, which incorporates individual case planning with a family and community perspective. The program stresses a mix of intensive surveillance and services, and a balance of incentives and graduated consequences coupled with the imposition of realistic, enforceable conditions. There is also "service brokerage," in which community resources are used and linkage with social networks established.[153]

The IAP initiative was designed to help correctional agencies implement effective aftercare programs for chronic and serious juvenile offenders. After more than 12 years of testing, the program is now being aimed at determining how juveniles are prepared for reentry into their communities, how the transition is handled, and how the aftercare in the community is provided.[154] The Focus on Delinquency box entitled "The Intensive Aftercare Program (IAP) Model" illustrates how the model is being used in three state jurisdictions and reports on the latest evaluation results.

Aftercare Revocation Procedures

Juvenile parolees are required to meet established standards of behavior, which generally include but are not limited to the following:

▌ Adhere to a reasonable curfew set by youth worker or parent.

▌ Refrain from associating with persons whose influence would be detrimental.

▌ Attend school in accordance with the law.

▌ Abstain from drugs and alcohol.

Aftercare—the juvenile equivalent of parole in the adult criminal justice system—includes a range of services designed to help juveniles adjust to community life upon release from an institution. Here, Tristan Cassidy, 17 (top) and Scott Epperley, 15, work on a project for their geography class at the Northwest Regional Learning Center (NRLC) in Everett, Washington. The NRLC is a detention school for juveniles on probation or in aftercare that serves as a last chance for some to earn their high school diploma if their former schools will not accept them back.

© AP Images/Chris Goodenow

How has the IAP model been used around the nation and has it proven effective?

The Intensive Aftercare Program (IAP) Model

COLORADO

Although adolescents are still institutionalized, community-based providers begin weekly services (including multifamily counseling and life-skills services) that continue during aftercare. Sixty days prior to release, IAP youths begin a series of step-down measures, including supervised trips to the community and, 30 days before release, overnight or weekend home passes. Upon release to parole, most program youths go through several months of day treatment programming that, in addition to services, provides a high level of structure during the day. As a youth's progress warrants, the frequency of supervision decreases.

NEVADA

Once the parole plan is finalized, all IAP youths begin a 30-day prerelease phase, during which IAP staff provide a series of services that continue through the early months of parole. These consist primarily of two structured curriculums on life skills (Jettstream) and substance abuse (Rational Recovery). The initial 30 days of release are considered an institutional furlough (youths are still on the institutional rolls) that involves intensive supervision and service; any time during this period the youth may be returned to the institution for significant program infractions. During furlough, youths are involved in day programming and are subject to frequent drug testing and evening and weekend surveillance. Upon successful completion of the furlough, the IAP transition continues through the use of phased levels of supervision. During the first three months, three contacts per week with the case manager or field agent are required. This level of supervision is reduced to two contacts per week for the next two months, and then to once per week during the last month of parole.

VIRGINIA

Virginia's transition differs from the other two sites in that its central feature is the use of group home placements as a bridge between the institution and the community. Immediately after release from the institution, youths enter one of two group homes for a 30- to 60-day period. The programs and services in which they will be involved in the community are initiated shortly after placement in the group home. Virginia uses a formal step-down system to ease the intensity of parole supervision gradually. In the two months following the youth's release from the group home, staff are required to contact him

five to seven times per week. This is reduced to three to five times per week during the next two months, and again to three times per week during the final 30 days.

DOES THE IAP MODEL WORK?

In each state one site was chosen to assess the effectiveness of the IAP model: Denver, Colorado; Las Vegas, Nevada; and Norfolk, Virginia. An experimental evaluation that randomly assigned juveniles to the program or to a control group was used to assess the model's effectiveness on recidivism. As shown in Table 16-A, the program produced some benefits in Norfolk, but in Denver program youths were more likely than their control counterparts to recidivate and be sentenced to a period of incarceration. The researchers call for caution in interpreting these results. In the case of Denver, control group youths received services similar to those in the IAP. They also note that this was the first test of a "very complex intervention." Suggestions for improvement to the IAP include: maximizing parental involvement, emphasizing education and employment skills, and strengthening community support networks.

TABLE 16-A THE IAP MODEL'S EFFECTS ON RECIDIVISM

	Denver		Las Vegas		Norfolk	
	IAP	Control	IAP	Control	IAP	Control
Arrested (%)	69	65	77	77	60	67
Convicted (%)	42	33	59	60	44	59
Incarcerated (%)	41	26	45	41	56	58

Critical Thinking

1. What is the importance of reducing the number of supervision contacts with the juvenile offender toward the end of the aftercare program?

2. Should juvenile offenders who have committed less serious offenses also have to go through intensive aftercare programs?

SOURCE: Richard G. Wiebush, Dennis Wagner, Betsie McNulty, Yanqing Wang, and Thao N. Le, *Implementation and Outcome Evaluation of the Intensive Aftercare Program* (Washington, DC: OJJDP, 2005); Steve V. Gies, *Aftercare Services* (Washington, DC: OJJDP Juvenile Justice Bulletin, 2003); Richard G. Wiebush, Betsie McNulty, and Thao Le, *Implementation of the Intensive Community-Based Aftercare Program* (Washington, DC: OJJDP Juvenile Justice Bulletin, 2000).

I Report to the youth worker when required.

I Refrain from acts that would be crimes if committed by an adult.

I Refrain from operating an automobile without permission of the youth worker or parent.

I Refrain from being habitually disobedient and beyond the lawful control of parent or other legal authority.

I Refrain from running away from the lawful custody of parent or other lawful authority.

If these rules are violated, the juvenile may have his parole revoked and be returned to the institution. Most states have extended the same legal rights enjoyed by adults at parole revocation hearings to juveniles who are in danger of losing their aftercare privileges, as follows:

I   Juveniles must be informed of the conditions of parole and receive notice of any obligations.

I   Juveniles have the right to legal counsel at state expense if necessary.

I   They maintain the right to confront and cross-examine witnesses against them.

I   They have the right to introduce documentary evidence and witnesses.

I   They have the right to a hearing before an officer who shall be an attorney but not an employee of the revoking agency.[155]

FUTURE OF JUVENILE CORRECTIONS

In the area of community sentencing, new forms of probation supervision have received greater attention in recent years. Intensive probation supervision, balanced probation, wilderness probation, and electronic monitoring have become important community-based alternatives over the last few years. Some studies report mixed results for these new forms of probation, but more experimentation is needed. Probation continues to be the single most important intermediate sanction available to the juvenile court system. It is anticipated that the cost and effectiveness of probation will underpin its usefulness in the coming years. In the future, look for probation caseloads to increase.

There exists much debate about the effectiveness of community versus institutional treatment. Considerable research shows that warehousing juveniles without proper treatment does little to prevent future delinquent activities. The most effective secure corrections programs are those that provide individual services for a small number of participants.[156] Evaluations of community treatment provide evidence of a number of successful ways to prevent delinquency without jeopardizing the safety of community residents.

There is also a long-standing debate about the effectiveness of correctional treatments compared with other delinquency prevention measures. In their assessment of the full range of interventions to prevent serious and violent juvenile offending, Rolf Loeber and David Farrington found that it is never too early and never too late to make a difference.[157] Though some critics believe that juveniles are being coddled, in the future it is likely that innovative treatment methods will be applied continually within the juvenile justice system.

On another front, deinstitutionalization has become an important goal of the juvenile justice system. The Office of Juvenile Justice and Delinquency Prevention provided funds to encourage this process. In the early 1980s, the deinstitutionalization movement seemed to be partially successful. Admissions to public juvenile correctional facilities declined in the late 1970s and early 1980s. In addition, the number of status offenders being held within the juvenile justice system was reduced. Following a substantial increase in the number of institutionalized children in the 1990s and the early 2000s, numbers have decreased of late. During these years, the majority of states achieved compliance with the DSO mandate (Deinstitutionalizing Status Offenders). Because juvenile crime is a high priority, the challenge to the states will be to retain a focus on prevention despite political, not necessarily public, assertions of the need for more punitive approaches. If that can be achieved, deinstitutionalization will remain a central theme in the juvenile justice system.

A more pressing problem is that a disproportionate number of minority youths continue to be incarcerated in youth facilities. The difference is greatest for African American youths, with the incarceration rate being almost four times greater than that for Caucasian youths. Of equal importance, minorities are more likely to be placed in secure public facilities rather than in open private facilities that might provide more costly and effective treatment. The OJJDP is committed to ensuring that the country address situations where there is disproportionate confinement of minority offenders in the nation's juvenile justice system. In the future, it is expected that this initiative will result in a more fair and balanced juvenile justice system.

Aftercare and reentry services represent crucial elements of a juvenile offender's successful transition back to the community. Correctional authorities recognize that juvenile offenders who are released from confinement are at heightened risk for returning to a life of crime without assistance in overcoming barriers with employment, education, and housing and dealing with mental health, substance abuse, and other problems. Many jurisdictions are experiencing success with halfway houses, reintegration centers, and other reentry programs, and the federal government's substantial investment in reentry programs through the Serious and Violent Offender Reentry Initiative offers to produce even more success stories in the years ahead.

Lastly, the future of the legal right to treatment for juveniles remains uncertain. The appellate courts have established minimum standards of care and treatment on a case-by-case basis, but it does not appear that the courts can be persuaded today to expand this constitutional theory to mandate that incarcerated children receive adequate treatment. Eventually, this issue must be clarified by the Supreme Court. Reforms in state juvenile institutions often result from class-action lawsuits filed on behalf of incarcerated youth.

Summary

1. **Be able to distinguish between community treatment and institutional treatment for juvenile offenders**

I Community treatment encompasses efforts to keep offenders in the community and spare them the stigma of incarceration. The primary purpose is to provide a nonrestrictive or home setting, employing educational, vocational, counseling, and employment services.

I Institutional treatment encompasses provision of these services but in more restrictive and sometimes secure facilities.

2. **Be familiar with the disposition of probation, including how it is administered and by whom and recent trends in its use**

I Probation is the most widely used method of community treatment.

I Youths on probation must obey rules given to them by the court and participate in some form of treatment program. If rules are violated, youths may have their probation revoked.

I Behavior is monitored by probation officers.

I Formal probation accounts for more than 62 percent of all juvenile dispositions and its use has increased significantly in the last decade.

3. **Be aware of new approaches for providing probation services to juvenile offenders and comment on their effectiveness in reducing recidivism**

I It is now common to enhance probation with more restrictive forms of treatment, such as intensive supervision and house arrest with electronic monitoring.

I Restitution programs involve having juvenile offenders either reimburse their victims or do community service.

I Residential community treatment programs allow youths to live at home while receiving treatment in a nonpunitive, community-based center.

I Some of these probation innovations, such as intensive supervision, get mixed reviews on their effectiveness in reducing recidivism, while others, such as restitution and restorative justice, show success.

4. **Understand key historical developments of secure juvenile corrections in this country, including the principle of *least restrictive alternative***

I The secure juvenile institution was developed in the mid-nineteenth century as an alternative to placing youths in adult prisons.

I Youth institutions evolved from large, closed institutions to cottage-based education- and rehabilitation-oriented institutions.

- The concept of "least restrictive alternative" is applicable in decisions on placing juvenile offenders to institutions to ensure that the setting benefits the juvenile's treatment needs.

5. Be familiar with recent trends in the use of juvenile institutions for juvenile offenders and how their use differs across states

- The juvenile institutional population has decreased in recent years.
- A large number of youths continue to be "hidden" in private medical centers and drug treatment clinics.
- There are wide variations in juvenile custody rates across states.

6. Understand key issues facing the institutionalized juvenile offender

- A disproportionate number of minorities are incarcerated in more secure, state-run youth facilities.
- Compared to males, female juvenile inmates are faced with many hardships.

7. Be able to identify the various juvenile correctional treatment approaches that are in use today and comment on their effectiveness in reducing recidivism

- Most juvenile institutions maintain intensive treatment programs featuring individual or group therapy.

- Little evidence has been found that any single method is effective in reducing recidivism.
- Rehabilitation remains an important goal of juvenile practitioners.

8. Understand juvenile offenders' legal right to treatment

- The right to treatment is an important issue in juvenile justice.
- Legal decisions have mandated that a juvenile cannot simply be warehoused in a correctional center but must receive proper care and treatment to aid rehabilitation.
- What constitutes proper care is still being debated, however.

9. Know the nature of aftercare for juvenile offenders and comment on recent innovations in juvenile aftercare and reentry programs

- Juveniles released from institutions are often placed on parole or in aftercare.
- There is little evidence that community supervision is more beneficial than simply releasing youths.
- Many jurisdictions are experiencing success with halfway houses, reintegration centers, and other reentry programs.

Key Terms

Viewpoint

As a local juvenile court judge you have been assigned the case of Jim Butler, a 13-year-old juvenile so short he can barely see over the bench. On trial for armed robbery, the boy has been accused of threatening a woman with a knife and stealing her purse. Barely a teenager, he has already had a long history of involvement with the law. At age 11 he was arrested for drug possession and placed on probation; soon after, he stole a car. At age 12 he was arrested for shoplifting. Jim is accompanied by his legal guardian, his maternal grandmother. His parents are unavailable because his father abandoned the family years ago and his mother is currently undergoing inpatient treatment at a local drug clinic. After talking with his court-appointed attorney, Jim decides to admit to the armed robbery. At a dispositional hearing, his attorney tells you of the tough life Jim has been forced to endure. His grandmother states that, although she loves the boy, her advanced age makes it impossible for her to provide the care he needs to stay out of trouble. She says that Jim is a good boy who has developed a set of bad companions; his current scrape was precipitated by his friends. A representative of the school system testifies that Jim has above-average intelligence and is actually respectful of teachers. He has potential, but his life circumstances have short-circuited his academic success. Jim himself shows remorse and appears to be a sensitive youngster who is easily led astray by older youths.

You must now make a decision. You can place Jim on probation and allow him to live with his grandmother while being monitored by county probation staff. You can place him in a secure incarceration facility for up to three years. You can also put him into an intermediate program such as a community-based facility, which would allow him to attend school during the day while residing in a halfway house and receiving group treatment in the evenings. Although Jim appears to be a possibility for rehabilitation, his crime was serious and involved the use of a weapon. If he remains in the community he may offend again; if he is sent to a correctional facility he will interact with older, tougher kids. What mode of correctional treatment would you choose?

▌ Would you place Jim on probation and allow him to live with his grandmother while being monitored?

▌ Would you send him to a secure incarceration facility for up to three years?

▌ Would you put him into an intermediate program such as a community-based facility?

Doing Research on the Web

Before you answer these questions, you may want to research the effectiveness of different types of correctional treatment for juvenile offenders. To learn more about juvenile treatment options, visit the following websites via **academic.cengage.com/criminaljustice/siegel**

California Department of Corrections and Rehabilitation, Division of Juvenile Justice

Center for the Study and Prevention of Violence

Washington State Institute for Public Policy on Juvenile Justice

The National Council on Crime and Delinquency and Children's Research Center

The Urban Institute

Questions for Discussion

1. Would you want a community treatment program in your neighborhood? Why or why not?

2. Is widening the net a real danger, or are treatment-oriented programs simply a method of helping troubled youths?

3. If youths violate the rules of probation, should they be placed in a secure institution?

4. Is juvenile restitution fair? Should a poor child have to pay back a wealthy victim?

5. What are the most important advantages to community treatment for juvenile offenders?

6. What is the purpose of juvenile probation? Identify some conditions of probation and discuss the responsibilities of the juvenile probation officer.

7. Has community treatment generally proven successful?

8. Why have juvenile boot camps not been effective in reducing recidivism?

Notes

1. Josh Richman, "Juvenile Prison Bill Inspired by Ward's Suicide Advances," *Inside Bay Area*, August 31, 2007; Kim McGill, "New Name, Same Pain—Another Young Person Dies Behind Bars in California," *Pacific News Service*, September 20, 2005.

2. Charles Murray and Louis B. Cox, *Beyond Probation* (Beverly Hills, CA: Sage Publications, 1979).

3. Robert Shepard, Jr., ed., *Juvenile Justice Standards, A Balanced Approach* (Chicago: ABA, 1996).

4. George Killinger, Hazel Kerper, and Paul F. Cromwell, Jr., *Probation and Parole in the Criminal Justice System* (St. Paul, MN: West, 1976), p. 45; National Advisory Commission on Criminal Justice Standards and Goals, *Corrections* (Washington, DC: U.S. Government Printing Office, 1983), p. 75.

5. Ibid.

6. Jerome Miller, *Last One over the Wall: The Massachusetts Experiment in Closing Reform Schools* (Columbus: Ohio State University Press, 1998).

7. Bureau of Justice Statistics, *Report to the Nation on Crime and Justice* (Washington, DC: U.S. Government Printing Office, 1988), pp. 44–45; Peter Greenwood, "What Works with Juvenile Offenders: A Synthesis of the Literature and Experience," *Federal Probation* 58:63–67 (1994).

8. Robert Coates, Alden Miller, and Lloyd Ohlin, *Diversity in a Youth Correctional System* (Cambridge, MA: Ballinger, 1978); Barry Krisberg, James Austin, and Patricia Steele, *Unlocking Juvenile Corrections* (San Francisco: National Council on Crime and Delinquency, 1989).

9. Personal correspondence, Taneekah Freeman, executive assistant, January 3, 2001; "Roxbury Agency Offers a Map for Youths at the Crossroads," *Boston Globe*, 18 February 1990, p. 32.

10. Howard N. Snyder and Melissa Sickmund, *Juvenile Offenders and Victims: 2006 National Report* (Pittsburgh, PA: National Center for Juvenile Justice, 2006), pp. 174–175.

11. Emily Gaarder, Nancy Rodriguez, and Marjorie S. Zatz, "Criers, Liars, and Manipulators: Probation Officers' Views of Girls," *Justice Quarterly* 21:547–578 (2004).

12. Snyder and Sickmund, *Juvenile Offenders and Victims*.

13. *In re J.G.*, 692 N.E.2d 1226 (Ill.App. 1998).

14. *In re Michael D.*, 264 CA Rptr 476 (CA App. 1989).

15. *Morrissey v. Brewer*, 408 U.S. 471, 92 S.Ct. 2593, 33 L.Ed.2d 484 (1972); *Gagnon v. Scarpelli*, 411 U.S. 778, 93 S.Ct. 1756, 36 L.Ed.2d 655 (1973).

16. Patricia McFall Torbet, *Juvenile Probation: The Workhorse of the Juvenile Justice System* (Washington, DC: Office of Juvenile Justice and Delinquency Prevention, 1996).

17. Richard Lawrence, "Reexamining Community Corrections Models," *Crime and Delinquency* 37:449–464 (1991).

18. See Matthew J. Giblin, "Using Police Officers to Enhance the Supervision of Juvenile Probationers: An Evaluation of the Anchorage CAN Program," *Crime and Delinquency* 48:116–137 (2002).

19. See Richard G. Wiebush, "Juvenile Intensive Supervision: The Impact on Felony Offenders Diverted from Institutional Placement," *Crime and Delinquency* 39:68–89 (1993); James Byrne, "The Control Controversy: A Preliminary Examination of Intensive Probation Supervision Programs in the United States," *Federal Probation* 50:4–16 (1986).

20. For a review of these programs, see James Austin, Kelly Dedel Johnson, and Ronald Weitzer, *Alternatives to the Secure Detention and Confinement of Juvenile Offenders* (Washington, DC: OJJDP Bulletin, 2005), pp. 18–19.

21. James Ryan, "Who Gets Revoked? A Comparison of Intensive Supervision Successes and Failures in Vermont," *Crime and Delinquency* 43:104–118 (1997).

22. Sheldon X. Zhang and Lening Zhang, "An Experimental Study of the Los Angeles County Repeat Offender Prevention Program: Its Implementation and Evaluation," *Criminology and Public Policy* 4:205–236 (2005).

23. Jodi Lane, Susan Turner, Terry Fain, and Amber Sehgal, "Evaluating an Experimental Intensive Juvenile Probation Program: Supervision and Official Outcomes," *Crime and Delinquency* 51:26–52 (2005).

24. Angela A. Robertson, Paul W. Grimes, and Kevin E. Rogers, "A Short-Run Cost-Benefit Analysis of Community-Based Interventions for Juvenile Offenders," *Crime and Delinquency* 47:265–284 (2001).

25. Richard Ball and J. Robert Lilly, "A Theoretical Examination of Home Incarceration," *Federal Probation* 50:17–25 (1986); Joan Petersilia, "Exploring the Option of House Arrest," *Federal Probation* 50:50–56 (1986); Annesley

Schmidt, "Electronic Monitors," *Federal Probation* 50:56–60 (1986); Michael Charles, "The Development of a Juvenile Electronic Monitoring Program," *Federal Probation* 53:3–12 (1989).

26. Joseph B. Vaughn, "A Survey of Juvenile Electronic Monitoring and Home Confinement Programs," *Juvenile and Family Court Journal* 40:1–36 (1989).

27. Sudipto Roy, "Five Years of Electronic Monitoring of Adults and Juveniles in Lake County, Indiana: A Comparative Study on Factors Related to Failure," *Journal of Crime and Justice* 20:141–160 (1997).

28. Marc Renzema and Evan Mayo-Wilson, "Can Electronic Monitoring Reduce Crime for Moderate- to High-Risk Offenders?" *Journal of Experimental Criminology* 1:215–237 (2005).

29. Heather Strang and Lawrence W. Sherman, "Restorative Justice to Reduce Victimization," in Brandon C. Welsh and David P. Farrington, eds., *Preventing Crime: What Works for Children, Offenders, Victims, and Places* (New York: Springer, 2006), p. 148; see also Lawrence W. Sherman, Heather Strang, Caroline Angel, Daniel Woods, Geoffrey C. Barnes, Sarah Bennett, and Nova Inkpen, "Effects of Face-to-Face Restorative Justice on Victims of Crime in Four Randomized, Controlled Trials," *Journal of Experimental Criminology* 1:367–395 (2005); Lawrence W. Sherman and Heather Strang, *Restorative Justice: The Evidence* (London: The Smith Institute, 2007).

30. Strang and Sherman, "Restorative Justice to Reduce Victimization," pp. 152–156.

31. Nancy Rodriguez, "Restorative Justice, Communities, and Delinquency: Whom Do We Reintegrate?" *Criminology and Public Policy* 4:103–130 (2005).

32. Andrew J. DeAngelo, "Evolution of Juvenile Justice: Community-Based Partnerships Through Balanced and Restorative Justice," *Corrections Today* 67(5):105–106 (2005); Dennis Mahoney, Dennis Romig, and Troy Armstrong, "Juvenile Probation: The Balanced Approach," *Juvenile and Family Court Journal* 39:1–59 (1988).

33. Gordon Bazemore, "On Mission Statements and Reform in Juvenile Justice: The Case of the Balanced Approach," *Federal Probation* 61:64–70 (1992); Gordon Bazemore and Mark Umbreit, *Balanced and Restorative Justice* (Washington, DC: Office of Juvenile Justice and Delinquency Prevention, 1994).

34. Gordon Bazemore, *Guide for Implementing the Balanced and Restorative Justice Model* (Washington, DC: Office of Juvenile Justice and Delinquency Prevention, 1998).

35. Office of Juvenile Justice and Delinquency Prevention, *The 8% Solution* (Washington, DC: OJJDP Fact Sheet, 2001).

36. Ibid., pp. 1–2.

37. Peter R. Schneider and Matthew C. Finkelstein, eds., *RESTTA National Directory of Restitution and Community Service Programs* (Washington, DC: Office of Juvenile Justice and Delinquency Prevention, U.S. Department of Justice, 1998).

38. Gordon Bazemore, "New Concepts and Alternative Practice in Community Supervision of Juvenile Offenders: Rediscovering Work Experience and Competency Development," *Journal of Crime and Justice* 14:27–45 (1991).

39. Anne Schneider, "Restitution and Recidivism Rates of Juvenile Offenders: Results from Four Experimental Studies," *Criminology* 24:533–552 (1986).

40. Shay Bilchik, *A Juvenile Justice System for the 21st Century* (Washington, DC: Office of Juvenile Justice and Delinquency Prevention, 1998).

41. Schneider and Finkelstein, *RESTTA National Directory of Restitution and Community Service Programs*, tables 12, 15.

42. Anne Schneider, "Restitution and Recidivism Rates of Juvenile Offenders," *Directory of Restitution Programs* (Washington, DC: OJJDP Juvenile Justice Clearinghouse, 1996). This directory contains information on more than 500 restitution programs across the country.

43. H. Ted Rubin, "Fulfilling Juvenile Restitution Requirements in Community Correctional Programs," *Federal Probation* 52:32–43 (1988).

44. Shelley Zavlek, *Planning Community-Based Facilities for Violent Juvenile Offenders as Part of a System of Graduated Sanctions* (Washington, DC: OJJDP Bulletin, 2005), p. 5; Peter W. Greenwood, "Juvenile Crime and Juvenile Justice," in James Q. Wilson and Joan Petersilia, eds., *Crime: Public Policies for Crime Control* (Oakland, CA: Institute for Contemporary Studies, 2002), pp. 90–91.

45. Sharon F. Mihalic, Abigail Fagan, Katherine Irwin, Diane Ballard, and Delbert Elliott, *Blueprints for Violence Prevention* (Washington, DC: OJJDP Report, 2004).

46. Patricia Chamberlain and John B. Reid, "Comparison of Two Community Alternatives to Incarceration," *Journal of Consulting and Clinical Psychology* 66:624–633 (1998).

47. Lamar T. Empey and Maynard Erickson, *The Provo Experiment* (Lexington, MA: D. C. Heath, 1972); Paul Pilnick, Albert Elias, and Neale Clapp, "The Essexfields Concept: A New Approach to the Social Treatment of Juvenile Delinquents," *Journal of Applied Behavioral Sciences* 2:109–121 (1966); Yitzhak Bakal, "Reflections: A Quarter Century of Reform in Massachusetts Youth Corrections," *Crime and Delinquency* 40:110–117 (1998).

48. Ira Schwartz, *Juvenile Justice and Public Policy* (New York: Lexington Books, 1992), p. 217.

49. Dan Macallair, "Reaffirming Rehabilitation in Juvenile Justice," *Youth and Society* 25:104–123 (1993).

50. Doris Layton MacKenzie, *What Works in Corrections: Reducing the Criminal Activities of Offenders and Delinquents* (New York: Cambridge University Press, 2006).

51. Barry Krisberg, Elliot Currie, and David Onek, "New Approaches in Corrections," *American Bar Association Journal of Criminal Justice* 10:51 (1995).

52. U.S. Department of Justice, *Children in Custody 1975–85: Census of Public and Private Juvenile Detention, Correctional, and Shelter Facilities* (Washington, DC: U.S. Department of Justice, 1989), p. 4.

53. For a detailed description of juvenile delinquency in the 1800s, see J. Hawes, *Children in Urban Society: Juvenile Delinquency in Nineteenth Century America* (New York: Oxford University Press, 1971).

54. Dwight C. Jarvis, *Institutional Treatment of the Offender* (New York: McGraw-Hill, 1978), p. 101.

55. Margaret Werner Cahalan, *Historical Corrections Statistics in the United States, 1850–1984* (Washington, DC: U.S. Department of Justice, 1986), pp. 104–105.

56. Clemons Bartollas, Stuart J. Miller, and Simon Dinitz, *Juvenile Victimization: The Institutional Paradox* (New York: Wiley, 1976), p. 6.

57. LaMar T. Empey, *American Delinquency—Its Meaning and Construction* (Homewood, IL: Dorsey, 1978), p. 515.

58. Edward Eldefonso and Walter Hartinger, *Control, Treatment, and Rehabilitation of Juvenile Offenders* (Beverly Hills: Glencoe, 1976), p. 151.

59. Ibid., p. 152.

60. M. Rosenthal, "Reforming the Justice Correctional Institution: Efforts of U.S. Children's Bureau in the 1930s," *Journal of Sociology and Social Welfare* 14:47–73 (1987).

61. Bureau of Justice Statistics, *Fact Sheet on Children in Custody* (Washington, DC: U.S. Department of Justice, 1989); Barbara Allen-Hagen, *Public Juvenile Facilities—Children in Custody, 1989* (Washington, DC: Office of Juvenile Justice and Delinquency Prevention, 1991); James Austin et al., *Juveniles Taken into Custody, 1993* (Washington, DC: Office of Juvenile Justice and Delinquency Prevention, 1995).

62. National Conference of State Legislatures, *A Legislator's Guide to Comprehensive Juvenile Justice, Juvenile Detention and Corrections* (Denver: National Conference of State Legislators, 1996).

63. Ibid.

64. Snyder and Sickmund, *Juvenile Offenders and Victims: 2006 National Report*, ch. 7.

65. Ibid., pp. 198–199.

66. Ibid., p. 201.

67. Daniel P. Mears, "Exploring State-Level Variation in Juvenile Incarceration Rates: Symbolic Threats and Competing Explanations," *The Prison Journal* 86:470–490 (2006).

68. Ira Schwartz, Marilyn Jackson-Beck, and Roger Anderson, "The 'Hidden' System of Juvenile Control," *Crime and Delinquency* 30:371–385 (1984).

69. Rebecca Craig and Andrea Paterson, "State Involuntary Commitment Laws: Beyond Deinstitutionalization," *National Conference of State Legislative Reports* 13:1–10 (1988).

70. Robert Pear, "Many Youths Reported Held Awaiting Mental Help," *New York Times*, 8 July 2004.

71. Richard Lezin Jones and Leslie Kaufman, "New Jersey Youths Out of Foster Homes End Up in Detention," *New York Times*, 31 May 2003.

72. Melissa Sickmund, *Juvenile Residential Facility Census, 2002: Selected Findings* (Washington, DC: OJJDP Bulletin, 2006), p. 2; see also Snyder and Sickmund, *Juvenile Offenders and Victims*, p. 223.

73. Sickmund, *Juvenile Residential Facility Census, 2002*, p. 9.

74. John M. Broder, "Dismal California Prisons Hold Juvenile Offenders: Reports Document Long List of Maltreatment," *New York Times*, 15 February 2004, p. 12.

75. Snyder and Sickmund, *Juvenile Offenders and Victims*, pp. 209, 215.

76. Gail A. Wasserman, Peter S. Jensen, Susan J. Ko, Joseph Cocozza, Eric Trupin, Adrian Angold, Elizabeth Cauffman, and Thomas Grisso, "Mental Health Assessments in Juvenile Justice: Report on the Consensus Conference," *Journal of the American Academy of Child and Adolescent Psychiatry* 42:752–761 (2003), p. 752.

77. Gail A. Wasserman, Susan J. Ko, and Larkin S. McReynolds, *Assessing the Mental Health Status of Youth in Juvenile Justice Settings* (Washington, DC: OJJDP Bulletin, 2004), p. 1.

78. Deborah Shelton, "Patterns of Treatment Services and Costs for Young Offenders with Mental Disorders," *Journal of Child and Adolescent Psychiatric Nursing* 18:103–112 (2005).

79. Wasserman, Jensen, Ko, Cocozza, Trupin, Angold, Cauffman, and Grisso, "Mental Health Assessments in Juvenile Justice: Report on the Consensus Conference," p. 752.

80. Michael D. Pullman, Jodi Kerbs, Nancy Koroloff, Ernie Veach-White, Rita Gaylor, and DeDe Sieler, "Juvenile Offenders with Mental Health Needs: Reducing Recidivism Using Wraparound," *Crime and Delinquency* 52:375–397 (2006).

81. Snyder and Sickmund, *Juvenile Offenders and Victims*, p. 213.

82. Michael J. Leiber and Kristan C. Fox, "Race and the Impact of Detention on Juvenile Justice Decision Making," *Crime and Delinquency* 51:470–497 (2005).

83. Snyder and Sickmund, *Juvenile Offenders and Victims*, p. 212.

84. Rodney L. Engen, Sara Steen, and George S. Bridges, "Racial Disparities in the Punishment of Youth: A Theoretical and Empirical Assessment of the Literature," *Social Problems* 49:194–220 (2002).

85. Snyder and Sickmund, *Juvenile Offenders and Victims*, p. 211; see also National Council on Crime and Delinquency, *And Justice for Some: Differential Treatment of Youth of Color in the Justice System* (San Francisco, CA: Author, 2007).

86. John F. Chapman, Rani A. Desai, Paul R. Falzer, and Randy Borum, "Violence Risk and Race in a Sample of Youth in Juvenile Detention: The Potential to Reduce Disproportionate Minority Confinement," *Youth Violence and Juvenile Justice* 4:170–184 (2006).

87. Heidi M. Hsia, George S. Bridges, and Rosalie McHale, *Disproportionate Minority Confinement: 2002 Update: Summary* (Washington, DC: Office of Juvenile Justice and Delinquency Prevention, 2004).

88. Ibid., pp. 16–17.

89. Emily R. Cabaniss, James M. Frabutt, Mary H. Kendrick, and Margaret B. Arbuckle, "Reducing Disproportionate Minority Contact in the Juvenile Justice System: Promising Practices," *Aggression and Violent Behavior* 12:393–401 (2007).

90. See David M. Halbfinger, "Care of Juvenile Offenders in Mississippi Is Faulted," *New York Times*, 1 September 2003.

91. Snyder and Sickmund, *Juvenile Offenders and Victims*, p. 206.

92. Bartollas, Miller, and Dinitz, *Juvenile Victimization*.

93. Christopher Sieverdes and Clemens Bartollas, "Security Level and Adjustment Patterns in Juvenile Institutions," *Journal of Criminal Justice* 14:135–145 (1986).

94. Snyder and Sickmund, *Juvenile Offenders and Victims*, p. 206.

95. Several authors have written of this sexual double standard. See E. A. Anderson, "The Chivalrous Treatment of the Female Offender in the Arms of the Criminal Justice System: A Review of the Literature," *Social Problems* 23:350–357 (1976); G. Armstrong, "Females under the Law: Protected but Unequal," *Crime and Delinquency* 23:109–120 (1977); M. Chesney-Lind, "Judicial Enforcement of the Female Sex Role: The Family Court and the Female Delinquent," *Issues in Criminology* 8:51–59 (1973); M. Chesney-Lind, "Juvenile Delinquency: The Sexualization of Female Crime," *Psychology Today* 19:43–46 (1974); Allan Conway and Carol Bogdan, "Sexual Delinquency: The Persistence of a Double Standard," *Crime and Delinquency* 23:13–35 (1977); Medna Chesney-Lind and Randall G. Shelden, *Girls, Delinquency, and the Juvenile Justice System*, 3rd ed. (Belmont, CA: Wadsworth, 2004).

96. Snyder and Sickmund, *Juvenile Offenders and* Victims, p. 209.

97. Kristi Holsinger and Alexander M. Holsinger, "Differential Pathways to Violence and Self-Injurious Behavior: African American and White Girls in the Juvenile Justice System," *Journal of Research in Crime and Delinquency* 42:211–242 (2005).

98. Sara Goodkind, Irene Ng, and Rosemary C. Sarri, "The Impact of Sexual Abuse in the Lives of Young Women Involved or at Risk of Involvement

with the Juvenile Justice System," *Violence Against Women* 12:465–477 (2006); see also Emily Gaarder and Joanne Belknap, "Tenuous Borders: Girls Transferred to Adult Court," *Criminology* 40:481–518 (2002).

99. Leslie Acoca, "Outside/Inside: The Violation of American Girls at Home, on the Streets, and in the Juvenile Justice System," *Crime and Delinquency* 44:561–589 (1998).

100. Barbara Bloom, Barbara Owen, Elizabeth Piper Deschenes, and Jill Rosenbaum, "Improving Juvenile Justice for Females: A Statewide Assessment in California," *Crime and Delinquency* 48:526–552 (2002), p. 548.

101. For a historical analysis of a girls' reformatory, see Barbara Brenzel, *Daughters of the State* (Cambridge, MA: MIT Press, 1983).

102. Ilene R. Bergsmann, "The Forgotten Few Juvenile Female Offenders," *Federal Probation* 53:73–79 (1989).

103. *Justice by Gender: The Lack of Appropriate Prevention, Diversion and Treatment Alternatives for Girls in the Justice System: A Report* (Chicago: American Bar Association and National Bar Association, 2001), pp. 27–29.

104. Doris Layton MacKenzie, "Reducing the Criminal Activities of Known Offenders and Delinquents: Crime Prevention in the Courts and Corrections," in Lawrence W. Sherman, David P. Farrington, Brandon C. Welsh, and Doris Layton MacKenzie, eds., *Evidence-Based Crime Prevention* (New York: Routledge, 2006, rev. ed.), p. 352.

105. Patrick A. Langan and David J. Levin, *Recidivism of Prisoners Released in 1994* (Washington, DC: Bureau of Justice Statistics, 2002).

106. David Farabee, *Rethinking Rehabilitation: Why Can't We Reform Our Criminals?* (Washington, DC: American Enterprise Institute, 2005); for a rebuttal of this view, see James M. Byrne and Faye S. Taxman, "Crime (Control) is a Choice: Divergent Perspectives on the Role of Treatment in the Adult Corrections System," *Criminology and Public Policy* 4:291–310 (2005).

107. Mark W. Lipsey and David B. Wilson, "Effective Intervention for Serious Juvenile Offenders: A Synthesis of Research," in Rolf Loeber and David P. Farrington, eds., *Serious and Violent Juvenile Offenders: Risk Factors and Successful Interventions* (Thousand Oaks, CA: Sage, 1998).

108. Steve Aos, Roxanne Lieb, Jim Mayfield, Marna Miller, and Annie Pennucci, *Benefits and Costs of Prevention and Early Intervention Programs for Youth* (Olympia, WA: Washington State Institute for Public Policy, 2004); Brandon C. Welsh, "Monetary Costs and Benefits of Correctional Treatment Programs: Implications for Offender Reentry," *Federal Probation* 68(2):9–13 (2004).

109. Michael F. Caldwell, Michael Vitacco, and Gregory J. Van Rybroek, "Are Violent Delinquents Worth Treating: A Cost-Benefit Analysis," *Journal of Research in Crime and Delinquency* 43:148–168 (2006).

110. Louise Sas and Peter Jaffe, "Understanding Depression in Juvenile Delinquency: Implications for Institutional Admission Policies and Treatment Programs," *Juvenile and Family Court Journal* 37:49–58 (1985–1986).

111. See, generally, William Glasser, "Reality Therapy: A Realistic Approach to the Young Offender," in Robert Schaste and Jo Wallach, eds., *Readings in Delinquency and Treatment* (Los Angeles: Delinquency Prevention Training Project, Youth Studies Center, University of Southern California, 1965); see also Richard Rachin, "Reality Therapy: Helping People Help Themselves," *Crime and Delinquency* 16:143 (1974).

112. Helen A. Klein, "Toward More Effective Behavior Programs for Juvenile Offenders," *Federal Probation* 41:45–50 (1977); Albert Bandura, *Principles of Behavior Modification* (New York: Holt, Rinehart & Winston, 1969); H. A. Klein, "Behavior Modification as Therapeutic Paradox," *American Journal of Orthopsychiatry* 44:353 (1974).

113. Thomas J. Dishion, Joan McCord, and François Poulin, "When Interventions Harm: Peer Groups and Problem Behavior," *American Psychologist* 54:755–764 (1999); Joan McCord, "Cures that Harm: Unanticipated Outcomes of Crime Prevention Programs," *Annals of the American Academy of Political and Social Science* 587:16–30 (2003).

114. Larry Brendtero and Arlin Ness, "Perspectives on Peer Group Treatment: The Use and Abuses of Guided Group Interaction/Positive Peer Culture," *Child and Youth Services Review* 4:307–324 (1982).

115. Elaine Traynelis-Yurek and George A. Giacobbe, "Communication Rehabilitation Regime for Incarcerated Youth: Positive Peer Culture," *Journal of Offender Rehabilitation* 26:157–167 (1998).

116. Bruno Bettelheim, *The Empty Fortress* (New York: Free Press, 1967).

117. California Youth Authority, "Ventura School for Juvenile Female Offenders," *CYA Newsletter* (Ventura, CA: Author, 1988).

118. Kate O'Sullivan, Nancy Rose, and Thomas Murphy, *PEPNet: Connecting Juvenile Offenders to Education and Employment* (Washington, DC: OJJDP Fact Sheet, 2001), p. 1.

119. Doris Layton MacKenzie, "Reducing the Criminal Activities of Known Offenders and Delinquents," p. 355; Doris Layton MacKenzie, "Evidence-Based Corrections: Identifying What Works," *Crime and Delinquency* 46:457–471 (2000), p. 466.

120. Thomas Castellano and Irina Soderstrom, "Therapeutic Wilderness Programs and Juvenile Recidivism: A Program Evaluation," *Journal of Offender Rehabilitation* 17:19–46 (1992).

121. MacKenzie, "Reducing the Criminal Activities of Known Offenders and Delinquents," p. 355.

122. Sandra Jo Wilson and Mark W. Lipsey, "Wilderness Challenge Programs for Delinquent Youth: A Meta-Analysis of Outcome Evaluations," *Evaluation and Program Planning* 23:1–12 (2003).

123. Jerald Burns and Gennaro Vito, "An Impact Analysis of the Alabama Boot Camp Program," *Federal Probation* 59:63–67 (1995).

124. Ronald Corbett and Joan Petersilia, eds., "The Results of a Multi-Site Study of Boot Camps," *Federal Probation* 58:60–66 (1995).

125. Doris Layton MacKenzie, Angela R. Gover, Gaylene Styve Armstrong, and Ojmarrh Mitchell, *A National Study Comparing the Environments of Boot Camps with Traditional Facilities for Juvenile Offenders* (Washington, DC: NIJ Research in Brief, 2001), pp. 1–2.

126. David B. Wilson and Doris Layton MacKenzie, "Boot Camps," in Brandon C. Welsh and David P. Farrington, eds., *Preventing Crime: What Works for Children, Offenders, Victims, and Places?* (New York, Springer, 2006), p. 80, table 2.

127. Ibid., p. 80.

128. Ibid.; Doris Layton MacKenzie, *What Works in Corrections: Reducing the Criminal Activities of Offenders and Delinquents* (New York: Cambridge University Press, 2006), p. 294.

129. Megan Kurlychek and Cynthia Kempinen, "Beyond Boot Camp: The Impact of Aftercare on Offender Reentry," *Criminology and Public Policy* 5:363–388 (2006).

130. MacKenzie, "Reducing the Criminal Activities of Known Offenders and Delinquents," p. 348.

131. Dale G. Parent, *Correctional Boot Camps: Lessons Learned from a Decade of Research* (Washington, DC: National Institute of Justice, 2003).

132. Anthony Salerno, "Boot Camps—A Critique and Proposed Alternative," *Journal of Offender Rehabilitation* 20:147–158 (1994).

133. Joanne Ardovini-Brooker and Lewis Walker, "Juvenile Boot Camps and the Reclamation of Our Youth: Some Food for Thought," *Juvenile and Family Court Journal* 51:12–28 (2000).

134. Morton Birnbaum, "The Right to Treatment," *American Bar Association Journal* 46:499 (1960).

135. See, for example, *Matter of Welfare of CAW*, 579 N.W.2d 494 (MN App. 1998).

136. *Inmates of the Boys' Training School v. Affleck*, 346 F. Supp. 1354 (D.R.I. 1972).

137. Ibid., p. 1343.

138. *Nelson v. Heyne*, 491 F.2d 353 (1974).

139. *Morales v. Turman*, 383 F. Supp. 53 (E.D. Texas 1974).

140. *Pena v. New York State Division for Youth*, 419 F. Supp. 203 (S.D.N.Y. 1976).

141. *Ralston v. Robinson*, 102 S.Ct. 233 (1981).

142. Patricia Puritz and Mary Ann Scali, *Beyond the Walls: Improving Conditions of Confinement for Youth in Custody* (Washington, DC: Office of Juvenile Justice and Delinquency Prevention, 1998).

143. Joan McCord, Cathy Spatz Widom, and Nancy A. Crowell, *Juvenile Crime, Juvenile Justice*, Panel on Juvenile Crime: Prevention, Treatment, and Control (Washington, DC: National Academy Press, 2001), p. 194.

144. David M. Altschuler and Rachel Brash, "Adolescent and Teenage Offenders Confronting the Challenges and Opportunities of Reentry," *Youth Violence and Juvenile Justice* 2:72–87 (2004), p. 72.

145. Daniel P. Mears and Jeremy Travis, "Youth Development and Reentry," *Youth Violence and Juvenile Justice* 2:3–20 (2004), p. 3.

146. Edward J. Latessa, "Homelessness and Reincarceration: Editorial Introduction," *Criminology and Public Policy* 3:137–138 (2004).

147. Joan Petersilia, *When Prisoners Come Home: Parole and Prisoner Reentry* (New York: Oxford University Press, 2003).

148. Margaret Beale Spencer and Cheryl Jones-Walker, "Interventions and Services Offered to Former Juvenile Offenders Reentering Their Communities: An Analysis of Program Effectiveness," *Youth Violence and Juvenile Justice* 2:88–97 (2004), p. 91.

149. Pamela K. Lattimore, "Reentry, Reintegration, Rehabilitation, Recidivism, and Redemption," *The Criminologist* 31(3):1, 3–6 (2006), p. 1.

150. Michael Norman, "Discretionary Justice: Decision Making in a State Juvenile Parole Board," *Juvenile and Family Court Journal* 37:19–26 (1985–1986).

151. James Maupin, "Risk Classification Systems and the Provisions of Juvenile Aftercare," *Crime and Delinquency* 39:90–105 (1993).

152. David M. Altschuler and Troy L. Armstrong, "Juvenile Corrections and Continuity of Care in a Community Context–The Evidence and Promising Directions," *Federal Probation* 66:72–77 (2002).

153. David M. Altschuler and Troy L. Armstrong, "Intensive Aftercare for High-Risk Juveniles: A Community Care Model" (Washington, DC: Office of Juvenile Justice and Delinquency Prevention, 1994).

154. David M. Altschuler and Troy Armstrong, "Reintegrating Juvenile Offenders: Translating the Intensive Aftercare Program Model into Performance Standards," paper presented at the annual meeting of the American Society of Criminology, San Francisco, November 2000.

155. See *Morrissey v. Brewer*, 408 U.S. 471, 92 S.Ct. 2593, 33 L.Ed.2d 484 (1972).

156. Peter W. Greenwood, "Juvenile Crime and Juvenile Justice," in James Q. Wilson and Joan Petersilia, eds., *Crime: Public Policies for Crime Control* (Oakland, CA: Institute for Contemporary Studies, 2002), pp. 90–91.

157. Rolf Loeber and David P. Farrington, "Never Too Early, Never Too Late: Risk Factors and Successful Interventions for Serious and Violent Juvenile Offenders," *Studies on Crime and Crime Prevention* 7:7–30 (1998).

Delinquency and Juvenile Justice Abroad

17

Chapter Outline

Delinquency around the World

Europe
The Americas
Australia and New Zealand
Asia

FOCUS ON DELINQUENCY: Youth Violence on the Rise in Japan

Africa

International Comparisons

Problems of Cross-National Research
Benefits of Cross-National Research
Juvenile Violence
Juvenile Property Crime
Juvenile Drug Use
Conclusion: What Do the Trends Tell Us?

Juvenile Justice Systems across Countries

Juvenile Policing
Age of Criminal Responsibility: Minimum and Maximum
Presence of Juvenile Court
Transfers to Adult Court
Sentencing Policies

POLICY AND PRACTICE: Precourt Diversion Programs around the World

Incarcerated Juveniles
Aftercare

POLICY AND PRACTICE: The Changing Nature of Youth Justice in Canada

A Profile of Juvenile Justice in England

Apprehension and Charge
Bail
Precourt Diversion
Prosecution
Youth Court
Sentencing

Future of International Juvenile Justice

Chapter Objectives

1. Have a grasp of some of the different delinquency problems facing the regions of the world
2. Be able to identify the main challenges of conducting international comparisons of delinquency
3. Be able to identify the benefits of international comparative research
4. Be able to comment on trends in juvenile violence, property crime, and drug use in Europe and North America
5. Understand the key explanations for changes in these types of delinquency in Europe and North America
6. Know about the work of the United Nations to help countries improve their juvenile justice systems
7. Be familiar with differences and similarities on key issues of juvenile justice around the world
8. Understand the key stages of juvenile justice in England
9. Be able to comment on the differences and similarities in juvenile justice in the United States and in England

Toxic pet food, lead paint in toys, faulty automobile tires, and dangerous chemicals in specialty foods have led to widespread consumer safety alerts and large-scale recalls by companies in the United States and caused many local problems in China where these goods are manufactured. These events are not the result of delinquent acts perpetrated by Chinese youths. But they do signal the changing times in China, which also appear to be behind a growing problem with crime and juvenile delinquency in this country.

These events, shaped by globalization, a rapidly expanding Chinese economy, and a fiercely competitive manufacturing sector, follow on the heels of one of the worst individual atrocities committed in China in recent memory. Dubbed the "Kindergarten Killer" by the Chinese media, Fu Hegong, age 31, was recently convicted and sentenced to death for the brutal murder of a teacher and a 5-year-old boy. Fu had broken into a Beijing kindergarten to rob it. Discovered by the teacher, he killed her by smothering her with a quilt. He then took the life of the young student who was with the teacher at the time. Beijing's No. 2 Intermediate Court also found the "Kindergarten Killer" guilty of three other, unrelated murders, one of a security guard in a botched robbery.

Although rare, it is atrocities like these that have brought further national and international attention to China's growing problem with crime and delinquency of late, and prompted the Chinese government to take a number of steps to improve school security as well as community safety. The rise in crime and delinquency in China has been linked to the country's ongoing social and economic upheaval that began in 1979 when the country first adopted its reform policies and embraced the outside world. Though the rapid economic growth has transformed society, rapid change has strained traditional norms, values, and ethics.

China is not alone in experiencing some of these social and economic shifts and the associated problems. Many nations around the world are experiencing an upsurge in juvenile problem behavior, including gang violence, prostitution, and drug abuse. In response to the growing number of delinquent acts, some nations are now in the process of revamping their juvenile justice systems in an effort to increase their effectiveness and efficiency. This chapter addresses these issues by looking at international perspectives of delinquency and juvenile justice systems. The chapter begins by providing a snapshot of juvenile delinquency around the world. We discuss the challenges and benefits of making comparisons across nations and examine trends in delinquency rates in different countries compared with the United States. Next we provide a review of juvenile justice systems in **developed countries**, organized around important issues facing juvenile justice today, such as minimum age of criminal responsibility, transfers to adult court, and maximum length of sentence for incarcerated juveniles. The chapter concludes with a profile of the juvenile justice system in England, examining the many different stages that juveniles may face as they go through the system.

DELINQUENCY AROUND THE WORLD

There has been a noted upswing in juvenile delinquency around the world. Where has this occurred, and what has been the cause? Examples are found in all major areas of the world, and though there are many reasons, some common themes emerge.

Europe

Teen violence has been on the rise in Europe. This increase in violence is evident in both the absolute rate of offending and the proportion of total offenses committed.[1] One of the most alarming developments has been the involvement of children in the international sex trade. Russia is plagued with Internet sex rings that involve youths in pornographic pictures. In Moscow, more than 800 tapes and videos were seized during Operation Blue Orchid, a joint operation conducted by Russian police and U.S. Customs agents.[2] Operation Blue Orchid led to criminal investigations against people who ordered child pornography in more than 20 nations. Equally disturbing has been the involvement of European youths in global prostitution rings. Desperate young girls and boys in war-torn areas such as the former Yugoslavia and in impoverished areas such as eastern Europe have become involved with gangs that ship them around the world. In one case, an organized crime group involved in wildlife smuggling of tiger bones and skins to Asian markets began a sideline of supplying sex clubs with young Russian women.[3] In another case, as a result of a 12-nation crackdown on the trafficking of women for sex commerce, the Southeast European Cooperative Initiative in Bucharest, Romania, identified 696 victims of trafficking and 831 suspected traffickers.[4] Illicit drug use has also become more problematic in eastern Europe, and is partly responsible for a large-scale increase in HIV infection in Estonia.[5]

Western Europe has recently experienced an alarming amount of teen violence. France is one of the countries where youth unrest has led to increased violence in the streets. Here, youths try to block a road after a demonstration against a controversial government youth jobs plan on April 4, 2006, in the city of Lille. The unrest later spread to the streets of Paris, where large numbers of youths hurled stones and bottles at riot police.

© Philippe Huguen/AFP/Getty Images

Western Europe has also experienced a surprising amount of teen violence. On April 26, 2002, in Erfurt, Germany, a 19-year-old male, armed with a pump-action shotgun and a handgun, entered his high school and shot dead 14 teachers, two students, and a police officer; he then took his own life. The youth had just been expelled from the school. It was the worst mass killing in Germany since World War II.[6]

Germany has also been plagued with skinhead violence since reunification in 1989. Most German skinheads are social misfits, with minimal education and few employment opportunities. Because unemployment is high, they feel helpless and hopeless regarding their future, and many resort to physical violence in reaction to their plight.[7] Most of the increase in German youth violence has been encountered in what was communist East Germany before the reunification. Youth violence in the east is 70 percent higher than in the west, a factor linked to the exposure of eastern youth to greater poverty and unemployment than their West German peers.[8]

France too has experienced a surge in violent hate crimes, as well as (to a lesser extent) street crime in Paris.[9] A more modest increase in juvenile violence has been reported across the country.[10] On October 27, 2005, riots erupted in the suburbs of Paris and quickly spread to other regions of the country. The immediate cause of the riots was the death of two teenage boys of African descent who were believed to have been chased by police and were electrocuted upon entering a power substation in the suburb of Clichy-sous-Bois. The larger cause was escalating tension between the government and immigrant populations who charge that the government is to blame for their communities' high rates of unemployment because of long-standing discrimination against them and their French-born children.[11] The rioting lasted for three weeks and caused immense property damage: 10,000 vehicles, 255 schools, and 233 government buildings were burned, and 51 post office and 140 public transportation vehicles were damaged by stone throwing. Of the 498 juveniles who were apprehended by the police and referred to youth court, 108 were held in police custody to await trial.[12]

What has fueled this increase in teen violence? Although each nation is quite different, all share an explosive mix of racial tension, poverty, envy, drug abuse, broken families, unemployment, and alienation. Some of the areas hardest hit have been undergoing rapid social and economic change—the fall of communism, the end of the Cold War, the effects of the global economy, an influx of multinational immigration— as they move toward increased economic integration, privatization, and diminished social services. In Europe, the main reason for an increase in teen violence is believed to be the tremendous growth in immigrant youth populations. This is not because immigrants are more prone to violence, but rather because of the relative poverty and social disintegration they face upon arriving in very homogenous countries such as Sweden, the Netherlands, and Germany.[13] This view has also been advanced as one of the main reasons for the growth in rates of total violent crime (adult plus juvenile) in Europe during the early 1990s to early 2000s.[14] The result of these rapid changes has been the development of personal alienation in an anomic environment. (See Chapter 4 for more on the effect of anomie.) Kids become susceptible to violence when institutional and interpersonal sources of stability, such as schools and parents, are weak and/or absent.[15]

The Americas

Shocking stories of teen violence are also not uncommon in North America and South America. In Canada, there has been a rash of school shootings in recent years. Many have resulted in death and serious injury of other students and teachers. School shootings in Canada increased substantially immediately following the massacre at Columbine High School in the United States in 1999, prompting some Canadian social scientists to speculate that these were copycat crimes. But other research points to the growing number of students who have access to guns and carry them to school,[16] as well as an increase in school violence in general.[17]

In Mexico, violent crime is one of the biggest problems facing the country. One study found more than 1,500 street gangs in Mexico City, the country's capital. Gang names include *Verdugos* (Executioners), *Malditos Ratas* (Damned Rats), *Niños Podridos* (Rotten Children), and *Cerdos* (Pigs). Most of the gangs are made up of teenagers, and each gang is accompanied by what is referred to as their "diaper brigade," the equivalent of a "minor league" for children under age 12.[18]

South America has a long history of violent uprisings, police abuse, and political unrest. Some countries are more violent than others. In Brazil, violence is the second leading cause of death behind heart disease; there are more deaths each year by murder than by cancer. Young people are responsible for a disproportionate number of these homicides.[19] Drug trafficking gangs are largely responsible for the violence. In Rio de Janeiro, the country's showcase city, these heavily armed gangs, referred to as "organized terrorist groups" by the head police authority, have taken to bombing government buildings, shopping centers, and tourist attractions. This is being done to cause the government to ease up on its long-standing campaign against these criminal groups.[20]

Among the more recent atrocities in South America is a government cover-up of killings of juvenile and other gang members in a prison in El Porvenir, Honduras, and in Guatemala.[21] The killing of street children continues to take place in many South American cities. These are children who leave home at a very young age because of abuse, neglect, or the loss of their parents, and earn their living largely by committing petty delinquent acts, begging, and selling garbage. In Rio de Janeiro, killings of street children are commonplace. Death squads, drug lords, juvenile gangs, and sometimes the police are behind these killings.[22]

death squads
Common to South America, organized government or criminal groups that selectively kill members of opposing groups and incite fear in those groups and among their supporters.

Australia and New Zealand

Although not normally associated with high crime and delinquency rates, these island nations have had their share of youth crime, ranging from graffiti to homicide. In fact, the graffiti problem has become so serious in New Zealand that some police departments have been forced to use photographs to prepare victim damage estimates. In one police office, 135 different incidents were investigated before the culprits, a youth group, were finally arrested.[23]

Australia has experienced a wide range of juvenile crime. As in Europe, child prostitution has become a significant problem, and an estimated 4,000 children, some as young as 10 years old, are involved in selling sex for money and drugs.[24] Australia has also experienced juvenile violence. Youths are the offenders (and/or victims) in about one-third of all the murders occurring in Australia.[25] Youth homicides tend to occur among strangers, with the youngest offenders (10 to 14 years) killing people they had never met before and older teens victimizing acquaintances. One reason for this trend is that the Australian juvenile is more likely to kill while committing another crime such as a robbery. Juveniles are also more likely to kill for revenge than are adults.

Asia

Crime rates are at an all-time high in Japan, reaching a post–World War II peak in 2002 and coming down slightly since then.[26] According to the National Police Agency in Japan, juvenile crime and foreign criminal gangs are the "twin causes" of the rising crime rates.[27] Between 1994 and 2003 (latest data available for juvenile crime), juvenile arrests for violent crime increased 60 percent, and the number of arrests for homicide by juveniles increased by one-quarter (24 percent, from 75 to 93); homicide arrests are down from a 1998 peak of 115.[28] Police in the Fukushima Prefecture, located north of Tokyo, arrested a 15-year-old boy for killing his father. The 15-year-old punched his 61-year-old father in the face and stomped on his stomach until he was dead. The incident was extremely shocking because it occurred one day after a 13-year-old was arrested for beating his mother to death because he objected to the meal she had cooked![29] The term *hikikomori* (those who isolate themselves) has been coined to describe troubled youth who commit crimes and engage in other antisocial acts.[30] The overall increase in teen violence and particularly heinous crimes like these were behind the Japanese government's get-tough measures introduced to the Juvenile Act (*Shônen-hô*), the first revisions to the act in 50 years.[31] The Japanese experience with delinquency and youth violence is the topic of the accompanying Focus on Delinquency.

Japan is not the only Asian nation experiencing an uptick in juvenile crime. Chinese authorities have found that juvenile delinquency has been on the increase for several years, with violence being a major component of juvenile crime.[32] The rise in delinquency has been linked to China's ongoing social and economic upheaval that began in 1979 when the country first adopted its reform policies and embraced the outside world.[33] Though the rapid economic growth has transformed society, rapid change has strained traditional norms, values, and ethics. Although China is often known for its ruthless suppression of crime and liberal use of the death penalty, the government has adopted a more humane approach to treating delinquents. The aim is to act as a wise and concerned pseudoparent, emphasizing prevention and education rather than punishment and repression.

Africa

Juvenile crime and gang violence are growing problems in many African countries. In the city of Dakar, Senegal, on the western coast of the continent, youth gang problems are out of control. Youth gangs with English names taken from American television and movies, such as the Hooligan Boys, the Mafia Boys, and the Eagles, prey on different segments of the population. The Hooligan Boys, for example, are best known for the violence they inflict at dance parties organized by other young people. This gang has also developed a type of violence market in which they "buy a fight." This involves gang members offering to take over a fight that has already started and then fighting the weaker of the two parties. Many of the younger boys growing up in Dakar look up to the gangs; this admiration serves as an important tool in recruiting future gang members.[34]

Abject poverty, ethnic tensions, and an ever-growing gap between the haves and have-nots underlie much of the violence throughout Africa. In Nairobi, the capital of Kenya and one of the largest cities in Africa, up to 70 percent of residents live in slums on the outskirts of the city; 80 percent of residents are low-income earners; the rich occupy 60 percent of the city's land; and two-thirds of the population does not have access to clean water.[35]

INTERNATIONAL COMPARISONS

How does youth crime around the world compare to what we are experiencing here in the United States? There have been numerous efforts to compare delinquency across different countries.[36] Social scientists have carried out international comparisons for many reasons, including to test theories of delinquency; to compare delinquency and punishment over long periods of time; to investigate the effects of government policies on delinquency, such as gun control or child welfare benefits; to examine why some countries have very low delinquency rates; or just for general interest.[37] (Concept Summary 17.1 reviews the key reasons for making cross-national comparisons.) Advocacy organizations as well as governments sometimes point to events or trends in other countries to show how the United States is doing better or sometimes worse than other countries.

Youth Violence on the Rise in Japan

Japan has long been considered a low-crime country. Despite its industrial might and highly urbanized population—trademarks of high-crime countries in the developed world—Japan has maintained extremely low delinquency and crime rates in the post–World War II era. But in recent years this trend has changed, with a dramatic upsurge in violence among young people. As shown in Figure 17-A, police arrests of 15- to 19- year-olds for violent offenses started to climb in 1996, following years of stability. (Although these figures are not expressed as rates per juvenile population, the increase in arrests between 1996 and 2003 far surpasses any increase in the juvenile population.) In 1997, the peak year, 2,263 arrests were made for juvenile violence.

Shocking events, rarely experienced before in Japan, are starting to become more common. Japanese youth gangs have started to carry out what they call "uncle hunting," whereby four or five gang members single out a lone businessman walking home, rob him, and beat him to the ground. Victim reports claim that gangs are not only doing this for the money, but also for the thrill of inflicting pain on others. Other events include a 13-year-old boy murdering his female schoolteacher and a 16-year-old boy stabbing his girlfriend when she tried to end the relationship.

So what is causing this rise in youth violence in Japan? Japanese social scientists, politicians, leaders of business, and the public are all weighing in on the debate. One of the more controversial views is that the increase in juvenile violence and crime in general is being fueled by an increase in the number of multinational immigrants (for the most part other Asians) who have come to find work in Japan. As in Europe, it is not that these new populations are more prone to violence, but rather that they are less well off financially, due in part to work being scarce, and are disconnected from familial and social groups.

Other views point to a decline in cultural values and societal norms, which are widely regarded as being fundamental to the economic success and crime-free lifestyle that Japan has long enjoyed. Conformity, sense of community, belonging to a group, honor or "face," and respect for authority are all believed to have declined in recent years, especially among young people. Economic stagnation has also played a role in the rise in youth violence. A higher unemployment rate and fewer opportunities have left many young people feeling marginalized and frustrated. It is also estimated that 45 percent of all crimes in Japan are committed by people under age 20, about double what it is in the United States. Because so much of Japanese crime is committed by youths and the rate of juvenile crime and violence is escalating, experts predict no slow-down in the present trends in youth violence.

Critical Thinking

1. What are some other possible reasons for Japan's increase in youth violence?

2. What type of action should Japan take to address this rise in youth violence? And how can young people be part of the solution?

SOURCES: Trevor Ryan, "Creating 'Problem Kids': Juvenile Crime in Japan and Revisions to the Juvenile Act," *Journal of Japanese Law* 10:153–188 (2005); Aki Roberts and Gary LaFree, "Explaining Japan's Postwar Violent Crime Trends," *Criminology* 42:179–209 (2004); Nobuo Komiya, "A Cultural Study of the Low Crime Rate in Japan," *British Journal of Criminology* 39:369–390 (1999); Minoru Yokoyama, "Juvenile Justice and Juvenile Crime: An Overview of Japan," in John Winterdyk, ed., *Juvenile Justice Systems: International Perspectives*, 2nd ed. (Toronto: Canadian Scholars' Press, 2002); Hans Joachim Schneider, "Crime and Its Control in Japan and the Federal Republic of Germany," *International Journal of Offender Therapy and Comparative Criminology* 36:307–321 (1992); Freda Adler, *Nations Not Obsessed with Crime* (Littleton, CO: Rothman, 1983).

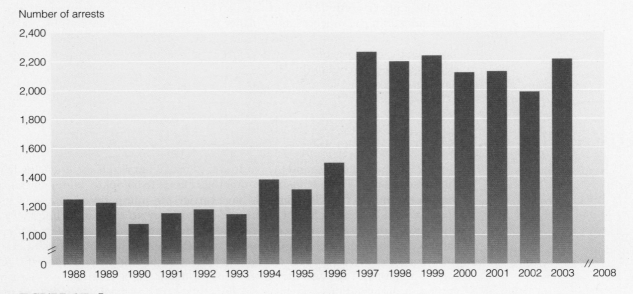

Number of arrests

FIGURE 17-A

Juvenile Arrests for Violent Offenses

SOURCE: Shinpei Nawa, "Postwar Fourth Wave of Juvenile Delinquency and Tasks of Juvenile Police," in *Current Juvenile Police Policy in Japan* (Tokyo: Police Policy Research Center, National Police Academy of Japan, 2006), table 1.

Concept Summary 17.1

Key Reasons for Cross-National Comparisons

Focus		Scope
Delinquency	▮	To assess which countries have high and low delinquency rates
Theories of delinquency	▮	To determine if similar theories can be used to explain delinquency in different countries
Juvenile justice system	▮	To compare differences in juvenile justice philosophy and administration
Treatment and prevention	▮	To compare different responses to juvenile delinquency and evaluate their effectiveness across countries

Problems of Cross-National Research

Unlike comparisons of delinquency in different cities or parts of the same country, international comparisons involving two or more countries demand that researchers pay a great deal more attention to what is being compared, what countries are being compared, and so on.[38] Comparing delinquency rates across countries can be difficult because of three main problems:

▮ The legal definitions of juvenile crime vary from country to country.[39]

▮ The measurement of juvenile crime varies across countries. In the United States, arrests are used to measure juvenile crime, while in many European countries, the number of cases solved by the police measures crime.[40]

▮ The age group defined as "juvenile" is not always the same.[41]

Despite these problems, valid comparisons of delinquency across different countries can still be made. The key is to acquire valid data and then make comparisons between nations that utilize similar methods of measuring youth crime. The best data sources are listed in Table 17.1.[42]

The United Nations Survey of Crime Trends and Operations of Criminal Justice Systems (UNCJS) provides data on juvenile delinquency and adult crime, as well as data on juvenile justice and criminal justice systems. Conducted every five years since 1977, the UNCJS survey makes it possible to look at changes over time and for a very large number of countries around the world. However, because the data are

TABLE 17.1

International Sources of Delinquency Data

Data Source	Type of Delinquency Data Collected	Organization in Charge of Data Collection	Number of Countries Represented	Frequency of Data Collection
UNCJS	Police statistics	United Nations	103	Every five years (since 1977)
INTERPOL	Police statistics	International Criminal Police Organization	179	Annually
WHO	Medical certified homicides	World Health Organization	191	Annually
European Sourcebook of Crime and Criminal Justice Statistics	Police statistics	Consortium of government agencies	37 European countries	Annually
International Self-Report Delinquency Study	Self-reports	Netherlands Ministry of Justice	12	One time only (early 1990s)

SOURCES: Josine Junger-Tas, Gert-Jan Terlouw, and Malcolm W. Klein, eds., *Delinquent Behavior among Young People in the Western World: First Results of the International Self-Report Delinquency Study* (New York: Kugler Publications, 1994); Graeme Newman and Gregory J. Howard, "Introduction: Data Sources and Their Use," in Graeme Newman, ed., *Global Report on Crime and Justice* (New York: Oxford University Press, 1999), pp. 3–12; Martin Killias et al., *European Sourcebook of Crime and Criminal Justice Statistics—2006*, 3rd ed. (The Hague, Netherlands: Research and Documentation Centre, Ministry of Justice, 2006).

a collection of statistics sent to the United Nations by individual countries, they are really no better than using official data provided by individual countries. The *European Sourcebook of Crime and Criminal Justice Statistics*, an initiative of the Council of Europe, is very similar to the UNCJS, but is limited to official statistics from Europe. Where the two data sources differ is that the Council of Europe is trying to develop a uniform system in the way official statistics on delinquency and crime are collected and reported.

The International Criminal Police Organization (INTERPOL) and the World Health Organization (WHO) are two other sources of official statistics on delinquency and crime at the international level. The two sources differ in a number of ways. INTERPOL compiles police crime statistics (completions and attempts) received from countries that are members of the organization. WHO, on the other hand, compiles homicide statistics (completions only) based on medical records received from countries that are affiliated with the organization. WHO's measure of homicide, which is based on the "classification of causes of death worldwide" and determined by medical practitioners,[43] is considered the most accurate source of homicide statistics[44] and is used in many international studies of homicide.[45] The main reason for WHO being the most accurate source of homicide data is that medical doctors and coroners are trained to determine cause of death.

The International Self-Report Delinquency (ISRD) study, which was carried out in 12 developed countries in the early 1990s, was the first attempt to measure self-reported delinquency at an international level using a standard questionnaire.[46] Because the same questionnaire was used for all subjects, delinquency rates could be compared in a more valid way across countries. Because the study has not been repeated, it is not possible to look at changes over time. A second sweep of the ISRD is planned.[47]

Benefits of Cross-National Research

Are juvenile offenders in the United States more violent than those in Japan? Are delinquents in western Europe more likely to steal cars? How does Australia's juvenile justice system differ from that of the United States? Knowledge of the nature of juvenile delinquency and how juvenile justice systems operate in other countries is not only beneficial for the concerned citizen, but also important to social scientists and government policy makers. Investigating whether juvenile offenders in the United States are more violent than, say, juveniles in Canada may lead to important discoveries to help explain any differences that exist. These discoveries may in turn be useful to policy makers and lead to action; for example, more funding for problem-solving policing tactics to reduce gun violence by juveniles.[48] (See Chapter 14 for examples of police efforts to reduce juvenile gun violence.)

Another value served by cross-national comparisons, whether it is delinquency rates or the treatment of incarcerated juvenile offenders, is to let a country know how well or how poorly it is doing relative to other countries. On the one hand, a poor international rating for the United States on juvenile homicides by an international agency, such as the United Nations, may prompt the U.S. government to take action to address this problem. On the other hand, a good international rating on, say, the legal rights afforded to detained juveniles demonstrates that the United States is on the right track. This, in turn, could lead to other countries making changes to follow the U.S. example.

Other benefits from cross-national comparisons can come from studying low-crime countries.[49] Examining these countries to find out how they maintain low delinquency rates may yield important insights for countries with higher delinquency rates. According to Harry Dammer, Erika Fairchild, and Jay Albanese, another good reason to make cross-national comparisons is the need to address transnational and international crime problems.[50] Transnational crimes are those activities that extend into two or more countries and violate the laws of those countries, such as illegal

To read more about the **United Nations**, go to their website via academic.cengage.com/criminaljustice/siegel.

To read more about **INTERPOL**, go to their website via academic.cengage.com/criminaljustice/siegel.

transnational crime
Crime that is carried out across the borders of two or more countries and violates the laws of those countries.

migration, trafficking in body parts, trafficking in illegal drugs and weapons, and theft and trafficking in automobiles.[51] Through the National Institute of Justice's International Center, the United States is playing an important role in addressing transnational crime problems.[52]

international crime
Crime that is punishable under international law.

International crimes are those that are recognized by international law, such as war crimes.[53] Criminal activities that take place across borders have grown considerably in the last two decades. "The end of the Cold War, the collapse of state authority in some countries and regions, and the process of globalization—of trade, finance, communications and information—have all provided an environment in which many criminal organizations find it more profitable and preferable to operate across national borders than confine their activities to one country."[54] This phenomenon has become known as the globalization of delinquency and crime.[55]

To read more about the **National Institute of Justice's International Center**, go to academic .cengage.com/criminaljustice/siegel.

The best method of comparing the level of delinquency across countries is to use data that have been collected in a uniform way, such as using a standard questionnaire that asks young people in different countries the same questions about their involvement in delinquency. At present, the best and most up-to-date source of delinquency rates is police statistics available from individual countries.

German social scientist Christian Pfeiffer examined trends in juvenile crime and violence in 10 European countries and the United States.[56] The European countries were England, Sweden, Germany, the Netherlands, Italy, Austria, France, Denmark, Switzerland, and Poland. A more recent study conducted by the European Crime Prevention Network (ECPN) examined trends in juvenile violence in countries that are members of the European Union.[57] Delinquency data were available from police statistics from the mid-1980s to the early-2000s. Three main findings emerged from the Pfeiffer study:

I Juvenile violence, especially robbery and offenses involving serious bodily harm, increased substantially over this period of time in almost all of the countries.

I Total juvenile crime, which includes burglary, motor vehicle theft, larceny, and vandalism, increased very little over this period of time, with some countries showing no increase or an actual decrease.

I Crimes of violence committed by young adults (18 to 20) or by adults in general have increased far less rapidly since the mid-1980s than have those committed by juveniles, and in some countries they have not increased at all.[58]

The main finding to emerge from the ECPN study was that the upward trend in juvenile violence in Europe has continued into the early 2000s. As previously noted, this increase in teen violence is evident in both the absolute rate of offending and the proportion of total offenses committed.[59] What does this international data tell us about the differences in delinquency trends between the United States and similar nations?

Juvenile Violence

The increase in juvenile violence between the mid-1980s and mid-1990s was greater in European countries than it was in the United States. (See Table 17.2.) However, while juvenile violence continued to increase in many European countries throughout the rest of the 1990s and into the early 2000s, teen violence in the United

Juvenile violence is a problem in all parts of the world. Here, two American teens, covering their faces on the tables, sit by their lawyers in the Darmstadt, Germany, state court before hearing their sentence. The teenagers were convicted of murder for dropping stones from a highway overpass onto passing cars. Two women were killed, and four other motorists were injured.

© AP Images/Axel Seidemann

TABLE 17.2

Juvenile Violent Crime in Europe and North America

Country	Years	Age of Juveniles (years)	Percentage Change in Rate
Austria	1991–1995	14–18	+20
Canada	1995–2006	12–17	−16
	1986–1995	12–17	+130
Denmark	1980–1994	15–17	+146
England	1986–1994	10–16	+53
European Union	1995–2000	12–17	+15
France	1984–1994	10–17	+87
Germany	1984–1995	14–17	+150
Italy	1986–1993	14–17	+175
Netherlands	1986–1995	12–17	+163
Switzerland	1980–1995	15–17	+200
United States	1994–2005	10–17	−46
	1985–1994	10–17	+73

NOTE: The increase in juvenile violence in European Union countries is an estimate based on data provided in the report by Fitzgerald, Stevens, and Hale.

SOURCES: Warren Silver, *Crime Statistics in Canada, 2006* (Ottawa: Canadian Centre for Justice Statistics Juristat, 2007), p. 14, table 5; Howard N. Snyder, *Juvenile Arrests 2005* (Washington, D.C.: Office of Juvenile Justice and Delinquency Prevention, U.S. Department of Justice, 2007); Marian Fitzgerald, Alex Stevens, and Chris Hale, *A Review of the Knowledge on Juvenile Violence: Trends, Policies and Responses in the EU Member States* (Brussels, Belgium: European Crime Prevention Network, European Commission, 2004), pp. 50–51; Christian Pfeiffer, "Juvenile Crime and Violence in Europe," in Michael Tonry, ed., *Crime and Justice: A Review of Research*, vol. 23 (Chicago: University of Chicago Press, 1998), pp. 263–291; Rebecca Kong, *Canadian Crime Statistics, 1996* (Ottawa: Canadian Centre for Justice Statistics Juristat, 1997), p. 17, table 4.

States dropped precipitously. Between the peak year of 1994 and 2005 (the latest data available), the American juvenile arrest rate for violent crime decreased by almost half (46 percent).[60] (See Chapter 2 for more details on trends in juvenile violence in the United States.)

One of the exceptions to this continued upward trend in European juvenile violence was the Netherlands. Between 1996 and 2000, juvenile violence rates decreased 13 percent in the Netherlands.[61] On the other hand, in Germany and Italy, rates of juvenile violence continued to climb into the late 1990s.[62]

Canada, the other North American country for which data were available to add to this comparison, showed a similar pattern to the United States: a substantial increase in juvenile violence between the mid-1980s and mid-1990s followed by a substantial decline up to 2006 (the latest data available). During the upward trend period (1986 to 1995), rates of all categories of juvenile violence in Canada showed a marked increase: homicide up 50 percent, assault up 150 percent, sexual assault up 40 percent, and robbery up 160 percent.[63]

This substantial increase in all violence categories was not the case in all of the European countries, with the increase in juvenile violence rates being largely driven by robbery and offenses involving serious bodily harm.[64] For example, in the Netherlands, during the mid-1980s to mid-1990s, increases in the rates of robbery (+297 percent) and violence against a person (+123 percent) were the driving forces behind the substantial increase in juvenile violence.[65] Russia too experienced a significant increase in juvenile violence over this period of time.[66]

Juvenile Property Crime

Juvenile property crime rates (including burglary, motor vehicle theft, larceny, and vandalism) increased very little in Europe and North America from the mid-1980s to the mid-1990s, and in the case of England, Denmark, and Switzerland, rates decreased or did not change at all (see Table 17.3). On the other hand, like juvenile violence, property crime rates increased substantially in two countries during this period of time: Germany with a 75 percent increase and Italy with a 140 percent increase. It is not altogether clear why total juvenile crime rates in these two countries increased as much as this. Perhaps the factors that were driving the increases in juvenile violence in these countries were also having an effect on less serious forms of delinquency, such as theft, burglary, and motor vehicle theft.

More recent data on juvenile property crime in Canada show that the slight increase in rates during the mid-1980s to mid-1990s changed to a 65 percent decrease between 1995 and 2006.[67] This reversal was also found in the United States, whereby juvenile property crime rates decreased by more than half (51 percent) between the peak year of 1994 and 2005.[68] European Union countries also experienced a drop, albeit much smaller than in Canada and the United States, in juvenile property crime from the mid-1990s into the early 2000s.[69] This is in sharp contrast to the increase in juvenile violence that most European countries experienced over the same time period.

Juvenile Drug Use

The latest comparative study of teenage drug use in the United States and Europe found that two in five American students (41 percent) compared to one in five European students (22 percent) had used illicit drugs over their lifetime.[70] Comparisons across European countries of the percentage of students who have ever used illicit drugs are just as striking, ranging from a low of 3 percent in Romania to a high of 44 percent in the Czech Republic (see Figure 17.1). Carried out in conjunction with a consortium of European agencies including the Council of Europe and the University of Michigan's Monitoring the Future project, 16,244 10th-grade students in 129 schools in the United States and more than 100,000 10th-grade students in 35 European countries responded to the survey.

TABLE 17.3

Juvenile Property Crime in Europe and North America

Country	Years	Age of Juveniles (years)	Percentage Change in Rate
Austria	1991–1995	14–18	+31
Canada	1995–2006	12–17	−65
	1986–1995	12–17	+5
Denmark	1980–1994	15–19	+30
England	1986–1994	10–16	−9
European Union	1995–2000	12–17	decrease
France	1984–1992	10–18	−30
Germany	1984–1995	14–17	+75
Italy	1986–1993	14–17	+140
Netherlands	1985–1995	12–17	+4
Switzerland	1980–1995	15–17	0
United States	1994–2005	10–17	−51
	1985–1994	10–17	+7

NOTE: A percentage decrease in juvenile property crime in European Union countries was not specified.

SOURCES: Warren Silver, *Crime Statistics in Canada, 2006* (Ottawa: Canadian Centre for Justice Statistics Juristat, 2007), p. 14, table 5; Howard N. Snyder, *Juvenile Arrests 2005* (Washington, DC: Office of Juvenile Justice and Delinquency Prevention, U.S. Department of Justice, 2007); Marian Fitzgerald, Alex Stevens, and Chris Hale, *A Review of the Knowledge on Juvenile Violence: Trends, Policies and Responses in the EU Member States* (Brussels, Belgium: European Crime Prevention Network, European Commission, 2004), p. 49; Christian Pfeiffer, "Juvenile Crime and Violence in Europe," in Michael Tonry, ed., *Crime and Justice: A Review of Research*, vol. 23 (Chicago: University of Chicago Press, 1998), pp. 263–291; Rebecca Kong, *Canadian Crime Statistics, 1996* (Ottawa: Canadian Centre for Justice Statistics Juristat, 1997), p. 17, table 4.

Country

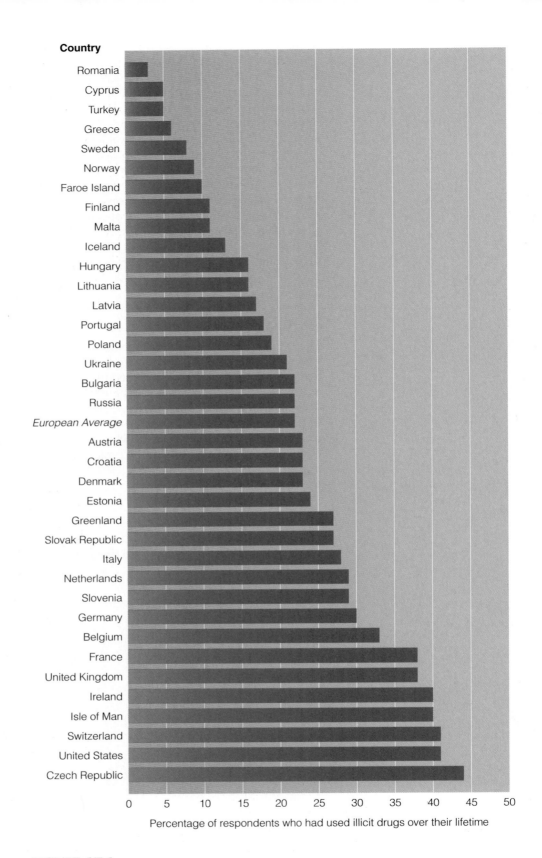

Percentage of respondents who had used illicit drugs over their lifetime

FIGURE 17.1

Lifetime Teenage Illicit Drug Use in the United States and Europe

NOTE: Illicit drugs include marijuana or hashish, LSD, amphetamines, crack, cocaine, heroin, and ecstasy.

SOURCE: Björn Hibell et al., *The ESPAD Report 2003: Alcohol and Other Drug Use Among Students in 35 European Countries* (Stockholm: The Swedish Council for Information on Alcohol and Other Drugs, Council of Europe, and Pompidou Group, 2004), table 27c.

The latest comparative study of teenage drug use found that one in five European students (22 percent) had used illicit drugs over their lifetime. Teen drug use is even higher in the United Kingdom (38 percent) and among certain groups in the country. The Bangladeshi community has been particularly hard hit by an influx of drugs. Here, Bangladeshi youths smoke crack on a stairway in east London.

Although American students are more likely to use marijuana and other illicit drugs over their lifetime, European students are more likely to smoke cigarettes and use alcohol over their lifetime. In England, underage drinking (the legal drinking age is 18) and drinking overall has become a "national crisis," which has resulted in the government considering a range of new measures, including tougher penalties for drunken behavior and making pubs pay for some of the costs of extra police officers.[71] In the United States, 66 percent of students report any alcohol use, while in the Czech Republic, the country with the highest rate, 98 percent of students report any alcohol use. Of the 36 countries, the United States has the second lowest rate of teenage alcohol use (Turkey has the lowest rate) and the lowest rate of cigarette smoking.[72]

Past studies of teenage drug use in Europe show rates climbing (between 1995 and 1999), particularly in eastern European countries,[73] while in the United States, the rate of teenage drug use shows declines from the recent peak years of 1996 and 1997 (see Chapter 11).

Conclusion: What Do the Trends Tell Us?

Throughout the world, juvenile delinquency is a serious problem. Although there are many differences in the nature and character of juvenile delinquency in the different regions and countries of the world, there are a number of common threads. One is that juveniles account for a disproportionate amount of total crime. A second is the presence of violent youth gangs. Most European countries report that juvenile violence is much higher today than it was 10 and 15 years ago. The question of greatest interest is why this has occurred.

As noted above, all countries share an explosive mix of racial tension, poverty, envy, drug abuse, broken families, unemployment, and alienation. Some countries are also feeling the impacts of rapid social and economic change. The end of apartheid in South Africa has left many broken promises for its youth, with access to education being severely limited and unemployment at an all-time high. The transition from communism to democracy in many eastern European countries has had profound effects. For example, neighboring countries have had to cope with a tremendous increase in immigrant youth populations in search of jobs and better lives, but because of difficulties in finding jobs and social isolation from family and friends, many of these youths turn to delinquency. Over the same period of time in the United States, rates of juvenile violence increased, but not as much as in most European countries. One possible explanation for this is that the United States did not experience some of the rapid social and economic changes that took place in Europe.

In some countries these trends in delinquency have begun to change. In other countries these trends have continued, and it is very likely that they will not be reversed unless governments are willing to tackle the many causal factors that give rise to juvenile delinquency. In some cases, this will mean countries working together to control the flow of immigration and providing assistance to new populations. In

To read more about delinquency across countries and what is being done to prevent it, visit the **International Centre for the Prevention of Crime** via academic.cengage.com/criminaljustice/siegel.

other cases, it will mean investing greater resources in education, employment training programs, and assistance programs for unemployed young people. It will also be important for countries to have effective and fair juvenile justice systems. In the next section we look at juvenile justice systems in different countries.

JUVENILE JUSTICE SYSTEMS ACROSS COUNTRIES

Many countries in the world have formal juvenile justice systems, but many do not. The presence of juvenile justice systems is strongly associated with a country's level of development; that is, developed or industrialized countries all have juvenile justice systems, while a smaller number of **developing** and **least developed countries** have juvenile justice systems. Part of the reason for countries not having separate justice systems to deal with juvenile delinquency and adult crime is the lack of importance placed on the special needs of juveniles who come in conflict with the law. Another reason is that developing and least developed countries have fewer financial resources to spend on a juvenile justice system, especially the building of separate correctional and treatment facilities.

developing countries
Recognized by the United Nations as countries that are showing signs of improved economic growth and are making the transition from low income to high income.

least developed countries
Recognized by the United Nations as being the poorest countries in the world and suffering from long-term barriers to economic growth.

In an effort to get more countries around the world to develop juvenile justice systems and improve the administration of juvenile justice, in 1985 the United Nations adopted the "Standard Minimum Rules for the Administration of Juvenile Justice" (see Exhibit 17.1). Also known as the "Beijing Rules" of juvenile justice because they were developed at a meeting in Beijing, these rules set out minimum standards for countries to follow in the administration of juvenile justice.[74]

There are many features of juvenile justice that are of interest to compare across countries. This section looks at the key features of juvenile justice systems in a number of developed countries: specialized police services for juveniles, age of criminal responsibility, presence of juvenile court, transfers to adult court, sentencing, treatment of incarcerated juveniles, and aftercare services.

Juvenile Policing

Specialized policing services for juveniles is an important but relatively recent addition to the repertoire of services offered by juvenile justice systems in many developed countries. The number of police officers assigned to juvenile work has increased in recent years. The International Association of Chiefs of Police found that of the 1,400 departments surveyed in 1960, approximately 500 had juvenile units. By 1970, the number of police departments with a juvenile specialist doubled.[75] Few developing or least developed countries have police officers trained specifically to deal with juvenile offenders.

In the United States, juvenile officers operate either as specialists within a police department or as part of the juvenile unit of a police department. Their role is similar to that of officers working with adult offenders: to intervene if the actions of a citizen produce public danger or disorder. (See Chapter 14 for more information on juvenile policing in the United States.) In Australia and New Zealand, police departments have established specialized youth aid sections, and in New Zealand it is reported that this national unit is responsible for diverting more than half of all juvenile offenders out of the juvenile justice system.[76]

In Austria an innovative delinquency prevention project involves specially trained police to deal with violent juvenile gangs. The gang unit works to establish an open dialogue with juvenile gangs to help get leaders of opposing gangs to meet and work out their conflicts in a nonviolent way. A four-year assessment of the program found that it

Special Austrian police detain a youth after his arrival by train from Germany at Salzburg's main railway station. Austrian police were on high alert with a European Union economic summit about to take place in the city. Riots by youths and others have disrupted other European Union summits.

EXHIBIT 17.1

Highlights of the "Standard Minimum Rules for the Administration of Juvenile Justice"

These rules were adopted by the U.N. General Assembly on November 29, 1985, on the recommendation of the Seventh U.N. Congress on the Prevention of Crime and the Treatment of Offenders (resolution 40/33).

Part 1: General Principles

▌ Member states shall seek to further the well-being of juveniles and their families.

▌ Member states shall try to develop conditions to ensure meaningful lives in the community for juveniles.

▌ Sufficient attention should be given to positive measures involving mobilization of resources, such as the family, volunteers and community groups, to promote the well-being of juveniles.

▌ Juvenile justice shall be an integral part of the national development process of each country.

▌ In legal systems recognizing the concept of an age of criminal responsibility for juveniles, such an age level shall not be fixed too low, bearing in mind emotional, mental, and physical maturity.

▌ Any reaction by the juvenile justice system to juvenile offenders shall be in proportion to both the offenders and the offense.

▌ Appropriate scope for the exercise of discretionary powers shall be allowed at all stages of legal processing affecting juveniles.

▌ Efforts shall be made to ensure sufficient accountability at all stages in the exercise of such discretion.

▌ Basic procedural safeguards, such as the presumption of innocence, the right to be notified of charges, the right to remain silent, the right to counsel, the right to the presence of a parent or guardian, the right

to confront and cross-examine witnesses and the right to appeal, shall be guaranteed at all stages of proceedings.

▌ The juvenile's right to privacy shall be respected at all stages.

Part 2: Investigation and Prosecution

▌ Upon the apprehension of a juvenile, parents or guardians shall be notified as soon as possible.

▌ Consideration shall be given to dealing with juvenile offenders without resort to trial, and any diversion to appropriate community or other services shall require consent of the juvenile or parents.

Part 3: Adjudication and Disposition

▌ The placement of a juvenile in an institution shall always be a disposition of last resort and for the minimum necessary period.

Part 4: Non-Institutional Treatment

▌ Efforts shall be made to provide necessary assistance, such as lodging, education, vocational training and employment, to facilitate the rehabilitation process.

Part 5: Institutional Treatment

▌ Juveniles in institutions shall be kept separate from adults, and special attention shall be used to the greatest extent possible.

Part 6: Aftercare

▌ Efforts shall be made to provide semi-institutional arrangements, such as halfway houses, educational homes, and daytime training centers, to assist juveniles in their reintegration into society.

SOURCE: Abridged from United Nations, *The United Nations and Crime Prevention: Seeking Security and Justice for All* (New York: United Nations, 1996), pp. 78–82.

---

was extremely successful in reducing juvenile violence.[77] Canada has also developed special juvenile gang units as part of police departments. Juvenile gang units exist in all of the police departments of the biggest Canadian cities, such as Montreal, Toronto, Vancouver, and Halifax, as well as in many medium-sized and smaller cities and towns.[78]

In Japan, police boxes (*koban*) in urban areas and police houses (*chuzaisho*) in rural areas have special officers who deal with juvenile delinquency. Because of the sheer number of these police stations in the country—about 6,600 *koban*s and 8,100 *chuzaisho*s—the police have a very good understanding of conditions that might give rise to juvenile delinquency and violence problems in the community. This knowledge assists them in intervening before problems get out of control. In addition to juvenile police officers, there is a police-established system of volunteers to aid the police in dealing with juvenile delinquency. There are three types of voluntary systems:

▌ Guidance volunteers

▌ Police helpers for juveniles

▌ Instructors for juveniles

Guidance volunteers work with the police in providing advice to young people about the dangers of being involved in gangs or using drugs; they also provide some counseling services to young people in trouble with the law. Police helpers are mostly retired police officers in charge of dispersing large groups of juvenile delinquents, such as gangs. They are not a riot squad, but simply assist the police in dealing with large groups of young people who may be looking for trouble or are involved in delinquent acts. Instructors are authorized by the 1985 Law on Regulation of Business Affecting Public Morals to protect juveniles from unsafe environments; that is, where young people are being abused or neglected.[79] In many ways, these individuals act as child or juvenile protection agents.

The **International Association of Chiefs of Police** is the world's oldest and largest nonprofit membership organization of police executives, with over 18,000 members in over 100 different countries. Visit their website via academic.cengage.com/criminaljustice/siegel.

Age of Criminal Responsibility: Minimum and Maximum

Across the world there is a great deal of variation in the minimum age a person can be held responsible for his or her criminal actions, ranging from a low of 6 years in Sri Lanka to a high of under 21 years in Indonesia. In the majority of countries around the world, full adult criminal responsibility begins at age 18 years or older.[80] This general pattern is the same for the developed countries listed in Table 17.4. Switzerland has the lowest minimum age of criminal responsibility at 7 years, and Belgium has the highest at 16 to 18 years. Interestingly, in the United States, 36 states have no set minimum age that a young person can be held criminally responsible. By common law, states may use 7 years as the minimum, but in practice children under the age of 10 are rarely brought before a juvenile court.[81]

In those countries in which the minimum age is quite high, such as Belgium (16 to 18 years), Denmark (15 years), or Sweden (15 years), what happens to young people below the minimum age who commit delinquent acts? Doing nothing is not an option in any of the developed countries. Instead, these young people are dealt with under various forms of child or social welfare or child protection legislation. Under these laws young people may be placed in state-run homes, undergo counseling, or report to a social worker on a regular basis.

In some countries the minimum age can be lowered. This is typically done when the offense is very serious; for example, in New Zealand, the minimum age is 14, but if the offense is murder or manslaughter, the minimum age becomes 10. In Romania, the minimum age can be dropped from 16 to 14 if the young person is capable of understanding right from wrong.[82]

Presence of Juvenile Court

The majority of the developed countries have courts specifically for juveniles (see Table 17.4), and they operate pretrial diversion programs. (See the Policy and Practice box entitled "Precourt Diversion Programs around the World.") Only Denmark, Russia, and Sweden do not have juvenile courts. In each of these countries, juveniles appear before regular adult criminal courts. However, in Denmark, the Administration of Justice Act provides special rights for juveniles who appear in court; for example, closing the proceedings to the public and press.[83] Swedish courts also try to protect the identity of juvenile offenders if the court believes that publicity may be harmful to the juvenile.[84] In Russia too there are some protections afforded the juvenile: Age must be taken into account as a mitigating factor, the juvenile's living conditions must be considered, and whether or not the offense was committed with an adult.[85]

Transfers to Adult Court

Transfers of juvenile offenders to adult court are a widely accepted practice in developed countries (see Table 17.4). In all of the countries in which transfers are allowed, the main criterion is that the offense was of a very serious or violent nature. Other criteria can include the youth's record of delinquency and the use of weapons. But in these cases, the evidence must be particularly strong for a transfer to take place.

In the developed countries of Austria, France, Hungary, Italy, and Switzerland, transfers of juveniles to adult court are not permissible. Typically, this is because youths can receive an adult sentence while still under the authority of the juvenile court. This is also the case in Canada, where, until recently, transfers of juveniles to adult court were allowed. Under the new Youth Criminal Justice Act there is a procedure that allows a juvenile to stay in youth court and be dealt with as a juvenile, and in the case of serious offenses the juvenile can receive an adult sentence.[86]

TABLE 17.4

International Comparisons of Juvenile Justice Systems

Country	Minimum Age of Criminal Responsibility	Age of Adult Criminal Responsibility	Court That Handles Juveniles	Transfer to Adult Court Allowable?	Maximum Length of Sentence for a Juvenile	Separation of Incarcerated Juveniles from Adults
Australia	10*	16–17**	Children's courts	Yes, for serious felonies	2–7 years	Not mandatory, generally separated in practice
Austria	14	19	Special sections in local and regional courts; youth courts	No	Half of adult sentence	Yes
Belgium	16–18	18	Special juvenile courts	Yes	No juvenile incarcerations in juvenile court	Not mandatory, generally separated in practice
Canada	12	18	Youth courts	Yes	10 years	Yes
Denmark	15	18	No juvenile court	N/A	8 years	Yes
England	10	18	Youth courts	Yes	2 years	Yes
France	13 (unofficial)	18	Children's tribunals; youth courts of assizes	No	Half of adult sentence	Yes
Germany	14	18	Single-sitting judge; juvenile court; juvenile chamber	Yes	10 years	Yes
Hungary	14	18	Special sections of regular court	No	15 years	Yes
Italy	14	18	Separate juvenile courts	No	One-third of adult sentence	Yes
Japan	14	20	Family courts	Yes	Lifetime sentence	Yes
The Netherlands	12	18	Special juvenile courts	Yes	Lifetime sentence	Yes
New Zealand	14; 10 for murder and manslaughter	18	Youth courts	Yes	No juvenile Incarcerations in youth court	No (some exceptions)
Russia	16; 14 for certain crimes	18	No juvenile court	N/A	10 years	Yes
Sweden	15	18	No juvenile court	N/A	No lifetime sentence	Yes
Switzerland	7	18	Special juvenile courts and/or juvenile prosecutors	No	1 year	Yes
United States	6–10 for 14 states; 36 other states have no set minimum but may use age 7	15 for 3 states; 16 for 10 states; 17 for 37 states	Juvenile courts	Yes	Lifetime	Yes

NOTES: * The lower age limit is 7 in Tasmania; ** Age of full criminal responsibility differs by state; N/A = not available.

SOURCES: Adapted from Joan McCord, Cathy Spatz Widom, and Nancy Crowell, eds., *Juvenile Crime, Juvenile Justice*. Panel on Juvenile Crime: Prevention, Treatment, and Control (Washington, DC: National Academy Press, 2001), pp. 18–20, table 1–1. Canadian data adapted from Brandon C. Welsh and Mark H. Irving, "Crime and Punishment in Canada, 1981–1999," in David P. Farrington and Michael Tonry, eds., *Cross-National Studies in Crime and Justice. Crime and Justice: A Review of Research*, Volume 33 (Chicago: University of Chicago Press, 2005). U.S. data adapted from Janet K. Wig, "Legal Issues," in Rolf Loeber and David P. Farrington, eds., *Child Delinquents: Development, Intervention, and Service Needs* (Thousand Oaks, CA: Sage Publications, 2001), p. 324.

Sentencing Policies

The maximum sentence length for juvenile offenders varies considerably across developed countries. In Belgium and New Zealand there can be no sentence of incarceration for youths who appear before juvenile court; instead, youths must be transferred to adult court to receive custodial sentences. Some countries, such as Austria, France, and Italy, specify that sentences can only be for one-half or one-third of what an adult would receive for a similar offense. In Italy, juveniles who are sentenced to custody can receive

Precourt Diversion Programs around the World

Keeping youths who have become involved in minor delinquent acts from being formally processed through the juvenile justice system is a top priority of many countries around the world. This is because they recognize the need to protect young people against the stigma and labeling that can occur from being "processed" through a juvenile court. In many ways, entering the juvenile justice system is viewed as a last resort to dealing with juvenile delinquency. Informal processing or precourt diversion programs, which vary from country to country, also represent a cost savings from the expense of paying for juvenile court judges, prosecutors, public defenders, and other justice personnel and administrative costs. These alternative approaches are more often used in European, particularly western European, countries than in the United States. These programs are also very popular in Australia and New Zealand. Part of the reason for the greater use of these programs outside of the United States is that these countries are less punitive toward juvenile offenders than the United States. What follows are profiles of the use of precourt diversion programs in the Netherlands, France, and Australia.

NETHERLANDS

In response to a sharp rise in juvenile vandalism and its associated costs, the government of the Netherlands implemented a precourt diversion program called *Het Alternatief* (the alternative) or HALT. Begun in the 1970s in the city of Rotterdam, the program quickly spread throughout the country and is now a national program in 65 locations. Accountability and assistance are at the center of the program. Young people age 12 to 18 years caught for the first or second time committing an act of vandalism (the program is now used for other offenses as well) are offered the chance to avoid formal prosecution by participating in the program. Juveniles who go through the program must repair the vandalism damage they have caused, and counselors work with the young people to assist them with employment, housing, and education issues. If the program is successfully completed, police charges are dropped and the case is dismissed, and in those cases that are not successful, an official report is sent to the prosecutor. An evaluation of the program in three cities (Rotterdam, Eindoven, and Dordrecht) found the program to be very effective in reducing future acts of vandalism. Juvenile offenders in the treatment group were 63 percent less likely to be rearrested versus a comparison group that were 25 percent less likely to be rearrested.

FRANCE

Maisons de justice, or community justice centers, are one of the most well known pretrial diversion programs for juvenile offenders in France. Set up by the Ministry of Justice and community associations across the country, the centers address minor offenses and other legal problems through alternative justice approaches. One of these alternative approaches is victim-offender mediation, whereby a trained staff member works with the offender, the victim, and sometimes the victim's family to settle a dispute without the need for formal justice proceedings. An apology or an order of restitution or compensation is commonly reached as part of victim-offender mediation. Although there has been no formal evaluation of community justice centers, they are widely credited as helping to relieve some of the backlog in the courts and to settle cases much faster than traditional means.

AUSTRALIA

Precourt diversion programs have gone through extensive changes in Australia in recent years. Up to the early 1990s, there were two types of juvenile diversion programs: police cautions, which involve the police more or less warning offenders that the next time they are caught, formal action will be taken; and children's panels, made up of police and social workers who admonish a young person for his or her delinquent behavior. Today, precourt diversion programs for juvenile offenders include an expanded use of police cautions and the addition of restorative justice–based programs known as family group conferences (FGCs). These conferences bring together the juvenile offender and his or her family, the victim, and a professional coordinator to discuss the problem caused by the juvenile offender and to agree on a mutually acceptable resolution that will benefit all parties and the wider community. FGCs attempt to provide the victim with restoration and restitution and the offender with rehabilitation and reintegration. An evaluation of an FGC program in Queensland showed that reoffending rates were reduced by 44 percent three to five years postconference, and 82 percent of the conference participants, victims included, were satisfied with the agreed outcomes.

Critical Thinking

1. What are some of the problems with precourt diversion programs?
2. Should these programs also be used for serious and violent juvenile offenders? Explain.

SOURCES: T. Wing Lo, Gabrielle M. Maxwell, and Dennis S. W. Wong, "Diversion from Youth Courts in Five Asia Pacific Jurisdictions: Welfare or Restorative Solutions," *International Journal of Offender Therapy and Comparative Criminology* 50:5–20 (2006); Josine Junger-Tas, "Youth Justice in the Netherlands," in Michael Tonry and Anthony N. Doob, eds., *Youth Crime and Youth Justice: Comparative and Cross-National Perspectives. Crime and Justice: A Review of Research*, vol. 31 (Chicago: University of Chicago Press, 2004); Irvin Waller and Brandon C. Welsh, "International Trends in Crime Prevention: Cost-Effective Ways to Reduce Victimization," in Graeme Newman, ed., *Global Report on Crime and Justice* (New York: Oxford University Press, 1999); Lynn Atkinson, "Juvenile Justice in Australia," in John A. Winterdyk, ed., *Juvenile Justice Systems: International Perspectives* (Toronto: Canadian Scholars' Press, 1997).

up to one-third of the same sentence for adults but, unlike adults, can be conditionally released at any stage of the sentence regardless of the amount of time spent in custody.[87]

The countries with the harshest sentence for juvenile offenders are the United States, Japan, and the Netherlands; here, juvenile offenders can receive lifetime sentences. In Japan, a life sentence may mean spending between 10 and 15 years in a correctional facility with or without forced labor, while in the Netherlands, a life sentence may mean serving as much as 20 years.[88] In Russia, the maximum sentence length for juveniles is 10 years, and in recent years it has made extensive use of incarceration (or commitment), with 50 to 60 percent of all adjudicated juvenile offenders receiving some form of this disposition.[89] Switzerland, on the other hand, is the most lenient country: One year is the longest period of time that a juvenile offender can be sentenced to custody, and transfers to adult court are not allowed.

Finding an appropriate balance between punishment (in the form of secure commitment) and treatment for juvenile offenders is more difficult for some countries than others. This is the subject of the Policy and Practice box entitled "The Changing Nature of Youth Justice in Canada."

Incarcerated Juveniles

The separation of juveniles from adults in correctional facilities is an important rule under the U.N.'s "Standard Minimum Rules for the Administration of Juvenile Justice," because juveniles are susceptible to negative influences of more seasoned and crime-prone adult offenders. In many ways, juvenile offenders become the apprentices of adult offenders, learning about new techniques to commit delinquent and criminal acts. Another reason for separating adults and juveniles in correctional institutions is for the physical safety of juveniles. With the average juvenile offender having less physical strength than the average adult offender, adults often prey upon juveniles.

To read more about **juvenile justice in Australia**, go to academic.cengage.com/criminaljustice/siegel.

In almost all of the developed countries, incarcerated juveniles are kept separate from incarcerated adults. In Australia and Belgium, separate incarceration is not mandatory, but in practice this is generally done. In New Zealand, the practice differs from all of the other countries. Incarcerated juveniles are not separated from incarcerated adults. But there are a few exceptions. For example, a juvenile offender who has been transferred to adult court and sentenced to a term of imprisonment may be held at the discretion of the Director General of Social Welfare and the Secretary for Justice in a social welfare facility until age 17. The reason for the government generally not housing juvenile and adult inmates in separate facilities is that there are no separate correctional facilities for juvenile offenders. The government claims that the country is too small and there are too few juvenile inmates to justify building a separate correctional facility.[90] But this view is changing. As part of the new government's "tougher approach to crime," construction has been proposed for at least two youth justice residences.[91]

In Scandinavian countries (Denmark, Finland, Norway, and Sweden), youths may be held in a prison or secure social institution. The prison is mainly focused on security and the institution is focused on treatment, addressing the individual needs of juvenile offenders through social skills training, counseling, and education. Wherever possible the treatment option is utilized throughout Scandinavia.[92] This is not the case in some European countries that once placed a special emphasis on treatment over security, as well as on the minimal use of incarceration for juvenile offenders. The Netherlands is one example. Between 1990 and 2003 (the most recent data available), institutional placements of juvenile offenders grew from 700 to 2,400.[93]

Aftercare

When juveniles are released from an institution, they may be placed in an aftercare program of some kind, rather than simply returned to the community without transitional assistance. This transitional assistance can take the form of halfway houses,

The Changing Nature of Youth Justice in Canada

Canada, a welfare state that has an extensive social safety network that includes among other benefits universal health care coverage and year-long maternity leave, is well known for its liberal views on social issues. Some of these include efforts to limit the use of prisons for offenders, the implementation of a national gun registry and other tough gun control laws, partial legalization of marijuana use, and support for same-sex marriage. But this liberal view may be changing somewhat with respect to the government's response to juvenile delinquency.

In 1984, the Young Offenders Act (YOA) replaced the Juvenile Delinquents Act (JDA), which had been the legislative framework for youth justice in Canada since 1908. In addition to numerous legal and procedural changes, the movement from the JDA to the YOA marked a change in principles of youth justice, from a welfare orientation to a more legalistic orientation. (Like the United States, Canada adheres to the *parens patriae* treatment philosophy. This did not change under the new law and continues to this day.) Some of the YOA's important provisions included:

▌ A minimum age of criminal responsibility of 12 years (it was 7 years) and a uniform age of adult criminal responsibility of 18 years.

▌ Youthful offenders are entitled to child care/youth care experts as well as lawyers for counsel.

▌ The primary purpose of intervention is a balance between penalizing delinquent behavior and providing appropriate treatment.

Over the years, academics and juvenile justice practitioners alike criticized the YOA for not providing clear legislative direction to guide appropriate implementation in several key areas, such as transfers to adult court. This lack of clear legislative direction was thought to be an important factor contributing to problems and deficiencies in Canada's youth justice system. Furthermore, as Canadian criminologists Anthony Doob and Jane Sprott point out,

> there are two substantial problems with the YOA on which almost all policy and academic observers agreed: the youth justice system is being overused for minor offenses, and too many youths are going to custody, especially for relatively minor offenses.

These concerns were at the heart of the federal government's new youth justice law, the Youth Criminal Justice Act (YCJA), which was proclaimed into force in April 2003. Also important to this new law was a get-tough approach or at least the appearance of this. Some of these get-tough measures included a greater focus on holding youths accountable for their actions, making it easier to impose adult sanctions on the most serious and violent juvenile offenders, and publishing the offender's identity, again in the most serious cases. Interestingly, the new law also established specific guidelines for police use of discretion in dealing with juvenile offenders.

The YCJA also greatly expanded aftercare programs for juvenile offenders. For example, it is now mandatory that all periods of time spent in an institution be followed by a period of intensive supervision in the community. The length of time of supervision is also stipulated in the law: It must be no less than half the time spent in custody. Thus, a juvenile offender who spends 12 months in an institution must then spend 6 months in intensive supervision while in the community. Under the old law, there were no requirements for supervision following a custodial sentence.

Another important change to the juvenile aftercare system introduced by the new law is that there are a number of conditions, both mandatory and optional, that the judge can impose on the youth as part of supervision orders. Mandatory conditions include keeping the peace and reporting to authorities. Optional conditions include attending school, getting a job, adhering to a curfew, abstaining from alcohol and drugs, and not associating with gang members.

Critical Thinking

1. How would you characterize the changes in Canada's youth justice laws over the last century?

2. Could juvenile justice in the United States benefit from incorporating some of the recent changes to Canada's youth justice laws? Explain.

SOURCES: Jennifer L. Schulenberg, "Police Culture and Young Offenders: The Effect of Legislative Change on Definitions of Crime and Delinquency," *Police Quarterly* 9:423–447 (2006); Brandon C. Welsh and Mark H. Irving, "Crime and Punishment in Canada, 1981–1999," in Michael Tonry and David P. Farrington, eds., *Crime and Punishment in Western Countries, 1980–1999. Crime and Justice: A Review of Research*, vol. 33 (Chicago: University of Chicago Press, 2005); Anthony N. Doob and Jane B. Sprott, "Youth Justice in Canada," in Michael Tonry and Anthony N. Doob, eds, *Youth Crime and Youth Justice: Comparative and Cross-National Perspectives. Crime and Justice: A Review of Research*, vol. 31 (Chicago: University of Chicago Press, 2004), pp. 224–225; John A. Winterdyk, "Juvenile Justice and Young Offenders: An Overview of Canada," in John A. Winterdyk, ed., *Juvenile Justice Systems: International Perspectives*, 2nd ed. (Toronto: Canadian Scholars' Press, 2002), pp. 66–68; Department of Justice Canada, "Fact Sheets: *Youth Criminal Justice Act*" (Ottawa: Department of Justice, March 1999).

educational homes, and daytime training centers. The U.N.'s "Standard Minimum Rules for the Administration of Juvenile Justice" recommend that all countries implement aftercare programs to help juveniles prepare for their return to the community.

All developed countries provide juveniles with a wide range of aftercare programs. In Hong Kong, now part of the People's Republic of China, supervision orders are the most commonly used aftercare program to help juvenile offenders make a successful transition from the correctional institution to their community. Juveniles are first granted early release from a correctional facility, with the provision that they must abide by a number of conditions. These conditions differ according to the nature of the delinquent act they committed, but almost always involve regular visits with their parole officer. Some juveniles will have to attend drug addiction treatment centers.[94]

In many developed countries, juvenile offenders are eligible for early release or parole much earlier than adult offenders sentenced to the same amount of time in institutions. In Germany, for example, a juvenile may be released to the community upon serving one-third of his or her sentence, while an adult must serve at least half of the sentence before being paroled.[95]

The next section profiles the juvenile justice system in England. It looks at the many different stages that juveniles may face as they go through the system, from arrest through sentencing. Comparisons are made with the U.S. juvenile justice system. One reason for making England the subject of this profile is that like the United States, it is a highly developed industrialized country and so comparisons are more meaningful. Another reason is the long-standing shared history between the two countries: Much of U.S. common law is derived from English law.

A PROFILE OF JUVENILE JUSTICE IN ENGLAND

In 1908, England passed legislation that established for the first time that young offenders were to be treated separately from adult offenders; the law was known as the Children Act. Like the United States, England adheres to the *parens patriae* treatment philosophy, which recognizes that youth are in need of special consideration and assistance. The Children Act was founded on three main principles:

1. Juvenile offenders should be kept separate from adult criminals and should receive treatment differentiated to suit their special needs.
2. Parents should be made more responsible for the wrongdoing of their children.
3. The imprisonment of juveniles should be abolished.[96]

Many changes have since taken place in juvenile justice in England. The following discussion of the different stages that juveniles may face as they go through the system reflects the way things are today. (See Figure 17.2.)

Police cautions—the police issuing a warning to a young person involved or suspected of being involved in a delinquent act—are by far the most widely used and important precourt diversion measure in England. Here London police officers question two boys who have been expelled from school.

© Simon Wheatley/Magnum Photos

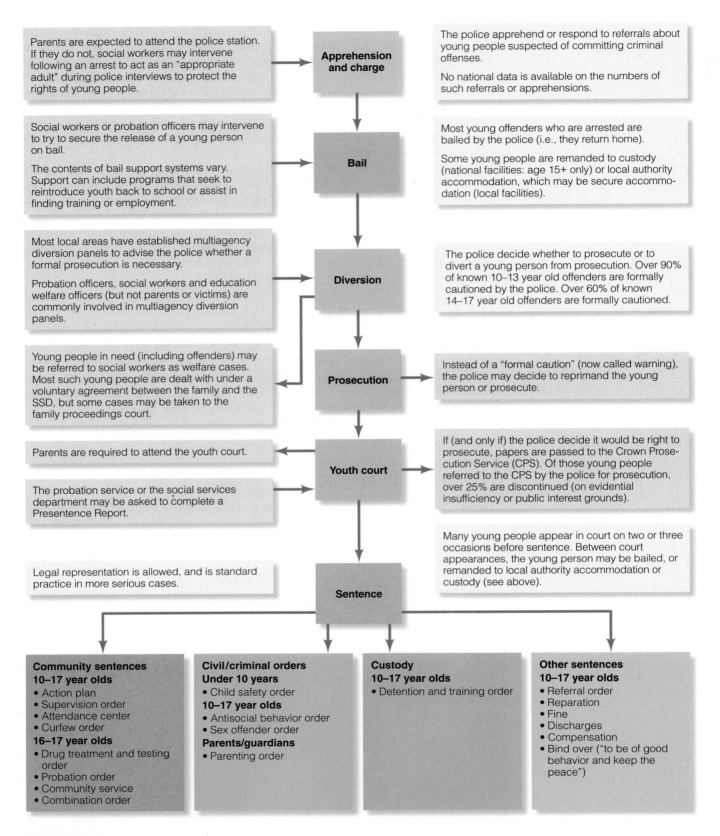

Apprehension and charge

Parents are expected to attend the police station. If they do not, social workers may intervene following an arrest to act as an "appropriate adult" during police interviews to protect the rights of young people.

The police apprehend or respond to referrals about young people suspected of committing criminal offenses.

No national data is available on the numbers of such referrals or apprehensions.

Bail

Social workers or probation officers may intervene to try to secure the release of a young person on bail.

The contents of bail support systems vary. Support can include programs that seek to reintroduce youth back to school or assist in finding training or employment.

Most young offenders who are arrested are bailed by the police (i.e., they return home).

Some young people are remanded to custody (national facilities: age 15+ only) or local authority accommodation, which may be secure accommodation (local facilities).

Diversion

Most local areas have established multiagency diversion panels to advise the police whether a formal prosecution is necessary.

Probation officers, social workers and education welfare officers (but not parents or victims) are commonly involved in multiagency diversion panels.

The police decide whether to prosecute or to divert a young person from prosecution. Over 90% of known 10–13 year old offenders are formally cautioned by the police. Over 60% of known 14–17 year old offenders are formally cautioned.

Prosecution

Young people in need (including offenders) may be referred to social workers as welfare cases. Most such young people are dealt with under a voluntary agreement between the family and the SSD, but some cases may be taken to the family proceedings court.

Instead of a "formal caution" (now called warning), the police may decide to reprimand the young person or prosecute.

Youth court

Parents are required to attend the youth court.

The probation service or the social services department may be asked to complete a Presentence Report.

If (and only if) the police decide it would be right to prosecute, papers are passed to the Crown Prosecution Service (CPS). Of those young people referred to the CPS by the police for prosecution, over 25% are discontinued (on evidential insufficiency or public interest grounds).

Sentence

Legal representation is allowed, and is standard practice in more serious cases.

Many young people appear in court on two or three occasions before sentence. Between court appearances, the young person may be bailed, or remanded to local authority accommodation or custody (see above).

Community sentences
10–17 year olds
- Action plan
- Supervision order
- Attendance center
- Curfew order
16–17 year olds
- Drug treatment and testing order
- Probation order
- Community service
- Combination order

Civil/criminal orders
Under 10 years
- Child safety order
10–17 year olds
- Antisocial behavior order
- Sex offender order
Parents/guardians
- Parenting order

Custody
10–17 year olds
- Detention and training order

Other sentences
10–17 year olds
- Referral order
- Reparation
- Fine
- Discharges
- Compensation
- Bind over ("to be of good behavior and keep the peace")

FIGURE 17.2
The Juvenile Justice System in England

SOURCE: Loraine Gelsthorpe and Vicky Kemp, "Comparative Juvenile Justice: England and Wales," in John A. Winterdyk, ed., *Juvenile Justice Systems: International Perspectives*, 2nd ed. (Toronto: Canadian Scholars' Press, 2002), figures 5.1, 5.2, pp. 129, 146.

Apprehension and Charge

The process of juvenile justice begins when police apprehend and charge a young person suspected of committing a delinquent act. The police are not the only ones involved at this stage. Parents or guardians of the young person are contacted and requested to attend the police station. If they cannot attend, social workers may offer assistance to the juvenile once an arrest has been made. The role of social workers at this stage is to act as an "appropriate adult" to help safeguard the legal rights of the juvenile. Alternatively, the juvenile may be represented by a defense attorney. The right to have legal representation exists throughout all stages of the juvenile justice system.[97] This is the same as in the U.S. juvenile justice system.

Bail

Once a decision has been made by the police to charge the juvenile, a bail hearing must take place to determine whether the juvenile can go home or be remanded to custody. This differs from the practice in the United States, where relatively few juveniles hold the right to be released on bail; in fact, most states refuse juveniles the right to bail. This is because detention is seen as rehabilitative, not punitive, and statutory provisions allow juveniles to be released into the custody of their parents. (See Chapter 15 for more information on bail for juveniles in the United States.)

In England, most juvenile offenders who are arrested are granted bail. For those who are denied bail, there are two options for where they will be held. National custody facilities can be used for juveniles 15 years and older, or local authority (local government) facilities may be used. For juveniles without legal representation, social workers or probation officers may assist the juvenile to be released on bail.

Precourt Diversion

Police "cautions"—the police issuing a warning to a young person involved or suspected of being involved in a delinquent act—is by far the most widely used and important precourt diversion measure in England. Begun in the 1970s, police cautions quickly became an essential component of the juvenile justice system. Although important administratively, so as to avoid the youth courts from becoming backlogged, police cautions were designed first and foremost with the best interests of the young person in mind: "Prosecution should not occur unless it was 'absolutely necessary' or as 'a last resort' and that the prosecution of first-time offenders where the offence was not serious was unlikely to be 'justifiable' unless there were 'exceptional circumstances.' Prosecution was to be regarded as a 'severe step.'"[98]

Instead of a formal caution (now called a warning under the "final warning scheme"), the police may issue a "reprimand" to a suspected juvenile delinquent or prosecute. Reprimands involve the police making a verbal admonition. They may go something like this: "I want you to behave properly from now on and do not get yourself involved in anything that requires us to bring you down to the station." These are not recorded by police and, therefore, cannot be used in court.

In the United States, police do not use a system of formal or other cautions per se; instead, they must rely on their discretionary authority. (See Chapter 14 for more details.) Upon the arrest of a juvenile, the police have the following options: refer to juvenile court; handle informally and release; refer to criminal court; refer to welfare; or refer to another police department. It is estimated that 20 percent of all juvenile arrests are handled informally within the police department or are referred to a community service agency.

Prosecution

Crown Prosecution Service
The national agency in England that is in charge of all criminal prosecutions of juveniles and adults.

In England the prosecution of a juvenile offender is the mandate of the **Crown Prosecution Service**. The CPS is a national agency established by statute in 1985. It is headed by the director of public prosecutions, who is accountable to the attorney general.[99] In the United States, each jurisdiction has its own prosecuting attorney who oversees public prosecutions; with England having a central government system (there are no states), the reporting structure is somewhat different.

Importantly, in England a prosecution can only take place once the police have recommended to the CPS that it be done. This differs slightly from the practice in the United States in that the prosecutor has the power either to initiate or discontinue allegations against a juvenile. In England the prosecutor does, however, have the right to dismiss a case (allegation), and this is done in more than 25 percent of the cases that the police recommend to the CPS. There are two reasons that a prosecutor may dismiss a case: (1) There is insufficient evidence, or (2) it is not in the public interest. The latter is done when it is felt that the harm to the offender that comes from prosecuting him or her will outweigh any benefit to society from doing so. In the event that the prosecution dismisses a case because it is not in the public interest, the prosecution may recommend to the police that they issue a formal caution.[100]

Youth Court

Like the United States and most other developed countries, England has a special court that handles juveniles; it is called a youth court. Even before the commencement of trial a juvenile may have already had a number of hearings before youth court, such as a bail hearing or a hearing on transfer to adult court. In most instances, trials of juveniles are presided over by a three-member panel of youth court lay magistrates or judges. In urban areas it is common for a trial to be presided over by a single professional or more qualified judge. Juries are not used in English youth courts. The lay or nonprofessional youth court judges are elected to a three-year term by and from the court district in which they presently serve. These judges receive special training in the juvenile offender laws. During trials they are often assisted by a legally trained court clerk.[101]

In the United States, only one juvenile court judge presides over a trial in the juvenile courtroom. Judges are assisted by court clerks, but unlike in England, court clerks in the United States rarely have law degrees and do not advise judges on legal matters. In the United States, juvenile court judges are either elected or appointed to that position, but when they are elected, it is by the public, not their fellow judges, as in England. In the United States, trial by jury in a juvenile court is seldom used; the majority of states do not allow for it.

Social workers and probation officers are other important actors in the English juvenile courtroom. Once a finding of guilt has been rendered, either party may be asked by the court to prepare a presentence report to assist the judge in sentencing. This is similar to a predisposition report in the U.S. juvenile justice system. As in the United States, plea bargaining is allowed for juveniles in England and is used extensively.

As in the United States, juveniles in England can be transferred to adult court— what is referred to as **Crown Court**. A juvenile can be transferred to Crown Court for two main reasons: (1) The juvenile is charged with a heinous crime, such as murder, or (2) the juvenile is charged with a serious crime in conjunction with an adult.[102]

Crown Court
In England, the criminal court that deals with adult offenders or juveniles who have been transferred from youth court.

Sentencing

Once the juvenile has been convicted, the youth court judge passes sentence, either immediately following conviction or at a special hearing a short time later. As in the United States, sentences (dispositions) for juvenile offenders are much more punitive in England today than they were 10 or 20 years ago. In the early 1980s, England changed its approach to the sentencing of juvenile offenders dramatically, moving away from a focus on institutional placements toward community-based sanctions. The murder of James Bulger by two 10-year-olds and an upsurge of juvenile violence in the country led to the passage of the Criminal Justice and Public Order Act in 1994. This made incarceration of juvenile offenders the preferred choice once again; it also increased the maximum sentence length and made it easier for very young juvenile offenders to be placed in correctional facilities. This punitive approach to dealing with juvenile offending, especially serious and violent juvenile offending, was continued with the passage of the Crime and Disorder Act in 1998 and the Youth Justice and Criminal Evidence Act in 1999.

As shown in Figure 17.2, a wide range of sentencing options is available to the youth court judge, including custodial sentences, community sentences, civil/criminal orders, and a general category of other sentences, which includes fines and compensation. Interestingly, juvenile boot camps modeled on the U.S. experience have received some interest in England, with two being introduced on a demonstration basis. One offered a high intensity treatment regime coupled with work or training placement on release, while the other offered more of a military-style regime. The former program showed more favorable recidivism results and was more cost-effective,[103] but public support for boot camps proved unfavorable, and the programs were shut down.

England's punitive approach to juvenile offending is somewhat tempered by the availability of a wide range of community sentences like probation and aftercare services. For example, attendance center orders require juvenile offenders to report to a specified place in the community once a week for a range of activities, including recreation, social skills training, and vocational skills training. There are also community punishment orders, which require juvenile offenders to perform various work-related activities in the community, and community punishment and rehabilitation orders that combine community service with increased supervision.[104]

FUTURE OF INTERNATIONAL JUVENILE JUSTICE

Harry Dammer, Erika Fairchild, and Jay Albanese argue that there are three issues that are at the heart of the future of juvenile justice around the world: visibility, community, and anticipating trends.[105] Visibility has to do with the openness of the juvenile justice system, from hearings being open to the public to the need for greater oversight to safeguard juvenile offenders who are in institutions. In the case of the second issue the authors argue that it is crucial that the "future of juvenile justice be guided by the recognition that communities are essential to producing delinquency, and they are essential in its prevention and in the reintegration of delinquents in society."[106] This second part of this view takes us back to Chapters 12 and 13, which highlighted the benefits of community-based prevention in the early and teen years and the need for a comprehensive juvenile justice strategy. Restorative justice and victim-offender mediation, both of which have received increased support over the last 20 years in many Western nations,[107] are also crucial to this cause.

On the matter of the key issue of anticipating trends that will impact juvenile justice, the authors contend that more needs to be done by national governments to be better informed about future potential problems and the best courses of action. This calls for more timely and high-quality research on the causes and correlates of juvenile offending. A great deal can be learned about studying past and current events that may help to ameliorate looming social problems. Comparative research among similar nations may also go some way toward informing governments of shared future problems, whether they be new forms of delinquency or crises facing the juvenile justice system, such as overcrowding or declining resources for treatment services.

This knowledge-based approach is applicable to current events in many countries around the world. For example, in recent years, a number of developed countries have taken measures to get tough on juvenile offending. In some cases, this is being done because of a real increase in delinquency, particularly violence. In other cases, this is being done because of a perceived increase in delinquency coupled with a political response to a "punitive public" (at least for violent juvenile offenders).[108] And while a more punitive juvenile justice system seems to be the future for many countries, a number are also making concerted efforts to reserve punitive sanctions for only the most serious and violent juvenile offenders and to provide more effective treatment, reentry, and aftercare services.

Summary

1. Have a grasp of some of the different delinquency problems facing the regions of the world

I Juvenile delinquency poses a serious problem to all regions of the world.

I Violent hate crimes plague many European countries.

I Gang violence is prevalent in the Americas and is a growing concern in parts of Africa.

I Juvenile crime is on the rise in Japan and China.

2. Be able to identify the main challenges of conducting international comparisons of delinquency

I There is a long history of comparing delinquency and juvenile justice systems across different countries, but many important issues need to be considered in making international comparisons. Differences in legal systems, culture, language, and so on, demand that close attention be paid to what is being compared and what countries are being compared.

I Comparing delinquency rates across countries has three main challenges:

  I Legal definitions of juvenile crime vary from country to country.

  I Measurement of juvenile crime varies across countries.

  I Age group defined as "juvenile" is not always the same.

3. Be able to identify the benefits of international comparative research

I Knowledge of the nature of juvenile delinquency and how juvenile justice systems operate in other countries can be useful for concerned citizens, social scientists, and policy makers.

I Comparative research can provide information on how well or how poorly one country is doing relative to other countries.

I Comparative research can lead to important discoveries that lead to action; for example, more funding for problem-solving policing tactics to reduce juvenile gun violence.

4. Be able to comment on trends in juvenile violence, property crime, and drug use in Europe and North America

I Juvenile violence in Europe and North America increased substantially between the mid-1980s and the mid-1990s.

I From the mid-1990s to the early 2000s, the upward trend in juvenile violence in Europe continued, while this trend was reversed in North America, with rates continuing to drop into the mid-2000s.

I During the first time period, juvenile property crime increased very little, with some countries showing no increase or a small decrease, followed by a downward trend in juvenile property crime across Europe and North America into the early 2000s.

I Recent figures for teenage drug use reveal that American students are more likely to use marijuana and other illicit drugs over their lifetime, while European students are more likely to smoke cigarettes and use alcohol.

5. Understand the key explanations for changes in these types of delinquency in Europe and North America

I Key explanations for the increase in teen violence include an explosive mix of racial tension, poverty, envy, drug abuse, broken families, unemployment, and alienation.

6. Know about the work of the United Nations to help countries improve their juvenile justice systems

I Many countries in the world have formal juvenile justice systems, but many do not.

I In an effort to get more countries around the world to develop juvenile justice systems and improve the administration of juvenile justice, in 1985 the United Nations adopted the "Standard Minimum Rules for the Administration of Juvenile Justice."

7. Be familiar with differences and similarities on key issues of juvenile justice around the world

I Juvenile justice systems in developed countries have many commonalities but also differ in many respects.

I Some of the key issues include juvenile policing, age of criminal responsibility, presence of juvenile court, transfers to adult court, sentencing, treatment of incarcerated juveniles, and aftercare programs.

8. Understand the key stages of juvenile justice in England

I The juvenile justice system in England was developed at the beginning of the twentieth century.

I The key stages of juvenile justice in England include:

  I Apprehension and charge

  I Bail

  I Precourt diversion

  I Prosecution

  I Youth court

  I Sentencing

9. Be able to comment on the differences and similarities in juvenile justice in the United States and England

I Like the United States, England adheres to the treatment philosophy known as *parens patriae*, which recognizes that youth are in need of special consideration and assistance.

- There are many other similarities between the British and U.S. juvenile justice systems, such as the use of bail hearings, plea bargaining, and the ability to transfer youths to adult court.

- There are also a number of important differences in juvenile justice between the two countries. For example, in England police use a system of formal or other cautions to divert juveniles from youth court, while in the United States police rely on their discretionary authority. In England, trials of juveniles in youth court are presided over by a three-member panel of youth court judges. In the United States, only one juvenile court judge presides over a trial in the juvenile courtroom.

- As in the United States, sentences for juvenile offenders are much more punitive in England today than they were 10 or 20 years ago.

Key Terms

developed countries, p. 576
death squads, p. 578
transnational crime, p. 582

international crime, p. 583
developing countries, p. 583
least developed countries, p. 588

Crown Prosecution Service, p. 597
Crown Court, p. 598

Viewpoint

As the recently elected prime minister of England you are faced with having to deal with national and international implications arising from the following case. In August 2001, two British teenagers, Jon Venables and Robert Thompson, were granted parole after serving eight years for the brutal murder of 2-year-old James Bulger. On February 12, 1993, these two boys, then 10 years old, abducted James from a mall just outside Liverpool, England. James's mother had stopped to look at a display window of one of the stores, letting go of James's hand for a few seconds. When she turned around James was gone. The whole event was caught on the mall's surveillance system. The horrifying video showed the two boys walking up to James and calmly leading him out of the mall. The 2-year-old's badly beaten body was found a short time later near railway tracks, a short distance from the mall. Because of the video, the two child killers were quickly apprehended and taken into custody. Throughout England there was a kind of collective agony for the death of the boy and the mother's loss of her young son.

The capture and subsequent trial of these two boys sparked national and international attention and debate. Immediately, England and other countries began to reconsider the minimum age when children can be held responsible for their delinquent or criminal actions. Fortunately for this case, in England the minimum age was 10 years. But in other countries, such as Canada, Italy, Japan, and Russia, the minimum age is much higher.

Like the capture and trial of these child killers, their release and events leading up to it caused national and international debate over the administration of juvenile justice. In January 1994, it was learned that the decision of Lord Justice Morland to detain the boys "at Her Majesty's pleasure"—the equivalent of a life sentence—had been recommended to be no higher than eight years. As a discretionary sentence, this was legal, but was it too lenient for the crime? England and other countries were soon contemplating mandatory minimum sentences for juvenile offenders, and in England the then home secretary, Michael Howard, tried unsuccessfully to have the boys serve a minimum of 15 years. Then, in the early months of 2001, the public learned that the two boys were to be paroled sometime in the summer. In addition, their identities were to be changed to protect them from reprisal from the public, and there were rumors about them being sent to another country.

These events put England's juvenile offender laws and juvenile justice system to an extreme test in trying to balance the rights of the offender with the rights of the community and the moral and public outrage caused by this violent act. The international implications of these events were wide reaching, causing some countries to reexamine their juvenile offender laws and how they deal with violent juvenile offenders. As prime minister, how would you answer these questions from the media?

- Did the English juvenile justice system fail the victim's family and society as a whole?

- Should England have done more to keep these juveniles locked up for a longer time, or was the sentence appropriate?

- What can the English government do to try to prevent this from happening again? Should they change their juvenile offender laws and policies?

Doing Research on the Web

Before you answer these questions, you may want to research how other Western countries respond to juvenile violence and delinquency. To learn more about juvenile treatment options, visit the following websites via

academic.cengage.com/criminaljustice/siegel

I Campbell Collaboration Crime and Justice Group

I International Centre for the Prevention of Crime

I European Institute for Crime Prevention and Control

I World Health Organization Department of Injuries and Violence Prevention

I United Nations Office on Drugs and Crime

Questions for Discussion

1. International comparisons of delinquency and juvenile justice systems are best done "like-with-like." What are some of the things that need to be considered in order to produce valid comparisons across countries?

2. What are some of the benefits and challenges in making international comparisons of delinquency?

3. Between the mid-1980s and the early 2000s, juvenile violence increased substantially in most European countries, and started to decline in the mid-1990s in the United States and Canada. What are some of the reasons for this rise and fall in juvenile violence in these different regions?

4. Across the world there is a great deal of variation in the minimum age a person can be held responsible for his or her criminal actions. What are the advantages and disadvantages of having a low minimum age?

5. Which developed countries appear to be the most lenient in their treatment of juvenile offenders, and which appear to be the most punitive?

6. What are some of the differences between juvenile justice systems in the United States and England? Identify two or three key differences and discuss how these differences could benefit the other country.

Notes

1. Marian FitzGerald, Alex Stevens, and Chris Hale, *A Review of the Knowledge on Juvenile Violence: Trends, Policies and Responses in the EU Member States* (Brussels, Belgium: European Crime Prevention Network, European Commission, 2004), p. 51.

2. "Pornography Cartel Broken," *Crime and Justice International* 17:13 (2001).

3. Sarah Shannon, "The Global Sex Trade: Humans as the Ultimate Commodity," *Crime and Justice International* 17:5–7 (2001).

4. David Binder, "12 Nations in Southeast Europe Pursue Traffickers in Sex Trade," *New York Times*, 19 October 2003, p. 6.

5. Lizette Alvarez, "H.I.V. Surge Catches Tradition-Bound Estonia Off Guard," *New York Times*, 15 February 2004, p. 6.

6. Reuters, "18 Dead in Shooting at High School in Eastern Germany," *New York Times*, 26 April 2002; Edmund L. Andrews, "Deep Shock in Germany, Where Guns Are Rare," *New York Times*, 28 April 2002, p. 15.

7. Stephan Lhotzky, "Will Kai Become a Skinhead? Cultures of Hate Germany the New Europe," *Reclaiming Children and Youth* 10:86–91 (2001).

8. Christian Pfeiffer, "The Impoverishment of the Lower Classes Is Increasing Juvenile Aggressivity," *European Education* 32:95–100 (2000).

9. John Tagliabue, "Synagogue in Paris Firebombed; Raids Go On," *New York Times*, 5 April 2002, p. 5; John Tagliabue, "Paris Takes Aim at Its Crime Rate," *New York Times*, 24 August 2003, p. 3, section 5.

10. Sophie Gendrot, "France: The Politicization of Youth Justice," in John Muncie and Barry Goldson, eds., *Comparative Youth Justice: Critical Issues* (Thousand Oaks, CA: Sage, 2006), p. 58.

11. Associated Press, "As Anniversary of Riots Nears, Suburban Youths March on Paris," *New York Times*, 26 October 2006.

12. Gendrot, "France: The Politicization of Youth Justice," p. 59.

13. Richard Bernstein, "Crimes Most Outlandish, but Why in Germany?" *New York Times*, 11 February 2004; Christian Pfeiffer, "Juvenile Crime and Violence in Europe," in Michael Tonry, ed., *Crime and Justice: A Review of Research*, vol. 23 (Chicago: University of Chicago Press, 1998), p. 300.

14. FitzGerald, Stevens, and Hale, *A Review of the Knowledge on Juvenile Violence*; Martin Killias and Marcelo F. Aebi, "Crime Trends in Europe from 1990 to 1996: How Europe Illustrates the Limits of the American Experience," *European Journal on Criminal Policy and Research* 8:43–63 (2000).

15. John Hagan, Hans Merkens, and Klaus Boehnke, "Delinquency and Disdain: Social Capital and the Control of Right-Wing Extremism among East and West Berlin Youth," *American Journal of Sociology* 100:1028–1053 (1995).

16. Sandra Gail Walker, *Weapons Use in Canadian Schools* (Ottawa: Solicitor General Canada, 1994).

17. John A. Winterdyk, "Juvenile Justice and Young Offenders: An Overview of Canada," in John A. Winterdyk, ed., *Juvenile Justice Systems: International Perspectives*, 2nd ed. (Toronto: Canadian Scholars' Press, 2002), p. 74; Thomas Gabor, "Trends in Youth Crime: Some Evidence Pointing to Increases in the Severity and Volume of Violence on the Part of Young People," *Canadian Journal of Criminology* 41:385–392 (1999), p. 389.

18. Héctor Castillo Berthier, "Popular Culture among Mexican Teenagers," *The Urban Age* 1:14–15 (1993).

19. Franz Vanderschueren, "From Violence to Justice and Security in Cities," *Environment and Urbanization* 8: 93–112 (1996).

20. Larry Rohter, "Rio's Drug Wars Begin to Take Toll on Tourism," *New York Times*, 27 April 2003, p. 3, section 5; Larry Rohter, "As Crime and Politics Collide in Rio, City Cowers in Fear," *New York Times*, 8 May 2003.

21. Tim Weiner, "Cover-Up Found in Honduras Prison Killings," *New York Times*, 20 May 2003; Ginger Thompson, "Guatemala Bleeds in Vise of Gangs and Vengeance," *New York Times*, 1 January 2006, p. 4.

22. José Carvalho de Noronha, "Drug Markets and Urban Violence in Rio de Janeiro: A Call for Action," *The Urban Age* 1:9 (1993).

23. "Graffiti, New York to New Zealand," *Crime and Justice International* 14:22 (1998).

24. "Child Prostitution on the Rise," *Crime and Justice International* 18:21 (2002).

25. Carlos Carcach, "Youth as Victims and Offenders of Homicide," *Crime and Justice International* 14:10–14 (1998).

26. Reuters, "Japan PM's Values Agenda Resonates After Crime Shocks," *New York Times*, 22 May 2007.

27. Norimitsu Onishi, "Crime Rattles Japanese Calm, Attracting Politician's Notice," *New York Times*, 6 September 2003.

28. Shinpei Nawa, "Postwar Fourth Wave of Juvenile Delinquency and Tasks of Juvenile Police," in *Current Juvenile Police Policy in Japan* (Tokyo: Police Policy Research Center, National Police Academy of Japan, 2006), table 1.

29. "Japan Again Hit by Incidents of Violent Teen Crime," *Crime and Justice International* 17:15 (2001).

30. Horace Lyons, "Hikikomori and Youth Crime," *Crime and Justice International* 17:9–10 (2001).

31. Trevor Ryan, "Creating 'Problem Kids': Juvenile Crime in Japan and Revisions to the Juvenile Act," *Journal of Japanese Law* 10:153–188 (2005), p. 153.

32. Dawei Wang, "The Study of Juvenile Delinquency and Juvenile Protection in the People's Republic of China," *Crime and Justice International*, 22(94):4–13 (2006), p. 5.

33. Liling Yue, "Youth Injustice in China," in Winterdyk, ed., *Juvenile Justice Systems: International Perspectives*, 2nd ed.

34. Mademba Ndiaye, "Dakar: Youth Groups and the Slide toward Violence," *The Urban Age* 1:7–8 (1993).

35. Otula Owuor, "City Residents Meet in Nairobi," *The Urban Age* 1:8 (1993).

36. For a general overview, see Piers Beirne, "Cultural Relativism and Comparative Criminology," *Contemporary Crises* 7:371–391 (1983); James Lynch, "Crime in International Perspective," in James Q. Wilson and Joan Petersilia, eds., *Crime: Public Policies for Crime Control* (Oakland, CA: Institute for Contemporary Studies, 2002).

37. John Henry Sloan et al., "Handgun Regulation, Crime, Assaults, and Homicide: A Tale of Two Cities," *New England Journal of Medicine* 319:1256–1262 (1988); Martin Killias, John van Kesteren, and Martin Rindlisbacher, "Guns, Violent Crime, and Suicide in 21 Countries," *Canadian Journal of Criminology* 43:429–448 (2001); Richard R. Bennett, "Constructing Cross-Cultural Theories in Criminology," *Criminology* 18:252–268 (1980); David Shichor, "Crime Patterns and Socioeconomic Development: A Cross-National Analysis," *Criminal Justice Review* 15:64–77 (1990); David P. Farrington, Patrick A. Langan, and Per-Olof H. Wikström, "Changes in Crime and Punishment in America, England and Sweden between the 1980s and the 1990s," *Studies on Crime and Crime Prevention* 3:104–131 (1994); Patrick A. Langan and David P. Farrington, *Crime and Justice in the United States and in England and Wales, 1981–96* (Washington, DC: Bureau of Justice Statistics, 1998); Joanne Savage and Bryan Vila, "Lagged Effects of Nurturance on Crime: A Cross-National Comparison," *Studies on Crime and Crime Prevention* 6:101–120 (1997); Marshall B. Clinard, *Cities with Little Crime: The Case of Switzerland* (New York: Cambridge University Press, 1978); Freda Adler, *Nations Not Obsessed with Crime* (Littleton, CO: Rothman, 1983); Manuel Eisner, "Crime, Problem Drinking, and Drug Use: Patterns of Problem Behavior in Cross-National Perspective," *Annals of the American Academy of Political and Social Science* 580:201–225 (2002).

38. Graeme Newman and Gregory J. Howard, "Introduction: Data Sources and Their Use," in Graeme Newman, ed., *Global Report on Crime and Justice* (New York: Oxford University Press, 1999), p. 18.

39. Jan van Dijk and Kristiina Kangaspunta, "Piecing Together the Cross-National Crime Puzzle," *National Institute of Justice Journal* 242:34–41 (2000).

40. Joan McCord, Cathy Spatz Widom, and Nancy Crowell, eds., *Juvenile Crime, Juvenile Justice*. Panel on Juvenile Crime: Prevention, Treatment, and Control (Washington, DC: National Academy Press, 2001), p. 17.

41. Pfeiffer, "Juvenile Crime and Violence in Europe," p. 261.

42. For more detail on the different international sources, see Gregory J. Howard, Graeme Newman, and William Alex Pridemore, "Theory, Method, and Data in Comparative Criminology," in David Duffee, ed., *Measurement and Analysis of Crime and Justice: Volume 4. Criminal Justice 2000* (Washington, DC: National Institute of Justice, 2000).

43. Newman and Howard, "Introduction: Data Sources and Their Use."

44. Gary LaFree, *Losing Legitimacy: Street Crime and the Decline of Social Institutions in America* (Boulder, CO: Westview Press, 1997), p. 29.

45. See, for example, Franklin E. Zimring and Gordon Hawkins, *Crime Is Not the Problem: Lethal Violence in America* (New York: Oxford University Press, 1997).

46. Josine Junger-Tas, Gert-Jan Terlouw, and Malcolm W. Klein, eds., *Delinquent Behavior among Young People in the Western World: First Results of the International Self-Report Delinquency Study* (New York: Kugler Publications, 1994).

47. Rosemary Barberet, Benjamin Bowling, Josine Junger-Tas, Cristina Rechea-Alberola, John van Kesteren, and Andrew Zurawan, *Self-Reported Juvenile Delinquency in England and Wales, the Netherlands and Spain* (Helsinki, Finland: European Institute for Crime Prevention and Control, 2004), p. iii; see also Josine Junger-Tas, Ineke Haen Marshall, and Denis Ribeaud, *Delinquency in International Perspective: The International Self-Reported Delinquency Study* (Monsey, NY: Criminal Justice Press, 2003).

48. See also Philip L. Reichel, *Comparative Criminal Justice Systems: A Topical Approach*, 3rd ed. (Upper Saddle River, NJ: Prentice Hall, 2002), pp. 4–5.

49. See, for example, Clinard, *Cities with Little Crime: The Case of Switzerland*; Adler, *Nations Not Obsessed with Crime*.

50. Harry R. Dammer and Erika Fairchild, with Jay S. Albanese, *Comparative Criminal Justice Systems*, 3rd ed. (Belmont, CA: Wadsworth, 2006), p. 10.

51. Phil Williams, "Emerging Issues: Transnational Crime and Its Control," in Newman, ed., *Global Report on Crime and Justice*, p. 222.

52. James O. Finckenauer, "Meeting the Challenge of Transnational Crime," *National Institute of Justice Journal* 244:2–7 (2000).

53. Williams, "Emerging Issues: Transnational Crime and Its Control," p. 222.

54. Ibid., p. 221.

55. Mark Findlay, *The Globalisation of Crime: Understanding Transnational Relationships in Context* (Cambridge, England: Cambridge University Press, 1999).

56. Pfeiffer, "Juvenile Crime and Violence in Europe."

57. Fitzgerald, Stevens, and Hale, *A Review of the Knowledge on Juvenile Violence: Trends, Policies and Responses in the EU Member States*.

58. Pfeiffer, "Juvenile Crime and Violence in Europe," p. 256.

59. Fitzgerald, Stevens, and Hale, *A Review of the Knowledge on Juvenile Violence: Trends, Policies and Responses in the EU Member States*, p. 51.

60. Howard N. Snyder, *Juvenile Arrests 2005* (Washington, DC: Office of Juvenile Justice and Delinquency Prevention, U.S. Department of Justice, 2007).

61. Josine Junger-Tas, "Youth Justice in the Netherlands," in Michael Tonry and Anthony N. Doob, eds., *Youth Crime and Youth Justice: Comparative and Cross-National Perspectives. Crime and Justice: A Review of Research*, vol. 31 (Chicago: University of Chicago Press, 2004).

62. Hans-Jörg Albrecht, "Juvenile Crime and Juvenile Law in the Federal Republic of Germany," in Winterdyk, ed., *Juvenile Justice Systems: International Perspectives*, 2nd ed.; Uberto Gatti and Alfredo Verde, "Comparative Juvenile Justice: An Overview of Italy," in Winterdyk, ed., *Juvenile Justice Systems: International Perspectives*, 2nd ed.

63. Warren Silver, *Crime Statistics in Canada, 2006* (Ottawa: Canadian Centre for Justice Statistics Juristat, 2007), p. 14, table 5; Rebecca Kong, *Canadian Crime Statistics, 1996* (Ottawa: Canadian Centre for Justice Statistics Juristat, 1997), p. 17, table 4.

64. Pfeiffer, "Juvenile Crime and Violence in Europe," p. 256.

65. Ibid., p. 279.

66. James O. Finckenauer, *Russian Youth: Law, Deviance, and the Pursuit of Freedom* (New Brunswick, NJ: Transaction Publishers, 1995), pp. 71–73.

67. Silver, *Crime Statistics in Canada, 2006*, p. 14, table 5; Kong, *Canadian Crime Statistics, 1996*, p. 17, table 4.

68. Snyder, *Juvenile Arrests 2005*.

69. Fitzgerald, Stevens, and Hale, *A Review of the Knowledge on Juvenile Violence: Trends, Policies and Responses in the EU Member States*, p. 49.

70. Björn Hibell, Barbro Andersson, Thoroddur Bjarnason, Salme Ahlström, Olga Balakireva, Anna Kokkevi, and Mark Morgan, *The ESPAD Report 2003: Alcohol and Other Drug Use Among Students in 35 European Countries* (Stockholm: The Swedish Council for Information on Alcohol and Other Drugs, Council of Europe, and Pompidou Group, 2004), table 41c; Monitoring the Future, *Excerpts from the 2003 European School Survey Project on Alcohol and Other Drugs (ESPAD)* (Ann Arbor, MI: Author, 2004).

71. Sarah Lyall, "British Worry that Drinking has Gotten Out of Hand," *New York Times*, 22 July 2004.

72. Björn Hibell et al., *The ESPAD Report 2003: Alcohol and Other Drug Use Among Students in 35 European Countries*, table 41c.

73. Kate Zernike, "Study Finds Teenage Drug Use Higher in U.S. than in Europe," *New York Times*, 21 February 2001.

74. Elmar G. M. Weitekamp, Hans-Juergen Kerner, and Gernot Trueg, *International Comparison of Juvenile Justice Systems: Report to the National Academy of Sciences Commission on Behavioral and Social Sciences and Education* (Tuebingen, Germany: Institute of Criminology, University of Tuebingen, July 1999), p. 13.

75. National Advisory Commission on Criminal Justice Standards and Goals, *Task Force Report on Juvenile Justice and Delinquency Prevention* (Washington, DC: Law Enforcement Assistance Administration, 1976), p. 258.

76. Dammer and Fairchild, with Albanese, *Comparative Criminal Justice Systems*, pp. 340–341.

77. Pfeiffer, "Juvenile Crime and Violence in Europe," p. 314.

78. John A. Winterdyk, "Juvenile Justice and Young Offenders: An Overview of Canada," in Winterdyk, ed., *Juvenile Justice Systems: International Perspectives*, 2nd ed., p. 91.

79. Minoru Yokoyama, "Juvenile Justice and Juvenile Crime: An Overview of Japan," in Winterdyk, ed., *Juvenile Justice Systems: International Perspectives*, 2nd ed., pp. 337–338.

80. Satyanshu Mukherjee and Philip Reichel, "Bringing to Justice," in Newman, ed., *Global Report on Crime and Justice*, p. 79.

81. McCord, Spatz Widom, and Crowell, eds., *Juvenile Crime, Juvenile Justice*, p. 20.
82. Winterdyk, ed., *Juvenile Justice Systems: International Perspectives*, p. xviii.
83. Weitekamp, Kerner, and Trueg, *International Comparison of Juvenile Justice Systems*, p. 83.
84. Ibid., p. 268.
85. Ibid., p. 253.
86. Doob and Sprott, "Youth Justice in Canada," p. 232.
87. Uberto Gatti and Alfredo Verde, "Comparative Juvenile Justice: An Overview of Italy," in Winterdyk, ed., *Juvenile Justice Systems: International Perspectives*, 2nd ed., p. 305.
88. Weitekamp, Kerner, and Trueg, *International Comparison of Juvenile Justice Systems*, pp. 208, 223.
89. James L. Williams and Daniel G. Rodeheaver, "Punishing Juvenile Offenders in Russia," *International Criminal Justice Review* 12:93–110 (2002), p. 104.
90. Weitekamp, Kerner, and Trueg, *International Comparison of Juvenile Justice Systems*, p. 243.
91. Trevor Bradley, Juan Tauri, and Reece Walters, "Demythologising Youth Justice in Aotearoa/New Zealand," in John Muncie and Barry Goldson, eds., *Comparative Youth Justice: Critical Issues* (Thousand Oaks, CA: Sage, 2006), p. 80.
92. Anette Storgaard, "Juvenile Justice in Scandinavia," *Journal of Scandinavian Studies in Criminology and Crime Prevention* 5:188–204 (2004), pp. 198–199.
93. John Muncie and Barry Goldson, "States of Transition: Convergence and Diversity in International Youth Justice," in John Muncie and Barry Goldson, eds., *Comparative Youth Justice: Critical Issues* (Thousand Oaks, CA: Sage, 2006), p. 206.
94. Harold Traver, "Juvenile Delinquency in Hong Kong," in Winterdyk, ed., *Juvenile Justice Systems: International Perspectives*, 2nd ed., p. 211.
95. Hans-Jörg Albrecht, "Youth Justice in Germany," in Tonry and Doob, eds., *Youth Crime and Youth Justice: Comparative and Cross-National Perspectives. Crime and Justice: A Review of Research*, vol. 31, p. 473.
96. Loraine Gelsthorpe and Vicky Kemp, "Comparative Juvenile Justice: England and Wales," in Winterdyk, ed., *Juvenile Justice Systems: International Perspectives*, 2nd ed., p. 130.
97. Weitekamp, Kerner, and Trueg, *International Comparison of Juvenile Justice Systems*, p. 90.
98. Gelsthorpe and Kemp, "Comparative Juvenile Justice: England and Wales," p. 138.
99. Weitekamp, Kerner, and Trueg, *International Comparison of Juvenile Justice Systems*, p. 90.
100. Ibid., p. 103.
101. Ibid., p. 100.
102. Ibid., p. 90.
103. David P. Farrington, John Ditchfield, Gareth Hancock, Philip Howard, Darrick Jolliffe, Mark S. Livingston, and Kate A. Painter, *Evaluation of Two Intensive Regimes for Young Offenders*, Home Office Research Study No. 239 (London: Home Office, 2002).
104. Gelsthorpe and Kemp, "Comparative Juvenile Justice: England and Wales," pp. 149–150.
105. Dammer and Fairchild, with Albanese, *Comparative Criminal Justice Systems*, p. 349.
106. Ibid., pp. 349–350.
107. Muncie and Goldson, "States of Transition: Convergence and Diversity in International Youth Justice," p. 209.
108. Julian V. Roberts, "Public Opinion and Youth Justice," in Tonry and Doob, eds., *Youth Crime and Youth Justice: Comparative and Cross-National Perspectives. Crime and Justice: A Review of Research*, vol. 31, pp. 509–510.

Excerpts from the U.S. Constitution

Amendment I (1791)
Congress shall make no law respecting an establishment of religion, or prohibiting the free exercise thereof; or abridging the freedom of speech, or of the press; or the right of the people peaceably to assemble, and to petition the government for a redress of grievances.

Amendment II (1791)
A well-regulated militia, being necessary to the security of a free state, the right of the people to keep and bear arms, shall not be infringed.

Amendment III (1791)
No soldier shall, in time of peace, be quartered in any house, without the consent of the owner, nor in time of war, but in a manner to be prescribed by law.

Amendment IV (1791)
The right of the people to be secure in their persons, houses, papers, and effects, against unreasonable searches and seizures, shall not be violated, and no warrants shall issue, but upon probable cause, supported by oath or affirmation, and particularly describing the place to be searched, and the persons or things to be seized.

Amendment V (1791)
No person shall be held to answer for a capital, or otherwise infamous, crime unless on a presentment or indictment of a grand jury, except in cases arising in the land or naval forces, or in the militia, when in actual service in time of war or public danger; nor shall any person be subject for the same offense to be twice put in jeopardy of life or limb; nor shall be compelled in any criminal case to be a witness against himself, nor be deprived of life, liberty, or property; without due process of law; nor shall private property be taken for public use without just compensation.

Amendment VI (1791)
In all criminal prosecutions, the accused shall enjoy the right to a speedy and public trial, by an impartial jury of the state and district wherein the crime shall have been committed, which district shall have been previously ascertained by law, and to be informed of the nature and cause of the accusation; to be confronted with the witnesses against him; to have compulsory process for obtaining witnesses in his favor, and to have the assistance of counsel for his defense.

Amendment VII (1791)
In suits at common law, where the value in controversy shall exceed twenty dollars, the right of trial by jury shall be preserved, and no fact tried by a jury shall be otherwise reexamined in any court of the United States, than according to the rules of common law.

Amendment VIII (1791)
Excessive bail shall not be required, nor excessive fines imposed, nor cruel and unusual punishment inflicted.

Amendment IX (1791)
The enumeration in the Constitution of certain rights shall not be construed to deny or disparage others retained by the people.

Amendment X (1791)
The powers not delegated to the United States by the Constitution, nor prohibited by it to the states, are reserved to the states respectively, or to the people.

Amendment XIV (1868)
Section I. All persons born or naturalized in the United States, and subject to the jurisdiction thereof, are citizens of the United States and of the state wherein they reside. No state shall make or enforce any laws which abridge the privilege or immunities of citizens of the United States; nor shall any state deprive any person of life, liberty, or property, without due process of law; nor deny to any person within its jurisdiction the equal protection of the laws.

abandonment Parents physically leave their children with the intention of completely severing the parent-child relationship.

academic achievement Being successful in a school environment.

active speech Speech involving actual language, expression, or gesture.

addict A person with an overpowering physical or psychological need to continue taking a particular substance or drug.

addiction-prone personality A personality that has a compulsion for mood-altering drugs, believed by some to be the cause of substance abuse.

adjudicatory hearing The fact-finding process wherein the juvenile court determines whether there is sufficient evidence to sustain the allegations in a petition.

adolescent-limited offenders Kids who get into minor scrapes as youths but whose misbehavior ends when they enter adulthood.

advisement hearing A preliminary protective or temporary custody hearing in which the court will review the facts and determine whether removal of the child is justified and notify parents of the charges against them.

aftercare Transitional assistance to juveniles, equivalent to adult parole, to help youths adjust to community life.

age of onset Age at which youths begin their delinquent careers; early onset is believed to be linked with chronic offending patterns.

aging-out process (also known as desistance from crime or spontaneous remission) The tendency for youths to reduce the frequency of their offending behavior as they age; aging out is thought to occur among all groups of offenders.

alcohol Fermented or distilled liquids containing ethanol, an intoxicating substance.

alexithymia A deficit in emotional cognition that prevents people from being aware of their feelings or being able to understand or talk about their thoughts and emotions; sufferers from alexithymia seem robotic and emotionally dead.

anabolic steroids Drugs used by athletes and bodybuilders to gain muscle bulk and strength.

anesthetic drugs Central nervous system depressants.

anomie Normlessness produced by rapidly shifting moral values; according to Merton, anomie occurs when personal goals cannot be achieved using available means.

appellate process Allows the juvenile an opportunity to have the case brought before a reviewing court after it has been heard in juvenile or family court.

arousal theorists Delinquency experts who believe that aggression is a function of the level of an individual's need for stimulation or arousal from the environment. Those who require more stimulation may act in an aggressive manner to meet their needs.

arrest Taking a person into the custody of the law to restrain the accused until he or she can be held accountable for the offense in court proceedings.

at-risk youth Young people who are extremely vulnerable to the negative consequences of school failure, substance abuse, and early sexuality.

authority conflict pathway Pathway to delinquent deviance that begins at an early age with stubborn behavior and leads to defiance and then to authority avoidance.

bail Amount of money that must be paid as a condition of pretrial release to ensure that the accused will return for subsequent proceedings. Bail is normally set by the judge at the initial appearance, and if unable to make bail, the accused is detained in jail.

balanced probation Programs that integrate community protection, accountability of the juvenile offender, competency, and individualized attention to the juvenile offender; based on the principle that juvenile offenders must accept responsibility for their behavior.

balancing-of-the-interests approach Efforts of the courts to balance the parents' natural right to raise a child with the child's right to grow into adulthood free from physical abuse or emotional harm.

barrio A Spanish word meaning "district."

battered child syndrome Nonaccidental physical injury of children by their parents or guardians.

behaviorism Branch of psychology concerned with the study of observable behavior rather than unconscious processes; focuses on particular stimuli and responses to them.

behavior modification A technique for shaping desired behaviors through a system of rewards and punishments.

best interests of the child A philosophical viewpoint that encourages the state to take control of wayward children and provide care, custody, and treatment to remedy delinquent behavior.

bifurcated process The procedure of separating adjudicatory and dispositionary hearings so different levels of evidence can be heard at each.

biosocial theory The view that both thought and behavior have biological and social bases.

blended families Nuclear families that are the product of divorce and remarriage, blending one parent from each of two families and their combined children into one family unit.

boot camps Juvenile programs that combine get-tough elements from adult programs with education, substance abuse treatment, and social skills training.

broken home Home in which one or both parents are absent due to divorce or separation; children in such an environment may be prone to antisocial behavior.

chancery courts Court proceedings created in fifteenth-century England to oversee the lives of highborn minors who were orphaned or otherwise could not care for themselves.

child abuse Any physical, emotional, or sexual trauma to a child, including neglecting to give proper care and attention, for which no reasonable explanation can be found.

Children's Aid Society Child saving organization that took children from the streets of large cities and placed them with farm families on the prairie.

child savers Nineteenth-century reformers who developed programs for troubled youth and influenced legislation creating the juvenile justice system; today some critics view them as being more concerned with control of the poor than with their welfare.

chivalry hypothesis (also known as paternalism hypothesis) The view that low female crime and delinquency rates are a reflection of the leniency with which police treat female offenders.

choice theory Holds that youths will engage in delinquent and criminal behavior after weighing the consequences and benefits of their actions; delinquent behavior is a rational choice made by a motivated offender who perceives that the chances of gain outweigh any possible punishment or loss.

chronic delinquent offenders (also known as chronic juvenile offenders, chronic delinquents, or chronic recidivists) Youths who have been arrested four or more times during their minority and perpetuate a striking majority of serious criminal acts. This small group, known as the "chronic 6 percent," is believed to engage in a significant portion of all delinquent behavior; these youths do not age out of crime but continue their criminal behavior into adulthood.

classical criminology Holds that decisions to violate the law are weighed against possible punishments, and to deter crime the pain of punishment must outweigh the benefit of illegal gain; led to graduated punishments based on seriousness of the crime (let the punishment fit the crime).

cliques Small groups of friends who share intimate knowledge and confidences.

cocaine A powerful natural stimulant derived from the coca plant.

cognitive theory The branch of psychology that studies the perception of reality and the mental processes required to understand the world we live in.

collective efficacy The ability of communities to regulate the behavior of their residents through the influence of community institutions, such as the family and school.

Residents in these communities share mutual trust and a willingness to intervene in the supervision of children and the maintenance of public order.

community policing Police strategy that emphasizes reducing fear, organizing the community, and maintaining order rather than fighting crime.

community service restitution The juvenile offender is required to assist some worthwhile community organization for a period of time.

community treatment Using nonsecure and noninstitutional residences, counseling services, victim restitution programs, and other community services to treat juveniles in their own communities.

complaint Report made by the police or some other agency to the court that initiates the intake process.

conditions of probation The rules and regulations mandating that a juvenile on probation behave in a particular way.

confidentiality Restriction of information in juvenile court proceedings in the interest of protecting the privacy of the juvenile.

continuity of crime The idea that chronic juvenile offenders are likely to continue violating the law as adults.

control group The comparison group of subjects that does not receive the program.

controversial status youth Aggressive kids who are either highly liked or intensely disliked by their peers and who are the ones most likely to become engaged in antisocial behavior.

cottage system Housing juveniles in a compound containing a series of cottages, each of which accommodates 20 to 40 children and is run by a set of cottage parents who create a homelike atmosphere.

covert pathway Pathway to a delinquent career that begins with minor underhanded behavior, leads to property damage, and eventually escalates to more serious forms of theft and fraud.

crack A highly addictive crystalline form of cocaine containing remnants of hydrochloride and sodium bicarbonate, which emits a crackling sound when smoked.

crime mapping A research technique that employs computerized crime maps and other graphic representations of crime data patterns.

criminal atavism The idea that delinquents manifest physical anomalies that make them biologically and physiologically similar to our primitive ancestors, savage throwbacks to an earlier stage of human evolution.

critical feminists Hold that gender inequality stems from the unequal power of men and women and the subsequent exploitation of women by men; the cause of female delinquency originates with the onset of male supremacy and the efforts of males to control females' sexuality.

crowds Loosely organized groups who share interests and activities.

Crown Court In England, the criminal court that deals with adult offenders or juveniles who have been transferred from youth court.

Crown Prosecution Service The national agency in England that is in charge of all criminal prosecutions of juveniles and adults.

cultural deviance theory A unique lower-class culture develops in disorganized neighborhoods whose unique set of values and beliefs puts residents in conflict with conventional social norms.

cultural transmission Cultural norms and values that are passed down from one generation to the next.

culture of poverty View that lower-class people form a separate culture with their own values and norms, which are sometimes in conflict with conventional society.

cumulative disadvantage A condition whereby serious delinquency in adolescence undermines things such as employability and social relations and helps increase the chances of continued offending in adulthood.

custodial interrogation Questions posed by the police to a suspect held in custody in the prejudicial stage of the juvenile justice process; juveniles have the same rights against self-incrimination as adults do when being questioned.

death squads Common to South America, organized government or criminal groups that selectively kill members of opposing groups and incite fear in those groups and among their supporters.

degradation ceremony Going to court, being scolded by a judge, or being found delinquent after a trial are examples of public ceremonies that can transform youthful offenders by degrading their self-image.

deinstitutionalization Removing juveniles from adult jails and placing them in community-based programs to avoid the stigma attached to these facilities.

delinquency control or delinquency repression Involves any justice program or policy designed to prevent the occurrence of a future delinquent act.

delinquency prevention Involves any nonjustice program or policy designed to prevent the occurrence of a future delinquent act.

designer drugs Lab-made drugs designed to avoid existing drug laws.

detached street workers Social workers who go out into the community and establish close relationships with juvenile gangs with the goal of modifying gang behavior to conform to conventional behaviors and help gang members get jobs and educational opportunities.

detention Temporary care of a child alleged to be delinquent who requires secure custody in physically restricting facilities pending court disposition or execution of a court order.

detention hearing A hearing by a judicial officer of a juvenile court to determine whether a juvenile is to be detained or released while juvenile proceedings are pending in the case.

determinate sentence Specifies a fixed term of detention that must be served.

developed countries Recognized by the United Nations as the richest countries in the world.

developing countries Recognized by the United Nations as countries that are showing signs of improved economic growth and are making the transition from low income to high income.

developmental theory The view that delinquency is a dynamic process, influenced by social experiences as well as individual characteristics.

differential association theory Asserts that criminal behavior is learned primarily within interpersonal groups and that youths will become delinquent if definitions they have learned favorable to violating the law exceed definitions favorable to obeying the law within that group.

differential opportunity The view that lower-class youths, whose legitimate opportunities are limited, join gangs and pursue criminal careers as alternative means to achieve universal success goals.

disaggregated Analyzing the relationship between two or more independent variables (such as murder convictions and death sentence) while controlling for the influence of a dependent variable (such as race).

discretion Use of personal decision making and choice in carrying out operations in the criminal justice system, such as deciding whether to make an arrest or when to accept a plea bargain.

disorganized neighborhood Inner-city areas of extreme poverty where the critical social control mechanisms have broken down.

disposition For juvenile offenders, the equivalent of sentencing for adult offenders; however, juvenile dispositions should be more rehabilitative than retributive.

disposition hearing The social service agency presents its case plan and recommendations for care of the child and treatment of the parents, including incarceration and counseling or other treatment.

diversion Official halting or suspending of a formal criminal or juvenile justice proceeding at any legally prescribed processing point after a recorded justice system entry, and referral of that person to a treatment or care program or a recommendation that the person be released.

dramatization of evil The process of social typing that transforms an offender's identity from a doer of evil to an evil person.

drift Idea that youths move in and out of delinquency and that their lifestyles can embrace both conventional and deviant values.

dropping out To leave school before completing the required program of education.

drug courts Courts whose focus is providing treatment for youths accused of drug-related acts.

due process Basic constitutional principle based on the concept of the primacy of the individual and the complementary concept of limitation on governmental power; safeguards the individual from unfair state procedures in judicial or administrative proceedings. Due process rights have been extended to juvenile trials.

egalitarian families Husband and wife share power at home; daughters gain a kind of freedom similar to that of sons, and their law-violating behaviors mirror those of their brothers.

ego identity According to Erik Erikson, ego identity is formed when a person develops a firm sense of who he is and what he stands for.

electronic monitoring Active monitoring systems consist of a radio transmitter worn by the offender that sends a continuous signal to the probation department computer, alerting officials if the offender leaves his or her place of confinement. Passive systems employ computer-generated random phone calls that must be responded to in a certain period of time from a particular phone or other device.

enculturated The process by which an established culture teaches an individual its norms and values, so that the individual can become an accepted member of the society. Through enculturation, the individual learns what is accepted behavior within that society and his or her particular status within the culture.

equipotentiality View that all people are equal at birth and are thereafter influenced by their environment.

euthanasia The act or practice of ending the life of an individual suffering from a terminal illness or an incurable condition.

evolutionary theory Explaining the existence of aggression and violent behavior as positive adaptive behaviors in human evolution; these traits allowed their bearers to reproduce disproportionately, which has had an effect on the human gene pool.

experimental group The group of subjects that receives the program.

extravert A person who behaves impulsively and doesn't have the ability to examine motives and behavior.

familicide Mass murders in which a spouse and one or more children are slain.

family group homes A combination of foster care and a group home in which a juvenile is placed in a private group home run by a single family rather than by professional staff.

Federal Bureau of Investigation (FBI) Arm of the U.S. Department of Justice that investigates violations of federal law, gathers crime statistics, runs a comprehensive crime laboratory, and helps train local law enforcement officers.

final order Order that ends litigation between two parties by determining all their rights and disposing of all the issues.

focal concerns The value orientation of lower-class culture that is characterized by a need for excitement, trouble, smartness, fate, and personal autonomy.

foster care Placing a child in the temporary care of a family other than its own as a result of state intervention into problems that are taking place within the birth family; can be used as a temporary shelter while a permanent adoption effort is being completed.

free will View that youths are in charge of their own destinies and are free to make personal behavior choices unencumbered by environmental factors.

gang Group of youths who collectively engage in delinquent behaviors.

gang sweep A method of enforcement in which police, armed with arrest and search warrants, enter a neighborhood in force in an operation to make as many arrests as possible.

gateway drug A substance that leads to use of more serious drugs; alcohol use has long been thought to lead to more serious drug abuse.

gender-schema theory A theory of development that holds that children internalize gender scripts that reflect the gender-related social practices of the culture. Once internalized, these gender scripts predispose the kids to construct a self-identity that is consistent with them.

general deterrence Crime control policies that depend on the fear of criminal penalties, such as long prison sentences for violent crimes; the aim is to convince law violators that the pain outweighs the benefit of criminal activity.

General Strain Theory (GST) According to Agnew, the view that multiple sources of strain interact with an individual's emotional traits and responses to produce criminality.

General Theory of Crime (GTC) A developmental theory that modifies social control theory by integrating concepts from biosocial, psychological, routine activities, and rational choice theories.

globalization The process of creating a global economy through transnational markets and political and legal systems.

graffiti Inscriptions or drawings made on a wall or structure and used by delinquents for gang messages and turf definition.

group homes Nonsecured, structured residences that provide counseling, education, job training, and family living.

group therapy Counseling several individuals together in a group session; individuals can obtain support from other group members as they work through similar problems.

guardian *ad litem* A court-appointed attorney who protects the interests of the child in cases involving the child's welfare.

guided group interaction (GGI) Through group interactions a delinquent can acknowledge and solve personal problems with support from other group members.

hallucinogens Natural or synthetic substances that produce vivid distortions of the senses without greatly disturbing consciousness.

harm reduction Efforts to minimize the harmful effects caused by drug use.

hashish A concentrated form of cannabis made from unadulterated resin from the female cannabis plant.

hearsay Out-of-court statements made by one person and recounted in court by another; such statements are generally not allowed as evidence except in child abuse cases wherein a child's statements to social workers, teachers, or police may be admissible.

heroin A narcotic made from opium and then cut with sugar or some other neutral substance until it is only 1 to 4 percent pure.

house arrest An offender is required to stay at home during specified periods of time; monitoring is done by random phone calls and visits or by electronic devices.

House of Refuge A care facility developed by the child savers to protect potential criminal youths by taking them off the street and providing a family-like environment.

identity crisis Psychological state, identified by Erikson, in which youth face inner turmoil and uncertainty about life roles.

indeterminate sentence Does not specify the length of time the juvenile must be held; rather, correctional authorities decide when the juvenile is ready to return to society.

individual counseling Counselors help juveniles understand and solve their current adjustment problems.

individualized treatment model Each sentence must be tailored to the individual needs of the child.

informant A person who has access to criminal networks and shares information with authorities in exchange for money or special treatment under conditions of anonymity.

inhalants Volatile liquids that give off a vapor, which is inhaled, producing short-term excitement and euphoria followed by a period of disorientation.

in loco parentis In the place of the parent; rights given to schools that allow them to assume parental duties in disciplining students.

intake Process during which a juvenile referral is received and a decision is made to file a petition in juvenile court to release the juvenile, to place the juvenile under supervision, or to refer the juvenile elsewhere.

integrated theories Theories that incorporate social, personal, and developmental factors into complex explanations of human behavior.

Intensive Aftercare Program (IAP) A balanced, highly structured, comprehensive continuum of intervention for serious and violent juvenile offenders returning to the community.

international crime Crime that is punishable under international law.

interstitial group Delinquent group that fills a crack in the social fabric and maintains standard group practices.

intrafamily violence An environment of discord and conflict within the family; children who grow up in dysfunctional homes often exhibit delinquent behaviors, having learned at a young age that aggression pays off.

juvenile court judge A judge elected or appointed to preside over juvenile cases and whose decisions can only be reviewed by a judge of a higher court.

juvenile defense attorney Represents children in juvenile court and plays an active role at all stages of the proceedings.

juvenile delinquency Participation in illegal behavior by a minor who falls under a statutory age limit.

juvenile intensive probation supervision (JIPS) A true alternative to incarceration that involves almost daily supervision of the juvenile by the probation officer assigned to the case.

juvenile justice process Under the paternal (*parens patriae*) philosophy, juvenile justice procedures are informal and nonadversarial, invoked for the juvenile offender rather than against him or her; a petition instead of a complaint is filed; courts make findings of involvement or adjudication of delinquency instead of convictions; and juvenile offenders receive dispositions instead of sentences.

juvenile justice system The segment of the justice system, including law enforcement officers, the courts, and correctional agencies, designed to treat youthful offenders.

juvenile officers Police officers who specialize in dealing with juvenile offenders; they may operate alone or as part of a juvenile police unit within the department.

juvenile probation officer Officer of the court involved in all four stages of the court process—intake, predisposition, postadjudication, and postdisposition—who assists the court and supervises juveniles placed on probation.

juvenile prosecutor Government attorney responsible for representing the interests of the state and bringing the case against the accused juvenile.

klikas Subgroups of same-aged youths in Hispanic gangs that remain together and have separate names and a unique identity in the gang.

labeling theory Posits that society creates deviance through a system of social control agencies that designate (or label) certain individuals as delinquent, thereby stigmatizing youths and encouraging them to accept this negative personal identity.

latent delinquents Youths whose troubled family life leads them to seek immediate gratification without consideration of right and wrong or the feelings of others.

latent trait A stable feature, characteristic, property, or condition, such as defective intelligence or impulsive personality, that makes some people delinquency-prone over the life course.

Law Enforcement Assistance Administration (LEAA) Unit in the U.S. Department of Justice established by the Omnibus Crime Control and Safe Streets Act of 1968 to administer grants and provide guidance for crime prevention policy and programs.

learning disability (LD) Neurological dysfunction that prevents an individual from learning to his or her potential.

least detrimental alternative Choice of a program for the child that will best foster the child's growth and development.

least developed countries Recognized by the United Nations as being the poorest countries in the world and suffering from long-term barriers to economic growth.

least restrictive alternative Choosing a program with the least restrictive or secure setting that will best benefit the child.

legalization of drugs Decriminalizing drug use to reduce the association between drug use and crime.

liberal feminism Asserts that females are less delinquent than males, because their social roles provide them with fewer opportunities to commit crimes; as the roles of girls and women become more similar to those of boys and men, so too will their crime patterns.

life-course persisters Delinquents who begin their offending career at a very early age and continue to offend well into adulthood.

life-course theory Theory that focuses on changes in criminality over the life course; developmental theory.

mandatory sentence Defined by a statutory requirement that states the penalty to be set for all cases of a specific offense.

marijuana The dried leaves of the cannabis plant.

masculinity hypothesis View that women who commit crimes have biological and psychological traits similar to those of men.

meta-analysis A research technique that uses the grouped data from several different studies.

middle-class measuring rods Standards by which teachers and other representatives of state authority evaluate students' behavior; when lower-class youths cannot meet these standards they are subject to failure, which brings on frustration and anger at conventional society.

milieu therapy All aspects of the environment are part of the treatment, and meaningful change, increased growth, and satisfactory adjustment are encouraged; this is often accomplished through peer pressure to conform to the group norms.

minimal brain dysfunction (MBD) Damage to the brain itself that causes antisocial behavior injurious to the individual's lifestyle and social adjustment.

Miranda warning Supreme Court decisions require police officers to inform individuals under arrest of their constitutional rights; warning must also be given when suspicion begins to focus on an individual in the accusatory stage.

monetary restitution A requirement that juvenile offenders compensate crime victims for out-of-pocket losses caused by the crime, including property damage, lost wages, and medical expenses.

mood disorder A condition in which the prevailing emotional mood is distorted or inappropriate to the circumstances.

multisystemic therapy (MST) Addresses a variety of family, peer, and psychological problems by focusing on problem-solving and communication skills training.

National Crime Victimization Survey (NCVS) The ongoing victimization study conducted jointly by the Justice Department and the U.S. Census Bureau that surveys victims about their experiences with law violation.

nature theory Holds that low intelligence is genetically determined and inherited.

near-groups Clusters of youth who, outwardly, seem unified but actually have limited cohesion, impermanence, minimal consensus of norms, shifting membership, disturbed leadership, and limited definitions of membership expectations.

negative affective states Anger, depression, disappointment, fear, and other adverse emotions that derive from strain.

neglect Passive neglect by a parent or guardian, depriving children of food, shelter, health care, and love.

neurological Pertaining to the brain and nervous system structure.

neuroticism A personality trait marked by unfounded anxiety, tension, and emotional instability.

neutralization techniques A set of attitudes or beliefs that allow would-be delinquents to negate any moral apprehension they may have about committing crime so that they may freely engage in antisocial behavior without regret.

nonresidential programs Juveniles remain in their own homes but receive counseling, education, employment, diagnostic, and casework services through an intensive support system.

nuclear family A family unit composed of parents and their children; this smaller family structure is subject to great stress due to the intense, close contact between parents and children.

nurture theory Holds that intelligence is partly biological but mostly sociological; negative environmental factors encourage delinquent behavior and depress intelligence scores for many youths.

Office of Juvenile Justice and Delinquency Prevention (OJJDP) Branch of the U.S. Justice Department charged with shaping national juvenile justice policy through disbursement of federal aid and research funds.

orphan trains The name for trains in which urban youths were sent west by the Children's Aid Society for adoption with local farm couples.

overt pathway Pathway to a delinquent career that begins with minor aggression, leads to physical fighting, and eventually escalates to violent delinquency.

parens patriae Power of the state to act on behalf of the child and provide care and protection equivalent to that of a parent.

parental efficacy Families in which parents are able to integrate their children into the household unit while at the same time helping assert their individuality and regulate their own behavior

parole guidelines Recommended length of confinement and kinds of aftercare assistance most effective for a juvenile who committed a specific offense.

Part I crimes Offenses including homicide and non-negligent manslaughter, forcible rape, robbery, aggravated assault, burglary, larceny, arson, and motor vehicle theft; recorded by local law enforcement officers, these crimes are tallied quarterly and sent to the FBI for inclusion in the UCR.

Part II crimes All crimes other than Part I crimes; recorded by local law enforcement officers, arrests for these crimes are tallied quarterly and sent to the FBI for inclusion in the UCR.

passive speech A form of expression protected by the First Amendment but not associated with actually speaking words; examples include wearing symbols or protest messages on buttons or signs.

paternalistic family A family style wherein the father is the final authority on all family matters and exercises complete control over his wife and children.

persistence The process by which juvenile offenders persist in their delinquent careers rather than aging out of crime.

petition Document filed in juvenile court alleging that a juvenile is a delinquent, a status offender, or a dependent and asking that the court assume jurisdiction over the juvenile.

plea bargaining The exchange of prosecutorial and judicial concessions for a guilty plea by the accused; plea bargaining usually results in a reduced charge or a more lenient sentence.

pledge system Early English system in which neighbors protected each other from thieves and warring groups.

Poor Laws English statutes that allowed the courts to appoint overseers over destitute and neglected children, allowing placement of these children as servants in the homes of the affluent.

positive peer culture (PPC) Counseling program in which peer leaders encourage other group members to modify their behavior, and peers help reinforce acceptable behaviors.

posting A system of positions, facial expressions, and body language used by gang members to convey a message.

power-control theory Holds that gender differences in the delinquency rate are a function of class differences and economic conditions that influence the structure of family life.

precocious sexuality Sexual experimentation in early adolescence.

predatory crime Violent crimes against people, and crimes in which an offender attempts to steal an object directly from its holder.

prestige crimes Stealing or assaulting someone to gain prestige in the neighborhood; often part of gang initiation rites.

pretrial conference The attorney for the social services agency presents an overview of the case, and a plea bargain or negotiated settlement can be agreed to in a consent decree.

preventive detention Keeping the accused in custody prior to trial because the accused is suspected of being a danger to the community.

primary deviance Norm violations that have very little influence on the actor and can be quickly forgotten and/or overlooked.

primogeniture During the Middle Ages, the right of firstborn sons to inherit lands and titles, leaving their brothers the option of a military or religious career.

probable cause Reasonable grounds to believe that an offense was committed and that the accused committed that offense.

probation Nonpunitive, legal disposition for juveniles emphasizing community treatment in which the juvenile is closely supervised by an officer of the court and must adhere to a strict set of rules to avoid incarceration.

problem behavior syndrome (PBS) A cluster of antisocial behaviors that may include family dysfunction, substance abuse, smoking, precocious sexuality and early pregnancy, educational underachievement, suicide attempts, sensation seeking, and unemployment, as well as delinquency.

problem-oriented policing Law enforcement that focuses on addressing the problems underlying incidents of juvenile delinquency rather than the incidents only.

procedural justice An evaluation of the fairness of the manner in which an offender's problem or dispute was handled by police.

protective factor A positive prior factor in an individual's life that decreases the risk of occurrence of a future delinquent act.

psychodynamic theory Branch of psychology that holds that the human personality is controlled by unconscious mental processes developed early in childhood.

psychopathic personality (also known as sociopathic personality) A person lacking in warmth and affection, exhibiting inappropriate behavior responses, and unable to learn from experience.

psychotherapy Highly structured counseling in which a skilled therapist helps a juvenile solve conflicts and make a more positive adjustment to society.

public defender An attorney who works in a public agency or under private contractual agreement as defense counsel to indigent defendants.

racial threat theory As the size of the black population increases, the perceived threat to the white population increases, resulting in a greater amount of social control imposed against blacks.

randomized experimental design Considered the "gold standard" of evaluation designs to measure the effect of a program on delinquency or other outcomes. Involves randomly assigning subjects either to receive the program (the experimental group) or not receive it (the control group).

reality therapy A form of counseling that emphasizes current behavior and that requires the individual to accept responsibility for all of his or her actions.

reentry The process and experience of returning to society upon release from a custody facility postadjudication.

reform schools Institutions in which educational and psychological services are used in an effort to improve the conduct of juveniles who are forcibly detained.

reintegrative shaming Techniques used to allow offenders to understand and recognize their wrongdoing and shame themselves. To be reintegrative, shaming must be brief and controlled and then followed by ceremonies of forgiveness, apology, and repentance.

representing Tossing or flashing gang signs in the presence of rivals, often escalating into a verbal or physical confrontation.

residential programs Placement of a juvenile offender in a residential, nonsecure facility such as a group home, foster home, family group home, or rural home where the juvenile can be closely monitored and develop close relationships with staff members.

resource dilution A condition that occurs when parents have such large families that their resources, such as time and money, are spread too thin, causing lack of familial support and control.

restorative justice Using humanistic, nonpunitive strategies to right wrongs and restore social harmony.

retrospective reading The reassessment of a person's past to fit a current generalized label.

review hearings Periodic meetings to determine whether the conditions of the case plan for an abused child are being met by the parents or guardians of the child.

right to treatment Philosophy espoused by many courts that juvenile offenders have a statutory right to treatment while under the jurisdiction of the courts.

risk factor A negative prior factor in an individual's life that increases the risk of occurrence of a future delinquent act.

role conflicts Conflicts police officers face that revolve around the requirement to perform their primary duty of law enforcement and a desire to aid in rehabilitating youthful offenders.

role diffusion According to Erik Erikson, role diffusion occurs when youths spread themselves too thin, experience personal uncertainty, and place themselves at the mercy of leaders who promise to give them a sense of identity they cannot develop for themselves.

routine activities theory View that crime is a "normal" function of the routine activities of modern living; offenses can be expected if there is a motivated offender and a suitable target that is not protected by capable guardians.

rural programs Specific recreational and work opportunities provided for juveniles in a rural setting such as a forestry camp, a farm, or a ranch.

school failure Failing to achieve success in school can result in frustration, anger, and reduced self-esteem, which may contribute to delinquent behavior.

search and seizure The U.S. Constitution protects citizens from any search and seizure by police without a lawfully obtained search warrant; such warrants are issued when there is probable cause to believe that an offense has been committed.

secondary deviance Deviant acts that define the actor and create a new identity.

sedatives Drugs of the barbiturate family that depress the central nervous system into a sleeplike condition.

self-control theory The theory of delinquency that holds that antisocial behavior is caused by a lack of self-control stemming from an impulsive personality.

self-fulfilling prophecy Deviant behavior patterns that are a response to an earlier labeling experience; youths act out these social roles even if they were falsely bestowed.

self-report survey Questionnaire or survey technique that asks subjects to reveal their own participation in delinquent or criminal acts.

sentencing circle A peacemaking technique in which offenders, victims, and other community members are brought together in an effort to formulate a sanction that addresses the needs of all.

shame The feeling we get when we don't meet the standards we have set for ourselves or that significant others have set for us.

shelter care A place for temporary care of children in physically unrestricting facilities.

siege mentality Residents become so suspicious of authority that they consider the outside world to be the enemy out to destroy the neighborhood.

situational crime prevention Crime prevention method that relies on reducing the opportunity to commit criminal acts by (a) making them more difficult to perform, (b) reducing their reward, and (c) increasing their risks.

skinhead Member of a white supremacist gang, identified by a shaved skull and Nazi or Ku Klux Klan markings.

social bond Ties a person to the institutions and processes of society; elements of the bond include attachment, commitment, involvement, and belief.

social capital Positive relations with individuals and institutions, as in a successful marriage or a successful career, that support conventional behavior and inhibit deviant behavior.

social conflict theory Asserts that society is in a state of constant internal conflict, and focuses on the role of social and governmental institutions as mechanisms for social control.

social control Ability of social institutions to influence human behavior; the justice system is the primary agency of formal social control.

social control theory Posits that delinquency results from a weakened commitment to the major social institutions (family, peers, and school); lack of such commitment allows youths to exercise antisocial behavioral choices.

social disorganization theory The inability of a community to exert social control allows youths the freedom to engage in illegal behavior.

social ecology Theory focuses attention on the influence social institutions have on individual behavior and suggests that law-violating behavior is a response to social rather than individual forces operating in an urban environment.

social investigation report, predisposition report Developed by the juvenile probation officer, this report consists of a clinical diagnosis of the juvenile and his or her need for court assistance, relevant environmental and personality factors, and any other information that would assist the court in developing a treatment plan for the juvenile.

socialization The process by which human beings learn to adopt the behavior patterns of the community in which they live, which requires them to develop the skills and knowledge necessary to function within their culture and environment.

social learning theory Hypothesizes that delinquency is learned through close relationships with others; asserts that children are born "good" and learn to be "bad" from others.

social structure theories Explain delinquency using socioeconomic conditions and cultural values.

Society for the Prevention of Cruelty to Children First established in 1874, these organizations protected children subjected to cruelty and neglect at home or at school.

specific deterrence Sending convicted offenders to secure incarceration facilities so that punishment is severe enough to convince offenders not to repeat their criminal activity.

status frustration A form of culture conflict experienced by lower-class youths because social conditions prevent them from achieving success as defined by the larger society.

status offense Conduct that is illegal only because the child is under age.

status symbol Something, such as a possession, rank or activity, by which one's social or economic prestige is measured.

stigmatize To mark someone with disgrace or reproach; to characterize or brand someone as disgraceful or disreputable.

stimulants Synthetic substances that produce an intense physical reaction by stimulating the central nervous system.

strain theory Links delinquency to the strain of being locked out of the economic mainstream, which creates the anger and frustration that lead to delinquent acts.

stratified society Grouping society into classes based on the unequal distribution of scarce resources.

street efficacy Using one's wits to avoid violent confrontations and to feel safe.

substance abuse Using drugs or alcohol in such a way as to cause physical, emotional and/or psychological harm to yourself.

subterranean values The ability of youthful law violators to repress social norms.

suppression effect A reduction in the number of arrests per year for youths who have been incarcerated or otherwise punished.

swaddling The practice during the Middle Ages of completely wrapping newborns in long bandage-like clothes in order to restrict their movements and make them easier to manage.

symbolic interaction The concept of how people communicate via symbols—gestures, signs, words, or images—that stand for or represent something else.

systematic review A research technique that involves collecting the findings from previously conducted studies, appraising and synthesizing the evidence, and using the collective evidence to address a particular scientific question.

target-hardening technique Crime prevention technique that makes it more difficult for a would-be delinquent to carry out the illegal act, for example, by installing a security device in a home.

teen courts Courts that make use of peer juries to decide nonserious delinquency cases.

tracking Dividing students into groups according to their ability and achievement levels.

trait theory Holds that youths engage in delinquent or criminal behavior due to aberrant physical or psychological traits that govern behavioral choices; delinquent actions are impulsive or instinctual rather than rational choices.

tranquilizers Drugs that reduce anxiety and promote relaxation.

transfer hearing Preadjudicatory hearing in juvenile court for the purpose of determining whether juvenile court should be retained over a juvenile or waived and the juvenile transferred to adult court for prosecution.

transfer process Transfer of a juvenile offender from the jurisdiction of juvenile court to adult criminal court.

transitional neighborhood Area undergoing a shift in population and structure, usually from middle-class residential to lower-class mixed use.

transnational crime Crime that is carried out across the borders of two or more countries and violates the laws of those countries.

truant Being out of school without permission.

truly disadvantaged According to William Julius Wilson, those people who are left out of the economic mainstream and reduced to living in the most deteriorated inner-city areas.

turning points Positive life experiences such as gaining employment, getting married, or joining the military, which create informal social control mechanisms that limit delinquent behavior opportunities.

underachievers Those who fail to meet expected levels of school achievement.

underclass Group of urban poor whose members have little chance of upward mobility or improvement.

Uniform Crime Report (UCR) Compiled by the FBI, the UCR is the most widely used source of national crime and delinquency statistics.

utilitarians Those who believe that people weigh the benefits and consequences of their future actions before deciding on a course of behavior.

victimization The number of people who are victims of criminal acts; young teens are 15 times more likely than older adults (age 65 and over) to be victims of crimes.

victim service restitution The juvenile offender is required to provide some service directly to the crime victim.

waiver (also known as bindover or removal) Transferring legal jurisdiction over the most serious and experienced juvenile offenders to the adult court for criminal prosecution.

watch system Replaced the pledge system in England; watchmen patrolled urban areas at night to provide protection from harm.

wayward minors Early legal designation of youths who violate the law because of their minority status; now referred to as status offenders.

widening the net Phenomenon that occurs when programs created to divert youths from the justice system actually involve them more deeply in the official process.

wilderness probation Programs involving outdoor expeditions that provide opportunities for juveniles to confront the difficulties of their lives while achieving positive personal satisfaction.

writ of habeas corpus Judicial order requesting that a person detaining another produce the body of the prisoner and give reasons for his or her capture and detention.

zero tolerance policy Mandating specific consequences or punishments for delinquent acts and not allowing anyone to avoid these consequences.

Budtz-Jorgensen, E., 110n78
Buerger, Michael, 482
Buffet, Warren, 128
Bugh, Henry, 437
Bullington, B., 525n47
Bumphus, Vic, 213n99
Burch, James H., 321; 329n110; 330n118
Burgess, Robert, 284nn138, 139
Burghardt, John, 428nn88, 90
Burke, Jeffrey, 94
Burnett, Darla M., 526n65
Burns, Elizabeth, 365n68
Burns, Jerald, 572n123
Burns, Shelley, 365n68
Burruss, George W., Jr., 525n11
Bursik, Robert, 150nn30, 34, 38; 151n78;
    213nn92, 124
Burt, Callie Harbin, 213n118; 281n4
Burt, Cyril, 224; 243n49
Burton, Velmer, 66n62; 151n103; 243n25
Bushman, Brad, 46; 65n31; 97; 112n185
Bushway, Shawn D., 109nn16, 19; 179n55;
    212n62; 285n178
Bussman, K., 284n124
Butterfield, Fox, 395n19; 397nn85, 109; 456n44;
    482
Butts, Jeffrey A., 450–451; 456n42; 527n123
Bynum, Timothy, 150nn9, 46;
    329nn90, 100
Byrne, James M., 150n48; 489n120; 570n19;
    572n106
Byrnes, Hilary, 150n27

C
Cabaniss, Emily R., 571n89
Cadoret, Remi, 111n132
Caeti, Troy, 26
Cahahn, Sorel, 113n227
Cahalan, Margaret Werner, 571n55
Cai, Bo, 110n86
Cain, Colleen, 111n132
Caldwell, M. G., 113n222
Caldwell, Michael F., 556; 572n109
Caldwell, Roslyn, 282n54; 364n3
Calhoun, George, 244n96
Callahan, Charlene M., 450–451
Callahan, S., 244n69
Calonge, Ned, 427n33; 457n51
Campbell, Anne, 213n91; 243nn15, 48; 244n58;
    329n82
Campbell, Suzanne, 109n37
Campos-Flores, Arian, 329n102
Cancino, Jeffrey Michael, 151nn62, 66
Canela-Cacho, Jose, 110n53
Canfield, Richard L., 110n85
Cannon, Jill, 364nn11, 12, 16
Cantor, David, 384; 397n87
Capaldi, Deborah, 211n20; 328n27; 396n41
Capowich, George E., 152n104
Carbonell, Joyce, 113n211
Carcach, Carlos, 602n25
Cardwell, Timothy J., 270
Carlson, Bonnie, 112n175
Carnagey, Nicholas, 112n179
Carrano, Jennifer, 282n55
Carrington, Kerry, 218; 243n3; 245n142
Carrozza, Mark, 153nn171, 183;
    283nn76, 79
Carter, David, 26–27

Carter, Deborah Brown, 476; 488n94
Cartwright, Desmond, 152n150; 292
Carvalho de Noronha, José, 602n21
Caspi, Avshalom, 111nn123, 129; 211nn9, 19, 25;
    212nn43, 52, 67; 214nn137, 139; 244n63;
    282n41
Castellano, Thomas, 572n120
Catalano, Richard F., 191; 214n140; 281n2;
    328n30; 330n115; 364n17; 397n96; 427n56;
    428nn96, 97, 101, 103, 105
Catalano, Shannan, 65n19; 66n97
Cauffman, Elizabeth, 112n163; 214n130; 244n80;
    282n70; 526n65; 571nn76, 79
Cavanagh, Shannon E., 428n100
Cernkovich, Stephen, 65n13; 150n6; 153n182;
    179n51; 211n12; 212n70; 214n139; 328n37
Chachere, Gregory, 112n182
Chaiken, Marcia, 396nn71, 72, 75, 79
Chakrabarti, Nandini, 84
Challinger, D., 283n78
Chamberlain, Patricia, 427n37; 571n46
Chamberlain, Robert, 427n27
Chamlin, Mitchell, 202; 214n126
Chapin, Deborah A., 525n46
Chapman, Derek A., 526n63
Chapman, John F., 571n86
Chappel, Duncan, 64n5
Charlebois, P., 66n89
Chart-Wierschem, Deborah, 330n157
Chase-Lansdale, P. Lindsay, 427n44
Chen, Aimin, 110n86
Chen, C.-Y, 150n50
Chen, Fengling, 244n96
Chen, Yi-Fu, 112n167; 151n100
Cheng, Zhongqi, 110n80
Cherlin, Andrew, 282nn52, 53
Chesney-Lind, Meda, 229; 238, 239; 245nn121,
    131, 132, 135, 139, 140; 328n3; 329n83; 475;
    488nn86, 88; 571n95
Chidi, George, 328n1
Chien, I., 396n49
Chiesa, James, 427nn31, 38
Chilcoat, Howard, 211n34
Chilton, Roland, 178n14; 282n30
Chiricos, Ted, 46
Chiu, Tina, 25
Chou, Chih-Ping, 328n36
Christakis, Dimitri, 112n184
Christakos, Antigone, 396n76
Christenson, R. L., 152n134
Christiansen, B. A., 396n67
Christiansen, Karl O., 111n134
Chung, He Len, 211n32
Chung, Ick-Joong, 212n45
Cicchetti, Dante, 283n108
Cicourel, Aaron, 488n72
Cimmarusti, Rocco, 365n83
Cirillo, Kathleen, 113n203
Clapp, Neale, 571n47
Clark, John, 65n15; 487n28
Clarke, Gregory N., 94
Clarke, Ronald, 110n59
Clayton, Richard, 365n48; 391
Cleckley, Hervey, 100; 113n218
Cleveland, H. Harrington, 113n225
Clinard, Marshall B., 603n37
Clingempeel, W. Glenn, 212n39; 397n122
Cloward, Richard, 133–134; 152nn123–128; 313;
    396n44; 404

Coates, Robert, 570n8
Cochran, John, 113n238; 153n177; 213n92
Cocozza, Joseph, 571nn76, 79
Cohen, Albert K., 131–133; 152nn114–117,
    119–121; 313; 330n139; 341; 364n30
Cohen, Debra, 488nn112, 117, 118
Cohen, Jacqueline, 65n26; 110n53
Cohen, Lawrence, 66n67; 73; 109n20, 28;
    112n140
Cohen, Mark A., 402; 409; 426nn2–4, 6, 7
Cohen, Nora, 113n227
Cohen, Patricia, 46; 112n185; 211n26
Cohen, Robert, 328n28
Cohn, Ellen, 65n32
Coie, John, 58; 328nn9–11, 26
Colden, Cadwallader, 434
Colditz, Graham, 150n7
Cole, Kristin C., 428nn81–83
Coley, Rebekah Levine, 151n72
Colletti, Patrick, 110n93; 113n221
Collins, Mark, 212n63
Collins, Rebecca, 32n6
Collins-Hall, Lori, 396n66
Colman, Adrian, 365n72
Colman, Robyn, 365n72
Colvin, Mark, 204
Comings, David, 244n65
Conger, Dylan, 525n28
Conger, Rand, 152n131; 178n25; 213n120;
    282nn38, 56
Conley, Dalton, 110n71
Conley, Darlene, 488n91
Connell, Patricia, 527n115
Conrad, John, 66nn71, 86
Conway, Allan, 571n95
Cook, Glenn, 365n81
Cook, Philip, 243n8
Cook, William, 452; 457n66
Cooley, Charles Horton, 178n3; 179n44
Coomer, Brandi Wilson, 65n25
Coon, Dennis, 395n6
Cooper, Edith Fairman, 457n54
Cooper, Harris, 428n70
Cooper, Sara, 433
Coppa, Frank J., 456n3
Corbett, Ronald, 560; 572n124
Cordella, Peter, 111n109
Cornell, Amy, 244n82
Cornell, Claire Pedrick, 283n100
Cornwell, Benjamin, 152n136; 328n6
Corrado, J., 396n47
Cortese, Samuele, 110n78
Cory, Stella, 508–509
Costa, Francis, 211n18
Costa, Joseph J., 281n13; 284n142
Costanzo, Philip, 328n9
Cota-Robles, Sonia, 282n58
Cottler, Linda, 396n27
Cotton, Edward, 157
Coupe, Richard Timothy, 109nn25, 36
Cowie, John, 244nn57, 89
Cowie, Valerie, 244nn57, 89
Cox, Louis B., 163; 179n53; 530; 570n2
Craig, Rebecca, 571n69
Craig, Wendy M., 243n23; 427nn24, 25, 42
Creamer, Vicki, 152n144
Cressey, Donald, 136–138; 152n142
Cretacci, Michael, 153n174

Crimmins, Susan, 32*n*7
Croisdale, Tim, 110*n*55
Cromwell, Paul F., 570*nn*4, 5
Crosby, Alex, 508–509
Crosby, L., 212*n*41
Crosby, Rick, 211*n*21
Crosnoe, Robert, 153*nn*162, 163
Cross, Tim, 428*nn*93, 94
Crowder, Martin J., 84
Crowe, Raymond, 111*n*132
Crowell, Nancy A., 427*n*25; 428*nn*61, 70, 71, 87;
    457*nn*60, 63; 487*n*63; 488*n*107; 572*n*143;
    591; 603*n*40; 604*n*81
Cuellar, Alison Evans, 525*n*50
Cuevas, Maribel, 187
Cullen, Francis T., 64*n*4; 66*n*62; 132; 151*n*103;
    152*nn*106, 132; 153*nn*165, 170, 171, 183;
    178*n*8; 202; 214*nn*126–128;
    243*n*25; 282*nn*51, 72; 283*nn*76, 79; 364*n*32;
    409; 457*n*61
Culliver, Concetta, 111*n*103
Culross, Patti L., 426*n*1; 427*n*26
Cummings, Scott, 328*n*2
Cunningham, Lea, 330*n*113
Cunningham, Phillippe B., 397*n*121
Curran, F. J., 284*n*160
Currie, Elliot, 526*n*93; 571*n*51
Currie, Janet, 405; 457*n*50
Curry, G. David, 151*n*56; 292; 330*nn*111, 154;
    331*n*180
Curtis, Lynn A., 428*n*89
Cuzzola-Kern, Amy, 245*n*130

D

Daigle, Leah, 64*n*4; 214*nn*127, 128
D'Alessio, Stewart, 65*nn*43, 47; 282*n*40
Dal Forno, Gloria, 213*n*116
Dalton, Katharina, 227; 244*n*73
Daly, Kathleen, 179*n*79; 245*n*121
Daly, Martin, 66*n*73; 112*n*141; 151*nn*52, 85;
    213*n*115; 284*nn*133–135
Dammer, Harry R., 582–583; 603*nn*50, 76;
    604*nn*105, 106
Dan, Heather, 244*n*82
Daniele, Antoinietta, 184*n*135
Dannefer, Dale, 65*n*36; 488*nn*77, 81
Dannerbeck, Anne, 283*n*92
Dassey, Brendan, 101
Datesman, Susan, 33*nn*56, 57
Datta, Geetanjali Dabral, 150*n*7
Davidson, Howard, 525*n*13
Davies, Mark, 396*n*45
Davies, Scott, 179*n*58
Davies, Susan, 211*n*21
Davies-Netley, Sally, 283*n*117
Davis, Carla, 245*n*137; 281*n*22
Davis, Kenneth Culp, 476; 487*n*55; 488*n*96
Davis, Lonna, 276
Davis, Nanette, 9; 32*n*5
Davis, Samuel M., 487*n*40
Davison, Elizabeth, 109*n*26
Dawkins, Marvin, 396*n*84
Dawley, David, 328*n*39
Dawson, Robert O., 520; 527*n*128
Day, H. D., 113*nn*235, 236
Day, L. Edward, 364*n*17
Day, Nancy, 283*n*89
Dean, Charles W., 211*n*17; 212*n*51; 488*n*107
Deane, Glenn, 64*n*3

DeAngelo, Andrew J., 570*n*32
DeBaryshe, Barbara, 211*n*14
Deboutte, Dirk, 282*n*54
Decker, Scott H., 65*n*11; 311; 329*nn*90, 100;
    330*nn*111, 129; 482
De Coster, Stacy, 112*nn*168, 169; 150*n*37;
    151*n*102
Dedel, Kelly, 489*n*119, 525*n*1; 570*n*20
DeFina, Robert, 44; 46; 179*n*78
DeFronzo, James, 152*n*129
de Goede, Martijn, 244*n*79
de Gruyter, Aldine, 284*n*124
DeJong, Christina, 65*n*45; 109*n*47; 178*n*17;
    282*n*34
DeKeseredy, Walter, 243*n*36
De Li, Spencer, 109*n*46; 212*n*61
Delisi, Matt, 402; 426*n*5; 488*n*94
Delon, Jeremy, 199
DeLone, Miriam, 65*n*39; 66*n*49; 488*n*84
Deluca, Stefanie, 151*n*60
Demaray, Michelle Kilpatrick, 365*n*47
Dembitz, Nanette, 284*n*131
Demos, John, 32*n*42
Den, Xiaogang, 213*n*95
Dentler, Robert, 66*n*61
Deptula, Daneen, 328*n*28
DeRios, M. D., 396*n*50
Desai, Rani A., 571*n*86
Deschenes, Elizabeth P., 213*n*121; 526*n*74;
    572*n*100
Des Jarlais, Don, 395*n*7
Devlin, Daniel, 486*n*2
Diaz, Rafael, 33*nn*54, 55; 244*n*61
DiClemente, Ralph, 211*n*21
Dietrich, Kim N., 110*nn*85, 86
Dietz, Robert D., 152*n*109
DiGiuseppe, David, 112*n*184
DiLalla, Lisabeth Fisher, 111*n*112
Di Luigi, Massimo, 213*n*116
DiMilio, Lisa, 450–451
Dinitz, Simon, 66*nn*71, 86; 152*n*159; 571*nn*56, 92
Dintcheff, Barbara, 109*n*24
Dionne, Ginette, 111*n*128
Dishion, Thomas J., 152*n*138; 291; 328*nn*27, 38;
    396*n*41; 426*n*15; 427*n*37; 428*n*64; 572*n*113
Ditchfield, John, 694*n*103
Dixon, Angela, 244*n*97
Dobkin, Patricia, 396*nn*56, 62
Dobrin, Adam, 214*nn*127, 128
Dodge, Douglas C., 525*n*17
Dodge, Kenneth A., 111*n*129; 113*n*195; 151*n*69;
    212*n*44; 282*n*73; 283*n*75; 291; 328*n*38
Dodge, Mary, 466; 487*nn*32, 33
Dohrenwend, Bruce, 178*n*8
Dolce, Philip, 456*n*3
Dominici, Cinzia, 213*n*116
D'Onfrio, Brian, 111*n*114
Donker, Andrea, 212*n*50
Donohue, John J., III, 45; 46
Donovan, John, 211*n*18
Donziger, Steven R., 397*nn*128, 132
Doob, Anthony N., 364*n*40; 409; 592; 593;
    603*n*61; 604*n*86
Dorn, Sherman, 338–339; 364*n*15
Dornfeld, Maude, 284*n*149
Downey, Douglas, 150*n*14; 283*n*77
Downs, William, 283*nn*106, 117
Doyle, Joseph, 260; 283*n*99
Draper, Patricia, 284*nn*138, 139

Drevon, Christian, 110*n*72
DuBois, David L., 428*n*70
Duggan, Anne K., 427*n*35; 457*n*51
Dumond, Doris, 488*n*107
Dunaway, R. Gregory, 66*n*62; 213*n*93; 243*n*25
Duncan, Greg J., 150*nn*16–20; 151*n*60; 284*n*161;
    427*n*44
D'Unger, Amy, 212*n*46
Dunlap, Earl, 525*n*37
Dunn, Melissa, 245*nn*120, 141
Dunworth, Terence, 463; 487*nn*19, 20
Durant, Lynne, 214*n*142
Durkheim, Émile, 126
Durrant, Lynne, 214*n*142
Dussault, Monique, 112*n*181
Dwiggins, Donna, 243*n*6
Dwyer, John, 153*n*191
Dwyer, Kevin, 347
Dyer, James, 397*n*113

E

Earls, Felton, 66*n*91; 151*n*67
Earnest, Terri, 150*n*48
Easson, W. M., 284*n*161
Eccles, Jacquelynne, 110*n*89; 244*n*60
Eck, John E., 285*n*178; 467; 487*nn*24, 37; 489*n*123
Edelson, Jeffrey I., 230–231; 235
Edwards, Leonard P., 285*n*175; 525*n*21; 527*n*128
Eels, Kenneth, 113*n*226
Eftekhari-Sanjani, Hossain, 243*n*26
Eggebeen, David, 32*n*14
Eggleston, Carolyn, 243*n*6
Eghigian, Mars, 329*nn*79, 80
Egley, Arlen, Jr., 329*nn*58, 61; 330*n*111
Einarsson, Emil, 113*n*216
Eisenberg, Marla, 345
Eisenbraun, Kristin, 364*n*2; 365*n*56
Eisner, Manuel, 603*n*37
Eitle, David, 65*nn*43, 47
Eldefonso, Edward, 571*nn*58, 59
Elder, Glen, 153*n*178; 213*n*120
Elder, Rob, 109*n*22
Elias, Albert, 571*n*47
Ellickson, Phyllis, 397*n*114
Elliott, Amanda, 151*nn*79, 80
Elliott, Delbert S., 65*n*36; 150*n*45; 151*nn*79,
    80; 178*n*27; 213*n*112; 375; 385; 396*n*39;
    397*nn*92, 93; 424; 427*n*55; 570*n*45
Elliott, Marc, 32*n*6
Ellis, Lee, 111*n*109; 112*nn*144, 145; 113*nn*239,
    240; 212*n*72; 213*n*87; 244*nn*70, 76–77
Ellison, Christopher, 282*n*62
Elonheimo, Henrik, 281*n*24
Empey, LaMar T., 65*n*22; 571*nn*47, 57
Engels, Rutger, 112*n*161
Engen, Rodney L., 65*nn*42, 46; 571*n*84
Englebrecht, David, 316
Ennett, Susan, 66*n*50; 397*n*112
Ensminger, Margaret, 281*n*2; 282*nn*52, 53
Epstein, Kitty Kelley, 179*n*75
Erickson, Kai, 157; 178*n*5
Erickson, Maynard, 65*n*22; 109*n*45; 571*n*47
Erikson, Erik, 4; 32*n*8; 91–92; 112*n*150
Eron, L., 113*n*198
Esbensen, Finn-Aage, 151*n*58; 213*n*121;
    329*nn*77, 101, 109; 330*n*154; 486*n*11;
    488*nn*101–103
Espelage, Dorothy, 112*n*163; 244*n*80
Estes, Richard J., 263; 284*n*126
Evans, Gary, 32*n*15; 150*n*20

Evans, Kristy, 330n117
Evans, Michelle, 45; 152n105
Evans, T. David, 66n62; 151n103; 243n25
Everingham, Susan S., 427n31
Eves, Anita, 84
Ewing, Darlene, 526n55
Eysenck, Hans, 100; 113nn208, 212
Eysenck, M. W., 113n212
Ezell, Mark, 525n49

F
Factor-Litvak, Pam, 110n80
Fader, James, 66n90
Fagan, Abigail A., 111n122; 243n12; 283n94; 424; 570n45
Fagan, Jeffrey, 66n94; 150n36; 152n113; 297; 329nn66, 67; 488n81; 525n43; 526n74
Fain, Terry, 570n23
Fairchild, Erika, 582–583; 603nn50, 76; 604nn105, 106
Fairman, Edith, 428n62
Falzer, Paul R., 571n86
Farabee, David, 572n106
Faraone, Stephen, 87
Farnworth, Margaret, 66n63; 191; 364n19
Farr, Kathryn Ann, 397n136
Farrall, Stephen, 212nn40, 55
Farrell, Graham, 397n98
Farrell, Michael, 109n24; 153n192; 243n33; 282n39
Farrington, David P., 65n18; 66nn65, 68, 71, 83, 86; 87–88; 109n21; 110nn60–62; 111nn117, 119, 121; 113nn209, 234; 188–189; 211nn16, 25, 35; 244nn86, 87; 258; 281n10; 283nn82–85, 93; 328n35; 397n118; 397nn114, 118; 408; 414; 426n6; 427nn22–25, 31, 43; 428nn70, 97, 111, 113; 457nn47–49; 467; 489n122; 546; 556; 566; 570nn29, 30; 572nn104, 107; 573n157; 591; 593; 603n37; 694n103
Farris, Elizabeth, 365n80
Fass, Simon M., 457n67
Fastabend, Annemarie, 110n81
Faulkner, Guy, 153n191
Faupel, Charles, 396n82
Faust, Frederick L., 427n20
Fein, Robert, 365n50
Feinberg, Seth, 152n109
Feingold, AlanMoffitt, Terrie, 213n106
Fejes-Mendoza, Kathy, 243n6
Feld, Barry C., 33n70; 469–470; 487n51; 520; 522; 526nn62, 78, 85; 527nn126, 127
Feldman, Marilyn, 111n98
Feldman, S. Shirley, 33nn54, 55; 244n61
Felson, Marcus, 73; 109nn20, 28; 110n57
Felson, Richard, 64n3; 152n112; 328n21; 364n28
Fendrich, Michael, 65n24; 374; 396nn36, 70
Ferdinand, Theodore, 437; 456nn24, 33; 487n61
Fergusson, David, 211n28; 212n44
Fergusson, L., 46
Ferrero, William, 224; 243nn2, 45–47
Ferri, Enrico, 80
Feucht, Thomas, 365n49
Feyerherm, William, 66n56
Fiedler, Mora, 150n47
Fienberg, Stephen, 110n83
Figlio, Robert, 55–56; 65n37; 109nn3, 41, 43; 211n5; 364nn22, 23

Figuerdo, Aurelio Jose, 112nn142, 143
Finckenauer, James O., 603n51; 603n65
Findlay, Mark, 603n55
Finkelhor, David, 218; 243n5; 284n127
Finkelstein, Matthew C., 543; 570nn37, 41
Finnegan, T., 517; 526nn75, 77
Firestone, Philip, 111n136
Fischer, Mariellen, 87
Fishbein, Diana, 110n73; 244nn71, 74
Fisher, Bonnie, 64n4; 213n84
Fisher, Deborah A., 426n7
Fisk, Wendy, 283n109
Fitzgerald, Marian, 584; 602nn1, 14; 603nn57, 59, 69
Fitzpatrick, Kevin, 329n110
Flaming, Karl, 150n47
Flanagan, Edward, 205
Flannery, Daniel J., 212n73; 243n34; 427n59
Flaving, Jeanne, 488n76
Fleisher, Mark, 300–301; 329nn81, 86
Fleming, Charles, 281n2
Fletcher, Kenneth, 87
Flewelling, Robert, 65n16; 66n50
Flitter, Jill Klotz, 283n119
Florin, Paul, 428n98
Flowes, Lucy, 433
Fogelson, Robert, 486n2
Foley, Michael, 32n7
Ford, Jason A., 385; 397n94
Forde, David, 212n81
Forehand, Rex, 396nn57, 58
Forero, Juan, 397nn100, 101
Forgays, Deborah Kirby, 450–451
Formoso, Diana, 282n44
Forrest, Walter, 213n119
Fort, Jeff, 305
Fortas, Abe, 358; 438
Fortson, Edward, 66n59; 150n12
Foster, Holly, 211n13
Fowler, Tom, 111n113
Fox, James A., 48; 65n27
Fox, Kristan, 65n44; 571n82
Fox, Sanford J., 456nn7, 10, 18, 19, 26, 27, 29; 526nn54, 91
Frabutt, James M., 571n89
Frank, James, 486n10
Franklin, J. M., 113nn235, 236
Fraser, Brian G., 283n103
Fraser, Matthew, 358
Frazee, Sharon Glave, 109n26
Frazier, Charles E., 473–474, 475; 488nn82, 83, 87; 526n82
Frease, Dean, 364nn30, 33
Freedman, Jonathan, 112nn187, 188
Freeman, Taneekah, 570n9
Freeman-Gallant, Adrienne, 111n120
Freemon, Melinda, 65n9
Frehsee, D., 284n124
Freisthler, Bridget, 151n59
Freng, Adrienne, 488nn101, 103
Freud, Anna, 514–515; 526n98
Freud, Sigmund, 91; 112n149; 225; 244n53
Frick, Paul, 244n82
Friedman, Ruth J., 427n44
Friedman, Samuel, 395n7
Friedrich-Cofer, Lynette, 112n182
Fritsch, Eric, 26
Frost, Laurie, 113n210
Frost, Martin, 526n74

Frydl, Kathleen, 475; 486nn7, 8; 487nn37, 69; 488n71; 489n123
Fuddy, Loretta, 427n35; 457n51
Fuentes, Angel Ilarraza, 525n32
Fukurai, Hiroshi, 178nn29, 36
Fulkerson, Andrew, 110n58
Fullilove, Mindy, 508–509
Fuqua-Whitley, Dawna, 482
Fyfe, James, 109n37; 488n76

G
Gaarder, Emily, 230–231; 244nn100, 101, 104; 526n69; 570n11; 572n98
Gabor, Thomas, 428n109; 602n17
Gabrielli, William, 111n135
Gadd, David, 212n40
Gadow, Kenneth, 112n181
Gaffney, Michael, 151n62
Gagnon, C., 66n89
Gaines, Larry K., 488n113
Gainey, Randy, 151n73
Gall, Carlotta, 397n103
Galvin, Jim, 178n14
Gamble, Thomas J., 245n130
Gamble, Wendy, 282n58
Ganousis, Jeanette, 527n115
Gant, Charles, 87
Garces, Eliana, 405; 457n50
Garcia, Crystal A., 365n69
Garcia, Robert, 329n87
Gardner, William, 244n67
Garfinkel, Harold, 163; 179n48
Garfinkel, Robin, 110n82
Garland, Ann, 244n81
Garner, Bonnie Chenoweth, 153nn165, 170
Garnier, Helen, 153n168
Garofalo, Rafaele, 80; 110n68
Garrett, Ronnie, 396n27
Garrison, Arthur H., 450–451
Gatling, Jewel M., 402; 426n5
Gatti, Uberto, 330n112; 603n62
Gaylor, Rita, 571n80
Geis, Gilbert, 64n5; 525n48
Geller, Susan Rose, 214n141
Gelles, Richard, 262–263; 283n100; 284nn136, 121–123, 157
Gelsthorpe, Loraine, 596; 604nn96, 98, 104
Gendrot, Sophie, 602nn10, 12
Gerard, D. L., 396n49
Gerber, Jurg, 397n134
Gerdes, D., 110n88
Gerstein, Dean, 211n26; 282n35
Gerstein, Steven, 527n110
Gerstenblith, Stephanie A., 427nn79, 85
Gertz, Marc, 457n62; 521–522; 527nn139, 140
Gesch, C. Bernard, 84
Gesiriech, Sarah, 284n148
Giacobbe, George A., 572n115
Giacomazzi, Andrew, 331n175
Gibbons, Donald C., 113n206; 244n94; 525n47
Gibbs, Jack, 109n45; 179n52
Gibbs, John, 213n98; 243n25
Giblin, Matthew, J., 570n18
Gibson, Chris, 151n62
Giddings, Martha, 475
Gies, Steve V., 565
Giever, Dennis, 213n88; 213n98; 243nn11, 25

Henderson, Charles R., 427*nn*27, 28
Hendriks, Jan, 113*n*213
Henggeler, Scott W., 113*nn*193, 194; 212*n*39; 281*n*7; 282*n*27; 390; 397*nn*121, 122; 546
Hennessy, James, 282*n*68
Hernandez, Daphne, 151*n*72
Hernandez, Rudy, 428*n*95
Herrenkohl, Todd, 58; 211*n*35; 212*n*38
Herrera, Veronica, 244*n*98; 282*n*46
Herrnstein, Richard, 102–103; 109*n*8; 111*n*137; 112*n*139; 113*n*232; 196; 212*nn*74–76
Herz, Denise C., 487*n*27; 525*n*12
Hessing, Dick, 213*n*94
Hetherington, E. Mavis, 253
Hetherington, Joshua, 365*n*83
Hibell, Björn, 586; 603*nn*70, 72
Hickey, J., 113*n*192
Hickman, Matthew J., 487*nn*17, 18; 488*n*100
Higgins, James, 284*n*130
Hilbert, Richard, 151*n*88
Hill, Andreas, 110*n*94
Hill, Karl G., 212*n*45; 328*n*30; 330*n*115
Hindelang, Michael, 65*nn*26, 33; 102; 113*n*230; 153*n*184
Hinshaw, S. P., 87
Hipple, Natalie Kroovand, 174
Hirschel, J. David, 488*n*107
Hirschfield, Paul, 94; 112*n*172
Hirschi, Travis, 65*nn*26, 33; 66*nn*66, 67; 102; 113*n*230; 141–144; 152*nn*160, 161; 196–203; 202, 203; 211*n*24; 212*nn*77–79, 82, 83; 213*nn*86, 90, 102, 109; 256; 290; 328*n*23; 364*nn*27, 38
Ho, Ching-hua, 112*n*160
Hochhauser, Lois, 283*n*101
Hodge, Carole, 178*n*9
Hodges, Jill, 284*n*167
Hoepner, Lori, 110*n*82
Hoffman, Beth, 328*n*36
Hoffman, Harry, 112*n*144
Hoffman, John, 211*n*26; 282*n*35
Hoffman, Joseph, 109*n*24
Hogan, Michael, 150*n*42
Hoge, Robert, 212*n*64
Holleran, Lori K., 397*n*117
Hollist, Dusten, 66*n*59; 150*n*12
Holloway, Bruce E., 428*n*70
Holmes, Malcolm, 153*n*167
Holsinger, Alexander M., 275; 285*n*174; 571*n*97
Holsinger, Kristi, 245*n*120; 245*n*141; 275; 285*n*174; 571*n*97
Holttum, S., 345
Holtz, Larry, 487*n*54
Homes, Malcolm, 169*nn*68, 69
Honig, Alice S., 427*n*40
Hook Edward, III, 211*n*21
Hope, Trina, 153*n*173
Horn, W., 284*n*124
Horney, Julie, 65*n*17; 213*n*115; 244*n*75
Hornung, Richard, 110*n*85
Horowitz, Ruth, 331*n*174; 385; 396*nn*46, 68, 69, 73; 397*n*89
Horvath, John, 33*n*82
Horwood, L. John, 46; 211*n*28; 212*n*44
Hoshi, Akemi, 397*n*118; 428*n*70
Hoskin, Anthony, 64*n*3
Houbè, Jill, 427*n*31
Hough, Richard, 244*n*81; 283*n*117
Houston, James, 331*n*179

Howard, Gregory J., 211*n*24; 581; 603*nn*38, 42, 43
Howard, Philip, 694*n*103
Howell, James C., 66*nn*92, 96; 328*n*40; 330*nn*118, 122–125; 397*n*124; 427*n*60; 428*n*104; 449; 457*nn*46, 55; 526*nn*72, 74
Howes, Paul, 150*n*6; 281*n*23
Howie, Pauline, 244*n*97
Hsia, Heidi M., 571*nn*87, 88
Huange, Bu, 397*n*96
Huebner, Beth, 150*nn*9, 46
Huesmann, L., 113*n*198
Huff, C. Ronald, 330*n*138
Hughes, Thomas, 527*n*121
Huh, David, 256
Huizinga, David, 65*n*36; 66*n*96; 151*nn*58, 79, 80; 281*n*16; 282*n*28; 329*n*77; 330*n*154; 385; 396*n*39; 397*nn*88, 92, 93
Hulse-Killacky, Diana, 61
Hummer, Don, 489*n*121
Hummer, R. A., 151*n*86
Hung, Geoffrey, 330*n*117
Hunt, Dana, 395*n*18
Hunt, Geoffrey, 329*n*82; 330*nn*156, 162
Hunter, John, 178*n*9
Hurlburt, Michael, 283*n*117
Hurst, Hunter, 521; 527*nn*131, 138
Hurst, Yolander G., 486*n*10; 487*n*12
Hurwitz, Emanuel, 365*n*79
Hussmann, Judith, 244*n*79
Husted, David, 211*n*22
Huston, Aletha, 112*n*182
Hutchings, Bernard, 89; 111*n*134
Hutchinson, Delyse, 328*n*8
Hutson, H. Range, 330*n*131

I

Iacono, William, 111*n*127
Ialongo, Nicholas, 211*n*34
Ildefonso, Gilbert, 395*n*7
Immarigeon, Russ, 179*n*79
Inciardi, James A., 381; 385; 395*n*7; 396*nn*27, 46, 68, 69, 73, 82; 397*n*89
Inglis, Ruth, 281*n*11; 283*n*105
Ingraham, James, 360
Inkpen, Nova, 570*n*29
Iovanni, Leeann, 179*n*56
Ireland, Jane, 345
Ireland, Timothy, 285*n*172; 396*n*48
Irving, Hyacinth, 153*n*191
Irving, Mark H., 591; 593
Irwin, John, 488*n*90
Irwin, Katherine, 424; 570*n*45
Ishikawa, S., 113*n*221

J

Jacklin, Carol, 244*n*66
Jackson, Kenneth, 65*n*45; 124; 178*n*17; 282*n*34
Jackson, Linda, 178*n*9
Jackson, Lori, 111*n*98
Jackson, Pamela Irving, 329*n*57
Jackson-Beck, Marilyn, 571*n*68
Jacob, Ayad, 396*n*76
Jacobs, Bruce, 109*n*38; 365*n*74
Jacobs, Nancy, 488*nn*115, 116
Jacobson, Kristen, 111*n*124; 283*n*88
Jacobson, Ronald, 345
Jaffe, Peter, 282*n*45; 572*n*110

Jaffee, Sara R., 111*nn*123, 129; 252, 254; 282*n*41
Jameson, Elizabeth, 525*n*41
Jang, Sung Joon, 282*n*48; 282*n*60; 283*n*74; 364*n*19
Jarjoura, G. Roger, 66*n*64; 152*n*134
Jarvis, Dwight C., 571*n*54
Jay, Carter, 527*nn*139, 140
Jenkins, Jennifer, 364*n*40
Jenkins, Pamela, 26–27
Jenkins, Patricia, 153*n*172, 364*n*40
Jensen, Eric L., 109*n*41; 397*n*134
Jensen, Gary, 153*n*185; 245*n*127
Jensen, Peter S., 428*n*110; 571*nn*76, 79
Jesilow, Paul, 152*n*130; 179*n*95
Jessor, Richard, 211*nn*18, 23
Joe, Karen A., 487*n*31
Johansson, Peter, 113*n*217
Johnsen, Matthew, 364*n*20
Johnson, Brian D., 397*n*88; 526*n*67
Johnson, Bruce, 66*n*79; 384–385; 396*nn*71, 72, 75, 79
Johnson, Charlotte, 111*n*101
Johnson, Christine, 213*n*120
Johnson, Courtney, 328*n*9
Johnson, Dale L., 427*n*41
Johnson, James, 244*n*65
Johnson, Jeffrey, 46; 112*n*185
Johnson, Jo, 270
Johnson, Kelly Dedel, 489*n*119, 525*n*1; 570*n*20
Johnson, Lee Michael, 178*n*25
Johnson, Lloyd D., 395*n*1; 395*nn*8, 16
Johnson, Mark, 65*n*9
Johnson, Robert, 178*n*36; 211*n*26; 282*n*35; 508–509
Johnston, Lloyd D., 65*nn*23, 38; 109*n*10; 244*n*106; 373; 395*n*24; 396*mm*25, 26
Johnston, N., 282*n*33
Johnstone, J., 152*n*122
Jolliffe, Darrick, 211*n*16; 694*n*103
Jones, Judith B., 525*n*5
Jones, Lisa, 284*n*127
Jones, Marshall B., 428*n*84
Jones, Peter, 66*n*90
Jones, Richard Lezin, 571*n*71
Jones, Sharon, 525*n*25
Jones, Shayne, 150*n*49
Jones, Stephanie M., 405
Jones-Walker, Cheryl, 573*n*148
Jorgensen, Jenel S., 94
Jorgensen, P. J., 110*n*78
Joscelyne, T., 345
Judah, Richard, 87
Junger, Marianne, 153*n*179; 211*n*24; 213*n*94
Junger-Tas, Josine, 153*n*179; 581; 592; 603*nn*46, 47, 61
Jurgens, Janelle, 244*n*96
Jurich, Sonia, 450–451
Justice, Blair, 284*n*131
Justice, Rita, 284*n*131

K

Kaduce, Lonn, 526*n*82
Kahan, Dan M., 488*n*79
Kalb, Larry, 211*n*16
Kaltiala-Heino, Riittakerttu, 112*n*158
Kandel, Denise, 396*n*45
Kandel, E., 113*n*231
Kane, Candice, 321
Kane, Robert, 151*n*76

Kang, W., 517; 526nn75, 77
Kangaspunta, Kristiina, 603n39
Kanouse, David, 32n6
Kantor, Glenda Kaufman, 284n123
Kao, Grace, 127–128; 151n90
Kaplan, Howard, 178nn29, 30, 36; 179nn37, 39, 40; 211n26
Karoly, Lynn A., 364nn11, 12; 427n31
Karp, David R., 179n94
Kasen, Stephanie, 46; 112n185
Kassebaum, Nancy, 405
Katkin, D., 525n47
Katz, Charles, 65n11; 111n108; 330n170; 331n178
Kauffman, K., 113n192
Kaufman, Jeanne, 283n115
Kaufman, Joanne, 150n8; 365n49
Kaufman, Leslie, 525n27; 571n71
Kaufman, Robert L., 488n78
Kawachi, Ichiro, 150n7
Kay, Barbara, 152n159
Kaysen, Debra, 243n22
Kazdin, Alan E., 428n110
Kazemian, Lila, 65n18; 66n68
Keels, Micere, 151n60
Keenan, Kate, 58; 211n30; 328n25
Keilitz, Ingo, 111nn104, 107
Keith, Bruce, 254; 282n49
Kellam, Sheppard, 211n34
Kellerman, Arthur L., 482
Kellett, Sue, 113n220
Kelley, Thomas, 33n73
Kelling, George, 487n14
Kelly, Delos, 33n83; 109n45; 292; 364nn34, 37
Kelly, John, 253
Kelly, Marion R., 457n46
Kelly, Tara, 416
Kemp, Vicki, 596; 604nn96, 98, 104
Kempe, C. Henry, 261; 283nn102, 107; 284nn128, 129
Kempe, Ruth S., 283n107
Kempf-Leonard, Kimberly, 56–57; 66nn88, 92, 93; 109n48; 153n181; 245n130; 525n11
Kempinen, Cynthia, 572n129
Kendrick, Mary H., 571n89
Kennedy, David M., 482; 486n2; 488n114
Kennedy, Leslie, 212n81
Kennedy, Mike, 365n70
Kennedy, Randall, 473; 488n80
Kerbs, Jodi, 571n80
Kerbs, John Johnson, 522
Kerner, Hans-Juergen, 603n74; 604nn83–85, 88, 90, 99–102
Kerpelman, Jennifer, 244n105
Kerper, Hazel, 570nn4, 5
Kerr, Margaret, 113n217
Ketchum, Sandy, 49
Khoury, Jane, 110n85
Kidd, Sean, 33n71
KiDeuk, Kim, 109n44
Kierkus, Christopher, 282n50
Kiernan, Kathleen, 427n44
Kilburn, Karoly, 364n16
Kilburn, M. Rebecca, 364nn11, 12; 427n31
Killias, Martin, 581; 602n14; 603n37
Killinger, George, 570nn4, 5
Kilpatrick, Dean, 61; 365n54
Kim, Julia Yun Soo, 65n24; 374; 396n36
King, C., 284n161

Kingree, J. B., 112n160
Kinlock, Timothy, 211n33
Kinsman, Jayne, 365n83
Kirby, Katherine, 329nn79, 80
Kirk, David, 39; 65n10
Kistner, Janet, 283n112
Kitzman, Harriet, 427n28
Kiviouri, Janne, 112n158
Kjelsberg, Ellen, 94; 112n158
Kleck, Gary, 46
Kleiman, Mark A. R., 330n171
Klein, Dorie, 244n54
Klein, Helen A., 572n112
Klein, Jody, 487n67
Klein, Malcolm W., 292; 293; 302–303; 312; 313; 328n43; 329nn 49, 50, 89; 330nn113, 132, 133, 141, 151; 581; 603n46
Kline, Jennie, 110n80
Klinger, David, 151n75; 488nn74, 76
Klockars, Carl, 396n82
Klugel, J., 525n47
Knoofal, Eric, 110n79
Knox, George, 328n2; 329nn72, 73; 330n136
Knupfer, Anne Meis, 456n6
Ko, Susan J., 571nn76, 77, 79
Kobrin, Solomon, 33n83
Kochanek, Kenneth, 32n22
Kocieniewski, David, 486n1
Koebel, LaDonna, 364n17
Kohlberg, Lawrence, 98–99; 113nn191, 192
Kokkevi, Anna, 603nn70, 72
Komiya, Nobuo, 579
Kong, Rebecca, 584; 603n63
Konofal, Eric, 110n78
Koons, Barbara, 150n41
Kopczynski, Mary, 428n102
Koper, Christopher S., 487n38
Koroloff, Nancy, 571n80
Kort-Butler, Lisa, 151n102
Kosterman, Rick, 211n35; 212n38; 214n140; 397n96; 427n56
Kovandzic, Tomislav V., 109n35
Koziey, Lynne, 178n1
Kraemer, Helena Chmura, 428n110
Krahn, Harvey, 153n184
Kramer, John, 65n47
Krämer, Ursula, 110n81
Krauss, Clifford, 397n100
Krienert, Jessie, 300–301; 329nn81, 86
Krisberg, Barry, 66n96; 179n61; 331n173; 426n9; 526n93; 547; 570n8; 571n51
Krivo, Lauren, 45
Krohn, Marvin, 65n35; 66n63; 109n27; 110n63; 111n120; 153n186; 160; 178nn21, 33, 34; 179n58; 189; 191; 211nn6, 19, 23; 328n27; 330nn119, 121, 148, 152, 157; 364nn19, 20; 396nn43, 66
Kroovand, Natalie, 179n98
Krueger, P. M., 151n86
Kruttschnitt, Candace, 212nn63, 66; 284n149
Ksander, Margaret, 66n79
Kubrin, Charis, 150nn24, 44
Kuck, Sarah, 395n18
Kumpfer, Karol L., 152n133; 396n53; 426n18
Kumpulkinen, Kirsti, 281n24
Kupchik, Aaron, 526n66
Kurlychek, Megan C., 179n55; 526n67; 572n129
Kurtz, David, 475
Kurtz, Don, 150n8

Kurtz, Ellen, 150n41
Kurtz, Steven P., 396n27

L
Lab, Steven, 32n24
Lacasse, Lori, 110n93; 113n221
Lafazia, Andrea M., 428n105
LaFree, Gary, 66n51; 150nn4, 10; 364n9; 579; 603n44
LaGrange, Randy, 153n188; 397n95
LaGrange, Teresa, 153nn169, 180
La Greca, Annette, 328n7
Lahey, Benjamin, 111n114
Laidler, Karen Joe, 329nn82, 83; 330nn117, 156, 162
Laird, Robert, 212n44
Lally, J. Ronald, 427n40
LaMay, Mary, 243n19
Lambert, Sharon, 211n34
Lanctôt, Nadine, 163; 179n51
Land, Kenneth, 66n67; 109n28; 151n53; 212n46
Landsheer, Johannes, 243n37
Lane, Jodi, 330n165; 570n23
Lane, Roger, 486n2
Langan, Patrick A., 572n105; 603n37
Lange, James, 416; 428n63
Langhinrichsen-Rohling, Jennifer, 364n29
Langley, Kate, 111n113
Lanphear, Bruce P., 110n85
Lansford, Jennifer E., 291; 328n38
Lansing, Amy, 244n81
Lanyado, Monica, 284n167
Lanza-Kaduce, Lonn, 65n35
Laplante, David, 111n128
LaPrairie, Carol, 179n92
Larivee, S., 66n89
LaRosa, John, 66n74
Lascala, Elizabeth, 151n59
Lasley, James, 153n187
Latessa, Edward J., 573n146
Lattimore, Pamela K., 109n49; 330n128; 573n149
Laub, John, 66n70; 111n115; 178n28; 178n32; 190–195; 211n15; 212nn56, 57, 68; 252; 282n33; 283n91
Laucht, M., 110n88
Laufer, William, 213n85
Lauritsen, Janet, 396nn80, 81
Law, Fergus, 211n18
Lawrence, Richard, 364nn6, 41; 365n63; 570n17
Lazoritz, Martin, 211n22
Le, Thao N., 565
Leaf, Philip, 211n34
Lebel, Thomas, 179nn57, 60
LeBlanc, Marc, 66nn78, 89; 153n166; 211n35; 213n92
Lecendreux, Michel, 110nn78, 79
Lee, Leona, 109n39; 525n45
Lee, Matthew, 113n221; 150n48
Lee, Ruth, 244n92; 396n49
Lee, Shawna, 61
Lefforge, Noelle, 282n54
Leiber, Michael, 65nn44, 47; 571n82
Leiter, Jeffrey, 364n20
Lemert, Edwin E., 150nn3, 5; 158; 161; 178nn11, 12; 525n46
Lencz, Todd, 110n93; 113n221
Lengua, Liliana, 211n35; 212n38
Lero, Cheryl N., 409; 457n61
Leschied, Alan, 212n64

Whyatt, Robin W., 110n82
Whyte, William, 41
Wiatrowski, Michael, 153nn164, 185
Wiebe, Richard, 214n129
Wiebush, Richard G., 565; 570n19
Wieczorek, William, 396n74
Wiederman, Michael, 283n117
Wiener, Jög-A., 110n81
Wiersema, Brian, 402; 426n2
Wiesner, Margit, 211n29
Wig, Janet K., 591
Wikström, Per-Olof H., 212n53; 603n37
Wilbanks, William, 66n48
Wilcox, Pamela, 150n49; 214n136; 365n48
Wilder, Esther, 153n173
Wilens, Timothy, 87
Wilhelm, C., 110n88
Will, Joseph, 491
Williams, Bryn, 284n167
Williams, Catrina, 365n68
Williams, James L., 604n89
Williams, Kirk R., 427n55; 546
Williams, Linda Meyer, 230–231; 235; 245n122;
    283n118; 284n166
Williams, Mark, 113n196
Williams, Nicholas, 364n32
Williams, Phil, 603nn51, 53, 54
Williams, Stephanie, 153n176
Williamson, Deborah, 450–451
Wilson, B., 396n82
Wilson, David B., 397n114; 414; 451; 457n59;
    556; 572nn107, 126–128
Wilson, G. T., 396n51
Wilson, James Q., 102–103; 109n8; 111n137;
    112n139; 113n232; 196; 212nn74–76;
    365n57; 427n25; 457n56; 486n9; 487n14;
    570n44; 603n36
Wilson, Janet, 109n10; 244n106
Wilson, John, 66n96
Wilson, Margo, 66n73; 112n141; 151n52;
    213n115; 284nn133–135
Wilson, O. W., 486n6
Wilson, Robin Fretwell, 284n145
Wilson, Sandra Jo, 559; 572n122
Wilson, Susan, 282n45
Wilson, William Julius, 150n22; 151nn79, 80,
    85; 167–168; 179nn76, 77; 300; 329nn59,
    60, 74, 75

Wilver, Warren, 584
Windham, Amy, 427n35; 457n51
Windle, Michael, 244n83
Wines, Enoch, 433
Winfree, L. Thomas, Jr., 329n101; 330n161;
    486n11
Wingood, Gina, 211n21
Winick, Charles, 396n38
Winneke, Gerhard, 110n81
Winner, Lawrence, 526n82
Winterdyk, John A., 579; 592; 593; 602n17;
    603n78; 604n82
Wish, Eric, 397nn88, 97
Wislar, Joseph S., 65n24; 374; 396n36
Wissow, Lawrence, 282n63
Witner, Helen, 64n8
Wittekind, Janice Clifford, 213n94
Wittinger, Naureen, 111n113
Wittrock, Stacy, 150n37
Wolfe, David, 282n45
Wolfgang, Marvin, 55–56; 65n37; 66nn71, 71, 84,
    85, 87; 109n3; 110n66; 183; 211n5; 282n33;
    339; 364nn22, 23
Wolfinger, Nicholas, 254
Wolford, Bruce, 364n17
Womer, Shannon C., 85; 427nn79,
Wong, Dennis S. W., 592
Wong, Frank, 112n182
Wood, Peter, 113n238; 213nn92, 93
Wood, Wendy, 112n182
Woods, Daniel, 570n29
Woolard, Jennifer, 525nn9, 10; 526n65
Woolfenden, Susan R., 546
Wooton, Barbara, 111n115; 283n80
Worden, Robert E., 471; 487n59, 64; 488n75
Wordes, Madeline, 525n25
Wormith, J. Stephen, 113n206
Worrall, John L., 488n113
Wright, Bradley Entner, 204; 211nn9, 19; 212n67;
    214nn137, 139
Wright, Claudia, 33n61
Wright, Darlene, 329n110
Wright, Daryl, 428nn93, 94
Wright, Jack, 243n40
Wright, John Paul, 132; 152nn106, 132;
    153nn171, 183; 202; 213n89; 214n126; 256;
    282n51; 283nn76, 79, 86; 328n20; 364n32
Wright, Lloyd, 397n90

Wright, Nat, 397nn129–131
Wright, Richard, 396nn80, 81
Wu, B., 475; 525n32
Wu, Chyi-In, 152n131
Wundram, Sabine, 110n81
Wung, Phen, 211n30

Y
Yablonsky, Lewis, 113n219; 313–314; 329n69;
    330nn149, 150
Yang, Yaling, 110n93
Yeh, Stuart, 365n82
Yeung, W. Jean, 150nn18, 19
Yili, Xu, 150n47
Yisrael, Donnovan Somera, 33nn54, 55; 244n61
Yokoyama, Minoru, 579; 603n79
Yolton, Kimberly, 110n85
Young, Kimball, 113n229
Yue, Liling, 603n33
Yun, Steve Chong, 329n105

Z
Zaff, Jonathan, 153n176
Zak, Lydia, 282n45
Zakriski, Audrey, 243n40
Zatz, Marjorie S., 329n53; 570n11
Zavlek, Shelley, 457n55; 570n44
Zawacki, Susanna, 33n62
Zeeb, Linda, 281n26
Zehr, Howard, 179n80
Zernike, Kate, 395n19; 603n73
Zhang, Lening, 178n24; 213n95; 396n74; 570n22
Zhang, Quanwu, 328n25
Zhang, Sheldon X., 570n22
Zhao, Jihong, 151n62
Zheng, Yan, 110n80
Zhong, Hua, 65n34; 243n43
Zigler, Edward, 285nn177, 179; 405; 427n54
Zimmerman, Frederick, 112n184
Zimmerman, Grégoire, 112n159
Zimmerman, Joel, 111nn104, 107
Zimmerman, Rick, 391
Zimring, Franklin E., 487n36; 503; 510; 525n52;
    526n82; 527n133; 603n45
Zingraff, Matthew, 285n171; 364n20; 488n78
Zlotnick, S. Jack, 112nn147, 155, 164
Zongping, Xiang, 427n50
Zurawan, Andrew, 603n47

Court Appointed Special Advocates (CASA) program, 493
court-ordered school attendance, 515
courts, 11. *See also* due process; juvenile courts; waiver
  abused children and, 271–272
  chancery courts, 15
  children, testimony by, 271–272
  drug courts, 450–451
  in England, 598
  removal of juveniles to, 19
  in restorative justice approach, 173
  teen courts, 450–452
covert pathway, 185
crack, 368–369
  dealers, 381
CRASH (Community Resources Against Street Hoodlums), 321–322
Creating the Dropout (Dorn), 338
crime. *See also* homicides; property crimes; schools; UCR (Uniform Crime Report)
  cleared crimes, reporting, 36
  in differential association theory, 137
  evolutionary theory, 89–90
  gangs and, 10, 133–134, 309–310
  international crime, 583
  mapping, 42
  maternal rejection and, 83
  National Crime Victimization Survey (NCVS), 40
  NIBRS (National Incident-Based Reporting System), 38
  pathways to, 185–186
  physical basis of, 80
  predatory crime, 73
  prestige crimes, 311
  self-reports, 39–40
  transnational crime, 582–583
  trends, 42–48
Crime, Shame, and Reintegration (Braithwaite), 169–170
Crime and Disorder Act, England, 599
Crime and Human Nature (Wilson & Herrnstein), 102, 196
Crime and the American Dream (Messner & Rosenfeld), 128
Crime in the Making (Sampson & Laub), 190–191
criminal atavism, 80
criminal justice *vs.* juvenile justice, 446–447
criminal laws, 18–19
Crips, 287, 291, 294, 305
  colors of, 303
Crips gang, 535
crisis, youth in, 4–5
critical theory. *See* social conflict theory
crop eradication, 387
cross-examination, right to, 444
cross-national research, 580–588
  benefits of, 582–583
  on drug use, 585–587
  problems of, 581–582
  on property crime, 584–585
  on social bond theory, 143
  trends in delinquency and, 587–588
  on violence, 583–584
crowds, 288
Crown Court, England, 598
Crown Prosecution Service (CPS), England, 597–598
cult of individualism, 9

cultural deviance theories, 120, 130–134
  delinquent subcultures theory, 131–133
  differential opportunity theory, 133–134
cultural transmission, 120
culture. *See also* anomie; cultural deviance theories; race/ethnicity
  American Dream culture, 128
  conflict, 137
  gender differences and, 221
  general theory of crime and, 202
  of poverty, 117
  self-control theory and, 199
cumulative disadvantage, 191
  increasing levels of, 193
curfews
  and community-based policing service, 480
  laws, 26–27
custodial interrogation, 469–470
cynicism, 4, 117
Czech Republic, alcohol use in, 587

D

damaged identity, 160
dance programs, 420
D.A.R.E. (Drug Abuse Resistance Education), 389, 390–391, 461
data mining, 42
date-rape drug, 388
dating violence, 236
day care programs, 249–250, 410–411
day treatment programs, 449
Dead Boys, 292
Dead Rabbits, 293
dealers. *See* drug dealers
death penalty, 16, 157, 517–518
decarceration policy, 537, 548
decent values, 132
defense attorneys, 492–493
defiance, 204
degradation ceremonies, 163
deinstitutionalization, 24, 566
delinquency
  concept of, 17–19
  control, 400
  control squads, 460
  correlates of, 48–55
  developmental view of, 54
  findings, 511
  legal status of, 17–18
  and *parens patriae*, 17
  repression, 400
  sanctions and, 18–19
Delinquency and Opportunity (Cloward & Ohlin), 133–134
Delinquency in a Birth Cohort (Wolfgang, Figlio & Thorsten), 55–56, 339
delinquency prevention, 400–401
  after-school programs, 419–420
  Big Brothers Big Sisters (BBBS) program, 417
  Boys and Girls Clubs of America, 419
  CASASTART program, 422
  classifying, 406
  community-based policing and, 480
  comprehensive community-based programs, 421–423
  contemporary preventive approaches, 404–405
  daycare programs, 410–411

developmental perspective on, 406
early prevention programs, 407–408
federally funded programs, 404
future of, 423
history of, 403–406
home-based programs, 407–408
job training programs, 420–421
and juvenile justice, 447–448
mentoring, 415–417
parenting skills, improving, 410
PATHE (Positive Action Through Holistic Education) program, 418
police work and, 477–481
preschool programs, 411–413
problem-oriented policing, 480–481
public health approach, 406
public support for, 409
Quantum Opportunities Program (QOP), 416–417
schools, 413–415
  primary grade programs, 413–415
  teens, programs for, 417–418
in teenage years, 415–423
violence prevention curricula, 418
delinquent boy role, 133
Delinquent Boys (Cohen), 131–133
delinquent children, 441
The Delinquent Girl (Vedder & Somerville), 229
delinquent subcultures theory, 131–133
dementia and diet, 84
Denmark
  incarcerated juveniles in, 594
  juvenile courts in, 590
  juvenile justice system, 591
  juvenile violence in, 584
  minimum/maximum ages of responsibility, 590
  property crime in, 585
Department of Health and Human Services, 405
Department of Justice, 441
  Civil Rights Division of, 562
depression, 3
  alienation and, 290
  bullying and, 345
  gender differences and, 219
  school shooters and, 346
designer drugs, 372
desistance from crime, 54, 187–188
  reasons for, 194–195
desistance remission, 11
detached street workers, 319–320, 404
detention. *See also* juvenile institutions
  in adult jails, 499–500
  increase in, 498
  juvenile court decision, 497–500
  national trends in, 498
  preventive detention, 501
  race/ethnicity and, 498, 499
  of status offenders, 500
detention boarding homes, 497
detention centers, 446
Detention Diversion Advocacy Program (DDAP), 499, 500
detention hearing, 444
determinate sentences, 516
deterrence theories
  general deterrence theory, 74–75
  specific deterrence theory, 76
  summary of, 79

developmental aphasia, 85
developmental delinquency
    prevention, 406
developmental theory, 54, 182. *See also* latent
    trait theory; life-course theory
    public policy and, 204–206
deviance
    Cambridge Study in Delinquent
        Development, 188–189
    cliques, deviant, 160–161
    divorce and, 252–253
    intergenerational deviance,
        258–259
    primary/secondary deviance,
        158–159, 161
    secondary deviance, 161
    in social reaction theory, 157
deviance amplification effect, 158
Deviant Peer Influences in Programs for Youth:
    Problems and Solutions
        (Dodge, Dishion & Lansford), 291
deviant peers/parents, 144
deviant subcultures theory, 132–133
Dexamyl, 371
Dexedrine, 371
diet and delinquency, 81, 82, 84
differential association theory, 137–138
differential coercion theory, 204
differential labeling, 159
differential opportunity theory,
    133–134
direct appeals, 518–519
disaggregated statistics, 43. *See also* UCR
    (Uniform Crime Report)
discipline. *See also* punishment
    in America, 16
    child-parent conflict and, 255
    chronic offenders and, 188
    inconsistent discipline, 257
    in Middle Ages, 13
    Oregon Social Learning Center (OSLC)
        and, 410
    parental responsibility laws, 26–27
    in schools, 360
discretion. *See also* discretionary justice
    of police, 470
    of prosecutors, 495
discretionary justice, 470–476
    bias and, 473–476
    environmental factors and, 471
    gender bias, 474–475
    limits on, 476
    organizational bias, 476–477
    procedural justice, 471
    public policy and, 472
    racial bias and, 473, 475
    situational factors, 472–473
disjunction of expectations/achievements,
    129
dismissals at intake, 501
disorganized neighborhoods, 295–296
    police in, 466
displacement effect, 26
disposition, 512–513. *See also* sentencing
    juvenile court dispositions, 513
    predisposition reports, 512–513
disposition hearing, 270–271
disproportionate minority confinement
    (DMC), 552
disruptions in life transitions, 183–184
disruptive behavior disorder (DBD), 94

dissociative identity disorder (DID),
    262
district attorneys, 494
    waiver decision by, 509
diversion, 502–503
    in England, 597
    international comparisons, 592–593
    issues in, 503
divorce, 7, 251–254
    children, effects on, 253
    chronic offenders and, 188–189
    gender and effects of, 228–229
    parental deviance and, 252–253
dizygotic (DZ) twins, 88, 89
dog sniffs at schools, 350
domestic violence. *See also* child abuse;
    sexual abuse
    divorce and, 252
dopamine and ADHD (attention deficit/
    hyperactivity disorder), 86
Dorchester Community Roundtable, 276
dower system, 13
dowry, 13
dramatization of evil, 162
drift process, 138
drive-by shootings, 299, 316, 317
driving while black, 473
dropping out, 336–339
    ADHD (attention deficit/hyperactivity
        disorder) and, 87
    rates, 44
    reasons for, 337–338
drug courts, 450–451
drug dealers, 9, 379–382, 383
    Brazil, trafficking in, 578
    immigration and, 44
    law enforcement and, 388
    profits of, 393
drug use, 7. *See also* gangs; specific drugs
    Across Ages program, 206–207
    ADHD (attention deficit/hyperactivity
        disorder) and, 87
    anesthetic drugs, 369–370
    balanced and restorative justice (BARJ)
        method, 391–392
    border control and, 387–388
    child abuse and, 266
    and chronic offenders, 384–385
    cigarettes, 372
    community strategies, 389
    control strategies, 386–393
    crop eradication and, 387
    cross-national research, 585–587
    and delinquency, 384–386
    designer drugs, 372
    in eastern Europe, 576
    education strategies, 388–389
    emotional problems and, 378, 381
    family factors and, 376
    and gangs, 294–295, 299–300, 382
    gateway drugs, 379
    genetics and, 376, 378
    hallucinogens, 370–371
    harm reduction efforts, 392–393
    human trafficking and, 230
    inhalants, 370
    law enforcement strategies, 386–388
    legalization of drugs, 393
    lifetime teenage illicit use, 586
    and losers, 382
    multiple crimes and, 382

    by parents, 250–251
    pathways to, 379–384
    peer pressure and, 375–376
    persistence and, 194
    persistent offenders and, 383–384
    problem behavior syndrome and, 378,
        380–381
    as rational choice, 378
    reasons for, 374–378
    schools, 348
        drug testing in, 357
        failure and drug use, 380–381
        violence at, 346, 347
    sedatives, 370
    SMART Moves (Self-management and
        Resistance Training) program, 419
    social capital, negation of, 194
    social disorganization and, 375
    source control strategy, 386–387
    steroids, 371
    stimulants, 371
    testing in schools, 357
    tranquilizers, 370
    treatment strategies, 390–392, 515
    trends in, 45, 372–374
    as type of delinquency, 385–386
Drum Power program, 340
due process
    discipline in schools, 360
    drug testing in schools and, 357
    in juvenile justice system, 440
    prosecutors, role of, 495
    in transfer to adult courts, 505–507
    trial, rights at, 511
    variances in, 510
dyslexia, 85

E
early puberty, 225–226
eastern Europe, delinquency in,
    576
eating disorders, 93
ecological patterns and general theory
    of crime, 200
economic factors. *See also* poverty;
    socioeconomic status (SES)
    and choice theory, 72
    and delinquency trends, 44
    and family, 250, 251
    and gangs, 300
    and general theory of crime, 202
Ecstasy, 372
    availability of, 388
    profits from selling, 393
education. *See also* school failure; schools
    and American Dream culture, 128
    at-risk children, 336
    development of, 13–15
    as drug prevention strategy, 388–389
    inadequate opportunity for, 7–8
    juvenile institutions, educational
        programs in, 558
    race and, 52
    retention rates, 8
    socioeconomic status (SES) and,
        334–335
    spending on, 335–336
    trends in, 335–336
EEG (electroencephalogram) and
    delinquency, 83
egalitarian families, 237

sexual abuse and, 262
steroid use and, 371
home-based prevention programs, 407–408
Homeboy Industries, 145
homeboys, 298–299
home detention, 515
homelessness, 7
Home Street, 305
home visitor program, 399–400, 408
homicides
cleared crimes, 37
drug use and, 384
familicide, 265
and gangs, 295, 310–311
honor killing, 235
immigration and, 44
street children, killings of, 578
honor and gangs, 311
honor killings, 235
hormones
and delinquency, 82–83
gender and, 226–227
house arrest, 538
House Committee on Government Reform, 549
House of Reformation, 434
House of Refuge, 433, 434–435, 547
housing
child poverty and, 118
and social ecology theory, 122
Houston Parent-Child Development Center, 411
human agency, 191–192
human nature, 196
and general theory of crime, 202
human trafficking, 217, 230–231, 576
and children, 230–231
Hungary, juvenile justice system, 591
hustlers, 298–299
hybrid gang culture, 297
hypnosis as drug treatment, 391

I
Ice methamphetamine, 371
id, 91, 92
identical twins, 88, 89
identity crisis, 91–92
Illinois Juvenile Court Act of 1899, 438
illness, child poverty and, 118
immigration
anomie and, 127–128
and delinquency trends, 44
impulsivity
causes of, 197
and general theory of crime, 197
genetics and, 256
incapacitation policy, 76–77, 79
incorrigible child, 21
indeterminate sentences, 515–516
individualized treatment model, 515–516
individual-level theories, 103–104
individual treatment techniques, 557
Industrial Revolution, 16
policing and, 460
industrial schools, 558
infant mortality, 8, 10
in Middle Ages, 12–13
informal consent decrees, 515
informal social control, 124

informants, use of, 465–466
information processing, 99
inhalants, 370
injunctions against gangs, 316–317
injury, denial of, 138–139
in loco parentis, police acting in, 468
innovation as social adaptation, 127
institutional anomie theory, 128
institutional facilities. See juvenile institutions
institutional social control, 125
intake process
in juvenile courts, 501–502
for probation, 535
integrated theories, 190
intelligence. See also latent trait theory
adoption studies and, 89
chronic offenders and, 188
controversy over delinquency and, 103
and delinquency, 101–103
nature theory of, 102
nurture theory of, 102
risk for crime and, 81
and trait theory, 80
Intensive Aftercare Program (IAP) model, 563–564, 565
interactional theory, 191
intergenerational deviance, 258–259
International Association of Chiefs of Police, 460, 588
international crime, 583
international gangs, 296–297
international perspective, 575–580. See also cross-national research
on aftercare, 594–595
on diversion programs, 592–593
future of juvenile justice, 599
incarcerated juveniles, 594
on juvenile courts, 590
on minimum/maximum ages, 590
on policing, 588–589
on sentencing, 591–594
on transfers of juveniles to adult courts, 590
International Self-Report Delinquency Study, 581, 582
Internet drug traffickers, 387–388
interpersonal interactions, 116
Interpol, 581, 582
interstitial area, 293
interstitial group, 292
intervention programs, 449
interview research, 41
intrafamily violence, 254
involvement in social bond theory, 142, 143
IQ. See intelligence
iron, 84
isolation and school violence, 347
Italy
juvenile justice system, 591
juvenile violence in, 584
property crime in, 585

J
Jacob Wetterling Crimes Against Children Law, 35
jails. See prisons and jails
Jamaican gangs, 296, 305
Japan
crime in, 578–580

juvenile justice system, 591
policing in, 589
sentencing in, 593–594
"Jena Six" incident, 141
Job Corps, 420–421, 449
Jo Boys, 307
jobs. See employment
job training programs, 420–421
jock identity, 144
jointure, 13
Jordan, honor killing in, 235
judges in juvenile courts, 496–497
judicial waiver, 505–506
jurisdiction
concurrent jurisdiction, 505
oldest age for juvenile court jurisdiction, 18
waiver of, 19
jury trial, right to, 444
Justice Policy Institute, 322, 477
gangs, report on, 323–324
justice system. See also juvenile justice system
social conflict theory and, 165–166
juvenile courts. See also hearings; juvenile justice system; petitions; probation; sentencing; trial; waiver
abolishment of, 522
appeal, right to, 518–519
appointed private counsel, 494
bail, 501
case flow in, 492
confidentiality of proceedings, 519–520
Court Appointed Special Advocates (CASA) program, 493
defense attorneys in, 492–493
detention, decision for, 497–500
and deterrence theory, 75
dispositions, 513
diversion by, 502–503
early system, 439
in England, 598
first courts, establishment of, 20
future of, 520–522
guardians ad litem, 493
history of, 437–439
Illinois Juvenile Court Act of 1899, 438
intake process, 501–502
international court systems, 590
judges, role of, 496–497
oldest age for jurisdiction, 18
plea bargaining, 504
prosecutors in, 494–496
public defenders in, 493–494, 495
reforming system, 439–441
reform of, 520–522
release, decision for, 497–500
summons, issuance of, 503
teen courts, 450–452
transfer to adult courts, 505–510
juvenile defense attorneys, 492–493
juvenile delinquency
as label, 162–163
study of, 10–11
trends in, 43–48, 45
Juvenile Delinquency Prevention and Control Act of 1968, 440
Juvenile Gangs in Context (Klein), 293
juvenile institutions. See also aftercare
boot camps, 559–560
civil rights and, 561–562

juvenile institutions *(continued)*
  coed institutions, 555
  comprehensive strategy for improving, 449–450
  correctional treatment in, 555–558
  detention decision and, 497
  educational programs, 558
  effectiveness of treatment in, 556
  female inmates, 554–555
  future of, 566–567
  gender differences and, 229
  group therapy in, 557–558
  history of, 547–548
  incapacitation policy, 76–77
  individual treatment techniques, 557
  international comparisons, 594
  male inmates, 554
  minimum standards for, 561
  in nineteenth century, 435–436
  physical conditions of, 549, 551
  population trends, 549
  private institutions, 548–549
  public institutions, 548–549
  race/ethnicity and, 552–554
  reentry programs, 562–566
  right to treatment concept, 560–562
  state comparisons of, 550–551
  suicide in, 529–530
  suppression effect, 530
  treatment options, 445–446
  twentieth-century developments, 547–548
  typical residents of, 551–555
  vocational training in, 558–559
  wilderness probation, 559
juvenile intensive probation supervision (JIPS), 537–538
Juvenile Justice Alternative Education Program, 445
Juvenile Justice and Delinquency Prevention Act (JJDPA) of 1974, 449, 499, 500
Juvenile Justice and Delinquency Prevention Act of 2002, 552
Juvenile Justice Reform Act of 1977 (Washington), 516
juvenile justice system, 11. *See also* child protection system; hearings; juvenile courts
  adjudication, 444
  adjudicatory hearings, 444
  alternative courts, 450–452
  "Beijing Rules" of juvenile justice, 588, 589
  benefits of comprehensive strategy, 449
  bifurcated processes, 444
  case flow, diagram of, 443
  Children's Aid Society, 436
  child saving movement, 433–435
  comparison of adult/juvenile terms, 447
  comprehensive strategy, 447–452
  conflict of values in, 446
  criminal justice *vs.*, 446–447
  degradation ceremonies, 163
  detention centers, 446
  detention hearing, 444
  differences from adult justice system, 448
  disposition in, 444–445
  drug courts, 450–451
  England, system in, 591, 595–599
  federal commissions on, 440–441
  future of, 452–453
  gender and, 238–239

graduated sanction programs, 449
House of Refuge, 433, 434–435
institutional programs, 449–450
international perspective on, 588–595
intervention programs, 449
and labeling, 162–163
maximum ages for, 442
in nineteenth century, 432–437
petitions in juvenile courts, 446
police investigation, 442, 444
pretrial procedures, 444
prevention and, 447–448
process, 442–446
racial bias in, 51–52
reforming, 439–441
restitution in, 542
similarities to adult justice system, 448
social conflict theory and, 165–166
Society for the Prevention of Cruelty to Children (SPCC), 436–437
status offenders in, 22–24
teen courts, 450–452
timeline of, 446
toughness on crime position, 409, 452–453, 521
treatment options, 445–446
urbanization and, 432–433
Juvenile Mentoring Program (JUMP), 415–416
juvenile officers, 465
Juvenile Residential Facility Census, 551

K
Kenya, poverty in, 580
Kids at Risk programs, 320
king's conscience, 15
kleptomania, 225
klikas, 302
known group method, 39

L
L.A. Brims, 294
labeling theory, 156. *See also* social reaction theory
  and delinquency prevention, 423
lack of capable guardians, 73–74
Lady Disciples, 300
language
  gender differences in, 219
  verbal skills studies, 88
latent delinquents, 92
latent trait theory, 182, 195–203
  evaluation of, 203–204
Latin America. *See* South America
Latin Kings, 291, 299
  hand signs, 303
Latino/a Americans. *See* Hispanic Americans
Latino Homicide: Immigration, Violence, and Community (Martinez), 127
law enforcement, 11. *See also* police
  drug control strategies, 386–388
  and school security, 352–353
Law Enforcement Assistance Administration (LEAA), 440, 441
  and police operations, 460–461
Law Enforcement Management and Administrative Statistics (LEMAS) survey, 462–463
Law on Regulation of Business Affecting Public Morals, Japan, 589

laws. *See also* specific laws
  curfew laws, 26–27
  in differential association theory, 137
  social conflict theory and, 165–166
leadership of gangs, 302–303, 307
lead exposure and antisocial behavior, 82
learning disabilities, 85
  school failure and, 341
learning in differential association theory, 136–140
least detrimental alternative standard, 514–515
legalization of drugs, 393
legal protections, 19
liberal feminism, 233–234
Librium, 370
life-course persisters, 188–190, 200
life-course theory, 182–184
  adolescent-limited offenders, 188–190
  age-graded theory, 190–195
  age of onset in, 186–187
  Cambridge Study in Delinquent Development, 188–189
  concepts of, 184–190
  continuity of crime, 186–187
  desistance from crime, 187–188
  disruptions in transitions and, 183–184
  evaluation of, 203–204
  fundamentals of, 183–184
  pathways to delinquency, 185–186
  problem behavior syndrome (PBS), 184–185
life crises, 4
lighting at schools, 350
living conditions, substandard, 7
LoJack tracking system, 78
losers, drug-involved, 382
"Lower Class Culture as a Generating Milieu of Gang Delinquency" (Miller), 130–131
low-visibility decision making, 470
LSD (lysergic acid diethylamide), 371
lying, neurological dysfunction and, 83
Lyman School for Boys, 547

M
magnesium, 84
Maine Boys' Training School, 547
Main Street Crips, 305
Malditos Ratas (Damned Rats), 578
malicious acts at school, 349
malnourishment, 84
management training programs, 447
mandatory sentences, 516
marijuana, 368
  alcohol use and, 385
  availability of, 388
  problem behaviors and, 380
marriage
  desistance and, 195
  quality of, 252, 254
  as turning point, 191
Marxist feminist view, 235–236
masculinity hypothesis, 218, 224–225
Massachusetts experience, 532
Master Tobacco Settlement Agreement, 372
materialism, 128
maternal rejection, 83
math education, 335–336, 337
maturation and delinquency, 54–55

maximum ages. *See* minimum/
maximum ages
media. *See also* television
and gangs, 291
social learning theory and, 95–98
trends in delinquency and, 45
medications, psychotropic, 104
Medieval Children (Orme), 12
Megan's Law, 35
mental disorders, 93–94
mental health. *See also* depression;
neurological dysfunction;
schizophrenia
bullying and, 345
child abuse and, 262
and juvenile institutions, 549,
551–552
nutrients and, 84
Mentoring Initiative for System Involved
Youth (MISIY), 415–416, 449
mescaline, 371
mesomorph physique, 183
meta-analysis, 41
of drug courts, 451
metal detectors at schools, 350
Metedrine, 371
methadone maintenance clinics, 392
methamphetamines, 388
Mexico, delinquency in, 578
Miami, gang control efforts in, 323
Mid-City Project, Boston, 404
Middle Ages, childhood in, 11–13
middle class
measuring rods, 131, 133
in social conflict theory, 166
migration of gangs, 296–297
milieu therapy, 558
military as turning point, 191, 193
Miltown, 370
minerals, 84
minimal brain dysfunction (MBD), 83
minimum/maximum ages, 442
international perspective, 590
Minnesota Study of Twins Reared Apart,
88, 89
minorities. *See* race/ethnicity
minors. *See also* children
defined, 17–18
in need of supervision, 21
minutes of silence, 359
Miranda warnings, 469–470
missing cases phenomenon, 39
Mobilization for Youth (MOBY) program,
404, 421–422
Model Youth Correction Authority Act,
548
Monitoring the Future (MTF), 46–47, 49
and African American
delinquency, 51
on drug use, 372–373
on gender patterns, 224
monozygotic (MZ) twins, 88, 89
Montreal Longitudinal-Experimental Study,
414
moods
and delinquency, 82
disorders, 93
moral development theory, 98–99
moral entrepreneurs, 157
moral outrage, 219
moral reasoning, 19

morals
in differential association theory, 137
general theory of crime and, 201
subterranean values, 138
motivated offenders, presence of, 73–74
motivation, unconscious, 91
motor coordination and learning disabilities,
85
motor vehicle theft
cleared crimes, 37
tracking systems, 78
MS-13 gang, 291, 296, 306–307
multidimensional treatment foster care
(MTFC) program, 544–545
multiple personality disorder
(MPD), 262
multi-systemic therapy (MST), 390,
545, 546
murders. *See* homicides
music programs, 420
Muslim gangs, 296
mythical punitive public, 409

N
National Advisory Commission on Criminal
Justice Standards and Goals, 24, 440
National Bar Association on girls in
institutions, 555
National Council of Juvenile and Family
Court Judges, 496
National Council on Crime and
Delinquency, 24, 555
civil rights in juvenile institutions,
561–562
National Crime Victimization Survey
(NCVS). *See* NCVS (National Crime
Victimization Survey)
National Incident-Based Reporting System
(NIBRS), 38
National Institute of Justice
Arrestee Drug Abuse Monitoring
(ADAM) program, 384
International Center, 583
National Institute on Fatherhood and
Domestic Violence, 276
nationality. *See* race/ethnicity
National Organization for Women (NOW),
233–234
National Survey on Drug Use and Health
(NSDUH), 373–374
National Youth Employment Coalition
(NYEC), 559
National Youth Gang Survey (NYGS),
294–295
Native Americans
police, attitudes about, 462
sentencing circles, 172
victimization and, 61
nature theory, 102
NCVS (National Crime Victimization
Survey), 40
compatibility of data, 47
on victims and offenders, 59–60
near-groups, 299–300
needle exchange programs, 392
needs in differential association theory, 138
negative affective states, 129
negative stimuli, 129
neglect. *See also* child abuse
defined, 261
and guardians *ad litem*, 493

Neighborhood, 305
neighborhoods. *See also* community;
disorganized neighborhoods
supervision programs, 497
The Netherlands
diversion programs in, 592
incarcerated juveniles in, 594
juvenile justice system, 591
juvenile violence in, 584
property crime in, 585
sentencing in, 593–594
neurological dysfunction, 83, 85–86. *See also*
ADHD (attention deficit/hyperactivity
disorder)
learning disabilities, 85
research supporting theory, 83
twin studies, 88
neuroticism, 100
neutralization theory, 138–140
techniques of, 138–139
testing, 139–140
New Frontier program, 404
New Zealand
delinquency in, 578
incarcerated juveniles in, 594
juvenile justice system, 591
minimum/maximum ages of
responsibility, 590
policing in, 588
NIBRS (National Incident-Based Reporting
System), 38
Niños Podridos (Rotten Children), 578
No Child Left Behind (NCLB) Act of 2001,
353–354
nonchronic recidivists, 56
non-crime, 196
nondealing gangs, 299–300
nonjustice delinquency prevention, 400–401
nonoffenders, 189
nonresidential treatment, 530, 545–547
norepinephrine, 86
Northwest Regional Learning Center
(NRLC), 564
Norway, incarcerated juveniles in, 594
not-guilty pleas, 504
Nurse-Family Partnership, 400, 408
The Nurture Assumption (Harris), 256
nurture theory, 102
nutrients and mental health, 84

O
observational research, 41
obsessions and gender, 228
Office of Community Oriented Policing
Services (COPS), 463–464
Office of Juvenile Justice and Delinquency
Prevention (OJJDP), 22, 24, 415–416,
441
Evaluation of Teen Courts Project, 451
jails, detention in, 499
on juvenile institutions, 548
Operation Ceasefire, Boston and, 481
status offenders, detaining, 500
omega-3 fatty acids, 84
Omnibus Safe Streets and Crime Control
Act, 440
once an adult/always an adult
program, 521
Operation Blue Orchid, 576
Operation Ceasefire, 319, 481, 482
Operation Gray Lord, 388

Operation Hammer, 321–322
Operation Night Light, 320
Operation Peacekeeper, 321
Operation Webslinger, 388
Operation Weed and Seed, 134
opportunity and general theory
    of crime, 198
oppositional defiant disorder (ODD), 94
oppression, feelings of, 92
Orange County's Family Keys program, 25
Oregon Social Learning Center
    (OSLC), 410
organizational bias, 476–477
organized crime, 312
organized gangs, 297
Oriana House, 318
orphans
    in American colonies, 15
    trains, 436
outpatient psychotherapy, 515
outsiders, 290, 348
overcrowding in juvenile institutions, 548
overt pathway, 185
OxyContin, 373

P
Pacatal, 370
panic disorder, 262
paranoia and gender, 227
parens patriae, 15, 437
    in Canada, 593
    and child saver movement, 435
    conflict of values and, 446
    delinquency and, 17
    and deterrence theory, 75
    and divorce, 252
    in England, 595
    and judges, 496
    juvenile court movement and, 438
    noncriminal behavior, control
        over, 21
    and trial rights, 511
    waiver of, 19
parental efficacy, 135, 254–255
    general theory of crime and, 201
parents. See also child abuse
    absent parents, 252
    and choice theory, 72
    chronic offenders and, 188
    deviance, parental, 258–259
    early maturity and, 226
    general theory of crime and, 201
    improving parenting skills, 410
    inconsistent discipline, 257
    influences of, 247–248
    intergenerational deviance and, 259
    labeling by, 160
    Oregon Social Learning Center
        (OSLC), 410
    resource dilution, 258
    responsibility laws, 26
    and routine activities theory, 74
    similarities, parent-child, 87–88
    support, perception of, 256
    termination of parental rights, 273
parking lots of schools, 349
parole. See also aftercare
    programs, 445
    reentry services, 573
Participate and Learn Skills (PALS)
    program, 419–420

Part I crimes, 36
    UCR (Uniform Crime Report) on, 43
Part II crimes, 36
    UCR (Uniform Crime Report) on, 43
party gangs, 297
passive speech, 356, 358
passive systems, 540
paternalism hypothesis, 225
paternalistic family, 11
PATHE (Positive Action Through Holistic
    Education) program, 418
pathways to delinquency, 185–186
patriarchy, 235–236
PCBs (polychlorinated biphenyls), 82
PCP (phencyclidine), 369–370
Peace-Builders, 414–415
peers. See also gangs; schools
    chronic offenders and, 189
    and delinquency, 289
    deviance and, 160–161
    in differential association
        theory, 137
    drug use and, 375–376
    general theory of crime and, 201
    impact of, 290
    positive peer culture (PPC), 558
    public policy and, 290–291
    relationships among, 288–291
    selection, 290
    in social bond theory, 143–144
    socialization and, 135
    susceptibility to influence by, 289
penis envy, 225
People Nation, 287
    national symbols of, 303
Perry Preschool, Michigan, 412
persistence, 11
persistent offenders
    child abuse and, 274
    drug users as, 383–384
    school achievement and, 339, 341
personal factors
    and choice theory, 72
    in integrated theories, 190
    school failure and, 341
personality
    addiction-prone personality, 378
    antisocial personality, 100–101, 378
    chronic offenders and, 188
    and delinquency, 99–101
    drug use and, 378
    gender differences, 220
    and general theory of crime, 197
    maturity and, 55
    and psychodynamic theory, 91–93
    risk for crime and, 81
    school failure and, 341
Peru and drug control, 386–387
pesticide exposure, 82
petitions, 503–504
    detention, filing on, 498
    in juvenile courts, 446
petty drug dealers, 379
physical basis of crime, 80
physical child abuse, 261
physical relocation, 189
picture IDs at schools, 350
PINS (person in need of supervision), 25,
    440, 441
Piru Street Boys, 294
Pittsburgh Youth Study, 402

placasos/placa, 303
place and delinquency, 48
placing-out plan, 436
plain view searches, 469
Plan Colombia, 387
plea bargaining, 444, 504
pleadings, 444
pleas in juvenile courts, 504
pledge system, 460
Plug Uglies, 293
plunder, 204
PMS (premenstrual syndrome), 227
police. See also community policing;
        discretionary justice;
        problem-oriented policing
    arrest, role in, 467–468
    bias and, 473–476
    closed-circuit television (CCTV), use of,
        482–483, 484
    complaint reports, 503
    and curfew laws, 26
    custodial interrogation, 469–470
    delinquency prevention and, 477–481
    and deterrence theory, 75
    future of juvenile policing, 481–484
    gangs, law enforcement efforts and,
        317–319
    history of, 460–461
    informants, use of, 465–466
    international perspective on, 588–589
    investigations by, 442, 444
    in loco parentis, action in, 468
    Miranda warnings, 469–470
    organizational bias, 476–477
    procedural justice, 471
    programs, list of, 467
    Rampart Scandal, 322
    in restorative justice approach, 173
    role conflicts for, 465
    roles of, 465–466
    and rule of law, 467–470
    in schools, 477–480
    search and seizure, role in, 468–469
    social conflict theory and, 165
    technology and, 482–483
    urban police department organization,
        464–465
    and violent juvenile crime, 466
police athletic leagues, 461
Police Executive Research Forum, 481
Police Working with Youth, 480
political unrest, 116
polyunsaturated fatty acids, 84
poorhouses, 14
Poor Laws, 13, 14
    of American colonies, 15
population trends
    by age, 5
    by gender and age, 6
positive life experiences, 191
positively valued stimuli, 129
positive peer culture (PPC), 558
positivism, 80
postadjudication stage of probation, 535
postdisposition stage of probation, 535
posting, 304
post-traumatic stress disorder (PTSD), 61
poverty, 6, 116–118. See also social
        disorganization
    in Africa, 580
    age, rates by, 119

reading, 8
  performance levels, 335
reality therapy, 557
rebellion as social adaptation, 127
recidivism
  boot camps and, 560
  electronic monitoring and, 540
  Intensive Aftercare Program (IAP) model
    and, 565
  mental health and, 551
  Repeat Offender Prevention Program
    (ROPP), Los Angeles, 538
  teen courts and, 451
  wilderness programs and, 550
reconciliation in restorative approach, 172
reentry programs, 562–566
  future of, 567
reformatories, 434
reform schools, 435–436, 547
rehabilitation
  decline of, 546–547
  and juvenile institutions, 556
  programs, 104
reintegrative shaming, 169–170
rejection
  in cognitive theory, 99
  and school violence, 347
release, decision for, 497–500
religion
  House of Refuge movement, 434
  and institutional social control, 125
  school prayer, 359
Repeat Offender Prevention Program
  (ROPP), Los Angeles, 538
reports. See also self-reports; UCR (Uniform
    Crime Report)
  compatibility of data sources, 47
  National Crime Victimization Survey
    (NCVS), 40
  NIBRS (National Incident-Based
    Reporting System), 38
representing, 304
research. See also cross-national research;
    reports
  on ADHD (attention deficit/hyperactivity
    disorder), 87
  cohort research data, 40–41
  compatibility of data sources, 47
  crime mapping, 42
  data mining, 42
  on diet and delinquency, 84
  experimental data, 41
  interview research, 41
  meta-analysis, 41
  Monitoring the Future (MTF) survey,
    46–47
  on neurological dysfunction link, 83
  observational research, 41
  on social bond theory, 142–143
  on social reaction theory, 164
  of socioeconomic status (SES), 53
  systematic review, 41
  on television violence, 97
residential treatment, 390, 543–545
  commitment to program, 515
  pros and cons of, 545–547
resource dilution, 258
respect and code of the streets, 132
responsibility, denial of, 138
restitution programs, 542–543
  success of, 543

restorative justice, 168–169, 540–541
  balanced and restorative justice
    (BARJ), 174
  family group conferencing (FGC),
    173–174
  juvenile community restoration example,
    175
  process of restoration, 171–172
  programs, 172–173
restricted scope of social bond
    theory, 144
retention rates, 8
retreatism as social adaptation, 127
retreatist gangs, 134
retrospective cohort studies, 41
retrospective reading, 161–162
reunification goals, 270
revenge and gangs, 311
review hearings, 271
revocation of aftercare, 565–566
right to counsel, 444, 492
  public defenders in, 493–494, 495
right to treatment concept, 560–562
risk factors, 406
risk-taking, 9
  and general theory of crime, 197
Ritalin, 104
ritualism as social adaptation, 127
Roach Guards, 293
robbery
  as cleared crime, 37
  gender and, 60
Rochester Youth Development Study
    (RYDS), 88, 310
role conflicts for police, 465
role diffusion, 4
Romania, minimum/maximum ages of
    responsibility in, 590
routine activities theory, 73–74
Roxbury Comprehensive Community
    Health Services, 276
Roxbury Youthworks, 532
rules of procedure, 510
rural programs, 545
Russia
  courts in, 590
  delinquency in, 576
  juvenile justice system, 591
  mafiya, 296
  Revolution, gangs and, 313
  sentencing in, 594

S
SafeFutures Initiative, 422
Safe Harbor program, 354
Safe School study, 343
same-sex parents, 254
Samoan gangs, 307
S.A.R.A. (Scanning, Analysis, Response, and
    Assessment), 480–481
saturated fats, 84
Savage Nomads, 294
Savage Skulls, 294
S.A.V.E. (Stop Active Vandalism
    Everywhere), 323
Scarface, 315
schizophrenia, 93
  bullying and, 345
  diet deficits and, 84
  and gender, 227
Scholastic Aptitude Test (SAT), 220

School Collaborations' Substance Abuse
    Program, 205
school failure, 85, 341
  alienation and, 342–343
  class and, 341–342
  correlates of, 341–343
  drug use and, 380–381
  personal problems and, 342
  tracking and, 342
schools, 333. See also delinquency
    prevention; drug use; education; school
    failure
  academic performance and delinquency,
    339–343
  after-school programs, 419–420
  at-risk children, 336
  attacks on teachers, 343, 344
  bullying in, 345, 347
  causes of crime, 346–350
  chronic offenders and, 189
  climate
    improving, 353
    and violence, 347–349
  community and crime at, 348–350
  court-ordered school attendance, 515
  desegregation of, 335
  discipline in, 360
  dropping out, 336–339
  free speech and, 356, 358–359
  gang-control programs, 321
  guards at, 78
  and institutional social control, 125
  labeling, consequences of, 159–160
  legal rights in, 355–360
  No Child Left Behind (NCLB) Act of 2001,
    353–354
  physical condition of, 348
  poverty and crime, 349
  prayer in, 359
  privacy rights and, 356
  profile of school shooters, 346
  reducing crime, 350–352
  in restorative justice approach, 173
  role in delinquency prevention, 353–355
  Safe Harbor program, 354
  safety measures, 348–349, 350
  searches on school premises, 467
  security measures in, 348–352
  sex, teacher-student, 333–334
  shootings in, 333, 343–346
  socialization and, 135, 334–335
  social programs and, 353
  spending on, 335–336
  survival value and crime, 350
  tracking, 342
  trends in education, 335–336
  types of prevention programs, 354–355
  victimization at, 60
science education, 335–336
scripts and gender, 221
search and seizure, 19, 468–469
  warrantless searches, 469
search incident to arrest, 469
Seattle Social Development Project (SSDP), 413
Seconal, 370
secondary delinquency prevention, 406
secondary deviance, 158–159, 161
second-generation bullies, 258
secret deviants, 158–159
secure corrections, 547. See also juvenile
    institutions

Sparine, 370
SPCA (Society for the Prevention of Cruelty to Animals), 261
specific deterrence theory, 76, 79
Spectrum Wilderness Program, 559
speedballing, 368
spontaneous remission, 11, 54
sports. *See* athletics
Sri Lanka, minimum/maximum ages of responsibility, 590
Standard Minimum Rules for the Administration of Juvenile Justice (United Nations), 588, 589, 594
standards of living and globalization, 167
stare-downs, 307
State Agricultural and Industrial School, New York, 547
state attorneys, 494
statistics. *See* reports
status dropout rates, 337
status frustration, 131
status offenses, 19–22, 441
    detention for, 500
    girls and, 554
    history of, 20–22
    and juvenile justice system, 22–24
    probation for, 532
    reforming laws, 24–26
    separate categories for offenders, 21
    substitution of delinquency charge, 22
    types of, 20
status quo and social conflict theory, 165
status symbols, 156–157
statutory exclusion policies, 505, 521
stepparents, 251
    and child abuse, 265
steroids, 371
stigmatization, 158
    and delinquency prevention, 423
    intergenerational deviance and, 259
    shaming and, 169
stimulants, 371
stoners, 309
stop-and-frisk actions, 469
strain theory, 119–120. *See also* anomie
    elements of, 126
    general strain theory, 129–130
stratified society, 116
street children in South America, 578
Street Corner Society (Whyte), 41
street crimes, 165
street efficacy, 125
street gangs, 299–300
street values, 132
stress, 3
    and general strain theory, 129
    and sexual abuse, 262
stubborn child laws, 16, 20
stun guns, 482
subcultures
    delinquent subcultures theory, 131–133
    values, 120
submission, 204
substance abuse, 367. *See also* alcohol use; drug use
    and ADHD (attention deficit/hyperactivity disorder), 87
    child abuse and, 265, 266
    intergenerational deviance and, 258–259
    victimization and, 61

substandard living conditions, 7
subterranean values, 138
suicide
    in juvenile institutions, 529–530
    pacts, 3
    rates of, 3–4
    school shooters and, 346
    twin studies, 88
suitable targets, availability of, 73–74
summons, issuance of, 503
superego, 91, 92
supervised visitation centers (SVCs), 276
supervision in family, 257
suppression effect, 530
Supreme Court. *See* U.S. Supreme Court
surveillance lighting, 78
susceptibility rationale, 85
swaddling, 13
sweatshops, 230
Sweden
    courts in, 590
    incarcerated juveniles in, 594
    juvenile justice system, 591
    minimum/maximum ages of responsibility, 590
Switzerland
    juvenile justice system, 591
    juvenile violence in, 584
    minimum/maximum ages of responsibility, 590
    property crime in, 585
    sentencing in, 594
symbolic interaction, 156–157
Syracuse University Family Development Research Program, 410–411
systematic review, 41
    of drug courts, 451

T
targets
    hardening techniques, 78
    and routine activities theory, 74
tasers, 482
Task Force on Community Preventive Services, 508–509
Tasmania, minimum age of responsibility in, 591
tattoos and gangs, 304, 306
tautology and general theory of crime, 200
teachers. *See* schools
technology
    crime mapping, 42
    in police work, 482–483
teenage pregnancy. *See* pregnancy
teen courts, 450–452
Tegretol, 87
television
    closed-circuit television (CCTV), 78, 271–272, 482–483, 484
    trends in delinquency and, 45
    violence in, 95–98
temperature and delinquency, 48
termination of parental rights, 273
territoriality and gangs, 301–302
terrorism and social conflict theory, 165
tertiary delinquency prevention, 406
Teslac, 371
testosterone, 82–83
tetrahydrocannabinol (THC), 368

theft, 9. *See also* motor vehicle theft
    cleared crimes, 37
    at schools, 348
theories of delinquency. *See also* specific theories
    classical theories, 71
    controlling delinquency, theories for, 74–79
    evaluating, 103–104
    general deterrence concept, 74–75
    individual-level theories, 103–104
    nature theory, 102
    nurture theory, 102
    routine activities theory, 73–74
Thorazine, 370
thrill-seeking theory, 85–86
thug lifestyle, 315
time and delinquency, 48
time out technique, 410
tobacco use. *See* cigarettes
tongs, 307
tossing gang signs, 304
toughness as lower-class concern, 131
toughness on crime position, 409, 452–453, 521
toys in Middle Ages, 12
tracking in schools, 342
tracking systems, 78
Trafficking Victims Protection Act of 2003, 231
trait theory, 70, 79–81
    and abuse and delinquency, 273
    origins of, 80–81
    and preventing delinquency, 104–105
tranquilizers, 370
transfer hearings, 507
transfers to adult courts, 19, 505–510. *See also* waiver
    international perspective, 590
    and violence, 508–509
transitional neighborhoods, 120
transitions
    in adolescence, 4
    in life-course theory, 183
transnational crime, 582–583
treatment programs, 172, 445–446. *See also* community treatment; residential treatment
    developmental models for, 204–205
    legal right to treatment, 560–562
    nonresidential treatment, 530, 545–547
trial, 510–514. *See also* sentencing
    confidentiality of, 519–520
    constitutional rights at, 511–512
    disposition at, 512–513
    public access to, 519–520
trouble as lower-class concern, 131
truancy, 10, 336–337
    court-ordered school attendance, 515
truly disadvantaged children, 118
Tuinal, 370
turning points, 191, 193
twins, 88–89
The Two Sexes: Growing up Apart, Coming Together (Maccoby), 221

U
UCR (Uniform Crime Report), 36–38
    compatibility of data, 47
    compilation of, 36

© AP Images/Michael Dwyer

1971

Mckeiver v. Pennsylvania establishes that a jury trial is not constitutionally required in a juvenile hearing but states can permit one if they wish.

The Twenty-Sixth Amendment to the Constitution is passed, granting the right to vote to 18-year-olds.

1972

Wisconsin v. Yoder gives parents the right to impose their religion on their children.

Wolfgang publishes *Delinquency in a Birth Cohort*.

1973

In re Snyder gives minors the right to bring proceedings against their parents.

San Antonio Independent School District v. Rodriguez establishes that differences in education based on wealth were not necessarily discriminatory.

1974

Federal Child Abuse Prevention Act.

Buckley Amendment to the Education Act of 1974, the Family Education Rights and Privacy Act. Students have the right to see their own files with parental consent.

Juvenile Justice and Delinquency Prevention Act.

1970

In re Winship establishes that proof beyond a reasonable doubt is necessary in the adjudicatory phase of a juvenile hearing. A juvenile can appeal on the ground of insufficiency of the evidence if the offense alleged is an act that would be a crime in an adult court.

White House Conference on Children.

1965

1970

1969

Tinker v. Des Moines School District establishes that the First Amendment applies to juveniles and protects their constitutional right to free speech.

1968

Ginsberg v. New York establishes that it is unlawful to sell pornography to a minor.

1967

President's Commission on Law Enforcement recognizes the problems of the juvenile justice system.

In re Gault, a U.S. Supreme Court decision establishes juveniles have the right to counsel, notice, confrontation of witnesses, and the avoidance of self-incrimination. In general, the court holds that Fourteenth Amendment due process applies to the juvenile justice system, specifically in adjudicatory hearings.

1966

Kent v. United States—initial decision to establish due process protections for juvenile at transfer proceedings.

1975

Goss v. Lopez establishes that a student facing suspension has the right to due process, prior notice, and an open hearing.

1977

Report of the Committee of the Judiciary, especially concerning the rights of the unborn and the right of 18-year-olds to vote.

Juvenile Justice Amendment of 1977.

Ingraham v. Wright establishes that corporal punishment is permissible in public schools and is not a violation of the Eighth Amendment.

American Bar Association, Standards on Juvenile Justice.

Washington State amends its sentencing policy.

1979

International Year of the Child.

...continued from front endsheets

© AP Images/Color China Photo

1980
National concern over child
abuse and neglect.

1981
Fare v. Michael C. defines *Miranda*
rights of minors.

1982
Efforts to decarcerate status offenders
escalate.

1984
Schall v. Martin allows states to use
preventive detention with juvenile
offenders.

Juvenile Delinquents Act replaced
by Young Offenders Act, making
juvenile justice in Canada uniform
across the country.

1990
Maryland v. Craig allows
child abuse victims to
testify on closed-circuit
television.

1991
Juvenile violence rate hits
an all-time high at 430 acts
per 100,000 adolescents.

1994 and 1998
Criminal Justice and Public Order Act
and Crime and Disorder Act expand
use of incarceration of juvenile
offenders in England.

1995
Reported child abuse
cases top 3 million.

1980

1990

1989
Supreme Court upholds death penalty for
children over 16.

1988
Re-emergence of nationwide gang problem.

1987
Conservative trends result in 10,000 juvenile waivers to adult courts.

1986
Juvenile offenders waived to adult court are executed, focusing
attention on the death penalty for children.

1985
New Jersey v. T.L.O. allows teachers to search students without a warrant or
probable cause.

Wilson and Herrnstein publish *Crime and Human Nature,* focusing attention
on biological causes of delinquency.

United Nations General Assembly adopts "Standard Minimum Rules for the
Administration of Juvenile Justice."

© Corbis RF/Alamy